ZAGATSURVEY®

FIFTH EDITION
1998/99

U.S. HOTELS, RESORTS & SPAS

Edited by David Doty

Hotel research coordinated by Susan Safronoff

Published and distributed by
ZAGAT SURVEY, LLC
4 Columbus Circle
New York, New York 10019
Tel: 212 977 6000
E-mail: zagat@zagatsurvey.com

Sixth Printing
© 1997 Zagat Survey, LLC
ISBN 1-57006-081-9

Acknowledgments

We would like to thank the following for all their help: Stan Arnold, Karen Berk, Anthony Dias Blue, Olga Boikess, Kimmy Brauer, Meg Brazill, Cindy Butler, Amy Cates, John Christensen, Millard Cohen, Suzanne and Norman Cohn, Betty Cook, Christopher Cook, Susan Cramer, Laurie Dayton, Pat Denechaud, Terry Byrne-Dodge, Shelia Donnelly, Maryellen Duckett, Margot and John Ernst, John Farrell, Karen Feldman, Skye Ferrante, Suzanne Fitzgerald, Hal Foster, Valerie Foster, Gerry Frank, Eunice Fried, Heather Gedlen, Kay Goldstein, Norma Gottlieb, Nic Gough, Vivian Hager, Lisa Shara Hall, Robert Hosman, Bobbye Hughes, Jan Johnson, Lynda Jones, Scott Joseph, Dick Kagan, Ivan Karp, Marty Katz, Mike Klein, Gretchen Kurz, Jane Lavine, Nancy Leson, William Levit, Jr., Sharon Litwin, John Long, Donna Maroni, John Martellaro, John McDermott, Cynthia McFadden, Carolyn McGuire, Leroy Meshel, Charles Monaghan, Mike Munday, Kristine Nickel, Jerome Oestreich, Ann Orton, Mike Paskevich, Neil Peck, Joe Pollack, Eric Redman, Steve Reidman, Jennifer Reinsdorf, Joan Reminick, Elizabeth Rhein, Robert Rich, Shelley Sawyer, John Schell, Jesica Seacor, Brenda and Earl Shapiro, Merrill Shindler, Mary Stagaman, Ila Stanger, Al Stankus, Debra Stantic, Muriel Stevens, Susan Stiger, Evan Smith, Bill St. John, Steve Stover, Howard Stravitz, Polly Summar, Valerie Tamis, Paul Uhlmann III, Phil Vettel and Carla Waldemar.

Special thanks to Cynthia Baker and Thomas Brown.

Contents

Introduction

Here are the results of our new *U.S. Hotels, Resorts & Spas Survey*, covering over 2,100 hotels, resorts, spas and hotel chains across the country, as well as 60 airlines and 11 car rental companies. It shows that the United States currently has the world's premier travel facilities and values.

This *Survey* is based on voting by over 12,300 people. Since the average participant stayed at hotels upwards of 34 nights per year, the *Survey* is based on roughly 420,000 nights at hotels per year – or viewed another way, 1,150 visits per night.

Among the surveyors, there were over 1,500 travel professionals (e.g. travel agents, meeting planners and corporate travel managers) who brought their combined expertise to this project. As far as we are aware, there has never before been such a sharing of knowledge and experience by travel industry experts. We especially thank the following organizations for their support: American Society of Association Executives (ASAE), American Society of Travel Agents (ASTA), Meeting Professionals International (MPI), Professional Convention Management Association (PCMA) and Society of Incentive Travel Executives (SITE).

By surveying large numbers of regular travelers and travel professionals, we think we have achieved a uniquely current and reliable guide. After looking up the hotels, airlines and car rental companies that you know, we hope you will agree. On the assumption that most people want a "quick fix" on the places at which they are considering staying, we have also tried to be concise and to provide handy indexes.

Knowing that the quality of this *Survey* is the direct result of their thoughtful voting and commentary, we sincerely thank each participant. This book is dedicated to all of them; they are its real authors.

We are especially grateful to our editor, David Doty, a writer and editor with many years of experience in travel journalism, and our coordinator, Susan Safronoff, who provided invaluable knowledge of the hotel market. They made the daunting job of surveying the constantly changing travel industry almost seem easy and made sure that the information contained in this guide is as up-to-date as possible. The factual information, including addresses, phone numbers and specifics on facilities, was gathered directly from the hotels, resorts, spas, airlines and car rental companies.

We invite you to be a reviewer in our next *Hotels, Resorts & Spas Survey*. Just send a stamped, self-addressed, business-size envelope marked "Travel" to ZAGAT SURVEY, 4 Columbus Circle, New York, NY 10019. Each participant will receive a free copy of the next *Survey* when it is published.

Your comments, suggestions and even criticism of this *Survey* are also solicited. There is always room for improvement – with your help.

New York, New York   Nina and Tim Zagat
July 8, 1997

Foreword

The US lodging industry is at its highest level of profitability – ever. That picture is quite different from the one we presented in our last edition two years ago, when hotels with large inventories of empty rooms struggled to entice guests with deep discounting. Back then, as a result of the extensive building boom begun in the 1980s, the supply of rooms exceeded demand and travelers found themselves in a buyer's market. For a while.

Recently, occupancy rates have risen. According to press reports early in 1997, occupancy in Honolulu was at 82.5 percent, in New York 81.5 percent, in Chicago 75.8 percent and in New Orleans 73.3 percent. In the high season, it is difficult to find a room in many locales.

While inflation may be generally under control in America, higher hotel occupancy has produced rapidly rising room rates. According to our *Survey,* the most expensive hotels are in New York City, where already steep rates jumped 16 percent between 1995 and 1997, and are continuing to climb as travelers struggle to book rooms well in advance. However, New York's price increase over the past two years is minimal when compared to destinations such as Fort Lauderdale (41 percent), Miami (40 percent) and Tampa Bay (37 percent).

To some extent, these sharply rising prices reflect a correction from the buyer's market of the early '90s. Inevitably, high occupancy rates and increasing demand have restored profitability to the hotel construction industry, and a new cycle of building has begun.

Of course this is good news for the hotel industry, but what does it mean for the traveler? As evidenced by this *Survey,* there is now an unprecedented variety of hotels, resorts, inns and spas to choose from. And despite rising prices and occupancy rates, with a little savvy you can still keep travel costs in line.

The main rule: **Don't be shy – negotiate!** Even if there's less leeway than in the past in cutting front-desk deals, there are usually plenty of rooms to haggle over. Always ask about "special rates" – if rooms are empty, the front desk is often authorized to cut prices. And discounts come in many other ways: corporate rates, society membership rates (such as AARP), even frequent-flier specials. When a rate is tendered by a hotel, always ask the $64-dollar question: "Is this the lowest price you have?" See our Travel Tips on the next two pages for more ways to navigate the current market.

As you will note from reviewing the Travel Tips, the travel industry has gotten pretty clever – perhaps too clever – about maximizing revenues. In the absence of government regulation to require simpler pricing, *you* will have to be equally clever to protect yourself and minimize expenses.

At Zagat Survey we will continue to look for your input on these and other trends. If you enjoy this book and find it useful, we invite you to join our army of surveyors, who will be on the front line of travel-industry transitions over the next few years.

New York, New York
July 8, 1997

David Doty
Susan Safronoff

Travel Tips

HOTELS, RESORTS & SPAS

■ Costs listed in this guide are based on surveyors' estimates for one night in a double room. Since rates are rapidly rising and vary according to many factors, use them as a benchmark and call ahead to confirm current pricing.

■ Call the hotel directly rather than its 800 number so you can make the best deal with people on the scene. Or try hotel discounting services like Quikbook (800-789-9887), which offers competitive rates in Atlanta, Boston, Chicago, Los Angeles, New York, San Francisco and Washington, D.C.

■ Don't be shy – ask about special rates, packages and upgrades. You can still cut deals, especially in city hotels on weekends and weekend destinations during the week. Seasonal places may offer discounts of up to 50 percent off-season.

■ Always ask the bottom-line question: "Is this the lowest price you have?" Reservation agents are not required to quote you the lowest price and they are trained to sell the highest prices first. So keep asking for a lower price; you'll be surprised how much you'll save.

■ When reserving, ask for details on the rooms. Which have the best views? The most sunlight? Do you want to overlook the golf course, the pool – or the parking lot?

■ Ask if the hotel will be undergoing renovations during your stay.

■ If there are empty rooms on the day of your arrival, the front desk is sometimes authorized to slash rates. BUT YOU MUST ASK – they won't volunteer the information. At the least you might get an upgrade.

■ Check carefully what is included in room rates for resorts and spas; often such items as meals and sports facilities are extra. As for hotels, many include continental breakfast and other amenities in rates. Value-added packages (which include benefits such as parking or use of the fitness center) may cost a few dollars more but may be the best bargain.

■ Ask about special features such as business/concierge floors, no-smoking rooms and floors, secretarial help, child care, two-line phones, dataports that accommodate computer modems, etc.

■ Access is important to travelers with special needs. Pose specific questions, not only about the kinds of access but the kinds of rooms outfitted for accessibility. Hypoallergenic items such as pillows and sheets are also often available. Don't be afraid to tell the hotel what you need.

■ If your room is not satisfactory, immediately call the front desk and ask for another. Explain carefully what the problem is. If something needs to be repaired, ask when you can expect it to be fixed.

■ To avoid surprises at check-out, find out about hotel taxes (some cities charge over 10 percent), phone charges (if you have a long-distance calling card, use the room phone only for the local call to your carrier) and fax charges (some hotels charge for receiving a fax).

■ Carefully read any room-service bill to see if a tip has been added before you hand out any more money.

CAR RENTALS

■ Declining certain insurance options may make sense if the coverage is duplicated by your own auto policy or credit cards, but get specifics from your insurance agent or credit-card company first.

■ Take a few minutes to refuel the car yourself because rental agencies charge an outrageous price for gasoline.

■ Except in big East Coast cities, weekend rates are often drastically lower than weekday charges. When you rent in a city, compare downtown vs. airport and suburban rates, which are often lower.

■ When you get to the counter, don't be afraid to ask for a free upgrade, especially on weekends or if you're a regular customer.

■ Return the car on time, since hourly fees are assessed at whopping rates. However, if you return a weekly rental early, you might be charged the higher daily rate.

■ Inquire about taxes, mileage fees, other-city drop-off charges and any other costs that may dramatically boost your bill. Ask about instant-rental programs that allow you to bypass the line at the counter.

AIRLINES

■ Always book ahead, using the best travel agent you can find or by doing your own research. In general, the lowest fares in any market require an advance purchase of 14 to 30 days and a Saturday-night stay.

■ Bargains are sometimes available at the less-traveled local airports of major destinations (e.g. Midway in Chicago or Dulles in Washington, DC).

■ Since airline prices soar and descend as often as the planes themselves, one good way to keep up is to sign on to an Internet page that gives up-to-date flight options and prices. You might try AirWatcher (http://www.webflyer.com) for its FareTracker. Other Web addresses include www.travelocity.com, www.thetrip.com, www.travelbug.com and www.itn.com. A fair number of airlines also offer "Internet-only" discounts, which are usually valid for last minute, weekend travel.

■ When an agent quotes you a price, ask for the rates for other flights that same day. You can sometimes save as much as 50 percent just by leaving or arriving a few hours earlier or later; a change of plane en route may also produce a big savings over the price of a nonstop flight.

■ Join frequent-flier programs and use "affinity" cards. But be aware their "free" miles come with lots of restrictions and some headaches.

■ Ask about airport taxes and any other surcharges for your destination, especially overseas.

■ Watch for discounts even after you have booked. Unless your reservation is nonrefundable, you may be better off taking advantage of last-minute offerings.

Key to Ratings/Symbols

This sample entry identifies the various types of information contained in your Zagat Survey.

(1) Hotel/Resort/Spa Name, Address & Phone Number

(2) Rooms & Suites

(3) ZAGAT Ratings

R	S	D	P	$

		R	S	D	P	$
Tim & Nina's Inn 20R (10S)		▽	18	8	13	16	$80

4 Columbus Circle (8th Ave.), 212-977-6000

☑ Despite dazzling views of Central Park, surveyors split over this "minuscule", "mini-priced" Midtown B&B; fans tout its handy location and kitchenettes; however, critics knock "rooms that are too small to change your mind", a restaurant "outshone by the corner hot-dog stand" and staff that "makes Sing Sing guards look hospitable"; free bedtime cookies and ice cream are a plus, but not the "nonpaying guests they attract."

(4) Surveyors' Commentary

The names of hotels, resorts, inns and spas with the highest overall ratings are printed in **CAPITAL LETTERS**. Addresses and phone numbers are in *italics*.

(2) Rooms & Suites

The number of rooms and suites in each hotel, resort, inn or spa is indicated after its name. For example:

20R (10S)................*the property has 20 one-room accommodations and 10 additional suites, villas, condos or cabins*

(3) ZAGAT Ratings

Rooms, Service, Dining and **Public Facilities** are rated on a scale of **0** to **30**:

R	S	D	P	$

R...........................Rooms
S...........................Service
D...........................Dining
P...........................Public Facilities
$ ....Cost

18	8	13	16	$80

0 - 9	*poor to fair*
10 - 15	*fair to good*
16 - 19	*good to very good*
20 - 25	*very good to excellent*
26 - 30	*extraordinary to perfection*

▽	18	8	13	16	$80

▽ ....,................*Low number of votes*

The **Cost ($)** column shows our surveyors' estimated price of a double room for one night. **N.B.** Rates may vary seasonally and are rising markedly of late.

10

A hotel, resort, inn or spa listed without ratings is either an important **newcomer** or a popular **write-in**. The estimated cost is indicated by the following symbols.

VI .... *below $65*
I .... *$65 – $99*
M .... *$100 – $149*
E .... *$150 – $199*
VE .... *$200 and up*

The **Best Overall** hotels, resorts, inns and spas are listed at the beginning of their respective directory sections. Also listed for major cities and states are **Best Values** (derived by dividing the cost of a room into the hotel's overall rating, i.e. the average of its R, S, D and P ratings).

Airlines, car rental companies and **hotel chains** are also reviewed in the front of the book, along with their top overall and best value listings.

Airlines are rated on their:

C.............................. Comfort
S.............................. Service
T.............................. Timeliness
F.............................. Food
$ .... Cost

Car rental companies are rated on their:

V.............................. Vehicles
S.............................. Service
C.............................. Convenience
A .... Availability
$ .... Cost

(4) Surveyors' Commentary

Surveyors' comments are summarized, with literal comments shown in quotation marks. The following symbols indicate whether responses were mixed or uniform.

◪............................. *mixed*
■............................. *uniform*

Top Ratings*

Top 100 U.S. Hotels

28 Mansion on Turtle Creek/Dallas, TX
Bel-Air/Los Angeles, CA
Windsor Court/New Orleans, LA
Halekulani/Oahu, HI
Ritz-Carlton/San Francisco, CA
Four Seasons/Chicago, IL
Peninsula Beverly Hills/Los Angeles, CA
Four Seasons/New York City, NY
27 Four Seasons/Los Angeles, CA
Little Nell/Aspen, CO
Four Seasons/Boston, MA
Four Seasons/Philadelphia, PA
Ritz-Carlton Buckhead/Atlanta, GA
Ritz-Carlton/Chicago, IL
Ritz-Carlton/Aspen, CO
Ritz-Carlton Huntington/Los Angeles, CA
Marquesa/Key West, FL
Four Seasons/Palm Beach, FL
St. Regis/New York City, NY
Ritz-Carlton/Houston, TX
Four Seasons/Washington, DC
Deer Valley Lodging/Park City, UT
26 Regent Beverly Wilshire/Los Angeles, CA
Ritz-Carlton Pentagon City/Washington, DC
Four Seasons/Newport Beach, CA
Ritz-Carlton/Phoenix, AZ
Mandarin Oriental/San Francisco, CA
Four Seasons Olympic/Seattle, WA
Ritz-Carlton/St. Louis, MO
Four Seasons/Austin, TX
Four Seasons/Atlanta, GA
Grand Bay/Miami, FL
Carlyle/New York City, NY
Ritz-Carlton/Philadelphia, PA
Four Seasons/Houston, TX
Crescent Court/Dallas, TX
Plaza Athénée/New York City, NY
Ritz-Carlton Marina del Rey/Los Angeles, CA
Lowell/New York City, NY
Ritz-Carlton/Boston, MA
Shutters on the Beach/Los Angeles, CA
Ritz-Carlton Atlanta/Atlanta, GA
Ritz-Carlton/Cleveland, OH
25 Hyatt Regency/Beaver Creek, CO
Grand Hyatt/Atlanta, GA
Boston Harbor/Boston, MA
Willard Inter-Continental/Washington, DC
Beverly Hills/Los Angeles, CA
Rittenhouse/Philadelphia, PA
Hana-Maui/Maui, HI

Monaco Hotel/San Francisco, CA
Ritz-Carlton Dearborn/Detroit, MI
Woodmark Hotel/Seattle, WA
L'Auberge de Sedona/Sedona, AZ
Pierre/New York City, NY
Williamsburg Inn/Williamsburg, VA
Campton Place/San Francisco, CA
Ritz-Carlton Tysons Corner/Washington, DC
Ritz-Carlton Washington/Washington, DC
Grand Hotel/Mackinac Island, MI
Harbor Court/Baltimore, MD
Peninsula/New York City, NY
Jefferson/Richmond, VA
Park Hyatt/Washington, DC
Townsend/Detroit, MI
St. James/Red Wing, MN
Mark/New York City, NY
Peabody/Orlando, FL
Pan Pacific/San Francisco, CA
Hotel du Pont/Wilmington, DE
Jerome/Aspen, CO
24 Hay-Adams/Washington, DC
Clift/San Francisco, CA
Nikko Beverly Hills/Los Angeles, CA
Hilton/Short Hills, NJ
Tremont House/Galveston, TX
Adolphus/Dallas, TX
Ritz-Carlton/Kansas City, MO
Jefferson/Washington, DC
Siena Hotel/Raleigh-Durham, NC
Waldorf Towers/New York City, NY
Fairmont/Chicago, IL
Arizona Inn/Tucson, AZ
Stanhope/New York City, NY
Royal Hawaiian/Oahu, HI
Ritz-Carlton/New York City, NY
Disney's BoardWalk Inn/Orlando, FL
Delano/Miami, FL
Westin River North/Chicago, IL
Le Meridien/San Diego, CA
Huntington/San Francisco, CA
Alexis/Seattle, WA
Renaissance Stanford Court/San Francisco, CA
Palace/San Francisco, CA
Argyle/Los Angeles, CA
Sorrento/Seattle, WA
Omni/Houston, TX
Wyndham Checkers/Los Angeles, CA
Park Hyatt/San Francisco, CA
Charleston Place/Charleston, SC

---

* Based on overall ratings derived by averaging ratings for rooms, service, dining and
public facilities; these lists exclude places with low voting (▽).

Top 100 U.S. Resorts

29 Lodge at Koele/Lanai, HI
28 Four Seasons Resort/Maui, HI
 Ritz-Carlton/Naples, FL
 Ritz-Carlton Laguna Niguel/Dana Point, CA
 Boulders Resort/Phoenix, AZ
 Manele Bay/Lanai, HI
 Mauna Lani Bay/Big Island, HI
 Inn at Spanish Bay/Pebble Beach, CA
27 Rancho Valencia Resort/San Diego, CA
 Phoenician/Scottsdale, AZ
 Ritz-Carlton/Amelia Island, FL
 Greenbrier/White Sulphur Springs, WV
 Four Seasons/Dallas, TX
 Ritz-Carlton Rancho Mirage/Palm Sprgs., CA
 Ritz-Carlton/Palm Beach, FL
 Lodge at Pebble Beach/Pebble Bch., CA
 Grand Wailea/Maui, HI
 Cloister/Sea Island, GA
 Ritz-Carlton Kapalua/Maui, HI
 Stein Eriksen Lodge/Park City, UT
 Fisher Island Club/Miami, FL
 Mauna Kea Beach Hotel/Big Island, HI
26 American Club/Kohler, WI
 Ihilani Resort & Spa/Oahu, HI
 Hyatt Regency/Kauai, HI
 Meadowood/St. Helena, CA
 Orchid Mauna Lani/Big Island, HI
 Four Seasons Biltmore/Santa Barbara, CA
 Princeville/Kauai, HI
 Kahala Mandarin Oriental/Oahu, HI
 Scottsdale Princess/Scottsdale, AZ
 Arizona Biltmore/Phoenix, AZ
 Disney's Grand Floridian/Orlando, FL
 Loews Ventana Canyon/Tucson, AZ
 Peaks at Telluride/Telluride, CO
 Hyatt Regency Grand Cypress/Orlando, FL
 Broadmoor/Colorado Springs, CO
 Kea Lani/Maui, HI
 Nemacolin Woods/Farmington, PA
 Lodge at Cordillera/Edwards, CO
 Quail Lodge/Carmel, CA
 Enchantment Resort/Sedona, AZ
 Renaissance Vinoy Resort/Tampa Bay, FL
25 J. Gardiner's Tennis/Carmel Valley, CA
 Turnberry Isle Resort & Club/Miami, FL
 Registry Resort/Naples, FL
 Hyatt Regency Hill Country/San Antonio, TX
 Villas of Grand Cypress/Orlando, FL
 Carmel Valley Ranch/Carmel, CA
 Hyatt Regency/Maui, HI

 Salishan Lodge/Gleneden Beach, OR
 Hyatt Regency/Scottsdale, AZ
 Alyeska Prince/Girdwood, AK
 Kapalua Bay/Maui, HI
 Boca Raton Resort/Boca Raton, FL
 Gardiner's Resort/Phoenix, AZ
 Homestead/Hot Springs, VA
 Lodge at Ventana Canyon/Tucson, AZ
 Disney's Wilderness Lodge/Orlando, FL
 Breakers/Palm Beach, FL
 La Quinta/Palm Springs, CA
 Westin La Paloma/Tucson, AZ
 Hapuna Beach Prince/Big Island, HI
 Pinehurst Resort/Pinehurst, NC
 Wigwam/Phoenix, AZ
24 Biltmore/Miami, FL
 Sanderling Inn/Duck, NC
 El Conquistador/Fajardo, PR
 Sonnenalp Resort/Vail, CO
 Disney's Yacht Club Resort/Orlando, FL
 Renaissance/Maui, HI
 Marriott's Desert Springs/Palm Springs, CA
 Inn & Club/Ponte Vedra Beach, FL
 Westin Mission Hills/Palm Springs, CA
 Sun Mountain Lodge/Winthrop, WA
 Rancho Bernardo Inn/San Diego, CA
 Renaissance Esmeralda/Palm Springs, CA
 Barton Creek/Austin, TX
 Loews Coronado Bay/San Diego, CA
 Black Butte Ranch/Black Butte, OR
 L'Auberge Del Mar/San Diego, CA
 Disney's Old Key West/Orlando, FL
 Sundance Resort/Provo, UT
 Disney's Beach Club Resort/Orlando, FL
 Hilton Waikoloa Village/Big Island, HI
 Grove Park Inn/Asheville, NC
 Jekyll Island Club/Jekyll Island, GA
 Marriott/Kauai, HI
 Tides Inn/Irvington, VA
 Woodstock Inn/Woodstock, VT
 Westin/Maui, HI
 Balsams Grand/Dixville Notch, NH
 Sea Pines Resort/Hilton Head, SC
 Black Point Inn/Scarborough, ME
 Resort at Longboat Key/Longboat Key, FL
 Marriott's Grand/Point Clear, AL
 Sun Valley Resort/Sun Valley, ID
 Hyatt Grand Champions/Palm Springs, CA
 Sheraton Grande Torrey Pines/San Diego, CA
23 La Casa del Zorro/Borrego Springs, CA

Top 50 U.S. Inns & B&Bs

29 Twin Farms/Barnard, VT
Point/Saranac Lake, NY
28 Château du Sureau/Oakhurst, CA
Inn at Blackberry Farm/Walland, TN
27 Post Ranch Inn/Big Sur, CA
Auberge du Soleil/Rutherford, CA
Inn at Little Washington/Washington, VA
Fearrington House/Pittsboro, NC
Mayflower Inn/Washington, CT
Blantyre/Lenox, MA
Sherman House/San Francisco, CA
Keswick Hall/Keswick, VA
Horned Dorset Primavera/Rincon, PR
Little Palm/Little Torch Key, FL
26 Ventana Inn/Big Sur, CA
Wauwinet/Nantucket, MA
Stonepine Resort/Carmel Valley, CA
Inn at Perry Cabin/St. Michaels, MD
Highlands Inn/Carmel, CA
San Ysidro Ranch/Montecito, CA
Inn of the Anasazi/Santa Fe, NM
Canyon Villa B&B/Sedona, AZ
Inn at Sawmill Farm/West Dover, VT
Monmouth Plantation/Natchez, MS
Inn at Shelburne Farms/Shelburne, VT

Inn on Mt. Ada/Avalon, CA
25 Greystone Inn/Lake Toxaway, NC
Timberhill Ranch/Cazadero, CA
Tu Tu'Tun Lodge/Gold Beach, OR
Goldener Hirsch/Park City, UT
Charlotte Inn/Martha's Vineyard, MA
White Barn Inn/Kennebunkport, ME
Salish Lodge/Snoqualmie, WA
Wheatleigh/Lenox, MA
Albion River Inn/Albion, CA
Richmond Hill Inn/Asheville, NC
Evermay on-the-Delaware/Erwinna, PA
Gastonian/Savannah, GA
24 Morrison House/Alexandria, VA*
Jenny Lake Lodge/Moran, WY
Inn at National Hall/Westport, CT
Rhett House/Beaufort, SC
Norumbega Inn/Camden, ME
Ballastone Inn/Savannah, GA
Sardy House/Aspen, CO
1842 Inn/Macon, GA
Château Elan/Braselton, GA
Rose Inn/Ithaca, NY
Mainstay Inn/Cape May, NJ
Rusty Parrot Lodge/Jackson, WY

Top 10 U.S. Spas

28 Golden Door/ Escondido, CA
26 Canyon Ranch/Tucson, AZ
Canyon Ranch/Lenox, MA
Givenchy/Palm Springs, CA
25 Spa Internazionale/Fisher Island, FL

Spa at Doral/Miami, FL
24 Rancho La Puerta/Baja, Mexico
Sonoma Mission Inn/Sonoma, CA
23 La Costa Spa/Carlsbad, CA
22 Lake Austin Spa Resort/Austin, TX

---

* Listed in Washington, DC section.

Important 800 Numbers

AIRLINES

Aer Lingus	223-6537
Aero California	237-6225
Aeroflot	995-5555
Aeromexico	237-6639
Air Canada	776-3000
Air France	237-2747
Air India	255-3191
Air New Zealand	262-1234
Alaska Airlines	426-0333
Alitalia	223-5730
Aloha Airlines	367-5250
American	433-7300
America West	235-9292
ANA	235-9262
Ansett Australia	888-442-9626
Asiana Airlines	227-4262
Austrian Airlines	843-0002
Avianca	284-2622
British Airways	247-9297
BWIA	538-2942
Carnival Airlines	437-2110
Cathay Pacific	233-2742
China Airlines	227-5118
Continental	525-0280
Delta	221-1212
El Al	223-6700
Finnair	950-5000
Garuda Indonesia	342-7832
Hawaiian Airlines	367-5320
Iberia	772-4642
Icelandair	223-5500
Japan Airlines (JAL)	525-3663
Kiwi International	538-5494
KLM Royal Dutch	374-7747
Korean Air	438-5000
Lufthansa	645-3880
Mexicana Airlines	531-7921
Midway Airlines	446-4392
Midwest Express	452-2022
Northwest Airlines	225-2525
Olympic	223-1226
Philippine Airlines	435-9725
Qantas	227-4500
Reno Air	736-6247
Royal Jordanian	758-6878
Sabena	955-2000
SAS	221-2350
Singapore Airlines	742-3333
South African Airways	722-9675
Southwest Airlines	435-9792
Swissair	221-4750
TAP Air Portugal	221-7370
Thai Airways	426-5204
Tower Air	348-6937
Turkish Airlines	874-8875
TWA	221-2000
United	241-6522
US Airways	428-4322
Valujet	825-8538
Varig	468-2744
Virgin Atlantic	862-8621

RAILROADS

Amtrak	872-7245

BUS LINES

Bonanza	556-3815
Greyhound/Trailways	231-2222

CAR RENTAL

Alamo	327-9633
Avis	331-1212
Budget	527-0700
Dollar	800-4000
Enterprise	325-8007
Hertz	654-3131
National	227-7368
Payless	729-5377
Rent-A-Wreck	535-1391
Thrifty	367-2277
U-Save	272-8728
Value	327-2501

HOTEL CHAINS

Adam's Mark	444-2326
Best Western	528-1234
Budgetel	428-3438
Clarion	252-7466
Comfort Inns	228-5150
Courtyard by Marriott	321-2211
Crown Sterling Suites	433-4600
Days Inn	325-2525
Doubletree	222-TREE
Econo Lodge	446-6900
Embassy Suites	362-2779
Fairfield Inns	228-2800
Fairmont	527-4727
Four Seasons	332-3442
Hampton Inn	426-7866
Harvey Hotels	922-9222
Hilton	445-8667
Holiday Inn	465-4329
Homewood Suites	225-5466
Howard Johnson	446-4656
Hyatt	233-1234
Inter-Continental	327-0200
La Quinta Inns	531-5900
Leading Hotels**	223-6800
Loews Hotels	235-6397
Marriott	228-9290
Motel 6	466-8356
Omni	843-6664
Preferred Hotels**	323-7500
Quality Inns	228-5151
Radisson	333-3333
Ramada	272-6232
Red Lion Hotels & Inns	547-8010
Red Roof Inns	843-7663
Relais & Châteaux**	212-856-0115*
Renaissance	468-3571
Residence Inns	331-3131
Ritz-Carlton	241-3333
Sheraton	325-3535
Small Luxury Hotels**	525-4800
Sonesta	766-3782
Super 8	800-8000
Travelodge/Thriftlodge	578-7878
Westin	228-3000
Wyndham	822-4200

---

* Not a toll-free number.
** Indicates a marketing/reservations service, rather than a chain.

Alphabetical Directory

Airlines

DOMESTIC AIRLINES

BEST OVERALL	BEST VALUES
24 Midwest Express	Midwest Express
21 Alaska Airlines	Alaska Airlines
17 American	Kiwi International
United	Reno Air
Delta	Midway Airlines
Kiwi International	Southwest Airlines
16 Midway Airlines	American
Reno Air	United
Northwest Airlines	Delta
Aloha Airlines	Aloha Airlines

INTERNATIONAL AIRLINES

BEST OVERALL	BEST VALUES
27 Singapore Airlines	Singapore Airlines
25 Cathay Pacific	Cathay Pacific
Swissair	Virgin Atlantic
24 Japan Airlines	Thai
Thai	Swissair
ANA	Air New Zealand
Qantas	Asiana
23 Air New Zealand	Qantas
SAS	ANA
Virgin Atlantic	Japan Airlines

C = Comfort, S = Service, T = Timeliness, F = Food, $ = Cost.

C	S	T	F	$

Aer Lingus
(800) 223-6537

C	S	T	F	$
20	22	21	16	M

■ Experience "a touch of Ireland as soon as you board" this "caring, experienced" airline that surveyors call a "wonderful way to start a trip" to the "old sod"; they report that it offers "high quality" and "courteous" service at a "moderate price", and would like it still better but for its leprechaun-size "small seats."

Aero California
(800) 237-6225

C	S	T	F	$
13	14	15	10	I

☑ Flying from Los Angeles and Tucson to Mexico's resort cities, this carrier pleases budget-minded sun-seekers with reasonable prices, but even admirers feel compelled to qualify their praise: "a nice friendly little airline – when they actually show up"; critics gripe about "frequent overbookings and poor, unresponsive service."

Aeroflot
(800) 995-5555

C	S	T	F	$
5	5	7	4	M

■ Surveyors may not enjoy flying this "nightmare" of an airline (our lowest-rated), but they love bashing it: "quicker than Kevorkian", "equipment older than Methuselah", "a basket of apples for food", "water as the beverage – if they don't run out" and "one community towel in the bathroom"; still, it's the only way to go in Russia.

Aeromexico
(800) 237-6639

C	S	T	F	$
14	15	14	12	M

☑ Admirers of this Mexican carrier applaud "surprisingly good service" and "free drinks" that can create a "party" atmosphere; but critics say "they give you the liquor so you don't care" about "cramped" seating and a "we-have-a-schedule-but-so-what?" attitude; still, the "price is right."

Air Canada
(800) 776-3000

C	S	T	F	$
19	20	20	16	M

■ "No frills, no problems" are what you can expect from this "dependable", "no-nonsense" carrier offering "quick, on-time flights" to and from Canada; most find it "organized and friendly", with "convenient" scheduling, "roomy" seats and "edible" food.

C S T F $

Air France
(800) 237-2747

21 21 21 22 E

■ "The French have style", and it shows in "ooh-la-la food" and "civilized service" that make for "classy", comfy flying; a few Francophobes call it "snooty" and as "efficient as the French government", but most shout "vive la différence", pronouncing it "about as good as it gets five miles high."

Air India
(800) 255-3191

12 13 11 13 M

☑ Some business and first-class passengers may consider this Indian carrier a "decent" performer, but as ratings attest, it doesn't curry favor with everyone: "adequate in every way", "overcrowded", "late", "chaos."

Air New Zealand
(800) 262-1234

23 25 24 21 M

■ "Comfort is a lambswool-covered seat" report business travelers, and even those in economy enjoy "civilized" conditions aboard this airline that's "like the country it represents: clean, efficient, friendly"; "phenomenal service" by some of "the best flight attendants anywhere" is cheered as is "delicious food", but the coach seating may be "uncomfortable" for long hauls to and from Auckland.

Alaska Airlines
(800) 426-0333

21 23 23 18 M

■ "The other US airlines are lucky these guys don't fly everywhere" is a typical rave for this West Coast regional carrier "that could teach the big boys something", especially when it comes to "people-oriented service": "clean planes", "more room between seats" and "far above average" food are more reasons why it's a "damn good airline."

Alitalia
(800) 223-5730

17 17 16 17 M

☑ Depending on whom you ask, this is either "*la bella Italia*" or an "Italian cattle car"; while some praise "*molto bene*" service, "fine food" and "comfortable seating", others give it the boot for "too many smokers", "chaotic boarding" and a "nonchalant attitude toward rules", not to mention "random annoying strikes – their specialty."

Aloha Airlines
(800) 367-5250

15 17 20 11 I

☑ A "quick, cheap way to island-hop" thanks to "an efficient, frequent schedule" and "good" if "basic" service ("hello and goodbye, that's about it"); while it's not exactly paradise on this "volume-oriented", often "cramped, crowded" Hawaiian puddle jumper, Aloha clearly "serves a purpose" and surely "beats swimming."

American
(800) 433-7300

18 19 19 14 M

☑ "Consistent performance" throughout its "large route system", "efficient" service and a "super frequent-flier program" have loyalists pledging allegiance to this "class act", rated for the fourth time in a row as the best major US airline; critics counter that "penny-pinching" "cutbacks in food and on-board services are obvious" and wonder "are the seats getting smaller?"

America West
(800) 235-9292

16 17 17 12 I

☑ "Go [America] West, young man" is the rallying cry for fans of this "nice, clean" regional airline praised for its "inexpensive flight options", "good connections" and "young, upbeat staff"; detractors irritated by "cramped seats" ("leave your legs at home") and "peanuts and pop" cuisine dub it "America Worst", but most still rank it as one of "the best of the cheapies."

ANA
(800) 235-9262

24 25 24 21 E

■ "Everything about this airline is top quality" say devotees who deem All Nippon Airways "the only way to go to Japan", with nonstop flights from NYC, LA and DC; "superior food and wine", comfortable seating and "amazing but not doting service" by "attendants who whisper to passengers" make for the "best long flights ever"; some surveyors "prefer their first class to heaven – or maybe they're the same."

Ansett Australia
(888) 442-9626

20 21 22 17 M

■ A "favorite domestic down under" that's a "great way to get around Australia" (and New Zealand) thanks to "unbelievably friendly, perky staff", "clean aircraft", "comfortable seats" and "good food"; it's an exemplar of an "efficient", "on-time" operation.

Asiana Airlines
(800) 227-4262

23 | 23 | 22 | 21 | M

■ "Good competition" for other carriers on Far East routes, offering "on-time" performance, "excellent service" and "lots of food and drink" on flights linking Seoul with LA, SF, NYC, Detroit, Seattle and Honolulu; some think there's too much smoking, but US airlines might "take some lessons" here.

Austrian Airlines
(800) 843-0002

20 | 22 | 22 | 20 | M

◪ Loyalists yodel about the "super food and service" as well as the "very comfortable" business class where "gifts keep coming"; "solid" and "dependable", it's especially "good for short European hops", but to naysayers it's "an old airline with old ideas" and "uninspired in all departments."

Avianca
(800) 284-2622

17 | 17 | 17 | 15 | M

◪ Its ratings have improved since our last *Survey*, but according to irate clock-watchers this Colombian carrier is "never on time"; still "if you have to fly to Colombia" it will get you to Bogotá from NYC, LA and Miami.

British Airways
(800) 247-9297

22 | 23 | 23 | 19 | M

■ "Brittania still rules on the NYC-London route" say devotees of this British carrier; "regal treatment" even "for the untitled", "Anglo punctuality" and "good food" add up to "top-drawer" flying, made even better by "sensational" first-class sleeper seats; aside from a few jabs at "snippy service" and "no legroom", most agree "the Queen would be proud."

Bwia
(800) 538-2942

15 | 16 | 13 | 13 | M

◪ The crew's "West Indian charm" and the fact that they take you "to paradise" is enough to put some fliers in a festive mood; however, others complain that "service has gone downhill" and suggest that the name stands for "but will it arrive?"

Carnival Airlines
(800) 437-2110

13 | 14 | 14 | 11 | I

◪ Though "tight seating" is a common complaint, this carrier principally plying the Northeast/Florida/Nassau/Puerto Rico corridor is "convenient and cheap"; others claim "you get what you pay for", citing "shabby planes", "poor service" and "bad on-time" performance.

CATHAY PACIFIC
(800) 233-2742

25 | 26 | 24 | 24 | E

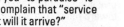

■ "You have not flown a first-class airline until you've flown Cathay" is how enthusiasts (i.e. just about everyone) see it; its completely nonsmoking flights between Hong Kong and NYC (one stop in Vancouver) and LA (nonstop) with "wondrous service", "roomy" seating and "outstanding food" "make a long flight over the Pacific pass quickly."

Continental
(800) 525-0280

15 | 16 | 16 | 11 | M

◪ This airline produces a true "Continental divide" among its passengers: fans find it "much improved" and "getting better", with "affordable" fares, "excellent" business and first-class service and "the best frequent-flier program"; but to foes it's "the Greyhound of air travel" – "like all the big [airlines] – mixed pleasure and pain."

Delta
(800) 221-1212

18 | 19 | 18 | 13 | M

◪ Judging from widely mixed comments, Delta is Greek to most surveyors: "Southern hospitality" vs. "understaffed and rushed", "above-average food" vs. "bring a doggy bag", "solid" vs. "spotty"; "cost-cutting has perhaps gone too far", resulting in "falling standards"; still, it's "one of the best" domestics and "gets it right more often than not."

El Al
(800) 223-6700

17 | 18 | 19 | 15 | M

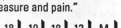

■ "Best security in the sky" is the unanimous opinion on this Israeli airline, and despite complaints that it's "always changing schedules" and "never on time", most don't mind because they've "never felt safer"; once airborne, however, some object to being "crammed in like gefilte fish" and shout "oy vey" about the service and food.

Airlines

	C	S	T	F	$

Finnair
(800) 950-5000

22 | 24 | 23 | 20 | M

■ "A great introduction to a fascinating country" is the consensus on this "first-class" Finnish airline that links Helsinki with NYC and SF; "good food" (who else would offer a "reindeer meat appetizer"?) and "excellent", "personable" service are strong points, though some charge there's not enough lap land.

Garuda Indonesia
(800) 342-7832

15 | 17 | 15 | 14 | M

◪ Some passengers enjoy "unexpectedly delightful" flights aboard this Indonesian airline, however, modest ratings are more in line with those who say it "leaves a lot to be desired"; the discrepancy may be partly explained by reports that "international is ok" (LA and Honolulu are its US gateways). but flights within Indonesia may be less impressive.

Hawaiian Airlines
(800) 367-5320

15 | 17 | 18 | 12 | I

◪ "A model of efficiency on interisland flights", Hawaiian also flies to and from the mainland; "good schedules", "friendly staff" and "reasonable prices" get most fliers into the aloha spirit; critics claim that "behind the bright Polynesian-style paint job, it's just another airline."

Iberia
(800) 772-4642

16 | 16 | 15 | 15 | M

▣ A few defenders cite "polite" crew and "decent food", but most voters are less bullish about Spain's national airline; "poor service and connections" and "tight seating" irk critics, as do planes that resemble "flying smoke chambers"; there are also complaints that it's "often late", but "so is most of the country."

Icelandair
(800) 223-5500

16 | 19 | 18 | 17 | I

■ One of "the best ways to Europe" (from Baltimore, Boston, NYC, Orlando and Ft. Lauderdale) for those looking for "excellent economy travel"; "good food", "clean" planes and "efficient" service make transatlantic flights "most pleasant", especially for those who "love the stopover" in Reykjavík.

Japan Airlines (JAL)
(800) 525-3663

24 | 26 | 24 | 23 | E

■ The rising sun shines on this "wonderful" if pricey airline with "very gracious service", "excellent food" and even "shiatsu massage in first class" that makes it "tops for long flights"; but several caution "you'd better fly first or business class unless you're tiny" and wish they'd "get rid of smokers."

Kiwi International
(800) 538-5494

17 | 18 | 17 | 15 | I

◪ Budget-minded fliers appreciate the "cheap" rates and "friendly, upbeat staff" on this "no-frills" carrier that, despite its name, flies only as far as Florida, PR and Chicago from its Newark hub; while it's a "pleasant surprise" and "new favorite" to some, other travelers say Kiwi, a "flightless bird", is an apt appellation.

KLM Royal Dutch
(800) 374-7747

22 | 23 | 23 | 20 | M

■ For a "Dutch treat", take advantage of this "reliable", "well-run" operation where the "gracious staff" "makes you feel like first class in economy" and where you'll land at the "best airport" (Schiphol) with its "great system of connections"; a minority worries that "quality is diminishing" since partnering with Northwest.

Korean Air
(800) 438-5000

19 | 20 | 20 | 18 | M

◪ Admirers say the "excellent nonstop flights" to Seoul are a good deal due to "fine service" by a "hardworking staff" that "makes the long trip very comfortable"; despite a few gripes, most agree this carrier is "decent to the Far East" "on a budget."

Lufthansa
(800) 645-3880

22 | 23 | 24 | 20 | E

■ "Like a well-oiled machine", Lufthansa enjoys near universal praise for "timeliness", "cool" but "efficient" service, "clean" cabins and "comfortable seats" (although a few claim Airbus seating is "cramped"); it's a "professional and confidence-inspiring" airline.

	C	S	T	F	$

Mexicana Airlines
(800) 531-7921

| 14 | 15 | 14 | 13 | M |

☑ Though "it gets you to Mexico" "cheaply" and the "free beer" ensures a "festive atmosphere", comments such as "sloppy service", "lack of security in Mexico", "terrible food" crop up concerning this south-of-the-border alternative.

Midway Airlines
(800) 446-4392

| 17 | 18 | 18 | 13 | I |

■ This "humble but lovable underdog" is considered one of "the best bargains around" for its "leather seats in coach", "good legroom", "friendly service" and "nice, new" aircraft; but "limited destinations" may mean "you'll save money but lose patience."

MIDWEST EXPRESS
(800) 452-2022

| 26 | 25 | 24 | 23 | M |

■ Adulation for the *Survey*'s highest-rated US airline is near unanimous as devotees of this democratic, single-class carrier tout "first-class seating", "first-class service" and "first-class food" at "coach prices"; "they're reinventing airline travel" with "two-by-two leather seating", "on-time travel" and "china and champagne service"; fans sum it up as "the only domestic airline that deserves loyalty."

Northwest Airlines
(800) 225-2525

| 16 | 17 | 17 | 13 | M |

☑ Despite "improvements" and the "best economy flights" to Asia, "bad choices of hub cities" (Detroit and Minneapolis), "aging equipment" and "surly" staff cause complaints; while a few note "first class can be great", coach is "just a bus ride."

Olympic
(800) 223-1226

| 12 | 12 | 12 | 12 | M |

■ This "disorganized", "bare-bones" Greek carrier earns brass medals for "discomfort", "horrible service", "nasty personnel" and "terrible food"; its motto could be "sit down, shut up and hang on"; P.S. "smoking is required."

Philippine Airlines
(800) 435-9725

| 18 | 20 | 15 | 16 | M |

☑ Fans flying to Manila enjoy being pampered by the "pleasant, competent" staff that provides "surprisingly good service and food"; there are "no frills" but the consensus is that "decent prices" and "comfortable seats" make the long flight enjoyable.

Qantas
(800) 227-4500

| 24 | 25 | 24 | 22 | M |

■ It's "the best way to fly Down Under" according to blissful travelers who report that Qantas "really distinguishes itself" by offering "the best customer service", "excellent food", "comfortable seats" and "good solid performance" in both first class and economy; it turns "long-distance flight into an art form."

Reno Air
(800) 736-6247

| 17 | 18 | 19 | 11 | I |

☑ "The price is right and so is the service" at this "good small airline" – it's "reliable" and "pleasant" for "short, local hops" on the West Coast; critics, a minority, zoom in on "seats for Lilliputians" and "run-down aircraft."

Royal Jordanian
(800) 223-0470

| 16 | 16 | 16 | 14 | M |

☑ Opinions vary on this Jordan-based airline: fans cite "inexpensive flights" and the "best security" making it "an excellent choice for Mideast travel"; foes fault "too many connections" and service that's "not exactly the world's friendliest."

Sabena
(800) 955-2000

| 18 | 19 | 19 | 17 | M |

☑ Surveyors say Belgium's national airline waffles between "friendly service" vs. "rudeness" and "good food" vs. "like-army" rations; most agree that "Brussels is a good hub" and overall this carrier is "clean", "comfortable" and "decent."

SAS
(800) 221-2350

| 23 | 24 | 24 | 22 | M |

■ Here's "an airline one can love" because of "special touches" that include "roomy" "sleeper seats" with "comfort even in coach", "wonderful service" that's also "great for kids" and "very good food and wine"; many tout this "class act" as the only way to fly to Scandinavia.

	C	S	T	F	$

SINGAPORE AIRLINES
(800) 742-3333

	27	28	26	26	E

■ Top-rated again in our *Survey*, "everybody's favorite" "best-in-the-world" airline "sets the standard" with riders raving over "perfection from security to accommodations"; passengers report "marvelous food", attendants who "act like they are glad you're flying" and an economy class that's "equal or superior to US carriers' first class"; some simply "don't want to get off the plane."

South African Airways
(800) 722-9675

	21	23	22	20	M

■ "All the expected amenities are present" on this "well-run", "dependable" airline making the long flight to Johannesburg "comfortable" and "pleasant" for all, with "great food and wines" and "good service even in the back of the plane"; some claim "first class is an experience of a lifetime."

Southwest Airlines
(800) 435-9792

	14	18	22	8	I

☑ "What they do, they do so well", and what they do is "cheap fares" ("buddy fares are a great value") and "on-time service"; but they also do "zip amenities" and "no assigned seats" so be ready for "stampedes" and minimal snacks on this "Greyhound of the air."

SWISSAIR
(800) 221-4750

	25	26	26	24	E

■ "Like clockwork", this "reliable and professional" airline, again the *Survey*'s top-rated European carrier, "feels solid, safe and secure" to travelers who enjoy "comfortable" if "slightly chilly" Swiss hospitality and "great food" all the way to Zurich, where you'll arrive "on-time" "to the nanosecond."

TAP Air Portugal
(800) 221-7370

	17	18	17	16	M

☑ While "inexpensive", Portugal's national airline "could be better organized", seating is "cramped unless in first class" and service is variable; but a minority reports "warm crew, good flight" and perhaps more tellingly: "we love Portugal so all is forgiven."

Thai Airways
(800) 426-5204

	24	26	23	23	M

■ A "lower-cost alternative to Singapore Airlines", this "consistently great" carrier boasts "excellent" "on-time international and domestic" flights and one of the "most caring staffs aloft", offering "first-class food, hot towels and big smiles."

Tower Air
(800) 348-6937

	11	11	11	9	I

■ "Cheap and they put you through the wringer" sums up surveyor scorn for "the world's noisiest airline", where "cancellations" and "delays", "cramped cabins", "old planes", "poor quality food" and "overworked staff" are all risks; "business class is a bargain" and the only way to fly this airline.

Turkish Airlines
(800) 874-8875

	16	17	17	14	M

☑ While ratings are hardly stellar, travelers say this airline is "really a pleasant surprise"; once past the "disorganized check-in and boarding" you'll find "clean cabins", "big tourist-class seats", "wonderful food" and "good service"; dissenters cite "rickety", "shabby" planes on domestic runs and "poor ventilation."

TWA
(800) 221-2000

	17	16	15	12	M

☑ Partisans feel that TWA is "trying hard to rebuild" by offering the "best comfort" with "fantastic legroom" ("the larger seat pitch is really true"), "a great frequent-flier program" and "fairly attentive service" by the employee-owner staff; but trying isn't the same as succeeding: "never leaves on time", "cranky attendants", "horrible food."

United
(800) 241-6522

	18	18	18	14	M

☑ Many still consider this "basic US airline" "reliable" for "great routes", "good scheduling" and the "best frequent-flier program"; but to the less impressed, "the friendly skies have given way to the balance sheet" – "cutbacks in onboard services are obvious" and "cramped seating" in coach draws yelps; still, it's "always good but not great" unless you "upgrade."

US Airways
14 | 15 | 15 | 11 | M

(800) 428-4322

☑ "Everywhere in the East" and "seeming to go places no other airline does", US Airways is "like the common cold, unavoidable, but tolerable"; the "quick", "no-frills shuttles are reliable", but "erratic" service, "canceled flights", "long delays" and "poor" food on longer flights "could improve"; laid-back passengers like the "generous frequent-flier" program and "cheap flights that get you there", even if seemingly "never on time."

Valujet
10 | 11 | 11 | 6 | I

(800) 825-8538

☑ This "good-price" airline is back and flying out of its Atlanta hub, providing loyalists a "much-needed discount airline" with "upbeat" service; still, many are "nervous to fly" these "cattle cars of the sky" citing "prehistoric planes" and "safety record" concerns.

Varig
20 | 20 | 18 | 18 | M

(800) 468-2744

■ It's "Brazil from the time you step aboard" this "sweet and functional" "choice to South America" whose "employees seem to genuinely enjoy serving"; "very comfortable, even in economy" say passengers who report "wonderful service", "dependable timetables", "good food" and "movie after movie" on the road to Rio.

Virgin Atlantic
23 | 25 | 23 | 21 | M

800-862-8621

■ Studio 54 in the sky" is how many view the "hip", "youthful" "alternative to British Airways", where "they pamper you" "even in coach" (and "upper class is so good it's scary"); respondents "love the personalized movie screens", "headphones, slippers and eyeshades you can keep" and, most of all, "the cheap prices to London."

Car Rental Companies

BEST OVERALL
- *23* Hertz
- *22* Avis
- *20* National
- *18* Budget
- *17* Enterprise

BEST VALUES
- Hertz
- Avis
- National
- Enterprise
- Budget

**V = Vehicles, S = Service, C = Convenience,
A = Availability, $ = Cost.**

V	S	C	A	$

Alamo
(800) 327-9633

18	15	14	17	I

☑ "Good prices on tiny cars" plus airline mileage deals please renters, who rate this a "friendly", "good value" operation; but disgruntled drivers cite "excruciating waits", "too far" off-airport "locations" and "bait and switch" tactics by "hard sell" counter clerks who "push upgrades and insurance" on cars that "could be cleaner"; ergo, some would "rather not remember the Alamo."

Avis
(800) 331-1212

23	21	23	21	M

■ Though no longer employee owned, its "gracious staff" still provides "pain-free check-in and fast, easy return" at "always convenient" sites; "solid, reliable" and "fabulously adequate", this outfit with its GM cars "tries hard to be No. 1", but rolls on as the perennial No. 2 in our *Survey*.

Budget
(800) 527-0700

20	17	18	18	M

☑ "Clean vehicles", "fast, efficient service", a "good selection of cars" (mostly Ford and Mercury) and numerous airport locations suit many, but not all, surveyors: "inconvenient pick-up/drop-off locations", "rates do not reflect the name", "all budget, no value"; still, its fans like Budget "better than the big guys."

Dollar
(800) 800-4000

18	16	16	17	I

☑ "You get what you pay for – a dollar's worth of service and value" say those who bemoan "long waits" for "cars that are often not cleaned" at sites that are "difficult to find"; but experience "varies", with "excellent rates" ("best value" on Chryslers) causing many to opt for this "low-price competitor" that has 270 locations, 100 of them on-airport.

Enterprise
(800) 325-8007

18	18	16	17	I

☑ "Home pick-up and drop-off service is a big plus" for this "consumer-friendly" company that's "good with insurance loaners" and "repair shop situations"; it "fills a need", but perhaps too specifically, as some suggest it's "strictly for when your car is in the shop" – this, despite having the largest fleet and number of locations (none airport) and trailing only Hertz in revenues.

Hertz
(800) 654-3131

24	22	24	22	E

■ The "king of the car-rental companies" reigns for the fourth *Survey* in a row as voters proclaim its "No. 1 position is well deserved"; "clean cars", "fast service" at "convenient pick-up/drop-off sites" (1,200 in the US) paired with the "#1 Club Gold" make it the frequent traveler's dream"; "they set the standard" and are "worth the cost."

National
(800) 227-7368

22	20	20	20	M

☑ "Best if you're in the Emerald Club" say members who "love the option of picking your own car on the lot" at the *Survey*'s No. 3–rated firm's 950 locations (more than 500 on-airport); nonmembers also enjoy "good prices and good service", but assert that a "better choice of cars is needed", especially after a "long wait on a long check-in line."

Payless
(800) 729-5377

17	15	14	16	I

■ "No thanks" say regretful renters who report that "you don't pay as 'less' as you used to" at this "inconvenient" (65 US, 23 international locations) franchise operator; others come upon "cars in poor condition" and say "the discount is not worth the aggravation."

Car Rental Companies

V S C A $

Rent-A-Wreck
10 13 10 13 I

(800) 535-1391

■ "The name says it all", but "at least they're honest"; "drivers with no ego and no vanity" can rent "four wheels and an engine" at this no-frills company; seekers of the better things in life advise: "do yourself a favor – pay the extra buck and get a real car."

Thrifty
18 16 14 16 I

(800) 367-2277

☑ "Bargain hunters who are happy to get what they pay for" will be happy here; however, other folks question the thrift of "long, long lines" at "inconvenient locations" and suggest that "cheap" may mean "not dependable."

Value
18 14 14 16 I

(800) 327-2501

☑ This company "deserves credit" for its "rent by the hour concept that works" and for "good cars [many Mitsubishis] at good value"; but those on tight schedules warn about "glacial service" due to "no express check-in/check-out" at "not-convenient locations."

Hotel Chains*

R	S	D	P	$

Adam's Mark
(800) 444-2326

18	18	17	17	$130

☑ "They vary", which may explain differing views of this chain of 14 "centrally located" hotels; some hit the mark with "lovely public facilities", "consistent" restaurants, "good business atmosphere" and "friendly staff"; others are judged "off the mark": "standard rooms" "are a big disappointment" and there's "always a problem and never anyone who seems to care"; ratings support those who find it generally "solid", though better quality control might help this "poor man's Hyatt."

Best Western
(800) 528-1234

15	14	11	12	$85

☑ The 3,400 "clean", "straightforward" albeit "charmless" independently owned and operated Best Westerns are "a good value", but with so many franchisees it's "a crapshoot – some are lovely, others atrocious"; even if "you can't rely on name alone", most agree that "the meat-and-potatoes of motels" is "functional" and "inexpensive."

Budgetel
(800) 428-3438

14	12	8	10	$58

☑ "Clean" but "spartan" rooms that "seem built out of cardboard" "serve the purpose, nothing more", but many find them "ideal for quick stops while driving distances"; despite "no frills" and "no service", the 140 "reasonable" Eastern and Midwestern sites get nods for "high security" ("lots of desk personnel" and "no outside entry") and free "breakfast delivered to your door."

Clarion
(800) 252-7466

16	15	13	13	$94

☑ While "nothing special", the nearly 100 Clarion hotels offer "pleasant", "adequate" rooms that are "affordable" for "a night in transit", some featuring on-premises restaurants and complimentary breakfasts; enthusiasts consider it a "best value in comfort and price" – just be prepared for "no extras" and "indifferent service."

Comfort Inn
(800) 228-5150

15	15	11	12	$70

■ "Clean", "convenient" and "cheap" sum up the virtues of the US' fifth largest lodging chain (with 1,600 locations worldwide) that offers "a basic room for a good price", with "discounts for older travelers", "good value for family trips", swimming pools and complimentary breakfast; "you can count on a decent minimum standard" at this budget chain that's among the more "dependable."

Courtyard by Marriott
(800) 321-2211

19	18	14	16	$100

■ The "modern", "clean" Courtyard chain (250 properties) is a "reliable friend for the traveler", offering "polite, well-trained staff" and "well-maintained" accommodations that work equally well "for families and business folk alike" (breakfast buffets, minigyms with pools and large rooms with work desks are among the amenities at most locations); it's a "great alternative to fancy hotels", especially if you can take advantage of the frequent stay programs.

---

* Because most chains have franchises, their operations are not necessarily uniform.
**A marketing/reservations group, not a chain.

Hotel Chains

	R	S	D	P	$

Days Inn
(800) 329-7466

☑ A much-cited "lack of quality control" means "you never know what you'll get" at the more than 1,700 "cheap places to sleep" offered by this "bare-bones" chain; while "ubiquitous" and "adequate", here's more proof that "you get what you pay for."

R 12 | S 12 | D 9 | P 10 | $ $69

Doubletree Hotels and Guest Suites
(800) 222-TREE

■ The merger of Doubletree with Guest Quarters Suites resulted in an expanded chain of some 250 "competent", "good-value", "modern" lodgings that are "very livable for business trips" and "spacious" enough to "accommodate families"; the hotels feature "reliable", "attractive" rooms while the Guest Suites are the "best of the [all-suites] concept" – "a notch above" others "in their price range."

R 20 | S 19 | D 17 | P 18 | $ $115

Econo Lodge
(800) 446-6900

☑ "If you're just looking for a place to sleep", economizers say this chain's "cheap", "functional" 700-plus sites are "ok for an overnight stay"; but to others the "depressing", "run-down" rooms are "not worth the lower cost" – "you have to be pretty desperate."

R 11 | S 11 | D 9 | P 10 | $ $57

Embassy Suites
(800) 362-2779

■ "Excellent" – "you always know what to expect" at the largest all-suite hotel chain (140-plus): two "clean", "spacious" rooms "for the price of one" and "great amenities", including kitchenettes in each suite plus complimentary cooked-to-order breakfasts and afternoon cocktails; "a good value" for "families and business alike", it's also "ideal for people relocating."

R 22 | S 19 | D 17 | P 18 | $ $118

Fairfield Inn by Marriott
(800) 228-2800

■ "One of the better chains in the inexpensive category", these almost 250 "cookie-cutter" inns provide "nice, clean" rooms and the "best continental breakfast", making it "a surprisingly good value"; but as one reviewer notes, it's "the least desirable of properties carrying the Marriott name."

R 18 | S 17 | D 13 | P 14 | $ $71

FAIRMONT HOTELS
(800) 527-4727

■ This "professionally run" chain of five "elegant", "refined" hotels is "a class act" – "never a disappointment"; Fairmont guests "count on impeccable luxury" in the "spacious rooms and bathrooms" and can expect "unbeatable personal service" that's "done the old-fashioned way", with skill and "charm."

R 25 | S 25 | D 24 | P 24 | $ $184

FOUR SEASONS
(800) 332-3442

■ "Bravo" – rated the *Survey*'s top overall chain, the "fabulous" Four Seasons hotels and resorts define "real luxury", especially in terms of service from "the best-trained staff" that pays "impeccable attention to detail" and makes guests "feel totally pampered"; "beautiful lobbies", "elegant public spaces" and "deluxe rooms" combine with "superb food and room service" to make this chain with 18 US locations (over 40 worldwide) "truly fit for royalty"; "go ahead and splurge – it's worth it."

R 29 | S 28 | D 28 | P 28 | $ $237

Hampton Inns
(800) 426-7866

■ A stay at these "functional", "clean" inns is a "cost-cutter's dream": "inexpensive suites", "large" "dependable rooms", "pleasant service" and a "very good" free continental breakfast buffet add up to an "excellent value" for "business and family travel"; the 100-percent-satisfaction guarantee ('clean, comfortable, friendly and efficient') at the 500-plus "convenient" locations makes it a "safe" choice.

R 18 | S 17 | D 13 | P 14 | $ $76

Harvey Hotels
(800) 922-9222

☑ Citing "reasonable rates", "large clean rooms" and an "excellent free breakfast", admirers call this Southwest chain with 13 hotels (seven in Dallas) "good overall" and "a cut above" competitors in its class; few argue with a staff that's "very customer oriented", though some contend the "older" properties "need renovating."

R 18 | S 18 | D 16 | P 16 | $ $108

Hilton

<u>19</u>   <u>19</u>   <u>17</u>   <u>19</u>   <u>$139</u>

(800) 445-8667

☑ "Mainstays for business trips", the "ubiquitous" Hiltons (with some 200 US locations) are still considered a "sure bet" by many for "comfortable" rooms and "good service"; but while "the best are top-notch", a sizable number of critics claim "they're not the chain they used to be"; the US Hiltons and Hilton International (with another 200-plus properties) are separately owned – a few reviewers opine that "International is better."

Holiday Inn

<u>14</u>   <u>14</u>   <u>12</u>   <u>13</u>   <u>$95</u>

(800) 465-4329

☑ With more than 1,600 properties under the Holiday Inn name, the "once reliable" lodgings have become for some "a cliché of mediocrity" with "uneven accommodations" packed with "plastic and polyester"; others see "signs of life" at the "old standby" which has recently become niche oriented: SunSpree Resorts, Express, newer Select hotels (with special amenities for business travelers) and top-of-the-line Crowne Plaza Hotels ("consistent" and "generally better").

Homewood Suites

<u>22</u>   <u>19</u>   <u>–</u>   <u>17</u>   <u>$99</u>

(800) 225-5466

■ Reviewers "like the concept" of this fast-growing chain of more than 30 residential properties (with another 30 scheduled to open soon), finding the "great suites" "clean" and "roomy"; it's "wonderful for families" or "those on a budget" looking for a place that "will make you feel at home"; two-room suites with kitchens as well as an exercise room, pool and laundry make it "good for a long stay" despite no on-site restaurants.

Howard Johnson

<u>12</u>   <u>12</u>   <u>10</u>   <u>11</u>   <u>$85</u>

(800) 446-4656

■ Those who "keep remembering better rooms and food" are "sad to see" the decline of this one-time "symbol of quality"; despite the chain's efforts to upgrade by introducing full-service Howard Johnson Plaza Hotels (currently 40 of its 600-plus properties), most agree only "the ice cream is good" at this "shadow of its former self."

Hyatt

<u>22</u>   <u>22</u>   <u>20</u>   <u>22</u>   <u>$155</u>

(800) 233-1234

■ The "wonderful standards" of a "reliable" "full-service" chain (more than 100 US hotels) with "user-friendly rooms" and "lots of lobby action" make these "flashy" Goliaths "excellent for the business traveler"; although basic Hyatts take a few knocks as "ordinary" and "overblown" (they "spend more on the lobbies than the rooms"), the Grand Hyatts "exude luxury" and the "exclusive Park Hyatts are superb"; most agree you "can count on a pleasant stay" at any location.

Inter-Continental

<u>23</u>   <u>23</u>   <u>22</u>   <u>23</u>   <u>$178</u>

(800) 327-0200

■ Since "you can rely on great service", "it always feels special" at the more than 25 "classy" US properties (175 international) that offer "lots of European touches", "beautiful flowers", "wonderful restaurants" and "rooms with character"; although a few find the atmosphere "stuffy", ratings agree with fans who say "always good, sometimes superb."

ITT Sheraton

<u>20</u>   <u>19</u>   <u>18</u>   <u>19</u>   <u>$139</u>

(800) 325-3535

☑ Because "quality is never uniform" at the 250 US hotels of the ITT Sheraton chain, reviewers ring in that "only the high-end" "luxury resorts" and "renovated properties" are "good choices"; while most agree that these "standard business hotels" offer "good frequent-user perks", that's not enough to offset perceptions that the "chain lacks definition" and is "being overshadowed by new rivals."

La Quinta

<u>16</u>   <u>16</u>   <u>12</u>   <u>14</u>   <u>$76</u>

(800) 531-5900

☑ Many are "surprised" and "impressed" by the "helpful" service, "nicely decorated rooms" with a SW motif and cleanliness at these 240 "budget-minded" hotels where "inexpensive" rates include a continental breakfast; although detractors sneer it's for those "partial to painted cinder block", others respond it "meets our needs when we are on a tight budget."

LEADING HOTELS OF THE WORLD

<u>28</u>   <u>27</u>   <u>26</u>   <u>27</u>   <u>$244</u>

(800) 223-6800

■ Not a true hotel chain, this marketing and reservations company represents "a great collection" of "luxurious", "expensive" hotels (300 worldwide, including Ritz-Carltons, Four Seasons, LA's Bel-Air, New Orleans' Windsor Court et al.) that offer "a guaranteed level" of "absolutely trusted service", "superb accommodations" and "excellent quality"; each "distinctive" property "pleases even the most discriminating traveler", making this one organization that "lives up to its name."

Loews
(800) 235-6397

☑ Loews is "hard to rate" as a chain because while its two resorts earn unanimous kudos as "attractive" and "top of the line", its eight hotels are "not consistent", varying from "first-rate" to "needs work"; but surveyors agree that the majority are "well-run" facilities with "surprisingly good" service in "very comfortable" surroundings.

23 | 23 | 22 | 22 | $174

Marriott
(800) 228-9290

☑ Admirers of this "dependable" "business hostelry" say the 275-plus locations (or 1,075 locations, if you count divisions like Courtyard by Marriott) uphold an "excellent standard", garnering "high marks for amenities and service" and "immaculate facilities"; but others sigh over an "old standby" that's "basic vanilla" – "you know what you're going to get" and it's "not necessarily exciting"; still, "you can't go wrong" and the chain's frequent-stay and air-mile bonuses are pluses.

21 | 21 | 19 | 20 | $141

Motel 6
(800) 437-7486

☑ "When price is of the utmost importance", penny-pinchers see the "bare-bones basic" rooms in the more than 760 locations as "fine for stopovers" ("what do you want for cheap?") and note that some even "have indoor pools"; but many "would rather pay a little more to get much more" than what's currently offered by these glorified "truck stops" – "don't leave the light on for me."

9 | 10 | 7 | 7 | $51

Omni
(800) 843-6664

☑ Despite the name, Omnis are "tough to find" (only 35 US locations), but those who do are often rewarded with a "surprisingly good" experience: "well-decorated rooms", "pampering" and "nice touches for the business traveler"; still, reports of "variable quality" abound and doubters consider them "pricey for second-tier hotels."

21 | 20 | 19 | 20 | $148

PREFERRED HOTELS
(800) 323-7500

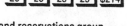

■ The "high-class independent" members of this marketing and reservations group (110 properties, 63 in the US) are names equated with such phrases as "consistently wonderful" and "always elegant" (Hawaii's Lodge at Koele, DC's Hay-Adams Hotel, etc.) and they also provide "superb service" by an "excellent staff" that must pass Preferred's criteria; it's "a safe bet" that stays will be "memorable" at this "welcome change from chain-type hotels."

26 | 26 | 25 | 25 | $214

Quality Inns
(800) 228-5151

☑ "Average in all respects" is the verdict on this "satisfactory", "middle-of-the-road" midpriced chain; while "usually a safe choice" "for overnight", the large number of "centrally located" properties (approximately 735) means "you need to know which are better" because "Quality varies"; several surveyors note these are "almost a duplicate of Comfort Inns" which are also part of the Choice Hotels group.

14 | 14 | 12 | 13 | $75

Radisson
(800) 333-3333

☑ The more than 200 Radisson inns, hotels, suites and resorts in the US generally offer a "decent, attractive setting" with "comfortable", "well-appointed rooms" and "great summer sales"; although many warn that "quality varies" (some say "wildly"), the majority is usually "very pleased" with these "solid, practical business hotels" that are a "good choice within this price range."

18 | 18 | 16 | 17 | $116

Ramada
(800) 272-6232

☑ Despite scattered compliments that some sites are "clean" and "reasonable", most surveyors are "disappointed" and view this 900-property chain as "on a downhill run"; "shame on Ramada" for letting the hotels "get run-down" – they need to "upgrade", "spend money on the chain, not a TV campaign" and stop "riding on name recognition."

14 | 14 | 12 | 13 | $90

Red Lion
(800) 547-8010

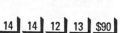

■ Red Lion's 50 hotels in 11 Western states became part of Doubletree in late 1996, so watch for name changes and expansions at this "good regional chain"; "you can count on a good night's sleep" in "consistently clean", "comfortable" and "well-appointed rooms" which, at "reasonable rates", have reviewers purring it's a "pleasant surprise."

18 | 18 | 16 | 17 | $109

Hotel Chains

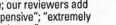

Red Roof Inns
(800) 843-7663

R	S	D	P	$
12	12	9	10	$60

☑ For those seeking "economical", "basic accommodations" that are "very reliable" and "always clean"; but as mediocre scores attest, even "good rates" cannot totally offset "primitive", "dorm-quality" rooms with "furniture built to take a beating."

RELAIS & CHÂTEAUX
(212) 856-0115

28	28	28	27	$276

■ "Absolutely the best" is the unequivocal reaction to this collection of "unique, memorable" "outstanding" properties (27 hotels in the US, over 400 worldwide) offering "old-world charm" in "beautiful settings"; each lodging (The Point in NYS, the Inn at Little Washington or Little Nell in Aspen, for example) must pass the chain's "rule of five Cs" – character, courtesy, calm, charm and cuisine; our reviewers add five Es – "excellent", "elegant", "exquisite", "expensive" and "expensive"; "extremely high standards" make them "a real reference book of romantic places."

Renaissance
(800) 468-3571

23	22	21	22	$156

■ Once Stouffer, then Stouffer Renaissance, and then (until 1997) all 35 properties carried only the Renaissance name when they were bought again, this time by Marriott; surveyors report that the chain, already "a cut above other second-tier hotels", has been "really improving in all categories" and "looking for an upscale identity"; despite gripes about "high prices", no one's complaining about the "impressive rooms and amenities" and "unsurpassed service."

Residence Inn by Marriott
(800) 331-3131

23	19	14	18	$112

■ "God's gift for families traveling together" and business folk "on extended stays", these approximately 200 inns offer "huge rooms" and "apartments at bargain prices" with "home-away-from-home comfort" including kitchens with microwaves and coffeemakers; "great free breakfast buffet" and happy hours add to the "excellent value."

RITZ-CARLTON
(800) 241-3333

28	28	28	27	$230

■ Enthusiasts spread it on thick, gushing about the Ritz's 25 "splendid", "luxurious", English-style US properties that offer "class all the way" with "fabulous food" and "comfortable", "beautiful rooms"; "the most customer-oriented hotel company" (now nearly half-owned by Marriott) "puts service as the central theme", and surveyors are nearly unanimous in putting this "top-of-the-line" chain near the top of our *Survey* – "expensive, but deservedly so."

SMALL LUXURY HOTELS OF THE WORLD
(800) 525-4800

28	27	26	26	$239

■ "You can't make a mistake" at any of the 36 "intimate", "lovely" US members of this "sleeper" of a reservations and marketing association; while the privately owned "idiosyncratic lodgings" include some "undiscovered gems", others are better known (e.g. Dallas' Mansion on Turtle Creek, Vermont's Woodstock Inn, The Peaks at Telluride), but all are "definitely the way to go" when you want to "indulge yourself."

Sonesta
(800) 766-3782

23	22	21	22	$161

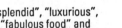

■ Alas, there are only four of these "well-run" hotels and "fine resorts" in the US (16 worldwide); admirers praise them as "airy", "beautifully decorated and enchanting" with an "outstanding staff-to-guest ratio" that results in "wonderful treatment"; it pays "attention to detail" and serves "great food", ergo, "you can book with confidence."

Super 8
(800) 800-8000

12	12	8	9	$57

☑ Most surveyors agree that the 1,400 franchises "get the job done" by offering "all the basics" in "stripped-down" "clean rooms" at "good value" prices; critics charge that older properties are "going downhill fast", but the consensus is that this "very affordable chain" should change its name to Super Rate.

Travelodge/Thriftlodge
(800) 578-7878

12	12	10	10	$69

☑ For "cheap travel" with "no frills", this "dowdy but dependable" chain is "generally ok"; but some surveyors feel it "needs a new image and new properties", along with better overall standards that could smooth out "inconsistent quality" at the 450 locations.

Westin
(800) 228-3000

23 | 22 | 21 | 22 | $166

■ An "upscale business-oriented" operation with more than 40 "good locations" in the US (and over 50 others worldwide) that provides a "comfortable, indulging feeling" in its "well-furnished", "high-quality rooms"; "trying harder" to "compete with the next level", this "upper middle class of hotel chains" "pays attention to details in the dining room" and "provides first-rate amenities" and a "helpful staff."

Wyndham
(800) 822-4200

21 | 20 | 18 | 20 | $136

☑ The "great locations" of Wyndham's approximately 90 US and Caribbean hotels and resorts are backed up by "stylish", "comfortable" and generally pleasant rooms; but while "better than standard", some claim this "coming on strong" chain "can't decide between budget and upscale", which may explain why penny-pinchers call it "overpriced" while others consider it "a good value"; but most agree "they try hard" and usually come out a "winner."

Individual Hotels, Resorts and Inns

Alabama

R S D P $

Victoria, The 56R (4S)
▽ 25 | 23 | 24 | 21 | $100

PO Box 2213, 1604 Quintard Ave., Anniston; (205) 236-0503; (800) 260-8781;
FAX: (205) 236-1138

■ "Great atmosphere", "good service" and "extremely well-appointed rooms" (think individual decor, period antiques and some working fireplaces) characterize this 1888 Victorian; about 60 miles from Birmingham, it's nestled in "beautiful grounds" that include a courtyard, pool and gardens; don't miss cocktails in the piano lounge and gourmet breakfast on the glass-enclosed veranda.

Birmingham

Radisson Hotel Birmingham 285R (13S)
14 | 15 | 11 | 13 | $99

808 S. 20th St., Birmingham; (205) 933-9000; (800) 333-3333; FAX: (205) 933-0920

☑ "The basics – no more, no less" say some surveyors about this Downtown business/convention hotel within walking distance of the medical center; others aren't so charitable, warning "only if desperate"; then again, if you "don't expect much" you may be "pleased."

Sheraton Birmingham 727R (43S)
18 | 17 | 15 | 17 | $106
(fka Sheraton Civic Center Hotel)

2101 Civic Ctr. Blvd., Birmingham; (205) 324-5000; (800) 325-3535; FAX: (205) 307-3045

☑ Corporate travelers craving a "good location" next door to the civic center find this Downtown high-rise makes for a "comfortable stop near business, malls and sports venues", but reactions are mixed for everything else; where some enjoy a "well-run change of pace" with "very nice" accommodations, others are startled by "frightening service" (employees "need social skills"), "tacky" rooms and "poorly managed food service."

Tutwiler Hotel 95R (52S)
22 | 22 | 21 | 21 | $129

2021 Park Pl. N., Birmingham; (205) 322-2100; (800) 745-1787: FAX: (205) 325-1183

■ "The Tut is still king in Birmingham" assert assessors who crown this "charming piece of the Old South" an "oasis of civility"; a 1986 re-creation of the 1914 original, this "rejuvenated grande old dame" features "fine decor" and "fine dining" in a "good business location central to Downtown"; fans advise "spring for a balcony suite", which affords a romantic panorama of the city.

Wynfrey Hotel 319R (10S)
23 | 20 | 19 | 21 | $120

1000 Riverchase Galleria, Birmingham; (205) 987-1600; (800) 476-7006; FAX: (205) 987-0454

■ "Beautifully decorated" throughout, the "most upscale hotel in Alabama" earns praise for its "Southern hospitality", "first-class restaurant", good-size meeting facilities and abundance of amenities including a fitness center and outdoor pool; yet many maintain the property's most notable feature is its location at Riverchase Galleria ("mall elegance at its best"), one of the Southeast's largest shopping malls.

Eufaula

Kendall Manor Inn 6R
- | - | - | - | I

534 W. Broad St., Eufaula; (334) 687-8847; FAX: (334) 616-0678

A stately National Register Italianate manor in southeast Alabama that's a relaxing base for strolls through the nearby historic district or sipping lemonade on the veranda; those who would like a bit more exertion can make the climb up to the belvedere, worth the heavy breathing for its miles of views and – Kilroy, take note – its 100 years worth of visitors' graffiti scribbled on the walls; the individually decorated rooms feature four-poster beds and private baths, and breakfast is included.

Eutaw

Kirkwood B&B 4R ⊅
- | - | - | - | I

111 Kirkwood Dr., Eutaw; (205) 372-9009

This antebellum treasure buried in east-central Alabama, 90 miles from Birmingham, whisks visitors back to the Old South circa 1860; the Greek Revival architecture has been attentively restored, and the antique furnishings and fixtures reflect a rich Southern tradition; rates include full breakfast.

Fairhope

Malaga Inn 35R (3S)   21 | 19 | 17 | 21 | $92
359 Church St., Fairhope; (334) 438-4701; (800) 235-1586; FAX: (334) 438-4701
■ "Casual perfection" and "old-time charm" mark this "always wonderful" 1862 inn in a "fabulous" Historic District location; a "friendly and accommodating staff" and "great food" round out the "pretty" albeit "pricey" picture.

Mobile

Adam's Mark Riverview Plaza 375R (12S)   18 | 18 | 16 | 18 | $99
64 S. Water St., Mobile; (334) 438-4000; (800) 444-2326; FAX: (334) 415-3060
■ A modern high-rise that enjoys the "best location in Mobile" – "on the water", attached to the convention center and across from the Amtrak station; it "does its job in terms of a place to stay" – service is "friendly", rooms are "comfortable" and the concierge floor is "great" – but it doesn't work overtime.

Radisson Admiral Semmes 148R (22S)   19 | 17 | 16 | 17 | $90
251 Government St., Mobile; (334) 432-8000; (800) 333-3333; FAX: (334) 405-5942
☑ From one viewpoint, this '40s art deco–style hotel with a marble lobby, "huge, comfortable" guestrooms and an "excellent Downtown location" exudes "old-fashioned charm"; from another, the "remake didn't improve matters" and the Admiral is fighting a losing battle "to appear classy"; in sum, it's an "adequate, not delightful," stopover.

Orange Beach

Perdido Beach Resort 333R (12S)   23 | 22 | 21 | 25 | $122
27200 Perdido Beach Blvd., Orange Beach; (334) 981-9811; (800) 634-8001;
FAX: (334) 981-5672
■ The beach isn't *perdido* here – it's in full sight and "fabulous"; as if the "pristine white sand" isn't enough, this Mediterranean-style resort has a health club, tennis, pools, an "incredible" restaurant and a piano bar; regulars rave it's "just like being in a movie with all the celebs and would-be celebs hobnobbing"; N.B. rooms are on the "small" side, but they come with a view of the Gulf.

Point Clear

Marriott's Grand Hotel 284R (22S)   23 | 24 | 22 | 25 | $158
1 Grand Blvd., Point Clear; (334) 928-9201; (800) 544-9933; FAX: (334) 928-1149
☑ Sentimentalists say this "old glory" bayside resort dating back to 1847 "has aged like a fine wine", pointing to the "warm, charming staff", "gorgeous setting" on 550 "out-of-the-way" acres and "fabulous water sports, golf and tennis"; harsher critics contend that the "rooms need to be redone" and the "food could be better", yet it's still considered "delightful for a family vacation, romantic getaway" or business meeting.

Tuscaloosa

Sheraton Capstone Inn 148R (4S)   18 | 17 | 17 | 19 | $109
320 Bryant Dr., Tuscaloosa; (205) 752-3200; (800) 477-2262; FAX: (205) 759-9314
■ It may be "the only game in town" (as long as you're not talking football), but surveyors still find this hotel "quite nice"; perhaps it's the recently redone rooms, decent-size meeting facilities, outdoor pool or proximity of the Paul 'Bear' Bryant Museum and historic buildings on the University of Alabama campus.

Tuskegee

Kellogg Executive Conference Center 98R (10S)   – | – | – | – | M
Tuskegee Univ., E. Campus Ave., Nurse's Home Rd., Tuskegee; (334) 727-3000;
(800) 949-6161; FAX: (334) 727-5119
On-site tennis and swimming plus 54 holes of golf nearby keep conferees occupied between meetings at this Georgian-style property; on the business side, there's a 300-seat amphitheater, teleconference studio, state-of-the-art computer lab, executive boardroom and meeting rooms of various sizes to accommodate a wide range of formats.

Alaska

R S D P $

Captain Cook Hotel 489R (77S)
21 20 19 19 $153
Fifth Ave. & K St., Anchorage; (907) 276-6000; (800) 843-1950; FAX: (907) 278-5366
☑ "An oasis in the frozen North", this "big, sophisticated", "first-class hotel" has a "warm, cozy interior" and an array of shops ("could have spent three nights shopping"); "good facilities" include an extensive athletic club, and "don't miss" the "incredible" "views in all directions", especially from the "dependably good rooftop restaurant"; however, more than a few recommend "a spruce-up", as rooms "vary in quality" from "spacious" and "elegant" to "shabby" and "worn."

Hilton Anchorage Hotel 568R (23S)
20 19 18 18 $147
500 W. Third Ave., Anchorage; (907) 272-7411; (800) HILTONS; FAX: (907) 265-7140
☑ While a coterie contends this Anchorage high-rise is "better than expected" and "a nice way to ease into any Alaskan experience", more suggest that apart from the "beautiful view" of the Chugach Range and Cook Inlet, this "cookie-cutter" Hilton "could be in Kansas"; the Downtown site is "convenient for tour groups", which may be why the "lobby is always full of suitcases"; the overall impression is "basic" and "ordinary", with some snipes about "no air-conditioning" in August.

Regal Alaskan Hotel 245R (3S)
19 20 17 18 $158
4800 Spenard Rd., Anchorage; (907) 243-2300; (800) 544-0553; FAX: (907) 243-8815
■ A "beautiful setting" on the east shore of Lake Spenard – reputedly the world's busiest float-plane base – adds to the charm of this midsize, close-to-the-airport hotel; there's a "great view from the meeting rooms" and many of the guestrooms too; "nice moose heads" and other stuffed wildlife accent the lobby, and the colorful Fancy Moose lounge and cafe is a focus of the "fun atmosphere"; "outstanding in its field" say fans, "overpriced" counter a few dissenters.

Sheraton Anchorage Hotel 375R
19 18 17 19 $145
401 E. Sixth Ave., Anchorage; (907) 276-8700; (800) 325-3535; FAX: (907) 276-7561
☑ You "won't ever forget the jade staircase" in the lobby or the extensive displays of "wonderful Native Alaskan artwork" at this otherwise "functional" Sheraton on the outskirts of Downtown; the site garners complaints for being "too far from the main drag" and "on the wrong side of everything"; a staff that "needs a lesson in customer service" and "food that is fair" at best add credence to an overall impression: the "best thing about this hotel is that it's in Alaska."

Kenai Princess Lodge 64R (4S)
– – – – M
Sterling Hwy., Cooper Landing; (907) 595-1425; (800) 426-0500; FAX: (907) 595-1424
A tranquil base from which to savor majestic Alaskan vistas: perched on a bluff in the Chugach National Forest overlooking the Kenai River, this rustic yet elegant lodge, a scenic two-hour drive south of Anchorage, offers guestrooms in secluded bungalows, each with wood stove, vaulted ceiling and private sun porch from which to take in the mountain views; active types can arrange for hiking, river-rafting or fishing trips; closed January and February.

Camp Denali 17R ⌿
15 17 14 16 $125
PO Box 67, Denali National Park; (907) 683-2290; FAX: (907) 683-1568

North Face Lodge 14R (1S) ⌿
18 21 20 20 $293
PO Box 67, Denali National Park; (907) 683-2290; FAX: (907) 683-1568
■ "The way to see Mt. McKinley" say wilderness seekers who feel that "no visit to Alaska is complete without staying" at this remote lodge and cabins in a "stunning" site 90 miles into Denali National Park; its "basic" charms aren't for everyone, as "adequate amenities in hiking accommodations" in cabins mean wood stoves, propane lamps and outhouses, though lodge rooms have central heating and toilets; "excellent service" includes three-squares, and the nature center offers naturalist programs and guided hikes: open early June–early September, cash only.

Denali Princess Lodge 275R (6S)
16 | 18 | 17 | 19 | $147

PO Box 110, Denali National Park; (907) 683-2282; (800) 462-0500; FAX: (907) 683-2545

☑ It's "not the Ritz", but the "rustic luxury" here is as ritzy as it gets at Denali; run by Princess Tours, which also operates the Midnight Sun Express (with a train/hotel deal that accounts for the "captive audience"), this park-entrance lodge offers quarters "like a cruise room – pretty but with few amenities"; foes grouse it's "not only rustic but primitive", while fans cheer "the beauty of the setting", which often includes a "great view of a bear from the dining room."

McKinley Chalet Resort 20R
17 | 16 | 16 | 17 | $127

Mile 239, George Parks Hwy., Denali National Park; (907) 683-2215; (800) 276-7234; FAX: (907) 258-3668

■ "Rustic", "rustic", "rustic" say one and all after sampling "the basic necessities" and "minimal attention to personal needs" found at this visitors' base camp at Denali National Park; there's "no phone or TV, just gorgeous scenery", and expect to "stand in line everywhere" since this resort is "designed for large numbers of guests"; cabins are "small and comfortable" ("request the new chalets"), and wildlife expeditions and river-rafting trips can be arranged.

Fairbanks

Captain Bartlett Inn 195R (2S)
13 | 15 | 12 | 12 | $116

1411 Airport Way, Fairbanks; (907) 452-1888; (800) 544-7528; FAX: (907) 452-7674

☑ Despite its "interesting frontier ambiance" – a "woody, Western, gold-rush setting" viewed variously as "hokey but clean" and "rugged but charming" – a pack of nonamused voters claims this "modest" "hole-in-the-wall" with "small", "low-budget rooms at high prices" just might be "the most squalid hotel on all the tour-bus itineraries"; a big-time '95 decor overhaul could have remedied those complaints, but ratings seem to suggest otherwise.

Fairbanks Princess Hotel 198R (2S)
20 | 19 | 17 | 19 | $132

4477 Pikes Landing. Fairbanks; (907) 455-4477; (800) 426-0500; FAX: (907) 455-4476

☑ Though surveyors "don't expect much from this very sleepy town", most find this up-to-date Princess Cruises landlubber to be "refreshed and stylish", making it "the only good hotel in Fairbanks"; there's a "lovely lobby and restaurant", "a great pub and bar" with live entertainment and an outdoor deck that extends to the banks of the Chena River; a minority moans about soaring "prices during high season" and "rudeness" because the "staff knows" this is the "only game in town."

Girdwood

ALYESKA RESORT & THE WESTERN ALYESKA PRINCE HOTEL 303R (4S)
26 | 23 | 24 | 27 | $184

1000 Arlberg Ave., Girdwood; (907) 754-1111; (800) 880-3880; FAX: (907) 754-2200

■ For true "luxury in the wilderness", consider this "little piece of heaven in the backwoods", a scenic 40-mile drive from Anchorage; whether used as a romantic getaway, corporate retreat or a chance to ski Mt. Alyeska (the lifts are just outside the door), this "fabulously appointed resort" in a "heavenly setting" with "incredible alpine vistas" provides "fine" rooms, a "spectacular restaurant" and "super facilities" including an "incredible" spa and fitness center; the only caveat concerns "oversized mosquitos."

Gustavus

Glacier Bay Lodge 56R (12S)
20 | 20 | 22 | 22 | $144

PO Box 199, Bartlett Cove, Gustavus; (907) 697-2226; (800) 451-5952; FAX: (907) 697-2408

☑ Perhaps this "gorgeous setting deserves better accommodations", but most agree that the "picturesque, comfortable" rooms at the only hotel in Glacier Bay National Park are "fine" and, what's more, the "excellent dining room" serves "superfresh seafood"; "lots of action" for guests includes sport fishing, whale-watching excursions and glacier cruises, and the remote location (arrival by float plane or boat) is so "outstanding" that folks just "don't want to leave."

Arizona

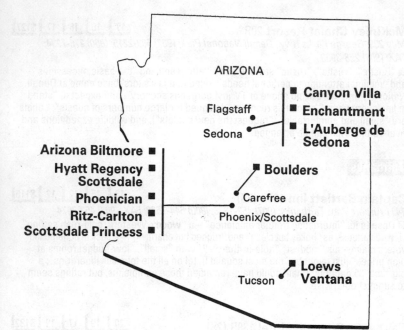

ARIZONA

■ Canyon Villa
■ Enchantment
■ L'Auberge de
Sedona

Flagstaff
Sedona

Arizona Biltmore ■
Hyatt Regency ■
Scottsdale
Phoenician ■
Ritz-Carlton ■
Scottsdale Princess ■

■ Boulders

Carefree
Phoenix/Scottsdale

■ Loews
Ventana

Tucson

BEST OVERALL
28 Boulders/Phoenix
27 Phoenician/Scottsdale
26 Ritz-Carlton Phoenix
Scottsdale Princess/Scottsdale
Arizona Biltmore/Phoenix
Loews Ventana Canyon/Tucson
Canyon Villa B&B/Sedona
Enchantment Resort/Sedona
25 L'Auberge de Sedona/Sedona
Hyatt Regency/Scottsdale

BEST VALUES
Sheraton Mesa/Phoenix
Wahweap Lodge/Page
Sheraton Crescent/Phoenix
Arizona Inn/Tucson
Doubletree Reid Parks/Tucson
Holiday Inn SunSpree/Scottsdale
Marriott Scottsdale
Doubletree Paradise Val./Scottsdale
Crowne Plaza/Phoenix
Westward Look Resort/Tucson

Bisbee

R | S | D | P | $

Copper Queen Hotel 47R
11 Howell Ave., Bisbee; (520) 432-2216; (800) 247-5829; FAX: (520) 432-4298
The Copper Queen mine may have closed in the 1970s, but this 1902 antiques-filled
Victorian lives on, giving visitors to this historic boomtown a taste of the rustic grandeur
that copper brought to way-south Arizona; a pool and a/c keep guests cool in summer,
and the on-site CQ Saloon offers a chance to rub shoulders with Teddy Roosevelt's
ghost; more spooky info: several murder mystery weekends are planned each year.

Douglas

Gadsden Hotel 130R (20S)

– | – | – | – | |

1046 G Ave., Douglas; (520) 364-4481; FAX: (520) 364-4005
Pancho Villa was still riding when the splendid, 42-foot Tiffany stained-glass window (depicting saguaro, ocotillo and other local flora), huge marble columns and grand marble staircase were set up in this barely-north-of-the-border hotel; today, it offers spare but comfortable rooms and a modest dining room, and guests can check out the hundreds of registered cattle brands painted on the walls of the Famous Saddle and Spur Lounge.

Gold Canyon

Gold Canyon Resort 57R

▽ 24 | 19 | 18 | 22 | $169

6100 S. Kings Ranch Rd., Gold Canyon; (602) 982-9090; (800) 624-6445;
FAX: (602) 830-5211
■ This "clubby, comfortable" golf resort nestled in the foothills of the Superstition Mountains (site of the legendary Lost Dutchman's Mine) is in the midst of a complete overhaul, putting a question mark next to the above ratings; so far, the rooms have been renovated, nine holes of golf have been added and a new facility for group functions has been built; plans for 1997 call for the construction of 50 rooms and another nine holes of golf; hopefully, it will remain a "great deal."

Grand Canyon

El Tovar Hotel/Grand Canyon National Park Lodges 66R (12S)

18 | 20 | 20 | 22 | $155

PO Box 699, Grand Canyon; (520) 638-2631; Reservations: (303) 297-2757;
FAX: (303) 297-3175
■ "Location, location, location" is the calling card of this "rustic mansion" perched on the south rim of the Grand Canyon, boasting "the most spectacular view one will ever behold" complemented by a "superb restaurant" and "marvelous lobby" with massive stone fireplace; surveyors "can't help but love it despite the second-rate rooms"; P.S. "frequent cancellations can make the terraced rim-view suites available without a two-year wait."

Grand Canyon National Park Lodges 900R (4S)

15 | 15 | 14 | 20 | $100

PO Box 699, South Rim, Grand Canyon; (520) 638-2991; Reservations: (303) 297-2757;
FAX: (303) 297-3175
■ Tourists who can't get into, or can't afford, El Tovar can take their pick of seven other "very plain" but "adequate" lodges on the south rim: Bright Angel, Kachina and Thunderbird (on the rim), Maswik (a quarter-mile from the rim), Yavapai (one mile from the rim), Moqui (just outside the park's south entrance) and Phantom Ranch (at the foot of the inner gorge, accessible only by foot, mule or raft); there are "no amenities at all", but no one seems to mind since the "views are magnificent."

Holiday Inn Express 163R (3S)

14 | 14 | 12 | 14 | $118

PO Box 3245, Hwy. 64, Grand Canyon; (520) 638-3000; (800) 465-4329;
FAX: (520) 638-0123
◧ Some say the newest hotel at the south rim of the Grand Canyon is "better than most" with "clean, comfortable rooms", "good service" and complimentary continental breakfast, while others insist that "service could not be slower" and they're "taking advantage of a captive market"; if you decide to go, be sure to "make reservations early."

Page

Wahweap Lodge & Marina 372R (3S)

18 | 18 | 17 | 19 | $114

100 Lake Shore Dr., Page; (520) 645-2433; (800) 528-6154; FAX: (520) 645-1031
◧ There's "nothing spectacular" about this "moderately priced" "motel-like" lodge "except the spectacular view" of Lake Powell; yet "people on tour buses" continue to come because the rooms are "comfortable", service is "adequate", the food is "good" and there's "no other choice" in the area.

TOP 10 OVERALL

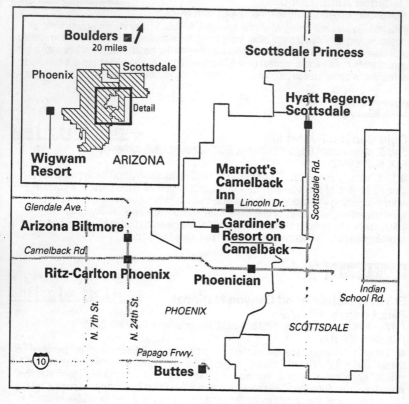

BEST OVERALL

28 Boulders
27 Phoenician
26 Ritz-Carlton Phoenix
   Scottsdale Princess
   Arizona Biltmore
25 Hyatt Regency Scottsdale
   Gardiner's Resort on Camelback
   Wigwam Resort
23 Marriott's Camelback Inn
22 Buttes

BEST VALUES

Sheraton Mesa
Sheraton Crescent
Holiday Inn SunSpree
Marriott Scottsdale
Doubletree Paradise Valley
Crowne Plaza Phoenix
Doubletree La Posada
Buttes
Radisson Scottsdale
Pointe Hilton South Mtn.

R	S	D	P	$

ARIZONA BILTMORE 532R (18S)
| 26 | 26 | 25 | 27 | $223 |

24th St. & Missouri Ave., Phoenix; (602) 955-6600; (800) 950-0086; FAX: (602) 381-7600
■ "Frank Lloyd Wright lives" at this "grand old lady" recently "renovated to an even grander scale"; nearly 1,400 reviewers cast their ballots for the "architectural gem" dating back to 1929, most raving about the "absolutely beautiful decor", "impeccable service", "delicious food" and "spectacular grounds" that define "manicured"; "room quality varies dramatically", however, so try to "get an upgrade."

Arizona Golf Resort 90R (96S)
▽ | 21 | 18 | 19 | 23 | $155 |

425 S. Power Rd., Mesa; (602) 832-3202; (800) 528-8282; FAX: (602) 981-0151
■ Located on 150 lush acres in the fast-growing East Valley, the "outstanding golf facilities" at this resort can be combined with play at any of 10 other nearby courses to create a "grand golf experience"; nonlinksters can take a dip in the outdoor pool, play tennis or work up a sweat in the fitness center: P.S. the rooms with kitchenettes are a particularly "good value."

R	S	D	P	$

BOULDERS, THE 160R (3S)

| 29 | 28 | 27 | 28 | $300 |

34631 N. Tom Darlington Dr., Carefree; (602) 488-9009; (800) 553-1717; FAX: (602) 488-4118

■ The No. 1 resort in the state, and one of the top five in the country, is a "very serene" spot that "blends perfectly" into the "magnificent" natural rock formations of the Sonoran Desert; "fabulous" casitas with wood-burning fireplaces, "off-the-chart service", "exquisite" dining, "breathtaking grounds" and the "great feeling of isolation from other guests" add up to "a place to call home – if you can afford it" – and a "yardstick" to measure "world class"; N.B. it's now open during the summer.

Buttes, The 345R (9S)

| 22 | 23 | 22 | 23 | $163 |

2000 Westcourt Way, Tempe; (602) 225-9000; (800) 843-1986; FAX: (602) 431-8433

■ A "convention-goer's paradise" "surrounded by highways" sums up this 25-acre mountaintop "oasis" offering 40,000 square feet of meeting space and easy airport access along with myriad amenities including a "gorgeous" free-form pool, "neat hot tubs built in the rocks", sand volleyball courts, a fully equipped fitness center, "elegant dining" and "top-notch service"; rooms are "pleasant" as long as you "don't get one facing the freeway."

Crowne Plaza Phoenix 447R (86S)

| 18 | 18 | 15 | 17 | $118 |

(fka Holiday Inn Phoenix Crowne Plaza)

100 W. First St., Phoenix; (602) 257-1525; (800) 359-7253; FAX: (602) 254-7926

◪ Thanks to a recent renovation of the lobby and guestrooms, scores for this Downtown convention hotel have improved slightly since our last *Survey*; reviewers report it's "better than expected" – "bright, airy and extremely clean" with "well laid-out rooms" and a "great pool"; if only they'd "improve the food."

Doubletree La Posada Resort 252R (10S)

| 21 | 21 | 20 | 22 | $153 |

(fka Red Lion La Posada Resort)

4949 E. Lincoln Dr., Scottsdale; (602) 952-0420; (800) 222-TREE; FAX: (602) 852-0151

■ "Everything revolves around the pool" at this "better than average" resort hotel straddling the border of Scottsdale and Paradise Valley – a "magnificent" lagoon pool fed by four waterfalls that dips and twists across more than half an acre; it's "great for families" as well as meetings with "large, comfortable rooms", "convenient" roomside parking and "very pretty grounds"; N.B. 10 golf courses are within a few minutes drive.

Doubletree Paradise Valley Resort 370R (17S)

| 20 | 19 | 17 | 20 | $135 |

(fka Wyndham Paradise Valley Resort)

5401 N. Scottsdale Rd., Scottsdale; (602) 947-5400; (800) 222-TREE; FAX: (602) 946-1524

■ "Better than average rooms" at "reasonable prices" and a "well-trained staff" make this "very attractive" resort hotel situated on 22 acres "adequate for an unpretentious business meeting"; there's "no golf course", but there are "great pools" to chase away the winter blues and, of course, "great" chocolate-chip cookies to satisfy sweet tooths.

Embassy Suites Phoenix - Biltmore (233S)

| 21 | 20 | 15 | 20 | $150 |

(fka Crown Sterling Suites)

2630 E. Camelback Rd., Phoenix; (602) 955-3992; (800) 362-2779; FAX: (602) 224-9061

■ The "fabulous large rooms" come with a "plentiful" cooked-to-order breakfast at this "cheerful, airy" all-suiter; rates are "reasonable" and it's in a "super location for shopoholics" (adjacent to Biltmore Fashion Park) and "within walking distance of great restaurants"; a $4.5-million renovation in 1996 should address concerns that it's "not aging well."

Embassy Suites Resort - Scottsdale (310S)

| 20 | 19 | 17 | 17 | $126 |

5001 N. Scottsdale Rd., Scottsdale; (602) 949-1414; (800) 528-1456; FAX: (602) 947-2675

◪ Near the heart of Downtown Scottsdale, this "reasonably priced" resort hotel is as "comfortable as an old shoe" with "spacious" two-room suites suitable "for a family of four" and a sprinkling of amenities including two pools, two tennis courts and an exercise room; "free booze" (at cocktail hour) and a "great full breakfast" included in the rate make it a "good value" despite claims that it "needs a major rehab."

GARDINER'S RESORT ON CAMELBACK 55R (45S)

| 25 | 25 | 24 | 25 | $255 |

5700 E. McDonald Dr., Scottsdale; (602) 948-2100; (800) 245-2051; FAX: (602) 483-3386

■ Not just for "tennis types", this "hidden gem" in the shadow of Camelback Mountain "scores an ace in every category" with "gorgeous casitas" featuring a fireplace, living room, dining area and kitchen, "outstanding" service, "lovely" food and grounds encompassing eight swimming pools; private or group lessons on 21 state-of-the-art courts make it one of the "best tennis camps in the US"; N.B. closed July and August.

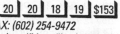
Hermosa Inn 27R (8S)
$-$ | $-$ | $-$ | $-$ | M

5532 N. Palo Cristi Rd., Paradise Valley; (602) 955-8614; (800) 241-1210;
FAX: (602) 955-8299

In the quiet desert enclave of Paradise Valley, on the outskirts of Phoenix, lies this beautiful inn reopened in 1994 after a major restoration; the sister to the Royal Palms caters to couples as well as corporate types with individually decorated adobe casitas, featuring vaulted ceilings, beehive fireplaces, hand-painted Mexican tiles and private patios, scattered on six-and-a-half acres of grounds marked by towering palms and stone walkways lined with flowers; rates include a continental breakfast.

Holiday Inn SunSpree
Resort Scottsdale 183R (17S)
18 | 18 | 16 | 18 | $117

7601 E. Indian Bend Rd., Scottsdale; (602) 991-2400; (800) 852-5205; FAX: (602) 998-2261

◪ "A motel maybe – not a resort" is the consensus on this "comfortable" but "undistinguished" property popular with the group-tour crowd; still, families find it a "surprisingly nice bargain" since kids up to 19 stay free in their parents' room and kids up to 12 eat free in the restaurant; sedentary types gripe that it's "too spread out – you have to hike to your room."

Hyatt Regency Phoenix 668R (44S)
20 | 20 | 18 | 19 | $153

122 N. Second Ave., Phoenix; (602) 252-1234; (800) 233-1234; FAX: (602) 254-9472

◪ Solid scores aside, surveyors say this "serviceable business hotel" in a "boring part of town" "should only be used for a convention across the street" at the Civic Plaza; it's "clean" and "friendly", and the rooms were recently redone, but overall it's "no great shakes" and "not up to most Hyatt Regencys"; yet some say it's the "best bet for Downtown Phoenix."

HYATT REGENCY SCOTTSDALE 461R (25S)
25 | 25 | 24 | 27 | $212

7500 E. Doubletree Ranch Rd., Scottsdale; (602) 991-3388; (800) 233-1234; FAX: (602) 483-5550

■ There's "water, water everywhere" at this "posh but family-oriented" resort with an "outrageous" two-and-a-half-acre aquatic playground featuring a sand beach, waterfalls and a three-story water slide (for landlubbers there's tennis, bicycling, 27 holes of championship golf and a fitness center); an "obliging staff", three "great restaurants" and "wonderful public spaces" complete the "beautiful" picture; compared to the "fantastic" facilities, however, the rooms are "only slightly above average."

Inn at the Citadel (11S)
▽ 27 | 24 | 23 | 21 | $155

8700 E. Pinnacle Peak Rd., Scottsdale; (602) 585-6133; (800) 927-8367; FAX: (602) 585-3436

■ Much to the disappointment of devotees, this "intimate charmer" nestled in a cozy complex of art galleries and shops in North Scottsdale is no longer an "out-of-the-way desert oasis"; others have discovered the romantic suites appointed with antiques, original artwork, fireplaces and balconies or terraces; continental breakfast is included.

Marriott's Camelback Inn Resort, Golf Club
& Spa 405R (22S)
24 | 23 | 22 | 24 | $199

5402 E. Lincoln Dr., Scottsdale; (602) 948-1700; (800) 242-2635; FAX: (602) 951-8469

◪ This "graceful lady" celebrated her 60th birthday in 1996 by unveiling a $3.5-million pool complex featuring tiered sundecks, a shaded trellis area, children's play area, two whirlpools, fitness room, cafe and an outdoor fireplace; the "spacious" adobe-style casitas also were revamped and the "heaven on earth" spa was expanded, addressing customer concerns that the resort is "living on its reputation"; some things remain the same, however, namely the "ultrafriendly staff", "beautiful grounds" and "picture-perfect" golf courses.

Marriott's Mountain Shadows Resort &
Golf Club 301R (36S)
21 | 22 | 20 | 21 | $175

5641 E. Lincoln Dr., Scottdale; (602) 948-7111; (800) 228-9290; FAX: (602) 951-5430

◪ Though this "very distant cousin to the Camelback" "has seen better days" and "pales in comparison" to the newer niches in town, it's still a "nice place to go if you're on a budget"; there's a "fabulous pool area", "great tennis", an "excellent executive golf course" and a "friendly staff"; "come here if you can't afford Camelback."

Marriott Suites Scottsdale (251S)
24 | 20 | 18 | 19 | $138

7325 E. Third Ave., Scottsdale; (602) 945-1550; (800) 228-9290; FAX: (602) 945-2005

◀ Other all-suiters "should take lessons" from this exemplar in the heart of Scottsdale ffering "huge", "nicely appointed" rooms, "friendly" service and a "wonderful pool"; s "good for those not needing a resort" and one of the "best values" in town.

Orange Tree Golf & Conference Resort (160S)   24 | 21 | 18 | 21 | $157

10601 W. 56th St., Scottsdale; (602) 948-6100; (800) 228-0386; FAX: (602) 483-6074

☑ An "oasis" in the suburbs where it's a 30-foot putt from one end of your suite to the other and the country club–like golf facilities include 18 holes, a driving range, chipping and putting greens, a pro shop and locker rooms; linksters laud the "fantastic service" and "moderate" prices, but lament the "poor restaurant."

PHOENICIAN, THE 567R (73S)   28 | 27 | 26 | 28 | $260

6000 E. Camelback Rd., Scottsdale; (602) 941-8200; (800) 888-8234; FAX: (602) 947-4311

■ The second-ranked resort in Arizona, and one of the top 20 in the US, is "everything they say it is and then some" – a "king's palace" that "celebrates the decadent '80s" with the "biggest, most beautiful rooms in the world", "phenomenal bathrooms", "wonderful works of art" and a "magical mother of pearl pool"; add "excellent service", "exceptional food", "glorious" grounds (including a two-acre cactus garden) an "incredible spa", golf and tennis and "you'll never want to leave."

Pointe Hilton Resort at Squaw Peak (564S)   22 | 21 | 20 | 23 | $164

7677 N. 16th St., Phoenix; (602) 997-2626; (800) 934-1000; FAX: (602) 997-2391

■ They've "perfected the suites formula" at this "relaxing" "one-stop resort" that caters to both conferences and families with 48,000 square feet of meeting space, a full-service spa and salon, "fantastic" eight-acre water park and year-round children's program; "well-decorated" rooms, an "outstanding staff" and an overall "hacienda ambiance" enhance the attraction.

Pointe Hilton Resort at Tapatio Cliffs (591S)   23 | 22 | 21 | 23 | $166

11111 N. Seventh St., Phoenix; (602) 866-7500; (800) 934-1000; FAX: (602) 993-0276

■ If you can handle the "climb to the rooms" at this "hilly property", you'll be rewarded with "lovely" suites, "lots of activities" (golf, tennis, horseback riding, mountain biking, spa services) and a "terrific restaurant overlooking the city" – all in a "beautiful" Spanish-Mediterranean setting; for the ultimate in luxury, reserve a private poolside cabana equipped with refreshments, newspapers and magazines, robes, ceiling fan, refrigerator, cable TV, telephone and dataport.

Pointe Hilton Resort on South Mountain (636S)   23 | 21 | 20 | 23 | $159

7777 South Pointe Pkwy., Phoenix; (602) 438-9000; (800) 934-1000; FAX: (602) 431-6535

■ It's the "fun surroundings" – six swimming pools (including a few for adults only), golf, tennis, racquetball, riding stables and a state-of-the-art sports club – that keep conventioneers and vacationers coming back to this all-suiter seven miles from the airport; admirers also appreciate the "comfortable, well-appointed" accommodations, "friendly staff" and "good variety" of restaurants on-site, but even they admit that it can be "hard to find your way around" the "lovely grounds."

Radisson Resort Scottsdale 277R (41S)   20 | 20 | 18 | 21 | $144

7171 N. Scottsdale Rd., Scottsdale; (602) 991-3800; (800) 333-3333; FAX: (602) 948-9843

■ "There are better options in Scottsdale", but this resort nestled between the Sonoran Desert and McDowell Mountains happens to be an "outstanding value" given the scope of its recreational amenities – three pools, two golf courses, 21 tennis courts and fitness facilities; "nice rooms", an "eager to please" staff and a "quiet Southwestern atmosphere" make it a "relaxing" destination for both business and leisure groups.

Regal McCormick Ranch 125R (3S)   20 | 21 | 20 | 20 | $166

7401 N. Scottsdale Rd., Scottsdale; (602) 948-5050; (800) 222-8888; FAX: (602) 991-5572

■ A pair of 18-hole championship courses are the main attraction at this "golfer's home away from home" situated on a 40-acre man-made lake overlooking the McDowell Mountains; both tourists and meeting-goers maintain it's a "good spot for the money" with recently renovated rooms, "fantastic" lakeside villas and "good Southwestern food" at Piñon Grill.

Renaissance Cottonwoods Resort 65R (106S)   22 | 22 | 19 | 21 | $167
(fka Stouffer Cottonwoods Resort)

6160 N. Scottsdale Rd., Scottsdale; (602) 991-1414; (800) 468-3571; FAX: (602) 951-3350

☑ This "little gem in a great location" adjacent to the Borgata rates raves for its "ample yet cozy" "casita-style" suites featuring a "hot tub for two" on a "private walled-in patio" – "perfect for romance"; compared to the competition there "aren't many on-site amenities", however, mainly a "mellow pool area", four tennis courts, putting green, croquet court and shuffleboard.

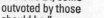

RITZ-CARLTON PHOENIX 267R (14S)

| 27 | 28 | 26 | 25 | $217 |

2401 E. Camelback Rd., Phoenix; (602) 468-0700; (800) 241-3333; FAX: (602) 468-0793
■ Expect the "typical Ritz" experience at this "urban gem" in the heart of the Camelback Corridor – "luxurious rooms", an executive floor where you're "pampered like royalty", "outstanding service" and "delightful" dining at the new and popular Bistro 24; some say it's "too uptight for casual Phoenix", but they're outvoiced and outvoted by those who maintain it's the "elegant business choice" and "what a hotel should be."

Royal Palms Hotel and Casitas 34R (82S)

| – | – | – | – | E |

5200 E. Camelback Rd., Phoenix; (602) 840-3610; (800) 672-6011; FAX: (602) 840-0233
This gracious Mediterranean-style hideaway in the Camelback Corridor reopened in April 1997, showing off the results of a year-long overhaul; the multimillion-dollar project created 19 sumptuous designer showcase casitas and added four executive suites, a small spa and fitness center, reflecting pools, romantic gardens, cocktail lounge, library, cigar room (with a leather floor), outdoor cafe, six outdoor fireplaces and 14 fountains, turning the once-tired property into a place of intimate splendor and understated luxury; at press time, only 48 rooms were completed, with the remaining expected to be available in August '97; rates include a full breakfast.

San Carlos Hotel 92R (23S)

| – | – | – | – | I |

202 N. Central Ave., Phoenix; (602) 253-4121; (800) 537-8483; FAX: (602) 253-6668
So this strictly-business hotel near the Civic Plaza "isn't fancy" – the "rooms are passable", service is "good" and the "rates are irresistible"; plus it's only six miles from the airport and easily accessible to all major highways; for post-convention relaxation there's a rooftop pool, three eateries and an exercise room.

Scottsdale Conference Resort 304R (21S)

| 20 | 21 | 20 | 21 | $178 |

7700 E. McCormick Pkwy., Scottsdale; (602) 991-9000; (800) 528-0293; FAX: (602) 596-7422
■ "A well-oiled machine for conferences" is the take on this mostly meetings facility featuring 50-plus function rooms, a business center, media center and "comfortable" guestrooms in a "beautiful location"; options for after-hours unwinding include golf, tennis, swimming, jogging and "outstanding dining" at the Palm Court.

Scottsdale Hilton Resort & Villas 178R (9S)

| 19 | 19 | 17 | 19 | $142 |

6333 N. Scottsdale Rd., Scottsdale; (602) 948-7750; (800) 528-3119; FAX: (602) 443-9702
☑ "Location" is the chief asset of this group-oriented resort hotel within walking distance of more than 100 shops and restaurants; otherwise it's "just ok", with lukewarm praise for the "nice pool area", "attentive service" and "good food"; despite recent renovations, only "if on a budget" remains the bottom line.

Scottsdale Plaza Resort 224R (170S)

| 21 | 20 | 18 | 21 | $178 |

7200 N. Scottsdale Rd., Scottsdale; (602) 948-5000; (800) 832-2025; FAX: (602) 951-5100
■ Admirers appreciate the wide range of accommodations – from "large, comfortable" standard rooms to "romantic" patio, bi-level and villa suites – at this "medium-fancy resort right on Scottsdale Road"; guests also give a nod to the "alluring", "well-equipped grounds" featuring swimming pools, tennis and racquetball courts, a health club and "excellent" Regional American cuisine at Remington's.

SCOTTSDALE PRINCESS 459R (191S)

| 27 | 26 | 25 | 27 | $226 |

7575 E. Princess Dr., Scottsdale; (602) 585-4848; (800) 344-4758; FAX: (602) 585-0086
■ "Away from the tourist crowds", though still in Scottsdale, this "excellent destination resort" catering to conventions is "lush, luxurious and laudable in every way" – from its "impeccable grounds" and casitas with wood-burning fireplaces that "make you want to forget about going home" to its "wonderful service" and "magnificent" Catalan cuisine at Marquesa; with two 18-hole golf courses, one the site of the PGA Tour's Phoenix Open, it's also "heaven for golfers."

Sheraton Crescent Hotel 330R (12S)

| 22 | 21 | 19 | 21 | $131 |

2620 W. Dunlap Ave., Phoenix; (602) 943-8200; (800) 423-4126; FAX: (602) 371-2856
■ You get "a lot for your money" at this "reliable mid-range" business hotel in northwest Phoenix – "spacious rooms", extensive meeting facilities and a surprisingly wide array of recreational offerings including swimming, tennis, sand volleyball, basketball, racquetball/squash and a fitness center; plus it's adjacent to the largest shopping and entertainment complex in the state.

Sheraton Mesa Hotel 264R (9S)

| 21 | 21 | 18 | 20 | $116 |

200 N. Centennial Way, Mesa; (602) 898-8300; (800) 456-6372; FAX: (602) 964-9279
■ The "only game in town" is a "better than average" "convention-type" hotel that receives approval for its "excellent" rooms and service, "good restaurants" and 52,000 square feet of function space; it's an "inexpensive alternative to Scottsdale" in a "great location for baseball spring training."

Sheraton San Marcos Golf Resort & Conference Center 280R (15S)

16 | 18 | 15 | 17 | $131

1 San Marcos Pl., Chandler; (602) 963-6655; (800) 528-8071; FAX: (602) 899-5441

■ "An affordable resort in the middle of nowhere" (about a half hour from the airport) is the take on this "oldie" but goodie built in 1913 and listed on the National Register of Historic Places; thanks to a recent renovation and expansion project, the 123-acre property now features spiffed-up guestrooms and function space along with a new 7,200-square-foot meeting pavilion and poolside cabana bar and grill.

WIGWAM RESORT 275R (56S)

25 | 24 | 23 | 25 | $211

300 Indian School Rd., Litchfield Park; (602) 935-3811; (800) 327-0396; FAX: (602) 935-3737

■ Solitude seekers say the "out-of-the-way site makes for a peaceful stay", while action-oriented types insist it's "too remote"; regardless, this "top-notch property" built by Goodyear in 1919 and opened to the public in 1929 earns plaudits for its "gorgeous", "large" casitas, "excellent service" and "one of the best Southwestern restaurants" (Arizona Kitchen); it's also the only resort in the area with 54 links of golf on-site.

Prescott

Hassayampa Inn 58R (10S)

– | – | – | – | M

122 E. Gurley St., Prescott; (520) 778-9434; (800) 322-1927; FAX: (520) 445-8590

Period oak furnishings and lace curtains lend an Old West air to the guestrooms at this local institution in a three-story 1927 brick building listed on the National Historic Register; adjacent to Prescott's courthouse square, it's a good base for exploring the town's attractions and the reasonable rates include breakfast in the Peacock Dining Room.

Scottsdale

See Phoenix/Scottsdale.

Sedona

CANYON VILLA BED & BREAKFAST INN 11R

28 | 26 | 24 | 25 | $167

125 Canyon Circle Dr., Sedona; (520) 284-1226; (800) 453-1166; FAX: (520) 284-2114

■ "Everything is done smoothly and graciously" at this "plush, modern" B&B – one of the top 20 in the US – offering unobstructed views of the red rocks from its "luxurious" rooms (most of which have whirlpool tubs and balconies or patios); amenities include "beautifully appointed" public spaces, a heated outdoor pool and complimentary full breakfast, late-afternoon hors d'oeuvres and "sweet dreams" before bedtime.

ENCHANTMENT RESORT 106R (56S)

26 | 25 | 24 | 27 | $229

525 Boynton Canyon Rd., Sedona; (520) 282-2900; (800) 826-4180; FAX: (520) 282-9249

■ "Heaven couldn't be more beautiful" than this "aptly named" resort in an "unmatched setting" amidst the red rocks; customers come here to "watch the stars" (both the celestial and celebrity types), and enjoy the "breathtaking facilities" including four pools, "superb tennis", spa and fitness center; all this – plus "wonderful" adobe-style casitas, "thoughtful service" and a "terrific dining room" – and it's "well worth the price."

Garland's Oak Creek Lodge 16R

23 | 23 | 24 | 22 | $173

PO Box 152, 8067 N. Hwy. 89-A, Sedona; (520) 282-3343; FAX: (520) 282-5920

■ "Don't spread the word – it's already too hard to get a reservation" at this "jewel" of a "hideaway" eight miles north of Sedona in Oak Creek Canyon; it's a "neat old spot" sporting "cabins with no phone, TV or radio" in a "very peaceful" setting; the inclusion of a full breakfast, afternoon tea, cocktails and gourmet dinner in the rate makes it the "best value" in the area "bar none"; a few find it "a bit regimented."

Graham Bed & Breakfast Inn 5R (5S)

▽ 28 | 27 | 26 | 24 | $147

150 Canyon Circle Dr., Sedona; (520) 284-1425; (800) 228-1425; FAX: (520) 284-0767

■ "What a find!" declare devotees of this "charming, gorgeous", "truly luxe" B&B touting "beautiful rooms" (each with a VCR and video library), "friendly, helpful hosts" and "excellent breakfasts" and afternoon refreshments included in the rate; "great golf" is nearby, an outdoor pool is on-site, "magnificent scenery" is everywhere.

L'AUBERGE DE SEDONA 95R (3S)

26 | 25 | 26 | 24 | $216

PO Box B, 301 L'Auberge Ln., Sedona; (520) 282-1661; (800) 272-6777; FAX: (520) 282-2885

◪ Though "a little incongruous" – a Country French inn in the middle of the desert – this "bit of Provence" "tucked into the side of a mountain" has legions of loyal fans who gush about the "marvelous cuisine", "standout" service and "terribly romantic cottages by the creek that will revive any marriage" (all with wood-burning fireplaces and covered porches, no TVs); best advice: "don't stay in the annex to save a few bucks" – it has a "motel feel that designer bedspreads don't hide."

Los Abrigados Resort & Spa (172S)
23 | 21 | 21 | 22 | $190

160 Portal Ln., Sedona; (520) 282-1777; (800) 521-3131; FAX: (520) 282-2614

☑ A "great location" in red rock country next to a "lovely self-contained shopping village" boosts the appeal of this "comfortable" all-suite resort; guests also give a nod to the "large suites", "accommodating service" and "outstanding food" courtesy of Scott Uehlein; for some, however, the experience is "marred by time-share sales attempts."

Poco Diablo Resort 135R (2S)
17 | 17 | 16 | 18 | $150

PO Box 1709, 1752 S. Hwy. 179, Sedona; (520) 282-7333; (800) 528-4275; FAX: (520) 282-2090

☑ Voters have mixed emotions about this recently redone resort hotel on the banks of Oak Creek; fans feel it's an "excellent value" with "delightful rooms", "fine service" and "beautiful facilities", while critics call it a "glorified motel" that's "still tacky after the redo" and "expensive for what you get" – "average" accommodations, "second-rate food" and uneven service; your call.

Tucson

ARIZONA INN 69R (14S)
23 | 26 | 24 | 25 | $161

2200 E. Elm St., Tucson; (520) 325-1541; (800) 933-1093; FAX: (520) 881-5830

■ On 14 acres of "gorgeous" lawns and gardens right "in the middle of the city" lies this "refreshing, graceful, peaceful throwback in time", a "true home away from home" with individually decorated guestrooms in "charming" pink stucco cottages, a "beautiful" sitting room and "excellent lounge for relaxing"; add "superb service", "marvelous food" clay tennis courts and a heated pool and you're in for a "real urban surprise."

Doubletree Hotel at Reid Park 287R (8S)
18 | 18 | 16 | 17 | $115

445 S. Alvernon, Tucson; (520) 881-4200; (800) 222-TREE; FAX: (520) 323-5225

■ A "modern room at a fair price" and meeting space for groups of 10 to 1,200 can be found at this "pleasant", "comfortable" Midtown hotel offering easy access to the airport, Downtown, major shopping areas and University of Arizona; it may be "nothing special", but with a jogging track, 25 tennis courts and 36 holes of golf just a chip shot away, customers consider it an "excellent value."

El Presidio Bed & Breakfast Inn 1R (3S) ⊄
– | – | – | – | M

297 N. Main Ave., Tucson; (520) 623-6151; (800) 349-6151; FAX: (520) 623-3860

Step back in time at this "beautiful" Victorian "overflowing with warmth" where accommodations filled with antiques, original artwork and fresh flowers surround shaded cobblestone courtyards; a gourmet breakfast is served on fine china and linens, and complimentary beverages and "goodies" are offered in the PM; "try it" and see if you agree that it's one of the "best B&Bs in the US."

LODGE AT VENTANA CANYON (49S)
26 | 25 | 24 | 25 | $231

(fka Ventana Canyon Golf & Racquet Club)

6200 N. Clubhouse Dr., Tucson; (520) 577-1400; (800) 828-5701; FAX: (520) 577-4065

■ There are almost as many holes of golf as guest suites at this recently refurbished country club and lodge nestled in the foothills of the Santa Catalina Mountains; expect nothing less than "excellent rooms" with spacious terraces and memorable touches like spiral staircases and old-fashioned footed bathtubs, "great service" and "top-of-the-line amenities" such as a 24-hour fitness center, 12 lighted tennis courts and, of course, "fabulous golf."

LOEWS VENTANA CANYON RESORT 371R (27S)
26 | 26 | 25 | 27 | $214

7000 N. Resort Dr., Tucson; (520) 299-2020; (800) 23-LOEWS; FAX: (520) 299-6832

■ This "spectacular oasis" set into the foothills of the Santa Catalinas is at "perfect peace with the desert", featuring a natural 80-foot waterfall, a pair of "otherworldly" golf courses "complete with cacti" and "exquisite rooms" (with tubs built for two) that look like they're "carved into the rock"; a "pampering staff", "absolutely fantastic" food at the Ventana Room and a "wonderful" new full-service spa add up to a "superb place to get away from it all."

Omni Tucson National Golf Resort & Spa 34R (109S)
24 | 22 | 20 | 22 | $177

(fka Tucson National Golf & Conference Resort)

2727 West Club Dr., Tucson; (520) 297-2271; (800) 528-4856; FAX: (520) 742-2452

☑ With three nine-hole courses, home of 21 PGA Tour events, this resort just northwest of Tucson is a "super choice for golf"; it's also a "great deal" given the "pretty rooms", "lovely grounds" and myriad nongolf offerings such as swimming, tennis, mountain biking, asketball, volleyball and a full-service spa; too bad the food is just "ok" in comparison

Sheraton El Conquistador 428R (100S)
24 | 23 | 22 | 24 | $178

10000 N. Oracle Rd., Tucson; (520) 544-5000; (800) 325-7832; FAX: (520) 544-1228
■ Conventioneers can't get enough of this recently renovated yet still "moderately priced" resort "surrounded by the beautiful Sonoran Desert", raving about the "extra-large rooms", "terrific service" and "extensive facilities" including 45 holes of golf, tennis, basketball, racquetball, volleyball and an "idyllic pool nestled against the mountains"; critics have only one complaint: "the food could improve."

SunCatcher B&B 4R
– | – | – | – | E

105 N. Avenida Javalina, Tucson; (520) 885-0883; (800) 835-8012; FAX: (520) 290-8821
Guestrooms at this "outstanding" B&B are furnished in the style of four of the world's greatest hotels – The Connaught in London, The Regent in Hong Kong, The Oriental in Bangkok and The Four Seasons in Chicago – and equipped with VCRs; the nonsmoking facility is far enough from town to offer a quiet setting yet close to major roadways and "outdoor activities"; a full breakfast is included.

Tanque Verde Guest Ranch 55R (13S)
22 | 23 | 21 | 24 | $206

14301 E. Speedway Blvd., Tucson; (520) 296-6275; (800) 234-DUDE; FAX: (520) 721-9426
■ "Horseback riding followed by herbal tea" – "the best of the dude ranches" is a "perfect place for New Yorkers to discover the outdoors"; it's a "same time next year" spot offering "plain but fine rooms" ("no TV!"), "generous portions of down-home food" (all meals are included) and "nonstop activities" (hiking, fishing, swimming, tennis) in the foothills of three colorful mountains; "friendly" staffers and "real wranglers" enhance the Wild West experience.

Triangle L Ranch (4S)
– | – | – | – | M

PO Box 900, Oracle; (520) 896-2804; FAX: (520) 623-6732
Accommodations at this 1890s homestead 35 miles east of Tucson consist of four private cottages (one with a fireplace, two with kitchenettes, none with TVs or telephones) furnished with antiques and shaded by giant oaks; the 80-acre ranch is a perfect place to do nothing – except relax on the porch, watch the wildlife, visit the resident chickens, gaze at the starry skies and listen to the calls of the great horned owls; a buffet-style continental breakfast is included.

WESTIN LA PALOMA 456R (31S)
25 | 24 | 23 | 26 | $208

3800 E. Sunrise Dr., Tucson; (520) 742-6000; (800) 228-3000; FAX: (520) 577-5878
■ "All the amenities you need or want" are available at this "architecturally striking" "jewel of a resort" – "spacious, luxurious rooms" with private balcony or patio, "magnificent grounds" and "delectable food" plus "great golf" (27 holes), tennis, a fitness center and a free-form pool with a swim-up bar and 177-foot water slide; no wonder it's "paradise" for conferences.

Westward Look Resort 236R (8S)
21 | 21 | 20 | 21 | $151

245 E. Ina Rd., Tucson; (520) 297-1151; (800) 722-2500; FAX: (520) 742-1573
■ Reviewers "can't rave enough" about this "older" but recently "redone" resort in the foothills of the Santa Catalinas, calling it a "perfect desert hideaway" ("and not too expensive") with "large, comfortable, suite-like rooms", "outstanding service" and "lots of well-maintained facilities" including three pools, eight tennis courts and a new wellness center offering everything from massages and facials to yoga and tai chi.

Wickenburg

Merv Griffin's Wickenburg Inn, Dude Ranch & Tennis Club 23R (40S)
21 | 20 | 18 | 20 | $197

(fka Wickenburg Tennis & Guest Ranch)
8 mi. north of Hwy. 89, Wickenburg; (520) 684-7811; (800) 942-5362; FAX: (520) 684-2981
■ This "wonderful" dude ranch on a 4,700-acre private preserve in "nowhere land" (70 miles northwest of Phoenix) rates raves from families for its "outstanding" hillside casitas with fireplaces, "beautiful desert scenery", "casual, laid-back, very relaxing" atmosphere and a host of things to do including horseback riding, tennis, nature hikes, trail rides, cattle drives, cowboy cookouts, roping lessons and gold panning; N.B. rates for the "fantastic experience" include three meals a day.

Arkansas

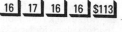

R S D P $

Dairy Hollow House 3R (3S)

– – – – E

515 Spring St., Eureka Springs; (501) 253-7444; (800) 562-8650; FAX: (501) 253-7223
Nouveau 'Zarks cuisine – a fusion of French and Ozarks – made chef Crescent
Dragonwagon famous; she also runs this intimate B&B fashioned partly from an 1880s
farmhouse near northwest Arkansas' Eureka Springs, a restored Victorian town and
home to much of the state's alternative-living set (witness Ms. D's adopted name); a
huge breakfast is delivered to guestrooms each AM, and though dinner is no longer
served nightly, it's worth finding out when the next seasonal feast is planned.

Palace Hotel & Bath House (8S)

16 17 16 16 $113

135 Spring St., Eureka Springs; (501) 253-7474
■ A 1901 Victorian in the Historic District of Eureka Springs that "inspires dreaming of
bygone days" while offering such modern comforts as whirlpool tubs, refrigerators and
cable TV in each suite; yet it's the "wonderful baths" attached to the hotel that are the
real draw, with such spa treatments as massage, mineral baths, eucalyptus steams
and clay-mask facials; there's no restaurant, but continental breakfast is included.

Hot Springs

Arlington Resort Hotel & Spa 469R (15S)

17 19 18 20 $105

239 Central Ave., Hot Springs; (501) 623-7771; (800) 643-1502; FAX: (501) 623-6191
◢ Soakers seek out the natural thermal baths at this "grande old dame", a 1923 resort
in the "pleasant setting" of Hot Springs National Park; while some are warmed by its
"terrific staff", "homey feel" and "fantastic food", others simmer over what they call a
"doddering" diva that's "begging for a major renovation"; in sum, "the spa is great",
but it may help to "have a taste for faded splendor."

Hot Springs Park Hilton 196R (4S)

17 16 15 16 $98

305 Malvern Ave., Hot Springs; (501) 623-6600; (800) 844-7275; FAX: (501) 624-7160
◢ Surveyors run hot and cold about this Hot Springs chain hotel-cum-spa: is it "better
than most Hiltons" with "great service" and "good food", or an "ordinary" place that
prompts "no rush to return"?; "clean", modern rooms appeal to those who note it's
the "only new hotel in town", but traditionalists prefer to "take advantage of historic
lodgings" in the area.

Lake Hamilton Resort (104S)

▽ 17 16 15 18 $99

2803 Albert Pike Rd., Hot Springs; (501) 767-5511; (800) 426-3184; FAX: (501) 767-8576
◢ All the "very comfortable" accommodations have private balconies and lake views
at this suburban all-suite resort and modest conference center on 10 acres; its setting
"right on" Lake Hamilton means it's just steps to swimming at the private beach, boating,
fishing and jet skiing (indoor and outdoor pools are also on-site); only a few surveyors
complain of "poor service" and "dark" rooms.

Majestic Hotel 232R (16S)

▽ 18 21 16 19 $93

101 Park Ave., Hot Springs; (501) 623-5511; (800) 643-1504; FAX: (501) 624-4737
■ The "best bath and massage in town" – and that's in a town with lots of baths and
massages – says one fan of this 1823 Downtowner (sister to the Arlington) in Hot Springs
National Park; catering to an "older clientele", it offers "super service" by the "nicest
people", and if some judge the rooms "so-so", others are too busy reveling in thermal
mineral soaks, rubdowns and spa retreat packages to notice.

Lakeview

Gaston's White River Resort 34R (40S)

▽ 16 22 24 24 $88

1 River Rd., Lakeview; (501) 431-5202; FAX: (501) 431-5216
■ "World-class trout fishing" is the raison d'être for this family resort spread along the
White River in northern Arkansas; if the cottage accommodations aren't to everyone's
liking ("rustic" vs. "ugly"), the "gorgeous river valley" makes it "well worth the trip"; a
tennis court, outdoor pool and American restaurant are on-site, but clearly it's "great
fishing" that brings 'em back hook, line and sinker.

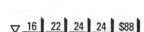

Arkansas Excelsior Hotel 396R (21S)

19 | 17 | 17 | 17 | $106

3 Statehouse Plaza, Little Rock; (501) 375-5000; (800) 527-1745; FAX: (501) 375-4721
■ A onetime haunt of Bill Clinton and still the "biggest game in town"; its exec-friendly rooms are "large" ("get a river view") and the staff is "nice", and while it's "bustling with activity" from conventions (18 meeting rooms), they know how to "handle crowds"; the hordes like to head to its Sunday brunch buffet.

Capital Hotel 118R (5S)

24 | 23 | 22 | 21 | $118

111 W. Markham St., Little Rock; (501) 374-7474; (800) 766-7666; FAX: (501) 370-7091
■ You don't need to be a friend of Bill's to get "good value" in Little Rock – it's offered to everyone at this "elegant" 1876 Downtowner, listed on the National Register of Historic Places and full of "old-world charm"; "huge, airy", "beautiful" rooms, "old-time service" and a "great restaurant" (Ashley's) add up to "one of the best in the US"; P.S. "tremendous elevators" (perhaps "largest in the US") give guests a lift.

Doubletree Hotel Little Rock 287R (11S)
(fka Camelot)

16 | 18 | 16 | 15 | $101

424 W. Markham St., Little Rock; (501) 372-4371; (800) 222-TREE; FAX: (501) 372-0518
▣ Doubletree felt your pain, took over the Camelot and undertook an $8-million redo; ratings have risen since the brand change, yet voters still aren't wholly convinced by this Downtowner overlooking the Arkansas River: "fine" views from "nice rooms" and a "great location" next to the convention center make it a natural "business trip" base, but some cite "microscopic rooms" and rate it overall "just average."

Little Rock Hilton Inn 256R (7S)

13 | 14 | 12 | 12 | $98

925 S. University Ave., Little Rock; (501) 664-5020; (800) HILTONS; FAX: (501) 664-3104
▣ This Midtowner is called "ok by Little Rock standards", but as ratings attest, that doesn't make much of an impression on surveyors – critics knock it as "busy and congested" with "poor service"; there are meeting rooms capable of handling 500, and for after-work relaxing there's an outdoor pool and fitness center plus nearby shopping, golf and tennis.

California

BEST OVERALL

28 Château du Sureau/Oakhurst
   Bel-Air/Los Angeles
   Ritz-Carlton Laguna Niguel/Dana Point
   Ritz-Carlton/San Francisco
   Peninsula Beverly Hills/Los Angeles
   Inn at Spanish Bay/Pebble Beach
27 Rancho Valencia/San Diego
   Post Ranch Inn/Big Sur
   Four Seasons/Los Angeles
   Auberge du Soleil/Rutherford
   Ritz-Carlton Huntington/Los Angeles
   Ritz-Carlton Rancho Mirage/Palm Spr.
   Lodge at Pebble Beach/Pebble Beach
   Sherman House/San Francisco
26 Ventana Inn/Big Sur
   Regent Beverly Wilshire/Los Angeles
   Meadowood/St. Helena
   Four Seasons Biltmore/Santa Barbara
   Four Seasons/Newport Beach
   Mandarin Oriental/San Francisco

BEST VALUES

Country Side Inn/Costa Mesa
Clarion Bedford/San Francisco
Apple Farm Inn/San Luis Obispo
Lafayette Park/Lafayette
de Anza, Hotel/San Jose
Doubletree/Anaheim
Gramma's Rose Garden/SF
Mission Inn/Riverside
Renaissance/Long Beach
Gosby House Inn/Pacific Grove
Majestic/San Francisco
Marriott/Costa Mesa
Red Lion/Costa Mesa
Monaco, Hotel/San Francisco
Palos Verdes Inn/Los Angeles
Juliana Hotel/San Francisco
Kensington Park/San Francisco
Doubletree Del Mar/San Diego
Vintage Court/San Francisco
Marriott Mission Valley/San Diego

Albion

ALBION RIVER INN 20R 26 | 24 | 25 | 24 | $176
3790 Hwy. 1 N., Albion; (707) 937-1919; (800) 479-7944; FAX: (707) 937-2604
■ On 10 acres of "ultra-scenic" northern coastline near Mendocino lies this "romantic", "exquisite" inn with "the ocean at your back door", where "charming" self-contained cottages with fireplaces and decks offer "unsurpassed" views (binoculars provided for whale-watching); a staff that "can't do enough" and "terrific" Cal cuisine (full breakfast included) work their "magic."

Anaheim

Disneyland Hotel 1075R (61S) 18 | 19 | 16 | 21 | $155
1150 W. Cerritos Ave., Anaheim; (714) 778-6600; FAX: (714) 956-6597
☑ The "amusement park spirit pervades" this "big", "strictly-for-Disneyland" hotel, a "madhouse" that's "fun for kids" with "all the Disney touches" including a direct entrance to the park via monorail, "enormous" rooms, "decor from Pluto", a Team Mickey workout center and the "friendliest staff around"; skeptics insist "Mickey would never take Minnie" to this "commercial" operation.

Disneyland Pacific Hotel 487R (15S) 18 | 19 | 17 | 18 | $144
(fka Pan Pacific Hotel)
1717 S. West St., Anaheim; (714) 999-0990; FAX: (714) 776-5763
■ Built in 1984, this new member of Disneyland Resorts is reportedly "very improved" after extensive renovations by the mouse empire; a "nice alternative to the huge Disneyland Hotel", it offers a quieter "oasis just steps from the action" and within walking distance of the monorail; but while its "spiffy" if "simple" rooms win ears from most and it's a "good buy for those on a budget", some note guest quarters are "smaller" than at its sibling and cite a "utilitarian" feel.

Doubletree Hotel 435R (19S) 19 | 20 | 18 | 18 | $115
100 The City Dr., Orange; (714) 634-4500; (800) 222-TREE; FAX: (714) 978-3839
■ "Modern rooms at a fair price" distinguish this contemporary 20-story high-rise near Anaheim that's also applauded for "convention center convenience" (two miles away) and, invariably, for the chain's complimentary chocolate-chip cookies that are "heaven" to hungry travelers; after the frequent shuttles deposit all the families at Disneyland, execs just might have the tennis courts, outdoor pool, spa and jogging track to themselves.

Hilton & Towers Anaheim 1480R (96S) 20 | 19 | 18 | 20 | $148
777 Convention Way, Anaheim; (714) 750-4321; (800) 222-9923; FAX: (714) 740-4252
☑ "Bland but well run", this "typical, huge convention hotel", a "bustling" operation next to the convention center and two blocks from Disneyland, boasts a "terrific" 25,000-square-foot fitness center featuring a full basketball court and indoor/outdoor pools; otherwise, it's considered "dependable" with "standard" rooms, though a few cite uneven service ("helpful" vs. "they don't care"); N.B. a "badly needed" $18.5-million total makeover in '96 could lift scores in the next *Survey*.

Hyatt Regency Alicante 384R (16S) 20 | 20 | 18 | 20 | $148
100 Plaza Alicante, Anaheim; (714) 750-1234; (800) 233-1234; FAX: (714) 740-0465
☑ "Down the street from Disneyland but enough removed for some quiet time", this "real find for Anaheim" earns kudos from some for "spacious" rooms and "outstanding" service, plus a complimentary Disneyland shuttle for Mouseketeers; but most agree that despite a "nice pool" and "pretty atrium" it's a fairly "boring convention hotel" that "needs upgrading."

Inn at the Park 488R (12S) 14 | 14 | 12 | 13 | $121
1855 S. Harbor Blvd., Anaheim; (714) 750-1811; (800) 421-6662; FAX: (714) 971-3626
■ A two-year total rehab is underway and none too soon, since despite a "killer" convention center/Disneyland location and facilities for medium-size conferences, along with 11 landscaped acres and an Olympic-size outdoor heated pool, this 14-story tower gets low ratings from surveyors who are of one mind: "needs refurbishing."

Marriott Anaheim 1003R (36S) 19 | 20 | 18 | 18 | $144
700 W. Convention Way, Anaheim; (714) 750-8000; (800) 228-9290; FAX: (714) 750-9100
■ Like most Marriotts, Anaheim's is "solid", "standard" and "reliable"; "a stone's throw" from the convention center, it's another "huge" operation that's "well run" by "friendly people", offering a "relaxing antidote to the hysteria" of nearby Disneyland (complimentary shuttle available) as well as a "lovely pool"; "superior food" pleases carnivores at J.W. Steakhouse, but as always with this chain, some shrug "ordinary."

| | R | S | D | P | $ |

Sheraton Anaheim 452R (39S)
1015 W. Ball Rd., Anaheim; (714) 778-1700; (800) 325-3535; FAX: (714) 778-5666

19 | 18 | 17 | 18 | $129

■ Sleeping Beauty might tuck in her kids at this Tudor-style castle across from Disneyland, where enormous medieval-style murals adorn the lobby; "great" service, a unique garden/courtyard setting, "nice pool facilities" and the "most spacious" rooms conjure up a "very comfortable" "good family hotel"; though it's "no big deal", those hopping the complimentary theme park shuttle seem more than satisfied.

Avalon

INN ON MT. ADA 4R (2S)
398 Wrigley Rd., Avalon; (310) 510-2030; (800) 884-1186; FAX: (310) 510-2237

26 | 26 | 24 | 26 | $249

■ The Wrigley family developed Catalina Island and built a "magnificent" Georgian colonial mansion in 1921 "high on a mountain overlooking the island"; it's now a "premium-priced" B&B appreciated for its "quiet" ambiance, pre-dinner cocktail hour ("complimentary champagne on the terrace") and "beautifully served" meals that are included in the "expensive-but-worth-it" rate; most agree "from the moment you arrive it's an experience", as in "outstanding"; children 14 and over only.

Big Sur

Big Sur Lodge 61R
Pfeiffer Big Sur State Park, Hwy. 1, Big Sur; (408) 667-3100; (800) 4-BIGSUR; FAX: (408) 667-3110

18 | 17 | 16 | 21 | $132

◪ "A great bargain in a beautiful setting", these "minimalist" cabins (many with fireplaces but no TVs, phones or views) offer a quiet, inexpensive getaway for meetings, hiking or horseback riding in a "breathtaking natural" area of coastal mountains and redwood forests close to the Pacific Ocean; critics gripe about "garage sale" furnishings and "nonexistent service", but nature lovers reply that the state park "is the attraction."

Big Sur River Inn 14R (6S)
Hwy. 1 at Pheneger Creek, Big Sur; (408) 667-2700; (800) 548-3610; FAX: (408) 667-2743

▽ **17 | 18 | 16 | 19 | $142**

■ Serving as a laid-back "love-inn" for locals, weddings and family gatherings, this veteran Big Sur resort provides "simple lodgings" in a "great rustic setting" among the redwoods; Adirondack chairs are set out in the river so guests can wiggle their toes in the water while sharing cocktails, and feet made for walking wander through excellent hiking trails nearby; the dining room overlooks the river and outdoor pools.

Deetjen's Big Sur Inn 20R
Hwy. 1, Big Sur; (408) 667-2377; FAX: (408) 667-0466

17 | 19 | 21 | 18 | $128

◪ This "hippie time warp" is a registered national historic site offering "terrific" American-French dining in the Norwegian-style main building and "funky" cabin-like quarters (11 with "great, romantic fireplaces" but no TVs) that "define rustic" but have a definite following for their "crunchy, warm New Age feel"; it's "quirky to say the least", and with about four to six rooms per building the "paper-thin" walls spell "not much privacy", but it's "worth a stop if you don't mind the lack of amenities."

POST RANCH INN 30R (2S)
PO Box 219, Hwy. 1, Big Sur; (408) 667-2200; (800) 527-2200; FAX: (408) 667-2824

28 | 27 | 27 | 27 | $349

■ New Age "heaven on the California coast" is found in an ecologically sensitive "architectural wonder" built into a "cliff overlooking the Pacific"; a "delight in every way", this "summer camp for billionaires" (the state's second-highest-rated inn) provides "exquisite" accommodations (all with stereos, fireplaces and whirlpools), "beyond-belief pampering" (including "in-room massages"), outdoor swimming and 'basking' pools, and "thrilling" views from "unique" rooms ("stay in the tree houses"); don't miss the glass-walled Sierra Mar Restaurant; N.B. "book well in advance."

VENTANA INN 54R (5S)
Hwy. 1, Big Sur; (408) 667-2331; (800) 628-6500; FAX: (408) 667-2287

28 | 26 | 26 | 27 | $274

■ "All the creature comforts" in "one of California's most beautiful settings" high above the ocean ensure that "relaxation just happens" at this "aging but still spectacular" adults-only "mountain retreat with class" and a "not-snobby" attitude; a "winner all around", this "haven for lovers" provides "huge", "lovely" rooms (many with fireplaces and hot tubs), "pampering" service, "million-dollar" views and an "exceptional" Cal-Med restaurant, plus a new fitness center and spa.

Bodega Bay

Inn at the Tides 86R
22 | 20 | 19 | 20 | $149

PO Box 640, 800 Hwy. 1, Bodega Bay; (707) 875-2751; (800) 541-7788; FAX: (707) 875-3285
■ "A wonderful place to relax and do nothing", this "cozy" collection of "delightful rustic lodges" sits on the Sonoma coast 40 miles north of San Francisco; "spectacular" views ("watch the fog roll in") and fireplaces in nearly half the rooms are the main draw, but there's also a pool as well as nearby wineries, golf, horseback riding, beachcombing or even bird-watching (the restaurant was a backdrop in Alfred Hitchcock's *The Birds*); only a few who cite a "dated look" find it a "little disappointing."

Borrego Springs

La Casa del Zorro Desert Resort 4R (77S)
25 | 24 | 21 | 25 | $179

3845 Yaqui Paso Rd., Borrego Springs; (619) 767-5323; (800) 824-1884; FAX: (619) 767-4782
■ "Everyone's so friendly" at this "romantic" "desert retreat" about 60 miles northeast of San Diego, a "gorgeous" "low-key" "getaway" built in the '30s on 33 "wonderful" acres in Anza Borrego Desert State Park; the marks of this Zorro are its "huge" suites and casitas (many with fireplaces), three outdoor pools, six tennis courts and championship golf nearby, plus meeting facilities for groups of up to 250, "fine" Continental dining at Butterfield and live blues and jazz weekends.

Capitola by the Sea

Inn at Depot Hill 12R
▽ 26 | 26 | 24 | 25 | $183

250 Monterey Ave., Capitola by the Sea; (408) 462-3376; (800) 572-2632; FAX: (408) 458-2490
■ "Nothing but beautiful memories" are reported from guests of this recently (and "elegantly") restored railroad depot turned "quiet", "romantic" B&B; set on a hill above a seaside town on Monterey Bay (a location offering a beach, shops and galleries as well as wineries and redwood forests nearby), its "gorgeous" "individually decorated rooms" and suites – all with fireplaces and luxe amenities – plus "incredible" breakfasts and wine tastings make it "expensive but worth it" to sybarites who already place it among the "very best in California."

Carlsbad

La Costa Resort and Spa 402R (77S)
23 | 24 | 22 | 25 | $253

2100 Costa del Mar Rd., Carlsbad; (619) 438-9111; (800) 854-5000; FAX: (619) 931-7585
☑ Although ratings support loyalists who laud the "spacious, comfortable" rooms, "wonderful" golf and tennis, "fantastic" food and "dynamite" spa in a "perfect, relaxed setting" north of San Diego, a sizable contingent of critics insists this resort, unrenovated since '87, "desperately needs to be refurbished", citing quarters that are "getting run-down" and a spa that "looks shabby"; fortunately, you'll "still feel pampered", but with "many specials", bargain hunters urge "don't pay full price."

Carmel

CARMEL VALLEY RANCH (100S)
27 | 25 | 23 | 26 | $236

1 Old Ranch Rd., Carmel; (408) 625-9500; (800) 422-7635; FAX: (408) 624-2858
■ The "perfect small resort" for "the golf-and-Chardonnay set" amid the "gorgeous" Santa Lucia Mountains boasts a "challenging", recently renovated Pete Dye–designed golf course and 12 tennis courts; "personalized" service, "spacious", "extravagant" recently refurbished suites (all with fireplaces, some with whirlpools), "good" Cal cuisine and "flower-filled" grounds all win raves, plus there's a new fitness center and nearby seaside towns offering the usual distractions; the heated outdoor pool helps in the foggy Carmel climate, as do "warm cookies and hot cider at bedtime."

Cobblestone Inn 20R (2S)
23 | 24 | 21 | 20 | $150

Junipero St., Carmel; (408) 625-5222; (800) 833-8836; FAX: (408) 625-0478
☑ Surveyors unanimously praise the "excellent" in-town location and the "fabulous" included breakfast at this "quaint" and "comfortable" English country inn, part of the small Four Sisters Inns chain, with "perfectly charming" individually decorated rooms (all with stone fireplaces) and a "friendly staff"; but some guests caution that "rooms vary in size", others grouse "too many teddy bears", "not enough parking."

HIGHLANDS INN 37R (105S)

| 26 | 25 | 26 | 25 | $253 |

PO Box 1700, Hwy. 1, Carmel; (408) 624-3801; (800) 682-4811; FAX: (408) 626-1574

■ Take the "great rat-race cure" at this Monterey Peninsula "couples' paradise" with a fireplace in every room and a whirlpool for two as the "centerpiece of each suite"; "sylvan forest and ocean vistas" from the decks are so "spellbinding" that some feel there's "no reason to leave the room when the sun's out" – but hiking, bicycling and an outdoor pool appeal to active types, and California fare as "breathtaking" as the view is a powerful lure at Pacific's Edge restaurant: a few barbs for "commercial" furnishings may change since rooms were "wonderfully redone" in '96.

JOHN GARDINER'S TENNIS RANCH 7R (7S)

| 25 | 26 | 25 | 26 | VE |

114 Carmel Valley Rd., PO Box 228, Carmel Valley; (408) 659-2207; (800) 453-6225; FAX: (408) 659-2492

■ Match point goes to the "rustic splendor", "spectacular view", "fine dining" and "excellent tennis instruction" on 14 courts (one for each guestroom) at this pricey 25-acre flower-filled resort where "it's like being a personal guest of the Gardiners" in the Carmel Valley sun; well-rated rooms include private patios and fireplaces, and while they may be "getting a little old-fashioned", that's a minor matter for serious players who swear it's "the best tennis camp there is"; basic rates include lodging and meals (jacket and tie for dinner) and tennis clinic packages are available.

La Playa Hotel 73R (7S)

| 21 | 22 | 21 | 22 | $172 |

PO Box 900, Carmel; (408) 624-6476; (800) 582-8900; FAX: (408) 624-7966

■ An "old California feel" and "quiet, peaceful, pretty" gardens right in Carmel make this "charming, historic" (circa 1904) Mediterranean-style hotel a "great place for small, classy business meetings" and a "perfect setting for a wedding"; just two blocks from the beach, it offers an outdoor pool, six tennis courts and five "terrific" cottages, but the rooms in the "beautiful" pink main building run from "pleasant" to "so-so" – although an early '97 room renovation may address some concerns.

Los Laureles 25R (5S)

▽ | 17 | 22 | 21 | 21 | $167 |

313 W. Carmel Valley Rd., Carmel Valley; (408) 659-2233; FAX: (408) 659-0481

■ While it's not widely known to surveyors, a few say Muriel Vanderbilt's former horse-breeding estate (some buildings date from 1890) offers a "fine" "down-home" "vacation spot" on 10 manicured acres at moderate prices for Carmel Valley; simple pine-paneled accommodations in several converted former stables include a few suites featuring fireplaces, whirlpools and kitchens, plus there's an outdoor pool, restaurant and lounge presenting live country music some evenings; golf packages are available for area courses, and a small spa opens in '97.

QUAIL LODGE (16S)

| 26 | 26 | 25 | 26 | $239 |

8205 Valley Greene Dr., Carmel; (408) 624-1581; (800) 538-9516; FAX: (408) 624-3726

■ "Country club peace and harmony" create a "top-notch, low-key resort" that's "the place to go in Carmel Valley" – a "posh", "delightful" "haven" with "always helpful" staff, "comfortable", "well-maintained" rooms and "the hardest golf course on the Monterey Peninsula" (tennis courts and two pools give nonduffers something to do); to some, the inland location is "its only drawback", but others welcome the "grand comfort away from the fog" and the "lush" wildlife preserve setting (and Carmel is just five minutes away); P.S. its Covey Restaurant is "wonderful."

STONEPINE RESORT 8R (6S)

| 26 | 26 | 24 | 28 | $346 |

150 E. Carmel Valley Rd., Carmel Valley; (408) 659-2245; FAX: (408) 659-5160

■ It's "worth taking out a second mortgage" for this "very formal but fabulous" Carmel Valley Relais & Châteaux estate on 330 acres catering especially to "the horsey set", providing a full-service equestrian center plus "luxurious", "unique" accommodations (whirlpools, fireplaces, etc.); service is "accommodating" if a tad "stuffy" to some – why not ask Brooke Shields and Andre Agassi, who had their wedding reception here?; N.B. the porcelain-and-crystal-filled Château Noël is off-limits to children under 12, but they're welcome in the more relaxed ranch-style quarters.

Cazadero

TIMBERHILL RANCH (15S)

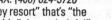

| 25 | 27 | 25 | 25 | $318 |

35755 Hauser Bridge Rd., Cazadero; (707) 847-3258; FAX: (707) 847-3342

■ Up for "roughing it gourmet-style in the middle of nowhere"? – this "special" Relais & Châteaux "get-away-from-it-all splurge" on 6,000 wilderness acres a half-mile from Sonoma County's coast offers upscale "rustic", "romantic", individually decorated cabins with fireplaces, handmade quilts and private decks along with an included six-course dinner prepared nightly by an "outstanding" chef (plus breakfast delivered to your door); there's also a heated pool, tennis, hiking and nearby Sea Ranch golf.

Costa Mesa

Country Side Inn & Suites 176R (124S)
19 | 19 | 17 | 18 | $105
325 Bristol St., Costa Mesa; (714) 549-0300; (800) 322-9992; FAX: (714) 662-0828
◪ A "pleasant surprise" in the shopping epicenter of Orange County, this Euro-style member of a small SoCal chain features mahogany furnishings, four-poster beds, a full fitness center, garden courtyard, two outdoor pools, comp breakfast and shuttle service to Newport Beach, Irvine and central Costa Mesa; the unimpressed complain that it "promises ambiance" but is really just "pretentious."

Marriott Suites Costa Mesa (253S)
20 | 18 | 16 | 17 | $114
500 Anton Blvd., Costa Mesa; (714) 957-1100; (800) 228-9290; FAX: (714) 966-8495
◼ In a "beautiful", "convenient OC location" within walking distance to shopping at South Coast Plaza, this "handy", "functional" all-suiter is a "nice change" from the "hustle-bustle" of full-size Marriotts; recently redone rooms (not reflected in scores), pool and complimentary shuttle service to John Wayne Airport are more pluses.

Red Lion Orange County Airport 474R (10S)
18 | 18 | 17 | 19 | $116
3050 Bristol St., Costa Mesa; (714) 540-7000; (800) 733-5466; FAX: (714) 540-9376
◪ This big business hotel that's "convenient" to the airport, South Coast Plaza and Disneyland offers "basic comfort", a recently expanded fitness center and "great" meeting facilities and prices, but "that's about all"; for most, it's "a place to put your head on a business trip", although a recent redo may add a little more pizazz.

Westin South Coast Plaza 373R (17S)
21 | 21 | 19 | 19 | $145
686 Anton Blvd., Costa Mesa; (714) 540-2500; (800) 937-8461; FAX: (714) 622-6695
◪ "Ready, aim, shop!" at "beautiful" South Coast Plaza, then "walk across the street to sleep" in what most tag a "commercial" but "luxurious" "modern" hotel with "nice" rooms, "good" food and pool area, and guest privileges at The Spa at South Coast Plaza; more jaded travelers sigh it's just "another hotel" – "journeyman-like."

Dana Point

Laguna Cliff Marriott 333R (17S)
21 | 20 | 19 | 23 | $161
(fka Dana Point Resort)
25135 Park Lantern, Dana Point; (714) 661-5000; (800) 533-9748; FAX: (714) 661-3688
◪ Admirers cheer this "relaxing" "California-casual" resort in a "spectacular" setting overlooking the Pacific halfway between LA and San Diego where the "friendly" staff, "rooms with views" (renovated in '96) and "excellent" Sunday brunch at Watercolors also win approval; a vocal minority complains that its "beauty is marred by a sterile, conventioneers' environment", but the fitness center, tennis courts, swimming pools and beach (within "walking distance") keep most guests happy.

RITZ-CARLTON LAGUNA NIGUEL 362R (31S)
28 | 28 | 27 | 29 | $265
1 Ritz-Carlton Dr., Dana Point; (714) 240-2000; (800) 241-3333; FAX: (714) 240-0829
◼ The state's top-rated resort is awash in tributes as an "unequaled", "special-occasion" splurge in a "glorious" SoCal setting on an oceanside bluff; the "gracious", "well-appointed" public areas, "fantastic" rooms, "impeccable" service, "amazing" views and "impressive" Dining Room add up to "everything a luxury hotel should be" – "it defines world-class"; of course it offers all the usual amenities (pools, tennis courts, championship golf) and it's especially "gorgeous at Christmas time."

Death Valley

Furnace Creek Inn 64R (2S)
18 | 20 | 18 | 21 | $169
PO Box 1, Hwy. 190, Death Valley; (619) 786-2345; (800) 236-7916; FAX: (619) 786-2423
◪ Some prefer the inn, some the adjacent ranch at this 70-year-old Death Valley resort, a "big surprise" on a "beautiful palm-tree oasis" "in the middle of nowhere"; now open year-round, the relatively formal Spanish villa–style inn is "great for romance" and while surveyors spar over whether the rooms are "lovely" or "average", all find the dining room "surprisingly gracious" (jackets required); the "homey" ranch is "more laid-back" with "basic" rooms, but it's a "better value", for families.

Eureka

Carter House Victorians 20R (12S)   22 23 22 20 $151
301 L St., Eureka; (707) 444-8062; (800) 404-1390; FAX: (707) 444-8067
■ "Victorian sumptuousness" permeates this "haven between Napa and Portland, Oregon" in Eureka's Old Town district; the three-building "gingerbread confection" includes two modern Victorian reproductions – the more intimate Carter House and the 20-room Hotel Carter – as well as an 1889 cottage; guests laud the "spacious", "well-appointed" rooms (some with fireplaces and whirlpools), "personal service" and gourmet breakfast, and rave over Restaurant 301.

Fish Camp

Tenaya Lodge at Yosemite 238R (6S)   20 20 19 22 $149
(fka Marriott Tenaya Lodge at Yosemite)
1122 Hwy. 41, Fish Camp; (209) 683-6555; (800) 635-5807; FAX: (209) 683-8684
☑ Reviewers agree that this ex-Marriott, built in 1990 "on the doorstep" of Yosemite National Park but "away from the tourist crowd", provides a "marvelous setting" for fishing, hiking, horseback riding, x-country skiing, swimming in the "nice pool", etc.; but they draw swords on whether it's a "well-run" facility that's "perfect for families" with "nicely appointed" rooms and "great" food or "mediocre" with "small" rooms and "poor" dining; scores back up the advocates, but in any case "it's a captive market."

Fresno

4 Points Hotel by ITT Sheraton 201R (3S)   15 16 12 13 $105
(fka Sheraton Smuggler's Inn)
3737 N. Blackstone Ave., Fresno; (209) 226-2200; (800) 325-3535; FAX: (209) 222-7147
☑ Totally renovated in 1994, and rebranded by Sheraton in late '95, this property adjacent to Fresno's business district offers "oversize rooms" but draws mixed reviews overall: "very good quality", "above average" vs. "disappointing"; similarly, the pool area is either "cramped" or the "most relaxed I know of"; ratings are middling, but it may be worth a try considering it's only five miles from the airport.

Garberville

Benbow Inn 52R (3S)   21 22 22 24 $155
445 Lake Benbow Dr., Garberville; (707) 923-2124; (800) 355-3301; FAX: (707) 923-2122
■ "Escape from the modern world" at this "rustically elegant" 1926 Tudor mansion, a "delight in the redwoods" north of SF, where surveyors enjoy the "first-class", "very comfortable", "charming" rooms (some are "tiny" so "be choosy"), "magnificent grounds" and "very sophisticated yet casual" dining; "great Christmas decorations" make it a "holiday must" after which it closes till mid-April.

Gualala

St. Orres 8R (11S)   22 22 24 20 $160
36601 Hwy. 1 S., Gualala; (707) 884-3303; FAX: (707) 884-1543
☑ "An unbelievable setting in the redwoods" hosts this "romantic gourmet getaway", an "unusual" 42-acre mock-Russian estate centered around three-story towers topped by stained glass and copper onion domes; about three hours north of SF, it offers small European-style rooms in the main building and a variety of cottages, from rustic to "luxurious" (some with ocean views, decks and skylights); fans say "to stay is fun, to dine divine"; but for a few it's "too much like staying at an old hippie colony."

Whale Watch Inn 18R   26 25 22 23 $196
35100 Hwy. 1, Gualala; (707) 884-3667; (800) 942-5342; FAX: (707) 884-4815
■ A contemporary cluster of five clapboard buildings offers "romance to the max" in a "beautiful", "isolated" beachfront location three hours north of SF; "beautifully appointed" rooms where you "gaze at the stars through your own personal skylight", whirlpools for two, fireplaces, decks with "spectacular views" (including whale sightings) and a "fabulous" full bedside breakfast make this B&B both "charming" and "reviving."

Guerneville

Applewood Inn 9R (7S)   ▽ 24 | 25 | 23 | 23 | $193
13555 Hwy. 116, Guerneville; (707) 869-9093; (800) 555-8509; FAX: (707) 869-9170

■ This "lovingly restored" pair of 1922 Mediterranean-style villas in the heart of Sonoma's vineyards enchant guests who recommend you "pamper yourself with food, wine and luxury" in uniquely decorated rooms and suites; the recently added terraced gardens lend more pleasure, and there's a pool and spa on-site and a beach just a short drive away, as well as "imaginative" regional fare at the eponymous restaurant.

Healdsburg

Madrona Manor 18R (3S)   23 | 23 | 25 | 21 | $169
1001 Westside Rd., Healdsburg; (707) 433-4231; (800) 258-4003; FAX: (707) 433-0703

◪ Though it's not for everyone, most find "gothic charm" in a "priceless" Sonoma wine country setting at this "quaint", "historic house with a great restaurant"; to critics the possibly "haunted" 1881 Victorian structure is "dusty" and "in need of updating", but more appreciate "homey", "low-key" accommodations (most with fireplaces, all with private baths), "lovely" service, "wonderful grounds", a heated pool and the ability to "walk downstairs to dinner", which just happens to be "top-notch."

Irvine

Hilton Orange County Airport 284R (5S)   18 | 17 | 16 | 15 | $132
18800 MacArthur Blvd., Irvine; (714) 833-9999; (800) 445-8667; FAX: (714) 833-3317

■ Scores reveal that the huge meeting facilities, "close-to-the-airport" location, "great motel-like rooms", heated pool, twin tennis courts and reasonable rates combine to make this hotel a "functional" choice for business; it's certainly serviceable for "a nap between planes."

Hyatt Regency Irvine 536R (20S)   20 | 20 | 19 | 19 | $144
17900 Jamboree Blvd., Irvine; (714) 975-1234; (800) 233-1234; FAX: (714) 863-0531

■ Conventions and shopping – for these alone, this "clean", "comfortable", "typical Hyatt Regency" close to OC's John Wayne Airport (where the hotel maintains a convenient check-in desk) "does the trick"; it's a "good business hotel" that can also be "fun for family weekends" when there are "good deals", and its already decent ratings may really take off next time due to a total renovation completed in early '97; seismophobes take note: "it sways well."

Irvine Marriott 461R (24S)   19 | 19 | 18 | 19 | $133
18000 VonKarman Ave., Irvine; (714) 553-0100; (800) 228-9290; FAX: (714) 261-7059

◪ "Excellent" for business trips and "right in the heart of great shopping", this chainer near OC's John Wayne Airport with four tennis courts, indoor/outdoor pool, "alluring" weekend specials and a "great" sushi bar is "better than ok" to many, though to a sizable minority, it's "standard", "functional" and "needs some sprucing up" (which the concierge level got in '96).

Lafayette

Lafayette Park Hotel 129R (10S)   25 | 22 | 22 | 22 | $139
3287 Mt. Diablo Blvd., Lafayette; (510) 283-3700; (800) 368-2468; FAX: (510) 284-1621

■ A three-story French-Norman–style "gem" built in 1985 provides a "civilized oasis" in the East Bay with an "elegant yet comfortable" ambiance and service and decor that are the "same as SF's best"; accommodations featuring cherrywood furniture and Italian granite baths (some with fireplaces and sitting areas), plus three courtyards, a pool, a "cozy, romantic" bar and "high-quality" California cuisine at the Duck Club add up to "top-notch all the way."

Laguna Beach

Surf & Sand Hotel 153R (4S)   23 | 22 | 23 | 22 | $204
1555 S. Coast Hwy., Laguna Beach; (714) 497-4477; (800) 664-7873; FAX: (714) 494-7653

■ "The view, the view, the view" – and a "perfect" beachfront location – equals bliss for guests of this "small", "romantic", "wonderful" hotel where the "lovely" rooms with balconies "open to crashing waves"; Splashes restaurant is "practically in the water" and serves "awesome lunches", while dinner at The Towers is "perfect"; umbrellas, towels and chairs are complimentary for beachcombers, and there's a pool for those who prefer calmer waters.

Lake Arrowhead

Lake Arrowhead Resort 240R (21S)   18 | 18 | 17 | 20 | $143
27984 Hwy. 189, Lake Arrowhead; (909) 336-1511; (800) 800-6792; FAX: (909) 336-1378
▣ "One way to gain access to the lake is to stay here", which may be the chief attraction of this "great escape" set on "beautiful", "serene" Lake Arrowhead in the San Bernardino Mountains; but surveyors clash over the service ("good" vs. "ha!") and most dismiss the "basic motel-style" rooms (although deluxe suites and lakeside villas are available); still, the "great health club" and spa, tennis, heated pool, video arcade, children's programs and restaurants provide plenty of distractions, and Lake Arrowhead Village next door offers myriad shopping and dining options.

Little River

Heritage House 55R (11S)   25 | 23 | 24 | 24 | $228
5200 N. Hwy. 1, Little River; (707) 937-5885; (800) 235-5885; FAX: (707) 937-0318
■ Overlooking the "majestic" Mendocino coast, this "self-contained", "lovely and rustic" "hideaway" on 37 acres provided the "very special", "romantic" setting for the film *Same Time Next Year*; most agree the "food and scenery are divine" (star chef Lance Dean Velasquez presides), but while a few also claim "all rooms are fantastic", more say they "vary in size, style and comfort" so it's "best to look before you book" (many are in cottages offering Pacific views, fireplaces and decks); breakfast and dinner are included, and there are no phones or televisions in guestrooms to disturb your newfound "piece of paradise."

Little River Inn 63R (2S)   21 | 22 | 22 | 20 | $151
7751 N. Hwy. 1, Little River; (707) 937-5942; (888) INN-LOVE; FAX: (707) 937-5942
■ Built by a Maine lumberman in 1853, this white coastal residence with picket fence may look "like New England", but it's actually "old California" just two miles south of Mendocino; still run by the same family, the "charming" inn has expanded to multiple units but remains a "romantic" setting with "great" ocean views, "very friendly" staff and a "beautiful" bar and restaurant, along with tennis, a beach and a nine-hole golf course; all in all, it's a "relaxing", "comfortable" getaway.

Long Beach

Queen Mary, Hotel 348R (17S)   18 | 18 | 18 | 21 | $139
1126 Queens Hwy., Long Beach; (310) 435-3511; (800) 437-2934; FAX: (310) 437-4531
▣ Take a "nostalgia trip" "without the seasickness" in this "splendid conversion" of the ocean liner *Queen Mary*, permanently berthed in Long Beach Harbor since 1967; but "be prepared for small quarters" (although they vary in size) that many say are "starting to get frumpy and dumpy"; the experience is "fun" and "unique for a night", especially for kids who like to "look through the portholes", but many agree that "once is enough" – "the idea is better than the reality."

Renaissance Long Beach Hotel 367R (7S)   21 | 19 | 18 | 19 | $121
111 E. Ocean Blvd., Long Beach; (310) 437-5900; (800) HOTELS-1; FAX: (310) 499-2509
■ A "great job of restoration" in '96, plus a staff that "works very hard to please" and "excellent" rooms and views for a "decent" price earn lots of compliments for this "well-located", mostly business hotel in Long Beach that's directly across the street from the convention center and within walking distance of restaurants, shops and other amusements in this "wonderful town"; a heated outdoor pool, two restaurants and a health club are among the on-site amenities.

Sheraton Long Beach Hotel 430R (30S)   18 | 17 | 16 | 17 | $131
333 E. Ocean Blvd., Long Beach; (310) 436-3000; (800) 325-3232; FAX: (310) 436-9176
■ The "comfortable", "relaxing" rooms and a "hard-working", "remarkably friendly" staff make this "dependable" hotel across from the convention center a "good compromise between Downtown and the beach" that's serviceable for both business and pleasure; "nice" ocean views, an "excellent" meetings and banquet department plus a pool and fitness center are more assets.

TOP 10 OVERALL

BEST OVERALL

28 Bel-Air
   Peninsula Beverly Hills
27 Four Seasons
   Ritz-Carlton Huntington
26 Regent Beverly Wilshire
   Ritz-Carlton Marina del Rey
   Shutters on the Beach
25 Beverly Hills
24 Nikko Beverly Hills
   Argyle

BEST VALUES

Palos Verdes
Barnabey's
Hilton Long Beach
Renaissance Los Angeles
Marriott Warner Center
Doubletree LAX
Wyndham LAX
Sheraton Industry Hills
Beverly Prescott
Ritz-Carlton Huntington

R	S	D	P	$

ARGYLE, THE 21R (43S) | 23 | 24 | 27 | 23 | $201 |
8358 Sunset Blvd., West Hollywood; (213) 654-7100; (800) 225-2637; FAX: (213) 654-9287
☑ "Hollywood '30s glamour is beautifully revisited" in this "knockout" West Hollywood art deco "in-spot", once the haunt of Errol Flynn and Jean Harlow; some find the quarters "well appointed" (if "small") and applaud the "memorable" skyline views and "great" service, others say the rooms "need TLC" and the staff is "a little snobbish" "unless you're in show business"; but most agree that chef Ken Frank's Franco-Californian fare at the "lovely" Fenix is "the best."

Barnabey's Hotel 122R | 20 | 20 | 19 | 17 | $129 |
3501 Sepulveda Blvd., Manhattan Beach; (310) 545-8466; (800) 545-8466; FAX: (310) 545-8621
☑ Anglophiles dub this Victorian-decorated, '70s-built hotel in a beach community near LAX "a haven in crazy LA", finding it to be an "animated but comfortable" "oasis" of "unexpected 19th-century European charm" with a heated outdoor pool and an English-style pub; though a few Scrooges sniff at its "kitschy Dickens" style, "dark, corny" rooms and "clutter, clutter, clutter", most consider it "good for a change" of pace.

BEL-AIR, HOTEL 52R (40S)   28 | 28 | 28 | 28 | $310

701 Stone Canyon Rd., Los Angeles; (310) 472-1211; (800) 648-4097; FAX: (310) 476-5890
■ Once again LA's top-rated hotel, this "Hollywood-style fantasy" come true is nestled in a 12-acre "sumptuous sanctuary" of gardens, villas and a lake where white swans swim; "amazingly private" bungalows and "discreet" service create an "idyllic" "hideaway" that's "lush, plush, and worth the $$$" for "perfection in every detail"; there's "superior" Cal-French dining at The Restaurant, and you can atone afterward in the fitness center housed in what was once known as the Marilyn Monroe Cottage.

BEVERLY HILLS HOTEL 157R (37S)   26 | 26 | 24 | 26 | $282

9641 Sunset Blvd., Beverly Hills; (310) 276-2251; (800) 283-8885; FAX: (310) 887-2887
☑ Since its '94 revamp, fans find "the magic has returned" to this "pretty as a picture", legendary "pink palace" and its famous bungalows, where you can "see and be seen" while enjoying "consummately discreet" "movie star attention"; "the grounds are still glorious, the pool peerless" and many enjoy dining at the Polo Lounge, but critics, a minority, cry "the glamour's gone" in "a sad renovation" that's "all glitz, no substance."

Beverly Hilton 501R (80S)   21 | 21 | 19 | 20 | $195

9876 Wilshire Blvd., Beverly Hills; (310) 274-7777; (800) 922-5432; FAX: (310) 285-1313
☑ "Big, brassy" and "impersonal" but "good for stargazing", this busy, "well-oiled, full-service" hotel owned by Merv Griffin is "perfectly located" and comes "at a really fair price"; there's an Olympic-size outdoor pool and dining at the "classic" Trader Vic's, but those distractions don't quiet critics who pronounce this star "washed up", finding the rooms "boring" (albeit "well laid out"), service "a little offhand" and the lobby "shabby."

Beverly Prescott Hotel 119R (20S)   23 | 22 | 20 | 19 | $160

1224 S. Beverwil Dr., Los Angeles; (310) 277-2800; (800) 421-3212; FAX: (301) 203-9537
■ "One of the West Side's best-kept secrets" is a "trendy but comfortable", "charming boutique hotel" set "a little off the beaten path" on the edge of Beverly Hills; assets include "innovative" decor, "large", "warm" rooms and "professional, considerate" service – and it's "a bargain" to boot; the latest effort in its ever-changing restaurant space is The Chez (Regional American cuisine) – "good" so far, say boosters.

Century Plaza Hotel & Tower 994R (78S)   23 | 22 | 20 | 22 | $201

2025 Ave. of the Stars, Los Angeles; (310) 277-2000; (800) 228-3000; FAX: (310) 551-3355
☑ This "large, bustling", "upscale" hotel has an "ideal location" in Century City and draws "lots of big shots", yet voter comments are mixed: "pretty", "classy", "efficient" vs. "convenient but humdrum", "always reliable and perfectly mediocre"; the explanation may be that Tower rooms ("worth the extra dollars") are said to "tower over" lodgings in the more "mundane" original building (an exception may be the latter's top-floor suites, which just had a $2.5-million redo); either way, "excellent meeting facilities" make it a "delight" for business.

Chateau Marmont 11R (52S)   21 | 21 | 18 | 21 | $210

8221 Sunset Blvd., Hollywood; (213) 656-1010; (800) CHATEAU; FAX: (213) 655-5311
☑ A "European, arty feel" mixes with a "Hollywood atmosphere" in this "fun", "funky", "hip place to stay", a "castlelike" setting where Harlow and Gable rendezvoused way back when; long a "show biz favorite", it dazzles admirers with fine views, "beautiful grounds" and a "lovely" pool, but others find "great nostalgia, nothing else", citing "dated" rooms and "tag sale" furniture; one thing's for sure: it's "unique."

Clarion Hollywood Roosevelt Hotel 272R (48S)   14 | 15 | 14 | 16 | $143
(fka Radisson Hollywood Roosevelt)
700 Hollywood Blvd., Hollywood; (213) 466-7000; (800) 950-7667; FAX: (213) 466-9376
☑ Changing its brand name as often as some stars change hair color, this "legendary" "old Hollywood" hotel charms cinema buffs as a "place of history" (the first Academy Awards were held here) located "in an improving neighborhood" overlooking Mann's Chinese Theater; it's "perfect for tourists", but if you're not a film fanatic, you may find it to be just an "old-timer" with "aches and pains."

Doubletree Hotel at LAX 680R (42S)   19 | 18 | 17 | 17 | $127

5400 W. Century Blvd., Los Angeles; (310) 216-5858; (800) 222-TREE; FAX: (310) 645-8053
■ "Nice for the night before you leave" from LAX, especially "if price is the most important factor", this airport hotel may be "nothing out of the ordinary", but it's "efficient and friendly", offering "functional" lodgings, a "convenient" location near freeways, "great views", good meeting facilities, a fitness center and pool; "pleasant" if "typical" sums it up.

FOUR SEASONS HOTEL 179R (106S)

28	28	27	27	$266

300 S. Doheny Dr., Los Angeles; (310) 273-2222; (800) 332-3442; FAX: (310) 859-9048

■ "Rub shoulders with celebs" or "see and be seen" over a "power breakfast" at the "ne plus ultra" in "chic", a "posh and swanky", "romantic" Beverly Hills retreat where surveyors swoon over "low-key high-class comfort" and "spiffy" service; "innovative" Mediterranean cuisine at Gardens makes for "divine" dining and the "bar is wall-to-wall stars" – "Dustin, Jodie and Jack blend in with the upscale lounge crowd"; with scores like these, "what's not to like?" (except maybe the cost).

Georgian 56R (28S)

▽	20	20	16	21	$145

1415 Ocean Ave., Santa Monica; (301) 395-9945; (800) 538-8147; FAX: (301) 451-3374

■ This "cross between old Hollywood and Rick's" Cafe is "perfectly located" near Santa Monica's restaurants and street life and features a "fabulous" wicker-laden beach-viewing veranda; an "old-fashioned, deco"-style hotel, it was built as the Lady Windemere in 1933, and though the "funky" rooms are "on the small side", they're "very clean" and come with "big" bathrooms, making it a "great deal for the money"; N.B. a/c arrives in '97.

Hilton & Towers Los Angeles Airport 1181R (55S)

18	17	15	16	$135

5711 W. Century Blvd., Los Angeles; (310) 410-4000; (800) HILTONS; FAX: (310) 410-6250

☑ "Fascinating views" of LAX takeoffs and landings can be enjoyed from "nicely soundproofed" rooms at this "clean and quiet", "industrial-strength", "well-managed" airport hotel; critics report a bumpier ride, citing "out-of-style" rooms in a "boring factory" that's "strangely lacking in amenities" (despite a pool and fitness facility), but "if you have an early flight" it'll do just fine.

Hilton Long Beach 387R (6S)

20	19	18	18	$129

2 World Trade Ctr., Long Beach; (310) 983-3400; (800) 445-8667; FAX: (310) 983-3478

■ Though some surveyors can't quite stifle a "ho hum", most consider this "pleasant" if "typical commercial hotel" to be a "good utilitarian" choice in Long Beach and "very handy" for business (with good-size meeting facilities) or for Grand Prix fans; rooms are "comfortable" (many with "a view of the water"), the pool area is "nice" and workout facilities are extensive, but overall some feel it "needs an overhaul."

Hyatt Regency Los Angeles 442R (43S)

20	20	18	18	$167

711 S. Hope St., Los Angeles; (213) 683-1234; (800) 233-1234; FAX: (213) 612-3179

☑ This "clean, classy" place in an "excellent" location for Downtown business meetings is "all that's needed" when a "steady, businessperson's hotel" is on the agenda; rooms are "very comfy" (though some report "small" beds) and in general it's "well maintained" for a "big", "high-use" hotel; the consensus: "nothing special" but "dependable."

Inter-Continental Los Angeles 415R (18S)

23	22	20	21	$172

251 S. Olive St., Los Angeles; (213) 617-3300; (800) 442-5251; FAX: (213) 617-3399

■ "Perfect for art lovers" (next to MOCA) and also a "nice place to stay for business", so this "clean", "bright", "up-to-date" place gets painted by some admirers as the "No. 1 Downtown value"; it's "well run" by an "attentive" staff and rooms are "lovely", though some may be "small"; the only debate seems to be over dining: "good" vs. "so-so."

Le Parc Hotel (154S)

21	19	15	15	$158

733 N. West Knoll Dr., West Hollywood; (310) 855-8888; (800) 5-SUITES; FAX: (310) 659-7812

■ Musicians and entertainers "love the privacy" of this "out-of-the-way", "quiet and comfortable" West Hollywood suite "surprise" that's "like staying in an apartment building" – one that happens to have a "great rooftop pool" and an "enthusiastic" staff; on a sour note, an "immediate improvement" is needed in the food, and some say avoid "le dark" (rooms in the back) – but "you'll love it if you get a suite facing west."

Loews Santa Monica Beach Hotel 326R (24S)

23	22	21	23	$201

1700 Ocean Ave., Santa Monica; (310) 458-6700; (800) 235-6397; FAX: (310) 458-6761

☑ "Fantastic" architectural design in a "spectacular" beachfront site with "gorgeous" ocean views creates "a dynamite first impression" at this "airy", "fast-paced" property that's "very accommodating to business" travelers yet just right for sand-and-sunning too; naysayers see it differently ("industrial and institutional", "like staying at a mall" with "ok" rooms near a "seedy" stretch of beach), but they're outvoted.

Malibu Beach Inn 44R (3S)

21	20	15	19	$172

22878 Pacific Coast Hwy., Malibu; (310) 456-6444; (800) 4-MALIBU; FAX: (310) 456-1499

■ "You can hear the waves from your bed", and possibly the smart set air-kissing, in this "way cool, fun-and-sun" "beachfront getaway" for the "LA overworked" crowd; it's a "charming, clean little inn" featuring "beautifully decorated, oversize" rooms, each with a fireplace, VCR, coffeemaker and private balcony; while there's no restaurant, there are many nearby and the included continental breakfast is "excellent."

Mansion Inn 38R (5S)

| – | – | – | – | M |

327 Washington Blvd., Marina del Ray; (310) 821-2557; (800) 828-0688; FAX: (310) 827-0289
"A very European atmosphere" appeals to a plethora of overseas travelers, and budget-minded prices draw value seekers to this B&B just a few blocks from the marina and the ever-changing exotica of the Venice Beach Boardwalk; breakfast, served outdoors in the Cobblestone Cafe, is included.

Marriott LAX 991R (19S)

| 17 | 17 | 15 | 15 | $129 |

5855 W. Century Blvd., Los Angeles; (310) 641-5700; (800) 228-9290; FAX: (310) 337-5358
☑ "Just another bland airport hotel", this "big", "busy", "efficient" facility with a "huge" lobby and "surprisingly nice grounds" has "a great location for LAX", but according to critics "convenience is the only good thing"; it's "getting a little shabby" with "gloomy", "worn" rooms and the food is "absolutely forgettable"; "functional" but "uninspired" is the consensus.

Marriott Marina Beach 353R (18S)
(fka Doubletree Marina del Rey)

| 18 | 20 | 17 | 18 | $144 |

4100 Admiralty Way, Marina del Rey; (310) 301-3000; (800) 228-9290; FAX: (310) 448-4825
☑ Optimists expect "good value" from this "fun place for a weekend" now that a major overhaul by Marriott is complete; "convenient freeway access", a "comfortable feel" and "nice setting" next to the Marina del Rey beach are assets, and rooms that were said to "need work" have presumably been spruced up; but will the redo cure what some describe as "surly", "poor" service?

Marriott Warner Center 455R (8S)

| 19 | 20 | 17 | 19 | $133 |

21850 Oxnard St., Woodland Hills; (818) 887-4800; (800) 228-9290; FAX: (818) 340-5893
☑ This "pleasant" "workhorse of a hotel" is "convenient" for suits on working trips to the Valley and for shoppers bound for mall and discount outlets; "good meeting rooms", a "knowledgeable" staff, "clean" but "plain" guestrooms that had a "nice face-lift" in '94–'95 plus "adequate" food equal an "average Marriott", which in most people's books equals a "good business hotel."

Miramar Sheraton Hotel 208R (62S)

| 22 | 22 | 19 | 22 | $180 |

101 Wilshire Blvd., Santa Monica; (310) 576-7777; (800) 325-3535; FAX: (310) 458-7912
■ "Lots of history", including a "spectacular" century-old banyan tree in the "beautiful gardens", resides at this "prettyish", "relaxing" hotel in a "great out-of-LA" location near the Santa Monica Pier and "tons" of restaurants; once a private mansion, it offers "comfortable" lodgings in the original building as well as a 10-story tower and bungalows near the pool; a recent renovation enhanced the "old charm" for some, but to others it "still feels cold"; N.B. a 4,000-square-foot "great health club" is a recent addition.

Mondrian Hotel 53R (192S)

| 20 | 19 | 18 | 17 | $184 |

8440 Sunset Blvd., West Hollywood; (213) 650-8999; (800) 525-8029; FAX: (213) 654-5804
☑ A total renovation by new owner Ian Schrager and designer Philippe Starck was completed too late for surveyor assessment, but this "ultracool" West Hollywood hotel was already a "gorgeous world" ideal for "stargazing" – "how much hipper could Schrager make it?"; its "artsy" aura has long been a draw, but some voters are chilled by service that combines "ineptitude with attitude" and roll their eyes at the "tragically hip" clientele: "bring your clip-on dreadlocks"; Coco Pazzo serves Italian fare and the Sky Bar is *the* place to hang out.

New Otani Hotel & Garden 413R (21S)

| 21 | 22 | 22 | 20 | $177 |

120 S. Los Angeles St., Los Angeles; (213) 629-1200; (800) 421-8795; FAX: (213) 622-0980
■ The only mainland-US outpost of this Japanese chain is a "pretty" hotel that provides "a little bit of Tokyo in Downtown LA" via "comfortable" rooms, fine service and a "peaceful", "austere" atmosphere complete with a beautiful Japanese garden; there's also "excellent", authentic Japanese cuisine at A Thousand Cranes; for real pampering, try a shiatsu massage followed by a session in the sauna or Jacuzzi at the on-site Sanwa Health Spa.

NIKKO AT BEVERLY HILLS 238R (62S)

| 26 | 25 | 23 | 24 | $203 |

465 S. La Cienega Blvd., Los Angeles; (310) 247-0400; (800) NIKKO-US; FAX: (310) 247-0315
■ For "quiet elegance amid the frenzy" of LA, surveyors bow to this "sleek" (some say "sterile") Japanese-style hotel with "elegant", "beautiful" public areas and "exquisite" ambiance; the "cool", "high-tech" rooms (with CD players, VCRs, modem and fax hookups, etc.) are "soothing for business", but nontechies moan they "need a user's manual" (there's state-of-the-art gadgetry in the health club too); Pangaea offers "great" Asian-Cal-French dining and a Sunday big-band brunch.

Oceana, Hotel (63S)
– – – – VE

849 Ocean Ave., Santa Monica; (310) 393-0486; (800) 777-0758; FAX: (310) 458-1182
For something different in LA, this upscale all-suiter, which underwent a stunning
'96 renovation designed by Cheryl Rowley, offers a residential Santa Monica address
on a bluff a block from the beach, fully equipped kitchens in all suites plus marble
baths, terry robes and executive work areas, private lanais in the inner courtyard
surrounding the pool, a fitness center, complimentary in-room breakfast and newspaper
plus room service from the Wolfgang Puck cafe; just remember: it costs plenty to get
into yuppie heaven.

Omni Los Angeles Hotel & Centre 865R (35S)
19 18 18 19 $149

930 Wilshire Blvd., Los Angeles; (213) 688-7777; (800) THE-OMNI; FAX: (213) 612-3989
■ "Not very flashy but reliable" and "fine for the price" with "good, basic" service is the
consensus on this "clean and comfortable" hotel in an "excellent business location"
near the LA Merchandise Mart; it's home to the spacious, opulent and expensive new
Korean restaurant Seoul Jung as well as the Italian Cardini; N.B. renovation of rooms
(which some critics found "boring") came too late to be reflected in ratings.

Palos Verdes Inn 109R (1S)
16 18 22 15 $115

1700 S. Pacific Coast Hwy., Redondo Beach; (310) 316-4211; (800) 421-9241; FAX: (310) 316-4863
◪ A "basic", "pleasant" place that's lifted out of the ordinary by the "glorious" restaurant
Chez Melange; popular with airline crews, it boasts a good location three blocks from
the beach, "nice rooms" (some with ocean-view balconies), a pool, sun deck and free
bike use plus passes to a nearby Bally's health club; still, doubters think it should be
"classified a motel", calling it "noisy" and "overpriced."

Park Hyatt Los Angeles 178R (189S)
24 23 20 22 $198

(fka J.W. Marriott)
2151 Ave. of the Stars, Los Angeles; (310) 277-2777; (800) 233-1234; FAX: (310) 785-9240
■ This "beautiful", "elegant" hotel is "a great place to stay and shop" (you can take
their limo to Rodeo Drive) with a "lovely" lobby (a place "to be seen"), "spacious", "nicely
decorated" rooms and a "well-trained" staff offering "superb" service; there are indoor
and outdoor pools and guests enjoy privileges at nearby golf, tennis and racquetball
facilities; N.B. those who hope Hyatt "will keep up Marriott's high standard" should
know that some recent visitors attest "Hyatt made it even better."

PENINSULA BEVERLY HILLS 148R (48S)
28 28 27 27 $287

9882 Little Santa Monica Blvd., Beverly Hills; (310) 551-2888; (800) 462-7899;
FAX: (310) 788-2319
 "Stunning" sums up this "very chichi", "savvy" outpost of the elite Hong Kong–
based chain, offering "unbelievable luxury" at the "best address in Beverly Hills", just
a stroll from Rodeo Drive; it earns LA's second-highest overall ratings, and no wonder:
rooms are "beautifully appointed", the "spacious" villas are "gorgeous" and service is
"first-rate" (if perhaps "slightly snooty"); beautiful people make the "trendy scene" at
The Belvedere, a "hot, hot" power-dining spot.

Ramada West Hollywood 130R (45S)
– – – – M

8585 Santa Monica Blvd., West Hollywood; (310) 652-6400; (800) 845-8585; FAX: (310) 652-4207
If a Ramada could ever approach hipness, it might be this one smack in the middle of
stylish West Hollywood; rooms vary from spartan doubles to two-level suites with wet
bars, refrigerators, coffeemakers and microwave ovens; it's handy to Melrose Avenue
shopping and the Pacific Design Center, though guests may want to lounge in the
lobby Starbucks watching the sidewalk action or take in some rays at the outdoor pool.

Regal Biltmore Hotel 620R (63S)
22 23 23 24 $180

(fka Biltmore Los Angeles)
506 S. Grand Ave., Los Angeles; (213) 624-1011; (800) 245-8673; FAX: (213) 612-1545
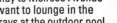 "A must if you love beautiful old hotels" sums up sentiment toward Downtown
LA's "classy" "landmark", a neoclassical "treasure" built in 1923 and famed for its
"breathtaking" lobby, "stunning" ballroom and "excellent" French dining at Bernard's;
service is "special" and the spa "is right out of a movie set"; N.B. Regal took over in
1996 and is renovating most of the rooms in '97, which should please those who find
them "matchbook-size" and "disappointing."

REGENT BEVERLY WILSHIRE 206R (69S)
27 27 26 26 $274

9500 Wilshire Blvd., Beverly Hills; (310) 275-5200; (800) 427-4354; FAX: (310) 274-2851
■ At the "epicenter of Beverly Hills" (Wilshire and Rodeo), this "classy" and "unfailingly
elegant" "mainstay of hospitality" is a "beautiful", "well-run" "grande dame still in her
glory" and "worth the splurge"; "pamper yourself" and enjoy its "huge", "magnificent"
rooms (with bathrooms "to die for"), "fantastic" service and stellar Cal-Continental
cuisine in the Dining Room; all in all, it's "bliss in a crazy place."

63

Renaissance Los Angeles Hotel 445R (60S) ⬛ 22 ⬛ 21 ⬛ 19 ⬛ 20 ⬛ $141 ⬛

9620 Airport Blvd., Los Angeles; (310) 337-2800; (800) HOTELS-1; FAX: (310) 216-6681
■ The "smartest of the airport hotels" offers the "best" location and "one of the best restaurants" (The Conservatory) for the LAX crowd, along with "friendly" service, "nice" soundproofed rooms featuring voicemail, dataports and other business amenities, and "great" meeting space; "if you have to go to a convention in LA, this is as good as any."

RITZ-CARLTON HUNTINGTON 355R (28S) ⬛ 27 ⬛ 27 ⬛ 26 ⬛ 28 ⬛ $215 ⬛

1401 S. Oak Knoll Ave., Pasadena; (818) 568-3900; (800) 241-3333; FAX: (818) 568-1842
■ "It's worth the commute to LA" (a whopping 15 minutes or so away) to stay at the "essence of elegance", a "wonderfully secluded", "very sophisticated but not stuffy" 1907-built masterpiece that "evokes a kinder, gentler era"; the "breathtaking" 23-acre Pasadena setting is "to die for", service is "truly excellent", rooms are "attractive" and "big" and there's "elegant" dining on "fine" Continental fare; N.B. a spa opens in late '97.

RITZ-CARLTON MARINA DEL REY 294R (12S) ⬛ 27 ⬛ 26 ⬛ 25 ⬛ 26 ⬛ $227 ⬛

4375 Admiralty Way, Marina del rey; (310) 823-1700; (800) 241-3333; FAX: (310) 823-8421
☑ Get a "beautiful" room facing the marina and "knockout sunsets" and you'll agree with those who call this "the best property near LAX by far"; for most guests its "magnificent" Marina del Rey setting and "formal yet friendly" ambiance make it "a typical Ritz", i.e. "close to perfect", yet despite high scores critics call it "the weak sister of the LA Ritzes" and say it's "showing some wear and tear" in looks and service ("well intentioned" but "harried"); on the bright side, you can "fall off your yacht and into brunch" here.

Shangri-La Hotel 12R (43S) ⬛ 19 ⬛ 17 ⬛ 13 ⬛ 15 ⬛ $151 ⬛

1301 Ocean Ave., Santa Monica; (310) 394-2791; (800) 345-7829; FAX: (310) 451-3351
■ "Gorgeous" ocean views and "always friendly" service in an "unpretentious" location add up to what many call the "best value in Santa Monica"; this "funky old" art deco landmark "fits into SM's happening Downtown" and offers "apartment-size" accommodations that are "tacky but roomy" and also done up in deco style; there's no restaurant, but continental breakfast is included and some rooms have kitchenettes.

Sheraton Grande Hotel 400R (69S) ⬛ 22 ⬛ 21 ⬛ 19 ⬛ 20 ⬛ $166 ⬛

333 S. Figueroa St., Los Angeles; (213) 617-1133; (800) 325-3535; FAX: (213) 613-0291
■ This "big", "well-located", "comfortable and efficient" Downtowner "serves the business client well" with "detailed, discreet" service from a "wonderful" staff – guests "love the butlers" who bring AM coffee, press clothes and shine shoes; rooms are "nicely appointed" and the "beautiful" lobby features "terrific" art; in all, "a good deal for the money and the location."

Sheraton Resort & Conference Center Industry Hills 284R (10S) ⬛ 19 ⬛ 18 ⬛ 16 ⬛ 19 ⬛ $130 ⬛

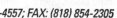

1 Industry Hills Pkwy., City of Industry; (818) 965-0861; (800) 524-4557; FAX: (818) 854-2305
☑ A "resortlike setting" in a "crazy" location "miles from anywhere but surprisingly good" is "hog heaven" for golf-playing business types thanks to two "tough" courses and "good meeting facilities"; there are also 17 tennis courts, an Olympic-size pool and on-site horseback riding, but even that doesn't stop critics from calling this a "typical corporate meeting center" that's mostly "just ok – not at all special."

Sheraton Universal 417R (25S) ⬛ 19 ⬛ 19 ⬛ 18 ⬛ 19 ⬛ $153 ⬛

333 Universal Terrace Pkwy., Universal City; (818) 980-1212; (800) 325-3535; FAX: (818) 985-4980
☑ In a "handy location" for the Universal Studios, CityWalk shopping and Valley business, this "family-oriented", "all-around nice hotel" is "pleasant" and even "above average" with "friendly staff", a "great pool" and "good value" rates; but for surveyors unmoved by its theme-park proximity, it can seem "merely adequate" and "touristy."

SHUTTERS ON THE BEACH 186R (12S) ⬛ 27 ⬛ 25 ⬛ 25 ⬛ 26 ⬛ $246 ⬛

1 Pico Blvd., Santa Monica; (310) 458-0030; (800) 334-9000; FAX: (310) 458-4589
■ "Airy and beautiful", this "intimate, romantic jewel" shines in a "sun-drenched beach location", offering "relaxed elegance" and "service second to none"; "shutter yourself off from the world" in a "bright, fresh room" with the "best bedding in the West" and "fabulous" bathrooms with large whirlpool tubs – "too romantic to go alone"; those who do leave their room find imaginative Cal-French cuisine at One Pico Restaurant; one quibble: you may "shutter" at the cost.

Sofitel Hotel Los Angeles 298R (13S) ⬛ 22 ⬛ 21 ⬛ 20 ⬛ 19 ⬛ $173 ⬛
(fka Ma Maison Sofitel)

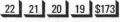

8555 Beverly Blvd., Los Angeles; (310) 278-5444; (800) 521-7772; FAX: (310) 657-2816
☑ "Liking it is easy", given its "convenient" location "across from mall heaven" (Beverly Center), "unthreateningly competent" staff, "very French" decor, "charming", "quiet" rooms and "low-key" atmosphere – not to mention its "good value"; those who murmur that the hotel is "a little past its prime" may change their minds after a '97 redo.

Summit Hotel Bel-Air 110R (51S)   16 | 16 | 15 | 13 | $137
(fka Radisson Bel-Air Summit)
11461 Sunset Blvd., Los Angeles; (310) 476-6571; (800) HOTEL-411; FAX: (310) 471-6310
☑ It's "not glamorous", but "big" rooms, "reasonable" rates, "decent" service and an on-site pool and tennis courts make this "small" hotel in residential Bel Air "satisfactory", especially "for tourists on a budget"; Radisson's departure and a 1997 redecoration might signal different scores next time out.

Summit Rodeo Drive 80R (6S)   17 | 20 | 18 | 15 | $151
360 N. Rodeo Dr., Beverly Hills; (310) 273-0300; (800) HOTEL-411; FAX: (310) 859-8730
■ "Cheap digs on America's most expensive street" sums up this value-minded option; hardly anyone comments on rooms or service because the main appeal is a "great location" in the "middle of the action" – you can "fall out your door and shop till you drop"; breakfast is included.

Sunset Marquis Hotel & Villas (114S)   20 | 20 | 18 | 20 | $201
1200 N. Alta Loma Rd., West Hollywood; (310) 657-1333; (800) 858-9758; FAX: (310) 657-1330
☑ "Spot celebs" at this "pretty, comfy, upscale" "hideaway" "crawling with rock 'n' rollers", a "very in, very LA" "fabulous oasis tucked behind hotel walls"; the suites are "big" and "roomy" and "the villas are amazing", offering privacy as they do, but those looking for a crowd should note "the bar is a scene on weekends" ("too much of a scene" for some); detractors deem the place "overblown" with "bad" service and "rip-off" food; N.B. all suites in the main building were renovated in '95.

Westin Bonaventure 1211R (157S)   17 | 18 | 17 | 18 | $166
404 S. Figueroa St., Los Angeles; (213) 624-1000; (800) 228-3000; FAX: (213) 612-4800
☑ "Everybody knows this place" – a Downtown "city within a city" with "great" views and "unusual" (some say "tiny") "pie-shaped rooms"; but what's a "modern" "landmark" to some is an "eyesore" to others – an "unruly", "soulless" "big barn" where it's "easy to get lost" in public areas that have "all the warmth of a prison yard"; N.B. "redesigned" rooms are said to be "much improved" after a late '96–early '97 renovation.

Westwood Marquis Hotel & Gardens (257S)   24 | 24 | 22 | 21 | $209
930 Hilgard Ave., Los Angeles; (310) 208-8765; (800) 421-2317; FAX: (310) 824-0355
■ "See and be seen" or enjoy "privacy and pampering" at Westwood's "hidden gem", a "classy", "charming" Westside all-suiter near the UCLA campus; lodgings are "huge" and "apartmentlike" and the "very helpful" staff "makes you feel at home"; the "lovely" Dynasty Room offers "top-notch" Cal-French dining; N.B. numerous "needs a makeover" critiques could vanish after a '97 floor-by-floor refurbishment.

Wyndham Bel Age Hotel (200S)   23 | 22 | 22 | 20 | $198
(fka Le Bel Age Hotel)
1020 N. San Vicente Blvd., West Hollywood; (310) 854-1111; (800) WYNDHAM;
FAX: (310) 854-0926
■ "All spruced up" after its takeover by Wyndham, this "gorgeous, gracious" all-suiter in a "great" West Hollywood location is "popular with Hollywood deal makers" yet "surprisingly affordable"; "beautiful" city views can be enjoyed from some of the "wonderfully redone", "comfortable" quarters as well as the "gorgeous" rooftop pool, and there's "amazing artwork" in the public areas; a resounding *da* goes to the "world-class" Diaghilev with its sumptuous French-Russian cuisine and romantic setting.

WYNDHAM CHECKERS HOTEL 173R (15S)   23 | 24 | 26 | 21 | $191
535 S. Grand Ave., Los Angeles; (213) 624-0000; (800) WYNDHAM; FAX: (213) 626-9906
■ A "first-rate" boutique hotel in a "convenient business location" Downtown, this "luxurious jewel" is "tasteful, elegant and restrained", offering "great value" with "small but well-appointed" rooms and "attentive service"; a few vocal critics contend the place has "lost its zing" and is "in need of some rehab", but more prounounce it "very well done"; check out the "outstanding" Checkers restaurant for Californian dining and power breakfasting.

Wyndham Hotel at LAX 579R (12S)   17 | 17 | 16 | 16 | $120
(fka Hyatt at Los Angeles Airport)
6225 W. Century Blvd., Los Angeles; (310) 670-9000; (800) WYNDHAM; FAX: (310) 670-7852
☑ Admirers call this a "surprising airport property" offering a "very relaxed atmosphere", "quality" service, good value and guestrooms remodeled in '96; another faction rates it merely "so-so" all-around, but the bottom line is it's "a good place to sleep before an early-morning flight" – "step out your door and you're at the gate."

Los Olivos

Los Olivos Grand Hotel 20R (1S)   25 | 21 | 21 | 20 | $174
2860 Grand Ave., Los Olivos; (805) 688-7788; (800) 446-2455; FAX: (805) 688-1942
◪ This "rare beauty" in the "pleasant setting" of the Santa Barbara wine country pleases most travelers with its "country charm", "large", "beautifully decorated" rooms (all with fireplaces), "friendly" staff and "grand" dining at the "excellent" Remington's; for a few hard-to-please types, the "best in the area" is "good but not great"; it's a member of the well-regarded Four Sisters Inns group.

Mendocino

Hill House Inn of Mendocino 40R (4S)   22 | 22 | 21 | 20 | $151
10701 Palette Dr., Mendocino; (707) 937-0554; (800) 422-0554; FAX: (707) 937-1123
■ As featured in the TV series *Murder She Wrote* (Mendocino substitutes in TV land for the coast of Maine), this modern but "comfortable and quaint" Cape Cod–style inn on a "dramatic" hilltop offers "wondrous" ocean views (when the fog permits) from many of the "lovely rooms"; dining gets mixed reactions, from "great food and wine" to "a disappointment", but it's "convenient to town" and other eatery options; if the "romantic" locale gets the better of you, an on-site wedding chapel awaits.

Mendocino Hotel & Garden Suites 26R (25S)   18 | 19 | 19 | 18 | $152
PO Box 587, 45080 Main St., Mendocino; (707) 937-0511; (800) 548-0513; FAX: (707) 937-0513
◪ "If you like old" you'll enjoy this "beautiful, restored" 1878 Victorian located Downtown "in the middle of things", a "true-to-its-origins" antiques-filled period piece in a "beautiful little town" full of "Western seacoast charm"; although a few gripe about "hot, noisy", "cramped" quarters and call it an option "only for easily impressed tourists", the majority uses other adjectives: "cozy, nostalgic, warm" – and some "did not want to leave."

Stanford Inn by the Sea 23R (4S)   23 | 23 | 19 | 22 | $182
Comptche-Ukiah Rd. & Hwy. 1, Mendocino; (707) 937-5615; (800) 331-8884; FAX: (707) 937-0305
■ Look for llamas and an organic nursery on the "charming grounds" of this "small, unpretentious" inn (with "perfect views" overlooking Mendocino) that's as much "like a comfortable farm" as a favorite B&B; "antiques-filled rooms" (all with fireplaces) are "great for a first, second or third honeymoon", the staff is "accommodating" and guests can work off the included champagne breakfast, afternoon tea and PM hors d'oeuvres at the fitness center, in the greenhouse-enclosed pool and spa, or by canoeing Big River or cycling the coast (rentals available on-site); no restaurant, but there are plenty nearby.

Menlo Park

Stanford Park Hotel 162R (8S)   22 | 22 | 20 | 20 | $157
100 El Camino Real, Menlo Park; (415) 322-1234; (800) 368-2468; FAX: (415) 322-0475
■ The "best place to stay if visiting Stanford" University is this "very comfortable", "surprisingly luxurious" "quiet" hotel with "class, efficiency and low-key ambiance all in one package"; the "lovely rooms" are well appointed with contemporary furnishings and come in a variety of sizes and styles – one surveyor suggests you "heat up your romance with a fireplace room"; "close to lovely Palo Alto and the Stanford shopping center", it also offers an outdoor pool and fitness center plus well-regarded Californian cuisine at the Duck Club.

Montecito

Montecito Inn 50R (10S)   18 | 22 | 22 | 19 | $169
1295 Coast Village Rd., Montecito; (805) 969-7854; (800) 843-2017; FAX: (805) 969-0623
■ Built in 1928 by Charlie Chaplin as a hideaway for the Hollywood crowd, and now something of a shrine to the Little Tramp (it's decorated with posters from his films and has a library of his works for viewing), this "cute", "casual" inn just two blocks from the beach offers "small but nicely decorated" French Provincial–style rooms in a "great" Montecito Village location; guests also enjoy dining at the "friendly, popular" cafe, and there's a pool, sauna and fitness room; one naysayer growls "trying to be a country inn in the city doesn't work", but the majority disagrees.

SAN YSIDRO RANCH 42R   25 | 26 | 26 | 25 | $275
900 San Ysidro Ln., Santa Barbara; (805) 969-5046; (800) 368-6788; FAX: (805) 565-1995
■ For "a great escape from LA . . . or anywhere", head to the Montecito hills where you'll find this "first-class hideaway", an upscale dude ranch that "defines rustic elegance"; Hollywood honchos come to enjoy its "wonderful" just-renovated cottages (all with fireplaces), "beautiful" grounds, "extremely accommodating" staff, spa services (many available in your room), pool and tennis courts, plus fine dining at the "exciting" but "pricey" Stonehouse.

Monterey

Doubletree at Fisherman's Wharf 364R (9S) | 20 | 19 | 18 | 19 | $150 |
2 Portola Plaza, Monterey; (408) 649-4511; (800) 222-TREE; FAX: (408) 649-4115
☑ The "good Downtown location" ("ideal for Cannery Row" and "right at" the convention center) and "always great" chocolate-chip cookies agree with everybody, but reactions are mixed when it comes to the rooms ("spacious" and "above average" vs. "mediocre") and service ("good" vs. "stale"); in sum, this "everyday hotel" could be "one of the chain's better properties", but it's "not Monterey's best."

Hyatt Regency Monterey 555R (20S) | 19 | 20 | 18 | 20 | $162 |
Old Golf Course Rd., Monterey; (408) 372-1234; (800) 233-1234; FAX: (408) 375-3960
☑ "Golf, seafood and more golf" are the main attractions at this "convention hotel in a nice setting" overlooking a championship course where "helpful", "friendly" service and "good" exercise facilities (two pools, six tennis courts, fitness machines) also get nods; surveyors disagree on whether rooms are "charming" or "tired", but as one guest notes "in Monterey who cares about the room? – there's so much to do outside."

Marriott Hotel Monterey 341R | 20 | 20 | 18 | 19 | $150 |
350 Calle Principal, Monterey; (408) 649-4234; (800) 228-9290; FAX: (408) 375-4313
☑ "Walk to everything in town" from this "very friendly" "great buy" with "good facilities for conferences"; while some call it "comfortable and pleasant" with "good service", many also view it as a "boring corporate hotel that's incongruous with Monterey"; an early '97 renovation might improve views about the "so-so" accommodations.

Monterey Plaza Hotel 278R (7S) | 24 | 22 | 21 | 23 | $179 |
400 Cannery Row, Monterey; (408) 646-1700; (800) 631-1339; FAX: (408) 646-5937
■ "Watch the otters at play" from one of the "fabulous", "well-appointed" rooms overlooking Monterey Bay (you'll have to request one, some face inland) or from an ocean-view table at the "excellent" Duck Club restaurant at this upscale hotel on Cannery Row that recently added a bistro; even the sea lions might clap for the "gracious", "very accommodating" staff at what one voter insists is "the best place to stay in Monterey"; N.B. guestrooms and 16,000 square feet of indoor meeting facilities are newly renovated.

Old Monterey Inn 8R (2S) | 24 | 23 | 22 | 21 | $175 |
500 Martin St., Monterey; (408) 375-8284; (800) 350-2344; FAX: (408) 375-6730
■ Away from the surf and four blocks from the center of town is a "marvelous" English Tudor "lovers' spot" known for its "superb hosts" who are "very helpful with sight-seeing suggestions"; guests who remain on-site relish the acre-plus of "beautiful grounds", "quaint" rooms and "great food"; to a small but vocal minority, it's "overrated", but those who think it "one of the best" win out.

Pacific, Hotel (105S) | 25 | 21 | 18 | 19 | $153 |
300 Pacific St., Monterey; (408) 373-5700; (800) 554-5542; FAX: (408) 373-6921
■ "Space, style, character and a happy staff" single out this Spanish-style "find" "close to the wharf" in Monterey featuring "bright" "adobe-style" suites with "wonderful furnishings" such as fireplaces and featherbeds ("one of the best I've ever slept in") plus private patios or balconies and "delightful" breakfast and afternoon tea (included in rates); the only complaint focuses on "road noise", but on the Pacific side, others report it's "charming seals that keep you awake."

Spindrift Inn 42R | 26 | 22 | 19 | 21 | $190 |
652 Cannery Row, Monterey; (408) 646-8900; (800) 841-1879; FAX: (408) 646-5342
■ Be "comfortable on Cannery Row" and enjoy "excellent" service in a "romantic", "delightful" setting where a rooftop garden offers lovely views of Monterey Bay; each "beautifully decorated", "suite-like" and "homey" room is equipped with a fireplace and a four-poster – the site of the "ultimate luxury: breakfast in bed"; N.B. the "street-side rooms can be noisy."

Morro Bay

Inn at Morro Bay 96R | 19 | 20 | 19 | 20 | $148 |
60 State Park Rd., Morro Bay; (805) 772-5651; (800) 321-9566; FAX: (805) 772-4779
■ "Charming, gracious service" in a "beautiful setting" on Morro Bay (halfway between SF and LA) makes this "relaxing little hotel" ideal for a "romantic hideaway"; the adjacent bird sanctuary is "a plus", as are the "spectacular" views of the bay and of seals sunning on the rocks at this "lovely site" close to Hearst Castle and just across the street from golf (there's a pool on-site); a '97 renovation may improve "ordinary" rooms (though the higher-priced options feature ocean views and fireplaces).

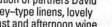

Napa

Embassy Suites Napa Valley (205S)
20 | 20 | 19 | 19 | $154
(fka Inn at Napa Valley)
1075 California Blvd., Napa; (707) 253-9540; (800) 433-4600; FAX: (707) 253-9202
☑ A "good wine-tasting location" in Napa Valley adds tourist appeal to this "utilitarian but comfortable" "standard business hotel" that offers "reasonable value" in the form of two-room suites with kitchenettes, indoor and outdoor pools, meeting facilities for groups of up to 250 and complimentary breakfast ("a godsend"); N.B. a complete redo, not reflected in the scores, accompanied the '96 renaming.

La Residence 20R
– | – | – | – | E
4066 St. Helena Hwy. N., Napa; (707) 253-0337; FAX: (707) 253-0382
Two buildings, one an 18-century Revival–style mansion with period antiques and the other a structure resembling a French barn, house the individually designed luxury accommodations of this Napa Valley inn; the 1980 megabucks creation of partners David Jackson and Craig Claussen, 'La Res' offers fireplaces, Laura Ashley–type linens, lovely grounds, a heated outdoor pool and sauna, complimentary breakfast and afternoon wine hour, all in addition to a perfect location for exploring the region's vineyards.

Marriott Napa Valley 187R (4S)
17 | 17 | 15 | 16 | $132
(fka The Sheraton Inn)
3425 Solano Ave., Napa; (707) 253-7433; (800) 228-9290; FAX: (707) 258-1320
☑ "Trying hard" with "lovely grounds", an outdoor pool and two tennis courts in a "great location for wine tastings", this Marriott is still panned as a "cookie-cutter" operation, with "unaccommodating" service drawing several comments; those who see the bright side consider it "a way to stay in Napa and get [frequent-stay] points" and note "they're working on eliminating the Holiday Inn look."

Silverado Country Club & Resort (280S)
21 | 21 | 21 | 24 | $206
1600 Atlas Peak Rd., Napa; (707) 257-0200; (800) 532-0500; FAX: (707) 257-5400
☑ This "luxurious" golf/tennis/conference resort in an "idyllic" setting on 360 "beautifully maintained" acres earns praise for its "privacy" and "great" amenities (including two golf courses, nine pools and 23 tennis courts), as well as "stunningly appointed" individually owned condos (all with fireplaces); but dissenters say "forget it unless you golf or have to attend a conference", citing variable quarters, a "snooty" staff ("everything is a hassle") and even "overplayed" greens; most praise the "good" dining options and ratings overall are high, but it seems wise to proceed with caution.

Newport Beach

FOUR SEASONS NEWPORT BEACH 192R (93S)
27 | 26 | 26 | 26 | $227
690 Newport Ctr. Dr., Newport Beach; (714) 759-0808; (800) 332-3442; FAX: (714) 759-0568
■ "Luxurious", "elegant" and "very accommodating" are the usual Four Seasons hallmarks, and this business/vacation hotel is no exception, offering "all the class" expected: "top-notch" rooms, "superior" service, "beautiful" public areas and "imaginative" Cal-Continental cuisine at the "stunning" Pavilion restaurant – and for shopaholics, there's even "a great view of Neiman-Marcus" across the street at chic Fashion Island Mall; there's a fitness center and lovely outdoor pool area "with cabanas" for those who don't drop while shopping, and the Pelican Hill Golf Course is nearby.

Hyatt Newporter 389R (21S)
19 | 20 | 19 | 21 | $162
1107 Jamboree Rd., Newport Beach; (714) 729-1234; (800) 233-1234; FAX: (714) 644-1552
☑ "Hawaii-like grounds" make surveyors feel "relaxed" at this "modest" Mediterranean-style resort complex in a "good" location on Newport's Back Bay; the facilities were upgraded in 1995 so "service and amenities are better now" and it's "sensibly priced" with an "attentive" staff, "great meeting rooms" and "lots of activities", including 16 tennis courts, a nine-hole pitch-and-putt golf course and three outdoor pools; one minor critique: "paper-thin" walls.

Marriott Hotel & Tennis Club
Newport Beach 562R (8S)
20 | 20 | 18 | 20 | $151
900 Newport Ctr. Dr., Newport Beach; (714) 640-4000; (800) 228-9290; FAX: (714) 640-5055
■ "A happening hotel in a happening area", this chainer is considered "a cut above other Marriotts"; although convention-oriented, it's in a "good location for shopping" at Fashion Island and is also "great for after the beach"; the recently renovated rooms are "clean" and "comfortable" (if "ordinary") and afford "terrific" views, while the "excellent" service and "lovely" grounds, which include eight tennis courts, an outdoor pool and a fitness center, score extra points; a few naysayers insist it's "just ok."

Marriott Suites Newport Beach (250S) 22 | 20 | 16 | 18 | $134
500 Bayview Circle, Newport Beach; (714) 854-4500; (800) 228-9290; FAX: (714) 854-3937

■ "Good value for the area" is found in these Marriott all-suite accommodations, which "are a great plus for a little extra money"; the "airy", "clean", "large" and "sunny" quarters are perfect for families, the staff is "friendly" and the facilities include a health club and indoor/outdoor pools; all in all, it's "worth the short trip to the beach."

Sutton Place Hotel 406R (29S) 22 | 22 | 22 | 20 | $165
4500 MacArthur Blvd., Newport Beach; (714) 476-2001; (800) 243-4141; FAX: (714) 476-0153

■ "A fine place" despite what some term an "awkward" location near the airport, this former Meridien "has kept its high standards of aiming to please" as a "beautiful" and "very good" business hotel; praise centers on the "kind, professional" staff, "clean" rooms and especially "large corner suites with huge terraces"; a "relaxing" pool and an "outstanding" Sunday brunch add to the aura, but some regulars lament the passing of the stellar Antoine's restaurant – Accents, offering good Cal-French cuisine, is the only dining option.

Oakhurst

CHÂTEAU DU SUREAU 9R 30 | 28 | 28 | 27 | $344
48688 Victoria Ln., Oakhurst; (209) 683-6860; FAX: (209) 683-0800

■ "So this is how fairy-tale princesses live" exclaim surveyors enchanted by California's "fabulous" top-rated lodging, a "French paradise" on seven flower-filled acres where "your every need" is met; "splurge for a special time" and enjoy "Yosemite by day", "deluxe" surroundings by night (think goose-down bedding, marble baths, fireplaces) at this example of "perfection" where "unbelievable style, service and setting" blend with "superior" Cal-French food and ambiance at Erna's Elderberry House, always among the state's top-rated restaurants.

Oakland

Waterfront Plaza 117R (27S) ▽ 17 | 16 | 16 | 17 | $130
10 Washington St., Oakland; (510) 836-3800; (800) 729-3638; FAX: (510) 832-6228

☑ Convenient to two Downtowns – Oakland's and San Francisco's – and overlooking the Bay, this small, modern property at the shopping- and eatery-filled Jack London Square is a modest hostelry working hard to attract business and vacation travelers alike, offering a pool, fitness center and bistro on-site; ferries to SF leave from the next-door dock, making this an economical and unexpected option for visitors to the San Francisco Bay Area.

Ojai

Ojai Valley Inn 192R (15S) 22 | 24 | 22 | 25 | $195
Country Club Rd., Ojai; (805) 646-5511; (800) 672-2822; FAX: (805) 646-7969

■ "Great" golf on an "enticing" PGA tour site, "serene surroundings" and a 28,000-square-foot spa make this "lovely", "peaceful" Spanish Colonial–style resort just south of Santa Barbara "excellent" for both group meetings and individual vacationers; the setting for the '30s classic *Lost Horizon*, it offers "lots of recreation", good kids' programs and "well-appointed" rooms, with praise for the fine renovation of the 1923 Hacienda section (four-poster beds, original tiles, etc.) that preserves "the old feeling" of "pure California"; a minority thinks the place "could still use more refurbishing."

Olympic Valley

Plumpjack's Squaw Valley Inn 55R (5S) 18 | 17 | 14 | 19 | $150
(fka Squaw Valley Inn)
1920 Squaw Valley Rd., Olympic Valley; (916) 583-1576; (800) 323-7666; FAX: (916) 583-7619

■ A "cool", "complete" rustic/modern renovation, along with a new name, has transformed this near–Lake Tahoe "gem", a famed wood-shingled inn originally built to house participants in the '60s Olympics; "nothing beats it for ski-in/ski-out" convenience, and on-site it offers a pool, tennis, whirlpools, its own pizza oven and a bar with fireplace, plus ice skating, tennis, golf, bicycling and other sports nearby.

Resort at Squaw Creek 203R (200S)　　23　23　21　26　$201
400 Squaw Creek Rd., Olympic Valley; (916) 583-6300; (800) 3-CREEK-3;
FAX: (916) 581-6632

■ Ski-in/ski-out convenience, ice skating, golf, tennis, pool and a children's program make this "classy", "all-inclusive", "first-class" operation in a "gorgeous" 620-acre Sierra Nevada setting near Lake Tahoe a "great all-year resort"; most find it "terrific" for small business groups and families thanks to "nicely furnished" quarters and "friendly", "alert" staff; a few protest that some rooms are "tiny", but larger options are available.

Oxnard

Embassy Suites Mandalay Beach Resort (250S)　19　16　15　20　$147
(fka Crown Sterling Suites Mandalay Beach Resort)
2101 Mandalay Beach Rd., Oxnard; (805) 984-2500; (800) EMBASSY;
FAX: (805) 984-8339

◪ "Spacious suites" and a "magnificent beach setting" work in favor of this "casual" resort that's undergoing a total rehabilitation since its takeover by Embassy Suites in 1997; the makeover comes just in time since many report it was "beginning to show its age"; nine acres of oceanfront property, extensive conference facilities and Southern California's largest free-form swimming pool add to the basic appeal.

Pacific Grove

Gosby House Inn 22R　　24　24　21　20　$138
643 Lighthouse Ave., Pacific Grove; (408) 375-1287; (800) 527-8828; FAX: (408) 665-9621

◪ Admirers of this historic 1888 B&B overlooking the Pacific near Monterey and brimming with teddy bears (a signature of the Four Sisters Inns chainlet) call it "very sweet and homey" – a "comfy, cozy", "perfect little Victorian" with a "warm and friendly" staff, peaceful porches, a "beautiful garden" and English antiques; a few warn that its "cheaper rooms" can be "teeny tiny", but others claim "it's worth the room rate just for afternoon tea [and wine] and breakfast", all included; N.B. nearly half the rooms feature fireplaces.

Green Gables Inn 10R (1S)　　25　24　21　23　$162
104 Fifth St., Pacific Grove; (408) 375-2095; (800) 722-1774; FAX: (408) 375-5437

◪ "I want to move in" exclaim devotees of this "charming" Victorian, another "very cozy" Four Sisters Inn with a teddy bear in each room; the "pretty-on-the-outside" 1888 mansion in a "fabulous" near-Monterey location with ocean views has guests gushing over gourmet breakfasts, afternoon wine or tea and home-baked cookies; a few dissenters complain that it's "overdone" to the point of being "terribly cute."

Martine Inn 17R (3S)　　▽ 21　22　18　16　$168
255 Ocean View Blvd., Pacific Grove; (408) 373-3388; (800) 852-5588;
FAX: (408) 373-3896

◪ An "incredible collection" of "museum-quality" antiques, California collectibles and classic cars grace this Monterey-area circa 1890 B&B that also pleases with "fabulous" ocean views, "very attentive, friendly" service and "sumptuous" included breakfast; renovations in the past year may appease a minority that's "not overly impressed with the rooms" – others call the accommodations "incomparable", especially the "spectacular" rooms facing the coast.

Seven Gables Inn 14R　　–　–　–　–　VE
555 Ocean View Blvd., Pacific Grove; (408) 372-4341

You might recognize from TV commercials this circa 1886 waterside Victorian treasure on a cliff overlooking Monterey Bay; furnished in Victorian style with many antiques, it offers spectacular views from every room and is a short drive from Monterey's Fisherman's Wharf, Cannery Row and other attractions; a full breakfast and afternoon tea are included in rates.

TOP 10 OVERALL

BEST OVERALL

27 Ritz-Carlton Rancho Mirage
25 La Quinta
24 Marriott's Desert Springs
    Westin Mission Hills
    Renaissance Esmeralda
    Hyatt Grand Champions
23 Two Bunch Palms
22 Indian Wells Resort
    Marriott's Rancho Las Palmas
21 Ingleside Inn

BEST VALUES

Doubletree Palm Springs
Wyndham Palm Springs
Hyatt Regency Palm Springs
Hilton Palm Springs
Indian Wells Resort
Marquis Palm Springs
Westin Mission Hills
Renaissance Esmeralda
Spa Hotel & Casino
Marriott's Rancho Las Palmas

R	S	D	P	$

Doubletree Palm Springs 276R (77S)

21	19	18	20	$140

67-967 Vista Chino, Cathedral City; (619) 322-7000; (800) 222-TREE; FAX: (619) 322-6853

◪ "The price is right" at this "relaxing", "best-bargain" resort for families or meetings that draws much praise for the "helpful, friendly" staff, "gorgeous" grounds and golf and tennis available at the adjoining Desert Princess Country Club (guests can use all the club's extensive facilities for a fee); but there are mixed reactions to accommodations that range from "ordinary" rooms to "terrific" fairway condos, and "mediocre" food gets a thumbs down; desert winds prompt warnings to "watch anything not tied down."

Hilton Resort Palm Springs 190R (70S)

18	18	17	18	$143

400 E. Tahquitz Canyon Way, Palm Springs; (619) 320-6868; (800) 522-6900; FAX: (619) 320-2126

◪ Even though most agree it's "just your basic Hilton" – "generic" but "clean" and "serviceable" – the "wonderful" management and staff help ensure a "pleasant experience" at this "professionally run", "good-value" resort in "convenient" Downtown; scores are creeping upward thanks to a "good job" on renovating public areas and the '96 addition of meeting rooms and a fitness center.

HYATT GRAND CHAMPIONS RESORT (336S)   24   23   21   26 $210
44-600 Indian Wells Ln., Indian Wells; (619) 341-1000; (800) 233-1234; FAX: (619) 568-2236
■ A "golfers' heaven" (36 holes) and "tennis players' paradise" (12 courts) mix it up at this "enormous" "island of elegance in the desert" where "lots to do" make it grand "not only for sports"; "large", "gracious", "comfortable" suites and villas delight devotees who also praise the "excellent" food (several options), "gorgeous" pools (four), conference facilities (20 rooms with nearly 8,000 square feet) and "quiet" location at this "superb vacation find"; N.B. all guestroom and restaurant furniture has recently been replaced.

Hyatt Regency Suites Palm Springs (192S)   23   21   18   21 $163
285 N. Palm Canyon Dr., Palm Springs; (619) 322-9000; (800) 233-1234; FAX: (619) 322-6009
 A "central" locale near the convention center and next to Desert Fashion Plaza shopping means "no car is necessary" to enjoy this "comfortable" all-suiter where every accommodation boasts a private balcony with "nice views"; a "good" if sometimes "packed" pool is another plus, but some complain of an "awkward" "layout" and "poor food", saying "not as good as it could have been."

Indian Wells Resort Hotel 129R (26S)   22   22   21   24 $182
(fka Radisson Resort Indian Wells)
76-661 Hwy. 111, Indian Wells; (619) 345-6466; (800) 248-3220; FAX: (619) 772-5083
 A "smaller, more personalized" resort than its Indian Wells neighbors gets the nod as a "good business" choice with its two tennis courts, pool and "convenient location" next door to a 36-hole public golf course; "casual" and "comfortable" describe it for most, though a few see a "resort-cum-motel" that's "not great, not bad."

Ingleside Inn 10R (20S)   20   22   23   19 $188
200 W. Ramon Rd., Palm Springs; (619) 325-0046; (800) 772-6655; FAX: (619) 325-0710
 Built in 1925 and a longtime hostelry to the stars, this Downtown B&B is a "romantic" "getaway" secluded behind Spanish adobe walls; although appreciated as a "friendly little place" that treats guests like "members of the family", its '94 renovation has failed to stem criticisms about "run-down" rooms with "antique a/c" and "thrift-shop" furnishings (but all have Jacuzzis and 20 offer fireplaces as well); for "wonderful", "old-style" Continental dining, don't miss Melvyn's, a popular time-warp hangout.

Inn at the Racquet Club (72S)   19   18   17   19 $160
2743 N. Indian Canyon Dr., Palm Springs; (619) 325-1281; (800) 367-0946; FAX: (619) 325-3429
 Actors Charlie Farrell and Ralph Bellamy caused a racket in 1934 when they opened this "low-key, relaxed" resort as a tennis getaway for their pals; today its loyalists find "good value" in the "comfortable", "spacious" villas, condos and suites (some with private pool and Jacuzzi), indoor/outdoor pools and 11 tennis courts (with 60 links of golf just a mile away); but a vocal contingent laments it's a "sad reminder" of "old Palm Springs" that's overdue for "some sprucing up."

La Mancha Private Villas 13R (53S)   22   19   16   20 $228
444 N. Ave. Caballeros, Palm Springs; (619) 323-1773; (800) 255-1773; FAX: (619) 323-5928
 "Wonderfully romantic" one-, two- and three-bedroom villas, most "like a home" with private pools, attract celebs, honeymooners and families; yet despite the "great" location with "perfect" views, as well as tennis courts, a nine-hole putting course, 68-foot pool and croquet, less starry-eyed surveyors aren't just tilting at windmills when they describe La Mancha as a "period piece" (built in the '70s) in need of "updating."

LA QUINTA RESORT & CLUB 613R (27S)   25   25   23   26 $225
49-499 Eisenhower Dr., La Quinta; (619) 564-4111; (800) 598-3828; FAX: (619) 564-7656
■ For a "taste of old Palm Springs" that "feels small although it's huge", seekers of "glitz and glamour" (or the "best convention spot in the desert") reserve at this Spanish-style "getaway", a "romantic tribute to a more elegant era"; guests tarry in "great casitas" offering "breathtaking" Santa Rosa mountain views or enjoy "lovely" manicured grounds encompassing 25 pools, 38 hot spas, "top-flight tennis" (30 courts), four championship golf courses and four restaurants; just a few whisper "they really should redo the rooms."

L'Horizon Garden Hotel 22R   –   –   –   –   M
1050 E. Palm Canyon Dr., Palm Springs; (760) 323-1858; (800) 377-7855; FAX: (760) 327-2933
Those seeking privacy can find it at this two-acre compound of palm trees and flower beds in a residential area of Old Palm Springs at the foot of Mt. San Jacinto; the pool is the centerpiece, around which are scattered seven buildings, each with several units featuring private terraces and large wooden shutters; a newspaper and continental breakfast are brought to each terrace, although those craving a little society can breakfast poolside; quiet is also a keyword: no kids on the horizon, please.

Marquis Crowne Plaza Resort & Suites
Palm Springs 163R (101S)

| 22 | 20 | 16 | 19 | $158 |

150 S. Indian Canyon Dr., Palm Springs; (619) 322-2121; (800) 223-1050; FAX: (619) 322-2380
■ Conventioneers and fellow travelers "love the location" ("convenient to shopping" and Downtown attractions) of this business-oriented property with over 23,000 square feet of meeting space, two pools and two tennis courts; all the rooms in the modern three-story Mediterranean-style buildings feature standard amenities (refrigerator, coffeemaker, hair dryer) plus private balconies or patios, and the suites have fireplaces and wet bars; a few dismiss a "disguised Holiday Inn", but ratings suggest otherwise.

MARRIOTT'S DESERT SPRINGS
RESORT & SPA 833R (51S)

| 24 | 24 | 23 | 26 | $201 |

74855 Country Club Dr., Palm Desert; (619) 341-2211; (800) 331-3112; FAX: (619) 341-1872
■ "What a show!" – this "immense", "glorious" (some label it "gaudy") golf and tennis resort (36 links, 20 courts) located 13 miles outside Palm Springs on 23 "beautiful" acres is an "H2-oh!" world of pools, ponds, fountains and waterways ("too much water for the desert" scold conservationists); small boats glide guests to and from "on-the-small-side" rooms, the "excellent" Tuscany's Ristorante and the "extraordinary" 30,000-square-foot spa; overall the "jolly giant" is "accommodating and welcoming" but "very busy", especially since it's "great for business" too.

Marriott's Rancho Las Palmas Resort 422R (22S)

| 22 | 22 | 20 | 23 | $180 |

41000 Bob Hope Dr., Rancho Mirage; (619) 568-2727; (800) 458-8786; FAX: (619) 568-5845
■ Surveyors scoop up "lots of luxury for a few bucks" at this "casual", "comfortable" spot known for "high-level", "very cordial" service and "well-maintained", "beautiful" grounds; "a perfect site for midsize meetings" (20,000 square feet of space), it's also "great for golfers" (27 holes) and tennis players (25 courts); but several guests note it's "fading a bit" and "rooms could use a face-lift."

Monte Vista 25R (6S)

| – | – | – | – | M |

414 N. Palm Canyon, Palm Springs; (619) 325-5641; (800) 789-3188; FAX: (619) 325-0571
The oldest hotel in Palm Springs, a neoclassic structure that welcomed its first overnighter in 1919, reopened in September 1996 after a complete renovation; most of the individually decorated rooms have kitchens, pets are allowed, there's an outdoor pool and rates are remarkably reasonable for the area; no restaurant.

RENAISSANCE ESMERALDA RESORT 538R (22S)

| 25 | 24 | 22 | 26 | $198 |

(fka Stouffer Esmeralda Resort)
44-400 Indian Wells Ln., Indian Wells; (619) 773-4444; (800) 552-4386; FAX: (619) 773-9250
■ "Count on an overall good stay" at this "lush oasis" that's "great for conferences" and "families with kids" due to three "unbeatable" pools (one with a "mock" sand beach), "cool California-style" rooms that are "spacious and bright", "excellent" public areas and a "friendly" staff (while a few feel "service is not the same since Renaissance took over", ratings are actually up); "lots of amenities" include two Ted Robinson–designed golf courses, nine tennis courts and a choice of Californian or Mediterranean dining.

RITZ-CARLTON RANCHO MIRAGE 220R (19S)

| 27 | 27 | 26 | 27 | $242 |

68-900 Frank Sinatra Dr., Rancho Mirage; (619) 321-8282; (800) 241-3333; FAX: (619) 321-6928
■ Luckily this Mirage is real, a "splendid" "getaway" (top-rated in Palm Springs) offering "elegant, sweeping" views over the Coachella Valley; although several find the traditional decor "too formal and stuffy for the desert", Ritz acolytes sigh over the "stunning" lobby and "superior" rooms as well as the usual "good pampering" and "very fine" dining; a new spa, tennis, croquet, pool and nature trails all add to the feeling that "you've arrived" – it "can't get better than this."

Riviera Resort Palm Springs 441R (36S)

| 14 | 15 | 12 | 17 | $127 |

1600 N. Indian Canyon Dr., Palm Springs; (619) 327-8311; (800) 444-8311; FAX: (619) 778-2560
■ "Sit by the big pool at night – it's lovely" is all we hear about this convention complex (21 meeting rooms) within walking distance of Downtown; despite the on-site tennis, fitness center, 18-hole putting course, croquet, bocce and lawn bowling, surveyors only remember "the best pool ever", which may be a blessing, considering ratings.

Shadow Mountain Resort (136S)

| 18 | 18 | 15 | 20 | $156 |

45750 San Luis Rey, Palm Desert; (619) 346-6123; (800) 472-3713; FAX: (619) 346-6518
■ "Still holding its head up against tough competition", this "relaxed" 1946 tennis resort wins points for Owen Gillen's USPTA-staffed Desert Tennis Academy (16 courts, six lighted); guests have "mixed" responses to accommodations which range from "nicely furnished" to "run-down", but note approvingly that "roomy apartment-style" lodgings are available; off-court action can be found at five whirlpool spas, four pools and the nearby El Paseo shopping district.

Spa Hotel & Casino 190R (20S) | 17 | 18 | 16 | 18 | $142 |
100 N. Indian Canyon Dr., Palm Springs; (619) 325-1461; (800) 854-1279; FAX: (619) 325-3344
A new casino adds to the "throwback to the glam days" feel of this "inexpensive" Downtown spa whose hot mineral springs gave the town its name; this "healthy getaway" is "a good deal" to some, with "decent rooms", "great massages", outdoor pools and "friendly people"; yet despite what a few call a "well-done" '93 renovation, ratings side with critics who insist the rooms are "tired"; one high roller says the addition of a casino "has given this hotel new life" yet "doesn't intrude" on the health aspect.

Sundance Villas (19S)   ▽ | 21 | 20 | 21 | 20 | $194 |
303 W. Cabrillo Rd., Palm Springs; (619) 325-3888; (800) 455-3888; FAX: (619) 323-3029
"Total peace and privacy" is provided by "large" privately owned villas, each equipped with a kitchen and its own pool and/or spa; the 3.5-acre complex located at the foot of the San Jacinto Mountains near Downtown also has a tennis court and plenty of golf nearby, should you ever wish to leave your hideaway.

Two Bunch Palms 23R (10S) | 22 | 24 | 23 | 24 | $226 |
67-425 Two Bunch Palms Trail, Desert Hot Springs; (619) 329-8791; (800) 472-4334; FAX: (619) 329-1317
"Escape from pressure" and "pamper yourself" at this "private, restful" historic hideaway (which, legend has it, hid Al Capone); Hollywood movers and moguls steal away to this "very romantic and lovely" resort to relax in the rock grotto pools and at the "heavenly" full-service spa offering some "mind-blowing" New Age treatments – reflexology, sea-algae mud wraps, etc.; "a private villa is a must" since the "small" rooms can be "disappointing"; closed in August.

WESTIN MISSION HILLS RESORT 472R (39S) | 24 | 24 | 23 | 26 | $198 |
Dinah Shore & Bob Hope Dr., Rancho Mirage; (619) 328-5955; (800) 228-3000; FAX: (619) 321-2955
Golf is key – Pete Dye and Gary Player each designed an 18-hole course – at this "very well-run" 360-acre resort that makes the grade with "A-plus" "friendly" service, "lovely" rooms and "great" views; it's "terrific" for families who find "plenty to do" off the greens (three pools, water slide, seven tennis courts, "outstanding" dining); overall it's "as good as a large golf/tennis resort can get."

Wyndham Palm Springs Hotel 253R (157S) | 19 | 19 | 17 | 20 | $137 |
888 Tahquitz Canyon Way, Palm Springs; (619) 322-6000; (800) 996-3426; FAX: (619) 325-0130
"There's not much character", but those who don't mind large hotels appreciate the "huge", "magnificent" pool, "lush" landscaping, "moderate" pricing and "good" service at this otherwise "functional" Spanish colonial–style Downtown hotel adjacent to the convention center; reactions to rooms range from "beautiful" to "average" to "dreary" – a '96 renovation came too late for surveyors to reflect it in their scores.

Palo Alto

Garden Court Hotel 50R (11S) | 25 | 23 | 22 | 19 | $188 |
520 Cowper St., Palo Alto; (415) 322-9000; (800) 824-9028; FAX: (415) 324-3609
A "quaint, charming" and "very quiet" hotel that brings "medium luxe" to a "terrific" Downtown location, ideal for shopping or visiting Stanford U; the Mediterranean-style structure houses "big", "beautiful" rooms and a flower-filled courtyard, with amenities including a 24-hour concierge, passes to a fitness center and "great room service" from the "consistently good" Il Fornaio Italian restaurant.

Pasadena

Doubletree Pasadena 350R | 20 | 21 | 19 | 19 | $136 |
191 N. Los Robles, Pasadena; (818) 792-2727; (800) 222-TREE; FAX: (818) 795-7669
A "stone's throw" from "hopping" Old Town, this "well-run", "reliable" hotel provides "perfectly nice business accommodations" with "friendly" service and "gorgeous" views, and who doesn't "love" the famed chocolate-chip cookies?; it's also a "terrific hang for the beach", although foes find the decor "sterile" and cry out for more "personality."

Pebble Beach

INN AT SPANISH BAY 244R (16S) | 28 | 27 | 26 | 28 | $276 |
2700 17 Mile Dr., Pebble Beach; (408) 647-7500; (800) 654-9300; FAX: (408) 649-2790
"A hole in one!" rave surveyors over this "dramatic", "luxurious" golf paradise (with access to four courses), sister to The Lodge at Pebble Beach and the second-highest-rated resort in the state; it's worth it "even if you don't play golf", with its "big", "elegant", "comfortable" rooms, all with fireplaces and balconies (get one with "an ocean view"), "unbelievably attentive" staff, eight lighted tennis courts, outdoor pool, spa and "great people-watching"; Pacific Rim dining at Roy's "makes your taste buds come alive" at this "benchmark by which other resorts should be judged."

LODGE AT PEBBLE BEACH 152R (9S)

27 | 27 | 26 | 28 | $293

1700 17-Mile Dr., Pebble Beach; (408) 624-3811; (800) 654-9300; FAX: (408) 625-8598

■ "Still the darling of senior CEOs", this "breathtaking, romantic" "dream destination" boasting a "very special" oceanside setting has inspired worship since 1919 as "the cathedral of golf" with three courses on-site including the world-class namesake Pebble Beach Golf Links; but it's also "heaven on earth" for nonduffers thanks to the "enormous rooms with fireplaces", "feeling of old luxury" and "unforgettable" scenery; when it comes to dining, "class oozes out the doorways" of the Cal-French restaurant Club XIX, and you can work it off at the beach club with its spa, pool, tennis and fitness center.

Redwood City

Sofitel Hotel, San Francisco Bay 291R (28S)

– | – | – | – | E

223 Twin Dolphin Dr., Redwood City; (415) 598-9000; (800) 763-4835; FAX: (415) 598-9383

This quiet, elegant oasis overlooking a lagoon in the heart of a mid-Peninsula business park is technologically friendly, befitting its proximity to some of America's largest high-tech firms; its staff serves guests admirably, and Baccarat restaurant offers Cal-French dining, no surprise at this French-owned chain property.

Riverside

Mission Inn 202R (33S)

22 | 21 | 21 | 24 | $138

3649 Mission Inn Ave., Riverside; (909) 784-0300; (800) 843-7755; FAX: (909) 784-5525

☑ Voters' reactions to the architecture – domes, clock towers, flying buttresses, stained-glass windows – of this "unique" 1876 landmark that took 30 years to build and fills an entire city block range from "fabulous" to "bizarre", but most say it's "worth a visit if in the area"; the "treasure-filled" historic structure underwent a "very interesting" $42-million renovation in '92 and now boasts its own museum ("take the docent's tour") plus a health club and Olympic-size pool; one guest grouses that some rooms are "the smallest I've ever seen", but in every respect it's "one of a kind."

Rutherford

AUBERGE DU SOLEIL 31R (19S)

28 | 26 | 27 | 27 | $310

180 Rutherford Hill Rd., Rutherford; (707) 963-1211; (800) 348-5406; FAX: (707) 963-0283

■ It's surveyors who shine on this patch of sun in the Napa Valley, an "elegant, rich", "dreamy" "Riviera in the hills" with a "trendy restaurant in a magnificent setting"; the "fantastic, well-appointed" rooms (all with fireplaces) create a "wonderfully romantic feeling" and the "heavenly" restaurant "offers everything but ambrosia and nectar"; three tennis courts, an outdoor pool and extensive spa services add to the "experience for the senses", but alas, there can be a chill in the air at this Relais & Châteaux affiliate, with more than one comment on "snobby service" suggesting "you could suffer frostbite at the front desk."

Rancho Caymus (26S)

19 | 16 | 15 | 16 | $152

1140 Rutherford Rd., Rutherford; (707) 763-1777; (800) 845-1777; FAX: (707) 763-5387

☑ Its "central location" in Napa Valley is "good" for visiting the wineries, and the "small", "pleasant" all-suite inn, designed to resemble a Spanish hacienda with an interior garden courtyard, offers "nicely decorated" rooms, each individually done, with hand-carved furnishings, high-beamed ceilings, fireplaces, Latin American fabrics and private balconies, along with an "above-average" included breakfast; a very few chide the lack of indoor public areas as "motel-like."

Sacramento

Hyatt Regency Sacramento 476R (24S)

20 | 21 | 19 | 19 | $141

1209 L St., Sacramento; (916) 443-1234; (800) 233-1234; FAX: (916) 321-6631

☑ "Rub elbows with the pols" in a "home for lobbyists" across from the capitol building; it's generally praised as "reliable" with a "friendly, helpful staff", an outdoor pool and meeting space for 1,700, although a few lob nays for the "uneven Downtown area" and "sterile" ambiance; realists point out it's a "decent hotel in a hotel wasteland" – probably "best in town."

Radisson Sacramento 282R (25S)

17 | 19 | 18 | 19 | $124

500 Leisure Ln., Sacramento; (916) 922-2020; (800) 333-3333; FAX: (916) 649-9432

■ There are "pretty" views of the lake on this 18-acre property close to Downtown Sacramento, plus a pool and "good" conference facilities, but still most surveyors suggest this "convention hotel" is merely a "so-so" business stop with "average" rooms that are getting "run-down."

San Diego

TOP 10 OVERALL

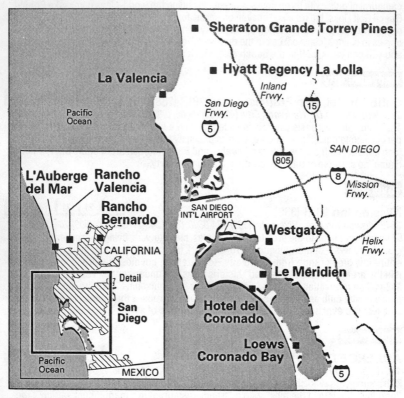

BEST OVERALL
- **27** Rancho Valencia
- **24** Rancho Bernardo
  - Loews Coronado Bay
  - L'Auberge del Mar
  - Le Meridien
  - Sheraton Grande Torrey Pines
- **23** La Valencia
  - Del Coronado, Hotel
  - Hyatt Regency La Jolla
  - Westgate

BEST VALUES
- Doubletree Hotel del Mar
- Marriott Mission Valley
- Embassy Suites San Diego Bay
- Horton Grand
- Catamaran Resort
- Kona Kai Plaza
- Westin San Diego
- Radisson Harbor View
- U.S. Grant Hotel
- Marriott La Jolla

R	S	D	P	$

Catamaran Resort Hotel 265R (50S)   18 | 19 | 17 | 21 | $132
3999 Mission Blvd., San Diego; (619) 488-1081; (800) 288-0770; FAX: (619) 488-1387
☑ "Noisy" talking parrots in the lobby are part of the "fun" "for kids" at this "funky" "waterfront" resort in a "lovely, lush" setting on Mission Bay; some squawk about "indifferent service" and rooms that "don't live up to the marvelous bay view" from their balconies – but "if you don't have time for Hawaii", it just might be the nest for you.

Del Coronado, Hotel 620R (80S)   22 | 24 | 22 | 26 | $201
1500 Orange Ave., Coronado; (619) 435-6611; (800) HOTEL-DEL; FAX: (619) 522-8262
☑ "What a treasure!" – this "one of a kind" "slice of vanishing Americana" is a "delight despite the tourists", with a "smashing" oceanfront location and a "small jewel of a beach"; rooms in the "timelessly elegant" Victorian main building (circa 1888, no a/c) have "charm and character" but "vary widely" and are "showing their age", while the modern Ocean Towers rooms (with a/c) can be "bland" but have a fine "view of the old building"; overall, it's "a real treat – everyone should stay at least once", and one fanatic urges "if necessary, swim across San Diego Bay for the Sunday brunch."

Doubletree Hotel Del Mar 216R (4S)   19   19   16   17 $116
11915 El Camino Real, Del Mar; (619) 481-5900; (800) 222-TREE; FAX: (619) 481-0990
◪ "Serviceable" for business in the "boonies" 20 miles north of San Diego near Del Mar racetrack and "convenient" to La Jolla, this "good-value" hotel earns limited praise as "aesthetically pleasant but sterile", offering "friendly" service, "good" rooms and a "beautiful" pool area (though a few feel it's "beginning to need a renovation"); food passes as "acceptable" – except for those cookies, which "hit the spot."

Embassy Suites San Diego Bay (337S)   22   20   17   20 $132
601 Pacific Hwy., San Diego; (619) 239-2400; (800) EMBASSY; FAX: (619) 239-1520
■ A "real bargain" for families and business travelers is the take on these "spacious", "clean and comfortable" suites with a "good" location convenient to Horton Plaza shopping, Seaport Village and the convention center, plus perks such as free AM breakfast and PM cocktails (though some note "long lines" for the drinks); most find the "common spaces very pleasant", as is "typical" for Embassy Suites.

Gaslamp Plaza Suites 26R (32S)   ▽ 20   19   14   19 $112
520 E St., San Diego; (619) 232-9500; (800) 874-8770; FAX: (619) 238-9945
■ The historic Downtown Gaslamp Quarter is home to a completely revamped 1913 "peaceful" Victorian hotel with economical time-share accommodations and a rooftop terrace but little else in the way of amenities (although for a fee guests have access to health club facilities at the Westin across the street); diners find creative SW food at the adjacent Dakota Grill & Spirits.

Hilton Beach & Tennis Resort San Diego   21   20   19   22 $158
340R (17S)
1775 E. Mission Bay Dr., San Diego; (619) 276-4010; (800) 445-8667; FAX: (619) 275-7991
◪ "Nice remodeling job" cheers one repeat guest about the 1995 redo of this "relaxing" resort that's "great for families" with a "wonderful" pool, kids' programs, tennis, marina, full-service spa and fitness center; its "beautiful" tropical grounds and location "right on Mission Bay" are more pluses.

Horton Grand Hotel 108R (24S)   21   21   19   19 $139
311 Island Ave., San Diego; (619) 544-1886; (800) 542-1886; FAX: (619) 544-0058
■ "The most erotic hotel in San Diego" purr surveyors about this "quaint", "historic", relocated hotel connected to a "former cathouse" (which now provides the suite accommodations) in the "seedy but fun" Gaslamp District; there's still some hanky-panky going on in this "very romantic" Victorian's "grand" rooms, each with a queen-size bed and gas fireplace; but while the building has "loads of personality", the food is only "bland" – though there's "good afternoon tea."

Hyatt Islandia 281R (141S)   19   19   17   20 $146
1441 Quivira Rd., San Diego; (619) 224-1234; (800) 233-1234; FAX: (619) 224-0348
◪ Its proximity to Sea World draws families to this "touristy but nice" Hyatt with "pretty" grounds, "spacious" rooms, a "very friendly" staff and "wonderful" ocean and sunset views (along with water sports, an on-site marina, an outdoor pool and kids' programs); but some shrug "nothing out of the ordinary", noting that rooms are "getting a little old" – at least the tower accommodations got an uplift in '96.

Hyatt Regency La Jolla 375R (25S)   23   23   22   23 $171
3777 La Jolla Village Dr., La Jolla, (619) 552-1234; (800) 233-1234; FAX: (619) 552-6066
◪ Whether architect Michael Graves' creation is "dramatic" and "beautiful" or "ugly" and "inappropriate" may depend on your affection for "postmodern pastiche", but surveyors agree on the "terrific" 32,000-square-foot fitness club ("jock heaven") and spa ("great massage"), as well as the "hip" "adventure in Pacific Rim" dining at Cafe Japengo; the "large, comfortable" rooms are "pleasant" to some, "average" to tougher critics, but overall most judge it an "excellent choice in La Jolla."

Hyatt Regency San Diego 819R (56S)   23   23   22   23 $176
1 Market Pl., San Diego; (619) 232-1234; (800) 233-1234; FAX: (619) 233-6464
■ "Breathtaking views", perhaps "the most beautiful in San Diego" (especially from the top-floor bar), are the highlight here, though it's a different experience looking at, rather than from, this "grain elevator"–like convention tower; even sans the views, the "first-rate" concierge service, "good rooms", extensive meeting space (capacity 2,700) and fitness and spa facilities make it "great for business travelers" and "solid and reliable" overall – no wonder the Republicans made it their official hotel HQ during the 1996 convention.

Inn at Rancho Santa Fe 17R (90S) | 22 | 24 | 22 | 23 | $195 |
5951 Linea Del Cielo, Rancho Santa Fe; (619) 756-1131; (800) 654-2928; FAX: (619) 759-1604

☑ "This is what I've been waiting for" says one devotee of this "dream of 1930s California" in "charming" Rancho Santa Fe; "historically interesting" and "comfortable", this "lovely old inn" is above all a "quiet golf getaway" where "the chief attraction is 'tee time'" and most accommodations are in cottages scattered throughout the 20-acre estate; also offering walking trails, croquet and its own cottage at Del Mar beach with showers and a private patio, it's a "hyperrelaxed" "hideaway for quiet reflection and elegance" – perhaps "a time warp, but we love it."

Kona Kai Plaza Las Glorias Resort & Marina | 20 | 21 | 18 | 21 | $143 |
176R (35S)
1151 Shelter Island Dr., San Diego; (619) 222-1191; (800) 566-2524; FAX: (619) 222-9738

■ Scores have soared since this "wonderful small hotel on the beach" with an Old Mexico theme underwent a total renovation in 1994-95; a candidate for "the most romantic" resort hotel, it stands out for its island setting across the bay that's like "a little bit of Hawaii" and for "huge", "quiet" rooms, "caring", "interested" service, its own marina and abundant activities – two tennis courts, boating, fishing, two heated pools and fitness facilities.

La Jolla Beach & Tennis Club 35R (55S) | 20 | 22 | 21 | 24 | $192 |
2000 Spindrift Dr., La Jolla; (619) 454-7126; (800) 624-2582; FAX: (619) 456-3805

■ "Superior" tennis facilities take center court at this historic Spanish-style "getaway" in a "magnificent" location 15 miles north of San Diego on its own "beautiful" beach – a 14-acre "perfect" place for a "relaxed family vacation"; in addition to 14 tennis courts are nine links of golf and an outdoor pool, as well as kitchenettes in most quarters (a $1-million renovation in '96 may address complaints of "blah" rooms); the "pleasant" surfside Marine Room restaurant lures a "preppy crowd" with reportedly improving Continental-French cuisine – in fact, "all changes have been pluses."

L'Auberge Del Mar Resort & Spa 112R (8S) | 25 | 24 | 23 | 25 | $203 |
1540 Camino Del Mar, Del Mar; (619) 259-1515; (800) 553-1336; FAX: (619) 755-4940

☑ "Splendid facilities match the ocean view" at this "low-key" resort on the site of a former historic movie star "hangout" (the Del Mar Inn) in a "beautiful" central village location; with five acres of gardens, an "excellent" spa, two "especially nice" outdoor heated pools and two tennis courts, it soothes relaxation seekers, and while most praise "comfortable", "charming" rooms (especially around the "lovely garden courtyard"), a minority murmurs they're "getting tired" – perhaps they visited before the 1995 redo.

La Valencia Hotel 87R (19S) | 22 | 25 | 24 | 23 | $202 |
1132 Prospect St., La Jolla; (619) 454-0771; (800) 451-0772; FAX: (619) 456-3921

■ "Glory and beauty from the golden days" with a "gorgeous Mediterranean motif" is the stuff of which this "classy" 1926 "throwback" is made; the "superior" La Jolla location on a bluff overlooking the Pacific, "outstanding service", "gustatory delights" served in the "wonderful dining room with a terrific ocean view" (especially from the patio), beach access and an outdoor pool make it "a keeper" that's "worth the money", even if many note some "very minute rooms" – "choose with care"; a few feel this "elegant grandmother" may be "a little stiff for children."

LE MERIDIEN SAN DIEGO AT CORONADO | 25 | 23 | 24 | 24 | $186 |
265R (35S)
(nka Coronado Marriott)
2000 Second St., Coronado; (619) 435-3000; (800) 543-4300; FAX: (619) 435-3032

■ A French "Fantasy Island–type" ambiance pervades this highly rated, "very well-run" "restful getaway" that "caters to an international" clientele, offering "across-the-bay" views "to die for", "beautiful" grounds, "big", "well-appointed" rooms with "gorgeous bathrooms" and terraces and an "impeccable" staff; in addition to three heated outdoor pools, six tennis courts, meeting facilities and extensive spa services, there's "wonderful" Provençal cuisine at the "superb" Marius restaurant; in the words of one blissful guest: "it doesn't get any better."

Lodge at Torrey Pines 73R | 22 | 21 | 19 | 21 | $162 |
11480 N. Torrey Pines, La Jolla; (619) 453-4420; (800) 288-0770; FAX: (619) 452-0691

☑ "Golf next to the Pacific" is the main claim to fame of this small "rustic" property on the famed scenic PGA Torrey Pines course, but surveyors also praise "very comfortable" rooms (although some grouse about "cardboard-thin walls"), a location convenient to La Jolla and "spectacular hiking up the road"; there's an outdoor pool and two restaurants, but otherwise amenities are limited.

LOEWS CORONADO BAY RESORT 403R (37S)   25 | 24 | 23 | 25 | $184

4000 Coronado Bay Rd., Coronado; (619) 424-4000; (800) 23-LOEWS; FAX: (619) 424-4400

☑ Whether the location is "fantastic" or "too far off the beaten path", most surveyors agree this 1991 Mediterranean-style resort features a "beautiful" 80-slip marina, "gorgeous" views, "gracious" service, "superb rooms", "nice conference facilities" and "fine" Pacific Rim dining at trendy Azzura Point; there's "water, water everywhere" (and its attendant sports), five tennis courts, three pools, nearby golf and kids' programs that make it a "good family hotel" too; detractors, a minority, find the layout "confusing" and say it's "too noisy and crowded."

Marriott Hotel & Marina San Diego 1302R (52S)   22 | 22 | 20 | 23 | $155

333 W. Harbor Dr., San Diego; (619) 234-1500; (800) 228-9290; FAX: (619) 234-8678

☑ "Location, location, location" means "great views" and nearby shops at this two-tower convention magnet, a "better-than-average" but "very busy" place for meetings (42 rooms, capacity 2,500) with "efficient, pleasant" service; despite good scores, several describe rooms as "small and in need of updating", but an on-site marina, health club and six tennis courts add appeal; "for a large city hotel they do a very good job", yet despite all the amenities, some feel it's no more than "typical Marriott."

Marriott La Jolla 349R (11S)   21 | 20 | 18 | 19 | $141

4240 La Jolla Village Dr., La Jolla; (619) 587-1414; (800) 228-9290; FAX: (619) 546-8518

☑ This "all-in-one" suburban business/vacation hotel splits surveyors; the ayes proclaim it "better than many Marriotts" and in a "beautiful area" (across from University Towne Center shopping mall) with "great service" and "tastefully decorated", "above-average" rooms; but the nays nix a "run-of-the-mill" operation with "tiny", "plastic" rooms, suggesting you might want to check out your quarters carefully; indoor and outdoor pools and a health club are pluses.

Marriott Mission Valley 344R (6S)   20 | 21 | 18 | 19 | $129

8757 Rio San Diego Dr., San Diego; (619) 692-3800; (800) 842-5329; FAX: (619) 692-0769

■ Located by Jack Murphy Stadium 20 minutes northeast of the city and near suburban shopping, this "average Marriott" is "ok for basic needs", offering "very good" service and "attractive" grounds, as well as a health club, two tennis courts and an outdoor pool; N.B. the $1.2-million '96 room upgrade came too late for this *Survey*'s scores.

Princess Resort San Diego 359R (103S)   18 | 20 | 17 | 22 | $157

1404 W. Vatican Rd., San Diego; (619) 274-4630; (800) 344-2626; FAX: (619) 581-5977

☑ "The Love Boat on land" is "great for kids of all ages", which means either a "terrific family resort" or "tacky beyond belief" (or both); set on a 44-acre island in Mission Bay, it offers "beautiful grounds" with five pools, a beach, six tennis courts, biking trails, mini golf and a marina, plus meeting space for 1,100; despite a '94 guestroom renovation, those ready to jump ship claim "the Princess has become a chambermaid" and its "standard rooms are dark little tunnels – most guests try to upgrade immediately" (perhaps to the "beautiful bay suites.")

Radisson Harbor View 313R (20S)   18 | 17 | 17 | 17 | $124

1646 Front St., San Diego; (619) 239-6800; (800) 333-3333; FAX: (619) 238-9461

☑ "There really is a harbor view" from this strictly business Downtowner, but as some surveyors note, the water is six blocks away; while a few praise "clean" accommodations in a "great" corporate location (just five minutes from the airport) with a heated outdoor pool and health club on-site, critics say it's getting "seedy" and gripe about "terrible service"; reasonable rates help keep it afloat.

RANCHO BERNARDO INN 227R (58S)   23 | 25 | 25 | 24 | $193

17550 Bernardo Oaks Dr., Rancho Bernardo; (619) 675-8500; (800) 323-7500; FAX: (619) 675-8501

■ "Secluded" in the San Pasqual Mountains north of San Diego, this "very, very comfortable", "elegant" and "relaxing" resort offers "a great all-around vacation" with "excellent golf and tennis packages", "spectacular" views and "friendly" service, along with "superb" French cuisine at El Bizcocho; a golf course, 12 tennis courts and two outdoor pools keep sporty guests and their kids bouncing back (there are tots' programs too), though several suggest some rooms are just "so-so."

RANCHO VALENCIA RESORT (43S)   29 | 27 | 27 | 27 | $280

5921 Valencia Circle, Rancho Santa Fe; (619) 756-1123; (800) 548-3664; FAX: (619) 756-0165

■ "More than sheer perfection, this place is heaven" – so go the accolades that abound in every category for San Diego's top-rated "small and stylish", "exquisite" resort in Rancho Santa Fe, providing the "best vacation on the mainland, ever"; praise is piled on the "beautiful setting", "silver-spoon service", "spacious casitas (all with fireplaces), "tennis heaven" (18 courts), an adjacent golf course, a pro croquet lawn and "truly wonderful" Cal-Med food; in sum, "from orange juice to orange sunsets, all is perfect."

Sea Lodge Hotel 121R (7S)
20 | 20 | 18 | 21 | $163

8110 Camino del Oro, La Jolla; (619) 459-8271; (800) 237-5211; FAX: (619) 456-9346

■ Boasting an "incredibly beautiful" setting on La Jolla's beach, this Old Mexico–style "perfect family destination" is "laid-back" and "informal" with an outdoor pool, two tennis courts and "loads of entertainment" on-site or nearby; after "walks on the beach" the "pounding surf lulls you to sleep" in "comfortable" rooms (renovated in 1996), and the "beach view from the dining room at breakfast is a California event."

SHERATON GRANDE TORREY PINES 375R (17S)
24 | 24 | 22 | 25 | $187

10950 N. Torrey Pines Rd., La Jolla; (619) 558-1500; (800) 762-6160; FAX: (619) 558-1131

◪ Located on the 18th fairway of the Torrey Pines course, this golf resort's solid scores reflect the opinions of those who remember "beautiful" ocean views and rooms, "very comfortable" rooms, "attentive" service and "excellent" food at Torreyana Grille; but an undercurrent murmurs about an "overblown", "charmless" property that "seems like a fancy hotel" but is "not as grand as they [Sheraton] would like to think"; a guestroom renovation was completed in 1996.

Sheraton San Diego Hotel & Marina 1004R (43S)
21 | 20 | 18 | 21 | $151

1380 Harbor Island Dr., San Diego; (619) 291-2900; (800) 325-3535; FAX: (619) 692-2338

■ A "long overdue" and "well-done" renovation makes this "high-end Sheraton" on Harbor Island "excellent" for conferences (42 rooms, capacity 7,900) and "convenient for an early-morning flight" while also serving as "a perfect place for the whole family"; there are "superb views of the marina and bay", "large" though "standard" rooms, a "friendly" staff, two oceanfront pools and a health club – still, the 'b's are buzzing: "blah", "boring", "too busy."

U.S. Grant Hotel 220R (60S)
21 | 21 | 21 | 20 | $148

326 Broadway, San Diego; (619) 232-3121; (800) 237-5029; FAX: (619) 232-3626

◪ Colonnades, crystal chandeliers and Dutch and Venetian paintings contribute to the "very stately, grand" ambiance at this "lovingly refurbished" 1910 hotel in a "convenient" Downtown location next to Horton Plaza; there may be no sports facilities, but guests enjoy a "bit of history" and "old-world charm" in the public areas and "great" guestrooms (all have new furnishings), and there's good Continental fare at Grant Grill; rates are "a bargain for San Diego."

Westgate Hotel 214R (9S)
24 | 23 | 22 | 22 | $182

1055 Second Ave., San Diego; (619) 238-1818; (800) 221-3802; FAX: (619) 557-3737

◪ This "intimate and sophisticated" "step back in time" is actually a modern rendition of "a taste of France in Downtown San Diego"; reviewers revel in the "great-looking" lobby, "superb", "huge" rooms (no two alike), "charming", "friendly" staff, "special" teatime and "first-class" Fontainebleau restaurant; a few demanding critics contend that it "needs some work."

Westin San Diego 450R (14S)
20 | 19 | 16 | 18 | $132

(fka Doubletree Hotel at Horton Plaza)
910 Broadway Circle, San Diego; (619) 239-2200; (800) 228-3000; FAX: (619) 239-1730

◪ A "great location for shopping" at Horton Plaza is the major selling point of this Downtown chainer, and "friendly" service, "pretty" common areas, a "lively" lobby and those "good" chocolate-chip cookies just up the demand; though a few cite a "commercial feel", most agree it's a "comfortable", "convenient" choice.

Wyndham Emerald Plaza 413R (20S)
21 | 20 | 19 | 19 | $149

(fka Pan Pacific Hotel)
400 W. Broadway, San Diego; (619) 239-4500; (800) 626-3988; FAX: (619) 239-3274

◪ An "eye-popping futuristic" lobby is the chief attraction at this multitower high-rise, a "well-managed" business/convention Downtowner that's "anxious to please" and "comfortable" for work; basically it's "nothing special" aside from the business center with private offices and a law library, and the rooms apparently vary: "big, bright and sunny" vs. "dreary", "be selective"; the Emerald Fitness Club has an outdoor lap pool and complete workout equipment.

San Francisco Bay Area

TOP 10 OVERALL

BEST OVERALL

- **28** Ritz-Carlton
- **27** Sherman House
- **26** Mandarin Oriental
- **25** Monaco Hotel
- Campton Place
- Pan Pacific
- **24** Clift Hotel
- Huntington Hotel
- Renaissance Stanford Court
- Palace Hotel

BEST VALUES

- Clarion Bedford
- Majestic
- Monaco Hotel
- Juliana Hotel
- Kensington Park
- Vintage Court
- Tuscan Inn
- Savoy Hotel
- Milano Hotel
- White Swan

R	S	D	P	$

ANA Hotel San Francisco 641R (26S)   22 | 20 | 19 | 19 | $176

50 Third St., San Francisco; (415) 974-6400; (800) ANA-HOTELS; FAX: (415) 543-8268

☑ "Very classy in its own way", this "all-around good", "well-located" business hotel in the Financial District wins kudos for its "exceptionally professional" approach, "reasonable rates" and "great views from some rooms"; less-enthused respondents find it "efficient but not very colorful", and a few outright critics pan the place as "sterile" with service that "could be better and friendlier" and parking that's "expensive."

Archbishop's Mansion 10R (5S)   26 | 24 | 17 | 22 | $188

1000 Fulton St., San Francisco; (415) 563-7872; (800) 543-5820; FAX: (415) 885-3193

■ "What a dream" – this "very romantic" 1904 belle epoque landmark, a "lovely hideaway" with "enchanting", "exquisitely appointed" rooms, strikes many as a "fantasy come true"; alas, the "only-average" food falls short and the dicey Alamo Square neighborhood is too "off the beaten track" for some, though nearby is a much-photographed 'Postcard Row' of Victorians.

Bohème, Hotel 15R   ▽ 23 | 21 | 18 | 17 | $164
(fka Millefiori Inn)
444 Columbus Ave., San Francisco; (415) 433-9111; FAX: (415) 362-6292
■ "The way to do North Beach", this small new offering in SF's classic bohemian neighborhood has been redone as a Beat-gone-upscale oasis where guests groove to its "great beds and showers and location"; depending on your familiarity with Ferlinghetti, it's either a "nice hideaway" or "an adventure" or both.

CAMPTON PLACE HOTEL 107R (10S)   25 | 26 | 27 | 23 | $241
340 Stockton St., San Francisco; (415) 781-5555; (800) 235-4300; FAX: (415) 955-5536
■ "Perfection, professional, superb" and "most sublime" sigh surveyors about this "exquisitely maintained" "boutique hotel" "in SF's hub"; "exceptionally attentive service" is a given, and "serious foodies" can "dine gloriously" at what devotees call "the most gracious restaurant in the country"; a few gentle quibblers refer to somewhat "cramped elegance" at this "charming gem" with "room size to match."

Cathedral Hill Hotel 390R (10S)   16 | 14 | 13 | 13 | $122
1101 Van Ness Ave., San Francisco; (415) 776-8200; (800) 622-0855; FAX: (415) 441-1174
■ "Cheap, clean" and just "adequate" is the take on this "functional business hotel" near City Hall, which makes it "great for government" but "out of the way" for tourists; "nice gardens" and a "good coffee shop" are pluses, but some of the rooms, though "large", are "very tired."

Chancellor Hotel 135R (2S)   15 | 18 | 14 | 14 | $116
433 Powell St., San Francisco; (415) 362-2004; (800) 428-4748; FAX: (415) 362-1403
☑ "Being hard of hearing helps" if your room faces bustling Union Square, but "location is everything" at this "relatively cheap", "no-nonsense place to sleep" that's been owned by the same family for 80 years; however, what some characterize as a "lovely old hotel" with "charming" accommodations is to others "only passable" with "adequate" but "tiny" quarters that lack a/c.

Claremont Resort & Spa 204R (35S)   21 | 22 | 21 | 24 | $175
41 Tunnel Rd., Berkeley; (510) 843-3000; (800) 551-7266; FAX: (510) 848-6208
☑ "Handsome elegance abounds" at this "beautiful white castle in the Berkeley hills" offering guests "wonderful" views of SF and the Bay, "magnificent" grounds and "excellent facilities" including a "fabulous spa", an Olympic-size pool and 10 "world-class" tennis courts; "great service" also helps make this "grand" "Victorian" "remnant of a past age" "always enjoyable", but many also point out that "some of the rooms disappoint" and "need refurbishing."

Clarion Bedford Hotel 137R (7S)   19 | 21 | 19 | 17 | $113
(fka Hotel Bedford)
761 Post St., San Francisco; (415) 673-6040; (800) 227-5642; FAX: (415) 563-6739
☑ "Close to Downtown", "good value" but "not spiffy" capsulizes comments about this renamed Kimpton-operated veteran that attracts a government trade and other economy-minded visitors; while ratings have risen since our last *Survey*, a few surveyors still cite "substandard housekeeping" and a "shaky" front desk; an evening wine hour is included in the "reasonable" rate.

CLIFT HOTEL 297R (32S)   24 | 26 | 25 | 23 | $224
(fka Four Seasons Clift Hotel)
495 Geary St., San Francisco; (415) 775-4700; (800) 65-CLIFT; FAX: (415) 441-4621
☑ "Bright and beautiful", "ultraspacious" rooms, "very personal" service, a "great central location" not far from Union Square, the historic Redwood Room for drinks and the French Room for dinner make this an "extra-special" bastion of "true luxury" for many partisans; now that talented hotelier Ian Schrager has taken over, maybe the chorus of laments such as "iffy" management and "once great, now slipping" will quiet as he puts his stylish, sophisticated stamp on this "queen of hotels."

Diva Hotel 110R (1S)   17 | 18 | 14 | 14 | $133
440 Geary St., San Francisco; (415) 885-0200; (800) 553-1900; FAX: (415) 885-3268
☑ This "small, artsy" place is definitely "not for everyone" but "ok if you like art deco", "Italian design", "tiny rooms" and a location that's "in the heart of everything" – that is, "on the border of Hell and the Theater District"; some patrons describe it as "fun and funky", a "nice hotel if you are young", although the disenchanted wail that it "wants to be cool but ends up cheap"; N.B. there's a California Pizza Kitchen on-site.

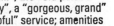
R	S	D	P	$

Donatello, The 86R (8S)

| 22 | 21 | 22 | 18 | $179 |

501 Post St., San Francisco; (415) 441-7100; (800) 227-3184; FAX: (415) 885-8842

■ "Always a treat" rave business travelers and tourists alike about this "charming, contemporary", Italian-themed "great small hotel for the money"; there are also bravissimos for the "wonderful location" a block from Union Square, "beautiful rooms" and Zingari, a "great restaurant" for "serious Italian foodies"; all in all, "they do you right."

Fairmont Hotel San Francisco 530R (62S)

| 23 | 24 | 23 | 23 | $207 |

950 Mason St., San Francisco; (415) 772-5000; (800) 527-4727; FAX: (415) 781-3929

■ "Elegance, elegance, elegance" chant fascinated fans of this "classic, beautiful" "grande dame" poised "like a castle" at "the crown of Nob Hill"; the "old palace" boasts "large, high-ceilinged rooms", "the best views in the city", a "gorgeous, grand" lobby that's perfect for "people-watching" plus "polite and helpful" service; amenities include eight restaurants and lounges, as well as nightly entertainment in the New Orleans Room; while a few dub it "a bit long in the tooth", many more say it's "still going strong after all these years."

Galleria Park Hotel 162R (15S)

| 17 | 19 | 18 | 15 | $135 |

191 Sutter St., San Francisco; (415) 781-3060; (800) 792-9639; FAX: (415) 433-4409

■ "A lovely, friendly, small hotel" that's a "good buy" in an "excellent Financial District location"; the 1996 "nice redecoration" of this "quaint" art nouveau Kimpton unit adds a bit of ambiance to otherwise "very plain", "very tiny" quarters; along with advising newcomers that there's a third-floor jogging track, regulars say "request an inside room" to avoid street noise and tout Perry's, a popular watering hole and eatery.

Gramma's Rose Garden Inn 40R

| 19 | 18 | 18 | 19 | $114 |

2740 Telegraph Ave., Berkeley; (510) 549-2145; FAX: (510) 549-1085

☑ "Where flower children go when they grow up", this "sweet retreat in Berkeley" offers "a nice change of pace" from the big hotels, with "beautiful" gardens and "quaint" antiques-filled rooms, some featuring stained-glass windows (one guest was particularly taken by the "romantic cottage out back"); but while "nice overall", like all roses this one has thorns, including "very variable" accommodations that can be "disappointing", and despite university "convenience", the neighborhood "puts off" some guests.

Grand Hyatt San Francisco 662R (31S)

| 22 | 21 | 20 | 20 | $188 |

345 Stockton St., San Francisco; (415) 398-1234; (800) 233-1234; FAX: (415) 391-1780

☑ "Walk to everything" from this "modern, sleek and well-staffed" "megahotel" in Union Square – a "terrific location if you're a shopper" or a conventioneer; many value the "friendly, helpful staff" and "very comfortable", "good but plain" rooms, some with views of the Bay; an inevitable few nonfans find it a "faceless", "basic business hotel" with a "factory atmosphere" and a "hectic" lobby, but boosters counter that "the name says it all – grand."

Griffon, Hotel 59R (3S)

| 19 | 20 | 24 | 16 | $142 |

155 Steuart St., San Francisco; (415) 495-2100; (800) 321-2201; FAX: (415) 495-3522

☑ "Old-world charm" and "small but well-decorated rooms" (eight with Bay views) bring business travelers and weekenders to this "good-value" hostelry with an "offbeat location" on San Francisco's waterfront Embarcadero; a few find the accommodations "sad", but everyone seems upbeat about the "excellent" bistro/grill, Roti, which provides room service, and the extensive YMCA gym next door (complimentary for Griffon guests).

Handlery Union Square Hotel 357R (20S)

| 16 | 18 | 15 | 14 | $126 |

351 Geary St., San Francisco; (415) 781-7800; (800) 843-4343; FAX: (415) 781-0269

☑ "Good prices", "clean and airy" rooms and "friendly" service satisfy the clientele of this Union Square hotel that's near the theaters; but scores support the view that this "modest and noisy" "older" place "has gone downhill" (a just-completed renovation might change that), and there are complaints about the old-line Italian fare at New Joe's; however, the rare (for SF) outdoor heated pool makes a nice splash.

Harbor Court Hotel 130R (1S)

| 20 | 21 | 20 | 20 | $154 |

165 Steuart St., San Francisco; (415) 882-1300; (800) 346-0555; FAX: (415) 882-1313

■ "An often overlooked alternative in the Financial District", this "comfortable", "good-value" Kimpton-run 1907 landmark has "beautifully decorated" albeit "small" rooms (some do provide "great water views"), a pool and afternoon tea or wine; perennially popular Harry Denton's Bar & Grill gives guests the option to mix with fun-loving locals, and an "outstanding fitness facility" (complimentary for guests) is adjacent.

Hilton & Towers San Francisco 1790R (110S)   19 | 19 | 17 | 18 | $165
333 O'Farrell St., San Francisco; (415) 771-1400; (800) 445-8667; FAX: (415) 771-6807
◪ "Bring a compass" to navigate this "big, brassy, busy" and "cavernous hotel"; raves abound for "million-dollar views", but what is "very courteous" service to some is "consistent in messing up" to others; likewise, dining is seen as "fair" to "good" and room assessments vary from "nice" to "bland" to "dumpy", with some also irked by a somewhat "seedy area"; nevertheless, most feel that "despite the immediate surroundings, it's a good convention hotel."

HUNTINGTON HOTEL 110R (30S)   25 | 26 | 24 | 21 | $229
1075 California St., San Francisco; (415) 474-5400; (800) 227-4683; FAX: (415) 474-6227
■ "Quiet and conservative, with great service" and "understated elegance" sums up responses to "one of the old greats" atop "divine" Nob Hill; a "clubby, intimate" ambiance pervades, from the "aristocratic accommodations" to the "world-class" Big Four Restaurant; guests who "don't need a lot of action" call it a "home away from home" that's "sedate and comfortable" (though it "needs a/c"); "if you can afford it, stay here" – "you feel special."

Hyatt at Fisherman's Wharf 305R (8S)   20 | 20 | 19 | 19 | $163
555 Northpoint St., San Francisco; (415) 563-1234; (800) 233-1234; FAX: (415) 749-6122
■ "The best hotel on the Wharf", this "oasis among the kitschy spots" is "surprisingly quiet for being in the heart of the tourist area"; "the staff tries hard", it's "nicely appointed", there's an outdoor pool and also the "cheerful" Knuckles Sports Bar to boot; nevertheless, some critics say don't expect old-time SF ambiance, and a few phobes pan the place as "positively charmless."

Hyatt Regency San Francisco 760R (45S)   21 | 21 | 19 | 21 | $182
5 Embarcadero Ctr., San Francisco; (415) 788-1234; (800) 233-1234; FAX: (415) 398-2567
◪ "Vibrant" and "well-situated" in a "great location for business", this Hyatt impresses guests with its "movie-set-perfect" atrium lobby and "great views of the Bay if you're in the right room" (or in Equinox, its revolving rooftop restaurant); while this "convention-type" "sleek facility" might be "big and busy" and "too commercial for a romantic weekend", a crew of "concierges who come through beautifully" have conference attendees feeling they are "treated like royalty."

Hyde Park Suites (24S)   26 | 23 | 21 | 20 | $187
2655 Hyde St., San Francisco; (415) 771-0200; (800) 227-3608; FAX: (415) 346-8058
■ The "very homey", "pleasant suites" with full kitchens in a "great location near Fisherman's Wharf" are "excellent for families", and biz types find them "great for longer stays"; pluses include continental breakfast, 24-hour concierge and free morning limos to Downtown, while afternoon tea and an evening wine hour are appreciated pick-me-ups.

Inn at the Opera 30R (17S)   21 | 23 | 23 | 20 | $172
333 Fulton St., San Francisco; (415) 863-8400; (800) 325-2708; FAX: (415) 861-0821
■ "If you hate chains" this "charming" 1927 inn is likely to satisfy; it's a "pampering place" offering an "intimate", "cozy" and "old-fashioned setting" near the civic center along with "lots of value"; there are fanfares for the "lovely" Act IV dining room, and even if the "minute", "cramped" rooms ring a few sour notes they are still "amenity-filled" and "nicely appointed."

Inn at Union Square 23R (7S)   22 | 23 | 18 | 17 | $157
440 Post St., San Francisco; (415) 397-3510; (800) 288-4346; FAX: (415) 989-0529
■ "A true gem" "in the midst of everything", this "always cozy", "high-class personalized inn" with "lots of character" is "very European" in its "superb" service; while it lacks a restaurant, there are "lovely breakfasts" (included, as are afternoon tea and evening wine/hors d'oeuvres) and room service is available from area eateries; for big spenders, there's a penthouse with fireplace, whirlpool and sauna; overall, a "great place to begin and end a day."

Juliana Hotel 81R (25S)   19 | 22 | 18 | 17 | $122
590 Bush St., San Francisco; (415) 392-2540; (800) 328-3880; FAX: (415) 391-8447
■ "What a wonderful little hotel" gush fans of this "quaint and comfortable" turn-of-the-century "boutique" stopover that's "around the corner from the Fairmont at one-third the price", offering "Euro-style ambiance" that makes it "like being in Paris"; the only meal is continental breakfast, but afternoon tea, evening wine and twice-daily limo service to the Financial District are offered; a late-1996 renovation may make "more than adequate rooms" an understatement.

Kensington Park 85R (1S)
19 | 22 | 18 | 18 | $124

450 Post St., San Francisco; (415) 788-6400; (800) 553-1900; FAX: (415) 399-9484

☑ It "feels very Old English" at this "nonluxury", "inexpensive gem" in a "unique old building" near Union Square; owned by the same group as the Diva, it's applauded by many for its "cordial staff", "lovely accommodations" and "good value" that includes continental breakfast and afternoon tea and sherry; a naysaying minority dubs the rooms "dated and small."

Majestic, The 48R (9S)
23 | 23 | 24 | 21 | $146

1500 Sutter St., San Francisco; (415) 441-1100; (800) 869-8966; FAX: (415) 673-7331

■ "Canopy-covered beds" in "very ornate", "romantic rooms" and the "great" Californian cuisine at the "famous" Cafe Majestic make this "off-the-beaten-path", 1902 Edwardian-style "fine old hotel" "well worth the trip"; "have an affair here with your spouse" suggest second-honeymooning surveyors; if you do go out, the Cathedral Hill/Lower Pacific Heights neighborhood is "great for walking."

MANDARIN ORIENTAL 154R (4S)
28 | 27 | 26 | 23 | $257

222 Sansome St., San Francisco; (415) 885-0999; (800) 526-6566; FAX: (415) 433-0289

■ A "dazzling" Downtown hotel with an Asian accent and a "dedicated staff" that "couldn't be more accommodating"; the "plush", "stylish", "comfortable" guestrooms come with "fabulous, unbelievable bathrooms" in which you can "perch above the city [it's the third-tallest building in SF] in a bubble bath with a skyline view and check your voicemail"; given that there's also "great contemporary dining" on Cal-Asian food at Silks, it's easy to agree that "it doesn't get much better than this."

Mansions Hotel 15R (6S)
21 | 22 | 21 | 20 | $162

2220 Sacramento St., San Francisco; (415) 929-9444; (800) 826-9398;
FAX: (415) 567-9391

☑ "Funky, charming" Pacific Heights Victorian offering what fans call "a magical experience" – including a magic show with dinner; depending on personal tastes, decor is either "beautiful and artsy" or "gimmicky" – "like staying in a wax museum"; in fact there are five mini-museums on-site, so when guests tire of the International Pig Museum they can check out the collection of antique purses; some conclude it's "fun to be in once", but they've "no desire to return."

Mark Hopkins Inter-Continental 362R (28S)
22 | 23 | 22 | 22 | $201

1 Nob Hill, San Francisco; (415) 392-3434; (800) 662-4455; FAX: (415) 421-3302

■ This Nob Hill "fading beauty in need of a little nip and tuck" is scheduled for floor-by-floor major surgery in '97 and '98; for now, top marks go to the "enthusiastic staff" and "incomparable views"; "Sunday brunch is worth the wait" at the just-redone Top of the Mark – and so is the intended fulfillment of the "great potential" of this "wonderful old treasure" whose name "everybody knows."

Marriott Fisherman's Wharf 274R (11S)
19 | 19 | 17 | 17 | $155

1250 Columbus Ave., San Francisco; (415) 775-7555; (800) 525-0956;
FAX: (415) 771-9076

☑ Visitors who think "the Wharf is really great" call this "tourist-oriented property" "very comfortable" and praise the "friendly, excellent service"; dissenters note a "trace of seediness", "sterile, basic rooms" and a "dark interior" – "nothing special in such a special city"; N.B. 30 rooms were added in 1996.

Marriott San Francisco 1365R (133S)
21 | 21 | 19 | 20 | $170

55 Fourth St., San Francisco; (415) 896-1600; (800) 228-9290; FAX: (415) 896-6176

■ "If you love big conference/convention hotels", this "glitzy" "jukebox building" adjoining Moscone Center is "a great place to stay"; it's a "convention machine" with 52 "slick and modern" meeting venues but with "small guestrooms"; the "area borders on the seedy" but is "improving", and the views from the rooftop bar are "not to be missed."

MAXWELL HOTEL 151R (2S)
– | – | – | – | M

(fka Raphael Hotel)

386 Geary St., San Francisco; (415) 986-2000; (888) 734-6299; FAX: (415) 397-2447

Locally based Joie de Vivre took over the Raphael in late '96 and spent the next six-plus months on a floor-to-ceiling renovation of this 1919-built art deco/Victorian property between Union Square and the Theater District; the restaurant is now called Gracie's and offers American classics and live entertainment.

Milano, Hotel 108R   21 | 19 | 23 | 18 | $142
55 Fifth St., San Francisco; (415) 543-8555; (800) 398-7555; FAX: (415) 543-5843
■ The "tastefully minimalist" modern Italian "decor is fun" at this SOMA "trendy place" fashioned from a 1929 neoclassical building; film crews are known to fill the beds – maybe they relax with the Nintendo installed in every "small but stylish" room of this "great find"; surveyors differ only on the service: some note a "helpful staff" while others sigh "it seemed like no one was in charge"; celeb chef Michel Richard's Bistro M is closed and will be replaced by a new entry.

MONACO, HOTEL 169R (32S)   25 | 26 | 24 | 26 | $163
501 Geary St., San Francisco; (415) 292-0100; (800) 214-4220; FAX: (415) 292-0111
■ After a debut "with great style" in June 1995, this Kimpton property (a French-inspired remake of a 1910 beaux arts edifice that was once the Hotel Bellevue) continues to win praise as "a masterpiece of decorating" with "lots of personality" that "uplifts spirits" – and bodies, too, in a 4,700-square-foot on-site fitness center; "smallish" rooms are nevertheless "gorgeous" and a "friendly staff" gives "great service"; the Grand Cafe also boasts "eclectic decor" as well as "unique" dining and "prime people-watching."

Mosser Victorian Hotel 164R (2S)   – | – | – | – | M
(fka Victorian Hotel)
54 Fourth St., San Francisco; (415) 986-4400; (800) 227-3804; FAX: (415) 495-7653
This 1913 Victorian-style Downtown building had been 100-percent residential until converted in 1995 to a "nice, small hotel" that's a real bargain as well as being close to Moscone Center, Nordstrom, SOMA, MOMA and Yerba Buena; Annabelle's Bar & Bistro, under the same ownership, is next door; N.B. only 85 rooms have private bath.

Nikko Hotel San Francisco 501R (22S)   23 | 23 | 21 | 21 | $183
222 Mason St., San Francisco; (415) 394-1111; (800) 645-5687; FAX: (415) 394-1106
☑ An "austere" "haven of peace and quiet" done in "elegant Japanese style" that strikes some as "beautiful", many as "stark but comfortable" and a few as "cold and sterile"; but there's agreement on two things: "gracious" service and "great sushi" at the lobby bar; the "very clean, bright" accommodations (with "great bathrooms") are being redone in '97 and '98, but they'll still be "small and compact" – though guests can stretch out in the indoor pool or relax with a shiatsu massage.

PALACE HOTEL 517R (33S)   23 | 24 | 23 | 25 | $195
(fka Sheraton Palace Hotel)
2 New Montgomery St., San Francisco; (415) 512-1111; (800) 325-3589; FAX: (415) 543-0671
■ With "stunningly beautiful public areas", "gracious", "well-equipped rooms" (that can "range from closet-size to large") and a "close-to-everything" location just off Market, this "gorgeously redone" 1875 "landmark" on the National Register of Historic Places is "truly a palace"; there's royal praise for both the "finest Sunday champagne brunch in the USA" at the "very impressive" Garden Court and the "melt-in-your-mouth" sushi at Kyo-Ya; N.B. all this "almost-affordable luxury" is now part of the premium ITT Sheraton Luxury Collection.

PAN PACIFIC SAN FRANCISCO 296R (33S)   26 | 26 | 24 | 23 | $200
500 Post St., San Francisco; (415) 771-8600; (800) 533-6465; FAX: (415) 398-0267
■ "Asian serenity" abounds in the "quiet sophistication" of this "service-oriented", "elegant, modern hotel" near Union Square; respondents acclaim the "comfortable and personalized" design, "well-appointed" public areas and "pretty rooms", as well as the "outstanding in every way" contemporary fare at Pacific restaurant; complimentary Rolls-Royce transportation rounds out the "understated luxury and pampering"; altogether a "very pleasant experience."

Parc Fifty-Five 989R (20S)   20 | 19 | 18 | 18 | $150
55 Cyril Magnin St., San Francisco; (415) 392-8000; (800) 650-7272; FAX: (415) 403-6602
☑ "A very busy business hotel" that "does a good job for convention groups"; along with "excellent value" and a "stunning lobby", the "nice central location" makes it "convenient for sight-seeing" (for those who manage to skip out of the 21 meeting rooms); still, a cheerless contingent claims it's merely "functional."

PARK HYATT SAN FRANCISCO 323R (37S)   25 | 25 | 23 | 22 | $209
333 Battery St., San Francisco; (415) 392-1234; (800) 323-7275; FAX: (415) 421-2433
■ "The most relaxing place to stay in the heart of the Financial District" is an "elegant, polished" "gem" that provides "superb, wonderful rooms", many with "a great view of the Bay"; there are also kudos for "classic", "attentive", "intimate" service and the "top-notch" Park Grill for power-lunching; this "best-of-breed" Hyatt "does the chain proud."

Petite Auberge 25R (1S)   24 | 25 | 22 | 21 | $165
863 Bush St., San Francisco; (415) 928-6000; (800) 365-3004; FAX: (415) 775-5717
■ A "countrified" "corner of France" has been transported to Nob Hill, where "teddy bears and warm fuzzies abound" at a "charming, romantic getaway" that "fortunately stops short of being too cute"; rooms are "quaint and comfortable", although some can be "a little frilly" and at times "noisy"; however, "romantic fireplaces" help keep nights cozy, and days begin with an included "delicious gourmet breakfast."

Phoenix Hotel 41R (3S)   ▽ 16 | 19 | 21 | 18 | $124
601 Eddy St., San Francisco; (415) 776-1380; (800) CITY-INN; FAX: (415) 885-3109
■ The "perfect place for young nip travelers" turns out to be a "quintessential '50s motel" in a "funky" civic center locale; rooms are "clean" but, some say, "feel confusing" at this Joie de Vivre–run "rock 'n' roller haven" patronized by entertainment-biz types; the on-site eatery is the "very good" Jamaica-themed Miss Pearl's Jam House, nominated as the "best place to eat by a motel swimming pool"; free parking is a plus.

Prescott Hotel 128R (37S)   21 | 24 | 27 | 20 | $178
545 Post St., San Francisco; (415) 563-0303; (800) 283-7322; FAX: (415) 563-6831
■ Cheers abound for this "pricey but charming" "bandbox of a hotel" just off Union Square, where the rooms are "small but very well appointed" and "truffles and Pellegrino before bed ease any sting"; the staff is "friendly and warm", especially the "fabulous", "helpful" concierge and the dispensers of "personal service" at the Club Level; raves are loudest for Wolfgang Puck's "exceptional" Postrio (SF's most popular restaurant) and "if you stay here, you get in", so "who can complain?"

Queen Anne Hotel 41R (7S)   20 | 21 | 17 | 18 | $150
1590 Sutter St., San Francisco; (415) 441-2828; (800) 227-3970; FAX: (415) 775-5212
◪ A "lovely", "charming" B&B in an 1890 Victorian with a "quiet" Lower Pacific Heights setting that's beyond the hassle of city hustle (though morning limo service takes you to the bustle); guests disagree on decor at this former girls' finishing school – "well appointed" with antiques vs. "old and tired" – but the continental breakfast and afternoon tea earn curtsies all-around, and there's "easy neighborhood parking" too.

Radisson Miyako Hotel 183R (9S)   21 | 22 | 22 | 18 | $152
(fka Miyako Hotel)
1625 Post St., San Francisco; (415) 922-3200; (800) 333-3333; FAX: (415) 921-0417
■ The arrival of the Radisson flag in 1996 brought no substantive changes to the "unusual but refreshing", "tranquil Japanese gardens and rooms" at this "well-run", "worthwhile", "good-value" hostelry in Japantown; a few naysayers view it as "more austere than Asian", but any need for more warmth can be remedied by requesting a room with a furo tub or sauna; the popular but pricey Yoyo Bistro (formerly Elka's) features "cutting-edge" French-Asian cuisine.

RENAISSANCE STANFORD COURT HOTEL   24 | 25 | 24 | 23 | $225
361R (32S)
(fka Stouffer Renaissance Stanford Court Hotel)
905 California St., San Francisco; (415) 989-3500; (800) 468-3571; FAX: (415) 391-0513
◪ "Elegance prevails" at this "oasis of calm" where the cable-car lines cross at the top of Nob Hill; while many find it "gracious" with "well-appointed" rooms and the "best convention staff anywhere", several skeptics contend it's been "overrated" so "let's see if Renaissance does better"; however, it remains "the place to go for Ferrari-watching", and visiting and local gourmands insist that the "superb" contemporary cuisine at Fournou's Ovens alone "makes it worthwhile."

Rex, Hotel 92R (2S)   ▽ 20 | 20 | 18 | 18 | $147
(fka Orchard Hotel)
562 Sutter St., San Francisco; (415) 433-4434; (800) 433-4434; FAX: (415) 433-3695
■ Decent scores for rooms and service from surveyors who've visited this "quiet, cozy", circa 1907 vet since it was renovated and renamed by the local Joie de Vivre group portend that the Rex is on the road to being the small, solid Downtown business hotel it aims to be; it's a "comfortable place" to park your bags, and though there's no restaurant, breakfast is available in the lobby or via room service.

RITZ-CARLTON SAN FRANCISCO 292R (44S)   28 | 28 | 28 | 27 | $249
600 Stockton St., San Francisco; (415) 296-7465; (800) 241-3333; FAX: (415) 291-0147
■ "Absolutely outstanding in every respect", this "cosmopolitan" sophisticate with a "timeless feel" on the slope of Nob Hill is for many the "favorite choice in SF" (and top-rated overall), with devotees deeming it "simply one of the best hotels in the world"; the concierge floor is "heaven", the Dining Room "seals the deal" and "luxury abounds"; some respondents suggest it's "for high rollers only" and to a few it "feels stodgy", but all others opine that "if you can survive the climb", "you won't be disappointed."

Savoy Hotel 78R (5S)
17 | 20 | 21 | 15 | $127

580 Geary St., San Francisco; (415) 441-2700; (800) 227-4223; FAX: (415) 441-2700

▣ To boosters it's "a good bargain", a "small business/tourist" base that's "quaint", "classic" and "friendly beyond compare"; critics, however, pounce on "another feeble boutique hotel" with "depressing decor" and "small rooms"; the Theater District neighborhood can be iffy, but Brasserie Savoy does serve "excellent pre-theater dinners."

Sheraton at Fisherman's Wharf 517R (7S)
17 | 17 | 15 | 16 | $150

2500 Mason St., San Francisco; (415) 362-5500; (800) 325-3535; FAX: (415) 956-5275

▣ "Clean and well-run" but "bare-bones" describes this "glorified motel" that respondents note is "good for families" and "very convenient" to cable cars and the Wharf; "stay here for the location only" say those who find it merely "respectable", offering a "great breakfast buffet" but "lacking local charm."

SHERMAN HOUSE 8R (6S)
27 | 27 | 27 | 26 | $328

2160 Green St., San Francisco; (415) 563-3600; (800) 424-5777; FAX: (415) 563-3600

▪ Fans of this 1876 "black-tie mansion" in "out-of-the-way" Pacific Heights sigh that "hotel heaven" comes to earth at this "secluded and peaceful" "luxurious hideaway" where the "lovely" public places and rooms are "stuffed with antiques"; although a very few find it "vastly overrated and overpriced", the majority view is "expensive but worth it"; meals in the highly rated guests-only dining room are an additional charge.

Sir Francis Drake Hotel 412R (5S)
19 | 20 | 19 | 18 | $168

450 Powell St., San Francisco; (415) 392-7755; (800) 227-5480; FAX: (415) 391-8719

▣ There's virtually universal praise for the "greatest" Union Square location of this "golden oldie" that loyalists call "a classic, wonderful hotel" offering "quiet elegance"; but despite the 1994 redo of the beaux arts building, others suggest that "Sir Francis could use a haircut" and "needs a face-lift" to boot; the "small" rooms and "old decor" of public spaces is scored "a bit under par"; N.B. more renovations are coming in '97.

Triton, Hotel 133R (7S)
21 | 19 | 18 | 20 | $147

342 Grant Ave., San Francisco; (415) 394-0500; (800) 433-6611; FAX: (415) 394-0555

▣ "A little quirky" perhaps, but enthusiasts dig the "fun, funky" designer rooms (including the new Santana Suite, complete with meditation area, prayer pillow and incense), the "friendly but confused service", the on-site health club and the "gates of Chinatown" location of this "trendy" choice; yet disenchanted visitors moan that you get art deco style "instead of space" and you "need a shoehorn to get from the bed to the bath", not to mention that service is "hoity-toity" – "hipness doesn't make a quality hotel."

Tuscan Inn 221R
21 | 21 | 22 | 19 | $140

235 Northpoint St., San Francisco; (415) 561-1100; (800) 648-4626; FAX: (415) 561-1199

▪ "Far enough from the hubbub so you can relax", this "nice surprise" near Fisherman's Wharf and the piers is a "comfy, intimate" "European-style seaside retreat" providing "small, quiet" rooms done in "attractive decor"; what's more, the "huge portions" of Italian seafare in the restaurant are "wonderful"; possibly because of the location, a few sniff that this is also "the essence of San Francisco for tourists."

Victorian Inn on the Park 10R (2S)
▽ 23 | 20 | 15 | 22 | $141

301 Lyon St., San Francisco; (415) 931-1830; (800) 435-1967; FAX: (415) 931-1830

▣ "Haight-Ashbury meets Laura Ashley" quip style-conscious surveyors about this tiny, century-old B&B near the "great culture" (and ace jogging expanses) of Golden Gate Park; otherwise, opinion splits: supporters declare "this place feels good" and "nobody swarms on you", but detractors decry "a cramped room, cheap towels, no air, too loud"; N.B. streetside rooms were soundproofed in 1996.

Villa Florence Hotel 180R
16 | 20 | 23 | 15 | $134

255 Powell St., San Francisco; (415) 397-7700; (800) 553-4411; FAX: (415) 397-1006

▣ "Cozy" quarters in a "good location" by Union Square please some respondents, but many others describe the rooms here as "tiny" and "noisy" with "paper walls"; yet even those who say "there are better places to stay" tend to agree that the "wonderful" Kuleto's Italian Restaurant is a "great meeting place" (and therefore usually mobbed).

Vintage Court, Hotel 106R (1S)   16 | 20 | 24 | 16 | $128
650 Bush St., San Francisco; (415) 392-4666; (800) 654-1100; FAX: (415) 433-4065

☑ "We need more hotels like this" say partisans of this "nicely refurbished" older Kimpton Downtowner that provides "good value"; but others cite "cramped" rooms and say unless you get one in front "you wake up to garbage can" clatter; while some enjoy the "fun" early evening Napa Valley wines reception, foodies snipe that the hotel is "not worthy of being home to Masa's" (the perennially high-rated, "superb" New French restaurant) – the main gripe is that guests don't have an edge in getting a reservation.

Warwick Regis Hotel 54R (16S)   ▽ 20 | 21 | 18 | 18 | $136
490 Geary St., San Francisco; (415) 928-7900; (800) 827-3447; FAX: (415) 441-8788

☑ This "family-style", "small and cheap" hotel in the Theater District draws applause for antiques-filled rooms and public areas decorated in Louis XVI style; La Scene Cafe & Bar is a hot pre- and post-theater scene, but it might get hot upstairs too: "help – no a/c!"

Washington Square Inn 15R   21 | 22 | 19 | 21 | $148
1660 Stockton St., San Francisco; (415) 981-4220; (800) 388-0220; FAX: (415) 397-7242

☑ You can "watch tai chi in the park from your window" at this North Beach B&B that's a "great escape" and a "great value"; it's "romantic", "comfortable" and "full of charm" with "small, nicely appointed rooms", and the "helpful staff" provides "wonderful tea service" as well as PM wine and cheese; accommodations vary, and a few disappointees say "beware" of some quarters that are "matchbox-size" and "sparse."

Westin St. Francis 1109R (83S)   22 | 23 | 21 | 23 | $191
Union Sq., 355 Powell St., San Francisco; (415) 397-7000; (800) 228-3000; FAX: (415) 774-0124

■ Cable cars stop at the front door of this "grande dame" where a "wonderful" $50-million 1996 renovation has "made it better" while "retaining its charm"; faithful fans rate this "historic beauty" attached to a modern tower as "the best centrally located hotel in the city", but while "classy and comfortable" there's a "great variance" in room size and quality ("tower rooms are superior"); socially smart surveyors tout the "people-watching" lobby and add that "cocktails are a must" in the Compass Rose lounge.

White Swan Inn 23R (3S)   24 | 24 | 21 | 21 | $160
845 Bush St., San Francisco; (415) 775-1755; (800) 999-9570; FAX: (415) 775-5717

■ A "wonderful hidden jewel" whisper regulars who covet the "British charm" of hunting prints, "large rooms with cozy fireplaces", "very personal" service and afternoon tea with "delish" cookies – this "romantic hideaway" is "as cute as an inn can be in the heart of a city"; as if all that weren't enough, the full breakfast (included) "is worth the stay."

York Hotel 91R (5S)   ▽ 16 | 19 | 15 | 16 | $128
940 Sutter St., San Francisco; (415) 885-6800; (800) 808-YORK; FAX: (415) 885-2115

■ Still remembered by movie buffs as a primary setting in the Hitchcock classic *Vertigo*, this "small, quiet, charming" and reasonably priced "gem" in Lower Nob Hill was entirely renovated in 1995 and shines a bit more with "nice touches"; alas, the limo service and wine hour are gone, but the Plush Room remains: by day a meeting venue, by night a high-end cabaret (no meals) featuring the likes of Michael Feinstein and Andrea Marcovicci.

San Jose

de Anza Hotel 92R (8S)   24 | 23 | 23 | 22 | $142
233 W. Santa Clara St., San Jose; (408) 286-1000; (800) 843-3700; FAX: (408) 286-0500

■ For an "old-world feeling done right", book a room at this 1931 art deco "gem" "hidden" in Downtown San Jose; the "charming" 10-story landmark features all the modern amenities plus a "good" Italian restaurant, La Pastaia; one late-night eater "loved" the help-yourself "kitchen cupboard for complimentary midnight snacks."

Fairmont Hotel San Jose 500R (41S)   24 | 23 | 22 | 23 | $160
170 S. Market St., San Jose; (408) 998-1900; (800) 527-4727; FAX: (408) 287-1648

■ "Pure elegance and style" equal "graciousness personified" to friends of this "well-managed", "first-class business hotel" in Downtown San Jose; a "young, energetic" staff provides "attentive" service, the rooms are "spacious and modern", the lobby is "beautiful" and Pagoda Restaurant "is the next best thing to eating in Hong Kong"; to a hard-to-please few, there's "nothing really memorable" ("public rooms have the comfort of a mausoleum"), but plenty of others vehemently disagree.

R	S	D	P	$

Hayes Conference Center 113R (22S)

| – | – | – | – | VE |

200 Edenvale Ave., San Jose; (408) 226-3200; (800) 420-3200; FAX: (408) 362-2388
The 1905 Hayes Mansion, completely and elegantly updated with high-tech features befitting the Silicon Valley location, is the core of this all-business hotel and conference center opened in 1994; the new incarnation maintains the architectural integrity of the old, while adding meeting space, a pool and exercise facilities; there's fine dining at Orlo's, a favorite with local movers and shakers.

Hyatt Saint Claire Hotel 153R (17S)
(fka Hilton Saint Claire)

| 18 | 19 | 19 | 17 | $140 |

302 S. Market St., San Jose; (408) 295-2000; (800) 223-1234; FAX: (408) 977-0403
■ Satisfied business travelers admire the "gorgeous" public spaces and rooms "full of charm" at this small-for-a-Hyatt, "beautiful" 1926 Euro-style hotel adjacent to the San Jose Convention Center; fans swear "you won't forget the [down] comforters" or "the best minibar in the world"; Il Fornaio restaurant serves "consistently good" Italian fare.

San Luis Obispo

Apple Farm Inn 69R

| 22 | 22 | 19 | 20 | $127 |

2015 Monterey St., San Luis Obispo; (805) 544-2040; (800) 255-2040; FAX: (805) 546-9495
◪ "If you love quaint" you "can't go wrong" according to admirers of this Victorian "decorator's dream" of an inn/restaurant/gift shop, located midway between SF and LA; in addition to tours of the cider press, there are "charming" fireplaced rooms with canopied beds and a "homey restaurant", but a whole barrel of sour apples grumps over "kitschy", "cutesy" decor that's like "Laura Ashley gone wild"; overall, it's "largely a tourist stop", but "good for one night" seems to be the consensus.

Madonna Inn 69R (40S)

| 21 | 17 | 15 | 18 | $145 |

100 Madonna Rd., San Luis Obispo; (805) 543-3000; (800) 543-9666; FAX: (805) 543-1800
◪ "What *is* this place?" – surveyors are still pondering this "wacky", '50s-era, husband-and-wife-built "fantastyland", a "kitsch to the max", "tacky, tacky, tacky" motel with "one-of-a-kind" thematically decorated rooms ranging from Old West and caveman to Hawaiian and neo-Hapsburg, and a pink, gilded lobby so "garish" it requires "a sense of humor to enjoy"; a "must to see", it can be "fun for one night", but "if nothing else, stop and use the men's room" – its "waterfall urinal is the eighth wonder of the world."

Santa Barbara

El Encanto Hotel & Garden Villas 55R (29S)

| 20 | 22 | 23 | 21 | $190 |

1900 Lasuen Rd., Santa Barbara; (805) 687-5000; (800) 346-7039; FAX: (805) 687-3903
◪ Set on a hilltop overlooking Santa Barbara, the ocean and coastal islands, this "enchanting" "true hideaway" commands "a view that will take your breath away" and offers its "el contento" guests "cozy", "romantic" accommodations (many with fireplaces) in the main inn and cottages, "superior service", 10 "beautiful" gardened acres with pergola and lily pond, tennis, pool and "good" Cal-French dining at the "charming" restaurant; despite warnings that there are "all sorts of rooms" and some "need a face-lift", this old favorite is still "the place Angelenos run to for a quick escape."

Fess Parker's Red Lion Resort 337R (23S)

| 20 | 19 | 17 | 20 | $169 |

633 E. Cabrillo Blvd., Santa Barbara; (805) 564-4333; (800) RED-LION; FAX: (805) 962-8198
◪ "A good family resort" and convention facility in "charming Santa Barbara" offering a "superb" location on 24 acres near Downtown and across the street from the beach; those with modest expectations (and/or kids in tow) applaud its "basic comfort at a reasonable rate", "well-maintained" facilities (including a pool and three tennis courts), "nice" public areas and "decent" rooms, all with balconies; but critics looking for charm gripe that it's too "big" and "impersonal" with rooms "one step above a standard motel."

FOUR SEASONS BILTMORE 217R (17S)

| 25 | 27 | 26 | 27 | $251 |

1260 Channel Dr., Santa Barbara; (805) 969-2261; (800) 332-3442; FAX: (805) 969-4682
■ "The '20s come roaring back to life" at this seaside Spanish Colonial "classic", an "elegant" "treasure" that "retains its tradition" of "easy luxury", "impeccable" service and "world-class" dining, including "the best Sunday brunch in California"; besides the beach, the "beautiful" 21-acre getaway has "amazing grounds", two health clubs, two outdoor pools and three tennis courts; rooms might "vary" from "large and lovely" to "small and old-fashioned" ("take a casita" urge some) but all agree "it's worth the splurge" – "if you can't be happy here, give up."

Santa Clara

Westin Hotel Santa Clara 500R (20S)   _ | _ | _ | _ | E
5101 Great America Pkwy., Santa Clara; (408) 986-0700; (800) 937-8461; FAX: (408) 986-3990
This modern, well-run business/convention hotel in the heart of Silicon Valley, connected to the Santa Clara Convention Center and adjacent to Paramount's Great America theme park as well as golf and tennis, offers technologically friendly rooms and staff, certainly appropriate for its techie clientele.

Santa Cruz

Chaminade Conference Center 142R (10S)   20 | 22 | 21 | 23 | $163
1 Chaminade Ln., Santa Cruz; (408) 475-5600; (800) 283-6569; FAX: (408) 476-4942
☑ "Serene and easy", this executive conference facility on "beautiful" grounds in the Santa Cruz Mountains is an "excellent retreat" for corporate think fests, with "lots of redwood trees" and a view of Monterey Bay as antidote to 12,000 square feet of indoor meeting space equipped with the latest in conference technology; although some say guestrooms "are just adequate", a full array of sports facilities, including pool, four lighted tennis courts, a fitness center and nearby golf, all help CEOs unwind, as do outdoor ropes courses; the resort also hosts individual guests, based on room availability.

Santa Rosa

La Rose, Hotel 38R (11S)   ▽ 20 | 21 | 20 | 16 | $103
308 Wilson St., Santa Rosa; (707) 579-3200; (800) LA ROSE-8;
FAX: (707) 579-3247
■ This "attractively" renovated 1907 landmark hotel is a terrific value in a "good" location for shopping and dining in the redeveloped historic Railroad Square of this Sonoma Valley town; visitors report "extra-large" and "charming" rooms, "friendly" service and a "lovely" Continental restaurant, with a restored carriage house offering additional accommodations with balconies around a garden courtyard.

Vintners Inn 39R (5S)   24 | 23 | 25 | 21 | $167
4350 Barnes Rd., Santa Rosa; (707) 575-7350; (800) 421-2584; FAX: (707) 575-1426
■ "Provence in America" wins a following for this "low-key", "friendly" French-style hostelry in a "beautiful", "dynamite location" "surrounded by vineyards" and adjacent to the "magnificent" John Ash & Co. restaurant ("the main attraction" for many); value seekers note "sleek", "spacious", "comfortable" rooms, half with fireplaces, that are "the equal of places costing twice as much"; a tiny minority gripes there's "no pool."

Sausalito

Alta Mira Hotel 30R   18 | 20 | 21 | 20 | $165
125 Bulkley Ave., Sausalito; (415) 332-1350; FAX: (415) 331-3862
☑ "Stupendous" views of the SF skyline and the Bay from both the "great, funky" rooms and the outdoor dining terrace are this Spanish-style Sausalito landmark's strengths; yet despite a loyal following that enjoys its "faded" "charm", many note it's getting "down at the heels" – although the inn did refurbish public areas in '96; boosters call Sunday brunch "the best breakfast in the US."

Casa Madrona Hotel 33R (1S)   23 | 23 | 24 | 20 | $185
801 Bridgeway, Sausalito; (415) 332-0502; (800) 567-9524; FAX: (415) 332-2537
■ "Refreshing, cozy and romantic", this Downtown Sausalito hotel combines an 1885 Victorian with a New England–style inn, and each has "terrific, unusual rooms" ("decorated by different designers with varying themes"); its position "stacked on a hillside" provides "spectacular views", especially from Mikayla restaurant featuring a health-oriented American menu by a "great new chef"; an outdoor Jacuzzi, gardens and included breakfast and evening wine and cheese are more reasons treasure hunters deem it "one of the best finds in Northern California."

Shell Beach

Cliffs at Shell Beach 137R (28S)   20 | 19 | 19 | 21 | $146
2757 Shell Beach Rd., Shell Beach; (805) 773-5000; (800) 826-7827;
FAX: (805) 773-0764
☑ "Breathtaking views and it has a/c" are enough to attract guests to this "delightful" Mediterranean-style hotel on the Pacific, a "peaceful", "weekend escape" that's "about as good as you can find" in the Hearst Castle/Central Coast region, offering an outdoor heated pool, Jacuzzis, fitness equipment and, of course, the beach; to a smattering of critics it's "dated" and "overpriced", but the "oceanfront saves it."

Solvang

Alisal Guest Ranch & Resort 36R (37S)   20 | 24 | 21 | 24 | $231
1054 Alisal Rd., Solvang; (805) 688-6411; (800) 425-4725; FAX: (805) 688-2510
■ Kids' programs so "terrific you'll wish you had a parent cool enough to take you" make for "an excellent family vacation" at this half-century-old working ranch on 10,000 acres near Santa Barbara; besides "good horseback riding", there's an "ultrabroad choice of activities" (seven tennis courts, boating, recently refurbished golf courses, pool, playground area and more), along with "rustic but comfortable" cottages with fireplaces and "good" dining; a few whinny about "old" furnishings and "yuppies from LA taking over", but some "return every year"; N.B. rates include breakfast and dinner.

Sonoma

El Dorado Hotel 26R   21 | 20 | 22 | 18 | $137
405 First St. W., Sonoma; (707) 996-3030; (800) 289-3031; FAX: (707) 996-3148
■ A "great central location" on the plaza in Downtown Sonoma within "walking distance to just about everything" (including "top restaurants") distinguishes this "sunny, bright" 19th-century hotel with "character", where "balcony rooms overlook the action"; also "convenient for touring the Sonoma Valley wineries", it will start you on your way with a "lovely" included breakfast in the courtyard, and at dinnertime, check out its branch of the "lively, comfortable" Cal-Ital chain Piatti; there's also a heated pool on-site.

St. Helena

Harvest Inn 46R (8S)   23 | 21 | 18 | 21 | $163
1 Main St., St. Helena; (707) 963-9463; (800) 950-8466; FAX: (707) 963-4402
☑ Guests praise the "quaint and relaxing atmosphere" of this "wonderful retreat" built in English Tudor style on seven acres of "expansive beautiful grounds" overlooking a working vineyard; a "romantic hideaway", it offers lots of "privacy", two heated swimming pools and "not fancy, but sparkling clean and so comfy" rooms (most with fireplaces) along with a "generous continental breakfast"; a few growl that the "barnlike rooms could use a decorator", but others fondly recall the "Jacuzzi at midnight under the stars."

MEADOWOOD, NAPA VALLEY 24R (62S)   27 | 26 | 26 | 27 | $272
900 Meadowood Ln., St. Helena; (707) 963-3646; (800) 458-8080; FAX: (707) 963-3532
■ "The most romantic hideaway available" twitter lovebirds about a Napa wine country "jewel" on 250 acres where "they can't do enough for you"; it's a "golfer's dream" that also features "first-class" tennis, "beautiful" croquet, an "excellent" spa, "incredible cabinlike rooms" and a "terrific eating adventure" at the "very elegant" eponymous restaurant and its casual sibling, The Grill; to a few skeptics, it's "preppy beyond belief" ("everyone wears white"), but scores support those who sing the praises of this "pricey paradise."

Wine Country Inn 21R (3S)   21 | 21 | 19 | 19 | $162
1152 Lodi Ln., St. Helena; (707) 963-7077; FAX: (707) 963-9018
☑ "Right in there with the vineyards" in a "tranquil" spot away from but between the two main wine country highways, this "lovely" inn offers "rural comfort", a "very helpful" staff and a "tasty" included breakfast, as well as an outdoor pool and hot tub; but this "secluded getaway for a romantic weekend" can be soured for a few by "paper-thin walls" and just "ok" rooms; the "wine tastings are a real plus."

Truckee

Northstar-at-Tahoe 30R (260S)   21 | 18 | 17 | 23 | $171
Hwy. 267 & Northstar Dr., Truckee; (916) 562-1010; (800) GO-NORTH; FAX: (916) 562-2215
☑ "Great for a family ski trip" with shuttles that transport guests to the slopes, this "well-run" year-round resort complex consists of a main lodge and clusters of condos along with 30 mountain homes, and offers tennis, golf, outdoor pools and a fitness center; but while some report "very comfortable" condos, others note "quality varies a lot" – still, "it's the amenities you go for, not the accommodations."

Ventura

Cliff House Inn 20R (4S)

▽ | 15 | 15 | 17 | 20 | $119

6602 W. Pacific Coast Hwy., Ventura; (805) 652-1381; (800) 892-5433; FAX: (805) 652-1201
☑ Surveyors lament that the "ocean at your feet" doesn't make up for the "faded elegance" of this tiny three-story B&B with pool on a romantic Rincon Coast bluff near Ventura; Shoals Restaurant is "great" to some, "overpriced" to others, but the good news is that breakfast is included and every room faces the ocean.

Yosemite

Ahwahnee Hotel 119R (4S)

22 | 22 | 22 | 27 | $196

Yosemite National Park, Yosemite; (209) 372-1407; FAX: (209) 372-1463
☑ The "consummate National Park–style lodge" is a "grand, luxury" "living piece of American history" (circa 1927) that's "the best way to see Yosemite" if seeking "fancy rusticity" or "one of the world's true great views"; the "dramatic" dining room is "an awesome sight" that "shouldn't be missed", but there's dissension over service ("professional" vs. "don't give a damn"), food ("surprisingly good" vs. "terrible") and lodgings ("cozy and rustic" vs. "spartan"); yet most agree it's "a national treasure to be preserved at all costs" – "everyone should stay here at least once" (judging by the demand, everyone is trying).

Yountville

Vintage Inn - Napa Valley 68R (12S)

25 | 22 | 19 | 21 | $170

6541 Washington St., Yountville; (707) 944-1112; (800) 351-1133; FAX: (707) 944-1617
☑ This "charming" French country–style hotel is among the "pick of the crop" on the Napa Valley Wine Trail, a "refined, modern escape" offering "large, lovely", "very romantic" rooms (fireplaces in each "add a great touch"), a "good" included champagne continental breakfast, outdoor pool and two tennis courts; gripes center on "unresponsive management" and "noisy" highway-side accommodations.

Colorado

TOP 10 OVERALL

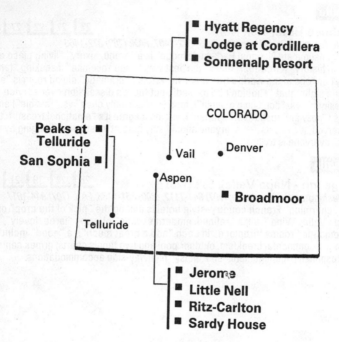

- **Hyatt Regency**
- **Lodge at Cordillera**
- **Sonnenalp Resort**

COLORADO

Peaks at Telluride ■

San Sophia ■

- Vail
- Denver
- Aspen
- Telluride

■ **Broadmoor**

- ■ **Jerome**
- ■ **Little Nell**
- ■ **Ritz-Carlton**
- ■ **Sardy House**

BEST OVERALL

27 Little Nell/Aspen
Ritz-Carlton/Aspen
26 Peaks at Telluride/Telluride
Broadmoor/Colorado Springs
Lodge at Cordillera /Edwards
25 Hyatt Regency/Beaver Creek
Jerome/Aspen
24 Sonnenalp Resort/Vail
Sardy House/Aspen
San Sophia/Telluride

BEST VALUES

Inverness Hotel/Denver
Strater Hotel/Durango
Doubletree/Denver
Antlers Doubletree/Col. Springs
Marriott/Denver (Southeast)
Embassy Suites/Denver
Burnsley Hotel/Denver
Oxford Hotel/Denver
Sheraton/Colorado Springs
Loews Giorgio/Denver

Aspen

| R | S | D | P | $ |

Aspen Club Lodge 84R (6S)

| 20 | 21 | 19 | 19 | $201 |

709 E. Durant Ave., Aspen; (970) 925-6760; (800) 882-2582; FAX: (970) 925-6778

☑ This lodge boasts one of the most "desirable" locations in Aspen (Downtown, at the base of Aspen Mountain), and no one minds free use of the "terrific" fitness facilities at the Aspen Club (though a few grumble about its being nearly a mile away); a complimentary breakfast buffet and "simple, casual" atmosphere are assets, but regulars say stick with the "nice, newer rooms" over "dingy" older ones (and even then, some say they're "rather small").

| R | S | D | P | $ |

Gant, The 120R

22 | 20 | – | 19 | $215

610 S. West End St., Aspen; (970) 925-5000; (800) 345-1471; FAX: (970) 925-6891
■ A venerable old-timer (for Aspen, that is), this complex of "large", privately owned condos is "perfect for families" and "extended vacations"; it sports five tennis courts, two pools and free shuttle service around town, should you ever care to leave its "beautiful setting" near the slopes; there are no dining facilities, but each unit has a kitchen plus a fireplace and balcony; a few say varying condo quality makes it "a crap shoot", and rates range from "economical" to "pricey."

Inn at Aspen 114R (5S)

22 | 22 | 21 | 22 | $179

38750 Hwy. 82, Aspen; (970) 925-1500; (800) 952-1515; FAX: (970) 925-9037
■ "Moderate" prices ("especially off-season") distinguish this "lovely", well-located, ski-in/ski-out choice from most Aspen lodgings; most rooms have kitchenettes, making it a good option for families and longer stays; some may find the quarters "small" and a bit "worn" but there's "good food" and "great" service plus a year-round heated outdoor pool and Jacuzzi.

JEROME, HOTEL 77R (16S)

25 | 25 | 24 | 24 | $233

330 E. Main St., Aspen; (970) 920-1000; (800) 331-7213; FAX: (970) 925-2784
■ If what you're after is "luxury and convenience", then this "elegant", "beautifully restored" 1889 Downtown Victorian is the ticket; its antiques-furnished rooms exude "the feel of old-time Aspen" (except "the Wild West was never this classy"), the staff "treats you like royalty" and the famously lively J-Bar still defines "the scene" in Glitter Gulch; a few traitors find it "pricey" and "overhyped."

Lenado, Hotel 19R

22 | 24 | 23 | 20 | $209

200 S. Aspen St., Aspen; (970) 925-6246; (800) 321-3457; FAX: (970) 925-3840
■ It may call itself a hotel, but it acts more like a "pleasant B&B"; set in a contemporary building in central Aspen, it manages to have the "true feel of a mountain inn" thanks to "wood appointments" (including carved wood beds), wood-burning stoves in some rooms and a "great location" on the town park; guests enjoy a full complimentary breakfast each day, and locals frequent the restaurant for dinner.

LITTLE NELL 78R (14S)

28 | 28 | 27 | 27 | $293

675 E. Durant St., Aspen; (970) 920-4600; (800) 525-6200; FAX: (970) 920-4670
■ "Aspen's classiest act" is the consensus on this "cushy" Relais & Châteaux member that earns Colorado's top overall ratings; "impeccable in every way", it offers "huge" rooms with "lavish bathrooms" and fireplaces, "exceptional service", a "phenomenal" American restaurant and a "great location" (Aspen's lift #1 is right outside); a pool and ski concierge add to the "pampering environment"; the only question is whether it's even better off-season, when "nothing beats" the summer mountain view and lower prices.

RITZ-CARLTON ASPEN 231R (26S)

27 | 27 | 27 | 27 | $282

315 E. Dean St., Aspen; (970) 920-3300; (800) 241-3333; FAX: (970) 920-7353
■ "Chintz meets the slopes and it works perfectly" at this glitzy yet "elegant" central Aspen standout; "beautiful" appointments, "service at its best" and lavish fitness facilities are hallmarks, and there's "excellent" regional cuisine and "the best Sunday brunch in the universe" at The Terrace; it also receives a few typical Ritz digs ("close your eyes and you could be in any Ritz", "not worth the money"), but to most it's "as good as it gets."

SARDY HOUSE HOTEL 14R (6S)

25 | 25 | 25 | 22 | $216

128 E. Main St., Aspen; (970) 920-2525; FAX: (970) 920-4478
■ "Guests do not come to this romantic inn for the slopes", necessarily, but rather to enjoy the "charm" and "character" of its setting: an 1892 Queen Anne Victorian in central Aspen; though a few critics fume "nowhere but in Aspen could they charge this much" for "cramped" rooms, most agree with the fan who says "if they're booked, we cancel our trip"; N.B. ask about ski-for-free packages in January and early February.

Beaver Creek

Charter at Beaver Creek (135S)

24 | 23 | 22 | 23 | $213

PO Box 5310, 120 Offerson Rd., Beaver Creek; (970) 949-6660; (800) 525-6660; FAX: (970) 949-6709
■ Guests stay in privately owned, "Architectural Digest"–like condos at this resort, so "be ready for eclectic decorating", but they're "comfortable and clean", each with kitchen, fireplace and balcony; three restaurants offer "delicious food" and you'll find "the nicest people" at the front desk; après-ski muscle aches can be soothed at the spa and fitness center and the first tee of a Robert Trent Jones golf course is just 100 yards away.

Embassy Suites - Beaver Creek Lodge (76S)   – | – | – | – | VE
(fka Beaver Creek Lodge)
PO Box 2578, 26 Avondale Ln., Avon; (970) 845-9800; (800) EMBASSY; FAX: (970) 845-8242
Take "an ordinary Embassy Suites" and plop it into "a great location" and you have this ski-sloper – a "very convenient", comfy all-suites hotel, "one of the cheapest" options in Beaver Creek with a "nice outdoor pool and hot tub"; while full breakfast is included, each suite has a kitchenette, making it good for longer stays (six luxury condos please larger groups); N.B. a complete redo was finished in '96.

HYATT REGENCY BEAVER CREEK 288R (7S)   26 | 26 | 23 | 27 | $247
PO Box 1595, 50 W. Thomas Pl., Avon; (970) 949-1234; (800) 233-1234; FAX: (970) 949-4164
■ Though some describe the decor as "Laura Ashley meets *Twin Peaks*", most find the rooms "gorgeous" at this big "hunting lodge"–like Hyatt with arguably the "best ski-in/ski-out service" in the Rockies thanks to its smack-in-central-Beaver Creek location; a "cheerful staff" provides "top-flight service" and the "great public spaces" include an enormous lobby that's perfect après-ski; there's also a spa, tennis, indoor/outdoor pool and more, yet some cavil there's "not much to do at night."

Inn at Beaver Creek 42R (3S)   25 | 23 | 21 | 24 | $207
10 Elk Track Ln., Beaver Creek; (970) 845-7800; (800) 859 8242; FAX: (970) 845-5279
■ An "alpine-style", "comfy, cozy" inn conveniently located on Beaver Creek's slopes for "great" ski-in/ski-out access (a chair lift is just yards from the door); in addition to the "rustic" ambiance, surveyors praise its "clean", "good-sized" lodgings (top-floor rooms are "wonderful"), "friendly, attentive service" and "beautiful views" of Gore Range.

Pines Lodge 60R (8S)   ▽ 25 | 22 | 25 | 21 | $195
141 Scott Hill Rd., Beaver Creek; (970) 845-7900; (800) 859-8242; FAX: (970) 845-7809
☑ Spectacular views of Beaver Creek Valley, summer or winter, can be savored from this "cozy, small" ski-in/ski-out hotel with warm Southwestern decor; lodgings range from rooms to condos (all with balcony), service is "friendly" and the award-winning Grouse Mountain Grill serves New American cooking (and lots of it) for dinner; afternoon tea, a ski concierge and heated outdoor pool are bonuses.

Boulder

Boulderado, Hotel 135R (21S)   20 | 21 | 21 | 20 | $145
2115 13th St., Boulder; (303) 442-4344; (800) 433-4344; FAX: (303) 442-4378
☑ "As much a center of activity" in central Boulder as a hotel, this "piece of history" that "oozes" "old-world charm" is "a great fit" for this 'crunchy', post-hippie town; the "magnificent lobby" is a must-see, and while some say rooms "in the old section" have the most "character", others think they "desperately need upgrading" (a '96 renovation may have helped); there's "excellent" New American cuisine at Q's Restaurant.

Breckenridge

Breckenridge Mountain Lodge 71R   22 | 20 | 20 | 22 | $168
600 South Ridge St., Breckenridge; (970) 453-2333; (800) 800-7829; FAX: (970) 483-5426
■ An "excellent view of the Rockies" is enough to make this a "skier's dream lodge" in the eyes of enthusiasts, but it's basically a "comfortable" if not spectacular motel-like option that earns solid ratings across the board and is good for families; après-ski relaxation might include a dip in the outdoor hot tub.

Hilton Resort Breckenridge 201R (7S)   19 | 20 | 18 | 20 | $141
PO Box 8059, 550 Village Way, Breckenridge; (970) 453-4500; (800) 321-8444; FAX: (970) 453-0212
☑ Guests at this Breckenridge behemoth relish its "magnificent" vistas and proximity to the slopes; but while some call it a "well-run resort" with "nice rooms", others contend it "needs sprucing up" and gripe about "poor food" and a "functional but confusing" layout; N.B. the Jack Nicklaus–designed Breckenridge Golf Course is nearby.

Village at Breckenridge 50R (222S)   19 | 19 | 17 | 20 | $159
PO Box 8329, 535 S. Park Ave., Breckenridge; (970) 453-2000; (800) 800-7829; FAX: (970) 453-3116
☑ The price is right at this "centrally located" resort "convenient" to Breckenridge Mountain and in-town sights; lodgings range from rooms to "funky condos for ski bums", and reactions vary accordingly ("spacious, well-equipped" vs. "dorm style"); there are lots of facilities (fitness center, pool, nine hot tubs, several restaurants), but some say it can seem like a "crowded" "zoo"; N.B. 30,000 square feet of meeting space makes it a popular summer seminar site.

Clark

Home Ranch, The 6R (8S)
– – – – VE

PO Box 822, Clark; (970) 879-1780; FAX: (970) 879-1795

Families and city folk with a taste for cowboy living favor this Relais & Châteaux dude ranch near Steamboat Springs, where guests rustle themselves up a good time horseback riding, fly fishing, x-country skiing and country dancing; accommodations include cozy rooms in the main lodge and lovely private one- to three-bedroom cabins with hot tubs and wood-burning stoves; rates are steep, but they cover superlative everything, including memorable meals; closed mid-October to mid-December: children six or older (only) find it awesome.

Colorado Springs

Antlers Doubletree Hotel 284R (6S)
20 | 20 | 18 | 20 | $129

4 S. Cascade Ave., Colorado Springs; (719) 473-5600; (800) 222-TREE; FAX: (719) 389-0259

☑ A "great way to wake up" is to peek at the mountains outside the west-facing windows of this "typical convention hotel" in Downtown Colorado Springs (even the health club sports mountain views); most find the staff "friendly" and the rooms "clean and comfortable", but detractors say it's "as bland as Pikes Peak is grand" and claim room service pales next to the "great" signature chocolate-chip cookies.

BROADMOOR, THE 610R (90S)
25 | 26 | 25 | 27 | $220

1 Lake Avenue, Colorado Springs; (719) 634-7711; (800) 634-7711; FAX: (719) 577-5779

■ Like "a dream come true", this "classy old resort" at the foot of Cheyenne Mountain has it all; "beautiful grounds" with "grand views of Pikes Peak", "wonderful" facilities, especially the spa and three world-class golf courses, the fine Charles Court restaurant and "superior" service with a "concierge staff beyond compare"; also on-site: 12 tennis courts and indoor and outdoor pools; if a few grumble that older rooms "need updating", more call it "a must" that harks back to "a more glamorous time."

Cheyenne Mountain Conference Resort 271R (5S)
22 | 23 | 22 | 25 | $170

3225 Broadmoor Valley Rd., Colorado Springs; (719) 527-1308; (800) 428-8886; FAX: (719) 576-4711

☑ More of an "excellent conference center" than a vacation spot, it nonetheless offers "great golf", 18 tennis courts, four pools and "spectacular views" of the Rockies plus "spacious, attractive" rooms at value-conscious prices; predictably, noncorporate types gripe that it's "obsessively functional" and clearly "geared more toward business."

Hearthstone Inn 20R (3S)
▽ 21 | 21 | 19 | 18 | $125

506 N. Cascade Ave., Colorado Springs; (719) 473-4413; (800) 521-1885; FAX: (719) 473-1322

■ A "beautiful" 1885 Queen Anne home, completely furnished in antiques (and completely smoke- and TV-free), is the setting for this Downtown inn that fans call "simply one of the finest in the country"; guests like the "coziness and warmth" of its rooms (some with working fireplace or porch), the "nice people" who staff it and the full complimentary breakfast; ideal for couples, it also works for small corporate retreats; N.B. a few rooms have shared baths.

Sheraton Hotel 500R (16S)
18 | 17 | 17 | 17 | $118

2886 South Circle Dr., Colorado Springs; (719) 576-5900; (800) 981-4012; FAX: (719) 576-0507

☑ While some surveyors appreciate this "serviceable" Sheraton for its "moderate prices", handy location just off I-25 and mountain views, others wince at "poor service" and departments that "do not work well together", especially for a business-oriented hotel; a $4-million renovation in 1996 may have resolved complaints about "dingy" rooms and common areas "in need of a face-lift."

Copper Mountain

Copper Mountain Resort (750S)
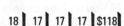
19 | 19 | 17 | 19 | $157

PO Box 3001, Copper Mountain; (970) 968-2882; (800) 458-8386; FAX: (970) 968-6227

☑ You want it, you got it at this "self-contained" Summit County resort where lodgings range from rooms to condos and there's lots to do year-round; in winter it's a "superb ski" base (you can schuss "right out the door") and in summer it has golf, fishing, boating and biking, not to mention "great rates"; glitz seekers aren't thrilled by what they call its "community college campus" looks and say "bunker-like" buildings "do not match the beauty of the mountain."

Denver

	BEST OVERALL		BEST VALUES
23	Brown Palace		Holtze
22	Inverness		Inverness
	Loews Giorgio		Doubletree
	Westin–Tabor Ctr.		Embassy Suites
21	Oxford		Marriott

Brown Palace Hotel 205R (25S) 22 | 24 | 23 | 23 | $173
321 17th St., Denver; (303) 297-3111; (800) 321-2599; FAX: (303) 293-9204
☑ A "sense of history permeates" Denver's top-rated hotel, a 105-year-old Downtown US presidents' favorite that fairly "screams Molly Brown" with its "gotta-see" glass-domed lobby and overall "comfort, charm and class"; Continental dining is "superb" at the Palace Arms, Ellyngton's is *the* place for power breakfast, and Churchill's cigar bar is a trendy place to light up; a few groan that the old girl "needs a redo, like most legends" but a '96 renovation may change their minds.

Burnsley Hotel (82S) 21 | 21 | 19 | 17 | $130
1000 Grant St., Denver; (303) 830-1000; (800) 231-3915; FAX: (303) 830-7676
■ "Nice for business travelers" looking for a "quiet" place to unwind, this near-Downtown all-suiter offers "spacious", kitchenette-equipped quarters, free weekday happy hour and a full free breakfast buffet (plus the "best Sunday brunch"); if a few find it "cold", more consider it a "great off-the-beaten-path place" and a "value" to boot.

Cambridge Hotel (25S) ▽ 21 | 19 | 16 | 19 | $151
1560 Sherman St., Denver; (303) 831-1252; (800) 877-1252; FAX: (303) 831-4724
■ "Like home" is one of the highest compliments anyone can pay a hotel, and that's what fans say about this Downtown all-suite old-timer; its "quiet, well-decorated" lodgings resemble a "private apartment" (most with kitchenette), continental breakfast is included and limo service is available; P.S. turndown service includes Godiva chocolates.

Doubletree Hotel - Denver Southeast 244R (4S) 20 | 19 | 16 | 18 | $116
13696 E. Iliff Pl., Aurora; (303) 337-2800; (800) 222-TREE; FAX: (303) 752-0296
■ High fives go to this East Denver suburbanite in a "convenient" location just off I-225 and near the Denver Tech Center; "more than adequate" rooms (with coffeemakers and ironing boards), exercise facilities, an indoor pool, "great Sunday brunch" and those signature "warm cookies on arrival" add up to a "good value" made even better by golf and tennis privileges at the Heather Ridge Country Club.

Embassy Suites Denver Place (337S) 21 | 19 | 16 | 18 | $124
1881 Curtis St., Denver; (303) 297-8888; (800) 733-3366; FAX: (303) 298-1103
☑ An "excellent bargain" in a central Downtown location handy for shopping and business; to fans it's the "perfect family pleaser" thanks to "comfortable" all-suite lodgings (each with three TVs), an outdoor pool and complimentary breakfast buffet; still, picky palates prefer to "eat elsewhere" and critics find the hotel overall "sort of blah" and "tired."

Holtze Executive Place 125R (119S) ▽ 22 | 20 | 15 | 20 | $115
818 17th St., Denver; (303) 607-9000; (800) 422-2092; FAX: (303) 607-0101
■ New to central Downtown is this "businessperson's nirvana" with "livable" rooms plus apartment-like suites with full kitchens for extended stays; guests applaud its "quiet, understated elegance", "great" staff and "nice amenities" such as a complimentary breakfast buffet and weekday happy hour; there's no on-site restaurant, but there is room service and java junkies like the Starbucks off the lobby; N.B. you can work off your caffeine buzz at the recently opened fitness center.

Hyatt Regency Denver Downtown 476R (25S) 20 | 20 | 18 | 19 | $147
1750 Welton St., Denver; (303) 295-1234; (800) 233-1234; FAX: (303) 292-2472
☑ The strong suits of this "effective business hotel" in central Downtown are its meeting facilities and convention center convenience; though it strikes critics as a "typical Hyatt" that's "lost its edge", to the majority it's a "clean, functional" place with a "courteous" staff and a "spiffed-up" renovated lobby; N.B. a room redo was finished in early '97.

Hyatt Regency Denver Tech Center 436R (12S) 20 | 20 | 17 | 19 | $146
7800 E. Tufts Ave., Denver; (303) 779-1234; (800) 233-1234; FAX: (303) 850-7164
■ It may be "too far from everything" for some, but most find this SE Denver "basic business hotel" at the junction of two major highways "convenient" and pleasant; "corner rooms are beautiful", the staff is "very welcoming" and the rooftop restaurant, Centennial, has "a wonderful view" of the Rockies; a pool, sauna, tennis court and other fitness facilities make it good for "exercise buffs."

Inverness Hotel & Golf Club 284R (18S) $\boxed{22}$ $\boxed{23}$ $\boxed{22}$ $\boxed{23}$ $\boxed{\$139}$

200 Inverness Dr. W., Englewood; (303) 799-5800; (800) 346-4891; FAX: (303) 397-7148

◪ Way down south of Denver, this meeting specialist offers "extremely comfortable", "spacious" rooms and "high-tech" facilities, making it "great for conferences" with the area's "best seafood buffet" (weekends) at the Garden Terrace and fine New American fare at The Swan; those who faulted "cold" decor may want to check out the big recent redo; an 18-hole golf course, tennis courts and Olympic-size pool keep athletes busy while the acquisitive head to the Park Meadows Shopping Center nearby.

Loews Giorgio Hotel 168R (18S) $\boxed{23}$ $\boxed{22}$ $\boxed{23}$ $\boxed{21}$ $\boxed{\$156}$

4150 E. Mississippi Ave., Denver; (303) 782-9300; (800) 345-9172; FAX: (303) 758-6542

■ "Such elegance in such a wasteland of an area" is how some react to this Italian-style "hidden treasure" of a "good business hotel" in SE Denver; it may be "hard to find", but that means "no convention crowds" and its proximity to the Cherry Creek Shopping Center pleases browsers; "lavish rooms", "high-class service" and a "lovely" Italian dining room, Tuscany, are further assets, and though there's no pool there is free access to nearby Bally's Total Fitness.

Marriott City Center Denver 599R (14S) $\boxed{19}$ $\boxed{20}$ $\boxed{17}$ $\boxed{18}$ $\boxed{\$142}$

1701 California St., Denver; (303) 297-1300; (800) 228-9290; FAX: (303) 298-7474

◪ "No complaints" but no swoons either for a "cookie-cutter", "basic Marriott"; "well-located" in the center of Downtown, it earns kudos from some for "comfortable" rooms and "friendly, helpful" service – and gripes from others for "boring" quarters and "rude" staff; a 10-minute walk from the convention center, it sees stampedes of name tags and so may be close to "needing renovation" (and it was just redone in '94).

Marriott Southeast Denver 578R (17S) $\boxed{18}$ $\boxed{18}$ $\boxed{16}$ $\boxed{16}$ $\boxed{\$113}$

6363 E. Hampden Ave., Denver; (303) 758-7000; (800) 228-9290; FAX: (303) 691-3418

◪ Other than the "nice location" (off I-25 and near the Denver Tech Center in SE Denver) and a "spectacular view" of the Rockies from the "lodge-like lobby", this is your "standard issue", "clean, basic Marriott", high on "function over style" – but that's enough to make it "pretty good" according to most surveyors; "big, well-furnished rooms" are appreciated, but some deduct points for "bland food."

Marriott Tech Center Denver 615R (12S) $\boxed{18}$ $\boxed{17}$ $\boxed{16}$ $\boxed{16}$ $\boxed{\$130}$
(fka Sheraton Denver Tech Center)

4900 S. Syracuse St., Denver; (303) 779-1100; (800) 228-9290; FAX: (303) 740-2523

◪ A former Sheraton in SE Denver that's now "a typical Marriott", i.e. "plain vanilla", "average" and "handy"; 25 meeting rooms and an all-night desk for late arrivals please business travelers, but less-satisfied voters say rooms off the atrium "can be noisy", service is "well-meaning but inefficient" and the whole place "needs an upgrade"; a 1996 renovation may quell those complaints.

Oxford Hotel 71R (10S) $\boxed{20}$ $\boxed{21}$ $\boxed{21}$ $\boxed{19}$ $\boxed{\$141}$

1600 17th St., Denver; (303) 628-5400; (800) 228-5838; FAX: (303) 628-5413

◪ Take a trip "back to the turn of the century" via this "elegant yet funky" restored Victorian, one of the "best of the bygoners" with a "great location" in Lower Downtown near Coors Field; there's a fine bar (the art deco Cruise Room) and good seafood at McCormick's Fish House, but critics cite "haphazard service" and "gloomy" rooms, saying the old bird "could work on its decor"; N.B. the Oxford Club fitness center and Aveda City Spa are next door.

Renaissance Denver Hotel 390R (10S) $\boxed{20}$ $\boxed{19}$ $\boxed{15}$ $\boxed{18}$ $\boxed{\$138}$
(fka Stouffer Renaissance Denver)

3801 Quebec St., Denver; (303) 399-7500; (800) HOTELS-1; FAX: (303) 321-1783

◪ Once in the thick of things due to its location near now-defunct Stapleton Airport, this business-oriented, center-atrium hotel remains "surprisingly good for meetings"; rooms were redone in '96 and all have balconies (some with mountain views), but the lobby and bar can seem "cavernous and noisy" and critics rate the whole place "ho-hum"; AARP members can get "great" discounts and all guests enjoy a free shuttle to the new airport.

Residence Inn by Marriott - Denver Downtown (156S) $\boxed{\triangledown}$ $\boxed{17}$ $\boxed{18}$ $\boxed{13}$ $\boxed{13}$ $\boxed{\$105}$

2777 Zuni St., Denver; (303) 458-5318; (800) 331-3131; FAX: (303) 458-5318

■ Downtown all-suiter with "spacious", kitchenette-equipped accommodations and helpful staff ("they made our family get-together very comfortable"); proximity to Coors Field, Mile High Stadium and Larimer Square (and comp shuttle service) is a plus, though some feel it's in a "tough area"; continental breakfast and weekday dinners are included.

Warwick Hotel 142R (49S)

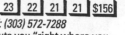

1776 Grant St., Denver; (303) 861-2000; (800) 525-2888; FAX: (303) 839-8504

☑ Admirers say "don't overlook" this high-rise hotel that offers "baronial rooms" (with evening turndown service), a rooftop pool, health club privileges, a complimentary European-style breakfast buffet and free transportation around Downtown and to the Cherry Creek Shopping Center; critics counter that it's "too expensive for the ho-hum decor and service" (but weekend packages offer discounts).

Westin Hotel Tabor Center 407R (13S)

| 23 | 22 | 21 | 21 | $156 |

1672 Lawrence St., Denver; (303) 572-9100; (800) 228-3000; FAX: (303) 572-7288

■ A "great location" between central and lower Downtown puts you "right where you want to be" for the Denver Center for the Performing Arts, Shops at Tabor Center, Coors Field and much more; most consider this modern, business-oriented hotel an "oasis of quality" with "first-class everything", from the "spacious rooms" and "good service" to the "beautiful restaurant", Augusta; N.B. the on-site fitness center has racquetball courts as well as the usual facilities.

Durango

General Palmer 36R (3S)

| 21 | 21 | 17 | 17 | $132 |

567 Main Ave., Durango; (970) 247-4747; (800) 523-3358; FAX: (970) 247-1332

■ All aboard Downtown Durango's 1898 Victorian gem with a "gracious country" ambiance that's a "welcome change from the chains"; the "lovingly restored", "frontier-style rooms" have "rustic appeal", the "staff is incredibly nice" and continental breakfast is included; being "right in the center of things", it's "convenient" to the Durango & Silverton narrow gauge choo-choo, but that means mornings can be "noisy" because of the whistles.

Rochester Hotel 13R (2S)

| – | – | – | – | M |

726 E. Second Ave., Durango; (970) 385-1920; (800) 664-1920; FAX: (970) 385-1967

Built in 1892, this recently restored Downtown Durango landmark is a relic of the real West, but the indoor decor is a tribute to the reel West, with rooms designed to reflect Hollywood Westerns filmed in the area; complimentary breakfast includes regional specialties such as eggs with green chiles and black beans; Leland House, under the same ownership and across the street, offers more Western-accented accommodations, including six three-room suites.

Strater Hotel 93R

| 21 | 21 | 17 | 21 | $125 |

699 Main Ave., Durango; (970) 247-4431; (800) 227-4431; FAX: (970) 259-2208

☑ Take a trip "back to the last century" at this atmospheric "alternative to modern hotels" in central Durango; its Victorian trappings are "bordello beautiful", both in the rooms and in public spaces like the Diamond Belle Saloon – the "best place in the West" if you like costumed staff and old-time pianists; cynics say it's a "slice of the Old West with the emphasis on 'old'" and claim "rooms and closets are the same size."

Tall Timber (10S)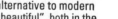

| ▽ | 24 | 25 | 24 | 24 | $253 |

PO Box 90, Silverton Star Rte., Durango; (970) 259-4813

■ A retreat in the true sense, this "remote, relaxed" condo-style hideaway deep in the San Juan National Forest is accessible only via the Durango & Silverton railway or by helicopter; no TVs, radios or phones makes it a "perfect getaway" with all the activities you'd expect in such a setting; it's unique for small corporate retreats and "great for kids", and while rates are steep they cover most everything for stays of three to six nights.

Tamarron Hilton Resort 100R

| 22 | 21 | 20 | 24 | $163 |

(fka Tamarron Resort)
40292 US Hwy. 550 N., Durango; (970) 259-2000; (800) 678-1000; FAX: (970) 259-0745

■ Duffers delight in the "spectacular golf course" at this "peaceful, scenic" resort, especially because the thin Colorado air makes "your golf ball go forever"; children's programs, swimming pools, white-water rafting, tennis courts and the like please families, and it's a good location for a conference or that "perfect small board meeting"; rooms and condo units are "big and beautiful", though sometimes a "long walk from dining."

Wit's End Guest Ranch & Resort (37S)

| – | – | – | – | VE |

254 County Rd. 500, Vallicito Lake; (970) 884-4113; FAX: (970) 884-3261

A historic ranch, now done up as a family-friendly getaway with 37 log cabins in a rural setting; "worth the high price" say those who find lots to do on-site and nearby: fishing in trout-rich ponds, swimming in the outdoor pool, tennis, horseback riding, ice skating; it's also close to major southwest Colorado attractions such as the Durango & Silverton railway; N.B. weeklong all-inclusive stays are the only option in peak summer months.

Edwards

LODGE AND SPA AT CORDILLERA 49R (7S)   26 | 24 | 26 | 27 | $259
PO Box 988, Cordillera Way, Edwards; (970) 926-2200; (800) 877-3529; FAX: (970) 926-2486
◪ In a "magnificent setting" a few miles from Beaver Creek, atop a ridge overlooking Vail Valley, this "remote but first-class" "refuge" has many fans for its "excellent restaurant", Picasso, hillside golf courses and super European-style spa with a 25-meter indoor pool; but it's also knocked for "ups and downs in service" and while some find the rooms "luxurious", others think they're rather "spartan" given the "big-bucks" prices; N.B. 28 rooms are to be added by late summer '97.

Granby

C Lazy U Ranch 41R (3S) ⊟   ▽ 25 | 28 | 26 | 28 | $308
PO Box 379, 3640 Colorado Hwy. 125, Granby; (970) 887-3344; FAX: (970) 887-3917
■ "Super children's programs" make for "terrific family vacations" at this rustic ranch where horseback riding and skeet shooting augment the usual activities; set near Rocky Mountain National Park, it earns yee-haws from pardners who say it "could become a habit" thanks to "the best food" (included in rates) and service, but lonesome doves say you'd better be ready to "turn a deaf ear to other people's kids"; cash only, open June–late September and mid-December–March; minimum stays vary by season.

Keystone

Keystone Resort 152R (753S)   23 | 22 | 20 | 24 | $164
PO Box 38, Hwy. 9, Keystone; (970) 496-2316; (800) 468-5004; FAX: (970) 496-4343
■ In a "beautiful setting amid the majestic mountains", this "self-contained" resort offers "something for everyone" summer or winter: swimming, skiing, nearby golf and more; lodgings include rooms, suites and condos with decor ranging "from lovely to awful", but "service is terrific" and there are "wonderful" eats 12,000 feet up at the Alpenglow Stube; "package deals" add to the "good value"; the resort also operates the nearby Ski Tip Lodge, a Victorian B&B with excellent dining.

Mosca

Inn at Zapata Ranch 15R (1S)   – | – | – | – | E
(fka Great San Dunes Country Club & Inn)
Zapata Ranch, 5303 Hwy. 150, Mosca; (719) 378-2356; (800) 284-9213; FAX: (719) 378-2428
Offering breathtaking views of one of the country's natural wonders, the Great Sand Dunes National Monument, this deluxe ranch is a "great place to escape and watch the buffalo roam" – it has its own bison herd, and some of them even show up in the award-winning restaurant (on the plate, that is); "rooms are well done but small" and for amusement there's golf, trout fishing, horseback riding and a health club and spa services, but no TVs or smoking; open April–October.

Mt. Crested Butte

Grande Butte Hotel 158R (52S)   22 | 20 | 18 | 21 | $163
500 Gothic Rd., Mt. Crested Butte; (970) 349-4000; (800) 544-8448; FAX: (970) 349-2397
◪ The rooms are "large" and "comfortable", but the best feature of this Crested Butte hotel is its "great location" – you "ski in and out" to lifts 100 yards away; special packages offer free lift tickets very early and late in the season and there's a free shuttle to town; while it has "all the basics", some feel it "lacks charm" and is just a "typical hotel in a fantastic setting."

Redstone

Redstone Inn 31R (4S)   – | – | – | – | I
82 Redstone Blvd., Redstone; (970) 963-2526; (800) 748-2524; FAX: (970) 963-2527
The spectacular Maroon Bells Snowmass Wilderness Area is the backyard of this 1902 English Tudor–style mountain resort decorated with Stickley furniture, handcrafted wrought-iron fixtures and stone masonry and offering two restaurants, sleigh rides, x-country skiing on-site and downhill skiing at Aspen just 45 minutes away; summer brings trout fishing, mountain biking, rock climbing, tennis and relaxing at the outdoor pool; N.B. dormer rooms have showers across the hall and Clock Tower rooms have shared baths.

Snowmass Village

Silvertree Hotel 247R (15S)   20 21 19 22 $205
100 Elbert Ln., Snowmass Village; (970) 923-3520; (800) 525-9402; FAX: (970) 923-5494
◪ "Location" is this large Snowmass hotel's main claim to fame; nothing beats "skiing right off" onto the slopes – you can see them from nearly every "small but efficient" room; surveyors applaud "good service", but some knock "poor food" from the lackluster restaurants; check out the atrium lobby for après-ski musical entertainment.

Snowmass Lodge & Club 76R (4S)   23 22 22 25 $207
PO Box G-2, 239 Snowmass Club Circle, Snowmass Village; (970) 923-5600; (800) 525-0710; FAX: (970) 923-0944
■ A "relaxing" mountain melange with accommodations in a "cozy lodge" or privately owned villas ("rent one and live it up!"); lodge rooms are "large, clean and tasteful, if not exciting", but "service is great" and it's a "good value" for the Aspen area, with amenities including x-country skiing, 18 holes of golf, 13 tennis courts and two outdoor pools; a new ski lift two minutes from the door should please those who find it a "little far" from the slopes.

Steamboat Springs

Sheraton Steamboat Resort 270R (3S)   18 18 18 20 $174
PO Box 774808, 2200 Village Inn Ct., Steamboat Springs; (970) 879-2220; (800) 325-3535; FAX: (970) 879-7686
◪ Steps from the Silver Bullet gondola and thus boasting the "best ski-in/ski-out location", this Sheraton also has amenities aplenty – fireplaces and kitchenettes in some rooms, conference facilities, a fitness center and nearby golf and hot mineral springs; still, complainers find it "a little worn" with a "plastic, industrial" feel, calling it an "ordinary resort in an extraordinary town."

Telluride

Columbia Hotel 20R (1S)   – – – – VE
300 W. San Juan Ave., Telluride; (970) 728-0660; (800) 201-9505; FAX: (970) 728-9249
Just a push of the ski poles away from Telluride's new gondola and two blocks from Downtown shops, restaurants and nightspots, this intimate hostelry offers all the amenities of a full-service hotel; shivering skiiers can warm up in rooms outfitted with fireplaces, steam showers and six-foot-long clawfoot tubs, or head for the rooftop hot tub and take in the scenery as they soak.

PEAKS AT TELLURIDE 149R (28S)   27 26 24 27 $257
PO Box 2702, 136 Country Club Dr., Telluride; (970) 728-6800; (800) 789-2220; FAX: (970) 728-6567
■ Truly a peak experience according to surveyors who shower superlatives on this "ultimate luxury ski resort" with a "fab", 42,000-square-foot European-style spa in the "Shangri-la" setting of Telluride; there's "no need to go anywhere else" given lovely rooms with "breathtaking" views, "fantastic service" and innovative regional cuisine; snow buffs enjoy ski-in/ski-out access in winter, and in summer there's biking, golf, swimming, tennis – you name it.

SAN SOPHIA, THE 16R   24 25 23 23 $163
PO Box 1825, 330 W. Pacific Ave., Telluride; (970) 728-3001; (800) 537-4781; FAX: (970) 728-6226
■ New owners are emphasizing the culinary by offering on-site dinner as well as "delicious breakfasts" at this centrally located, nonsmoking Victorian-style B&B in Telluride; "beautifully appointed" with "lovely rooms", it's praised for its "restful" atmosphere and "friendly staff" as well as the "wonderful hosts"; some say summers can be sticky due to no a/c.

Vail

Christiana at Vail 15R (42S)   21 19 17 20 $227
356 E. Hanson Ranch Rd., Vail; (970) 476-5641; (800) 530-3999; FAX: (970) 476-0470
■ Like a "transplanted European ski lodge" in a "good location" near the slopes, which means ski-in/ski-out access in winter; though rooms (in the main hotel or condos) receive reviews ranging from "charming" to "need upgrading", most visitors enjoy the pleasant ambiance and amenities such as an outdoor pool, sun deck and hiking and mountain biking just out the door; only continental breakfast is served, but there are many lunch and dinner options nearby.

Lodge at Vail 60R (40S)
23 | 23 | 23 | 23 | $238

174 E. Gore Creek Dr., Vail; (970) 476-5011; (800) 331-5634; FAX: (970) 476-7425
■ An Orient-Express property, this hotel dates from Vail's first days and hence enjoys a prime location at the base of lift #1; "pleasant" rooms and condos with "beautiful views" offer "upscale cozy comfort à la Ralph Lauren and Laura Ashley", and "fabulous wine and food events" routinely take place in the "superb" American restaurant, Wildflower; N.B. construction of a new wing is scheduled to be completed in early '98.

Marriott's Mountain Resort at Vail 311R (38S)
– | – | – | – | M

715 W. Lionshead Circle, Vail; (970) 476-4444; (800) 648-0720
Well-located (150 yards from Vail's Eagle Bahn gondola) and well-equipped, with indoor and outdoor pools, two tennis courts, a health club, Jacuzzis, nearby golf and more, this full-service Marriott covers the bases year-round; but it isn't just for sporty types: it has the largest conference facilities in the Vail Valley, with over 16,000 square feet of meeting space.

Marriott's Streamside at Vail (150S)
21 | 20 | 18 | 20 | $171

2284 S. Frontage Rd. W., Vail; (970) 476-6000; (800) 223-8245; FAX: (970) 476-4463
■ A "very friendly, helpful" staff manages this "convenient" Marriott time-share property a five-minute drive from Vail; fitness facilities include pools, racquetball courts, whirlpools and exercise rooms, and a shuttle transports guests from the "terrific" studio, one- and two-bedroom condos to town and lifts.

Mountain Haus at Vail 10R (64S)
21 | 19 | 15 | 19 | $234

292 E. Meadow Dr., Vail; (970) 476-2434; (800) 237-0922; FAX: (970) 476-3007
■ This mix of rooms and "spacious, very private" kitchenette-equipped condos in the heart of Vail impresses surveyors as a "no-frills" "good value" in a "perfect location"; the sauna and heated outdoor pool appeal to skiers, as does the continental breakfast (free in winter); a renovation of the lobby was completed in 1996.

Sitzmark Lodge 35R
20 | 22 | 22 | 17 | $164

183 Gore Creek Dr., Vail; (970) 476-5001; FAX: (970) 476-8702
■ "Now this is my idea of a ski lodge" cheers a fan of this "cozy", "hospitable" alpine-style lodge in a "fantastic location" on Vail's main pedestrian mall; "unpretentious by Vail standards", it has whirlpools, a sauna and heated outdoor pool, plus "excellent" French cuisine at the on-site Left Bank, arguably "the best restaurant" in town; no wonder it's called "the best value I've seen in a while."

SONNENALP RESORT OF VAIL 92R (94S)
25 | 25 | 24 | 24 | $260

20 Vail Rd., Vail; (970) 476-5656; (800) 654-8312; FAX: (970) 476-8066
■ Guests find plenty of "alpine charm" at this "sparkling", "very European" resort in a "wonderful location" in the heart of Vail; "beautiful rooms" in three buildings ("Bavaria Haus is best", some claim), "superb service" and "fantastic" food (light Bavarian cuisine at Ludwig's and "fabulous fondue at the Swiss Chalet") are among its assets, and you'll find plenty of "beautiful people" pampering themselves at the spa; about the only complaint heard is "overpriced."

Vail Athletic Club Hotel & Spa 36R (2S)
21 | 22 | 22 | 21 | $224

352 E. Meadow Dr., Vail; (970) 476-0700; (800) 822-4754; FAX: (970) 476-6451
■ "Pretend you're an upscale jock" at this "expensive-but-worth-it" hotel where the nearly 20,000 square feet of "great athletic facilities" are the draw: an indoor rock-climbing wall, lap pool, yoga, aerobics and more plus a full range of spa treatments; rooms may be "tiny", but there are "mountain views" and "good" low-fat American food at Terra Bistro; a few say the place "can't decide what it is", calling it "very Vail, but not so athletic or clubby."

Vail Cascade Hotel & Club 260R (29S)
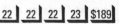
22 | 22 | 22 | 23 | $189

1300 Westhaven Dr., Vail; (970) 476-7111; (800) 420-2424; FAX: (970) 479-7020
■ Although "kind of remote", this resort is "worth the short, free bus ride" to town say those who enjoy its "lovely rooms", "anxious-to-please" staff, "comfy piano bar" and private ski lift up Vail Mountain; facilities include two outdoor pools, 14 tennis courts and a 75,000-square-foot fitness center; a few find it "a bit too corporate" and say quality is "sliding downhill", but they're outvoted; N.B. the adjacent "babbling" Gore Creek is renowned for trout fishing.

Connecticut

TOP 10 OVERALL

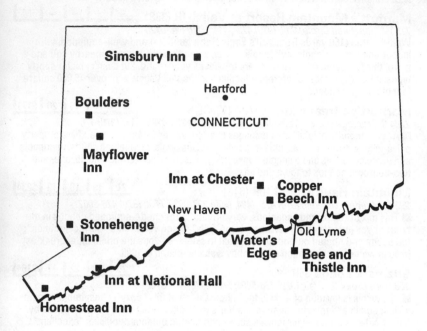

BEST OVERALL
- **27** Mayflower Inn/Washington
- **24** Inn at National Hall/Westport
- **23** Copper Beech Inn/Ivoryton
- **22** Bee and Thistle Inn/Old Lyme
  Stonehenge Inn/Ridgefield
  Boulders/New Preston
- **21** Homestead Inn/Greenwich
  Simsbury Inn/Simsbury
  Inn at Chester/Chester
- **20** Water's Edge/Westbrook

BEST VALUES
Simsbury Inn/Simsbury
Bee and Thistle Inn/Old Lyme
Inn at Chester/Chester
Lighthouse Inn/New London
Griswold Inn/Essex
White Hart Inn/Salisbury
Heritage Inn/Southbury
Old Lyme Inn/Old Lyme
Copper Beech Inn/Ivoryton
Two Trees Inn/Ledyard

Chester | R | S | D | P | $ |

Inn At Chester 41R (1S) | 20 | 21 | 22 | 19 | $142 |

318 W. Main St., Chester; (203) 526-9541; (800) 949-7829; FAX: (860) 526-4387

■ This "modern inn with an 'old' look" on a 200-year-old homestead is lauded for its "warm staff" and "great location" near the Goodspeed Opera and Gilette's Castle; most guests also enjoy the reproduction 18th-century decor combined with such 20th-century amenities as TVs, a/c and business facilities as well as biking, tennis and croquet; an old barn houses the "excellent" Post and Beam restaurant.

Essex

Griswold Inn (28S) | 18 | 21 | 21 | 19 | $138 |

36 Main St., Essex; (860) 767-1776; FAX: (860) 767-0481

☑ Continuously operating since 1776, the Gris charms its longtime loyalists like a "favorite old shoe" with "classic Connecticut" "colonial ambiance", "cozy rooms" and a "distinctive restaurant" where the housemade "sausage alone is worth the trip"; others sniff at the "verging on shabby" decor, "polyester express-bus" crowd and "noisy" scene.

Greenwich

Homestead Inn 17R (6S)   20 | 22 | 24 | 20 | $175
420 Field Point Rd., Greenwich; (203) 869-7500; FAX: (203) 869-7500

■ Closing in on its 200th birthday, this "charming" country manse with cupola top, wide porches and shade trees is "perfect" "for a relaxing, elegant weekend", with "accommodating" staff and "excellent" "white linen" dining at its pricey French restaurant, La Grange; despite a caution that rooms can be "inconsistent", nearly everyone (including the business crowd) is pleased with this "long-running class act."

Hartford

Goodwin Hotel 113R (11S)   20 | 19 | 20 | 17 | $147
1 Haynes St., Hartford; (860) 246-7500; (800) 922-5006; FAX: (860) 247-4576

☑ Arguably the "best in Hartford", this "potentially great" Downtown hotel built by J.P. Morgan offers "classic old-world" ambiance and "sophisticated dining" at Pierpont's; yet many complain of "small" rooms and "nonexistent" service – "too bad it doesn't have any competitors."

Ivoryton

Copper Beech Inn 13R   23 | 22 | 25 | 21 | $172
46 Main St., Ivoryton; (860) 767-0330; FAX: (860) 767-4840

■ A "lovely" Victorian inn (the former home of an ivory importer) "nestled in a beautiful spot" in the Connecticut River Valley lulls guests with "exquisite" country French dining and "pretty", "spacious" rooms (many with canopy beds, TVs, whirlpools and some private decks) in both the main inn and Carriage House; only a few find it "a bit too stuffy."

Lakeville

Interlaken Resort & Conference Center 73R (7S) 16 | 17 | 17 | 17 | $145
74 Interlaken Rd, Lakeville; (860) 435-9878; (800) 222-2909; FAX: (860) 435-2980

☑ The good news about this "clean", "quiet" "getaway" on 30 acres set between two lakes is the whirlwind of outdoor activities it offers serious sports enthusiasts, ranging from water sports and racquetball to tennis, golf, skiing and even race-car training at the nearby Skip Barber school; but some shudder at "tired", "motelish" rooms, "mediocre" food and "couldn't-care-less" service.

Ledyard

Foxwoods Resort Casino 272R (40S)   18 | 18 | 16 | 19 | $147
PO Box 410, Rte. 2, Ledyard; (860) 885-3000; (800) 369-9663; FAX: (860) 885-4040

☑ A "mini-Vegas in the NE", this "glitzy" casino resort run by the Mashantucket Pequot tribe is a good bet for admirers who find it "pretty and convenient" with a "tastefully done Indian theme", "great entertainment", "unexpectedly good food" and a "good game room for kids"; but critics call it a losing wager – "ugly" and "cheaply done" with an "amusement park" atmosphere and "average everything"; your call.

Two Trees Inn 220R (60S)   19 | 19 | 15 | 18 | $138
PO Box 410, Rte. 2, Ledyard; (860) 885-3000; (800) FOXWOOD; FAX: (203) 885-4050

■ An alternative to the main hotel at the Foxwoods Casino, this "quiet oasis" offering refuge "from the hectic scene" is nevertheless "convenient" to the action, with "pleasant service" and "comfortable" accommodations; an indoor pool and workout room may relieve blackjack-induced tension, but the "subpar" food can be irritating.

Mystic

Inn at Mystic 67R   20 | 19 | 20 | 19 | $151
(fka Mystic Motor Inn)
PO Box 216, Jct. Rtes. 1 & 27, Mystic; (860) 536-9604; (800) 237-2415; FAX: (860) 572-3516

☑ This "cozy, elegant, turn-of-the-century inn" with a less charming motor court addition offers the pleasures of a "tranquil setting" overlooking the harbor and Long Island Sound, "lovely gardens", "comfortable rooms" (many with fireplace and/or Jacuzzi) and "excellent" Continental dining; but several warn the "main house is the only place to stay for a romantic getaway", otherwise it's "ok – that's all."

New Haven

Three Chimneys Inn 10R
– – – – M

(fka Inn at Chapel West)
1201 Chapel St., New Haven; (203) 789-1201; FAX: (203) 776-7363
Just one block from the Yale campus, this 1870 Victorian mansion is a newly renovated haven for visiting parents who can relax in front of period fireplaces surrounded by such 19th-century details as high ceilings and oak millwork, or in rooms luxuriously furnished with canopy beds, Oriental rugs and period furniture; computer hookups and conference rooms are 20th-century touches.

New London

Lighthouse Inn 45R (5S)
21 21 19 19 $141

6 Guthrie Pl., New London; (860) 443-8411; FAX: (860) 437-7027
◪ "Stunning views" from a "nice location by the water" as well as "large" "beautiful rooms" and a "nice Sunday brunch" draw surveyors to this "conglomeration" where some claim the "newer building has the best amenities"; others yawn "pretty good" but "like being in a motel."

New Preston

Boulders, The 7R (10S)
20 22 23 22 $173

PO Box 2575, E. Shore Rd./Rte. 45, New Preston; (860) 868-0541; (800) 55-BOULDERS; FAX: (860) 868-1925
■ "One of the most romantic inns around" in a "beautiful setting" along Lake Waramaug enchants city escapees with its "attention to details" and "rustic" charm aplenty, especially its "unique", "homey" antiques-filled rooms (renovated in 1996) and "serious" New American food (terrace dining is "exhilarating"); despite a few gripes about "snooty service", "lovely" is the consensus.

Inn on Lake Waramaug 22R (1S)
16 18 20 17 $156

107 N. Shore Rd., New Preston; (860) 868-0563; (800) 525-3466; FAX: (860) 868-9173
◪ "The charming setting on the lake" "makes an average stay unique and pleasant, otherwise accommodations are standard" at this "quaint" colonial mainstay in the Litchfield Hills antiques region; but while the majority agrees that rooms need both an 'overhaul' and "housekeeping", the heated indoor pool, tennis courts, private beach and "delightful terrace" dining help account for its longevity.

Norfolk

Blackberry River Inn 16R (3S)
▽ 15 19 15 16 $131

536 Greenwoods Rd. W./Rte. 44, Norfolk; (860) 542-5100; (800) 414-3636; FAX: (860) 542-1763
■ This recently restored lakeside inn (circa 1763) features some rooms with working fireplaces (one with Jacuzzi), three sitting rooms and library, all with fireplaces, complimentary breakfast and afternoon tea; situated in the foothills of the Berkshires, its 27 acres yield such country pleasures as boating, fishing and nature walking, and there's plenty of antiquing and culture fixes (Tanglewood, etc.) within a short drive.

Old Lyme

Bee And Thistle Inn 11R (1S)
21 23 24 20 $149

100 Lyme St., Old Lyme; (860) 434-1667; (800) 622-4946; FAX: (860) 434-3402
■ Starry-eyed surveyors gush "if you're not in love when you arrive, you will be when you leave" this "romantic" 1756 colonial in the "quaint" Old Lyme historic district; well-known for New American "country dining at its best", it boasts "extremely gracious hosts", "lovely antiques", rooms with canopied beds and a "highly recommended afternoon tea"; enthusiasts advise "go in autumn to see the leaves."

Old Lyme Inn 13R
20 21 22 18 $148

85 Lyme St., Old Lyme; (860) 434-2600; (800) 434-5352; FAX: (860) 434-5352
◪ Oh so "New Englandy", this restored 1850 Empire-style farmhouse next door to the Lyme Historical Society "takes you back to a lovely era" with a "charming" setting, "fine" rooms (with a/c, private baths and antique furnishings) and "wonderful" New American cuisine; but while most consider it a "classic", a vocal minority complains of "too much attitude."

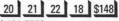

Ridgefield

Stonehenge Inn 12R (4S)   21 | 22 | 24 | 20 | $183
PO Box 667, Rte. 7, Ridgefield; (203) 438-6511; FAX: (203) 438-2478
■ "Small, pleasant and old-fashioned", this "picturesque inn" with three buildings in "beautiful" "lakeside surroundings" is a "quiet getaway" where swans glide across a trout-filled lake and gastronomes dote on the "exceptional", highly regarded French-Continental cuisine (a new terrace dining room opened in '95); although a few suggest the "large" "old rooms" "border on seedy", they do come with a/c, private baths and TVs.

Salisbury

White Hart Inn 23R (3S)   18 | 21 | 22 | 19 | $146
Village Green, Salisbury; (860) 435-0030; (800) 832-0041; FAX: (860) 435-0040
■ This "cozy", "quintessential" Federal-style inn is a "nice place to stop" when passing through "beautiful" Salisbury, with "small" "but cute" rooms, "fine food", a "lovely staff" and a "relaxed" ambiance complete with a front porch dressed up in wicker; while a few shrug "average", overall it's "very pleasant" and the "pub is the spot to be (a local hangout)."

Simsbury

Simsbury Inn 90R (8S)   21 | 21 | 21 | 21 | $138
397 Hopmeadow St./Rte. 10, Simsbury; (860) 651-5700; (800) 634-2719;
FAX: (860) 651-8024
■ "Geared to businesspeople who work in Hartford", this "comfortable" faux-Federalist facility near Bradley Airport offers "spacious public rooms" and views over Farmington Valley plus lots of sports facilities (tennis, indoor pool, health club, etc.) all serviced by a "friendly" staff; while "unremarkable" to a few, it's "comfortable" and as realists note, practically "the only game in town."

Southbury

Heritage Inn 158R (5S)   20 | 20 | 18 | 20 | $142
Heritage Rd., Southbury; (203) 264-8200; (800) 932-3466; FAX: (203) 264-6910
☑ While a few still cheer this resort hotel as "a great conference and training facility" offering 25 meeting rooms plus tennis, golf, indoor/outdoor pools and a health club, others say "it was once" outstanding but now suffers from "run-down rooms" and "terrible food"; yet even critics think it "has potential."

Washington

MAYFLOWER INN 17R (8S)   28 | 27 | 26 | 27 | $300
PO Box 1288, 118 Woodbury Rd./Rte. 47, Washington; (860) 868-9466; FAX: (860) 868-1497
■ The "crème de la crème" sums it up for this Relais & Châteaux "movie-set perfect", 28-acre hideaway in Litchfield County with "pampering" service, "luxurious" rooms (many boasting fireplaces, balconies, Tabriz rugs, canopy beds) and "excellent" Continental–New England cuisine along with gardens, hiking trails, an outdoor heated pool, tennis court and a fitness center for the active set; all in all, "pure heaven."

Westbrook

Water's Edge Resort 20R (15S)   21 | 20 | 20 | 22 | $159
PO Box 688, 1525 Boston Post Rd., Westbrook; (860) 399-5901; (800) 222-5901;
FAX: (860) 399-6172
■ "A gorgeous location on Long Island Sound" is the chief asset of this "great seaside spot" with spa facilities, tennis, swimming pools and "terrific views" from the dining room; a few cast it off as "average" and warn "it's turning into a wedding factory", but kitchenettes in condo units make it "super for families" and just about everyone loves "a walk along the beach."

Westport

INN AT NATIONAL HALL 8R (7S)   26 | 24 | 25 | 23 | $269
2 Post Rd. W., Westport; (212) 221-1351; (800) 628-4255; FAX: (212) 221-0276
■ Virtually "perfect on all counts" after a five-year restoration, this brick Italianate/Victorian former bank merited a cover story in *Architectural Digest*; our surveyors are wowed by its "stately" luxury, proclaiming "every room a gem", the service "outstanding" and Restaurant Zanghi "gorgeous"; "everything is impressive" – "including the bill!"

Delaware

R **S** **D** **P** **$**

Addy Sea 13R ▽ 17 | 16 | 12 | 12 | $120
99 Oceanview Pkwy., Bethany Beach; (302) 539-3707; (800) 418-6764
■ Surveyors "can't believe" the *Survey* "found this funky old" Victorian B&B "with a marvelous location" right on the beach; it has just 13 rooms, so reserve early in order to enjoy its antiques-filled ambiance and ocean-view porch with rockers overlooking a quiet stretch of sand; when the mood for noisier beach scenes strikes, Rehoboth Beach and Ocean City are close at hand.

Dover

Sheraton Inn & Conference Center 153R (3S) 14 | 15 | 11 | 14 | $103
1570 N. Dupont Hwy., Dover; (302) 678-8500; (800) 325-3535; FAX: (302) 678-9073
☑ It may be "convenient for South Delaware" destinations and its large-scale convention facilities make it a "good commercial hotel", but otherwise most reviewers brand this a "run-of-the-mill" chain offering "no fluff" accommodations – "just someplace to crash"; check out the "wild and crazy" lounge, which some call a "local hot spot."

Lewes

New Devon Inn 24R (2S) ▽ 20 | 20 | 22 | 18 | $132
PO Box 516, 142 Second St., Lewes; (302) 645-6466; (800) 824-8754; FAX: (302) 645-7196
■ Built in 1926, this "quaint" inn, listed on the National Register of Historic Places, brings a sense of history to the seaside pleasures of the nearby beach and wildlife refuge; antiques-furnished rooms and Continental dining add up to "as good value as can be had" in a picturesque 17th-century town, especially with off-season package deals.

Montchanin

Inn at Montchanin Village (22S) − | − | − | − | E
Rte. 100 & Kirk Rd., Montchanin; (302) 888-2133; (800) COWBIRD; FAX: (302) 888-0389
A unique setting for a getaway, Montchanin Village is an 1800s hamlet of 11 buildings (on the National Historic Register) that once housed laborers at Brandywine Valley factories; charming guestrooms (by '98, there should be 37) are set in nine restored buildings and vary in size and price, but all feature private marble baths, period and reproduction furniture and modern conveniences; landscaped gardens, peaceful porches and fine dining (breakfast included) round out the pleasant picture.

Newark

Christiana Hilton Inn 262R (4S) 21 | 20 | 16 | 18 | $115
100 Continental Dr., Newark; (302) 454-1500; (800) HILTONS; FAX: (302) 454-0233
■ A suburban option offering "solid comfort" that blends Old Williamsburg architectural styling, "pleasant service" and "fair" dining with corporate amenities such as computer jacks and meeting space; there's a pool and fitness room on-site plus "easy access" to golf, horse racing and nearby Wilmington's tourist sights; most call it a "good value" and a "nice experience", though some ask "why 'inn'?" – "it's just another roadside property."

New Castle

Armitage Inn 5R − | − | − | − | M
2 The Strand, New Castle; (302) 328-6618; FAX: (302) 324-1164
Steeped in colonial lore, this house-turned-B&B dating from 1732 sets the stage for exploring the historic town of New Castle as well as nearby Wilmington, the Winterthur Museum, Longwood Gardens and more; rooms blend period decor and unique features (a river-view bay window, a canopy bed) with modern musts like computer jacks, earning it accolades such as "best in town" and "favorite for a weekend away from the city."

Rehoboth Beach

Boardwalk Plaza Hotel 27R (57S) <u>21</u> <u>20</u> <u>19</u> <u>19</u> <u>$164</u>
2 Olive Ave., Rehoboth Beach; (302) 227-7169; (800) 33-BEACH; FAX: (302) 227-0561
☑ It was built in 1991, but this oceanfront hotel sports a Victorian look, from the pink and white exterior to the period decor; some guests "like" its style, others say "too much" Victoriana, but the "best location" at the state's most popular beach is hard to argue with; rooms feature antique and reproduction touches and there are some kitchen-equipped suites; pluses include an indoor/outdoor spa pool, rooftop sun deck, Continental dining and even a talking parrot in the lounge.

Corner Cupboard Inn 18R ▽ <u>18</u> <u>22</u> <u>18</u> <u>14</u> <u>$136</u>
50 Park Ave., Rehoboth Beach; (302) 227-8553; FAX: (302) 226-9113
■ An "old-fashioned" Rehoboth mainstay, run for 60 years by the same family, that evokes a bygone era with its "cozy" rooms and "good" "home cooking"; a few find it "quaint to excess", but most enjoy its "comfortable, informal" feel and such simple pleasures as walks "in the woods" or on the beach (a block and a half away); summer rates cover breakfast and dinner, which enhances the sense of visiting old friends.

Wilmington

Boulevard Bed & Breakfast 6R <u>-</u> <u>-</u> <u>-</u> <u>-</u> <u>I</u>
1909 Baynard Blvd., Wilmington; (302) 656-9700; FAX: (302) 656-9701
Sample the lifestyle of Wilmington's mercantile heyday by overnighting at this Historic District 1913 mansion (on the National Register of Historic Places); rooms are furnished with family antiques and a full breakfast (included in rates) is served in the formal dining room or on the screened-in porch – an elegant prelude to anything from a Downtown business meeting to a visit to the Brandywine River Museum.

HOTEL DU PONT 206R (10S) <u>25</u> <u>25</u> <u>25</u> <u>23</u> <u>$177</u>
11th & Market Sts., Wilmington; (302) 594-3100; (800) 441-9019; FAX: (302) 594-3108
■ Being "treated like a du Pont" is reason enough to visit this Wilmington showpiece – though its grand lobby and ballroom, "elegant service" and "outstanding" Continental dining in the Green Room are also worth the trip; it offers "old-time luxury in a modern mode" ("fluffy robes", computer jacks, the "best wake-up call ever") in "lovely" (if sometimes "small") rooms, making it "perfect for business functions" and a terrific "weekend buy" for visits to nearby Winterthur and other attractions.

Florida

TOP 10 OVERALL

Ritz-Carlton Amelia Island

Tallahassee

FLORIDA

Disney's Grand Floridian ■
Hyatt Regency Grand Cypress ■

Orlando

Tampa

Lake Okeechobee

Four Seasons ■
Ritz-Carlton ■

Palm Beach

Boca Raton

Naples

Ritz-Carlton ■

Miami

Grand Bay ■
Fisher Island Club ■

Marquesa   **Little Palm**

BEST OVERALL
28 Ritz-Carlton/Naples
27 Ritz-Carlton/Amelia Island
    Marquesa/Key West
    Four Seasons/Palm Beach
    Ritz-Carlton/Palm Beach
    Fisher Island Club/Miami
    Little Palm/Little Torch Key
26 Grand Bay/Miami
    Disney's Grand Floridian/Orlando
    Hyatt Reg. Grand Cypress/Orlando

BEST VALUES
Disney's All-Star Music/Orlando
Disney's All-Star Sports/Orlando
Disney's Port Orleans/Orlando
Holiday Inn SunSpree/Orlando
Disney's Dixie Landings/Orlando
Radisson Plaza/Orlando
Disney's Caribbean/Orlando
Marriott's Bay Point/Panama City
Sheraton Grand/Tampa Bay
Hyatt Reg. Westshore/Tampa Bay

Amelia Island

R	S	D	P	$
23	22	21	24	$192

Amelia Island Plantation 130R (358S)
PO Box 3000, Amelia Island Plantation, Fernandina Beach; (904) 261-6161; (800) 874-6878; FAX: (904) 277-5945

☑ It's "life in the slow lane" for lollygaggers who ease toward this "well-run" 1,250-acre island resort that's "good for adults and families", offering "roomy accommodations", a "lovely beach" and "spectacular facilities", including "great golf", tennis, pools, bicycling, horseback riding and a fitness center, plus "lots of activities for kids"; some say the "kinda-spread-out" setting on the Florida-Georgia border is "not easy to get around on foot", but even those who say it's "aging" call it "terrific."

RITZ-CARLTON AMELIA ISLAND 404R (45S) 28 28 27 27 $217

4750 Amelia Island Pkwy., Amelia Island; (904) 277-1100; (800) 241-3333; FAX: (904) 261-9063
■ "Silver service on a desolate beach – this must be nirvana" sighs one admirer of this island R-C (the state's No. 2 resort) blending "big-time elegance", a "spectacular setting", "delightful rooms" and "service too good to be true"; an indoor pool supplements a "beach at its best", and out of the water there's championship golf, tennis, even cooking classes, as well as "very impressive" dining at The Grill; although a "first-class operation", a few casual types find the highly attentive Ritz service just "too much."

Boca Raton

BOCA RATON RESORT & CLUB 864R (39S) 24 25 24 26 $244

501 E. Camino Real, Boca Raton; (561) 395-3000; (800) 327-0101; FAX: (561) 391-3183
◪ "Class and tradition" live on in the "old-world elegance" of this "spread-out" 365-acre 1926 Mediterranean-style resort with a half-mile of private beach; longtime fans say the "beautiful rooms and grounds" and extensive sports and spa facilities mean it "will always be a favorite", and children's and teens' programs provide family appeal; but while admirers swear "they do the best they can to make guests feel special", critics grouse about "pompous" ambiance.

Marriott Boca Raton 240R (16S) 20 19 18 19 $155

5150 Town Center Circle, Boca Raton; (561) 392-4600; (800) 228-9290; FAX: (561) 368-9223
◪ "Fine lodging in an upscale shopping area" gives credit-card flashers a workout at this "very corporate" property in the heart of Boca Raton; while considered "average", it's viewed favorably by surveyors who find it "comfortable" and friendly – "we stayed seven weeks and were treated like family."

Captiva Island

South Seas Plantation Resort & Yacht Harbour 106R (563S) 23 22 20 24 $206

5400 Sanibel Captiva Rd., Captiva Island; (941) 472-5111; (800) 227-8482; FAX: (941) 472-7541
◪ The "ultimate beachfront escape from reality" lies on 330 acres at the northern tip of Captiva Island, a paradise of "shells, shells, shells", tennis, golf, a marina, swimming pools and kids' programs; many appreciate the "helpful staff" and "well-appointed" accommodations (hotel rooms, villas and beach cottages) scattered throughout the estate, but for some it's "too large", "too crowded" and "a bit isolated" – though for others that's exactly the point.

Clearwater

Belleview Mido Resort Hotel 202R (40S) – – – – E

25 Belleview Blvd., Clearwater; (813) 442-6171; (800) 237-8947; FAX: (813) 441-4173
Opened in 1897, this gabled white Victorian, listed on the National Register of Historic Places, remains true to its history with Tiffany-style windows, crystal chandeliers and period furniture; the rambling wooden structure overlooks the Intracoastal Waterway, and Gulf beaches are five miles away; on-site amenities include championship golf, tennis, a spa and fitness center, six pools and six restaurants.

Destin

Hilton Golf & Tennis Resort Sandestin Beach 385R (15S) 22 21 19 23 $153

4000 Sandestin Blvd., Destin; (904) 267-9500; (800) 367-1271; FAX: (904) 267-3076
■ The star of this "complete resort" on the Panhandle coast may be the "spectacular beach" of white sand and emerald water, but there's much more to please surveyors here: "big rooms" (all junior suites with balconies), "lots of activities" (including golf, tennis and a spa) and "good small convention facilities" – in all, "very nice as Hiltons go"; what's more, "bunk beds", kitchenettes and an indoor pool for rainy days "make this a perfect place to take the kids."

Fort Lauderdale

Doubletree Guest Suites (254S) 18 16 14 15 $138

(fka Guest Quarters Suite Hotel)
555 NW 62nd St., Fort Lauderdale; (954) 772-5400; (800) 222-TREE; FAX: (954) 772-5490
■ "Decent", "spacious suites" with computer jacks and kitchenettes are an "excellent value that's hard to beat", serving the needs of both business travelers as well as parents with tots in tow; located near I-95 in Uptown Fort Lauderdale, it has pleasant public facilities including a "light and airy atrium" and a lagoon-shaped outdoor pool, and beyond its doorsteps there's easy access to outlet shopping.

111

Hyatt Regency Pier 66 380R (8S)   22 | 21 | 20 | 22 | $171
(fka Pier 66 Resort & Marina)
2301 SE 17th St. Causeway, Fort Lauderdale; (954) 525-6666; (800) 327-3796; FAX: (954) 728-3541
◪ "Renovations have done wonders to this landmark" high-rise on the Intracoastal Waterway; a marina-equipped yachter's haven, it offers "delightful" rooms with "beautiful views", four restaurants (plus a revolving rooftop bar), a fitness center and spa, three outdoor pools, a location three blocks from the beach ("fun water taxis" whisk you there) and 22 acres of "tropical", "exquisite gardens" that provide relief from sessions in the 22 meeting rooms; while a few still insist it's "resting on its laurels", far more say "Hyatt's putting class back in this property."

Lago Mar Resort 32R (123S)   22 | 22 | 20 | 24 | $182
1700 S. Ocean Ln., Fort Lauderdale; (954) 523-6511; (800) 524-6627; FAX: (954) 524-6627
◪ "A guest is still a guest" at this "genteel" "throwback to the '50s", an "on the beach and private" "grand old" Mediterranean-style resort providing "wonderful rooms" for both business travelers and families; in a Downtown locale that's near tony Las Olas shopping but still "off the beaten path", it has facilities including four tennis courts, a fitness center and outdoor pool; while a few complain that "older rooms could be better", others note "frequent upgrades" and consider it "well managed."

Little Inn by the Sea 10R (19S)   ▽ 19 | 18 | 18 | 17 | $116
4546 El Mar Dr., Lauderdale by the Sea; (954) 772-2450; (800) 492-0311; FAX: (954) 938-9354
■ "A nice change from high-rise, commercial hotels", this "funky" deco-style inn stakes its claim "right on the beach" in a wealthy, walled-off community; its international clientele appreciates the "charming interiors", "clean rooms" (most with kitchenettes, some with balconies), outdoor pool and rooftop spa, not to mention the "good prices."

Marriott Fort Lauderdale Marina 563R (17S)   20 | 20 | 18 | 20 | $152
1881 SE 17th St., Fort Lauderdale; (954) 463-4000; (800) 433-2254; FAX: (954) 527-6705
◪ We hear the usual complaints – "standard", "typical", "a Marriott is a Marriott" – but just as many compliments about this "friendliest of Marriott properties" boasting a "beautiful" Port Everglades setting with "wonderful" marina views (you can "dream of your yacht"), "good service", a "great pool" and "fabulous early-bird dinner with sunset over the waterway"; it's very convenient for pre- and post-cruise passengers too.

Marriott's Harbor Beach Resort 589R (35S)   23 | 22 | 21 | 24 | $182
3030 Holiday Dr., Fort Lauderdale; (954) 525-4000; (800) 222-6543; FAX: (954) 766-6152
■ It's not a mirage – this "big", "luxurious" "oasis" earns its ranking as Fort Lauderdale's top lodging by being both an "excellent convention hotel" and "the best affordable family resort in the area"; while rooms are "nice" (dissenters say "average"), what really excites surveyors are the "beautiful grounds", "service-oriented staff", "wonderful oceanfront setting" with a "great beach", "fantastic", "plush" pool area and five tennis courts; "complete and friendly", it feels "like an island resort."

Radisson Bahia Mar Beach Resort 299R (1S)   18 | 17 | 17 | 18 | $152
801 Seabreeze Blvd., Fort Lauderdale; (954) 764-2233; (800) 327-8154; FAX: (954) 524-6912
◪ Smack on the Downtown beachfront sits this high-rise resort with "perfect views" and a landmark 350-slip marina on a site that's been attracting sailors since 1875, when it was a haven for shipwreck survivors; these days there's tennis, fishing, an outdoor pool, a fitness center and waterskiing, yet some rate it all only "so-so" – critics note that though "rooms have been freshened" by a recent renovation (they're now "bright and airy"), the staff still "needs to work on service "

Riverside Hotel 102R (7S)   16 | 20 | 18 | 16 | $121
620 E. Las Olas Blvd., Fort Lauderdale; (954) 467-0671; (800) 325-3280; FAX: (954) 462-2148
◪ "Right on revitalized Las Olas Boulevard", this '30s "jewel in an area of glitz" with Cuban terra-cotta floors, Jacobian oak furnishings and native coral fireplaces is getting some much-needed revitalizing of its own, which may address low room scores and gripes about "shabby" accommodations; the "friendly, helpful" staff and the "excellent new Indigo restaurant" serving Indonesian cuisine are more signs of a brighter future.

Westin Hotel Fort Lauderdale 260R (33S)   21 | 20 | 18 | 20 | $142
(fka Westin Hotel Cypress Creek)
400 Corporate Dr., Fort Lauderdale; (954) 772-1331; (800) 228-3000; FAX: (954) 772-6867
■ A "good business hotel", this glass structure in the Uptown office district right off I-95 is equipped with extensive meeting facilities and enhanced by an "excellent staff, large rooms and a good restaurant", the Cypress Room; yet even with the "beautiful setting" among gardens adjacent to a three-acre lagoon, a few gripe about the "terrible location" surrounded by busy highways.

Wyndham Hotel Fort Lauderdale Airport
17 | 17 | 15 | 16 | $126

244R (6S)
(fka Sheraton Design Center)
1825 Griffin Rd., Dania; (954) 920-3500; (800) 325-3535; FAX: (954) 920-3571

■ "If you must stay at the airport, this is the place to be" is the consensus on this "adequate and comfortable" chainer that's also just steps from the Design Center of the Americas; tennis, racquetball, a "tiny" outdoor heated pool and 11 meeting rooms (capacity 500) round out the facilities, but everyone agrees about its "best feature": five minutes to your flight.

Fort Myers

Sanibel Harbour Resort & Spa 320R (122S)
22 | 21 | 20 | 22 | $159

17260 Harbour Pointe Dr., Fort Myers; (941) 466-4000; (800) 767-7777; FAX: (941) 466-6050

◪ A "relaxing, comfy" resort that's "great for families", located at the tip of the mainland before the Sanibel Causeway; the tennis center (13 courts) and a "great spa" – 40,000 square feet including an extensive fitness center with indoor and outdoor pools – help vacationers work off the "great cuisine" found at Chez le Bear and Promenade restaurants; but a few critics cite a "minute beach" and "uncaring staff."

Gasparilla Island

Gasparilla Inn & Cottages 80R (50S) ⊄
23 | 24 | 22 | 23 | $196

500 Palm Ave., Gasparilla Island; (941) 964-2201; FAX: (941) 964-2733

■ "Step back in time" at this "old-fashioned" 1912 landmark, a "unique", somewhat "formal" Old Southern Florida–style beachfront resort "catering to generations" of families who would like it to "be kept a secret"; golf, tennis, swimming and croquet are on-site, while tarpon, grouper and snook wait to be caught nearby; N.B. the social season (mid-December to mid-April) sees the full American plan in effect (with jackets and ties after 6 PM); things get just a bit looser in tarpon season (mid-April to mid-June) – and all year it's cash only.

Haines City

Grenelefe Golf & Tennis Resort (900S)
20 | 19 | 15 | 21 | $144

3200 State Rd. 546, Haines City; (941) 422-7511; (800) 237-9549; FAX: (941) 421-5000

◪ "A golfer's paradise" with a total of 54 holes also diverts guests with tennis, bicycling and boating; it's a "good family resort" (a half hour to Disney) that has meeting facilities too (capacity 1,300); but a few warn that while some of the condos are "well kept", others are "poorly maintained" and the "out-of-the-way" location has one duffer commenting "I'd hate to be a golfer's widow."

Howey-in-the-Hills

Mission Inn Golf & Tennis Resort 132R (44S)
20 | 23 | 22 | 23 | $144

10400 Country Rd. 48, Howey-in-the-Hills; (352) 324-3101; (800) 874-9053; FAX: (352) 324-2636

◪ "The El Campeon course is a must do" say fans of the Charles E. Clarke–designed course at this "delightful" Spanish colonial–style "getaway" that also offers a popular newer Gary Koch–designed course; eight tennis courts, boating, cycling and a pool offer other challenges, and execs can share the pain during the 'experiential' outdoor training course (and also in the 15 meeting rooms); while some call it "wonderful even if you don't play golf", a few dismiss it as "mostly for business meetings" and in the "middle of nowhere" (actually it's about a half-hour from Orlando).

Islamorada

Cheeca Lodge 139R (64S)
22 | 23 | 23 | 24 | $223

Mile Marker 82, Islamorada; (305) 664-4651; (800) 327-2888; FAX: (305) 664-2893

■ A "fisherman's paradise" that's also "great for kiddies", this 27-acre "service-oriented" "oasis" in an "incredible" "lovely beach setting" in the casual Keys offers a nine-hole golf course, boating, tennis, waterskiing, swimming and kids' programs as well as "outstanding food" at Atlantic's restaurant ("best-ever Key lime pie"); while the "large, homey rooms" get several calls for "updating", most guests are pleased overall, though one angler advises "if you don't fish, stay away", but if you do, "it's heavenly."

Jacksonville

Club Hotel by Doubletree 164R (3S)
▽ 18 | 16 | 17 | 16 | $106

4700 Salisbury Rd., Jacksonville; (904) 281-9700; (800) 222-TREE; FAX: (904) 281-1957

◪ "Fairly priced" "pleasant rooms" can be expected at this "business hotel" with on-site exercise equipment and an outdoor pool, but the "out-in-the-sticks" suburban location (25 miles from the airport) doesn't thrill everyone.

Marriott Jacksonville 250R (6S)   20 | 20 | 17 | 17 | $125
4760 Salisbury Rd., Jacksonville; (904) 296-2222; (800) 228-9290; FAX: (904) 296-7561
☑ All the "typical Marriott" features are here: a "basic room", indoor/outdoor pools, a weight room, meeting facilities, even tennis courts; and all the typical voter reactions too, from "a solid hotel" to "nothing special."

Omni Jacksonville Hotel 350R (4S)   20 | 19 | 18 | 18 | $130
245 Water St., Jacksonville; (904) 355-6664; (800) THE-OMNI; FAX: (904) 791-4809
■ Recently renovated rooms get positive reviews at this "standard business hotel" that is nevertheless Jacksonville's "best Downtown" with a "very friendly staff" and "good food" at Juliette's as well as a rooftop pool and fitness room; a handful of critics claim the riverfront location is its "only asset", but they're a minority.

Jupiter

Jupiter Beach Resort 182R (4S)   19 | 18 | 19 | 20 | $150
5 North A1A, Jupiter; (561) 746-2511; (800) 228-8810; FAX: (561) 744-1741
☑ A "small beach club atmosphere" prevails at this resort in a "great location" north of Palm Beach; on the ocean and adjacent to seven miles of publicly protected undeveloped beachfront, the locale is favored by endangered turtles for laying eggs and by humans for "ocean walks"; indoors, a '96 $2.5-million guestroom renovation earns compliments for "nice rooms", and though a few toss barbs at "nonexistent service", just as many praise "eager to please" staff; at press time, the property was in the process of being converted to a time-share resort.

Key Largo

Marriott's Key Largo Bay Beach Resort 133R (20S)   21 | 20 | 19 | 22 | $171
103800 Overseas Hwy., Key Largo; (305) 453-0000; (800) 932-9332; FAX: (305) 453-0093
☑ We wonder if surveyors stayed at the same place – devotees declare it "the best resort in the upper Keys", a "place to relax" with "good service", plenty of activities (including a kids' program) and a "beautiful location"; but naysayers slam an "old facility on an old island"; ratings side with the ayes, and a health club and convention facilities, scheduled to open in 1997, should liven things up even more.

Ocean Reef Club 143R (147S)   23 | 23 | 22 | 25 | $223
31 Ocean Reef Dr., Key Largo; (305) 367-2611; (800) 741-REEF; FAX: (305) 367-2224
■ Privacy is the name of the game, so the only guests here are members and their invitees; once in, you find out "what a resort should feel like" – there's the "beautiful setting" on 4,000 acres and "wonderful facilities" (including two golf courses, 11 tennis courts, outdoor pool, a marina and even a private airstrip); the closed-door policy and strict dress code inspire a few sniffs of "snobbish" – but isn't that the point?

Key West

Banana Bay Resort - Key West 30R (12S)   – | – | – | – | M
2319 North Roosevelt Blvd., Key West; (305) 296-6925; (800) BANANA-1; FAX: (305) 296-2004
This intimate, adults-only resort overlooking the Gulf of Mexico opened in 1995 and offers a three-night Romantic Escape package for R&R around the pool (though dive trips and other water sports can also be arranged); a fitness center is on-site, and suites are equipped with kitchenettes; while within walking distance of Old Town, it's a mile from Duval Street, which may inconvenience those whose collection of gaudy T-shirts could use another entry.

Cuban Club Suites (8S)   – | – | – | – | E
1102-1108 Duval St., Key West; (305) 296-4065; (800) 432-4849; FAX: (305) 293-7669
Set amongst the T-shirt hawkers on Key West's main drag, this 19th-century Bahamian-style landmark seems a world away; many of the one- and two-bedroom suites open onto the wraparound balcony, where antique Cuban rockers invite lazybones to sit and watch the town walk by; all suites have microwaves and most feature full kitchens; there's a museum of Key West history in the lobby.

Holiday Inn La Concha 150R (10S)   17 | 18 | 16 | 18 | $140
430 Duval St., Key West; (305) 296-2991; (800) 745-2191; FAX: (305) 294-3283
☑ "Comfortable and conveniently located" in the heart of Key West's historic district, this 1920s art deco landmark listed on the National Register affords a "great rooftop view" of the southernmost sunset in the country; the "pleasant" indoor pool and "friendly service" get nods, but the hotel promotes and revels in its Duval Street location, which can mean "dreadful noise" and definitely means "avoid during spring break."

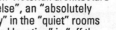
Hyatt Key West 110R (10S)   22 | 22 | 21 | 22 | $208
601 Front St., Key West; (305) 296-9900; (800) 233-1234; FAX: (305) 292-1038

■ "Watch the sun go down from your balcony" at this "posh destination" in Key West's historic district, so "close to the nightlife that there's no need to drive"; for many fans this is the "favorite choice in Key West", but value-driven voters groan it's "overpriced" considering the "small, undistinctive rooms", "bathtub-size beach" and "teeny pool."

MARQUESA HOTEL 25R (2S)   27 | 28 | 28 | 26 | $192
600 Fleming St., Key West; (305) 292-1919; (800) 869-4631; FAX: (305) 294-2121

■ Florida's top-rated hotel, this "sublime" "little jewel" of conch-Victorian architecture strikes surveyors as "head and shoulders above anywhere else", an "absolutely charming", "wonderful respite" "offering peace and tranquility" in the "quiet" rooms and around the two pools in the "beautiful" courtyard; the "good location" is "off the beaten path" and yet a short walk to noisy Duval Street dives; even better, the on-site Cafe Marquesa offers "impeccable" Eclectic–New World dining.

Marriott Reach Resort 70R (79S)   22 | 21 | 20 | 21 | $189
1435 Simonton St., Key West; (305) 296-5000; (800) 874-4118; FAX: (305) 296-3008

■ On a 700-foot private Atlantic beach, this "pretty in pastel" Marriott prompts division all around, beginning with that beach ("best in Key West" vs. "small") and continuing on to the rooms ("well kept" vs. "need refurbishing") and the staff ("such service!" vs. "snotty"); some debaters maintain it's "best for the younger nightlife crowd."

Marriott's Casa Marina Resort 240R (71S)   21 | 21 | 20 | 23 | $188
1500 Reynold's St., Key West; (305) 296-3535; (800) 626-0777; FAX: (305) 296-3008

■ Admirers say this 1921 Spanish-style property "captures the Key West flavor" in a "terrific beach setting" that's "away from the hubbub but close enough"; the resort "caters to families" with an array of sports and kids' programs, and to conference planners who can book the 12 meeting rooms; but critics gripe that the "fancy facade obscures the ordinary" (including "plain" rooms that need a "spruce-up"); more jolly-minded vacationers shrug it off at the Sun Sun – "the best bar to watch sunsets."

Ocean Key House Suite Resort and Marina   25 | 22 | 21 | 22 | $208
28R (68S)
Zero Duval St., Key West; (305) 296-7701; (800) 328-9815; FAX: (305) 292-7685

■ An "elegant resort" in a "terrific" location at the base of Duval Street provides a primo spot for viewing "pretty sunsets", and the romantic ambiance continues in the suites, where "huge" Jacuzzis are "great for loving couples"; all surveyors aren't as affectionate about the staff, however, which can be "very helpful" or offer "skimpy service"; "delicious" local cuisine at Zeros and at the raw bar and grill helps create good memories.

Pier House 130R (12S)   22 | 21 | 22 | 22 | $209
1 Duval St., Key West; (305) 296-4600; (800) 327-8340; FAX: (305) 296-7568

■ It's hard to beat the Gulf location of this recently renovated hip resort in Old Town for inspiring contemplation of "the best sunset in Florida" amid "tropical, laid-back surroundings" that include a small beach, outdoor pool and full-service spa; although reactions to rooms range from "comfortable" to "minimal", most agree on the "good" dining at the Pier House Restaurant and Harborview Cafe; shy types and extroverts take note: it's home to one of the world's great costume extravaganzas during October's Fantasy Fest.

Lake Wales

Chalet Suzanne 30R   19 | 20 | 26 | 19 | $165
3800 Chalet Suzanne Dr., Lake Wales; (941) 676-6011; (800) 433-6011;
FAX: (941) 676-1814

■ "A charming oasis where everything is tasteful" or a "wonderfully crackpot" hideaway – either way, many are seduced by this "unique" Bavarian-style inn (complete with its own soup cannery and private airstrip) run since 1931 by the Hinshaw family; service is "outstanding" and most agree the restaurant serves "delicious and original" Continental food with a Florida touch; but rooms are the only sticking point, with some finding them "funky" but "beautiful", others giving an "ok" at best.

Little Torch Key

LITTLE PALM ISLAND (30S)   27 | 26 | 27 | 25 | $322
28500 Oversea Hwy., Little Torch Key; (305) 872-2524; (800) 343-8567; FAX: (305) 872-4843
■ "You'll think you've landed in heaven" at "Gilligan's Island for millionaires" three miles off the main string of Keys; the thatched-roof villas and sandy beach make for a "sophisticated hideaway" where even the Professor could "unwind and relax", and Gilligan himself would find that it's a "great place to do nothing" – except maybe eat, since there's "exquisite dining" on French-Caribbean cuisine; some (obviously not Thurston or Lovey Howell III) sneer that it's "impossibly pretentious", but ratings support those who ask "who needs Tahiti?"

Longboat Key

Colony Beach & Tennis Resort (235S)   22 | 21 | 22 | 22 | $209
1620 Gulf of Mexico Dr., Longboat Key; (941) 383-6464; (800) 4-COLONY; FAX: (941) 383-7549
■ Living up to its name, the Colony offers a "beautiful stretch of beach" and "great tennis" (21 courts) as well as food that ranges from "good" to "incredible"; however, its other features draw mixed responses, with some applauding the "wonderful condos" and critics warning of "hit or miss" units; N.B. room renovations began in late 1996, after most surveyors had already cast their votes.

RESORT AT LONGBOAT KEY CLUB (232S)   26 | 23 | 21 | 25 | $235
301 Gulf of Mexico Dr., Longboat Key; (941) 383-8821; (800) 237-8821; FAX: (941) 387-1617
■ This "wonderful resort" "pampers you" with "understated elegance" and "spacious" suites equipped with kitchens and washer/dryers; adding even more attraction are the "beautiful beach", "good golf" (45 championship holes), "very fine tennis" on 38 courts (the staff "is conscientious about getting you games") and a new, fully equipped fitness center; parents, heads up: it's "great for kids, tennis and Sunday brunch."

Marathon

Hawk's Cay Resort 157R (19S)   19 | 20 | 19 | 21 | $174
Mile Marker 61, Marathon; (305) 743-7000; (800) 432-2242; FAX: (305) 743-5215
◪ "The seals and dolphins give a fine show" at the "interesting dolphin center", part of this resort with marina on a private island that's "as close to the Caribbean as the Keys get"; there's "family appeal" aplenty ("good kids' programs") and it's also a "fun place for a meeting" with a "nice pool" and "beautiful beach", but doubters dismiss a "dated" facility with a "Middle America feel" that has "seen better days."

Marco Island

Marco Island Hilton Beach Resort 265R (33S)   22 | 21 | 20 | 22 | $172
560 S. Collier Blvd., Marco Island; (941) 394-5000; (800) 443-4550; FAX: (941) 394-5251
■ "There's no better place when the snow falls up north" than on the beach at this "perfect medium-size resort" on the Gulf of Mexico; "large rooms" and a "really clean" look make it "a good choice", and "wonderful amenities" include boating, fishing, swimming, tennis and waterskiing.

Marriott's Marco Island Resort and Golf Club 673R (62S)    21 | 22 | 20 | 23 | $174
400 S. Collier Blvd., Marco Island; (941) 394-2511; (800) 438-4373; FAX: (941) 642-2688
■ A "beautiful and well-kept beach" on the Gulf of Mexico affords "spectacular sunset" views, and the meeting space for 2,300 has business travelers vying with families for the "large", "good" rooms (the North Tower rooms were renovated in the summer of '96); in addition to 18 links of golf, the "natural setting" on 30 acres offers biking, boating, fishing, swimming, waterskiing and tennis; simply put, it's "very comfortable, with no attitude."

Radisson Suite Beach Resort 52R (217S)   20 | 18 | 16 | 19 | $151
600 S. Collier Blvd., Marco Island; (941) 394-4100; (800) 333-3333; FAX: (941) 394-0262
◪ Vacationers particularly like the "awesome view of the Gulf from spacious suites" at this high-rise where all accommodations have screened-in porches and all suites have kitchenettes; and when they head downstairs there's a "great pool" and a "stunning beachfront with water sports galore" including boating, fishing, jet skiing and waterskiing; Mango Leone's also earns kudos for "surprisingly good" Florida fare, but naysayers complain that the "converted condos" are "not classy."

Miami/Miami Beach
TOP 10 OVERALL

BEST OVERALL

27 Fisher Island Club
26 Grand Bay
25 Turnberry Isle Resort & Club
24 Biltmore Hotel & Golf Resort
   Delano
   Mayfair House
23 Omni Colonnade
22 Doral Golf Resort & Spa
   Hyatt Regency Coral Gables
   Sonesta Beach Resort

BEST VALUES

Omni Colonnade
Crowne Plaza Miami
Hyatt Regency Coral Gables
Marriott Biscayne Bay
Biltmore Hotel & Golf Resort
Mayfair House
Sheraton Biscayne Bay
Park Central
Inter-Continental Miami
Hyatt Regency Miami

R	S	D	P	$
–	–	–	–	E

Albion, The 95R (15S)
1650 James Ave., Miami Beach; (305) 913-1000; (888) 665-0008; FAX: (305) 674-0507
After a $10-million redo, the 1939 art deco Albion reopened in early '97, heating up the hype-heavy 'battle' between its owners, the heirs of Steve Rubell and Rubell's former partner Ian Schrager, owner of SoBe's previously unchallenged kingdom of hip, the Delano; designed by Carlos Zapata, it offers rooms with minimalist decor and maximum amenities and a 'vertical pond' in the lobby; though aimed at beautiful young things, its proximity to the ocean and convention center should give it wider appeal.

Alexander All-Suite Luxury Hotel (152S)

22	21	22	20	$222

5225 Collins Ave., Miami Beach; (305) 865-6500; (800) 327-6121; FAX: (305) 864-8525
☑ A "gracious old-world hotel" with a "great lobby", this beachfront neo-deco complex offers only suites, all with balconies and kitchens; while they earn solid ratings, comments indicate that units vary ("lovely", "well appointed" vs. "old bathrooms", "poor furnishings"), perhaps due to the fact that all are privately owned condos; "swank" French-Continental Dominique's wins points for its "magnificent ocean view."

Astor Hotel 26R (15S) ▽ 25 | 21 | 26 | 24 | $200
956 Washington Ave., Miami Beach; (305) 531-8081; (800) 270-4981; FAX: (305) 531-3193
■ One starstruck surveyor reports "lots of celebrities" at the "tastefully elegant" Astor, a historic boutique hotel with outdoor pool that's an oasis of "quiet" "in the center of activity"; within walking distance of sandy shores and chic South Beach nightlife, it's also a destination for "great dining" in "one of South Beach's finest restaurants", the very hip Astor Place Bar & Grill.

BILTMORE HOTEL & GOLF RESORT 244R (35S) 24 | 24 | 24 | 26 | $195
1200 Anastasia Ave., Coral Gables; (305) 445-1926; (800) 727-1926; FAX: (305) 448-9976
■ "Return to elegance" in a "beautifully redone" 1926 Mediterranean-revival resort famous for its "magnificent architecture" and "romantic grandeur", not to mention the "most beautiful pool in the USA" – all of which once attracted the Windsors and Howard Hughes and today sets the stage for frequent modeling shoots; "spectacular rooms" are "well priced" ("the lobby ceilings alone are worth the room rate"), and the French-Italian Il Ristorante offers "excellent dining" and service; an 18-hole golf course and full-service spa complete the "glamorous" picture.

Casa Grande Hotel (33S) ▽ 27 | 22 | 23 | 21 | $194
834 Ocean Dr., Miami Beach; (305) 672-7003; (800) 688-7678; FAX: (305) 673-3669
■ "Where civilization meets the South Beach scene" is one voter's take on this "pampering", "very elegant" all-suite boutique hotel built in 1993; accommodations, each with a kitchenette, are "indeed grand", and the "great location" plants guests at the epicenter of SoBe life; the on-premises restaurant Mezzaluna serves Italian fare.

Crowne Plaza Miami 470R (58S) 19 | 18 | 18 | 19 | $140
1601 Biscayne Blvd., Miami; (305) 374-0000; (800) 2-CROWNE; FAX: (305) 374-0020
◪ While some say this hotel's Downtown setting near the Port of Miami is "very nice, especially if you're staying near the water to go on a cruise", others question the safety of the location; its "big rooms" and public spaces were recently renovated, though the "disorganized" staff could also use polish according to critics; a big plus: the on-site restaurant The Fish Market serves some of "the best fish in Miami" plus "scrumptious desserts."

DELANO HOTEL 171R (16S) 24 | 22 | 24 | 25 | $219
1685 Collins Ave., Miami Beach; (305) 672-2000; (800) 555-5001; FAX: (305) 532-0099
◪ "Not just a hotel – an experience" that's "dramatically theatrical, like a stage set" designed in "sexy" "all-white" by Philippe Starck to "make you feel cool" while mingling with South Beach scene makers in the "ethereal lobby" of this "chic" oceanfront happening; rooms are "small but nice" and the Blue Door restaurant is known for "excellent" French–Middle Eastern food; detractors grouse about "snooty" service, but realists shrug "of course" – "even the beautiful people get attitude" here.

Doral Golf Resort & Spa 600R (94S) 22 | 21 | 20 | 24 | $215
4400 NW 87th Ave., Miami; (305) 592-2000; (800) 71-DORAL; FAX: (305) 594-4682
◪ A "golfer's dream" plus a "world-class spa" make a happy marriage at this recently renovated complex; set amidst "attractive grounds", the resort boasts five championship courses, tennis, indoor and outdoor pools and proximity to the Miami airport (but no beach), and if that's not enough, the "gorgeous" Doral Saturnia spa across the street "offers everything"; some respondents say "if you don't play golf it's deadly" (but it's "heaven" if you do) and many complain of "ancient rooms", but a $30-million redo may soften critics who warn "choose your room with care."

Doubletree Grand Hotel 126R (26S) ▽ 21 | 19 | 21 | 21 | $142
1717 N. Bayshore Dr., Miami; (305) 372-0313; (800) 222-TREE; FAX: (305) 372-9455
■ This modern half-condo, half-hotel complex with tower views of Biscayne Bay is "fine" for a Downtown base with a skywalk connection to Omni International Mall; if guests are determined not to step outside, they'll find American (Blue Water Bistro), Chinese (Tony Chen's Water Club) and Italian (Cafe Bolla) food on-site; "try one of the suites – a great value" advises one satisfied surveyor.

Doubletree Hotel at Coconut Grove 173R (19S) 18 | 18 | 18 | 17 | $154
2649 S. Bayshore Dr., Coconut Grove; (305) 858-2500; (800) 222-TREE; FAX: (305) 858-9117
◪ "A very trendy location" in smart Coconut Grove is the chief lure of this neighbor of the Grand Bay Hotel and Mayfair House shops; while some find it "pleasant" and "good for a business trip", no one is overly excited, with critics opining it "survives on location and cookies" and suggesting "bring a cleaning service before you check in"; N.B. high floors may have views, but they'll be closer to the throbbing rooftop disco.

Eden Roc Resort & Spa 300R (49S)
| 18 | 18 | 17 | 19 | $178 |

4525 Collins Ave., Miami Beach; (305) 531-0000; (800) 525-8353; FAX: (305) 538-4227

◪ "Remodeled to look as bad as it did in the '50s" say critics of this 40-year-old art deco "relic"; while some get a kick out of bashing its "deliriously tacky lobby" and "ingeniously hideous" decor, others claim it's "getting better all the time" (scores are indeed up since our last *Survey*), with "nice" views from "clean" rooms plus a "great health club" with spa services; expect "crowds" ("if you like being a sardine at the pool it's for you") and "noise" and note that some complain of "rude" staff.

FISHER ISLAND CLUB (60S)
| 27 | 27 | 25 | 27 | $319 |

1 Fisher Island Dr., Fisher Island; (305) 535-6020; (800) 537-3708; FAX: (305) 535-6003

■ "World-class perfection", "outstanding in every way", "the lap of luxury" gush voters who rate this retreat tops in the Miami area; "lifestyles of the rich and famous" are played out on a "secluded" island in Biscayne Bay (accessible only by air or boat) where guests stay in "extraordinary" 1920s cottages surrounding a former Vanderbilt mansion; it has "every amenity", including "delicious" food from two restaurants, a full spa, fitness center, 18 "first-class" tennis courts, complimentary cabanas, a golf course (complimentary cart) and boating; expensive, yes, but "the only way to go."

Florida Suites (175S)
| – | – | – | – | M |

169 Lincoln Rd., Ste. 324, Miami Beach; (305) 673-5390; (800) 327-1039; FAX: (305) 672-9010

Few surveyors have tried this all-suiter, despite the fact that it's "priced nicely" and families and pets are welcome; a modern, oceanfront property in the heart of South Beach, it features kitchenettes in all accommodations, making it a good choice for longer stays, plus a fitness center and outdoor pool.

Fontainebleau Hilton Resort 1146R (60S)
| 19 | 18 | 18 | 21 | $186 |

4441 Collins Ave., Miami Beach; (305) 538-2000; (800) 548-8886; FAX: (305) 531-9274

◪ "Ya want big and sassy? – this is it", the eccentric epitome of what people love to hate and hate to love about old-time Miami Beach; this '50s-era beachfront behemoth is "an attraction in itself", lauded by loyalists as "a Miami staple" with an "amazingly vibrant" ambiance, but dismissed by critics as a "monstrosity" – "too big, too loud, too everything", in "need of a face-lift" and "professional staff"; it has Vegas-style entertainment, 10 restaurants, multiple "fantastic" pools, a large beach, tennis courts, a spa and fitness center – "you've got to try it once."

GRAND BAY HOTEL 131R (47S)
| 27 | 26 | 26 | 26 | $233 |

2669 S. Bayshore Dr., Coconut Grove; (305) 858-9600; (800) 327-2788; FAX: (305) 854-7998

■ "Elegant, contemporary rooms" (all with terraces), a "fantastic pool" and "excellent service" bring surveyors back to "the most stylish Euro act in town"; a "luxurious", "exceptionally well-run" hotel overlooking Dinner Key in "cool Coconut Grove", it's "comfortable, not stuffy" with "a real happening lobby and bar scene" and "impeccable" regional Florida fare in the highly rated Grand Cafe; overall it puts on "a class act – and you pay for it."

Greenview Hotel (44S)
| – | – | – | – | M |

1671 Washington Ave., Miami Beach; (305) 531-6588; FAX: (305) 531-4580

Yet another noted art deco renovation, the spare, elegant Greenview angles to attract the fashion trade with a rooftop photo deck and solarium, wardrobe rooms and a periodical library as well as custom-designed furniture, luxe bedding and fine toiletries; assets include a central location across from the convention center and two blocks from the beach, and complimentary breakfast.

Grove Isle Club & Resort 40R (9S)
| 23 | 20 | 23 | 20 | $227 |

4 Grove Isle Dr., Coconut Grove; (305) 858-8300; (800) 88-GROVE; FAX: (305) 858-5908

■ "A glass of champagne" at check-in lets "you know you're in for a treat" at this "very romantic" hotel in a "fantastic" waterside setting on a private island; "great big beautiful rooms" with private balconies, "excellent" gourmet fare, "nice grounds", an outdoor pool, 12 tennis courts and a fitness center plus "sumptuous" special touches like terra-cotta floors explain why it has a loyal return crowd that ranges from "entertainers who don't want to be seen" to business groups; for a few dissenters the "off-the-beaten-path" locale is "too isolated."

Hyatt Regency Coral Gables 192R (50S)   23 | 22 | 21 | 21 | $167
50 Alhambra Plaza, Coral Gables; (305) 441-1234; (800) 233-1234; FAX: (305) 441-0520
■ "Old-world atmosphere with modern conveniences" is nice enough at this "relaxing hotel" with an "accommodating" staff, "charming lobby" and "great rooftop pool", but what really gets shoppers' pulses pumping is its location within walking distance of Miracle Mile; execs appreciate its 12 meeting rooms, new business center and computer hookups in rooms, and when work is done, there's Spanish and Pacific Rim fare at the "gourmet-all-the-way" Two Sisters restaurant and a big "singles scene" at the popular Alcazaba nightclub.

Hyatt Regency Miami 557R (58S)   19 | 18 | 17 | 17 | $152
400 SE Second Ave., Miami; (305) 358-1234; (800) 233-1234; FAX: (305) 374-1728
☑ Business travelers can check in to a "solid, dependable hotel" at the Miami Convention Center that provides "spacious, well-appointed rooms", some with "pleasant balcony vistas", plus a "very helpful staff", 40 meeting rooms, an exercise center, outdoor pool and two tennis courts; while it's also "convenient for the first night before a cruise", some feel it has "no personality" and, as with many Downtown hotels, a few say "be careful outside."

Indian Creek Hotel 55R (6S)   – | – | – | – | M
2727 Indian Creek Dr., Miami Beach; (305) 531-2727; (800) 491-2772; FAX: (305) 531-5651
The few surveyors who have ferreted out this 1936 art deco Central Beach landmark report it's a "totally film noir great place" whose careful restoration, complete with the original Norman Bel Geddes–designed furniture, has won accolades from architects and preservationists; close to both the convention center and hot SoBe, it's just one block from the beach and offers an outdoor pool, business center and Pan Court, a Pan Asian–Caribbean eatery serving "terrific dinners"; a/c in some rooms.

Inter-Continental Miami, Hotel 610R (34S)   21 | 19 | 19 | 20 | $168
100 Chopin Plaza, Miami; (305) 577-1000; (800) 327-0200; FAX: (305) 577-0384
☑ This "top-flight business hotel for Downtown Miami" puts up guests in "spacious", "comfortable rooms" with "fine water views" of Biscayne Bay and the "best bathrooms anywhere"; a "terrific" outdoor pool and Le Pavillon restaurant are other pluses, but the place "needs a real gym" and a better-prepared staff – "train them!" pleads one critic.

Lafayette Hotel 50R (5S)   – | – | – | – | E
944 Collins Ave., Miami Beach; (305) 673-2262; (800) 673-2262; FAX: (305) 534-5399
While unknown to our reviewers, the family-owned Lafayette is a quiet and affordable Mediterranean-style getaway within the pulsating South Beach scene, providing simple, pine-furnished rooms that appeal to an international clientele (the library stocks books and magazines in English, French, Spanish and Italian); there's no pool on-site, but it's only a block to the beach; all rooms have a/c.

Marlin Hotel (12S)   21 | 19 | 20 | 21 | $181
1200 Collins Ave., Miami Beach; (305) 673-8770; (800) 688-7678; FAX: (305) 673-9609
☑ "Very cool, very hip" and perhaps the primo place to be snubbed by a model, the art deco Marlin is "more arty than comfortable", but the Euros staying at party central aren't here to sleep and probably don't notice that the brightly decorated suites (all with kitchenettes) are "not as terrific as expected" – but "cute"; the Leslie Cafe serves light fare (designer pizzas, burgers) in a great spot for observing South Beach passersby, while the rooftop terrace is more private.

Marriott Hotel & Marina Biscayne Bay 582R (21S)   20 | 18 | 17 | 18 | $144
1633 N. Bayshore Dr., Miami; (305) 374-3900; (800) 228-9290; FAX: (305) 375-0597
☑ Like other Downtowners, this modern high-rise on Biscayne Bay provides "great views" in a "not-great neighborhood"; "comfortable" and "clean", "it serves its purpose" for those heading for cruise ships and conventions, but it's a "standard" Marriott and some wish they'd "redecorate soon."

Mayfair House Hotel (185S)   26 | 24 | 23 | 21 | $193
3000 Florida Ave., Coconut Grove; (305) 441-0000; (800) 433-4555; FAX: (305) 447-9173
■ "Private hot tubs on balconies" – "hot dang!" shout the amorous in love with the "romantic" ambiance of the "elegant", "unique" suites (each with terrace, "lots of mahogany" furnishings, stocked minibar and sitting area) in this "eclectic and fun" Coconut Grove hotel; the shopping mall locale lends an "odd atmosphere", but most agree it's "a beautiful place" with "terrific" New World food at the Mayfair Grill; one problem – those "steamy" tubs seem to create a "mildew smell" in some rooms, according to several surveyors.

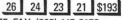

Miami Beach Ocean Resort 238R (6S)   ▽ 19 | 19 | 17 | 18 | $130
3025 Collins Ave., Miami Beach; (305) 534-0505; (800) 550-0505; FAX: (305) 534-0515
■ Just north of the art deco district, this European-style hotel with a landscaped tropical pool area is "good for families" since it's "on the beach and not too expensive"; it's exec friendly too, with five meeting rooms (capacity 200) and a business center; the International food is "tasty and plentiful" at the Palm Garden.

Occidental Plaza Hotel 44R (90S)   – | – | – | – | M
(fka H.J. Occidental Plaza Hotel)
100 SE Fourth St., Miami; (305) 374-5100; (800) 521-5100; FAX: (305) 381-9826
Having experienced yet another name change since our last *Survey*, this "serviceable", inexpensive Downtown high-rise doesn't draw many surveyors despite its being next to the James L. Knight Convention Center and within walking distance of the financial center; it's a good bunk for business stays, with a business center and meeting facilities for up to 300 plus an on-site restaurant and cafe, but a few voters urge caution when walking in the area.

Ocean Front Hotel 8R (19S)   – | – | – | – | E
1230-38 Ocean Dr., Miami Beach; (305) 672-2579; (800) 783-1725; FAX: (305) 672-7665
"Fabulous French style on South Beach" raves one fan of this 1936 Mediterranean grande dame whose 1994 renovation won honors; French fare and seafood are on the moderately priced menu at Les Deux Fontaines restaurant, which offers "great dining in the courtyard."

Omni Colonnade Hotel 140R (17S)   23 | 22 | 22 | 23 | $167
180 Aragon Ave., Coral Cables; (305) 441-3929; (800) THE-OMNI; FAX: (305) 445-3929
◩ Admirers are plentiful for this "comfortable", "well-located" Mediterranean-style hotel "in the center of Coral Gables" featuring "decent" rooms, a rooftop pool and fitness center and a historic (1926) rotunda; it manages to be "very accommodating to the business crowd" and "good for young kids", although comments vary concerning service ("friendly and courteous" vs. "lagging"); Doc Dammer's serves Miami nueva cocina for dinner.

Park Central Hotel 112R (8S)   15 | 15 | 17 | 18 | $138
(fka Park Central & Imperial Hotel)
640 Ocean Dr., Miami Beach; (305) 538-1611; (800) PARK CENTRAL; FAX: (305) 534-7520
◩ A "hip scene" animates the "beautiful" public spaces (with airy tropical ambiance) and "great pool" at this "nicely renovated" 1937 art deco beachfront landmark, a member of the Historic Hotels of America; while a few find some of the pleasant, retro rooms "too small and basic", suites with kitchenettes are available, and there's a/c in all quarters ("a plus for those hot Miami days"), a "good" restaurant (the Casablanca), fitness facilities, an open-air sculpture garden, a rooftop garden deck and a "terrific" location on Ocean Drive.

Place St. Michel, Hotel 24R (3S)   ▽ 21 | 23 | 27 | 21 | $137
162 Alcazar Ave., Coral Gables; (305) 444-1666; (800) 848-HOTEL; FAX: (305) 529-0074
■ Offering "a welcome change" from the typical Miami scene, this small, 1926 Mediterranean-style landmark refreshes weary wayfarers with a "wonderful ambiance" that's "like being in Provence"; "charming but small rooms" and "personal service" bring fans back to this "old favorite", as does the "terrific" Restaurant St. Michel serving Contemporary American fare.

Radisson Mart Plaza 309R (25S)   ▽ 16 | 15 | 13 | 15 | $129
711 NW 72nd Ave., Miami; (305) 261-3800; (800) 333-3333; FAX: (305) 261-7665
■ Unless proximity to the airport and Merchandise Mart are important, this glass high-rise strikes surveyors as "inconvenient"; but to execs, it's an "ok" convention hotel with meeting space for 2,500, a business center and in-room computer hookups; a fitness center, outdoor pool and tennis and racquetball courts provide stress-reducing recreation.

Raleigh Hotel 93R (14S)   17 | 18 | 19 | 20 | $167
1775 Collins Ave., Miami Beach; (305) 534-6300; (800) 848-1775; FAX: (305) 538-8140
◩ "The most beautiful pool I've ever seen" agree bathing beauties, but when it comes to this circa 1941 oceanfront hotel's other qualities, surveyors tread water: some see a "sharp look" in the art deco decor and commend the "great staff", while others deem the rooms "too minimalist and cold" and the service "snotty"; the New American–Continental dining room is noted for "consistently good" food.

Ritz Plaza Hotel 128R (4S) ▽ 21 21 21 24 $203
1701 Collins Ave., Miami Beach; (305) 534-3500; (800) 522-6400; FAX: (305) 531-6928
■ Ground zero for the fashion faction, whose models and photographers fill this oceanfront 1940 art deco classic affiliated with the Historic Hotels of America; the on-site Ritz Cafe serves American fare, while Harry's Bar features lighter food selections; the few surveyors who have stayed here give it decent ratings, but some find it "disappointing compared to its reputation"; an outdoor pool and a/c in rooms help keep things even cooler.

Sheraton Bal Harbour Beach Resort 603R (26S) 20 20 18 21 $178
9701 Collins Ave., Bal Harbour; (305) 865-7511; (800) 999-9898; FAX: (305) 868-2571
☑ Its location "away from all the noise down on Collins Avenue" and across the street from the "sharp" Bal Harbour Shops draws kudos for this beachfront veteran; in addition to "great rooms", there's a "superb" new pool area thanks to a $12-million renovation that added a water slide, lagoon-style pools, waterfalls and restaurants: the Al Carbon serves steak and seafood with a Latin flavor, while the Bal Harbour Beach House offers oceanfront seafood dining.

Sheraton Biscayne Bay 582R (16S) 17 16 15 17 $135
495 Brickell Ave., Miami; (305) 373-6000; (800) 325-3535; FAX: (305) 372-9808
☑ "Adequate in all respects" sums up sentiments about this Downtown chainer, a "decent hotel in a good location" (though some think the "neighborhood is getting dangerous at night"); though "needs updating" is a common complaint, most voters wrote in before completion of the major 1996 renovation that refurbished all rooms and grounds and brought a new marina, from which a complimentary water shuttle ferries guests to coastal hot spots.

Sonesta Beach Resort Key Biscayne 280R (15S) 22 22 20 23 $195
350 Ocean Dr., Key Biscayne; (305) 361-2021; (800) SONESTA; FAX: (305) 361-3096
☑ "A gem on the island" is how escapists who "want to relax, not sightsee" describe this "beautiful but isolated" Key Biscayne resort; everyone likes the "great" white-sand beach, outdoor pool, 10 tennis courts and the 10 AM–10 PM kids' program, but while rooms are "pleasant" and boast "ocean views", some surveyors think it's time for an "upgrade"; the "fabulous staff" is a plus.

Tides, The 42R (3S) – – – – VE
1220 Ocean Dr., Miami Beach; (305) 604-5000; (800) OUTPOST; FAX: (305) 604-5180
South Beach's newest luxury hotel opened in May 1997 in an elegantly restored 1936 art deco landmark; all rooms feature VCRs, CD players and modem hookups plus full ocean views, and the Mediterranean dining room overlooks the hip street life on Ocean Drive; there's a heated pool (topless sunbathing permitted) on the mezzanine terrace and a full exercise facility on the ninth-floor terrace.

TURNBERRY ISLE RESORT & CLUB 298R (42S) 27 25 24 26 $251
19999 W. Country Club Dr., Aventura; (305) 932-6200; (800) 327-7028; FAX: (305) 933-6560
■ "Pure elegance" permeates this "touch of the Riviera in Florida" rave admirers of its "lovely rooms", "superb service" and "great food" at The Veranda; with million-dollar renovations on its two golf courses complete, the Mediterranean-style resort is more than ever "a hole-in-one for golfers", and its "best facilities" also include 24 tennis courts, a "wonderful pool", a complete fitness center and meeting rooms for 1,000; all in all, "fantastic in every way."

Westin Resort Miami Beach 371R (46S) 19 19 18 19 $186
(fka Doral Ocean Beach Resort)
4833 Collins Ave., Miami Beach; (305) 532-3600; (800) 203-8368; FAX: (305) 532-2334
☑ Westin took over this "comfy" but "tired" '60s beachfront resort in late 1996 and is doing a $10.5-million restoration, starting with the exterior and pool (which will be closed in summer '97, though guests can use another pool) and upgrading interiors in late '97; with 18 meeting rooms, a new rooftop restaurant (Hibiscus Court) and a health club with sauna, Jacuzzi and new equipment, many surveyors are confident that this well-located property not only "can be salvaged" but "will be great again."

Mount Dora

Lakeside Inn 70R (18S)
– | – | – | – | I
100 N. Alexander St., Mount Dora; (352) 383-4101; (800) 556-5016; FAX: (352) 735-2642
Listed on the National Historic Register, this 1883 Victorian and English Tudor–style retreat built for bird-watchers and fishermen now offers on-site tennis, swimming, sailing, croquet and canoeing; for relaxing, there are rocking chairs on the verandas, parlor games and tea dances in the ballroom lobby, cocktails in the lounge and Regional American candlelit dining in the Beauclaire restaurant; golf, horseback riding and antiques shopping are nearby, and Orlando's attractions are only 30 miles away.

Naples

Edgewater Beach Hotel (124S)
22 | 20 | 19 | 19 | $195
1901 Gulf Shore Blvd. N., Naples; (941) 262-6511, (800) 821-0196; FAX: (941) 262-1243
■ In "a quiet part of Naples", this all-suiter with kitchenettes is "the complete Florida resort", offering "a caring, experienced, professional staff" and "beach walks" in a "relaxing, beautiful" setting overlooking the Gulf – note the Club Dining Room "has a great view"; bicycling, exercise equipment and a pool are on-site.

La Playa Beach Resort 187R (4S)
19 | 19 | 18 | 18 | $178
9891 Gulf Shore Dr., Naples; (941) 597-3123; (800) 237-6883; FAX: (941) 597-6278
☑ Sporting $15 million in renovations, this late-'60s specimen has a new lobby, "beautifully refurbished rooms", most with water view, and a 'renourished' beach; on-site diversions include two pools and four tennis courts, and Cafe La Playa serves "good" Continental food with a tropical flair; but a few dissenters feel the ambiance is "diminished" since the redo and find "service lacking."

Naples Bath & Tennis Club (38S)
18 | 20 | 19 | 22 | $184
4995 Airport Blvd. N., Naples; (941) 261-5777; (800) 225-9692; FAX: (941) 649-2072
☑ A private country club that welcomes overnight guests, this resort in central Naples offers an "excellent tennis facility" with 37 courts and a "helpful tennis staff"; other activities include swimming and fishing, and it's not far from the beach, shopping or the Everglades; while some stay in "nice condominiums", others gripe the club is "coasting on past glory" and its public spaces are "faded"; N.B. a 48-unit expansion is planned.

Naples Beach Hotel & Golf Club 265R (50S)
19 | 20 | 19 | 19 | $163
851 Gulf Shore Blvd. N., Naples; (941) 261-2222; (800) 237-7600; FAX: (941) 261-7380
☑ "Gulf beach, pools, golf – something for everyone" is one voter's take on this 50-year-old fixture on the Naples beachscape; its championship golf course is the site of the Florida State PGA Seniors Open, and other amenities include tennis (four courts) and two restaurants; a $10-million renovation and a beach renourishment project, both recently completed, may quiet calls for "updating"; one fan insists "it may be a little threadbare, but it's still Florida at its best."

REGISTRY RESORT 396R (29S)
26 | 25 | 24 | 26 | $203
475 Seagate Dr., Naples; (941) 597-3232; (800) 247-9810; FAX: (941) 566-7919
■ "One of the most spectacular facilities in the continental US" delivers an "elegant, ritzy but not overdone" ambiance, "nurturing service" and a "beautiful view from every room"; situated on a protected mangrove sanctuary, the "grounds are beautiful" with on-site tennis and pool and a "good" beach (although it's "a hike" to get there); a "super staff" and "great restaurants" round out a stay that's "first class all the way"; N.B. new Club Zanzibar brings a hot dance spot to sleepy Naples.

RITZ-CARLTON NAPLES 435R (28S)
28 | 28 | 27 | 28 | $252
280 Vanderbilt Beach Rd., Naples; (941) 598-3300; (800) 241-3333; FAX: (941) 598-6690
■ "A first-class city hotel somehow put on the beach" makes for "luxury", "elegance and solitude" – a "wonderful-in-every-way" vacation among "beautiful" surroundings where one can enjoy "incredible, impeccable service", "outstanding rooms" (each with Gulf view), "excellent dining", afternoon tea and myriad outdoor activities; while it's too "stuffy" for some who frown on "too much dark wood for Florida", the majority agrees the Sunshine State's top-rated resort gleams like a "dream of a perfect hotel."

Orlando

TOP 10 OVERALL

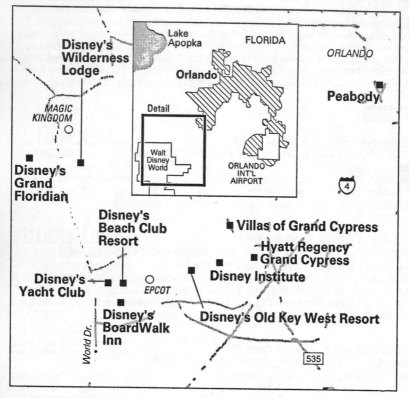

BEST OVERALL

26 Disney's Grand Floridian
Hyatt Regency Grand Cypress
25 Villas of Grand Cypress
Disney's Wilderness Lodge
Peabody
24 Disney's Yacht Club
Disney's BoardWalk Inn
Disney's Old Key West Resort
Disney's Beach Club Resort
23 Disney Institute

BEST VALUES

Disney's All-Star Music
Disney's All-Star Sports
Disney's Port Orleans
Holiday Inn SunSpree
Disney's Dixie Landings
Radisson Plaza
Disney's Caribbean Beach
Travelodge
Disney's Fort Wilderness
Clarion Plaza

R	S	D	P	$

Buena Vista Palace Resort & Spa 887R (127S) | 21 | 20 | 20 | 21 | $159 |

1900 Buena Vista Dr., Lake Buena Vista; (407) 827-2727; (800) 327-2990; FAX: (407) 827-6034
☑ Perhaps "not a palace", but this Disney resort has a handy location (a short free shuttle ride from Walt Disney World), "roomy" suites that are "great for small families", "good food" at Arthur's 27 and The Outback Restaurant and "wonderful package deals" including programs at the 9,000-square-foot spa; 40 meeting rooms make it an "excellent conference facility", while "the best children's programs" please parents; doubters knock "worn out" rooms that "need a makeover", but recent renovations may have helped.

Clarion Plaza Hotel 778R (32S) | 17 | 17 | 16 | 18 | $118 |

9700 International Dr., Orlando; (407) 352-9700; (800) 627-VALUE; FAX: (407) 351-9111
☑ "Good for those on business and on a budget" is the positive take on this "convention central" Clarion; critics say it has "little to offer besides location", citing "so-so" rooms and "get 'em in, get 'em out" service, but the fact that it's "convenient to the convention center" counts for a lot (and explains why it can be "noisy").

Disney Institute 457R
23 | 24 | 22 | 25 | $200

(fka Disney's Village Resort)

1960 Magnolia Way, Lake Buena Vista; (407) 934-7639; FAX: (407) 939-4898

■ A "fabulous concept" say alumni of this new Disney entry that's like a "banquet of continuing education" where guests choose from an array of "fun and illuminating" personal growth programs ranging from animation and computers to cooking, gardening and more; suites (sleeping four to six) in modern townhouses and bungalows "make you feel comfortable and cozy" and are good for families, and there's "wonderful" American and International food at Seasons; P.S. package deals are a fine "value."

Disney's All-Star Music Resort 1920R
17 | 19 | 15 | 18 | $84

1801 W. Buena Vista Dr., Lake Buena Vista; (407) 939-6000; FAX: (407) 939-7222

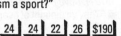 "You get what you pay for" at this "mob-scene", music-themed budget resort, but while fans say that makes it the "best bargain at WDW", hecklers call it "the cheesiest place in Mickey Mouse land"; expect "basic, clean rooms" in buildings with names like Calypso and Jazz, a food court and "crazy touches" like "huge music props" (a 40-foot-tall sax); "great for kids", but a few adults find it off-key.

Disney's All-Star Sports Resort 1920R
18 | 19 | 16 | 21 | $90

1701 W. Buena Vista Dr., Lake Buena Vista; (407) 939-5000; FAX: (407) 827-8555

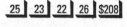 A companion to the All-Star Music Resort (this time with "huge sports props" and an athletic motif) that also wins votes as the "best value at Disney"; rooters rate it "lots of fun" as long as you don't mind "basic" rooms and service; spoilsports say "avoid unless you're with a male child under 10" and wonder "is tacky tourism a sport?"

DISNEY'S BEACH CLUB RESORT 563R (20S)
24 | 24 | 22 | 26 | $190

1800 Epcot Resorts Blvd., Lake Buena Vista; (407) 934-8000; FAX: (407) 934-3850

■ Beach lovers like to slip on their flip-flops at "one of Disney's better resorts", which gets countless cheers for its "sensational" three-acre water sports complex with a lagoon, whirlpools, a 'shipwreck' with water slides and a "fabulous" sand-bottomed pool; some surveyors even have energy left to do backflips for the "excellent rooms and service", the "wonderful buy" at Cape May Cafe's nightly clambake and the divine desserts dispensed at the soda shop.

DISNEY'S BOARDWALK INN & VILLAS
25 | 23 | 22 | 26 | $208

350R (552S)

2101 N. Epcot Resorts Blvd., Lake Buena Vista; (407) W-DISNEY; FAX: (407) 932-5100

■ "Disney's newest [opened July 1996] is also its best" according to admirers who laud this "fun property" adjacent to Epcot; while the boardwalk that sets the theme is "phony" (this is Disney, after all), the "great villas" and rooms, "nice decor", "convenient transportation" and two noteworthy restaurants – Flying Fish Cafe for seafood and Spoodles, serving fine Mediterranean fare – make the place "worth it."

Disney's Caribbean Beach Resort 2112R
21 | 22 | 18 | 23 | $126

900 Cayman Way, Lake Buena Vista; (407) 934-3400; FAX: (407) 934-3288

■ Among the moderately priced Disney resorts, this one scores as fine "for kids and adults" and "a good deal for the money"; the "colorful" Caribbean theme plays out in the architecture and the complex's island-like layout, and bathers love its "several pools"; rooms are "clean and comfortable", the staff is "superfriendly" and "food and entertainment are reasonably priced", with a choice of several eateries.

Disney's Contemporary Resort 969R (72S)
20 | 21 | 18 | 22 | $180

4600 N. World Dr., Lake Buena Vista; (407) W-DISNEY; FAX: (407) 824-3539

 "Contemporary? – not!" scoff critics of this "very busy" Disney resort built in '71 and now "a little tired-looking"; even so, it has plenty going for it: the location is "great" (especially "for kids"), the California Grill offers "excellent" food and views, and the monorail running through the lobby "is a major plus"; as for the rooms, some say "clean and spacious", others find the whole place "dated" – "needs more pixie dust."

Disney's Dixie Landings Resort 2048R
21 | 22 | 19 | 24 | $124

1251 Dixie Dr., Lake Buena Vista; (407) 934-6000; FAX: (407) 934-5777

■ Disney meets Huckleberry Finn at this "clever", "cute and clean" Southern-themed resort on the Sassagoula River, where good Cajun food, "friendly, accommodating service" and ersatz "rustic room decor" keep both kids and their elders happy; you get "more than your money's worth" here – "Walt would be proud"; a veteran's tip: "the Magnolia Bend rooms are best."

Disney's Fort Wilderness Resort   23 | 22 | 20 | 25 | $152
& Campground (1192S)
4510 N. Ft. Wilderness Trail, Lake Buena Vista; (407) 824-2900; FAX: (407) 824-3508

■ "Davy Crockett wanna-bes" call this 750-acre wooded park with campsites, RV hookups and furnished homes a good place "to vacation with children"; "roughing it Disney-style" can mean "less stress than at a hotel" and "like all of Disney, it's spotless and people try hard" – one happy camper even cites "the cleanest, roomiest, best campground restrooms ever"; dining options include the Hoop-Dee-Doo Musical Revue with an all-you-can-eat meal and Western show.

DISNEY'S GRAND FLORIDIAN   27 | 26 | 24 | 27 | $241
BEACH RESORT 839R (61S)
4401 Grand Floridian Way, Lake Buena Vista; (407) 824-3000; FAX: (407) 824-3186

■ The "grande dame" of WDW resorts, and the top-ranked property in Orlando, is a Victorian-style beauty standing proud on the Magic Kingdom's monorail route; it's a "nice family" place, of course, but couples can have a "pampered adult Disney trip" here too, enjoying its brand of "turn-of-the-century elegance", "large, well-decorated rooms" and dining options that include Victoria & Albert's, "the best"; some find it "too expensive", but others don't mind paying for "the ultimate Disney fantasy."

DISNEY'S OLD KEY WEST RESORT (709S)   27 | 24 | 21 | 25 | $208
(fka Disney's Vacation Club)
1510 N. Cove Rd., Lake Buena Vista; (407) 827-7700; FAX: (407) 827-7710

■ "They've thought of everything" at this Key West–themed resort where guests stay in "well-stocked" one-, two- and three-bedroom town houses and chalet-style villas that offer "all the convenience of being at a Disney property plus a separate bedroom for the kids"; the grounds are "lovely" and depending on the unit, amenities may include "the most complete kitchens you'll ever find", Jacuzzis, VCRs and more; it's a "good value", especially for extended stays.

DISNEY'S POLYNESIAN RESORT 841R (12S)   21 | 22 | 20 | 23 | $193
1600 Seven Seas Dr., Lake Buena Vista; (407) 824-2000; FAX: (407) 824-3174

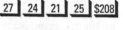 "Children will think they're in heaven" at Walt's Polynesian village, which "scores high for convenience" (it's a monorail ride to attractions) and for its "beautiful tropical setting" (a "good fake"); some adults, however, are brought down to earth by rooms variously described as "small for families" and "spacious but unexceptional", and dining that varies from "excellent" to "so awful I let my kids start a food fight"; we also hear reports that the resort "looks a bit tired" and "needs updating."

Disney's Port Orleans Resort 1008R   21 | 22 | 19 | 23 | $119
2201 Orleans Dr., Lake Buena Vista; (407) 934-5000; FAX: (407) 934-5353

■ "A clean French Quarter in pastels" describes this "affordable" Disney resort that's "charming and romantic" while still being a "great family experience"; "functional", "clean" rooms and "great swimming pool facilities" keep most guests happy, and there are two restaurants offering Creole and American fare, as well as "the best breakfast for the buck in WDW"; N.B. though it's not on the monorail route, voters still think it has a good location.

DISNEY'S WILDERNESS LODGE 722R (6S)   24 | 25 | 23 | 27 | $181
901 W. Timberline Dr., Lake Buena Vista; (407) 824-3200; FAX: (407) 824-3232

■ A re-creation of Wyoming's Old Faithful Inn, complete with geyser and a stream running through the lobby; it's "a theme park in itself" yet offers "a change from Disney cuteness" – admirers call it "romantic" and "nice for couples" as well as families, with food that's "daring" for Disney, from roasted and smoked meats at the Whispering Canyon Cafe to a wealth of fish at the Artist Point Seafood Grille; a few find it "too frenetic" with public spaces that are "impossible" because of the crowds.

DISNEY'S YACHT CLUB RESORT 610R (20S)   25 | 25 | 22 | 26 | $203
1800 Epcot Resorts Blvd., Lake Buena Vista; (407) 934-7000; FAX: (407) 934-3450

■ "Only a rung below the Grand Floridian, plus it's closer to Epcot and Disney-MGM" are reasons for casting anchor at this nautical-themed option that shares facilities with the Disney Beach Club Resort, including "the pool to end all pools"; it's "kid friendly", "very relaxing" and offers "great rooms and service"; also onboard are two restaurants and the Ship Shape Health Club; the few mutineers who knock the "artificial environment" may be missing the point of WDW.

Doubletree Guest Suites Resort (229S)   `22` `18` `16` `17` `$138`
(fka Guest Quarters Suite Resort)
2305 Hotel Plaza Blvd., Lake Buena Vista; (407) 934-1000; (800) 222-TREE; FAX: (407) 934-1011
■ A "two-story tropical aviary in the lobby sets the Disney tone", as do the "alert young staff" and "comfortable, spacious suites" at this option "close to all attractions" at WDW; they "give you all they promise", including "reasonable" packages and "easy access" to selected theme park sights, making it "good for families."

Grosvenor Resort 619R (7S)   `16` `17` `16` `16` `$132`
1850 Hotel Plaza Blvd., Lake Buena Vista; (407) 828-4444; (800) 624-4109; FAX: (407) 827-6314
◪ Elementary is an apt description of this hotel tribute to Arthur Conan Doyle offering "simple", "adequate" lodgings plus a Sherlock Holmes museum, Saturday night murder mystery shows at Baskervilles Restaurant and a WDW location convenient to Pleasure Island and other Disney attractions; despite its "good value", some surveyors detect that it's "old and tired", with areas that "need soapy water and a little paint."

Hilton at Walt Disney World Village 787R (27S)   `19` `20` `18` `19` `$156`
1751 Hotel Plaza Blvd., Lake Buena Vista; (407) 827-4000; (800) 782-4414; FAX: (407) 827-3890
◪ While surveyors seem to agree on this Hilton's "nice grounds" and "staff that works harder to keep up with the Disney properties", they differ on other issues: "good location" (near the Disney Village Marketplace and Pleasure Island) vs. "inconvenient", "large, spacious" rooms vs. "claustrophobic"; oh yes, there's also agreement that you should "watch out for conventioneers" (meeting space for 2,350).

Holiday Inn Main Gate East 609R (5S)   ▽ `20` `19` `18` `18` `$104`
5678 Irlo Bronson Memorial Hwy., Kissimmee; (407) 396-4488; (800) HOLIDAY; FAX: (407) 396-1296
■ "Quite comfortable" for families needing a place to crash between visits to the Magic Kingdom, this "pleasant" but "basic" HI features a "nice pool" and kids' suites in some rooms; a few find service "impersonal", but many like the "good price."

Holiday Inn SunSpree Resort 416R (91S)   `19` `19` `17` `19` `$106`
13351 State Rd. 535, Lake Buena Vista; (407) 239-4500; (800) HOLIDAY; FAX: (407) 239-7713
◪ "The kids will never forget being tucked in by their animal mascot" vs. "great only if you're under 15 years old" sums up two views of this family-friendly resort just over a mile from WDW; most agree it's "good for what it is", i.e. a "place to stay with children – they really care", as evident from such features as a special kids-only check-in, "oversized" rooms with child-proofing kits and extensive children's programs.

Hyatt Orlando 900R (22S)   `19` `19` `18` `18` `$136`
6375 W. Irlo Bronson Hwy., Kissimmee; (407) 396-1234; (800) 233-1234; FAX: (407) 396-5090
◪ With 30 meeting rooms (capacity 2,000), this Hyatt is "good for conventions", and being "close to Disney (two miles away) also makes it "easy for families"; most find it "convenient, reasonable and aging well", with "helpful, cooperative" staff, "lots of pools" on its 56 acres and two restaurants, Summerhouse (American) and Fio Fio (Italian); but foes pronounce it "dull" with a "confusing layout" and rooms that "need upgrading."

HYATT REGENCY GRAND CYPRESS 676R (74S)   `26` `25` `25` `28` `$209`
1 Grand Cypress, Orlando; (407) 239-1234; (800) 233-1234; FAX: (407) 239-3800
■ Superlatives abound for the "classy" resort ranked No. 2 overall in Orlando, from its "astounding decor", "luxurious" rooms and "superb service" to its "magnificent grounds" and "beautiful pool with caverns and bridges"; offering "a break from Mickey Mouse" (yet close to WDW sights), it caters to conventions and is a "dream" for golfers (45 holes) and other active types (tennis, racquetball, horseback riding, biking, boating and more); dining options include the highly rated La Coquina, serving New World fare.

Hyatt Regency Orlando   `–` `–` `–` `–` `E`
International Airport 423R (23S)
9300 Airport Blvd., Orlando; (407) 825-1234; (800) 233-1234; FAX: (407) 856-1672
It would be hard to sleep closer to baggage check than at this modern, tropically decorated Hyatt atop the main terminal at Orlando International; rooms encircle a six-story atrium with palm trees and fountain, and facilities include a fully equipped fitness room, lovely outdoor pool area, two restaurants, an amphitheater and meeting space for up to 700 conferees.

Marriott Orlando Downtown 280R (10S)   `16` `17` `14` `15` `$129`
400 W. Livingston St., Orlando; (407) 843-6664; (800) 574-3160; FAX: (407) 839-4982
◪ If bound for Downtown rather than Disney, this "comfortable" high-rise is deemed "the only decent place for business" in the area near the Sports Arena and Carr Performing Arts Centre; facilities include 24 meeting rooms (capacity 2,000), a fitness center, an outdoor pool and two restaurants, but unfortunately no boot camp for a staff that some find in need of "basic training."

Marriott Orlando - International Drive 1048R (16S) 19 19 17 19 $136
8001 International Dr., Orlando; (407) 351-2420; (800) 421-8001; FAX: (407) 351-5016
☑ A "good central location" near Sea World and Universal Studios and eight miles from Disney is a plus here, and admirers also laud "quiet", "decent-size" rooms, "reliable service" and a "great pool"; but critics call it "an aging relic that needs a real goosing" (a recent redo of guestrooms may have helped) and say the "heavy traffic" and "all-tourist" crowd can make it feel "like staying in a bus station."

Marriott's Orlando World Center 1418R (85S) 23 23 21 25 $170
8701 World Center Dr., Orlando; (407) 239-4200; (800) 621-0638; FAX: (407) 238-8777
■ Like a Marriott "on steroids", but rooms are "large" too at this "humongous", "complete resort" with golf, tennis, "the best" pools, a health club, even volleyball and basketball courts, plus a location near all attractions; extensive conference facilities (53 rooms with a capacity of 6,100) can mean "a zoo of meetings", but "outstanding service" keeps chaos at bay; with several on-site restaurants, it may be for the best that "you can sweat off five pounds just walking in from the parking lot."

Omni Rosen 1254R (80S) 18 19 19 19 $139
9840 International Dr., Orlando; (407) 354-9840; (800) 800-9840; FAX: (407) 354-3169
☑ A newcomer to the city's convention hotel scene and "surprisingly good" for the genre, this suburban giant is "comfortable" and "refreshing", a "great value" that's even "sort of elegant"; if 24 meeting rooms (capacity 5,000) aren't enough, the gold-hued high-rise is "close to the convention center"; there's a health club, tennis courts and pools, and dining options range from deli eats to regional fare at The Everglades; less-impressed guests call it "nothing spectacular."

PEABODY ORLANDO 834R (57S) 25 25 24 25 $176
9801 International Dr., Orlando; (407) 345-4540; (800) PEABODY; FAX: (407) 363-1505
■ "Just ducky" quip voters, and not just for the twice-daily duck parade at this "upscale but comfortable" modern version of the Memphis original: "rooms are large and properly equipped", the staff has a "very upbeat attitude", the fitness center is top-notch and there's "great" New American dining at Dux; a "convenient" location (across from the convention center) draws business travelers, as does meeting space for 3,000; while most find it "a pleasure in every way", a few quack "overpriced."

Radisson Barcelo Hotel 297R (2S) ▽ 16 15 14 14 $104
(fka Radisson Inn on International Drive)
8444 International Dr., Orlando; (407) 345-0505; (800) 304-8000; FAX: (407) 425-7440
☑ Only a few surveyors have experienced this suburbanite that caters primarily to vacationers with its minutes-away proximity to WDW, Universal Studios, Sea World and Wet 'n' Wild; golf is also nearby and, in addition to on-site pools and tennis, the adjacent YMCA has two Olympic-size pools and more workout facilities; service gets varying reviews: "good", "friendly" vs. "indifferent."

Radisson Plaza Hotel Orlando 313R (27S) 20 19 16 19 $110
60 S. Ivanhoe Blvd., Orlando; (407) 425-4455; (800) 333-3333; FAX: (407) 425-7440
☑ "An oasis" Downtown and "one of Orlando's best" to some, "big and cold", "nothing special" to others, but despite the debate this Radisson on Lake Ivanhoe gets respectable grades for its "nice clean rooms" and "good service", and execs say the "convenient" location and concierge floor make it "good for business"; tennis, a pool and health club with sauna are all on-site.

Radisson Twin Towers Hotel & 15 16 13 15 $111
Convention Center 741R (19S)
(fka Twin Towers Hotel & Convention Center)
5780 Major Blvd., Orlando; (407) 351-1000; (800) 327-2110; FAX: (407) 363-0106
☑ The "best-located hotel for Universal Studios fans" (it's across the street) offers "good views", especially of the Universal fireworks displays, at a "good price"; but even those attributes don't prevent critics from calling it "very dated" with "only so-so" rooms, though recent renovations may upgrade those reactions.

Renaissance Orlando Resort 716R (64S) 22 21 21 22 $158
(fka Stouffer Renaissance Orlando Resort)
6677 Sea Harbor Dr., Orlando; (407) 351-5555; (800) 327-6677; FAX: (407) 351-9994
■ This "huge hotel" across from Sea World and near Universal Studios is "convention city" (185,000 square feet of meeting space); but even with "too many conventioneers", most consider it a "nice place" and especially like its "amazing" 10-story atrium lobby with tropical birds, rare fish and a waterfall; "very spacious rooms" and good service are noted too, and the restaurants Atlantis and Haifeng are "worth every penny."

Residence Inn by Marriott (688S) | 20 | 17 | 14 | 17 | $119 |
8800 Meadow Creek Dr., Orlando; (407) 239-7700; (800) 331-3131; FAX: (407) 239-7605

■ "The converted apartments are anything but fancy", but they're "economical" and "work for a family" – full kitchens in each and washer/dryers in some can make it seem like "home away from home for longer stays"; there are pools and fitness equipment on-site, and access to the facilities at the adjacent Marriott's Orlando World Center adds even more appeal; a recent renovation may sway those who say it "needs a rehab."

Sheraton World Resort 754R (34S) | 16 | 18 | 16 | 17 | $122 |
10100 International Dr., Orlando; (407) 352-1100; (800) 327-0363; FAX: (407) 352-3679

◪ Twenty-eight acres of "nice grounds" and "three good-size swimming pools" make this villa-style resort a "comfortable" "place to rest" after a day at WDW or the next-door Sea World; while the "meeting facilities are great" (capacity 800) and the restaurant serves "a wonderful brunch", many nevertheless find it "old", "impersonal and plastic."

Travelodge Hotel | 17 | 17 | 15 | 16 | $107 |
Walt Disney World Village 321R (4S)
2000 Hotel Plaza Blvd., Lake Buena Vista; (407) 828-2424; (800) 348-3765; FAX: (407) 828-8933

■ An 18-story tower that manages to sport a Barbados plantation house theme, this lakeside resort in WDW Village is "good for families on a budget", offering "functional", "comfortable" rooms (each with private balcony) and pleasant public areas; there's a free shuttle to Disney attractions and a splendid view of nightly fireworks from the top-floor Toppers nightclub.

VILLAS OF GRAND CYPRESS (146S) | 28 | 25 | 24 | 25 | $227 |
1 N. Jacaranda, Orlando; (407) 239-4700; (800) 835-7377; FAX: (407) 239-7219

■ "If you live for golf", this is the life – 45 holes on Jack Nicklaus–designed courses surround this "quiet" enclave of Mediterranean-style villas, part of the Grand Cypress Resort (as is the Hyatt Regency Grand Cypress, at the other end of the complex); besides "excellent accommodations", "good service" and a "secluded" setting near Disney, it has a golf academy, equestrian center, tennis and "wonderful" Continental dining at the Black Swan; in sum, a place to "retreat in style."

Vistana Resort (1100S) | 27 | 22 | 19 | 24 | $173 |
8800 Vistana Centre Dr., Orlando; (407) 239-3376; (800) 877-8787; FAX: (407) 239-3062

■ "Beautiful accommodations", "excellent amenities" (several pools, 13 tennis courts, mini golf, basketball courts and more) and children's programs make this "lovely" resort "good for a family vacation"; the "huge condos" sleep six to eight and come with full kitchens and VCRs, and most have whirlpools; all in all "a nice place to relax after Disney."

Walt Disney World Dolphin 1509R (130S) | 22 | 22 | 20 | 24 | $187 |
1500 Epcot Resorts Blvd., Lake Buena Vista; (407) 934-4000; (800) 227-1500; FAX: (407) 934-4884

◪ Fans call it "whimsical" and "cute for kids", while critics claim Disney made a "big mistake" with the design for this "garish", "seriously tacky" building festooned with giant dolphins; still, rooms are "comfortable and quiet", service is "good" and there's a range of sports facilities, but "even adults need a map to get around"; the place was "built for conferences, which can overwhelm food and beverage" services, so some say vacationers "beware."

Walt Disney World Swan 703R (55S) | 21 | 22 | 21 | 23 | $192 |
1200 Epcot Resorts Blvd., Lake Buena Vista; (407) 934-3000; (800) 248-SWAN; FAX: (407) 934-4499

◪ Either a "lovely" "ode to teal and peach" or an "architectural travesty", depending on your taste, but most agree this Westin-affiliated sibling to the WDW Dolphin (both designed by Michael Graves) provides "well-appointed rooms", "excellent" service and "wonderful" Italian food at Palio; like the Dolphin, it "caters to conferences" so there'll often be more briefcases than babies.

Westgate Lakes Resort (320S) | ▽ 23 | 22 | 21 | 22 | $166 |
10000 Turkey Lake Rd., Orlando; (407) 345-0000; (800) 424-0708; FAX: (407) 345-5384

■ A "nice resort run by nice people", this Mediterranean-style lakefront property lodges guests in pleasant villas, each with kitchenette; all-age activities include bicycling, boating, fishing and waterskiing, but it's especially appealing to those with children given extensive children's programs, the ubiquitous costumed mascot Sunny the Seal, an on-site Pizza Hut and easy access to WDW.

Palm Beach

Brazilian Court 60R (43S)

19 | 20 | 19 | 18 | $192

*301 Australian Ave., Palm Beach; (561) 655-7740; (800) 552-0335;
FAX: (561) 655-0801*

■ A total interior renovation has added even more charm to this "classy old dowager", a "relaxing, historic" Spanish-style hotel with "lovely grounds", a "beautiful courtyard", heated pool, restaurants and round-the-clock room service in a residential area near Worth Avenue; while the overhaul is aimed in part at attracting more year-round residents (kitchenettes and more closets were added to an expanded number of suites), it remains open to the public, which should please the many admirers who consider it "a gem" (it's "a bit stuffy" for others).

BREAKERS, THE 524R (48S)

24 | 25 | 23 | 27 | $250

1 S. County Rd., Palm Beach; (561) 655-6611; (800) 833-3141; FAX: (561) 659-8403

■ Following an "outstanding" $75-million renovation, "the grande dame is glorious again" exult well-heeled devotees of this "distinguished" 1926 beachfront landmark that delivers "Gatsby-like" "luxury in a castle by the sea"; the "ultimate Palm Beach experience" means "luxurious" rooms, "gorgeous public areas", "wonderful" dining options, a "terrific beach" and pool area, 14 tennis courts, two golf courses, even fine children's programs; "a treat", "marvelous" – the superlatives go on and on.

Chesterfield Hotel 42R (11S)

21 | 23 | 21 | 20 | $179

363 Coconut Row, Palm Beach; (561) 659-5800; (800) 243-7871; FAX: (561) 659-6707

■ "A decent base" for exploring Palm Beach, this "small", elegant, circa 1926 hotel with a British club ambiance and individually decorated rooms is praised for "great service" and is a local favorite for afternoon tea (perhaps to relax after a credit-card frenzy in the Worth Avenue shopping district three blocks away); an on-site restaurant, spa and outdoor pool provide more comforts, although other recreational activities are somewhat sparse in this residential neighborhood.

Colony Hotel 67R (14S)

19 | 22 | 21 | 19 | $193

155 Hammon Ave., Palm Beach; (561) 655-5430; (800) 521-5525; FAX: (561) 659-8104

■ "Beautiful and homey public spaces" and "friendly service" win admirers for this British colonial–style boutique hotel that appeals to "a very European, sophisticated crowd"; its location "footsteps from great shopping" on Worth Avenue in Downtown Palm Beach is another plus, and there are pools and tennis courts on-site, along with the Polo Lounge and Restaurant serving "excellent" Continental fare; a room renovation in 1996 may dispel criticisms that the hotel "needs refurbishing."

FOUR SEASONS RESORT PALM BEACH

27 | 28 | 27 | 27 | $273

198R (12S)
(fka Four Seasons Ocean Grand)
*2800 S. Ocean Blvd., Palm Beach; (561) 582-2800; (800) 432-2335;
FAX: (561) 547-1374*

■ "The place to be seen" in Palm Beach is this "elegant, classy getaway" in a "dreamlike setting" "secluded on a private oceanfront"; top-rated in Palm Beach (and the state's No. 2 hotel), it's where "the rich and famous relax" in "beautiful rooms" (the rare complaint is that some are "a little small") and "fabulous public areas" while being coddled by "super service" (staff will even "spritz" you at the beach) and enjoying "superb if pricey dining"; a 6,000-square-foot spa and fitness center, tennis courts and pool round out the "first-class" amenities.

Palm Beach Polo & Country Club (55S)

▽ 21 | 23 | 21 | 23 | $252

11809 Polo Club Rd., West Palm Beach; (561) 798-7020; FAX: (561) 798-7345

■ "It's hard to ask for more in a resort", since there's "tennis, golf, polo, good food and service" at this modern condo complex amid landscaped grounds and waterways; it hosts polo clinics and international high-goal polo matches on its 10 fields, and year-round events at the world-class equestrian center (including Grand Prix and World Cup competitions); the out-of-the-saddle set settles happily for 45 holes of championship golf, 24 tennis courts, six pools, and croquet (it's HQ of the US Croquet Association) and squash courts.

PGA National Resort & Spa 339R   21   21   20   23 $188
400 Ave. of Champions, Palm Beach Gardens; (561) 627-2000; (800) 633-9150; FAX: (561) 691-9133

☑ "A fitness fantasy" in Palm Beach Gardens combining a "golfer's paradise" (five courses), a "fabulous spa" and 19 tennis courts appeals to both conventioneers and couples; there are also three pools, boating on a 26-acre lake and seven lounges and restaurants, as well as a landing pad for your 'copter; but while "relaxed", most agree it's "long on golf, short on luxury", and one voter warns that while cottage suites are good for longer stays, "look at a few" as quality varies; a large croquet complex suits those who can't stop swinging.

RITZ-CARLTON PALM BEACH 214R (56S)   28   27   26   27 $253
100 S. Ocean Blvd., Manalapan; (561) 533-6000; (800) 241-3333; FAX: (561) 588-4202

■ The "usual exemplary Ritz-Carlton standards", including "impeccable service" and "elegant four o'clock tea", are maintained at this Mediterranean-style oceanfront resort where "humongous rooms" and "lots of sunlight streaming into halls" create a "delightful" ambiance; "excellent restaurants" and activities galore help make up for a location eight miles from the heart of Palm Beach, and those who enjoy "long walks on the beach" see the "out-of-the-way" setting as a "restful" plus; the only quibbles are over "typical Ritz decor" that a few find "somewhat out of place at the beach."

Panama City Beach

Marriott's Bay Point Resort 277R (78S)   22   23   22   25 $141
4200 Marriott Dr., Panama City Beach; (904) 234-3307; (800) 874-7105; FAX: (904) 233-1308

■ An "absolutely beautiful golf resort", this "well-kept secret" also offers "every amenity you could think of" including 12 tennis courts, boating, a health club, 36 golf holes, pools, children's programs and even a post office; it's situated on a tropical wildlife sanctuary, replete with canals and ponds, overlooking St. Andrews Bay.

Ponte Vedra Beach

Lodge & Beach Club at Ponte Vedra Beach   24   22   23   24 $210
42R (24S)
607 Ponte Vedra Blvd., Ponte Vedra Beach; (904) 273-9500; (800) 243-4304; FAX: (904) 273-0210

■ Classic Mediterranean-style architecture on the beachfront provides "a beautiful, romantic setting" for "big", well-appointed rooms with balconies that offer "wonderful views" of the Atlantic (many feature fireplaces and Jacuzzis, as well as kitchenettes in the suites); "good service" is a plus, along with 10 tennis courts, three outdoor pools, a fitness center, two restaurants and 6,500 square feet of meeting space for groups of up to 350.

Marriott at Sawgrass 407R (21S)   23   23   20   24 $171
1000 TPC Blvd., Ponte Vedra Beach; (904) 285-7777; (800) 457-4653; FAX: (904) 285-0906

☑ There's "incredible golf" on five championship courses, including the PGA's TPC Stadium Course; but this "beautiful hotel" with "nice public spaces" is also a "place to unwind", whether that entails American dining at Cafe on the Green or limbering up at the 19 tennis courts, pools and health club (there are kids' programs to occupy the younger set); but while there's praise for the "wonderfully expansive grounds", critics gripe that it's "too far from the beach" and, despite good ratings, many frown on "small", "utilitarian" rooms.

PONTE VEDRA INN & CLUB 182R (20S)   23   25   23   25 $185
200 Ponte Vedra Blvd., Ponte Vedra Beach; (904) 285-1111; (800) 234-7842; FAX: (904) 285-2111

■ A "great vacation spot for families", although business travelers also seek out this north Florida "low-key genteel sporting club" for its "super services" and "spacious rooms" in six two-story Mediterranean-style buildings on 300 "fabulous" acres with "easy beach and golf access"; upholding "the tradition of the Old South", it offers an "unhurried" ambiance, "great staff" and "marvelous cuisine", along with a 10,000-square-foot spa (opened in 1996), 34 links, a fitness center, boating, fishing, four pools and 15 tennis courts; a few find the "old-line" atmosphere "somewhat stuffy."

Port St. Lucie

Club Med Sandpiper 331R
▽ 20 | 20 | 19 | 21 | $200
3500 SE Morningside Blvd., Port St. Lucie; (561) 335-4400; (800) CLUBMED;
FAX: (561) 335-9497
■ "If you have kids, it beats Disney World" rave parental units about Club Med's foray into an all-inclusive (except golf and bar bill) "terrific family resort"; the "modest accommodations" are "ok", since guests "spend most of the time away from their rooms", joining "great" kids' programs such as a circus workshop or making use of the 19 tennis courts, four pools, 36 holes of golf and boating; the "typical Club Med" experience includes "mountains of good (not great) food", but some "don't know what all the fuss is about, it isn't even on the beach."

Sanibel Island

Casa Ybel Resort (114S)
24 | 21 | 21 | 24 | $189
2255 W. Gulf Dr., Sanibel Island; (941) 472-3145; (800) 276-ISLE; FAX: (941) 472-2109
■ Each of the "well-equipped" one- and two-bedroom condos has a screened porch overlooking the Gulf and a "great beach" that's a "shell collector's dream" (just plan to "wear sandals"); "restful" and "quiet" with tropically landscaped grounds, it's "wonderful for families" with boating, fishing, tennis and a pool plus access to golf and extensive bicycling trails nearby.

Sanibel Inn 49R (47S)
20 | 20 | 18 | 19 | $166
937 Golf Dr., Sanibel Island; (941) 472-3181; (800) 237-1491; FAX: (941) 472-5234
☑ Boasting a "beautiful location" along the Gulf of Mexico on Sanibel Island, this "great family resort" delivers a "good beach" and "adequate if not luxurious" rooms (including one- and two-bedroom quarters) plus amenities such as bicycling, kayaking and tennis, with golf five minutes away; critics call for "better housekeeping" and soundproofing to address "thin walls"; although some feel the "quiet location" can mean idle rainy days, children's programs and the complimentary Disney Channel keep the little ones occupied.

Sundial Beach Resort (270S)
21 | 21 | 18 | 21 | $191
1451 Middle Gulf Dr., Sanibel Island; (941) 472-4151; (800) 237-4184; FAX: (941) 481-4947
☑ If it's time for a "quiet pool area", "great shelling on the beach", "excellent children's programs" and "a staff that goes overboard to please", check out Sundial; there's "terrific tennis" on 12 courts, plus five pools, a fitness center, boating and bicycling, with golf nearby; but surveyors note that the privately owned condo "accommodations can vary" from "bare-bones" to "very nice."

Siesta Key

Captiva Beach Resort 16R (4S)
▽ 24 | 23 | – | 21 | $123
6772 Sara Sea Circle, Siesta Key; (941) 349-4131; (800) 349-4131; FAX: (941) 349-8141
This modern family-run resort on Siesta Key, about three miles from Sarasota, features kitchenettes in every room, an outdoor pool and a white-sand beach, but low voter turnout indicates it doesn't have a captive audience; it may be a good choice for getting away from it all, but you'll have to cook or join the masses at dinnertime since there's no restaurant on-site.

Stuart

Indian River Plantation 180R (125S)
21 | 21 | 20 | 22 | $156
555 NE Ocean Blvd., Hutchinson Island, Stuart; (561) 225-3700; (800) 444-3389;
FAX: (561) 225-0003
■ "Combining a fine hotel, condos, marina, golfing and dining in one resort", this "place away from Florida crowds" is good for "long stays" with kitchenettes in many accommodations; a "great beach", "lovely golf course", four pools and 13 tennis courts provide plenty of activity and "if you like to fish, it's mecca"; while the privately owned units may vary, most are satisfied ("get a room facing the golf course") and the "beautiful location" "makes up" for minor deficiencies; N.B. turtle watch programs are underway May through August.

Tampa Bay

TOP 10 OVERALL

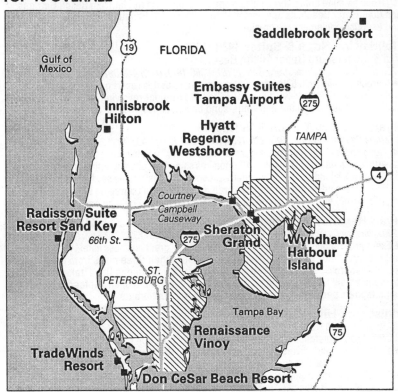

BEST OVERALL

26 Renaissance Viney
23 Don CeSar Beach Resort
   Hyatt Regency Westshore
22 Saddlebrook Resort
21 Sheraton Grand
   Innisbrook Hilton
   Wyndham Harbour Island
20 Embassy Suites Tampa Airport
19 Radisson Suite Resort Sand Key
19 TradeWinds Resort

BEST VALUES

Sheraton Grand
Hyatt Regency Westshore
Embassy Suites Tampa Airport
Radisson Suite Resort Sand Key
Sheraton Sand Key
Renaissance Vinoy
TradeWinds Resort
Marriott Tampa Westshore
Wyndham Harbour Island
Saddlebrook Resort

R	S	D	P	$

Don CeSar Beach Resort & Spa 232R (43S)

| 23 | 23 | 23 | 25 | $182 |

3400 Gulf Blvd., St. Petersburg Beach; (813) 360-1881; (800) 282-1116; FAX: (813) 367-6952
■ "You can almost see F. Scott and Zelda" at "Florida's pink palace", a 1928 Moorish marvel overlooking a "gorgeous beach" with "spectacular sunsets"; luxe amenities at this "quintessential grand beach resort" include extensive spa services, tennis courts and two pools, and on Sundays there's "a brunch to die for" at the Mariana Grill; although most agree the rooms are "very small", "everything else is fabulous", especially since a "wonderful renovation" "restored its long-ago elegance."

Doubletree Guest Suites Tampa Bay (203S)

| 20 | 17 | 15 | 16 | $102 |

(fka Guest Quarters Suite Hotel Tampa Bay)
3050 N. Rocky Point Dr. W., Tampa; (813) 888-8800; (800) 222-TREE; FAX: (813) 888-8743
☑ "Peacefully nestled away from the nearby Business District" in "a preferred location", this all-suiter pleases those who like the "spaciousness", "nice pool" and fitness facilities that make it a "good value"; a '96 redo may sweeten up critics who insist "the cookie has crumbled – it needs renovation immediately."

133

EMBASSY SUITES TAMPA AIRPORT (221S)

| 23 | 22 | 19 | 19 | $131 |

555 N. Westshore Blvd., Tampa Bay; (813) 875-1555; (800) EMBASSY; FAX: (813) 287-3664

■ Business travelers are the primary clientele of this "typical" branch of the well-regarded all-suite chain; three miles from the airport and not far from Busch Gardens and Clearwater Beach, its accommodations all have kitchenettes, and an outdoor pool and exercise equipment are on-site.

Holiday Inn Hotel & Suites 143R (13S)

▽ | 18 | 18 | 14 | 17 | $133 |

(fka St. Petersburg Beach Hilton Resort)

5250 Gulf Blvd., St. Petersburg Beach; (813) 360-1811; (800) 448-0919; FAX: (813) 360-6919

■ All rooms come with balconies and refrigerators at this resort on Boca Ciega Bay, and for an even better view, guests head to the 11th-floor revolving lounge; despite an outdoor pool, fitness center and white-sand beach, all we hear is "ordinary."

Hyatt Regency Tampa 502R (16S)

| 19 | 19 | 17 | 18 | $142 |

2 Tampa City Ctr., Tampa; (813) 225-1234; (800) 233-1234; FAX: (813) 273-0234

☑ "Good and reliable" but "nothing out of the ordinary" when it comes to Hyatts, which nevertheless means that Downtown Tampa has some "excellent meeting facilities" in a high-rise with "good service", "standard accommodations" (some say "slightly worn"), a fitness center and an outdoor pool; overall, surveyors can't agree on whether it's "an island of luxury in a sea of low-level motels" or "so blah it could be anywhere."

Hyatt Regency Westshore 391R (54S)

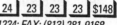

| 24 | 23 | 23 | 23 | $148 |

6200 Courtney Campbell Cswy., Tampa; (813) 874-1234; (800) 233-1234; FAX: (813) 281-9168

■ Execs crow about this "gem in the Hyatt chain", a "great business hotel" with "super service" and "unexpectedly beautiful rooms" less than three miles from the airport yet adjacent to a "beautiful" 35-acre bird sanctuary on Tampa Bay ("take a walk on the nature trail"); meeting rooms can handle a flock of 2,000, and at feeding time name-taggers peck at "very good" food from three restaurants.

Innisbrook Hilton Resort (1000S)

| 21 | 21 | 20 | 23 | $176 |

36750 US Hwy. 19 N., Palm Harbor; (813) 942-2000; (800) 456-2000; FAX: (813) 942-5577

☑ With three "outstanding" courses, Innisbrook is the "golf capital of the world" for some linksters; more diversified athletes indulge in the "great health club", 15 tennis courts and biking, hiking and water sports, while kids' programs amuse the younger set; to some it's "like a small resort city" with meeting space for 2,000, but there's debate over the all-suite lodgings – "gorgeous" vs. due for "remodeling."

Marriott Tampa Westshore 305R (2S)

| 18 | 19 | 16 | 17 | $128 |

1001 N. Westshore Blvd., Tampa Bay; (813) 287-2555; (800) 228-9290; FAX: (813) 289-5464

☑ This "basic business hotel" offers corporate types "a pleasant stay in Tampa" with its "convenience to both the airport and Downtown", "great pool area" and "attentive staff"; but pickier travelers see an "average" Marriott at work – "ho hum."

Radisson Suite Resort On Sand Key (220S)

| 21 | 20 | 18 | 20 | $129 |

1201 Gulf Blvd., Clearwater; (813) 596-1100; (800) 333-3333; FAX: (813) 595-4292

■ Overlooking Clearwater Bay on a barrier island, this resort offers "a nice break from it all" with "comfortable rooms" boasting "nice bay views"; the 10-story complex has a boardwalk with 25 shops and is across from Sand Key Beach, ranked among the nation's best; the large outdoor pool, spa/fitness center and six restaurants appeal to both vacationers and business travelers, as does the "very helpful, courteous staff."

RENAISSANCE VINOY RESORT 340R (20S)

| 26 | 25 | 26 | 25 | $179 |

(fka Stouffer Renaissance Vinoy Resort)

501 Fifth Ave. NE, St. Petersburg; (813) 894-1000; (800) 468-3571; FAX: (813) 822-2785

■ "A great mix of past and present" makes this "beautifully restored" 1920s pink Mediterranean-style complex "a treasure" and the *Survey's* top-ranked Tampa Bay–area property; "fabulous rooms", "excellent service" and an "ornate" lobby attract a classy clientele that basks in the spa, "great hot tubs", "gorgeous pool" and bay views; active guests head for golf, 14 tennis courts or the 74-slip marina – all of which adds up to "the ultimate Florida resort"; yet despite high ratings, a few find some rooms "average", advising "the place to stay is in the Towers."

Saddlebrook Resort Tampa 375R (415S)

| 22 | 22 | 20 | 23 | $165 |

5700 Saddlebrook Way, Wesley Chapel; (813) 973-1111; (800) 729-8383; FAX: (813) 973-4504

☑ This "ranch-style complex" north of Tampa offers "great conference services and facilities", a pool the size of a football field and "exceptional condo suites", but the main draws are golf and tennis (36 holes and 45 courts), including tutoring at the on-site Arnold Palmer Golf or Harry Hopman Tennis academies; while many suggest the food "could improve" and some object to the "hike" around the "beautiful" but "voluminous" grounds, pluses far outweigh minuses at this "relaxing, comfortable place" – one tongue-in-cheek fan says even the alligators are "friendly."

Sheraton Grand Hotel 302R (22S)   22 | 22 | 21 | 21 | $134
4860 W. Kennedy Blvd., Tampa; (813) 286-4400; (800) 866-7177; FAX: (813) 286-4053
☑ "Beautiful rooms and public areas" greet guests at this well-rated modern hotel; near the airport on Tampa Bay, it offers a free shuttle to your flight, plus an outdoor pool, meeting space for 500 and "great food" at Don Shula's Steak House; still, a few respondents consider it "limited."

Sheraton Sand Key Resort 375R (15S)   19 | 20 | 17 | 20 | $132
1160 Gulf Blvd., Clearwater; (813) 595-1611; (800) 325-3535; FAX: (813) 596-8488
☑ Combine a '70s-era chain high-rise with a beautiful location on the Gulf of Mexico and the result, depending on your perspective, is either "a great" beach base "with all the amenities" or "an old hotel trying desperately to be a resort"; "a pleasant hotel in a pleasant place" seems a safe summation, but "the beach certainly helps its rating."

Tradewinds Resort 370R (200S)   18 | 20 | 18 | 21 | $140
5500 Gulf Blvd., St. Petersburg Beach; (813) 367-6461; (800) 237-0707; FAX: (813) 562-1222
☑ A happy "surprise" to plenty of surveyors who laud this "elegant hideaway" with a "great beach", "beautiful views" and "good rooms" (a suite with a Gulf view is "worth the extra money"), along with 30,000 square feet of meeting space; a variety of water sports, outdoor pools and tennis along with kids' programs and several dining options help make it a "good value" to many, though less so to those stuck "in the wing that has not been renovated" where accommodations are "getting a little tired."

Wyndham Harbour Island Hotel 280R (20S)   23 | 21 | 19 | 22 | $154
725 S. Harbour Island Blvd., Tampa; (813) 229-5000; (800) WYNDHAM; FAX: (813) 229-5032
■ "Isolated" (nearly always used in a positive sense) is how respondents describe this "pleasant" if "innocuous" hotel's "great secluded setting" on its own island "just over a bridge" from Downtown; others commend "spacious", "comfortable" rooms and "excellent service" that caters especially to "convention center business travelers"; an on-site marina and privileges at Harbor Island Athletic Club (tennis, racquetball, lap pool) don't hurt either.

Winter Park

Park Plaza Hotel 16R (11S)   18 | 21 | 23 | 16 | $139
307 Park Ave. S., Winter Park; (407) 647-1072; (800) 228-7220; FAX: (407) 647-4081
☑ Surveyors run hot and cold over this B&B in trendy Winter Park; some find "small-town charm amidst an area covered with Disney plastic" (although the theme parks are 25 miles away) in a "hospitable", "intimate" "hideaway" with a "lovely lobby" and "superb" American-Continental dining in the Park Plaza Gardens; but others call it a "big disappointment", advising "stay only in suites because rooms and bathrooms are very small and antiquated."

Georgia

R S D P $

── ── ── ── I

Windsor Hotel 45R (8S)
125 West Lamar St., Americus; (912) 924-1555; FAX: (912) 924-1555 x113
"The only place to stay" in Downtown Americus, an 1892 Victorian remodeled and reopened in 1991, is a unique blend of old and new; the lobby features a three-story atrium of carved oak, and the period-style guestrooms and suites (no two are exactly alike) feature 12-foot ceilings, ceiling fans, VCRs and coffeemakers; the home of former president Jimmy Carter is just nine miles away.

Atlanta

TOP 10 OVERALL

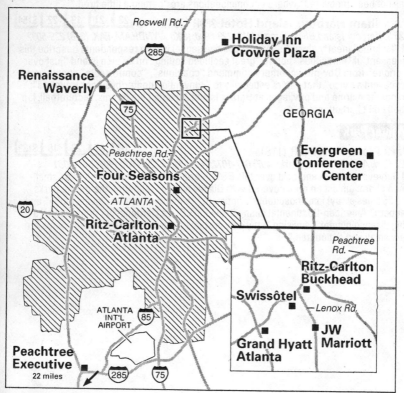

BEST OVERALL
27 Ritz-Carlton Buckhead
26 Four Seasons Atlanta
    Ritz-Carlton Atlanta
25 Grand Hyatt Atlanta
23 Renaissance Waverly
    Swissôtel
22 J.W. Marriott
    Peachtree Executive Conf. Ctr.
21 Holiday Inn Crowne Plaza
    Evergreen Conference Ctr.

BEST VALUES
Renaissance Waverly
Embassy Suites Perimeter Ctr.
Holiday Inn Crowne Plaza
Sheraton Gateway
Evergreen Conference Ctr.
Marriott Perimeter Ctr.
Wyndham Garden Vinings
Westin Perimeter Ctr.
Wyndham Garden Midtown
Peachtree Executive Conf. Ctr.

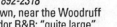

Ansley Inn 19R (4S)
▽ 20 | 21 | 15 | 20 | $117
253 15th St. NE, Atlanta; (404) 872-9000; (800) 446-5416; FAX: (404) 892-2318
■ The "lovely residential neighborhood" of Ansley Park in Midtown, near the Woodruff Arts Center and Atlanta Botanical Gardens, is home to this 1907 Tudor B&B; "quite large" rooms (all with Jacuzzis, some with kitchenettes or fireplaces), a "very helpful innkeeper" and 24-hour room service add up to a comfortable stay.

Biltmore Suites 8R (65S)
▽ 14 | 16 | 15 | 12 | $147
30 Fifth St. NE, Atlanta; (404) 874-0824; (800) 822-0824; FAX: (404) 458-5384
■ This small, affordable, mostly suites hotel housed in a 1924 Georgian structure features "old" touches like hardwood floors, 10-foot ceilings and crown moldings as well as contemporary conveniences such as full kitchens in most rooms and Jacuzzis in some; a long-term lease option makes it a good choice for extended Midtown stays; N.B. a sister property, the Biltmore Peachtree Hotel, is located Downtown.

Buckhead B&B 19R
▽ 23 | 21 | 23 | 20 | $134
70 Lenox Pt. NE, Atlanta; (404) 261-8284; (888) 224-8797; FAX: (404) 237-9224
■ Travelers searching for a "homey" alternative to the business hotels in town look to this 1995 newcomer "off the beaten path" in affluent Buckhead; with its columned porches and balconies, and individually decorated guestrooms featuring four-poster beds, it has all the "charm" of an antebellum mansion, but also offers '90s niceties such as computer jacks and a conference room; continental breakfast is included.

Doubletree Guest Suites (224S)
▽ 20 | 18 | 15 | 17 | $149
(fka Guest Quarters)
6120 Peachtree Dunwoody Rd., Atlanta; (770) 668-0808; (800) 222-TREE; FAX: (770) 668-0008
■ Buttoned-down types contend that the "convenient location" of this "elegant" Perimeter Center all-suiter is enhanced by "well-appointed rooms" – king-size bed, oversized work desk, complimentary coffee and tea, refrigerator, hair dryer and more; there's also a fitness center and pool plus free transportation within a three-mile radius.

Embassy Suites Perimeter Center (241S)
22 | 19 | 17 | 19 | $125
1030 Crown Pointe Pkwy., Atlanta; (404) 394-5454; (800) EMBASSY; FAX: (404) 396-5167
■ The corporate crowd applauds this suburban all-suite hotel, but families also find it fits the bill for extended stays; with "clean rooms" that are "great to stretch out in" (perhaps after the free evening cocktail reception), in-room kitchenettes and a restaurant, fitness center and indoor pool all on-site, it's like "a self-contained village."

Evergreen Conference Center & Resort 238R
20 | 22 | 18 | 23 | $140
(11S)
1 Lakeview Dr., Stone Mountain; (770) 879-9900; (800) 722-1000; FAX: (770) 413-9052
■ "If you want a quiet, private place, this is it" declare devotees of this "great conference center" located on 3,200 acres in historic Stone Mountain Park; service is "super" and the "excellent grounds" include attractions and activities for the entire family – golf, tennis, swimming, fishing and canoeing just to name a few.

FOUR SEASONS HOTEL ATLANTA 226R (18S)
27 | 26 | 25 | 26 | $192
(fka Grand Hotel Atlanta)
75 14th St., Atlanta; (404) 881-9898; (800) 952-0702; FAX: (404) 870-4289
■ "The Taj Mahal of Atlanta", "where no wish goes ungranted", indulges guests with "impeccable service", "gorgeous rooms", "elegant and lush" surroundings and fine dining; despite "beautiful everything" at this "grand favorite", the wary warn that the Midtown neighborhood, though "up and coming", can be "a bit frightening at night"; N.B. the Four Seasons takeover may mean changes.

French Quarter Suites Hotel (155S)
▽ 18 | 18 | 15 | 16 | $124
2780 Whitley Rd., Atlanta; (770) 980-1900; (800) 843-5858; FAX: (770) 980-1528
■ It "feels like New Orleans" at this North Atlanta all-suite hotel sporting warm pastel tones, wrought iron balconies, Cajun-Creole cuisine and live jazz; it's "greatly improved after renovations" in 1995, with bedrooms that feel "almost like your own" – as long as yours has a whirlpool tub built for two.

GRAND HYATT ATLANTA 418R (22S)
26 | 26 | 25 | 25 | $188
(fka Nikko Atlanta)
3300 Peachtree Rd. NE, Atlanta; (404) 365-8100; (800) 233-1234; FAX: (404) 233-5686
■ "This hotel believes in perfect service" and a whole lot more according to loyalists who say it offers "elegance at its best" in Buckhead; rooms are "beautifully furnished", the restaurants are "exceptional" and the "striking" lobby overlooks a three-story waterfall and Japanese garden; a few feel it's "cold" and "stark", but most maintain a stay here is "well worth it" – especially "if you're on an expense account"; N.B. Grand Hyatt's takeover may spell changes.

Hilton & Towers Atlanta 1180R (42S)   18 | 18 | 17 | 17 | $148
255 Courtland St. NE, Atlanta; (404) 659-2000; (800) HILTONS; FAX: (404) 222-2868

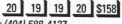 A "vast, rambling", "sterile" Downtown hotel nevertheless captures compliments for its "wonderful rooftop Russian restaurant", "extraordinary meeting space" and direct access to the World Congress Center; critics who claim it "needs a face-lift, tummy-tuck and lots more" may be mollified by a recent (post-*Survey*) $18-million renovation.

Hilton & Towers Atlanta Airport 498R (5S)   20 | 18 | 17 | 17 | $128
1031 Virginia Ave., Atlanta; (404) 767-9000; (800) 445-8667; FAX: (404) 768-0185

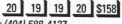 "As an airport hotel it's in a class by itself" vs. "convenient to the airport but that's all" sums up the debate about this "big, very impersonal" property offering a complimentary 24-hour shuttle to Hartsfield; the middle ground maintains it's "generic but clean" with "nice rooms" and "fairly efficient" service.

Holiday Inn Crowne Plaza Ravinia 462R (33S)   22 | 20 | 20 | 21 | $140
4355 Ashford-Dunwoody Rd., Atlanta; (707) 395-7700; (800) 392-9864; FAX: (770) 396-5167

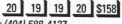 While many crown this Perimeter Center hotel the chain's "showpiece" – "not the Holiday Inn you expect" – a few detractors dismiss it as only "basic for business travel" and say it was "built to impress the yokels"; regardless, raves are in order for the "beautiful ravine", "fabulous grounds", "spectacular gardens" and convenience to "excellent shopping", restaurants and entertainment.

Hyatt Regency Atlanta 1206R (58S)   20 | 19 | 19 | 20 | $158
265 Peachtree St., Atlanta; (404) 577-1234; (800) 233-1234; FAX: (404) 588-4137

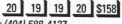 "The original and still the best" sigh supporters of this "solid, dependable" convention hotel that makes its mark with 180,000 square feet of function space, a "great revolving rooftop restaurant" and "convenient" Downtown location ("close to Macy's" and MARTA); but cynics say the rooms could use "a bit of sprucing up", there "aren't enough elevators" and the 23-story atrium "is like an echo chamber."

Hyatt Regency Suites Perimeter NW (200S)   ▽ 22 | 22 | 18 | 17 | $141
2999 Windy Hill Rd., Marietta; (770) 956-1234; (800) 233-1234; FAX: (770) 916-1120

■ This newly renovated, "well-managed" suburban all-suiter delivers "excellent service" "even when it's packed"; those looking for "very healthy food choices" will find them, along with the "best pancakes in the US"; "perfect for a short stay", the hotel blends business and pleasure by offering convenience to attractions like historic Marietta, White Water and Six Flags.

J.W. Marriott - Lenox 361R (10S)   24 | 23 | 21 | 22 | $158
3300 Lenox Rd. NE, Atlanta; (404) 262-3344; (800) 228-9290; FAX: (404) 262-8689

■ Surveyors who "love this hotel" in the heart of upscale Buckhead offer comments ranging from "a first-class property" to "one of the best around"; it's a "pricey" "place to mix business and pleasure", providing over 15,000 square feet of meeting space and a "great shopping location" with direct access to Lenox Square; N.B. there's a MARTA station opposite the hotel for easy airport transportation.

Marietta Conference Center & Resort 190R (9S) ▽ 21 | 23 | 21 | 23 | $146
500 Powder Springs St., Marietta; (770) 427-2500; FAX: (770) 429-9577

■ "It's about time they put a decent hotel in Marietta" rejoice reviewers about this modern newcomer with "spacious rooms" built on the site of the old Marietta Country Club; a "killer breakfast" is only part of the "great Southern hospitality" served up at this resort located 20 minutes north of Atlanta – gardens provide space for parties and receptions, and the antebellum Brumby Hall is being renovated for a 1997 opening.

Marque of Atlanta 120R (154S)   ▽ 19 | 18 | 16 | 16 | $123
111 Perimeter Ctr. W., Atlanta; (770) 396-6800; (800) 683-6100; FAX: (770) 399-5514

■ "An unknown bargain – keep it a secret" say those who know this 12-story suburbanite within walking distance of restaurants and shopping at Perimeter Mall; amenities include full kitchens in balconied suites, in-room computer jacks, a business center, outdoor pool and exercise room; small meetings are a specialty.

Marriott Atlanta Airport 640R (16S)   – | – | – | – | E
4711 Best Rd., College Park; (404) 766-7900; (800) 228-9290; FAX: (404) 209-6838

Surrounded by 14 wooded acres, this airport hotel offers a business center, airline desk and express video check-out only five minutes from the runways; layovers are made easier by the health club as well as basketball, tennis and racquetball facilities.

Marriott Marquis Atlanta 1600R (71S)   21   21   19   20 $156
265 Peachtree Ctr. Ave., Atlanta; (404) 521-0000; (800) 228-9290; FAX: (404) 586-6247
■ It's "convention city" at this "humongous" Downtowner sporting a 50-story atrium
that visitors either love or hate: "spectacular" vs. "hideous"; expect "standard big-
city Marriott rooms", a "courteous staff", attached shopping and a choice of five
restaurants along with "the weaknesses of a big hotel" – "slow check-in" and an
atmosphere that "lacks warmth."

Marriott North Central Atlanta 282R (5S)   ▽ 16   16   14   15 $115
(fka Sheraton Century Center)
2000 Century Blvd., Atlanta; (404) 325-0000; (800) 325-7224; FAX: (404) 325-4920
■ "Average" sums up participants' opinions on this business-only high-rise hotel
surrounded by corporate offices in Century Center; a jogging trail, tennis court,
outdoor pool and exercise room don't prevent grousing about "no real facilities."

Marriott Northwest Atlanta 397R (3S)   16   17   15   17 $117
200 Interstate North Pkwy., Atlanta; (770) 952-7900; (800) 228-9290; FAX: (770) 952-1468
■ "Clean rooms", a "friendly staff", easy access to major highways and easy-on-the-
wallet prices make this Northwest suburbanite a "great place to stay if you're watching
your budget"; business travelers take note: there's a "special dining area" for solo seaters.

Marriott Perimeter Center Atlanta 396R (4S)   20   20   17   18 $127
246 Perimeter Ctr. Pkwy., Atlanta; (770) 394-6500; (800) 228-9290; FAX: (770) 394-4338
■ Considering the "well-appointed rooms", "great service", indoor/outdoor pool, tennis
courts and "convenient location" near restaurants, entertainment and Perimeter Mall,
devotees deem this Dunwoodyan an "altogether average to above-average" hotel – a
"good place to send visiting relatives."

Marriott Suites Midtown Atlanta (254S)   22   20   16   18 $141
35 14th St., Atlanta; (404) 876-8888; (800) 228-9290; FAX: (404) 888-3667
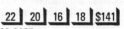 A "great location for business or pleasure" (walking distance to the High Museum of
Art and Woodruff Arts Center and convenient to Georgia Tech, Piedmont Park and the
Fox Theatre) and "spacious suites" (with work desks, wet bars, refrigerators and two
phones with call waiting and dataports) add up to a "superb value" at this Midtowner;
"good service" may help offset the "ho-hum" ambiance.

Omni Hotel at CNN Center 446R (12S)   19   18   17   17 $159
100 CNN Ctr., Atlanta; (404) 659-0000; (800) THE-OMNI; FAX: (404) 818-4322
■ Newshounds report "it's fun to be involved with CNN" whose studios occupy part
of the atrium lobby of this "great-for-conventions" hotel next to the World Congress
Center and Omni Sports Arena; the scoop is that there are "great views" of the skyline
or CNN Center – but from "small" albeit recently revamped rooms; some say it's a
"tough, tough neighborhood."

Peachtree Executive Conference Center   23   23   21   21 $154
244R (6S)
2443 GA Hwy. 54 W., Peachtree City; (770) 487-2000; (800) PEACH-11; FAX: (770) 487-4428
■ "Hotel amenities", "food galore" and "excellent meeting space" (24 rooms for up to
600) characterize this 19-acre campus south of the airport designed with corporate
America in mind; rain or shine, activities prevail inside and out – health club with indoor
and outdoor pools, billiard tables, golf course, 72 miles of bike trails and "wonderful
walking paths", even a team-building ropes course.

Renaissance Hotel - Downtown Atlanta   16   16   15   16 $152
480R (24S)
590 W. Peachtree St. NW, Atlanta; (404) 881-6000; (800) 633-0000; FAX: (404) 815-5010
■ The Renaissance appears to be faltering to most respondents, evidenced by a drop in
ratings since our last *Survey*; critics claim this "average hotel" is "frayed" and "a bit
dumpy inside", and some surveyors "don't feel safe" in the Downtown location near
the World Congress Center and Underground Atlanta.

Renaissance Waverly 504R (24S)   24   23   22   23 $151
(fka Stouffer Waverly Hotel)
2450 Galleria Pkwy., Atlanta; (770) 953-4500; (800) HOTELS-1; FAX: (770) 953-0740
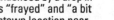 "A bit off the beaten path", this "totally adequate suburban hotel" pleases patrons
with "large rooms" and "convenience to shops and restaurants" at the adjacent Cobb
Galleria Center and nearby Cumberland Mall; admirers adore the "best Sunday brunch in
town", but a few late-night revelers claim "there's nothing to do in the hotel after 10 PM."

RITZ-CARLTON ATLANTA 425R (22S)

26	26	26	24	$198

181 Peachtree St. NE, Atlanta; (404) 659-0400; (800) 241-3333; FAX: (404) 688-0400

■ "One of the country's best" exclaim enthusiasts of the "hedonism" that abounds at this "oasis of civilization" that's a "quiet escape" despite its "perfect location" Downtown; "beautiful rooms", "awesome high tea" and fine dining at The Cafe and The Restaurant make it a "gem in the tradition of this first-class chain"; most agree "the staff defines good service", but the attention is "almost too much" for some.

RITZ-CARLTON BUCKHEAD 524R (29S)

27	28	27	26	$207

3434 Peachtree Rd. NE, Atlanta; (404) 237-2700; (800) 241-3333; FAX: (404) 239-0078

■ Atlanta's top-rated hotel (and one of the top 20 in the country) is "close to perfect" and "one of the best R-Cs anywhere", with a "staff that treats every guest like royalty", "superb dining" at The Cafe and The Dining Room, "spectacular" public spaces and proximity to posh shopping at Phipps Plaza and Lenox Square; though some say "such a special place ought to have bigger rooms", no one can deny they're "beautiful."

Sheraton Colony Square Hotel 431R (31S)

17	17	16	16	$134

188 14th St. NE, Atlanta; (404) 892-6000; (800) 422-7895; FAX: (404) 876-3276

◪ The Midtown "location cannot be beat" and the rooms and service are "ok", but the attached mini-mall "is the saving grace" of this "basic business hotel"; naysayers claim it's a "has-been" in "dire need of remodeling"; they're being heard – a renovation is scheduled to be completed in 1997.

Sheraton Gateway Hotel 384R (11S)

18	20	17	17	$122

1900 Sullivan Rd., College Park; (770) 997-1100; (800) 784-9400; FAX: (770) 991-5906

■ "Airport accessibility" and direct access to the Georgia International Convention Center are the hallmarks of this otherwise "ok" business hotel; recreational amenities include an indoor/outdoor swimming pool and a workout room equipped with weights, Lifecycles and a sauna.

Summerfield Suites Hotel (122S)

▽ 22	17	15	14	$107

760 Mt. Vernon Hwy. NE, Atlanta; (404) 250-0110; (800) 833-4353; FAX: (404) 250-9335

■ This "spacious" all-suiter inspires nods for its "great breakfast and happy hour" (both complimentary); while a few find the suburban setting a "lousy area at night", most praise this "deal of the century" for amenities like kitchens and VCRs in every suite.

Swissôtel Atlanta 349R (16S)

24	24	23	23	$171

3391 Peachtree Rd. NE, Atlanta; (404) 365-0065; (800) 253-1397; FAX: (404) 365-8787

■ "European flavor" combines with "very New York" style to create a "cosmopolitan" feel at this "first-class" Buckhead hotel; reviewers loll in "lovely rooms" when they're not working out in the "great" fitness center or taking advantage of the "fabulous shopping next door"; most give kudos to the "fabulous artwork" and "sleek, sexy" decor, though some are chilled by the "cold, impersonal" character.

Terrace Garden Hotel - Buckhead 363R (5S)

15	15	14	13	$118

3405 Lenox Rd. NE, Atlanta; (404) 261-9250; (800) 866-ROOM; FAX: (404) 848-7301

◪ "Moderately priced lodging in a good location" sums up the sentiment about this "great place for a shopping tour of Lenox Square and Phipps Plaza"; though many accuse this Buckhead budgeteer of being "a bit shabby", 1997 will bring improvements to rooms and business facilities following a 1996 renovation of the lobby, lounge and exterior.

Westin Atlanta North at Perimeter 364R (6S)
(fka Doubletree at Concourse, Atlanta)

21	21	19	20	$137

7 Concourse Pkwy., Atlanta; (770) 395-3900; (800) WESTIN-1; FAX: (770) 395-3935

◪ Boosters cheer the "Southern hospitality", "great public spaces" and "unbelievable health club" ($10 a day) at this "beautiful", "very classy" North Atlanta business abode; but where some sleep in "very nice large rooms", others bide their time in "drab, gray, small" quarters; N.B. at press time, improvement plans were on the drawing board.

Westin Hotel Atlanta Airport 498R (3S)
(fka Renaissance College Park)

19	18	15	17	$128

4736 Best Rd., College Park; (404) 762-7676; (800) 228-3000; FAX: (404) 559-7330

■ A recent redo of this airport property created guestrooms designed with business travelers in mind; amenities include a printer/fax/copier, speakerphone with dataport, complimentary 800, local and credit card calls, and complimentary office supplies; to help corporate types unwind after hours there's an indoor/outdoor pool, basketball court, sauna, whirlpool and health club.

Westin Peachtree Plaza 1020R (48S)
19 | 19 | 18 | 18 | $161

210 Peachtree St. NW, Atlanta; (404) 659-1400; (800) WESTIN-1; FAX: (404) 589-7424

◪ The "wedge-shaped rooms" that make up this John Portman–designed 73-story glass cylinder are "comfortable" and "cozy" to some but leave many others feeling "like pepperoni on a pizza" given "closet-sized" dimensions; but the staff "tries hard" and the Downtown location is "convenient"; for vertiginous views, "check out the Sun Dial Restaurant where you spin around 360 degrees while seeing the sites of Atlanta."

Wyndham Garden Hotel - Midtown Atlanta
19 | 19 | 17 | 17 | $124
190R (1S)

125 10th St. NE, Atlanta; (404) 873-4800; (800) WYNDHAM; FAX: (404) 870-1530

■ On-site exercise equipment and easy access to the Georgia Dome, Olympic Park and Woodruff Arts Center redeem this otherwise "ho-hum" Midtowner; rooms are "comfortable", but there's "no room-service breakfast" ("good grits" are available at the Juniper Cafe); the bottom line: "ok for sleeping", just "don't meet any clients" here.

Wyndham Garden Hotel - Vinings 151R (8S)
18 | 18 | 14 | 15 | $110

2857 Paces Ferry Rd., Atlanta; (770) 432-5555; (800) WYNDHAM; FAX: (770) 436-5558

■ Recent renovations may satisfy mumblers who find "nothing special" about this suburban business hotel with a New England–inspired design; guestrooms are supplied with hair dryers, two phones and work areas, and there's an outdoor pool, two lighted tennis courts and three meeting rooms.

Augusta

Partridge Inn 114R (41S)
▽ 18 | 19 | 18 | 19 | $101

2100 Walton Way, Augusta; (706) 737-8888; (800) 476-6888; FAX: (706) 731-0826

◪ Constructed in the 1890s by a New York hotelier and now listed in the National Register of Historic Places, this "charming" inn marked by terraces, balconies and verandas "takes you back to the Old South" (perhaps too far back for those who say it's "worn at the edges" and has "rooms on the small side"); some suites have kitchens, and dining options also include the casual Veranda and more upscale Dining Room.

Braselton

CHÂTEAU ELAN WINERY & RESORT 263R (43S)
26 | 23 | 23 | 25 | $165

100 Rue Charlemagne, Braselton; (770) 932-0900; (800) 233-9463; FAX: (770) 271-6005

◪ "A winery in Georgia?" sneer skeptics who've never heard of this country inn 30 minutes north of Atlanta; 200 acres planted with varietal grapes surround the "beautiful facility", and the local product is served in several full-service restaurants; amenities include a spa, three 18-hole golf courses, tennis courts and swimming pools.

Jekyll Island

JEKYLL ISLAND CLUB HOTEL 114R (20S)
24 | 24 | 23 | 25 | $149

371 Riverview Dr., Jekyll Island; (912) 635-2600; (800) 535-9547; FAX: (912) 635-2818

◪ Once a magnet for the upper crust (i.e. the Vanderbilts, Pulitzers, Rockefellers), this "mini Hotel del Coronado" on one of Georgia's Golden Isles sends guests "back in time" to "old-fashioned island living"; expect "beautiful interiors", "fantastic food" and a "well-rounded" list of diversions including golf, tennis, swimming, croquet and jet skiing; to a minority, it's "long on historic charm, short on creature comforts."

Lake Lanier Islands

Renaissance Pineisle Resort 241R (9S)
21 | 22 | 19 | 23 | $161
(fka Stouffer Renaissance Pineisle Resort)

9000 Holiday Rd., Lake Lanier Islands; (770) 945-8921; (800) HOTELS-1; FAX: (770) 945-1024

■ Vacationers seeking a "well-hidden getaway" favor the "beautiful lake and scenery" surrounding this newly renovated island resort in the foothills of the Blue Ridge Mountains, 45 minutes from Downtown Atlanta; a beach, water park and 1,200-acre forest make it a "great place for kids"; golf and tennis get high scores from parents, as does the "extremely hospitable staff"; overall, it's a "fun place to be."

Macon

1842 INN 21R
26 | 26 | 22 | 23 | $133

353 College St., Macon; (912) 741-1842; (800) 336-1842; FAX: (912) 741-1842

■ This 1842 Greek Revival home with an adjoining Victorian house ranks as a "delightful antebellum property" with "wonderful antiques-filled rooms", some featuring fireplaces and whirlpool tubs; its brand of "warm, friendly service" includes complimentary continental breakfast (with morning newspaper), evening hors d'oeuvres in the library and nightly turndown service; towel warmers are "a nice touch" too.

Peachtree City

Aberdeen Woods Conference Center 230R (3S) ▽ | 19 | 20 | 19 | 20 | $134
201 Aberdeen Pkwy., Peachtree City; (770) 487-2666; FAX: (770) 631-4096
■ Twenty-five minutes from Hartsfield Airport, this 38-acre campus neatly wraps up conference packages in facilities that include 59 meeting rooms, an auditorium and two amphitheaters plus a wide variety of recreational activities including basketball, bicycling, billiards, swimming, tennis and volleyball; conferees agree it's a "great place for a meeting" though "not a luxury spot."

Pine Mountain

Callaway Gardens 349R (293S) | 19 | 22 | 19 | 24 | $141
US Hwy. 27, Pine Mountain; (706) 663-2281; (800) CALLAWAY; FAX: (706) 663-5090
■ A man-made "garden of Eden" with 14,000-plus acres of gardens, woodlands, lakes, a horticultural center, the largest free-flight butterfly conservatory in North America and "wonderful recreational facilities" (golf, tennis, swimming, canoeing, fishing, biking); the food's kinda "dull", but the staff is "charming" and lodgings range from "motel-type rooms" to "lovely" cottages that are "a steal" for families; it just may be the "best value in Southern resorts" and is "a quick trip from Atlanta."

Savannah

BALLASTONE INN 14R (3S) | 27 | 25 | 21 | 24 | $167
14 E. Oglethorpe Ave., Savannah; (912) 236-1484; (800) 822-4553; FAX: (912) 236-4626
■ This 1838 B&B with "disarming Southern charm" and a "gorgeous garden" rewards guests with "wonderfully and differently decorated rooms" replete with antiques and most with fireplace – "even the tiny rooms have charm"; this "gem" serves up "every creature comfort" in a "consistently gracious" manner including complimentary breakfast in bed, "tea in the parlor" and hors d'oeuvres in the lounge on Friday and Saturday nights.

Eliza Thompson House 23R | 25 | 24 | 22 | 23 | $127
5 W. Jones St., Savannah; (912) 236-3620; (800) 348-9378; FAX: (912) 238-1920
■ "Very lovely rooms", many equipped with working fireplaces, entice romantics to one of Savannah's oldest inns, a "charming" antebellum abode redecorated in 1996; its Historic District location makes it easy to "walk around old Savannah"; before strolling, surveyors enjoy an "excellent breakfast" served by "gracious" staffers, and a wine and cheese reception welcomes them back in the evening.

GASTONIAN, THE 10R (3S) | 27 | 25 | 23 | 23 | $169
220 E. Gaston St., Savannah; (912) 232-2869; (800) 322-6603; FAX: (912) 232-0710
■ This "B&B puts everything together" – "excellent service", "wonderful breakfasts" and "lovely rooms" all with fireplaces and decorated with English Georgian and Regency antiques; the 1868 Italianate mansion on "the far edge of the Historic District" is "a pure delight" and "just what Savannah should be"; an added attraction: the "most unusual tubs", some of which "require a short ladder."

Hyatt Regency Savannah 318R (28S) | 20 | 20 | 18 | 20 | $137
2 W. Bay St., Savannah; (912) 238-1234; (800) 233-1234; FAX: (912) 944-3678
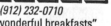 A "good choice if visiting Savannah with kids" as well as "a terrific business hotel" say those who like this recently renovated (1996) Downtowner with an indoor pool and 16 meeting rooms; the "prime location" overlooks the revitalized Riverfront Plaza district, so "get a room with a river view and watch the ships go by"; ditto at dinner: aim for "a window table" at Windows; "except for the view", however, it's a "typical Hyatt."

Kehoe House 13R (2S) ▽ | 24 | 27 | 23 | 24 | $185
123 Habersham St., Savannah; (912) 232-1020; (800) 820-1020; FAX: (912) 231-0208
■ Built in 1892 and located in the Historic District, this "gorgeous", "utterly charming" B&B offers a panoramic view of Downtown from individually designed guestrooms and suites (insiders advise "book the enormous rooms facing Columbia Square"); rates include full breakfast and wine and hors d'oeuvres.

Magnolia Place Inn 13R ▽ | 23 | 23 | 18 | 21 | $150
503 Whitaker St., Savannah; (912) 236-7674; (800) 238-7674; FAX: (912) 236-1145
■ This 1878 Victorian is "exactly what a B&B should be": "completely charming", "very atmospheric" and equipped with "up-to-date amenities"; "comfortable rooms" are individually decorated with English antiques and period prints, and many have canopied four-poster beds; rates include continental breakfast served in the parlor, in your room or on the veranda overlooking Forsyth Park.

Marriott Savannah Riverfront 337R (46S)   19 | 18 | 16 | 18 | $133
(fka Radisson Plaza Savannah)

100 General McIntosh Blvd., Savannah; (912) 233-7722; (800) 228-9290; FAX: (912) 233-3765

■ It has a "great location" and offers "river views", but the "beautiful surroundings" at this Riverfront neighbor aren't enough to offset "below-average" service and limited dining options ("T.G.I. Friday's for dinner?"); adults may find it on the "pedestrian" side but admit it's a "good kids' place" – there are indoor and outdoor pools to splash around in.

Mulberry Holiday Inn 96R (26S)   20 | 21 | 16 | 19 | $127
601 E. Bay St., Savannah; (912) 238-1200; (800) HOLIDAY; FAX: (912) 236-2184

■ Erected in 1860 as a livery stable and later serving as a cotton warehouse and a Coca-Cola bottling plant, this Holiday Inn acquisition receives contrary remarks; some call it "pleasant as a tourist base" with "beautiful rooms" and "old-fashioned courteous service", while others say it has "seen better days" and is, after all, "a Holiday Inn" – but, according to one sanguine soul, "the nicest one I've been to."

Planters Inn - Savannah 55R (1S)   ▽ 21 | 22 | 17 | 16 | $113
29 Abercorn St., Savannah; (912) 232-5678; (800) 554-1187; FAX: (912) 232-8893

■ Live oaks, flowering azaleas and horse-drawn carriages set the mood at this "historic B&B" in an 1812 Victorian on Reynolds Square, where visitors plant themselves for "terrific service" and "wonderful rooms"; Baker furnishings, complimentary continental breakfast and afternoon tea add charm and make it "an excellent value."

President's Quarters 9R (7S)   ▽ 26 | 22 | 21 | 16 | $137
225 E. Presidents St., Savannah; (912) 233-1600; (800) 233-1776; FAX: (912) 238-0849

■ An "absolutely delightful" pair of 1855 Greek Revival townhouses in the Historic District commemorating the past visits of 20 commanders in chief with presidential memorabilia throughout; guests enjoy "the charm of the Old South" not only in the "large, comfortable rooms" and ornate balconies overlooking a beautifully landscaped courtyard, but also at the afternoon tea served after a day of sight-seeing.

17 Hundred 90 Inn & Restaurant 13R (1S)   ▽ 23 | 22 | 22 | 18 | $128
307 E. Presidents St., Savannah; (912) 236-7122; (800) 487-1790; FAX: (912) 236-7123

■ Lunch at this inn's Garden Room is as much a part of Savannah life as the squares laid out by General Oglethorpe; history buffs will relish the huge brick fireplaces in the restaurant and the antiques throughout the two joined 1790s houses; the innkeepers offer a complimentary bottle of wine in each room, and continental breakfast is included.

Sea Island

CLOISTER, THE 234R (28S) 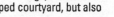   26 | 27 | 26 | 28 | $263
Sea Island; (912) 638-3611; (800) 732-4752; FAX: (912) 638-5823

■ Most say this "classic American resort" in a "country club setting" "has everything" – "beautiful, spacious rooms", "superb service", "terrific dining" (included in the rates) and "excellent facilities" for the entire family including golf, tennis, a full-service spa and five miles of private beach; while some grow weary of "silly formalities" (coat and tie required at dinner in the main dining room), most maintain "it doesn't get any better than this."

St. Simons Island

King and Prince Beach & Golf Resort 94R (91S) 20 | 21 | 19 | 22 | $157
201 Arnold Rd., St. Simons Island; (912) 638-3631; (800) 342-0212; FAX: (912) 634-1720

■ "The way it used to be along the barrier islands", this example of 1930s Spanish-style architecture lures families with on-site recreation including swimming, sailing, tennis and a secluded stretch of white-sand beach; though the "food needs improving" and the "rooms in the old section" are "small", the two- and three-bedroom villas are "terrific" (offering "superb views of sunrise") and the atmosphere is "personal and intimate."

Lodge at Little St. Simons Island 13R (2S)   – | – | – | – | VE
PO Box 21078, St. Simons Island; (912) 638-7472; FAX: (912) 634-1811

Ten thousand acres capped by a seven-mile beach bring nature lovers to this island camp/resort where guests can rent any of several houses and cottages or even the entire island (accommodations for 30); there's horseback riding, fishing and boating, but many come to bird-watch and witness sea-turtles nesting (staff naturalists offer nature walks); rates include three meals a day, and there's now a/c in some accommodations.

Sea Palms Golf & Tennis Resort 130R (30S)   22 | 20 | 20 | 23 | $173
5445 Frederica Rd., St. Simons Island; (912) 638-3351; (800) 841-6268; FAX: (912) 634-8029

■ Twenty-seven holes of golf, 12 tennis courts, two swimming pools, a private beach club and many children's activities keep guests entertained when they aren't attending a meeting, relaxing in renovated ('96) "comfy condos" or sampling the restaurant's American fare; golf packages include accommodations, greens fees and a golf cart.

Hawaii

TOP 20 OVERALL

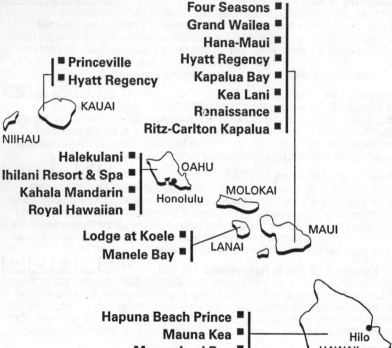

Four Seasons ■
Grand Wailea ■
Hana-Maui ■
Hyatt Regency ■
Kapalua Bay ■
Kea Lani ■
Renaissance ■
Ritz-Carlton Kapalua ■

■ **Princeville**
■ **Hyatt Regency**

KAUAI

NIIHAU

Halekulani ■
Ihilani Resort & Spa ■
Kahala Mandarin ■
Royal Hawaiian ■

OAHU

MOLOKAI

Honolulu

Lodge at Koele ■
Manele Bay ■

LANAI

MAUI

Hapuna Beach Prince ■
Mauna Kea ■
Mauna Lani Bay ■
Orchid Mauna Lani ■

Hilo
HAWAII

BEST OVERALL
- **29** Lodge at Koele/Lanai
- **28** Four Seasons/Maui
  Halekulani/Oahu
  Manele Bay/Lanai
  Mauna Lani Bay/Big Island
- **27** Grand Wailea/Maui
  Ritz-Carlton Kapalua/Maui
  Mauna Kea/Big Island
- **26** Ihilani Resort & Spa/Oahu
  Hyatt Regency/Kauai
  Orchid Mauna Lani/Big Island
  Princeville/Kauai
  Kahala Mandarin/Oahu
  Kea Lani/Maui
- **25** Hana-Maui/Maui
  Hyatt Regency/Maui
  Kapalua Bay/Maui
  Hapuna Beach Prince/Big Island
- **24** Renaissance Wailea/Maui
  Royal Hawaiian/Oahu

BEST VALUES
Kauai Coconut Beach/Kauai
Outrigger/Kauai
New Otani/Oahu
Outrigger Reef/Oahu
Kaanapali/Maui
Royal Waikoloan/Big Island
Hilton Turtle Bay/Oahu
Outrigger Waikiki/Oahu
Pacific Beach/Oahu
Hawaii Prince/Oahu
Waikiki Parc/Oahu
Sheraton Moana Surfrider/Oahu
Hawaiian Regent/Oahu
Aston Kaanapali/Maui
Hilton Hawaiian/Oahu
Marriott/Maui
Ala Moana/Oahu
Marriott/Kauai
Hyatt Regency Waikiki/Oahu
Sheraton Princess/Oahu

Big Island

FOUR SEASONS RESORT HUALALAI 212R (31S) — — — — VE
PO Box 1269, Kailua, Kona, Big Island; (808) 325-8000; (888) 340-5662;
FAX: (808) 325-8056
Sure to make big waves in our next *Survey*, Hawaii's newest beachside resort (opened September '96) offers luxury low-rise bungalows with private entrances and lanais, all with breathtaking ocean views, clustered around lovely oceanside pools and gardens; add a Jack Nicklaus golf course, eight tennis courts, fitness center and spa, three restaurants, a complimentary children's program and Four Seasons' renowned service, and the question is inevitable: what's not to like?

HAPUNA BEACH PRINCE HOTEL 314R (37S)   26 24 24 25 $258
62-100 Kauna'oa Dr., Kohala Coast, Big Island; (808) 880-1111; (808) 882-6060;
FAX: (808) 880-3200
■ "Mauna Kea's big, beautiful, more contemporary sister" on 32 terraced acres overlooking "the best beach in the islands" wins enthusiastic applause for its "panoramic ocean views", "amazing public areas" and "classy rooms with bathrooms you could get lost in"; the "gorgeous" pool, "magnificent gardens", Arnold Palmer–designed golf course and "signing privileges at both hotels" add appeal, but even some ardent admirers censure its "too austere" architecture.

Hawaii Naniloa Resort 306R (19S)   ▽ 14 16 15 16 $124
(fka Hawaii Naniloa Hotel)
93 Banyan Dr., Hilo, Big Island; (808) 969-3333; (800) 367-5360; FAX: (808) 969-6622
◪ This well-established hotel in "a beautiful setting" near Liliuokalani Gardens offers "postcard-perfect" views of the bay and "small, comfortable rooms" (though some say they cry out for "an overhaul"); customers consider it "typical" for Hilo and urge "get a balcony room."

HILTON WAIKOLOA VILLAGE RESORT   23 23 23 26 $219
1186R (55S)
425 Waikoloa Beach Dr., Kamuela, Big Island; (808) 885-1234; (800) HILTONS;
FAX: (808) 885-2900
■ "Disneyland in Hawaii" best describes this "megaresort for megacrowds"; "tastefully overdone" and "definitely entertaining", it has "something for everyone": "monorail and gondola rides" (great for kids), "snorkeling with paid-to-smile tropical fish in a man-made lagoon", "better-than-average food" at six restaurants, access to "great golf", a 25,000-square-foot spa, extensive meeting facilities, "many secluded pools" on "stunning grounds", even interactive "encounters with the dolphins"; there's "so much visual stimulation that you hardly notice there's no beach."

Kona Village Resort 125R   24 24 22 24 $280
PO Box 1299, Kaupulehu, Kona, Big Island; (808) 325-5555; (800) 367-5290;
FAX: (808) 325-5124
■ Habitués "kick back and chill out" at Kona's "ultimate Polynesian hideaway", "a great oasis" that inspires reactions like "am I in Bora Bora?"; the thirtysomething resort has "friendly employees" (some around for "15-plus years") and "cuisine so surprisingly imaginative" that it "gives the American plan a good name"; the accommodations in "wonderful" "thatched-roof huts" attract families and fans of South Pacific ambiance who note that "no in-room phone, TV or radio" means it's "not for everyone, thank God."

MAUNA KEA BEACH HOTEL 300R (21S)   26 27 26 28 $286
62-100 Mauna Kea Beach Dr., Kohala Coast, Big Island; (808) 882-7222; (808) 882-6060;
FAX: (808) 882-7007
■ The Queen Mother of the Kohala Coast is back and "better than ever" with "just the right blend of casual and class" after a "long overdue face-lift" to restore her "understated elegance"; although the redecorated rooms might seem "small" by '90s standards, stellar scores for the "grande dame" mean that to many she remains "an all-time favorite": "superb service", "fabulous food", "magnificent public facilities" and "the best beach on the island" sustain her reputation.

MAUNA LANI BAY 351R (45S)   27 | 27 | 27 | 28 | $293
68-1400 Mauna Lani Dr., Kohala Coast, Big Island; (808) 885-6622; (800) 367-2323; FAX: (808) 885-1484

■ "Beautiful", "elegant", "tasteful", this Kohala Coast fave rates "a perfect 10" for "luxury personified"; "outstanding rooms" (the butler-serviced bungalows are "the jewels in an impressive crown"), "excellent" food, "off-the-scale service" and access to "two superb golf courses" carved from a 16th-century lava flow make "this gorgeous hotel" "a hedonist's paradise"; you'll feel as if you had "died and gone to heaven."

ORCHID AT MAUNA LANI 485R (54S)   – | – | – | – | VE
(fka Ritz-Carlton, Mauna Lani)

1 N. Kaniku Dr., Kohala Coast, Big Island; (808) 885-2000; (800) 782-9488; FAX: (808) 885-5778
"Jeans-clad conventioneers and Chippendale don't mix" our snoops snort and the new Sheraton management seems to concur; so it's out with the weirdly awkward Bostonian touches that used to characterize this former Ritz-Carlton and in with Hawaiiana-like lush landscaping, island art and artifacts and greater emphasis on the property's historic sites; stuffiness is also out and the once-formal dining room has been claimed by an expanded spa and fitness center; looks like "Hawaii's best location is getting better."

Royal Waikoloan 508R (14S)   21 | 22 | 20 | 22 | $172
69-275 Waikoloa Beach Dr., Kamuela, Big Island; (808) 885-6789; (800) 922-5533; FAX: (808) 885-7852

☑ A "beautiful beach" and "relatively inexpensive rates" please price-sensitive sun seekers who note that this "relaxing, remote" resort "lacks the glitz of neighboring five-star properties" yet is "very comfortable" with "nice rooms", "warm and friendly" service and a "reasonably priced restaurant"; more discriminating types could do without "the Bud crowd" and complain it "needs refurbishing"; N.B. at press time, it was up for sale.

Kauai

HYATT REGENCY KAUAI RESORT & SPA   27 | 26 | 25 | 28 | $238
559R (41S)

1571 Poipu Rd., Lihue, Kauai; (808) 742-1234; (800) 228-9000; FAX: (808) 747-1557
■ Enthusiasts gush about this "large Hyatt that's done right" and spread over 50 acres on the lee coast of Kauai: there's a "gorgeous lobby", "magnificent grounds", "terrific staff", "out-of-a-dream pools and lagoons" (including an "adults-only pool"), "exemplary food", "fantastic golf" and a "luxurious spa – a near out-of-body experience at a fair price"; the rooms are "beautiful" too.

Kauai Coconut Beach Resort 283R (28S)   20 | 20 | 19 | 20 | $143
PO Box 830, Royal Coconut Coast, Kapaa, Kauai; (808) 822-3455; (808) 760-8555; FAX: (808) 822-0035

☑ Adjacent to the Coconut Plantation Marketplace, this "midpriced" property exemplifies "what a good average hotel is like" – "pleasant" and "comfortable" with "no pretension"; "beautiful" grounds, an "attentive staff" and "good package deals" complete the picture; critics who grouse about "faded glory" and "rooms that could use some updating" should note that the entire resort was refurbished in 1995.

Kiahuna Plantation (226S)   23 | 21 | 20 | 24 | $201
2253 Poipu Rd., Koloa, Kauai; (808) 742-6411; (800) OUTRIGGER; FAX: (808) 742-1698

☑ "Families with kids" have discovered "Kauai's best-kept secret", a "spacious, well-maintained" condo compound on 35 acres of "majestic grounds" on the "sunny side" of the island; the atmosphere is "casual", it's "close to a wonderful beach" and it's an "excellent value", yet these attributes are insufficient to quell complaints that it's "crowded and noisy" and the "units are too close together."

MARRIOTT RESORT & BEACH CLUB KAUAI   24 | 24 | 22 | 26 | $212
345R (243S)
(fka Westin Kauai)

Kalapaki Beach, Lihue, Kauai; (808) 245-5050; (800) 220-2925; FAX: (808) 245-5049
■ The Westin's glitz "has been toned down by Marriott" with warm Hawaiian touches including the transformation of the once-gaudy lobby into a garden with waterfall setting; the "great public spaces", "beautiful pool" and "incredible grounds" remain and a first-rate health club has been added, compensating for a location "too close to the airport"; two golf courses and a tennis complex abut the property.

Outrigger Kauai Beach 341R (6S)

| 19 | 19 | 18 | 21 | $145 |

4331 Kauai Beach Dr., Lihue, Kauai; (808) 245-1955; (800) OUTRIGGER; FAX: (808) 246-9085

■ This "mid-level" property in a "great location" is "overall nice and clean" with "spacious" if "simple rooms" at a "good price"; though the beach is coral, not sand, three lagoon-style pools connected with waterfalls, tennis courts, nearby golf and a "beautiful setting" ensure a "lovely experience"; N.B. guestrooms and public spaces were renovated in 1996, new concierge floors are expected in '97.

PRINCEVILLE HOTEL 201R (51S)

| 27 | 26 | 25 | 28 | $260 |

PO Box 3069, 5520 Kahaku Rd., Princeville, Kauai; (808) 826-9644; (800) 826-1166; FAX: (808) 826-1166

■ With its "breathtaking location" "overlooking Hanalei Bay" and "fabulous rooms" "built along the hill descending to the water", the "most beautiful place on earth" ("also the wettest place on earth") reminds respondents of the "majestic splendor of Bali Hai"; this is "where angels come when they die" and you too can have "every whim catered to", watch "dramatic sunsets", enjoy "excellent food" and perhaps even wing through 45 holes of "outstanding golf"; it's "not very Hawaiian" ("too formal"), but guests "love it anyway."

Lanai

LODGE AT KOELE 88R (14S)

| 29 | 29 | 28 | 29 | $309 |

PO Box 310, 1 Keomoku Hwy., Lanai City, Lanai; (808) 565-7300; (800) 321-4666; FAX: (808) 565-3868

■ "Unique in America", the *Survey*'s overall top-rated resort offers a "taste of absolute paradise" at 1,500 feet; this "10-star lodge" reminiscent of a "country manor" is home to exquisite plantation-style guestrooms, a "great hall with two huge stone fireplaces", "impeccable service", "unbelievable food" and a Greg Norman–designed golf course; enjoy "sunsets seen through pine trees from a rocking chair on the wide veranda" or "croquet followed by high tea in the lounge" – just be sure to "bring a lot of money."

MANELE BAY HOTEL 224R (26S)

| 28 | 27 | 27 | 28 | $303 |

PO Box 310, Lanai City, Lanai; (808) 565-7700; (800) 321-4666; FAX: (808) 565-2483

■ "Killer views" and "amazing food" in "drop-dead gorgeous surroundings" are just some of the attributes of the Lodge at Koele's sister, a Mediterranean-style property perched atop dramatic red lava cliffs overlooking the sapphire sea; there's also a spa and fitness center, tennis courts, courtyard gardens and a Jack Nicklaus–designed golf course with an ocean view from every hole; the one caveat: "bring a friend or loved one – there's nothing to do at night."

Maui

Aston Kaanapali Shores 463R

| 20 | 18 | 16 | 19 | $159 |

3445 Honoapiilani Hwy., Lahaina, Maui; (808) 667-2211; (800) 922-7866; FAX: (808) 661-0836

◪ "Comfortable", "spacious condos" with kitchens and microwave ovens (you'll use them since the "beachfront restaurant" is only "adequate") in an "intimate setting" with a "nice pool, grounds and beach" offer "great value for the money" to vacationing families; others find it "too close to other hotels" and the "rooms in poor repair."

Aston Wailea Resort 470R (46S)

| 20 | 21 | – | 21 | $195 |

(fka The Maui Inter-Continental Resort)
3700 Wailea Alanui Dr., Wailea, Maui; (808) 879-1922; (800) 367-2960; FAX: (808) 874-8331

◪ Voters have mixed emotions about this Wailea landmark, with fans giving it high marks for "excellent rooms" and "great service" and foes taking away points for merely "ok rooms", "almost nonexistent service" and food that "could stand improvement"; still, it's a "best buy" in a "great location."

Embassy Suites - Maui (413S)

| 24 | 21 | 19 | 23 | $208 |

104 Kaanapali Shores Pl., Lahaina, Maui; (808) 661-2000; (800) GO-2MAUI; FAX: (808) 667-5821

◪ "Large suites" equipped with a "full home theater", miniature golf, a video game room, a one-acre pool with water slide and a year-round children's program make this high-rise "the best" place to take the kids on Kaanapali Beach (of course, there are those who grouse about "too many brats running around"); aside from the "excellent breakfast buffet" included in the rate, reviewers recommend dining "off the premises."

R | S | D | P | $

FOUR SEASONS RESORT MAUI 305R (75S)
28 | 29 | 27 | 28 | $302

3900 Wailea Alanui Dr., Wailea, Maui; (800) 874-8000; (800) 334-6284; FAX: (804) 874-6449

■ "The most amazing place in the world" and "absolute perfection" is what pampered patrons have to say about the country's second-highest-rated resort; the poolside service receives raves ("being sprayed with Evian water is the ultimate in sybaritic pleasure") as do the "huge" rooms ("I've never seen bigger bathrooms"), "stunning grounds", "excellent food" and "gracious and charming staff"; no wonder "I'd like to retire here" comments are the norm – with one caveat: "*if* I could afford it."

GRAND WAILEA RESORT, HOTEL & SPA 708R (53S)
28 | 26 | 25 | 28 | $307

3850 Wailea Alanui Dr., Wailea, Maui; (808) 875-1234; (800) 888-6100; FAX: (808) 879-4077

■ This "big birthday cake of marble" on 42 acres with an "amazing" river-pool that "must be seen to be believed" (there are water slides, waterfalls, caves, a rope swing and white-water rapids) makes guests of all ages "act like a kid again"; boasting "grand rooms", "spectacular public areas", a "perfect spa" and "fabulous art", it's "one of the most expensive hotels ever built and it shows"; but it just may be "too big and too busy for some tastes."

HANA-MAUI HOTEL 93R
27 | 26 | 23 | 26 | $317

PO Box 9, Hana Hwy., Hana, Maui; (808) 248-8211; (800) 321-HANA; FAX: (808) 248-7202

■ "The ultimate in relaxation" in "Hawaii's most peaceful spot" on the east end of Maui inspires oceans of praise for its "romantic sea ranch cottages at the edge of the ocean", rooms "with private hot tub on a secluded lanai" and "fab setting"; it's "a welcome reminder of what Hawaii used to be" ("a great break from the standard marble and glitz") and the majority agrees there's "still no better place to get away from it all"; "rain is the only drawback"; N.B. Amans Resort is expected to take over management in '97.

HYATT REGENCY MAUI 782R (33S)
25 | 24 | 24 | 27 | $235

200 Nohea Kai Dr., Lahaina, Maui; (808) 661-1234; (800) 223-1234; FAX: (808) 667-4499

■ "The first and still the best of Hawaii's whimsical resorts" sports a "spectacular lobby atrium" filled with "exotic birds, Asian art and waterfalls", "magnificent grounds" including a Japanese garden and a swan lake, and a "surreal swimming pool" featuring "waterfall-protected caves" and "the greatest water slide ever seen"; there are also "breathtaking views" from high-rise guestrooms and three restaurants, the star being the "magnifico", "romantic" Swan Court.

Ka'anapali Beach Hotel 416R (14S)
22 | 22 | 20 | 22 | $176

2525 Ka'anapali Pkwy., Lahaina, Maui; (808) 661-0011; (800) 262-8450; FAX: (808) 667-5978

☑ One of the golden oldies on the "most beautiful" stretch of Kaanapali Beach has "a real Hawaiian atmosphere" and offers "lots of traditional Hawaiian activities" including lei making and hula lessons; in terms of lodgings it "doesn't measure up" to its newer neighbors – the rooms are just "average" – but it still represents "the best value on Maui"; N.B. families favor the all-you-can-eat buffets for breakfast, lunch and dinner.

KAPALUA BAY HOTEL 191R (3S)
25 | 25 | 24 | 26 | $258

1 Bay Dr., Kapalua, Maui; (808) 669-5656; (800) 367-8000; FAX: (808) 669-4694

■ While "somewhat remote" and "north of the action", that's all the better for surveyors who swoon over this "peaceful" resort's "pristine location" – the bay is "movie-set material"; rooms are "spacious" and "well appointed", but visitors spend most of their time outside since it's "heaven for golfers" and features "top-notch tennis facilities" and "stunning snorkeling from the beautiful beach"; dart throwers who say "needs a face-lift" will be happy to know the hotel's been taken over by Halekulani management, with extensive renovations underway at press time.

KEA LANI HOTEL SUITES & VILLAS (413S)
27 | 26 | 24 | 26 | $270

4100 Wailea Alanui Dr., Wailea, Maui; (808) 875-4100; (800) 882-4100; FAX: (808) 875-2250

■ Get past the eye-popping "unusual Moorish architecture" and you'll find a family-friendly all-suite hotel with a staff that "welcomes you as though you've arrived home", "wonderful public areas", "drop-dead accommodations and bathrooms big enough for aerobic classes" – an "incredible value" for Wailea; "splurge for a villa and you'll feel like a sheik" as you dally shamelessly in your private plunge pool; N.B. mountain-view suites also overlook the parking lot.

Marriott Maui 701R (19S)
21 | 22 | 20 | 23 | $191
100 Nohea Kai Dr., Lahaina, Maui; (808) 667-1200; (800) 763-1333; FAX: (808) 667-8192
◪ A "predictable Marriott" (but with "wonderful views") that wins praise from vacationers and conventioneers for its "great location" on Kaanapali Beach, "extremely pleasant staff" and buffets that you'll have to "pull yourself away from"; the less enthused claim the "food is only fair" and "tiny rooms" "in need of major upgrading" encourage you "to stay outdoors", but even they can't deny it's one of the "best buys on the island."

Maui Prince Hotel 291R (19S)
22 | 23 | 23 | 22 | $212
5400 Makena Alanui, Makena, Maui; (808) 874-1111; (800) 321-MAUI; FAX: (808) 879-8763
■ "Quiet", "remote" and "good for isolation freaks" is the overwhelming consensus on this "deluxe" 420-acre resort at the virtual end of the southernmost road on Maui; "all rooms have an ocean view and surround a stunning open-air atrium", two Robert Trent Jones golf courses give nongolfers "the hotel to themselves" by day and the attraction by night is "excellent cuisine" – the "Prince Court is a gem" – served by a "wonderful staff."

RENAISSANCE WAILEA BEACH RESORT
24 | 25 | 23 | 25 | $232
333R (12S)
(fka Stouffer Renaissance Wailea Beach Resort)
3550 Wailea Alanui Dr., Wailea, Maui; (808) 879-4900; (800) 9-WAILEA; FAX: (808) 879-6128
■ "Superb in all respects" sums up this "wonderful" Wailea "sleeper" now managed by Marriott; the "perfect beachfront location" and "beautiful grounds" are "very private", and the "sublime service" soothes as do the "top-notch rooms" and "fine dining" in four restaurants ("the Maui Onion is not to be missed"); "you'll never want to say aloha!"

RITZ-CARLTON KAPALUA 492R (58S)
27 | 27 | 26 | 27 | $271
1 Ritz-Carlton Dr., Kapalua, Maui; (808) 669-6200; (800) 262-8440; FAX: (808) 665-0026
■ "Breathless adulation", inspired by "typically terrific Ritz service, food and swank", abounds for "this lovely resort amid the misty hills of Kapalua" "away from Kaanapali clutter"; the "awesome grounds", "beautiful pool" and "great golf" add up to a "grand" vacation; there's some criticism for its location "too far from the beach" and "standard Ritz interior" ("could be Boston"), but most surveyors seem to think it "absolutely flawless."

Royal Lahaina Resort 434R (26S)
18 | 19 | 18 | 20 | $170
2780 Kekaa Dr., Lahaina, Maui; (808) 661-3611; (800) 447-6925; FAX: (808) 661-6150
■ This first-on-the-beach hotel opened 35 years ago as a private club and has been "a longtime favorite" for its "fine beach, gracious staff", "decent rooms" and "local color"; if now "past its prime", it's "an inexpensive alternative" for groups and families who want golf, tennis and the action of Kaanapali; it serves "the best piña colada on Maui", stages a "great beach luau" and, a boon for nonsmokers, prohibits lighting up in all public areas.

Sheraton Maui Hotel 464R (46S)
– | – | – | – | E
2605 Ka'anapali Pkwy., Lahaina, Maui; (808) 661-0031; (800) STAY-ITT; FAX: (808) 661-0458
Reopened in November 1996 after a two-year, $150-million redo, this 23-acre resort retained the best of its original features: guestrooms built into and around a legendary lava cliff called Black Rock, a lovely beach and cliff divers who still welcome the sunset by lighting tiki torches to strums of Hawaiian guitars; new are the low-rise guestroom wings set amid landscaped gardens, a flowing river-pool, three restaurants and conference facilities.

WESTIN MAUI 733R (28S)
23 | 24 | 23 | 26 | $231
2365 Ka'anapali Pkwy., Lahaina, Maui; (808) 667-2525; (800) WESTIN-1; FAX: (808) 661-5831
■ A "museum-quality art collection", "gorgeous" open-air lobby, five "fabulous" "fantasy pools", "killer ocean views" and a "truly gracious staff" add up to a "we don't want to leave" experience at this "first-class" "convention city" on Kaanapali Beach; rooms are "small", but they're no longer "outdated" thanks to a mid-1996 refurbishment.

149

Oahu

TOP 10 OVERALL

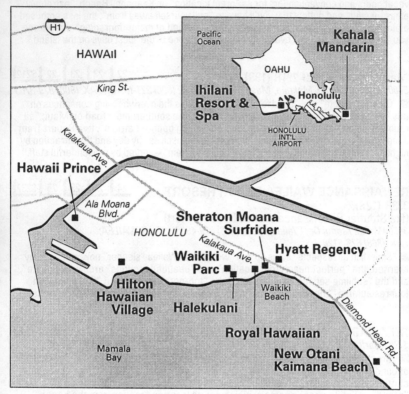

BEST OVERALL

- **28** Halekulani
- **26** Ihilani Resort & Spa
  Kahala Mandarin
- **24** Royal Hawaiian
- **23** Sheraton Moana Surfrider
- **22** Hyatt Regency Waikiki
  Hilton Hawaiian Village
  Hawaii Prince Waikiki
- **21** Waikiki Parc
- **20** New Otani Kaimana Beach

BEST VALUES

New Otani Kaimana Beach
Outrigger Reef
Hilton Turtle Bay
Outrigger Waikiki
Pacific Beach
Hawaii Prince Waikiki
Waikiki Parc
Sheraton Moana
Hawaiian Regent
Hilton Hawaiian Village

R	S	D	P	$

Ala Moana Hotel 1105R (64S)

18	18	17	18	$154

410 Atkinson Dr., Honolulu, Oahu; (808) 955-4811; (800) 367-6025; FAX: (808) 944-2974
☑ "Very nice for a basically commercial business hotel" sums up this longtime high-rise located midway between Waikiki and Downtown (across from the Hawaii Convention Center scheduled to open in 1998) and connected by skybridge to the mammoth Ala Moana Center; it's "convenient" for shopaholics and "business travelers", but sun seekers say it "suffers from not being on the beach."

Aston Waikiki Beach Tower (140S)

19	19	15	16	$161

2470 Kalakaua Ave., Honolulu, Oahu; (808) 926-6400; (800) 922-7866; FAX: (808) 926-7380
■ A towering "top-of-the-line" all-suiter across the street from Waikiki Beach offering "views to die for" from many of its 40 stories; the one- and two-bedroom suites come complete with full kitchens, "comfortable furnishings", "huge lanais" and "space to hold a football game"; guests can also expect "excellent service" but no on-site restaurant.

HALEKULANI 412R (44S)
28 | 28 | 27 | 27 | $291

2199 Kalia Rd., Honolulu, Oahu; (808) 923-2311; (800) 367-2343; FAX: (808) 926-8004

■ "An island of civility in Oahu" and "an oasis of seclusion on Waikiki Beach" vouches the very enthusiastic majority about the island's top-rated property; the "impeccable service" that makes it "a class act from check-in to check-out" is the work of "the lady general manager" (Patricia Tam) who "keeps guests and staff smiling; "breakfast is out of this world", dining at "La Mer is like being on a movie set" and the rooms are "incredible" – "with prices to match."

Hawaiian Regent 1334R (12S)
21 | 20 | 19 | 20 | $171

2552 Kalakaua Ave., Honolulu, Oahu; (808) 922-6611; (800) 367-5370; FAX: (800) 921-5255

☑ Despite solid scores, reviewers have mixed reactions about this across-the-street-from-the-beach giant: a "good value" with "comfortable" rooms and "great service" vs. a "tour operator's warehouse" that's "too big and impersonal" with "lots of concrete"; N.B. special packages are available for the hotel's 25th anniversary in 1997.

Hawaiian Waikiki Beach 675R (41S)
18 | 19 | 18 | 19 | $145

2570 Kalakaua Ave., Honolulu, Oahu; (808) 922-2511; (800) 877-7666; FAX: (808) 923-3656

■ Other than approving this property's "nice location" across the street from Waikiki Beach and its "low price for the area", respondents throw zingers like "dingy rooms", "uncomfortable beds", "stuffy smell" and "average food."

Hawaii Prince Hotel Waikiki 464R (57S)
23 | 23 | 22 | 20 | $185

100 Holomoana St., Honolulu, Oahu; (808) 956-1111; (800) 321-OAHU; FAX: (808) 946-0811

■ "The best big hotel built here in years" provides travelers with a "central location" between Waikiki and the Ala Moana Center (there's a free shuttle to the beach) as well as "great views of the ocean" from "beautiful rooms" with floor to ceiling windows; service is "excellent" and some voters would do the hula at noon on Diamond Head Road for the "outstanding buffet" and "great sushi bar" at the Prince Court, which "can't be beat" for its regional cuisine.

Hilton Golf & Tennis Resort Turtle Bay 370R (115S)
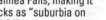 20 | 20 | 18 | 22 | $167

57-091 Kamehameha Hwy., Kahuku, Oahu; (808) 293-8811; (800) HILTONS; FAX: (808) 293-1286

☑ This North Oahu retreat that "sits by itself on a peninsula one hour from town" provides a "wonderful hideaway" with its "perfectly protected beach and lovely grounds"; a large tennis center and "two windy golf courses" are abetted by children's programs and nearby attractions such as the Polynesian Cultural Center and Waimea Falls, making it a "great hotel for families" – perhaps that's why it gets some knocks as "suburbia on the North Shore"; another caution: "the rooms could use a little TLC."

Hilton Hawaiian Village 2182R (363S)
22 | 21 | 21 | 24 | $193

2005 Kalia Rd., Honolulu, Oahu; (808) 949-4321; (800) HILTONS; FAX: (808) 947-7914

☑ It's so "biggggg" and "busy, busy, busy" with conventioneers that it "should be eligible for statehood in its own right", but many maintain this megaresort "on the good end of the beach" is also a "superlatively run self-contained village" with "fabulous grounds" including two large pools, "first-class shows" and "good restaurants"; some advise "book the Alii Tower" with its own private pool, workout room and concierge.

Hyatt Regency Waikiki 1205R (25S)
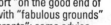 23 | 23 | 21 | 23 | $201

2424 Kalakaua Ave., Honolulu, Oahu; (808) 923-1234; (800) 233-1234; FAX: (808) 923-7839

■ "Comfortable though mammoth", this "fun destination across from the beach" is a "classic Hyatt Regency" with an "impressive open-air lobby atrium" three stories tall; "good rooms" and "excellent service" make it "more than ok for an aging megahotel", while a "stay on the Regency Club floors is a fantastic experience"; the Chinese-Italian cuisine at Ciao Mein is not only "good" but also "truly unusual."

IHILANI RESORT & SPA 351R (36S)
29 | 27 | 25 | 26 | $265

92-1001 Olani St., Kapolei, Oahu; (808) 679-0079; (800) 626-4446; FAX: (808) 679-0080

■ "It feels like you're in the outer islands" claim boosters, even though Waikiki is only 30 minutes away; many agree that it's nice to be "out of the hustle and hassle" and in a "relaxing, classy" and even "exquisite" resort – "from the moment you walk in the lobby it is incredible"; "luxurious rooms with peaceful views" add to the ease, as do a "dynamite" "spa that's heaven", "wonderful dining" and "great golf"; all in all, "magnificent."

Ilikai Hotel Nikko Waikiki 732R (50S)
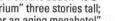 20 | 20 | 19 | 20 | $197

1777 Ala Moana Blvd., Honolulu, Oahu; (808) 949-3811; (800) NIKKO-US; FAX: (808) 947-4527

■ "Mucho dinero was spent on much-needed renovations" at this three-decades-old landmark, and more is being laid out to continue upgrades; "although not deluxe, certainly adequate" and "comfortable" say nostalgic loyalists who "love the public areas around sunset", not to mention the Hawaiian entertainment in the courtyard and the nightly torch-lighting ritual; added bonuses are "great local food at the buffet", a "good beach" and five rooftop tennis courts.

KAHALA MANDARIN ORIENTAL 341R (29S)   26 | 26 | 25 | 26 | $283
5000 Kahala Ave., Honolulu, Oahu; (808) 739-8888; (800) 367-2525; FAX: (808) 739-8800
■ "The diamond is shining brightly again" enthuse returnees upon entering the "elegant" lobby of the reopened "stately" fave of dignitaries and celebs in the heart of residential Kahala; the $84-million redo enhanced both the fine and casual dining spaces with oceanfront views, further improved the "gorgeous guestrooms" with Hawaiian koa furniture and "his and her bathrooms", and also added a "great new health club"; for a memorable moment, "communing with the three resident dolphins from your balcony" is something special.

New Otani Kaimana Beach Hotel 94R (30S)   19 | 22 | 21 | 19 | $159
2863 Kalakaua Ave., Honolulu, Oahu; (808) 923-1555; (800) 356-8264; FAX: (808) 922-9404
■ "Small, lovely" oceanfronter that's recommended for vacationers seeking a "quiet spot" "away from the hustle of Waikiki", but within walking distance on the "great" Sans Souci Beach just opposite "terrific" Kapiolani Park; this "simple but clean place for a stopover in Honolulu" may have "tiny rooms", but that's offset by the "lovely location" and "good price", as well as the "good food and service" at the "beautiful" alfresco Hau Tree Lanai restaurant; N.B. all the nice-size lanais were redone in '96.

Outrigger Prince Kuhio 616R (7S)   – | – | – | – | M
2500 Kuhio Ave., Honolulu, Oahu; (808) 922-0811; (800) OUTRIGGER; FAX: (808) 923-0330
The locally owned Outrigger's conference hotel, located a block from Waikiki Beach, offers groups an assortment of meeting facilities including a lovely waterfall/garden space; loners will find solace in guestrooms on the four Voyagers Club floors; quite decent all-American and Chinese restaurants are on-site.

Outrigger Reef 838R (45S)   18 | 18 | 15 | 17 | $135
2169 Kalia Rd., Honolulu, Oahu; (808) 923-3111; (800) 688-7444; FAX: (808) 924-4957
☑ This could be the "best buy on Oahu for a beachfront hotel" even though "the rooms are small" and the staff gets mixed reviews ("surly" vs. "helpful"); most seem to agree that in addition to "low rates", "the location is a plus" and the broil-your-own-steak restaurant is "great" and a lively perch for the beach action; N.B. the hotel shares facilities with Outrigger Waikiki across the street.

Outrigger Waikiki 520R (10S)   18 | 17 | 16 | 16 | $141
2335 Kalakaua Ave., Honolulu, Oahu; (808) 923-0711; (800) 688-7444; FAX: (808) 921-9749
☑ Fans say "so what if the room is narrow – the view is wide" at this "good-for-the-price" hotel with "clean, simple rooms, helpful staff" and a "primo location, directly across from International Market Place" and at the center of Waikiki Beach; others are less thrilled, calling it "a tourist" stop on "a miserable, crowded beach" with "no food served at late hours" and "no service to speak of."

Pacific Beach Hotel 823R (8S)   19 | 19 | 16 | 18 | $151
2490 Kalakaua Ave., Honolulu, Oahu; (808) 922-1233; (800) 367-6060; FAX: (808) 922-8061
■ Those who've been to this convenient Waikiki two-tower hotel urge all to "check out the huge Oceanarium", a dramatic three-story salt-water fish tank that's the backdrop for two of the hotel's three restaurants; as for the drier precincts, surveyors find "clean, plain-Jane rooms" and note a "great location."

ROYAL HAWAIIAN HOTEL 470R (56S)   24 | 24 | 23 | 25 | $238
2259 Kalakaua Ave., Honolulu, Oahu; (808) 923-7311; (800) 325-3535; FAX: (808) 931-7840
■ "Historic and classy with a feel for yesteryear", the built-in-1927 and "gracefully aging" "Pink Lady" still charms because management knows how to "pamper guests"; surveyors split on where to stay: "get a room in the original building" say some, "love the new tower rooms" opine others; the faithful also love the "great bar and breakfast buffet", but a few warn that, despite "elegant grounds", "it's a pink dollhouse surrounded by urban renewal."

Sheraton Moana Surfrider 746R (45S)   23 | 24 | 22 | 25 | $202
2365 Kalakaua Ave., Honolulu, Oahu; (808) 922-3111; (800) 782-9488; FAX: (808) 923-0308
■ The "old, charming, beautifully restored" 1901 landmark facility (on the National Register of Historic Places) and the postwar Surfrider section offer "a hodgepodge of styles, comforts and experiences", with traditionalists insisting "ask for a room in the original building" as "the new tower is just another place"; you can "relax in your rocker and look out to the turquoise Pacific", enjoy "high tea" on "the loveliest veranda" or discover "the secret Edwardian beauty of Honolulu" in the "wonderful public areas" – and of course, service is "just right."

Sheraton Princess Kaiulani Hotel 13R (1137S) 17 | 19 | 18 | 18 | $161

120 Kaiulani Ave., Honolulu, Oahu; (808) 922-5811; (800) 782-9488; FAX: (808) 931-4577

▨ This "hotel for the masses", catering to "loud, rowdy conventions" and Asian tour groups, has a "pretty lobby though spartan rooms" that some dismiss as "run-down"; regulars tout it as "the best value of the moderately priced hotels" due to its "great location and convenience to shops and the beach", but none of that comforts sleepless critics who contend that the "walls are so thin you can hear the guy next door snoring."

Sheraton Waikiki 1647R (130S) 19 | 20 | 19 | 20 | $182

2255 Kalakaua Ave., Honolulu, Oahu; (808) 922-4422; (800) 325-3535; FAX: (808) 923-8785

▨ "Basically a convention and Asian tour group hotel", this "behemoth" has "all the intimacy of Grand Central Station" albeit in an "excellent centralized location"; the '70s-era, 30-story "mega-resort" is upgrading its accommodations and public spaces in an ongoing $20-million program – even now "the suites are awesome", though regular rooms run the gamut from "pleasant" to "dreary"; a "stellar Sunday brunch" at the penthouse Hanohano Room is a decided plus, but overall, whether "Coney Island revisited" is "lots of fun" or "a zoo" is your call.

Waikiki Parc Hotel 298R 21 | 23 | 22 | 17 | $176

2233 Helumoa Rd., Honolulu, Oahu; (808) 921-7272; (800) 422-0450; FAX: (808) 923-1336

■ "Excellent" describes the value, food, service and "small but clean rooms" at this "quiet and sophisticated enclave" across the street from the beachside Halekulani, its big sister; there's "not much luxury" but it is "smart looking", "comfortable" and "well maintained", and respondents dub it "one of the better nonbeachfront properties."

Idaho

Boise

R | S | D | P | $

Doubletree Club Hotel 156R (2S)
▽ 18 | 18 | 16 | 15 | $95
475 W. Park Center Blvd., Boise; (208) 345-2002; (800) 222-TREE; FAX: (208) 345-8354
◪ "The basics, just the basics" suffice at this "clean, convenient, good value" where weary working stiffs are greeted with chocolate-chip cookies, complimentary continental breakfasts and late-night snacks; this "well-run" business-oriented chain member may be a "bland hotel in an even blander industrial park", but it's "not bad for Idaho."

Idanha Hotel 40R (2S)
▽ 20 | 23 | 18 | 17 | $97
928 Main St., Boise; (208) 342-3611; (800) 714-7346; FAX: (208) 383-9690
■ "Dated but wonderful", the capital's turn-of-the-century "historic landmark" is "charming but not fancy", offering "quaint rooms" and turret suites with claw-foot tubs and antique furnishings; the hotel also houses one of "Boise's best restaurants, Peter Schott's", featuring New American food; all in all a "great find in a great location."

Owyhee Plaza Hotel 98R (2S)
▽ 14 | 17 | 15 | 12 | $96
1109 Main St., Boise; (208) 343-4611; (800) 233-4611; FAX: (208) 381-0695
◪ The few surveyors who've made it to this well-situated Downtowner can't muster much excitement, but perhaps recent renovations will assuage those who say it's "long overdue for a face-lift"; penny-pinchers will find rooms in the poolside wing priced just right and enjoy in-room coffeemakers with complimentary coffee; meeting space for up to 250 and a central location appeal to business travelers.

Red Lion Boise Riverside 269R (35S)
17 | 18 | 15 | 16 | $112
2900 Chinden Blvd., Boise; (208) 343-1871; (800) 547-8010; FAX: (208) 331-4994
■ Yawning it's "almost as boring as the city", Boise-bashers still allow that this "utilitarian", "good business" hotel on the Boise River offers "decent rooms", an outdoor pool and proximity to the airport and Downtown – but that's not enough to stifle complaints about "weak food" and "slow service"; one surveyor sighs there's "not much to comment on other than its cheap price."

Coeur d'Alene

Blackwell House B&B 5R (3S)
– | – | – | – | E
820 Sherman Ave., Coeur d'Alene; (208) 664-0656; (800) 899-0656
"Traditional and special", this stately Victorian with two downstairs fireplaces caters to the wedding crowd with the requisite flowers-and-lace receptions; B&B guests find the quarters (some with private bath) "quaint", the facilities "well maintained" and the Downtown location on the City by the Lake's main drag a plus.

Coeur d'Alene Resort 315R (22S)
23 | 23 | 23 | 25 | $181
115 S. Second St. (on the lake), Coeur d'Alene; (208) 765-4000; (800) 365-8338; FAX: (208) 667-0217
◪ "A wonderful surprise" for most, this lakeside golfer's and skier's full-service resort with an unusual "floating golf green" offers varied "upscale accommodations in the rugged Northwest", with highest praise going to "beautifully decorated" tower rooms with "incredible" lake views; other assets: "fantastic meeting spaces", a "best-ever" spa "terrific restaurant", children's programs and 30 shops for browsing; a few naysayers find it "too touristy and convention-like" – "great for golfers, not for others."

Gregory's McFarland House Bed & Breakfast (5S)
– | – | – | – | M
601 Foster Ave., Coeur d'Alene; (208) 667-1232
This charming, turn-of-the-century Downtown B&B pampers skiers with individually decorated rooms featuring private baths with claw-foot tubs, an entertainment room with VCR, video library and pool table, and full gourmet breakfast and afternoon tea with homemade cakes in the all-glass conservatory overlooking the gardens and deck; if you happen to meet Mr. or Ms. Right, the resident minister/photographer will get you hitched and documented; N.B. no smoking, children under the age of 14 or pets.

Ketchum

Knob Hill Inn 20R (4S)   ▽ 25 | 22 | 25 | 21 | $203
960 N. Main St., Ketchum; (208) 726-8010; (800) 526-8010; FAX: (208) 726-2712
◪ At a "fabulous in-town location" within walking distance of Downtown Ketchum, this luxe Relais & Châteaux alpine-style inn is inviting to upscale schussers who eschew the ski resort scene; the day starts with free breakfast in the cafe and may end at the "excellent" Mediterranean restaurant, Felix's, after a stint in the sauna, indoor/outdoor pool or Jacuzzi, or a private soak in the in-room oversize tubs (all rooms have balconies and wet bars, and suites also offer fireplaces); only a few frown at "big-city prices and attitude that are out of order in Sun Valley."

McCall

Shore Lodge 53R (63S)   ▽ 17 | 19 | 18 | 23 | $112
501 W. Lake St., McCall; (208) 634-2244; (800) 657-6464; FAX: (208) 634-7504
◼ Expect a "family feel" and "small-town touch" at this upscale but rustic Payette Lake lodge in a "beautiful" site that draws fishers, boaters and those skiing nearby Brundage Mountain; though rooms strike a few as "small" and "nondescript", many, especially suites, feature balconies with lake views and some are large enough for families; two heated pools, a sauna, fitness center, tennis and racquetball courts, a NW steak-and-seafood restaurant and a casual cafe with deck for cocktails round out the amenities, along with meeting space and a ballroom that can seat 300.

Priest Lake

Hill's Hospitality, Inc. (72S)   - | - | - | - | E
(fka Hill's Resort)
HCR5, Box 162A, Priest Lake; (208) 443-2551; FAX: (208) 443-2363
Owned and run by the Hill family for 50 years, this sprawling, rustic, "beautiful" old North Idaho resort evokes fond memories of "great food", "great service" and "orchids galore"; bring the extended family: cabins and chalets (all with kitchenette, some with fireplace) "out in the woods" on the bay at Priest Lake can sleep plenty, there are children's programs and Bowser's welcome, too; it's a year-round base for anything from fishing and cycling to x-country skiing and snowmobiling, and its homey, lake-view restaurant is open daily mid-May–mid-October and on weekends the rest of the year.

Sun Valley

SUN VALLEY RESORT 261R (272S)   23 | 24 | 22 | 26 | $196
Sun Valley Rd., Sun Valley; (208) 622-4111; (800) 786-8259; FAX: (208) 622-3700
◼ This "historic" "grand ski" complex in "a spectacular setting" offers "civilization far from civilization" and "hasn't lost an appreciation for fine service"; the slopes may rule, but two heated pools beckon, as does an ice rink, shops, a game room, movie house, golf, tennis and horseback riding; though a few gripe it's "living on past reputation", citing "dreary", "tattered" accommodations in inn, lodge and condo quarters, they're overruled by loyalists who admit it's "slightly fading" but insist it's still a "first-class operation" that "you hate to leave"; N.B. children's programs available.

Tetonia

Teton Ridge Ranch 1R (7S) ⌀   - | - | - | - | VE
200 Valley View Rd., Tetonia; (208) 456-2650; FAX: (208) 456-2217
"Old-money atmosphere and armchair comfort" are the hallmarks of this sterling lodge on a 4,000-acre ranch in the shade of the Tetons; all activities are individually arranged (riding, hunting, fishing, skiing or hiking, including trips to Yellowstone with a naturalist), suites are equipped with whirlpool, wood-burning stove and private porch, and a hearty three-squares are provided (wine is served at dinner, but it's BYO otherwise); come with lots of cash (in rather large denominations) or checkbook in hand since credit cards are plastica-non-grata.

Illinois

R | S | D | P | $

Indian Lakes Resort 284R (24S)

17 | 17 | 15 | 18 | $127

250 W. Schick Rd., Bloomingdale; (630) 529-0200; (800) 537-8483; FAX: (630) 529-9271

☑ Sporting an unusual design featuring hexagonal buildings connected by walkways and surrounded by landscaped grounds and two golf courses, this resort 30 minutes west of O'Hare airport earns points for its "convenient" location and meeting facilities (capacity 1,200) that are "a cut above"; admirers further find it "well run", but to critics it's "institutional" – "where's the luxury?"; a '96 room redo may up scores next time around.

Chicago

TOP 10 OVERALL

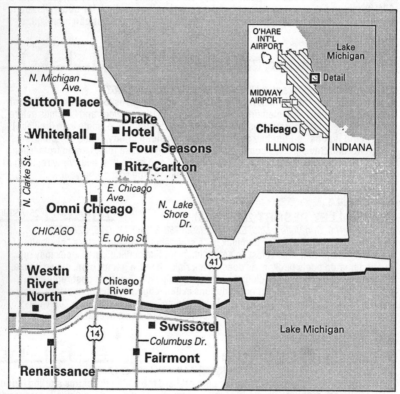

BEST OVERALL

28 Four Seasons
27 Ritz-Carlton
24 Fairmont
 Westin River North
23 Drake Hotel
 Renaissance
22 Sutton Place
 Omni Chicago
 Whitehall
21 Swissôtel

BEST VALUES

Rosemont Suites
Radisson Chicago
Marriott Suites O'Hare
Doubletree Guest Suites
Claridge
Sheraton Chicago
Westin River North
Renaissance
Sofitel
Fairmont

Ambassador West 170R (50S)
18 | 20 | 19 | 18 | $168

1300 N. State Pkwy., Chicago; (312) 787-3700; (810) 300-WEST; FAX: (312) 640-2967

▲ An "excellent location" on the Gold Coast and near Magnificent Mile shops is a big plus for this "stately", circa 1924 veteran; while rooms draw mixed response ("tiny though pretty" vs. "tired"), suites are "great" and come at a fairly "reasonable price", and most guests enjoy its "warm" service and "old-school atmosphere"; still, to a few it's simply "over the hill."

Best Western Inn of Chicago 358R (22S)
14 | 16 | 12 | 13 | $117

162 E. Ohio at Michigan Ave., Chicago; (312) 787-3100; (800) 557-BEST; FAX: (312) 573-3140

■ "No thrills" here, just "large, comfortable, quiet rooms" in a "great location" half a block from the Magnificent Mile – so what you save thanks to its "bargain" rates you can blow on shopping; 'nuff said.

Blackstone Hotel 285R (20S)
14 | 17 | 12 | 14 | $121

636 S. Michigan Ave., Chicago; (312) 427-4300; (800) 622-6330; FAX: (312) 427-4736

▲ "Even though it isn't all spiffed up", partisans like this parkside old-timer because it "has personality" ("like stepping back into the '20s"), not to mention "bargain" rates (continental breakfast included); naysayers, meanwhile, concede it has "character, but is missing" niceties: "poor decor", "no room service" (though there is American fare at the on-site Blackstone Grill).

Claridge 162R (6S)
17 | 20 | 17 | 15 | $134

1244 N. Dearborn Pkwy., Chicago; (312) 787-4980; (800) 245-1258; FAX: (312) 266-0978

■ Scores may be modest and some cite "close quarters", but this "small hotel" in a "nice area" on the Gold Coast is considered "a find" thanks to its "personal service" and "cozy" rooms; add complimentary continental breakfast and you have an all-around "good buy."

Clarion Executive Plaza 358R (59S)
20 | 18 | 14 | 15 | $142

71 E. Wacker Dr., Chicago; (312) 346-7100; (800) 621-4005; FAX: (312) 346-1721

■ A "central location", spacious accommodations (some with "spectacular" Chicago River views) and "good prices" (especially with package deals) make this 39-story tower near the Loop's north edge "hard to beat" for admirers; rising room ratings are a testament to recent renovations, but a few aesthetes still grumble about "Archie Bunker" decor; a fitness room and business center are pluses.

Doubletree Guest Suites (345S)
22 | 19 | 20 | 18 | $149

(fka Guest Quarters Suite Hotel)

198 E. Delaware Pl., Chicago; (312) 664-1100; (800) 222-TREE; FAX: (312) 664-8627

■ "Comfy, large", "well-appointed" suites deliver "value for your money", and the location (next to the John Hancock Center, a block off the Magnificent Mile) is handy for business and shopping; what's more, this Doubletree has "crisp, friendly" service, a rooftop health club and pool with terrific views, "well-designed" meeting space and two "excellent" restaurants: the chic Park Avenue Cafe and more casual Mrs. Park's Tavern; a room renovation completed in spring '97 is more good news.

Drake Hotel 467R (68S)
22 | 24 | 23 | 23 | $197

140 E. Walton Pl., Chicago; (312) 787-2200; (800) 55-DRAKE ; FAX: (312) 787-1431

▲ The "grand old lady of the lake keeps getting grander" declare devotees of this "American classic" whose "charm and elegance" evoke "another era"; while some salute a "great comeback" after a $30-million renovation, others still say rooms "vary" and can be "smallish", but no one denies the appeal of its "beautiful public spaces", "gracious" service and "unbeatable location" on the Magnificent Mile; "power breakfasts" in the Oak Terrace, a "lovely high tea" in the Palm Court, seafood in the Cape Cod Room and drinks at the Coq d'Or are more reasons it's "a must for Chicago visits."

FAIRMONT HOTEL 626R (66S)
25 | 24 | 24 | 23 | $190

200 N. Columbus Dr., Chicago; (312) 565-8000; (800) 527-4727; FAX: (312) 856-1032

■ "Up-to-the-minute luxury", "style and class all the way", "every detail in place" – and so the praise goes for this modern high-rise; there's some debate about the east-of-Downtown locale ("terrific" vs. "out of the way") and a few find it "sterile", but those quibbles are drowned out by praise for its "huge", "business-friendly" rooms, "gorgeous" lake views and fine service; guests can use the sports facilities at the adjacent Illinois Center for a fee, and there's "outstanding" French-American food at Entre Nous plus Italian fare at Primavera.

FOUR SEASONS HOTEL CHICAGO 176R (167S) `28` `28` `27` `27` `$251`
120 E. Delaware Pl., Chicago; (312) 280-8800; (800) 332-3442; FAX: (312) 280-9814
■ "A little nicer than paradise" sums up the "Windy City's winner", a "precision-run" phenom that sweeps top honors across the board; "in the heart of it all" on the Magnificent Mile, it's "everything a city hotel should be", with "sumptuous" rooms, "unflappable" service, "magnificent" views, an "outstanding" health club and chic "shopping without leaving the hotel" (take the elevator to Bloomie's, Bendel's, etc.), all "topped off by great food" at Seasons; in sum: "bliss!", especially if "someone else is footing the bill."

Hilton & Towers Chicago 1400R (143S) `21` `20` `19` `21` `$165`
720 S. Michigan Ave., Chicago; (312) 922-4400; (800) HILTONS; FAX: (312) 922-5240
☑ It may be a "mega" convention hotel "teeming with people" (meeting space for 2,400) and the location across from Grant Park is "too far south of the action" for some, but this Hilton upholds a "high level of service" (especially in the elite Towers) and has "lots of character" thanks to a "truly grand restoration" that enhanced the "charming architecture" of the original 1927 building; "small" rooms draw a few grumbles, but doubles with two bathrooms are "a definite plus", ditto the "superb fitness facility"; "surprisingly good" says the majority.

Hilton O'Hare 827R (31S) `17` `16` `15` `15` `$156`
O'Hare International Airport, Chicago; (312) 686-8000; (800) 445-8667; FAX: (312) 601-2339
☑ "Any closer to the runways and this place would have its own jetway", so you "can't beat the convenience" of the only hotel on O'Hare property; it's "very basic" but rooms are "decent" ("no airplane noise"), service is "friendly" and there's a "good health club" – "makes sense" for "fly-in/fly-out meetings" and if you're "stranded by weather" you'll be "glad it's there."

Holiday Inn Chicago City Centre 491R (9S) `17` `16` `15` `15` `$129`
300 E. Ohio St., Chicago; (312) 787-6100; (800) HOLIDAY; FAX: (312) 787-6259
■ "Don't expect anything special" and odds are you'll be content at this "decent" hotel that's "nice for a Holiday Inn", offering Downtown convenience at moderate rates plus "excellent views of Lake Michigan" from some quarters; a $3-million '95 redo may mute reports of "shopworn" rooms, and though some cite "spotty service", the "great health club" (including pools, racquetball and tennis courts) "makes up for a lot."

Hyatt on Printers Row 157R (4S) `20` `19` `21` `15` `$147`
500 S. Dearborn St., Chicago; (312) 986-1234; (800) 233-1234; FAX: (312) 939-2468
■ "An unexpected surprise – a Hyatt with personality" thanks to its "intimate" setting in a restored landmark building in the South Loop financial district; "spacious, high-ceilinged rooms", "helpful staff" and one of Chicago's "best" Regional American restaurants, the Frank Lloyd Wright–style Prairie, make it "actually charming"; though there are no fitness facilities on-site, guests have access to those at the City Club.

Hyatt Regency Chicago 1844R (175S) `20` `19` `18` `19` `$167`
151 E. Wacker Dr., Chicago; (312) 565-1234; (800) 233-1234; FAX: (312) 565-2966
☑ "Convention city", which means different things to different folks: "where the action is", "efficient for business meetings" (capacity 3,000), "no surprises" vs. "size run amok", "human warehouse"; but for most, this "glitzy" giant "works" thanks to its "perfect location" close to Downtown and Magnificent Mile shops, "comfortable" (some say "boring") newly redone rooms, "beautiful" airy lobby and "friendly" staff; guests can work out at the adjacent Illinois Center Athletic Club for a fee.

Hyatt Regency O'Hare 1057R (42S) `17` `16` `16` `15` `$154`
9300 W. Bryn Mawr Ave., Rosemont; (847) 696-1234; (800) 233-1234; FAX: (847) 698-0139
☑ It's "close to" O'Hare and connected by skywalk to the Rosemont Convention Center, and its "functional, cookie-cutter rooms" and service are "good enough for an expeditious in-and-out" trip; but this Hyatt also stirs up turbulence among those who find it too "huge and impersonal" (meeting space for 5,300!) and claim a '96 renovation "only helped a little"; as one surveyor sees it, "they're trying, but it's a factory."

Inter-Continental Chicago, Hotel 824R (20S) `21` `20` `19` `20` `$173`
505 N. Michigan Ave., Chicago; (312) 944-4100; (800) 233-1234; FAX: (312) 944-3050
☑ Despite solid scores, comments on this 1929 landmark on the Magnificent Mile swing from "fabulous rooms", "fine service", "first class" to "ordinary", "misses the mark in every way"; reports that the old section is "terrific" while the new tower (formerly the Forum Hotel) is "not nearly as nice" may explain the discrepancy; on two things all concur: the "ideal" location and the "amazing" vintage pool surrounded by majolica tiles.

La Salle Club Hotel 19R (3S)
▽ | 21 | 25 | 21 | 20 | $196

440 S. La Salle, Chicago; (312) 663-8910; (800) 338-8910; FAX: (312) 663-8909
■ The few surveyors who know this "unique" small hotel situated on the 40th floor of a Loop financial tower give it high marks for "excellent service" and "beautiful rooms" with "great views" of the lakefront ("especially in suites"); the fact that the "superb" French restaurant Everest (perennially one of Chicago's top-rated) occupies the same floor works in its favor, too.

Marriott Chicago Downtown 1147R (25S)
18 | 19 | 17 | 17 | $160

540 N. Michigan Ave., Chicago; (312) 836-0100; (800) 228-0265; FAX: (312) 836-9290
■ "It is what it is" – a "giant", "bustling", business-oriented Marriott (meeting space for 1,900) – but it's "good for the price", "very efficient for its size" and right on the Magnificent Mile, thus "close to everything"; there are "great gym facilities" and while the "standard" rooms don't excite, those on "high floors have spectacular views" and the "concierge level is worth the difference" in cost.

Marriott O'Hare 659R (22S)
16 | 17 | 16 | 16 | $138

8535 W. Higgins Rd., Chicago; (312) 693-4444; (800) 228-9290; FAX: (312) 714-4297
☑ A "clean, nothing special" but "reliable" O'Hare-area Marriott that's a "convenient" place to hang your hat before or after flights and well equipped for business confabs (meeting space for 1,000); it has an impressive array of fitness facilities including two tennis courts and an indoor/outdoor pool.

Marriott Suites O'Hare (256S)
22 | 19 | 17 | 17 | $141

6155 N. River Rd., Rosemont; (847) 696-4400; (800) 228-9290; FAX: (847) 696-4122
■ "If space and rooms matter" for airport-area sojourns, this "comfortable", newly refurbished all-suiter is likely to satisfy; all accommodations feature a living room, bedroom and marbled bathroom, plus extras like two TVs and two phones; a health club with indoor pool adds to what most call a "pleasant experience" and a "good value."

Midland Hotel 253R (4S)
15 | 19 | 17 | 15 | $133

172 W. Adams at LaSalle, Chicago; (312) 332-1200; (800) 621-2360; FAX: (312) 332-5909
■ "One of the bargains of Chicago" say fans of this 1929 art deco business specialist in the "heart of the Loop"; the staff "tries hard to please" and the place has a "fun '20s" feel, so few mind if rooms are "unexciting and small"; making a good deal even better: complimentary breakfast, PM cocktail hour and English taxi service within Downtown.

Omni Ambassador East 223R (52S)
18 | 19 | 21 | 18 | $165

1301 N. State Pkwy., Chicago; (312) 787-7200; (800) THE-OMNI; FAX: (312) 787-4766
☑ A "classy old hotel that still has it" is how admirers see this 1926 grande dame in a tree-lined Gold Coast neighborhood; to them it's "charming, quiet" and "aging gracefully", with "excellent bellmen" and suites that are "great for a romantic weekend"; critics, meanwhile, say it's "getting tired" with rooms that "need help" and staff that's "hard to find", but even they concede there's "excellent" dining at the Pump Room, one of Chicago's most fabled eateries.

Omni Chicago Hotel (347S)
25 | 22 | 20 | 20 | $178

676 N. Michigan Ave., Chicago; (312) 944-6664; (800) THE-OMNI; FAX: (312) 266-3015
■ "First-rate" all around, this "very classy" Omni is arguably the "best suite hotel in town"; providing "a sense of quiet" in the midst of the Magnificent Mile, it's "ideal for business" or pleasure, offering "attentive" service and "lovely" accommodations that feel "like libraries", adorned with "cherry-colored wood" and soothing shades of rose and green; add a fully equipped fitness center and good Mediterranean fare at Cielo and you have a "great find" and "excellent value."

Palmer House Hilton 1559R (88S)
19 | 20 | 19 | 21 | $165

17 E. Monroe St., Chicago; (312) 726-7500; (800) 445-8667; FAX: (312) 917-1707
☑ "Grand old Chicago" lives on at this "enormous" 19th-century Loop "landmark" with an "incredibly ornate lobby" that conjures up the "ghosts of Capone" and others; today it caters to conventions and tour groups and does a good job by most accounts, but some report a "wide variation in rooms" (the Towers is "highly recommended") and others find it "dowdy" despite ongoing renovations; there's meeting space for 1,500 and a full-service fitness club, though you may get a workout just "walking from your room to the street."

Radisson Hotel & Suites Chicago 245R (96S)
20 | 18 | 16 | 16 | $130

160 E. Huron St., Chicago; (312) 787-2900; (800) 333-3333; FAX: (312) 787-6093
■ A $9-million renovation has pushed room scores up a notch at this "very clean and comfortable" hotel; "convenient to the Magnificent Mile", it's a "good value" offering such pluses as in-room coffeemakers, dataports and Nintendo, an exercise room, rooftop outdoor pool and Southwestern and steakhouse fare at the Red Rock Grill, which has one of the city's most appealing outdoor cafes.

Radisson Hotel Lincolnwood 270R (24S)   ▽ 14 | 13 | 13 | 13 | $117

4500 W. Touhy Ave., Lincolnwood; (847) 677-1234; (800) 333-3333 ; FAX: (847) 677-0234
◨ Its "convenient Chicago North location" (in the suburb of Lincolnwood, eight miles from Downtown and an equal distance from O'Hare) would seem to be this Radisson's main selling point – that, and "reasonable" prices; otherwise it receives middling scores, though a '96 renovation may add some oomph.

Raphael 100R (72S)   21 | 21 | 17 | 16 | $151

201 E. Delaware Pl., Chicago; (312) 943-5000; (800) 821-5343; FAX: (312) 943-9483
■ Those tired of convention mills appreciate this "comfy, cozy, quiet" smaller hotel with a "European" ambiance in a "walk-to-anywhere" location near the Magnificent Mile; though a few find it "a bit tired", most think the rooms have "character" and are a "good value"; in sum, it's an "understated" "find" that "feels like home."

Regal Knickerbocker 228R (26S)   18 | 18 | 17 | 17 | $147
(fka Knickerbocker Chicago Hotel)

163 E. Walton Pl., Chicago; (312) 751-8100; (800) 621- 8140; FAX: (312) 751-0370
◨ Regal took over this "charming older hotel" (circa 1927) in '96 and embarked on a $15-million renovation; while the jury is still out on the results, fans hope it will remain an "excellent value" staffed by "nice people" – and one thing that definitely won't change is the "great location" off the Magnificent Mile.

Renaissance Chicago Hotel 521R (32S)   24 | 23 | 21 | 22 | $176
(fka Stouffer Renaissance Chicago Hotel)

1 W. Wacker Dr., Chicago; (312) 372-7200; (800) 468-3571; FAX: (312) 372-0093
■ "Low-key class" sums up this luxury hotel that has "a lot to offer": a "perfect" Theater District location between the Loop and Magnificent Mile, "gorgeous" public spaces, "tasteful" rooms with "good amenities" (especially on Club Floors), a "wonderful health club" and "excellent" service; an award-winning wine list at Cuisines is another plus; try for an upper-floor room with a river view – "it doesn't get any better."

RITZ-CARLTON CHICAGO 327R (82S)   28 | 28 | 27 | 26 | $249

160 E. Pearson St., Chicago; (312) 266-1000; (800) 621-6906; FAX: (312) 266-1194
■ "Heaven" in a high-rise, Chicago's second-highest-rated hotel is an "elegant" "class act" that "knows how to pamper guests" from the moment they step into the "stunning" lobby; a member of the Four Seasons chain, it "simply has everything": "beautiful rooms", service "with a personal touch", "superb" New French fare at the Dining Room, a sybaritic spa, "amazing views" to "soothe the business beast" and shops galore at the attached Water Tower Place; "what's not to like, except the prices?"

Rosemont Suites Hotel O'Hare (296S)   19 | 17 | 15 | 16 | $121
(fka Radisson Suite Hotel O'Hare)

5500 N. River Rd., Rosemont; (847) 678-4000; (888) 4ROSEMONT; FAX: (847) 928-7659
◨ Ratings have risen across the board for this O'Hare-area all-suiter that was renovated in Frank Lloyd Wright style in early '96; "nice big rooms", "easy access to the airport" and meeting space for 1,000 remain its main appeals, and there's a skywalk to the Rosemont Convention Center; guests can work out on-site or at a nearby private club for a fee.

Sheraton Chicago Hotel & Towers 1152R (52S)   22 | 21 | 20 | 21 | $164

301 E. North Water St., Chicago; (312) 464-1000; (800) 233-4100; FAX: (312) 464-1940
■ "A cut above the usual Sheraton", this "spanking new" (built in '92) convention hotel is "surprisingly nice for being so large"; "pretty if a bit cold", it offers "modern" "roomy" quarters, an "elegant conference center", "good exercise facilities" (including an atrium pool) and service by a staff that "really does like working there"; its east-of-Downtown riverside setting may seem a bit "far from Michigan Avenue", but most find it a "great location" and it yields "beautiful views."

Sheraton Gateway Suites (297S)   21 | 19 | 18 | 18 | $155

6501 N. Mannheim Rd., Rosemont; (847) 699-6300; (800) 325-3535; FAX: (847) 699-0391
◨ "Rises above other airport hotels" say boosters of this O'Hare-area all-suiter with "bright, clean" accommodations (all with kitchenette and Nintendo) and such pluses as an indoor pool, 24-hour room service and convenience to the Rosemont Convention Center; still, the less-impressed report suites resembling "a hotel room with a divider."

Sofitel Hotel 296R (8S)   21 | 21 | 20 | 19 | $162

5550 N. River Rd., Rosemont; (847) 678-4488; (800) 233-5959; FAX: (847) 678-4244
■ "Not the usual cold hotel-type atmosphere" but rather a "French feeling" is what admirers find at this chain import near O'Hare, where "pleasant, comfortable" rooms come at "moderate prices" and are augmented by "very accommodating" service and "well-kept facilities" including meeting space for 800 and a 24-hour pool and exercise room; the French bread given at check-out is a "nice touch."

Summerfield Suites Hotel (120S)
▽ 22 | 17 | 16 | 17 | $130

(fka Barclay Chicago)
166 E. Superior St., Chicago; (312) 787-6000; (800) 833-4353; FAX: (312) 787-4331
■ "Perfect when traveling on business" as well as "great for families" thanks to "enormous" all-suite accommodations that are "comfortable" and "reasonably priced", with a full breakfast included; in a prime location just a half-block east of the Magnificent Mile, it boasts a 29th-floor rooftop fitness center, kitchenettes in most units and an on-site convenience store and coin-op laundry, making it an efficient "lower-cost alternative."

Sutton Place Hotel 206R (40S)
26 | 23 | 20 | 19 | $177

21 E. Bellevue Pl., Chicago; (312) 266-2100; (800) 606-8188; FAX: (312) 266-2141
■ "A bargain based on the quality and location", this "unique boutique" hotel is "wonderfully located" in the Gold Coast and offers "elegant" (if "smallish") rooms outfitted with CD players, VCRs, three phones, voicemail, "great bathrooms and the most comfortable beds on earth"; "attentive" service and good dining at Brasserie Bellevue help make it "a delight."

Swissôtel 595R (35S)
23 | 22 | 20 | 21 | $174

323 E. Wacker Dr., Chicago; (312) 565-0565; (800) 644-7263; FAX: (312) 565-0540
■ "Like a dependable watch" say surveyors of this triangular glass high-rise that's as "efficient" as one would expect of the Swiss; located on the New East Side fronting the Chicago River, it offers "heart-stopping views" from the penthouse health club as well as the rooms, which are "spacious" and "very tastefully decorated" with "large marble bathrooms"; though a few find it "somewhat sterile", more consider it a "classy" "good value"; it's also a carnivore's dream, thanks to The Palm restaurant.

Tremont, The 109R (20S)
20 | 22 | 20 | 18 | $180

100 E. Chestnut St., Chicago; (312) 751-1900; (800) 621-8133; FAX: (312) 280-1304
■ This "intimate, classy" hotel "makes you feel you're in Europe", but in fact you're a half-block off the Magnificent Mile "in the middle of everything"; built in 1923 and "nicely restored", it offers "tasteful", "elegant" rooms that may be "a bit small" but feature "great amenities" (CD players, VCRs, dual-line phones), and the "excellent staff" treats guests "as individuals"; for some devotees it's a "first choice in Chicago" and "nicer than the giant chains."

Westin Hotel Chicago 700R (43S)
18 | 19 | 18 | 18 | $163

909 N. Michigan Ave., Chicago; (312) 943-7200; (800) 879-5444; FAX: (312) 943-9347
◪ All agree it has a "great location" "right on the Magnificent Mile in the heart of Downtown"; but beyond that surveyors split between those who call this a "comfortable" hotel that's "ideal" for business travelers (meeting space for 1,500) with "very nice rooms", "helpful staff" and a "good health club", and those who yawn "just another convention hotel"; a '96 renovation may win more converts.

Westin Hotel O'Hare 496R (29S)
19 | 19 | 17 | 17 | $148

6100 River Rd., Rosemont; (847) 698-6000; (800) 879-5444; FAX: (847) 698-4591
◪ To supporters this O'Hare-area Westin is among the "best of the [airport] lot", thanks to "attractive" soundproof rooms and good service; others say "no complaints, but nothing to rave about", though if looking for a "convenient meeting" site (capacity 1,500) or a place "to get over jet lag" it will do just fine, judging from its solid scores; proximity to the Rosemont Convention Center and a full-service health club with indoor pool are pluses.

WESTIN RIVER NORTH, CHICAGO 401R (21S)
25 | 24 | 24 | 23 | $187

(fka Hotel Nikko Chicago)
320 N. Dearborn Ave., Chicago; (312) 744-1900; (800) WESTIN-1; FAX: (312) 527-2664
■ This highly rated Nikko became a Westin post-*Survey*, but it remains a "classy-looking" contemporary Downtowner that's "sleek and elegant" yet "very comfortable"; "discerning business travelers" appreciate its "understated", spacious and "well-appointed" rooms (some with lovely views), business center and meeting space for 900, as well as its "bend-over-backwards" service, fully equipped health club and "good location" in River North; Celebrity Cafe is still serving a stellar Sunday brunch.

Whitehall Hotel 213R (8S)   22 | 24 | 21 | 20 | $197
105 E. Delaware Pl., Chicago; (312) 944-6300; (800) 948-4255; FAX: (312) 573-6250
■ This "small, elegant, upper-crust" hotel has the "atmosphere of a private residence", no surprise since it began life as an apartment building in 1928; today it pleases business travelers and vacationers alike with "impressive room decor", "excellent service" ("they really try to solve problems") and a prime Gold Coast address steps from the Magnificent Mile; though some find it "expensive", weekend packages are a good deal and in any case, aficionados "don't want too many people to find out about it."

Galena

Eagle Ridge Inn & Resort 78R (352S)   23 | 21 | 19 | 23 | $159
PO Box 777, Rte. 20, Galena; (815) 777-2444; (800) 892-2269; FAX: (815) 777-0445
■ "Wonderful small-town service in a complete resort" is what most find at this getaway geared for golfers (63 holes, including The General, a new championship course opened in '96); set on 6,800 "beautiful" acres eight miles east of historic Galena, it offers "comfortable" lodgings (in the main inn or privately owned one- to five-bedroom homes) and lots to do even for nonduffers: tennis, hiking, kids' programs, etc.; a few beef about "mediocre" food, but guests can head into Galena for more options.

Itasca

Nordic Hills Resort 212R (8S)   15 | 16 | 14 | 16 | $123
1401 Nordic Rd., Itasca; (630) 773-2750; (800) 334-3417; FAX: (630) 773-3622
☑ Sister to Indian Lakes Resort and also close to O'Hare aiport (about 20 minutes west), this "low-key" complex centered around two hexagonal mid-rise towers strikes some as a "golf lover's delight" thanks to a challenging 18-hole course; there's also tennis, swimming and other sports plus "nice" staff, but while some find the rooms "rustic and cozy", others cry "paint me please" – presumably, a '96 room redo has helped.

Wyndham Hotel NW Chicago 408R (29S)   ▽ 21 | 20 | 20 | 19 | $128
(fka Wyndham Hamilton Hotel)
400 Park Blvd., Itasca; (630) 773-4000; (800) 822-4200; FAX: (630) 773-4088
■ A "classy" 12-story modern business-oriented hotel in a "pretty area" 12 miles west of O'Hare airport and about 30 minutes from Downtown Chicago; it earns solid marks across the board and has all the requisite facilities: meeting space for 1,000, a business center, indoor pool, health club, two tennis courts and American fare at Ondine restaurant.

Lake Forest

Deer Path Inn 28R (26S)   – | – | – | – | E
255 E. Illinois Rd., Lake Forest; (847) 234-2280; (800) 788-9480; FAX: (847) 234-3352
Less than an hour north of Chicago in the affluent Lake Forest community is a 1929 Tudor inn listed on the National Register of Historic Places and modeled after a circa 1450s English manor house; guestrooms with four-poster beds and chintz trimmings appeal to weekend retreaters, while meeting rooms (capacity 350) attract conference-goers; rates include a full breakfast buffet.

Lincolnshire

Marriott's Lincolnshire Resort 384R (6S)   19 | 20 | 18 | 21 | $153
10 Marriott Dr., Lincolnshire; (847) 634-0100; (800) 228-9290; FAX: (847) 634-1278
☑ To boosters this Marriott is a "full resort with golf, etc." (tennis, racquetball, indoor and outdoor pools, health club), all "topped off by an excellent in-the-round theater"; to doubters it's "nice but not spectacular" and even "boring"; mixed notices also go to its location 25 minutes north of O'Hare ("convenient" vs. "middle of nowhere"), but it's judged "very good for conventions" (capacity 500) and a '96 renovation is welcome news.

Oak Brook

Oak Brook Hills Hotel & Resort 344R (38S)   22 | 22 | 20 | 24 | $154
3500 Midwest Rd., Oak Brook; (630) 850-5555; (800) 445-3315; FAX: (630) 850-5569
■ A "relaxing" "retreat for a Chicagoland weekend or holiday" is how most surveyors see this "resort-type hotel" near the affluent suburb of Oakbrook west of the city; "beautiful", "large and clean" rooms provide a pleasant base for those attending corporate conferences (meeting space for 1,200) or enjoying the "great on-site activities" (including golf, tennis and swimming); American-Continental dining at Waterford restaurant is a "gourmet's delight" (if "expensive").

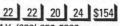

St. Charles

Pheasant Run Resort & Convention Center   15 | 17 | 15 | 17 | $126
423R (50S)

4051 E. Main St., St. Charles; (630) 584-6300; (800) 474-3272; FAX: (630) 584-4693
☑ It strike some as "unremarkable", but this "complete resort" an hour west of Chicago is "fine for conventions" (able to handle up to 4,000) and offers "good weekend getaway packages"; in addition to a usual-suspects roster of activities (golf, tennis, swimming, a fitness center) it has a not-so-usual dinner theater; those who say it seems to have hosted "one too many conferences" may be heartened by '95/'96 renovations.

Whittington

Rend Lake Resort 45R (4S)   _ | _ | _ | _ | I
11712 E. Windy Ln., Whittington; (618) 629-2211; (800) 633-3341; FAX: (618) 629-2584
Calling all crappie anglers: Rend Lake is crawling with crappie and other fish, making this fairly new (built in '91) Southern Illinois lakeside resort fertile ground for fishing folk, hunters and other outdoorsy types; set in Wayne Fitzgerrell State Park, it puts guests up in cabins, rooms and waterside 'boatel' suites and keeps them moving with tennis, swimming, horseback riding, biking and nearby golf; rates are modest and boat docking is free (on a first-come, first-served basis).

Indiana

Bloomington

R | S | D | P | $

Fourwinds Resort & Marina 123R (3S) ▽ 18 | 19 | 18 | 18 | $106
PO Box 160, Fairfax Rd., Bloomington; (812) 824-9904; (800) 538-1187; FAX: (812) 824-9816
■ Set in wooded hills on Lake Monroe an hour south of Indianapolis, this '70s-era resort offers water sports of all sorts: sailing with pontoon boats, fishing, lake or pool swimming and an on-site full-service marina; landlubbers can opt for miniature golf, volleyball and basketball and there are many children's activities, so perhaps it doesn't matter if some surveyors say the "rooms need updating"; N.B. an extensive renovation was in the works at press time.

French Lick

French Lick Springs Resort 460R (25S) 16 | 18 | 18 | 20 | $126
8670 W. State Rd. 56, French Lick; (812) 936-9300; (800) 457-4042; FAX: (812) 936-2100
☑ "The grand old lady just keeps putting on makeup", yet still some say she "needs a major face-lift"; while fans of this vintage 1901 Southern Indiana resort like its "very warm atmosphere", "impressive public areas" and "ancient but stylish facilities", others call it a "faded token of a more elegant era" and "way past its prime"; at any rate, it offers lots to do with two 18-hole golf courses, tennis, horseback riding, a health club and even a bowling alley.

Indianapolis

Canterbury Hotel 84R (15S) 24 | 24 | 22 | 20 | $164
123 S. Illinois St., Indianapolis; (317) 634-3000; (800) 538-8186; FAX: (317) 685-2519
■ "If you require a classy hotel with personalized service", this "beautifully restored" historic beauty is "top-of-the-line by any city's standards" – and where else can you enjoy a "gracious", "European feel" so close to the Hoosier Dome? (it's handy to Union Station and the convention center too); the "wonderful atmosphere" is enhanced by "small but charming rooms" and "excellent" American-Continental dining at The Restaurant; devotees advise "don't stay anyplace else in this town."

Crowne Plaza Union Station 244R (32S) 21 | 20 | 17 | 21 | $124
(fka Holiday Inn Crowne Plaza Union Station)
123 W. Louisiana St., Indianapolis; (317) 631-2221; (800) 2-CROWNE; FAX: (317) 236-7474
■ "Love, love, love the ['96] renovation" toots a surveyor taken with this "fun hotel" attached to the Union Station rail and shopping complex where "sleeping in an old train car [26 Pullman cars now serve as suites] is the best"; "kids love it" and so do many adults, though a few dissenters deem it a "weird place" and say the staff, though "nice", could "pay more attention to details"; a word of advice: "make sure not to be over the real trains – noisy."

Embassy Suites Indianapolis Downtown (360S) 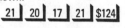 22 | 20 | 18 | 19 | $119
110 W. Washington St., Indianapolis; (317) 236-1800; (800) EMBASSY; FAX: (317) 236-1816
■ This Downtown high-rise may "inspire vertigo with its 15-story atrium" but even dizzy voters call it "an exceptionally good value"; what makes it "above average" is a "nice location" (it's "built into a shopping arcade"), an indoor pool, meeting space for medium to large groups and a $4.5 million renovation in '96; a full breakfast is included in the rate.

Hyatt Regency Indianapolis 474R (23S) 19 | 19 | 17 | 18 | $136
1 S. Capitol Ave., Indianapolis; (317) 632-1234; (800) 233-1234; FAX: (317) 231-7569
☑ A "functional Hyatt" that can also be "a great convention hotel"; this "all-purpose, moderately priced property" features "nice meeting rooms" and a "fantastic futuristic lobby", and though opinion is split on the rooms ("beautiful" vs. "ok"), all applaud the "wonderful Downtown location" near the capitol and Hoosier Dome and connected by skywalk to the convention center and Circle Centre Mall; check out "the view from the revolving rooftop restaurant."

Marriott Indianapolis 249R (3S)  18 | 18 | 17 | 16 | $124
7202 E. 21st St., Indianapolis; (317) 352-1231; (800) 228-9290; FAX: (317) 352-1231
■ "Typical", "standard", "dependable" echo surveyors who consider this "functional Marriott" eight miles east of Downtown to be "great for conventions" and "ok for business" (with meeting space for 1,500) but not particularly outstanding otherwise; leisure facilities include an indoor/outdoor pool, fitness room and a putting green; N.B. all guestrooms and public areas were renovated in 1996.

Omni Severin 386R (37S)   20   20   16   18 $121
40 W. Jackson Pl., Indianapolis; (317) 634-6664; (800) 834-6664; FAX: (317) 767-0003
■ This "nicely refurbished" 1913 hotel pleases most guests with its blend of historic details and modern style; there's a "beautiful" two-story skylit atrium lobby with waterfall and "a great view of the city" from suites (some with balconies), and the three business-class floors offer work desks, fax machines and computer hookups in every room; it's across from Union Station and connected to Circle Centre Mall, putting "lots of activities" within walking distance.

Radisson Plaza & Suite Hotel Indianapolis   17   18   16   17 $112
400R (159S)
8787 Keystone Crossing, Indianapolis; (317) 846-2700; (800) 333-3333; FAX: (317) 574-6402
◪ "Far from memorable" but "perfectly acceptable" are among the range of views on this northeast-of-Downtown property; while supporters call it "good for business" with a "great location for shopping and food", critics (backed by a drop in ratings) cite "shabby" public areas and "noisy", "dark" rooms (suites are "much nicer"); free access to the adjacent health club "is a plus."

Westin Hotel Indianapolis 534R (39S)   19   18   17   18 $131
50 S. Capitol Ave., Indianapolis; (317) 262-8100; (800) 228-3000; FAX: (317) 231-3928
◪ "Very satisfactory" say admirers of this Downtown option with a "convenient" location (linked by skywalk to the convention center and Hoosier Dome) and "excellent facilities" including an indoor pool and meeting space for up to 2,400; but while satisfied guests rate it "good overall", dissenters can muster only an "ok" and carp that the staff "needs some hospitality training", calling it a "typical Westin minus the good service."

Iowa

Bettendorf

Jumer's Castle Lodge 150R (60S)   19 | 19 | 20 | 18 | $104
900 Spruce Hills Dr., Bettendorf; (319) 359-7141; (800) 285-8637; FAX: (319) 359-7141
■ If you're hankering for "a castle without a moat" perhaps this ersatz alcazar, one of an eccentric chain of Midwestern hotels owned by the Jumer family, will do; surveyors say it's "wonderful", an "interesting" overnight experience with "old European flavor" – and speaking of flavor, the German restaurant has "wonderful food."

Cedar Rapids

Wyndham Five Seasons Hotel 270R (5S)   18 | 17 | 16 | 16 | $110
350 First Ave. NE, Cedar Rapids; (319) 363-8161; (800) WYNDHAM; FAX: (319) 363-1867
■ It may be as "plain as Iowa" – with "dreary rooms", "simple food" and an "early '70s" aura – yet this Downtown business hotel is the "best in the area" and "convenient" to shopping and dining via a 12-block skywalk system; execs should note that concierge-level accommodations include continental breakfast, evening cocktails and complimentary access to a nearby YMCA.

Des Moines

Embassy Suites (234S)   20 | 21 | 15 | 16 | $106
101 E. Locust St., Des Moines; (515) 244-1700; (800) EMBASSY; FAX: (515) 244-2537
■ The "best hotel in town" is "adequate" for business or pleasure, offering "comfortable" suites with kitchenettes, "friendly service" and a "nice complimentary happy hour"; convenience to the convention center is a plus, as are the indoor pool, workout room and full breakfast included in the rate.

Marriott Des Moines 416R (10S)   17 | 18 | 16 | 15 | $120
700 Grand Ave., Des Moines; (515) 245-5530; (800) 228-9290; FAX: (515) 245-5567
■ A "standard Marriott" but a "pleasant surprise in Des Moines" is how reviewers see this "big, clean", contemporary capital city standby; it's good for business since it's within walking distance of the convention center and has decent-sized conference facilities on-site, plus there's an indoor pool and fitness center.

Savery Hotel 209R (12S)   17 | 19 | 18 | 16 | $104
401 Locust St., Des Moines; (515) 244-2151; (800) 798-2151; FAX: (515) 244-1408
■ "Well located" in the Business District of Des Moines, this hostelry from 1861 is "a real jewel" that's "more like a country inn than a hotel" with "nice furnishings" that some find "a little too cutesy" and a staff that really makes you feel like "a guest"; amenities include two restaurants, a fitness center, indoor pool and sauna.

Dubuque

Redstone Inn 15R (12S)
504 Bluff St., Dubuque; (319) 582-1894; FAX: (319) 582-1893
This "gorgeous" 1894 Queen Anne Victorian "convenient to Downtown Dubuque" features fireplaces, whirlpools and kitchenettes in a number of rooms – "a most pleasant surprise"; an included full breakfast begins a day that might be spent shopping at nearby Cable Car Square or strolling through historic neighborhoods.

Richards House 5R (1S)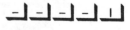
1492 Locust St., Dubuque; (319) 557-1492
Much of Dubuque's appeal is in its extensive stock of 19th-century architecture and this B&B on the north end of Downtown fits right into the period charm; built in 1883, the Stick-style Victorian still boasts the original ornate fireplaces, chandeliers and hand-painted tiles as well as dozens of stained-glass windows; the rooms (four with fireplaces) are furnished with antiques and have private baths; an included full breakfast is served in a lavish dining room.

Fort Madison
Kingsley Inn 14R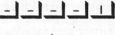
707 Avenue H, Fort Madison; (319) 372-7074; FAX: (319) 372-7096
Beyond the very 20th-century glass-atrium entrance lies this 19th-century brick-and-wrought-iron beauty featuring rooms that combine restored antiques with modern comforts like cable TV and whirlpools; a heart-of-the-city location puts guests steps from Mississippi River cruises and gambling boats; N.B. continental breakfast is included, smoking is prohibited.

Homestead
Die Heimat Country Inn 19R
Amana Colonies, Main St., Homestead; (319) 622-3937
In the Amana Colonies, where 19th-century German immigrants created a now-defunct communal religious society as well as the eponymous refrigerator company, this former stagecoach stop and communal kitchen is "home place" (or *heimat*–) for tourists who experience Amana life in "tiny" rooms filled with furniture and quilts created by Amana craftsmen; a full breakfast is included, and while no other food is served on-site, the area is rich with German restaurants.

Newton
La Corsette Maison Inn 5R (2S)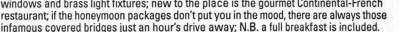
629 First Ave. E., Newton; (515) 792-6833
This Mission-style mansion is one of the more beautiful examples of Arts and Crafts design in the Midwest; built in 1909 by Iowa senator August Berman (the money man behind nearby Maytag), the house retains its original oak woodwork, stained-glass windows and brass light fixtures; new to the place is the gourmet Continental-French restaurant; if the honeymoon packages don't put you in the mood, there are always those infamous covered bridges just an hour's drive away; N.B. a full breakfast is included.

Walnut
Antique City Inn and B&B 4R (2S)
PO Box 584, 400 Antique City Dr., Walnut; (712) 784-3722
Surveyors browsing through intriguing shops in the antique-rich Walnut area might take a gander at this antique, a newly renovated 1911 Edwardian-style house where rates are so reasonable that guests might save enough to bring home an extra candelabra; a full breakfast is included, but there are no TVs in the rooms.

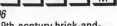

Kansas

Council Grove

R S D P $

Cottage House Hotel 26R (10S)

25 N. Neosho St., Council Grove; (316) 767-6828; (800) 727-7903; FAX: (316) 767-6414
Council Grove, once the last supply stop on the Santa Fe Trail between the Missouri River and Santa Fe, is home to this unusual Victorian-era two-story brick building boasting turrets and stained-glass windows; hallways with pressed-tin ceilings lead guests to individually decorated rooms with private baths; nearby are Old West historic sites and several parks and lakes, but porch sitting is the main activity in town; N.B. no on-site restaurant.

Fort Scott

Chenault Mansion 3R (2S)

820 S. National Ave., Fort Scott; (316) 223-6800; FAX: (316) 223-4212
A "convenient spot" for touring the Fort Scott National Historic Site – a frontier outpost in the mid–19th century (today it's five miles from the Missouri border) and a supply center for Union troops during the Civil War – this 1887 Queen Anne mansion embellished with stained glass and decorative woodwork receives guests in restful rooms outfitted with antiques, queen-size beds, private baths and air conditioning.

Lawrence

Eldridge Hotel (48S)
▽ 17 | 18 | 18 | 17 | $152
701 Massachusetts St., Lawrence; (913) 749-5011; (800) 527-0909; FAX: (913) 749-4512
☑ Some gripe the "rooms need work" and "public spaces are so-so", but others call the Eldridge the "only class act in town"; listed on the National Register of Historic Places, the red-brick Victorian-style all-suiter offers all the amenities of a full-service hotel: meeting space for 150, a fitness center and in-room wet bars, refrigerators, coffeemakers and dataports; Shalor's serves "good" New American fare, and the Jayhawker Pub is popular for watching the 'Hawks play hoops.

Lindsborg

Swedish Country Inn 19R

112 W. Lincoln St., Lindsborg; (913) 227-2985; (800) 231-0266; FAX: (913) 227-2795
An "interesting location" in Lindsborg, a central Kansas town 60 miles north of Wichita homesteaded by Swedish immigrants in the 1860s, heightens the "quaint" appeal of this turn-of-the-century feed store and Studebaker showroom converted into a hotel in 1930; "nice accommodations" (with hard-pine furniture, quilts and lace curtains), "good service" and a hearty Swedish buffet breakfast (included) ensure guests "never go away hungry"; N.B. no smoking.

Overland Park

See Kansas City, MO.

Topeka

Heritage House 10R (1S)

3535 SW Sixth St., Topeka; (913) 233-3800; (800) 582-1937; FAX: (913) 233-9793
☑ Some may find "nothing to write home about" here, but for others there's "no place else in Topeka" to stay besides this "supposedly haunted" turn-of-the-century farmhouse-turned-B&B, listed on the National Register of Historic Places; opinions on the individually decorated rooms range from "small and cozy" to "run-down", but all agree the restaurant is "great" (and the only class act in town); a full free breakfast fuels trips to area sites including the capitol, the Kansas State Historical Society Museum and the Potwin neighborhood of Victorian homes.

Inn at the Park 10R (2S)
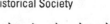
3751 E. Douglas Ave., Wichita; (316) 652-0500; (800) 258-1951; FAX: (316) 652-0610
A distinctive choice in the stylish College Hill area, this three-story 1909 Colonial Revival brick mansion offers striking rooms with decor ranging from English Victorian to French country to art nouveau; both weekday business travelers and amorous weekend couples appreciate the free continental breakfast, and some quarters also offer the opportunity to warm up beside a fireplace.

Senate Luxury Suites (52S)   – – – – I
900 SW Tyler St., Topeka; (913) 233-5050; (800) 488-3188; FAX: (913) 233-1614
This converted 1920s apartment building is a home-away-from-home to lawyers and lobbyists working at the nearby capitol and Kansas Supreme Court; all rooms have a balcony or porch, many have refrigerators and there are meeting facilities, a business center and exercise room; continental breakfast is included; tip: the Tiffany windows in the First Presbyterian Church across from the Capitol are worth a look.

Wichita

Castle Inn Riverside 13R (1S)   – – – – M
(fka The Campbell Castle)
1155 N. River Blvd., Wichita; (316) 263-9300; FAX: (316) 263-4998
Only a few voters know this 1886 castle built in Richardsonian Romanesque style, with a limestone exterior modeled after a Scottish château; on the National Register of Historic Places, it opened as a B&B in 1995, and if some say the guestrooms (filled with antiques plus modern musts like VCRs and dataports, most with working fireplace) are "not in keeping" with the grand public spaces graced with stained glass and carved woodwork, the overall effect is still "beautiful"; a full breakfast is included.

Hilton & Executive Conference Center   14 15 14 13 $93
Wichita Airport 291R (11S)
2098 Airport Rd., Wichita; (316) 945-5272; (800) 445-8667; FAX: (316) 945-7620
☑ What some call a "nice hotel close to the airport" others deem an "average Hilton" that just seems to wing it, judging by its modest ratings; still, this modern convention specialist is "convenient for short stays", offering meeting facilities for 1,000, an American restaurant, a nightclub and an indoor pool, plus privileges at a nearby health club.

Marriott Wichita 290R (4S)   19 18 16 17 $106
9100 Corporate Hills Dr., Wichita; (316) 651-0333; (800) 228-9290; FAX: (316) 651-0900
☑ "Best bet in Wichita" say boosters of this east-of-Downtowner that's "good for conventions" (15 meeting rooms for up to 1,000) and execs doing business at nearby companies' headquarters; though demanding types say it's "ok" with "little" by way of amenities, rooms are equipped with cable TVs, hair dryers, coffeemakers and the like, and facilities include a business center, indoor/outdoor pool, health club, jogging trails, nightclub and two restaurants; N.B. Toto-size pets permitted.

Kentucky

Berea

R S D P $

Boone Tavern Hotel 59R   19 | 21 | 23 | 18 | $66

Main & Prospect Sts., Berea; (606) 986-9358; (800) 366-9358; FAX: (606) 986-7711
■ "An unusual experience" that's both a "pleasant place" to stay and "a great cause",
this white-columned charmer a half-hour south of Lexington is "run by students" from
Berea College's Hotel School; they earn solid grades all-around and "do a great job in the
dining room", where the regional food is "very good" and the "simplicity is refreshing";
you can check out some "great arts and crafts" at the nearby Appalachian Museum;
N.B. there's an evening and Sunday dress code, no liquor and no tipping.

Harrodsburg

Beaumont Inn 33R   22 | 24 | 25 | 22 | $111

638 Beaumont Inn Dr., Harrodsburg; (606) 734-3381; (800) 352-3992; FAX: (606) 734-6897
■ "A classic inn" set on 30 acres in bluegrass country; it's been owned by the same
family for four generations, and they still draw guests with "good service" and "interesting
local food", including their celebrated country ham (reservations advised for the
restaurant); rooms in the "very nice" main inn (circa 1845) and three guest buildings
are furnished with antiques, and the grounds include tennis courts and an outdoor
pool; BYO – it's a dry county; N.B. closed mid-December–February.

Inn at Shaker Village of Pleasant Hill 76R (5S)   24 | 22 | 24 | 24 | $93

3501 Lexington Rd., Harrodsburg; (606) 734-5411; FAX: (606) 734-5411
■ "Oh no, you're going to tell people about this gem" sigh surveyors who "can't wait
to go back" to this "rocking-chair quaint" historic village with lodgings throughout its
33 restored Shaker buildings; repro Shaker furnishings set the stage for a "joyous" stay in
"a super place to relax" with "fabulous food" and "absolutely no noise" (no alcohol or
tipping either); you can tour the village or "spend an entire day walking" its 2,700 acres
of bluegrass farmland; just remember the Shaker tenet ' 'tis a gift to be simple' – "spartan"
rooms "are not for the luxury minded."

Lexington

Hilton Suites Lexington (174S)   19 | 20 | 16 | 17 | $106

3195 Nicholasville Rd., Lexington; (606) 271-4000; (800) 445-8667; FAX: (606) 273-2975
■ "So-so" but "good service and clean comfort for the business traveler" sums up
reviewer reaction to this all-suiter in an all-glass building; those who say you can expect
a "nice room, that's about it" must be discounting the outdoor pool, fitness center and
facilities for small conferences on-site, and the Whitley Museum and shopping nearby.

Hyatt Regency Lexington 356R (9S)   19 | 19 | 16 | 17 | $131

400 W. Vine St., Lexington; (606) 253-1234; (800) 233-1234; FAX: (606) 233-7974
■ "Best in town" trumpet bluegrass-country visitors who applaud this "fine Hyatt"
with a "friendly staff" and "Downtown convenience"; part of the Lexington Center
complex, which includes Rupp Arena and the Civic Center Shops, it's connected via
glass skywalks to shops and restaurants at Victorian Square and The Market Place;
some find the rooms "small" and "basic", but then again you probably "don't spend a
lot of time" in them.

Marriott Griffin Gate Resort 388R (21S)   21 | 22 | 21 | 22 | $137

1800 Newtown Pike, Lexington; (606) 231-5100; (800) 228-9290; FAX: (606) 231-5136
■ Lexington's biggest hotel is "a cut above the norm" and caters "extremely well to
business functions" with extensive meeting space and a variety of restaurants and
lounges (try the Mansion for "superb" steaks and fine dining); thoroughbreds graze in
bluegrass pastures near the "pretty grounds" and there's "lots to do" for humans: 18
holes of golf ("perhaps the best golf hotel around"), tennis, swimming or just exploring
horse country; tip: it's a "great location for going to the races."

Radisson Plaza Hotel Lexington 367R   20 | 20 | 18 | 19 | $133

369 W. Vine St., Lexington; (606) 231-9000; (800) 333-3333; FAX: (606) 281-3737
☑ Aimed at the business crowd, with 15 meeting rooms, in-room computer jacks and a
concierge floor, this Downtowner doesn't impress respondents who cite "thin walls" and
"rooms in need of maintenance", but the latter complaint may be remedied by a renovation
ongoing at press time, and solid ratings suggest that most visitors have few complaints.

Louisville

Camberly Brown Hotel 286R (6S)
21 | 21 | 21 | 19 | $144

(fka The Brown, A Camberly Hotel)
335 W. Broadway, Louisville; (502) 583-1234; (800) 555-8000; FAX: (502) 587-7006
☑ A "Louisville milestone" dating from the 1920s, this "restored Downtown hotel" exudes "old-world elegance" and has a "great old-money feeling"; while fans gush about "luxurious rooms", "a presidential suite to die for" and two floors of "sweet concierge accommodations", others say the place may be "historic" but is "somewhat faded" and "needs modern technology" (a renovation is ongoing); its three restaurants include the popular English Grill.

Club Hotel by Doubletree 399R (45S)
▽ 10 | 11 | 9 | 9 | $101

(fka Hurstbourne Hotel)
9700 Bluegrass Pkwy., Louisville; (502) 491-4830; (800) 222-TREE; FAX: (502) 499-2893
☑ Time will tell if the Doubletree acquisition and ongoing renovation will raise scores for the erstwhile Hurstbourne Hotel; Doubletree is turning it into a business-friendly place, with computer jacks and work desks in the guestrooms, a club room offering video, audio and modem connections and extensive conference facilities.

Galt House East Hotel (600S)
15 | 16 | 14 | 13 | $103

141 N. Fourth St., Louisville; (502) 589-3300; (800) 843-4258; FAX: (502) 585-4266
☑ Though unimpressed critics call this all-suite convention hotel "tacky", its location by the Ohio River is close to the arts center, shopping and museums, meeting facilities are huge and ongoing renovations may make a difference.

Galt House Hotel 700R
16 | 17 | 14 | 15 | $121

140 N. Fourth St., Louisville; (502) 589-5200; (800) 626-1814; FAX: (502) 589-3444
☑ This convention behemoth shares restaurants with sister property Galt House East and, like its sibling, draws a few darts for its atmosphere; defenders call it a "good commercial hotel" with "very spacious, clean rooms", but critics say it "could use a makeover" (a 1996 renovation could sway doubters); all agree it has some of the city's "best river views."

Hyatt Regency Louisville 376R (12S)
19 | 18 | 16 | 17 | $127

320 W. Jefferson St., Louisville; (502) 587-3434; (800) 523-1234; FAX: (502) 581-0133
■ "Nothing spectacular", but what more do you need besides "very nice rooms" and "good service and location"? – which is what you can expect at this "basic Hyatt" with an 18-story atrium, indoor pool and a tennis court; covered walkways lead to the Galleria mall and the Commonwealth Convention Center (the hotel has its own large conference facilities as well), and a revolving rooftop restaurant offers a panoramic view of Louisville and the nearby Ohio River.

Marriott East Louisville 252R (2S)
19 | 20 | 17 | 17 | $113

1903 Embassy Square Blvd., Louisville; (502) 499-6220; (800) 228-9290; FAX: (502) 499-2480
■ "Standard all the way" sums up surveyor sentiment on this East End business abode, and while that may not sound like resounding praise, respectable ratings suggest most are satisfied; 12 meeting rooms can handle up to 700 attendees, and for nonbusiness pursuits there's a "nice indoor pool" as well as a fitness room; N.B. some renovations took place in 1996.

Seelbach Hotel 288R (33S)
22 | 22 | 21 | 21 | $137

500 Fourth Ave., Louisville; (502) 585-3200; (800) 333-3399; FAX: (502) 587-6564
■ The "best hotel in town, with the best restaurant" is the verdict on Downtown's "historic, beautifully updated" circa 1905 "gentlemen's palace" that spreads on "old-world charm" and "grand style" "right down to the canopied beds"; it's "worth it for the Rathskeller alone", a room opulently fashioned from Rookwood pottery, though fine-dining aficionados wouldn't miss the "fabulous" Oakroom; a few doubters think the restoration "didn't go far enough", but for most it's a "nostalgic spot of hotel history."

Louisiana

Napoleonville

Madewood Plantation House 6R (2S)   ▽ 25 | 27 | 21 | 21 | $145
4250 Hwy. 308, Napoleonville; (504) 369-7151; (800) 375-7151; FAX: (504) 369-9848
■ "A charming trip back to the Old South" awaits visitors to this 1846 Greek Revival mansion – "this is the place to get a real sense of plantation life"; the "gracious" environment is enhanced by canopied beds in antiques-filled guestrooms and dinners by candlelight; no phones or TVs in rooms, but that's the way it was back then.

New Iberia

Inn at Le Rosier 4R   – | – | – | – | I
314 E. Main St., New Iberia; (318) 367-5306; (888) 804-ROSE; FAX: (318) 365-1216
Wake up and smell the roses in one of four guestrooms, each with antiques and private bath, in a reproduction Acadian raised cottage; one of the highlights of a stay at this romantic B&B is New American dining in the circa 1870 main building, as well as relaxing in the three parlors or on the veranda.

New Orleans

TOP 10 OVERALL

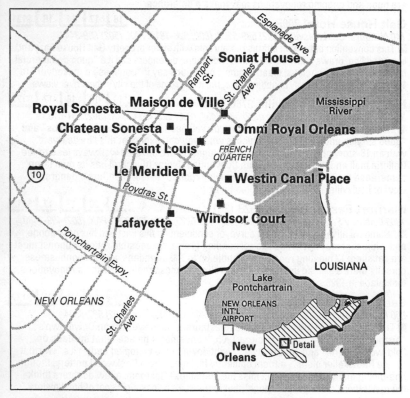

BEST OVERALL
28 Windsor Court
24 Maison de Ville
23 Chateau Sonesta
    Soniat House
    Westin Canal Place
    Omni Royal Orleans
22 Royal Sonesta
    Lafayette
    Saint Louis
    Le Meridien

BEST VALUES
Holiday Inn Chateau Le Moyne
Dauphine Orleans
Chateau Sonesta
Le Richelieu
De La Poste
Le Pavillon
St. Ann/Marie Antoinette
Prince Conti
Place d'Armes
Lafayette

Best Western Inn on Bourbon 184R (2S)
18 | 18 | 16 | 17 | $133

541 Bourbon St., New Orleans; (504) 524-7611; (800) 535-7891; FAX: (504) 524-8273

The rooms "could use a little updating" and the "confused staff" seems to run on "two speeds – slow and stop", yet the "spring break and Mardi Gras types" who frequent this "mediocre" hotel don't seem to mind since it's "right in the center of the action"; the Bourbon Street balconies open to all guests allow the interested to look down on a lot of hooting, staggering frat boys and out-of-control conventioneers.

Bienville House 80R (3S)
19 | 20 | 18 | 18 | $140

320 Decatur St., New Orleans; (504) 529-2345; (800) 535-7836; FAX: (504) 525-6079

This "cute little hotel" in an "ideal neighborhood" ("on the edge of the French Quarter") is "old but comfy" and "a pleasant change of pace from the big hotels" in town; surveyors who say it "seems seedy and run-down" and "needs major updating" should note that the lobby and guestrooms were refurbished post-*Survey*.

Bourbon Orleans Hotel 161R (50S)
21 | 21 | 20 | 20 | $148

717 Orleans St., New Orleans; (504) 523-2222; (800) 521-5338; FAX: (504) 525-8166

"Great location" is the real plus here: "close to the action" near Bourbon Street yet "quiet on the inside"; the legendary site of 19th-century quadroon balls is popular today with tourists and businesspeople alike for its "attentive staff", with "killer balconies", charming courtyard and "lovely pool"; rooms range from "small" standards to two-story suites that "work for families."

Chateau Sonesta Hotel New Orleans 232R (11S)
25 | 24 | 22 | 21 | $156

800 Iberville St., New Orleans; (504) 586-0800; (800) SONESTA; FAX: (504) 586-1987

A brand-new French Quarter hotel one block from both Bourbon and Canal Streets was fashioned from the beloved old D.H. Holmes department store building, and surveyors are sold on the "huge rooms" and "great service"; while a few don't cotton to the "sparse courtyard", most agree that "corporate types" will feel at home here, and it's hard to beat the "extremely convenient location" or the new Brennan restaurant, Red Fish Grill.

Cornstalk Hotel 14R
17 | 19 | 15 | 19 | $137

915 Royal St., New Orleans; (504) 523-1515; FAX: (504) 522-5558

Named for its extraordinary fence of cast-iron cornstalks (and morning glories and pumpkins), this "atmospheric" Victorian B&B with a "lovely location" in the heart of the Vieux Carré is "steeped in history"; but the "rooms are not so great", which may be why many enjoy their complimentary continental breakfast and morning newspaper on the porch or balcony.

Crowne Plaza New Orleans 435R (4S)
18 | 18 | 16 | 17 | $134

(fka Holiday Inn Crowne Plaza)

333 Poydras St., New Orleans; (504) 525-9444; (800) 777-7372; FAX: (504) 568-9312

It's "quiet and relaxed" at this 23-story business hotel "within walking distance" of the French Quarter, Riverwalk, Superdome and convention center; "nice rooms" and "friendly" service add up to an "adequate" experience, but "after a few drinks you'll forget where you're staying anyway"; P.S. "who would eat hotel food in New Orleans?"

Dauphine Orleans Hotel 103R (8S)
21 | 21 | 17 | 18 | $129

415 Rue Dauphine, New Orleans; (504) 586-1800; (800) 521-7111; FAX: (504) 586-1409

"Reasonable rates" and a "perfect" location "away from the noise and bustle" yet within "walking distance of the action" – that's what admirers appreciate about this "charming small hotel" in the French Quarter, constructed in the 1960s from a group of historic buildings; bonuses include "especially nice rooms" ("be sure to get a balcony"), "friendly" service, and complimentary continental breakfast and neighborhood shuttle.

De La Poste, Hotel 86R (14S)
20 | 21 | 21 | 17 | $135

316 Chartres St., New Orleans: (504) 581-1200; (800) 448-4927; FAX: (504) 522-3208

This "lovely little" "European-type hotel" that's "close to everything" delights respondents with its "comfortable rooms", "pretty courtyard" and fine Italian dining at Brennan-run Bacco; while a minority of sleepyheads notes it can be "noisy at night" – it's in the Quarter, after all – a "very accommodating" staff and "a bargain rate" help others get their rest.

Doubletree New Orleans 351R (12S)
17 | 18 | 16 | 16 | $122

300 Canal St., New Orleans; (504) 581-1300; (800) 222-TREE; FAX: (504) 522-4100

"Irresistible chocolate-chip cookies" "upon arrival" and an "excellent location" between the convention center and the French Quarter are the calling cards of this "comfortable, unpretentious" hotel "run by friendly people"; "moderate prices" mean "basic rooms, "ordinary food" and "limited public areas", though there's an on-site fitness center and outdoor pool to help sweet tooths work off the cookie calories.

Fairmont Hotel New Orleans 615R (85S)   20   21   21   21 $164
123 Baronne St., New Orleans; (504) 529-7111; (800) 527-4727; FAX: (504) 529-4775
📧 "Massive renovations" completed post-*Survey* "thankfully" have restored this "grande dame" to her former glory; reviewers report that the once "dreary, drab rooms" are now "beautifully decorated" and the staff's "attitude has improved as well" (the "charming old-world lobby" and "magnificent" Sazerac Restaurant and Bar were updated a few years ago); depending on whether you're a solitude seeker or party-goer, you'll find the location just across Canal Street from the French Quarter either "quiet and convenient" or "too far away" from action central.

Hilton Riverside New Orleans 1522R (78S)   20   20   19   21 $157
2 Poydras St., New Orleans; (504) 584-3999; (800) HILTONS; FAX: (504) 584-3979
■ "Huge but friendly" is the consensus on this "well-managed" "monster" "on the Mississippi" that's "convenient" to the Riverwalk and "within staggering distance of the Quarter"; escapees from the nearby convention center ease their worries in "above-average rooms" (ask for one with a river view), while the "great front desk staff", on-site health and racquet club and Pete Fountain playing in the third-floor club also do their part to shrink stress.

Holiday Inn Château Le Moyne 159R (12S)   19   19   16   18 $119
301 Dauphine St., New Orleans; (504) 581-1303; (800) HOLIDAY; FAX: (504) 523-5709
■ A "jewel of a place" in the heart of the French Quarter incorporating four restored Greek Revival townhouses and courtyards that give it an "old-world feel"; although "all rooms are not equal" and the "menu choices are poor", customers still consider it a "good value" in a "great location" – far enough from Bourbon Street to be "quiet, but close enough to the noise."

Hyatt Regency New Orleans 1084R (100S)   20   20   19   19 $158
500 Poydras Plaza, New Orleans; (504) 561-1234; (800) 233-1234; FAX: (504) 587-4141
📧 A "behemoth convention hotel" that "could be anywhere" ("a Hyatt is a Hyatt"), but this 32-story offering on the edge of the Central Business District happens to be "convenient" to the Superdome, convention center and New Orleans Centre; guests who grouse about being "too far from the action" can take advantage of the free shuttle to and from the Quarter; P.S. if revolving rooftop restaurants are "your thing", check out the Top of the Dome for cocktails and/or dinner.

Inter-Continental New Orleans, Hotel 446R (36S)   21   21   21   20 $160
444 St. Charles Ave., New Orleans; (504) 525-5566; (800) 327-0200; FAX: (504) 523-7310
■ This "glitzy, elegant" hotel in the Central Business District is "often overlooked because it's so out of the way", but what folks don't realize is that the St. Charles Avenue streetcar stops at the front door; surveyors say it's "nice and quiet", with "lovely rooms" and "friendly" service, and a "great place to stay during Mardi Gras" – "you can watch the parades in front of your door"; N.B. Rex toasts the queen of Carnival here.

Lafayette Hotel 24R (20S)   23   22   25   19 $158
600 St. Charles Ave., New Orleans; (504) 524-4441; (800) 733-4754; FAX: (504) 523-7327
■ "Old-fashioned graciousness with a vengeance" is demonstrated at this "stylish", "beautiful" "boutique hotel" at the edge of the Warehouse District on the St. Charles Avenue streetcar line; it's a "great location" for lawyers who need to be near the courthouse or for businesspeople with appointments on Poydras Street – and it's just around the corner from the Julia Street Arts District; P.S. there's an "incredible restaurant on premises" too – Mike's on the Avenue.

Le Meridien New Orleans 487R (7S)   23   22   22   21 $172
614 Canal St., New Orleans; (504) 525-6500; (800) 543-4300; FAX: (504) 525-1128
■ "Escape from the French Quarter to this lovely Parisian sanctuary" on Canal Street, an "attractive", "modern" business hotel offering "wonderful large rooms", "a friendly and helpful staff", "great jazz", a full-service fitness center and fine French fare at La Gauloise Bistro; a few feel that it's "lacking in character" – specifically, it could use "more New Orleans flavor."

Le Pavillon Hotel 219R (7S)   20   21   20   20 $139
833 Poydras St., New Orleans; (504) 581-3111; (800) 535-9095; FAX: (504) 529-4415
■ "Renovations have improved" the "best-kept secret in the center of the Business District", a "lovely old hotel" offering "charm and elegance at a great price"; guests gush that it's "absolutely gorgeous" with a "beautifully decorated" lobby filled with "fresh flowers" and spacious guestrooms featuring antiques and original artwork; a heated rooftop pool, free late-night PB&J sandwiches served in the lobby and "excellent service" make things go even easier in the Big Easy.

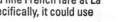

R	S	D	P	$

Le Richelieu in the French Quarter 70R (16S)

| 20 | 20 | 17 | 18 | $128 |

1234 Chartres St., New Orleans; (504) 529-2492; (800) 535-9653; FAX: (504) 524-8179

■ With its impressive lobby with black-and-white marble floors and mahogany-paneled walls, "old but terrific rooms" (all individually decorated) and the atmospheric appeal of an edifice dating back to 1845, this "charming" hotel in a quiet section of the French Quarter reminds visitors of "an Anne Rice novel"; free on-site parking, a godsend in the Vieux Carré, and free local calls help make it one of the "best values in New Orleans."

MAISON DE VILLE 14R (2S)

| 24 | 24 | 24 | 22 | $193 |

727 Toulouse St., New Orleans; (504) 561-5858; (800) 634-1600; FAX: (504) 528-9939

■ The "essence of New Orleans" is embodied in this "warm, cozy, intimate" Vieux Carré 'town house' – an "oasis" where "antiques and charm abound" in a "storybook setting"; rooms in the main building are "small" and "vary a lot", which is why the "very private" Audubon cottages (one of which was home to John James Audubon) "are the thing here"; "wonderful service" and "sublime" dining at The Bistro complete the "perfect" picture; N.B. Tennessee Williams is said to have completed *A Streetcar Named Desire* here.

Maison Dupuy Hotel 190R (8S)

| 21 | 21 | 20 | 20 | $146 |

1001 Rue Toulouse, New Orleans; (504) 586-8000; (800) 535-9177; FAX: (504) 525-5334

☑ Seven restored townhouses surrounding a "surprisingly secluded" courtyard with a heated pool and bar compose this "very French Quarter, very old school" hotel in a "very convenient location" ("just far enough off Bourbon Street to avoid crowds and noise"); rooms range from "big" to "tiny", and the decor swings from "seedy but charming" to "tacky, tacky, tacky", but "the staff is exceptionally friendly and service-oriented" and dining at Dominique's is a delight.

Marriott New Orleans 1236R (54S)

| 19 | 19 | 17 | 18 | $150 |

555 Canal St., New Orleans; (504) 581-1000; (800) 228-9290; FAX: (504) 523-6755

■ A "typical" Downtown convention hotel – "big and noisy", "bland and faceless" with the "slowest elevators in civilization" – sums up this "ugly monolith" "within stumbling distance of the French Quarter"; while "nothing to write home about", the "great location", "views of the river from upper floors" and "knowledgeable staff" make it "a cut above other Marriotts."

Melrose Mansion 4R (4S)

| ▽ 24 | 26 | 19 | 21 | $226 |

937 Esplanade Ave., New Orleans; (504) 944-2255; FAX: (504) 945-1794

■ This antiques-filled Victorian Gothic mansion on the National Register of Historic Places is "expensive" but "worth it" considering that rates include limo service to and from the airport, a full home-cooked Creole breakfast daily, nightly cocktail hour with hors d'oeuvres and "wonderful innkeepers" ladling out lots of "true Southern hospitality"; it's "a spectacular honeymoon spot" (ask for the Donecio Suite) on the downriver edge of the French Quarter, an iffy area at night.

Monteleone, Hotel 570R (28S)

| 18 | 20 | 18 | 19 | $144 |

214 Royal St., New Orleans; (504) 523-3341; (800) 535-9595; FAX: (504) 528-1019

☑ Despite a $15-million face-lift in 1995, reviewers remain split on this "well-situated" French Quarter grande dame: "great old hotel" with "raffish charm" vs. "lost its charm" and "old is not always wonderful"; fans ignore the "shoe-box-size" rooms in favor of "personal service", "good prices" and a "very cool" rooftop pool.

Omni Royal Crescent Hotel 91R (7S)

| ▽ 25 | 23 | 23 | 24 | $165 |

535 Gravier St., New Orleans; (504) 527-0006; (800) THE-OMNI; FAX: (504) 523-0806

■ This brand-new Central Business District hotel is getting favorable early returns, with voters' views ranging from "nice" to the "best of New Orleans"; a block from Canal Street makes it either "off the beaten path" or a "good location" depending on whether you're in town for pleasure or business (if the latter, take note of fax machines and dual dataport phones in every room); chef Kevin Graham's newest restaurant, Sapphire, is on-site.

Omni Royal Orleans 330R (16S)

| 22 | 23 | 23 | 23 | $174 |

621 St. Louis St., New Orleans; (504) 529-5333; (800) THE-OMNI; FAX: (504) 529-7089

■ A "classy, cozy" hotel that stands "right in the middle of the action" in the Quarter and yet is a "haven of calm" (and just around the corner from famous antiques stores); the rooms get a loud chorus of "small", but they're "clean" and service is "organized"; "great rooftop views from the pool" and the "best lobby in town" also keep the faithful coming, and the Rib Room "is a great place to network with the good ol' boys."

Pelham Hotel 60R   ▽ 19 | 18 | 21 | 13 | $123
444 Common St., New Orleans; (504) 522-4444; (800) 659-5621; FAX: (504) 539-9010
■ The few surveyors who've stayed at this former warehouse nestled between the French Quarter and Downtown love the "convenient location" but label the "small" rooms a "disappointment"; still, amenities like four-poster beds, antique furnishings and marble baths make this historic landmark an interesting place to stay.

Place d'Armes Hotel 70R (4S)   17 | 20 | 14 | 19 | $124
625 St. Ann St., New Orleans; (504) 524-4531; (800) 366-2743; FAX: (504) 581-3802
☑ It's the "best little hotel in the Quarter" with "lovely atmosphere" and a "quiet location" to some, but others raise arms against an "awful lobby" and rooms that "vary widely" and are "a little worn"; the "garden and patio are a delight", however, and this "historic bit of old New Orleans" just off Jackson Square is "close to everything"; continental breakfast is included.

Pontchartrain Hotel 69R (35S)   21 | 23 | 23 | 18 | $166
2031 St. Charles Ave., New Orleans; (504) 524-0581; (800) 777-6193; FAX: (504) 524-7828
☑ This Garden District old-timer on the St. Charles Avenue streetcar line is exactly how fans "imagined Southern hospitality" would be: "lovely antiques-filled rooms", "huge, sophisticated suites" and a "gracious" staff; "unforgettable food" is served at the Caribbean Room, and in the morning locals congregate to power-breakfast in the coffee shop; to a significant few it's "a little faded around the edges" – "a once great ship that has long since sailed."

Prince Conti Hotel 46R (4S)   20 | 20 | 18 | 16 | $128
830 Conti St., New Orleans; (504) 529-4172; (800) 366-2743; FAX: (504) 581-3802
☑ There "aren't many amenities" at this small hotel, just "charming rooms" at a "good price" furnished with "nice antiques", a "cooperative staff" and a French Quarter location; some say it's a "great place to relax" – perhaps they're thinking of the tony Bombay Club, which lures martini-mad locals who shun the area's downscale drinking holes.

Queen & Crescent 129R   − | − | − | − | M
344 Camp St., New Orleans; (504) 587-9700; (800) 975-6652; FAX: (504) 587-9701
The handful of reviewers who've been to this Central Business District hotel since its April 1996 debut report that it's "elegant" with "excellent" service; details include complimentary continental breakfast, plus minibars, coffeemakers, irons and ironing boards, safes and voicemail in each room.

Radisson Hotel New Orleans 737R (22S)   14 | 16 | 13 | 13 | $116
1500 Canal St., New Orleans; (504) 522-4500; (800) 333-3333; FAX: (504) 525-2644
■ "Old but adequate" is the best surveyors can say about this hotel convenient to the Superdome but not much else (a shuttle takes guests to the French Quarter); despite a $10-million renovation, you still "get to know your neighbors intimately" since "sound not only penetrates, it vibrates" through the walls; and it's still "not safe to walk around" the "awful" neighborhood at night.

Royal Sonesta Hotel   22 | 23 | 22 | 22 | $170
New Orleans 465R (35S)
300 Bourbon St., New Orleans; (504) 586-0300; (800) SONESTA; FAX: (504) 586-0335
■ "Location, location, location, noise, noise, noise" – "if you like Bourbon Street, go for it" advise party-goers; quieter types clamor it's "too noisy to sleep", though there are plenty of "nice but small" rooms facing the "beautiful courtyard", an "oasis" where visitors can better appreciate the hotel's "romantic", "elegant" ambiance; there's also a "terrific oyster bar" and "great" Creole eats at Begue's.

Saint Louis Hotel 45R (27S)   22 | 22 | 24 | 21 | $180
730 Rue Bienville, New Orleans; (504) 581-7300; (800) 535-9111; FAX: (504) 524-8925
■ The "handsome building" may be "slightly worn", but this small Vieux Carré hotel exudes "all the charm and uniqueness of old New Orleans"; devotees declare it's "just like a movie set" and a "relaxing place to visit" with a "delightful" courtyard and "fabulous" fare at Louis XVI, one of the top-rated French restaurants in the city.

Sheraton New Orleans Hotel 1065R (35S)   18 | 18 | 17 | 18 | $148
500 Canal St., New Orleans; (504) 525-2500; (800) 325-3535; FAX: (504) 561-0178
☑ A "big, sprawling convention mill" where you "feel like a computer chip" sums up this towering hulk of a hotel overlooking the French Quarter; yet it's "well run", rooms are "large" (some have river views), the meeting facilities are massive and it's "close enough, yet far away enough, from Bourbon Street" for guests to get a good night's sleep.

Soniat House 18R (13S)
24 | 25 | 20 | 23 | $183

1133 Chartres St., New Orleans; (504) 522-0570; (800) 544-8808; FAX: (504) 522-7208
■ It's the "Big Easy at its sultry best" – a "gorgeous", "totally romantic" restored 1829 townhouse on the edge of the French Quarter with a "charming courtyard" and rooms "uniquely decorated" with "the owner's antiques"; though breakfast is not included in rates, many remember the "fabulous biscuits and coffee served on the patio" every AM.

St. Ann/Marie Antoinette 66R
21 | 21 | 18 | 20 | $138

717 Conti St., New Orleans; (504) 525-2300; (800) 535-9111; FAX: (504) 524-8925
☑ Despite solid scores, mixed emotions greet the "sister to the Saint Louis" – "beautiful and intimate", "a real French Quarter experience" vs. "decent", "modest", "needs a face-lift badly"; all agree, however, that it's "a bargain" in a "terrific location."

Westin Canal Place 398R (41S)
24 | 23 | 22 | 23 | $180

100 Rue Iberville, New Orleans; (504) 566-7006; (800) 228-3000; FAX: (504) 553-5120
■ A "perfect location" at the foot of Canal Street – offering "unparalleled river views", "access to upscale shopping" at Canal Place (which houses the only movie theater in or near the Quarter) and "good proximity" to the Vieux Carré – sets this "sleek, modern", recently renovated business hotel apart from the waterside competition; "large", "well-decorated rooms", "great public areas", "exceptional service" and "marvelous" food also please the "trendy folks" who stay here.

WINDSOR COURT 58R (264S)
28 | 28 | 28 | 27 | $241

300 Gravier St., New Orleans; (504) 523-6000; (800) 262-2662; FAX: (504) 596-4513
■ Beaucoup de bouquets, as usual, for this Crescent City palace with a "pedigree": "amazing", "impeccable", "a real jewel", "the best in New Orleans" and third best in the country according to our *Survey*; rooms are "gorgeous", service is "excellent", afternoon tea in the Salon is "to die for" and dinner in the Grill Room is "outstanding in every way"; the price you pay for "perfection" is "high", of course, "but worth it."

Wyndham Riverfront New Orleans 200R (2S) ▽

24 | 24 | 22 | 23 | $139

701 Convention Ctr. Blvd., New Orleans; (504) 524-8200; (800) WYNDHAM; FAX: (504) 524-0600
■ Another "newish" hotel upriver from the French Quarter and in "the best location for the convention center" (it's across the street); "pleasant and quiet" with "good service" say the handful of participants who've tried it; N.B. notwithstanding the name, there's a street, streetcar line and shopping center between the hotel and the riverfront.

St. Francisville

Lodge at The Bluffs (39S)
▽ 23 | 21 | 21 | 23 | $141

PO Box 1220, St. Francisville; (504) 634-3410; (888) 634-3410; FAX: (504) 634-3528
☑ This all-suite getaway with an Arnold Palmer–designed golf course, tennis, pool and lakeside jogging path is close to antebellum homes and antiques stores and popular for small executive meetings; some rooms are furnished with antiques and Audubon prints; there's some disagreement over the Cajun-Continental food, with some saying "excellent" and others opining "could use a new chef."

White Castle

Nottoway Plantation 10R (3S)
24 | 22 | 21 | 23 | $147

PO Box 160, Mississippi River Rd., White Castle; (504) 545-2730; FAX: (504) 545-8632
■ "There's no more beautiful plantation mansion in America" sigh dreamy surveyors about this 1859 explosion of antebellum opulence an hour from New Orleans where "you expect Scarlett O'Hara to race down the driveway"; spacious rooms with private baths get the nod (hint: "the front two bedrooms are terrific") as do grounds facing the Mississippi and Creole-Cajun dining in a 19th-century setting.

Maine

TOP 10 OVERALL

Presque Island

MAINE

Norumbega Inn ■

Samoset Resort ■

Millinocket

Harraseeket

Bangor

Camden/Rockport

Castine Inn

Black Point Inn

Portland

Pilgrims Inn

Kennebunkport

Inn By The Sea

■ Captain Lord Mansion

■ Inn at Harbor Head

■ White Barn Inn

BEST OVERALL

25 White Barn Inn/Kennebunkport
24 Norumbega Inn/Camden
 Pilgrims Inn/Deer Isle
 Black Point Inn/Scarborough
23 Captain Lord Mansion/Kennebunkport
 Harraseeket Inn/Freeport
22 Inn By The Sea/Cape Elizabeth
 Inn at Harbor Head/Kennebunkport
21 Samoset Resort/Rockport
 Castine Inn/Castine

BEST VALUES

Castine Inn/Castine
Regency/Portland
Marriott/Portland
Pilgrims Inn/Deer Isle
Kennebunkport Inn/Kennebunk.
Bar Harbor Hotel/Bar Harbor
Harraseeket Inn/Freeport
Sheraton/Portland
Radisson/Portland
Bayview/Bar Harbor

Bar Harbor

R	S	D	P	$

Atlantic Oakes By-the-Sea 145R (5S)

20	20	19	21	$132

119 Eden St., Bar Harbor; (207) 288-5801; (800) 336-2463; FAX: (207) 288-8402
■ "A favorite year after year", the former mansion of Klondike millionaire Sir Harry Oakes is a "clean, comfortable" corporate and family resort set on 12 wooded acres just down the road from Bar Harbor's trendy shops and restaurants and "convenient to Acadia National Park"; return visitors come for the "good view of Frenchman's Bay", indoor/outdoor pools and five tennis courts; even so, a few tsk "lacks fine touches."

Bar Harbor Hotel/Bluenose Inn 55R (42S)

22	21	18	20	$146

90 Eden St., Bar Harbor; (207) 288-3348; (800) 445-4077; FAX: (207) 288-2183
■ "Numerous special touches" including rooms with fireplaces, "pretty furnishings" and the "best soap and shampoo anywhere" (Crabtree & Evelyn), a "beautiful lounge", fitness center and heated indoor/outdoor pools make this "well-located" place among "Bar Harbor's best" – not to mention a "good value"; the few who find it "unimpressive" probably haven't been back since the renovation; open May–October.

R	S	D	P	$

Bar Harbor Inn 153R

| – | – | – | – | M |

PO Box 7, Newport Dr., Bar Harbor; 207-288-3351; (800) 248-3351; FAX: 207-288-5296
Spectacular Frenchman Bay skirts this gracious eight-acre full-service resort on Mount Desert Island; accommodations are in the New England–style Main Inn, the contemporary Oceanfront Lodge (where all rooms have private ocean-view balconies) and in the Newport Building, built in 1994 and set back from the water; rates include continental breakfast and vacation packages are a good value.

Bayview, The 31R (1S)

| 22 | 21 | 20 | 20 | $157 |

111 Eden St., Bar Harbor; (207) 288-5861; (800) 356-3585; FAX: (207) 288-3173
■ Sink into "huge beds", "elegant style and homey comfort" at this "great summer resort" peeking at the Atlantic; it's a three-parter: an adults-only old-world–style inn (the original 1930 estate was host to Winston Churchill), a newer more upscale hotel and six townhouses; families favor the latter for "sweet service" ("couldn't have been nicer to us with a rambunctious three-year-old"), gourmet kitchens, laundries and fireplaces.

Boothbay Harbor

Spruce Point Inn 47R (17S)

| 18 | 20 | 20 | 20 | $156 |

Grandview Ave., Boothbay Harbor; (207) 633-4152; (800) 553-0289; FAX: (207) 633-7138
■ "Beautiful grounds" (100 acres with two outdoor pools – one freshwater, one saltwater – and two tennis courts) and "wonderful views" of the rocky coastline are the attraction at this "quiet", "peaceful" white clapboard inn one mile from town; though the accommodations "could use more sprucing up", most May–October visitors find it a "fantastic value"; N.B. there's a new Downtown annex.

Brunswick

Captain Daniel Stone Inn 30R (4S)

▽ | 22 | 19 | 18 | 19 | $142 |

10 Water St., Brunswick; (207) 725-9898; (800) 267-0525; FAX: (207) 725-9898
■ This Federal-style sea captain's mansion built in 1819 "tries hard" to please – and "never fails" – with period decorated rooms, complimentary light breakfast daily, an award-winning French-American restaurant featuring a double-hearth fireplace and spacious screened veranda; the 20-minute drive to L.L. Bean suits "camping sorts."

Camden

NORUMBEGA INN 9R (3S)

| 25 | 25 | 23 | 24 | $217 |

61 High St., Camden; (207) 236-4646; FAX: (207) 236-0824
■ "Feel like a Rockefeller" at this "gorgeous" 1886 fieldstone mansion (listed on the National Register of Historic Places) near the edge of Penobscot Bay that exemplifies "just what a lovely inn can be" with its "beautifully furnished" guestrooms, fireplaced parlors, sunlit conservatory, garden gazebos and "spectacular breakfasts" served by "friendly people"; "very expensive", yes, but worth it for a "romantic seaside castle."

Cape Elizabeth

Inn By The Sea 43R

| 23 | 20 | 23 | 24 | $207 |

40 Bowery Beach Rd., Cape Elizabeth; (207) 799-3134; (800) 888-4287; FAX: (207) 799-4779
■ "Lovely" old New England–style clapboard inn that pleases families and conference-goers year-round with "great" suites (featuring full kitchens and patios or porches), a "friendly, attentive staff", "beautiful beach" and array of activities from swimming to tennis to shuffleboard; a few feel "the beauty of the place is all in the outdoors", but many more maintain it's a "very satisfactory total experience."

Castine

Castine Inn 17R (3S)

| 20 | 21 | 21 | 21 | $124 |

PO Box 41, Main St., Castine; (207) 326-4365; FAX: (207) 326-4570
◪ "Quaint and charming" vs. "tired" and "needs refurbishing" reflects the debate about this 1898 hostelry hemmed by rose and perennial gardens in "a perfect New England town"; nevertheless, it's regarded as a "great value" near Acadia National Park.

Deer Isle

PILGRIMS INN 13R (1S)

| 23 | 24 | 25 | 23 | $169 |

Deer Isle; (207) 348-6615; FAX: (207) 348-7769
■ "Charming rooms, cordial hosts and a very good dinner" cap the compliments for this 1793 Dutch Colonial "gem" listed on the National Register of Historic Places; privacy seekers book Number Fifteen, a one-bedroom cottage featuring turn-of-the-century furnishings, a fireplace and a deck overlooking Northwest Harbor; rates include breakfast and dinner; open mid-May–mid-October.

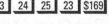

East Holden

Lucerne Inn 21R (4S)   – | – | – | – | M
PO Box 540, R.R. 3, East Holden; (207) 843-5123; (800) 325-5123; FAX: (207) 843-6138
On a knoll overlooking Phillips Lake lies this recently renovated 1814 country inn appreciated for its "good staff" and antique-appointed guestrooms with wood-burning fireplaces (some also have whirlpool tubs) and "magnificent views"; year-round packages including lodging, dinner and Sunday brunch are available.

Freeport

Harraseeket Inn 50R (4S)   22 | 22 | 24 | 22 | $164
162 Main St., Freeport; (207) 865-9377; (800) 342-6432; FAX: (207) 865-1684
■ After walking to L.L. Bean and 110 upscale outlet shops "it's so nice to come home to" "the best inn in the region"; this "clean", "comfortable", year-round colonial with a modern addition and five acres of grounds rates raves for its "charming lobby", "adorable rooms", "free snacks at teatime", "old Maine hospitality" and "restaurant equal to the shopping" – a "must for Sunday brunch."

Kennebunkport

Captain Lord Mansion 20R   25 | 24 | 22 | 22 | $180
PO Box 800, Kennebunkport; (207) 967-3141; FAX: (207) 967-3172
■ Overlooking the village green, this "top of the line" sea captain's mansion built during the War of 1812 earns accolades for its "huge", "romantic" "period rooms with high beds and fireplaces" (hint: "the Captain's Hideaway is best"); "wonderful" owners who "aim to please" and "superb" three-course breakfasts served family style in the country kitchen add to the appeal of this "perfect New England getaway."

Inn At Harbor Head 3R (2S)   23 | 21 | 21 | 23 | $177
41 Pier Rd., Kennebunkport; (207) 967-5564; FAX: (207) 967-1294
■ "A great location and beautiful view" are "what make it special" – snuggle into a king-size hammock and watch lobster boats riding the tide in Cape Porpoise Harbor from the sloping lawn of this "enchanting", "spotless and quiet" inn; some suggest it's "overpriced for the rest of its services", but the coddled majority appreciates the "special attention to detail" such as "rooms painted with local scenes."

Kennebunkport Inn 34R   20 | 21 | 21 | 19 | $146
1 Dock Sq., Box 111, Kennebunkport; (207) 967-2621; (800) 248-2621; FAX: (207) 967-3705
◪ "Understated elegance", "charming rooms and top food" served by a "caring staff" – that's what surveyors admire about this "quintessential New England inn", a 19th-century mansion adjoining the 1930s River House on Dock Square ("best outdoor patio restaurant in town"); a few fret "somewhat stodgy", though most maintain "if you're looking for a quiet weekend and hospitality at a great price, this is it."

WHITE BARN INN 17R (7S)   25 | 26 | 27 | 23 | $218
PO Box 560C, 37 Beach St., Kennebunkport; (207) 967-2321; FAX: (207) 967-1100
■ Prepare to be pampered with "unsurpassed" service at this "romantic" homestead built in the 1850s and now a Relais & Châteaux property; guests feel "welcomed like old friends", enjoying "complimentary afternoon tea and evening port" and "exquisite" food "in a converted barn" (a few find that the "charming albeit small rooms" "don't match the restaurant"); it may "cost a fortune", but "a visit will stay in your memory forever."

Newcastle

Newcastle Inn 14R (1S)   – | – | – | – | E
PO Box 24, R.R.2, River Rd., Newcastle; (207) 563-5685; (800) 832-8669; FAX: (207) 563-8677
Relax in a big wing chair in the living room, settle in by the fire with a good book, stretch out on the new deck overlooking the Damariscotta River, then enjoy a "wonderful" five-course dinner prepared by the "pleasant owners" of this "comfortable" white clapboard house – "a great getaway" between Camden and Boothbay Harbor.

Northeast Harbor

Asticou Inn 35R (15S)   19 | 20 | 20 | 22 | $198
PO Box 406, Rtes. 3 & 198, Northeast Harbor; (207) 276-3344; (800) 258-3373; FAX: (207) 276-3373
◪ The "classiest place on Mount Desert Island" is a "quiet, rustic" B&B "out of another era" known for its "magnificent location" ("book a room facing the water"), "friendly and helpful staff" and "good food"; P.S. a recent renovation has updated some of the "rooms my grandmother must have slept in", but the "stuffy guests" have yet to "lighten up."

Ogunquit

Cliff House 160R (2S)   20 | 21 | 20 | 21 | $162
1 Shore Rd., Ogunquit; (207) 361-1000; FAX: (207) 361-2122
☑ "Worth a stay for the view alone" sums up this sprawling "stress-buster retreat" (open since 1872) named for the "incomparable" vistas from its 90-foot perch near Ogunquit; given the "very romantic setting" with "waves crashing below and good times above" plus amenities like tennis courts and indoor/outdoor pools, many don't mind that the "rooms are too sparse and lacking in charm"; closed in winter.

Portland

Marriott at Sable Oaks 222R (5S)   18 | 20 | 17 | 17 | $128
200 Sable Oaks Dr., South Portland; (207) 871-8000; (800) 228-9290; FAX: (207) 871-7971
■ The rooms are "comfortable", the location is "convenient" to both the mall and the airport, and the breakfast buffet is "excellent", but it's the "remarkably friendly can-do attitude" of the staff that sets this link apart from the rest of the "typical" chain; "one of the nicest in Portland" is the majority view.

Radisson Eastland Hotel Portland 183R (21S)   15 | 17 | 13 | 13 | $109
157 High St., Portland; (207) 775-5411; (800) 333-3333
☑ Corporate types appreciate the "very nice conference space" at this otherwise "blah" harborview hotel in Portland's Arts and Theater District; others suggest it's "showing its age" with "very tiny bathrooms" and implore "please, restore the lobby"; your call.

Regency Hotel Portland 89R (6S)   21 | 21 | 19 | 19 | $132
20 Milk St., Portland; (207) 774-4200; (800) 727-3436; FAX: (207) 775-2150
■ "Nicely located in the middle of the Old Port" and a few blocks from the Civic Center, this "tastefully" converted late–19th-century armory combines "cozy, charming and relaxing" ambiance with biz needs (in-room computer jacks, meeting rooms) and a full-service fitness center; aside from the room with only "a skylight for a window", this "classic old-worlder" is "the only place to stay in Portland."

Sheraton Tara South Portland 216R (4S)   17 | 16 | 15 | 15 | $119
363 Maine Mall Rd., South Portland; (207) 775-6161; (800) 843-8272; FAX: (207) 775-0196
☑ The "huge pie-shaped rooms" with floor to ceiling windows at this "businessperson's hotel" rate raves from reviewers, as does its strategic location across from the Maine Mall and "near the camps for visiting day"; otherwise, there's "nothing to recommend it."

Rockport

Samoset Resort 132R (91S)   20 | 21 | 19 | 24 | $176
220 Warrenton St., Rockport; (207) 594-2511; (800) 341-1650; FAX: (207) 594-0722
☑ "The setting – a promontory in Penobscot Bay – couldn't be better" for vacationing or conferencing, according to aficionados of this "wonderful" year-round 19th-century resort; "go for the golf" (18 "sensational" oceanside links) and "abundance" of other activities including tennis, swimming and x-country skiing; just know there are "lots of kids" and conventions comprise more than half of the clientele.

Scarborough

BLACK POINT INN RESORT 74R (6S)   21 | 25 | 23 | 25 | $210
510 Black Point Rd., Scarborough; (207) 883-4126; (800) 258-0003; FAX: (207) 883-9976
■ Sojourning at this "lovely old inn in Winslow Homer territory" is "like staying with a favorite aunt who's a great housekeeper" – and just happens to have a golf course, 14 clay tennis courts and indoor and outdoor (saltwater) pools; the "authentic dignity" of the "charming" 1878 property appeals to both the "Harvard set" and corporate retreaters looking for a "restorative and calming" experience just outside Portland.

Maryland

Annapolis

	R	S	D	P	$

Loews Annapolis Hotel 205R (11S) | 21 | 21 | 20 | 19 | $132 |
126 West St., Annapolis; (410) 263-7777; (800) 526-2593; FAX: (410) 263-0084
■ This "upscale" property with "nice rooms", a lively bar and "romantic" dining is probably the closest one gets to contemporary "luxury" that's "within walking distance" of Annapolis town center and "convenient to the famous waterfront"; the "good" meeting facilities, service and parking also earn points, even with those critics who feel the hotel "doesn't have a lot of character."

Marriott Waterfront Annapolis 147R (3S) | 18 | 18 | 17 | 18 | $146 |
80 Compromise St., Annapolis; (410) 268-7555; (800) 336-0072; FAX: (410) 269-5864
◪ Whether you sail to this "simple" Annapolis docksider or drive in from Route 50, the "spectacular views of Chesapeake Bay" from its balconies and waterfront bar are likely to make you feel like a mariner; it's the "best spot for harbor action, boat shows or Fourth of July fireworks" – but not always for getting a good night's sleep ("noisy" harbor rooms) or a decent meal.

Maryland Historic Inn 127R (10S) | 20 | 20 | 21 | 18 | $145 |
58 State Circle, Annapolis; (410) 263-2641; (800) 847-8882; FAX: (410) 268-3813
◪ "Modern construction behind a historic facade" would be a blessing if the "quaint" 18th-century buildings that form this cluster were all comfortably revamped; but the rooms "vary" – some are "charming", others "musty" or "seedy" – and the staff can be "indifferent"; however, philosophic types say "a few creaks, a few flaws, but it's part of our past"; what's more, there's "wonderful food" in the Treaty of Paris restaurant, and weekend jazz in the tavern features the likes of Charlie Byrd.

Baltimore

BEST OVERALL	BEST VALUES
25 Harbor Court	Inn at Henderson's
22 Doubletree Colonnade	Marriott's Hunt Valley
21 Renaissance Harborplace	Clarion
Inn at Henderson's	Doubletree Colonnade
20 Hyatt Regency	Admiral Fell Inn

Admiral Fell Inn 74R (6S) | 21 | 21 | 19 | 19 | $144 |
888 S. Broadway, Baltimore; (410) 522-7377; (800) 292-4667; FAX: (410) 522-0707
◪ "In the heart of funky Fells Point", and not far from Little Italy and Johns Hopkins, this waterfront "favorite small hotel" inspires "love" for its "quaint" 18th-century mood, "gruff" friendliness and New Southern dining at Savannah, though a few guests are at sea about the "big difference" between the "old rooms" of "historical significance, but only average comfort" and the "new, which lack charm"; since "it's in the middle of everything", there can be wee hours "street noise" from revelers leaving area bars.

Ann Street B&B 2R (1S) ⌦ | – | – | – | – | M |
804 S. Ann St., Baltimore; (410) 342-5883
A circa 1780 Federal-style B&B in Historic Fells Point that attracts budget-minded visitors who enjoy the happening (if noisy) area and its local life but don't want to be too far from Inner Harbor tourist destinations; rooms are furnished with poster beds and antiques, and a full breakfast is served in the kitchen or, weather permitting, the private garden; N.B. cash only.

Brookshire Inner Harbor Suite Hotel (90S)   ▽ | 19 | 18 | 16 | 15 | $161 |
120 E. Lombard St., Baltimore; (410) 625-1300; (800) 647-0013; FAX: (410) 625-0912
◪ This "tasteful" recycled commercial space near "the middle of Inner Harbor life" provides "spacious" kitchenette-equipped suites; but other than noting the stellar "location" and "generous" elbow room, respondents seem at a loss for kind words: "pedestrian and ordinary come to mind", along with "poorly managed", "poor service" and "could use sprucing up."

182

Celie's Waterfront B&B 7R
▽ 24 | 24 | 23 | 16 | $129

1714 Thames St., Baltimore; (410) 522-2323; (800) 432-0184; FAX: (410) 522-2324

■ Its seven "charming" guestrooms are "always booked", which could be why more surveyors haven't stayed at this "top East Coast B&B" on the Fells Point waterfront; for "luxury in the midst of funk", it's hard to beat the antiques-filled rooms, "attention to detail", "helpful staff", "pretty" rooftop lounge and, depending on the season, breakfast in the private garden or by the dining room fireplace; N.B. don't be surprised by shoots for the TV show *Homicide* just outside the door.

Clarion Hotel at Mt. Vernon Square 103R (1S)
19 | 19 | 20 | 17 | $140
(fka Latham Hotel)

612 Cathedral St., Baltimore; (410) 727-7101; (800) 292-5500; FAX: (410) 789-3312

◪ "Once elegant", this Mt. Vernon luxury hotel's performance has seemed to "sink with each turnover of management", yet its 1923 neoclassical style and cityscape views (especially from "great" rooms on the concierge floor) still win approval, especially from those who manage "bargain" rates; the closing of the rooftop restaurant, Citronelle, bothers some regulars, but recent extensive renovations could renew spirits, if not its surrounding neighborhood.

Cross Keys Inn 134R (12S)
18 | 17 | 15 | 16 | $137

5100 Falls Rd., Baltimore; (410) 532-6900; (800) 756-7285; FAX: (410) 532-2403

■ A manicured, 72-acre secured community only minutes by shuttle from Downtown Baltimore, this "classy hideaway" boasts an "eager" staff, redone rooms, conference space and an "outstanding Sunday brunch"; diversions include outdoor swimming and a "good gym" complemented by shopping in an "upscale" mall; all the same, a disappointed few say it falls "short of its potential."

Doubletree Inn at the Colonnade 93R (32S)
21 | 23 | 23 | 20 | $147

4 W. University Pkwy., Baltimore; (410) 235-5400; (800) 222-TREE; FAX: (410) 235-5572

■ Unless "visiting Johns Hopkins" or "neighboring residences", this modish condo hotel's Midtown locale may seem out-of-the-way to out-of-towners, which is fine with local power sceners who treat its "great bar" and "great restaurant", Polo Grill, as their private club; visitors, however, quickly discover that the "attractive" quarters and public spaces, "very nice" staff and "convenient" gym make it "surprisingly nice for the price."

HARBOR COURT HOTEL 178R (25S)
26 | 25 | 25 | 24 | $187

550 Light St., Baltimore; (410) 234-0550; (800) 824-0076; FAX: (410) 659-5925

■ "Bawlmer's best" showcases "fabulous" Inner Harbor views in a "luxurious" setting with "handsome" rooms, "top-notch" fitness and business facilities (in-room fax, dataports and voicemail), plus "don't miss" New American dining at Hampton's; what's more, this "all-around excellent" hostelry provides "service as it should be" and is "very child-friendly" – "now I know why Baltimore is called Charm City."

Hyatt Regency Baltimore 461R (25S)
21 | 20 | 19 | 20 | $153

300 Light St., Baltimore; (410) 528-1234; (800) 233-1234; FAX: (410) 685-3382

■ "Panoramic views" from its lively rooftop restaurant and upper-floor rooms plus "good support staff" "help this typical Hyatt enormously", as does the "perfect convention location" (connected by bridgeways to the convention center and Harborplace); the Regency Club floor is "excellent", and other accommodations are "clean, serviceable" and brightened with an occasional "nice touch" like "roses with breakfast."

Inn at Henderson's Wharf 38R
24 | 21 | 19 | 19 | $123

1000 Fell St., Baltimore; (410) 522-7777; (800) 522-2088; FAX: (410) 522-7087

■ Set in a restored 19th-century warehouse on the Fells Point waterfront, this B&B makes adventurous "corporate" visitors "very comfortable" with "nice rooms", "harbor views" and convenient meeting space; guests commute to Downtown by water taxi, and special packages include neighborhood dinner/wine deals and a see-an-Orioles-game option; N.B. it serves "continental breakfast only", and it's not much.

Marriott Inner Harbor Baltimore 491R (34S)
20 | 20 | 18 | 19 | $150

110 S. Eutaw St., Baltimore; (410) 962-0202; (800) 228-9290; FAX: (410) 962-8585

◪ Baseball fans cheer this "heart of Downtown" hotel's "great access to Camden Yards" – you can watch an Orioles "game right from your window" or let the "accommodating" staff "help get tickets"; though it's a "long walk" to seaport sights and many find "nothing distinguishing" about the "standard" rooms, large-scale facilities or food, this "typical Marriott" is "reliable" and "always booked."

Marriott's Hunt Valley Inn 388R (2S) 19 | 20 | 18 | 19 | $124
245 Shawan Rd., Hunt Valley; (410) 785-7000; (800) 228-9290; FAX: (410) 785-0341
In a fast-growing 'burb north of Baltimore, this sprawling complex gears its boardroom comforts ("big upholstered chairs" and 16 meeting rooms) for seminar and golf agendas; however, the outdoor amenities ("patio room facing pool", tennis courts amid the "rolling hills" of "horse country") help make it "decent for families" also; the recently redecorated quarters, public areas, dining room and service are generically "pleasant", which for some urbanites translates as "too boring and white bread."

Mr. Mole B&B 3R (2S) – | – | – | – | M

1601 Bolton St., Baltimore; (410) 728-1179; FAX: (410) 728-3379
Guests at this antiques-filled Victorian row house on Bolton Hill slip back in time, occupying suites with four-poster bed, sitting room, bathroom and reading books (no TV); not far from antique shops, galleries, the Myerhoff Symphony Hall and the Lyric Opera, it's a favorite burrow for visiting art enthusiasts – but take a cab home at night; N.B. continental breakfast is included, exercise can be arranged.

Omni Inner Harbor Hotel 707R (22S) 18 | 18 | 16 | 17 | $138
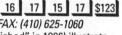
101 W. Fayette St., Baltimore; (410) 752-1100; (800) 344-2814; FAX: (410) 625-9646
It's "stretching the truth" to label this an Inner Harbor hotel, since the harbor is "a few blocks away" and a view "can be tough to find"; respondents still rate it "ok", if you're looking for discounted, "functional" accommodations and don't mind walking a "few blocks to the action" (cab it at night); but phobes dismiss it as overall "inefficient" and "a bad day for architecture", finding "not a single grace note in the rooms."

Radisson Plaza Lord Baltimore 395R (24S) 16 | 17 | 15 | 17 | $123
20 W. Baltimore St., Baltimore; (410) 539-8400; (800) 333-3333; FAX: (410) 625-1060
Comments on this Downtown 1928 landmark ("nicely refurnished" in 1996) illustrate that what some find "charming" in a vintage hotel (a "huge, old-time lobby", "large rooms" and "well-equipped" meeting space) can seem "merely old" to others – particularly if the service and food aren't right and some find the area iffy; N.B. the dining rating might improve now that its daytime deli morphs into an Italian trattoria at night.

Renaissance Harborplace Hotel 582R (40S) 22 | 21 | 20 | 22 | $158
(fka Stouffer Harborplace)
202 E. Pratt St., Baltimore; (410) 547-1200; (800) HOTELS-1; FAX: (410) 783-9676
"Hands down the Inner Harbor's best choice for location, amenities and cost", this "modern deluxe facility" offers "first-class" conference space and "comfortable rooms in an energized environment" (a skywalk connects with the Harborplace pavilions); its restaurant, Windows, not only has "the best views" but is "super for kids and picky eaters" thanks to "fantastic" dining room servers who, like other staff, seem to "actually enjoy" what they do – another reason why this is "what vacations are about."

Sheraton Baltimore North 289R (2S) 18 | 19 | 15 | 16 | $128
903 Dulaney Valley Rd., Towson; (410) 321-7400; (800) 433-7619; FAX: (410) 296-9534
"Nothing fancy" but "neat and useful", this Towson high-rise next to Goucher College is a "business travel" beacon due to its generous meeting space and backup services; diversions from commerce are supplied by a seafood restaurant, indoor pool, comp use of Bally's gym across the street and proximity to an enormous shopping mall.

Sheraton Inner Harbor Hotel 317R (20S) 20 | 20 | 18 | 19 | $148
300 S. Charles St., Baltimore; (410) 962-8300; (800) 325-3535; FAX: (410) 962-8211
"Exceptionally convenient to the best of Baltimore", including Camden Yards, this "big", "functional" chain hotel on the waterfront is a "prime" conference location and "family destination"; "large rooms", "good" public facilities, "friendly" staff and fair prices overshadow its "profoundly unexciting" atmosphere – and nearby restaurants remedy what some write off as "under-par" dining.

Berlin

Atlantic Hotel 16R (1S) – | – | – | – | M
2 N. Main St., Berlin; (410) 641-3589; (800) 814-7672; FAX: (410) 641-4928
Sample turn-of-the-century small-town life and some of the best cooking on the Eastern Shore at this handsomely restored Victorian B&B; its civilized accommodations provide a restorative prelude to observing nature at the nearby Assateague Wildlife Refuge, or catching the wild life at Ocean City bars and beaches.

Chestertown

Imperial Hotel 11R (2S)   ▽ 22 | 23 | 25 | 18 | $146
208 High St., Chestertown; (410) 778-5000; FAX: (410) 778-9662
■ A "marvelous renovation in a marvelous town", this 1903 Victorian in Chestertown's Historic District is also renowned for its "excellent, creative" Regional American dining and "wonderful" wines; the owners are "fabulous hosts", equally ready to arrange a "private wine tasting" or a bicycle tour of the countryside; one caveat: it may be too cosmopolitan for some – the "room felt like a city hotel [and] we expected a country experience."

Easton

Tidewater Inn & Conference Center 108R (6S)   19 | 21 | 20 | 20 | $137
101 E. Dover St., Easton; (410) 822-1300; (800) 237-8775; FAX: (410) 820-8847
■ Yes, there are kennels in the basement of this old-fashioned yet "inexplicably sophisticated" Eastern Shore hostelry that's a duck hunter's roost (hunt breakfasts are served at 4:30 AM); it also bags federal and corporate retreaters with good meeting rates and "recently redone" rooms; a few complaints that quarters are "spartan" compared to the "tasteful" lobby are muted by "friendly staff" and "decent" regional specialties in the Hunter's Tavern.

Ocean City

Coconut Malorie Hotel (85S)   ▽ 24 | 22 | 22 | 20 | $165
201 60th St., Ocean City; (410) 723-6100; (800) 767-6060; FAX: (410) 524-9327
■ "If there's class in Ocean City" you'll find it at this all-suites Caribbean-themed sleeper (and its sister, the Lighthouse Club); what awaits at an "off-the-strip, on-the-bay" setting (though no ocean views) are "beautiful" Jacuzzi-equipped quarters ("small for a family of four") decorated with original island art, plus "well-maintained" facilities and good dining; in winter it's a "very romantic" getaway.

Dunes Manor Hotel 160R (10S)   ▽ 20 | 19 | 16 | 19 | $144
2800 Baltimore Ave., Ocean City; (410) 289-1100; (800) 523-2888; FAX: (410) 289-4905
■ "Right on the beach in a good part of town", this contemporary grand hotel mixes "Victorian style" (wicker porch rockers, a complimentary "great afternoon tea") with enough modern facilities (indoor/outdoor pools, exercise equipment) and traditional seafood dining for a "fine" vacation or meeting; it's "clean", "quiet" and "hospitable" – and priced appropriately.

Lighthouse Club (23S)   ▽ 25 | 23 | 22 | 22 | $181
201 60th St., Ocean City; (410) 524-5400; (800) 767-6060; FAX: (410) 524-9327
■ In a "beautiful" octagonal lighthouse replica overlooking the bay at Ocean City, Coconut Malorie's suite sister beckons pleasure seekers with "great service" and romantic trappings like Jacuzzis and gas fireplaces in penthouse rooms; there's "sort of a party atmosphere" (to put it mildly) on the deck of its popular bar and restaurant, Fager's Island, which serves more than 100 varieties of beer.

Sheraton Fontainebleau 230R (63S)   17 | 18 | 13 | 17 | $163
10100 Coastal Hwy., Ocean City; (410) 524-3535; (800) 638-2100; FAX: (410) 524-3834
☑ A glossy high-rise "with the ocean at its door", this beachfronter has its own conference center, ballrooms, multiplex restaurants and is "fun for the family" too; but some rooms "lack a view", there's "no outdoor pool" and dining is "disappointing" – none of which bothers guests who proclaim that since there's a "nice beach and they accept dogs – what more can you ask?"

Oxford

Robert Morris Inn 35R   20 | 21 | 21 | 21 | $152
314 N. Morris St., Oxford; (410) 226-5111; FAX: (410) 226-5744
☑ "'Historic' is written in capital letters" all over this colonial-era Oxford mainstay, celebrated by author James Michener and local yachtsmen for its "lovely" harbor setting, "lots of" Chesapeake Bay "atmosphere" and "great seafood" dining (a leading candidate for best crab cakes); as one would expect in a hostelry dating back to 1710, its "varied accommodations" include quaint but "squeaking" rooms, many of which could use "some updating."

Stevensville

Kent Manor Inn 22R (2S)   _ | _ | _ | _ | M

500 Kent Manor Dr., Stevensville; 410-643-5757; (800) 820-4511; FAX: 410-643-8315
This beautifully restored 1820 mansion, once part of the Smithfield plantation (now known as Thompson's Creek), sits on 226 acres on Kent Island, across from Annapolis via the Chesapeake Bay Bridge; cozy rooms, some with fireplaces, are furnished with Victorian reproductions and all have a water view; activities include crabbing, paddle boating, biking, jogging and shopping at nearby factory outlets; the inn's dining rooms are overseen by chef Dennis Shakan, formerly of the well-regarded Tall Timbers Resort in Durango, Colorado.

St. Michaels

INN AT PERRY CABIN 38R (3S)    26 | 26 | 26 | 26 | $245

308 Watkins Ln., St. Michaels; (410) 745-2200; (800) 722-2949; FAX: (410) 745-3148
■ "Sublime" Eastern Shore waterfront "retreat" created by Sir Bernard Ashley (co-founder with his late wife of Laura Ashley Enterprises), where "lots of bucks buy incredible comfort, pampering, decor and wonderful food" in a "designer-perfect" country house environment; everything from the "charming" rooms, "formal" dining and "manicured" grounds to the boutique conference space and fitness center bespeaks "gentility" and tony staging – "splendid sets, great cast, top Broadway prices."

Taneytown

Antrim 1844 9R (5S)   _ | _ | _ | _ | M

30 Trevanion Rd., Taneytown; (410) 756-6512; (800) 858-1844; FAX: (410) 756-2744
"Lovely and secluded" 19th-century plantation in rolling mountain country near the Gettysburg battlefields that provides "wonderful service" and relaxing atmosphere; an "out-of-another-era" haven, its period appointments, full breakfasts and multicourse dinners, varied meeting facilities and outdoor diversions (swimming, tennis, croquet and nearby golf) make it "great for functions", business sessions or a "romantic" getaway.

Massachusetts

TOP 10 OVERALL

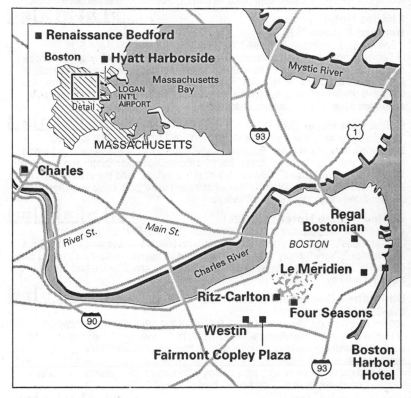

BEST OVERALL

27 Four Seasons
26 Ritz-Carlton
25 Boston Harbor
23 Le Meridien
    Regal Bostonian
    Renaissance Bedford
22 Charles/Harvard Square
21 Hyatt Harborside
    Fairmont Copley Plaza
    Westin Copley Place

BEST VALUES

Hyatt Harborside
Marriott Copley Place
Swissôtel
Lenox
Doubletree
Boston Park Plaza
Eliot Suite
Colonnade
Copley Square
Westin Copley Place

R	S	D	P	$

BOSTON HARBOR HOTEL 204R (26S)

26	25	25	26	$221

70 Rowes Wharf, Boston; (617) 439-7000; (800) 752-7077

■ An "elegant" contemporary waterside hotel where it's a "special treat" to "watch sunrise" from "beautiful rooms" and later dine on "consistently superb" New England cuisine at Rowes Wharf; extra kudos go to service that's "warm" and "accommodating" and for the "convenient water shuttle from Logan Airport"; on the downside is a less-than-central location.

Boston Park Plaza Hotel 936R (24S)

17	18	18	18	$148

64 Arlington St., Boston; (617) 426-2000; (800) 225-2008; FAX: (617) 423-1708

◪ A "well-run", "environmentally aware" oldie praised for its "convenient location near the Common", "grand public rooms", "gracious service" and reliable fare at Legal Sea Foods, but panned for "rooms that vary wildly" from "spacious" and "beautifully decorated" to "depressing" and "boxlike" plus "bathrooms and mattresses that qualify as historic"; still, in the silver lining department, it's a "good value for the money."

Chandler Inn 56R   ▽ 11 15 13 12 $113
26 Chandler at Berkeley, Boston; (617) 482-3450; (800) 842-3450; FAX: (617) 542-3428
◪ Some surveyors view this "basic", "gay-friendly" hotel as an "inexpensive" choice near Copley Place that's "clean" and within "a few blocks of a subway and the Amtrak station"; most, however, shudder at an experience beyond "spartan" – i.e. "gloomy" rooms in a "seamy" location with "difficult parking"; continental breakfast included.

Charles Hotel In
Harvard Square 252R (44S)   22 22 23 21 $192
1 Bennett St., Cambridge; (617) 864-1200; (800) 882-1818; FAX: (617) 864-5715
◪ Corporate execs and "Harvard mommies and daddies" say this "cool, crisp" Cambridge hotel is "as good as it gets – and at those prices it ought to be"; amenities include Bose Wave Radios and "great quilts" in the "distinctive" but "smallish" guestrooms, a state-of-the-art spa, two "wonderful" restaurants and a "sophisticated" jazz club; dissenters deem it "a bit cold and charmless."

Colonnade Hotel 273R (12S)   21 20 19 19 $165
120 Huntington Ave., Boston; (617) 424-7000; (800) 962-3030; FAX: (617) 424-0968
■ Business travelers like this "European-style" hotel for its "good value", "old-world elegance" and "great location" across from the Hynes Convention Center and Prudential Center; rooms are "quaint", "the rooftop pool is a delight" and the staff is "very accommodating"; a minority sniffs "not what it used to be", but a rise in ratings since our last *Survey* suggests it's still a "favorite."

Copley Square Hotel 131R (12S)   20 21 20 20 $173
47 Huntington Ave., Boston; (617) 536-9000; (800) 225-7062; FAX: (617) 267-3547
◪ A "gracious", "beautifully restored" historic hotel built in 1891 boasting a "great Back Bay location", "very friendly" staff and "marvelous Hungarian restaurant"; rooms can be "teeny", though, and "not up to the beautiful public areas" – too bad "you can't sleep in the lobby."

Doubletree Guest Suites 20R (290S)   20 19 17 17 $150
(fka Guest Quarters Hotel)
400 Soldiers Field Rd., Boston; (617) 783-0090; (800) 222-TREE; FAX: (617) 783-0897
◪ Families favor this "comfortable" all-suiter that's "convenient for visiting Harvard" but "within walking distance of nothing" else (there's complimentary scheduled van service to Downtown); respectable ratings suggest it pleases most, but those in search of charm and character come up empty, calling it "average in all respects" – "adequate rooms", "adequate service", "mediocre" food.

Eliot Suite Hotel 14R (82S)   24 22 17 18 $169
370 Commonwealth Ave., Boston; (617) 267-1607; (800) 44-ELIOT; FAX: (617) 536-9114
■ Expect "European charm" and "old-style elegance" at this "quiet retreat in the Back Bay", a 1925 neo-Georgian edifice with "wonderful personnel" and suites that are so "spacious and clean" "you'll probably never want to go home"; less-than-stellar dining ratings may get a boost when the Parisian-style supper club Clio opens in '97 – meanwhile, there are scads of options along Newbury Street just a short stroll away; N.B. a fitness center is planned for '97.

Fairmont Copley Plaza 347R (32S)   21 22 21 22 $181
138 St. James Ave., Boston; (617) 267-5300; (800) 527-4727; FAX: (617) 437-0794
◪ "This *is* Boston" rave reviewers charmed by the old-timer's "luxurious" public spaces replete with crystal chandeliers, marble floors and gilded coffered ceilings; there's also "indulgent service", a "lovely afternoon tea service" and a hot new steakhouse and cigar-friendly martini bar, the Oak Room (which replaced the Plaza Dining Room); complaints of "tired rooms", however, suggest this "grande dame" needs to "get her act together and renovate"; N.B. at press time, a guestroom refurbishment was under way and scheduled to be completed by 1998.

FOUR SEASONS HOTEL BOSTON 216R (72S)   28 28 27 26 $249
200 Boylston St., Boston; (617) 338-4400; (800) 332-3442; FAX: (617) 423-0154
■ The top-rated hotel in the city, and among the top 100 in the US, has it all – "a wonderful location" overlooking the Boston Common and Public Garden, "handsome", "spacious" rooms, a fabulous spa and 51-foot indoor pool, "heavenly" New French food at Aujourd'hui and a staff that "treats you like royalty"; it's "celebrity-spotting central" and, yes, it's "expensive."

Hilton Boston Back Bay 339R (3S)   19 19 16 16 $155
40 Dalton St., Boston; (617) 236-1100; (800) 874-0663; FAX: (617) 867-6104
◪ "Location, location, location" is the main draw at this "typical business traveler's hotel" just a short walk to Fenway Park or Newbury Street shops; rooms are "comfortable" and rates "reasonable", but most write it off as "just a place to sleep" and "not much else."

Hyatt Conference Center & Hotel Harborside 259R (11S)
22 | 22 | 21 | 21 | $168

101 Harborside Dr., Boston; (617) 568-6000; (800) 233-1234; FAX: (617) 568-6080
■ As an airport hotel, this one "leaves all the others near Logan at the gate", offering "wonderful views of the Boston skyline", "very comfortable" rooms, a "convenient" water shuttle to Downtown (for a fee) and nice facilities for business travelers; we hear only a few distant rumbles about "thin walls" and "an indifferent staff."

Hyatt Regency Cambridge 461R (8S)
20 | 20 | 19 | 19 | $163

575 Memorial Dr., Cambridge; (617) 492-1234; (800) 233-1234; FAX: (617) 491-6906
◪ Proponents of this pyramid-shaped property enjoy "walking along the Charles River", "swimming in the indoor pool" and service from a staff that "treats every guest like a VIP", while opponents bemoan the "out-of-the-way location" and judge the ambiance "sterile", the rooms "badly in need of remodeling" and the city's only revolving rooftop restaurant "not very special"; perhaps management is listening – a renovation of all rooms began in late '96.

Inn at Harvard 112R (1S)
21 | 22 | 19 | 20 | $173

1201 Massachusetts Ave., Cambridge; (617) 491-2222; (800) 222-8733; FAX: (617) 491-6520
■ This "charming" inn on Harvard Square is "a godsend to college families" who appreciate its "comfortable" "European ambiance", "lovely interior courtyard" and "smallish" but "pretty" rooms adorned with cherry furnishings and artwork from the Fogg Museum; for tuition-strapped parents, however, it may be too "high-priced."

Le Meridien 304R (22S)
23 | 24 | 24 | 22 | $200

250 Franklin St., Boston; (617) 451-1900; (800) 543-4300; FAX: (617) 423-2844
■ "Hidden in the Financial District" and well-suited to business travelers, this "unique" "fortresslike" hotel exemplifies the "elegant remodeling of a treasured old building" (a former Federal Reserve Bank); guests can bank on "beautiful public spaces", "small but wonderful rooms" and "lovely French pampering", which extends to the "excellent" Julien restaurant; a minority won't be making any deposits, calling the hotel "stuffy", "overpriced" and "overrated."

Lenox Hotel 211R (3S)
20 | 19 | 16 | 17 | $149

710 Boylston St., Boston; (617) 536-5300; (800) 225-7676; FAX: (617) 267-1237
■ "Visit Boston as it was at the turn of the century" at this recently renovated (to the tune of $20 million) "classic" offering "old-world drama" in the heart of the Back Bay; its "charming" rooms (some are "large", some are "small" and 30 feature fireplaces), "friendly" staff and "central location" that's "perfect" for shopping add up to a "great experience" at "bargain" rates.

Marriott Cambridge 418R (13S)
19 | 19 | 17 | 18 | $148

2 Cambridge Ctr., Cambridge; (617) 494-6600; (800) 228-9290; FAX: (617) 494-0036
◪ There's debate about the location of this "dependable" business hotel "in the shadow of MIT" – "a welcome alternative to staying Downtown" vs. "in the middle of nowhere"; otherwise, all agree it "may not be sexy" (it may even be "soulless"), but it's "priced right" and offers some "nice river views" and "comfortable rooms"; plus, you can just "walk right out of the lobby door to the subway."

Marriott Copley Place Boston 1100R (47S)
22 | 21 | 20 | 21 | $170

110 Huntington Ave., Boston; (617) 236-5800; (800) 228-9290; FAX: (617) 236-5885
■ A dream for shopaholics and conventioneers, this "sleek" high-rise is connected by covered walkway to a "fabulous" upscale mall (Neiman Marcus, Saks and more) and the Hynes Convention Center; "lovely public areas", "nice-size" quarters and "an attentive staff" make some see "no need to go outdoors"; request a room on one of the upper floors, where "views are awesome"; it's "hardly cozy, but you wouldn't expect it to be."

Marriott Long Wharf Hotel Boston 398R (4S)
21 | 20 | 18 | 20 | $181

296 State St., Boston; (617) 227-0800; (800) 228-9290; FAX: (617) 227-2867
◪ An "excellent" location, next door to the New England Aquarium and convenient to the North End and Faneuil Hall, is the main attraction of this "dramatic" hotel frequented by both tourists and corporate types; to some it has "all the charm of a cell block", but the staff is "friendly" and the rooms are "pleasant" with "wonderful harbor views."

Newbury Guest House 32R
▽ 20 | 20 | 17 | 17 | $116

261 Newbury St., Boston; (617) 437-7666; FAX: (617) 262-4243
■ Surveyors "hate for others to know about" this restored 1882 brownstone townhouse with a fashionable Newbury Street address; it's "the best bed and breakfast" in "the heart of Boston", a place chock-full of Victorian "elegance" yet almost "like being at home" – and comfortably priced too; continental breakfast (included) is served in the parlor or on the patio.

Omni Parker House 518R (17S)   15 | 18 | 17 | 17 | $156
60 School St., Boston; (617) 227-8600; (800) 843-6664; FAX: (617) 227-2120
☑ A "grande dame" that's "showing her age despite cosmetic surgery" sums up the longest continuously operated hotel in the US and the birthplace of Boston cream pie in 1855; a dip in ratings since our last *Survey* suggests that "personalized service", "wonderful Parker House rolls", "great martinis" and an "excellent location" along the Freedom Trail no longer make up for rooms that are "dark", "drafty" and "closet-size"; N.B. recent renovations may present a more encouraging picture.

Regal Bostonian 140R (12S)   23 | 24 | 24 | 22 | $210
(fka Bostonian Hotel, The)
Faneuil Hall Marketplace, Boston; (617) 523-3600; (800) 343-0922; FAX: (617) 523-2593
■ "Elegant and understated", this "little gem" near Quincy Market is "one of Boston's best small hotels"; some of the "well-appointed" but "small" rooms come equipped with fireplaces and whirlpool tubs, and the "terrific" Seasons restaurant touts a "beautiful" "rooftop view"; P.S. avoid rooms facing the market side – it's "very noisy at night."

Renaissance Bedford Hotel 276R (8S)   21 | 22 | 21 | 21 | $129
(fka Stouffer Renaissance Bedford Hotel)
44 Middlesex Tpke., Bedford; (617) 275-5500; (800) HOTELS-1; FAX: (617) 275-3042
■ "Recent renovations have brought back this facility" on 24 piney acres near historic Lexington and Concord; it's "well set up for kids" with "comfy, childproof rooms" despite being a business-oriented place with 23 meeting sites; amenities for all include a health club with indoor pool, sauna, Jacuzzi and tennis courts (two indoor, two outdoor).

RITZ-CARLTON BOSTON 231R (47S)   26 | 27 | 26 | 25 | $246
15 Arlington St., Boston; (617) 536-5700; (800) 241-3333; FAX: (617) 536-1335
■ The "last link to Boston's glittering past" is "flawless in every respect" and offers everything – "the Common, swan boats and afternoon tea", "unparalleled public spaces" filled with "exquisite flowers", "elegant rooms", "impeccable service" personified in "white-gloved elevator operators" and, of course, the just-renovated but "classic" Dining Room; if some sniff that it's all a bit too "stuffy", a contented majority revels in being "pampered" at "Boston's blue-blooded best."

Royal Sonesta Hotel Boston 377R (23S)   19 | 20 | 18 | 18 | $158
5 Cambridge Pkwy., Cambridge; (617) 491-3600; (800) SONESTA; FAX: (617) 661-5956
☑ Despite being "a little off the beaten track", this "handsome" hotel fits business folk as well as an Armani suit; there are "clean and comfortable" rooms, "great meeting facilities", "attractive public spaces" displaying contemporary art and "terrific views" of the Charles River and Boston skyline; notwithstanding, a sizable contingent finds the whole experience "nothing special"; N.B. a $7-million renovation is planned for '97.

Sheraton Boston Hotel & Towers 1035R (146S)   19 | 18 | 17 | 18 | $160
39 Dalton St., Boston; (617) 236-2000; (800) 325-3535; FAX: (617) 236-1702
☑ To pragmatists, this "centrally located" convention hotel is a businessperson's paradise – connected to the Hynes Convention Center and "well equipped" with 44 meeting rooms and an indoor pool and health club; charm-seekers shrug it off as "impersonal" and "overwhelming"; P.S. regulars report that "rooms in the tower are worth the upgrade."

Sheraton Commander Hotel 152R (23S)   16 | 17 | 15 | 14 | $143
16 Garden St., Cambridge; (617) 547-4800; (800) 535-5007; FAX: (617) 868-8322
☑ Opinions differ dramatically on this "Harvard Square tradition"; the ayes favor its "quiet" "convenience", calling it "charming and comfortable" with "unexpectedly fine rooms" (some featuring four-poster beds) and "moderate prices"; the nays grade it merely "functional" and "strictly for Harvard parents – eat somewhere else"; N.B. recent renovations may not be reflected in the ratings.

Swissôtel 458R (42S)   21 | 20 | 20 | 18 | $162
1 Ave. de Lafayette, Boston; (617) 451-2600; (800) 621-9200; FAX: (617) 451-0054
☑ "From the jar of chocolates at the reception desk to the plush rooms" upstairs, this "luxurious" European-style hotel is typically Swiss in its "very personal service"; alas, the "terrible location next to a bankrupt mall" in "a neighborhood that's experiencing growing pains" leaves little to yodel about; executive floors, 17 function rooms and a business center with PCs and fax machines make work a pleasure.

Tremont House Hotel 310R (12S)   14 | 16 | 12 | 14 | $127
275 Tremont St., Boston; (617) 426-1400; (800) 331-9998; FAX: (617) 338-7881
☑ Theater buffs are hopeful that this "once-grand" "old" hotel two blocks from the Public Garden will emerge from its current $10-million renovation as the "luxurious hideaway" it has the potential to be; at press time, the consensus remains "nothing special."

Westin Hotel Copley Place 755R (45S)   22 | 21 | 20 | 21 | $181
10 Huntington Ave., Boston; (617) 262-9600; (800) WESTIN-1; FAX: (617) 424-7483
■ This "massive" "conventioneer's delight" has a "prime location" attached to the Copley Place Mall and Hynes Convention Center; an underwhelmed minority shrugs it off as "too loud", "too busy" and "too impersonal" – the "General Motors of hotels" – but for most its "glitzy public spaces", "comfortable rooms" with "inspiring views" and "great food" at Turner Fisheries and The Palm drive it to higher ratings.

Westin Hotel Waltham 313R (33S)   20 | 19 | 18 | 17 | $133
70 Third Ave., Waltham; (617) 290-5600; (800) 228-3000; FAX: (617) 290-5626
☑ Positive reports on this "surprisingly good" suburban hotel on "the outskirts of Boston" stress that it's "conveniently located" with "lovely rooms" and "reasonable prices"; others find it "serviceable" but "bland" and claim that "when the corporate clientele leaves for the weekend, so does the service"; respondents who say there's a "need for a makeover" might be glad to know one was recently completed.

Cape Cod

Brass Key 30R (4S)   ▽ 24 | 24 | 20 | 22 | $151
12 Carver St., Provincetown; (508) 487-9005; (800) 842-9858; FAX: (508) 487-9020
■ One key to the success of this "lovely", "gay-friendly B&B" is staff that "spells hospitality with a capital H"; quiet yet "in the heart of Provincetown action", it offers rooms in several restored 19th-century buildings (including a Federal-style whaling captain's home and a Victorian house), each with period decor as well as modern touches (VCR, voicemail) and some with fireplace and whirlpool· there's an outdoor pool too; check for seasonal opening/closing dates.

Cape Codder 253R (8S)   17 | 18 | 17 | 17 | $126
Rte. 132 & Bearse's Way, Hyannis; (508) 771-3000; (800) THE-TARA; FAX: (508) 771-6564
■ Soothe your frazzled nerves swinging on the porch of this "old-time resort" in a "gorgeous" "cliffside setting" where "down-home, customer-friendly" ways make it a fine "family destination"; if rooms are merely "adequate" and bathrooms "ancient", nobody seems to mind much.

Chatham Bars Inn 135R (20S)   22 | 23 | 22 | 24 | $216
Shore Rd., Chatham; (508) 945-0096; (800) 527-4884; FAX: (508) 945-5491
■ On an eastern Cape Cod hilltop overlooking the ocean is this "stately" shingled "dowager" exuding "old-line" "elegance" from the "romantic" main house to the "lovely" rooms and cottages; admirers say it has it all – "the beach, a nine-hole golf course, good food" and "gorgeous views"; a few mutter "stuffy" (there's a dining-room dress code in season) and "expensive", but "off-season rates make it affordable", and a '96 redo may hush whispers that it's "somewhat worn"; P.S. "cottages on the beach are a dream."

Coonamessett Inn (26S)   19 | 20 | 21 | 20 | $162
311 Gifford St., Falmouth; (508) 548-2300; FAX: (508) 540-9831
☑ For those who think "lots of red yachting pants and Talbots dresses" are a good thing, there's "charm aplenty" at this "old-fashioned" 18th-century Falmouth clapboard inn with "attractive grounds" ("nice for a wedding") and a "great Cape menu" in a choice of dining rooms; antiprepsters call it "stuffy" and say the "rooms are nothing great", but recent renovations may put things in new perspective.

Dan'l Webster Inn 37R (9S)   23 | 22 | 22 | 21 | $160
149 Main St., Sandwich; (508) 888-3622; (800) 444-3566; FAX: (508) 888-5156
■ A "nice old New Englandy" inn that some call "deceptively historic", possibly because its 1692 birthdate is belied by such modern amenities as an outdoor pool and meeting facilities; Dan'l himself, though, would find little reason to debate surveyors who praise the inn's "cozy", "old-world" atmosphere and "good food" served in three dining rooms, including a "beautiful" glass conservatory looking out onto "pretty gardens"; only a few devil's advocates gripe "overrated, overpriced."

Dunscroft by the Sea 7R (3S)   – | – | – | – | M
24 Pilgrim Rd., Harwich Port; (508) 432-0810; (800) 432-4345; FAX: (508) 432-5134
On a quiet street within walking distance of the beach at Nantucket Sound, Alyce and Wally Cunningham encourage romance at their 1920 Dutch Colonial inn, not only with their Sweetheart Package (a basket filled with chocolates, strawberries, champagne and a rose) but also with a famous-lovers theme in the Laura Ashley–style rooms, each with private bath; there's a sitting room and screened porch, and beach chairs and full breakfast are complimentary; children over 12 only.

High Brewster Inn 3R (3S) ▽ 22 | 20 | 24 | 20 | $178
964 Satucket Rd., Brewster; (508) 896-3636; (800) 203-2634; FAX: (508) 896-3734
■ In a "beautiful setting" on a high bluff in Brewster's Historic District, this "authentic historic inn" overlooking a scenic pond offers rooms in an "elegant" main house (built in 1738) as well as cottage accommodations plus "excellent dining" in its classic American restaurant; to devotees it's like a "good private club."

New Seabury Cape Cod (130S) 23 | 19 | 18 | 22 | $200
Rock Landing Rd., Mashpee; (508) 477-9111; (800) 999-9033; FAX: (508) 477-9790
☑ Teeing off is a prime activity at this 2,000-acre all-villas complex in a "quaint Cape Cod setting" on Nantucket Sound, where "great golf" on two "beautiful courses" scores a hole in one; New England's largest waterfront resort also boasts 16 tennis courts, an outdoor pool, a marina and three miles of private beach, not to mention a "party atmosphere"; though room ratings are high, comments ranging from "lovely" to "tired" suggest that some "need an uplift"; kitchenettes in each are a plus.

Ocean Edge Resort & Golf Club 238R (2S) 22 | 21 | 19 | 24 | $182
2907 Main St., Brewster; (508) 896-9000; (800) 343-6074; FAX: (508) 896-9123
■ Admirers of this "unusual family-oriented" resort on Cape Cod Bay say it "has everything": "exquisite" grounds surrounding the main 19th-century mansion and carriage house, "good-size rooms" as well as kitchen-equipped contemporary villas, a "wonderful" private beach and "caring employees"; though a few find fault with "average food" and "disjointed", "spread-out" facilities, most are too busy with golf, tennis, swimming and other activities to notice.

Sea Crest Resort 260R (6S) 17 | 17 | 17 | 19 | $139
350 Quaker Rd., North Falmouth; (508) 540-9400; (800) 225-3110; FAX: (508) 548-0556
☑ "Popular" with families and also "a super place for a meeting or convention" offering a complete range of resort facilities, including tennis, indoor/outdoor pools, a white-sand beach and 14 meeting rooms; contrarians cite "weak" dining and find it generally "uninspiring", but recent renovations could promise a rosier future.

Wequassett Inn 97R (7S) 23 | 23 | 22 | 24 | $217
Rte. 28, Pleasant Bay, Chatham; (508) 432-5400; (800) 225-7125; FAX: (508) 432-5032
■ "Quaint but modern", this "luxurious" resort, "spread out" on 22 acres of "beautiful" grounds, is deemed "the diamond of Cape establishments" by voters who give it the Cape's highest overall marks; a "lovely complex" of 20 colonial and modern buildings, it's lauded for its "friendly service", "spectacular view and food" in the main dining room, "great tennis" and other "good facilities"; gripes that "rooms need updating" may be quieted by a recent redo; N.B. a private 18-hole championship golf course is scheduled to open in 1998.

Whalewalk Inn 7R (5S) ▽ 21 | 19 | 17 | 19 | $135
220 Bridge Rd., Eastham; (508) 255-0617; FAX: (508) 240-0017
■ The few surveyors who have discovered this "charming", "comfortable" Eastham hideaway (an 1830s whaler's home with a barn and two cottages) enjoy its "peaceful setting", "wonderful service" and such simple pleasures as strolling to nearby Cape Cod Bay and afternoon hors d'oeuvres on the patio; for a truly "secluded" experience, insiders recommend the studio cottage.

Danvers

Tara's Ferncroft Conference Resort 350R (17S) 20 | 20 | 18 | 22 | $109
(fka Sheraton Tara Hotel)
50 Ferncroft Rd., Danvers; (978) 777-2500; (800) THE TARA; FAX: (978) 750-7991
■ A "better than average business hotel", this "wonderful suburbanite with European flair" is "one of those special properties that's worth the trip"; the "excellent" amenities include 22 function rooms, an "exceptional health club" and numerous sports options – eight tennis courts (four clay), a putting green and driving range, indoor and outdoor pools, racquetball courts, an outdoor skating rink and x-country skiing; guestrooms may be "forgettable", but they are "comfortable."

Deerfield

Deerfield Inn 23R 20 | 21 | 21 | 21 | $155
81 Old Main St., Deerfield; (413) 774-5587; (800) 926-3865; FAX: (413) 773-8712
■ "You'll love it, ghosts and all" say antiquity buffs who delight in "the spooky feeling" of "the historical architecture" of this "charming", "well-restored" 1884 inn at the center of a 300-year-old New England village; there also happen to be "lovely rooms", "wonderful food" and "excellent service" that, best of all, come at a "reasonable cost"; N.B. it's a no-smoking establishment.

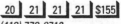

Lenox

BLANTYRE 16R (7S)   27 | 27 | 27 | 27 | $308
16 Blantyre Rd., Lenox; (413) 637-3556 (Summer), (413) 298-1661 (Winter);
FAX: (413) 637-4282

■ In a "baronial setting" near Tanglewood, this "breathtaking" 1901 replica of a "Scottish castle" sits regally amid acres of "magnificent grounds"; expect "luxury throughout" – "gorgeous", "treasure-filled" rooms, "pampering" from a staff that "knows your name", "superb food" (jacket and tie at dinner, please) – and "zillions of things to do nearby" (tennis and swimming on-site); while a few grumble "too stuffy" and "too expensive", most see this Relais & Châteaux member as a "pricey" "once in a lifetime treat" that makes you feel "it's good to be king."

Cranwell Resort & Golf Club 50R (15S)   23 | 21 | 20 | 25 | $212
55 Lee Rd., Lenox; (413) 637-1364; (800) CRANWEL; FAX: (413) 637-4364

■ This "gem in the heart of the Berkshires" is praised for "spectacular views" and "huge", "beautiful rooms", especially "in the main house" (an 1853 Tudor mansion); along with "great golf", there are the Fredrick Law Olmsted–designed grounds and a new x-country ski center to please outdoors folk; an unimpressed few, who compare it to "an impersonal large motel", might feel differently after recent multimillion-dollar renovations; P.S. "rates vary greatly depending on when you go" and where you stay.

Gables Inn 15R (3S)   21 | 22 | 20 | 21 | $173
81 Walker St., Lenox; (413) 637-3416; (800) 382-9401; FAX: (413) 382-9401

■ An 1885 Queen Anne cottage in Lenox village that was the family home of author Edith Wharton is now a "romantic" B&B offering "beautifully furnished rooms", many with fireplaces; service is "personal", distractions are plentiful: there's a heated outdoor pool and newly installed tennis court, Tanglewood is minutes away and "all the Berkshires' cultural activity" is just a bit further; tip: "the room with the balcony is the best."

WHEATLEIGH, THE 17R   24 | 24 | 26 | 25 | $278
Hawthorne Rd., Lenox; (413) 637-0610; (800) 321-0610; FAX: (413) 637-4507

■ Guests "live out fantasies" at this "magnificent" monument to the Gilded Age, a Florentine-style palazzo where you can "enjoy the sounds of Tanglewood from your balcony"; the "exceptional" "elegance" encompasses "incredible rooms with marble baths and fireplaces", "spectacular food", "superior service" and "beautiful grounds"; a few naysayers find it "overpriced, stuffy" and due for a redo, but the clear consensus is "perfect, pricey and worth it."

Martha's Vineyard

CHARLOTTE INN 23R (2S)   26 | 25 | 26 | 24 | $246
27 S. Summer St., Edgartown, Martha's Vineyard; (508) 627-4751; FAX: (508) 627-4652

■ "Extraordinary!" rave surveyors smitten with this "quaint" yet "elegant" 1860s Victorian inn, a "world-class" "romantic" haven (no groups or meetings here) that earns the Vineyard's top overall ratings; the "fabulous", antiques-filled rooms are right "out of *Architectural Digest*" and the French fare at this Relais & Châteaux property is "wonderful"; a few carp about "high prices" and service that's "a tad pretentious", but to most "there's not a thing that could be improved"; gentler rates prevail off-season.

Daggett House 21R (4S)   20 | 21 | 22 | 20 | $165
59 N. Water St., Edgartown, Martha's Vineyard; (508) 627-4600; (800) 946-3400;
FAX: (508) 627-4611

■ Rumors that it's haunted don't scare away guests who enjoy the "homelike" atmosphere, "enticing breakfasts" and "remarkable water views" at this "simple New England island inn" comprised of three 17th-century buildings in a harborside garden setting; it's "not fancy" and "some rooms can be noisy", but it's a "reliable friend" and a "best value in Edgartown"; N.B. no smoking allowed.

Harbor View Hotel 113R (11S)   20 | 21 | 19 | 22 | $201
131 N. Water St., Edgartown, Martha's Vineyard; (508) 627-7000; (800) ISLANDS;
FAX: (508) 627-8417

■ "Sitting on a rocking chair on the porch watching the sun set" in full "view of the Edgartown lighthouse" equals "heaven" at this "friendly" waterside "Vineyard classic"; open year-round, it boasts "mouthwatering food", on-site tennis, "caring staff", "some super rooms" in the stately Victorian main building and several "charming" one- and two-bedroom cottages; a few faultfinders call it "overpriced and overrun" and don't like the "cell-phone" ambiance around the pool.

Outermost Inn 5R (2S)   ▽ 22 | 22 | 21 | 24 | $217

1 Lighthouse Rd., R.R.# 1, Gay Head, Martha's Vineyard; (508) 645-3511; FAX: (508) 645-3514

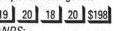 Secluded on the western tip of Martha's Vineyard is this "tranquil" shingled inn admired by some as "the prettiest spot on the beach at sunset", offering lovely "views from every room", "friendly" service, "hearty" homestyle meals and daily catamaran sails; the less impressed say it's "too expensive" and has "no style to speak of" plus "mediocre food"; open April to October.

Thorncroft Inn 14R   ▽ 26 | 26 | 24 | 21 | $192

PO Box 1022, 460 Main St., Vineyard Haven, Martha's Vineyard; (508) 693-3333; (800) 332-1236; FAX: (508) 693-5419

■ A "beautiful find" for romantic getaways; set in a secluded, tree-filled setting a block from the ocean, this "quality" country inn impresses surveyors with its antiques-filled rooms ("every one different", including some with Jacuzzi and wood-burning fireplace), "friendly", "helpful" owners and "delicious" "homemade" breakfasts and afternoon teas; there's even a private cottage with garage for those who really want to get away from it all; N.B. no smoking.

Tuscany Inn 8R   ▽ 25 | 25 | 27 | 24 | $202

22 N. Water St., Edgartown, Martha's Vineyard; (508) 627-5999; FAX: (508) 627-6605

■ *La bella Italia* meets New England at this renovated 19th-century sea captain's home in the heart of Edgartown; when Laura Sbrana-Scheuer, a native of Tuscany, and husband Rusty bought the property a few years ago, they gave it an elegant makeover that reflects Laura's heritage and the Vineyard's rustic charm; the few voters who have visited call it one of "the best on the island" and rave over Laura's "out-of-this-world" food (ask about her La Cucina cooking school packages).

Nantucket

Beachside at Nantucket 87R (3S)   ▽ 16 | 19 | 17 | 14 | $178

30 N. Beach St., Nantucket; (508) 228-2241; (800) 322-4433; FAX: (508) 228-8901

■ Known above all as a "good value", this gray-shingled four-building resort offers "cute rooms" done in wicker and florals, an outdoor pool plus a "great location" in a pretty residential neighborhood a short walk to town and the beach; it's popular with families (kids under 16 stay free with parents) as well as small corporate groups (meeting rooms for up to 40 people).

Centerboard Guest House 5R (2S)   – | – | – | – | M

8 Chester St., Nantucket; (508) 228-9696; FAX: (508) 228-1963

In a convenient location in the Historic District, this lovely restored Victorian offers charm and hospitality, along with period decor and, as a nod to modern comforts, a/c in all rooms; a separate cottage is also available for rental, and continental breakfast is included in the rates.

Cliffside Beach Club 21R (6S)   ▽ 21 | 22 | 21 | 23 | $223

PO Box 449, Nantucket; (970) 920-4175; (800) 932-9645 (OFF-SEASON ONLY); FAX: (508) 325-4735

■ "Breezy, easy and comfortable – the epitome of summer" describes "the only place on the beach in Nantucket", a combination private beach club/public resort; in a tony north shore area a 15-minute stroll from town, it offers "charm" and "convenience", whether in a room (with furnishings by Nantucket craftsmen), two-story suite or rental apartment; a few beef that "beach club members may take priority over hotel guests."

Harbor House Hotel 111R (2S)   19 | 20 | 18 | 20 | $198

PO Box 1139, S. Beach St., Nantucket; (508) 228-1500; (800) ISLANDS; FAX: (508) 228-7639

◪ Surveyors are of two minds about this sibling to the White Elephant Resort and the Vineyard's Harbor View Hotel; partisans applaud its "Nantucket atmosphere" and "great location" "handy to Downtown" shopping, adding that you're certain to find "a good New England meal"; the discontented shrug it off as "boring for the price", griping about "tiny", "spartan" rooms in "need of a face-lift"; open April–December.

Jared Coffin House 60R   22 | 23 | 23 | 22 | $185

29 Broad St., Nantucket; (508) 228-2400; (800) 248-2405; FAX: (508) 228-8549

■ "Taste without pretense" is the hallmark of this "comfortable", "antiques-galore" inn steeped in "Nantucket tradition" (it's in the Downtown Historic District) and all the more enjoyable thanks to "a staff that really tries"; for maximum "charm" and "character", cognoscenti advise reserving a room in the 1845 red-brick main house rather than in one of the five outlying buildings; only a few malcontents pan it as "too primitive" and burdened with a "stuffy attitude."

R	S	D	P	$

Nantucket Inn & Conference Center 94R (6S) | 21 | 21 | 21 | 19 | $167 |
27 Macy's Ln., Nantucket; (508) 228-6900; (800) 321-8484; FAX: (508) 228-9861
▣ "Near the airport", this "nice", modern resort facility built in traditional Nantucket style offers lots to do – there are two lighted tennis courts, indoor and outdoor pools, exercise facilities, supervised children's programs and meeting rooms for 150; the catch is that it's a couple of miles from Downtown, but a free shuttle bus transports town- and beach-goers.

Summer House 5R (3S) | 22 | 22 | 25 | 24 | $245 |
PO Box 880, 17 Ocean Ave., Siasconset, Nantucket; (508) 257-4577; FAX: (508) 257-4590
■ A "quaint", "summery" and above all "romantic" cluster of rose-covered cottages perched on a bluff overlooking the Atlantic; amenities include a well-regarded New American restaurant (some surveyors call it "best on the island") and a pool nestled among the dunes; off-season can be even "more enjoyable", especially if you "ask for the room with a fireplace."

WAUWINET, THE 28R (5S) | 26 | 26 | 27 | 26 | $322 |
120 Wauwinet Rd., Nantucket; (508) 228-0145; (800) 426-8718; FAX: (508) 228-6712
■ Accolades are nearly unanimous for this "luxurious", "secluded" "Nantucket dream", offering "small but wonderful" rooms in a 19th-century main inn and smaller outlying buildings; "a slice of heaven" one fan sighs, while another asks "can I live here?"; the "spectacular" setting has two private beaches, the staff is adept at "pampering" and the "spectacular" restaurant, Topper's, is the talk of the island; a disenfranchised few call it an "overpriced", "uppity snob heaven"; open May–late October.

White Elephant Resort 48R (53S) | 20 | 22 | 20 | 21 | $233 |
PO Box 1139, Easton St., Nantucket; (508) 228-2500; (800) ISLANDS; FAX: (508) 325-1195
▣ "Enjoy brunch on the patio and linger all day" say admirers of this "peaceful", "romantic" place with a "terrific" location right on Nantucket harbor; guests can stay in the main building, one- to three-bedroom cottages or in The Breakers, set apart from the main grounds and with more elegant lodgings; critics, while refraining from making puns of the name, say "some rooms could use remodeling" and it's "expensive for what you get", but to most it's "a great spot on a great island"; open May–October.

Northampton

Northampton, Hotel 69R (4S) | 19 | 20 | 19 | 18 | $136 |
36 King St., Northampton; (413) 584-3100; (800) 547-3529; FAX: (413) 584-9455
■ "Remarkably renovated", this Laura Ashley-esque hotel is "probably the best place" in a "charming town" in Western Massachusetts and popular with visitors to area colleges; "tastefully done" rooms are "small" but "delightful", and dining is in a transplanted 200-year-old tavern or a new glassed-in porch; there's a chandeliered grand ballroom for weddings and other special occasions.

Peabody

Marriott Peabody 253R (3S) | 19 | 19 | 17 | 17 | $133 |
8A Centennial Dr., Peabody; (978) 977-9700; (800) 801-0099; FAX: (978) 977-0297
▣ This "well-run" suburbanite close to historic Salem and Marblehead pleases budget-minded surveyors undeterred by an "out-of-the-way location" – the "short drive Downtown" is "well worth the savings" if one doesn't expect sheer luxe; N.B. a full renovation was completed in '96.

Rockport

Yankee Clipper Inn 21R (6S) | 20 | 20 | 20 | 20 | $144 |
96 Granite St., Rockport; (978) 546-3407; (800) 545-3699; FAX: (978) 546-9730
■ A "wonderful inn overlooking the ocean" that consists of four distinctive estate buildings with "lots of personality" (the main house is an 1840s Greek Revival manse designed by Charles Bulfinch, one of the architects of the US Capitol); set among "award-winning gardens" in a "great location in funky Rockport", this seacoaster is "reasonably priced" and "may be haunted!"

Salem

Hawthorne Hotel 83R (6S)
– – – – M
18 Washington Sq., Salem; (978) 744-4080; (800) SAY-STAY; FAX: (978) 745-9842
The hunt for which hotel to stay in was ended by the citizens of Salem when they built this Federal-style property in the 1920s; it offers a restaurant and tavern, room service, exercise equipment, a ballroom and conference facilities, and its location on Salem Common, just a stone's throw from the Heritage Trail and within walking distance of museums, shopping centers and the waterfront, makes it popular with tourists; book early for Halloween festivities.

Stockbridge

Red Lion Inn 91R (20S)
18 20 19 20 $156
Main St., Stockbridge; (413) 298-5545; FAX: (413) 298-5130
☑ It's "a very Berkshires experience" to "sit on the front porch", "people-watch" and soak up the "creaky gentility" and Stockbridge "spirit" at this "Rockwellian" "throwback to the 19th century"; the food is "quintessential New England" and the "small rooms" are filled with "ancient charm", which translates to "seedy" and "dingy" for some; sure, it's "touristy" and may "have slipped somewhat" in recent years, but many still feel that "in fall, everyone must spend a weekend at the Red Lion."

Sturbridge

Publick House Historic Inn 112R (12S)
19 20 21 20 $135
Rte. 131, Sturbridge; (508) 347-3313; (800) PUBLICK; FAX: (508) 347-5073
☑ Somewhere between "commercialized" and "quaint", this "well-kept" 1771 lodging in a popular "historic village" is known for the "wonderful sticky buns" and "dependable", "old-fashioned food" in its restaurant; the inn itself is "attractive" and "comfortable", with "antiques-filled" rooms, two outdoor pools and tennis courts; but the downside is "lots of noise" from "people, people, people everywhere."

Williamstown

Orchards, The 47R (2S)
24 22 20 21 $171
222 Adams Rd., Williamstown; (413) 458-9611; (800) 225-1517; FAX: (413) 458-3273
☑ A "cozy", "pretty" "gem", this courtyard-style inn near Williams College is "elegant without being stuffy", sporting English country manor decor in "big", "comfortable" rooms, as well as providing "excellent" New England cuisine; so while a few detractors mutter "don't bother" and insist that "service and food leave something to be desired", enthusiasts look forward to the "wonderful fireplace to relax in front of at teatime."

Michigan

TOP 10 OVERALL

Houghton

Grand Hotel ■
Iroquois ■

Sault Ste. Marie

Marquette

Mackinac Island

Boyne Highlands ■
Stafford's Bay View ■

Shanty Creek ■

Grand Traverse ■

MICHIGAN

Ludington

Saginaw

Amway Grand Plaza ■

Marriott Dearborn Inn ■
Ritz-Carlton Dearborn ■
Townsend ■

Detroit

BEST OVERALL

25 Ritz-Carlton Dearborn/Detroit
Grand Hotel/Mackinac Is.
Townsend/Detroit
22 Stafford's Bay View/Petoskey
Iroquois/Mackinac Is.
Shanty Creek/Bellaire
Grand Traverse/Acme
Amway Grand Plaza/Grand Rapids
Marriott Dearborn Inn/Detroit
21 Boyne Highlands/Harbor Springs

BEST VALUES

Shanty Creek/Bellaire
Boyne Highlands/Harbor Springs
Boyne Mountain/Boyne Falls
Amway Grand Plaza/Grand Rapids
Marriott/Ypsilanti
Stafford's Bay View/Petoskey
Hilton Novi /Detroit
Grand Traverse/Acme
Ritz-Carlton Dearborn/Detroit
Marriott Dearborn Inn/Detroit

Acme

R	S	D	P	$
22	22	20	24	$155

Grand Traverse Resort 506R (244S)
100 Grand Traverse Village Blvd., Acme; (616) 938-2100; (800) 748-0303
■ Some feel the main glass tower at this condo resort is an "eyesore", but in this "lovely area" few pay attention to the building, diverted as they are by extensive fitness and spa facilities, indoor and outdoor pools, hiking, x-country skiing and a Jack Nicklaus–designed course ("come for the golf, not the rooms"); Interlochen Center for the Arts and spectacular Sleeping Bear Dunes are also nearby; all in all, it may be "too big" and "slightly tacky" but it's "comfortable" and "great for northern Michigan."

Bellaire

Shanty Creek 340R (240S)   21 | 22 | 21 | 24 | $117
1 Shanty Creek Rd., Bellaire; (616) 533-8621; (800) 678-4111; FAX: (616) 533-7001
☑ A "great location" in northern Michigan with an Arnold Palmer–designed course, two other 18 holers and 29 downhill ski runs please outdoorsy types, while stuffed suits are at home in the extensive meeting facilities at this resort blending European and contemporary styling in the Village accommodations (which have easy access to skiing) as well as in the rooms and condos overlooking Lake Bellaire; on the downside, a few report that the rooms are "much in need of updating."

Boyne Falls

Boyne Mountain Resort 90R   20 | 21 | 19 | 22 | $120
Boyne Mountain Rd., Boyne Falls; (616) 549-6000; (800) GO-BOYNE; FAX: (616) 549-6094
☑ "Good for sports", this alpine-style resort development offers two championship golf courses and 37 runs of downhill skiing plus snowboarding, x-country trails and fishing; ski schools, a heated outdoor pool, children's ski packages and day care make it attractive for families but a few warn that some accommodations can be "rustic."

Detroit

BEST OVERALL	BEST VALUES
25 Ritz-Carlton	Hilton Novi
Townsend	Mayflower B&B
22 Marriott Dearborn	Marriott Dearborn
19 Hyatt Regency	Ritz-Carlton
18 River Place	Marriott Southfield

Atheneum Suite Hotel (174S)   21 | 18 | 15 | 16 | $140
1000 Brush St., Detroit; (313) 962-2323; (800) 772-2323; FAX: (313) 962-2424
■ "All the glory that was Greece" is found at this all-suite "well-kept secret" that fans applaud as the "best place to stay Downtown" due to its "grand luxe rooms" and "great location in Greektown" near the city's best ethnic restaurants plus its extensive meeting facilities just seconds from the Business District; although a few (Trojans, no doubt) attack "spotty service" and consider it "isolated", the majority agrees it's a "treat."

Crowne Plaza Pontchartrain 392R (20S)   18 | 17 | 16 | 16 | $143
2 Washington Blvd., Detroit; (313) 965-0200; (800) 227-6963; FAX: (313) 965-9464
☑ It may be "as tired as the city itself", but the "good central location" across from Cobo Hall convention center keeps execs booking the "tiny" but "nice rooms"; yet even with a 1995 redo critics say the place "still needs a makeover to make it tenable", citing "poor climate control", uneven service, and, despite valet parking, some question security; the Mesquite Creek Steakhouse is on-site.

Doubletree Hotel Detroit 239R (16S)   16 | 14 | 13 | 13 | $133
(fka Omni International Hotel)
333 E. Jefferson Ave., Detroit; (313) 222-7700; (800) 222-TREE; FAX: (313) 222-8517
☑ A "good business location" that's "convenient to the Renaissance Center", along with "large rooms" and a "nice health spa" are not enough to lift ratings at this former Omni; while "passable if you must stay Downtown", it's derided by critics who say "new name, same hotel" and cite "rude" service and poor food; a '95-'96 renovation of lobby, ballroom, guestrooms and the restaurant may improve scores next time around.

Hilton Novi 234R (5S)   19 | 18 | 16 | 18 | $119
21111 Haggerty Rd., Novi; (810) 349-4000; (800) HILTONS; FAX: (810) 349-4066
☑ This "beautiful hotel" in a "convenient location" close to freeways in a NW upscale suburb earns kudos for its "spacious rooms" and "some of the best meeting facilities in the area"; but critics cite erratic housekeeping ("forgot to clean my room") as proof there's "no one in charge."

Hyatt Regency Dearborn 746R (25S)   20 | 19 | 19 | 18 | $144
Fairlane Town Ctr., Dearborn; (313) 593-1234; (800) 233-1234; FAX: (313) 593-3366
☑ A quick drive from Ford HQ guarantees that this "excellent, not-your-average chain hotel" is "full of auto industry people", and its proximity to Greenfield Village and monorail ride to Fairlane Town Center mall draws tourists as well; "redone" rooms are "nicely appointed" (although others can be "worn") and there's "always good food" at Guilio's, but some grumble about a "noisy and crowded" "convention" ambiance.

Marriott Dearborn Inn 192R (30S) 22 | 21 | 21 | 22 | $153
20301 Oakwood Blvd., Dearborn; (313) 271-2700; FAX: (313) 271-7464
■ "Marriott did a fine restoration on this old beauty", a 1931 Georgian built by Henry Ford that's now a "tastefully decorated" hotel with a "beautiful lobby and grounds" and a "good restaurant"; worthy conference facilities and an "extraordinary staff" make it "a meeting planner's dream" and the "historical setting" also adds up to a "best bet for Greenfield Village" visitors.

Marriott Southfield 219R (3S) 17 | 18 | 15 | 15 | $117
27033 Northwestern Hwy., Southfield; (810) 356-7400; (800) 228-9290; FAX: (810) 356-5501
☑ "A good solid deal" describes this "upscale for Marriott" suburbanite with a "very laid-back" ambiance that makes it "just the place while visiting relatives"; although others are lukewarm ("ok") there are no loud complaints either.

Mayflower B&B 66R (8S) – | – | – | – | M
827 W. Ann Arbor Trail, Plymouth; (313) 453-1620; FAX: (313) 453-0193
Midway between Detroit and Ann Arbor in the leafy suburb of Plymouth sits this "very pleasant" 1927 Victorian with smallish but charming rooms that are scheduled for a '97 redo; in addition to complimentary breakfast, there are two on-site restaurants – the Mayflower Dining Room and the Steakhouse – and the London Pub for imbibing.

Radisson Plaza Hotel 343R (42S) 19 | 19 | 16 | 17 | $145
1500 Town Center Dr., Southfield; (810) 827-4000; (800) 333-3333; FAX: (810) 827-1364
☑ "If you want to stay in Detroit" this chain operation in a "good location" on the NW side is an "adequate convention hotel" with "big rooms", an indoor pool and a fitness center; foes frown on the food and paint the place "dark and musty", although a '96 renovation may have brightened things up.

RITZ-CARLTON DEARBORN 293R (15S) 26 | 26 | 25 | 24 | $179
Fairlane Plaza, 300 Town Center Dr., Dearborn; (313) 441-2000; (800) 241-3333; FAX: (313) 441-2051
■ All agree – the "best Motown has to offer" provides an "oasis" of "traditional Ritz charm", "the most attentive service" and "excellent dining"; the rooms are "small" but "good", especially if you "spring for a Club room", and "be sure to use the wonderful pool and Jacuzzi"; although "not the group's shining statement", "you'll know it's a Ritz" ("plenty of Ford execs" park here), with "reasonable prices" for this level of "class."

River Place, A Grand Heritage Hotel 90R (18S) 21 | 17 | 17 | 17 | $153
1000 River Place Dr., Detroit; (313) 259-9500; (800) 890-9505; FAX: (313) 259-0657
■ A 1902 "jewel in the city" that shines in a redeveloped condo and loft area on the Detroit River east of Downtown, where the "superb accommodations" include large, "individually decorated rooms" with river views, plus an indoor pool and two tennis courts; despite middling ratings for service and facilities, loyalists consider this "very quiet" "sleeper" "the only place" to stay in town.

ST. REGIS, HOTEL 212R (20S) 18 | 18 | 17 | 16 | $135
3071 W. Grand Blvd., Detroit; (313) 873-3000; (800) 848-4810; FAX: (313) 872-2574
☑ Proximity to the Detroit Institute of Arts with skywalk access to the Fisher Theater and GM's former headquarters (America's corporate giant is slated for a move Downtown to the RenCen) is the St. Regis' chief asset; but while some call it a "gracious place to stay", underwhelmed critics say "only if you must."

TOWNSEND HOTEL 38R (49S) 27 | 25 | 24 | 24 | $207
100 Townsend St., Birmingham; (810) 642-7900; (800) 548-4172; FAX: (810) 645-9061
■ This "charming, boutique hotel" "for the rich and famous" nestled in the heart of an upscale suburb is "expensive but worth it" for its "European-style elegance", "intimate rooms" (more than half of them "lovely suites"), proximity to galleries and shops and "comfortable, superior dining" in the Rugby Grille; a few naysayers gripe that it's "understaffed" but "they try hard."

Westin Hotel Renaissance Center 1340R (52S) 17 | 14 | 15 | 15 | $141
Renaissance Ctr., Detroit; (313) 568-8000; (800) 228-3000; FAX: (313) 568-8146
☑ "The best view" of Detroit's skyline and river and an "excellent location" don't appease critics who call this soaring riverfront monolith in a mall and office complex a "motel in the sky" with poor service and the "longest lines of any major hotel chain"; foes further blast it as a "conference hotel that can't handle crowds."

199

Grand Rapids

Amway Grand Plaza 652R (30S)      22   22   22   21 $132
187 Monroe St. NW, Grand Rapids; (616) 774-2000; (800) 253-3590; FAX: (616) 776-6489
■ "Grand Rapids is blessed with this world-class hotel", a 1913 building restored and grafted to a contemporary tower; the "superior lobby" has a fountain, balcony and gold-leaf ceiling with period details, rooms are "large" and "elegant" and there's "excellent dining" (the Lumber Baron bar is a "must"); but guests differ on where to sleep: "stay in the old wing" advises one; "new sections extremely well done" declares another.

Harbor Springs

Boyne Highlands Resort 222R (126S)   21   21   19   23 $118
600 Highlands Dr., Harbor Springs; (616) 526-2171; (800) GO-BOYNE; FAX: (616) 526-3095
■ "A place to be no matter the season", Boyne Mountain's sister resort just north of Petoskey is a "beautiful" golf-and-ski haven with four courses, 42 downhill runs, three heated outdoor pools, children's programs, an exercise center and plenty of other amenities; enthusiasts like it "more and more every trip", and though a few offer more tepid praise ("ok"), ratings back up the boosters.

Mackinac Island

Bay View B&B 17R (3S)   –   –   –   –   M
PO Box 448, Mackinac Island; (906) 847-3295
Perspectives vary over this 1890 Victorian on the horse-and-buggy island; advocates point to "good food, good views, a good location" and "reasonable rates"; critics report a "tacky, touristy" feel, "small rooms" and practically "no service"; N.B. closed in winter.

GRAND HOTEL 312R (12S)   23   26   24   27 $237
Mackinac Island; (906) 847-3331; (800) 33-GRAND; FAX: (906) 847-3259
■ With "no prettier setting in the US", this "stately", "marvelous" 1887 "jewel of Mackinac Island" on a bluff overlooking the straits is renowned for "a front porch that goes on forever", not to mention "white-glove service" and "excellent" food (breakfast and five-course, jacket-and-tie dinner included in the rate); while a few grouse about "garish" period decor and "sky-high prices", most find it perfect for a "romantic getaway" in "vintage elegance"; open early May through late October; N.B. the "step back in time" includes no a/c in rooms.

Iroquois Hotel 41R (6S)   23   22   22   22 $178
298 Main St., Mackinac Island; (906) 847-3321
■ "Shh! don't tell anyone" plead surveyors about this "stunning" turreted lakeside Victorian that impresses the few who've visited with "beautiful rooms", a "responsive and accommodating staff", "a good bar" and the Carriage House, which some consider the "best restaurant on the island"; open May to mid-November.

Mission Point Resort 200R (36S)   ▽ 20   19   19   21 $167
1 Lakeshore Dr., Mackinac Island; (810) 488-3200; (800) 833-5583; FAX: (810) 488-3222
■ Built in the '50s as a retreat to promote world peace, this waterfront resort with "great views" now promotes peaceful nights with "comfortable rooms" that suit both families and corporate groups; an on-site movie theater and playhouse, two tennis courts, a heated outdoor pool, health club, bicycle and in-line skate rentals along with a Kids Klub with kite flying, hayrides and other activities provide the recreation, 35,000 square feet of meeting space provides the work sites and two restaurants and a deli provide the fuel; open May through October.

New Buffalo

Harbor Grand Hotel Suites 41R (16S)      –   –   –   –   M
111 W. Water St., New Buffalo; (616) 469-7700; FAX: (616) 469-7386
New in 1996, this "small, quaint" harborside hotel built in Frank Lloyd Wright's Prairie School style features "low-cost" accommodations (some with kitchenettes, Jacuzzis and/or fireplaces) steps from a marina and charter boating on Lake Michigan; the "very friendly staff" serves complimentary breakfast and can give information about the area's galleries, wineries, shopping and antiquing; small meeting facilities, an indoor pool and fitness room are on-site.

Petoskey

Stafford's Bay View Inn 22R (11S)   22 | 22 | 23 | 22 | $148
613 Woodland Ave., Petoskey; (616) 347-2771; (800) 456-1917; FAX: (616) 347-3413
■ "All rooms have their own personality" at this "lovely", "kind of quaint" Victorian country inn "set in a picture-postcard town" on Little Traverse Bay – "for a taste of Petoskey, this is a tradition"; sans TV but with porch rockers, lawn croquet and quiet bike rides (along with modern amenities such as whirlpools and a/c), this place has guests' peace of mind on its mind, and surveyors urge "keep it a secret"; the dining room is noted for regional fare and Sunday brunch.

Saugatuck

Wickwood Country Inn 7R (4S)   ▽ 26 | 25 | 23 | 25 | $176
510 Butler St., Saugatuck; (616) 857-1465; FAX: (616) 857-1552
■ Located in a famed summer art colony and resort town on Lake Michigan, this "beautiful", romantic B&B has a "sweet atmosphere" and the "good location" at the edge of the village is "close to shopping too"; "friendly personnel" and "great food" by cookbook author–owner Julee Rosso Miller (of Silver Palate fame) make this one "worth a return trip"; all rooms have a/c but no TVs.

Thompsonville

Crystal Mountain Resort 82R (98S)   ▽ 18 | 21 | 18 | 19 | $137
12500 Crystal Mtn. Dr., Thompsonville; (616) 378-2000; (800) 968-7686; FAX: (616) 378-4594
■ A contemporary family resort 30 miles south of Traverse City offering 27 holes of golf and 25 ski runs, extensive x-country trails, a snowboard park, on-site tennis, indoor/outdoor pools, a fitness center, and if execs can find the time, a meeting center that can handle up to 300; surveyors claim "some of the rooms are tiny", but condos and resort homes are also available; an additional 28-suite inn will open in fall 1997.

Traverse City

Waterfront Inn 122R (6S)   ▽ 21 | 20 | 20 | 21 | $127
2061 US 31 N., Traverse City; (616) 938-1100; (800) 551-9283; FAX: (616) 939-9711
☑ This boldly colored inn with a "beautiful lake view" and beach on East Grand Traverse Bay is really a surf 'n' turf kind of place: anglers charter boats for chasing Chinook salmon or stay right on-site and fish the natural trout stream, while golfers choose from many nearby courses; après tee, a heated pool awaits; while surveyors praise "friendly service", a few mutters are heard about "mediocre rooms" and food that "lacks creativity."

Ypsilanti

Marriott Ypsilanti 233R (3S)   18 | 19 | 18 | 21 | $117
(fka Radisson on the Lake)
1275 S. Huron, Ypsilanti; (313) 487-2000; (800) 228-9290; FAX: (313) 487-0773
■ "Beautiful grounds and golf course" on a man-made lake, proximity to the I-94 expressway, a big conference center, fitness center, indoor pool and major 1996 redo help this chainer just east of Ann Arbor rate as "first class all the way"; but while it may be "great for Michigan football/reunion weekends", those not into chanting 'Go Blue!' until they're blue in the face may think it's "in the middle of nowhere."

Minnesota

TOP 10 OVERALL

BEST OVERALL

25 St. James/Red Wing
24 Saint Paul/Minneapolis
23 Whitney/Minneapolis
22 Madden's on Gull Lake/Brainerd
21 Sofitel/Minneapolis
  Arrowwood Radisson/Alexandria
20 Kahler Plaza/Rochester
  Hilton & Towers/Minneapolis
19 Marriott City Center/Minneapolis
  Marquette/Minneapolis

BEST VALUES

St. James/Red Wing
Madden's on Gull Lake/Brainerd
Arrowwood Radisson/Alexandria
Radisson Metrodome/Minn.
Saint Paul Hotel/Minneapolis
Embassy Suites/Minneapolis
Kahler Hotel/Rochester
Sheraton Park Place/Minn.
Radisson Hotel South/Minn.
Doubletree Grand Hotel/Minn.

Alexandria

R	S	D	P	$
20	21	19	23	$129

ARROWWOOD - A RADISSON RESORT
182R (18S)
2100 Arrowwood Ln., Alexandria; (320) 762-1124; (800) 333-3333; FAX: (320) 762-0133
■ This getaway 130 miles NW of the Twin Cities hosts "lots of families" and also "handles [business] groups well" in a 450-acre setting on the shores of Lake Darling; though some find the country-decor rooms "outdated", they're "spacious" and in any case people come here for the myriad year-round activities, including skiing, tennis (indoor and outdoor), "great golf", biking and fishing, plus a children's program (ages 4-12) at Camp Arrowwood; many packages and discounts are available.

Brainerd

Madden's On Gull Lake 249R (40S)   21 23 21 24 $124
8001 Pine Beach Peninsula, Brainerd; (218) 829-2811; (800) 247-1040; FAX: (218) 829-6583

■ Families and groups dive into this sprawling, "regionally popular" resort that appeals "for fun and business": croquet, lawn bowling, 63 holes of golf, five pools, a marina and kids' programs plus meeting space for up to 825 are all available on its 1,000-acre setting on the shores of Gull Lake; the rooms ("lakeside villas have the best") offer "traditional charm" (but no TVs), and though "old" the facilities (and grounds) are "very well kept"; open late April to late October.

Hibbing

Kahler Park Hotel 120R (3S)   – – – – |
1402 E. Howard St., Hibbing; (218) 262-3481; (800) 262-3481; FAX: (218) 262-1906

■ Prospectors strike it rich, relatively speaking, at "about the only game in town" when it comes to lodging in Northern Minnesota's historic Iron Range; it's a "comfortable place near the pits" of Hull-Rust (the world's largest open-pit iron mine) and attractions such as Ironworld USA, and the surrounding region rich with lakes and forests offers abundant recreation possibilities; in chilly weather, an indoor pool and sauna help guests thaw out.

Lutsen

Lutsen Resort 49R (57S)   ▽ 21 22 20 24 $120
PO Box 9, Hwy. 61, Lutsen; (218) 663-7212; (800) 258-8736; FAX: (218) 663-7212

■ It's Highway 61 revisited for the many who travel yearly to stay in the "historical lodge", waterside villas or cliff house of this "beautiful, scenic" resort on Lake Superior; six new two-bedroom log cabins were recently added, expanding the choice of "rustic, comfy" lodgings, and the rural setting means no shortage of year-round outdoor activities (downhill and x-country skiing, kayaking, biking, swimming) on-site or within a mile; "ambiance that won't quit" and "the best service" make it "a dream."

Minneapolis/St. Paul

Doubletree Grand Hotel/Mall of America   19 18 17 18 $114
315R (6S)
(fka Mall of America Grand Hotel)
7901 24th Ave. S., Bloomington; (612) 854-2244; (800) 222-TREE; FAX: (612) 854-4421

■ "Directly across the street from the best mall ever", this "pleasant" if "busy" Bloomington hotel is a handy place to recharge after you've "shopped till you drop" at the Mall of America (think of it as a "retail resort"); "good location" aside, a few gripe that it's only "so-so" with a "poorly laid-out lobby", but maybe they just had a bad day at the racks; does any mall-maven care that there's an indoor pool and exercise equipment?

Embassy Suites Minneapolis (218S)   20 18 17 18 $115
(fka Crown Sterling Suites)
425 S. Seventh St., Minneapolis; (612) 333-3111; (800) EMBASSY; FAX: (612) 333-7984

■ This "functional" all-suite Downtowner changed hands and underwent a complete redo of its rooms (all with kitchenette, voicemail and modem capacity) and six-story atrium lobby; "comfortable" if "nothing too spectacular", it's linked to the business and shopping districts via the skyway and is near the Metrodome, IDS Crystal Court and City Center shops; complimentary breakfast, newspaper and PM cocktails boost the value.

HILTON & TOWERS MINNEAPOLIS 764R (52S)   21 20 18 19 $145
1001 Marquette Ave., Minneapolis; (612) 376-1000; (800) HILTONS; FAX: (612) 397-4875

◪ A "central location" Downtown allows guests to "get anywhere indoors" via the skyway from this convention giant (biggest in the state) that's "very well organized for a large hotel"; most give it solid ratings and judge it "good" for conferences (meeting space for 2,500), but it also draws a few knocks for "small rooms", "long waits for elevators" and an ambiance "slightly warmer than a cold Minnesota night"; pluses include a health club, indoor pool and Carvers, serving American food with a Continental flair.

Hyatt Regency Minneapolis 512R (21S)   20 19 18 18 $144
1300 Nicollet Mall, Minneapolis; (612) 370-1234; (800) 233-1234; FAX: (612) 370-1463

◪ The "excellent" fitness center (including a pool, tennis and racquetball courts) is a highlight at this "well-maintained", "well-run" Downtown business base with "good-size rooms" and "nice views"; some are less impressed ("cookie-cutter", "basic"), but overall "it does the job"; "skyway access to the convention center is a plus", as are amenities such as in-room fax and 24-hour access to printers and copiers on Business Plan floors.

Marquette Hotel 264R (14S)   21 20 18 18 $146
710 Marquette Ave., Minneapolis; (612) 333-4545; (800) 32-VISTA; FAX: (612) 376-7418
■ "Large", "very luxurious" rooms and "huge bathrooms" motivate business travelers to overnight at this "comfortable and charming" Downtowner; a "very friendly, welcoming" staff makes conferences (24 meeting rooms, capacity 300) as well as getaways gratifying, and the skyway system connects it to 50 blocks of offices, shopping, dining and entertainment; there's a fitness center on-site, and "up-to-date" American fare at Basil's.

Marriott City Center Minneapolis 471R (82S)   20 20 18 19 $143
30 S. Seventh St., Minneapolis; (612) 349-4000; (800) 228-9290; FAX: (612) 332-7165
☑ Those who call the glass half full say this Downtown triangular glass tower connected to the City Center shopping complex "provides everything the traveler needs" and is a "solid" convention hotel with "impressive facilities" (20 meeting rooms for up to 1,800) and skyway access; those who call it half empty find it "ok" with "poor food", but most toast typical "Marriott quality" – "reliable and clean"; N.B. ongoing renovations should further brighten the picture.

Radisson Hotel & Conference Center 237R (6S)   19 19 17 18 $124
3131 Campus Dr., Plymouth; (612) 559-6600; (800) 333-3333; FAX: (612) 559-1053
☑ In the suburban Northwest Business Campus overlooking 25 acres of woods and wetlands, this "self-contained facility" recently underwent a $2.5-million redo, upgrading its 44 meeting rooms with more than $1.5-million worth of audio-visual equipment; though it strikes some as simply "typical", rooms offer "lots of space" and sporty types will find a full range of fitness facilities including an indoor pool plus racquetball, basketball and tennis courts.

Radisson Hotel Metrodome 288R (16S)   19 19 19 18 $115
615 Washington Ave. SE, Minneapolis; (612) 379-8888; (800) 822-6757; FAX: (612) 379-8682
☑ The location on the U of Minnesota campus is "perfect, if that's where you want to be", making this Radisson popular with parents of Gophers who dig its "good value" and "large rooms" (with dataports, voicemail and, in executive suites, whirlpool baths), even if some cite "friendly but not entirely competent service"; there's an exercise room on-site and guests can use the U of M's facilities next door; a complimentary shuttle transports visitors within a five-mile radius.

Radisson Hotel South & Plaza Tower 568R (13S)   19 19 16 17 $111
7800 Normandale Blvd., Bloomington; (612) 835-7800; (800) 333-3333; FAX: (612) 893-8431
☑ Most surveyors toss bouquets at this Bloomington operation, calling it an "atypical convention hotel with nice rooms and public areas", "good" fitness facilities and, of course, a "wide selection of meeting rooms" (capacity 2,400); a few wince at "small" quarters (tip: ask for an oversized Plaza Tower room) and "impersonal" ambiance, but overall it makes a good impression.

Radisson Plaza Hotel Minneapolis 329R (28S)   20 19 18 18 $132
35 S. Seventh St., Minneapolis; (612) 339-4900; (800) 333-3333; FAX: (612) 337-9766
■ A "serviceable hotel when traveling for business" that springs "no surprises" on guests who find all the "expected" qualities – it's "reliable" and "clean", with a fitness center and a "great location Downtown" connected to the skyway; veterans recommend rooms on the executive level – they "offer more" for your money.

SAINT PAUL HOTEL 224R (30S)   23 24 25 22 $147
350 Market St., St. Paul; (612) 292-9292; (800) 292-9292; FAX: (612) 228-9506
■ Apostles preach the virtues of this "beautifully maintained", "glorious" Italian Renaissance–style old-timer, a "Downtown jewel" since 1910; it offers "excellent rooms and service", a "fabulous lobby" and "incredible" American food at the St. Paul Grill, all within walking distance of the convention center, Ordway theater and Landmark Center; exercise equipment delivered to your door is another reason why this "classic" is top-rated in the Twin Cities – "as perfect a hotel as one can find."

Sheraton Park Place Hotel 262R (29S)   18 19 17 18 $113
1500 Park Pl. Blvd., Minneapolis; (612) 542-8600; (800) 542-5566; FAX: (612) 542-8068
☑ Voters don't have much to say about this Sheraton except that it's in a "good location if you want to be out of the city center" (Downtown is four miles away, the Mall of America is 12 miles) and the "very helpful" staff can make events here enjoyable; there's plenty of meeting space (18,000 square feet) and business services, and the 30 lanai suites fronting the indoor pool are an interesting touch; a recent refurnishing could raise ratings next time around.

Sofitel, Hotel 271R (11S)
22 | 22 | 23 | 19 | $137

5601 W. 78th St., Minneapolis; (612) 835-1900; (800) 876-6303; FAX: (612) 835-2696

This "touch of France" brings "chic" to the southwest suburbs of Minneapolis say those who enjoy its pleasant rooms, "best weekend" packages and good dining at three French-inspired restaurants, highlighted by Chez Colette (some also cite "the best cup of coffee I ever woke up to"); critics call it a "typical commercial hotel" that's "not exactly central to much of anything" (though the airport and Mall of America are nearby), but the *ouis* carry the vote.

Whitney Hotel 56R (40S)
24 | 23 | 23 | 21 | $165

150 Portland Ave., Minneapolis; (612) 339-9300; (800) 248-1879; FAX: (612) 339-1333

"A top-notch renovation" converted an 1879 flour mill on the Mississippi River into "the only hotel with character in Minneapolis", which accounts for the "hip crowd"; the lobby's grand staircase and rich appointments exude "lovely old-world charm" that carries through to the "sumptuous" suites, but we also hear reports of "small" and even "really weird" rooms ("unless on the river side, they're very dark"); the "great" Whitney Grille is an asset, but the location is "too far from the sights" for some.

Pine River

McGuire's Piney Ridge Lodge (30S)
– | – | – | – | I

Rte. 1, Pine River; (218) 587-2296; FAX: (218) 587-4323

About three hours north of the Twin Cities on the Whitefish Chain (the state's largest chain of lakes), this former lumber camp is now a beautiful and welcoming resort offering spacious accommodations in villas and cabins plus much to do, including fishing with excellent guides, swimming, golf, many children's activities and regional dining at its best at the on-site McGuire's; no in-room phones or TVs add to the getaway feel – no wonder it's one of Northern Minnesota's most popular resorts.

Red Wing

ST. JAMES HOTEL 60R
25 | 26 | 23 | 24 | $122

406 Main St., Red Wing; (612) 388-2846; (800) 252-1875; FAX: (612) 388-5226

Minnesota's highest overall ratings go to this "beautifully restored" 1875 hotel that maintains its "Victorian elegance", as does much of Downtown Red Wing; rooms adorned with period antiques and reproductions (some with Mississippi River views) and a welcome bottle of champagne make it ideal "for romance", and "surprisingly good food" is found at the Port of Red Wing Restaurant and the Veranda.

Rochester

Kahler Hotel 680R (15S)
17 | 20 | 17 | 16 | $110

20 SW Second Ave., Rochester; (507) 282-2581; (800) 533-1655; FAX: (507) 285-2775

A less-expensive alternative to its sibling Kahler Plaza, this old world–style (simply "old" to some), circa 1921 Downtowner is geared for visitors to the Mayo Clinic (reachable via pedestrian tunnel and skyway), which can give it the feel of "a hospital"; but while some cite "small rooms" and "depressing hallways", others say it offers "many comforts and conveniences" (a domed rooftop pool, Continental fare at the Elizabethan Room) plus "good service", making it "pleasing in an unexpected way."

Kahler Plaza Hotel 194R
20 | 21 | 18 | 19 | $135

101 SW First Ave., Rochester; (507) 280-6000; (800) 733-1655; FAX: (507) 280-8531

"Upscale" and "much more contemporary" than its sibling the Kahler Hotel, this modern chrome-and-glass edifice caters to execs and also gets its share of Mayo Clinic visitors and medical personnel (it's linked to the complex by pedestrian tunnel); "comfortable" and "pleasant", it offers "great service", "excellent food", an atrium pool and fitness center, plus proximity to shopping and nearby sites including historic Mayowood (family home of the Mayos).

Stillwater

Lumber Baron's Hotel (36S)
▽ 17 | 17 | 11 | 13 | $142

101 Water St. S., Stillwater; (612) 439-6000; FAX: (612) 430-9393

Though it began as a hotel in the 1890s, this Victorian in Downtown Stillwater (a 20-minute drive from the Twin Cities) lived other lives before being renovated and reopening as a hotel in November '95; guests stay in antiques-filled suites, each with fireplace and whirlpool bath, and can watch the St. Croix River roll by from the 300-foot patio; while there are no on-site sports facilities, the exercises of choice in this historic town are shopping, antiques hunting and wine tasting; breakfast included.

Mississippi

	R	S	D	P	$

Grand Casino 491R (9S)   – | – | – | – | M

265 Beach Blvd., Biloxi; (601) 432-2500; (800) 946-2946; FAX: (601) 435-8901
You can bet on being jolted if you haven't been to the Mississippi Gulf Coast in a while: the once-quiet beach has been transformed into a gambling strip, with this casino hotel leading the way; meeting facilities, a shopping arcade and the beautiful white sands outside offer distraction, but gaming is the real deal here; those with Biloxi blues from bad-luck blackjack can seek solace in the pool, fitness center, whirlpool or sauna.

Gulfport

Grand Casino 361R (46S)   – | – | – | – | M

3215 W. Beach Blvd., Gulfport; (601) 870-7777; (800) 946-7777; FAX: (601) 870-7220
If the slot machines and other gambling diversions aren't enough to keep you occupied at this waterside casino hotel, there's always the option of exploring the Gulf Islands National Seashore; meeting facilities and modem hookups make life easy for business travelers, while others enjoy the indoor pool, wading pool and fitness center.

Jackson

Millsaps Buie House 10R (1S)   – | – | – | – | M

628 N. State St., Jackson; (601) 352-0221; (800) 784-0221; FAX: (601) 352-0221
In the same family for five generations, this 1888 antiques-filled Victorian provides comfortable rooms, some with private balconies or patios, allowing quiet reflection after the complimentary full Southern breakfast; while only one small meeting room is available, business travelers appreciate modem hookups and the Downtown location.

Natchez

Briars Inn & Gardens 11R (3S)   ▽ 24 | 22 | 21 | 23 | $150

PO Box 1245, 31 Irving Ln., Natchez; (601) 446-9654; (800) 634-1818; FAX: (601) 445-6037
■ This "historic", circa 1812 mansion with "lovely antiques" is where Jefferson Davis wed Varina Howell and is still serving up "Southern hospitality" as a "beautiful" B&B that's distinctive even in a town overflowing with antebellum beauty; "great staff", extensive gardens and a "nice view of the Mississippi" are appeals, and while there's no restaurant, a "wonderful" four-course plantation breakfast is included; all in all, a "true Southern experience."

Burn, The 6R (1S)   ▽ 23 | 24 | 21 | 21 | $126

712 N. Union St., Natchez; (601) 442-1344; (800) 654-8859; FAX: (601) 445-0606
■ "Feel the history" at this B&B set in a "lovely", "tastefully furnished" Greek Revival mansion, once a headquarters for Confederate troops ("welcome to 1860"); surveyors are seduced by this "Southern charm" as well as the "comfortable", "luxurious" antiques-filled rooms and "plantation breakfasts served around an incredible mahogany table" (no restaurant); an outdoor pool, wine on arrival and a "good location" in Natchez's historic district earn extra points.

Dunleith 11R   – | – | – | – | M

84 Homochitto St., Natchez; (601) 446-8500; (800) 433-2445
An 1856 Greek Revival stately home that's a National Historic Landmark and favorite subject for photographers thanks to its lovely colonnaded facade and interiors that capture the "Old South"; "hospitable folks", "great breakfasts" in the restored poultry house, in-room fireplaces and 40 acres of grounds add to the appeal of this B&B that's also popular for executive retreats; tip: be choosy as "the right room makes the difference"; children under 18 not welcome.

Linden Bed & Breakfast 7R ⌷   – | – | – | – | M

1 Linden Pl., Natchez; (601) 445-5472; (800) 2LINDEN; FAX: (601) 445-5472
The owner's family has lived for six generations in this circa 1790 Federal-style plantation listed on the National Register of Historic Places, and guests say they make you "feel like it's your home"; the "gorgeous" surroundings feature a notable collection of Sheraton and Chippendale furniture and a front doorway that was used as a model for Tara in *Gone with the Wind*; N.B. no phones or TVs in rooms.

MONMOUTH PLANTATION 13R (14S)

27 25 24 27 $159

36 Melrose Ave., Natchez; (601) 442-5852; (800) 828-4531; FAX: (601) 446-7762

■ "Breathtaking beauty" marks both the "lovely grounds" and "magnificent" 1818 Greek Revival estate at this "classy" B&B that earns Mississippi's top overall ratings; visitors looking to savor "a page from the past" laud guestrooms decked out in period finery (in the main house, carriage house and other buildings), "wonderful" staff that "coddles you" and "great dining" (one admirer "spent hours in the kitchen with the chef watching her cook"); in sum, the "perfect romantic getaway."

Natchez Eola Hotel 118R (7S)

16 19 15 18 $134

110 N. Pearl St., Natchez; (601) 445-6000; FAX: (601) 446-5310

■ Despite modest ratings, surveyors consider this "old-timey" hotel (dating from 1927) to be an "all-around good" "alternative to B&Bs"; in Downtown Natchez, it's a short walk from riverboat gambling, historic homes and antique shops and has meeting rooms for up to 325; though not without faults ("not for those in a hurry", "rooms small"), devotees say it's "so charming you don't care."

Oxford

Barksdale-Isom House 5R

– – – – E

(fka Isom Place)

1003 Jefferson Ave., Oxford; (601) 236-5600; (800) 236-5696; FAX: (601) 236-6763

Said to be the setting for William Faulkner's *A Rose for Emily*, this antebellum Greek Revival mansion is steeped in history, from its early years as a medical center to its housing of General Grant during the Union occupation to its present incarnation; it offers those on the Faulkner trail, as well as history buffs and parents of Ole Miss students, rooms with period decor and private baths, a veranda, gardens and afternoon wine as well as a full Southern breakfast preceding days of touring local landmarks or browsing through the house's library of Southern authors.

Robinsonville

Harrah's Mardi Gras Casino & Hotel 200R (20S)

– – – – I

1100 Casino Strip Blvd., Robinsonville; (601) 363-7777; (800) HARRAHS; FAX: (601) 387-2420

It's Fat Tuesday every day for lucky gamblers attended to by "caring staff" at this "spread-out" casino hotel featuring a variety of restaurants, meeting rooms for 1,000, entertainment for adults and fun-filled programs for the kids; a golf course is scheduled for early 1998, and the attractions of Memphis are just a short drive away.

Hollywood Casino Hotel & RV Park 473R (33S)

– – – – I

1150 Casino Strip Blvd., Robinsville; (601) 357-7700; (800) 871-0711; FAX: (601) 357-7800

Surveyors are at odds over this casino hotel in northwestern Mississippi's Tunica County: "a fun place to stay, like being in Hollywood" vs. "has gotten tacky"; those who say "rooms need redoing" will be happy to know that more than 350 rooms (plus an indoor pool and Jacuzzi) were added in 1996; P.S. "the giant King Kong hanging outside the window is kind of creepy."

Horseshoe Casino & Hotel 200R

– – – – VI

1021 Casino Ctr. Dr., Robinsonville; (601) 357-5576; (800) 303-SHOE; FAX: (601) 357-5600

Built in '95 and already undergoing a significant expansion, this blend of Mississippi riverboat flash and casino glitz has obviously caught on in Tunica County; scheduled to be completed in late summer '97, the redo will add luxury suites equipped with wet bars and Jacuzzi tubs, more casino space and a new Bluesville entertainment complex, including a museum, blues club, cafe and gift shop.

Sam's Town Hotel & Gambling Hall 823R (34S) ▽

20 19 15 17 $77

1477 Casino Strip Blvd., Robinsonville; (601) 363-0711; (800) 456-0711; FAX: (601) 363-0896

■ A "country-western theme" pervades this "great value", which claims to be the largest hotel/casino complex in the South; behind its Old West facade are "large" guestrooms, a variety of restaurants and gaming tables spread out over a space of two football fields; when you need a break from the action, there's an outdoor pool and live entertainment; even so, some quibble there's "nothing to do outside the hotel."

Tupelo

Mockingbird Inn Bed & Breakfast 6R (1S)

– – – – M

305 N. Gloster, Tupelo; (601) 841-0286; FAX: (601) 840-4158

The King's birthplace is also home to this vintage 1925 B&B (Elvis attended grade school across the street); designed in Arts and Crafts/art deco style, it offers individually decorated rooms, each keyed to a different geographic theme (Paris, Africa, etc.), plus a landscaped backyard that's a perfect backdrop for mockingbird-watching; amenities include in-room massages (by appointment), bountiful breakfasts and evening snacks.

R | S | D | P | $

Vicksburg

Cedar Grove Mansion Inn 16R (17S)
▽ 23 | 22 | 19 | 22 | $142
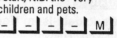
2200 Oak St., Vicksburg; (601) 636-1000; (800) 862-1300; FAX: (601) 634-6126
■ "Johnny Reb never had it so good" attest admirers of this "beautiful antebellum mansion" built in 1840 and listed on the National Register of Historic Places; rooms (in the mansion or cottages) are individually named ("ask for General Grant's room" – he really slept there), and touches like period antiques and a Union cannonball embedded in a parlor wall convey "a true sense of history"; the "lovely grounds" include a pool and Victorian tennis court.

Corners Bed & Breakfast Inn 13R (2S)
– | – | – | – | VE
601 Klein St., Vicksburg; (601) 636-7421; (800) 444-7421; FAX: (601) 636-7232
Resting on one of Vicksburg's highest bluffs, this 1872 Louisiana-style raised cottage pleases guests with "nice, roomy", antiques-filled quarters and views of the Mississippi and Yazoo rivers; the setting in the "historic" Garden District makes for good exploring, and a hearty plantation breakfast gets the day off to a delicious start; N.B. the "very nice proprietors" are among the few in Vicksburg who accept children and pets.

Duff Green Mansion 6R (2S)
– | – | – | – | M
114 First East St., Vicksburg; (601) 636-6968; FAX: (601) 634-1061
This circa 1856 example of Palladian architecture served as a hospital during the Civil War and now administers to both the B&B crowd and business travelers; rooms feature a blend of antiques and modern amenities, with fireplaces in most, and there's an outdoor pool, meeting space for 100 and full breakfasts; the Garden District location is ground zero for Southern-architecture buffs, and the Vicksburg National Military Park is nearby.

Missouri

TOP 10 OVERALL

BEST OVERALL
26 Ritz-Carlton/St. Louis
24 Ritz-Carlton/Kansas City
22 Crowne Plaza Majestic/St. Louis
Seven Gables Inn/St. Louis
21 Westin Crown Center/Kansas City
Raphael/Kansas City
Hyatt Regency/St. Louis
Lodge of Four Seasons/Lake Ozark
Hyatt Regency Crown Ctr./Kansas City
20 Marriot's Tan-Tar-A/Osage Beach

BEST VALUES
Crowne Plaza Majestic/St. Louis
Drury Inn/St. Louis
Marriott/Kansas City
Sheraton West Port/St. Louis
Westin Crown Center/Kansas City
Seven Gables Inn/St. Louis
Adam's Mark/Kansas City
Holiday Inn/Kansas City
Doubletree/St. Louis
Marriott's Tan-Tar-A/Osage Beach

Branson

R	S	D	P	$

Best Western Knights Inn 161R (5S) ▽ | 17 | 17 | 14 | 15 | $91 |

3215 W. Hwy. 76, Branson; (417) 334-1894; (800) 528-1234; FAX: (417) 334-3437
■ In the heart of Branson, which draws more than five million visitors a year for its country-western music and family entertainment, this budget operation offers an indoor/outdoor pool and whirlpool, exercise equipment and sauna; showgoers can purchase tickets at the service desk on the premises; complimentary breakfast is included.

Best Western Mountain Oak Lodge 147R (3S)   –|–|–|–|I
PO Box 1106, Hwy. 76W, Branson; (417) 338-2141; (800) 865-6625; FAX: (417) 338-8320
Family vacationers comin' 'round the mountain from Silver Dollar City (free shuttle service) and down the road a piece from Country Music Boulevard ($5 shuttle service) arrive at this motel-like lodge nestled in the woods on the quiet side of Highway 76; amenities include an indoor pool, two tennis courts and an electronic ticket service for Branson shows; children under 18 stay free.

Best Western Music Capital Inn 89R (4S)

3257 Shepherd of the Hills Expy., Branson; (417) 334-8378; (800) 528-1234; FAX: (417) 334-8855
The central location (across from Shoji Tabuchi's Theater) and many comforts (indoor pool, whirlpool, sauna, exercise room) of this three-story hotel are why it's the best of the area's Best Westerns even though some find the rooms merely "ok" ("the reason you're in Branson is the music, not the room"); there's no restaurant on-site, but continental breakfast is included and there are lots of dining options nearby.

Branson Hotel B&B Inn 7R (2S)

214 W. Main St., Branson; (417) 335-6104
This historic Downtown Victorian landmark, built in 1903 to house railroad passengers, is now a B&B where C&W fans get R&R between shows at Branson theaters; guests relax in Adirondack chairs on the two verandas or sip a drink in the antiques-filled parlor; a glass-enclosed breakfast room is the setting for the complimentary full breakfast.

Branson House B&B Inn 6R (1S)

120 Fourth St., Branson; (417) 334-0959
One of Branson's noblest old homes, now converted into a B&B, occupies a hillside overlooking Downtown and the bluffs of Lake Taneycomo; the fieldstone walls, old oaks and flower gardens lend an English country touch to the seven-room property (the Tapestry Suite has a private entrance); complimentary breakfast starts the day.

Chateau on the Lake Resort Hotel and Convention Center 245R (57S)

415 N. Hwy 265, Branson; (417) 334-1161; (888)333-LAKE; FAX (417) 339-5566
Five minutes from the hustle and bustle lies this comfortably elegant newcomer, a mountaintop resort overlooking Table Rock Lake that caters to both families and conferees with a variety of restaurants, indoor/outdoor pools, tennis courts, a fitness center, salon and spa, full-service marina, children's program, playground, 40,000 square feet of meeting space and a business center; the centerpiece of the 10-story property is a skylit atrium courtyard filled with meandering streams, lush foliage and towering trees around which most guestrooms are situated.

Clarion at Fall Creek Resort (220S)

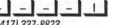

1 Fall Creek Dr., Branson; (417) 334-6404; (800) 56-CONDO; FAX: (417) 335-4652
An alternative to area motels, this "well-maintained" full-service resort on Lake Taneycomo combines a "great location" two-and-a-half miles south of Country Music Boulevard with accommodations ranging from studios to three-bedroom condos, many with kitchenettes; on-site boating and fishing, mini-golf, basketball, indoor and outdoor pools, tennis courts and a fitness center offer guests something other than the music, scenery and shopping that has made Branson famous.

Red Bud Cove Bed & Breakfast Suites (8S)

162 Lakewood Dr., Branson; (417) 334-7144; (800) 677-5525; FAX: (417) 337-8823
A lovely setting on Table Rock Lake serves up a full plate of activities (hiking, biking, boating, fishing) to keep vacationers busy; guests not wishing to partake of the full complimentary breakfast can prepare their own in the kitchenette included in each suite; scenic access roads to all the Branson-area attractions make this B&B on a quiet cove an attractive alternative to the motels along Highway 76.

Hannibal

Fifth Street Mansion 6R (1S)

213 S. Fifth St., Hannibal; (573) 221-0445; (800) 874-5661; FAX: (573) 221-3355
This 1858 mansion listed on the National Register of Historic Places is full of history: Mark Twain dined here during his last visit to Hannibal and it was a stop in the underground railroad during the Civil War; the Italianate home with two parlors, a library and a wraparound porch also features eight fireplaces, its original chandeliers and a cupola that overlooks Downtown and the Mississippi River; a full breakfast is included.

Garth Woodside Mansion 8R

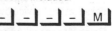

PO Box 578, R.R. 3, Hannibal; (573) 221-2789; FAX: (573) 221-2789
The 'flying staircase', which winds up three stories with no apparent support, is the focal point of the carefully restored 1871 country estate where Mark Twain twice stayed; the original furnishings and 19th-century knickknacks in the eight guestrooms offer a nostalgic glimpse of life in a Victorian home; in the heart of the historic district, it's conveniently located to the many attractions of Twain's real and fictional worlds; a full breakfast is included.

Kansas City*

Adam's Mark Hotel 366R (8S)
19 | 20 | 19 | 18 | $122

9103 E. 39th St., Kansas City; (816) 737-0200; (800) 444-ADAM; FAX: (816) 737-4713

☑ The Eastside location, directly across from the Chiefs and Royals stadiums, makes this "plain vanilla" property "convenient for baseball and football games" but "inconvenient for anything else"; nevertheless, the well-equipped health club, indoor and outdoor pools and tennis courts are a hit, and the hotel scores extra points for the "excellent food" at Remington's; of course "weekends can be a nightmare during football season."

Doubletree Corporate Woods 340R (17S)
21 | 21 | 19 | 19 | $109

10100 College Blvd., Overland Park, KS; (913) 451-6100; (800) 222-TREE; FAX: (913) 451-6463

⬛ "Wonderful all around" sums up the majority opinion on this "comfortable", "moderately priced" high-rise with a "nice suburban location" in the booming Corporate Woods business complex on the Kansas side of Kansas City; "modern", "businesslike" rooms, "polished service", "good menu choices", "great meeting facilities" (capacity: 1,000), a fitness center with indoor pool and jogging trails make it a favorite choice for business travelers.

Historic Suites of America (100S)
▽ 25 | 20 | 19 | 20 | $99

612 Central St., Kansas City; (816) 842-6544; (800) 733-0612; FAX: (816) 842-0656

⬛ A "beautiful renovation" has turned an "old warehouse" into an "exceptional" Victorian-looking hotel; its mostly corporate clients find suites that are "as big as a house" complete with "fully equipped kitchens"; there's no restaurant on-site, but daily breakfast is provided and it's close to many of Kansas City's finest restaurants (13 within three blocks).

Holiday Inn Crowne Plaza 278R (18S)
20 | 19 | 17 | 19 | $122

4445 Main St., Kansas City; (816) 531-3000; (800) 465-4329; FAX: (816) 531-3007

☑ Oversized rooms, a health club and an indoor lap pool are some of the jewels of the Crowne Plaza, a Midtown high-rise that's "well located" (Country Club Plaza is just two blocks away) and "has everything" for the business traveler; the thorns in the Crowne are a "sterile atmosphere" and food that could be better, yet most agree it's "very nice for the price."

Hyatt Regency Crown Center 689R (42S)
21 | 21 | 20 | 21 | $139

2345 McGee St., Kansas City; (816) 421-1234; (800) 233-1234; FAX: (816) 435-4190

☑ This "skyscraper of a hotel" linked to shops, restaurants and theaters is the "center of action in KC", baiting both execs and tourists with newly renovated rooms, a "beautiful lobby", "very accommodating staff" and "wonderful food" at the Peppercorn Duck Club (which offers a chocolate dessert buffet "that will leave you searching for insulin"); still, it strikes some as a "typical Hyatt" – "sterile and antiseptic."

Marriott Downtown 550R (23S)
21 | 22 | 19 | 19 | $128

200 W. 12th St., Kansas City; (816) 421-6800; (800) 548-4782; FAX: (816) 855-4418

⬛ A recent guestroom renovation spruced up this "above average" Downtowner in anticipation of the debut of a new 430-room tower in late 1997; meanwhile, meeting-goers try to ignore the "lovely view of the construction site" and focus on the easy access to the Bartle Hall convention center (via underground walkway) and Avenue of the Arts (home of the Folly Theater, Music Hall and Lyric Opera).

Marriott Hotel Overland Park 390R (7S)
20 | 20 | 18 | 18 | $112

10800 Metcalf Ave., Overland Park, KS; (913) 451-8000; (800) 228-9290; FAX: (913) 451-5914

☑ "One of the better Marriotts" to believers who find "good value" and "quiet" accommodations in "the best hotel in South Kansas City", but "nothing special" to the disenchanted who dismiss "small rooms" and "ok" quality; there's on-site dining at Parkside (Continental) and Nikko (a Japanese steakhouse), plus "lots of good restaurants" nearby; meeting space for 1,000 and a Johnson County location make it "good for business", but some note it "doesn't cater to tourists."

Radisson Suite Hotel (240S)
▽ 19 | 21 | 20 | 19 | $97

106 W. 12th St., Kansas City; (816) 221-7000; (800) 333-3333; FAX: (816) 221-3477

⬛ Hats off to the "nice renovation" of this historic Downtown landmark (original site of the Haberdashery hotel co-owned by Harry Truman) where the lobby maintains its old-world ambiance and the accommodations feature modern accoutrements such as large work desks and computer hookups; complimentary continental breakfast and cocktail reception, an exercise room and "fine" food at Bodine's Steakhouse cap off this all-suiter near Bartle Hall.

---

* Including Overland Park, KS.

Raphael Hotel 32R (91S)　　　22 23 21 20 $142
325 Ward Pkwy, Kansas City; (816) 756-3800; (800) 821-5343; FAX: (816) 756-3800
■ Participants paint a pretty picture of this "fine example of old-world elegance" in "the classiest area of the city" (Country Club Plaza); the composition embraces "comfortably understated" "apartmentlike rooms", "really fine" food, an "attentive staff" and an "intimate atmosphere"; it's a "good backup hotel when the Ritz is full" – with more "reasonable rates."

Ritz-Carlton Kansas City 345R (28S)　　25 25 24 24 $168
401 Ward Pkwy., Kansas City; (816) 756-1500; (800) 241-3333; FAX: (816) 531-1483
■ "Luxury abounds" at Kansas City's highest-rated hotel – from the "beautiful" "parlorlike" lobby (a favorite for afternoon tea replete with crystal chandeliers, antique oil paintings and fresh flowers) to the "excellent" recently refurbished guestrooms to the Rooftop Restaurant with its "great view" of Country Club Plaza; add "impeccable service" to the equation and this "high-class hotel" is, without a doubt, "tops for business" as well as pleasure.

Savoy, Hotel 9R (13S)　　　▽ 23 22 26 14 $113
219 W. Ninth St., Kansas City; (816) 842-3575; (800) 728-6922; FAX: (816) 842-3575
■ Surveyors have a stomping good time at the Savoy, a "wonderful, historic KC legend" operating Downtown since 1888 and under renovation at press time; stained-glass windows, high beamed ceilings, an enormous oak bar and the "best seafood in the Midwest" at the Savoy Grill (ask for booth four, host to Harding, Truman, Ford and Reagan) make for a "unique lodging experience"; an elaborate breakfast is included in the rate.

Sheraton Suites Kansas City (258S)　　▽ 21 19 17 19 $116
770 W. 47th St., Kansas City; (816) 931-4400; (800) 227-2416; FAX: (816) 561-7330
■ "Great value in a wonderful location" sums up reviewer reaction to this "reliable" all-suiter in the Country Club Plaza shopping and dining district; expect plenty of in-suite amenities, including refrigerators, coffeemakers, hair dryers and irons and ironing boards, plus a pool, exercise room and whirlpool for unwinding at the end of the day.

Southmoreland on the Plaza 12R　　　– – – – I
116 E. 46th St., Kansas City; (816) 531-7979; FAX: (816) 531-2407
Shade trees, formal gardens and sweeping lawns surround this 1913 Colonial Revival mansion, creating an unexpected country ambiance a five-minute walk from County Club Plaza; the individually decorated guestrooms, named after notable KC personalities, feature upscale touches like balconies or fireplaces, down duvets and Caswell-Massey toiletries; amenities include homemade breakfast, evening wine and cheese, business equipment and tennis and fitness privileges at a nearby club.

Westin Crown Center 676R (49S)　　21 21 21 22 $137
1 Pershing Rd., Kansas City; (816) 474-4400; (800) 228-3000; FAX: (816) 391-4438
■ A handy location at the Crown Center shopping-dining-business complex, along with on-site amenities like a full-service health club and "fantastic bars and restaurants", make this "always bustling" high-rise seem like a "self-contained resort"; the "solid property" also earns praise for its "beautiful lobby", "nicely decorated rooms" and "pleasant staff"; N.B. 31 meeting rooms make it a conference planner's dream.

Lake Ozark

LODGE OF FOUR SEASONS 314R (150S)　　20 21 20 23 $139
PO Box 215, State Rd. HH, Lake Ozark; (314) 365-3000; (800) THE-LAKE; FAX: (314) 365-8555
■ "Lots of activities" are available at this "Midwest jewel" boasting a "beautiful setting" on the Lake of the Ozarks; guests get busy with 45 holes of golf, 17 tennis courts, a 200-slip marina, riding stables, trapshooting, bowling, six restaurants, a movie theater and a spa; admirers also appreciate the "nice-size rooms" and "warm, pleasant" staff as well as the many packages that keep them coming back.

Osage Beach

Marriott's Tan-Tar-A Resort, Golf Club &　　20 21 18 23 $134
Spa 755R (175S)
State Rd. KK, Osage Beach; (573) 348-3131; (800) 826-8272; FAX: (573) 348-3206
■ "What a surprise in the middle of nowhere" cheer boosters of this "beautiful, well-run resort" that's "great for family vacations" as well as conventions; the hillside and lakeside setting ("too spread out" for some) "has everything" – from paddleboating to go-carting, from freshwater fishing to sea-salt massages – making it a "great escape" "with no reason to leave"; repeaters recommend "stay away from the noisy lodge" and spring for one of the condos surrounding the Hidden Lakes golf course.

Ridgedale

Big Cedar Lodge 124R (124S)
▽ 25 | 23 | 24 | 26 | $155
612 Devil's Pool Rd., Ridgedale; (417) 335-2777; FAX: (417) 335-2340

■ The few who know this "well-kept secret" cherish a "great getaway" – "if you can overlook all the dead animals on the walls"; you're in store for "fantastic" scenery and "incredible attention to detail" plus a wide variety of activities including boating, canoeing, waterskiing, fishing, horseback riding, tennis and golfing on a Jack Nicklaus–designed course; accommodations include rooms in three lodges, knotty pine cottages and log cabins on 250 acres; N.B. Branson is nine miles away.

St. Louis

Adam's Mark Hotel 814R (96S)
20 | 20 | 20 | 20 | $139
Fourth & Chestnut Sts., St. Louis; (314) 241-7400; (800) 444-ADAM; FAX: (314) 241-6618

■ It may "look like a prison on the outside", but the inside of this Downtowner is "lovely" with a "beautiful" lobby highlighted by two bronze horses and "tastefully decorated" rooms affording "spectacular" views of the Mississippi River and Gateway Arch; with indoor and outdoor pools, racquetball courts, a health club, top French–New American dining at Faust's, four lounges and 76,000 square feet of meeting space, it's no wonder surveyors say "it's all happening here", especially since the arrival of a new manager from the Ritz-Carlton who's taking a ritzy approach to service.

Cheshire Inn Motor Hotel 96R (10S)
19 | 18 | 16 | 17 | $123
6300 Clayton Rd., St. Louis; (314) 647-7300; (800) 325-7378; FAX: (314) 647-0442

☑ Voters can't make up their minds about this "old-world" mock-Tudor inn near Washington University and Forest Park; some see it as a "class act" with "excellent theme rooms", a "good restaurant" and a staff that "really makes you feel at home", while others write it off as "slightly run-down" with "cheesy" decor, "awful food" and "snooty service"; but detractors can't deny that the Fox and Hounds Pub is "purrfect in winter" and a happening place for singles; N.B. a shuttle service runs to Downtown and Clayton.

Crowne Plaza Majestic 89R (2S)
24 | 24 | 22 | 19 | $128
(fka The Hotel Majestic)
1019 Pine St., St. Louis; (314) 436-2355; (800) 451-2355; FAX: (314) 436-0223

☑ A "wonderfully restored" 1913 Renaissance Revival building, a national historic landmark, is the setting for this "little gem" in big Downtown; the "very pretty rooms" and "personal service and attention" justify reviewers who call it "the class act of the area"; despite the loss of the "good jazz bar" and "too many changes in the restaurant", ratings have held up for "this great place to get some peace."

Daniele Hotel 76R (6S)
19 | 21 | 19 | 18 | $134
216 N. Meramec Ave., Clayton; (314) 721-0101; (800) 325-8302; FAX: (314) 721-0609

■ This "quiet, peaceful" suburban hotel with a "European feel" in its public areas attracts business types with its "large rooms" and "super service", especially the chauffeured transportation to and from the airport, Galleria Shopping Center and Plaza Frontenac; there are no fitness facilities on-site, but bell captains are available to drop you off and pick you up at a nearby health club for a complimentary workout.

Doubletree Hotel & Conference Center 218R (5S)
20 | 20 | 18 | 20 | $126
16625 Swingley Ridge Dr., St. Louis; (314) 532-5000; (800) 222-TREE; FAX: (314) 532-9984

■ Groups seeking a combination of "excellent" business and sports facilities gravitate toward this "out of the way" property (25 miles west of Downtown) offering state-of-the-art meeting space along with indoor/outdoor pools and tennis, racquetball, volleyball, fitness equipment, an indoor driving range and more; guests give it extra points for "very good service" but take away a few for the fact that there's "no food service after 11 PM."

Drury Inn at Union Station 169R (7S)
20 | 19 | 18 | 20 | $114
201 S. 20th St., St. Louis; (314) 231-3900; (800) 325-8300; FAX: (314) 231-3900

☑ Fans feel they did a "beautiful job upgrading" the 1907 brick building that was once the YMCA Railroad Hotel, giving a nod to the "very comfortable rooms" (some with kitchenettes), fitness center, indoor pool and "nice facilities for dining"; critics claim the "convenient" Union Station location is "about all" the property has going for it, but solid scores coupled with a complimentary continental breakfast suggest it's worth a stay.

Embassy Suites - St. Louis (297S)
20 | 18 | 15 | 17 | $121

901 N. First St., St. Louis; (314) 241-4200; (800) 241-5151; FAX: (314) 241-6513

A "good location" in historic Laclede's Landing – within walking distance of the Gateway Arch, TWA Dome, convention center and Busch Stadium – makes this all-suiter "useful" for both business and leisure travelers; ambassadors report that the rooms are "nice" enough and the "rates are competitive for the area", but the staff seems "disinterested" and the "food isn't the best"; yet no one's complaining about the full breakfast included in the rate.

Frontenac Hilton 266R (42S)
18 | 18 | 17 | 16 | $120

1335 S. Lindbergh Blvd., St. Louis; (314) 993-1100; (800) 325-7800; FAX: (314) 993-8546

Even if not going to a convention, surveyors cite proximity to the "best shopping in town" at posh Plaza Frontenac as reason enough to overnight at this Mid County hotel; a relatively recent renovation resulted in a "beautiful exterior" and European-style lobby with a dual winding staircase and crystal chandeliers, and an upcoming expansion is scheduled to add 75 guestrooms and more meeting space; faultfinders fuss that "half the rooms are outside the main building."

Harley Hotel of St. Louis 187R (6S)
▽ 17 | 22 | 17 | 19 | $83

3400 Rider Trail S., St. Louis; (314) 291-6800; (800) 321-2323; FAX: (314) 291-4049

This business hotel with an "out of the way" location – closer to the Missouri than the Mississippi River, closer to the airport than the Arch – redeems itself by giving guests the best bang for the buck in St. Louis; facilities include a pool, tennis courts and a VIP floor featuring in-room steam baths, continental breakfast and evening cocktails.

Holiday Inn Riverfront 360R (96S)
16 | 16 | 15 | 15 | $105

200 N. Fourth St., St. Louis; (314) 621-8200; (800) 925-1395; FAX: (314) 621-8073

The "rooms are clean, the view is nice, the price is right" is the take on this former apartment building across from the Gateway Arch and within walking distance of Busch Stadium, Laclede's Landing and riverboat gambling; the "restaurants are lacking", but more than half the rooms have kitchenettes and first-rate restaurants are a short stroll away; a recent redo of the guestrooms should help future ratings.

Hyatt Regency St. Louis 526R (12S)
21 | 21 | 19 | 22 | $144

1 St. Louis Union Station, St. Louis; (314) 231-1234; (800) 233-1234; FAX: (314) 923-3970

"Go out of your way to stay" at this "beautiful hotel" within historic Union Station (two blocks from Kiel Center) boasting an "unbelievably gorgeous lobby" capped with a barrel-vaulted ceiling; "the best business accommodations in St. Louis" seal the deal with "excellent service", "very nice" though "smallish" rooms, a business center, health club and an outdoor pool; the "restaurants are ok, but the concierges can recommend better places" in the area.

Marriott Pavilion Hotel 649R (21S)
18 | 19 | 17 | 17 | $126

1 Broadway, St. Louis; (314) 421-1776; (800) 228-9290; FAX: (314) 331-9029

Baseball fans can "watch Cardinals games from the higher floors" or in the various bars and restaurants of this "fine but not special hotel" across the street from Busch Stadium; aside from sports, it's "convention heaven", catering to business travelers with executive-level rooms, in-room dataports, a health club and 28,000 square feet of meeting space; a spring 1996 refurbishment of the rooms should take care of complaints that it "really needs a face-lift."

Marriott West St. Louis 302R (3S)
17 | 18 | 14 | 15 | $122

660 Maryville Ctr. Dr., St. Louis; (314) 878-2747; (800) 352-1175; FAX: (314) 878-4513

To some explorers "it's too far from St. Louis attractions", but the "quiet location" in West County (17 miles from Downtown) provides the mostly corporate clientele with enough meeting space and recreational facilities to warrant the trip; those venturing out to discover better restaurants and activities will find Six Flags Over Mid-America and The Galleria within easy driving distance.

RITZ-CARLTON ST. LOUIS 269R (32S)
27 | 26 | 26 | 25 | $186

100 Carondelet Plaza, St. Louis; (314) 863-6300; (800) 241-3333; FAX: (314) 863-3525

The top-ranked showpiece of the 'Show Me State' garners reviewers' praise as "the only real hotel in St. Louis" (15 minutes from Downtown in suburban Clayton); the Persian carpets in the lobby and "gorgeous flowers all over the hotel" impart an upscale ambiance that continues in the "big", "beautiful", "well-appointed" rooms where marble bathrooms, terry bathrobes and vanity tables with lighted makeup mirrors are standard; the "best afternoon tea" is topped only by the "excellent food" at The Restaurant; in sum, "perfection in the Midwest."

Seven Gables Inn 28R (3S)
22 | 22 | 23 | 20 | $141

26 N. Meramec St., Clayton; (314) 863-8400; (800) 433-6590; FAX: (314) 863-8846

◪ Most tell stories of a "charming little" hostelry with "European ambiance", "a welcome alternative to the big hotels" in suburban Clayton, offering "top-notch cuisine" and a pleasant patio in back plus individually designed rooms furnished with country French antiques; a few spin yarns of a "tired", "overrated inn" with "small", "slightly threadbare" rooms, yet this "reasonably priced" property remains a best-seller.

Sheraton Plaza 194R (6S)
19 | 18 | 18 | 18 | $134

900 West Port Plaza, St. Louis; (314) 434-5010; (800) 325-3535; FAX: (314) 434-0140

■ This glass-and-concrete mid-rise in the heart of West Port Plaza, 20 minutes from Downtown, is smaller than its neighboring sibling and caters mostly to corporate clients combining business with pleasure; there aren't many diversions on-site, but shops, restaurants, clubs, movies and live theater are just steps away.

Sheraton West Port Inn 291R (9S)
19 | 18 | 17 | 17 | $113

191 West Port Plaza, St. Louis; (314) 878-1500; (800) 325-3535; FAX: (314) 878-2837

■ Despite decent ratings, voters don't have very many good things to say about this Tudor-style hotel – "ok rooms", "unimpressive public spaces"; the setting, in a 42-acre complex of shops and restaurants next to a five-acre lake. seems to be its saving grace.

Montana

Bigfork

R	S	D	P	$

Averill's Flathead Lake Lodge 18R (20S) ▽ 22 | 25 | 22 | 26 | $214
150 Flathead Lake Lodge Rd., Bigfork; (406) 837-4391; FAX: (406) 837-6977
■ Dust off your chaps for the "vacation of a lifetime" at this 2,000-acre dude ranch near Glacier National Park that "has a little bit of everything": wrangling, riding and rodeo along with sailing, fishing, white-water rafting and swimming in pristine Flathead Lake, tennis, barbecues and an on-site saloon; while lodge rooms and cottages are "simple" and "rustic", outdoor enthusiasts swear by this "highly recommended family adventure"; meals and other costs are included; open May–October.

Big Sky

Huntley Lodge/Shoshone   20 | 19 | 17 | 22 | $161
Condominium Hotel 200R (94S)
Big Sky Ski & Summer Resort, US Hwy. 191, Big Sky; (406) 995-5000; (800) 548-4486; FAX: (406) 995-5001
☑ "Instead of staying in the lodge", ski-happy voters "opt for" the newer, "comfortable", "spacious condos", chalets and townhouses with amenities like full kitchens, fireplaces, whirlpools, laundries and quick slope access; despite renovations, the "cardboard-box" lodge rooms "resemble a dorm", but at least they have "great panoramic views"; summer brings golf, mountain biking, tennis and breathtaking scenery for hiking.

Lone Mountain Ranch 24R   ▽ 23 | 25 | 24 | 26 | $211
PO Box 160069, Big Sky; (406) 995-4644; (800) 514-4644; FAX: (406) 995-4670
☑ The Schaap family and its "knowledgeable staff set the highest standards for service" at this "outstanding" naturalist-oriented ranch "in a spectacular location" close to Yellowstone, offering guided, informative hikes and rides, "unbeatable fly-fishing" and extensive trails for x-country skiing; the "small, older cabins are not very comfortable but the newer cabins are excellent" though "pricey" (raising a few eyebrows at "Holiday Inn–like toiletries"); three meals daily are included, and there are children's programs in summer.

Bozeman

Mountain Sky Guest Ranch 27R   ▽ 22 | 26 | 25 | 25 | $205
PO Box 1128, Big Creek Rd., Bozeman; (406) 587-1244 (Sept – May); (406) 333-4911 (May – Oct.); (800) 548-3392; FAX: (406) 587-3977 (Sept. – May); (406) 333-4911 (May – Oct.)
■ "We've been back five times" crows one happy camper, sold on this "fun" ranch near Yellowstone that features rustic cabin accommodations and less-rustic duplex units; the "terrific horse program" provides a mount for each guest, and prices for a weeklong stay include all "outstanding" meals, on-ranch activities (hiking, riding, fly-fishing, swimming, tennis, etc.), a "terrific kids' camp" and even dancing in the evening; N.B. one surveyor comments "as a couple without kids, we didn't enjoy it as much as we would have with them."

Darby

Triple Creek Ranch 18R   – | – | – | – | VE
5551 W. Fork Stage Rte., Darby; (406) 821-4600; FAX: (406) 821-4666
Some 75 miles south of Missoula is a rustic Relais & Châteaux ranch that doesn't skimp on service or amenities in accommodating executive retreats and romantic getaways; 18 log cabins are outfitted with indulgent touches such as fireplaces, outdoor hot tubs and showers built for two; the all-inclusive rates cover gourmet meals and activities, including tennis, swimming, fly fishing, x-country skiing and horseback riding.

Gallatin Gateway

Gallatin Gateway Inn 26R (9S)   20 | 19 | 21 | 20 | $134
PO Box 376, US Hwy. I91, Gallatin Gateway; (406) 763-4672; (800) 676-3522; FAX: (406) 763-4672
☑ "A luxurious surprise in the middle of nowhere", this grand Spanish Mission–style inn near Bozeman was built in 1927 as a railway stopover for folks headed to Yellowstone; now on the National Register of Historic Places, it's lauded for its "gorgeous interior", "large rooms" and "excellent" New American food; hiking, cycling, tennis, swimming and hot tub as well as Orvis-sponsored "fly-fishing packages" are a draw, while rear-facing rooms where "the racket is awful" are a drawback, along with variable service.

R | S | D | P | $

320 Guest Ranch 60R

– | – | – | – | E

205 Buffalo Horn Creek, Gallatin Gateway; (406) 995-4283; (800) 243-0320; FAX: (406) 995-4694
"Great package deals" make this "bargain right on the Gallatin River" particularly enticing to families, with kids' programs plus a full range of activities from guided horseback rides and trail barbecues to hayrides (sleighs in winter), x-country skiing, snowmobiling and trout fishing; the "rustic" but "nice" log cabins have porches, cable TVs and phones, and some offer fireplaces and complete kitchen facilities; there are extra charges for some activities.

Red Lodge

Pollard, The 25R (11S)

– | – | – | – | M

2 N. Broadway, Red Lodge; (406) 446-0001; (800) 765-5273; FAX: (406) 446-0002
The cornerstone of the historic district in Red Lodge is this 1893 red brick hotel listed on the National Historic Register; the place where Buffalo Bill, Calamity Jane and William Jennings Bryan once slumbered today offers comfy rooms (some with mountain views, hot tubs or balconies), fine dining, an exercise room, racquetball courts, a sauna and hot tub and conference space for 50; from the edge of town, the scenic Beartooth Highway leads nature lovers to Yellowstone and Grand Teton national parks; no smoking.

Whitefish

Grouse Mountain Lodge 124R (20S)

22 | 23 | 22 | 23 | $135

1205 Hwy. 93 W., Whitefish; (406) 862-3000; (800) 321-8822; FAX: (406) 862-0326
■ "Large", "modern" rooms with "warm furnishings" make this a "comfortable" four-season getaway, and the "marvelous", "convenient" Flathead Valley setting ("one of the most beautiful areas of the US") and "real Montana ambiance" are "a treat for city folk" who also appreciate "wonderful food" at the on-site restaurant and "genuinely friendly" service; "very nice facilities" include the 36-hole Whitefish Lake Golf Club, x-country ski trails, an indoor pool and outdoor hot tubs; the lodge can accommodate conventions and special events for up to 300 people.

North Forty Resort 14R (8S)

– | – | – | – | I

3765 Hwy. 40 W., Whitefish; (406) 862-7740; (800) 775-1740; FAX: (406) 862-7741
Summer or winter, the minutes-from-Glacier-National-Park location draws vacationers to this collection of modern log cabins with full kitchens and fireplaces complemented by the resort's open-air hot tubs and saunas; surveyors enjoy "wonderful service" when they're actually on-site and not out fly-fishing, hiking or downhill skiing at nearby Big Mountain ski area.

Nebraska

Beatrice   R   S   D   P $

Carriage House B&B 6R   _ _ _ _ I
Box 136B, Rte. 1, Beatrice; (402) 228-0356
Guests can pet the owners' five horses (they earn their keep during evening carriage rides) and check out a collection of carriages built from 1865 to 1902 at this turn-of-the-century B&B 45 miles south of Lincoln; a full five-course breakfast is included in the very reasonable rates; N.B. no kids under 10, no TVs or pets in rooms and most baths are shared; check-in from 4–9 PM only, unless arranged in advance.

Lincoln

Rogers House, The 10R (2S)   _ _ _ _ I
2145 B St., Lincoln; (402) 476-6961; FAX: (406) 476-6473
A standout mansion among the stately homes in Lincoln's historic Near South neighborhood; built in 1914, the brick Jacobean-style B&B has local landmark status and features individually decorated guestrooms graced with touches such as antique beds, sunrooms, working fireplace or clawfoot tub; rates include full breakfast.

Omaha

Marriott Hotel Omaha 297R (4S)   17   18   16   14 $115
10220 Regency Circle, Omaha; (402) 399-9000; (800) 228-9290; FAX: (402) 399-0220
☑ "Fine but nothing special" is the consensus on this business-oriented Downtowner in the Regency Office Park; some find the rooms "dreary", but "friendly, pleasant" staff and a "good buffet breakfast" compensate as do facilities including 12 meeting rooms for up to 600, a health club and indoor/outdoor pool; "if you get religious, Boys Town is just to the west" and if you're looking for worldly goods, the Westroads mall and Regency Fashion Court are nearby.

Offutt House 5R (2S)   _ _ _ _ I
146 N. 39th St., Omaha; (402) 553-0951; FAX: (402) 553-0704
Glory be, the Easter Sunday tornado of 1913 spared a few of Omaha's Gold Coast mansions, including this 1894 French chateau–like, red-slate-roof beauty near the Old Market area of shops and restaurants; it's now a B&B adorned with antiques and period furnishings from the guestrooms (all with private bath and some with fireplace) to the living room, sun porch and library; full breakfast is included.

Radisson Redick Tower Hotel 63R (25S)   ▽ 20   20   17   17 $107
1504 Harney St., Omaha; (402) 342-1500; (800) 333-3333; FAX: (402) 342-5317
■ "Nice art deco" decor in the lobby is the highlight at this Downtown "classic" geared to the biz traveler and "convenient" to sites such as the Henry Doorly Zoo and Heartland of America Park; rates include full breakfast and transportation to the airport and nearby businesses and attractions; unfortunately, some say the lobby's good looks "aren't carried through the rest of the hotel."

Red Lion Hotel/Omaha 413R (20S)   _ _ _ _ E
1616 Dodge St., Omaha; (402) 346-7600; (800) 847-5010; FAX: (402) 636-4936
The king of the business jungle is a Downtown high-rise offering 16 meeting rooms, three ballrooms, an indoor pool, fitness center and sauna, two restaurants and two lounges; a safari to this den in the heartland's heart wouldn't be complete without visits to the nearby Old Market historic district, Fontenelle Forest and the world's largest tropical rain forest at the Omaha Zoo.

Waterloo

J.C. Robinson House Bed & Breakfast 4R ⊟   _ _ _ _ VI
102 E. Lincoln Ave., Waterloo; (402) 779-2704; (800) 779-2705; FAX: (402) 779-2315
A 21-room, 1905 manse 16 miles from Omaha offering good-deal rates on its four restored, antiques-filled bedrooms (choice of continental or American breakfast included); the from-another-era ambiance is heightened by the owner's antique clock collection (no worries about wake-ups here), while modern pastimes include three golf courses and several restaurants within a few miles' drive; no smoking, no kids under 16 and cash only; only one room has a private bath.

Wilber

Wilber, Hotel 10R   _ _ _ _ I
PO Box 641, 203 S. Wilson St., Wilber; (402) 821-2020; (800) 609-4663
Check in to this 1895 B&B in the 'Czech Capital of the US' and you'll find accommodations with names like the "Zajicek Room", Pilsner Urquell on tap and Bohemian cooking in the dining room; about 40 minutes from Lincoln and 90 from Omaha, it's on the National Register of Historic Places and combines country charm and Victorian elegance in its 10 rooms (no private baths); full breakfast included; ask about special hunting packages and murder mystery weekends.

Nevada

	R	S	D	P	$

Cal-Neva Resort 176R (24S)   – | – | – | – | M
2 Stateline Rd., Crystal Bay; (702) 832-4000; (800) CAL-NEVA; FAX: (702) 831-9007
Straddling the California-Nevada border on Tahoe's north shore, the 'Lady of the Lake' once belonged to Old Blue Eyes (check out the Frank Sinatra Celebrity Showroom) but fell out of grace after a scandal involving Sam Giancana; it came back in the '80s under new owners who undertook a five-year renovation, and today puts guests up in a nine-story tower with lake views or in several cabins; the bark-clad lodge houses a spa, casino, video arcade, two restaurants and two bars; there's skiing at the High Sierra Ski Bowl, swimming, boating, tennis and plenty of other activities in the area.

Lake Tahoe

Caesars Tahoe 403R (37S)   23 | 21 | 20 | 22 | $139
55 Hwy. 50, S. Lake Tahoe; (702) 588-3515; (800) 648-3353; FAX: (702) 586-2056
■ Loyalists put a laurel wreath on this "grand refuge" with views of Lake Tahoe, awarding it the highest *Survey* ratings in the area; expect "recently redone" rooms, theme-decorated suites (Bahamas, Hollywood, Roman, etc.) and a "wonderful" spa – all "lovely areas to rest up" after a day of skiing, golfing or tennis; other offerings at this "gorgeous hotel" include a 24-hour casino, live shows at Circus Maximus and a Planet Hollywood restaurant.

Harrah's Lake Tahoe 454R (78S)   23 | 21 | 20 | 21 | $139
PO Box 8, Hwy. 50, Stateline; (702) 588-6611; (800) HARRAHS; FAX: (702) 586-6696
■ "Every room has two bathrooms" (each with a TV and telephone) at this "high-roller heaven" in "one of the world's most beautiful places" – "it doesn't get better than that"; year-round outdoor activities range from tee to ski, hiking to biking, boating to floating; the "best restaurants in the area", a family activity center and a glass dome–covered pool provide "diversions from the Lake."

Harvey's Resort Hotel Casino 704R (36S)   21 | 21 | 20 | 20 | $125
Hwy. 50, Stateline; (702) 588-2411; (800) HARVEYS; FAX: (702) 782-4889
■ "It gives you what you came for" – "breathtaking scenery", "nice large rooms", "food and drink galore", "the best service in the area" and a "comfortable place to bet"; the "lobby makeover", "beautifully refurbished rooms" and South Lake Tahoe location make it "a good bet that keeps getting better"; a golf course across the street, nearby ski slopes and lakeside recreational activities "help you forget the gambling."

Hyatt Regency Lake Tahoe 436R (22S)   21 | 21 | 20 | 21 | $154
PO Box 3231, Country Club at Lakeshore, Incline Village; (702) 832-1234; (800) 233-1234; FAX: (702) 831-7508
■ "Away from the hustle and bustle of the South Shore", this hotel's "secluded, rustic" setting has some surveyors calling it "the most beautiful location in the US to gamble"; the "wonderful lakeside suites" with fireplaces and kitchens are "the only way to go", otherwise reviewers report "rooms are typical"; "an incredible variety of activities" and "magnificent restaurant right on the lake" "add to the pleasure."

Lake Tahoe Horizon Casino Resort 513R (26S)   15 | 16 | 14 | 15 | $114
Hwy. 50, Lake Tahoe; (702) 588-6211; (800) 648-3322; FAX: (702) 588-0349
◪ Looking beyond the Horizon there's "plenty to do" (eight nearby ski resorts) around this lakeside property in a "good location" on the South Shore; once the sun sets, however, reviewers focus on "fair rooms" and "indifferent service"; "nothing to talk about" is the majority view.

Las Vegas

TOP 10 OVERALL

NEVADA

Detail

Las Vegas

Golden Nugget — 95

Charleston Blvd.

Sahara Ave.

Las Vegas Blvd. "The Strip"

15

LAS VEGAS

Treasure Island — ■ Desert Inn

Spring Mountain Rd.

Mirage ■

Rio Suite ■

Caesars Palace

Flamingo Rd.

Hard Rock ■

Harmon Ave.

Harmon Ave.

Tropicana Ave.

Monte Carlo ■

■ MGM Grand

Luxor ■

McCARRAN INT'L AIRPORT

BEST OVERALL	**BEST VALUES**
23 Rio Suite	Monte Carlo
Mirage	Lady Luck
Caesars Palace	Rio Suite
Monte Carlo	Four Queens
22 Hard Rock	Maxim Hotel
Golden Nugget	Harrah's Casino
21 Treasure Island	Sahara
20 MGM Grand	Hard Rock
Luxor	Excalibur
Desert Inn	Luxor

R	S	D	P	$

Aladdin Hotel & Casino 1050R (50S)   `11 | 12 | 11 | 13 | $85`
3667 Las Vegas Blvd. S., Las Vegas; (702) 736-0111; (800) 634-3424; FAX: (702) 734-3583
■ Ratings keep slipping for this "tired old hotel" that needs more than a genie and three wishes to change reviews of "tacky", "gaudy and run-down" and "perfect if you know you'll always be out of your room"; the "worn-out rugs" and "old setting" make "a face-lift" (at the least) "appropriate" for this '60s legend.

Alexis Park Resort (500S)   `20 | 18 | 18 | 18 | $140`
375 E. Harmon Ave., Las Vegas; (702) 796-3300; (800) 582-2228; FAX: (702) 796-3354
■ "If you want to stay away from the casinos", or simply need "a respite from the slots", check out this 20-acre complex "just off the Strip"; it's "a nongambling paradise" "on lovely grounds" with three pools, a nine-hole putting green, fitness center and lighted tennis courts; "big", "tasteful" one- and two-bedroom suites, many with whirlpools and fireplaces, make it "much nicer than a typical Las Vegas hotel" and "the only place to stay for serious business."

221

Bally's Las Vegas 2555R (259S)
19 | 18 | 17 | 19 | $116

3645 Las Vegas Blvd. S., Las Vegas; (702) 739-4111; (800) 634-3434; FAX: (702) 739-4405
Even after a $70-million renovation, this "legendary" Stripper is still "big", "noisy" and "cheesy" – "exactly what you want in a Vegas hotel"; slotsters and conventioneers consider it a "good value" given the "best-sized rooms in town" and "phenomenal suites" plus nongaming amenities like tennis courts, an Olympic-size pool, a full-service spa, two main showrooms and 175,000 square feet of meeting space; former fans feel "it used to be the best" but "time has passed it by."

Binion's Horseshoe Hotel and Casino 360R (8S) – | – | – | – | I

128 E. Fremont St., Las Vegas; (702) 382-1600; (800) 622-6468; FAX (702) 384-1574
While this glitzy, gaudy Vegas landmark may have seen better days, high rollers overlook its pint-size accommodations and furnishings – this is one of the best bets in town for real gaming action (with no maximum bet limitations) and top-of-the-line beef from Binion's Cattle Ranch at the Steakhouse.

Caesars Palace 1200R (300S)
23 | 21 | 22 | 24 | $160

3570 Las Vegas Blvd. S., Las Vegas; (702) 731-7110; (800) 634-6001; FAX: (702) 731-6636
With "round beds", "mirrors on the ceiling" and "marble everywhere", this "Vegas classic" is "still the king of glitz" and is about to become much glitzier given a massive renovation/expansion that will add a 1,130-room hotel tower, a 20,000-square-foot spa/fitness center, pools, convention space and 35 stores to the "fabulous" Forum Shops (where outposts of Chinois and the Cheesecake Factory will join Spago and The Palm); some say "it's gone downhill since ITT took over" and gripe about "arrogant personnel" (only high rollers should expect respect), but most applaud the "awesome combo of glitz and gambling" as "a wonder" that "everyone should experience."

Circus Circus Hotel/Casino/Theme Park
13 | 12 | 11 | 14 | $78

3658R (116S)
2880 Las Vegas Blvd. S., Las Vegas; (702) 734-0410; (800) 444-CIRCUS; FAX: (702) 734-2268
From one viewpoint, this "well-named" Strip property is a "cheap, clean, acceptable" place where "kids are welcome" and the "free circus acts" in the lobby and five-acre indoor theme park mean "fun, fun, fun"; from another, it's "punishment by tots" and proves that "a sucker *is* born every minute" with "tacky rooms" ("the wallpaper is visual torture"), "terrible service" and "the worst food" (aside from the "amazing steakhouse"); N.B. a 384-space RV park adjoins the hotel.

Desert Inn 445R (257S)
21 | 20 | 19 | 20 | $144

(fka Sheraton Desert Inn)
3145 Las Vegas Blvd. S., Las Vegas; (702) 733-4444; (800) 634-6906; FAX: (702) 733-4790
As we went to press, this "quiet, civil" "smaller hotel" on the Strip was "in a state of transition", but customers are confident that it "will be spectacular" and won't lose its "deluxe, old-money country-club feel" when a $160-million renovation is completed in 1997; stand-alone hotel wings, a championship golf course, full-service spa and new, comfortable European-style gaming arena create a "respite from all the [Vegas] glitz."

Excalibur Hotel/Casino 4018R (14S)
14 | 14 | 13 | 16 | $84

3850 Las Vegas Blvd. S., Las Vegas; (702) 597-7777; (800) 937-7777; FAX: (702) 597-7009
Surveyors joust about this "low-budget" medieval-themed sister to Circus Circus: "King Arthur would approve" vs. "they certainly have that dark, musty castle atmosphere down pat"; adults are turned off by rooms with "no bathtubs", "schlocky decor", "not much service" and "poor food" ("what can you say about a hotel whose Italian restaurant is Lance-A-Lotta Pasta?"), but while some steer clear, parents bear it because the fire-breathing dragon, tournament dinner show and motion-simulator theaters "are loads of fun" "for kids."

Flamingo Hilton Las Vegas 3466R (377S)
18 | 18 | 17 | 19 | $108

3555 Las Vegas Blvd. S., Las Vegas; (702) 733-3111; (800) 732-2111; FAX: (702) 733-3528
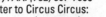 "The makeover worked" at "the original Las Vegas hotel and casino", in the pink once again with "bright rooms", "amazing gardens", "gorgeous pools" and "magnificent grounds" dotted with flamingos, penguins and Rockettes; Bugsy Siegel can rest easy knowing that it offers "everything you need" including "a variety of good restaurants", tennis courts, health club and "good price" for the "four-star location"; now if only they'd "do something about those horrible lines to check in and out."

Four Queens Hotel & Casino 662R (38S)
14 | 15 | 16 | 13 | $77

202 Fremont St., Las Vegas; (702) 385-4011; (800) 634-6045; FAX: (702) 387-5122
Despite a drop in ratings since our last *Survey*, this "good mid-level hotel" Downtown has loyal fans who laud the "comfortable, newly decorated rooms", "terrific restaurant" (Hugo's Cellar) and "great entertainment" at the French Quarter Lounge; though "not luxurious", it's "nice" for an "inexpensive weekend."

Frontier Hotel & Gambling Hall 586R (400S)   13 | 12 | 12 | 12 | $76
3120 Las Vegas Blvd. S., Las Vegas; (702) 794-8200; (800) 634-6966; FAX: (702) 794-8326
A "good location" (central Strip, next to the Fashion Show Mall) and "reasonably priced" suites in the recently renovated Atrium Tower aren't enough to overcome complaints of a "mediocre hotel" that "needs serious upgrading"; neighboring "glitzy brethren" only intensify its "very run-down" look.

Golden Nugget 1805R (102S)   23 | 22 | 21 | 22 | $107
129 E. Fremont St., Las Vegas; (702) 385-7111; (800) 634-3454; FAX: (702) 386-8362
Steve Wynn's opening volley in the war for Vegas (is it for families, gamblers or both?) is the "last of the great old hotels" and the "class act of Downtown"; it wins points for its "elegant" decor, employees who "make you feel at home", "excellent spa" and "fantastic food" at Stephano's; the "remote location" is "a drawback" to some, but others appreciate being "away from the mobs" on the Strip.

Hard Rock Hotel & Casino 312R (28S)   23 | 22 | 21 | 23 | $127
4455 Paradise Rd., Las Vegas; (702) 693-5000; (800) 693-7625; FAX: (702) 693-5010
"Much classier than one would expect", this cousin of the ubiquitous restaurant chain is an "electrifying" place where "hipness abounds" from the "cool leopard skin carpet" to the "faux sand beach" and "thirtysomething crowd" trying to out-trend one another; a huge array of rock memorabilia, an R&R–themed casino, 1,200-seat nightclub, Mortoni's restaurant and an athletic club are other reasons it's one of the "hottest" hotels in town, although insiders claim it's not for real players.

Harrah's Casino Hotel 2700R (108S)   19 | 19 | 18 | 19 | $103
3475 Las Vegas Blvd. S., Las Vegas; (702) 369-5000; (800) HARRAHS; FAX: (702) 369-6014
The longtime riverboat theme is gone, the carnival theme is in at this recently expanded "middle-of-the-Strip" property sporting a 10-ton globe, 32-foot-high court jesters, a Brazilian-themed indoor/outdoor lounge and a new 35-story guestroom tower; the $200-million project should quiet critics who say the hotel is "very dated" and "feels old inside"; those overcome by the party atmosphere can cool off in the Olympic-size pool.

Hilton Las Vegas 2600R (400S)   19 | 17 | 17 | 18 | $124
3000 Paradise Rd., Las Vegas; (702) 732-5111; (800) HILTONS; FAX: (702) 732-5834
Lots of toos ("too big", "too pricey", "too impersonal", "too much concrete", "too many conventioneers") about this "city within a city"; surveyors either love the location ("quiet", "true oasis in the desert", "near the convention center") or hate it ("far from the Strip", "away from the action", "not within walking distance of any other hotel"); even with on-site health clubs, restaurants, pools and tennis courts, party-goers prefer "more action-packed" surroundings.

Lady Luck Casino Hotel 651R (141S)   14 | 15 | 12 | 13 | $60
206 N. Third St., Las Vegas; (702) 477-3000; (800) LADYLUCK; FAX: (702) 477-7021
"You get an awful lot for very little" at this "poor man's luxury hotel" just off Glitter Gulch, rated the best bang for the buck in LV; "basically, it's an old lady" for "blue hairs" and "low-rent gamblers" lured by the "cheap, cheap" accommodations and "great free funbook" containing $350 worth of freebies and discounts; for post-slot unwinding there's an outdoor pool and three restaurants.

Luxor Las Vegas 3986R (488S)   21 | 19 | 18 | 22 | $119
3900 Las Vegas Blvd. S., Las Vegas; (702) 262-4000; (800) 288-1000; FAX: (702) 262-4404
This already "amazing" 30-story pyramid recently took the wraps off a $300-million expansion, which added 1,950 rooms, a life-sized replica of the Temple of Ramses II, a full-service spa and 20,000 square feet of meeting space; two new restaurants, a state-of-the-art showroom and 18 retail shops are expected to come on line by September 1997; surveyors say the rooms are "surprisingly nice" for such a "hokey" place; cynics find "more glitter than substance" – "don't expect personal service", "the food needs work", "leave a trail of bread crumbs from your room."

Maxim Hotel/Casino 757R (38S)   17 | 17 | 16 | 15 | $87
160 E. Flamingo Rd., Las Vegas; (702) 731-4300; (800) 634-6987; FAX: (702) 735-3252
Only in Las Vegas could an 800-room hotel be deemed "small", but this property is also considered a "nice, quiet" place and a "low-cost", "off-the-beaten-track" alternative to neighboring behemoths; lacking most of the amenities of the Strippers (no 'theme', health club or spa, though there are three restaurants and a rooftop pool), most guests take the short walk to Caesars' Forum Shops or cruise the 'giants'.

MGM Grand 4254R (751S)   21 | 19 | 20 | 22 | $139
3799 Las Vegas Blvd. S., Las Vegas; (702) 891-1111; (800) 929-1111; FAX: (702) 891-7676
☑ Vegas meets Hollywood at this "full Technicolor experience" featuring a 33-acre theme park, "exceptional dining choices" (including Emeril's New Orleans Fish House, Brown Derby, Coyote Cafe and Wolfgang Puck Cafe) and a "wonderful" four-acre pool complex; many maintain it's "a gimmick you never tire of", but just as many warn that it's "overrun with kids", there are "too many lines everywhere" and you "need a map to find your room."

Mirage, The 2763R (281S)   23 | 22 | 22 | 25 | $150
3400 Las Vegas Blvd. S., Las Vegas; (702) 791-7111; (800) 627-6667; FAX: (702) 791-7414
■ By all accounts, this is the one hotel that's "responsible for changing the face of LV"; it has "by far the prettiest lobby and casino area" and "the best landscaping", but the "breathtaking public spaces" are "so crowded with sightseers" that "guests have trouble" appreciating the indoor rain forest, "phenomenal" aquarium, white-tiger habitat and other "added attractions"; the rooms may be "basic", but the "pool alone is worth the price", plus there's "a spa to die for" and "superior food"; perhaps more to the point, it's known to offer good gaming for all levels of play.

Monte Carlo Resort & Casino 2800R (204S)   24 | 22 | 23 | 23 | $101
3770 Las Vegas Blvd. S., Las Vegas; (702) 730-7777; (800) 311-8999; FAX: (702) 730-7275
■ The newest offering from the Circus Circus crowd "bills itself as elegance for the budget traveler" and some surveyors affirm that the resort lives up to the claim, calling it "exquisite" and "beautiful" as well as "inexpensive"; the suites come with whirlpools and kitchenettes, and even the standard rooms are deemed "nice" and "large"; the "best pool on the Vegas Strip" swims in accolades, though sun worshippers warn "get in line early for a chaise."

New York-New York Hotel & Casino 2064R   – | – | – | – | I
3790 Las Vegas Blvd. S., Las Vegas; (702) 740-6969; (888) 693-6763; FAX: (702) 740-6700
A 150-foot-tall replica of the Statue of Liberty beckons the huddled masses yearning to gamble at LV's newest themery, a $460-million megaresort masquerading as NYC; a scaled-down 12-tower mock skyline, including the Empire State and Chrysler Buildings, contains guestrooms, the Brooklyn Bridge forms a sidewalk promenade and Little Italy houses a food court; amidst it all, Central Park serves as the casino.

Rio Suite Hotel & Casino (2554S)   25 | 22 | 23 | 21 | $109
3700 W. Flamingo Rd., Las Vegas; (702) 252-7777; (800) PLAY-RIO; FAX: (702) 252-8909
■ "A notch or two above the rest", this "un-Vegas oasis" just west of the Strip is once again the *Survey*'s top-rated Las Vegas property; "many devoted repeaters" samba into "spacious", "stupendous" rooms that are amenity rich (coffeemakers, refrigerators, safes, hair dryers) and feature floor-to-ceiling windows offering unsurpassed views, and "the friendliest staff" helps make it "the most fun in Vegas"; the new 41-story Masquerade Village tower adds 1,028 suites, nearly two dozen retail shops and seven restaurants, including Jean-Louis Palladin's highly praised Napa.

Riviera Hotel & Casino 1997R (103S)   15 | 15 | 14 | 14 | $97
2901 Las Vegas Blvd. S., Las Vegas; (702) 734-5110; (800) 426-4063; FAX: (702) 794-9410
■ With new megahotels opening nearby, this "misnamed" hotel's "heyday has passed"; surveyors say it "was probably top-shelf in 1965" but is now "lacking in class and amenities" – "tacky velvet rooms", "cattle car service", "nothing special food"; yet it fits the bill when what you're looking for is a "clean, reasonably priced room" in the center of the Strip.

Sahara Hotel & Casino 1628R (81S)   14 | 15 | 14 | 14 | $82
2535 Las Vegas Blvd. S., Las Vegas; (702) 737-2111; (800) 634-6666; FAX: (702) 737-1017
■ This oasis would seem to need replenishing given drooping ratings – reviewers insist the "once favorite Vegas hotel" "smack in the middle between Uptown and Downtown" is "past its prime", but renovations, including a new Strip-side facade, might quiet complaints that it "needs a complete redo" to "keep up with the times"; the consensus: "it ain't pretty, but it's cheap."

Stardust Resort & Casino 2340R (160S)   15 | 14 | 14 | 14 | $86
3000 Las Vegas Blvd. S., Las Vegas; (702) 732-6111; (800) 634-6757; FAX: (702) 732-6257
☑ Some reviewers refer to the Stardust as "a lesser cousin of the nearby fabulous hotels", but most see no relation, calling it "not much more than a big motel" with "threadbare" but "very cheap" motor inn rooms and "ok" tower rooms; the Strip location, famous race and sports book, choice of six restaurants and money-saving promotions are reasons enough for some to gamble on "a night or two."

Stratosphere 1444R
15 | 15 | 16 | 16 | $97

2000 Las Vegas Blvd. S., Las Vegas; (702) 380-7777; (800) 99-TOWER; FAX: (708) 383-4755

◪ New heights in "tackiness" were reached when the rebuilt version of Vegas World opened in 1996, at least according to critics who call it a "big eyesore" that "still hasn't worked out the kinks"; the few happy reports are from thrill-seekers who have "wonderful fun" taking in the "full Strip view" from the world's tallest free-standing observation tower and screaming on the Big Shot Ride.

Treasure Island At The Mirage 2679R (212S)
21 | 21 | 20 | 23 | $126

3300 Las Vegas Blvd. S., Las Vegas; (702) 894-7111; (800) 944-7444; FAX: (702) 894-7446

■ Another Steve Wynn-er on the Strip that's "a more family-oriented" and "less-expensive alternative to the Mirage", where the "atmosphere of excitement" starts out front at the live "Strip-stopping sea battle" between a pirate ship and British frigate; the "busy lobby" is crowded with tourists, but it's "quiet upstairs" in "great, comfortable rooms" "with super views"; a treasure chest of amenities, including seven restaurants, an the "excellent health club", a "fun game room" and the "fabulous" Cirque du Soleil, "puts it a cut above the rest."

Tropicana Resort & Casino 1855R (50S)
16 | 16 | 14 | 18 | $98

3801 Las Vegas Blvd. S., Las Vegas; (702) 739-2222; (800) 634-4000; FAX: (702) 739-3648

◪ "Some rooms are refurbished and some aren't", but that doesn't deter devotees who swear that being on the "tropical" grounds complete with "lots of birds and waterfalls" and a "luxurious" five-acre water park "is a vacation in itself" and reason enough to stay on the corner where the Strip begins; overall, guests are juiced about the "great health club" and "best comedy show in Las Vegas", insisting you can squeeze "a lot of fun" from the "best of the old hotels."

Laughlin

Don Laughlin's Riverside Resort Hotel & Casino 1374R (30S)
16 | 14 | 14 | 14 | $54

1650 Casino Dr., Laughlin; (702) 298-2535; (800) 227-3849; FAX: (702) 298-2614

■ Despite less than stellar scores, enthusiasts insist this "old" riverside resort is "still comfortable" and still offers "good value", "good restaurants" ("try the Gourmet Room"), headline entertainment and unique diversions including Colorado River cruises aboard the *USS Riverside*.

Flamingo Hilton Laughlin 1970R (30S)
18 | 17 | 16 | 18 | $72

1900 S. Casino Dr., Laughlin; (702) 298-5111; (800) FLAMINGO; FAX: (702) 298-5116

◪ "In a hot and dusty burg" along the Colorado River just down the road from Lake Mohave and Lake Havasu lies this "large, well-kept", "not too dazzling" hotel that's "perhaps the best bargain anywhere" (many packages are available); nearly every room has a river view, and there are tennis courts and an outdoor pool on-site plus easy access to the river for jet skiing, boating and fishing.

Golden Nugget 296R (4S)
20 | 18 | 17 | 19 | $67

2300 S. Casino Dr., Laughlin; (702) 298-7111; (800) 237-1739; FAX: (702) 298-7204

◪ "Magnificent indoor foliage" awaits guests entering this jungle-themed resort that's one of "the best in Laughlin" according to those who appreciate the "beautiful decor" and "comfortable, inexpensive rooms"; faultfinders feel it's "a disappointment" and "not up to the standards of its Vegas sister" with (heavens!) a "mediocre buffet"; N.B. ferry boats bring visitors from the Arizona side of the river.

Harrah's Laughlin Casino & Hotel 1619R (38S)
20 | 18 | 18 | 19 | $63

2900 S. Casino Dr., Laughlin; (702) 298-4600; (800) 447-8700; FAX: (702) 298-6827

■ "The most beautiful natural setting" with the only private sand beach in town has most voters calling this south-of-the-border-themed resort "easily the best in Laughlin" – "a real bargain" with "plenty of promotional deals" on "attractive" rooms affording "great views of the river and mountains"; the nonsmoking casino wins over health-conscious gamblers, as do "the best restaurants" and Club Philipe health and fitness center.

Mesquite

Players Island 478R (22S)
20 | 20 | 19 | 22 | $69

930 W. Mesquite Blvd., Mesquite; (702) 346-7529; (800) 896-4567; FAX: (702) 346-6888

■ A "terrific surprise in a little desert town" sums up reviewer reaction to this "inexpensive getaway" one hour north of Las Vegas that's "just like being on a tropical island" with its "wonderful" lagoon pool featuring a "cascading waterfall and water slide"; "very nice rooms", a "great" full-service spa and a Cal Olson–designed golf course also help "losers" take their minds off their troubles.

Reno

Circus Circus Hotel Casino 1548R (77S)

 – – – – 1

500 N. Sierra St., Reno; (702) 329-0711; (800) 648-5010; FAX: (702) 329-0599

Like its bigger Las Vegas sibling, this three-ring full-concept hotel in Reno attracts lots of families with lots of kids to its pandemonium-filled lobby with free circus acts overhead and a surrounding midway with rides, carnival games and clowns; to round it out, there are three full-size casinos, a wedding chapel, swimming pools and a Circusland RV Park (linked by Circus Skywalk, Sky Shuttles and minibuses) as well as restaurants, snack bars and shops – in other words, not for the faint of heart.

Eldorado Hotel Casino 690R (93S)

21 | 21 | 23 | 20 | $95

345 N. Virginia St., Reno; (702) 786-5700; (800) 777-5325; FAX: (702) 348-9250

■ "High marks all around", especially for the "delicious Italian restaurant" (La Strada), go to this "surprisingly good" Downtown high-rise; given the nonstop gaming action and myriad other activities available, guests don't spend much time in their rooms but are pleased to point out that they're "modern" and "reasonable"; another asset is the "friendly, helpful staff."

Flamingo Hilton Reno 604R (66S)

18 | 18 | 16 | 17 | $96

255 N. Sierra St., Reno; (702) 322-1111; (800) 648-4882; FAX: (702) 785-7057

◪ Reviewers have mixed emotions about this Downtowner, with proponents praising "huge rooms" with "terrific decor" and detractors deeming it "a run of the mill Hilton" that "needs remodeling"; "no pool" is a problem to some, but others just take advantage of the exercise equipment, free gaming lessons and "great views" of Reno and the Sierra Nevadas from the only rooftop restaurant in town.

Harrah's & Hampton Inn Reno 965R (8S)

19 | 20 | 19 | 18 | $111

(fka Harrah's Reno)

PO Box 10, 219 Center St., Reno; (702) 786-3232; (800) HARRAHS; FAX: (702) 788-3703

■ Three nightly shows, a variety of restaurants – including the Fresh Market Square Buffet (object of a recent $3.7-million upgrade), Harrah's Steak House and Planet Hollywood – and the biggest jackpots around are part of the "massive action" going on at this "good" Downtown hotel with "excellent rooms"; the world's largest Hampton Inn (connected to Harrah's Reno) is home to the first exhibit of original gaming art with sculptures throughout the 26-story tower.

John Ascuaga's Nugget 1376R (196S)

18 | 19 | 19 | 18 | $89

PO Box 30030, 1100 Nugget Ave., Reno; (702) 356-3300; (800) 648-1177; FAX: (702) 356-4198

■ A "wonderful family-run hotel" with "first-rate" facilities including the newly opened west tower, "many fine restaurants", a "beautiful indoor pool" and a "good health club"; the mother lode of activities and sight-seeing opportunities in the surrounding area, coupled with the "friendly staff", makes up for the "bit out-of-the-way location."

Peppermill Hotel Casino 945R (130S)

18 | 19 | 19 | 17 | $89

2707 S. Virginia St., Reno; (702) 826-2121; (800) 648-6992; FAX: (702) 826-5205

◪ This "average" hotel "isn't fancy" (unless you're staying in of the 4,000-square-foot 'super suites'), but it's "comfortable" and the "rooms are clean and cheap"; on-site diversions include a pool with an 'active volcano', a state-of-the art fitness center and nine themed lounges; for those venturing beyond the dimmed lights over the gaming tables, historic Virginia City and Lake Tahoe are nearby.

Silver Legacy Resort Casino 1556R (156S)

22 | 20 | 20 | 23 | $95

407 N. Virginia St., Reno; (702) 329-4777; (800) 687-8733; FAX: (702) 325-7474

■ Expect an "ultra experience" at Reno's newest Downtown resort, a Victorian-themed property built directly over an old silver mine; the "remarkable" automated mining-machine "centerpiece" in the casino and a high-tech laser light show add to the excitement, while a skywalk connection to the Eldorado and Circus Circus creates an entertainment complex that's a minicity in the world's biggest little city.

New Hampshire

Bretton Woods

R | S | D | P | $

1896 Bretton Arms Country Inn 31R (3S) ▽ 23 | 23 | 24 | 22 | $135
Rte. 302, Bretton Woods; (603) 278-1000; (800) 258-0330; FAX: (603) 278-3457
■ A "quaint historic inn", boasting "nicely refurbished" rooms, "inventive, exciting food", "great atmosphere and beautiful grounds", a snowball's throw from the Mount Washington Hotel with which it shares golf, tennis and other "wonderful amenities"; the lengthy ski season makes it "ideal" for x-country and alpine enthusiasts; so while a few dissenters murmur it's "not great", fans feel it often is.

Mount Washington Hotel & Resort 188R (7S)   19 | 21 | 21 | 25 | $175
Rte. 302, Bretton Woods; (603) 278-1000; (800) 258-0330; FAX: (603) 278-3457
■ "See how the wealthy used to live" at this "elegant dowager" with "big old-fashioned rooms" (tip: "get one in the new wing"), a "breathtaking" locale, "plenty of organized activities" (social and sporting) during the May–October season, plus "wonderful porches" on which sedentary guests can "rock around the clock"; P.S. "you still need to dress for dinner", and grousers grumble that "a lot of history was made here, and the hotel's plumbing was there when it happened."

Dixville Notch

BALSAMS GRAND RESORT HOTEL 227R (5S)   21 | 23 | 24 | 26 | $218
Rte. 26, Lake Gloriette, Dixville Notch; (603) 255-3400; (800) 255-0600; FAX: (603) 255-4221
■ "Old-world elegance, fabulous food and excellent service" lure travelers to this "grand old resort" on 15,000 acres hugging the shores of Lake Gloriette; "every need is taken care of", meaning that along with a "sensible" children's program ("you will never see your kids"), there are facilities including two golf courses, six tennis courts, alpine/ x-country skiing and an Olympic-size pool; a few sniff at "puritanical", "small" rooms and say the "decor could use updating", but who can pass up "the magic of Switzerland transported to the US"?

Franconia

Franconia Inn 31R (3S)   18 | 20 | 21 | 20 | $118
1300 Easton Valley Rd., Franconia; (603) 823-5542; (800) 473-5299; FAX: (603) 823-8078
☑ Devotees of "New England charm and hospitality" rave about the "incredible meals and lovely setting" at this "sweet country inn", even while other folks bemoan "ho-hum New England food", "no a/c" and suggest a "refurbishing"; many guests, however, confess they "love the midnight Jacuzzi" and find this "rustic" getaway "a great place to relax" when they're not playing tennis, hiking, biking, skiing or horseback riding in the "beautiful" countryside.

Hanover

Hanover Inn 69R (24S)   22 | 23 | 21 | 21 | $163
E. Wheelock & Main Sts., Hanover; (603) 643-4300; (800) 443-7024; FAX: (603) 646-3744
■ A "lovely little inn" "owned by Dartmouth College" and overlooking the campus and the Hanover Green; guests, who can avail themselves of college facilities, give good grades to the Georgian brick hostelry's "genteel elegance", "excellent dining" ("lunch is a bargain"), "cheerful staff" and "cozy rooms"; but be advised: "get the right room and you're in Early American heaven, get the wrong room and you're in a broom closet."

Holderness

Manor on Golden Pond 24R (3S)   ▽ 19 | 20 | 20 | 19 | $177
Rte. 3 & Shepard Hill Rd., Holderness; (603) 968-3348; (800) 545-2141; FAX: (603) 968-2116
■ "Out of a magazine on how the rich decorate" but still "comfortable and relaxing", this 1907 English-style manor house provides "lots" of activities year-round, including swimming, canoeing, fishing and ice skating on "splendid" Squam Lake (where parts of *On Golden Pond* were filmed); a few feel "it needs a renovation and dusting", but "each room has individual personality" and kudos confirm this inn is a "very gracious place"; children under 12 are not invited.

Jackson

Christmas Farm Inn 25R (11S)   21 23 22 23 $161
Box CC, Rte. 16B, Jackson; (603) 383-4313; (800) HI-ELVES; FAX: (603) 383-6495
■ A "really friendly" family resort that's "equally charming for adults and children" ("where else can you get a room called Blitzen?"); "good food and good value" keep spirits festive year-round: the original 1778 farmhouse, 1786 main inn and adjoining cottages serve as a "delightful winter retreat" and "home of x-country skiing", and the outdoor pool and "lovely setting" satisfy summer sojourners too.

Eagle Mountain House 93R (30S)   18 21 19 21 $120
Carter Notch Rd., Jackson; (603) 383-9111; (800) 966-5779; FAX: (603) 383-0854
■ "Fine, old-fashioned mountain hotel" done in white clapboard Victorian style that attracts business groups as well as families; in winter the "classic Currier & Ives setting" is "ideal for x-country skiing" (a trailhead is across the road), in summer there's trout fishing and golfing, and in every season it's "close to outlet shopping"; concerns that "rooms are a bit drab" are eased by the health club's cedar saunas and whirlpool or afternoon tea in the "great common area."

Lincoln

Mountain Club on Loon 117R (117S)   ▽ 26 21 19 22 $152
Rte. 112/Kancamagus Hwy., Lincoln; (603) 745-8111; (800) 229-STAY; FAX: (603) 745-2317
■ "Excellent ski-in/ski-out accommodations" at an "unbeatable price for the view you wake up with" are central to this "nature lover's paradise" – a modern, year-round resort aside Loon Mountain in the heart of the White Mountain National Forest; accolades abound for the "wonderful services" at this "secluded" corporate retreat that's also "family friendly"; the "many facilities available" range from tennis courts and mountain biking to indoor/outdoor pools and a spa center.

Meredith

Inn at Mill Falls 55R   ▽ 22 18 19 19 $147
Rtes. 3 & 25, Meredith; (603) 279-7006; (800) 622-6455; FAX: (603) 279-6797
■ "A whole self-sufficient complex" snug to the shores of Lake Winnipesaukee and centered around a historic linen mill transformed into a contemporary country inn; surveyors say it's "out of the way, but charming and a good place to hang 'em up"; along with "welcoming staff" and "excellent food", there's shopping at the Mill Falls Marketplace just a short walk across a covered bridge; be advised that during leaf-peeping season it's "kind of bus-toury."

North Conway

Four Points Hotel by Sheraton   21 19 17 19 $125
North Conway 189R (11S)
(fka Sheraton Inn North Conway)
PO Box 3189, Rte. 16 at Settlers' Green, North Conway; (603) 356-9300; (800) 648-4397; FAX: (603) 356-9300
☑ "Near all the outlets" in a "shopping-crazy town", boosters find this to be an oasis that's "comfortable and a good value" (especially the "midweek package") with "large rooms", a "nice health spa" and "great service", making it just possibly "the best of the chain"; critics with another point of view carry on that this "touristy" "plain-Jane hotel with no character" has "spartan rooms" and "needs to improve dining."

White Mountain Hotel and Resort 69R (11S)   22 22 21 20 $127
PO Box 1828, Hale's Location, West Side Rd., North Conway; (603) 356-7100; (800) 533-6301; FAX: (603) 356-7100
■ A "magnificent setting" at the base of Whitehorse Ledge and alongside Echo Lake State Park and "friendly service" are the stuff of fond memories for visitors to this modern white clapboard resort; family and corporate guests "would definitely return" to use the nine-hole golf course, tennis courts, fitness center and year-round-heated pool, though some caution that "rooms are a little small for a family of four."

Portsmouth

Sise Inn 29R (8S)   ▽ 22 | 20 | 16 | 20 | $120
40 Court St., Portsmouth; (603) 433-1200; (800) 267-0525; FAX: (603) 433-1200
■ "About perfect – everything looks good, everything works" say fans of this 1881 Queen Anne mansion set five blocks from the historic Strawberry Bank district and five minutes from the ocean; despite stray regrets about "small", "fairly nondescript" quarters and "no dining room" (although an "enormous self-serve breakfast" is complimentary), admirers who "aren't interested in too much luxury" applaud its "obliging staff" and "good public areas", calling it a "lovely place to stay", even "a treasure."

Waterville Valley

Snowy Owl Inn 80R (1S)   19 | 19 | 18 | 19 | $134
Village Rd., Waterville Valley; (603) 236-8383; (800) 766-9969; FAX: (603) 236-4890
■ A "gem in the White Mountains", this three-story barnlike timber lodge offers "comfortable rooms", "spacious public areas" (the lobby is warmed by five fieldstone fireplaces) and "beautiful scenery"; a few dissenters find the premises "dull" with only "adequate rooms", but execs vote with the majority, saying it's "very nice for meetings" and (although "pricey in season") generally a "good value."

Waterville Valley Resort & Conference Center 1000R   ▽ 18 | 18 | 17 | 19 | $121
PO Box 252, Town Sq., Waterville Valley; (603) 236-8311; (800) 468-2553; FAX: (603) 236-4344
■ After hopping off the "convenient shuttle bus to/from the slopes", skiers sink into the "nice heated outdoor pool in winter" at this resort/conference-center complex made up of five independent lodges in the heart of the White Mountain National Forest; golfers tee off on a nine-hole course and tennis buffs serve on 20 courts, while year-round conference-goers meet in 23 rooms (the largest seats 2,500); of course there are "good shops" for browsing.

New Jersey

	R	S	D	P	$

Atlantic Palace Suites (177S)
(fka Ramada Boardwalk Plaza Suite Hotel)

▽ 16 | 14 | 10 | 12 | $120

1507 Boardwalk, Atlantic City; (609) 344-1200; (800) 527-8483; FAX: (609) 348-8772

■ Although centrally located, this recently renamed property doesn't appear to have a large following, but most who know it like the "large, clean, condo-like" suites, all with "excellent Jacuzzis"; the current low rates, due largely to ongoing renovations of the restaurant and spa, also are appealing.

Bally's Park Place - Hilton Casino Resort
1095R (160S)

21 | 19 | 18 | 19 | $137

Boardwalk & Park Pl., Atlantic City; (609) 340-2000; (800) 772-7777; FAX: (609) 340-1725

☑ The "best of the Boardwalk" delights players with a 40,000-square-foot "incredible spa", an array of dining facilities (10 restaurants, including AC's highly rated Prime Place steakhouse) and a good, central location; while some get a kick out of "lots of glitter", especially in the casino, others complain about "bored staff" and many caution "avoid the old Dennis Hotel section" and "stick to the Tower", where rooms are "beautiful."

Caesars Atlantic City 447R (194S)

20 | 19 | 19 | 18 | $137

2100 Pacific Ave., Atlantic City; (609) 348-4411; (800) 443-0104; FAX: (609) 348-8830

☑ "Friends, countrymen, lend me your ears – Caesars has been the best in AC for years" rhapsodize those who favor its "flashy, exciting" ambiance; however, others chant "overdone", "cheesy" and turn thumbs down on the Roman-themed decor; a $280-million expansion project due for completion in 1998 will add another tower, more restaurants, a 20,000-square-foot ballroom and meeting space, plus expand the casino, perhaps changing the votes of those who lament it's "getting kind of shabby."

Claridge Casino Hotel 431R (75S)

16 | 17 | 16 | 15 | $119

Indiana Ave. & Park Pl., Atlantic City; (609) 340-3400; (800) 257-8585; FAX: (609) 340-3131

☑ "Decent and homey", this "old but pleasant" hostelry "with a warm, family feeling" and "pretty good rooms" is reportedly the "smallest of AC casinos", making it "AC's version of intimate"; the staff generally earns plaudits, but even they "can't help" according to critics who dismiss its charms as "below average."

Harrah's Casino Hotel 505R (240S)

21 | 21 | 19 | 20 | $132

777 Harrah's Blvd., Atlantic City; (609) 441-5000; (800) 427-7247; FAX: (609) 348-6057

■ "Far from the madding crowd" and therefore "more civilized", this recently expanded bayfront casino hotel (400 new rooms) offers a "nice setting" overlooking an active marina about a mile and a half from the Boardwalk; there are "nice rooms", "good service" and a "user-friendly atmosphere" enhanced by facilities for toddlers and teens (wall-to-wall video games, outdoor miniature golf); only a few world-weary critics sigh that "it's adequate, nothing special."

Hilton Atlantic City 293R (197S)
(fka Bally's Grand)

22 | 20 | 19 | 19 | $139

Boardwalk Ave. & Boston, Atlantic City; (609) 347-7111; (800) 257-8677; FAX: (609) 340-4858

■ Guests like this "grand" and glossy beachfront hotel (reminiscent of the showy caravansaries of 1960s Miami Beach) for its "large, spacious" accommodations with "terrific bathrooms" ("oo-la-la, don't miss those giant tubs for two"); a "first-rate staff" and "good spa" plus the "great dinner buffet" in the Cornucopia Cafe enhance the experience; but while "it's quieter at this end" of town, a few partyers are distressed that it's also "away from the action"; current construction is adding 300 rooms.

Marriott Seaview Resort 266R (34S)

21 | 23 | 21 | 23 | $176

401 S. New York Rd., Absecon; (609) 652-1800; (800) 932-8000; FAX: (609) 652-2307

☑ "Great for golfers" given 36 holes but "no slots" or casino at this "old-money", "country club–style", "beautiful shore resort" that fans call a "classy alternative" to "the AC action", a 15-minute free shuttle away; "nice facilities" include jogging trails, indoor/outdoor pools, 10 tennis courts and a fitness center, and the Brigantine Wildlife Refuge is nearby; there are a few plaints about "slightly weary furnishings" and those who booked it by mistake grumble "it's in the middle of nowhere."

Merv Griffin's Resorts Casino Hotel 517R (145S)   16 | 16 | 17 | 16 | $125
1133 Boardwalk, Atlantic City; (609) 344-6000; (800) 366-MERV; FAX: (609) 340-7684
☑ A "grand, old hotel with plenty of panache" proclaim partisans of the former Chalfonte-Haddon Hall (the belle of the Boardwalk before Miss America came on the scene); but despite several "superb restaurants" (including the highly rated French, Le Palais, plus "romantic" Capriccio and the Camelot steakhouse), a casino and a "nice" health club (offering Swedish and shiatsu massage), reactions vary wildly, from "beautiful rooms with good service" to "what a dump", "rude personnel", "get me outta here."

Sands Hotel & Casino 534R (56S)   18 | 18 | 19 | 18 | $133
Indiana Ave. & Brighton Park, Atlantic City; (609) 441-4000; (800) AC-SANDS; FAX: (609) 441-4180
☑ The "great location" (a block off the Boardwalk, near other big casinos and not far from the convention center) pleases players who want to spread their action around; admirers praise "good food" (including a "great spread" at Epic Buffet), "good shows", "friendly staff" and a "pleasant, comfortable" atmosphere; but other views range from "it serves its purpose" and "typical AC" to "it's seen better days", "run-down and cheesy."

Showboat Casino Hotel 800R   19 | 19 | 17 | 18 | $124
801 Boardwalk, Atlantic City; (609) 343-4000; (800) 621-0200; FAX: (609) 343-4057
■ Expanded in 1995, this New Orleans–themed casino hotel on the north end of the Boardwalk has "comfortable rooms", a "good staff" and a "fun, carnival atmosphere" accented by strolling Dixieland bands – it's like "a year-round Mardi Gras"; there's something for everyone, so "bring the kids if they like to bowl" and for grown-ups, "massage is a must"; it may not be a top choice for serious players, but "they insist you have a good time."

Tropicana Casino & Resort 1370R (254S)   18 | 17 | 16 | 18 | $124
(fka TropWorld Casino & Entertainment Resort)
Boardwalk & Brighton Ave., Atlantic City; (609) 340-4000; (800) THE-TROP; FAX: (609) 343-5211
☑ A $100-million expansion has made the Trop the largest hotel in NJ, but bigger isn't necessarily better according to skeptics who claim "the so-called 'all new' is really nothing new": 3,200 slots, 154 table games and the Poker/Keno/Simulcast Club can add up to "more activities than you need" and make for a "more chaotic" feel at this Tivoli Pier–themed resort on the south end of the Boardwalk; a plus for budget-watchers: it's one of AC's cheapest casino hotels.

Trump Plaza Hotel & Casino 792R (103S)   20 | 18 | 18 | 19 | $141
Boardwalk & Mississippi Ave., Atlantic City; (609) 441-6000; (800) 677-7378; FAX: (609) 441-6916
■ The Donald runs "a good casino hotel with nice amenities" according to many visitors who find it "glitzy" but "not excessively" so; the center-of-the-Boardwalk site connecting to the convention center wins approval as do "excellent" restaurants such as Ivanka's for Contemporary American fare and Max's for steaks; guests enjoy "beautiful ocean views" from some rooms and the staff is "helpful", but avoid the "3 PM check-in rush."

Trump's Castle Casino Resort 563R (162S)   21 | 19 | 18 | 19 | $130
(nka Trump Marina Hotel Casino)
Huron Ave. & Brigantine Blvd., Atlantic City; (609) 441-2000; (800) 777-8477; FAX: (609) 441-8541
☑ The "fanciful medieval" decor is "very Trumpian" at this away-from-the-Boardwalk casino hotel whose location in the Farley Marina area is considered "more relaxed"; the Portofino restaurant is hailed as a "class act with water views" and "you might even see Donald"; but critics rate the rooms only "ok" to "adequate", and there are a few who still wonder "what possesses this man to build these garish monuments?"

Trump Taj Mahal Casino Resort 980R (270S)   21 | 19 | 19 | 20 | $148
1000 Boardwalk, Atlantic City; (609) 449-1000; (800) 825-8888; FAX: (609) 449-6818
☑ "A spectacle" that's like "India in NJ", the casino-equipped Taj may appeal to those who like "glitzy fun", prefer "purple and pink" to beige and white and are willing to "just enjoy and don't take it seriously", but don't be fooled – serious gaming goes on here; opinions vary widely as to whether the "biggest Trump" is "too big" ("wear sneakers or you'll never make it back to your room") and service is "friendly" or "surly", but the majority wisdom seems to be that "if you go to AC, you might as well go the gaudiest."

Trump World's Fair Casino 462R (38S)   ▽ 15 | 12 | 13 | 14 | $137
(fka Trump Regency)
2500 Boardwalk, Atlantic City; (609) 441-6000; (800) 677-7378; FAX: (609) 441-7881
☑ With meeting rooms accommodating up to 2,000 and a location next door to the convention center, this casino hotel appeals largely to conventioneers; opinions vary from "a good choice at reasonable prices" to "depressing" with service to match; cynics say that "when Trump Plaza overbooks they put you here."

Basking Ridge

Olde Mill Inn 96R (6S)
16 | 16 | 17 | 15 | $128

225 Rte. 202, Basking Ridge; (908) 221-1100; FAX: (908) 221-1560

☑ "Back to earth and reality, this is a lovely stop" right off the multilane monotony of I-287; roving respondents report that this venerable inn is "a very nice facility with a caring staff", offering "a pleasant overnight stay" in a traditional-style property as well as a "charming restaurant" in an adjacent colonial-era grain house; others are less enthusiastic, finding it "nothing special" and "overpriced" for "small" guestrooms.

Beach Haven

Green Gables Inn & Restaurant 4R (2S)
▽ 18 | 22 | 22 | 20 | $144

212 Centre St., Beach Haven; (609) 492-3553; (800) 492-0492; FAX: (609) 492-2507

☑ "Very quaint and near everything", this oceanside 1890 Victorian inn on Long Beach Island is favored by fans as a "quiet", "romantic" summer destination; the prix fixe, five-course New American dinners prepared by innkeeper-chef Adolfo Martino are "fantastic" and there's a "lovely afternoon tea too"; however, a few voters aren't charmed by "little, musty, dusty" rooms with "not enough amenities."

Cape May

Abbey, The 12R (2S)
▽ 22 | 21 | 21 | 21 | $140

34 Gurney St., Cape May; (609) 884-4506; FAX: (609) 884-2379

☑ "Afternoon tea is highly recommended" at this Victorian Gothic B&B, originally an adjoining summer villa and cottage for a 19th-century coal baron and family (tours of the grand public rooms are offered to nonguests); period furnishings add to the charm.

Angel of the Sea 27R
24 | 23 | 23 | 22 | $179

5-7 Trenton Ave., Cape May; (609) 884-3369; (800) 848-3369; FAX: (609) 884-3331

■ "A gorgeous B&B in a prime location", this "dreamy" Angel "lives up to its name in many respects"; dating from 1850 and renovated in 1988, the double-winged Victorian beauty just may be "the most romantic place in Cape May"; while rooms are mostly "cute" and "quaint", there are stray cautions that "not all are great, especially when they don't overlook the ocean"; bikes are available for casual explorations.

Chalfonte, The 60R (2S)
15 | 19 | 20 | 19 | $128

PO Box 475, 301 Howard St., Cape May; (609) 884-8409; FAX: (609) 884-4588

☑ "Southern hospitality" and "delicious Southern cooking" in the Magnolia Room (breakfast and dinner are included in room rates) are the lure at this erstwhile boarding house built in 1876 by a Cape May Civil War hero; in the center of the Historic District, three blocks from the beach, its "great porch" is the place to rock but not roll; downers are "plain rooms with bathrooms down the hall" (only 11 have private bath) and "no a/c" or TV; open June to mid-September, then weekends to Columbus Day.

MAINSTAY INN 9R (7S)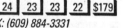
25 | 25 | 23 | 24 | $153

635 Columbia Ave., Cape May; (609) 884-8690

■ This "attractive Victorian inn" with "gorgeous" antiques-filled rooms is "a class act" – "the grand lady that sets standards and lets guests relax"; a block from the beach in the Historic District, it was built in 1872 as a gentlemen's gambling club, but today surveyors tout "tea on the veranda – it's a must" and "a great host and hostess"; a few warn that some rooms "lack a/c."

Queen Victoria, The 17R (6S)
24 | 23 | 22 | 21 | $152

102 Ocean St., Cape May; (609) 884-8702

■ "They could film a movie here it's so charming" say devotees of this trio of Historic District houses just one block from the beach; "the best B&B at the Jersey shore" say buffs, explaining that it "can't be beat" for "clean and pretty rooms" with "comfy beds"; while many jump into the swim and even advise to "splurge on a suite with whirlpool", a minority opines "too cutesy"; N.B. full breakfast and PM tea are included in rates.

Virginia Hotel 24R
23 | 23 | 26 | 20 | $182

PO Box 557, 25 Jackson St., Cape May; (609) 884-5700; (800) 732-4236; FAX: (609) 884-1236

■ A "luxurious" place with "warm ambiance and friendly staff", this small 1879 hotel in the Historic District, steps from the beach, has "nice" rooms (some with private porches) and conference space; it serves "the best breakfast in your room", "a wonderful afternoon tea" (pastry fanciers should "insist on the almond squares") and for dinner, the "fabulous" New American fare in the Ebbitt Room just could be "best in the area."

Hope

Inn at Millrace Pond 17R
▽ 23 | 23 | 25 | 23 | $116

PO Box 359, Rte. 519, Hope; (908) 459-4884; (800) 7-INNHOPE; FAX: (908) 459-5276
⬛ "Get away from it all" at this "great" inn, a picturesque (but not cutesy) Moravian settlement founded in 1769 and now on the National Register of Historic Places; "very sweet and tranquil", with period furnishings, fireplaces and surrounding landmark buildings that include an 18th-century limestone gristmill, it provides a real "step back in time", while the "terrific" regional cooking offers very of-the-moment satisfactions.

Lambertville

Inn at Lambertville Station 37R (8S)
20 | 20 | 19 | 18 | $129

11 Bridge St., Lambertville; (609) 397-4400; (800) 524-1091; FAX: (609) 397-9744
✓ "Every room is different" at this antiques-filled Victorian-style inn (built in 1986) overlooking the Delaware River just across from New Hope, PA; with "great food" and a lobby that "looks like an old-time lodge", it has the makings for "a perfect weekend getaway"; but what's "quaint and tasteful" to fans is a "glorified Holiday Inn" to phobes; be advised that "some rooms are way superior to others."

Long Beach

Ocean Place Hilton Resort & Spa 249R (5S)
19 | 18 | 18 | 20 | $135

1 Ocean Blvd., Long Beach; (908) 571-4000; (800) HILTONS; FAX: (908) 571-8974
✓ "Right on the beach", this mid-rise is "a pleasant surprise" for those who appreciate that each of the "good rooms" has a balcony "with great views"; health-conscious types like "the terrific spa", offering everything from mud baths to herbal wraps; but plenty of surveyors may need more than that to relax, given a "quite run-down neighborhood", "staff that's not very friendly" and a lobby that "screams wedding factory."

Morristown

Headquarters Plaza Hotel 252R (4S)
17 | 17 | 17 | 15 | $135

3 Headquarters Plaza, Morristown; (201) 898-9100; (800) 225-1942; FAX: (201) 292-0112
✓ This modern high-rise is called "the best in the area", especially for "business travelers" who appreciate its 23,000 square feet spread over 22 meeting venues and the "best banquet facilities"; although it offers "clean, comfortable rooms" and "very good" services, some correspondents contend it's "a suburban yawn" where "you have to walk through a busy shopping mall to get to the health club and pool."

Princeton

Chauncey Conference Center 96R (4S)
▽ 21 | 20 | 21 | 22 | $163

Rosedale Rd., Princeton; (609) 921-3600; FAX: (609) 683-4958
✓ "A great secluded place in a wooded setting" – "like a college dorm, but on a beautiful campus"; facilities for small- to mid-size meetings, an outdoor pool, tennis courts and "terrific service" help make it a good place to confer; but those who find it too quiet wind up sighing "dullsville."

Forrestal, The 281R (10S)
19 | 20 | 19 | 19 | $142

(fka Scanticon Hotel)
100 College Rd. E., Princeton; (609) 452-7800; (800) 222-1131; FAX: (609) 452-7883
✓ Partisans consider this facility near the Ivy League school "probably the best conference center we've ever seen", a "treasure in the woods" with "Scandinavian atmosphere"; "top-notch amenities" include a fully equipped fitness center and stunning glass-enclosed pool, and the "wonderful" food and service also win plaudits; critics, however, cavil that the place can be "crowded and noisy" and the rooms "dreary like a dorm", concluding "very ordinary."

Hyatt Regency Princeton 348R (14S)
19 | 20 | 18 | 18 | $138

102 Carnegie Ctr., Princeton; (609) 987-1234; (800) 233-1234; FAX: (609) 987-2584
✓ When it comes to Hyatt, "large and predictable" usually means a "good business hotel", so many execs like this entry in a 500-acre Princeton office park a mile from the university; "nice rooms" and a "gardenlike atmosphere" in the skylit atrium lobby also please some voters; but "predictable" can also mean to some an "impersonal", "sterile" facility that's "too corporate"; service ranges from "helpful" to "confused."

Marriott Princeton 290R (4S)   20 │ 20 │ 17 │ 19 │ $123
201 Village Blvd., Princeton; (609) 457-7900; (800) 242-8689; FAX: (609) 452-1223
☑ "Clean, crisp", "modern" and "surprisingly lovely for a business hotel", this facility is set in an imitation-village shopping mall dotted with "great factory outlets"; it attracts vacationers with "good weekend deals" and has "nice" restaurant options, including Japanese teppanyaki dining; however, guests disinterested in reliving academic days complain "the rooms are like college dorms", and business travelers say it's "just another cookie-cutter Marriott."

Nassau Inn 190R (26S)   17 │ 19 │ 18 │ 19 │ $147
10 Palmer Sq., Princeton; (609) 921-7500; (800) 862-7728; FAX: (609) 921-9385
☑ Reeking of "frayed gentility", "the old Nass" (an inn since 1756) "has a great location" surrounded by shops in the heart of Princeton, just a two-minute walk from the ivy-clad campus; "the great downstairs bar" (the Yankee Doodle Tap Room, with a famous Norman Rockwell mural) exudes colonial ambiance; but doubters say that guestrooms, while "charming", are "not very comfortable" (some "are the size of broom closets") and there are pros and cons about public spaces "overrun with loyal Princeton alumni."

Short Hills

HILTON AT SHORT HILLS 269R (31S)   25 │ 25 │ 25 │ 23 │ $179
41 JFK Pkwy., Short Hills; (201) 379-0100; (800) HILTONS; FAX: (201) 379-6870
■ "A luxury oasis amid the sprawl of NJ", this handsome hotel offers "opulence in the 'burbs" across the street from the "upscale" Mall at Short Hills; "attentive service", "top-notch rooms" and a "standout spa" all earn mountains of praise, as does the "exceptional" Dining Room, offering some of the state's best Continental fare; so while an unimpressed few call it "pretentious in the extreme", the consensus is "nothing less than a jewel."

Spring Lake

Breakers, The 64R   19 │ 20 │ 19 │ 19 │ $165
1507 Ocean Ave., Spring Lake; (908) 449-7700; FAX: (908) 449-0161
☑ "The setting could not be prettier" at this Victorian oceanfront resort with an outdoor pool "right across the street from the beach", and "picturesque" Spring Lake is replete with historic houses, good shops and a quiet air of affluence; but "a lot of weddings" (i.e. too many), "small rooms", only "ok" food (the restaurant is open only on weekends in winter and early spring) and a "stuffy crowd" ("someone ought to tell those people to lighten up") mean it's not for everybody.

Sea Crest by the Sea 10R (2S)   – │ – │ – │ – │ E
19 Tuttle Ave., Spring Lake; (908) 449-9031; (800) 803-9031; FAX: (908) 974-0403
With the emphasis on romantic ambiance (that means no kids or pets), this ornate 1885 Queen Anne inn an hour south of NYC aims to enchant with luxuriously decorated theme guestrooms (Victorian Rosebud, Casablanca, etc.), many with fireplaces and some with Jacuzzis and ocean views; the inn provides beach and tennis passes as well as bicycles for exploring the quiet Victorian town; afternoon tea and continental breakfast are included in rates.

Summit

Grand Summit Hotel 132R (13S)   16 │ 18 │ 17 │ 17 │ $148
570 Springfield Ave., Summit; (908) 273-3000; (800) 346-0773; FAX: (908) 273-4228
☑ Those who appreciate its "classy, old-world" ambiance call this recently renovated hotel "a hidden gem" in a "great location for a quick getaway" (an affluent suburban setting 45 minutes from NYC); the Tudor-style structure dating from 1929 is on the National Register of Historic Places, but one person's jewel is another's rhinestone, so those indifferent to its charms can only cite "standard rooms, standard service."

Vernon

Great Gorge Village Hotel (112S)   15 │ 15 │ 13 │ 17 │ $141
Rte. 94, Vernon; (201) 827-2222; FAX: (201) 827-8115
☑ There's "beautiful scenery" at this year-round resort offering skiing in winter, nearby golf in summer and Action Park (self-described as the world's largest water park) "right down the road"; but the "serene" setting in the northwestern corner of NJ (a little over an hour's drive from NYC) doesn't appease those who say the facilities "need another face-lift" and call the food "poor" and the kitchen-equipped condo-style lodgings "tired."

New Mexico

	R	S	D	P	$

Crowne Plaza Pyramid 252R (59S)   20 | 19 | 17 | 19 | $110
(fka Holiday Inn Pyramid)
5151 San Francisco Rd. NE, Albuquerque; (505) 821-3333; (800) HOLIDAY; FAX: (505) 822-8115
☑ A recent upgrade to Crowne Plaza status may generate more enthusiasm for this architecturally "interesting" modern 10-story rendering of an Aztec pyramid, housing a pleasant atrium with waterfall and piano, along with a health club, indoor/outdoor pool, 16,000 square feet of meeting space and a SW-oriented restaurant; room improvements include additional amenities such as irons and ironing boards, coffeemakers and robes, and "friendly", "helpful" service is another plus, but the location (despite its Journal Center complex setting) strikes some as "isolated."

Doubletree Albuquerque 281R (13S)   17 | 18 | 16 | 16 | $110
201 Marquette Ave. NW, Albuquerque; (505) 247-3344; (800) 222-TREE; FAX: (505) 247-7025
☑ Connected by walkway to the convention center, this "pleasant" but "average" hotel earns the most praise for its location "right in the Downtown business district"; otherwise, it's an "average" facility with "good" (if occasionally "harried") service, "clean, neat" accommodations, an indoor pool and, for a nominal fee, use of a nearby health club; "great cookies" are "what you expect from Doubletree."

Hilton Albuquerque 262R (2S)   17 | 17 | 18 | 17 | $115
1901 University Blvd. NE, Albuquerque; (505) 884-2500; (800) HILTONS; FAX: (505) 889-9118
☑ Despite middling ratings, "one of the best restaurants in Albuquerque" (the Rancher's Club) distinguishes this "comfortable, business-oriented facility" in the university area that recently renovated all public and meeting spaces; some praise the new decor as a "breath of Southwestern fresh air" and appreciate "good" Sandia mountain views from balconies on higher floors, and considering its heated indoor and outdoor pools, sauna, fitness center and tennis courts, even critics who call it "typical" admit "nice enough."

Hyatt Regency Albuquerque 381R (14S)   22 | 21 | 19 | 20 | $135
330 Tijeras Ave. NW, Albuquerque; (505) 842-1234; (800) 233-1234; FAX: (505) 766-6710
■ This "well-located", "large, busy, modern" Downtown hotel "close to restaurants and shops" may offer "a standard Hyatt experience – nothing special yet quite comfortable", but it's nevertheless top-rated in Albuquerque, providing "beautiful rooms", a "very good restaurant" (McGrath's), a "very nice lobby", health club, pool, sauna and "excellent service"; fans "wish the big city boys would take charm lessons here."

La Posada de Albuquerque 111R (3S)   19 | 19 | 18 | 18 | $127
125 Second St. NW, Albuquerque; (505) 242-9090; (800) 777-5732; FAX: (505) 242-8664
☑ The "wonderful lobby" (and its "bar with pianist") is the star of the show at this "historic" '30s Spanish-style hotel listed on the National Register that even locals favor for the "great happy hour"; but unfortunately, most agree the "really lovely public rooms" are contrasted by "really dreary" guestrooms – maybe a '96 renovation will restore their "quaint charm"; for now, optimists focus on the "potential" and "beautiful views from the higher floors"; Conrad's Downtown gets good notices for its Spanish cuisine.

Marriott Albuquerque 411R (6S)   20 | 20 | 18 | 17 | $116
2101 Louisiana Blvd. NE, Albuquerque; (505) 228-9290; (800) 334-2086; FAX: (505) 888-2982
■ Among the "best in Albuquerque", this "well-kept" Marriott high-rise with a "Southwest motif" offers "clean, comfortable, quiet" quarters, a "friendly" staff and a "wonderful indoor/outdoor pool" with health club; the "decent location" offers access to shopping malls, and while there's some controversy over the food ("one of the best meals we've had" vs. "don't even think about dinner here"), most would agree it's "fine for a night or two, even just to view the mountains in the distance"; N.B. continental breakfast is included in the rates.

Sheraton Old Town 168R (20S)   19 | 18 | 16 | 17 | $114
800 Rio Grande Blvd. NW, Albuquerque; (505) 843-6300; (800) 237-2133; FAX: (505) 842-9863
☑ A location "convenient to Old Town" is the chief, and some say "only asset", of this otherwise "undistinguished" chain link, although there are kind words for the "large rooms with SW decor", "good service" and "architectural look" that matches "its neighborhood"; but even critics who point to "so-so", "run-down" facilities admit the shops, museums, galleries and restaurants "within walking distance" are a powerful draw, and there's a pool, fitness center and meeting space for groups of up to 300.

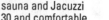

Chama

Lodge at Chama 9R (2S)

─|─|─|─| VE

PO Box 127, Chama; (505) 756-2133; FAX: (505) 756-2519
A small executive retreat also catering to those with deep pockets and a hankering for the great outdoors, this 32,000-acre working ranch and sporting lodge in the San Juan Mountains provides, for varying rates, rooms, meals, bar, guides, vehicles and equipment for hunting and fishing, and also offers horseback riding (including trail rides, cattle drives and sleigh rides), snowmobiling, hiking and more, with opportunities to observe diverse wildlife; the rock and timber lodge boasts a 20-foot wide fireplace, sauna and Jacuzzi (and lots of animal-head decor), meeting facilities for groups up to 30 and comfortable guestrooms including two suites with kiva fireplaces.

Chimayo

Hacienda Rancho de Chimayó 6R (1S)

─|─|─|─| I

PO Box 11, Chimayó; (505) 351-2222; FAX: (505) 351-4038
Run by the same family that serves up choice NM cooking at the renowned Rancho de Chimayó restaurant down the road, this restored adobe hacienda offers antiques-decorated rooms, each opening onto the courtyard and featuring a fireplace and private bath; on the scenic High Road to Taos, the mountain town of Chimayó is a center of Hispanic weaving, and its lovely Spanish Colonial church is known as the Lourdes of America for its associations with the miraculous; continental breakfast is included.

Cloudcroft

Lodge at Cloudcroft 42R (17S)

20 | 19 | 18 | 22 | $134

(fka The Lodge)
PO Box 497, 1 Corona Pl., Cloudcroft; (505) 682-2566; (800) 395-6343; FAX: (505) 682-2715
■ "Golf at 9,000 feet" is just one of the high-altitude year-round pleasures offered at this "perfect mountain retreat" in the southern Rockies; whether they stay in the "wonderful, restored" 1899 main lodge, the rustic Retreat (a four-bedroom home) or the Pavilion (a B&B), guests enjoy "nice rooms" (some with antiques and down comforters), "lovely public areas" and "good service and food" (the restaurant Rebecca's is named for the resident ghost), plus activities ranging from biking, hiking and swimming to nearby tennis, skiing and ice skating; in sum, "a real find."

Española

Rancho de San Juan 4R (4S)

─|─|─|─| E

PO Box 4140, Fairview Station, Española; (505) 753-6818; (800) 726-7121; FAX: (505) 753-6818
If looking for secluded luxury in a striking setting, look no further than this Relais & Châteaux member in the high desert foothills north of Santa Fe; centered around a Spanish/Pueblo–style hacienda, it coddles just a few guests at a time, putting them up in elegant, antiques–filled rooms and suites (all with fireplace and patio) and pampering them with the likes of massage and fine country French–Northern Italian dining; besides hiking, biking and lounging in the hot tub, the main activities here would seem to be contemplating mountain and river valley views and indulging in the good life.

Mescalero

Inn of the Mountain Gods 230R (13S)

20 | 19 | 18 | 24 | $122

PO Box 269, Carrizo Canyon Rd., Mescalero; (505) 257-5141; (800) 545-9011; FAX: (505) 257-6173
■ "The appeal is the scenery and gambling", not the "modest" lodgings offered at this "large-scale" mountain resort operated by the Mescalero Apache Tribe and set in the midst of their ruggedly "beautiful" reservation in south-central New Mexico (or, as some call it, "the middle of nowhere"); service could use some polish, but most are too busy enjoying the "fabulous" setting and hoping the mountain gods help them out at the casino to notice; for active types there's golf, tennis, swimming, boating and more.

Raton

Vermejo Park Ranch 50R (4S) ⌨

─|─|─|─| VE

W. Hwy. 555, Raton; (505) 445-3097; FAX: (505) 445-0545
As you'd expect from a property owned by Turner Enterprises, this ranch is *big*, set on close to 600,000 acres with 21 lakes and views of the Sangre de Cristo Mountains; comprised of eight stone Victorian houses and a log guest lodge, it's a paradise for sportsmen who head here to hunt and fish or simply take in the amazing scenery; rates include all meals; open seasonally.

Santa Fe
TOP 10 OVERALL

BEST OVERALL		BEST VALUES
26	Inn of the Anasazi	Grant Corner Inn
22	Bishop's Lodge	Radisson/Santa Fe
	Rancho Encantado	Santa Fe, Hotel
	Grant Corner Inn	Inn of the Governors
21	Eldorado Hotel	St. Francis, Hotel
	Inn on the Alameda	Inn at Loretto
20	Santa Fe, Hotel	Inn on the Alameda
	St. Francis, Hotel	Plaza Real, Hotel
19	Inn of the Governors	La Posada de Santa Fe
	La Fonda	Eldorado Hotel

R	S	D	P	$

Bishop's Lodge 70R (18S)   22 | 23 | 21 | 23 | $208
Bishop's Lodge Rd., Santa Fe; (505) 983-6377; (800) 732-2240; FAX: (505) 989-8739
■ "Authentic SW ambiance just an adobe's throw from the center of town" makes this historic ranch resort "the best choice in Santa Fe", especially for families, since there's "lots for kids and parents to do" including a highly praised children's program in summer; just minutes to Downtown, it offers what most call "great", "rustic" rooms, "lovely grounds, pool and hot tub", riding, fishing, tennis and much more; despite a few warnings about "cold staff", most praise this "magical blend of history, comfort and scenery."

Eldorado Hotel 201R (18S)   22 | 22 | 20 | 22 | $187
309 W. San Francisco St., Santa Fe; (505) 988-4455; (800) 955-4455; FAX: (505) 995-4543
◪ The Downtown location means you can "walk to everything" and the "large, beautiful lobby" is a "happy hour" favorite, but otherwise reactions are mixed for this "big hotel in a small city"; some praise "large rooms", "great butlers" (a complimentary service for deluxe rooms and suites) and "tasteful" SW decor, while others gripe about "tissue-paper walls", an "impersonal", "grand" ambiance "not in keeping with low-key Santa Fe" and a pool that's "way too small"; one thing most agree about is it's "great" for conferences.

237

Grant Corner Inn 9R (3S)
20 | 23 | 25 | 19 | $142
122 Grant Ave., Santa Fe; (505) 983-6678; FAX: (505) 983-1526
■ "If you like B&Bs", chances are "you'll like this" colonial manor (circa 1905) just two blocks from the Plaza in Downtown Santa Fe; "beautiful rooms, great location, fabulous [included] breakfasts" sum it up for many as the "ultimate feel-good experience", with antiques in the rooms, complimentary wine in the evenings, access to nearby fitness facilities (for a small fee) and local attractions to fill the day; the inn also operates a nearby SW-style condominium with two guestrooms, living room and kitchen.

Inn at Loretto 141R (6S)
20 | 19 | 18 | 19 | $153
211 Old Santa Fe Trail, Santa Fe; (505) 988-5531; (800) 727-5531; FAX: (505) 984-7988
☑ Under new ownership since '96 when it was purchased by Noble House Hotels & Resorts, this Downtown Pueblo-style hotel has recently completed a $3.7-million (post-*Survey*) renovation of lobby, guestrooms, restaurants and meeting space; already praised as a "lovely building" in an "excellent location" with "everything at your fingertips", its just "so-so" rooms may receive better notices next time around; it offers an outdoor pool, deli and restaurant, and shares grounds with the historic Loretto Chapel.

INN OF THE ANASAZI 59R
26 | 26 | 27 | 24 | $232
113 Washington Ave., Santa Fe; (505) 988-3030; (800) 688-8100; FAX: (505) 988-3277
■ Tops in Santa Fe as well as the state, this "beautiful, almost spiritual retreat" with "wonderful amenities and quality" offers a "whole new level of class for SF", from its "refined" but "authentic Southwestern style" and "great" central location to its "lovely", "comfortable" rooms and "fabulous food and service"; all of the "casually elegant" (if "smallish") accommodations feature gaslit fireplaces, four-poster beds, Indian rugs and organic toiletries, and the "superlative" Anasazi restaurant offers "outstanding" nouvelle Southwestern cuisine; this is one lodging where the chorus is unanimous: "magnificent."

Inn Of The Governors 94R (6S)
20 | 20 | 19 | 19 | $147
234 Don Gaspar Ave., Santa Fe; (505) 982-4333; (800) 234-4534; FAX: (505) 989-9149
☑ "Romantic rooms with fireplaces and balconies" are the top-drawer choice at this "pleasant", "smallish hotel" with "very Santa Fe decor" that's "close" to the Plaza "but not on top of it"; although it may be "average quality", the "inexpensive" rates, "well-kept" facilities, "nice staff" and "cozy" ambiance add up to "great value" for many.

Inn On The Alameda 58R (9S)
22 | 23 | 20 | 20 | $172
303 E. Alemeda St., Santa Fe; (505) 984-2121; (800) 289-2122; FAX: (505) 986-8325
■ "Comfortable and luxurious", this "lovely" Pueblo Revival–style inn offers "charming rooms", many with "romantic fireplaces", as well as balconies or patios facing the inner gardened courtyard; the "very hospitable staff" sets out a "magnificent breakfast" (included in rates), and this "absolutely pleasant, friendly place" is "within walking distance of the Plaza"; while there's no restaurant, there are two open-air whirlpools to ease those gams after a day of sight-seeing.

La Fonda 132R (21S)
19 | 20 | 18 | 21 | $154
100 E. San Francisco St., Santa Fe; (505) 982-5511; (800) 523-5002; FAX: (505) 982-6367
☑ "A classic", this historic "authentic adobe in a wonderful location" at the end of the Santa Fe Trail (an inn has been at this site since 1610, putting up many celebs over the years) may be "getting a bit run-down and crowded", but a host of defenders swears it "retains its rustic charm" with "funky", "unique" "period" rooms and suites (some with fireplaces) and a "great roof bar"; the hotel also offers an outdoor pool, hot tubs, restaurants and 13,000 square feet of meeting space, but critics who call it "tired" say it's also "too expensive and taken with itself" and leave it to "history buffs and bus tours."

La Posada de Santa Fe 79R (40S)
20 | 20 | 18 | 19 | $161
330 E. Palace Ave., Santa Fe; (505) 986-0000; (800) 727-5276; FAX: (505) 982-6850
☑ All are enchanted by the "beautiful grounds" of this historic hostelry, but variable accommodations bring a wide range of responses; comprised of adobe cottages surrounding an 1882 Victorian mansion, it has admirers who proclaim it a "gem in Santa Fe", applauding its "very romantic" "cute casitas with fireplaces" and "old-world charm"; others decry "small rooms" that are "slightly run-down" and "unimaginative"; the hotel is constantly renovating (20 rooms were completely redone in '96), so it seems safest to insist on the "remodeled rooms" that are "far superior."

Plaza Real, Hotel 12R (44S)
20 | 20 | 18 | 18 | $157
125 Washington Ave., Santa Fe; (505) 988-4900; (800) 279-7325; FAX: (505) 983-9322
☑ "Great value and location" equal "unpretentious charm" for most surveyors who seem satisfied with this small, SW-style hotel just a half-block from the Plaza; "nice suite rooms", nearly all with fireplaces and some offering balconies with views of the Sangre de Cristo Mountains, are part of the "very pleasant" ambiance, though a vocal minority insists it "needs refreshing" and cite variations in service.

Preston House 13R (2S)   ▽ 23 | 23 | 22 | 21 | $130
106 Faithway St., Santa Fe; (505) 982-3465; FAX: (505) 982-3465
■ A "lovely B&B within walking distance to town" has developed a small following
for its "fine rooms and location"; comprised of a restored Victorian house and an
adobe compound across the street, it offers lodgings that "vary greatly" both in style
and amenities (some with fireplace and private bath), with one guest favoring the
Southwestern "annex with more comfortable rooms and privacy"; continental breakfast
and afternoon tea with desserts is included in rates; no restaurant, but many nearby.

Radisson Hotel Santa Fe 116R (44S)   15 | 17 | 15 | 15 | $108
(fka Picacho Plaza Hotel)
750 N. St. Francis Dr., Santa Fe; (505) 982-5591; (800) 333-3333; FAX: (505) 988-2821
☑ With a location that's either "out of the way" or "great if you don't want to be in the
middle of things", this Southwestern "adobe-like construction blending in with super
mountain views is a relaxing setting" that's "reasonably priced" and "friendly"; but the
harsher view is that it's "pedestrian" ("you could be anywhere"); in either case, "they
try", offering a "fine pool", health club privileges next door, and accommodations ranging
from standard rooms to suites and condos featuring kivas, wet bars, decks and kitchens.

Rancho Encantado 29R (38S)   23 | 22 | 22 | 23 | $231
State Rd. 592, Santa Fe; (505) 982-3537; (800) 722-9339; FAX: (505) 983-8269
■ "Beautiful in every way", this "rural paradise" just outside Tesuque is "like it was in the
old days", offering "gorgeous villas" with Southwestern decor, "glorious desert views", a
"very helpful staff", "excellent food" and "whopper margaritas"; the ranch offers a wide
array of outdoor adventure, including horseback riding (natch), hiking, two tennis courts
and a pool, and almost all guestrooms have fireplaces; despite children's programs, some
say they "get bored" and it's "too far from the action" for a few city birds, but for "dazzling
natural beauty" it's tough to top; the "excellent" restaurant offers contemporary SW food.

Santa Fe, Hotel 40R (91S)   22 | 22 | 17 | 20 | $149
1501 Paseo de Peralta, Santa Fe; (505) 982-1200; (800) 825-9876; FAX: (505) 984-2211
■ "Great Native American decor" and storytelling by the lobby's kiva fireplace reflect
the part-ownership of the Picuris People at this "lovely and comfortable" Pueblo-style
hotel; while "a little out of the way" in the Guadalupe District, it's still "within walking
distance to the Plaza" (with a shuttle for those who disagree) and features "big suites for
the money" and a "small but pretty pool"; many praise the "pleasant help" and "nice
breakfast" (not included) and those who cry out it "desperately needs a restaurant"
will be happy to note the full-service Corn Dance Cafe, offering Native American fare.

St. Francis, Hotel 81R (2S)   18 | 21 | 20 | 21 | $152
210 Don Gaspar Ave., Santa Fe; (505) 983-5700; (800) 529-5700; FAX: (505) 989-7690
☑ This "small, elegant, historic hotel" offers "considerable charm and a super location" one
block from the Plaza; set in a '20s Federal-style National Register structure, it has a
"lovely" lobby combining SW touches such as clay tile floors with period furnishings,
and "small but well-appointed rooms" (each is unique); a "very helpful concierge" and
afternoon tea (not included in rates) on the veranda are winners, and the "marvelous"
restaurant, the Club, provides a "beautiful setting for dining" in the garden patio; on
the downside, some find the "cozy" quarters simply too "cramped" (although a range
of sizes is available) and in need of a "face-lift."

Taos

Casa Benavides 31R   24 | 22 | 22 | 15 | $153
137 Kit Carson Rd. E., Taos; (505) 758-1772; (800) 552-1772; FAX: (505) 758-5738
■ "In town but close enough to the mountains", this "well-run" B&B consists of a group
of historic buildings housing "huge rooms" "creatively decorated" with handmade
furniture, down comforters and interesting antiques; the "sensational hosts" serve a
"superb breakfast" and ensure that "all of your expectations" are met.

Fechin Inn 71R (14S)   ▽ 28 | 28 | 25 | 27 | $168
227 Paseo del Pueblo Norte, Taos; (505) 751-1000; (800) 811-2933; FAX: (505) 751-7338
■ Only a few reviewers had the pleasure of overnighting at this new two-story inn
bearing the name of one of the most gifted artists in Taos; located on the secluded
grounds of the Fechin Institute, two blocks north of the Taos Plaza, the pueblo-style
structure features "tasteful" guestrooms, a lounge and library area where breakfast
and evening cocktails and hors d'oeuvres are served, an exercise room and outdoor
hot tub; early reports indicate it's a "lovely entry into the market."

Historic Taos Inn 33R (3S)

19	20	21	21	$147

125 Paseo del Pueblo Norte, Taos; (505) 758-2233; (800) TAOSINN; FAX: (505) 758-5776
☑ Expect "lots of local color" at this 60-year-old inn where "Miss Kitty would feel right at home"; it's an "experience" in a "perfect location" with a "wonderful Old West atmosphere" and "terrific food" at Doc Martin's (named after the town's first physician); critics cry "old-world charm is not enough", complaining about "small and noisy" rooms in the main house; perhaps they haven't figured out that "the courtyard rooms are best."

Quail Ridge Inn 50R (60S)

18	19	17	19	$143

PO Box 707, Ski Valley Rd., Taos; (505) 776-2211; (800) 624-4448; FAX: (505) 776-2949
☑ Four miles north of Taos and 13 miles from Taos Ski Valley lies this "sprawling adobe-style" resort offering myriad recreational facilities including tennis, squash and racquetball courts, a fitness center, heated pool and hot tub; there's an equally wide range of accommodations – standard rooms, studios, suites, casitas – yet some say the place is "good only if you plan to spend most of your time skiing and not in your room."

Sagebrush Inn 68R (32S)

17	17	16	16	$97

PO Box 557, 1508 S. Santa Fe Rd., Taos; (505) 758-2254; (800) 428-3626; FAX: (505) 758-5077
☑ Despite a dip in ratings since our last *Survey*, reviewers recommend this "charmingly out of the way" "adobe-style" inn three miles south of Taos for its "small but romantic rooms" decorated with hand-carved furniture and "funky, rustic, homey, comfy" atmosphere; cynics say it's "tacky" and "a bit of a dump", but even they can't deny that "the price is right" and "watching the locals dance to the country-western band" is a hoot; a full breakfast is included

Taos Ski Valley

Edelweiss, Hotel 7R (3S)

17	23	22	19	$182

PO Box 83, 106 Sutton Pl., Taos Ski Valley; (505) 776-2301; (800) 458-8754; FAX: (505) 776-2533
☒ A "good location" offering ski-in/ski-out access to Taos Ski Valley is the calling card of this "cozy" hotel that reminds surveyors of a "Swiss chalet"; accommodations range from "just ok" rooms to two-bedroom condos equipped with a full kitchen, fireplace and whirlpool; weekly winter packages include a "memorable breakfast", lift tickets and ski lessons; N.B. though the restaurant was destroyed in a fire, breakfast and lunch buffets are still available.

St. Bernard, Hotel 27R (1S) ⌀

19	24	26	20	$189

PO Box 88, Ski Valley Rd., Taos Ski Valley; (505) 776-2251
☑ The "very best" food and service in the area can be found at this "classy joint on the slopes", the original hotel in Taos Ski Valley; the rooms pale in comparison, but the weekly packages including three meals a day, lift tickets and ski lessons are a good value; open Thanksgiving to Easter.

New York

Albany

Desmond, The 299R (21S)
20 20 19 20 $121
(fka The Desmond Americana)
660 Albany Shaker Rd., Albany; (518) 869-8100; (800) 448-3500; FAX: (518) 869-7659
■ Service is so "very good" that "10 conventions can be happening at once and you're treated like the only guest" at this "all-round excellent hotel" resembling a "small New England town"; a top business choice for Albany, it has family appeal as well, with "large rooms", "good food", a "great indoor pool" and fitness center and a "charming" 18th-century theme that "kids will find fun"; though airport "convenience" triggers a few grumbles about "noise", most find it a "refreshing change" from the chains.

Marriott Albany 356R (3S)
18 18 16 16 $117
189 Wolf Rd., Albany; (518) 458-8444; (800) 228-9290; FAX: (518) 482-7809
☑ While "otherwise standard", this "dependable", "convenient" chain link with both indoor and outdoor pools is singled out for its "pleasant staff" that's "accommodating to the business traveler" and "treats regular visitors with much courtesy"; although a few gripe it's "nothing special", citing "dark" interiors and "very thin walls", more realistic travelers shrug "ordinary but far from awful."

Omni Albany 369R (17S)
17 17 16 16 $118
State & Lodge Sts., Albany; (518) 462-6611; (800) 843-6664; FAX: (518) 462-2901
☑ Since it's "close to the capitol" it may be "the most convenient place for business", but where a few find "nice rooms" (especially those "newly renovated"), more decry "outmoded" accommodations as well as service that's sometimes "nonexistent" and food that's only "fair"; facilities include a "good pool" and 17 meeting rooms.

Alexandria Bay

Bonnie Castle Resort 126R (2S)
– – – – M
Holland St., Alexandria Bay; (315) 482-4511; (800) 955-4511; FAX: (315) 482-9600
It's all here: nightclub, hot tubs, riverboat, marina, pools, tennis, volleyball, "great views" and a conference center (it's "good at conventions"); close by in the Thousand Islands region are cruises, fishing, horseback riding, hayrides and a driving range; so while some knock "cheap, motel-type rooms", you probably won't spend a lot of time in them, and more upscale accommodations (many with Jacuzzis) are also available.

Riveredge Resort Hotel 92R (37S)
– – – – M
17 Holland St., Alexandria Bay; (315) 482-9917; (800) ENJOY-US; FAX: (315) 482-5010
This contemporary riverfront property with a small marina in the Thousand Islands area suits small conferences (meeting capacity up to 250) as well as individual vacationers; in addition to guestrooms with Jacuzzis and water views, there are indoor and outdoor pools, a fitness room and two restaurants, as well as the resort's own charter tour boat.

Amenia

Troutbeck 34R (8S)
21 25 26 24 $263
Leedsville Rd., Amenia; (914) 373-9681; (800) 978-7688; FAX: (914) 373-7080
■ Imagine "Edith Wharton and F. Scott Fitzgerald go country" and you can picture this "quiet, dignified" Tudor-style mansion on 442 "beautiful" acres, a historic '20s literati haunt that's "off-the-beaten-path" yet only two hours from NYC; guests relish the "wonderful rooms" ("every one different"), "exquisite service" and "great cuisine" and enjoy the ballroom and covered heated pool; it's "a great conference spot" that's corporate on weekdays but open to individuals on weekends.

Bolton Landing

Sagamore, The 174R (176S)
      23 | 22 | 21 | 25 | $204

(fka Omni Sagamore Resort)
110 Sagamore Rd., Bolton Landing; (518) 644-9400; (800) 358-3585; FAX: (518) 644-2626
☑ An 1883 "grand" "Victorian retreat" on a private island in Lake George with "great boating and fishing". "beautiful grounds and views", "the most bountiful buffet", a "fabulous fitness center" and an indoor/outdoor pool; rooms, however, vary greatly, with those in the original building rated "luxurious" and "spacious" and those in newer buildings "ugly" and "dungeonlike"; despite gripes about "second-rate service", this Adirondack "gem" is "still a favorite" in every season; P.S. "insist on a water view."

Cooperstown

Otesaga Hotel 110R (17S)
      20 | 22 | 20 | 24 | $178

PO Box 311, 60 Lake St., Cooperstown; (607) 547-9931; (800) 348-6222; FAX: (607) 547-9675
☑ A "classic historic resort" in "the most perfect village", this 1909 grande dame on Otsego Lake exudes "old-fashioned charm"; a "great golf course" and location near the National Baseball Hall of Fame, Glimmerglass Opera and the Fenimore House are added pluses; still some complain it "needs renovation" and "all meals are included so you can't eat elsewhere"; N.B. open late April to late October.

Dover Plains

Old Drovers Inn 4R
      22 | 23 | 24 | 18 | $199

Old Rte. 22, Dover Plains; (914) 832-9311; FAX: (914) 832-6356
■ An inn that greeted cattle drovers in 1750 and has never closed its doors since is today "a luxurious hideaway" affiliated with Relais & Châteaux; "unique" and "as authentic as it gets", the stone-and-wood colonial house has "wonderful rooms", "friendly service" and a "superb" New American–French restaurant; owners Alice Pitcher and Kemper Peacock help keep "history alive" at this pricey "charmer" that's "not to be missed."

Ellenville

Nevele, The 437R (5S)
      15 | 16 | 15 | 18 | $157

Rte. 209, Ellenville; (914) 647-6000; (800) 647-6000; FAX: (914) 647-9884
☑ Although everyone agrees this Catskill resort had its "heyday in the '60s" and "needs some serious updating", it still enjoys a loyal following who claim it's "old but nice and intimate" and "great for family vacations" since "it offers every amenity" and "lots of fun activities"; but the "beautiful grounds", 18-hole golf course, tennis courts, fitness center, ski slope and ice rink don't convince critics who call it a "shabby has-been."

Garden City

Garden City Hotel 264R (16S)
      24 | 24 | 24 | 23 | $189

45 Seventh St., Garden City; (516) 747-3000; (800) 547-0400; FAX: (516) 747-1414
■ The "best hotel in Nassau County" is "a lovely place" "with good ambiance", "wonderful service", "beautiful furnishings" and "spacious, modern rooms"; only 45 minutes from Manhattan and about 20 minutes to major airports, this "first-class suburban" also houses the "excellent" Polo Grill serving a "great brunch"; a few gripe "overpriced", but more think it's "the most desirable place for miles and miles."

Geneva

Geneva on the Lake (30S)
      ▽ 24 | 23 | 22 | 25 | $193

1001 Lochland Rd., Rte. 14S., Geneva; (315) 789-7190; (800) 3-GENEVA; FAX: (315) 789-0322
■ The "beautiful location" surrounded by formal gardens and overlooking Seneca Lake enchants guests at this 1911 Italian Renaissance–style villa, built as a private residence and once a Capuchin seminary; these days, "good food and service" make it a "great executive retreat", while kitchen-equipped suites appeal to families, as does easy access to Finger Lakes wineries, sports activities and the Corning Glass center; even with a jump in scores since our last *Survey*, a few continue to call for a "face-lift."

Glen Cove

Harrison Conference Center
at Glen Cove 195R (4S)
20 | 21 | 20 | 23 | $175

Dosoris Ln., Glen Cove; (516) 671-6400; (800) 422-6338; FAX: (516) 759-6725

■ Built in 1910, this suburban Long Island estate turned full-service conference center "still retains the elegance of the mansion" while offering "beautiful surroundings" for myriad amenities and a range of sports and recreational facilities; though some say "the rooms are like a cheap motel" and "service can be snippy", the majority finds it a "great place to have a good time."

Great Neck

Inn at Great Neck 79R (6S)
22 | 19 | 16 | 18 | $174

30 Cutter Mill Rd., Great Neck; (516) 773-2000; (800) 777-4151;
FAX: (516) 773-2020

■ "A classy hotel" is "what Great Neck always needed", and it's got one now in this neo-deco "elegant spot near NYC" and the major airports; "charming and convenient", it features "large rooms", all with VCRs, CD players and speakerphones, plus a "cordial staff", an on-site fitness room, four meeting rooms and "brand-new everything."

Hopewell Junction

Le Chambord 25R
19 | 20 | 23 | 17 | $131

2075 Rte. 52, Hopewell Junction; (914) 221-1941; (800) 274-1941;
FAX: (914) 221-1941

■ Those who know about this 1863 Georgian colonial inn in Dutchess County report a "very obliging staff" and "comfy" "period rooms" with "plenty of space for computers and printers"; guests can "R&R or work" in a "pretty country setting" and enjoy "fine dining" in the "wonderful" French restaurant; the Culinary Institute of America, Roosevelt and Vanderbilt estates and 21 wineries are within easy driving distance.

Ithaca

ROSE INN 12R (5S)
26 | 22 | 26 | 23 | $160

Box 6576, Rte. 34N, Ithaca; (607) 533-7905; FAX: (607) 533-7908

■ "I've died and gone to quaint B&B heaven" coos one devotee about this "beautiful, isolated" 1848 inn on 20 acres, "an exceptional place run by caring, wonderful people"; the rooms are "gorgeous", the service "friendly" and the food "fabulous", adding up to "total perfection with no detail overlooked"; it may be "a wonderful secret", but plenty of Cornell and Ithaca College parents have discovered it.

Statler Hotel 134R (16S)
20 | 23 | 21 | 19 | $127

11 East Ave., Ithaca; (607) 254-2602; (800) 541-2501; FAX: (607) 257-6432

■ "The students really try hard" at this "modern, elegant hotel", the training ground for Cornell's School of Hotel Administration and "located on the beautiful university campus"; while "you are part of the learning process", most give high scores, especially "for service – the professionalism and enthusiasm of youth outshines all other hotels"; we hear only scattered complaints: "rooms need renovating", "dining is sometimes spotty."

Kiamesha Lake

Concord Resort Hotel 1114R (36S)
14 | 16 | 16 | 18 | $168

Concord Rd., Kiamesha Lake; (914) 794-4000; (800) CONCORD;
FAX: (914) 794-7471

▨ "The place needs major renovations, but the food keeps coming" at this gargantuan, family-oriented "borscht belt time warp" on 2,000 Catskill acres; "every activity imaginable" is available, including the famed Monster Golf Course and two others, swimming, fitness center, nightclubs, 40 tennis courts, child care, the works, but "food is the primary activity" – "an orgy every day"; though many say this "dinosaur" is "past its prime", it's popular for holidays and singles weekends.

Lake Placid

Lake Placid Lodge 17R (5S)   23 | 23 | 23 | 23 | $205

PO Box 550, Whiteface Inn Rd., Lake Placid; (518) 523-2700; FAX: (518) 523-1124

■ "What the Adirondacks are all about" gush those enchanted by "one of the truly great American rustic resorts", an 1882 lodge in "beautiful" surroundings that's sister to the Point and a Relais & Châteaux member; many of the "luxurious", individually decorated rooms and cabins boast stone fireplaces and some have private porches overlooking the lake; besides "divine" New American cuisine, there's golf, fishing, hiking trails, canoes and mountain bikes on-site; N.B. not all rooms have a/c.

Mirror Lake Inn 109R (19S)   23 | 23 | 23 | 24 | $165

5 Mirror Lake Dr., Lake Placid; (518) 523-2544; FAX: (518) 523-2871

■ "A wonderful hideaway", this "elegant" 1924 hotel set amidst seven acres of "pine-scented heaven" delights with lake views and "old-world charm", from its "rich lobby", "beautiful wood-paneled rooms" (including duplex suites) and "helpful staff" to the "great food in a lovely dining room" where a spa-type menu is also available; "afternoon tea is the best time to hang out in the parlor", and there's also an on-site pub; indoor and outdoor pools and spa services lead a wide range of sports activities.

Lew Beach

Beaverkill Valley Inn 21R   ▽ 16 | 20 | 21 | 22 | $209

136 Beaverkill Rd., Lew Beach; (914) 439-4844; FAX: (914) 439-3884

■ This Rockefeller-owned "great nature spot", a cozy Victorian haven on 700 acres in Catskill State Park, two hours from NYC, is "great for kids" and for grown-ups too; a "fisherman's paradise", it offers a mile of Beaverkill River for fly fishing, plus x-country and downhill skiing, ice skating, miles of hiking trails, tennis courts, an indoor pool, self-service ice cream parlor and boating; there are conference facilities as well, and rates include three squares of Regional American fare per day.

Montauk

Montauk Yacht Club Resort & Marina 100R (7S)   20 | 18 | 19 | 20 | $201

PO Box 5048, Star Island Rd., Montauk; (516) 668-3100; (800) 832-4200; FAX: (516) 668-3303

☑ A "special place" is anchored at the east end of Long Island where "fresh air and fresh seafood" abound; guests enjoy "charming beachfront rooms" and "outstanding views of the boats" – in fact this resort especially attracts yacht owners since there's a 232-slip marina; but some are bothered by "unprofessional service" and food that only rates an "ok", finding that quality depends on the changing ownership.

Monticello

Kutsher's Country Club 400R (10S)   14 | 15 | 15 | 16 | $160

Kutsher's Rd., Monticello; (914) 794-6000; (800) 431-1273; FAX: (914) 794-0157

☑ "A typical Catskill property" that feels "vintage 1955" – meaning to many that it "needs a major renovation", though it's still "a fun family place", with enough "great athletic facilities" (including an 18-hole golf course), kiddie programs and evening entertainment to "keep one occupied"; the Kutsher family has been in charge since this "blast from the past" was built in 1907, still offering "plentiful" but not always beloved kosher food."

New Paltz

Mohonk Mountain House 273R (4S)   17 | 20 | 17 | 24 | $205

1000 Mountain Rest Rd., New Paltz; (914) 255-1000; (800) 772-6646; FAX: (914) 256-2161

☑ A turreted, landmarked "Victorian castle" within a two-hour drive from NYC, this "quaint, charming" "retreat" has been run by the Smiley family for 125 years; "fabulous summer and winter", it's where nature lovers can breathe "mountain air" and hike on miles of forest trails in an "unforgettable setting"; the "rooms are small" and "need major renovations" and the food (included in rates) gets "only passable" grades, but the "service is very good" and the "wonders of Mother Nature" override all complaints; N.B. "no TV" and "no a/c."

New York City
TOP 10 OVERALL

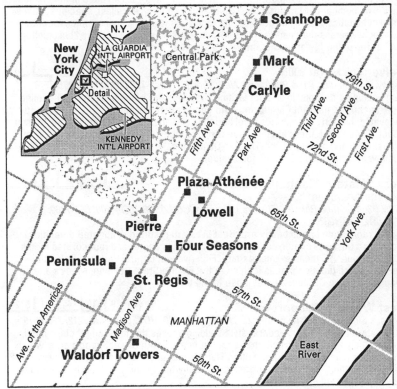

BEST OVERALL

28 Four Seasons
27 St. Regis
26 Carlyle
 Plaza Athénée
 Lowell
25 Pierre
 Peninsula
 Mark
24 Waldorf Towers
 Stanhope

BEST VALUES

Paramount
Millennium Broadway
Pickwick Arms
Eastgate Tower Suite
Renaissance
Mansfield
UN Plaza-Park Hyatt
Millenium Hilton
Tudor
Fitzpatrick Manhattan

R	S	D	P	$

Algonquin Hotel 142R (23S) | 16 | 19 | 19 | 19 | $190 |

59 W. 44th St. (bet. 5th & 6th Aves.), New York; (212) 840-6800; (800) 228-3000; FAX: (212) 944-1419

☑ "Literary types" find "a slice of history" and "great tradition preserved" at the one-time home of the Round Table; others find "an old, tired, expensive lady with an attitude", claiming "nostalgia is the only reason to go"; it does have a handy Theater District location, "enchanting old-world lobby" and "premier" cabaret acts in the Oak Room, and one can hope that a '96 renovation (and new owners as of early '97) will boost ratings for the "small", "uneven" rooms.

Barbizon 283R (17S) | 11 | 14 | 13 | 12 | $153 |

140 E. 63rd St. (Lexington Ave.), New York; (212) 838-5700; (800) 223-1020, FAX: (212) 888-4271

☑ A "great NYC feel", "good location" (near Bloomie's) and rich "history" (Grace Kelly, Candice Bergen and other celebs stayed here when it was a genteel ladies-only hostelry) have long been draws at this Eastsider; however, lately it's become "faded" and "shabby" with "postage-stamp rooms"; a $30-million redo (scheduled for completion in '97) portends improvements and will add meeting rooms and a pool.

Beekman Tower Hotel (172S)

19 | 18 | 16 | 15 | $178

3 Mitchell Pl. (1st Ave. & 49th St.), New York; (212) 355-7300; (800) ME-SUITE; FAX: (212) 753-9366

■ Like having your own "pied-à-terre in Manhattan", this 1928 art deco landmark near the UN (a member of Manhattan East Suite Hotels) offers "excellent, spacious" suites with kitchenettes, making it "good for the family" as well as a smart choice for eat-in-your-room, impress-the-bean-counters corporate travelers; don't miss the "best rooftop bar" at Top of the Tower restaurant, where the view "is worth it all."

Belvedere Hotel 300R

– | – | – | – | M

319 W. 48th St. (bet. 8th & 9th Aves.), New York; (212) 245-7000; FAX: (212) 265-7778

Fast becoming *the* hotel in NYC for visiting Brazilians (it's home to the up-and-coming churrascaria restaurant Plataforma) and popular with Europeans too, this recently renovated, formerly famous '30s hotel and then less-than-famous rental (there are still about 100 tenants) offers an attractive terrazzo lobby, clean, decent quarters with kitchenettes and a close-to-the-Theater-District locale; while there's no room service and few amenities, it's a definite good value.

Best Western Manhattan 141R (35S)

– | – | – | – | M

(fka The Aberdeen)

17 W. 32nd St. (bet. B'way & 5th Ave.), New York; (212) 736-1600; (800) 567-7760; FAX: (212) 563-4007

A total renovation of this beaux arts Best Western resulted in updated amenities, including a business center, conference room, fitness center and redecorated rooms based on four NYC themes: Empire State, Fifth Avenue, Central Park and SoHo; the Herald Square location places it close to the Empire State Building, Macy's and Madison Square Garden, but not close to the top.

Best Western Seaport Inn 66R

▽ 19 | 16 | – | 21 | $129

33 Peck Slip (Front St.), New York; (212) 766-6600; (800) HOTELNY; FAX: (212) 766-6615

◪ A restored 19th-century Federal-style building houses this low-budget chain hotel, the only lodging in Lower Manhattan's tourist-heavy South Street Seaport area, which puts it near the lively if pungent Fulton Fish Market and the Financial District; a "charming lobby" is a plus but critics cite "teeny tiny" rooms and the lack of room service, restaurant and bellhops.

Best Western Woodward 96R (35S)

▽ 11 | 11 | 6 | 12 | $121

210 W. 55th St. (B'way), New York; (212) 247-2000; (800) 336-4110; FAX: (212) 581-2248

◪ It's "clean and inexpensive" and has a "good location" near the Theater District, but ratings suggest there's lots of room for improvement at this beaux arts–style oldie; despite a complete '95 renovation critics still cite "tired decor", but on the plus side rooms may be "larger than average" and guests enjoy comp passes to Prescriptives Gym – a necessity given room service from the nearby Carnegie Deli.

Beverly, Hotel 30R (156S)

15 | 14 | 11 | 12 | $145

125 E. 50th St. (Lexington Ave.), New York; (212) 753-2700; (800) 223-0945; FAX: (212) 715-2452

◪ Offering what boosters call "real value especially on weekends" and a "good location" in East Midtown, this 1927-built hotel is best known locally as the home of Kaufman's drugstore (conveniently open to midnight, but no longer round-the-clock); rooms may be "basic" and "a little tired looking", but they're "large" and most have a kitchenette, upping its "bargain" appeal.

Box Tree, The 13R

25 | 23 | 25 | 21 | $272

250 E. 49th St. (bet. 2nd & 3rd Aves.), New York; (212) 758-8320; FAX: (212) 308-3899

■ "Take your amour" to what some consider "NYC's most romantic hotel", a "jewel box" in an East Side brownstone offering 13 "unique", "exotic" minisuites (each with fireplace) and "impeccable service"; the eponymous French dining room boasts "amazing food and beautiful decor", but "ouch, $86 per person for dinner" (to soften the blow, weekend hotel guests receive a $100 dining credit); a few dissenters find it "overdone" and precious; N.B. there's no elevator.

Broadway Bed & Breakfast Inn 30R (10S)

– | – | – | – | I

264 W. 46th St. (bet. B'way & 8th Ave.), New York; (212) 997-9200; (800) 826-6300; FAX: (212) 768-2807

The curtain went up two years ago on this well-priced B&B housed in a renovated 1918 building in the heart of the thriving Theater District and near the newly vibrant Times Square; free continental breakfast, concierge service, kitchenettes in the suites and a 20 percent discount at J. R.'s, the on-site Irish-American pub, add to the good value.

CARLYLE, THE 125R (45S)
26 | 27 | 26 | 25 | $303

35 E. 76th St. (bet. Madison & Park Aves.), New York; (212) 744-1600; (800) 227-5737; FAX: (212) 717-4682

■ "Grand and glorious" with "upper-crust elegance" and "old-world charm", this "classic" Upper Eastsider is in the "top echelon of NY hotels" drawing a top-echelon clientele; Bobby Short's singing in the "city's best nightclub" "sets the tone" for sophistication throughout, from the "exquisite" rooms to the "discreet", "sumptuous service" (a very few find it "snobbish"); just "bring lots of money", because the "crème de la crème" doesn't come cheap.

Casablanca Hotel 40R (8S)
– | – | – | – | VE

147 W. 43rd St. (bet. B'way & 6th Ave.), New York City; (212) 869-1212; (888) 922-7225; FAX: (212) 391-7585

In the center of the Theater District/Times Square action, this new luxury boutique hotel is set in a 1920s building with Moroccan-tinged decor: ceiling fans, imported tiles, hand-carved archways and doors; rooms are small but well appointed (marble bathrooms, voicemail, dataports) and perks include free continental breakfast at Rick's Cafe and use of the nearby New York Sports Club.

Chelsea Hotel 244R (6S)
10 | 12 | 10 | 13 | $139

222 W. 23rd St. (bet. 7th & 8th Aves.), New York; (212) 243-3700; FAX: (212) 243-3700

☑ "A glorious dive" in buzzing Chelsea, this 1884 Queen Anne/Victorian brick landmark "looks like it was lifted out of New Orleans and planted on 23rd Street for Tennessee Williams types" and other "artists" (past guests include Mark Twain, Dylan Thomas and Bob Dylan); about half residential, it's big on "pop-culture history", not amenities: "rooms tend to be large" but can be "gloomy" and public areas may be "creepy", but that only adds to its bohemian cachet.

Chelsea Savoy Hotel 90R
– | – | – | – | M

204 W. 23rd St. (7th Ave.), New York; (212) 929-9353; FAX: (212) 741-6309

Brand new in 1997, this modest, decent six-story hotel in Chelsea is a welcome option for budget-minded travelers; while amenities and furnishings are basic, the rooms are of reasonable size, and all feature private baths, a/c and TVs; Greenwich Village and the Flatiron District are within walking distance, as are the neighborhood's many restaurants and major sports complex, Chelsea Piers.

Crowne Plaza Manhattan 745R (25S)
20 | 18 | 18 | 18 | $184

(fka Holiday Inn Crowne Plaza)

1605 Broadway (bet. 48th & 49th Sts.), New York; (212) 977-4000; (800) 243-NYNY; FAX: (212) 977-5517

■ "Busy, busy, busy but good" sums up this 46-story glass tower that offers "an excellent way to stay" "in the heart" of the Theater District, close to B'way shows and in a "great location for the Thanksgiving Day parade"; rooms are "quiet, pleasant" and a "good value", even if some find service "indifferent"; the 29,000-square-foot fitness center may be "the best hotel gym in NYC" and is "reason alone to stay here."

Delmonico, Hotel (145S)
19 | 17 | 16 | 14 | $208

502 Park Ave. (59th St.), New York; (212) 355-2500; (800) 821-3842; FAX: (212) 755-3779

■ An "interesting old hotel" with "great atmosphere" in a "top location" near Barneys, Bloomie's and other chichi shopping; this 1929 Spanish-style, part-residential all-suiter has "reasonable rates" given its address, and newly renovated, kitchen-equipped quarters; other pluses: the lobby lounge is a "good watering hole" and guests can work out at the on-site New York Sports Club.

Doral Court 151R (47S)
17 | 18 | 17 | 15 | $184

130 E. 39th St. (Lexington Ave.), New York; (212) 685-1100; (800) 22-DORAL; FAX: (212) 779-8590

☑ To the majority this "small hotel with good service" is a "nice little sleeper with class and style that's relatively quiet and sophisticated"; assets include a "good location" in the Londonesque Murray Hill area, a courtyard cafe for breakfast and the Doral Fitness Center a block away; the consensus is "charming for NYC" even if a few find the rooms "small" and the overall performance "nothing special."

Doral Inn 610R (45S)
13 | 13 | 12 | 12 | $166

541 Lexington Ave. (bet. 49th & 50th Sts.), New York; (212) 755-1200; (800) 22-DORAL; FAX: (212) 319-8344

☑ An "impersonal" but "efficient tourist center", this Midtowner strikes critics as "functional at best" with "small", "noisy", "dreary" rooms, but it offers a "Waldorf locale at half-price", the "best squash facility" and an exercise room; it's either "a good value" or "forgettable" depending on who you ask.

Doral Park Avenue 170R (18S)   17 | 18 | 17 | 16 | $184
70 Park Ave. (38th St.), New York; (212) 687-7050; (800) 22-DORAL; FAX: (212) 808-9029
☑ The Murray Hill location "is just right" and "really great people work here" according to fans who consider this "an excellent value" and "good for small business meetings"; others see an "average" hotel with rooms "in need of refurbishing" and a staff that sometimes displays "NY attitude"; its fitness center, though a block away, is a plus.

Doral Tuscany 109R (12S)   18 | 18 | 16 | 16 | $181
120 E. 39th St. (Lexington Ave.), New York; (212) 686-1600; (800) 22-DORAL; FAX: (212) 779-7822
■ "An off-the-beaten-path gem – don't tell" plead admirers of this "small, comfortable" "Euro-style gem" that proves "good value can still be found in NYC"; some call the rooms "lovely" in a "classic blue-blood" way, others say they "need a face-lift", but the "good location" in Murray Hill, "nice staff" and use of the nearby Doral Fitness Center add up to a "big bargain in the Big Apple."

Doubletree Guest Suites (460S)   21 | 18 | 16 | 15 | $177
(fka Embassy Suites)
1568 Broadway (47th St.), New York; (212) 719-1600; (800) 222-TREE; FAX: (212) 921-5212
■ A few years ago, no one would have called Times Square a "fantastic location for families", but the area's rebirth means they do now, and this "convenient, inexpensive" choice is smack in the heart of Theater District action; a floor of childproof quarters plus special kids' programs boost its family appeal, and everyone appreciates its "spacious" suites (all with fridge and microwave), "nice amenities" and "helpful staff."

Drake Swissôtel 380R (107S)   19 | 20 | 19 | 17 | $210
440 Park Ave. (56th St.), New York; (212) 421-0900; (800) 637-9477; FAX: (212) 371-3820
☑ "Old-world charm" and "classic service" complete with a "fantastic concierge" make this Swiss-owned Midtown business hotel "feel like Europe without the jet lag"; its "Park Avenue locale and good bar" are pluses, and a $30-million renovation (nearly complete at press time) may swell the ranks of those who find the rooms "lovely and nicely decorated" and quiet those who call them "mediocre" and "closet-like."

Dumont Plaza Suite Hotel (247S)   20 | 18 | 14 | 14 | $163
150 E. 34th St. (bet. Lexington & 3rd Aves.), New York; (212) 481-7600; (800) ME-SUITE; FAX: (212) 889-8516
■ "One of NYC's best deals" has "a decent location" near the Empire State Building and, like its fellow Manhattan East Suite Hotels, is "great for an extended stay", offering "perfectly comfortable", "very large, well-equipped" suites, all with kitchenettes, an "excellent exercise facility" and a staff made up of – get this – "cordial New Yorkers."

Eastgate Tower Suite Hotel (188S)   18 | 18 | 15 | 15 | $155
222 E. 39th St. (bet. 2nd & 3rd Aves.), New York; (212) 687-8000; (800) ME-SUITE; FAX: (212) 490-2634
■ Another Manhattan East Suite property and candidate for "best bargain in NYC", this "comfortable and clean" if somewhat "blah" hotel on a quiet Murray Hill residential block offers "spacious" suites with "convenient" full kitchens (each with microwave) and computer jacks, plus a fitness center; best of all, the "price is right."

Edison Hotel 960R (40S)   12 | 13 | 11 | 12 | $127
228 W. 47th St. (bet. B'way & 8th Ave.), New York; (212) 840-5000; (800) 637-7070; FAX: (212) 596-6850
☑ "A no-frills" base off Times Square, the art deco Edison is "as basic as can be, but it has a great location for B'way shows" and is "cheap", thus "more than adequate" for theater buffs and bargain hunters; "tiny" quarters and "impersonal" service cause grumbling, but "renovated rooms are good" (the hotel revamps a few floors per year); the coffee shop is a longtime hangout for stage gypsies, complete with "pretty salty" service.

Elysée, Hotel 85R (14S)   20 | 21 | 19 | 19 | $210
60 E. 54th St. (bet. Madison & Park Aves.), New York; (212) 753-1066; (800) 535-9733; FAX: (212) 980-9278
■ The legendary Monkey Bar packs them in and the art deco–style restaurant rates a "wow", but there are other appeals too at this "chic" east Midtown "Eurostyle gem": its "central" location, "great service" and perks such as free continental breakfast, tea and cookies, and access to the nearby Cardio Fitness Center; rooms earn good marks, but some bleary-eyed voters aren't into the monkey business.

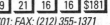

Essex House, Hotel Nikko 518R (197S)

23 | 23 | 24 | 22 | $233

160 Central Park S. (bet. 6th & 7th Aves.), New York; (212) 247-0300; (800) 645-5687; FAX: (212) 315-1839

■ "Like a good wine that gets better with age", Central Park South's "wonderfully" restored art deco beauty beguiles with its "stunning" public spaces, "plush" rooms and "impeccable" service, not to mention dining at the top-notch Les Célébrités and the "very fine" Café Botanica; you may "need a second mortgage" to cover the bill, but it's "worth it", especially if you "get a park-view room" – "fabulous."

59th Street Bridge Apartments 62R (3S)

– | – | – | – | M

351 E. 60th St. (1st Ave.), New York; (212) 754-9388; (888) 754-9389; FAX: (212) 754-9593

Near Bloomingdale's and the other tony East Side shops, this small, reasonably priced full-service hotel opened in 1996 with kitchens, voicemail and computer jacks in every room; while decor is spare, natural brick walls provide character and some rates include access to the Vertical Club fitness facility nearby; N.B. there's no elevator, only stairs, to all five floors, and be sure to ask for a room with a/c in summer.

Fitzpatrick Manhattan Hotel 40R (52S)

19 | 21 | 16 | 16 | $181

687 Lexington Ave. (57th St.), New York; (212) 355-0100; (800) 367-7701; FAX: (212) 355-1371

■ No blarney, just "excellent Irish hospitality" and "service with a genuine smile" that gives guests a "homey feeling" at this Irish-owned Eastsider, where "small but well-appointed rooms" (with voicemail and dataports) and a prime location near Bloomie's add up to "good value"; as might be expected of a place patronized by Emerald Isle expats, "the lobby pub is lively."

Flatotel International (169S)

▽ 22 | 15 | – | 12 | $194

135 W. 52nd St. (bet. 6th & 7th Aves.), New York; (212) 887-9400; (800) FLATOTEL; FAX: (212) 887-9442

☑ "A nice idea", this apartment-style (ergo, "flat"-hotel) all-suiter gets good scores for its "large" accommodations with full kitchens and marble whirlpool baths; however, the concept is "poorly executed" in the eyes of critics who knock "fair" service and aren't thrilled by the decor; a business center, fitness room and Midtown West location near Rockefeller Center work in its favor; no dining on-site, but lots nearby.

FOUR SEASONS 309R (61S)

29 | 27 | 27 | 27 | $334

57 E. 57th St. (bet. Madison & Park Aves.), New York; (212) 758-5700; (800) 332-3442; FAX: (212) 758-5711

■ "Supermodern" elegance and "attention to detail" suit the hotshots who wouldn't lay their important heads anywhere but at NYC's top-ranked hotel; this I. M. Pei "masterpiece" earns "bravos" for everything from its "magnificent rooms" with "unique bathtubs that fill in 60 seconds" to it's "superb" service, top-flight business center and health club, "fabulous" American fare at Fifty-Seven, Fifty-Seven, even the bar's "amazing" martinis; in short, "if you want to feel pampered, this is it" – "splurge and enjoy"; rooms on higher floors have spectacular city views.

Franklin Hotel 53R

▽ 16 | 19 | 14 | 15 | $155

164 E. 87th St. (bet. Lexington & 3rd Aves.), New York; (212) 369-1000; (800) 600-8787; FAX: (212) 369-8000

■ This small, sleekly furnished Upper East Side boutique hotel, run by the Gotham Hospitality Group, is an "attractive" "pied-à-terre" and "great bargain", with rooms that are "amazingly well designed" for their "Lilliputian" size; "proximity to Museum Mile" and free parking boost its appeal, and, while there's no restaurant, breakfast (included) is served to a stylish crowd in a stylish lounge.

Gorham, The 69R (45S)

19 | 17 | 15 | 14 | $163

136 W. 55th St. (bet. 6th & 7th Aves.), New York; (212) 245-1800; (800) 735-0710; FAX: (212) 582-8332

■ With its "charming European style" and "incredibly convenient" location near the Theater District and MoMA, this "small", older hotel is worth "recommending for the money"; it has kitchenettes in all its "efficient" recently renovated rooms, and noncooks can opt for the on-site Italian favorite Castellano or tackle a gargantuan sandwich at the nearby Carnegie Deli; a buffet breakfast and fitness center are pluses.

Gramercy Park Hotel 365R (144S)

12 | 12 | 12 | 12 | $142

2 Lexington Ave. (21st St.), New York; (212) 475-4320; (800) 221-4083; FAX: (212) 505-0535

☑ The location is "lovely", overlooking the "historic" and private Gramercy Park (guests have access) in a quiet area with many hip new restaurants on nearby streets; alas, this "old dowager in decline" takes a beating for its "small", "drab" rooms, "harried" service and general "frumpiness"; on the bright side, it's "cheap" and draws a "very international crowd", and some defenders like its "funky" yet "genteel" feel.

Grand Hyatt New York 1320R (87S)
18 | 17 | 17 | 18 | $197

Park Ave. at Grand Central (Lexington Ave. & 42nd St.), New York; (212) 883-1234; (800) 233-1234; FAX: (212) 697-3772

◪ It's hard to argue with the Midtown location, but voters find other bones to pick at this Trump behemoth that's "busy, like neighbor Grand Central Station"; some like its "huge, glitzy" lobby, others say "too glittery", service is either "good" or "impersonal", and a "mystery house of guestrooms" means you "can get a closet or a football field" – and some "need a redo "

Helmsley Middletowne Hotel 147R (43S)
17 | 17 | – | 14 | $162

148 E. 48th St. (bet. Lexington & 3rd Aves.), New York; (212) 755-3000; (800) 221-4982; FAX: (212) 832-0261

◪ Near Lexington Avenue's hotel gulch, this "reasonably priced", "functional" hotel has rooms that may be "small" but they please penny-pinchers looking for "value"; there's "no lobby" to speak of, no restaurant and no room service, but some suites in this former apartment building have full kitchens; those who find it "dreary" ("where are you Leona?") may be mollified by ongoing renovations.

Helmsley New York Hotel 789R (11S)
22 | 21 | 20 | 20 | $222

212 E. 42nd St. (bet. 2nd & 3rd Aves.), New York; (212) 490-8900; (800) 221-4982; FAX: (212) 986-4792

◪ This Midtowner means different things to different people: some enjoy "clean, prim rooms" that are "pleasant and cheery" with "nice extras" and service by "a staff that will go out in the middle of the night to get a sandwich", while others report doing hard time in "adequate" quarters with sometimes "surly" help; a "good Sunday brunch" is a plus.

Helmsley Park Lane Hotel 588R (40S)
22 | 21 | 19 | 19 | $234

36 Central Park S. (bet. 5th & 6th Aves.), New York; (212) 371-4000; (800) 221-4982; FAX: (212) 521-6666

◪ "Conveniently and beautifully located" at the south end of Central Park, this Helmsley is still a contender thanks to "comfortable rooms" that are "elegant and well appointed" with "fabulous views" – if facing the park; however, the generally "good service" sometimes slips ("disinterested and haughty", "worst desk clerks outside of Omsk").

Helmsley Windsor Hotel 191R (53S)
16 | 17 | 11 | 13 | $152

100 W. 58th St. (6th Ave.), New York; (212) 265-2100; (800) 742-4318; FAX: (212) 765-0371

◪ "Charming" residential-style lodgings close to Carnegie Hall prompt repeat visits from musicians and others who appreciate "good value" in a city better known for high prices; surveyors liken it to "a small European hotel" where "personal attention" is the norm, but they also caution the "rooms vary" with "some large and others quite small"; still, "what a location – the rest doesn't count."

Hilton and Towers, New York 1946R (95S)
18 | 17 | 16 | 17 | $193

1335 Sixth Ave. (bet. 53rd & 54th Sts.), New York; (212) 586-7000; (800) HILTONS; FAX: (212) 315-1374

◪ "Nonstop conventions and tours" lend a "tower of Babel" feel to this mammoth Midtown business "workhorse", which can host up to 3,300 people in its 45 meeting rooms; guestrooms, in contrast, are generally "small but nicely furnished and kept up well"; as you'd expect from its size, service varies from "efficient" to "abrasive" and the lobby can resemble "baggage claim at La Guardia"; for best results, "splurge" for a suite in the Towers, a calmer hotel-within-a-hotel.

Holiday Inn Downtown 211R (12S)
14 | 15 | 15 | 13 | $153

138 Lafayette St. (bet. Howard & Canal Sts.), New York; (212) 966-8898; (800) HOLIDAY; FAX: (212) 966-3933

◼ It's in an "odd location" in lower Manhattan at the crossroads of Chinatown, Little Italy and SoHo, but that means "wonderful restaurants abound", so "go, eat, and see the city" and use this Asian-accented HI with "average rooms" as a well-priced base.

Hotel 17 130R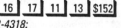
– | – | – | – | I

225 E. 17th St. (bet. 2nd & 3rd Aves.), New York; (212) 475-2845; FAX: (212) 677-8178

If even the Paramount isn't hip enough, Hotel 17 may fit the bill, filled as it is with rockers (Madonna and David Bowie staged photo shoots here), trendy fashion types and Euro artistes; there are few amenities, but its low rates (including weekly) for its spare, retro but functional rooms attract youngsters who haven't yet made the cover of *Vogue*.

Inn at Irving Place 5R (7S)   23 | 22 | 21 | 21 | $235
56 Irving Pl. (bet. 17th & 18th Sts.), New York; (212) 533-4600; (800) 685-1447; FAX: (212) 533-4611
■ Imagine staying at a rich friend's NYC townhouse and you get an idea of what this little known Gramercy Park inn is like; set in a pair of well-restored, 1834 landmark buildings, it offers "antiques-filled" rooms outfitted with modern amenities (VCRs, dataports), plus peace and quiet (no children under 12); if a few feel the rooms "don't justify the price", more consider it a special "place to indulge."

Inter-Continental Hotel New York 608R (82S)   20 | 20 | 19 | 20 | $210
111 E. 48th St. (bet. Park & Lexington Aves.), New York; (212) 755-5900; (800) 327-0200; FAX: (212) 644-0079
◪ "Much improved", this "well-located" Eastsider's ratings have risen after an overhaul including a $5-million lobby renovation that restored the marble floors and gold leaf moldings to their 1926 splendor; devotees dote on its "charming, old-world" ambiance and find the redone suites especially "beautiful", but others still complain of "matchbox-size" rooms, and reports on service vary from "excellent" to "slow."

Jolly Madison Towers Hotel 222R (5S)   ▽ 13 | 13 | 14 | 11 | $148
22 E. 38th St. (Madison Ave.), New York; (212) 802-0600; (800) 225-4340; FAX: (212) 447-0747
◪ You might not be terribly jolly after staying in "ok" rooms ("not great size", "not ma amenities") with service by a "staff that needs training"; but then again, you might cheer up when you get the bill, since some call this the "best buy in Midtown"; there's Italian fare at Cinque Terre on-site.

Kimberly, The 32R (160S)   21 | 17 | 15 | 15 | $191
145 E. 50th St. (bet. Lexington & 3rd Aves.), New York; (212) 755-0400; (800) 683-0400; FAX: (212) 486-6915
■ This "little jewel of a hotel" offers "more room and good value" than many an Eastsider, especially in its "huge", "beautifully furnished" suites complete with balconies, kitchens and fax machines; other pluses are the happening supper club Tatou, free access to the nearby New York Health & Racquet Club and a complimentary sunset cruise (weather permitting) around Manhattan.

Kitano New York 150R (8S)   23 | 24 | 23 | 22 | $252
66 Park Ave. (38th St.), New York; (212) 885-7000; (800) 548-2666; FAX: (212) 885-7100
■ A "gorgeous lobby and tranquil service" set the tone at this Murray Hill oasis of calm, where guests stay in recently renovated, "small but beautiful rooms" with soundproof windows, dual-line phones and fax and computer hookups; add in Nadaman Hakubai restaurant, known for its authentic megabucks kaiseki dinners, and the lovely Garden Cafe and you have an experience that's "first class all the way."

Larchmont Hotel 55R   – | – | – | – | I
27 W. 11th St. (bet. 5th & 6th Aves.), New York; (212) 989-9333; FAX: (212) 989-9496
It's not impossible to find a wonderful inexpensive hotel in NYC if you don't mind sharing a bathroom; more a B&B than a full-service hotel, the Larchmont offers small rooms (all with a/c) decorated with rattan furniture, complimentary breakfast in its private cafe and a location on a landmark Greenwich Village block of brownstones close to the shops, restaurants and action of the area.

Le Parker Meridien Hotel 617R (81S)   22 | 21 | 21 | 20 | $226
118 W. 57th St. (bet. 6th & 7th Aves.), New York; (212) 245-5000; (800) 543-4300; FAX: (212) 307-1776
■ A "touch of Paris" in Midtown? – *oui, oui* say Francophiles charmed by a "très chic", "international" ambiance, "pleasant" service and "nicely decorated, comfortable" rooms in a superb location for music, theater and shopping; athletes also applaud the "top-notch" gym with jogging track and the "best rooftop pool" in town; only a few Francophobes find it a bit "cold" with "snooty" staff: "if I wanted rude Parisians, I would have gone to Paris."

Le Refuge Inn Bed & Breakfast 9R   – | – | – | – | VE
620 City Island Ave. (Sutherland St.), City Island, Bronx; (718) 885-2478; FAX: (718) 885-1519
Can you find French countryside ambiance in The Bronx? – bien sûr, at this restored 19th-century Victorian sea captain's residence just 30 minutes from Manhattan on restaurant-crammed City Island; overlooking the 300-year-old harbor, it has pleasantly furnished rooms and a French owner who is an accomplished chef and cooks up the inn's highly praised French country cuisine.

Lexington, Hotel 686R (14S) | 11 | 13 | 11 | 12 | $157
511 Lexington Ave. (48th St.), New York; (212) 755-4400; (800) 448-4471; FAX: (212) 751-4091
☑ Relatively low rates (for Midtown) and a recent "well-done renovation" of the tower's 10th–24th floors are pluses, but otherwise surveyors criticize this veteran's "drab" rooms and less-than-stellar service; novel attributes are Denim 'n' Diamonds, a country-western dance club in the basement, and the elegant J. Sung Dynasty serving good Chinese fare on the mezzanine.

Loews New York Hotel 678R (44S) | 15 | 15 | 14 | 14 | $159
569 Lexington Ave. (51st St.), New York; (212) 350-6050; (800) LOEWS-23; FAX: (212) 758-6311
☑ "Catering mostly to budget-conscious tourists", this "bustling", "well-situated" utilitarian Midtowner does its job by providing "good value" and "friendly" service; a $26-million renovation in '96 may have brightened "drab", "smaller-than-a-closet" rooms, but some report "sleepless nights" due to police and fire-truck sirens from nearby stations; there's "decent" American food at the Lexington Avenue Grill.

Lombardy Hotel 40R (50S) | 19 | 20 | 17 | 15 | $225
111 E. 56th St. (bet. Park & Lexington Aves.), New York; (212) 753-8600; (800) 223-5254; FAX: (212) 754-5683
■ Consider it discovered: this "small, old-world"–style hotel in a prime East Side location doesn't have a high profile but pleases those who know it with its "nice" accommodations (all with kitchenettes), "friendly" staff, "good housekeeping" and value-minded weekend deals; though a few say rooms are a "mixed bag" and can be "small", most enjoy its "comfort" and "sense of privacy."

LOWELL, THE 21R (44S) | 27 | 28 | 25 | 23 | $308
28 E. 63rd St. (bet. Madison & Park Aves.), New York; (212) 838-1400; (800) 221-4444; FAX: (212) 319-4230
■ "Don't make me go home" is a typical reaction after a stay at this "most intimate European-style hotel" – it's like "living in a mansion with full staff" in posh East Side terrain; a few mention "attitude" and "small" quarters, but most simply marvel at "perfect personal service", "beautiful rooms" and knockout specialty suites (one has flower-filled terraces, another a private gym); red-blooded steak aficionados flash knives at the Post House downstairs.

Lucerne, The 210R (40S) | – | – | – | – | E
201 W. 79th St. (Amsterdam Ave.), New York; (212) 875-1000; (800) 492-8122; FAX: (212) 579-2408
Opened in March 1996 in a restored landmark Upper West Side building, this welcome addition to a lively residential neighborhood short on hotels is surrounded by cafes and boutiques, close to the Museum of Natural History and Central Park and not far from Lincoln Center; the on-site Chaz & Wilson Grill offers American food and live music.

Lyden Gardens Suite Hotel (131S) | 20 | 16 | 13 | 12 | $177
215 E. 64th St. (bet. 2nd & 3rd Aves.), New York; (212) 355-1230; (800) ME-SUITE; FAX: (212) 758-7858
■ Like having your own "NY apartment", this "no-frills" (read: little by way of services) all-suiter in a "great" East Side location offers "comfortable" quarters, all with fully equipped kitchens, that "make you feel at home"; like its fellow Manhattan East Suite properties, it's a fine choice for families and extended business stays.

Lyden House Suite Hotel (80S) | ▽ 22 | 17 | 17 | 15 | $147
320 E. 53rd St. (bet. 1st & 2nd Aves.), New York; (212) 888-6070; (800) ME-SUITE; FAX: (212) 935-7690
■ "A great way to taste the Big Apple" say fans of this "good", affordable all-suiter (another Manhattan East Suite member); assets include an "excellent location" near tony Sutton Place, a "pretty lobby" and a fully equipped kitchen in every suite.

Mansfield, The 96R (27S) | 19 | 18 | 16 | 19 | $173
12 W. 44th St. (bet. 5th & 6th Aves.), New York; (212) 944-6050; (800) 255-5167; FAX: (212) 764-4477
■ Rooms at this renovated hotel may still be "small" but they're now "sleek" and "cleverly furnished" with such extras as soundproof windows, VCRs and CD players; add "excellent service", "free breakfast", free parking and a location near theaters and you have "a real find" for "high style at a moderate price."

MARK, THE 120R (60S)
25 | 25 | 26 | 23 | $266

25 E. 77th St. (Madison Ave.), New York; (212) 744-4300; (800) THE-MARK; FAX: (212) 744-2749

■ "An oasis of elegance", a "haven of tranquillity", this "classy" Upper Eastsider exudes "European charm and taste"; high marks go to its rooms that some find "smallish" but all call "luxurious" and "well equipped" with "fine linens", oversize tubs and, in many, a kitchenette; other strengths include "fantastic service", "good breakfasts", a "charming" bar and "wonderful" contemporary French dining at Mark's; GM Raymond Bickson is one of the best in the business.

Marriott East Side, New York 656R (6S)
16 | 18 | 15 | 14 | $174

525 Lexington Ave. (49th St.), New York; (212) 755-4000; (800) 228-9290; FAX: (212) 980-6175

☑ Such notables as Errol Flynn and Houdini once played in its pool, however, today it's best "for businessmen on a budget" who value an "outstanding" Midtown East locale; service is "friendly", but rooms range from "spacious" and comfy (with "wonderful top-floor suites") to "cramped", "in need of refurbishing" (a recent redo may have helped).

Marriott Financial Center, New York 491R (13S)
19 | 19 | 17 | 18 | $182

85 West St. (bet. Albany & Carlisle Sts.), New York; (212) 385-4900; (800) 242-8685; FAX: (212) 227-8136

☑ "A very good choice if you need to be Downtown for business", this Marriott attracts moneymakers with its executive business center and "good location" a block from the World Trade Center and World Financial Center; rooms tend to be "small and nondescript", but some offer "great views of the Statue of Liberty" and the harbor.

Marriott Marquis, New York 1850R (61S)
20 | 19 | 18 | 20 | $194

1535 Broadway (bet. 45th & 46th Sts.), New York; (212) 398-1900; (800) 843-4898; FAX: (212) 704-8930

☑ This "glitzy" Time Square "monolith" with a 37-story atrium can resemble a "three-ring circus", but it's arguably the "best spot in town for theatergoers" and has "terrific views", especially from its revolving rooftop restaurant; a recent $20-million redo has some guests praising "well-decorated" rooms, but given its size it's no surprise that service varies ("well trained" vs. "impersonal") and it takes knocks for "endless elevator waits" and an "inconvenient" eighth-floor lobby; P.S. ask about "can't-be-beat" discounts.

Marriott World Trade Center 795R (25S)
19 | 19 | 18 | 18 | $188

(fka New York Vista Hotel)

3 World Trade Ctr. (bet. West & Liberty Sts.), New York; (212) 938-9100; (800) 550-2344; FAX: (212) 444-3444

■ A $60-million rehab after the Trade Center bombing brought this Lower Manhattan high-rise back to life; now a Marriott, it doesn't excite everyone ("typical convention hotel"), but it still "works well" for the "financial crowd", offering "large, modern, comfortable" rooms and "good" service that cause some to call it "best for business" Downtown; it's also "peaceful" on weekends and has great Hudson views.

Mayflower Hotel 165R (200S)
15 | 16 | 15 | 14 | $165

15 Central Park W. (bet. 61st & 62nd Sts.), New York; (212) 265-0060; (800) 223-4164; FAX: (212) 265-5098

☑ Musicians, TV folk and the budget-minded overnight at this venerable 1925 Westsider in a "perfect location" overlooking Central Park; it's a "cheap stay" "convenient to Lincoln Center" and "covers the basics", though "not much more"; ongoing renovations may address reports that rooms are "large and comfortable but worn", and while some find it "short on elegance", others like its "warm" staff and "gracious service"; the movie *Wolf* was filmed here.

Michelangelo, The 126R (52S)
24 | 23 | 20 | 20 | $226

152 W. 51st St. (bet. 6th & 7th Aves.), New York; (212) 765-1900; (800) 237-0990; FAX: (212) 541-6604

■ "Exquisite rooms" (some with computer, fax, printer and copier), "sophisticated suites" and a "lovely, quiet" ambiance make those longing for *la bella Italia* feel they're "back in the best of European hotels"; "super" service and free continental breakfast add to the pleasure, as do the "handy" Theater District locale and good Italian fare at Limoncello restaurant; a minority finds it "pompous" with "not enough staff."

Millenium Hilton 441R (120S)
24 | 22 | 21 | 20 | $210

55 Church St. (bet. Dey & Fulton Sts.), New York; (212) 693-2001; (800) HILTONS; FAX: (212) 571-2316

■ Bulls and bears take stock in a Hilton that's "efficient and in tune with Wall Street"; in "a great Downtown location" facing the World Trade Center and "convenient to the Financial District", it offers "sleek, well-equipped" rooms with "fabulous views", "first-class" service and a high-tech fitness facility; other pluses: a business center, free car service; good dining at Taliesin and weekend packages.

Millennium Broadway 620R (9S) | 22 | 22 | 21 | 20 | $190 |
(fka Macklowe Hotel)
145 W. 44th St. (B'way), New York; (212) 768-4400; (800) 622-5693; FAX: (212) 789-7698
■ A player in the Theater District/Times Square area where fans find the "perfect balance of room, service, location and dining"; its "striking", "updated art deco" design is "chic and modern" to most, "cold" and "dark" to a few, but rooms are "well decorated in European" style, the staff is "responsive" and meeting facilities are "excellent"; Charlotte restaurant serves eclectic American fare, and there's a fitness center.

Morgans 85R (28S) | 22 | 21 | 18 | 19 | $213 |
237 Madison Ave. (bet. 37th & 38th Sts.), New York; (212) 686-0300; (800) 334-3408; FAX: (212) 779-8352
■ Quiet modern chic reigns at Ian Schrager's first "cutting-edge" boutique hotel, where "kinky", "funky" Andrée Putman–designed rooms fit hip clients "like a custom-tailored suit" (though some find the fit a bit snug); the low-profile Murray Hill address belies a "classy place" known for its "jazzy" style and sharp service from "employees who look like models" (no surprise, it's a "fashion industry hangout").

Murray Hill East Suites (125S) | 19 | 16 | – | 13 | $158 |
149 E. 39th St. (bet. Lexington & 3rd Aves.), New York; (212) 661-2100; (800) 221-3037; FAX: (212) 818-0724
■ C'mon down – "the price is right" say low-maintenance types who don't mind if this "low-key" all-suiter in a Murray Hill residential area has no restaurant and few services and strikes some as "dowdy"; accommodations are "nice and big" and all have full kitchens, making it "a terrific bargain" and "convenient for families"; weekend packages sweeten the deal.

New York Palace Hotel 800R (100S) | 24 | 21 | 20 | 23 | $242 |
455 Madison Ave. (bet. 50th & 51st Sts.), New York; (212) 888-7000; (800) NY-PALACE; FAX: (212) 303-6000
■ Have "the Sultan of Brunei's big plans to wipe out garish days of yore" worked at Leona's former Midtown realm? – yes, say voters in awe of newly renovated "sumptuous" rooms and "remarkable" public spaces "fit for an archbishop" (apt as the site faces St. Pat's and the landmarked Villard Houses at the base formerly housed NYC's cardinals); service gets mixed votes ("you won't find better" vs. "God forbid you should be a mere paying guest when the Sultan is here"), but there's still a "great tea" at Istana and Le Cirque now feeds the fabled in eye-popping digs.

Novotel New York 472R (2S) | 17 | 17 | 15 | 15 | $161 |
226 W. 52nd St. (B'way), New York; (212) 315-0100; (800) 221-4542; FAX: (212) 765-5369
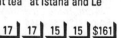 This Midtowner is perhaps "not very exciting", but its location on the northern edge of the Theater District and near Times Square, puts it in the middle of the action; it offers "good value for the money" and is "pet-tolerant" (bien sûr, it's a French import), so most don't mind if the "clean" rooms can be "petite" (some say like "camping in a closet").

Omni Berkshire Place Hotel 349R (47S) | 22 | 21 | 19 | 20 | $216 |
21 E. 52nd St. (Madison Ave.), New York; (212) 753-5800; (800) THE-OMNI; FAX: (212) 753-5800
■ Reopened in '95 after a "wonderful renovation", the Omni still exudes "old European elegance" and now boasts some of "the most modern rooms in the city"; "aristocratic" yet "comfortable", it makes habitués "feel at home" with its "quiet, refined" ambiance, "courteous" staff and "luxurious" lodgings with "beautiful marble bathrooms"; Kokachin restaurant, serving French-Asian cuisine, is just off the lobby.

Paramount 597R (13S) | 17 | 19 | 20 | 22 | $173 |
235 W. 46th St. (B'way), New York; (212) 764-5500; (800) 225-7474; FAX: (212) 575-4892
☑ The stylish Philippe Starck stamp is everywhere at this "ultracool" Theater District eyeful; it's "funky", "kooky" and "dripping with attitude" from a "staff of posers who wear black"; critics cry "all style, no substance", advising "don't pack more than a shoe box" as your room may be "the nicest closet you'll ever stay in", but you get a lot of chic for your dollar (tip: "a greasy ponytail guarantees a room upgrade"); the "oh so trendy" lounge is a B'way show in itself, ditto the sexy Whiskey Bar.

PENINSULA NEW YORK 200R (41S) | 25 | 26 | 24 | 24 | $293 |
700 Fifth Ave. (55th St.), New York; (212) 247-2200; (800) 262-9467; FAX: (212) 903-3943
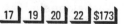 "Elegance and comfort personified" say admirers of this "absolutely grand" beaux arts landmark built in 1905: "posh" rooms and "pampering service" are complemented by a "super rooftop bar", "wonderful dining" at Adrienne and a top-floor spa and health club that "make even the lazy want to work out" while gazing at the spires of St. Pat's; it may be "very expensive", but it's "worth every penny."

Pennsylvania, Hotel 1675R (30S) | – | – | – | – | M |
401 Seventh Ave. (bet. 32nd & 33rd Sts.), New York; (212) 736-5000; (800) 223-8585;
FAX: (212) 502-8712
A bustling behemoth across from Madison Square Garden that's popular with sports
fans, tour groups and the canine and feline crowd (February and March are booked
months ahead for the dog and cat shows); although it's definitely not going to win any
'best of show' awards itself, it fills a niche providing beds for roving packs of tourists
and conventioneers (facilities for up to 1,000).

Pickwick Arms Hotel 300R | 11 | 13 | 11 | 10 | $101 |
230 E. 51st St. (bet. 2nd & 3rd Aves.), New York; (212) 355-0300; (800) 742-5945;
FAX: (212) 755-5029
■ Frugal and not-too-finicky travelers declare "if you want a reasonably priced hotel
in NYC, this is the one"; expect no frills, just "a clean, comfortable bed" in Midtown
for rates so amazingly "cheap" it seems silly to complain about "small" rooms.

PIERRE HOTEL 149R (53S) | 25 | 26 | 25 | 25 | $298 |
2 E. 61st St. (5th Ave.), New York; (212) 838-8000; (800) PIERRE-4; FAX: (212) 758-1615
■ "Old-world elegance and charm", "attention to detail" and Central Park panoramas –
this "fabulous" landmark with "superb service and a doorman who actually remembers
your name" offers for many "the best classic luxury in NYC"; its "gorgeous rooms" could
"use some modernizing, but the overall effect is dazzling"; "don't miss tea in the muraled
Rotunda" or a meal (with weekend dancing) at Café Pierre; true, it strikes a few as
"snobby" and is "super" costly, but it's the "crème de la crème."

PLAZA ATHÉNÉE 117R (36S) | 26 | 27 | 26 | 25 | $296 |
37 E. 64th St. (bet. Madison & Park Aves.), New York; (212) 734-9100; (800) 447-8800;
FAX: (212) 772-0958
■ "A touch of Paris in NYC" describes this "very deluxe, very tasteful", "beautiful small
hotel" on a quiet Upper East Side street; a celeb retreat, it has "class galore" from its
"discreet" service to its "elegant rooms" that may be "costly" (and, some say, "small")
but are "beautifully appointed", especially after a '95 rehab; fans cite Le Régence as
offering "everything you could want" in classic French dining.

Plaza Fifty Suite Hotel 74R (136S) | 19 | 17 | 15 | 14 | $184 |
155 E. 50th St. (3rd Ave.), New York; (212) 751-5710; (800) ME-SUITE;
FAX: (212) 753-1468
■ "Good clean rooms" and "spacious suites" in a "convenient" Midtown location
recommend this "no-frills", "very economical" hotel with "helpful staff" and a kitchen
in every room (plus room service); it's especially "good for families" and business
travelers on extended stays, with a fitness center and conveniences like grocery
shopping for a nominal charge.

Plaza Hotel 673R (133S) | 22 | 23 | 24 | 24 | $267 |
Fifth Ave. & Central Park S., New York; (212) 759-3000; (800) 759-3000; FAX: (212) 759-3167
◪ This "legendary grand hotel" is for many the "essence of NY", a "wonderland of the
rich and famous" with "constant hustle and bustle" and a "great location" overlooking
Central Park; rooms "vary widely", from "palatial" and "well appointed" to "tiny" and
"bland", and service also earns mixed marks, but it's "still thrilling" to see the "lovely
lobby", "incredible Palm Court" and "elegant" Edwardian and Oak Rooms; perhaps it's
"not as good as its rep, but nothing could be" and it remains a "true classic."

Quality Hotel & Suites Rockefeller Center | – | – | – | – | M |
172R (20S)
59 W. 46th St. (bet. 5th & 6th Aves.), New York; (212) 719-2300; (800) 567-7720;
FAX: (212) 921-8929
For inexpensive (by NYC standards), comfortable lodgings in Rockefeller Center, this
recently renovated 1902 hotel fits the bill; guestrooms feature early American decor,
cable TV, coffeemakers and hair dryers, and new meeting rooms, a business center
and conference center attract working travelers; the great location for Broadway
theaters, Fifth Avenue shopping and Times Square sightseeing has price-conscious
tourists booking well in advance.

Quality Hotel East Side 100R | – | – | – | – | M |
161 Lexington Ave. (bet. 30th & 31st Sts.), New York; (212) 545-1800; (800) 567-7720;
FAX: (212) 481-7270
A $4-million dollar renovation has transformed the dilapidated 90-year-old Americana
into a refurbished beaux arts hotel, making it a welcome addition to the Murray Hill
neighborhood; guestrooms (ask for East River or Empire State Building views) are
furnished in early American style and come equipped with coffeemakers and hair dryers.

Radisson Empire Hotel 348R (25S) 16 | 17 | 15 | 15 | $163
44 W. 63rd St. (B'way), New York; (212) 265-7400; (800) 333-3333; FAX: (212) 315-0349
■ Lovers of the performing arts to whom "location is all" put the spotlight on this affordable Westsider opposite Lincoln Center; rooms may be "closet size" but they're "tasteful, tidy" and equipped with VCRs and stereo systems; it's "perfect for opera weekends", but if high Cs aren't music to your ears, try the basement jazz club.

Ramada Milford Plaza Hotel 1290R (10S) 9 | 11 | 9 | 9 | $124
270 W. 45th St. (8th Ave.), New York; (212) 869-3600; (800) 221-2690; FAX: (212) 398-6919
☑ First, the good news: this Theater District vet is "an economical and superconvenient spot" for the B'way-bound; but as the *Survey*'s lowest overall scores attest, there's room for much improvement, with the chief complaint being that, "as the comics used to say, rooms are so small even the mice are hunchbacked"; new furnishings in '96 and the rehabilitation of the Times Square area can only help.

Regency Hotel 270R (94S) 24 | 25 | 24 | 21 | $263
540 Park Ave. (61st St.), New York; (212) 759-4100; (800) 233-2356; FAX: (212) 826-5674
■ "Location, style and quality" are hallmarks of the Loews flagship, which sails smoothly on offering "deluxe, comfortable rooms", "wonderful" service, an "elegant lobby" and what may be "NY's fastest check-in"; captains of industry still navigate its famed power breakfast scene alongside a "mix of foreign guests and rock stars", and The Library is a clubby place for light bites and drinks; factor in business and fitness centers and kitchens in nearly half the rooms and you have a taste of "NYC at its best."

Remington Hotel 80R – | – | – | – | E
129 W. 46th St. (bet. 6th Ave. & B'way), New York; (212) 221-2600; (800) 755-3194; FAX: (212) 764-7481
At press time, the 1936-built Remington was finishing a renovation of all rooms and bathrooms, which could establish it as a small, price-conscious theatergoer's boon; there's no restaurant on-site, but Restaurant Row (46th Street between 8th and 9th Avenues) is a block away, and it's close to both Times Square and Fifth Avenue.

Renaissance New York Hotel 295R (10S) 23 | 20 | 17 | 18 | $185
714 Seventh Ave. (bet. 47th & 48th Sts.), New York; (212) 765-7676; (800) 628-5222; FAX: (212) 956-1962
■ A "small", "beautiful" hotel "in the heart" of Times Square that's "amazingly quiet" with "surprisingly good rooms and friendly service"; its sleek black facade is so unobtrusive that "half the cabbies don't know it", but its prime location and spectacular views from Foley's Fish House could make it party central come December 31, 1999.

Rihga Royal Hotel (500S) 27 | 23 | 22 | 21 | $240
151 W. 54th St. (bet. 6th & 7th Aves.), New York; (212) 307-5000; (800) 937-5454; FAX: (212) 765-6530
■ "Fit for a king" proclaim partisans of this all-suiter that's "excellent for business or pleasure" with an "ideal" Midtown location "in walking distance of theaters"; quarters are "large" and "lovely", and other regal touches include "the world's best bathrooms", a 24-hour gym, fine American fare at Halcyon and a "power scene at the bar"; a few quibble with the "small lobby" and "uneven" service, but overall it's "a winner."

RITZ-CARLTON NEW YORK 183R (31S) 24 | 26 | 24 | 22 | $273
112 Central Park S. (bet. 6th & 7th Aves.), New York; (212) 757-1900; (800) 241-3333; FAX: (212) 757-9620
■ Devotees of this first-class chain cite its hallmark "incredible service", which is here enhanced by a "great location" on Central Park South that wins over sightseers and business travelers alike; the "elegant", "thoughtfully equipped" rooms at this "wonderful oasis" may be "small", but those overlooking the park afford "the best view in town"; on-site Italian dining at Fantino also gets high marks.

Roosevelt Hotel, The 1000R (40S) – | – | – | – | E
45 E. 45th St. (Madison Ave.), New York; (212) 661-9600; (888) TEDDY-NY; FAX: (212) 885-6168
Recently reopened after a two-year, $65-million renovation, this landmark Midtowner offers rooms with simple, traditional furnishings (mahogany wood, rich-toned floral bed coverings) and a cozy, residential feel, along with such amenities as 28,000 square feet of meeting space and valet parking; there are plans to add a restaurant in late 1997.

Royalton 140R (28S) 23 | 21 | 23 | 23 | $233
44 W. 44th St. (bet. 5th & 6th Aves.), New York; (212) 869-4400; (800) 635-9013; FAX: (212) 869-8965
■ Philippe Starck to the max, this "sleek" Midtowner has "elegantly modern everything", from the "uniquely contemporary lobby" to the "exciting high-tech rooms" and "awesome bathrooms" (those in the lobby are a "must-see"); "handsome staffers" clad in black may come off as "cold", but they add to the aura of the "sexiest hotel alive"; restaurant 44 is the place to watch Condé Nast biggies.

Shelburne Murray Hill (258S)
19 | 18 | 13 | 14 | $170

303 Lexington Ave. (bet. 37th & 38th Sts.), New York; (212) 689-5200; (800) ME-SUITE; FAX: (212) 779-7068

■ For "Uptown atmosphere at half the price", some recommend this Murray Hill all-suiter that offers "very nice, good-size" lodgings "with high ceilings" and kitchens plus such extras as a health club and grocery-shopping service along with a "staff that makes you feel welcome."

Sheraton Manhattan 650R (7S)
18 | 17 | 15 | 16 | $180

730 Seventh Ave. (51st St.), New York; (212) 581-3300; (800) 223-6550; FAX: (212) 315-4265

■ Smaller than its across-the-street sibling, but also well situated for both Midtown and the Theater District, with "comfortable" rooms, "a good bar", a fitness center and "nice pool" "to soothe the tired tourist" or business traveler; N.B. Sheraton plans to close the hotel briefly in '97 to convert it into a high tech business-oriented format.

Sheraton NY Hotel & Towers 1690R (53S)
18 | 18 | 16 | 17 | $186

811 Seventh Ave. (53rd St.), New York; (212) 581-1000; (800) 223-6550; FAX: (212) 315-4265

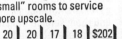 "Convention business is everything", or so it feels at this "huge", "mainstream" hotel in a "convenient" Midtown/Theater District site; fans call it a "serviceable" "good value", while critics feel "everything needs improvement", from the "small" rooms to service that can be "pleasant" or "impersonal"; N.B. Tower rooms are more upscale.

Sheraton Russell Hotel 146R (23S)
20 | 20 | 17 | 18 | $202

45 Park Ave. (37th St.), New York; (212) 685-7676; (800) 537-0075; FAX: (212) 889-3193

■ Reopened after a brief closure, this "well-kept secret" of a Sheraton in residential Murray Hill has been converted into the chain's business-oriented Corporate Club format, with such features as oversized desks, dataports, voicemail and printer/fax/copiers in each room, plus a fitness center; presumably, surveyors who gave it the above ratings will now be even more pleased.

Sherry Netherland 400R
25 | 25 | 22 | 22 | $280

781 Fifth Ave. (59th St.), New York; (212) 355-2800; (800) 247-4377; FAX: (212) 319-4306

■ Fifth Avenue's "grande old dame" feels "like a home", especially if the homes you're used to have a lobby modeled after the Vatican Library; largely residential, it provides its moneyed clientele with an "oasis in the city" permeated by "old-style elegance", from the "comfortable, understated" rooms and suites to the "very good service"; it also has a fitness center and the famously expensive Italian restaurant Harry Cipriani.

Shoreham Hotel 47R (37S)
20 | 21 | 16 | 16 | $187

33 W. 55th St. (bet. 5th & 6th Aves.), New York; (212) 247-6700; (800) 553-3347; FAX: (212) 765-9741

■ This "hip" yet "refined" Midtowner is a "nice change from the big guys", with "cool", "modern" ambiance, "good service" and rooms that may be "tiny" but have "great decor" and "lovely linens"; add free continental breakfast and after-theater desserts plus La Caravelle, one of NYC's finest French restaurants, and this "small gem" shines as a "total class act" and real "deal."

SoHo Grand Hotel 363R (4S)
– | – | – | – | VE

310 W. Broadway (bet. Canal & Grand Sts.), New York; (212) 965-3000; (800) 965-3000; FAX: (212) 965-3141

The first new hotel in SoHo in more than a century opened in August 1996, sporting a striking design that blends an edgy modern attitude with elements inspired by the area's turn-of-the-century cast-iron past; the sleek bedrooms, decorated in cool tones and featuring Frette linens and bathrooms with pedestal sinks, are filled with players from the art, fashion, design and advertising worlds. as is its Canal House restaurant.

Southgate Tower Suite Hotel (519S)
15 | 13 | 10 | 11 | $147

371 Seventh Ave. (31st St.), New York; (212) 563-1800; (800) ME-SUITE; FAX: (212) 714-2159

 The site is fine if you're into sports (Madison Square Garden), shopping (Macy's) or the rag trade (Garment District), but not so appealing if you aren't; still, "good rates" for "large" kitchen-equipped suites that are "old but comfortable" (and recently renovated) make this all suiter "good for families"; but remember it's just "the basics."

STANHOPE HOTEL 70R (70S)
25 | 25 | 24 | 23 | $278

995 Fifth Ave. (81st St.), New York; (212) 288-5800; (800) 828-1123; FAX: (212) 517-0088

■ Despite a change in owners, this "stylish little hideaway" across from the Metropolitan Museum and Central Park remains one of NYC's most "elegant" hotels, known for its "impeccable service", "lovely" antiques-filled lobby and "beautifully appointed rooms with many creature comforts"; yes, it's "expensive", but it epitomizes "luxurious European style" and you can't beat the sidewalk cafe for people-watching.

St. Moritz on the Park 560R (120S)   13 | 15 | 14 | 14 | $181

50 S. Central Park S. (6th Ave.), New York; (212) 755-5800; (800) 221-4774; FAX: (212) 752-5097

☑ Everyone loves the Central Park South location, some rooms have "stunning views" and budget-watchers rate it a "best bargain"; but this "slipping" saint would appear to need a miracle, or at least "a complete renovation", to quiet critics who berate it for "terminal dowdiness", "small" rooms and staff that at times "couldn't care less."

ST. REGIS, THE 221R (92S)   27 | 27 | 27 | 26 | $319

2 E. 55th St. (bet. 5th & Madison), New York; (212) 753-4500; (800) 759-7550; FAX: (212) 787-3447

■ "All the opulence you'll ever want", from "luxurious rooms with many amenities" to "unbelievably good" service (a "butler on every floor") makes this 1904 beaux arts belle the "ne plus ultra" of hotels for many (it's NYC's No. 2 overall best); "catering to the fastidiously rich as opposed to the filthy rich", it is, alas, "wildly expensive, but must be done at least once"; ditto its French-Asian Lespinasse restaurant.

Surrey Hotel (130S)   22 | 20 | 23 | 15 | $228

20 E. 76th St. (bet. 5th & Madison Aves.), New York; (212) 288-3700; (800) ME-SUITE; FAX: (212) 628-1549

■ "Spacious", "well-appointed" suites with kitchens give guests at this "small" Upper Eastsider the impression of "having their own apartment in the best part of NYC"; as if that's not enough, there's a "quiet, elegant" lobby, "helpful" staff, fitness center and room service from the highly acclaimed French restaurant Daniel; all in all, "an unbelievable find."

Trump International Hotel & Tower (168S)   – | – | – | – | VE

1 Central Park W. (Columbus Circle), New York; (212) 299-1000; (888) 44-TRUMP; FAX: (212) 299-1150

He's back and brash as ever: Donald Trump's latest is a 52-story glass-sheathed Columbus Circle condo tower with a luxury all-suite hotel on 15 floors; quarters feature floor-to-ceiling windows, full kitchens, CD players, VCRs, fax machines, even telescopes, and each guest is assigned a 'Trump attaché' as personal assistant; also on-site: a spa/fitness center with a 55-foot lap pool, plus the chic new restaurant Jean Georges, one of only five NYC restaurants to be given four stars by the *New York Times*.

Tudor, The 286R (14S)   17 | 17 | 16 | 15 | $159

304 E. 42nd St. (2nd Ave.), New York; (212) 986-8800; (800) 879-8836; FAX: (212) 297-3440

☑ Near the UN and Grand Central Station, the revamped Tudor is touted as a "best value" by boosters who cite "beautifully remodeled rooms" (with dataports and dual-line phones), "friendly, accommodating service" and a "pretty lobby"; critics point to "tiny, tiny" quarters and "mixed service", but the consensus is it's "a find for East Side visitors"; ratings may not reflect the complete redo.

UN Plaza - Park Hyatt Hotel 382R (45S)   23 | 23 | 21 | 20 | $213

(nka Regal UN Plaza Hotel)

1 United Nations Plaza (44th St. & 1st Ave.), New York; (212) 758-1234; (800) 233-1234; FAX: (212) 702-5051

■ At times resembling a "makeshift embassy for UN delegates" thanks to its "interesting clientele", this "cosmopolitan" high-rise across from the UN promotes its own kind of peace with "rooms from heaven", "superb service" and "spectacular" views; "an excellent health club", "terrific glass-enclosed pool" and indoor tennis court are further assets, and the Ambassador Grill serves "a fabulous brunch", making weekend package deals particularly satisfying.

Waldorf Astoria 1160R (50S)   21 | 22 | 22 | 23 | $233

301 Park Ave. (bet. 49th & 50th Sts.), New York; (212) 872-4534; (800) WALDORF; FAX: (212) 872-7272

☑ Pause in the "unsurpassed" art deco lobby with its "gorgeous flowers", dine at the "excellent" Peacock Alley, watch the "ladies in ball gowns" and "international dignitaries" – this Midtown legend is a world unto itself and "still the queen" for loyalists; perhaps "its reputation is better" than its "inconsistent" rooms ("elegant, spacious" vs. "microscopic") and service that sometimes slips, but the bottom line is "it's the Waldorf" and few places match its "aura of NY history."

WALDORF TOWERS 120R (75S)   26 | 25 | 23 | 24 | $296

100 E. 50th St. (bet. Park & Lexington Aves.), New York; (212) 355-3100; (800) WALDORF; FAX: (212) 872-4799

■ "If you can afford it, there's no alternative to the Towers", a 14-floor haven within the Waldorf Astoria with a separate entrance; the "Queen Mum of NYC hotels", it's "a sedate world" where presidents, and other "bigwigs" overnight in "unique rooms" with "the world's best beds"; a few brand it "stodgy" and claim staff are "uninterested unless they've seen you in *People* magazine", but most salute "class all the way."

Wales Hotel 46R (40S)   – | – | – | – | E

1295 Madison Ave. (92nd St.), New York; (212) 876-6000; (800) 428-5252; FAX: (212) 860-7000
This beautifully restored turn-of-the-century Victorian in the Upper East Side's quiet Carnegie Hill section is ideal for museum hopping and antique shopping; a Euro-style boutique hotel, it offers fireplaces and kitchenettes in some rooms, plus complimentary breakfast and afternoon tea complete with classical music recitals; on-site but not associated with the hotel is Sarabeth's Kitchen, a popular American restaurant.

Warwick, The 355R (70S)   16 | 17 | 15 | 14 | $176

65 W. 54th St. (6th Ave.), New York; (212) 247-2700; (800) 223-4099; FAX: (212) 957-8915
 Built by William Randolph Hearst in 1927, this veteran once hosted Cary Grant, the Beatles and Elvis Presley; today, it draws tourists and business travelers with its "good value" and "excellent location" near Carnegie Hall and Fifth Avenue; renovations haven't erased all complaints about the rooms ("so-so", "smallest bathroom in NYC") or "poor service at the desk", but in general it's a "comfortable, convenient" choice.

Washington Square Hotel 160R   11 | 11 | 11 | 11 | $111

103 Waverly Pl. (bet. 6th Ave. & MacDougal St.), New York; (212) 777-9515; (800) 222-0418; FAX: (212) 979-8373
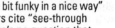 You "can't beat the price", so "teeny tiny rooms" and "average service" don't matter much – this family-operated hostelry on Washington Square has become the darling of foreign tourists, NYU parents and others seeking a "clean, quiet" base in Greenwich Village; the great rates even include continental breakfast.

Westbury Hotel 174R (54S)   24 | 24 | 22 | 21 | $253

15 E. 69th St. (Madison Ave.), New York; (212) 535-2000; (800) 321-1569; FAX: (212) 535-5058
■ "A gentle, charming hotel in a hustle-bustle town" with "English"-style service and elegance – no wonder it's "terribly popular with Brits"; it's "a vacation just to be in its beautiful", "well-appointed" rooms (even more "heavenly" after a '95 rehab, as a rise in ratings attests), but those who can bear to leave them also enjoy its modern fitness center, stylish Madison Avenue surroundings and New American dining at The Polo; N.B. the hotel plans to close in late '97 for a major renovation.

Wolcott, Hotel 100R (70S)   – | – | – | – | M

4 W. 31st St. (bet. 5th Ave. & B'way), New York; (212) 268-2900; FAX: (212) 563-0096
Providing "excellent value" near Herald Square shopping, Madison Square Garden and the Empire State Building, this beaux arts hotel renovated in 1995 appeals to students, group vacationers and business travelers on a tight budget; amenities are limited, though all rooms include color TV and direct-dial phones (some share a bath).

Wyndham Hotel 62R (60S)   17 | 17 | 11 | 12 | $159

42 W. 58th St. (bet. 5th & 6th Aves.), New York; (212) 753-3500; (800) 257-1111; FAX: (212) 754-5638
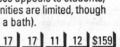 This "small, friendly hotel nestled near all the action of Fifth Avenue" "feels like a friend's apartment" or a pair of "favorite old shoes"; fans call it "a bit funky in a nice way" with rooms that are "old but clean, spacious and homey", others cite "see-through towels" and staff that "stays till death do they part"; still, there's no question that it's a "great value."

North Hudson

Elk Lake Lodge 6R (7S)   – | – | – | – | M

PO Box 59, Blue Ridge Rd., North Hudson; (518) 532-7616; FAX: (518) 532-9262
Set amid 12,000 acres of private Adirondack beauty, this 1904 lakeside lodge may offer only "basic" rooms and food, but there are also seven lovely, comfortable cottages with "unparalleled views" of what *National Geographic* has called "the jewel of the Adirondacks"; there's mountain lake swimming, canoeing, fishing, climbing and 45 miles of hiking trails, as well as an aura of wilderness peace without phones and TVs; open May–October; early word is that new cooks have enlivened the hearty three meals.

Old Chatham

Old Chatham Sheepherding Co. Inn 6R (2S)   ▽ 27 | 27 | 28 | 27 | $210

99 Shaker Museum Rd., Old Chatham; (518) 794-9774; FAX: (518) 794-9779
■ High ratings indeed for a working sheep farm, but this "romantic getaway" set in a "wonderful" restored 1790 Georgian manor offers "charming", individually decorated rooms, a "pastoral scene" of rolling hills, "grazing sheep" and a Shaker village across the road, it's above all a mecca for fine dining, with raves for "fantastic chef" Melissa Kelly's "glorious" American fare emphasizing local ingredients; for an extra treat, check out the "state-of-the-art barn at milking time"; breakfast included.

Poughkeepsie

Inn at the Falls 22R (14S) 22 | 21 | 17 | 20 | $143
50 Red Oaks Mill Rd., Poughkeepsie; (914) 462-5770; (800) 344-1466;
FAX: (914) 462-5943
☑ Built along the Wappinger Creek and Falls is an inn that respondents dub both an "efficient businessperson's delight" and a "great base station for antiquing" or "a weekend visiting Hyde Park and the Culinary Institute"; the "staff is friendly", but the rooms get mixed reactions: some find them "beautiful" and "thoughtfully furnished", others sigh "motel quality", but even so, "fine for Poughkeepsie."

Rhinebeck

Beekman Arms 57R (2S) 19 | 20 | 22 | 18 | $141
4 Mill St., Rhinebeck; (914) 876-7077; FAX: (914) 876-7077
☑ "Washington really did sleep" at this "cozy, friendly" 1766 Hudson Valley inn, a "great getaway with lots of style and old-world charm" where the "excellent" if "pricey" fare at An American Place Country Restaurant is cooked by star chef Larry Forgione; rooms in the original inn (renovated in 1995) are "historic" but "too small" for some, those in the adjacent motel are "comfortable" but lack the "charm of the colonial ones" and those in the circa 1844 Delamater House (with adjoining conference center) are "lovely" but about a block away.

Rye Brook

Doral Arrowwood 269R (3S) 19 | 19 | 19 | 22 | $167
Anderson Hill Rd., Rye Brook; (914) 939-5500; (800) 22-DORAL; FAX: (914) 323-5500
☑ "Good for corporate conferences – end of story" sums up reactions to this "modern" facility "close to NYC" that offers execs a "professional" resort conference center bolstered by "excellent" athletic facilities amid the Westchester countryside; but while "high on utility", most find it "low on charm", with many chilled by a "cold, impersonal" atmosphere and "functional" but "monastic" rooms; it's also a "good value on weekends" for adults but discourages bringing children.

Saranac Lake

POINT, THE 10R (1S) 29 | 29 | 28 | 28 | VE
Box 65, HCR 1, Saranac Lake; (518) 891-5674; (800) 255-3530; FAX: (518) 891-1152
■ Always among the top-ranked lodgings in the country, this Adirondack camp built by the Rockefellers is "superlative in every way" – so "fabulous" that you should "cancel 10 other vacations and go here once"; in an "out-of-this-world" setting on Saranac Lake and now affiliated with Relais & Châteaux, its "very special rooms" are "decorated in rustic elegance", the "food [included in rates] is superb", and the staff "cannot do enough for you"; yes, the "prices are breathtaking", but "heaven" is "well worth it."

Saranac, Hotel 92R ▽ 18 | 20 | 20 | 19 | $139
101 Main St., Saranac Lake; (518) 891-2200; (800) 937-0211; FAX: (518) 891-5664
■ Inspired by a Florentine palace, this "elegant" 1926 "center-of-town" hotel has "an old-fashioned feel with modern amenities"; since 1961 it's been owned and operated by Paul Smith's College and although a few say "rooms are cramped", the "helpful" student staff gets decent grades, as does the "good food" in the two on-site restaurants; a host of athletic options are nearby.

Saratoga Springs

Gideon Putnam Hotel and Conference Center 120R (12S) 19 | 20 | 19 | 22 | $174
Saratoga Spa State Park, Saratoga Springs; (518) 584-3000; (800) 732-1560; FAX: (518) 584-1354
☑ Set in the "gorgeous grounds" of a 2,000-acre park noted for its famed mineral waters, this Georgian-style "golden-age hotel" is "perfect during the races" and "convenient" to the Saratoga Performing Arts Center" as well as a place for "excellent golf", tennis and x-country skiing; still lots of guests know it best for the traditional Sunday brunch; for a few, it's a "creaky antique" whose "furnishings have seen better days", but even they admire the "beautiful setting"; conference center facilities and services are available.

Inn at Saratoga 34R (4S)
19 21 20 20 $154

231 Broadway, Saratoga Springs; (518) 583-1890; (800) 274-3573;
FAX: (518) 583-2543

☑ An 1850 Victorian with English gardens, this "well-kept" small inn boasts an "excellent location" that is "perfect for the races" as well as for the performing arts center and the mineral baths; although "service and accommodations are merely adequate", the food is "solid American" if "nothing unusual" (check out the Sunday jazz brunch); despite its modest size, it hosts "lots of meetings."

Sheraton Saratoga Springs Hotel & Conference Center 216R (24S)
18 18 16 18 $141

534 Broadway, Saratoga Springs; (518) 584-4000; (800) 325-3535; FAX: (518) 584-7430

☑ While some dismiss this "large and commercial" chainer as an "ordinary modern hotel in an extraordinary Victorian town", others take a more positive view, dubbing it a "modernized place to stay that's clean and pretty"; all agree its "center-city" location is convenient to racing and concerts, and there are meeting and conference facilities for groups of up to 800; the "huge, inexpensive Sunday brunch" is worth a try.

Shandaken

Shandaken Inn 11R (1S)
▽ 21 22 24 22 $177

Golf Course Rd./Rte. 28, Shandaken; (914) 688-5100

■ The rooms are "antiques-filled" at this 1870 converted dairy barn on 40 acres in the Catskills; besides having a "friendly" host and "really good home cooking" (well, it's home cooking if your home is in the French countryside), the inn is near all kinds of sporting activities including golf, hiking, "good" skiing and, especially, trout fishing in the wonderful Esopus Creek; open weekends only, rates include breakfast and dinner; N.B. plastic is now accepted.

Shelter Island

Chequit Inn 32R (3S)
– – – – M

23 Grand Ave., Shelter Island; (516) 749-0018; FAX: (516) 749-0183

North Ferry riders can't miss this 1872 SI Heights landmark, an imposing Victorian perched on a hill overlooking the harbor, and those looking for alfresco dining keep its outdoor tables filled all summer; under the same ownership as the Rams Head Inn, the Chequit is in the midst of a gradual, total renovation; it offers a convenient in-town location, a variety of individually decorated rooms (some newly redone and some with a/c), good New American dining in its downstairs restaurant and complimentary sherry by the fireplace in the lobby; continental breakfast included.

Ram's Head Inn 17R
18 21 23 22 $160

108 Ram Island Dr., Shelter Island; (516) 749-0811; FAX: (516) 749-0059

■ Shelter Island is "a short ferry ride to a better day", one where there are no TVs, radios or clocks in the guestrooms of this center-hall colonial inn, which may be why it's so "quiet and cozy" and filled with "old-fashioned charm"; most think "rooms are lovely" (a few find them small) and the "food is excellent" and enjoy the "sprawling lawn overlooking the bay" and 800 feet of beachfront; seafarers get to use sloops, sunfish, a paddleboat and a kayak, while landlubbers relax with croquet; N.B. don't miss dinner on the porch in summer.

Stony Brook

Three Village Inn 20R (6S)
20 22 21 20 $137

150 Main St., Stony Brook; (516) 751-0555; FAX: (516) 751-0593

■ The original 1750 farmhouse of this "charming and quaint" inn in a "cute village" is where you'll find a "superior restaurant", with American fare served by waitresses in period costume; the "cozy" rooms have "an old-world feel" while the newer but "charming" cottages overlook Stony Brook harbor; its "natural setting near the water" and "great service" make it both "pretty to look at" and a "delightful spot" to stay on Long Island.

Tarrytown

Castle at Tarrytown (7S)   ▽ 21 20 22 21 $199
400 Benedict Ave., Tarrytown; (914) 631-1980; FAX: (914) 631-4612
Yes, it's really a castle in suburban New York, built at the turn of the century in Sleepy Hollow country and opened in late 1996 as a seven-suite inn, with 24 more rooms and suites to come in '97; guests may sleep as well as Rip Van Winkle with walls as thick as three feet, and masterful execs feel like the kings they think they are in the Gothic, stained-glass Great Hall meeting room; on-site Equus restaurant offers Eclectic contemporary cuisine.

Marriott Westchester 439R (5S)   18 17 16 17 $133
670 White Plains Rd., Tarrytown; (914) 631-2200; (800) 228-9290; FAX: (914) 631-2832
☑ Tarrytown's Marriott has "decent facilities for business", and with space to accommodate 1,200, it's "great for conventions"; critics, however, note that while the hotel is "serviceable" it's just "basic Marriott – not very memorable."

Tarrytown House Executive Conference Center 146R (2S)   20 21 21 22 $166
E. Sunnyside Ln., Tarrytown; (914) 591-8200; (800) 553-8118; FAX: (914) 591-4014
☑ As an executive conference center that can accommodate 400, this 26-acre estate has a "great atmosphere", "surprising gourmet cuisine" and "wonderful facilities" surrounded by "picturesque" grounds with "lots of grass and woods"; the "elegant" main 1868 Victorian mansion and "Gatsby setting" makes for a "quaint and romantic" "weekend retreat", especially for those sans laptops, but a few critics say "standard rooms" are due for "renovation"; while mainly a conference facility weekdays, social guests are welcome if space allows and it's also a popular wedding site.

North Carolina

Asheville

R	S	D	P	$

Great Smokies SunSpree Golf & Tennis Resort 277R (3S)
| 16 | 15 | 16 | 17 | $97 |

1 Holiday Inn Dr., Asheville; (704) 254-3211; (800) 733-3211; FAX: (704) 254-1603
☑ This Holiday Inn–affiliate is located in a "beautiful area" but is otherwise regarded as fairly "basic"; recreation facilities including two outdoor pools, indoor and outdoor tennis courts, an 18-hole golf course and a Fun-Club for kids beckon families and tour groups, and it's a convenient base for outings to the Biltmore Estate.

GROVE PARK INN RESORT 486R (24S)
| 23 | 23 | 23 | 26 | $168 |

290 Macon Ave., Asheville; (704) 252-2711; (800) 438-5800; FAX: (704) 253-7053
■ "If going to see the grand old Biltmore Estate, why not stay in a picturesque grand hotel?"; this "historic" Asheville resort has a "top-of-the-world feel", from the Great Hall with huge stone fireplaces in the Arts and Crafts–furnished main building to the terrace with "incredible" mountain views; "stay in the old part for a real step back in time", but rest assured there are plenty of modern diversions (tennis, golf, etc.); "everyone deserves to be here once."

RICHMOND HILL INN 33R (3S)
| 25 | 24 | 25 | 24 | $172 |

87 Richmond Hill Dr., Asheville; (704) 252-7313; (800) 545-9238; FAX: (704) 252-8726
■ From the "impeccable service" to the location on a hill above Asheville, this "charming" inn is "tip-top" all-around; the main building, an "elegant" 1888 Queen Anne–style mansion, offers "lovely rooms", but some prefer the newer cottages, all with fireplace and porch; either way, life at the top is "extraordinary" – all the more so given "wonderful" nouvelle Southern cuisine at the "fine" on-site restaurant, Gabrielle's (full breakfast included).

Blowing Rock

Hound Ears Club 13R (15S)
| ▽ 21 | 21 | 21 | 21 | $166 |

PO Box 188, Hwy. 105 S., Blowing Rock; (704) 963-4321; FAX: (704) 963-8030
■ An intimate resort hidden on 700 acres near Grandfather Mountain; "beautiful scenery", "excellent service" and "fine dining" impress, as does what "could be the prettiest golf course in the US"; accommodations range from lodge rooms to clubhouse suites and privately owned chalets or condos, with panoramic Blue Ridge views from most balconies; for relaxing there's tennis, swimming and nearby hiking and horseback riding, but no alcohol, so BYO.

Cashiers

High Hampton Inn & Country Club 120R (40S)
| 20 | 23 | 19 | 24 | $149 |

PO Box 338, Hwy. 107 S., Cashiers; (704) 743-2411; (800) 334-2551; FAX: (704) 743-5991
☑ "Our favorite family vacation spot" proclaim partisans of this "laid-back resort" built in the 1930s; lodgings are "very plain", but it's "one of the most relaxing places" around and "very reasonably priced", offering golf, tennis, biking, hiking and more; the summer-camp ambiance includes buffet-style "good Southern" meals and group activities ("they made us Yankees sing 'Dixie' at a sing-along – wow!"); open April–November.

Charlotte

Adam's Mark Hotel 561R (37S)
| 18 | 18 | 16 | 17 | $120 |

555 S. McDowell St., Charlotte; (704) 372-4100; (800) 444-ADAM; FAX: (704) 348-4646
☑ This "standard" Uptown "commercial business hotel" inspires a wide range of reactions, from "great pool, food and room" and "warm, helpful service" to "mediocre", "beats sleeping in your car"; pluses include a fitness center, indoor and outdoor pools and meeting space for up to 2,000.

Dunhill Hotel 59R (1S)
| ▽ 23 | 22 | 19 | 19 | $103 |

237 N. Tryon St., Charlotte; (704) 332-4141; (800) 354-4141; FAX: (704) 376-4117
☑ "A continental jewel in the Queen City", this European-style hotel built in 1929 offers "old-world elegance" at affordable fares; surveyors laud the "friendly staff" and "efficient front desk", but a few knock "tiny rooms" and slow breakfast service; its Arts District locale means lots to do, with the Blumenthal Center for the Performing Arts a block away and the science museum Discovery Place next door.

Hyatt Charlotte 258R (4S)   21 | 20 | 19 | 19 | $125
5501 Carnegie Blvd., Charlotte; (704) 554-1234; (800) 233-1234; FAX: (704) 554-8319
■ "Excellent" is the verdict of surveyors impressed by this Hyatt's "large rooms", good service and "convenient" SouthPark business district location; while the flora-filled atrium and indoor pool invite relaxation, workaholics can head for the printer- and copier-equipped Business Plan floor where rooms have work stations and fax machines; shops and restaurants are across the street at SouthPark Mall.

Marriott City Center Charlotte 423R (8S)   19 | 19 | 18 | 18 | $129
100 W. Trade St., Charlotte; (704) 333-9000; (800) 228-9290; FAX: (704) 342-3419
☑ The phrase "standard Marriott" induces *Rashomon*-like reactions here: "above average" vs. "thoroughly mediocre"; "reliable" vs. "a disappointment"; "good service" vs. "a room, nothing else"; at least no one questions the "convenient" Downtown location, a stroll from Spirit Square and Discovery Place, and "nice pool and gym"; while it may be "typical", it can be "just right for a convention or business traveler."

Park Hotel, The 190R (4S)   24 | 23 | 22 | 22 | $138
2200 Rexford Rd., Charlotte; (704) 364-8220; (800) 334-0331; FAX: (704) 365-4712
■ The "best you can do in Charlotte" is a "jewel of a hotel in a suburbanlike setting" near tony SouthPark Mall; "upscale, clean and fashionable", it strikes most as an all-around "delight" with pleasant rooms and "friendly, personal service" from a "responsive staff"· "excellent" Southern-Continental dining at Morrocrofts restaurant is a plus.

Radisson Plaza Hotel Charlotte 336R (29S)   17 | 15 | 14 | 14 | $118
1 Radisson Plaza, 101 S. Tryon St., Charlotte; (704) 377-0400; (800) 333-3333; FAX: (704) 347-0649
☑ Despite moderate ratings, most consider this a "very nice" civic center option that rewards weary execs with "fine rooms", "Southern hospitality", a well-equipped fitness center and rooftop pool; while known as a "dependable business hotel", there's also family fun just a skywalk away at museums, shops and restaurants; special packages let you bring the brood without breaking the bank.

Westin Hotel Charlotte 398R (12S)   22 | 20 | 19 | 20 | $131
(fka Omni Charlotte Hotel)
222 E. Third St., Charlotte; (704) 377-1500; (800) WESTIN-1; FAX: (704) 377-4143
☑ "Excellent service", "good rooms" and a "suave" ambiance please most visitors to this "big Uptown hotel", but the less impressed find it "predictable" and "convenient – that's all, folks"; 14 meeting rooms hold up to 800 people who stay awake during presentations thanks to Starbucks coffee, which is served in the hotel; N.B. a revamp of all guestrooms. meeting spaces and public areas was completed in '96.

Duck

SANDERLING INN RESORT 77R (10S)   25 | 24 | 23 | 26 | $171
1461 Duck Rd., Duck; (919) 261-4111; (800) 701-4111; FAX: (919) 261-1638
■ For admirers, "the only place to stay on the Outer Banks" is this "luxurious yet understated" resort in a "great" oceanfront location at the edge of a bird sanctuary; "comfortable rooms", "excellent food" (served in a converted 1899 lifesaving station), "limitless beach" and a certain "indescribable charm" make for "blissful" stays; bonuses include free continental breakfast and afternoon tea, indoor and outdoor pools, tennis and nearby nature trails.

Edenton

Lords Proprietors' Inn 20R ⊟   – | – | – | – | E
300 N. Broad St., Edenton; (919) 482-3641; FAX: (919) 482-2432
Lords and ladies alike laze in this gracious B&B offering accommodations in three restored structures – a brick Victorian, an 1801 frame house and a converted tobacco-packing house – in historic Edenton; the pretty rooms feature such grace notes as four-poster beds, and guests can savor afternoon tea in the parlors or on the porches and sophisticated Southern cuisine in the Whedbee House dining room; no credit cards.

Fayetteville

Radisson Prince Charles Hotel 26R (57S)   ▽ 19 | 18 | 16 | 19 | $92
450 Hay St., Fayetteville; (910) 433-4444; (800) 333-3333; FAX: (910) 485-8269
■ The few surveyors who know this Colonial Revival–style hotel in Downtown Fayetteville call it a "nice stopover place" with spacious "refurbished rooms", an "excellent staff" and elaborate marble stairways and floors in the public areas; step back in time and up to the plate at Babe's, the hotel bar named for George Herman Ruth, who hit his first pro home run in this town.

Lake Toxaway

GREYSTONE INN 30R (3S)
26 | 25 | 25 | 27 | $237

Greystone Ln., Lake Toxaway; (704) 966-4700; (800) 824-5766; FAX: (704) 862-5689
■ The "closest place to heaven – period" is the kind of reaction provoked by this lakeside mountain retreat in western NC; a "lovely setting", "terrific food", "excellent service" and "large, luxurious rooms" make it a place "you don't want to leave"; while some find it "ridiculously expensive", everything is included, from full breakfast to "terrific" gourmet dinners, plus activities (like water skiing, fishing and tennis) to burn all those calories.

Nags Head

First Colony Inn 20R (6S)
– | – | – | – | M

6720 S. Virginia Dare Trail, Nags Head; (919) 441-2343; (800) 368-9390; FAX: (919) 441-9234
A 1930s shingled structure that was moved in 1988 from its original precarious location to a site offering more shelter from ocean storms; on the National Register of Historic Places, it lures those in search of a romantic Outer Banks escape with period decor and rooms that open onto wraparound porches; the beach locale inspires swimming and sunning, with sailing and windsurfing gear available for rent nearby.

Pinehurst

Holly Inn 44R (30S)
22 | 23 | 21 | 24 | $138

PO Box 2300, 2300 Cherokee Rd., Pinehurst; (910) 295-2300; (800) 682-6901; FAX: (910) 295-0988
☑ "Rest at its best" is enjoyed by admirers at this "sweetly decorated", Cape Cod–style inn, built in 1895 by the transplanted Bostonian who founded the village of Pinehurst; a "cute", "comfortable" charmer, it offers "tasteful rooms", "delicious meals" and "super service" and is "wonderful for small conference groups"; a very few critics beef about "poor dining and service", but most consider it "nicely done" overall.

PINEHURST RESORT & COUNTRY CLUB
23 | 25 | 24 | 27 | $199

220R (233S)
PO Box 4000, Carolina Vista, Pinehurst; (910) 295-8553; (800) ITS-GOLF; FAX: (910) 295-8503
☑ "First, shoot in the high 70s, then reserve a room" at a "genteel golfer's paradise" with eight 18-hole "world-class" courses; those who say there's "not much to do if you don't golf" must be ignoring the 24 tennis courts and water sports, plus the fact that you can play "Scarlett O'Hara for a day" enjoying "Southern hospitality" in an 1895 white clapboard hotel with elegant verandas; critics cite "nothing special" rooms and a "factory" feel, but they're outvoted.

Pittsboro

FEARRINGTON HOUSE 19R (9S)
28 | 27 | 28 | 26 | $187

2000 Fearrington Village Ctr., Pittsboro; (919) 542-2121; FAX: (919) 542-4202
■ A Relais & Châteaux "gem" in a "beautiful country" setting eight miles south of Chapel Hill ("great for Duke U" and UNC visitors); tucked away in a "wonderful" complex of quaint shops, it offers "pleasant, comfortable" rooms adorned with English pine antiques and fresh flowers, "European-style hospitality", "lovely" public areas and "exquisite dining" (a full breakfast is included); all in all, "a total joy."

Raleigh-Durham

Carolina Inn 177R (7S)
19 | 20 | 20 | 20 | $116

211 Pittsboro St., Chapel Hill; (919) 933-2001; (800) 962-8519; FAX: (919) 962-3400
☑ A major redo completed in 1995 "dramatically improved comfort" at this "quaint", vintage-1924 hotel with a "terrific" location on the UNC campus in the heart of Chapel Hill; now a Doubletree affiliate, it feels "like home" to admirers of its "Southern hospitality", lovely public rooms and floral arrangements, but critics gripe about "rooms like closets."

Four Points Hotel at Crabtree 308R (10S)
15 | 15 | 14 | 15 | $110

(fka Sheraton at Crabtree Valley)
4501 Creedmoor Rd., Raleigh; (919) 787-7111; (800) 325-3535; FAX: (919) 783-0024
☑ While some praise "good food and service" and "meetings done with flair", others call this suburbanite next to Crabtree Valley Mall "just another Sheraton" (it's still affiliated with the chain despite the name change) and "disappointing" at that; however, full exterior and interior renovations may change critics' minds; assets include an indoor pool, exercise equipment and meeting space for up to 500.

Hilton North Raleigh 339R (6S)   18 | 17 | 15 | 16 | $114
3415 Wake Forest Rd., Raleigh; (919) 872-2323; (800) HILTONS; FAX: (919) 876-0890
☑ Convenient to the capitol and Downtown business district, this hotel pleases some with "excellent" executive-level amenities, "good resources" for conferences (20 meeting rooms hold up to 1,000) and the "friendliest greeting ever"; but others grumble that even if it's "best in the area, that's not saying much", calling it "typical" except for the "nice bar scene" (at Bowties); a few reports of the "worst service" aren't encouraging.

Marriott at Research Triangle Park 220R (4S)   18 | 19 | 17 | 17 | $123
4700 Guardian Dr., Durham; (919) 941-6200; (800) 228-9290; FAX: (919) 941-6229
■ A "big-city feel in the middle of nowhere" is offered at this "very pleasant", "practical business hotel" with "clean, functional" rooms and "excellent facilities" for work and play; though adjacent to Research Triangle Park, some find the airport-area location somewhat "isolated" and the modern architecture a bit "cold"; overall it's "nice enough" and "service is very accommodating."

Marriott Raleigh 371R (4S)   19 | 20 | 17 | 18 | $110
4500 Marriott Dr., Raleigh; (919) 781-7000; (800) 228-9290; FAX: (919) 781-3059
☑ "Not plush or pretentious, but spacious, clean and friendly", this north Raleigh hotel is in a "great location" for business execs visiting Research Triangle Park; "good value" and "nice facilities" (including an indoor/outdoor pool and exercise room) boost its appeal, and shopaholics like its proximity to the Crabtree Valley Mall; still, critics rate it "nothing special."

Omni Chapel Hill 164R (4S)   18 | 18 | 15 | 16 | $113
(fka Omni Europa Hotel)
1 Europa Dr., Chapel Hill; (919) 968-4900; (800) THE-OMNI; FAX: (919) 968-3520
☑ A "nice small hotel for a nice small university town" is how admirers view this "comfortable and conveniently located" option near UNC, Duke and the Dean Smith Center; "good service" and "elegant decor" help put it on their dean's list; but another faction grades it "adequate", pointing to a "sterile" atmosphere and "impersonal" attitude.

SIENA HOTEL 68R (12S)   24 | 25 | 24 | 23 | $142
1505 E. Franklin St., Chapel Hill; (919) 929-4000; (800) 223-7379; FAX: (919) 968-8527
■ This "gem" modeled after a private Italian villa is a "surprise in Tar Heel country", with "quietly elegant" decor, "incredible free breakfasts" and an "outstanding restaurant", Il Palio, serving fine Italian cuisine; "excellent service" from a staff that "greets you by name" is another plus – now if only they could "say 'y'all come back' in Italian, it would be exceptional."

Washington Duke Inn & Golf Club 164R (7S)   22 | 23 | 21 | 24 | $147
3001 Cameron Blvd., Durham; (919) 490-0999; (800) 443-3853; FAX: (919) 688-0105
■ "If you like golf and are visiting Duke, it's the only place to stay", but remember there's "no room at the inn when Duke plays at home"; set "right on campus" with an 18-hole Robert Trent Jones course in back, this "elegant" hotel boasts a "country club setting", "lovely rooms" and "first-rate service"; there's "good food" at the Fairview restaurant, plus "beautiful" jogging paths and an outdoor pool to work off the calories afterward.

Wrightsville Beach

Blockade Runner Beach Resort 151R (2S)   15 | 16 | 15 | 15 | $130
275 Waynick Blvd., Wrightsville Beach; (910) 256-2251; (800) 541-1161; FAX: (910) 256-5502
☑ Rooms with "great views of either the Intracoastal Waterway or the Atlantic" make this oceanfront resort "the place to stay at Wrightsville Beach" for scenery seekers, but those more focused on interior comforts say the guest quarters and "unattractive" public spaces "need upgrading" (renovations are ongoing); six meeting rooms hold up to 300, and for relaxation there's a pool, fitness center and full range of water sports.

North Dakota

Bismarck

	R	S	D	P	$

Holiday Inn Hotel Bismarck 163R (52S)   ▽ | 14 | 16 | 12 | 14 | $82
605 E. Broadway, Bismarck; (701) 255-6000; (800) HOLIDAY; FAX: (701) 223-0400
☑ "The Downtown location is the real draw" say surveyors about this "average Holiday Inn" that serves businessmen coming to the state capitol; vacationers also find that recreational choices within two miles (fishing, boating, golf, tennis) and nearby points of interest (Dakota Zoo, Farwest Riverboat, Fort Lincoln) make this "clean facility" an ok choice, though there are a few who say it's "not up to HI standards."

Radisson Inn Bismarck 298R (8S)   ▽ | 18 | 17 | 13 | 15 | $85
800 S. Third St., Bismarck; (701) 258-7700; (800) 333-3333; FAX: (701) 224-8212
■ "Though not elegant", this "nice, medium-priced" Bavarian-style hostelry in the heart of the Capitol District "is the best place to stay in Bismarck", especially given its "very quiet rooms" and "large indoor pool"; while catering mainly to vacationers, its extensive meeting facilities can handle a 1,500-person conference; there are two restaurants on site, and the 120-store Kirkwood Mall is nearby.

Fargo

Best Western Doublewood Inn 160R (13S)   ▽ | 16 | 17 | 14 | 15 | $83
3333 13th Ave. S., Fargo; (701) 235-3333; (800) 433-3235; FAX: (701) 280-9482
☑ Despite modest ratings, rooms stocked with amenities (microwaves, refrigerators, hair dryers, dataports, coffeemakers) and a variety of special plans and discounts make this an "ok facility" for most surveyors; there's an indoor pool, lounge and casino, and the good-size meeting venues can handle 1,200; the state's largest shopping center is just two blocks away and Red River–area attractions (Children's Museum, Bonanzaville and Historic Downtown Fargo) are easily accessible.

Bohlig's B&B 3R ⌷ | – | – | – | – | VI
1418 Third Ave. S., Fargo; (701) 235-7867
A classic example of Prairie Georgian architecture built in 1909, this B&B in a college/residential neighborhood offers three rooms (one with private bath), plus the opportunity to relax in its two libraries, three porches and gardens; after breakfast and before PM tea (both included), guests can explore such nearby diversions as art galleries and shopping; N.B. no credit cards accepted.

Radisson Hotel Fargo 148R (3S) | 17 | 18 | 17 | 15 | $85
201 N. Fifth St., Fargo; (701) 232-7363; (800) 333-3333; FAX: (701) 298-9134
☑ All agree that this Downtown high-rise is "the best in Fargo", which for many means "an enjoyable stay" thanks to "really friendly" service, a "quite good" restaurant and "very good meeting facilities" (capacity 280); what's more, there's a lounge, casino and complete health club, and the Fargo Civic Auditorium is a skyway connection away; so while skeptics sniff that "the best in town" is, in this case, still a "generic experience", the consensus is "pleasantly surprising."

Jamestown

Country Charm 4R ⌷ | – | – | – | – | VI
PO Box 71, R.R. 3, Jamestown; (701) 251-1372
The rural setting provides undisturbed views from this 1897 farmhouse that became a B&B in 1990; vacationers enjoy fishing and boating on two nearby reservoirs, x-country skiing in winter and visits to the Buffalo Museum in Jamestown.

Luverne

Volden Farm B&B 2R (1S) ⌂

PO Box 50, R.R. 2, Luverne; (701) 769-2275

-|-|-|-|1

Situated on a 300-acre farm on the eastern prairie, this B&B's country-farmhouse accommodations include the Law Office, a separate 1880s cottage moved from the main street of nearby Cooperstown; outdoor activities include canoeing on the nearby Sheyenne River, biking, x-country skiing and hiking in the woods, and there's a playhouse and swings for children.

Medora

Rough Rider Hotel B&B 9R

301 Third St., Medora; (701) 623-4444; (800) 633-6721; FAX: (701) 623-4494

-|-|-|-|1

Most experience a smooth ride at this "Old West–style" B&B built in 1863, "the best place to stay" in Medora, a "great little", "real cowboy town" with a population of 98 (at last count); the "small-town hospitality" is especially evident at the family restaurant where home-cooked dinners are "a nice treat."

Ohio

Aurora

| R | S | D | P | $ |

Aurora Inn 69R

▽ 16 | 17 | 17 | 18 | $122

PO Box 197, Rtes. 306 & 82, Aurora; (216) 562-6121; (800) 444-6121; FAX: (216) 562-5249

☑ To admirers, this "homey", "quaint" inn 35 miles SE of Cleveland lights up Ohio's Western Reserve and is as "nice as any place could be" in the area; but others simply see an "old" hostelry built in 1927 and last renovated in 1963; assets include indoor and outdoor pools, two tennis courts and a "good golf course" next door; minutes away is Geauga Lake, Sea World and the Aurora Premium Outlet Center.

Cincinnati

BEST OVERALL	**BEST VALUES**
24 Cincinnatian	Doubletree Suites
21 Omni Netherland	Omni Netherland
20 Westin	Westin

Cincinnatian Hotel 143R (5S)

23 | 25 | 25 | 22 | $164

601 Vine St., Cincinnati; (513) 381-3000; (800) 942-9000; FAX: (513) 651-0256

■ This "wonderfully restored old lady", built in 1882 and elegantly reborn in 1987 after a full renovation, wears the crown as the Queen City's top-rated property; it's a "class act" in a "good Downtown location", with "lush public spaces", an impressive skylit atrium, "helpful" staff and rooms that range in size from "a bit small" to "very spacious", all with "great" oversized tubs; the "outstanding" Palace Restaurant serves "superb" American fare, breakfast through dinner; in short, "a gem."

Doubletree Guest Suites (151S)

▽ 21 | 20 | 17 | 20 | $104

(fka Guest Quarters Suites)

6300 E. Kemper Rd., Cincinnati; (513) 489-3636; (800) 222-TREE; FAX: (513) 489-8231

■ "As usual for this chain", you can expect "clean" lodgings, "well-done design" and "nice touches" ("free *USA Today*" weekdays), making this suburbanite a "big surprise" and at least one voter's "favorite suite hotel"; rooms feature voicemail and dataports, and there's an indoor/outdoor pool and a fitness center on-site.

Drawbridge Estate 500R (8S)

13 | 14 | 14 | 14 | $98

2477 Royal Dr., Ft. Mitchell, KY; (606) 341-2800; (800) 354-9793; FAX: (606) 341-5644

☑ On the Kentucky side of the Ohio River, five miles from Downtown Cincinnati and seven miles from the Cincinnati/Northern Kentucky airport, this full-service convention hotel has admirers who call it a "good airport property for meetings" (18 rooms, capacity 1,700) and a "worthwhile stop" if visiting nearby sites such as the Museum Center at Union Terminal and the Oldenberg Brewery; however, dissenters on the other side of the moat rate it just "ok for a medium-priced hotel."

Hyatt Regency Cincinnati 473R (12S)

20 | 19 | 18 | 18 | $131

151 W. Fifth St., Cincinnati; (513) 579-1234; (800) 233-1234; FAX: (513) 579-0107

☑ Surveyor comments are generally moderate ("pretty standard", "nothing special") regarding this "typical Hyatt", but there is enthusiasm for its "convenient location" "close to everything", including the convention center, shopping, and Reds and Bengal games; for best results, "ask for a river-view room", and to keep active, check out the fitness center and pool or do some elbow-bending at the Sungarden, an atrium lounge overlooking Downtown.

Marriott, Cincinnati 347R (5S)

16 | 17 | 15 | 14 | $118

11320 Chester Rd., Cincinnati; (513) 772-1720; (800) 228-9290; FAX: (513) 772-6466

☑ Business travelers rate this suburbanite "ok for meetings" since it can handle groups up to 1,100 and the Sharonville Convention Center is across the street; service is "helpful" and there's an indoor/outdoor pool, but the location (20 minutes north of Downtown) might deter those going to baseball or football games or the city's other attractions; it remains to be seen if a multimillion-dollar renovation completed in '96 will sway those who say "good for a night, no more."

Omni Netherland Plaza 600R (19S)

<u>20</u> <u>21</u> <u>22</u> <u>23</u> <u>$142</u>

35 W. Fifth St., Cincinnati; (513) 421-9100; (800) THE-OMNI; FAX: (513) 421-4291

◪ This "art deco treasure" listed on the National Register of Historic Places has enthusiasts who call it "the most stunningly beautiful city hotel in America", and it earns extra praise for its "cool" Palm Court Bar, "top-notch restaurant" (Orchids) and easy access to Tower Place shopping and the convention center; but comments on the guest quarters are less glorious, ranging from "fine" to "satisfactory" to "watch out for tiny old rooms"; the consensus: "beautiful bones but not yet great."

Regal Cincinnati Hotel 868R (12S)

▽ <u>10</u> <u>13</u> <u>15</u> <u>15</u> <u>$107</u>

150 W. Fifth St., Cincinnati; (513) 352-2100; (800) 876-2100; FAX: (513) 352-2148

◪ Despite the perfect Downtown location, a revolving restaurant with fabulous views, a "nice health club" and a 1994 renovation, ratings are less than regal for this convention center neighbor (they're linked by skywalk); rooms that "need spiffing up" and "inefficient" service are among the complaints lodged.

Vernon Manor Hotel 115R (58S)

<u>16</u> <u>18</u> <u>17</u> <u>15</u> <u>$112</u>

400 Oak St., Cincinnati; (513) 281-3300; (800) 543-3999; FAX: (513) 281-8933

◪ Built just north of Downtown in 1924 to emulate a stately British manor house (and recognizable as a location in *Rain Man*), Vernon Manor is "a good value" (check out the sports packages) and "always a pleasant experience", even if sliding ratings support the view that it's "showing its age"; it also earns a vote for "best brunch in town", and there's a free shuttle to nearby attractions; P.S. "the Beatles slept here", as did other notables.

Westin Hotel 430R (18S)

<u>21</u> <u>21</u> <u>19</u> <u>20</u> <u>$137</u>

Fountain Sq., 21 E. Fifth St., Cincinnati; (513) 621-7700; (800) 228-3000; FAX: (513) 852-5670

■ A "comfortable business hotel" overlooking Fountain Square at Cincinnati's busiest corner (Fifth and Vine), linked by skywalk to shopping and just three blocks from the convention center (a "great location" for execs); most find it "civilized, pleasant and comfortable" with "good service, amenities and meeting facilities", but a few doubters judge it simply "serviceable", with a "chain hotel atmosphere."

Cleveland

BEST OVERALL	BEST VALUES
26 Ritz-Carlton	Omni International
23 Baricelli Inn	Baricelli Inn
22 Renaissance	Embassy Suites

Baricelli Inn 7R

<u>22</u> <u>24</u> <u>26</u> <u>19</u> <u>$139</u>

2203 Cornell Rd., Cleveland; (216) 791-6500; FAX: (216) 791-9131

■ Called "a real find in a big city", this 1896 brownstone mansion in the University Circle area "improves with time" and is "excellent for romantics"; out-of-towners and locals alike vie for its seven "homey, comfy" rooms (three with fireplace) and enjoy its "superb" food and complimentary continental breakfast (served in the glass-enclosed porch); with "every need catered to", guests can relax and enjoy nearby museums, gardens and Severance Hall (home of the Cleveland Orchestra).

Embassy Suites Hotel (268S)

<u>21</u> <u>19</u> <u>16</u> <u>18</u> <u>$122</u>

(fka Radisson Plaza Suite Hotel)

1701 E. 12th St., Cleveland; (216) 523-8000; (800) EMBASSY; FAX: (216) 523-1698

◪ Grumblers may find it "ordinary", but ratings support those who like this Downtown family favorite for its "spacious" suites, "kid-friendly" ambiance, free full breakfast and "great location" within strolling distance of Jacobs Field, Gund Arena, the Rock and Roll Hall of Fame, Playhouse Square and The Flats; it's also "perfectly adequate" for businessfolk, offering rooms with voicemail and two dataports and convenience to the financial district and convention center.

Glidden House Inn 52R (8S)

<u>19</u> <u>19</u> <u>18</u> <u>18</u> <u>$118</u>

1901 Ford Dr., Cleveland; (216) 231-8900; FAX: (216) 231-2130

■ The careful restoration of an "absolutely elegant" French Gothic landmark mansion landed it on the National Register of Historic Places – and sightseers love to land in the "lovely" rooms of this "charming" B&B, a "perfect place to stay" near museums, Case Western Reserve and the medical district; continental breakfast is included.

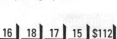

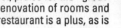
Marriott Downtown at Key Center 385R (15S) 19 | 19 | 17 | 18 | $133
(fka Marriott Society Center)
127 Public Sq., Cleveland; (216) 696-9200; (800) 228-9290; FAX: (216) 696-0966
◪ "Nothing to complain about, nothing to write home about" is one view of this convention-oriented high-rise, but most consider it "a fine Downtown hotel" for business travelers, with a "convenient" location, "good staff" ("did a meeting with no hitches") and "clean", well-appointed (some say "smallish") rooms; for free time there's an indoor pool, fitness center and a lobby piano bar, plus lake activities, golf and tennis nearby.

Omni International Hotel 258R (16S) ▽ 18 | 18 | 19 | 18 | $122
2065 E. 96th St., Cleveland; (216) 791-1900; (800) THE-OMNI; FAX: (216) 231-3329
◼ "Good accommodations and service" earn decent scores for this hotel located eight minutes from Downtown in the heart of the city's cultural district; praise for the "great upkeep" of common spaces may reflect the results of a '96 renovation of rooms and public areas; standout American-Continental fare at Classics restaurant is a plus, as is proximity to several world-class museums and theaters.

Renaissance Cleveland Hotel 441R (50S) 21 | 21 | 22 | 22 | $154
(fka Stouffer Renaissance Cleveland Hotel)
Tower City Ctr., 24 Public Sq., Cleveland; (216) 696-5600; (800) 468-3571; FAX: (216) 696-0432
◼ "Old elegance" is what the majority finds at this restored 1918 Downtown "treasure" with "grand public spaces" including a lovely lobby; there's further agreement on its "great restaurant" (Sans Souci, serving Mediterranean fare) and "great location" (with an indoor walkway to The Avenue mall, Jacobs Field and Gund Arena), but a few complain of "small" rooms and feel the place "needs major renovations."

RITZ-CARLTON CLEVELAND 181R (27S) 26 | 26 | 25 | 25 | $183
1515 W. Third St., Cleveland; (216) 623-1300; (800) 241-3333; FAX: (216) 623-0515
◼ Surveyors are jubilant that Cleveland "finally has a really fabulous", "first-class hotel" – a "picture-perfect" "breath of fresh air Downtown"; ranked No. 1 overall in the city (and the state), it "meets the chain's usual high standards", indulging guests with "lovely rooms", "terrific service" and "excellent food" plus luxuries like an indoor pool; built in 1990 as part of the restored Terminal Tower rail station, it's an "oasis" in a "reborn" area, prompting some to insist "if in Cleveland, stay here."

Sheraton Cleveland City Centre 425R (45S) 20 | 19 | 17 | 17 | $137
777 St. Clair Ave., Cleveland; (216) 771-7600; (800) 321-1090; FAX: (216) 566-0736
◼ A "beautiful" '96 renovation may explain improved ratings for this Downtown high-rise that earns such praise as "very good without pretense", "the city's midprice buy" and even the "showplace of Cleveland"; "rooms are ample and clean" and feature two phones, a computer hookup and oversize desk, and while the 20 meeting rooms (capacity: 1,000) attract execs, the "good location" also brings in vacationers heading to The Galleria, Jacobs Field, Gund Arena and other sites.

Wyndham Cleveland Hotel at 18 | 17 | 17 | 17 | $130
Playhouse Square 205R (13S)
1260 Euclid Ave., Cleveland; (216) 615-7500; (800) WYNDHAM; FAX: (216) 621-8659
◪ Opened in 1995, this Wyndham strikes some voters as "classy", others as "cold and drab", but all agree it has a "great Downtown" address in the business district and near major attractions like Jacobs Field and the Rock and Roll Hall of Fame; in-room amenities include voicemail, dataports, coffeemakers, irons and hair dryers, and in addition to an on-site lap pool and exercise room, guests can use the full fitness facility next door for a fee; the "nice" Sunday breakfast buffet is a plus.

Columbus

BEST OVERALL	BEST VALUES
22 Worthington Inn	Worthington Inn
20 Hyatt–Capitol Sq.	Holiday Inn Crowne Plaza
19 Sheraton Suites	Marriott North

Doubletree Guest Suites (196S) 21 | 18 | 15 | 17 | $117
50 S. Front St., Columbus; (614) 228-4600; (800) 222-TREE; FAX: (614) 228-0297
◪ "Above average but nothing special" is one take on this Downtown all-suiter offering "very nice" if "not posh" lodgings with "lots of room"; views on the service vary ("great staff" vs. "a little surly"), ditto dining ("good" vs. "below par"), but there's no arguing with its "convenient" location, connected by inside walkway to Huntington Center, the State Office Tower and the State Capitol Building and within walking distance of the Palace and Ohio theaters and City Center Mall.

Holiday Inn Crowne Plaza 283R (2S)   16 | 18 | 15 | 16 | $104

33 Nationwide Blvd., Columbus; (614) 461-4100; (800) 465-4329; FAX: (614) 461-4100

◪ This "adequate Downtowner" serves mostly business travelers and convention-goers (an enclosed walkway connects it to the convention center), but while "convenient" it doesn't arouse much surveyor enthusiasm and some complain of "indifferent staff"; there's a lap pool and exercise room on-site, and Crowne Plaza Club executive rooms offer perks such as complimentary breakfast and nightly hors d'oeuvres.

Hyatt on Capitol Square 387R (13S)   21 | 21 | 19 | 19 | $135

75 E. State St., Columbus; (614) 228-1234; (800) 233-1234; FAX: (614) 469-9664

■ One of Columbus' "best options" according to admirers who cite "clean, quiet, comfortable" rooms, "great service" and "lovely" views of the Capitol (especially from the penthouse fitness center); even those who call it "very generic" and note the absence of a pool admit it's generally "excellent", and its convenience to the City Center mall, Museum of Art and the Center of Science and Industry can't be denied.

Hyatt Regency Columbus 614R (16S)   19 | 19 | 18 | 18 | $131

350 N. High St., Columbus; (614) 463-1234; (800) 233-1234; FAX: (614) 463-9161

◪ Though it's a Hyatt Regency, some voters (backed by ratings) call this Downtown convention center hotel "the plainer of the two Hyatt sisters in town"; it's considered a "good meeting place" (31 rooms, capacity 1,200) with "pleasant rooms", but it also takes some flak for being "hopelessly average", "disorganized" and "noisy"; diversions include an indoor pool and a complimentary shuttle to City Center.

Marriott North, Columbus 300R (6S)   17 | 16 | 15 | 16 | $110

6500 Doubletree Ave., Columbus; (614) 885-1885; (800) 228-3429; FAX: (614) 885-7222

◪ Within the Busch Corporate Center (brewery tours available) on the north side of Columbus is a "typical Marriott", which for some means a "good business" hotel (meeting rooms for up to 600); there's an indoor/outdoor pool, sauna and jogging track on-site, and nearby attractions include The Continent (a complex of shops, clubs and movies), Ohio State Fairgrounds and Ohio Museum and Village.

Renaissance Dublin Hotel 207R (10S)   ▽ 18 | 21 | 18 | 19 | $104

600 Metro Place N., Dublin; (614) 764-2200; (800) HOTELS-1; FAX: (614) 764-1213

■ This modern low-rise caters mostly to business travelers visiting the suburban northwest Metro Center business park (home to Ashland Chemical, AT&T, Wendy's and more); though it doesn't inspire much surveyor excitement ("average", "fine"), it does offer such niceties as skylights or balconies in some rooms, free coffee and newspaper on weekdays, complimentary shoeshine and 24-hour room service; on-site facilities include an exercise room, sauna and indoor skylit pool.

Sheraton Suites Columbus (261S)   ▽ 21 | 18 | 17 | 19 | $126

201 Hutchinson Ave., Columbus; (614) 436-0004; (800) 325-3535; FAX: (614) 436-0926

■ Located near the Crosswoods Business Park in Columbus' northern suburbs (and just north of Worthington, which has a historic Downtown district), this all-suites hotel does double duty, hosting tourists on weekends (Polaris Amphitheater is nearby) and corporate types during the week; for relaxation, guests can head to the indoor and outdoor pools, fitness center and whirlpool or just unwind at the lobby bar.

Westin Hotel Columbus 168R (28S)   17 | 19 | 18 | 18 | $127

(fka Great Southern Hotel)

310 S. High St., Columbus; (614) 228-3800; (800) 228-3000; FAX: (614) 228-7666

◪ Renovations on this "lovely, historic hotel" have transformed an 1897 grande dame into a 21st-century "workable business hotel" (complete with dataports, voicemail and special 'Guest Office' rooms); cherrywood furnishings and marble baths aren't enough for faultfinders who feel "rooms could be better appointed", but for history lovers the "treasure" that was good enough for Teddy Roosevelt, Sarah Bernhardt and John Barrymore is good enough for them.

Worthington Inn 22R (4S)   24 | 23 | 25 | 19 | $128

649 High St., Worthington; (614) 885-2600; FAX: (614) 885-1283

■ "A country inn in a city" offers the best of both worlds to surveyors who recommend this "quaint" and "charming", circa 1831 Victorian/colonial inn, located in the Worthington historic district; "attention is paid to details" here, from the cocktails upon arrival to the "interesting" rooms done up with antiques to the "delicious" full breakfast (free); what's more, the Regional American Seven Stars restaurant is "excellent."

Dellroy

Atwood Lake Resort and   _ | _ | _ | _ | M
Conference Center 100R (4S)
2650 Lodge Rd., Dellroy; (330) 735-2211; (800) 362-6406; FAX: (330) 735-2562
There's no shortage of activities at this year-round resort nestled on a hilltop next to Atwood Lake and overlooking 8,000 acres of eastern Ohio countryside; x-country skiing, golf, tennis, swimming, biking and square dancing are all offered on-site, with boating and water skiing nearby; if the idea of all play and no work somehow doesn't appeal, there are six meeting rooms with a capacity of 250.

Granville

Granville Inn 27R (3S)   19 | 20 | 19 | 17 | $116
314 E. Broadway, Granville; (614) 587-3333; FAX: (614) 587-3333
■ The New England–style village of Granville (25 miles east of Columbus) is a fitting setting for this "quaint old" English Tudor–style manor house; built in 1924 from Ohio sandstone, it "looks like a movie set for a country inn" – a stone hearth in the pub, billiards in the lounge, an oak-paneled library and "lovely veranda" give it "unexpected elegance" and "old-fashioned charm", but nitpickers note "good not great food" and "dreary meeting space."

Huron

Sawmill Creek Resort 220R (20S)   ∇ 18 | 18 | 17 | 19 | $116
2401 Cleveland Rd. W., Huron; (419) 433-3800; (800) SAWMILL; FAX: (419) 433-7610
◪ On the shore of Lake Erie in the heart of Ohio's 'Vacationland' (close to Lake Erie Islands and Cedar Point Amusement Park), this full-service, "reasonable resort" is used as a retreat by corporate groups (13 meeting rooms) and also works for families; on-site attractions include an 18-hole golf course (check out the golf package deals), fishing, tennis, indoor and outdoor pools and a marina.

Marietta

Lafayette Hotel 77R (2S)   ∇ 15 | 18 | 20 | 16 | $84
101 Front St., Marietta; (614) 373-5522; (800) 331-9336; FAX: (614) 373-4684
■ An official stop for the American Queen, Mississippi Queen and Delta Queen riverboats, this 1892 Victorian Downtowner (on the National Historic Register) with views of the Ohio River serves the needs of business travelers in southeastern Ohio, and in tourist season (April to October) hosts those visiting nearby museums, crafts factories and other sights; two on-site restaurants serve steak and seafood fare, and calories can be worked off at the local YMCA, where guests have privileges.

Millersburg

Inn at Honey Run 33R (4S)   ∇ 25 | 24 | 25 | 25 | $113
6920 County Rd. 203, Millersburg; (330) 674-0011; (800) 468-6639; FAX: (330) 674-2623
■ The emphasis is on serenity at this "back-to-nature place with modern furnishings" in Amish country, where the ambiance is "cheerful" and the "scenery is great"; 25 rooms in the inn are supplemented by 12 earth-sheltered Honeycomb rooms and two guest cottages; watching birds, photographing sheep and observing horse-drawn carts add up to "rest and relaxation at its finest" – just "don't expect much excitement" (especially as there's no alcohol).

Painesville

Quail Hollow Resort & Country Club 165R (2S) ∇ 21 | 22 | 21 | 23 | $133
11080 Concord-Hambden Rd., Painesville; (216) 352-6201; (800) 792-0258; FAX: (216) 350-3504
◪ Two "excellent" golf courses (one designed by Bruce Devlin and Robert Von Hagge) are the main draw at this rural resort 30 miles east of Cleveland; though it posts solid all-around scores, some duffers slice it as "overrated" and "tired" (a 1996 spruce-up of public areas may have helped); the conference center can handle small to medium meetings, and for those not into golfing other recreation options include on-site tennis, indoor and outdoor pools and nearby antiquing and winery-touring.

Oklahoma

Afton

Shangri-La Resort 256R (144S)   16 | 18 | 15 | 21 | $121
Rte. 3, Afton; (918) 257-4204; (800) 331-4060; FAX: (918) 257-5619
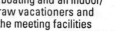 "Fairly nice" if not idyllic, this '70s-era resort on Grand Lake O' the Cherokees gets active families and meeting-goers moving with its "beautiful golf course", "good fishing", tennis, waterskiing and kids' program; the rooms are only "so-so" or "adequate" and the "food is not the greatest", "but the people are the best."

Bartlesville

Phillips, Hotel 121R (24S)   ▽ 18 | 20 | 18 | 16 | $94
821 S. Johnstone Ave., Bartlesville; (918) 336-5600; (800) 331-0706; FAX: (918) 336-0350
■ You'll find "quality in a surprising location" at this "good price performer" three blocks from Phillips Petroleum headquarters; "a friendly staff" offers "eager service" and if the Italian restaurant isn't a gusher, "it tries"; meanwhile, continental breakfast is included and the lounge offers a light bar menu.

Checotah

Fountainhead Resort Hotel 182R (4S)   – | – | – | – | I
Box 1355, HC 60, Checotah; (918) 689-9173; (800) 345-6343; FAX: (918) 689-9493
Plenty of activities – golf, tennis, racquetball, volleyball, hiking, boating and an indoor/outdoor pool – plus the "peaceful setting" on Lake Eufaula draw vacationers and conference-goers to this otherwise ordinary rural resort; N.B. the meeting facilities are extensive – 17 rooms with a capacity of 1,000.

Kingston

Texoma State Resort 100R (67S)   – | – | – | – | VI
PO Box 279, US 70, Kingston; (405) 564-2311; (800) 654-8240; FAX: (405) 564-2262
Looking for indoor fishing? – look no further than this state-park resort with an indoor fishing arena plus golf, tennis, biking, boating and horseback riding for those in the mood for more direct contact with Mother Nature; be sure to bring the kids: there are also go-carts, mini golf, a petting zoo and hayrides, even batting cages; accommodations are in rooms or cottages, and packages are available for golfers and anglers.

Norman

Holmberg House 4R   – | – | – | – | I
766 DeBarr St., Norman; (405) 321-6221; (800) 646-6221
On the National Register of Historic Places, this 1914 Craftsman-style house features handsome period decor and memorabilia, and its location across from the U of Oklahoma campus draws visiting scholars, alumni and parents; all rooms have private baths, and one has an old-fashioned tub charmingly set right in the bedroom; full breakfast is included and there are 15 restaurants within walking distance.

Oklahoma City

Marriott Oklahoma City 347R (7S)   18 | 17 | 16 | 15 | $105
3233 Northwest Expy., Oklahoma City; (405) 842-6633; (800) 228-9290; FAX: (405) 842-3152
 An "ok" place, so to speak, the capital city Marriott is a "good business hotel" with 11 meeting rooms (capacity 1,200), easy access to all major freeways and a fitness center with sauna and indoor/outdoor pool; like lots of Marriotts, it's called "reliable and comfortable" but also gets lukewarm reactions like "little to rave about."

Radisson Inn Oklahoma City 502R (7S)   ▽ 14 | 16 | 14 | 16 | $95
401 S. Meridian Ave., Oklahoma City; (405) 947-7681; (800) 333-3333; FAX: (405) 947-4253
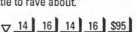 Though five miles from Downtown, the appeal here is still to business travelers – on a budget; they get an "adequate room" and "good facilities" that, for work, include 16 meeting rooms with a capacity of 900, and, for play, a fitness center, indoor/outdoor pools, sauna and two tennis courts.

Waterford Hotel 165R (32S)   22 | 22 | 21 | 20 | $129
6300 Waterford Blvd., Oklahoma City; (405) 848-4782; (800) 992-2009; FAX: (405) 843-9161
■ "A lovely place" all agree about this recently renovated Euro-style mid-rise that "puts the ok" in OK City's Nichols Hill area; with "great rooms" ("especially" the suites), a "very nice" staff, "always agreeable" dining and on-site squash, volleyball, exercise equipment and spa services, "it would be a bargain at twice the price."

Tulsa

Adam's Mark Tulsa 354R (8S)   _ | _ | _ | _ | M
100 E. Second St., Tulsa; (918) 582-9000; (800) 444-2326; FAX: (918) 560-2261
This modern high-rise Downtowner, seven blocks from the convention center, caters to business travelers with extensive meeting space (38,000 square feet) and multiuse areas that can be configured in 18 different ways; depending on the price of crude oil, speculators and futures traders can work out tension in the health club and pool, drown their sorrows in the Players Sports Bar or happily sing along with the performing waiters in Bravo! Ristorante.

Sheraton Tulsa Hotel 331R (5S)   _ | _ | _ | _ | M
(fka Tulsa Marriott)
10918 E. 41st St., Tulsa; (918) 627-5000; (800) 325-3535; FAX: (918) 627-4003
A business clientele fills up this East Tulsa high-rise during the week (there's meeting space for 900), but on weekends families check in, drawn by special packages and by the fact that 41st Street dead-ends at the Southroads Southland Shopping Center; nonshoppers can relax in the pool or take advantage of nearby golf and tennis.

Oregon

TOP 10 OVERALL

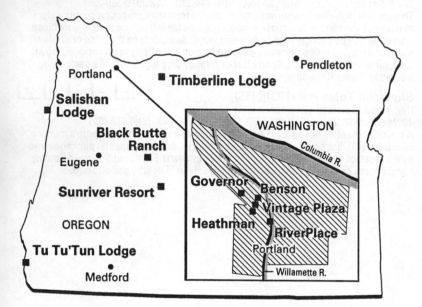

BEST OVERALL

25 Tu Tu'Tun Lodge/Gold Beach
   Salishan Lodge/Gleneden Beach
24 Black Butte Ranch/Black Butte
   Heathman/Portland
22 RiverPlace/Portland
   Benson/Portland
   Governor/Portland
   Vintage Plaza/Portland
   Sunriver Resort/Sunriver
21 Timberline Lodge/Timberline

BEST VALUES

Greenwood Inn/Portland
Tu Tu'Tun Lodge/Gold Beach
Valley River Inn/Eugene
Black Butte Ranch/Black Butte
Inn of Seventh Mtn./Bend
Timberline Lodge/Timberline
Inn at Spanish Head/Lincoln City
Embarcadero/Newport
Sunriver Resort/Sunriver
Vintage Plaza/Portland

Bend

R	S	D	P	$

Inn of the Seventh Mountain 260R

20	19	19	21	$129

18575 SW Century Dr., Bend; (541) 382-8711; (800) 452-6810; FAX: (541) 228-3598

■ This "interesting" "full-service resort" near Mt. Bachelor woos with "lots to do": it's "great for family ski vacations", ice skating and snowmobile tours (followed by a dip in the heated pool or hot tubs), and summer brings "great fishing and rafting" and "good children's activities"; though critics grumble about "functional" rooms with walls that "must be made of paper", "various-sized accommodations" help, as do "friendly" staff, fair prices and the "unbelievable location."

Black Butte Ranch

BLACK BUTTE RANCH (110S)   24 | 23 | 22 | 27 | $156
PO Box 8000, Hwy. 20, Black Butte Ranch; (541) 595-6211; (800) 452-7455; FAX: (541) 595-2077
☑ Possessive fans say "shhh, we don't want any more people to know about" this "clean, refreshing getaway" amidst "gorgeous surroundings" in the "amazing" Cascades; rental homes and condos on the 1,800-acre ranch are independently owned, so there's limited housekeeping services and, some say, architecture "too much like a faceless subdivision"; but a restaurant, lounge, "two cute golf courses", 22 tennis courts and other "wonderful facilities" are added reasons it might be "too crowded" during peak season.

Eugene

Valley River Inn 248R (9S)   19 | 19 | 19 | 20 | $124
1000 Valley River Way, Eugene; (541) 687-0123; (800) 543-8266; FAX: (541) 683-5121
☑ Comments are squarely divided between voters who find this Eugene hostelry a "good choice for a stopover" "near the U of Oregon" (and the area's major shopping mall), and those who say it's "just a renovated motel" with "a roof to keep the rain off, that's all"; many rooms overlook the Willamette, and the "very good" riverside restaurant has outdoor seating, weather permitting, and "excellent breakfasts" rain or shine.

Gleneden Beach

SALISHAN LODGE 202R (3S)   25 | 24 | 25 | 26 | $182
Hwy. 101, Gleneden Beach; (541) 764-2371; (800) 452-2300; FAX: (541) 764-3681
■ "*The* place on the Oregon Coast", this "classic in modern dress" with "beautiful" grounds and public spaces is perched in a "fabulous woodsy setting" overlooking a bay; the clusters of rooms have fireplaces and carports, and there's a "scenic golf course", an indoor tennis and fitness center, shops and galleries; while stray critics cry "overrated" and "disappointing", most rate it a "lovely, comfortable" experience; N.B. the restaurant was closed and undergoing changes at press time.

Gold Beach

TU TU'TUN LODGE 16R (2S)   25 | 26 | 27 | 24 | $163
96550 North Bank Rogue, Gold Beach; (541) 247-6664; FAX: (541) 247-0672
■ A "relaxing" "escape" in southernmost Oregon that's known as a "superb location" for fishing (there are also 104-mile white-water tours just outside the door); the "charming", "ever-present owners" pamper guests with "little touches that make a difference", and "inventive gourmet cuisine" is "served family-style"; "rooms with fireplace and outdoor tubs are the best" say insiders, but there are also two "well-appointed" houses.

Hood River

Columbia Gorge Hotel 42R   18 | 21 | 22 | 22 | $165
4000 Westcliff Dr., Hood River; (541) 386-5566; (800) 345-1921; FAX: (541) 387-5414
☑ Despite being "right on the highway", this vintage-1921 "Hollywood hideaway of yore" (Valentino slept here) is "still romantic" given its "spectacular" setting overlooking Columbia Gorge and some quarters with polished brass or canopy beds; though some gripe about rooms that are "old, old", many others "want to go back again" to enjoy "the views" of the Gorge – and gorge on the "excellent", lumberjack-worthy breakfast.

Lincoln City

Inn at Spanish Head 75R (45S)   19 | 20 | 18 | 18 | $125
4009 SW Hwy. 101, Lincoln City; (541) 996-2161; (800) 452-8127; FAX: (541) 996-4089
☑ Admirers "could live here" because "it's soooo romantic" say those for whom this Spanish-style oceansider is the "resort of choice in Oregon"; there's a heated pool and ocean access for whale-watching and beachcombing, yet plaintive cries of "going downhill" rise above the spectacular crash of the breakers below from respondents who are "not overly impressed" with rooms that "need to be updated desperately."

Newport

Embarcadero Resort Hotel & Marina 30R (45S)   20 | 19 | 17 | 17 | $124
1000 SE Bay Blvd., Newport; (541) 265-8521; (800) 547-4779; FAX: (541) 265-7844
☑ "The views across Yaquina Bay make the rooms" at what some describe as a "so-so facility in a fantastic harbor location"; some quarters are "motel-like", but there are also "very nice apartment-type units" (with fireplaces and kitchenettes) and meeting facilities; amenities such as an indoor pool, a private dock for crabbing and charter fishing from the resort's marina appeal to families, and Newport's shops are within walking distance.

Sylvia Beach Hotel 20R (2S)

▽ 19 | 21 | 21 | 20 | $109

267 NW Cliff St., Newport; (541) 265-5428

☑ Bookworms warm to the "fantastic atmosphere" at this historic, four-story oceanfront B&B devoted to all things literary (sorry, no phones, TVs or radios); the "interesting" rooms and suites are "uniquely" furnished (there are also separate women's and men's "bunk-bed dorms" at remainder rates); guests might chat over mulled wine served in the library before a family-style dinner in the Tables of Content seafood restaurant; quibblers find the place "run-down"; N.B. no smoking.

Portland

Benson Hotel 231R (56S)

22 | 23 | 22 | 22 | $161

309 SW Broadway, Portland; (503) 228-2000; (800)-426-0670; FAX: (503) 226-4603

■ This 1912 "grande dame" in Downtown Portland has been "restored with impeccable taste", making a great first impression with its "fantastic lobby" that boasts a "huge fireplace" and lots of "dark wood and comfy chairs"; what's more, the "great staff" includes a "helpful concierge", and there's "winning" NW fare in the London Grill; rooms can vary from "small" and "bland" to "spacious" and "elegant", but overall this is clearly a "class act" with "lots of character."

5th Avenue Suites Hotel 82R (139S)

– | – | – | – | E

506 SW Washington St., Portland; (503) 222-0001; (800) 711-2971; FAX: (503) 222-0004

A smart renovation has crafted a gorgeous Downtown jewel from the former Frederick & Nelson department store, producing huge sunny suites with floor-to-ceiling windows and decor in sophisticated warm yellow tones; just down the street from its sibling, Vintage Plaza, it offers complimentary morning coffee and juice and afternoon wine tastings, as well as in-house dining in the Red Star Tavern and Roast House (set on the first floor amidst the ghosts of the ladies' gloves and candy counters).

Governor Hotel 76R (24S)

22 | 23 | 22 | 21 | $160

611 SW 10th Ave., Portland; (503) 224-3400; (800) 554-3456; FAX: (503) 241-2122

■ "The best of old and new Portland", this "lovingly and accurately restored" Arts and Crafts–style "historic hotel" is a "very cozy and personal" "gem" with rooms that are "small but full of Old Town charm"; "eat at Jake's" say fans of the clubby American grill (and maybe work off the calories later at the well-equipped health club); the "great atmosphere" is made all the more pleasant by "outstanding service."

Greenwood Inn 225R (26S)

18 | 18 | 19 | 16 | $107

10700 SW Allen Blvd., Beaverton; (503) 643-7444; (800) 289-1300; FAX: (503) 626-4553

☑ You'll "need a car" because this "business-oriented" Beaverton "bargain" is "not near anything"; rooms are "motel-like" and, while some have kitchenettes, demanding types say "don't expect much" otherwise; all the same, the "wonderful restaurant staff" at the Pavilion Bar and Grill get appreciative nods, and admission to the nearby Griffith Park Athletic Club is complimentary.

HEATHMAN HOTEL 103R (47S)

22 | 25 | 25 | 22 | $169

1001 SW Broadway, Portland; (503) 241-4100; (800) 551-0011; FAX: (503) 790-7110

■ "As welcoming as the city it's located in", this Downtown "landmark" feels "more like a mansion than a hotel"; a sense of "understated elegance" pervades the "beautiful public areas", the "stately" lounge (site of "great jazz" every evening) and its "top-flight" restaurant, The Heathman; "service is superb in every respect" and complimentary movies from an "unsurpassed" video library "make rainy days a delight", even if guests are cloistered in "tiny suites" or "shoe-box rooms."

Marriott Portland 497R (6S)

19 | 20 | 17 | 18 | $133

1401 SW Front Ave., Portland; (503) 226-7600; (800) 228-9290; FAX: (503) 221-1789

■ Although a "strategic Downtown location" places this Marriott "within walking distance to tourist sites", it's more a "place for business"; some call it a "big hotel without personality", but what it "lacks in character" it makes up for with "spacious", "comfortable" guestrooms and meeting facilities, a "very helpful staff", plenty of eateries, a health club with indoor pool and a "stunning" overlook of the Willamette River.

Riverplace Hotel 39R (45S)

24 | 23 | 21 | 22 | $174

1510 SW Harbor Way, Portland; (503) 228-3233; (800) 227-1333; FAX: (503) 295-6161

■ "Out of the mainstream" yet close to Downtown, this "top-notch", "young-feeling", midsize "gem" on the Willamette wins kudos for its "modern, upscale decor" and "charming, attentive" service; continental breakfast is complimentary whether you stay in "sunny" rooms "decorated in pretty eggshell colors", suites (some have fireplaces and whirlpool baths) or condos that "meet every need"; the on-site Esplanade restaurant makes the most of the "fantastic" setting.

Vintage Plaza, Hotel 86R (21S)　　　23 | 23 | 22 | 20 | $154

422 SW Broadway, Portland; (503) 228-1212; (800) 243-0555; FAX: (503) 228-3598

■ Like its Vintage Park sister in Seattle, this "smallish Downtown hotel" is "charming, eclectic" and "first-class"; "rooms are comfortable" and some feature "unforgettable skylights" for stargazers ("isn't it romantic?"); the "accommodating" service extends to complimentary "nice touches" like an evening "wine reception" and a "good" continental breakfast (both in the luxe lobby); N.B. lots of locals favor Pazzo Ristorante for Italian fare with a NW accent.

Steamboat

Steamboat Inn 8R (11S)　　　– | – | – | – | M

42705 N. Umpqua Hwy., Steamboat; (800) 840-8825; (800) 840-8825; FAX: (541) 498-2230

Perched on the edges of the wild North Umpqua River, this rustic yet pretty retreat is an unspoiled paradise offering riverside suites and refurbished cottages; fishing is the sport of choice, but there's also wonderful hiking (check out the waterfalls nearby); after a day of exercise, the fabulous kitchen satisfies big appetites by bringing in top Portland chefs and Oregon wineries for winemaker dinners, as well as with its famous Friday night fisherman's dinner, with guests seated at long communal tables.

Sunriver

Sunriver Resort 134R (301S)　　　23 | 21 | 20 | 24 | $153

1 Center Dr., Sunriver; (541) 593-1000; (800) 547-3922; FAX: (541) 593-5458

■ While this "great family resort" is "close to Mt. Bachelor" and appeals to skiers, the facilities at this planned community make it "fantastic for kids of all ages" year-round with "biking, fishing, golfing and more"; guest sites include the newly refurbished Lodge Village and "comfortable" privately owned homes ("try for a two-story lodge"); activists urge others to "take advantage of the free bikes" to explore what just might be "the most beautiful location in the West."

Timberline

Timberline Lodge 60R (11S)　　　19 | 19 | 20 | 25 | $136

Timberline Rd., Timberline; (503) 272-3311; (800) 547-1406; FAX: (503) 272-3710

■ Expect a "wonderful homey feeling" with "limited comfort but great 1930s ambiance" at this "fabulous WPA" "work of art" perched 6,000 feet up Mt. Hood; boosters say "you can't beat the location or atmosphere", the "skiing and snowboarding all summer" and the "awesome chairlift ride"; stay in a "tiny" but "nice" guestroom in the lodge or rent a comfier fireplace unit, or consider a bunk room and meals at the restored Silcox Hut another 1,000 vertical feet above the timberline.

Warm Springs

Kah-Nee-Ta Resort 139R (63S)　　　▽ 17 | 17 | 17 | 20 | $120

PO Box K, Hwy. 3, Warm Springs; (541) 553-1112; (800) 554-4786; FAX: (541) 553-1015

■ In addition to kayaking, swimming and horseback riding, a slew of somewhat kitschy "cultural activities" beckons at this "friendly" high desert country retreat owned by the area's Confederated Tribes; sleeping options range from lodge rooms and suites to cottages to oversize teepees to an RV park; the "fun, safe camping environment" is a "nice change of pace" for families, but the resort also "caters to a lot of business groups", and they can unwind on the 18-hole golf course.

Welches

Resort at the Mountain 149R (11S)　　　▽ 21 | 19 | 20 | 21 | $132

68010 E. Fairway Ave., Welches; (503) 622-3101; (800) 669-7666; FAX: (503) 622-2222

◪ Comments such as "pleasant" "nice", "routine" and "ok" reflect mixed opinions on this continually updated, Scottish-themed, century-old resort on the west slope of Mt. Hood; reasons to return include "large rooms", a "gorgeous pool", 27 holes of golf and low-key pursuits such as croquet, badminton and hiking the nearby Oregon Trail; but even all that, plus proximity to year-round skiing and fishing, isn't enough for spoilsports who find "no nearby sites of interest."

Pennsylvania

R S D P $

Seven Springs Mountain Resort 385R (12S) ▽ | 18 | 20 | 20 | 22 | $147
RD #1, Champion; (814) 352-7777; (800) 452-2223; FAX: (814) 352-7911

☑ An "excellent family ski resort" report those who enjoy frolicking with the kids in the "rustic environment" of this mountain resort about an hour's drive from Pittsburgh; a "winter wonderland" that also offers a full menu of summer activities (tennis, golf, swimming, horseback riding), it strikes most as a "great weekend spot to relax" and an "ok conference facility", but a few dissenters yawn "ho hum."

Erwinna

EVERMAY ON-THE-DELAWARE 16R (1S) | 23 | 24 | 27 | 24 | $161
PO Box 60, River Rd., Erwinna; (610) 294-9100; FAX: (610) 294-8249

☑ "The staff makes you feel like a long-lost cousin" at this inn built in the 1700s in a "romantic location" in verdurous Bucks County; it's a "great place for an affair" and foodies are drawn by "terrific" New American dinners prepared by "an immensely talented chef", but while most guests are captivated by its "charming rooms", the sciatica set says "watch out for smallish beds with saggy mattresses"; continental breakfast and PM tea are included.

Farmington

NEMACOLIN WOODLANDS RESORT 98R (44S) | 27 | 25 | 24 | 27 | $186
PO Box 188, Rte. 40 E., Farmington; (412) 329-8555; (800) 422-2736; FAX: (412) 329-6153

■ "A fairy-tale resort in the middle of nowhere", this former lodge and game preserve in SW Pennsylvania's Laurel Mountains is one of the state's "best-kept secrets"; "rooms are the nicest anywhere" and facilities include the "spectacular" Mystic Rock golf course, an equestrian center, a "luxurious" full-service spa and (a recent addition) downhill skiing; N.B. another 124 rooms are planned for 1997.

Glen Mills

Sweetwater Farm 7R (5S) ▽ | 23 | 25 | 20 | 23 | $172
50 Sweetwater Rd., Glen Mills; (610) 459-4711; (800) SWEETWATER; FAX: (610) 358-4945

■ "Off the beaten path" but "near all Brandywine Valley attractions" (including Longwood Gardens and the Winterthur Museum) is this "very pleasant" B&B set in an 18th-century Georgian stone mansion; it's "like staying at a friend's home" replete with fireplaces in some quarters and "enchanting grounds" with pool; though some say the "rooms need freshening", admirers consider it the area's "best"; hint: "try the cottages."

Hershey

Hershey Lodge & Convention Center 437R (20S) | 19 | 20 | 18 | 20 | $136
W. Chocolate Ave. & University Dr., Hershey; (717) 533-3311; (800) 533-3131; FAX: (717) 534-8666

☑ A "logical home base" for families heading to local candy-coated attractions and also "a great place for meetings", able to handle groups of up to 2,300; while "not exciting", this "well-equipped resort" is a "comfortable" "good value" and offers on-site diversions including miniature golf, tennis and swimming; dissenters cite "a hike through long corridors" to rooms that "need sparkling up" and are put off by a "we-don't-care-if-you-stay-here-or-not attitude."

Hershey, The Hotel 223R (18S) | 22 | 22 | 22 | 24 | $168
PO Box 400, Hotel Rd., Hershey; (717) 533-2171; (800) 533-3131; FAX: (717) 534-8887

☑ More reminiscent of South Florida than heartland PA, this Med-style "palace" built in 1933 by chocolate king Milton Hershey boasts "magnificent grounds and gardens", a "very nice staff", nine holes of golf, tennis, space for midsize conferences and, of course, proximity to Hershey sights; "there are chocolate snacks everywhere you turn" and fans plant a kiss on its "elegance with a sense of fun", but others are soured by "small rooms" with "paper-thin walls" and "old bathrooms."

King of Prussia

Park Ridge at Valley Forge 262R (3S)   19 | 19 | 19 | 18 | $122
480 N. Gulph Rd., King of Prussia; (610) 337-1800; (800) 337-1801; FAX: (610) 337-4506
◪ "A bargain at a good location," this suburban hotel and conference center a half-hour drive from Downtown Philadelphia is just minutes from the historic site of George Washington's winter encampment as well as one of the nation's biggest malls; with a pool, two tennis courts and "state-of-the-art meeting facilities" for groups of up to 600, it may be "best in the area", but some find it "too much like a budget hotel."

Sheraton Valley Forge 349R (140S)   16 | 16 | 15 | 15 | $120
1160 First Ave., King of Prussia; (610) 337-2000; (800) 325-3535; FAX: (610) 768-0183
◪ "Love those fantasy-theme" suites say guests whose imagination is whetted by this hotel's 70 specialty suites done in motifs ranging from 18th century to futuristic (some with Jacuzzi – "yum!"); but what's "fun" to some is "garish" to others, and views of the service also veer from "very nice" to "stuck-up and inconsiderate"; most agree it's "ok for meetings" and has an "advantageous location" 20 minutes from Downtown Philadelphia.

Lahaska

Golden Plough Inn 41R (19S)   24 | 21 | 19 | 21 | $146
PO Box 218, Rte. 202 & Street Rd., Lahaska; (215) 794-4004; FAX: (215) 794-4008
◪ "Fantastic" cheer fans of this inn, part of a 42-acre complex of colonial-style buildings housing some 70 shops and eateries linked by garden-edged brick walkways; rooms, decked out in country decor, are located in the main inn as well as throughout the complex; the place is golden for shopaholics, but some find the surroundings "kitschy" and "cutesy" and the setting, two miles from New Hope, "crowded with tours."

Malvern

Desmond Hotel 186R (7S)   19 | 18 | 17 | 18 | $156
1 Liberty Blvd., Malvern; (610) 296-9800; (800) 575-1776; FAX: (610) 889-9869
◼ "A good meeting locale" for small conferences, this contemporary hotel in a suburban "office campus" west of Philadelphia has colonial-style decor, "lovely bedroom furnishings" and "service to please"; there's an indoor pool, tennis and volleyball courts, exercise equipment, a pub and restaurant, but some find the food "disappointing."

Mount Joy

Cameron Estate Inn 16R (1S)   ▽ 22 | 22 | 22 | 20 | $145
1855 Mansion Ln., Mount Joy; (717) 653-1773; (888) 722-6376; FAX: (717) 653-8334
◼ An 1805 manor that was once the home of Simon Cameron, Abraham Lincoln's Secretary of War, is now a "a quaint country inn" with "large, nice" rooms, some with four-posters and fireplaces; "midpoint between Lancaster and Hershey", it's handy if traveling to the Amish Country, and while most find "class all-around" and "great dining", a few encounter "overcooked food" and "inexplicable signs of bad maintenance"; "yummy" continental breakfast is included.

Mt. Pocono/Pocono Manor

Mount Airy Lodge Resort & Conference Center 465R (120S)   12 | 13 | 11 | 13 | $147
42 Woodland Rd., Mt. Pocono; (717) 839-8811; (800) 441-4410; FAX: (717) 839-3385
◪ This "supposedly great resort and honeymoon haven" in the Pocono Mountains is "rather disappointing" say polite surveyors who think less money should be spent on TV ads and more on "rooms that need to be refurbished"; sharper-tongued critics let loose with a barage of insults: "chintzy", "sloppy", "tacky" with "high-school cafeteria food"; on the bright side there's lots to do, including "great" golf.

Pocono Manor Inn & Golf Resort 250R (7S)   11 | 13 | 11 | 15 | $148
Rte. 314, Pocono Manor; (717) 839-7111; (800) 233-8150; FAX: (717) 839-0708
◪ "We had a pleasant surprise here" report those who find "terrific entertainment" and "lots of activities that kids love" at this 3,000-acre Pocono Mountains resort dating to 1902; others sigh "maybe 50 years ago" but today it's "a dump" with "awful" food and rooms despite a '96 renovation; at least the staff is "friendly" and there are two 18-hole golf courses, indoor and outdoor tennis courts and pools for diversion.

TOP 10 OVERALL

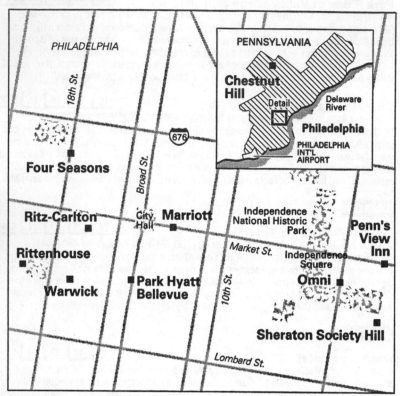

BEST OVERALL

27 Four Seasons
26 Ritz-Carlton
25 Rittenhouse
22 Park Hyatt Bellevue
21 Omni Independence Park
    Marriott Philadelphia
20 Penn's View Inn
    Sheraton Society Hill
    Chestnut Hill
18 Warwick

BEST VALUES

Chestnut Hill
Penn's View Inn
Marriott Philadelphia
Omni Independence Park
Sheraton Society Hill
Best Western
Doubletree Philadelphia
Korman Suites
Adam's Mark
Ritz-Carlton

	R	S	D	P	$

Adam's Mark Hotel 449R (66S)

17	17	17	16	$135

City Ave. & Monument Rd., Philadelphia; (215) 581-5000; (800) 444-ADAM; FAX: (215) 581-5069
☑ This "typical convention hotel" seven miles from Center City is "ok for meetings" "but not for tourists" because it's "a drive from historic Philadelphia sights"; to admirers it's a "good value" with "a nice health club and pool" and an "accommodating" staff, even though the rooms are "small" and "very tired"; to the less enchanted, the Marker restaurant is "its saving grace."

Best Western Independence Park Hotel 36R

18	18	17	17	$133

235 Chestnut St., Philadelphia; (215) 922-4443; (800) 624-2988; FAX: (215) 922-4487
☑ "A great old space with excellent management", this small hotel is set in a renovated Victorian building in the heart of the Historic District, an ideal location "for tourists"; while admirers find it "cute" and say it "doesn't feel like a chain hotel", dissenters call it "run-down" and long for liberty from "average rooms that could be a little cleaner"; on one point most surveyors agree: it's a "good value" that's made even better by complimentary continental breakfast.

Chestnut Hill Hotel 25R (3S)
| 21 | 20 | 19 | 19 | $129 |

8229 Germantown Ave., Philadelphia; (215) 242-5905; (800) 628-9744; FAX: (215) 242-8778
■ This "charming establishment" has seen a rise in ratings since our last *Survey*, supporting those who call it a "nice alternative" in an affluent setting 25 minutes from Downtown; "B&B-like" in feel, it offers rooms with 18th century–style furnishings plus proximity to antiques shops and cozy restaurants – there are also on-site dining options ranging from Italian to fondue; continental breakfast is included.

Doubletree Hotel Philadelphia 419R (8S)
| 19 | 18 | 16 | 17 | $139 |

Ave. of the Arts (Broad & Locust Sts.), Philadelphia; (215) 893-1600; (800) 222-TREE; FAX: (215) 893-1664
☑ Here's "a good deal": "surprisingly comfortable", "spacious" rooms at a "fair price" in a "super location" steps from the Academy of Music, Merriam Theater and, fortunately, top restaurants, since some surveyors find in-house dining "mediocre"; voters split on the service ("great" vs. "disappointing"), but overall most find "excellent quality for a standard chain hotel"; fitness facilities include an indoor pool and racquetball courts.

FOUR SEASONS PHILADELPHIA 261R (90S)
| 28 | 28 | 27 | 27 | $225 |

1 Logan Sq., Philadelphia; (215) 963-1500; (800) 332-3442; FAX: (215) 963-9506
■ "*The* place in Philly" surveyors agree about the city's top-rated hotel, a Four Seasons standout that can be summed up in "four words: nobody does it better"; "beautiful rooms" and suites, a "gracious staff" and "magnificent public facilities" (including "a great health club") make staying at this "deluxe" delight "always a treat"; a "lovely location" on Logan Circle midway between City Hall and the Museum of Art, and "a fabulous restaurant", the Fountain, are more reasons why this paragon of "classic elegance" is "worth the high tariff."

Korman Suites Hotel 100R (4S)
| 20 | 17 | 16 | 17 | $138 |

2001 Hamilton St., Philadelphia; (215) 569-7000; (800) 4-KORMAN; FAX: (215) 569-1422
☑ This high-rise can be "a great place to stay on an extended visit", as rooms feature coffeemakers, microwave ovens, refrigerators and washer/dryers; though critics label it "utilitarian" with a staff that's "slow on follow-through", supporters find it "pleasant" and note there's a "great exercise room", tennis courts and pool; north of Logan Circle, it's a bit "out of the way" but operates a shuttle bus to major Center City destinations.

Latham Hotel 136R (2S)
| 18 | 19 | 18 | 15 | $151 |

135 S. 17th St., Philadelphia; (215) 563-7474; (800) LATHAM-1; FAX: (215) 563-4034
☑ "A small, attractive European-style hotel" in "a good Center City location" that bids both for business travelers (modem hookups in rooms and *The Wall Street Journal* at the door each morning) and weekenders ("supervalue" packages); but rooms that some deem "charming" others find "so tired they yawn", and comments about service seesaw from "above average" to "erratic"; overall, though, the consensus is "very acceptable."

Marriott Philadelphia 1144R (56S)
| 22 | 21 | 19 | 21 | $155 |

1201 Market St., Philadelphia; (215) 625-2900; (800) 228-9290; FAX: (215) 625-6000
☑ By far the city's largest hostelry, this two-year-old colossus next to the convention center is "well above the usual Marriott" and "surprisingly good for a convention hotel" according to fans; they call it a "good value" that's "well run" by an "accommodating staff", though rooms get mixed reviews: "decent size, very well appointed" vs. "just ok"; still, "size is important" here (85,000 square feet of function space is a draw), though size also prompts critics to claim it's "too big to really be any good."

Omni At Independence Park 147R (3S)
| 23 | 22 | 20 | 21 | $160 |

401 Chestnut St., Philadelphia; (215) 925-0000; (800) THE-OMNI; FAX: (215) 925-1263
■ Overlooking Independence National Historical Park is a "wonderful hotel" in a "great location for families", close to major historic sites; though built in 1990, the high-rise has a traditional look and ambiance that's "like the loveliest private home"; in addition to "well-appointed rooms", guests can enjoy the indoor pool, "tasteful bar and lounge" and Regional American cookery in the Azalea dining room; service, while generally "caring" or at least "ok", occasionally lapses into "clueless."

Park Hyatt Philadelphia At The Bellevue
| 23 | 22 | 22 | 22 | $185 |

143R (27S)
(fka Hotel Atop the Bellevue)
1415 Chancellor Ct., Philadelphia; (215) 893-1776; (800) 221-0833; FAX: (215) 732-8518
☑ So she's "a bit worn" and "showing her age" – this "great lady" occupying the upper floors of the original beaux arts hotel (upscale shopping and various restaurants make up the lower levels) is still the epitome of "elegance" with "large, beautifully decorated rooms", "spectacular public spaces" and a top-floor dining room that's "one short level below heaven"; a location next to the Academy of Music and the "best gym in the city" are bonuses; perhaps new management will mollify those who say "service has slipped."

Penn's View Inn Hotel 38R (2S)   20 21 22 18 $142
14 N. Front St., Philadelphia; (215) 922-7600; (800) 331-7634; FAX: (215) 922-7642
☑ "The best deal" in town for some, this "lovely small hotel" in the Old City is "a short walk to fun eateries", but many opt to stay on-site to enjoy the "excellent" Ristorante Panorama and cozy wine bar (120 varieties by the glass); rooms furnished in colonial style generate opinions ranging from "pretty" to "no charm", but the sound-sensitive claim the main problem is the hum of traffic "noise" from I-95.

RITTENHOUSE HOTEL 102R (34S)   27 26 24 24 $212
210 W. Rittenhouse Sq., Philadelphia; (215) 546-9000; (800) 635-1042; FAX: (215) 732-3364
■ "A class act" on Rittenhouse Square; even if some find it a tad "overdone", this high- style hotel provides "a luxe" experience with "large, beautiful" rooms that are "tops", "service beyond fondest expectations" and a "wonderful" spa; if the American cuisine at TreeTops doesn't quite reach the same levels, it's still "creative and delicious" (and there's now also seafood and other fare at the new Nicholas Nickolas), and the overall package prompts some to say "if all hotels were this good I'd never go home."

RITZ-CARLTON PHILADELPHIA 273R (17S)   26 27 26 25 $212
17th & Chestnut Sts., Philadelphia; (215) 563-1600; (800) 241-3333; FAX: (215) 564-9559
■ This "classic" R-C tucked inside the glossy Liberty Place Center City office and shopping complex is "an elegant oasis" with an "outstanding, well-informed staff", "plush", "well-appointed rooms" and The Grill, which "stands as one of the finest" for American cuisine; the only drawback, albeit minor, seems to be that the "entrance is not very welcoming", but "the staff is, and the lobby [reached by elevator] is impressive once you find it"; the city's second-highest overall ratings speak volumes.

Sheraton Society Hill 351R (14S)   21 20 19 21 $153
1 Dock St., Philadelphia; (215) 238-6000; (800) 325-3535;
FAX: (215) 922-2709
☑ In a "wonderful" Society Hill location "close to historic sights" and surrounded by impeccably restored 18th-century houses, this 1980s-built hotel blends a colonial-style exterior with very 20th-century touches like a "lovely" atrium lobby and skylit indoor pool; with "comfortable rooms" and "a staff that tries its best", it may be "one of the nicer Sheratons", but, as with all Sheratons, a dissatisfied minority sniffs that although "reliable", it's "nothing special."

Thomas Bond House Bed & Breakfast 12R   – – – – M
129 S. Second St., Philadelphia; (215) 923-8523; (800) 845-BOND;
FAX: (215) 923-8504
Located in Independence National Historic Park, this 1769 Georgian overlooking Welcome Park (site of William Penn's home) recalls a more gracious time thanks to atmospheric common areas and guestrooms outfitted with period decor (two with fireplace); rates include continental breakfast during the week, a full gourmet breakfast on weekends and evening wine and cheese; many historic sights are within walking distance and guests can use a nearby health club for a fee.

Warwick Philadelphia 197R (3S)   18 19 17 17 $161
1701 Locust St., Philadelphia; (215) 735-6000; (800) 523-4210;
FAX: (215) 790-7766
☑ "Popular with long-term guests" as well as conventioneers, this Center City property a block from Rittenhouse Square can still evoke "old-style Philadelphia class and elegance", even if rooms vary from "bright and cheerful" to "musty"; admirers say it delivers "atmosphere and location at a fair price" and enjoy "cordial service" and "good" Mediterranean fare in Mia's restaurant, but some say "nothing lives up to the promise of its lovely lobby."

Wyndham Franklin Plaza Hotel 726R (32S)   17 17 15 17 $143
17th & Race Sts., Philadelphia; (215) 448-2000; (800) 996-3426;
FAX: (215) 448-2864
☑ The spacious "*Star Wars*–like lobby" strikes some as "lovely", others as "cold and unwelcoming" at this convention-friendly high-rise, which gets similarly mixed reviews across the board: the location at the northern edge of Center City is "convenient" or "iffy", rooms are "pretty clean" and "comfortable" or "small" and "seedy", and service is "efficient" or "sour"; on the plus side: an "excellent" brunch at Between Friends, a "fab health club" with racquetball courts and a jogging track, and "good prices."

Pittsburgh

BEST OVERALL	BEST VALUES
22 Priory–A City Inn	Priory–A City Inn
19 Westin William Penn	Radisson Hotel
Doubletree	Marriott Greentree

Doubletree Hotel Pittsburgh 576R (40S)

20 | 19 | 18 | 18 | $142

(fka Vista International Hotel)
1000 Penn Ave., Pittsburgh; (412) 281-3700; (800) 222-TREE; FAX: (412) 227-4504
◪ A "convenient" Downtown address with "views of the three rivers" pleases execs, as do "comfortable" rooms, making this "better than the usual business hotel" – perhaps because the place was totally renovated in '96 when it became a Doubletree; while some guests get their endorphins up in the "great workout" facility, others are brought down by service that "lacks polish", though at least it's "friendly."

Hilton & Towers Pittsburgh 681R (31S)

19 | 18 | 17 | 17 | $142

600 Commonwealth Pl., Pittsburgh; (412) 391-4600; (800) HILTONS; FAX: (412) 594-5161
◪ At Point State Park, the "best location" Downtown, Steel City's Hilton has "knockout views of the rivers" and "does a nice job of periodically updating its facilities"; as might be expected of "a good meeting place" that pays "attention to details", its "banquet staff aims to please" and there's a "good concierge floor"; still, critics say guests should steel themselves for "cramped" rooms that "feel like walk-in closets."

Marriott City Center Pittsburgh 399R (2S)

17 | 18 | 16 | 16 | $142

(fka Hyatt Regency Pittsburgh)
112 Washington Pl., Pittsburgh; (412) 471-4000; (888) 456-6600; FAX: (412) 394-1017
◪ It "was great as a Hyatt" and admirers say the quality continues under Marriott, listing a "good location" near the civic center, "good meeting" space (14 rooms equipped to handle large conferences), "good value" and a "good exercise room, pool and sauna" as reasons to stay; all those "goods", however, aren't enough for critics who rate it "inadequate in every way"; N.B. it was totally renovated in 1996.

Marriott Greentree Pittsburgh 465R (5S)

17 | 18 | 16 | 16 | $118

101 Marriott Dr., Pittsburgh; (412) 922-8400; (800) 525-5902; FAX: (412) 922-8981
◪ Another "cookie-cutter", "standard Marriott", which can mean many things: a "surprisingly charming" place with a "good staff" and "convenient" suburban location (off I-279 near the airport), or an "ok", "blah" conference hotel that's "mediocre at best" and, to some, "overpriced"; pluses include indoor and outdoor pools, tennis courts, an exercise room – even a "good bartender" in Cahoots lounge.

Priory - A City Inn 21R (3S)

24 | 25 | 18 | 20 | $119

614 Pressley St., Pittsburgh; (412) 231-3338; FAX: (412) 231-4838
◼ Built in 1888 to house traveling Benedictine clerics, this "beautiful, quiet and secluded" inn now welcomes travelers on different missions; furnished with period antiques, it's "quaint and comfortable" and "a fire is usually going in the lobby", making the free PM wine hour extra cozy (continental breakfast is also included); we hear differing accounts of the Deutschtown neighborhood ("nice" vs. "awful"), but there's AM limo service to Downtown (though it's "a surprisingly convenient walk").

Radisson Hotel Pittsburgh 322R (48S)

▽ 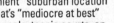 19 | 18 | 18 | 17 | $112

101 Mall Blvd., Monroeville; (412) 373-7300; (800) 333-3333; FAX: (412) 373-3915
◼ This contemporary hotel in a suburb 15 minutes from Downtown benefits from being "the only game" in that area (it adjoins the Pittsburgh Expo Mart and is across from the Monroeville Mall); the "newly renovated guestrooms are great" and the "staff is friendly", but some murmur that it's "anonymous and dull"; there's a pool on-site and guests enjoy tennis, squash and racquetball privileges at the nearby Pittsburgh Racquet Club.

Sheraton Hotel Station Square 297R (3S)

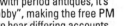 18 | 19 | 18 | 19 | $135

7 Station Square Dr., Pittsburgh; (412) 261-2000; (800) 255-7488; FAX: (412) 261-2932
◪ The only riverfront hotel in a city with three rivers is in "an interesting setting" across the Monongahela from Downtown; though opinions about rooms veer from "nice" to "adequate" to "ain't much", it boasts "accommodating staff" and a "surprisingly good" dining room; the adjoining restored historic rail facility offers more restaurants options plus "late-night action" at a comedy club, sports bar and several saloons.

Westin William Penn 544R (45S)
20 | 20 | 18 | 20 | $149

530 William Penn Pl., Pittsburgh; (412) 281-7100; (800) 228-3000; FAX: (412) 553-5252

✓ "A lovely", "grand" hotel with "character" and "smallish but immaculately decorated rooms", this "step back in time" was "nicely renovated" in '96; overlooking Mellon Square and within "walking distance" of the city's corporate towers, it pleases those seeking "turn-of-the-century elegance", but a more thoroughly modern minority moans "it's past its prime" and claim that service is "friendly but annoyingly incompetent."

Skytop

Skytop Lodge 164R (3S)
18 | 22 | 20 | 24 | $190

1 Skytop, Skytop; (717) 595-7401; (800) 345-7759; FAX: (717) 595-9618

■ "The grande dame of the Poconos", this circa 1928 fieldstone lodge is "a gem in a tacky area", like being "on a mountaintop cruise ship"; its 5,500 acres offer golf, tennis, fishing, hayrides, hiking, skiing and more, plus "lovely views"; but while most bask in its "casual yet elegant" ambiance, a few gripe that it's "rather pricey" for "small", "less-than-luxurious" rooms and claim that in summer it resembles "a geriatrics ward."

South Sterling

Sterling Inn 35R (16S)
▽ 18 | 20 | 20 | 21 | $138

Rte. 191, South Sterling; (717) 676-3311; (800) 523-8200; FAX: (717) 676-9786

✓ "A good find in the Poconos" offering "charming" (some say "small") rooms in several buildings including the main inn and individual cottages; in addition to hayrides, sleigh rides, fishing, x-country skiing and ice skating, folks enjoy its "away from everything" feel and the personal touch of the "exceptional hosts"; the food earns mixed reviews ("good" vs. "overrated"), but it's "plentiful" (gents are requested to don jackets for dinner).

St. Davids

Radnor Hotel 163R (7S)
16 | 18 | 17 | 15 | $118

591 E. Lancaster Ave., St. Davids; (610) 688-5800; (800) 537-3000; FAX: (610) 341-3299

✓ "One of the better suburban hotels" describes this "well-guarded Main Line oasis" west of Philadelphia with "a friendly sales staff that's a meeting planner's dream" plus "a lovely garden" and 24-hour fitness center; however, opinions on the rooms range from "nice" to "in need of a revamp" and critics contend that overall it's "not anything special" except you "can walk to the train station."

Strasburg

Historic Strasburg Inn 93R (8S)
21 | 19 | 19 | 19 | $117

1 Historic Dr., Strasburg; (717) 687-7691; (800) 872-0201; FAX: (717) 687-6098

✓ Surrounded by the Amish farms of Lancaster County, this "picturesque" inn has "nice, clean rooms" with colonial decor, "a wonderful staff" and "excellent dining"; for recreation there are carriage and hot-air balloon rides, a fitness center and outdoor pool; but while the inn's origins go back to 1793, critics grumble that the present circa 1972 facility is "neither historic nor an inn, just a group-infested motel."

Wayne

Wayne Hotel 30R (5S)
21 | 22 | 24 | 20 | $132

139 E. Lancaster Ave., Wayne; (610) 687-5000; (800) 962-5850; FAX: (610) 687-8387

■ "A thoughtful and loving" restoration of a hotel built in 1906, this "pretty place" on the Main Line with "charming Victorian rooms, all different" is "a great find in suburban Philadelphia" made even greater by a "fine restaurant", Taquet, serving contemporary French fare; a few nitpickers say rooms can be "musty" and "after 11 PM, the service staff fades", but you'll hear no complaints from those enjoying "cool summertime drinks on the white-wickered front porch."

Puerto Rico

TOP 10 OVERALL

BEST OVERALL

27 Horned Dorset/Rincon
24 El Conquistador/Fajardo
22 Hyatt Regency Dorado/Dorado
    El San Juan/San Juan
    Palmas del Mar/Humacao
    Hyatt Regency Cerromar/Dorado
21 El Convento/Old San Juan
20 Caribe Hilton/San Juan
    Condado Plaza/San Juan
18 Sands Hotel/San Juan

BEST VALUES

El Convento/Old San Juan
Sands Hotel/San Juan
Condado Plaza/San Juan
Condado Beach Trio/San Juan
Palmas del Mar/Humacao
Horned Dorset/Rincon
El San Juan/San Juan
Caribe Hilton/San Juan
Hyatt Regency Cerromar/Dorado
El Conquistador/Fajardo

`Dorado`

R	S	D	P	$

Hyatt Regency Cerromar Beach 460R (44S) | 21 | 21 | 20 | 25 | $236 |
Rd. 693, Dorado; (787) 796-1234; (800) 233-1234; FAX: (787) 796-4647

■ "What a pool!" (reputedly the world's largest, complete with flumes and slides) shout surveyors, but that's not the only thing this resort has going for it: "superb rooms and views", "lovely surroundings", "a magnificent beach" and "great golf" please even nonpool types; it's "good for families", which means "too many kids" to some, and there are scattered gripes about "cafeteria food at high prices" and "small" rooms "not up to par."

Hyatt Regency Dorado Beach 297R (1S) | 23 | 22 | 20 | 25 | $261 |
Rd. 693, Dorado; (787) 796-1234; (800) 233-1234; FAX: (787) 796-2022
■ "As far from the glitz of Puerto Rico as you can get", this "Caribbean paradise" is an "upscale" resort sharing facilities with the Cerromar; strengths include an "elegant lobby and lovely guestrooms", "excellent golf", tennis courts and "spectacular alfresco dining"; a few critics find it "overpriced" and target "mediocre food", but parents appreciate the "great set-up for kids in beachfront rooms", which are "worth the extra money."

Fajardo

EL CONQUISTADOR RESORT & COUNTRY CLUB 736R (214S) | 25 | 23 | 23 | 27 | $270 |
1000 El Conquistador Ave., Fajardo; (787) 863-1000; (800) 468-5228; FAX: (787) 863-6500
■ A "spectacular setting on a cliff with water views all around" sets apart this "dazzling" 500-acre complex, where guests stay in the main hotel or one of three different 'villages'; a "sports lover's paradise", it boasts "great tennis", six pools and "breathtaking views on the hilly golf course", and those who can keep their mind on business say it's super "for large meetings"; a few knock "inconsistent" food and service and say it's "too far from the beach", but the consensus is "what a palace!" – one of the "best in Puerto Rico."

Humacao

Palmas Del Mar Resort 100R (203S) | 23 | 20 | 20 | 25 | $211 |
PO Box 2020, Rd. 3, Humacao; (787) 852-6000; (800) PALMAS-0; FAX: (787) 852-6320
■ Recommended for a "restful" stay in "beautiful" surroundings, this "outstanding" if somewhat "isolated" resort has "something for everyone": 20 "terrific tennis" courts, a Gary Player golf course, four pools, pony rides, a casino and more, making for "a great family vacation"; most also extol "extraordinary food and service par excellence", and if some feel "far from San Juan" and "out of the action", that's just why others like it.

Old San Juan

El Convento Hotel 90R (9S) | 21 | 21 | 20 | 21 | $182 |
PO Box 1048, Hwy. 52, Old San Juan; (787) 723-9020; (800) 468-2779; FAX: (787) 721-2877
☑ A "great location" in Old San Juan has long been the main asset of this 17th-century former convent lauded for its "old-world charm" and "classy casino"; complaints that "the building's history doesn't compensate for small" quarters that "need an overhaul" may have been addressed by a redo completed in early '97; guestrooms now have a multi-line speaker phone, fax, VCR, CD player and refrigerator, and buffet breakfast is included in the rate.

Rincon

HORNED DORSET PRIMAVERA 22R (8S) | 27 | 28 | 26 | 26 | $259 |
PO Box 1132, Rd. 429, Rincon; (787) 823-4030; FAX: (787) 823-5580
■ Rated tops overall in Puerto Rico, this ""unique" "boutique hotel" is "out of the mainstream" on the island's west coast, making it a "true destination" for blissed-out vacationers in search of "a very peaceful escape" – "no children, radios, telephones or TVs, just the seduction of the area"; guests gush about the "huge rooms, comforting decor and ocean views" at this Mediterranean-style villa; as befits a Relais & Châteaux member, there's "excellent" French food and a "manager as polished as any anywhere."

San Juan

Caribe Hilton Hotel & Casino 629R (49S)   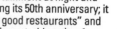 | 20 | 19 | 19 | 22 | $202 |
Calle Los Rosales, San Juan; (787) 721-0303; (800) 468-8585; FAX: (787) 722-2910
■ "A first-class, centrally located deluxe hotel with great entertainment at night and impeccable service" say admirers of this San Juan veteran nearing its 50th anniversary; it seduces with "stunning views from rooms with balconies", "very good restaurants" and super tennis, not to mention "great piña coladas" (reputedly invented here); a few foes find it "a bit shopworn" and "touristy", but the consensus is "still one of the best."

Condado Beach Trio Resort, Casino & Convention Center 463R (16S) | 18 | 18 | 18 | 19 | $172 |
1061 Ashford Ave., San Juan; (787) 721-6090; (800) 468-2775; FAX: (787) 722-3200
☑ An all-in-one complex consisting of the historic Condado Beach hotel (built by the Vanderbilts in 1919), the modern La Concha resort, and the El Centro convention facility; assets include a "good beachfront" site and "great lobby" in the older hotel, but some cite "disappointing rooms" and say it's "most remarkable for the casino"; both properties have their own pool and meeting facilities, and there's an extra 80,000 square feet of event space at El Centro.

Condado Plaza Hotel & Casino 508R (62S)

20 | 19 | 19 | 21 | $181

999 Ashford Ave., San Juan; (787) 721-1000; (800) 468-8588; FAX: (787) 722-7955

◪ "Geared for business travelers who still want to have a good time", this modern hotel earns praise for "wonderful rooms", "good service" ("club floor is best"), a "variety of restaurants" and a "nice casino"; some feel the public beach is "too close", but the on-site pool compensates.

El San Juan Hotel & Casino 356R (33S)

22 | 21 | 22 | 24 | $217

6063 Ave. Isla Verde, San Juan; (787) 791-1000; (800) 468-2818; FAX: (787) 791-6985

◼ "Lush grounds, a beautiful beach" and "excellent restaurants" are among the assets of this "classy", "well-run" veteran; "a great casino" and "hopping disco" mean there's "no need to leave the hotel for nightlife", which is another reason why fans "wouldn't stay anywhere else"; a few sigh "if only the rooms were as beautiful" as the "old-world lobby" and warn against booking "on the airport side"; N.B. stogie smokers can light up in the new cigar bar.

Sands Hotel & Casino Beach Resort 402R (10S)

19 | 19 | 18 | 19 | $163

E. La Verde Rd./Hwy. 187, San Juan; (787) 791-6100; (800) 468-9076; FAX: (787) 791-7540

◪ Finding a touch of Las Vegas in San Juan is fine with supporters of this "convenient, clean" casino hotel with a "helpful staff" and prices that make it a "terrific value"; nods also go to "good dining" and the "nice pool, bar and beach"; critics, however, rate it "adequate" with "poor service", and even fans cite "noisy rooms on the airport side", so "ask for a beach view."

Rhode Island

	R	S	D	P	$

Atlantic Inn 20R (1S)   19 | 21 | 22 | 20 | $161
PO Box 188, High St., Block Island; (401) 466-5883; (800) 224-7422; FAX: (401) 466-5678
■ A "relaxed, refined" 1879 Victorian inn on a Block Island hilltop with a "lovely" overlook of the ocean and village; guests enthuse about the "wonderful staff" that's "attentive to details" and "excellent" local seafood, as well as the "charming public spaces"; there are a few comments about "tiny rooms" with "thin walls", so "try for corner rooms"; open seasonally.

Manisses, Hotel 17R   20 | 22 | 23 | 21 | $157
PO Box I, Spring St., Block Island; (401) 466-2421; (800) MANISSE; FAX: (401) 466-2858
■ "Quaint", "friendly" and "casual", this "old-fashioned" Victorian sister of the 1661 Inn wins kudos for its "very personal" approach and "unusual", "eclectic" restaurant fare that boosters call the "best dining" on Block Island; a "sweet petting zoo" keeps kids occupied while parents partake of the afternoon wine-and-nibble hour; P.S. "rooms really vary – so ask."

1661 Inn 9R   18 | 21 | 20 | 18 | $169
PO Box I, Spring St., Block Island; (401) 466-2063; (800) MANISSE; FAX: (401) 466-2858
■ "Seaside relaxation" is a given at this white clapboard getaway named for the year Block Island was settled; what's "charming" to most is "a little too rustic" to a few comfort seekers, but overall reviewers relish an "amazing buffet breakfast" complete with "great views of the Atlantic", a "pretty setting" that's a "bird-watcher's paradise" and sangria-fueled walks on the beach at sunset.

Newport

Castle Hill Inn & Resort 37R (2S)   21 | 20 | 23 | 22 | $197
(fka Inn at Castle Hill)
590 Ocean Ave., Newport; (401) 849-3800; FAX: (401) 849-3838
☑ "Gorgeously located" on a 40-acre peninsula that's a 10-minute drive from Newport center, this 1874 Victorian manse (plus cottages with kitchen facilities on a private beach) is "a favorite" for "great" New England dining and "unbeatable sunset views"; but "quaint charm" can be offset by "condescending service", and some grumble that "expensive" rates don't jibe with rooms that "need refurbishing" and "vary significantly in size and decor."

Cliffside Inn 8R (7S)   – | – | – | – | VE
2 Seaview Ave., Newport; (401) 847-1811; (800) 845-1811; FAX: (401) 848-5850
Built in 1880 as a summer home for one of Maryland's governors, this Victorian beauty boasts a prime location a block from the spectacular Cliff Walk and short strolls to the beach and Newport's mansions; rooms are elegantly decorated (all with a/c and many with touches such as fireplaces and whirlpools) and a cottage houses two suites with cathedral ceilings; the inn's most distinctive aspect may be its many paintings by artist Beatrice Turner, a former owner; rates include full breakfast and afternoon tea.

Doubletree Islander Hotel, Newport 253R (17S)   19 | 19 | 17 | 19 | $173
Goat Island, Newport; (401) 849-2600; (800) 222-TREE; FAX: (401) 846-7210
■ "Outstanding" views of the bay and bridge and a "terrific location on Goat Island" (a two-minute walk across the causeway from Newport) crown this "friendly", "kid-oriented" hotel known for offering "cookies and comfort"; a few critics knock "small", "motel-like rooms" and "boxy architecture", but up-and-at-'em guests enjoy the pools (indoor freshwater, outdoor saltwater) and tennis courts and rate it "just plain excellent."

Elm Tree Cottage 5R (1S)   – | – | – | – | E
336 Gibbs Ave., Newport; (401) 849-1610; (888) ELM-TREE; FAX: (401) 842-2084
Two blocks from the beach and the Cliff Walk lies this casually elegant 1882 mansion featuring extraordinary public spaces and large, romantic guestrooms (most with fireplaces) filled with fine French and English antiques, stained glass and touches of whimsy; the impressive interior, combined with the graciousness of artist-owners Priscilla and Tom Mallone, is what turns first-time visitors into regulars; a full gourmet breakfast served at individual candlelit tables is included.

Inntowne Inn 17R (9S)　　　　　　　　17 | 17 | 14 | 15 | $158
6 Mary St., Newport; (401) 846-9200; (800) 457-7803; FAX: (401) 846-1534
■ This "just ok", "gray" hostelry with antique decor and a rooftop deck needs more than a "nice Old Newport location" to satisfy surveyors; critics contend that "very small rooms" and "very slow service" are "not what you come to Newport for."

Marriott Newport 310R (7S)　　　　　19 | 20 | 17 | 19 | $161
25 America's Cup Ave., Newport; (401) 849-1000; (800) 458-3066; FAX: (401) 849-3422
☑ An "ultramodern facility" overlooking Narragansett Bay, this newly renovated atrium hotel offers "attractive views", "good service", "fairly spacious rooms" and "beautiful public areas", as well as an indoor pool and fitness center; all the same, quaintness buffs cry "no charm", finding this chain hotel an "adequate" but "humdrum" "place to sleep and shower" – "if all the inns and B&Bs are booked."

Newport Harbor Hotel & Marina 132R (1S)　　19 | 19 | 18 | 19 | $181
49 America's Cup Ave., Newport; (401) 847-9000; (800) 955-2558; FAX: (401) 849-6380
☑ The "awesome location" in the heart of Newport is a main attraction here, although a full-service marina and a deck overlooking the "pretty" harbor please nautical types; there's also "nice service", but this veteran may be "showing its age and use", so "don't expect much from the rooms", which are "nothing special."

Vanderbilt Hall 42R (9S)　　　　　　– | – | – | – | VE
41 Mary St., Newport; (401) 846-6200; (800) VAN-HALL; FAX: (401) 846-0701
Once a Vanderbilt estate, this Colonial Revival landmark in Newport's Historic Hill District was set to make its debut as a hotel at press time, promising pampering that, if not quite in Gilded Age style, is surely a close approximation; after local house tours, guests can retreat to rooms with period furnishings or take a dip in the marble-decked pool, have a massage or savor cigars and brandy in the Billiards Room; dining venues include the grand dining room, an airy conservatory and, of course, room service.

Viking, Hotel 174R (8S)　　　　　　– | – | – | – | M
1 Bellevue Ave., Newport; (401) 847-3300; (800) 556-7126; FAX: (401) 849-0749
In 1926, the owners of the mansions along Bellevue Avenue chipped in to build the Viking to house their guests; today, this landmark is still hosting visitors here to tour the grand estates, putting them up in comfortable guestrooms oufitted in traditional decor; 22 meeting rooms (capacity 800) and a ballroom cater to those with business on their mind, and the rooftop bar (reputedly Newport's highest point) offers beautiful harbor views.

Providence

Biltmore Providence 220R (20S)　　　18 | 18 | 16 | 18 | $143
(fka Omni Biltmore)
Kennedy Plaza, Providence; (401) 421-0700; (800) 294-7709; FAX: (401) 455-3050
☑ "Enchanted" loyalists describe this neoclassical Downtown "grande dame" as "polished, sophisticated" and "good as Providence offers", gratefully citing "huge rooms"; complaints to the contrary about "food that could be better", a "mall-like" look "that's stuck in the '70s" and "rooms that are nothing special" could be annulled by a full restoration and renovation completed post-*Survey.*

Marriott Providence 339R (6S)　　　17 | 17 | 15 | 16 | $124
1 Orms St., Providence; (401) 272-2400; (800) 937-7768; FAX: (401) 421-8006
☑ "The staff is friendly" and the location near the Capitol and blocks from Brown U is "convenient"; but otherwise surveyors find "nothing special" about what some call the "runt of the Marriott litter" with "spartan rooms", "eat-elsewhere" food and a "very noisy disco" off the lobby.

Westin Providence 341R (22S)　　　　23 | 22 | 21 | 22 | $144
1 W. Exchange St., Providence; (401) 598-8000; (800) 228-3000; FAX: (401) 598-8200
■ "Everyone's first choice" in Providence, this "lovely, new" hotel is an oasis of "cool, calm comfort" where the "first-class" rooms are "light, airy" and "have all amenities" and the staff "treats guests with respect"; direct connection to the Convention Center is a plus for business travelers, as is the "good health club", even if the indoor "pool is amusingly small"; diners devour "superb", "innovative" seafood at Agora, the "chic" on-site restaurant.

South Carolina

Beaufort

R	S	D	P	$

RHETT HOUSE INN 10R
26 | 23 | 25 | 24 | $159

1009 Craven St., Beaufort; (803) 524-1310; FAX: (803) 524-1310
■ There's "no better spot to stay in the area" say admirers of this 1820 Greek Revival mansion near the waterfront in Downtown Beaufort; assets include "extra-large rooms" (some with fireplace), "gourmet dinners and a relaxing atmosphere", complete with wraparound porches, and rates include a full breakfast, afternoon tea and use of bicycles; if looking for the feel of "the Old South", this inn "is a true gem."

Charleston

Battery Carriage House Inn 11R
24 | 25 | 21 | 23 | $151

20 South Battery, Charleston; (803) 727-3100; (800) 775-5575; FAX: (803) 727-3100
■ A "quaint and lovely" inn set in a gracious 1843 home in Old Charleston near White Point Gardens and the waterfront; enthusiasts call it "perfect in every way", with "nicely furnished" rooms (some with Jacuzzis and computer hookups), and while there's no on-site restaurant, there are plenty in the area and continental breakfast is included.

CHARLESTON PLACE 394R (46S)
24 | 24 | 23 | 24 | $170

(fka Omni Hotel at Charleston Place)
130 Market St., Charleston; (803) 722-4900; (800) 611-5545; FAX: (803) 722-4074
■ Though it was built in 1986, this Historic District "delight" boasts "old South charm" and "a grand staircase Scarlett would have loved"; "beautifully appointed rooms" and public areas, "helpful" staff and an "ideal" location add up to what many consider "the best of the major hotels"; a fitness center and "excellent" Southern cuisine are bonuses.

Fulton Lane Inn 22R (5S)
– | – | – | – | M

202 King St., Charleston; (803) 720-2600; (800) 720-2688; FAX: (803) 720-2940
A "quiet location" in the Historic District makes this inn a "very pleasant" choice for a romantic getaway; built in the late 1800s by a former Confederate blockade runner, it offers lovely rooms (many with touches such as canopied beds, whirlpools and fireplaces) and niceties including breakfast in bed (served on silver trays), wine and sherry each evening and nightly turndown service; N.B. nonsmoking throughout.

Hilton Charleston 294R (2S)
20 | 20 | 19 | 19 | $123

(fka Charleston Marriott)
4770 Goer Dr., N. Charleston; (803) 747-1900; (800) HILTONS; FAX: (803) 744-6108
☑ It may be a "functional", "very generic" Hilton but it's "not bad considering the price"; near the airport and "far removed from historic Charleston", it focuses on business with "spacious" rooms, an executive floor and 11 meeting rooms, plus a pool and fitness center; N.B. guestrooms and public areas underwent a $3-million renovation in '96.

Indigo Inn 40R
22 | 21 | 18 | 18 | $150

1 Maiden Ln., Charleston; (803) 577-5900; (800) 845-7639; FAX: (803) 577-0378
■ "You feel like you're a houseguest" at this "charming, accommodating" antebellum inn with a Historic District location "within walking distance of everywhere"; continental breakfasts (included in rate) served in the courtyard "are done with Southern splendor", and while some find the rooms "small", satisfied surveyors pronounce it an "excellent value" and implore "keep the secret, it's so wonderful."

John Rutledge House Inn 16R (3S)
26 | 25 | 21 | 22 | $182

116 Broad St., Charleston; (803) 729-7999; (800) 476-9741; FAX: (803) 720-2615
■ "Restored elegance" permeates this "grand" and "historically significant" 1763 manse built by John Rutledge, a signer of the Constitution; "antiques-filled", "beautifully decorated rooms" in the main house and two carriage houses contribute to the "charming atmosphere", as does "gracious" service; complimentary continental breakfast and brandy nightcaps and a "perfect" Downtown location are pluses.

Kings Courtyard Inn 37R (4S)
21 | 22 | 19 | 20 | $138

198 King St., Charleston; (803) 723-7000; (800) 845-6119; FAX: (803) 720-2608
■ "Live like the gentry" at this "lovely" inn housed in an 1853 Greek Revival building with unusual Egyptian accents; reviewers relish the "excellent value and location" ("convenient for exploring Downtown") as well as the "charming" courtyards and garden; nicely decorated rooms, some with canopied beds and fireplaces, are havens in which to enjoy complimentary continental breakfast and evening brandy and chocolates.

Lodge Alley Inn 34R (61S)
24 | 20 | 19 | 19 | $144

195 E. Bay St., Charleston; (803) 722-1611; (800) 845-1004; FAX: (803) 722-1611

☑ This "pleasantly idiosyncratic" Downtown inn, created from a cluster of restored 18th-century warehouses surrounding a courtyard and gardens, is called a "wonderful find" by admirers who enjoy its brand of "Southern comfort" in "gorgeous" rooms, suites and lofts (many with fireplace and kitchen); unusual among Charleston inns, it has an on-site restaurant, The French Quarter; dissenters find it "stuffy" and "old-fashioned."

Mills House Hotel 195R (19S)
22 | 23 | 22 | 23 | $146

115 Meeting St., Charleston; (803) 577-2400; (800) 874-9600; FAX: (803) 722-2112

☑ "You can feel yourself relax as soon as you step through the doors" of this "beautifully restored old-timer", an antebellum charmer that happens to be affiliated with Holiday Inn; though some note "typical" rooms, others find them "nicely appointed" and just about everyone appreciates the "good location" in the Historic District and "lovely pool"; the breakfast buffet is noted throughout town and the on-site Barbadoes Room serves up seafood.

Planters Inn 35R (6S)
23 | 23 | 21 | 21 | $139

112 N. Market St., Charleston; (803) 722-2345; (800) 845-7082; FAX: (803) 577-2125

■ This "lovely", full-service 1841 inn is "right in the heart of things", across from City Market shops and sights; "beautiful rooms" furnished in period style tempt guests to sleep late (the "mattresses are the most comfortable" ever), or at least until breakfast arrives on a silver platter; evening is ushered in with "delicious" free hors d'oeuvres in the lobby, after which guests can opt for dinner in the newly renovated on-site restaurant.

Vendue Inn 22R (23S)
26 | 24 | 22 | 21 | $157

19 Vendue Range, Charleston; (803) 577-7970; (800) 845-7900; FAX: (803) 577-2913

■ "The best location in Charleston" say admirers of this "wonderful" inn's waterfront-area address; built in 1808 and once a warehouse for French traders, it has a "charming, quaint" ambiance, "lovely rooms" with period decor (some with fireplace), "friendly service" and "very good" complimentary continental breakfasts and afternoon wine and cheese receptions; tip: you can survey the city and harbor from the rooftop bar.

Victoria House Inn 14R (4S)
▽ 20 | 21 | 20 | 19 | $157

208 King St., Charleston; (803) 720-2944; (800) 933-5464; FAX: (803) 720-2930

■ "You know you're in Charleston" at this "beautiful" 1889 Romanesque-style inn (a YMCA in a former life) in the heart of the Historic District; all decked out in Victorian finery, it's a restful retreat with a "classic" lobby (where guests enjoy afternoon sherry) and comfortable rooms (some with fireplaces and whirlpool baths); a complimentary continental champagne breakfast gets the day off to a festive start.

Hilton Head

Crowne Plaza Resort 315R (25S)
21 | 23 | 22 | 24 | $161

(fka Crystal Sands)

130 Shipyard Dr., Hilton Head; (803) 842-2400; (803) 334-1881; FAX: (803) 842-9975

☑ A "bargain on Hilton Head" say fans of this group-oriented resort nestled inside quiet Shipyard Plantation; "wonderfully secluded, yet near everything", it boasts a "beautiful" 11-mile stretch of white sand beach and is "paradise" for golfers thanks to more than 20 area courses; dissenters cite "so-so rooms", "ok food" and a "small pool for too many people", but they're in the minority.

Disney's Hilton Head Island Resort (102S)
– | – | – | – | M

22 Harborside Ln., Hilton Head; (803) 341-4100; (800) 453-4911; FAX: (803) 341-4130

Opened in 1996, this Disney resort on 15 acres adjacent to Shelter Cove Harbor Marina is, not surprisingly, a family-friendly facility with kitchenettes in the spacious quarters (all villas), three outdoor heated pools, an arcade and children's play area, as well as an additional oceanfront site with beach house a mile away; for grown-ups there's a fitness center, fishing from the pier and golf, tennis, dining and shopping nearby.

Hilton Resort Hilton Head Island 296R (28S)
22 | 21 | 20 | 23 | $165

23 Ocean Ln., Hilton Head; (803) 842-8000; (800) 845-8001; FAX: (803) 842-9569

☑ "Oversized rooms", all with kitchenettes, "fabulous grounds" and "pleasant staff" add up to a "very satisfying" stay at this beachfront Hilton Head resort in the Palmetto Dunes community; "good value" is another asset and there's no shortage of activities, with over 20 tennis courts, two pools and three adjacent golf courses; a few critics yawn "ho-hum", but the fact that there are "no surprises" is a plus for most surveyors.

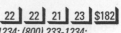

Hyatt Regency Hilton Head Resort 474R (31S) | 22 | 22 | 21 | 23 | $182

1 Hyatt Circle, Palmetto Dunes Resort, Hilton Head; (803) 785-1234; (800) 233-1234; FAX: (803) 785-2432

☑ Set on "one of the world's great beaches" in the tony Palmetto Dunes area, this "upscale" Hilton Head resort wins points for "excellent service", "wonderful grounds" and a full array of facilities including an Olympic-size pool, spa, bike trails and easy access to tennis and golf; however, rooms get mixed reviews ("top-notch", "great ocean view" vs. "dated", "typical") and some serenity seekers find the place "too bustling" and "chockablock with guests" and conventioneers.

Palmetto Dunes Resort (515S) | 23 | 21 | 20 | 24 | $179

4 Queens Folly Rd., Hilton Head; (803) 785-1199; (800) 845-6130; FAX: (803) 686-2877

■ "The ultimate in resorts" with "activities for the preschool to geriatric set" is a "diverse" collection of one- to four-bedroom villas and condos (all with full kitchen) set on 2,000 "rambling" oceanfront Hilton Head acres; "lose your car and get a golf cart" to explore the property's beaches, lagoons and harbor, five golf courses, 28 tennis courts and 20 restaurants; no one denies it's a "great family" destination, but a few feel it has become "very crowded and commercial."

SEA PINES RESORT (435S) | 25 | 23 | 22 | 26 | $185

32 Greenwood Dr., Hilton Head; (803) 785-3333; (800) 325-4653; FAX: (803) 363-4536

■ "Still the best in Hilton Head for home and condo rentals", the island's first gated and groomed development is the "perfect place for a family vacation" with "lots to do" for all: four miles of "fabulous" beach, "great bike trails", "terrific" world-class golf courses, 25 pools and 30 tennis courts; despite reports of a "huge variance" in lodgings – "some units are beautiful, others outdated" – overall it has all the makings for a "heavenly" getaway.

Westin Resort 382R (118S) | 23 | 22 | 22 | 25 | $198

2 Grasslawn Ave., Hilton Head; (803) 681-4000; (800) 228-3000; FAX: (803) 681-1017

☑ One of "the best on the Island" by most accounts, this beachfront Westin is "everything you want in a resort", with "beautiful grounds", "excellent" rooms (enhanced by a recent $2-million redo), "responsive staff", "exceptional" golf and tennis and a "reasonable seafood buffet" at the Carolina Cafe; a few critics call it a "letdown", citing "small, noisy rooms" and a "commercial" ambiance, but most are too busy enjoying "instant relaxation" to pay much mind.

Isle of Palms

Wild Dunes Resort (300S) | 24 | 21 | 21 | 24 | $164

5757 Palm Blvd., Isle of Palms; (803) 886-6000; (800) 845-8880; FAX: (803) 886-2916

■ "Highly recommended as a family destination" but good for corporate groups too, this beachfront island resort 20 minutes from Downtown Charleston offers "fabulous" villa lodgings that "suit all pocketbooks" plus a wealth of activities including biking, boating, fishing, golf, hiking and tennis; though some detect a "compound atmosphere – a little like a hostile foreign nation", most enjoy its isolation and security, calling it the "best resort in the Charleston area."

Kiawah Island

Kiawah Island Resort 150R (360S) | 23 | 22 | 20 | 24 | $185

12 Kiawah Beach Dr., Kiawah Island; (803) 768-2121; (800) 654-2924; FAX: (803) 768-9339

☑ "If you can't relax here", you should probably give up say fans of this "gorgeous" island complex of rooms, condos and houses situated around 10.5 miles of "the best beach around"; "if you love tennis, you'll love Kiawah", and if you're into golf it's "heaven" too; critics call it a "suburbia by the sea" that's "relaxing to the point of being boring", but those looking for "blissful isolation" say it "can't be beat" (and besides, Charleston is just 21 miles away).

Myrtle Beach

Hilton Myrtle Beach Oceanfront Golf Resort | 18 | 17 | 17 | 18 | $135
(nka Wyndham Myrtle Beach Resort & Arcadian
Shores Golf Club) 374R (11S)

10000 Beach Club Dr., Myrtle Beach; (803) 449-5000; (800) 248-9228; FAX: (803) 497-0168

☑ "If you're a golfer, you can't afford not to go" because the "package deals are terrific" at this oceanfront Myrtle Beach resort where the rooms offer "good views" and there are meeting facilities for up to 1,000; while some rate it only "so-so", links lovers retort "who spends time at the hotel when there are 80 golf courses" nearby? (plus on-site tennis, pool and beach); N.B. the Wyndham rebranding (Feb. '98) includes a planned $8.5 million redo.

Kingston Plantation - A Radisson Resort (715S) 22 | 19 | 18 | 22 | $156
9800 Lake Dr., Myrtle Beach; (803) 449-0006; (800) 333-3333; FAX: (803) 497-1017
■ "Myrtle minus the tackiness" is what most find at this "secluded, well-maintained resort", a "casual" yet "classy" all-suite option with three beachfront towers and villas spread out on 145 acres; "roomy" quarters and "many activities" (tennis, pools, a health club and more) make it a "great family" choice, while meeting space for up to 2,000 draws business groups; a few surveyors cite "somewhat tired" suites and claim the complex's size has "outstripped services."

Myrtle Beach Martinique Resort Hotel 196R (7S) – | – | – | – | M
7100 N. Ocean Blvd., Myrtle Beach; (803) 449-4441; (800) 542-0048; FAX: (803) 497-3041
A budget-minded alternative to Myrtle Beach's resort scene, this '70s-era hotel offers oceanfront rooms (many with kitchenette and all with private balcony), indoor and outdoor pools and meeting space for small conferences; while there's no golf on-site, courses abound in the area and golf packages are offered.

Ocean Creek Resort & Conference Center (420S)▽ 21 | 20 | 16 | 21 | $105
(fka Ocean Creek Plantation Resort)
10600 N. Kings Hwy., Myrtle Beach; (803) 272-7724; (800) 845-0353; FAX: (803) 272-9606
■ This "well-maintained, reasonably priced resort" earns points for "great public areas" and "excellent facilities", including eight pools, seven tennis courts and meeting space for up to 300; accommodations are in two beachfront condo towers and groupings of villas and townhomes throughout a "back-to-nature" setting on 57 acres of oaks and Carolina pines; slip on your sandals and head to nearby Barefoot Landing, home to 120 shops and restaurants.

Ocean Dunes Resort & Villas 138R (264S) 18 | 18 | 16 | 21 | $127
74th Ave. N., Myrtle Beach; (803) 449-7441; (800) 854-6701; FAX: (803) 449-1652
☑ Supporters say this Myrtle Beach resort provides "all you can ask for" with "clean rooms" and suites (many with kitchenette) in an oceanfront high-rise and surrounding villas, plus indoor and outdoor pools, a health club and facilities for medium-size meetings; it's also a "good golf getaway for a guys' weekend" (no on-site course, but plenty are nearby and there's a tee-time reservation service); critics find it "kind of plain" and "like all the others."

Sheraton Myrtle Beach Hotel 210R (9S) 18 | 18 | 17 | 18 | $149
2701 S. Ocean Blvd., Myrtle Beach; (803) 448-2518; (800) 992-1055; FAX: (803) 448-1506
☑ The million-dollar renovation completed in 1996 may bump some reviewers' "ok" assessments of this oceanfront high-rise up to the "above average" voiced by others; all rooms have refrigerators and coffeemakers, most have a private balcony, and there are indoor and outdoor pools in addition to the beach; it's close to the airport as well as more than 75 golf courses (golf packages available).

Pawleys Island

Litchfield Beach & Golf Resort (230S) 23 | 20 | 20 | 23 | $145
Hwy. 17 S., Pawleys Island; (803) 237-3000; (800) 845-1897; FAX: (803) 237-4282
■ "A bargain" and a "great deal for golfing" (with three courses on-site and access to over 80 more), this coastal resort is in the secluded Litchfield by the Sea area of Pawleys Island, near historic Georgetown; lodgings (in the all-suite oceanfront hotel or condos, villas and cottages) are "modern and comfortable", and the "wonderful beach" is perfect for jogging, biking or sunbathing; tennis, volleyball, pools and a kids' summer program keep families on the move.

Litchfield Plantation 8R (22S) ▽ 24 | 23 | 23 | 27 | $152
Kings River Rd., Pawleys Island; (803) 237-9121; (800) 869-1410; FAX: (803) 237-8558
■ An avenue of graceful oak trees leads to the romantic, circa 1750 manor house that's the showpiece of this "excellent" 600-acre Pawleys Island complex; guests stay in the main house or restful cottages and can enjoy on-site tennis, an oceanfront clubhouse, marina, a heated pool and "great dining" at the Carriage House Club, plus "outstanding golf" at nearby courses; continental breakfast is included; ask about special packages.

Seabrook Island

Seabrook Island Resort (175S) 25 | 22 | 22 | 24 | $179
1002 Landfall Way, Seabrook Island; (803) 768-1000; (800) 845-2475; FAX: (803) 768-3096
■ Surveyors "love the privacy" of the 2,200-acre barrier island that's home to this "quiet, clublike" resort 23 miles from Charleston; nature fans salute its "terrific beaches" and "sensitive to the environment" design (guest villas "snuggle" into the "beautiful" setting), golfers applaud its two championship courses, and business types like the meeting facilities; there are tennis courts, pools and an equestrian center too; a $2.2-million renovation was completed in 1996.

South Dakota

Chamberlain   R S D P $

Radisson Resort Hotel at Cedar Shore 95R (4S) – – – – M
PO Box 30, 101 George S. Mickelson Shoreline Dr., Chamberlain; (605) 734-6376;
(800) 333-3333; FAX: (605) 734-6854
On the banks of the Missouri River two hours west of Sioux Falls, this new (1995) resort
pitches the outdoor set such activities as jet skiing, fishing and sailing (there's a 100-slip
marina on-site), hiking, horseback riding, biking, tennis and nearby golf; if you must be
stuck inside, rooms are technologically friendly (Nintendo, dataports, microwaves and
refrigerators) and there's meeting space for groups from 10 to 300.

Custer

Custer Mansion B&B 2R (3S) ⊯   – – – – I
35 Centennial Dr., Custer; (605) 673-3333
A historic 1891 Victorian Gothic mansion listed on the National Register of Historic
Places is "a rustic dream" to escapists wanting an atmospheric base for exploring the
surrounding Black Hills; the day begins with a full home-cooked breakfast (included),
providing just the energy you'll need for hiking, biking and horseback riding and visiting
attractions such as Mt. Rushmore and Custer State Park; N.B. there's a two-night
minimum stay in summer; two rooms have shared bath.

State Game Lodge & Resort 5R (63S)   ▽ 17 18 21 20 $95
PO Box 74, HC 83, Custer; (605) 255-4541; (800) 658-3530; FAX: (605) 255-4706
■ "Right in the heart of" the wildlife action in Custer State Park, this "charming" resort
delights surveyors with its "presidential" history (the main wood-and-stone lodge was
Calvin Coolidge's Summer White House) and "lots of buffalo" and other four-legged
friends roaming freely nearby; plenty of activities (fishing, hiking, swimming and more)
plus "reasonable rates" make it "ideal for family vacations"; while the main lodge has
only five rooms and two suites (plus the Pheasant Dining Room, which cooks up local
game), there are also "great cabins" and motel rooms.

Gettysburg

Harer Lodge B&B 6R (1S)   – – – – M
PO Box 87A, R.R. 1, Gettysburg; (605) 765-2167; (800) 283-3356
The wide-open-spaces location of this modern prairie outpost means hunting season
(October–December) is prime time both for the lodge as well as for the deer and
pheasants that roam the area; summer brings great salmon and bass fishing along
the Oahe River; a full breakfast is included and a honeymoon cottage is available
for sporting couples.

Rapid City

Abend Haus Cottages and Audrie's B&B   – – – – M
6R (3S) ⊯

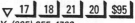

23029 Thunderhead Falls Rd., Rapid City; (605) 342-7788
A couples-only retreat in the Black Hills offering B&B-style accommodations surrounded
by thousands of acres of national forest lined with hiking and biking trails; rooms (set
in a trio of buildings) are decorated with antiques and each has a private entrance, hot
tub (indoor or outdoor) and amenities including cable TV, VCR and microwave; individual
log cottages are set in the forest and overlook Rapid Creek.

Alex Johnson, Hotel 124R (19S)   15 18 16 16 $95

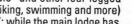

523 Sixth St., Rapid City; (605) 342-1210; (800) 888-2539; FAX: (605) 342-7436
▣ The National Register of Historic Places and some surveyors agree that this
"interesting" 1928 building blending German Tudor and Lakota Sioux styles has been
"faithfully restored" and "carefully maintains its Western flavor"; partisans praise its
"warm service" and call it a "fun old place with lots of history", but critics are on the
warpath against "dark", "spartan" rooms and "tiny" bathrooms; being the "only place
to stay in Rapid City" counts for a lot, though, and it's just 25 miles from Mt. Rushmore.

R S D P $

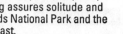

Willow Springs Cabins (2S)
11515 Sheraton Lk. Rd., Rapid City; (605) 342-3665
The Black Hills National Forest makes a romantic backdrop for this B&B's two fully equipped log cabins (each with a private bath and outdoor hot tub, color TV, VCR, microwave and refrigerator), and the secluded valley setting assures solitude and serenity but not isolation: it's not far to Mt. Rushmore, Badlands National Park and the historic gambling town of Deadwood; rates include full breakfast.

Spearfish

Eighth Street Inn B&B 4R (1S)
735 Eighth St., Spearfish; (605) 642-9812; (800) 642-9812
Each room of this 1900 Queen Anne–style B&B is filled with family heirlooms and special features (brass beds, bay windows, a carpenter's chest), making it a homey stopover for tourists visiting Mt. Rushmore and Black Hills National Forest or gambling in nearby Deadwood; a full breakfast is included. and guests are welcome to borrow the bicycles.

Yankton

Mulberry Inn 5R (1S)
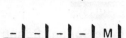
512 Mulberry St., Yankton; (605) 665-7116
Listed on the National Register of Historic Places, the Victorian Mulberry Inn was built in 1873 and sits in a residential neighborhood surrounded by other historic homes, within walking distance to the Missouri River and close enough to Lewis & Clark Lake that guests can take advantage of fishing, swimming and boating activities there; rooms are furnished in antiques and continental breakfast is included.

Tennessee

Fairfield Glade

R	S	D	P	$

Fairfield Glade Resort 160R (16S) ▽ | 24 | 21 | 19 | 23 | $112 |

101 Peavine Rd., Fairfield Glade; (615) 484-7521; FAX: (615) 484-3788
■ "Outstanding accommodations" at reasonable rates bring visitors to this quiet, family-friendly golf resort (four courses) on 12,000 acres in the Cumberland Plateau; though some say the "relaxing" atmosphere has the most appeal for "older groups or golfers", the pools, tennis courts, stable, a nearby marina and nearly a dozen lakes for boating and swimming assure "many activities" for all ages.

Fernvale

Lyric Springs Country Inn 3R — | — | — | — | M |

7306 S. Harpeth Rd., Fernvale; (615) 329-3385; (800) 621-7824
Twenty miles from Nashville glitz and just a holler from the scenic Natchez Trace parkway sits a homey log inn owned by songwriter Patsy Bruce (who penned *Mammas Don't Let Your Babies Grow Up to Be Cowboys*); Bruce's touch is everywhere, from the guestrooms with iron beds and antique quilts to the common areas featuring country music memorabilia; you can swim in the outdoor pool, have a massage or enjoy country cookin' with a nouvelle touch in the on-site dining room (dinner served weekends only).

Gatlinburg

Bent Creek Resort 88R (20S) ▽ | 22 | 22 | 22 | 24 | $131 |

3919 E. Pkwy., Gatlinburg; (423) 436-2875; (800) 251-9336; FAX: (423) 436-3257
■ This self-contained Gatlinburg resort on 109 well-landscaped valley acres pleases guests with "superb service" and large rooms, cabins, condos (some with fireplace) and "wonderful public spaces"; an 18-hole golf course, larger-than-Olympic-size outdoor pool, lighted tennis court and horseback riding beckon families who also appreciate the bargain rates.

Buckhorn Inn 6R (6S) ▽ | 21 | 21 | 21 | 21 | $125 |

2140 Tudor Mtn. Rd., Gatlinburg; (423) 436-4668; FAX: (423) 436-5009
■ Budget-minded romantics salute a "great little inn for the price", "impeccably maintained" with "wonderful rooms" (in the main building and cottages) and a "perfect setting" in the Great Smoky Arts and Crafts Community five miles from Gatlinburg; "service is excellent, food superb" (full breakfast is included), but at dinner "remember to bring wine, since none is served"; ask for a room with a view of Mt. LeConte.

Memphis

BEST OVERALL
23 Peabody
19 Embassy Suites
Marriott Memphis

BEST VALUES
Marriott Memphis
Embassy Suites
Peabody

Adam's Mark Hotel 366R (13S) 17 | 17 | 16 | 16 | $114 |

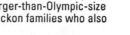

939 Ridge Lake Blvd., Memphis; (901) 684-6664; (800) 444-ADAM; FAX: (901) 762-7411
☑ Though it belongs to a group that some consider a "step above other chains for comfort" and customer attention, this outlying East Memphis hotel's "standard" rooms and service don't make much of a mark on surveyors; however, the "beautiful" 28-story gleaming glass tower rising above a three-acre lake does provide panoramic views of Downtown, just 15 minutes away.

Crowne Plaza Hotel 392R (10S) 18 | 18 | 15 | 16 | $119 |

(fka Holiday Inn Crowne Plaza Hotel)
250 N. Main St., Memphis; (901) 527-7300; (800) 465-4329; FAX: (901) 526-1561
☑ "Ho-hum" but "good value for the money" is the consensus on this "busy", 18-story, group-friendly option; it may be "your generic business hotel" but it has a decided plus: a "location bar none" overlooking the Mississippi River and close to the Cook Convention Center and Mud Island River Park; it's also handy to Beale Street.

Embassy Suites Memphis (220S)   22 | 19 | 17 | 19 | $122
1022 S. Shady Grove Rd., Memphis; (901) 728-4000; (800) EMBASSY; FAX: (901) 685-8185
◪ "Clean and adequate when visiting relatives" or hoping for a glimpse of the King at Graceland, and if that doesn't sound like lofty praise, "hey, you're here to see Elvis, not stay in the hotel"; this East Memphis all-suiter has "big enough rooms" that open onto an atrium with fish frolicking in a winding brook; a full free breakfast begins the day, and free PM cocktails and an indoor pool ease any pains from walking in Memphis.

French Quarter Suites Hotel (105S)   ▽ 20 | 18 | 17 | 17 | $130
2144 Madison Ave., Memphis; (901) 728-4000; (800) 843-0353; FAX: (901) 278-1262
■ "Comfortable rooms" and a "convenient location and parking" keep visitors satisfied at this Midtown all-suiter offering amenities like in-room whirlpool tubs and an outdoor pool; continental breakfast is included in the rate.

Marriott Memphis 316R (4S)   20 | 20 | 17 | 18 | $124
2625 Thousand Oaks Blvd., Memphis; (901) 362-6200; (800) 228-9290; FAX: (901) 362-7221
■ "You can't go wrong" with this "service-oriented hotel" that satisfies surveyors with "comfortable" rooms, "good weekend prices", "unusually attractive public areas" and "better food than most Marriotts"; set in southeast Memphis' suburban sprawl, next to the Mall of Memphis (the city's largest), it offers facilities that include meeting space for up to 1,000, a health club and indoor and outdoor pools.

Peabody Memphis Hotel 453R (15S)   22 | 24 | 23 | 24 | $156
149 Union Ave., Memphis; (901) 529-4000; (800) PEABODY; FAX: (901) 529-3600
■ "If it walks like a duck and quacks like a duck", it must be this historic "landmark", a "lovely grande dame" steeped in "Southern charm and tradition"; "beautiful rooms", "gracious service" and "great conference facilities" (for up to 1,600) earn praise, and "don't miss" the twice-daily parade of ducks to and from their penthouse pond to the massive marble fountain in "probably the best lobby anywhere" ("tip: follow them back up to the roof"); in sum, "why stay anywhere else in Memphis?"

Radisson Hotel Memphis 273R (8S)   16 | 15 | 12 | 14 | $116
185 Union Ave., Memphis; (901) 528-1800; (800) 333-3333; FAX: (901) 526-3226
◪ The "good location" works both for and against this Downtowner – it's engraved in some minds as "stepchild to The Peabody" directly across Union Avenue ("spend the extra money and cross the street"); supporters call it a "very nice hotel in the heart of the city", but others feel housekeeping could be improved and say "ask for a renovated room"; amenities include an outdoor pool and fitness equipment.

Nashville

BEST OVERALL	BEST VALUES
22 Hermitage	Embassy Suites
21 Opryland	Sheraton Music City
Sheraton Music City	Hermitage

Embassy Suites Nashville (296S)   22 | 20 | 18 | 18 | $114
10 Century Blvd., Nashville; (615) 871-0033; (800) EMBASSY; FAX: (615) 883-9245
◪ A "wonderful staff" offers "great Southern hospitality" in "very nice surroundings" croon fans of this Century City all-suiter just minutes from all the Nashville hot spots; the free breakfast buffet and cocktail hour send it up the charts for some, while others sing the blues, finding "all the charm of a dry cleaner" – but even they agree it's "functional."

Hermitage Suite Hotel (120S)   22 | 22 | 23 | 21 | $147
231 Sixth Ave. N., Nashville; (615) 244-3121; (800) 251-1908; FAX: (615) 254-6509
■ Like "a fish out of water, but what a fish", this beaux arts "Southern classic" recently emerged from a total redo that has surveyors raving over "beautifully refurbished, large, bright rooms" and the "magnificent museumlike lobby"; across from the capitol and near the Performing Arts Center, this historic place has heard its share of fish stories, having hosted presidents and celebs ranging from Greta Garbo to Gene Autry and his horse Champion.

Loews Vanderbilt Plaza Hotel 323R (12S)   22 | 21 | 19 | 20 | $143
2100 West End Ave., Nashville; (615) 320-1700; (800) 336-3335; FAX: (615) 320-5019
■ "The only place to stay in Nashville" for those who like this "excellent" hotel's "convenient" location next to Vanderbilt U (great for Vandy parents") in the heart of the business district; "always jumping but smoothly run", it attracts "music-biz moguls" and others with its "nice rooms", "good service" and necessities like voicemail and dual phone lines with computer jacks; the travertine lobby adds a note of elegance.

Marriott Nashville Airport 393R (6S)
19 | 18 | 16 | 17 | $125

600 Marriott Dr., Nashville; (615) 889-9300; (800) 228-9290; FAX: (615) 889-9315

☑ "One of the nicest Marriotts" proclaim partisans of this "well kept, up-to-date" hotel close to the airport and Opryland; some fliers find it a "homey place", others call it a "typical airport" option – "antiseptic and inoffensive"; tennis courts, saunas and indoor and outdoor pools help travelers keep fit.

Opryland Hotel 2663R (220S)
21 | 20 | 19 | 24 | $157

2800 Opryland Dr., Nashville; (615) 889-1000; FAX: (615) 871-7741

☑ "You must see it to believe" this "country-western blend of Disney and Vegas", an 8.5-acre "world under one roof"; "bring hiking shoes" to get around the maze-like "spectacle" of "fabulous" atriums, lush gardens and lobbies, and "leave bread crumbs to find your way back to your room" ("great" to some, "average" to others); long lines are a given (especially at restaurants), and while critics are harsh ("the evil biosphere", a "nightmare" of "schlock"), others say "heck, it's Nashville."

Renaissance Nashville Hotel 649R (24S)
21 | 20 | 18 | 18 | $138

(fka Stouffer Nashville)

611 Commerce St., Nashville; (615) 225-8400; (800) HOTELS-1; FAX: (615) 255-8163

☑ This "spacious" hotel attached to the Downtown convention center and Church Street shopping/entertainment complex is a "good business" base, offering execs "nice rooms and amenities" (including computer jacks and in-room coffeemakers), a "good Sunday brunch" and meeting space for 2,000; an indoor pool and health club help fill nonworking hours; although dissenters find it just "adequate", new Marriott management may bring changes.

Sheraton Music City 356R (56S)
21 | 22 | 20 | 20 | $129

777 McGavock Pike, Nashville; (615) 885-2200; (800) 325-3535; FAX: (615) 231-1120

■ "Old Southern charm" soothes surveyors at this "quiet oasis", a "lovely" Georgian manor–style convention mecca on 23 acres in Century City; "large" balconied rooms offer "comfort and value", and the "helpful concierge" and "friendly staff" pour on "wonderful hospitality"; amenities include indoor and outdoor pools and a fitness center, while hilltop views from the trellised veranda add to the ambiance.

Union Station Hotel 112R (12S)
20 | 19 | 21 | 22 | $129

1001 Broadway, Nashville; (615) 726-1001; (800) 331-2123; FAX: (615) 248-3554

☑ This "wonderfully restored" converted train station is an all-aboard experience for voters awed by its "great ambiance" and "grand" public spaces; a National Historic Landmark for its turn-of-the-century Romanesque style, the architecturally unique (some say "strange") guestrooms benefited from a '96 redo, and Arthur's restaurant is a perennial favorite with locals; a few gripe that it's on the wrong track with "rude staff" and "uneven service."

Pigeon Forge

Grand Resort Hotel & Convention Center
▽ 18 | 17 | 16 | 18 | $133

414R (11S)

3171 Pkwy., Pigeon Forge; (423) 453-1000; (800) 251-4444; FAX: (423) 428-3944

☑ If Tennessee-style glitter and glitz is what you're after, you'll probably find this concrete palace in Dollywood country "friendly and fun"; functional rooms provide "Smoky Mountain views galore", and there are pools, hot tubs, on-site dining options plus meeting facilities for up to 4,200.

Walland

INN AT BLACKBERRY FARM 26R (3S)
28 | 29 | 26 | 29 | $327

1471 W. Millers Cove Rd., Walland; (423) 984-8166; (800) 862-7610; FAX: (423) 984-5708

■ "The 'berry' best in relaxation" is found at this "picture-perfect" 1,100-acre Relais & Châteaux estate just outside Great Smoky Mountain National Park; "you won't want to change a thing" from the "luxurious rooms" and "caring staff" to the "creative" regional cuisine; it's ideal for romance or a corporate retreat, and guests undistracted by love or money can choose from "great hiking, fishing", swimming, tennis or simply toasting the sunset (BYO, it's a dry county) from a porch rocking chair; alas, it's "very expensive", but all meals and activities are included.

Texas

TOP 10 OVERALL

Four Seasons ■
Ritz-Carlton ■

Adolphus ■
Crescent Court ■
Four Seasons ■
Mansion on Turtle Creek ■

Fort Worth •   Dallas

Barton Creek ■
Four Seasons ■

Hyatt
Regency
Hill County ■

Austin •

Houston

Tremont
House

BEST OVERALL
28 Mansion on Turtle Creek/Dallas
27 Four Seasons/Dallas
   Ritz-Carlton/Houston
26 Four Seasons/Austin
   Four Seasons/Houston
   Crescent Court/Dallas
25 Hyatt Reg. Hill Country/San Antonio
24 Tremont House/Galveston
   Adolphus/Dallas
   Barton Creek/Austin

BEST VALUES
Westchase Hilton/Houston
Renaissance/Austin
Menger Hotel/San Antonio
Galvez, Hotel/Galveston
South Shore Harbour/Houston
Omni South Park/Austin
Embassy Suites/Dallas
Omni Parkwest/Dallas
Adam's Mark/Houston
Tremont House/Galveston

Austin

R	S	D	P	$

BARTON CREEK RESORT 143R (4S)
| 24 | 24 | 22 | 26 | $170 |

8212 Barton Club Dr., Austin; (512) 329-4000; (800) 336-6158; FAX: (512) 329-4597
■ "Spacious" rooms, "excellent sports facilities" (including three championship golf courses) and a notable spa make this country clubby estate of low-rise limestone buildings a "golfer's paradise" and can't-beat "white shoe" corporate retreat; it offers "quality everything", with a "nice staff", covey of well-rated restaurants and "beautiful views" of the Hill Country; one caveat: individual guests may feel they're at "a convention site, not a resort."

Driskill Hotel 169R (8S)
| 17 | 19 | 18 | 20 | $130 |

604 Brazos St., Austin; (512) 474-5911; (800) 252-9367; FAX: (512) 474-2188
☑ "Texas history has been plotted for 100 years" at this Austin "politico hangout" that combines Romanesque "19th-century elegance" with the "laid-back feel of the Old West" at a "great location" Downtown near the 6th Street music venues; so while detractors feel that "one night's enough", many boosters insist that ongoing "renovations will make it a place to stay", and until then there's the "wonderful lounge bar."

FOUR SEASONS HOTEL AUSTIN 267R (25S)   27 | 27 | 25 | 26 | $179
98 San Jacinto Blvd., Austin; (512) 478-4500; (800) 332-3442; FAX: (512) 478-3117
■ "Everything about this hotel is the best" from the "extremely helpful staff" to the "comfortable, well-appointed rooms" and "lovely location" on Town Lake; surveyors cite the "must view" of Austin's famous "nightly bat flight" as well as more predictable amenities like the "great lobby bar", "excellent restaurant" (The Cafe), "splendid" spa facilities and even the "best valet parking"; it's simply "the place to stay."

Hilton & Towers Austin North 234R (3S)   18 | 19 | 17 | 16 | $122
6000 Middle Forkville Rd., Austin; (512) 451-5757; (800) 347-0330; FAX: (512) 467-7644
☑ "Another Hilton": there are "no surprises" at this "generic" hostelry that "could be anywhere"; while the mid- to large-size meeting facilities are good for conventioneers, some travelers claim it's "inconvenient to Downtown" and "needs big improvements."

Hyatt Regency Austin 429R (17S)   20 | 19 | 19 | 19 | $129
208 Barton Springs Rd., Austin; (512) 477-1234; (800) 233-1234; FAX: (612) 480-2069
☑ "Great views of the city and Hill Country" and a lobby with "cowboy decor" make this huge Downtown atrium hotel just across Town Lake from the convention center "a pleasant place" to hang your hat; "recently redecorated rooms" are "large" and "stylish", meeting facilities are extensive and returnees hunger for the "best fajitas in town"; critics see a "noisy" chain hotel with service that "needs to improve", but "steady, predictable and nice location" sums up the middle ground.

Lakeway Inn 110R (27S)   16 | 16 | 16 | 19 | $133
101 Lakeway Dr., Austin; (512) 261-6600; (800) 525-3929; FAX: (512) 261-7311
☑ This Hill Country retreat boasts a "friendly staff" and a "pretty setting" on Lake Travis, about 20 miles west of Austin; with a meeting complex, on-site marina, two golf courses and 32 tennis courts, it's "great for groups" (especially for those in the two- or three-bedroom villas) and a generally "enjoyable experience"; doubters feel "it's less impressive for food and rooms", but perhaps the latter will improve with a 1997 renovation.

Marriott at the Capitol, Austin 361R (4S)   19 | 19 | 17 | 19 | $119
701 E. 11th St., Austin; (512) 478-1111; (800) 228-9290; FAX: (512) 478-3700
☑ "Totally Marriott" say respondents, who then split on what that means: "tiny" rooms that can be "musty" vs. a "bright, cheery hotel" with "great food" and a "friendly staff"; pluses include a "good location" close to the capitol and convention center, "ok" meeting facilities and a sports bar; however, "parking is a problem."

Omni Austin Hotel at South Park 311R (2S)   20 | 19 | 19 | 19 | $120
(fka Wyndham Austin)
4140 Governor's Row, Austin; (512) 448-2222; (800) THE OMNI; FAX: (512) 442-8028
■ "Good service" from a "friendly staff" wins friends for this "typical high-tech-area hotel" that's just minutes south of Downtown; the "excellent restaurant" and "pretty lobby" also please, and the fully equipped health club even includes a basketball court; a few comfort seekers wish they'd "make the rooms a little plusher."

Omni Austin Hotel Downtown 294R (10S)   21 | 20 | 18 | 19 | $129
700 San Jacinto Blvd., Austin; (512) 476-3700; (800) THE OMNI; FAX: (512) 320-1450
■ An "above average" "example of a corporate hotel" that's "geared to business travelers", this "large, not romantic but nice" glass-and-stone high-rise within steps of the capitol, convention center and 6th Street entertainment strip may have "the best location of any chain" in town; "rooms are fine" and guests appreciate the "beautiful atrium", "cool lobby dining", "good happy hour and pool"; all in all it's "good for the price."

Renaissance Austin Hotel 433R (45S)   23 | 23 | 20 | 23 | $133
(fka Stouffer Renaissance Austin Hotel)
9721 Arboretum Blvd., Austin; (512) 343-2626; (800) HOTELS-1; FAX: (512) 346-7953
■ "Absolutely top-notch" cheer respondents about the "superior accommodations" at this "prime location for conventions" in NW Austin's 95-acre Arboretum development of high-tech companies and "lots of shops, movies and restaurants"; kudos for the "very friendly staff", nine-story atrium and lobby bar outweigh the stray caveat about a "not-well-kept indoor pool", and a complete redo of all guestrooms can only improve matters.

Bandera

Mayan Dude Ranch 67R   ▽ 18 | 23 | 18 | 23 | $234
PO Box 577, Bandera; (210) 796-3312; FAX: (210) 796-8205
■ For the past half century the Hicks family has rustled up "a real Texas experience" at this Hill Country dude ranch in the heart of cowboy country; greenhorns who want to ride, rope and chow on Western grub can head here for a "great family vacation" with hayrides, horseback riding, tubing, dances, swimming, fishing, hiking and even golf and tennis; "comfortable cabins" are also good for bunking corporate conferees.

Cat Spring

Southwind Bed & Breakfast 2R (1S)   – – – – M
PO Box 15-C, Rte. 1, Sycamore Rd., Cat Spring; (409) 992-3270
Two rooms in the main house (a converted Dutch-style barn) and a cabin that's 'rustic Texas' but with modern conveniences offer guests intimate, restful times in this rural B&B less than an hour from Austin; private baths, a/c, microwaves and refrigerators plus private entrances for each room make longer stays easier, while antique reproductions, full breakfasts and a fireplace in one room add charm; you'll never forget you're in Texas with those views (especially from the porch) of longhorn cattle in the surrounding fields.

Corpus Christi

Omni Bayfront Marina 420R (54S)   18 18 16 18 $114
(fka Marriott Bayfront)
900 N. Shoreline Blvd., Corpus Christi; (512) 887-1600; (800) 843-6664; FAX: (512) 887-6715
■ "Not a jewel by the sea", but "the best CC can offer" – this "nice" property features "beautiful rooftop views" of the beach and a "great" Downtown location convenient to the state aquarium and the USS Lexington Aircraft Carrier Museum; if the rooftop restaurant's food is "overpriced", at least one fan recalls "one of the best steaks ever"; rooms are "typical" of a "convention-type hotel."

Dallas/Fort Worth
TOP 10 OVERALL

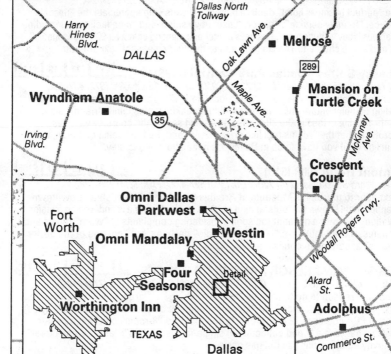

BEST OVERALL
28 Mansion on Turtle Creek
27 Four Seasons
26 Crescent Court
24 Adolphus
23 Omni Mandalay
21 Wyndham Anatole
Westin Galleria
Melrose
Worthington
Omni Dallas Parkwest

BEST VALUES
Embassy Suites
Omni Dallas Parkwest
Doubletree Lincoln Ctr.
Omni Mandalay
Melrose
Worthington
Radisson Plaza Ft. Worth
Sheraton Park Central
Wyndham Anatole
Doubletree Campbell Ctr.

ADOLPHUS, THE 287R (139S)
25 | 24 | 24 | 24 | $183

1321 Commerce St., Dallas; (214) 742-8200; (800) 221-9083; FAX: (214) 651-3563

■ "If you must stay Downtown, you must stay here", a "European oasis" built in 1912 by beer baron Adolphus Busch and now swathed in "classic Texas swank" from the "elegant old lobby" filled with Queen Anne and Chippendale to the "huge", "attractive" rooms to the "pinnacle of dining" at the French Room; service is "impeccable" – "even the doorman knows your name" – and it's two blocks from Neiman Marcus to boot.

CRESCENT COURT, HOTEL 188R (28S)
26 | 26 | 26 | 26 | $213

400 Crescent Court, Dallas; (214) 871-3200; (800) 654-6541; FAX: (214) 871-3272

■ "Elegance without glitz" is the hallmark of the "less-expensive sibling to the Mansion on Turtle Creek"; this north of Downtown hotel courts "business types, sheiks and families" with its "expansive rooms", "exceptional service" and "lovely large lobby" filled with Louis XV furnishings, not to mention the "outstanding" Beau Nash restaurant and "wonderful spa" with a new mind/body wellness center; "spectacular and worth every penny" is the majority view.

Doubletree Hotel at Campbell Centre 289R (13S)
18 | 18 | 15 | 14 | $121

8250 N. Central Expy., Dallas; (214) 691-8700; (800) 222-TREE; FAX: (214) 706-0187

☑ Comments like "good business" option vs. "ok freeway hotel" reflect the debate about this property near SMU, but there's no argument about the signature "great" chocolate-chip cookies received upon arrival; the Dart Light Rail stops two blocks away.

Doubletree Hotel Lincoln Centre 484R (18S)
21 | 21 | 19 | 20 | $126

5410 LBJ Frwy., Dallas; (972) 934-8400; (800) 222-TREE; FAX: (972) 701-5244

■ The "perfect business hotel" declare buttoned-downs who appreciate the "upscale" ambiance, "friendly service", "special" executive suites and "nice facilities" including a "spacious lobby", "huge pool", business center and meeting space for 900; "reasonable" rates and a free shuttle to The Galleria add to the "very pleasant" experience.

Embassy Suites - Dallas Park Central (279S)
21 | 21 | 17 | 18 | $119

13131 N. Central Expy., Dallas; (972) 234-3300; (800) EMBASSY; FAX: (972) 437-4247

☑ This North Dallas all-suiter has a "good location", "nice rooms" and "great services", including complimentary cocktail hour and full breakfast, plus family-friendly amenities like unbreakable dishes in the kitchens and a child seat in the courtesy van; despite a few protests that the "rooms feel like prison cells" and the food could be better, the bottom line is "if you have to be in Dallas, it's not a bad place to stay."

Fairmont Hotel 500R (51S)
20 | 21 | 21 | 20 | $166

1717 N. Akard St., Dallas; (214) 720-2020; (800) 527-4727; FAX: (214) 720-5282

☑ Next door to the Dallas Museum of Art, this "solid and dependable" Downtown convention hotel known for "outstanding cuisine" at The Pyramid is undergoing a major renovation – and not a moment too soon considering complaints of "worn" rooms and a "hopelessly tired look"; an "oldie but goodie" perhaps, but "not one of the better Fairmonts" according to critics.

FOUR SEASONS RESORT AND CLUB 301R (56S)
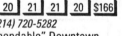
27 | 28 | 26 | 27 | $210

4150 N. MacArthur Blvd., Irving; (214) 717-0700; (800) 332-3442; FAX: (214) 717-2486

■ "The best reason to go to Dallas" "has everything" – "large, plush, comfortable rooms", "outstanding service", an "amazing health club" and "wonderful spa", "great golf" (two PGA courses), 12 tennis courts, four pools, a 28-room conference center and even a bar with a "good collection of single-malt scotches"; "ahhh, what a treat" sigh surveyors about this Las Colinas oasis.

Grand Kempinski Dallas 496R (32S)
21 | 21 | 20 | 20 | $153

15201 Dallas Pkwy., Dallas; (214) 386-6000; (800) 426-3135; FAX: (214) 404-1848

☑ A "renowned", "well-kept" North Dallas "convention hotel" providing "huge rooms", "fine European service", "a soaring lobby", "spacious conference rooms" and a Sunday buffet that's "the best in Dallas"; yet a few feel all this can't compensate for an "out-of-the-way" location "at the edge of the earth."

Green Oaks Park Hotel 236R (48S)
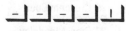
– | – | – | – | l

(fka Green Oaks Inn)

6901 West Frwy., Fort Worth; (817) 738-7311; (800) 433-2174; FAX: (817) 737-4486

This "very nice, almost elegant" business traveler's hotel offers good bang for the buck; it's conveniently located a short drive from Downtown Fort Worth and the Stockyards, with extensive meeting facilities, two outdoor pools, tennis courts and an adjacent golf course; activities aside, some squawk that the rooms "need reconditioning."

Hilton, Dallas Parkway 298R (12S)   18 | 19 | 17 | 16 | $129
4801 LBJ Frwy., Dallas; (972) 661-3600; (800) 345-6565; FAX: (972) 385-3156

☑ It's "in the middle of nowhere" – one of the reasons why this "typical business hotel" with "nice rooms" is such a "good value" – but van service takes civilization-starved guests to The Galleria and other destinations within five miles; despite solid scores, reviewers report "service leaves something to be desired."

Hyatt Regency Dallas 911R (28S)   19 | 19 | 17 | 18 | $151
300 Reunion Blvd., Dallas; (214) 651-1234; (800) 233-1234; FAX: (214) 742-8126

☑ You may need "bread crumbs to help find your way" back to your room at this "huge", "glitzy", 50-story Downtowner with a revolving restaurant; thanks to a recent redo of the lobby, guestrooms and meeting rooms, it's "a step up from most Hyatts", though "service can be slow if there's a convention in the hotel (which is almost always)"; "proximity to the hopping West End" is a plus.

Le Meridien Dallas 361R (35S)   20 | 21 | 20 | 19 | $161
(fka Plaza of Americas)
650 N. Pearl St., Dallas; (214) 979-9000; (800) 543-4300; FAX: (214) 953-1931

☑ What's "top shelf all the way" to some is "ordinary all around" to others, but there's nothing ordinary about a hotel with an ice-skating rink in its 15-story atrium (it's also attached to a shopping mall); located in the Downtown Arts District, it's just a short walk from the Symphony Center, Dallas Museum of Art, Majestic Theatre and Neiman Marcus.

MANSION ON TURTLE CREEK 126R (15S)   28 | 28 | 29 | 27 | $261
2821 Turtle Creek Blvd., Dallas; (214) 559-2100; (800) 527-5432; FAX: (214) 528-4187

■ "Luxury, luxury, luxury" sums up the *Survey*'s overall top-rated hotel, an "elegant, stately" Italian Renaissance–style residence that "lives up to its much-touted reputation"; rooms are "excellent", the "best staff of any hotel" "treats you like royalty" and world-famous chef Dean Fearing's SW cuisine is "to die for"; "pretentious", *mais oui*, but it's "as close to perfection as you can get."

Marriott Quorum by the Galleria, Dallas 538R (10S)   18 | 18 | 16 | 17 | $136
14901 Dallas Pkwy., Dallas; (972) 661-2800; (800) 228-9290; FAX: (972) 934-1731

■ "Good for what it is" – a "reliable, comfortable" convention hotel with "nice rooms" and "helpful personnel" – is the take on this North Dallas Marriott; what helps make it "above average for the chain" is a "convenient" location near The Galleria and Addison Airport; P.S. weekend packages provide "big value for a big city."

Melrose Hotel 163R (21S)   21 | 22 | 22 | 21 | $147
3015 Oak Lawn Ave., Dallas; (214) 521-5151; (800) 635-7673; FAX: (214) 521-2470

■ "An oasis of character in a city that desperately needs more", the "beautifully restored" circa 1924 Melrose offers as close to Downtown New York–style digs as you'll find in these parts; expect "wonderful" rooms (no two alike), "great" food and a staff that oozes "Southern charm"; the Library Bar is a magnet for Dallas Cowboys, fashion models and other night crawlers not especially interested in reading.

Omni Dallas Hotel At Parkwest 337R   22 | 21 | 20 | 20 | $127
(fka Doubletree Parkwest)
1590 LBJ Frwy., Dallas; (214) 869-4300; (800) THE OMNI; FAX: (214) 869-0215

■ "Surprisingly good" say surveyors about this "beautiful" hotel with "large, comfortable rooms", "nice service" and "great grounds" including a 125-acre lake and jogging trails plus nearby golf courses; it's close to the airport and Las Colinas but "way out from town – you gotta want to be there."

Omni Mandalay Hotel 304R (106S)   24 | 23 | 22 | 23 | $156
221 E. Las Colinas Blvd., Irving; (214) 556-0800; (800) THE-OMNI; FAX: (214) 869-9053

■ With its "spacious, well-appointed rooms", "A+" service and "picturesque canal location" near tony shops and restaurants, this Las Colinas Omni is "always a refreshing experience"; though a bit "out of the way", conference planners call it "the essence of a fine hotel for small meetings."

Radisson Park Central 431R (5S)   ▽ 16 | 18 | 20 | 15 | $120
(fka Dallas Park Central)
7750 LBJ Frwy., Dallas; (972) 233-4421; (800) 333-3333; FAX: (972) 701-8351

■ Near the LBJ loop in North Dallas, this recent addition to the Radisson chain struggles to find new footing; respondents report it has "no charm, but they're trying"; an ongoing $14-million makeover should help.

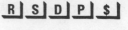
Radisson Plaza Hotel Ft. Worth 502R (15S) | 18 | 17 | 16 | 16 | $119 |
815 Main St., Fort Worth; (817) 870-2100; (800) 333-3333; FAX: (817) 882-1300
■ "Generic" ambiance, "nice service" and convenience to the Fort Worth Convention Center satisfy some surveyors, but others maintain this "older" (1921) convention hotel is "tired" and "very unexciting" – "it's like they've been renovating for 20 years and it's time to start all over again."

Renaissance Dallas Hotel 513R (27S) | 20 | 20 | 18 | 18 | $147 |
(fka Stouffer Dallas Hotel)
2222 Stemmons Frwy., Dallas; (214) 631-2222; (800) 468-3571; FAX: (214) 905-3814
■ Corporate travelers take note: this 30-story granite tower overlooking the Dallas Market Center (perhaps the largest wholesale market in the world) is "a real business address" with "character" and "beautifully appointed" rooms – a "great value" overall; N.B. rooms are larger along the center of the building's elliptical curve, smaller at the ends.

Sheraton Park Central Hotel 524R (21S) | 19 | 19 | 18 | 18 | $132 |
12720 Merit Dr., Dallas; (972) 385-3000; (800) 325-3535; FAX: (972) 991-4557
■ The "Texas-sized" rooms ("larger than my apartment") rate raves, as do the breakfast buffet, "beautiful" public spaces and nighttime view from the well-regarded Laurels restaurant (which will receive a makeover in '97) at this North Dallas business hotel.

Sheraton Suites Market Center (253S) | 20 | 16 | 15 | 15 | $140 |
2101 Stemmons Frwy., Dallas; (214) 747-3000; (800) 325-3535; FAX: (214) 742-3502
■ A "can't-beat location" in the heart of the Market Center is the key selling point of this SW-style all-suites hotel that offers corporate travelers "comfort" and "convenience"; respondents recall "very nice rooms" with wet bars, coffeemakers and free newspapers; "no good dining" is rectified by the property's proximity to Dallas' hip West End.

St. Germain Hotel (7S) | ▽ 29 | 29 | 29 | 25 | $216 |
2516 Maple Ave., Dallas; (214) 871-2516; (214) 683-2516; FAX: (214) 871-0740
■ Romance awaits at this "lovely small hotel", originally a residence built in 1906, where seven "beautiful" suites with canopied feather beds and fireplaces, "impeccable service" and a fine French-American restaurant add up to "perfection"; rates range from $200 to $600 and include breakfast, a glass of champagne and hors d'oeuvres.

Stockyards Hotel 44R (8S) | ▽ 19 | 20 | 18 | 19 | $120 |
109 E. Exchange Ave., Fort Worth; (817) 625-6427; (800) 423-8471; FAX: (817) 624-2571
■ Holy Cowtown! – "if you're in Fort Worth, this should be your only choice"; the venerable brick charmer has the market cornered on "Old West atmosphere" right down to the deer antlers on the wall and the saddle-topped bar stools; convenient to the Stockyards Historic District and Billy Bob's Texas, it's "fun and friendly" for vacationers and business travelers alike; N.B. lobby, bar and restaurant were renovated in '96.

Stoneleigh Hotel 99R (51S) | 18 | 19 | 18 | 15 | $140 |
2927 Maple Ave., Dallas; (214) 871-7111; (800) 255-9299; FAX: (214) 871-9379
■ With its "very large" rooms, "magnificent" suites and "Texas hospitality at its best", this "funky old dame of a hotel" is a "local fave" as well as a haunt for Hollywood types; dine at the "good restaurant" on-site (Ewald's) or at the Stoneleigh P, a quaint joint across the street that makes one of the city's best burgers; P.S. reviewers are pleased to report that recent renovations have "put it back in shape."

Westin Hotel Galleria Dallas 418R (13S) | 22 | 22 | 20 | 22 | $161 |
13340 Dallas Pkwy., Dallas; (214) 934-9494; (800) 228-3000; FAX: (214) 450-2979
■ "Probably the best in North Dallas" sits in "a spectacular location": the adjoining Galleria mall offers convenient shopping and eating plus access to the posh University Club fitness center; along with Big D glitz you get good service, including "superior" bellmen and valet crew, "lovely rooms" and a "great hot tub"; dissenters dismiss it as "impersonal" and "not up to Westin standards."

Worthington, The 460R (44S) | 23 | 22 | 20 | 20 | $150 |
200 Main St., Fort Worth; (817) 870-1000; (800) 433-5677; FAX: (817) 338-9176
■ "You can smell the old money" at this "pleasant" pyramid at Sundance Square, a "hidden jewel Downtown" that's "worth every penny" for its "extraordinary room service and health club", "very accommodating" staff and noteworthy Reflections restaurant; to most it's a "classy antidote to the Fort Worth blahs", but a few find it "a little too big and impersonal" and complain of "Houston hubris."

Wyndham Anatole Hotel 1491R (129S) | 22 | 20 | 21 | 23 | $158
(fka Loews Anatole)
2201 Stemmons Frwy., Dallas; (214) 748-1200; (800) WYNDHAM; FAX: (214) 761-7250
☑ It's "like a mini city" ("big enough to merit its own zip code") with 1,620 "nice" guest quarters, 58 meeting rooms, a lobby that "could house the Goodyear blimp", "the best hotel fitness center ever" and "first-rate food" at Nana Grill and 12 other restaurants on a 45-acre campus; some say it's all "too much", proving "big is not better."

Wyndham Garden 23R (45S) | ▽ 19 | 17 | 17 | 16 | $102
110 W. John Carpenter Frwy., Irving; (972) 650-1600; (800) WYNDHAM; FAX: (972) 541-0501
☑ This Las Colinas low rise built around a garden inspires some to say "more than adequate for a business trip", yet most maintain it's "nothing fancy"; critics complain it's "too big and spread out" and the food is "so-so"; "a basic midpricer" is the bottom line.

Galveston

Galvez, Hotel 225R (3S) | 18 | 19 | 18 | 19 | $112
2024 Seawall Blvd., Galveston; (409) 765-7721; (800) 392-4285; FAX: (409) 765-5780
☑ "A trip back to the early 1900s", this "beautiful" Castilian-style grande dame listed in the National Register of Historic Places was a hot spot in its heyday, and today charms surveyors with "antique furnishings", "beautiful landscaping" (thanks to a $6-million exterior redo in '95 that brought a pool with swim-up bar) and a location just steps from the beach; it's "relaxing" and "classy" despite "smallish" rooms "in need of an overhaul."

Harbor House 39R (3S) | ▽ 18 | 18 | 16 | 16 | $141
Pier 21 #28, Galveston; (409) 763-3321; (800) 874-3321; FAX: (409) 765-6421
■ Sea-ing is believing at this "very nautical" inn done up like a waterfront warehouse on the site of an early steamship terminal, part of a wharf development that includes shops and restaurants; maritime motifs dominate in the "cozy" bar as well as the handsome rooms (all with sitting areas and harbor views); nearby tourist attractions include the Texas Seaport Museum and the Strand Historic District – plus, of course, the beach; N.B. you can park your yacht in one of the nine boat slips next to the inn.

San Luis Resort 237R (7S) | 19 | 20 | 19 | 21 | $130
5222 Seawall Blvd., Galveston; (409) 744-1500; (800) 392-5937; FAX: (409) 744-8452
☑ "As good as it gets in Galveston if you want a view" (the Gulf of Mexico is across the street), this "pricey" but "beautiful property" recently completed a $10-million renovation and offers a "great pool area", two tennis courts, a health spa, sauna and restaurants so you can have "a fun vacation and never leave the grounds"; a few critics complain of "paper-thin walls" and, despite a/c, "humid rooms", but overall it looks like a good bet.

TREMONT HOUSE 102R (15S) | 26 | 24 | 24 | 24 | $151
2300 Ship's Mechanic Row, Galveston; (409) 763-0300; (800) 874-2300; FAX: (409) 763-1539
■ The "rooms ooze charm" at "the class act of Galveston", a former dry-goods store that's now an "elegant", "stately" Victorian-style hotel with "beautiful old-time decor" and "great" Continental dining in the Merchant Prince restaurant; the "extremely courteous" staff "understands romance", so "go there for your anniversary and they'll treat you like royalty"; although not on the beach, there's "lots of atmosphere" in its setting in The Strand Historic District (where Mardi Gras krewes parade), and some consider it "the only place to stay" when in town.

Horseshoe Bay

Horseshoe Bay Resort 140R (10S) | ▽ 18 | 18 | 18 | 23 | $131
1 Horseshoe Bay Blvd., Horseshoe Bay; (210) 598-2511; (800) 531-5105; FAX: (210) 598-5338
☑ A "golfer's paradise" with three Trent Jones–designed 18-hole courses, this Hill Country hideaway has an "attractive location" amid lovely gardens, plus 14 tennis courts, a large spa and even a private airport; but when not on the greens, some surveyors aren't as impressed, finding dining rooms "unnecessarily formal and stuffy" and the service in need of "fine-tuning."

Houston

TOP 10 OVERALL

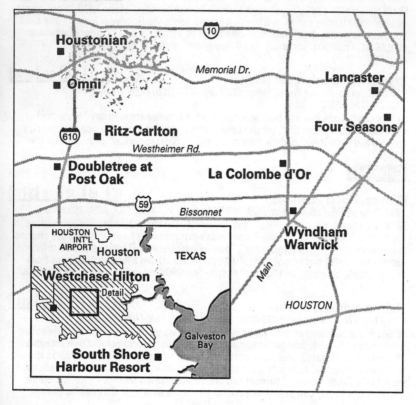

BEST OVERALL

27 Ritz-Carlton
26 Four Seasons
24 Omni Houston
23 Houstonian
    Lancaster
    South Shore Harbour
22 La Colombe d'Or
    Doubletree Post Oak
21 Wyndham Warwick
    Westchase Hilton

BEST VALUES

Westchase Hilton
South Shore Harbour
Adam's Mark
Crowne Plaza Galleria
Doubletree Post Oak
Wyndham Greenspoint
Marriott West Loop
Wyndham Warwick
Doubletree Guest Suites
Omni Houston

R	S	D	P	$

Adam's Mark Hotel 555R (49S) | 20 | 19 | 19 | 19 | $121 |

2700 Briarpark Dr., Houston; (713) 978-7400; (800) 436-ADAM; FAX: (713) 735-2727

☑ "Clean, bright and airy public spaces", including a 10-story atrium lobby with glass elevators, follow from a multimillion-dollar "just-finished rehab" that created a "modern hotel" on the West Side; "great convention facilities" along with "good room service" and a "responsive front desk" are pluses for business travelers; some surveyors find the place just "standard", but rates "can be a good bargain."

Crowne Plaza Galleria Area 471R (7S) | 21 | 21 | 19 | 19 | $126 |

(fka Holiday Inn Crowne Plaza Galleria Area)

2222 W. Loop S., Houston; (713) 961-7272; (800) 327-6213; FAX: (713) 627-0255

☑ A mostly business clientele checks in for "excellent", "clean and comfortable rooms with Galleria views" at a "good rate"; while there are swipes at "plastic food" and "tacky decor" that's "a bit run-down", many voters salute "gracious" treatment that includes "spectacular concierge services" and say "Texas hospitality and charm balance out any deficiencies"; free local phone calls help too.

Doubletree Guest Suites Hotel (335S)   22 | 21 | 20 | 19 | $139
(fka Guest Quarters Suite Hotel - Houston)
5353 Westheimer Rd., Houston; (713) 961-9000; (800) 222-TREE; FAX: (713) 877-8835
■ An all-suiter within eyeshot of the popular Galleria that wins a following for its "airy" and "very large rooms"; a "nice lobby" and Olympic-size pool are added attractions, and corporate types on extended stays appreciate the full kitchens, voicemail and computer jacks; an on-site convenience store extends the "good value" package.

Doubletree Hotel - Allen Center 341R (16S)   20 | 19 | 18 | 18 | $137
400 Dallas St., Houston; (713) 759-0202; (800) 222-TREE; FAX: (713) 752-2734
■ A "very convenient Downtown" choice on the edge of Sam Houston Park, offering "excellent views" of the city center; most respondents rate the rooms at this mid-rise glass hotel "nice" and find the staff "very friendly", and of course there are the chain's signature "great chocolate-chip cookies" on arrival; other assets include a fitness center and proximity to shops, restaurants and the Theater District, though "parking is ridiculous."

Doubletree Hotel At Post Oak 401R (48S)   23 | 22 | 21 | 21 | $137
2001 Post Oak Blvd., Houston; (713) 961-9300; (800) 222-TREE; FAX: (713) 961-1557
■ I.M. Pei designed this "overall treasure", which draws praise for "beautiful" facilities, "the best service" and "large rooms with amenities" as well as "wonderful" dining and "great entertainment in the lobby bar"; those at leisure take advantage of the "superb huge pool" and the "conveniently nearby" Galleria shopping area; unimpressed critics may gripe about "another typical business hotel" "without character", but devotees insist that this one is "underrated."

FOUR SEASONS HOTEL HOUSTON 387R (12S)   27 | 27 | 26 | 25 | $198
1300 Lamar St., Houston; (713) 650-1300; (800) 332-3442; FAX: (713) 650-8169
■ "Terrific in all respects", the city's "most comfortable business hotel" – across the street from the George R. Brown Convention Center – is also a "sleek and chic" place for leisure travelers: the "large, beautifully decorated rooms" have "the only beds as comfortable as home", there's "superb dining" in the DeVille restaurant and a "responsive and knowledgeable staff" "remembers your name throughout your stay"; in sum, "as good as it gets."

Hilton Houston Plaza 40R (141S)   ▽ 25 | 23 | 20 | 19 | $139
6633 Travis St., Houston; (713) 313-4000; FAX: (713) 313-4660
■ This "off-the-beaten-track" hotel near Rice U, the Texas Medical Center and the Astrodome impresses the few surveyors who know it; "suites here are larger than my house" says one ready-to-move respondent, and others name it "a real sleeper" with "very good rates"; the 141 well-equipped suites are particularly attractive to university and medical facility visitors needing lodging for a week or more.

Houstonian Hotel, Club & Spa 281R (10S)   23 | 24 | 22 | 25 | $163
111 N. Post Oak Ln., Houston; (713) 680-2626; (800) 231-2759; FAX: (713) 680-2992
◪ When he was President, George Bush claimed this stately standby as his Houston address; "old lodge decor with modern amenities" aptly describes a "true urban retreat" on 22 wooded acres; there's "an inviting lobby with a Texas theme", a "top health club" and 29 conference rooms; guestrooms can range from "lovely" to "plain", but service is "very pleasant" and the food is "good"; first-timers are known to say "solid, comfortable" and "big – everything I'd imagine from Texas."

Hyatt Regency Houston 926R (30S)   20 | 20 | 18 | 19 | $140
1200 Louisiana St., Houston; (713) 654-1234; (800) 233-1234; FAX: (713) 951-0934
◪ "Prototypical Hyatt atrium design" means "an overall nice property" with "innovative room layout", "good service" and a revolving rooftop restaurant, all of which please fans of this convention-oriented Downtown high-rise; but detractors say a "massive touch-up is needed" and complain about "long lines" and a "bland" quality that's "like a post office with beds."

La Colombe d'Or (6S)   23 | 22 | 23 | 21 | $208
3412 Montrose Blvd., Houston; (713) 524-7999; FAX: (713) 524-8923
■ "Definitely on the top end of quaint", this all-suiter in a "fabulous old" Montrose house could be perfect "for a splurge" on a romantic weekend; museum- quality antiques and artwork are sprinkled through the "charming" 1923 manse that's just down the street from Houston's chic Museum Row; the "wonderful food" spans "a reasonable value lunch menu" and, at night, "grand dining" – "then just wander upstairs to sleep it off": N.B. a brand-new ballroom accommodates 250.

Lancaster Hotel 87R (6S)

| 24 | 25 | 24 | 21 | $181 |

701 Texas Ave., Houston; (713) 228-9500; (800) 231-0336; FAX: (713) 223-4528

■ An "elegant", 1925 "European-style" rococo hotel in a "perfect Downtown location" near the theater and opera (performers stay here); surveyors sing about "beautifully appointed" rooms, lots of "nice extra amenities", "always great food" in the Bistro Lancaster and "great service" from "a friendly, solicitous staff"; guests feel "pampered, comfortable and safe" and so, despite high-ish prices, consider it a "best Houston value."

Marriott, J.W. 491R (12S)

| 21 | 20 | 18 | 20 | $140 |

5150 Westheimer Rd., Houston; (713) 961-1500; (800) 228-9290; FAX: (713) 961-5045

■ "Stetsons, Lucchese boots and Cadillacs" are abundant at this very Texas take on a "flagship" top-of-the-chain "good business hotel"; "above-average" rooms, "nice service", a "good health club" (with racquetball and basketball on-site) and, yup, proximity to the Galleria are crowd pleasers; while some regulars feel it "could use a good dining room", they also suggest that this might be "the cleanest hotel in Houston" and at day's end is "better than most" in the city.

Marriott Medical Center Houston 364R (22S)

| 17 | 18 | 16 | 16 | $120 |

6580 Fannin St., Houston; (713) 796-0080; (800) 228-9290; FAX: (713) 796-2201

■ "The only place to stay" for proximity-seeking outpatients and the families of anyone at the Texas Medical Center; it's "comfortable but average" with "cookie-cutter" rooms, "adequate food" and service that "leaves a lot to be desired", although the "rates are right" and some say "don't miss the health club"; clearly, the draw here is location – "unbelievable access" through an enclosed walkway to the hospitals.

Marriott West Loop Houston 300R (2S)

| 20 | 19 | 17 | 18 | $119 |

1750 W. Loop S., Houston; (713) 960-0111; (800) 469-1537; FAX: (713) 624-1568

☑ Another glass tower "ok business hotel" in the Galleria area that some call a "pleasant surprise" for its "consistent quality", "friendly staff" and "good room service", plus a health club and indoor pool; others rate their experience only "so-so" to "average", citing "worn rooms" and "standard"-at-best dining; on balance, however, most find it "good for a business stopover."

OMNI HOUSTON HOTEL 358R (10S)

| 24 | 23 | 24 | 24 | $163 |

4 Riverway, Houston; (713) 871-8181; (800) THE-OMNI; FAX: (713) 871-0719

■ "A memorable establishment" for its "unique design, landscaping" and "beautiful park setting" that includes a lake with "cute black swans"; what's more, there are "gorgeous rooms", a "great pool", an "innovative room service menu", a "lovely lobby for cocktails" and a "superb restaurant", La Réserve (top-rated for food in Houston); as for the staff, "these people must all be hotel school graduates – they act like they are so glad you came to visit."

Red Lion Hotel Houston 312R (6S)

| 17 | 17 | 16 | 17 | $128 |

(fka Sheraton Grand)

2525 W. Loop S., Houston; (713) 961-3000; (800) REDLION; FAX: (713) 961-1490

☑ This "nice hotel" might be "the best least-expensive place near the Galleria" according to fans who report that the happy hour buffet, "excellent health spa and pool" and convenient video check-out make it a "fun place for a convention" (there's a 600-person ballroom); critics charge it's "unremarkable" and "there's something about this place that doesn't click", but given recent management changes the jury is out.

Renaissance Houston Hotel 380R (9S)

| 19 | 19 | 16 | 16 | $132 |

(fka Stouffer Presidente Hotel)

6 Greenway Plaza E., Houston; (713) 629-1200; (800) 468-3571; FAX: (713) 629-4702

☑ Fly-ins for Rockets games can't get any closer to The Summit, where Hakeem and Sir Charles do their thing, than this midpriced mid-rise hotel across the street; along with the "convenient" location, there are complimentary coffee and newspapers to make mornings easier, and guests have access to the tony City Club fitness facility next door; still, there are a few complaints about an "aging building" and "mediocre service."

RITZ-CARLTON HOUSTON 208R (24S)

| 28 | 27 | 26 | 26 | $209 |

1919 Briar Oaks Ln., Houston; (713) 840-7600; (800) 421-3333; FAX: (713) 840-0616

■ "One of the most elegant urban hotels in America" and top-rated in Houston, this "luxurious" destination just across the freeway from the Galleria provides "typical Ritz quality" that "makes you feel like a million"; from "beautiful flower arrangements in the lovely marble entryways" to "spectacular rooms", "impeccable service" and "excellent food" in the highly rated Dining Room, it's "class from top to bottom" – "you feel like you're in some duke's Italian villa."

Sofitel, Hotel 335R (2S)
| 18 | 18 | 20 | 16 | $132 |

425 N. Sam Houston Pkwy. E., Houston; (713) 445-9000; (800) SOFITEL; FAX: (713) 445-9826

■ The "French atmosphere" includes "good food, hospitality and goodwill" at this Gallic chain hotel that's an "easy commute" (about 10 minutes) from Houston Intercontinental Airport – that plus 15 meeting rooms and related services make it a solid choice for business travelers; a recently completed renovation of all guestrooms should cure reports of "broken light fixtures, peeling wallpaper and worn carpeting"; the "interesting cuisine" options and "great long loaves" (given at check-out too) also help.

South Shore Harbour Resort & Conference Center 237R (13S)
| 24 | 22 | 21 | 23 | $138 |

2500 S. Shore Blvd., League City; (713) 334-1000; (800) 442-5005; FAX: (713) 334-1157

■ A "pleasant place to stay", this postmodern 12-story facility is equidistant from Houston and Galveston and convenient to the NASA/Clear Lake area, but with its 18 meeting rooms, on-site marina, golf, tennis, indoor/outdoor pools and 70,000-square-foot fitness center, some see little need to go anywhere else; "service, ambiance and food are excellent, and the rooms are one of a kind", leading enthusiasts to say it's "one of the few places I've had a meeting that I'd go on personal travel."

Westchase Hilton & Towers 259R (36S)
| 22 | 21 | 21 | 19 | $121 |

9999 Westheimer Rd., Houston; (713) 974-1000; (800) HILTONS; FAX: (713) 974-6866

◪ "Lovely rooms and suites, great staff" and an "at-home feel", plus a West Side location providing "excellent Beltway access", make this mirrored-glass high-rise a "favorite Houston hotel"; the Southwestern fare accompanied by Hill Country ambiance at the Rio Ranch restaurant also scores well; nevertheless, a covey of critics calls it an "ordinary" chain hotel with rooms that "need to be redone" and a "bad layout" on all but the tower floors.

Westin Galleria 445R (40S)
| 21 | 20 | 19 | 20 | $156 |

5060 W. Alabama St., Houston; (713) 960-8100; (800) 228-3000; FAX: (713) 960-6554

◪ With "direct access" to the lavish Galleria, this sibling of the Westin Oaks is "heaven for the shopping maven"; but is it "modern, elegant and comfortable" with "some of the largest rooms around", "good room service" and a "nice bar", or "tired, old", in need of "an overhaul" and "too expensive"?; on balance, most conclude that "if you like malls", this "can be an oasis in the city."

Westin Oaks 395R (11S)
| 20 | 20 | 17 | 19 | $155 |

5011 Westheimer Rd., Houston; (713) 960-8100; (800) 228-3000; FAX: (713) 960-6554

◪ Rated a tad lower and possibly "not as busy" as its sister Westin, this high-rise is just as convenient to the 350-plus shops and ice-skating rink in The Galleria – "you don't even have to go outside"; while supporters say it's "solid", showing off "Southern hospitality" and "class in every respect", detractors decry a "dingy, dark" place "in need of a renovation", which happens to be planned for 1997.

Woodlands Resort 150R (160S)
| 19 | 18 | 17 | 22 | $141 |

2301 N. Millbend Dr., The Woodlands; (713) 367-1100; (800) 433-2624; FAX: (713) 364-MEET

■ "A different experience" as corporate gathering places go, this retreat in Houston's fast-growing suburbs has "beautiful rooms in the forest" that "overlook greenery, lakes and ducks" – "a great change from glass-and-brass hotels"; there are 34 "wonderful meeting rooms", 24 tennis courts and "very good golf" on two 18-hole courses; so while it may be "lacking" foodwise and a few claim the place is "past its prime" and recent "renovations haven't helped much", many "remember it fondly."

Wyndham Greenspoint Hotel 422R (50S)
| 20 | 18 | 18 | 20 | $122 |

12400 Greenspoint Dr., Houston; (713) 875-2222; (800) WYNDHAM; FAX: (713) 875-1652

◪ In the shadow of Intercontinental Airport, this neo-Gothic stopover is called "a great hotel in a not-so-great area of town" by admirers of its "very impressive" one-acre atrium lobby, 24 meeting rooms and the 175-store Greenspoint Mall across the street; critics contend, though, that "this place needs help – they need to care for their rooms", which are called "adequate" or even "old and worn out."

Wyndham Warwick Hotel 263R (45S)
| 22 | 21 | 20 | 21 | $142 |

5701 Main St., Houston; (713) 526-1991; (800) WYNDHAM; FAX: (713) 639-4545

■ This "grand old hotel" in the middle of Hermann Park in the Arts District is a "romantic, upscale and luxurious getaway" that attracts an urbane clientele in town for business or a weekend of museum- and restaurant-going; the lobby "filled with antiques" has "that old-world, old-money feel", and the "excellent rooms" and "friendly, pleasant staff" win kudos; a few murmur that "bathrooms need to be updated" and the dining room is "poorly lit", but the overall sense is "elegance at its best."

Montgomery

Del Lago Golf Resort & Conference Center (357S)
▽ | 16 | 15 | 15 | 20 | $113

600 Del Lago Blvd., Montgomery; (409) 582-6100; (800) DEL-LAGO; FAX: (409) 582-4918
■ Houston business execs (and vacationers) can travel just 45 minutes north to this "very above-average corporate meeting facility" and full-service resort on 22,000-acre Lake Conroe; it boasts 22 meeting rooms, a full-service fitness center and a range of activities such as an 18-hole golf course, 11 tennis courts, bicycling, boating, an outdoor pool and a rigorous ropes course for suits needing postmeeting frustration outlets; all suites, villas and cottages feature kitchenettes and a/c, and many also offer fireplaces.

Rancho Viejo

Rancho Viejo Resort and Country Club 42R (20S)
_ | _ | _ | _ | M

1 Rancho Viejo Dr., Rancho Viejo; (210) 350-4000; (880) 531-7400; FAX: (210) 350-9681
With two fine courses and a golf school, teeing off is the main event at this Spanish-style resort and country club a few minutes from the border and South Padre Island; for time spent off the greens there are two tennis courts, an outdoor pool, a beauty salon, fitness room and formal dining room and clubhouse restaurant; Southwestern-style villas offer lodgings ranging from standard rooms to one-, two- and three-bedroom suites that include kitchens; N.B. good-value golf packages bring in club-wielding groups.

San Antonio

BEST OVERALL
25 Hyatt–Hill Country
24 Fairmount
22 Plaza San Antonio

BEST VALUES
Menger
Crowne Plaza
Plaza San Antonio

Crowne Plaza St. Anthony Hotel 308R (42S)
20 | 20 | 19 | 21 | $130

(fka St. Anthony Hotel)
300 E. Travis St., San Antonio; (210) 227-4392; (800) 2-CROWNE; FAX: (210) 227-0915
▨ This "charming historic hotel" near the Alamo and the famed Riverwalk has "one of the most beautiful lobbies in the world" (filled with antiques and chandeliers) and some "tasty" food in its restaurants; but renovations completed in 1995 apparently haven't satisfied those who say "everything seems old" and rooms "need a redo" – "hope it comes back to its former glory", but for now, "the saint be not praised."

Fairmount Hotel 20R (17S)
25 | 24 | 24 | 22 | $188

401 S. Alamo St., San Antonio; (210) 224-8800; (800) 642-3363; FAX: (210) 224-2767
■ There's "old Texas elegance" to spare at this "adorable", antiques-filled Italianate Victorian, built in 1906 and physically moved in 1985 six blocks from its original site; now minutes from the city center, it boasts an "intimate", "quiet" ambiance, "lovely" rooms "beautifully furnished" in a "trendy Old West" style, and Polo's, a "first-rate restaurant and bar" that makes a mean Bloody Mary; add "courteous", "responsive" service and it's clear why most feel it's "worth the high price."

Hilton Palacio del Rio 469R (12S)
20 | 20 | 19 | 20 | $147

200 S. Alamo St., San Antonio; (210) 222-1400; (800) HILTONS; FAX: (210) 270-0796
■ Location is the lure of this "typical Hilton" on the Riverwalk, "the site of all activity" in the Alamo City; you can "walk to restaurants and shopping" or "just sit and watch the river (and people) go by", though most guests spend their time in the convention center across the street; rooms are "small" but "nice" and surveyors also praise the "good staff" and "best lobby bar"; a few detractors complain of "dark, dreary" atmosphere.

HYATT REGENCY HILL COUNTRY RESORT 442R (58S)
26 | 26 | 23 | 27 | $178

9800 Hyatt Resort Dr., San Antonio; (210) 647-1234; (800) 233-1234; FAX: (210) 681-9681
■ San Antonio's highest overall ratings go to this "wonderful getaway", a 200-acre "Texas-size and -style" resort boasting "very attractive rooms" with "upscale Western decor" in low-rise limestone buildings, plus "excellent" service and food; Sea World is nearby, but there's "no need to leave" the premises given two pools, an artificial river for tubing, a kids' club, health club and golf course; "perfect for families", it's also popular with celebs and a meeting planner's favorite with conference space for 1,700.

Hyatt Regency San Antonio 604R (27S)   20 | 20 | 19 | 21 | $153
123 Losoya St., San Antonio; (210) 222-1234; (800) 233-1234; FAX: (210) 227-4925
◪ Even Davy Crockett and Santa Ana would agree that this Alamo-area hotel couldn't have a more "perfect" location on the Riverwalk; just a few blocks from the convention center, it has "good facilities" (including a jazz bar, fitness center and rooftop pool), "fine staff" and a "lovely setting" – the San Antonio River actually flows through the lobby; the less impressed call it a "drab", "cookie-cutter Hyatt" with "standard rooms", but they're definitely a minority.

La Mansion del Rio 326R (11S)   22 | 22 | 21 | 22 | $167
112 College St., San Antonio; (210) 225-2581; (800) 292-7300; FAX: (210) 226-0389
◪ Deserving of "a San Antonio rose (two dozen at least)" say admirers of this "quaint", "charming" circa 1852 hotel "smack in the middle of the action"; there's much to recommend here, from the "old-world" ambiance of the Spanish Colonial design to the "great food"; rooms are "small" but "beautiful", and ones with balconies overlooking the Riverwalk are "great"; a few surveyors say service is "pleasant but inefficient" and the place "needs renovation."

Marriott Rivercenter 920R (82S)   21 | 21 | 19 | 21 | $149
101 Bowie St., San Antonio; (210) 223-1000; (800) 228-9290; FAX: (210) 223-6239
■ There's "something for everyone" at this "big, bustling", "well-located" 38-story high-rise on the famed Riverwalk and connected to the Rivercenter shopping complex; "fast" elevators take you up to "comfortable rooms" or to such facilities as the "very good" fitness center or meeting space for 5,400; an "accommodating staff" and proximity to top city sights make it "fabulous for personal travel or conventions."

Marriott San Antonio 495R (5S)   21 | 21 | 20 | 21 | $147
(fka Riverwalk Marriott)
711 E. Riverwalk, San Antonio; (210) 224-4555; (800) 228-9290; FAX: (210) 224-2754
◪ This "convention mainstay" on the Riverwalk is "close to all the action" and offers what admirers call "very nice, big rooms" and "gracious service", making it a worthy alternative to its larger and busier Rivercenter sibling; others find it a "typical Marriott" with "ordinary" lodgings and a "loud crowd", but they do "handle people well."

Menger Hotel 304R (15S)   19 | 21 | 19 | 21 | $121
204 Alamo Plaza, San Antonio; (210) 223-4361; (800) 345-9285; FAX: (210) 228-0022
◪ You can't help but remember the Alamo since it's next door to this "cool" 1859 hotel, where Teddy Roosevelt recruited Rough Riders and Bill Clinton ate mango ice cream; besides the drop-dead Downtown location, assets include a "beautiful" antiques-filled restored lobby, an impressive three-story rotunda and "accommodating" staff; unfortunately, rooms are "small" and, some say, not up to par – insiders advise "stay in the old section" with antiques and canopied beds.

Plaza San Antonio, A Marriott Hotel 242R (10S)   22 | 22 | 22 | 22 | $142
(fka Plaza San Antonio Hotel)
555 S. Alamo St., San Antonio; (210) 229-1000; (800) 421-1172; FAX: (210) 229-1418
◪ A six-acre garden near La Villita (the Old Town) surrounds this "comfortable, quiet" Spanish-style luxury hotel that's like "a resort without the facilities" (though there is tennis and a "lovely" outdoor pool); "excellent food" at the Anaqua Grill and "great service" appeal to all, but 13 meeting rooms (renovated in 1996 along with guest quarters) keep the place business-oriented; check out bikes to explore the nearby historic King William district; overall, "a better San Antonio choice."

South Padre Island

Radisson Resort South Padre Island 128R (60S)   18 | 18 | 17 | 19 | $137
500 Padre Blvd., South Padre Island; (210) 761-6511; (800) 333-3333; FAX: (210) 761-1602
■ Life's a beach at this Gulf Coast hotel "in the heart of everything"; the issue isn't ritzy rooms or fabulous food (although ratings indicate they're decent) but rather location – and you get plenty of it on 10 beachfront acres; you can fish, sail, surf, swim in two pools or enjoy a host of other activities, including tennis, or you can just soak up the sun; N.B. South Padre Island is a madhouse during spring break.

Utah

TOP 10 OVERALL

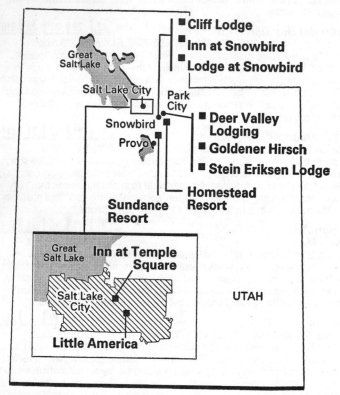

Great Salt Lake

Salt Lake City

Snowbird

Provo

Park City

■ Cliff Lodge
■ Inn at Snowbird
■ Lodge at Snowbird

■ Deer Valley Lodging
■ Goldener Hirsch
■ Stein Eriksen Lodge

Homestead Resort

Sundance Resort

Great Salt Lake

Inn at Temple Square

Salt Lake City

UTAH

Little America

BEST OVERALL
27 Stein Eriksen Lodge/Park City
Deer Valley Lodging/Park City
25 Goldener Hirsch/Park City
24 Sundance Resort/Provo
23 Homestead Resort/Midway
22 Cliff Lodge/Snowbird
21 Lodge at Snowbird/Snowbird
20 Inn at Snowbird/Snowbird
Inn at Temple Square/Salt Lake City
19 Little America/Salt Lake City

BEST VALUES
Bryce Canyon Lodge/Cedar City
Zion Lodge/Springdale
Peery/Salt Lake City
Little America/Salt Lake City
Inn at Temple Sq./Salt Lake City
Embassy Suites/Salt Lake City
Wyndham Hotel/Salt Lake City
Doubletree/Salt Lake City
Marriott/Salt Lake City
Hilton/Salt Lake City

Cedar City

R	S	D	P	$
18	17	15	20	$100

Bryce Canyon Lodge 110R (4S)
PO Box 400, Bryce Canyon National Park, Cedar City; (801) 834-5361; FAX: (801) 834-5464
■ Your tax dollars are at work at this "surprisingly comfortable" national park lodge 100 yards from the edge of spectacular Bryce Canyon, where 40 "rustic", "cozy and quaint cabins" and a "comfortable", "motel-like" main building look out to "incredible", "awesome scenery"; the only complaints are reserved for the food, but most agree "a log cabin with fireplace in a pine forest – what a deal!"; it's only open from mid-April through late-October.

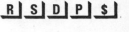
Midway

Homestead Resort 108R (9S)

| 21 | 23 | 23 | 25 | $148 |

PO Box 99, 700 N. Homestead Dr., Midway; (801) 654-1102; (800) 327-7220; FAX: (801) 654-5087
■ This 110-year-old "country home away from home" in "gorgeous surroundings" an hour east of Salt Lake offers year-round amenities in accommodations ranging from cottages and condos to a Victorian B&B; activities include sleigh rides, snowmobiling, skiing, horseback riding, tennis, mountain biking and an 18-hole golf course; although a very few find the rooms "so-so", "fantastic" food, in-room fireplaces, mineral baths and a "great pool and spa" provide plenty of pampering."

Ogden

Historic Radisson Suite Hotel 22R (122S)

▽ | 19 | 17 | 17 | 19 | $96 |

2510 Washington Blvd., Ogden; (801) 627-1900; (800) 333-3333; FAX: (801) 394-5342
■ "Great for Ogden", this 1927 grande dame with views of the Wasatch Mountains offers two TVs (with free Nintendo and HBO), a wet bar, refrigerator and large bathroom in every suite; complimentary breakfast buffet, covered parking, evening cocktails and numerous nearby attractions (fishing, golf, horseback riding, ice skating, swimming, tennis and waterskiing) add appeal.

Park City

DEER VALLEY LODGING (200S)

| 27 | 26 | 26 | 27 | VE |

PO Box 3000, 1375 Deer Valley Dr. S., Park City; (801) 649-4040; (800) 453-3833; FAX: (801) 645-8419
■ "Unbelievable in every category" swoon surveyors over this "skier's dream", a pricey but pristine mountain resort comprised of a stellar spread of luxury condos in an "idyllic location"; well-financed sybarites "go here to be pampered" with "unreal food", "exquisite accommodations", "superb service" ("valets for your skis") and abundant amenities: kitchenettes, fireplaces, washers and dryers, Jacuzzis, meeting rooms and an outdoor pool; it may be a little "too classy" for some, but "absolutely wonderful" is the consensus.

GOLDENER HIRSCH INN 8R (12S)

| 26 | 25 | 25 | 25 | $269 |

PO Box 859, 7570 Royal St. E., Park City; (801) 649-7770; (800) 252-3373; FAX: (801) 649-7901
■ "It's not Salzburg, but it comes close" say fanciers of this expensive but elegant doppelgänger of the Austrian original, set in the mountains outside Salt Lake near Sterling Chairlift; antiques, fireplaces and down comforters mark the "quaint, well-appointed rooms", with continental breakfast, indoor and outdoor hot tubs, a fireside lounge, sauna, heated underground parking and "an excellent hostess" all adding to the sense of well-being – "it's a joy to stay there."

1904 Imperial Hotel, A Bed and Breakfast Inn 8R (2S)

| – | – | – | – | E |

PO Box 1628, 221 Main St., Park City; (801) 649-1904; (800) 669-8824; FAX: (801) 645-7421
While not well known to our surveyors, this Park City landmark on historic Main Street is within minutes of three major ski areas and an hour from four more; features include complimentary breakfast, period decor and furnishings, and an indoor hot tub; the inn is nonsmoking and has no restaurant, but several are within walking distance nearby.

Olympia Park Hotel & Conference Center 199R (110S)

| 14 | 15 | 12 | 14 | $129 |

PO Box 4439, 1895 Sidewinder Dr., Park City; (801) 649-2900; (800) 234-9003; FAX: (801) 649-4852
■ Near, but not at, the slopes, this Prospector Square "ok place to stay" is "functional for winter trips", offering a main hotel and 100 privately owned condos for rent, with "good prices on packages" providing family ski appeal; but "thin walls" and "too many kids running wild" may make for "noisy" nights, and off-season travelers give it a thumbs down; 11 meeting rooms, computers, a fitness center and restaurants draw business groups looking for a full-service hotel.

Shadow Ridge Hotel (150S)

| 17 | 16 | 16 | 17 | $166 |

50 Shadow Ridge Dr., Park City; (801) 649-4300; (800) 451-3031; FAX: (801) 649-5951
☑ "Location, location, location" lures lodgers to this contemporary all-condo hotel "conveniently located" "slopeside", offering kitchenettes and fireplaces in some rooms, underground parking and an outdoor heated pool; but many gripe about "no amenities", "poor front desk service" and "unreliable maid service" – it's "all you need in a ski condo and no more "

STEIN ERIKSEN LODGE 81R (49S)
27 | 26 | 27 | 27 | $286

PO Box 3177, 7700 Stein Way, Park City; (801) 649-3700; (800) 453-1302; FAX: (801) 649-5825

■ It doesn't get much better than this "spectacular", ski-in/ski-out, "money-no-object" but "worth-the-expense" Norwegian-style ski lodge; almost everyone adores "a little Europe in Utah", with its "beautiful rooms" (many with fireplaces and all with Jacuzzis), "world-class restaurant" and "pampering" from an "excellent" staff; though a few find the "wealthy aura" "snooty", most sum it up as "fantastic" – "come for lunch and you'll never go back out."

Washington School Inn 12R (3S)
▽ 22 | 23 | 21 | 21 | $166

PO Box 536, 543 Park Ave., Park City; (801) 649-3800; (800) 824-1672; FAX: (801) 649-3802

■ "Beautifully renovate" a "very well-located" 1889 Victorian schoolhouse ("antiques in rooms"), staff it with "wonderful people" and serve "great, creative skier's breakfasts" and you have this "absolutely delightful" "B&B in the heart of Park City"; this "favorite of locals" even offers a "memorable downstairs spa."

Provo

SUNDANCE RESORT 35R (60S)
25 | 23 | 23 | 25 | $214

PO Box A-1, R.R. 3, Provo; (801) 225-4107; (800) 892-1600; FAX: (801) 226-1937

■ "See and ski" are the bywords for aficionados of Robert Redford's rustic-but-chic lodge, set on 5,000 "marvelous" acres of "mountains, forests and running rivers"; guests applaud "rooms with character" filled with Native American art and Western memorabilia, an "intelligent, energetic staff" and "innovative food" at the "superb" Tree Room; summer activities include horseback riding, hiking and cycling, and children's programs are offered; "limited room service" draws one of the few criticisms.

Salt Lake City

Doubletree Hotel Salt Lake 480R (16S)
17 | 17 | 15 | 16 | $112
(fka Red Lion Hotel Salt Lake)

255 S. West Temple St., Salt Lake City; (801) 328-2000; (800) 222-TREE; FAX: (801) 359-2938

☑ Despite tepid ratings, "unflaggingly pleasant" service and "large clean rooms" win smiles from some patrons of this "classic business hotel" near the convention center; recent renovations freshened public spaces and meeting rooms, and the fitness center keeps muscles toned with an indoor lap pool, Jacuzzi, exercise equipment and massages; while overall dining doesn't make a big impression, the Continental-American Maxi's is one of the city's top-rated restaurants.

Embassy Suites (241S)
21 | 18 | 15 | 17 | $115

110 W. 600 South, Salt Lake City; (801) 359-7800; (800) EMBASSY; FAX: (801) 359-3753

☑ "Convenience to skiing", "spacious rooms", discount lift tickets and complimentary cocktails and breakfast add up to a "great value" for snow bunnies at this all-suiter near Downtown that may be a "typical cookie-cutter Embassy", but still rates among "the best of a mediocre selection in town"; kitchenettes in every suite add appeal for families and those on extended business gigs.

Hilton Salt Lake 318R (33S)
16 | 17 | 15 | 15 | $117

150 W. 500 South, Salt Lake City; (801) 532-3344; (800) 421-7602; FAX: (801) 531-0705

☑ "Not remarkable but ok" typifies the lukewarm reaction to this "centrally located" Downtown Hilton that's "fair-priced for family ski vactions"; points go to the rooftop bar ("still the best in the city", especially for views of the Wasatch Mountains), a pool and sundeck, several restaurants and recently upgraded meeting spaces and fitness center; but critics deride "cold atmosphere" and "nondescript rooms", claiming it "just gets by."

INN AT TEMPLE SQUARE 85R (5S)
22 | 21 | 17 | 18 | $127

71 W. South Temple St., Salt Lake City; (801) 531-1000; (800) 843-4668; FAX: (801) 536-7272

■ "Gracious" and "elegant" but "sedate, even by SLC standards", with "entirely no-smoking, no-drinking" policies, this "quaint, comfortable" 1929 brick Downtowner offers discerning guests "cozy, welcoming rooms" with "spacious bathrooms"; surveyors concur "it's a great place", although a few Bacchus devotees sigh "a glass of wine would be nice"; a breakfast buffet is included.

Little America Hotel 850R
20 | 19 | 17 | 18 | $118

500 S. Main St., Salt Lake City; (801) 363-6781; (800) 453-9450; FAX: (801) 596-5911

☑ "Huge", "glitzy" rooms star at this "tacky but fun", family-appeal Downtown behemoth, a "trip back in time" (but only to the '70s) with indoor and outdoor pools, a "friendly staff", lobby shopping mall, extensive meeting facilities and "good value ski packages"; but some gripe that the building is "so big you get lost" and the "upscale brothel" decor complete with "fuzzy wallpaper" is getting "tattered"; tip: "stick with tower rooms, they're worth the price" (especially for the marble bathrooms with oval tubs).

Marriott Salt Lake City 509R (6S)   19 | 19 | 17 | 17 | $130
75 S. West Temple St., Salt Lake City; (801) 531-0800; (800) 345-ISKI; FAX: (801) 532-4127
☑ "The housekeeping is the best in the chain" and service is "good" say admirers of this Marriott convention mecca with a "great" Temple Square location "adjacent to the [Crossroads] mall", a complimentary airport shuttle, ski packages and a fitness area and pool with retractable roof; but "rooms are small" (although "suites are nice") and several note that while "adequate", it's "a typical Marriott" – "nothing to write home about."

Peery Hotel 71R (6S)   19 | 19 | 18 | 16 | $108
110 W. 300 South, Salt Lake City; (801) 521-4300; (800) 331-0073; FAX: (801) 575-5014
■ "Relaxed and old-fashioned", this Downtown landmark built in 1910 boasts a "responsive staff", "charming but tiny rooms" and continental breakfast on the house; location, meeting rooms, airport shuttle and reasonable rates make it a good deal for business travelers, with two rooms offering Jacuzzis for the super-stressed.

Wyndham Hotel 375R (6S)   19 | 18 | 16 | 17 | $114
(fka Doubletree Hotel)
215 W. South Temple St., Salt Lake City; (801) 531-7500; (800) 553-0075; FAX: (801) 328-1289
■ A "good location" Downtown is the most outstanding feature of this former Doubletree near Temple Square and the Delta Center; while "nothing exceptional", a few claim it's "wonderful compared to the alternatives", with pluses ranging from "excellent service", plenty of meeting space, a heated indoor pool and a revamped restaurant (post-*Survey*) to a "nice bar for a dry town"; N.B. a $4.5-million renovation of the guestrooms and lobby is scheduled for June 1997.

Snowbird

Cliff Lodge 484R (48S)   21 | 21 | 20 | 25 | $186
Snowbird Ski & Summer Resort, Little Cottonwood Canyon Rd., Snowbird; (801) 742-2222; (800) 453-3000; FAX: (801) 742-3204
■ "Be pampered in style" at this "simply great", ski-in/ski-out "beautiful mountain resort" on the slopes; surveyors gush over the "rooftop pool" under the stars, "spectacular scenery" of the Wasatch Mountains, "spartan but comfortable" and "spacious" rooms, "wonderful restaurants", "stupendous atrium"and "world-class health spa"; it even sports "great low-season prices" and children's programs are offered.

Inn At Snowbird 25R (12S)   20 | 20 | – | 22 | $171
Entry # 3, Snowbird; (801) 742-2222; (800) 453-3000; FAX: (801) 742-2211
☑ The advice from those in the know is "stay here cheaply" but "hang out at Cliff Lodge for drinks and the spa"; "convenience makes this a good, affordable option" and it's "comfortable", especially for families, but expect "no frills" and no restaurant – it's cook for yourself in the kitchenette-equipped condos or head to Snowbird Center; summer brings hiking, biking and great off-season rates.

Iron Blosam Lodge 123R (36S)   ▽ 19 | 21 | 18 | 23 | $192
PO Box 929000, Snowbird Resort, Snowbird; (801) 742-2222; (800) 453-3000; FAX: (801) 742-3445
■ In addition to its rooms and suites, this mountain aerie at 'The Bird' rents "great, spacious condos", many featuring full kitchens and fireplaces, and if you tire of cooking, bravos go to its "good" Wildflower Ristorante for Italian food; in summer, the lodge offers an abundance of recreation programs and lectures, but hereabouts winter's the thing and what could be better than the "world's best powder?"

Lodge At Snowbird 59R (61S)   20 | 21 | 20 | 22 | $175
Entry #3, Snowbird; (801) 742-2222; (800) 453-3000; FAX: (801) 742-3311
☑ "Awesome with or without snow" cheer all-season assessors who note "fabulous" bistro fare at the Lodge Club and rooms that are "noticeably larger" than others at Snowbird; all suites have kitchenettes and gas fireplaces, and a heated outdoor pool is a welcome amenity; a few critics are enthralled by the scenery only, calling the 1971 architecture "too modern and stark."

Springdale

Zion Lodge 75R (46S)   17 | 17 | 15 | 22 | $101
Zion National Park, Springdale; (303) 297-2757; FAX: (303) 338-2045
☑ Staying "at the floor of Zion Canyon is like being in a cathedral" and while this national park lodge hardly rivals its spectacular setting, many have ample praise for the "surprisingly comfortable", "nice and clean" "log cabinish" quarters and the "good" if "unremarkable" dining room – "for what it does, it's perfect"; N.B. cabin renovations are ongoing and planned through winter '97-'98.

Vermont

TOP 10 OVERALL

Lake Champlain

Newport

Inn at Essex

Inn on the Common

Burlington

Stowehof Inn

Inn at Shelburne Farms

VERMONT

Swift House Inn

Twin Farms

Rutland

Woodstock Inn

Old Tavern at Grafton

Equinox

Inn at Sawmill Farm

Bennington

Brattleboro

BEST OVERALL
29 Twin Farms/Barnard
26 Inn at Sawmill Farm/West Dover
Inn at Shelburne Farms/Shelburne
24 Stowehof Inn/Stowe
Woodstock Inn/Woodstock
23 Inn on the Common/Craftsbury Comm.
Equinox/Manchester
Inn at Essex/Essex
Old Tavern/Grafton
Swift House Inn/Middlebury

BEST VALUES
Inn at Essex/Essex
Green Mountain Inn/Stowe
Swift House Inn/Middlebury
Quechee Inn/Quechee
Middlebury Inn/Middlebury
Old Tavern/Grafton
Inn of the Six Mtns./Killington
Cortina Inn/Killington
Mountain Top Inn/Chittenden
Four Columns Inn/Newfane

Barnard

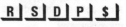

R	S	D	P	$

–	–	–	–	M

Maple Leaf Inn 7R
PO Box 273, Rte. 12, Barnard; (802) 234-5342; (800) 51-MAPLE
Sixteen acres of maple and birch trees surround this Victorian-style farmhouse nine miles north of Woodstock; embellished with gables, dormers, a gazebo and other turn-of-the-century touches, it offers seven spacious guestrooms (most with fireplace, some with whirlpool tub) and guests can also relax in the parlor or cozy library; rates include full breakfast, and the innkeepers can steer you to fine local restaurants (dinners served on-site by arrangement only); P.S. no smoking and no children.

TWIN FARMS (14S)

30 | 29 | 29 | 29 | $738

PO Box 115, Barnard; (802) 234-9999; (800) 894-6327; FAX: (802) 234-9990

■ "About as wonderful as you can get" say surveyors who give "highest praise" to the *Survey*'s top-rated B&B, a luxurious former vacation estate of Sinclair Lewis and Dorothy Thompson that's up the road a bit from Woodstock; 14 "sublime" suites and cottages decorated with antiques and fireplaces are set on 300 acres of mountain meadows and woods; "gourmet" meals, wines and an array of recreational amenities are included in the rates, making it all "worth every penny of its exorbitant price."

Brownsville

Ascutney Mountain Resort 100R (98S)

– | – | – | – | M

PO Box 699, Rte. 44, Brownsville; (802) 484-7711; (800) 243-0011; FAX: (802) 484-3117

It's "not high-end", but "the rooms are fresh" at this "family sort of place" that offers convenient kids' programs so parents can go off and play too; the resort's buildings include a village of restaurants, ski shops and a general store at the foot of Mount Ascutney; athletes crowd the extensive year-round sports facilities, but aesthetes seem to suffer from "college dorm" decor and "boring food."

Chittenden

Mountain Top Inn 29R (6S)

21 | 21 | 21 | 21 | $155

Mountain Top Rd., Chittenden; (802) 483-2311; (800) 445-2100; FAX: (802) 483-6373

☑ Perched at 2,000 feet in the Green Mountain National Forest, this "favorite vacation spot, both winter and summer" offers "country charm, modern amenities and excellent food" abetted by "good service"; "great x-country skiing and horse-drawn sleigh rides" are seasonally followed by mountain biking, fly-fishing and a "hike down" to the "beautiful lake" for boating and beach activities; while a few shrug that the inn "lacks a personality", most find it "warm, casual and classy."

Craftsbury Common

Inn On The Common 14R (2S)

23 | 24 | 24 | 21 | $175

N. Main St., Craftsbury Common; (802) 586-9619; (800) 521-2233; FAX: (802) 586-2249

■ A romantic getaway in a remote Northeast Kingdom village, this "simple, well-run inn" consisting of three Federal-style buildings wins friends with its "welcoming atmosphere in a lovely spot"; amenities range from the perennial gardens, swimming pool and clay tennis court to 60 miles of "excellent x-country skiing" in the colder months; although some say "the communal dining thing has to go", the Contemporary American food and award-winning wine list are "excellent."

Dorset

Dorset Inn 29R (2S)

20 | 23 | 23 | 20 | $165

Church & Main Sts., Dorset; (802) 867-5500; FAX: (802) 867-5542

■ Vermont's oldest continuously operating inn (200-plus years) carries on in a "charming setting" facing the village green of "one of the prettiest towns in New England"; "excellent" American dining – "as gourmet as any in NYC" – is important to its current popularity since the "quaint" rooms are "nice but not extraordinary"; there's a leading summer theater in town, sports facilities are nearby and five miles "down the road is Manchester – factory outlet heaven."

Essex

Inn At Essex 85R (12S)

24 | 24 | 25 | 20 | $138

70 Essex Way, Essex; (802) 878-1100; (800) 727-4295; FAX: (802) 878-0063

■ "A perfect colonial inn with charming rooms" near Burlington is also "worth a visit for dinner at Butler's", its "wonderful" New American restaurant (with bakery) run by the New England Culinary Institute; the "large and very clean" quarters, many with fireplace and two with Jacuzzi, prove pleasing, while minutes away Ben & Jerry's Ice Cream Factory and the Essex Outlet Fair offer other gratifications.

Goshen

Blueberry Hill Inn 12R

▽ 23 | 25 | 28 | 23 | $152

Green Mountain National Forest Rd. 32, Goshen; (802) 247-6735; (800) 448-0707; FAX: (802) 247-3983

■ "Charming and tasteful", this "first-rate inn" occupies a restored 1813 farmhouse in the Green Mountain National Forest; it's a "small gem" providing "exquisite rooms with antiques" (but no radio, TV or phone), "superb" four-course meals in the communal dining room, "great hors d'oeuvres" for cocktail hour (no liquor license, so bring your private stock) and "oh those hot cookies!"; guests work it all off hiking the adjacent Long Trail, casting for trout or enjoying "excellent x-country skiing" in winter.

Grafton

Old Tavern At Grafton 35R (31S)
22 | 23 | 23 | 23 | $162

Main St., Grafton; (802) 843-2231; (800) 843-1801; FAX: (802) 843-2245

☑ An 1801 stagecoach stop that's hosted the likes of Emerson, Thoreau and U.S. Grant (and still maintains a stable for guests' horses), this restored inn is a "friendly, well-priced" "true step back in time" set in a "quintessential New England village"; most enjoy its "good food" and "tastefully decorated rooms", although a few critics murmur "much charm but not much comfort", "aloof attitude", "for the blue-hair crowd"; but for sure, "if you want to relax in a rocker or hike in the woods, this is the place."

Highgate Springs

Tyler Place on Lake Champlain 50R
- | - | - | - | VE

PO Box 1, Old Dock Rd., Highgate Springs; (802) 868-4000; FAX: (802) 868-7602

"The best family vacation imaginable" cheer parents who cite the "good food" and "wonderful service" at this "favorite Eastern inn" where the staff is "fabulous with kids"; in addition to infant-to-teen programs (including newborn care), it boasts 165 acres of woods and meadows bordering Lake Champlain, heated indoor and outdoor swimming pools and a myriad of other sports facilities; rooms are "standard" but adequate.

Killington

Cortina Inn 90R (7S)
20 | 20 | 19 | 20 | $143

Rte. 4, Killington; (802) 773-3333; (800) 451-6108; FAX: (802) 775-6948

■ "A haven among the area's strip hotels" chirp snow buffs and corporate retreaters alike about this "large, handsome" central Vermont inn "close to the slopes"; many appreciate the "comfortable public areas" ("read the Sunday papers in front of the fire") and "good" American food (packages include a buffet country breakfast), although a few lament that the rooms are "just ok"; on-site distractions include spa and sports facilities, and there's a shuttle to the Killington and Pico ski trails.

Inn of the Six Mountains 99R (4S)
21 | 19 | 18 | 20 | $140

PO Box 2900, R.R. 1, Killington; (802) 422-4302; (800) 228-4676; FAX: (802) 422-4321

☑ "Location" – just one mile from Killington's base lodge – is a key virtue of this "casual, laid-back" modern inn with "lovely mountain views"; while those who appreciate the "downhill skiing ambiance" rate it "one of the nicest in Killington", others cite "tired rooms" and decide it's "an ok place to sleep, but nothing special."

Killington Resort 440R (110S)
20 | 18 | 18 | 21 | $156

Killington Rd., Killington; (802) 422-3333; FAX: (802) 422-4391

■ "Skiing to the slopes" may be the main attraction, but "it's wonderful to be right on the mountain summer or winter" and warm-weather rates are a "bargain"; this large, "pleasant" resort village has numerous restaurants and a "variety of accommodations" in condos, inns and more; although a few lodgings "need refurbishing", they're "clean" and "comfortable" (some with fireplaces and/or kitchenettes), and children's programs are available; N.B. a new Grand Hotel is scheduled to open in '97, adding some 200 units.

Trio of Inns 85R
- | - | - | - | M

PO Box 144, Killington Mtn. Rd., Killington; (802) 422-3451; (800) 451-4105; FAX: (802) 422-3971

The name says it all: the Killington Village Inn, Chalet Killington and Red Rob Inn comprise this reasonably priced trio convenient to the famous ski area; each has its own fireplace-equipped lounge, hot tub and dining options, and all offer shuttles to the nearby lifts; rates include breakfast and meal plans sweeten the deal; only the Red Rob Inn is open year-round.

Woods at Killington Resort & Spa (50S)
▽ 25 | 21 | 19 | 23 | $285

PO Box 2325, R.R. 1, Killington Rd., Killington; (802) 422-3244; (800) 438-1952; FAX: (802) 422-3320

■ "Scenic and close to the action", this "pleasant, convenient" resort's modern condo accommodations (all with fireplaces, kitchenettes and Jacuzzis) may well be "the nicest on the mountain"; "good facilities" include a Euro-style spa ("try a mud wrap"), "clean, beautiful grounds", outdoor tennis courts and an indoor pool and gym; all of which has boosters rating it a "perfect ski lodge getaway."

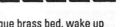
Lower Waterford

Rabbit Hill Inn 16R (5S)
▽ 25 | 26 | 25 | 24 | $204

Rte. 18 & Pucker St., Lower Waterford; (802) 748-5168; (800) 76-BUNNY;
FAX: (802) 748-8342

■ An "otherworldly experience" beckons at this 200-year-old "warm, wonderful" Federal-style inn set in a historic Northeast Kingdom village; a "very romantic" ambiance for honeymooners and other couples follows from candlelit dining on "wonderful" Contemporary American food, a library of films, books and games, turndown service, fantasy suites with Jacuzzis, and fireplaces in many rooms (though traditionalists insist "gas fireplaces don't cut it"); fresh-air distractions range from x-country skiing to swimming in the natural pond or wandering the unspoiled terrain.

Ludlow

Governor's Inn 8R (1S)
– | – | – | – | E

86 Main St., Ludlow; (802) 228-8830; (800) GOVERNOR

Sip afternoon tea by the fire, dive under a comforter in an antique brass bed, wake up to apple pancakes and coffee: such are the pleasures of a stay at this charming 1890 Victorian on Ludlow's village green; for sportier pursuits, Okemo Mountain and skiing are less than a mile away and the region boasts five lakes and year-round recreational activities; noted for its New England cuisine, the inn also offers gourmet six-course dinners and special cooking seminars.

Manchester

Equinox 147R (36S)
23 | 23 | 23 | 25 | $214

PO Box 36, Historic Rte. 7A, Manchester Village; (802) 362-4700; (800) 362-4747;
FAX: (802) 362-4861

■ "Classic New England charm and elegance" emanate from this "great old-style" resort in old Manchester Village; set in four "tastefully redone" historic buildings plus several newer townhouses, it's "large but homey" with "kind service", "very good food", "attractive public spaces" and "great amenities" on-site, including a "nice spa", "decent golf" and even a falconry school (first of its kind in the US); if a few snipe "stuffy", "a city slicker's idea of a Vermont country inn", far more rate it "superior" all-around.

Inn at Manchester 14R (4S)
▽ 21 | 23 | 21 | 21 | $202

PO Box 41, Historic Rte. 7A, Manchester Village; (802) 362-1793; (800) 273-1793;
FAX: (802) 362-3218

■ "Pretty, antiques-filled" rooms distinguish this inn (a National Historic Register entry), and while some find the quarters "small", that's in keeping with the 19th-century ambiance of the Queen Anne–style house; a full breakfast is included (don't miss co-owner "Harriet's cottage-cheese pancakes"), and for those who overindulge, privileges are available at two local spas; also nearby: downhill and x-country ski areas, lots of outlet shopping and Robert Todd Lincoln's Hildene homestead.

Inn at Willow Pond (40S)
▽ 22 | 20 | 22 | 21 | $141

PO Box 1429, Historic Rte. 7A N., Manchester; (802) 362-4733; (800) 533-3533;
FAX: (802) 362-4737

■ "Amazing suites" with "marble bathrooms" at "modest prices" are "welcome" finds at this modern complex (some see the exterior as a bit "motelish") on a former dairy farm just above Manchester Center; the restored farmhouse, with a 220-year-old, three-sided, walk-in fireplace, is now home to a "superb" Northern Italian restaurant; for those with a yen to shop, the local trove of designer outlets is just two miles away.

Reluctant Panther Inn 12R (4S)
– | – | – | – | E

1 West Rd., Manchester Village; (802) 362-2568; (800) 822-2331; FAX: (802) 362-2586

This 1850s inn is a more intimate alternative to the nearby grand dowager Equinox (and guests have access, for a fee, to its fitness facilities, spa and 18-hole PGA golf course); each attractively decorated guestroom has private bath and a/c, and the suites feature whirlpools, fireplaces and four-poster beds; nearby attractions include the Flyfishing Museum and outlet shopping in Manchester Center; full breakfast and à la carte dinner are included in rates.

Village Country Inn 18R (15S)
– | – | – | – | M

PO Box 408, Historic Rte. 7A, Manchester Village; (802) 362-1792; (800) 370-0300; FAX: (802) 362-7238

Set in the center of town, this romantic, historic 1921 inn with country French decor welcomes guests with rockers on its broad front porch, gracious and accommodating hosts, period furnishings in individually decorated rooms (some offering king-size beds, sitting rooms and fireplaces), lovely gardens in summer (along with a pool) and hot cider by the fire in winter; breakfast and gourmet French dinner are included in rates.

Wilburton Inn 20R (9S)
21 | 21 | 23 | 22 | $154

River Rd., Manchester Village; (802) 362-2500; (800) 648-4944; FAX: (802) 362-1107

■ A "great view" of the Battenkill Valley entrances breakfasting guests at this "wonderful turn-of-the-century" Tudor-style estate, the scene of many a "magical wedding"; it's called "the height of country elegance" by those who appreciate its "relaxing" rooms, "nicest staff", "grand country gourmet dinners" and overall "drop-dead charm"; tennis, swimming and biking are among the on-site activities and, yes, there's skiing nearby.

Middlebury

Middlebury Inn 68R (7S)
18 | 20 | 19 | 19 | $134

14 Courthouse Sq., Middlebury; (802) 388-4961; (800) 842-4666; FAX: (802) 388-4563

◪ Since 1827 this "quaint and friendly inn" has welcomed visitors to the "quintessential college town" of Middlebury; today "bare-bones rooms" that "often creak" may be too puritan for sybarites, and some say management is "coasting"; but fans insist that the "lovely colonial building and great dining room make up for" any shortcomings, adding that the "unpretentious" ambiance is just "what we anticipated New England would be."

Swift House Inn 21R
25 | 22 | 23 | 21 | $154

25 Stewart Ln., Middlebury; (802) 388-9925; FAX: (802) 388-9927

■ Respondents come upon a "treasure chest of country pleasures" at this "charming" inn composed of three buildings – an 1814 main house, an 1886 carriage house (renovated into "true luxury" quarters) and a turn-of-the-century turreted gatehouse; the "lovely grounds" and "warm people and atmosphere" make it an "oasis" that inspires return visits ("been seven times, all excellent"); "gourmet dinners" are a plus, although some say "the dining room could use more experienced help."

Waybury Inn 14R
– | – | – | – | I

PO Box 27, Rte. 125, E. Middlebury; (802) 388-4015; (800) 348-1810; FAX: (802) 388-1248

Off-the-beaten-path but right on the mark for relaxation, this 1810 colonial inn (which starred as the Stratford Inn on Bob Newhart's old TV show) soothes guests with its low-key pace: gazing at the gardens from the outdoor deck and napping in an old four-poster are typical activities, though there's also sledding, skating and skiing (x-country and downhill) nearby and culture vultures swoop in for auctions, theater, concerts and art exhibits; rates include breakfast.

Newfane

Four Columns Inn 10R (5S)
22 | 22 | 24 | 19 | $165

PO Box 278, West St., Newfane; (802) 365-7713; (800) 787-6633; FAX: (802) 365-0022

■ In a "wonderful little town" in southeastern Vermont, this "lovely and comfortable" inn adorned with Greek Revival columns has recently completed renovations to spruce up common areas and guest quarters; begin the evening with cocktails at the pewter-topped bar in the tavern before enjoying "creative" New American entrees in the "superb dining room"; a few bemoan "small rooms" and call the inn "uninspired in spite of an outstanding location", but as ratings attest they're widely outvoted.

Perkinsville

Inn at Weathersfield 9R (3S)
– | – | – | – | E

PO Box 165, Rte. 106, Weathersfield; (802) 263-9217; (800) 477-4828; FAX: (802) 263-9219

Set on 21 acres near the Connecticut River, this 200-year-old inn offers canopy beds, fireplaces and Victorian claw-foot tubs in most quarters; guests take tea in an antiques-laden parlor and dine to tunes from a Steinway grand; a tournament pool table, full exercise room and Finnish sauna augment the seasonal outdoor activities; rates include a full breakfast, afternoon tea and dinner in an award-winning dining room.

Plymouth

Hawk Inn and Mountain Resort 45R (42S)   ▽ 25 | 22 | 21 | 23 | $211
PO Box 64, HCR 70, Rte. 100, Plymouth; (802) 672-3811; (800) 685-HAWK; FAX: (802) 672-5067
■ Fervent fans "would love to be snowed in here" – a "cozy, beautifully decorated" colonial-style complex with a "friendly staff and "above-average food" (full breakfast included); 1,200 piney acres provide opportunities for virtually every summer and winter recreation; visitors also shuttle to skiing at nearby Okemo or Killington and afterward indulge in a sauna, swim or whirlpool in the spa; but despite the amenities, die-hard urbanites harp it's in "the middle of nowhere."

Quechee

Quechee Inn at Marshland Farm 22R (2S)   22 | 22 | 24 | 21 | $155
Clubhouse Rd., Quechee; (802) 295-3133; (800) 235-3133; FAX: (802) 295-6587
■ "A prime destination", this 1793 colonial farmhouse satisfies seekers of an inn that's "very country and cozy and low-key" with a "charming location" – in this case facing Dewey's Mill Pond, a wildfowl sanctuary; the "lovely but small" accommodations are "fine for the money" and can include breakfast, tea and dinner; there are golf and tennis privileges at the nearby private Quechee Club, and anglers advise "bring your fly rod."

Shelburne

INN AT SHELBURNE FARMS 24R   25 | 26 | 26 | 26 | $210
40 Shelburne Farms, Shelburne; (802) 985-8498; FAX: (802) 985-8498
■ "Perfection" purr respondents: a "remote and extraordinary setting" on Lake Champlain is home to this 1,400-acre working farm with a Queen Anne mansion built in the 1880s by a Vanderbilt that's now an inn offering "outstanding rooms and service" mid-May to mid-October; the "gracious palatial" landmark dazzles visitors with "original furnishings" and decor, while guided tours and a children's farmyard make things "chummy"; overall it's "spectacular and friendly, a rare combination."

Smugglers' Notch

Smugglers' Notch Resort (375S)   23 | 21 | 19 | 24 | $180
Rte. 108, Smugglers' Notch; (802) 644-8851; (800) 451-8752; FAX: (802) 644-2713
■ This "perfect family resort" nestled on an old smugglers' route to Canada provides "great value"; along with "plenty of activities for everyone", including programs for toddlers to teens, there's an "excellent restaurant", two outdoor hot tubs, a sauna and steam baths to add to the pampering; an occasional spoiler says the condos are "getting a little musty" and "room quality varies radically", but even so it's "a wonderful place for kids and friends to hang out."

Stowe

Green Mountain Inn 51R (14S)   20 | 21 | 21 | 20 | $135
PO Box 60, 1 Main St., Stowe; (802) 253-7301; (800) 253-7302; FAX: (802) 253-5096
◪ All aboard this "fun" inn stationed in a 19th-century train depot and an adjacent residence; the "great old place" with its "middle-of-town location" is "part of what makes Stowe the best in Vermont"; some of the "charming, quiet rooms" have fireplaces, Jacuzzis and kitchenettes, and guests enjoy use of the Stowe Athletic Club; a minority snipes that "rooms are run-down and musty", but boosters suggest they mellow out with a glass of cider and homemade cookies in the living room.

STOWEHOF INN & RESORT 50R   24 | 24 | 24 | 24 | $174
434 Edson Hill Rd., Stowe; (802) 253-9722; (800) 932-7136; FAX: (802) 253-7513
■ "Friendly and quaint", this "personal favorite" Swiss-Austrian–style chalet boasts "great panoramic views" from its crow's nest location atop a high hill as well as "pretty rooms" with antique accents, hand-hewn beams and wide pine flooring; four-season sportives enthuse about "great vacations, summer and winter" and enjoy fine dining fireside or lingering over pub fare in the Tyrolean Tap Room.

Stowe Motel & Snowdrift 49R (5S)   – | – | – | – | M
2043 Mountain Rd., Stowe; (802) 253-7629; (800) 829-7629; FAX: (802) 253-9971
This motel duo on 16 landscaped acres with views of Mt. Mansfield is "a nice place to relax" according to respondents who cite an "accommodating staff" and "good food and service"; quarters include rooms, two- or four-bedroom apartments and two- or four-bedroom houses; ultrapurists decide the compound is "too formal for a country inn", even if it has kind-to-a-student-budget prices.

Topnotch at Stowe Resort & Spa 83R (22S)   22   23   22   24 $205
PO Box 1458, 4000 Mountain Rd., Stowe; (802) 253-8585; (800) 451-8686; FAX: (802) 253-9263

■ "Topnotch is just that – food, inn and people" say fans who carry on about the "exceptional service", "terrific facilities and dining"; vigorous visitors enjoy "great tennis instruction", mountain biking and nearby skiing, as well as the "wonderful spa" offering fitness assessments and facials; while the budget-minded find it "a bit expensive", others advise "if you're looking for peace and quiet, this is the place."

Trapp Family Lodge 88R (105S)   21   22   22   23 $175
42 Trapp Hill Rd., Stowe; (802) 253-8511; (800) 826-7000; FAX: (802) 253-5740

■ "Right out of *The Sound of Music*" warble devotees of the Trapp family's famous bit of Austria in northern Vermont; the "nice, spacious rooms", "superb food" and "gorgeous setting" are a few of our respondents' favorite things; those naming it "Vermont's best x-country ski resort" say the 60k of trails "beat anything in the US and Europe", and summer folk enjoy "lovely mountain trails for hiking"; only a few critics claim it's "overdone, just like the movie" and "you have to like cute."

Stratton Mountain

Stratton Mountain Inn & Village Lodge   16   15   15   18 $156
207R (104S)
Middle Ridge Rd., Stratton Mountain; (802) 297-2500; (800) 777-1700; FAX: (802) 297-1778

☑ "No frills, but great skiing and golf school" sums up the reactions of surveyors who advise "stay at the mountain lodge" for ski-in/ski-out convenience; even though "the inn has dining", guests in lodge rooms get a microwave, coffeemaker, refrigerator and wet bar (plus charging privileges at the inn); while some find it "a good buy", about as many complain that it's "overpriced for what you get" – a "glorified motel" with "so-so service"; but "if you're looking for location, this is ok."

Vergennes

Basin Harbor Club 44R (77S)   21   22   21   23 $228
Basin Harbor Rd., Vergennes; (802) 475-2311; (800) 622-4000; FAX: (802) 475-6545

■ "Spectacular in every respect", this 700-acre "civilized old-fashioned resort" on Lake Champlain has been run by the Beach family since 1886; the "incredible food" and "fantastic location" earn points, and parents pipe up about "the classiest-run children's programs"; the 600-square-mile lake provides plenty of room for boating, fishing, waterskiing and swimming, and on-shore activities include golf and tennis; though a few call it "fussy" and think "it must have seen better days", a faithful clientele finds this getaway (open mid-May to mid-October) "overwhelmingly peaceful."

Warren

Sugarbush Resort 46R (250S)   20   19   21   22 $174
PO Box 350, Rte. 1, Warren; (802) 583-2381; (800) 53-SUGAR; FAX: (802) 583-6303

☑ An alpine-style "great ski destination", where the "very friendly" staff and "wonderful location" help make life sweet; however, a few critics are sour that "rooms are ill-stocked and uncomfortable" ("needs better lighting – used a flashlight to read my book") as well as "pricey" in high season; but dining scores well, health club membership is part of all packages and there are "nice tennis facilities across the street" too.

West Dover

INN AT SAWMILL FARM 10R (10S)   26   25   27   24 $273
PO Box 367, Crosstown Rd. & Rte. 100, West Dover; (802) 464-8131; (800) 464-8131; FAX: (802) 464-1130

■ One of the state's top-rated hostelries, this "sophisticated and elegant inn" fashioned from a 1797 barn may be "expensive", but some call it "the best Relais & Châteaux value"; the "finest foods and wines in Vermont" (a 36,000-bottle cellar) have epicureans whetting their appetites at the on-site swimming pool, tennis court and trout ponds or via nearby skiing and golf; two caveats: there are "no locks on the doors – my wife freaked" (no keys, just in-room latches for when guests retire), and gentlemen are requested to wear a jacket in all public areas after 6 PM.

Hermitage Inn 15R   ▽ 21 | 23 | 25 | 22 | $176
PO Box 457, Coldbrook Rd., Wilmington; (802) 464-3511; FAX: (802) 464-2688
■ A "perfect Vermont grand house" with a "huge wine cellar" and "top fo' 1"; the on-estate fowl farm puts "fabulous game" on the table each night, and hunters go after their own during the fall pheasant release or practice on a 15-field clays course (gun rental available); Delacroix prints and antique decoys share lodgings in the main house, once home to the editor of the Social Register; doubters find the place "a bit seedy, but very traditional", though the consensus is "delightful."

Woodstock

Kedron Valley Inn 25R (2S)   20 | 21 | 21 | 20 | $169
Rte. 106, S. Woodstock; (802) 457-1473; (800) 836-1193; FAX: (802) 457-4469
■ It's "a pleasure to stay at" this 19th-century Federal-style "charmer" that's convenient to "good horseback riding" and major ski areas; on-site are a "good, upscale restaurant" and swimming pond, and the "great hosts" have furnished the rooms with heirloom quilts, queen canopy beds and fireplaces or Franklin stoves (but some peak season visitors say "beware rooms facing the road"); animal lovers report that the inn "accepts and likes pets, a definite plus"; N.B. check out the midweek and nonpeak discounts.

WOODSTOCK INN & RESORT 139R (7S)   23 | 24 | 23 | 25 | $195
14 The Green, Woodstock; (802) 457-1100; (800) 448-7900; FAX: (802) 457-6699
■ "Classy, chic", the "best around" say admirers of this Rockefeller-owned "treasure", a complete resort built up from a modest 1793 tavern in one of New England's prettiest towns ("the village alone is worth the trip"); "everything was good, service was excellent" and "this place has it all", including a Robert Trent Jones, Sr. 18-hole golf course and fully equipped sports center plus x-country and downhill skiing for all ages and skill levels; "big hotel amenities with small inn charm" and "great off-season rates" make this "a winner."

325

Virginia

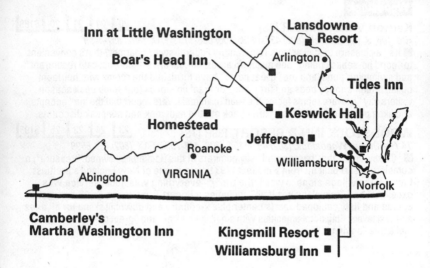

BEST OVERALL
- **27** Inn at Little Washington/Washington
  Keswick Hall/Keswick
- **25** Williamsburg Inn/Williamsburg
  Jefferson/Richmond
  Homestead/Hot Springs
- **24** Tides Inn/Irvington
- **23** Kingsmill Resort/Williamsburg
  Lansdowne Resort/Leesburg
- **22** Camberley's/Abingdon
  Boar's Head Inn/Charlottesville

BEST VALUES
Camberley's/Abingdon
Jefferson/Richmond
Marriott/Williamsburg
Marriott/Richmond
Williamsburg Hse./Williamsburg
Hilton/Virginia Beach
Hyatt/Richmond
Lansdowne Resort/Leesburg
Boar's Head Inn/Charlottesville
Omni/Richmond

Abingdon | R | S | D | P | $ |

Camberley's Martha Washington Inn 51R (10S) | 23 | 22 | 21 | 22 | $131 |
(fka Martha Washington Inn)
150 W. Main St., Abingdon; (540) 628-3161; (800) 555-8000; FAX: (540) 628-8885

■ A storybook wedding site, this "lovely old" antebellum mansion (once a women's college) is like a living museum offering "Southern hospitality", "good food" and "pretty" rooms in the historic district of a SW Virginia town; stoke up with a "great breakfast" (included) before heading off to one of many nearby activities, from biking, golf and fishing to a performance across the street at the Barter Theatre.

Charlottesville

Boar's Head Inn 162R (11S)
21 | 22 | 22 | 22 | $160

PO Box 5307, Charlottesville; (804) 296-2181; (800) 476-1988; FAX: (804) 972-6024

■ In a "beautiful", "gentleman farmer" setting outside Charlottesville, this "UVA-convenient" resort takes some knocks for its "slightly frayed" looks (perhaps a '96 redo helped), "corporate" orientation and somewhat "stuffy" vibes, but even so it's considered a "fine old-line VA" experience with colonial decor and "good service"; among its best features are the small- to mid-size conference facilities, sports options (including golf and 20 tennis courts) and "spectacular" Sunday brunch.

Hot Springs

HOMESTEAD, THE 430R (87S)
23 | 25 | 24 | 27 | $236

PO Box 2000, Rte. 220, Hot Springs; (540) 839-1766; (800) 838-1766; FAX: (540) 839-7670

■ Few places match this "lovely old" mountain resort for the "history, charm and elegance" of its imposing 1766 Georgian building and the many "fine activities and scenery" offered on its 15,000 acres; "if you get the right room, it's perfect", but they're said to "vary widely" (an ongoing major renovation may help); assets include "great breakfasts" (included), "wonderful" service and lots to do, from lectures and dancing to golf, bowling and horseback riding, but still some find it "sleepy."

Irvington

TIDES INN 108R (3S)
22 | 26 | 22 | 25 | $210

PO Box 480, King Carter Dr., Irvington; (804) 438-5000; (800) 843-3746; FAX: (804) 438-5222

■ At this "classic, old-fashioned family resort" on the Chesapeake Bay "everyone works hard to ensure your good time"; while rooms are "comfortable" and the traditional food is "good", it's the vanishing brand of "Southern relaxed hospitality", along with "challenging" golf and other sports, that are the keys to its appeal; "wonderful" moonlight Rappahannock River cruises on its yacht, Miss Ann, are not to be missed.

Tides Lodge Resort & Courtry Club 58R (14S) ▽ 23 | 24 | 19 | 24 | $188

PO Box 309, 1 St. Andrews Ln., Irvington; (804) 438-6000; (800) 248-4337; FAX: (804) 438-6000

■ Kin of the Tides Inn, this low-key resort is geared to families and sports enthusiasts, offering top-notch golf, tennis, swimming, a marina and a host of other activities; admirers call it a "class act" with "nice" country-modern accommodations and a "relaxed" atmosphere (though there are dress codes for the dining rooms); the veteran staff earns high marks, but food quality apparently ebbs and flows ("great brunch" vs. "so-so").

Keswick

KESWICK HALL 44R (4S)
28 | 27 | 24 | 27 | $252

701 Club Dr., Keswick; (804) 979-3440; (800) ASHLEY-1; FAX: (804) 977-4171

■ Drive up to your "own country mansion" at this "fabulously appointed", Sir Bernard Ashley–owned estate built in 1912 near Charlottesville; rooms ("uniquely decorated" with antiques and, of course, Laura Ashley fabrics) "couldn't be more beautiful", service is "exceptional" and everything, from afternoon tea in the lounge to the spa, Arnold Palmer golf course and other fitness facilities, is designed for a thoroughly "relaxing" time; so who cares if some say a few rooms and meals "aren't quite up to the fantasy"?

Leesburg

Lansdowne Resort 291R (14S)
23 | 22 | 23 | 25 | $169

44050 Woodridge Pkwy., Leesburg; (703) 729-8400; (800) 541-4801; FAX: (703) 729-4096

■ In the spreading sprawl between Dulles airport (eight miles away) and Leesburg, this manicured complex is a "place to have meetings and conferences" with "no distractions whatsoever" (except maybe for "terrific golf"); it also "works for a family" getaway thanks to "bike paths, a great gym and lap pool" and multiple dining options; however, some find it "sterile" and lacking in identity: "is it a conference center, a resort or a hotel?"

Paris

Ashby Inn & Restaurant 10R
▽ 23 | 25 | 26 | 25 | $173

692 Federal St., Paris; (540) 592-3900; FAX: (540) 592-3781

■ "Outstanding" New American dinners are the highlight of a "relaxing" stay at this "elegant" yet rustic small inn near Middleburg, where you spend the night in either the main building (a converted 1829 residence) or a former schoolhouse nearby; the "interesting, well-prepared" food and pastoral setting make it popular for weddings, while the taproom is a hitching post for the local horsey set; rates include a full breakfast.

Berkeley Hotel 54R (1S)

-　-　-　-　M

1200 E. Cary St., Richmond; (804) 780-1300; FAX: (804) 343-1885
Despite a great location in Shockoe Slip, this hotel built in 1988 hasn't caught the attention of many surveyors; it provides attentive service (including valet parking and a shuttle to Downtown), executive-class amenities and New American dining; those looking for Old Richmond–style cooking can choose from numerous nearby restaurants, not to mention one of the country's oldest farmers' markets.

Commonwealth Park Suites Hotel 10R (49S)

▽ 22　22　19　18　$164

901 Bank St., Richmond; (804) 343-7300; (888) 343-7301; FAX: (804) 343-1025
☑ Old-fashioned "elegance" matched by "white glove service" in a prime location near the capitol and Shockoe Slip (the historic commercial and entertainment district) are reasons why some consider this traditionalist a "great bargain"; accommodations are mostly handsome suites, and though it's unquestionably convenient for business (albeit with sparse meeting facilities), a few find it "fatigued" and prefer dining elsewhere.

Hyatt Richmond 361R (11S)

18　19　19　18　$127

6624 W. Broad St., Richmond; (804) 285-1234; (800) 233-1234; FAX: (804) 288-3961
☑ Renovations (in '95) spiffed up this standard Hyatt in a "nice setting" in the West End suburbs; its ability to host reasonably large meetings earns the loyalty of business travelers and conventioneers, even if overall some judge it "adequate but nothing special" and sometimes "low on service"; diversions include swimming, tennis, "good food" and entertainment and dancing in the lounge.

JEFFERSON HOTEL 248R (27S)

24　25　25　26　$151

Franklin & Adams Sts., Richmond; (804) 788-8000; (800) 424-8014; FAX: (804) 344-5162
■ Its "*Gone with the Wind* opulence and genteel quality" make this "beautifully run" 1895 Edwardian a must-see and a must-stay for those seeking an "experience in Old Virginia living"; aside from a few "shoe-box-size sleeping rooms" and the "inconvenient to Downtown" locale, it's "everything a hotel should be", with rich furnishings, "royal" service, "outstanding" Southern dining and "spectacular public spaces" including the Rotunda and Palm Court.

Linden Row Inn 64R (7S)

-　-　-　-　I

100 E. Franklin St., Richmond; (804) 783-7000; (800) 348-7424; FAX: (804) 648-7504
A series of neighboring Greek Revival townhouses built in 1847 make up this Downtown Richmond inn with an 'enchanted garden' courtyard that reputedly inspired Edgar Allan Poe; many of the houses' original features, such as fireplaces, mantels and chandeliers, remain intact and rooms are decorated in authentic and reproduction Victorian and Empire pieces; updated amenities for business travelers include in-room modem jacks and free transport to the business center.

Marriott Richmond 390R (10S)

19　18　17　18　$118

500 E. Broad St., Richmond; (804) 643-3400; (800) 228-9290; FAX: (804) 649-3725
☑ Through its skywalk link to the convention center flows the commercial lifeblood of this "large, conference-oriented" hotel; as one might expect, there is extensive meeting space (24 rooms holding from 15 to 2,000), a fully equipped health club, varied dining and "standard but attractive" rooms; revelry in the open bar and lobby space can be "loud", and some say that on "weekends or holidays it seems like all the staff is gone."

Omni Richmond Hotel 347R (6S)

21　20　19　19　$145

100 S. 12th St., Richmond; (804) 344-7000; (800) 843-6664; FAX: (804) 648-6704
■ "Great picture windows" overlooking the James River or Shockoe Slip let you plan a Downtown walking tour from your bedroom at this well-located base: primarily a "pleasant business hotel", it can "handle a convention professionally", provide "perfectly fine" lodgings (especially in "beautiful club floor rooms") and offers access to a nearby health club/spa for a fee; a few find service and parking "questionable."

Radisson Hotel 285R (14S)

▽ 17　17　17　17　$109

555 E. Canal St., Richmond; (804) 788-0900; (800) 333-3333; FAX: (804) 788-0791
☑ Mixed reviews go to this modern midpriced Downtowner near the James River (but "not in the historic area"), with some calling it "surprisingly pleasant" and "clean and bright", and others shrugging "so-so", "nothing special"; approached with scaled-down expectations it will probably do just fine, given its full range of business, function, dining, fitness and entertainment facilities.

Sheraton Park South Hotel 195R (1S) ▽ | 20 | 19 | 17 | 17 | $97 |
9901 Midlothian Tpke., Richmond; (804) 323-1144; (800) 525-9538; FAX: (804) 320-5255
■ Surrounded by Southside suburban office complexes and corporate centers, this businesslike response to the demand for conference and overnight accommodations anticipates nearly every office-away-from-home need: rooms are equipped with coffeemakers, computer ports, voicemail, two-line phones and more; other pluses are a "nice" indoor/outdoor pool and exercise room; serious sweats can be worked up at local sports and golf clubs.

Virginia Beach

Cavalier, The 400R (25S) | 18 | 19 | 19 | 21 | $157 |
Oceanfront at 42nd St., Virginia Beach; (804) 446-8199; (800) 980-5555; FAX: (804) 428-7957
☑ Guests can go traditional or contemporary at this two-parter consisting of a 1927 colonial-style "grande dame" plus a more modern beachfront addition; it boasts a kid-friendly game room, three restaurants, tennis, indoor and outdoor pools and a private beach ("away from obnoxious tourists"), but while some call it "still great" and a "beautiful setting for large parties", others say "a bit past its prime", "kind of woebegone."

Founders Inn 231R (9S) ▽ | 25 | 25 | 24 | 24 | $146 |
5641 Indian River Rd., Virginia Beach; (757) 424-5511; (800) 926-4466; FAX: (757) 366-5785
■ Inviting grounds and "attractive rooms" are strengths of this "simple, straightforward" hotel; though some interpret its "tranquil" atmosphere as "dull", others appreciate its north-of-town location ("a little out of the way" of Boardwalk spots) and full complement of dining, recreation and meeting facilities.

Hilton Inn Virginia Beach 124R | 19 | 18 | 14 | 18 | $117 |
Oceanfront at Eighth St., Virginia Beach; (757) 428-8935; (800) HILTONS; FAX: (757) 425-2769
☑ If "oceanfront rooms, family events" and "congenial" service are the basic needs for your sun-and-sand vacation, this contemporary-style resort may fit the bill; it offers family plans and packages in a quiet south-end beach location, and "good business rates" lend appeal to the midsize meeting rooms; still, less-impressed guests say "tacking 'inn' onto the Hilton name doesn't mean it's any less cookie-cutter."

Holiday Inn SunSpree Resort 211R (55S) ▽ | 18 | 18 | 16 | 18 | $107 |
3900 Atlantic Ave., Virginia Beach; (804) 428-1711; (800) 465-4329; FAX: (804) 475-5742
■ "Enormous" rooms and kitchenette-equipped suites not to mention the "ocean outside" draw sun seekers to this beach resort; rooftop dining, poolside relaxing and a kids' program keep vacationers happy while flexible meeting space attracts business groups; ratings suggest that most find it a solid if not stellar performer.

Pavilion Towers Resort & Conference Center 286R (6S) ▽ | 17 | 17 | 15 | 16 | $121 |
(fka Radisson Virginia Beach)
1900 Pavilion Dr., Virginia Beach; (804) 422-8900; (800) 313-0099; FAX: (804) 425-8460
■ Business groups appreciate the boardroom-like, full-service meeting facilities (capacity 700) at this modern high-rise adjacent to the Virginia Beach Pavilion Convention Center and eight blocks from the beach; newly renovated rooms ('96), tennis, an indoor pool, spa and exercise facilities are on-site assets and there's golf, deep-sea fishing and tourist attractions nearby.

Ramada Plaza Resort Oceanfront 211R (4S) ▽ | 17 | 17 | 15 | 15 | $114 |
(fka Ramada Oceanfront Tower)
Oceanfront at 57th St., Virginia Beach; (757) 428-7025; (800) 365-3032; FAX: (757) 428-2921
☑ It's "fun to watch the ships" from your oceanfront balcony or sample sushi, fresh seafood and sea breezes at this beachsider's lively outdoor cafe; there's lots of happening "stuff within walking distance", and if you must combine work with pleasure, a corporate center and meeting rooms are on-site; detractors say "not special."

Virginia Beach Resort Hotel & Conference Center (295S) ▽ | 16 | 18 | 16 | 18 | $140 |
2800 Shore Dr., Virginia Beach; (757) 481-9000; (800) 468-2722; FAX: (757) 496-7429
■ On a private Chesapeake Bay beach, this corporate-looking resort offers all-suite balconied lodgings plus activities ranging from windsurfing, sailing and volleyball to tennis (36 courts) and nearby golf; there's a fully equipped business center and conference facilities, plus restaurants, a health club and indoor and outdoor pools; the few surveyors who know it give it modest ratings, so moderate expectations are advised.

Washington

INN AT LITTLE WASHINGTON 9R (3S)   28 | 28 | 29 | 24 | $317
PO Box 300, Middle & Main Sts., Washington; (540) 675-3800; FAX: (540) 675-3100
■ Celebrated as "the best one-night stand in the US and maybe the world" (and "perfect" for longer stays too, if you can afford it), this "superb" inn near the Western VA foothills earns the state's top overall ratings thanks to sumptuous rooms that are a "decorator's dream" and Regional American dining that routinely sweeps top honors in the Washington DC restaurant *Survey*; service is indulgent yet "privacy is respected", making this Relais & Châteaux star "unforgettable" – "you'll want to return again and again."

White Post

L'Auberge Provençale 11R (3S)   ▽ 22 | 25 | 27 | 20 | $182
PO Box 119, White Post; (540) 837-1375; (800) 638-1702; FAX: (540) 837-2004
■ At their "peaceful" hunt country farmhouse, Alain Borel and his wife Celeste re-create the ambiance of a French inn, from the furnishings to the "superb" cuisine, starting with "the best breakfast ever" (included in rates); though some find rooms "smallish", most enjoy the elegant yet laid-back atmosphere and are "amazed" to "check out the paintings" and find works by Picasso and the like, not to mention amusing handicrafts and lovely antiques.

Williamsburg

Kingsmill Resort 237R (168S)   24 | 23 | 22 | 25 | $182
1010 Kingsmill Rd., Williamsburg; (804) 253-1703; (800) 982-2892; FAX: (804) 253-3993
■ One way "to enjoy Williamsburg [and Busch Gardens] and still feel like you're on a golf vacation" is to stay at this "beautiful" James River resort and conference complex with three championship courses plus tennis, swimming, spa facilities and much more; "well-maintained" lodgings include suites and condo rentals (ask for a river view) and there are dining options galore, but "if you don't golf or drink Bud" (it's an Anheuser-Busch property), you may find it "boring."

Marriott Williamsburg 283R (12S)   20 | 22 | 20 | 21 | $130
50 Kingsmill Rd., Williamsburg; (757) 220-2500; (800) 442-3654; FAX: (757) 221-0653
☑ Adjacent to Busch Gardens and near Colonial Williamsburg, this modern Marriott proves to be "better than expected" for convention-goers and those traveling with kids; "clean, neat rooms", extensive meeting space, "great golf" nearby and on-site swimming, tennis and exercise facilities outweigh its somewhat formulaic dining and tone; a major '96 renovation spiffed up the lobby and rooms.

Williamsburg Hospitality House 287R (11S)   19 | 19 | 17 | 19 | $124
415 Richmond Rd., Williamsburg; (757) 229-4020; (800) 932-9192; FAX: (757) 220-1560
☑ "Very nice", faux 18th-century public areas, modern conference facilities and a pretty fountain-centered courtyard are more impressive than the rather "plain" guestrooms and dining at this well-placed, well-priced Williamsburg hotel; its major attribute – "convenience" to William and Mary College and the Historic Area – sometimes cuts both ways: "seems to be run by students on summer break."

WILLIAMSBURG INN 221R (11S)   25 | 25 | 25 | 26 | $205
136 Francis St., Williamsburg; (804) 229-1000; (800) HISTORY; FAX: (804) 220-7096
■ "Staffed by courteous retainers and decorated in the historic Williamsburg style", this "beautiful" Georgian property, an official Colonial Williamsburg hotel, "seems a living part of the restoration", from the "fine" formal dining room to the "elegant" accommodations in the plush main inn or "small, authentic" cottages; meeting facilities, golf, tennis and fitness center privileges add "modern comfort" and help make it "absolutely worth the price."

Williamsburg Lodge 294R (21S)   20 | 21 | 19 | 21 | $161
PO Box 1776, S. England St., Williamsburg; (804) 220-7600; (800) 822-9127; FAX: (804) 220-7685
☑ On the edge of the Historic Area is this more "reasonably priced alternative" to the nearby Inn, a fellow official Colonial Williamsburg hotel; it's especially appealing if you're going to "take the kids" or host a meeting thanks to its more casual ambiance, a range of sports options and meeting facilities for 700-plus; some find the rooms "cozy" and "well appointed", while others call them "nondescript", but "good food" and "helpful", "friendly" service please most.

Wintergreen

Wintergreen Resort (320S)   21 21 18 23 $166
PO Box 706, Rte. 664, Wintergreen; (804) 325-2200; (800) 325-2200; FAX: (804) 325-8004
☑ An ambitious, 11,000-acre, year-round resort and conference center in the Blue Ridge Mountains below Charlottesville, where one can golf, ski, play tennis, swim, fish, go boating or develop corporate spirit through teamwork-building drills; accommodations are in condos and rental homes ranging from studios to six bedrooms and there's a variety of restaurants, but despite solid ratings some complain of "mediocre" food and "disorganized" management.

Woodstock

Inn at Narrow Passage 12R (2S)   _ _ _ _ _
PO Box 608, US 11 S., Woodstock; (540) 459-8000; (800) 459-8002; FAX: (540) 459-8001
A haven for travelers since the early 1740s and headquarters for Stonewall Jackson during the Valley Campaign of 1862, this log inn set on five acres along the Shenandoah River offers a sense of history along with comfortable lodgings in colonial-style rooms (all with a/c, most with private baths and fireplaces and some opening onto porches with river and mountain views); hearty fireside breakfasts (included) provide energy for hiking, fishing and touring nearby wineries and battlefields.

Washington

TOP 10 OVERALL

Inn at Semi-Ah-Moo
Bellingham
Sun Mountain Lodge
Port Angeles
Woodmark
Seattle
Spokane
Salish Lodge
WASHINGTON
Olympia
Skamania Lodge

Puget Sound
Four Seasons Olympic
Lake Washington
Inn at the Market
Sorrento
Alexis
Vintage Park
Seattle

BEST OVERALL

26 Four Seasons Olympic/Seattle
25 Woodmark/Seattle
Salish Lodge/Snoqualmie
24 Sun Mountain Lodge/Winthrop
Alexis/Seattle
Sorrento/Seattle
Inn at the Market/Seattle
23 Skamania Lodge/Stevenson
Vintage Park/Seattle
22 Inn at Semi-Ah-Moo/Blaine

BEST VALUES

Captain Whidbey Inn/Coupeville
Roosevelt/Seattle
Skamania Lodge/Stevenson
Lake Quinault Lodge/Lake Quinault
Sun Mountain Lodge/Winthrop
Kalaloch Lodge/Forks
Mayflower Park/Seattle
Woodmark/Seattle
Vintage Park/Seattle
Hyatt Regency Bellevue/Seattle

Blaine

R	S	D	P	$

Inn At Semi-Ah-Moo 176R (16S)

23	22	20	25	$164

9565 Semiahmoo Pkwy., Blaine; (360) 371-2000; (800) 770-7992; FAX: (360) 371-0151

☑ "As far into the NW corner of Washington as you can get", this resort beckons with "spacious rooms" and "beautiful surroundings"; guests "get away from it all" for "wonderful golfing" on the Arnold Palmer–designed course, plus boating, hiking, tennis, swimming in a heated outdoor pool and massages and body treatments – it's all "very NW: quiet, understated and relaxing", which to some means there's "nothing to do"; though critics are a definite minority, a few liken it to an "isolated glorified motel" with "spotty" service.

Coupeville

Captain Whidbey Inn 25R (7S)   20 | 22 | 23 | 23 | $122
2072 W. Captain Whidbey Inn Rd., Coupeville; (360) 678-4097; (800) 366-4097;
FAX: (360) 678-4110
■ For nature lovers seeking a "peaceful" getaway, this "sprawling resort" on Whidbey Island is "absolute paradise", with varied lodgings in either a "charming", somewhat "rustic" 1907 "log cabin"–style inn on Penn Cove or in individual cottages and cabins (all with feather beds and down comforters); there's "great hiking", boating, fishing and nearby horseback riding, tennis and golf, or for a "unique experience", catch a ride on the innkeeper's 52-foot ketch; the "creative, scrumptious" fare is "caught or grown down the road" (including the local treasure, Penn Cove mussels).

Eastsound

Rosario Resort 96R (19S)   16 | 18 | 18 | 21 | $144
1 Rosario Way, Eastsound, Orcas Island; (360) 376-2222; (800) 562-8820; FAX: (360) 376-3680
☑ "A little worn but still mystical", this "lovely old resort" facing Cascade Bay on Orcas Island ("prettiest place in the world") is "trying to bounce back" under new ownership, and some assert it "seems to have recovered from its bad rep", with special praise for the "balconies over the water"; unfortunately, organ recitals in the stately Moran Mansion ("for the over-60 crowd") and renovations (the spa and half of all rooms in the past two years) haven't erased all gripes about "shabby rooms" and poor facilities; one parent notes that "children are not permitted to use" the indoor spa pool, though an outdoor pool is available for families.

Forks

Kalaloch Lodge 14R (45S)   17 | 17 | 17 | 21 | $119
156151 Hwy. 101, Forks; (360) 962-2271; FAX: (360) 962-3391
■ "For an authentic Olympic Peninsula experience", surveyors insist "nothing beats the location" of this "incredible find high on the bluff overlooking the beach" in Olympic National Park; the "romantic setting" makes it easy to ignore the "worn furniture and dim bathrooms" in the '50s lodge, and couples prefer the "great" "cabins perched on the edge of the cliff" (they're "simple" too, but cozied-up in front of the fireplace after a day of beachcombing, few are complaining); N.B. cabins and rooms were recently outfitted with new carpets and furniture.

Lake Quinault

Lake Quinault Lodge 88R (4S)   18 | 19 | 18 | 23 | $126
345 S. Shore Rd., Lake Quinault; (360) 288-2900; (800) 562-6672; FAX: (360) 288-2901
☑ "Beautiful surroundings" and an "irresistibly rustic atmosphere" make this Olympic National Forest lodge "seem set in another era – with all the advantages and disadvantages that implies"; nostalgists prize its "quaint", "folksy" atmosphere warmed by the "very NW great hall" with a "giant stone fireplace", its "unique rainforest location", "clean, basic" quarters and "breakfast overlooking the lake", while the disaffected sniff it's "seen better days" and bash "national park food"; a heated indoor pool and sauna add points.

Port Angeles

Domaine Madeleine Bed & Breakfast 3R (2S)   – | – | – | – | M
146 Wildflower Ln., Port Angeles; (360) 457-4174; FAX: (360) 457-3037
This "superb B&B" just beyond the Olympic Peninsula gateway is a place to relax – "look for whales" while taking in the tranquil "view of the Strait of Juan de Fuca", hunt for mushrooms or hide away in one of the "beautiful rooms" with Jacuzzis and fireplaces; those seeking company can schmooze over an included "delicious five-course breakfast" prepared by "delightful hosts" Madeleine and John Chambers; N.B. no children under 12.

Port Ludlow

Inn at Ludlow Bay 34R (3S)   ▽ 24 | 23 | 22 | 23 | $174
1 Heron Rd., Port Ludlow; (360) 437-0411; FAX: (360) 437-0310
■ Developer Paul Schell's newest addition to the Peninsula's luxury lodging scene seems "bound for glory", a "restful and civilized" estatelike waterfront property with "great harbor views"; the day starts with a continental breakfast, then you might saunter to the adjacent marina and rent a kayak or sailboat, or head to the nearby Port Ludlow Golf Course; "excellent" dining awaits your return, as do "romantic" mountain-view guestrooms with down-filled duvets, whirlpool tubs and fireplaces.

Port Ludlow Resort & Conference Center ▽ 18 | 20 | 16 | 21 | $133
130R (53S)

9483 Oak Bay Rd., Port Ludlow; (360) 437-2222; (800) 732-1239; FAX: (360) 437-2482

▣ It may be a "great resort for a meeting", but a vocal contingent asserts that this '60s-style conference center "has fallen on bad times" "some rooms are old" and "dining facilities are limited – they know you are stuck"; water-view kitchen-equipped condos and "beautiful setting" aside, it's called "ordinary, except for the golf."

Seattle

ALEXIS HOTEL 65R (44S) 24 | 26 | 25 | 21 | $190
1007 First Ave., Seattle; (206) 624-4844; (800) 426-7033; FAX: (206) 621-9009

■ "Just the right balance between cozy European style and modern American conveniences" charms guests at this National Register historic Downtowner, where a "no tipping policy sets the service" tone; part of SF hotelier Bill Kimpton's growing empire, its '96 redo added meeting space and spa and refurbished all "luxuriously appointed" suites (some with Jacuzzis and fireplaces); but even devotees warn that the "classy" rooms offer "no views" and recommend the "quiet court" side to avoid "street traffic"; another "big plus" is The Painted Table's "standout" NW cuisine; breakfast included.

Doubletree Hotel Bellevue 353R (5S) 18 | 18 | 16 | 16 | $122
(fka Red Lion Hotel Bellevue)

300 112th Ave. SE, Bellevue; (425) 455-1300; (800) 222-TREE; FAX: (425) 455-0466

▣ Catering to "business types" with its high-capacity meeting facilities, and to the late-night crowd with its "great dance bar", this "big" suburbanite sports a lobby that looks like an "'80s disco" and other "gaudy public areas" dressed in "red velvet and chandeliers"; there's no accounting for taste – the hotel's or surveyors', whose reviews range from "surprisingly good" to "the worst ever"; as for the rooms, one voter's "nondescript" is another's "better than most."

Edgewater, The 232R (4S) 20 | 20 | 18 | 20 | $141
2411 Alaskan Way, Seattle; (206) 728-7000; (800) 624-0670; FAX: (206) 441-4119

▣ Nodding to "that Ralph Lauren Polo thing", this "homey" but modern hotel with a "tasteful lodge" look is a prized "gem that captures the essence of the city" in a "unique" waterfront location providing views of Puget Sound and the Olympics; "cozy and romantic" waterside rooms are perfect places to "lie in bed and watch the ships go by", but less dreamy types grouse about "tiny" accommodations and "noise" from trolleys and early rising seagulls; take in the "tremendous Sunday brunch" at Ernie's.

FOUR SEASONS OLYMPIC HOTEL 233R (217S) 26 | 27 | 26 | 26 | $208
411 University St., Seattle; (206) 621-1700; (800) 332-3442; FAX: (206) 682-9633

■ "Old-fashioned glamour" is only part of the charm at Seattle's "almost flawless", "majestic-yet-friendly" "grande dame", built in Italian Renaissance style in 1924; "delightful from start to finish", it wows guests with "elegant" rooms, grand public spaces, "superior" service and an "outstanding pool and fitness facility"; "dining is a dream from the past" in the Georgian Room, and afternoon tea in the graceful Garden Court is another treat; in short, a "top-notch" "hotel run as it should be."

Hilton Seattle 234R (3S) 18 | 19 | 17 | 16 | $142
1301 Sixth Ave., Seattle; (206) 624-0500; (800) 426-0535; FAX: (206) 682-9029

▣ Nods go to a "convenient location" "within walking distance of Pike Place Market and other attractions", and "views of the water", particularly from this high-rise's rooftop restaurant; but while some proclaim it "a solid choice" that's "a good value" ("you know what to expect of a Hilton"), critics say this "very ordinary" hotel with "small rooms" and "disorganized service" "needs redoing."

Hyatt Regency Bellevue 353R (29S) 22 | 22 | 20 | 21 | $152
900 Bellevue Way NE, Bellevue; (425) 462-1234; (800) 233-1234; FAX: (425) 451-3017

▣ "Convenient if you want to be on the Eastside" (though "tough traffic" slows the go to Seattle) or if you're a "shopping enthusiast" (it's opposite Bellevue Square and adjoins the boutiques at Bellevue Place), this "tasteful, business-oriented" high-rise offers a "great fitness center", myriad meeting spaces and an "elegant" restaurant; splurge for a Regency Club room on the "top floor, west side" since others are "standard."

INN AT THE MARKET 55R (10S) 24 | 24 | 23 | 22 | $176
86 Pine St., Seattle; (206) 443-3600; (800) 446-4484; FAX: (206) 448-0631

■ "It feels like the French countryside", but this "delightful" "small hotel" at Pike Place Market is "totally Seattle"; among the "very special" charms are a "wonderful view of Puget Sound from the rooftop terrace" "luxurious", "beautifully decorated rooms", a "helpful staff" and "great restaurants" (including "Euro-elegant" Campagne); quite simply, it's "recommended to everyone."

Mayflower Park 152R (20S) 21 22 21 19 $144
405 Olive Way, Seattle; (206) 623-8700; (800) 426-5100; FAX: (206) 382-6997
☑ "Top location" and "moderate prices" are draws at this "beautiful" "Euro-style" Downtowner steps from the shops at Westlake Center, a circa 1927 lodging that's "truly charming" albeit with the common drawback of historic hotels: its guestrooms are "pleasant" though "very small"; but there's no need to stay in your room when the "friendly bar" (Oliver's, renowned for martinis) and the "super new restaurant" (Mediterranean-inspired Andaluca) are right downstairs.

Renaissance Madison Hotel 465R (88S) 21 21 19 18 $145
(fka Stouffer Madison Hotel)
515 Madison St., Seattle; (206) 583-0300; (800) 278-4159; FAX: (206) 624-8125
■ "Fine all-around" is the genial verdict on this "very comfortable", "well-run" Downtown high-rise with "good rooms at a good price", though some note that Club Floor amenities (continental breakfasts, evening snacks and private concierge) are "worth the small premium" and that "upper rooms have great views"; businessfolk also appreciate "better-than-average" conference facilities and complimentary in-town transportation; be sure to check out the "high-altitude Italian" dining on the umpteenth floor at Prego.

Roosevelt, The 138R (13S) 19 20 17 18 $120
1531 Seventh Ave., Seattle; (206) 621-1200; (800) 426-0670; FAX: (206) 233-0335
☑ A 1929 "stately landmark" offering "a bit of art deco feeling" in the lobby – a "beautiful area" where a fireplace crackles and a pianist tickles the ivories nightly; guestrooms, while "comfortable and inexpensive", vary in size and amenities are nominal (there's a minuscule workout facility), but the Downtown location makes it a "great value" – it's adjacent to Niketown, Planet Hollywood, a 16-screen Cineplex and other vestiges of excess, and the hotel's own bustling Von's Grand City Cafe is a serious watering hole.

Sheraton Seattle Hotel & Towers 798R (42S) 21 21 21 20 $157
1400 Sixth Ave., Seattle; (206) 621-9000; (800) 204-6100; FAX: (206) 621-8441
■ "Headquarters for much that happens in Seattle", this "basic, well-run" "convention heaven" is gargantuan yet "friendly and personal"; rooms are "comfortable and modern", "nothing flashy", but those on "the concierge floor are the way to go" (patience, "the elevators need some caffeine"); just off the "wonderful lobby" (whose NW glass art "is like a minimuseum") are a new oyster bar and the "elegant" Fullers, "great for a power lunch"; relax in the pool at the health club on the 35th floor.

SORRENTO HOTEL 34R (42S) 23 26 24 22 $183
900 Madison St., Seattle; (206) 622-6400; (800) 426-1265; FAX: (206) 343-6155
■ "Absolutely gorgeous" enthuse fans of this "classic old-luxury hotel" whose First Hill locale, though close to Downtown, makes it "secluded and special"; expect "Italian villa elegance" and a "knockout lobby" "great for tea or drinks" "by the fireplace"; bargain hunters grouse "it's possible to spend $250 for a room the size of a shoe box", but "charming decor" (there was a major redo in '95) and a "friendly" staff that "warms the bed with a hot-water bottle" compensate; more kudos to "exquisite NW cuisine" at the "feels-like-London" Hunt Club.

Vintage Park, Hotel 125R (1S) 24 24 24 20 $160
1100 Fifth Ave., Seattle; (206) 624-8000; (800) 624-4433; FAX: (206) 623-0568
■ "A sleeper" and yet "another Kimpton success" (the savvy SF-based hotelier whose company also owns the Alexis); this "splendid hotel combines the feel of a large, efficient establishment and an intimate B&B", with a "subdued but first-class" Washington wines motif in the "small", "charming rooms", and evening wine tastings as part of the deal; "positively gushing service" extends to the "outstanding" Italian restaurant, Tulio; the Romance package includes champagne, rose petals on your bed and a satin kimono to take home.

Warwick Hotel 230R (4S) 17 20 17 14 $135
401 Lenora St., Seattle; (206) 443-4300; (800) 426-9280; FAX: (206) 448-1662
☑ "A nice view of the Space Needle" is the main charm of this "serviceable" "older" high-rise that the budget-conscious consider a "value" for its "ample" (if "typical") rooms, "good" restaurant, "great" balconies and location that's "a comfortable walking distance from Downtown" (there's also complimentary transportation "to pick you up after dinner"); but more demanding travelers groan that it's "greatly in need of refurbishment" – even the "lobby seemed tired."

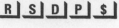
Westin Hotel Seattle 830R (35S)
21 | 21 | 19 | 20 | $162

1900 Fifth Ave., Seattle; (206) 728-1000; (800) 228-3000; FAX: (206) 728-2259

◪ "Comfortable", "well-appointed" rooms with "awesome views" earn praise for this Downtown "tourist-convention hotel" in "glass-sheathed silos" that may look "slick and corporate" but the attitude is warm: they "like kids and make parents feel welcome"; still, critics warns it's "getting old" – "make sure you get a renovated room"; "the staff is spread thin but they hustle", as do sushi lovers to in-house Nikko for "authentic Japanese fare without the jet lag", and newcomer Roy's for Pan-Asian with panache.

WOODMARK HOTEL 79R (21S)
25 | 25 | 24 | 26 | $177

1200 Carillon Pt., Kirkland; (425) 822-3700; (800) 822-3700; FAX: (425) 822-3699

■ On the eastern shore of Lake Washington at schmaltzy Carillon Point, this "peaceful and serene" "getaway" is "low-key" and "luxurious", but "not stuffy or formal"; the "beautiful rooms" offer "great views" and other pluses include nearby shops, a fitness facility, tennis courts and the independently operated Spa Csaba (à la carte but those who purchase spa services over $250 are entitled to special hotel rates); free 'Raid the Pantry' privileges mean "snacks all night long" – not that you'll need any after dining on eclectic NW bistro fare at Waters.

Silverdale

Silverdale on the Bay Resort Hotel 141R (9S)
▽ 18 | 19 | 16 | 16 | $99

3073 NW Bucklin Hill Rd., Silverdale; (360) 698-1000; (800) 544-9799; FAX: (360) 692-0932

◪ The price is right at this self-proclaimed resort hotel on the Olympic Peninsula that's more of a solid hotel than a resort (though there is an indoor pool); one surveyor describes "bad beds" but few complain about the "great dining room with a view" of the bay, which gets points for "excellent salads and seafood."

Snoqualmie

SALISH LODGE AT SNOQUALMIE FALLS
27 | 24 | 25 | 25 | $186

87R (4S)

6501 Railroad Ave. SE, Snoqualmie; (425) 888-2556; (800) 2SALISH; FAX: (425) 888-2420

■ "On the brink of Washington's most dramatic waterfront" – Snoqualmie Falls of *Twin Peaks* fame – lies a place so "altogether beautiful" it's "almost a crime to call it a lodge"; "understated luxury" extends to "hedonistic", "romantic rooms" with "wood-burning fireplaces and giant Jacuzzi tubs"; there's a new spa and a "superb" dining room with "inventive NW cuisine" and a "great wine list"; a few gripe that it's "expensive", but "top lodging experiences" usually don't come cheap.

Stevenson

Skamania Lodge 190R (5S)
24 | 22 | 22 | 25 | $152

1131 Skamania Lodge Way, Stevenson; (509) 427-7700; (800) 221-7117; FAX: (509) 427-2547

■ Columbia River Gorge, the windsurfing capital of North America, is the "magnificent setting" for this "wonderful" modern facility built in conjunction with the US Forest Service; most find it "charming and rustic" with "very pleasant" accommodations ("try for a riverside room"), but others cite "sterile architecture" and "a conference-center atmosphere" (there's meeting space for up to 600); nonsurfers tee off on an 18-hole golf course, lace up for "great hiking" or head to the fitness center for tennis, swimming and massages.

Winthrop

SUN MOUNTAIN LODGE 94R (8S)
25 | 23 | 23 | 26 | $160

Patterson Lake Rd., Winthrop; (509) 996-2211; (800) 572-0493; FAX: (509) 996-3133

■ Amid "spectacular mountain scenery", guests horseback ride, "ski from the front door, watch stars from the hot tub", play tennis, hike and revel in the "romantic" ambiance of this artfully rustic wilderness hotel set 3,000 feet above the Methow Valley; there are "attractions summer and winter" for corporate clients and vacationers alike, not the least of which are "charming Western rooms", lakeside cabins and "outstanding new units" with fireplace and whirlpool; "the first-rate staff can't do enough for you" and even the food is "incredible."

Washington, DC*

TOP 10 OVERALL

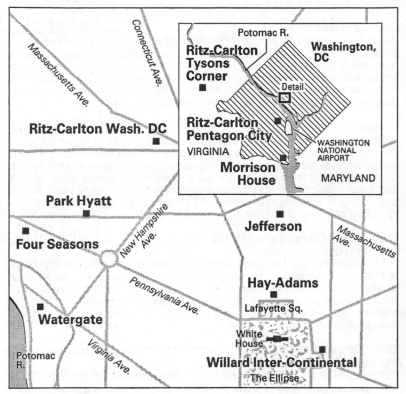

BEST OVERALL

27 Four Seasons
26 Ritz-Carlton Pentagon City
25 Willard Inter-Continental
   Ritz-Carlton Tysons Corner
   Ritz-Carlton Washington DC
   Park Hyatt
24 Morrison House
   Hay-Adams
   Jefferson
23 Watergate

BEST VALUES

River Inn
Tabard Inn
Morrison-Clark Inn
Henley Park
Phoenix Park
Sofitel
Embassy Suites Chevy Chase
Doubletree Guest Suites/NH Ave.
Washington Court
Canterbury

Washington, DC

R	S	D	P	$

ANA Hotel 406R (9S)

24	23	21	23	$182

2401 M St., NW, Washington; (202) 429-2400; (800) ANA-HOTELS; FAX: (202) 457-5010
■ One of DC's "best business hotels", a "top-of-the-line" "happy surprise", wins enthusiastic nods for its "large, spacious and relaxing rooms", "lovely" public spaces, serene courtyard and "solid staff" in a "close-to-Georgetown" West End location; savvy locals (and visiting celebs) do penance in its "outstanding" health club in order to splurge at a "great Sunday brunch"; N.B. management recruits some of the town's top young toques for its Bistro restaurant.

---

* Including Maryland and Virginia suburbs.

Canterbury Hotel (99S)
20 | 21 | 18 | 17 | $149

1733 N St., NW, Washington; (202) 393-3000; (800) 424-2950; FAX: (202) 785-9581
■ Satisfied loyalists "could live" at this "most hospitable" small hotel near Dupont Circle – its "spacious", refurbished junior suites are "slightly worn" but "comfortable" and sensibly priced, and each is equipped with a kitchenette, breakfast table and coffeemaker; a "charming" pub and a "great location" near public transportation and restaurants clinch the deal: a "real find."

Capital Hilton 505R (38S)
19 | 18 | 17 | 18 | $172

16th & K Sts., NW, Washington; (202) 393-1000; (800) HILTONS; FAX: (202) 639-5784
■ Close to the White House and the Downtown financial district, this veteran puts you "in the center of it all" for Capital biz; while some say the lobby's "marble and granite does not make up for small bathrooms and mediocre service", the property "still performs" for conventions and meetings, with renovated rooms ('95) and clubby steak and seafood dining at Fran O'Brien's – ergo, "if you can get a good rate", take it.

Carlton Hotel 180R (13S)
23 | 24 | 22 | 22 | $214

923 16th St., NW, Washington; (202) 638-2626; (800) 562-5661; FAX: (202) 638-4231
■ Only two blocks from the White House, this 1926 Italian Renaissance "classic" is "often overlooked" by tourists despite its "quiet" dignity and "incredible service" – and the fact that spotting famous faces in its "elegant" public rooms lends a "federal feeling" to one's stay; the only caution: some of its "subdued, comfortable rooms" "can be small"; N.B. the post-*Survey*, $5-million effort to replicate NYC's highly rated (and priced) Lespinasse restaurant adds new culinary interest.

Doubletree Guest Suites (101S)
(fka Guest Quarters Suites)
19 | 18 | 15 | 14 | $132

801 New Hampshire Ave., NW, Washington; (202) 785-2000; (800) 222-TREE; FAX: (202) 785-9485
☑ This "pleasant" residence's big pluses are "economy" and "location" – "hidden away" in Foggy Bottom "right by the Metro for the Smithsonian" and "convenient to George Washington University", the Kennedy Center and National Airport; but apart from full kitchens, "nice big apartments" and the chain's signature chocolate-chip cookies, there are few frills.

Doubletree Guest Suites (123S)
(fka Guest Quarters)
17 | 17 | 12 | 11 | $134

2500 Pennsylvania Ave., NW, Washington; (202) 333-8060; (800) 222-TREE; FAX: (202) 338-3818
☑ "A good buy for families" and business travelers, this all-suiter lets guests unwind in homelike surroundings, complete with kitchenettes; its "convenient location" not far from Foggy Bottom, Georgetown and the Metro turns the lack of on-site dining (apart from room service) into an opportunity to explore DC's varied restaurants and clubs; an off-site spa is available for guests' use.

Doubletree Hotel, National Airport, Pentagon City 480R (152S)
– | – | – | – | M

300 Army/Navy Dr., Arlington, VA; (703) 416-4100; (800) 222-TREE; FAX: (703) 416-4126
This Pentagon City eye-catcher parlays its minutes-from-National-Airport location and Metro and major shopping mall convenience into a bid for business meetings and sightseers; it ups the ante with refurbished ('96-'97) marble and mahogany appointments and guestrooms, up-to-date conference facilities, a rooftop swimming pool and health club and dancing in a revolving rooftop lounge accompanied by ambitious American dining with a view.

Doubletree Hotel Park Terrace 183R (36S)
– | – | – | – | M

1515 Rhode Island Ave., NW; (202) 232-7000; (800) 222-TREE; FAX: 202-332-8436
A recent redo of the public spaces and guestrooms has heightened the appeal of this conveniently located hotel (near the White House and three blocks from the Metro) catering to both the corporate and vacation crowds; add a California-French restaurant, exercise facilities and reasonable rates to the equation and it adds up to one of DC's best-kept secrets.

Embassy Row Hilton 157R (28S)
19 | 18 | 17 | 17 | $159

2015 Massachusetts Ave., NW, Washington; (202) 265-1600; (800) 424-2400; FAX: (202) 328-7526
☑ "Many international guests" find this "civilized" small hotel off Dupont Circle "adequate and reasonable for the area", providing a "very suitable" base for exploring this embassy neighborhood's galleries, bookstores and exciting restaurants; yet while "pleasant" and "comfortable", with "excellent" food at Bistro Twenty-Fifteen, it's "definitely not plush"; its recent acquisition by Hilton may mean changes.

Embassy Suites Chevy Chase Pavilion (198S)   23 | 19 | 17 | 19 | $147
4300 Military Rd., NW, Washington; (202) 362-9300; (800) EMBASSY; FAX: (202) 686-3405
■ Advocates claim you "can't beat" this "chic", atrium-centered, mall-based all-suiter for "family living" — not only does it offer "nice rooms" with kitchenettes, a well-equipped health club and a "great, free" full breakfast at a flat rate, but there's "lovely shopping", movies, eateries and the subway downstairs; the "deal" also appeals to commercial travelers who ride the Metro to Downtown offices and museums (it's "hard to get a cab").

FOUR SEASONS HOTEL 166R (30S)   27 | 27 | 26 | 26 | $256
2800 Pennsylvania Ave., NW, Washington; (202) 342-0444; (800) 332-3442; FAX: (202) 944-2076
■ "Quiet luxury" is the hallmark of DC's top-rated hotel, where the "superbly helpful" staff, round-the-clock room service, "lovely canal-view" rooms (request one), three-level fitness center and "peaceful" sense of seclusion draw a high-profile clientele; add a "good Georgetown location" and its excellence in event catering and it becomes "the capital choice" for many; good rubbernecking is guaranteed in its prestigious restaurant Seasons and garden terrace lounge.

Georgetown Dutch Inn (47S)   17 | 18 | 13 | 12 | $146
1075 Thomas Jefferson St., NW, Washington; (202) 337-0900; (800) 388-2410; FAX: (202) 333-6526
◪ "Nice enough" and relatively "cheap" for three rooms (including a kitchen), this "simple" side-street all-suiter offers "pleasant" service, free basement parking (for small and midsize cars) and decent value in Georgetown (which isn't easy to find); however, on weekends, raucous "late-night crowds outside your window" come with the territory.

Georgetown Inn 85R (10S)   19 | 19 | 18 | 17 | $170
1310 Wisconsin Ave., NW, Washington; (202) 333-8900; (800) 424-2979; FAX: (202) 625-1744
◪ Georgetown's nightlife, shopping and historic residential neighborhoods are this "decent, moderately priced" hotel's "biggest advantages"; while "teeny" bedrooms and "not great service" cause some to treat it merely as a roost, its devotees "really enjoy" the "almost European", "elegant ambiance", recently "enhanced" by room renovations and the fall '96 opening of a Mediterranean cafe.

George Washington University Inn 48R (47S)   17 | 19 | 16 | 14 | $146
(fka Inn at Foggy Bottom)
824 New Hampshire Ave., NW, Washington; (202) 337-6620; (800) 426-4455; FAX: (202) 298-7499
■ The major recommendations for this Foggy Bottom hostelry have always been its "peaceful" location "away from tourist crowds" (but near the Metro), budget rates and "friendly staff": now it's managed by nearby GWU, and the $3.5-million redo ('96) of the formerly "gloomy" rooms and kitchenette-equipped suites, along with the installation of a trendy Asian noodle bar, may prove it's really "worth a stay."

Grand Hyatt Washington 840R (60S)   23 | 22 | 20 | 22 | $179
1000 H St., NW, Washington; (202) 582-1234; (800) 233-1234; FAX: (202) 637-4797
■ A big, "beautiful atrium lobby sets the tone for the brightness" at "perhaps the best" of the convention center hotels; its "spacious", "excellent" office-equipped rooms (Regency Club rooms are best), large meeting facilities, "efficient" (if somewhat "impersonal") service, fitness center with indoor pool and varied dining options make it a good place to do business, albeit in an "iffy" part of town.

HAY-ADAMS HOTEL 124R (19S)   25 | 25 | 25 | 24 | $240
1 Lafayette Sq., Washington; (202) 638-6600; (800) 424-5054; FAX: (202) 638-2716
■ An "ambiance like no other" pervades this "well-tended" (and extensively refurbished) "grande dame" overlooking the White House — where else can you experience the "utter comfort" of "stately" digs (ask for a park-side room, others can be "small" and "stuffy") and "traditional", "attentive" service, while watching the "important and powerful" in its VIP-filled lobby and American dining room, Lafayette; one surveyor wistfully imagines: "if all of Washington were this classy . . . what a town."

Henley Park Hotel 90R (6S)   22 | 24 | 24 | 19 | $153
926 Massachusetts Ave., NW, Washington; (202) 638-5200; (800) 222-8474; FAX: (202) 638-6740
■ The "small but very elegant rooms" and "European warmth" at this "lovely" "little" Tudor-style restored hotel overcome its somewhat "isolated" Downtown environs, making it a "jewel among giants"; suits and suitors feel equally "at home" sipping tea in the parlor, dining on "delicious" New American food in the "romantic" restaurant, Coeur de Lion, or listening to "good bar music" later — but "not real late" in this early-to-bed town

Hilton Washington National Airport 379R (7S)   19 | 17 | 17 | 16 | $141
2399 Jefferson Davis Hwy., Arlington, VA; (703) 418-6800; (800) HILTONS; FAX: (703) 418-3763
☑ "Great service and a good location" (minutes from National Airport via shuttle bus) combined with dataport-equipped rooms, conference facilities, a health club and a pool should make this commercial property handy for fly-in meetings and short overnights if new management "can spruce it up"; some early reports on a 1996 revamping of the lobby, guestrooms and restaurant are promising, but others grade it "just ok."

Hyatt Dulles 314R (3S)   22 | 20 | 19 | 20 | $142
2300 Dulles Corner Blvd., Herndon, VA; (703) 713-1234; (800) 233-1234; FAX: (703) 713-3410
■ With its contemporary-style rooms (equipped with a work area and computer hookup, coffeemaker, iron and ironing board), workout facilities, full and continental breakfasts and a "very helpful staff", it's easy to get ready for a morning meeting at this "very good business hotel" not far from Dulles Airport; if you have an AM flight, note that "its physical proximity to the airport can be deceptive" so give yourself some extra time.

Hyatt Regency Bethesda 361R (10S)   21 | 20 | 18 | 19 | $149
1 Bethesda Metro Ctr., Bethesda, MD; (301) 657-1234; (800) 223-1234; FAX: (301) 657-6453
■ "Great for a weekend visit to DC", this "comfortable", "great value" suburbanite brings Downtown sight-seeing "Metro-close", yet it's in a "happening area with more restaurants in a four-block radius than anywhere else" in the district; on weekdays, "moderate accommodations" and "big hotel conveniences" keep it buzzing with government and business functions.

Hyatt Regency Crystal City 670R (15S)   20 | 19 | 17 | 17 | $147
2799 Jefferson David Hwy., Arlington, VA; (703) 418-1234; (800) 233-1234; FAX: (703) 418-1233
☑ "Nice rooms and conference facilities" put this modern high-rise near National Airport on meeting planners' lists; besides satisfying business needs, it offers moderate rates, mostly "good service", a health club with indoor pool, and rooftop dining; the fact that it's "a bit far from the Metro" keeps convention-goers on-site.

Hyatt Regency Reston 499R (13S)   22 | 22 | 21 | 22 | $143
1800 Presidents St., Reston, VA; (703) 709-1234; (800) 233-1234; FAX: (703) 709-2291
■ In Reston Town Center, a suburban complex near Dulles Airport with smart shops, restaurants, cinemas, outdoor concerts, an ice rink and hiking and biking trails, this "overall terrific" hotel's recently redone "large" guestrooms and its "great" meeting, dining and fitness facilities add a cosmopolitan dimension to business and tourist travel; a tiny minority harrumphs over a "Disney atmosphere", but to the majority it's "charming."

Hyatt Regency Washington 803R (31S)   20 | 20 | 18 | 19 | $171
400 New Jersey Ave., NW, Washington; (202) 737-1234; (800) 233-1234; FAX: (202) 737-5773
☑ The "best location" for "your congressional visit" or "legislative conference" is probably this "typical Hyatt" on Capitol Hill near the train station, even though its "sleek" lobby, meeting facilities and decent-size rooms generate little enthusiasm from surveyors; typical reactions are "noisy", "impersonal", "food could be better" and "adequate at best"; N.B. don't take advantage of its "walk-to-everything" convenience at night.

JEFFERSON HOTEL 68R (32S)   25 | 26 | 24 | 23 | $219
16th & M Sts., NW, Washington; (202) 347-2200; (800) 368-5966; FAX: (202) 331-7982
■ "Highly esteemed by the lords of Washington" for its "dignity" and "good dining", as well as the "personal attention" lavished upon its guests ("no better service anywhere"), this "beautifully furnished" small hotel with individually decorated rooms and suites (some with canopy beds and fireplaces) near the White House may be the "epitome" of a vanishing genre; go for tea or cocktails to "listen to all the politicians" cutting deals.

J.W. Marriott 738R (34S)   21 | 21 | 19 | 21 | $179
1331 Pennsylvania Ave., NW, Washington; (202) 393-2000; (800) 228-9290; FAX: (202) 626-6991
☑ "Big, bright, lively", this chain's flagship seemingly has it all – a "peerless" Downtown location "for sight-seeing" plus "all the Marriott basics": "courteous" staff, "clean, comfortable rooms", "good public areas and banquet facilities" and family appeal (kids "love the attached mall" and there's an indoor pool for relaxing as well as a full fitness center); although some "expect better" when paying a "luxury hotel" price, many enjoy the "good service and rooms without the pretension."

Latham Hotel Georgetown 122R (21S)   18 | 18 | 23 | 18 | $152
3000 M St., NW, Washington; (202) 726-5000; (800) LATHAM-1; FAX: (202) 337-4250
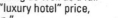
☑ Apart from chic California-French dining at one of DC's top restaurants, Citronelle, assets that explain why participants "would go back" to this Georgetowner are "reasonable" prices and a "four-star" location near nightlife and outdoor recreation; but on the downside are reports of "small", variable rooms and "indifferent" service that sometimes includes a "lack of honoring reservations."

Loews L'Enfant Plaza Hotel 350R (20S)

22 | 21 | 20 | 21 | $171

480 L'Enfant Plaza, SW, Washington; (202) 484-1000; (800) 23-LOEWS; FAX: (202) 646-4456

■ "Museum freaks" "walk to the Smithsonian" from this attractive "white palace" in SW Washington, while a "conveyor belt of conventions" takes advantage of its "pretty" rooms "with views", "good dining and meeting space" and mostly "accommodating" service; a few suggest housekeeping "could be better" and despite the blessing of a basement Metro stop, it is "isolated in the evening", but it "works well for family trips" with a staff that's "very hospitable to children."

Madison, The 314R (39S)

23 | 24 | 22 | 20 | $221

1177 15th St., NW, Washington; (202) 862-1600; (800) 424-8577; FAX: (202) 785-1255

☑ "Spectacular artwork" and museum-quality antiques set the tone at this "great old hotel" whose formal rooms, manners ("fine, but no one smiles, ever") and Continental dining prove that "venerable works" (especially when updated with computer hookups and a fitness facility next door); but "a taste of old DC" is not to everyone's taste: some assert the "tremendous service" is reserved for "diplomats – all others are hoi polloi."

Marriott Bethesda Hotel 400R (7S)

19 | 19 | 17 | 17 | $139

5151 Pooks Hill Rd., Bethesda, MD; (301) 897-9400; (800) 228-9290; FAX: (301) 897-4156

☑ "A homey alternative to Downtown Washington" for families with wheels and "those dealing with nearby National Institute of Health", this "older" suburbanite's "fine service" and facilities are boosted by tennis and swimming indoors and out; even those who say it's just "average" consider it "acceptable", although too far from the "heart of Bethesda" and the Metro.

Marriott Crystal Gateway 697R (71S)

20 | 19 | 18 | 19 | $146

1700 Jefferson Davis Hwy., Arlington, VA; (703) 920-3230; (800) 228-9290; FAX: (703) 271-5212

☑ A "dependable", "convenient" bivouac with access to a Metro stop and shopping mall near National Airport; it's a modern facility with a "lovely" lobby, some "huge, well-furnished rooms", "friendly" help, indoor pool and decent dining; in short "never bad", if a bit "nondescript" to some.

Marriott Fairview Park 394R (6S)

21 | 22 | 19 | 20 | $142

3111 Fairview Park Dr., Falls Church, VA; (703) 849-9400; (800) 228-9290; FAX: (703) 849-8692

☑ Handy for a "quick, clean business stop" in the Falls Church vicinity, this can be a "good convention hotel" (some fondly recall "great cocktail party food") with all the usual amenities, including a pool and lots of meeting spaces; otherwise, surveyors find it "too far outside DC to be convenient" and too "standard Marriott" to be worth that trip.

Marriott Key Bridge 565R (20S)

17 | 18 | 16 | 16 | $140

1401 Lee Hwy., Arlington, VA; (703) 524-6400; (800) 642-3234; FAX: (703) 524-8964

☑ "Low-budget businessmen and tourists" "enjoy DC without the hassle" from this "dated", "typical" Rosslyn facility whose major amenities are the "memorable" view from some bedrooms and its refurbished rooftop restaurant and lounge; still, staying here is "convenient" – "it's a quick walk over the bridge to Georgetown" or a short Metro ride Downtown – and a "tremendous value" (improved by a '94 redo), which explains why locals often "reserve here for guests."

Marriott Metro Center 444R (12S)

19 | 19 | 17 | 19 | $155

775 12th St., NW, Washington; (202) 737-2200; (800) 992-5891; FAX: (202) 347-0860

☑ Although this "modern", "convenient and reasonable" convention center hotel is loaded with "all sorts of useful things for business travelers" (including an executive floor and in-room computer jacks) and houses an ambitious American restaurant, a few critics gripe that it "still feels like the Holiday Inn it used to be" – "too busy and noisy"; "adequate" but "nothing special" sums it up.

Marriott Suites Bethesda (274S)

25 | 20 | 17 | 19 | $145

6711 Democracy Blvd., Bethesda, MD; (301) 897-5600; (800) 228-9290; FAX: (301) 530-1427

■ "This Beltway location combines comfort and economy" with "wonderful family accommodations" (microwaves on request), "great service and food", modern meeting facilities and a health club and pool; it's a suite deal "for anyone with wheels."

Marriott Tysons Corner 388R (2S)

19 | 20 | 17 | 18 | $137

8028 Leesburg Pike, Vienna, VA; (703) 734-3200; (800) 228-9290; FAX: (703) 734-5763

☑ Offering a "good night's sleep" in the "center of action for the Virginia suburbs", this "unexceptional" business-class veteran earns bonus points for its "very cooperative" desk and decent steakhouse dining, but not for "doll-sized rooms" that "need upgrading" (reportedly underway in 1996); on weekend nights, suburban singles stampede Studebakers, a bar adjacent to the hotel but not under Marriott management.

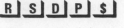

Marriott Washington 414R (4S)
19 | 19 | 17 | 18 | $152
1221 22nd St., NW, Washington; (202) 872-1500; (800) 228-9290; FAX: (202) 872-1424
■ "Centrally located" and a favorite site for "conducting business meetings", this "typical city hotel" with all the usual Marriott amenities charges "decent rates" commensurate with its "quiet, clean rooms" and "average" facilities and service; a big plus is that it's within "walking distance to Georgetown."

Marriott Westfields 318R (22S)
24 | 23 | 22 | 24 | $181
(fka Westfields International Conference Center)
14750 Conference Center. Dr., Chantilly, VA; (703) 818-0300; (800) 635-5666; FAX: (703) 818-3655
■ It's a "little far from DC action", yet close to Dulles Airport, which is a definite plus for conference planners who swear this "amazing" corporate complex "never misses a step"; its "lovely" facilities, "large rooms", colonial-style architecture and "great" contemporary Continental dining in the Palm Court as well as sports facilities ranging from indoor pool and spa to eight lighted tennis courts make it "a nice place to escape". even if it is "for business meetings."

Morrison-Clark Inn 41R (13S)
22 | 22 | 26 | 19 | $153
1015 L St., NW, Washington; (202) 898-1200; (800) 332-7898; FAX: (202) 659-8601
■ "Individually decorated bedrooms" reek of "old-fashioned charm" at this "lovely restored mansion" with a modern addition ("the old section has character" and is preferred by most), where period furnishings combine with modern amenities (dataports, minibars, hairdryers) to provide the best of both worlds; "good service" and a "terrific" Victorian dining room that redefines American home cooking are more pleasures that make staying here a "delight"; continental breakfast is included.

MORRISON HOUSE 42R (3S)
26 | 25 | 24 | 22 | $180
116 S. Alfred St., Alexandria, VA; (703) 838-8000; (800) 367-0800; FAX: (703) 548-2489
■ It's easy to "imagine yourself in Federalist America" while sipping tea in this "elegant", "romantic" Old Town Alexandrian – the "building fits into the setting beautifully" and the "service-oriented" staff has pampering down pat; this "truly classy" spot has "gorgeous but small" bedrooms and is "outstanding for private parties" and American-Eclectic dining at Elysium, yet it remains relatively "affordable" for luxury digs.

Normandy Inn 75R
▽ 20 | 19 | – | 15 | $125
2118 Wyoming Ave., NW, Washington; (202) 483-1350; (800) 424-3729; FAX: (202) 387-8241
■ Savvy execs on extended missions take up residence in this "quiet" and "very accommodating" Embassy Row lodging, finding the quaint library for sipping tea and the bedrooms with computer hookups, refrigerators and coffeepots "charming", "convenient" and a "good value"; with a health club close by, and Adams Morgan and Dupont Circle restaurants, museums, nightlife and the Metro just "a bit of a hike" away, what more do they need?; N.B. no dining, but continental breakfast is available for a fee.

Omni Shoreham 715R (55S)
17 | 16 | 16 | 18 | $157
2500 Calvert St., NW, Washington; (202) 234-0700; (800) THE-OMNI; FAX: (202) 234-2500
☑ Though some say the "glitter is gone from this fine old" art deco period hotel, it has good bones – "great views" over Rock Creek Park from upper rear floors, "high ceilings", "spacious rooms", Egyptian-Baroque public spaces, Metro convenience and a lovely outdoor pool and tennis courts – and a two-year $60-million renovation (to begin in August '97) should help boost ratings; service can "vary considerably", yet "history is alive in its meeting rooms" and few other places can handle really "large conferences."

One Washington Circle Hotel (151S)
19 | 18 | 18 | 14 | $150
1 Washington Circle, NW, Washington; (202) 872-1680; (800) 424-9671; FAX: (202) 223-3961
☑ While "not plush", this West Ender's "large" "old apartments" remade as suites (with full kitchens and two-line phones) prove "quite livable for a week or so", at least for those who prefer "comfortable" "good value" to luxury amenities; critics demand "better service" and insist "location is its saving grace", but advocates point to "decent" American food in the West End Cafe, "reasonable room rates", a middle-of-town locale and pool; N.B. the best piano player in town makes the bar the place to go after a show.

PARK HYATT WASHINGTON 92R (132S)
26 | 26 | 24 | 24 | $211
1201 24th St., NW, Washington; (202) 789-1234; (800) 233-1234; FAX: (202) 659-3724
■ Our surveyors can't find enough superlatives to describe this "outstanding", "first-class haven" near Georgetown: there's "superb service by employees who are obviously proud of their hotel", "large, fabulous", "well-kept" rooms and "suites to die for" with TV-equipped, marble bathrooms big enough to "raise a family in", "excellent" facilities including a full-service health club and pool, and for dining options, the "flawless" Melrose restaurant, a wine bar and a "fantastic afternoon tea"; some call it the "best Hyatt in the US."

Phoenix Park 141R (9S)   18 | 19 | 20 | 16 | $132
520 N. Capitol St., NW, Washington; (202) 638-6900; (800) 824-5419; FAX: (202) 638-4025
■ Revamped with a new tower of guestrooms, ballroom and banquet facilities, this "homey", "quaint Irish hotel", boasting a "fantastic" location across from Union Station and "tastefully furnished" (if "small") rooms, could rise to new prominence; its "interesting" and raucous Dubliner Pub is a magnet for legislative staffers.

Radisson Barceló Hotel Washington 232R (68S)   18 | 17 | 18 | 15 | $137
2121 P St., NW, Washington; (202) 293-3100; (800) 333-3333; FAX: (202) 857-0134
☑ What frequent travelers like about this revamped apartment house in an "interesting" Dupont Circle neighborhood are its "huge rooms like suites" with business amenities and a staff that "tries hard to make a stay very pleasant"; but a few don't like "poor" room care and feel it's "almost a government hotel – nothing special"; Gabriel, the handsome Spanish-Southwestern dining room with tapas bar, is a good buy.

Radisson Plaza Hotel at Mark Center 479R (16S)   22 | 19 | 19 | 22 | $140
5000 Seminary Rd., Alexandria, VA; (703) 845-1010; (800) 333-3333; FAX: (703) 845-7662
☑ "If you seek to be in DC without feeling the stress", some surveyors recommend this "impressive" Alexandria high-rise with good views that offers business-class accommodations (upgraded on the penthouse floor) as well as comprehensive conference facilities; there's an indoor/outdoor pool, four racquetball courts and good seafood dining; but despite its "excellent shuttle service", some find it "out of the way" "unless you drive"; N.B. the 50-acre Winkler Nature Park is adjacent.

Renaissance Mayflower Hotel 582R (78S)   23 | 23 | 21 | 23 | $199
(fka Stouffer Mayflower Hotel)
1127 Connecticut Ave., NW, Washington; (202) 347-3000; (800) 228-7697; FAX: (202) 776-9182
■ A "beautiful classic" – its breathtaking lobby, "luxurious" bedroom appointments and "superb service" (not to mention the first-class "political gossip on the elevators") compensate for a few "closet-size rooms" and the crowds generated by its tony meeting and banquet facilities, especially the lavish Grand Ballroom, scene of many an inaugural ball (beginning in 1925 when it opened for the Coolidge installation); listed on the National Register of Historic Places, it's set a few blocks from the White House, making breakfast a power scene; N.B. it's now under Marriott management.

Renaissance Washington DC Hotel 780R (21S)   19 | 19 | 17 | 17 | $155
999 Ninth St., NW, Washington; (202) 898-9000; (800) 468-3571; FAX: (202) 789-4213
☑ Rebranding (from Ramada) hasn't improved the "nondescript" rooms or service at this high-tech-looking overnight; its major asset remains convention-center convenience, which keeps it "catering to conferences, and it shows"; maybe Marriott management will succeed in giving this one a lift.

Residence Inn Bethesda (187S)   – | – | – | – | E
7335, Wisconsin Ave., Bethesda, MD; (301) 718-0200; (800) 331-3131; FAX: (301) 718-0679
This Downtown all-suiter satisfies families and execs on extended stay with fully equipped kitchens (plus a gratis grocery shopping service), complimentary continental breakfast and evening cocktails, an exercise room and a rooftop pool and sauna; a convenient location, one block from the Metro, adds to the attraction.

RITZ-CARLTON PENTAGON CITY 303R (42S)   27 | 27 | 26 | 25 | $195
1250 S. Hayes St., Arlington, VA; (703) 415-5000; (800) 241-3333; FAX: (703) 415-5061
■ The "essence of luxury" – derived from "the usual Ritz style", "unbelievable Ritz service", "plush" accommodations ("fantastically comfortable beds"), an up-to-the-minute fitness facility, "fabulous" indoor and rooftop pools, "elegant" meeting rooms and "great" dining at the Grill Room – is paired with Metro acess and shopping at the attached Fashion Centre mall; no wonder some consider this "airport hotel" (National is minutes away) "one of the best deals in the country."

RITZ-CARLTON TYSONS CORNER 366R (33S)   26 | 26 | 25 | 24 | $190
1700 Tysons Blvd., McLean, VA; (703) 506-4300; (800) 241-3333; FAX: (703) 506-4305
■ "Sitting on a mall but rising above it" is this "classy" "oasis of civilization in the suburbs", a unique Shangri-la where killer shopping combines with the "elegance and luxury one comes to expect" from a Ritz: "intimate" public spaces, state-of-the-art facilities (including multiline phones with computer and fax hookups) and "great food" at The Restaurant; locals come for tea when they "need to be pampered", stage "great parties and weddings" in the ballrooms and feast on its Friday night seafood buffet.

RITZ-CARLTON WASHINGTON DC 174R (32S) | 25 | 26 | 26 | 24 | $231 |
2100 Massachusetts Ave., NW, Washington; (202) 293-2100; (800) 241-3333; FAX: (202) 466-9867
■ A "sophisticated, small" and "dignified" "traditionalist" in a "renovated mansion" (a $15-million upgrade was just completed), this "choice" Embassy Row lodging for "high rollers who covet privacy and service" "understands elegance" and makes the most of its somewhat "cramped facilities", offering "pleasant rooms", "outstanding service" and "terrific food"; it's also "the place to corner pols", especially in the clubby Fairfax Bar and Jockey Club restaurant; as always, "quality wins friends but rich ones only."

River Inn (127S) | 22 | 19 | 20 | 17 | $133 |
924 25th St., NW, Washington; (202) 337-7600; (800) 424-2741; FAX: (202) 337-6520
■ Travelers visiting DC for "weeks at a time" enjoy "not feeling like a tourist" when ensconced in these "simple, clean and spacious" apartment-like suites near Kennedy Center and the Metro; added attractions are full kitchens (augmented by decent American dining downstairs), parking, "helpful staff" and a "fair price" that some consider an "unbelievable bargain" despite the "lack of ambiance."

Sheraton City Centre 337R (16S) | 17 | 18 | 17 | 16 | $140 |
1143 New Hampshire Ave., NW, Washington; (202) 775-0800; (800) 325-3535; FAX: (202) 331-9491
☑ Admirers say this standard's "good location" near Georgetown and "within walking distance to much of Downtown" makes it ideal for "both the business traveler and tourist", especially since it also offers "excellent value", including work-friendly facilities and "large rooms" that are "much improved" after a '95 rehab; the harder-to-please shrug "mediocre", "just a place to stay" – although even they might be impressed by the hundred-plus selection of single-malt scotches at the Grill bar.

Sheraton Premiere at Tysons Corner 419R (18S) | 23 | 19 | 18 | 19 | $146 |
8661 Leesburg Pike, Vienna, VA; (703) 448-1234; (800) 572-ROOM; FAX: (703) 893-8193
☑ A multimillion-dollar renovation revamped 300 rooms and added top-floor club facilities to the already extensive banquet and convention space (capacity 1,300) at this Tysons Corner tower that showcases "beautiful sunsets"; a "well-trained staff" and the "greatest workouts" at the fitness center make it "comfortable for business travelers", but while the rehab might address "run-of-the-mill rooms", complaints about the "too commercial" ambiance won't be so easy to repair; N.B. some of the area's best golf is nearby.

Sheraton Washington Hotel 1223R (125S) | 19 | 18 | 17 | 19 | $166 |
2660 Woodley Rd., NW, Washington; (202) 328-2000; (800) 325-3535; FAX: (202) 234-0015
☑ Most book this "faded" behemoth "if the convention meets there" or for the renovated Wardman Towers wing ("the only nice part"); otherwise one contends with "luck-of-the-draw rooms", a "cavernous" and "confusing" layout filled with "crowds", unimpressive dining and staff lacking in "guest courtesies"; compensations include strolls through its "beautiful grounds", outdoor swimming and a location near the Metro, interesting restaurants and the zoo.

Sofitel, Hotel 115R (30S) | 23 | 21 | 19 | 18 | $155 |
1914 Connecticut Ave., NW, Washington; (202) 797-2000; (800) 424-2464; FAX: (202) 328-1984
■ "Gallic charm" pervades this European-feeling perch above Dupont Circle; the "lovely" accommodations, "gracious help" (there's nightly turndown service with Evian water, rose and weather report) and regard for "good value" win *amis*, and the work areas in each room come with desks and hookups for modem and fax; its bistro is "surprisingly good", real praise considering the stiff competition in this nabe.

State Plaza Hotel (223S) ▽ | 16 | 15 | 13 | 13 | $109 |
2117 E St., NW, Washington; (202) 861-8200; (800) 424-2859; FAX: (202) 659-8601
■ "Clean, comfortable, cheap" and "charming" – small wonder that world-class performers at the Kennedy Center and visitors to the State Department, World Bank and GWU keep this Foggy Bottom suite secret under wraps; ordinary accommodations feature a bedroom, dressing area and eat-in kitchen, with deluxe rooms adding a sofa-bedded living room and dining area.

Tabard Inn 40R | 18 | 20 | 22 | 18 | $133 |
1739 N St., NW, Washington; (202) 785-1277; FAX: (202) 785-6173
☑ The funky "ambiance doesn't quit" at this Dupont Circle Victorian, a "stomping place" for the "bookish, artistic" and romantic who consider its "worn" but "comfortable" rooms and "laid-back" atmosphere "an antidote to all the wheeling, dealing and showiness" elsewhere and revel in its garden repasts and "inimitable breakfasts" ("who else gives you heavy cream for your morning granola?"); it's "love it or hate it", but definitely "one of a kind"; N.B. free passes are provided for a health club nearby.

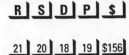
Washington Court Hotel 251R (13S)
21 | 20 | 18 | 19 | $156

525 New Jersey Ave., Washington; (202) 628-2100; (800) 321-3010; FAX: (202) 879-7918
As is common on Capitol Hill, there's a split ballot on this entry; yeas are logged for its "cheap", "big" luxury rooms, marble bathrooms with TVs (a "typical DC touch"), some of the "friendliest people anywhere", an "excellent location" and lobbying facilities; nays retort that the "rooms are tired, service is slow" and it's "scary" outside at night.

Washington Hilton & Towers 1041R (82S)
17 | 17 | 16 | 18 | $167

1919 Connecticut Ave., NW, Washington; (202) 483-3000; (800) HILTONS; FAX: (202) 265-8221
This bustling "convention megalopolis" above Dupont Circle can "handle anything" (its 31 meeting rooms accommodate up to 4,200) and hosts events "remarkably well"; considering the traffic, and the fact that its "rooms vary" widely (likewise service and food), it's a "functional" choice – especially in nice weather, when guests can take advantage of some of the best tennis and outdoor swimming facilities in town.

Washington, Hotel 334R (16S)
17 | 19 | 17 | 18 | $155

15th St. & Pennsylvania Ave., NW, Washington; (202) 638-5900; (800) 424-9540; FAX: (202) 638-4275
Regulars are fond of this "old-fashioned" historic hostelry (circa 1918) that offers good value (especially "off-season and weekends") and a location "near everything", notwithstanding a few service snafus, "tiny" rooms (the "small suites are worth the extra money") and the fact that it's showing its age and "needs renovations"; some say the rooftop terrace bar with matchless monument views is "what makes this hotel – it's *the* place to watch Fourth of July fireworks or a Pennsylvania Avenue parade.

Watergate Hotel 147R (85S)
24 | 24 | 24 | 22 | $223

2650 Virginia Ave., NW, Washington; (202) 965-2300; (800) 424-2736; FAX: (202) 337-7915
Quiet "views of sculls and spires", riverside suites that "provide enough room to jog indoors", fax machines in every guestroom and "royal" treatment – not to mention the "gorgeous lobby", "decent" health club and shopping mall downstairs – are among the reasons "anyone would want to break into" this "expensive" Nixon-era legend that attracts both foreign VIPs and Kennedy Center performers; its "fabulous" dining is a bit less so now that a Contemporary American restaurant replaced Jean-Louis Palladin's namesake dining rooms.

Westin City Center 387R (13S)
20 | 17 | 16 | 18 | $155

(fka Washington Vista Hotel)
1400 M St., NW, Washington; (202) 429-1700; (800) WESTIN-1; FAX: (202) 785-0786
This "impressive" atrium-centered hotel offers "spacious", "well-decorated" rooms (redone in '95), moderate rates and a location within "walking distance" of Downtown offices and tourist musts, all of which makes it a "good value"; but while Westin's takeover is unlikely to affect the "questionable neighborhood", it remains to be seen if they can perk up variable service and food.

Westin Hotel Washington, DC 246R (17S)
24 | 22 | 21 | 22 | $193

(fka The Grand Hotel)
2350 M St., NW, Washington; (202) 429-0100; (800) 228-3000; FAX: (202) 429-9759
The "best bathrooms of any business hotel in the country" are "a highlight" of this "elegant" if "commercial feeling" West End property, recently acquired by Westin (after it sold the ANA across the street); new management has done a "good job in updating" as well as improving service at this "small-meeting" specialist and there's extra praise for the "very comfortable rooms", yet a few say its restaurant still has a way to go.

WILLARD INTER-CONTINENTAL 305R (35S)
26 | 25 | 25 | 26 | $230

1401 Pennsylvania Ave., NW, Washington; (202) 628-9100; (800) 327-0200; FAX: (202) 637-7326
Known as the residence of presidents, this "superbly redone historic hotel" (circa 1904), an "impossibly opulent" Pennsylvania Avenue beaux arts "museum piece", remains a prime "place to dignitary-watch" or hold impressive meetings; securing its standing as the preeminent "status place to stay" are its "breathtaking" lobby, charming "nook-and-cranny" bedrooms (which "vary enormously" in size and comfort), "friendly" help and fine Contemporary French dining in the Willard Room; it's among "the best of DC, if you have bucks to spare."

Wyndham Bristol Hotel 200R (39S)
20 | 20 | 18 | 17 | $154

2430 Pennsylvania Ave., NW, Washington; (202) 955-6400; (800) WYNDHAM; FAX: (202) 775-8489
For an "affordable" bit of "luxury" near the Foggy Bottom Metro (halfway between Georgetown and the White House), consider booking a "roomy room" or suite (all with kitchenettes) at this "pleasant" apartment-building conversion; keep in mind, however, that the accommodations "vary considerably" and there's "not much to speak of" in the way of facilities or "real dining" (the lobby grill is best known for its "good weekend brunch"); N.B. special package deals often include "good weekend rates."

345

West Virginia

Berkeley Springs

R	S	D	P	$

Coolfont Resort 23R (202S)
1777 Cold Run Valley Rd., Berkeley Springs; (304) 258-4500; (800) 888-8768;
FAX: (304) 258-5499

16	17	15	17	$134

☑ On 1,200 "beautiful" secluded woodland acres, respite seekers find "minimalist alpine chalets, good hiking trails", tennis courts, an indoor pool plus an optional full-service spa with classes, scrubs, mind/body programs, etc.; it's a relatively cheap, democratic resort, "just this side of camping" and "not fancy at all", with "rustic" conference facilities (14 meeting rooms) patronized by Big "D" Democrats (as in the Gores) – so maybe it's Big "R" Republicans who find it "dark" and "buggy"; "mediocre buffet food" is one issue on which all parties agree.

Country Inn 65R (3S)
207 S. Washington St.. Berkeley Springs; (304) 258-2210; (800) 822-6630;
FAX: (304) 258-3986

▽ | 17 | 19 | 19 | 17 | $119 |
|---|---|---|---|---|

☑ There's a "modest small-town atmosphere" at this "downscale but nice" colonial-style inn that's a "getaway" for individuals or corporate execs; the healing waters of Berkeley Springs are a special draw and there's also a spa (providing massages, whirlpools and salon services), traditional dining and facilities for small meetings; nearby golf and Cacapon State Park offer enough activities for most outdoor types.

Charles Town

Hillbrook Inn 6R
Rte. 13, Summit Point Rd., Charles Town; (304) 725-4223; (800) 304-4223;
FAX: (304) 725-4455

–	–	–	–	E

Cascading down a wooded hillside near Charles Town, this richly appointed Tudor-style fantasy house with chimneys, gables and leaded-glass windows offers six unique and romantic guestrooms; its dining room and streamside porch are intimate backdrops for seven-course candlelit dinners and breakfasts (both included in rates), and there's a garden for postprandial strolls; it may be pricey, but you get a lot for your money.

Davis

Canaan Valley Resort 244R (6S)
Box 330, HC 70, Rte. 1, Davis; (304) 866-4121; (800) 622-4121;
FAX: (304) 866-2172

▽ | 16 | 19 | 19 | 24 | $83 |
|---|---|---|---|---|

■ "Scenic" and "woodsy" in keeping with its Canaan Valley State Park locale (the second largest wetland in the US), this year-round resort bubbles with outdoor activity: it's "good for skiing" as well as golf (18 links), fishing, ice skating, indoor/outdoor swimming, cycling and tennis (six courts); while decor in cabins, campsites and meeting rooms is "plain", the surroundings please the eye, and homey American dining and up-to-date meeting rooms for groups up to 500 are pluses.

Glen Ferris

Glen Ferris Inn 15R (2S)
Glen Ferris; (304) 632-1111; (800) 924-6093; FAX: (304) 632-0113

–	–	–	–	I

A former stagecoach stop that later served as housing for Civil War soldiers (it was fired upon in the process), this 1839 Federal-style mansion surrounded by gardens and overlooking picturesque Kanawha Falls is a comfortable retreat for both romantic getaways and business (ask about the spacious executive suites); rooms are individually decorated in styles ranging from Victorian to Shaker, and candlelit dinners can be enjoyed in the on-site dining room.

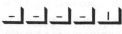

Harpers Ferry

Historic Hilltop House Hotel 54R (4S)   – – – – M
PO Box 900, 400 E. Ridge St., Harpers Ferry; (304) 535-2132; (800) 338-8319; FAX: (304) 535-6322
Majestic views of the Potomac River and three states from a scenic hilltop perch can be enjoyed along with homey comfort at this family-owned historic inn dating back to 1888; during the holidays, it's a popular base for multigenerational reunions, and year-round its reasonable prices, old-fashioned American food and low-key conference facilities make it a find.

Hedgesville

Woods Resort 60R (40S)   – – – – M
PO Box 5, Rte. 4, Mt. Lake Rd., Hedgesville; (304) 754-7977; (800) 248-2222; FAX: (304) 754-8146
Looking "like it was carved in the mountain", this Eastern Panhandle golf and small conference retreat offers "peaceful" isolation plus easy access to nearby Harpers Ferry, outlet malls, white-water rafting and the 23,000-acre Sleepy Creek wilderness area; even with all those nearby diversions, some prefer relaxing by the fireplace, lazing in the whirlpools of "nice, clean cabins or rooms", playing 27 holes of "great golf" or downing hearty American food.

Morgantown

Lakeview Resort 183R (4S)   17 20 18 20 $114
1 Lakeview Dr., Rte. 6, Morgantown; (304) 594-1111; (800) 624-8300; FAX: (304) 594-9472
■ This "plain" but "pleasant resort" on the oddly named Cheat Lake wins over sports fiends with two championship greens plus tennis, indoor/outdoor pools and an "extraordinary" fitness center; regional conveners find the "good" large-scale meeting rooms fair game, too, but there's nothing fancy about the "ok", "motel"-like lodgings ('96 renovations may perk things up); food choices include a lakeside dining room and a casual grill as well as a lounge for cocktails and entertainment.

Parkersburg

Blennerhassett Clarion Hotel 100R (4S)   – – – – I
320 Market St., Parkersburg; (304) 422-3131; (800) 262-2536; FAX: (304) 485-0267
Parkersburg's turn-of-the-century prosperity may have faded, but this 1889 Victorian hotel remains the town's showpiece; on the National Historic Register, it caters to area business bigwigs and Ohio Valley vacationers who appreciate its antiques-filled lobby and library, comfortable guestrooms, meeting space for 250 and fine American dining at Harman's Restaurant, not to mention its old-fashioned hospitality and reasonable prices.

Pipestem

McKeever Lodge/Pipestem Resort State Park 129R (14S)   ▽ 17 18 17 20 $85
PO Box 150, Rte. 20, Pipestem; (304) 466-1800; (800) CALL-WVA; FAX: (304) 466-2803
■ It's hard to beat this lodge on the lip of the Bluestone River Gorge, part of the Pipestem Resort State Park complex, for affordable "sight-seeing at its finest" or for an abundance of year-round sports, including hiking, horseback riding, boating and x-country skiing; rooms with "woodsy decor" are augmented by restaurants, meeting facilities and outdoor summer entertainment; N.B. associated property Mountain Creek Lodge, set 1,000 feet down at the base of Bluestone canyon, is accessible only by aerial tramway; the resort also offers cottage lodgings and campsites.

Shepherdstown

Bavarian Inn & Lodge 70R (2S)   23 20 24 20 $123
Box 30, Rte. 1, Shepherdstown; (304) 876-2551; FAX: (304) 876-9355
■ "Mouth-watering" German cooking – "the best food in the area" – brings 'em back *mach schnell* to this "nice but a bit pricey" well-groomed alpine lodge overlooking the Potomac River; also drawing guests are "wonderful" rooms, some with views, fireplaces, canopied beds and whirlpools; an outdoor pool, tennis court and exercise equipment are available to battle the wursts, and Civil War sites and outlet shopping are nearby.

Wheeling

Oglebay Resort and Conference Center 190R (64S) `17` `20` `17` `21` `$111`
Rte. 88 N., Wheeling; (304) 243-4000; (888) OGLEBAY; FAX: (304) 243-4070
✓ "Everyone loves" this "warm and casual" 150-acre year-round mountain resort in Wheeling for its "must-see" Christmas light show, "beautiful" grounds and "extensive sports facilities" including golf, tennis and swimming pools, plus a 35-acre zoo and nearby fishing and skiing; but even those who "grew up here" may find it "somewhat disappointing for food and lodging" (accommodations, including 50 cottages as well as the lodge, strike critics as "old and tired"); still, most rate it "surprisingly decent" – "a great family value" that can also host conference groups up to 300.

White Sulphur Springs

GREENBRIER, THE 518R (74S)　　　　　`27` `27` `26` `29` `$277`
300 W. Main St., White Sulphur Springs; (304) 536-1110; (800) 624-6070; FAX: (304) 536-7834
■ Few US resorts can match this "historic" Southern belle's magical combination of "cushy" accommodations, "excellent food" "never-ending variety of activities for all possible tastes", "every amenity you can imagine" and "spectacular" setting in the Allegheny Mountains; whether you enjoy the "regenerative spa", play championship golf or convene in "Southern comfort on a grand scale" (meeting capacity is 1,200), the pampering never stops; so while a minority finds it "a bit pricey" and "stuffy" (the "dress code is a little severe"), the majority agrees it's "one of the greats."

Wisconsin

Bailey's Harbor

Gordon Lodge 34R (6S)
20 | 22 | 20 | 22 | $150

1420 Pine Dr., Bailey's Harbor; (414) 839-2331; (800) 830-6235; FAX: (414) 839-2450

◪ Established in 1928, this "secluded" family-owned Door County resort on 130 acres along Lake Michigan offers a "quaint setting" and decent food, along with a "very friendly" ambiance, 18-hole putting green, two tennis courts, outdoor pool and many other activities that make it a "good getaway" for loyalists; but those looking for upscale call for an "update" of "tacky" "'60s" decor that looks to some "like a set from a *Brady Bunch* movie"; accommodations (all with a/c, some with fireplaces) include main lodge rooms, lakeside villas and cottages in the woods; open May to October.

Bayfield

Old Rittenhouse Inn 17R (3S)
▽ 27 | 24 | 28 | 23 | $144

PO Box 584, 301 Rittenhouse Ave./Hwy. 13, Bayfield; (715) 779-5111; FAX: (715) 779-5887

■ "Superb" American dining draws devotees to this "interesting", antiques-filled 1890 Victorian and its three sister properties (Le Château Boutin, the Grey Oak Guest House and the new Fountain Cottage) in historic Bayfield on the shores of Lake Superior; innkeepers Mary and Jerry Phillips offer year-round special occasion packages that range from Murder Mystery and Seasonal Wine weekends to B&B Business Basics seminars, and continental breakfast is included in the rates.

Delavan

Lake Lawn Lodge 256R (28S)
16 | 18 | 16 | 18 | $124

2400 E. Geneva St., Delavan; (414) 728-7950; (800) 338-5253; FAX: (414) 728-2347

◪ Approaching its 120th year, this self-contained year-round resort classic with "activities scheduled almost 'round the clock" on 275 acres at Lake Delavan keeps guests moving with three pools, tennis, an 18-hole golf course, volleyball, baseball, health club, sauna, hayrides, children's programs, several dining options and more; though some lament that this "formerly true individual rustic getaway now sadly caters to corporate groups", many insist it's still "fun for families" because children "love it so much"; new management in '96 has led to major and "much-needed renovation" (ongoing) that may lift scores next time around.

Eagle River

Chanticleer Inn 13R (63S)
▽ 16 | 17 | 18 | 18 | $123

1458 E. Dollar Lake Rd., Eagle River; (715) 479-4486; (800) 752-9193; FAX: (715) 479-0004

■ Golfing, fishing, snowmobiling and x-country skiing lure outdoorsy types to this "great family place", a year-round resort on Voyageur Lake, one of a chain of 28 lakes in the North Woods region; the waterside setting offers two private sand beaches and canoes and other boats for rent, along with accommodations ranging from comfortable motel rooms and suites to lakeside villas and condominiums, some with kitchenette, whirlpool and fireplace; a dining room with a summer beer garden is also on-site.

Fontana

Abbey Resort & Fontana Spa 324R (36S)
16 | 18 | 18 | 18 | $135

269 Fontana Blvd., Fontana; (414) 275-6811; (800) 558-2405; FAX: (414) 275-3264

◪ An "excellent spa" is the highlight of this Lake Geneva resort that pampers Chicago and Milwaukee residents escaping for "weekend and holiday" retreats; when they're not relaxing, guests enjoy the outdoor pool, six tennis courts and game room as well as boating and other water sports, along with "good food" at the formal La Tour de Bois (dress code in evening) and the casual Waterfront Cafe; yet despite a '95 renovation, many suggest it's "showing its age" and requires "guestroom attention"; meeting facilities for groups up to 1,300 draw lots of corporate groups.

Green Lake

Heidel House Resort & Conference Center   22 | 22 | 22 | 24 | $143
182R (18S)
643 Illinois Ave., Green Lake; (920) 294-3344; (800) 444-2812; FAX: (920) 294-6128
■ The "ideal weekend getaway", this "relaxing and refreshing" year-round resort 90 miles northwest of Milwaukee on Green Lake is "a wonderful place to wake up", with a private beach, marina, indoor/outdoor pools, tennis and 72 holes of golf on three nearby courses, plus "good food" in two lakeside settings and energetic staffers who "knock themselves out for the kids"; 20 acres of gardens and woods surround two main lodges and a variety of cottages; a new conference center and ballroom hold up to 350 people.

Kohler

AMERICAN CLUB, THE 234R (2S)   27 | 26 | 26 | 27 | $202
Highland Dr., Kohler; (920) 457-8000; (800) 344-2838; FAX: (920) 457-0299
■ Reviewers shower praise on "Wisconsin's best" resort, built in 1918 by Kohler (the plumbing giant) to house its immigrant workers; top-rated in the state, the red-brick Tudor complex offers "spectacular facilities" (two indoor pools, health club, tennis, etc.), "exceptional service", "pretty rooms" with whirlpools, "outstanding grounds", "great golf" at Blackwolf Run on courses designed by Pete Dye, shopping within walking distance and "gourmet dining" at the jackets-required Immigrant restaurant (plus other eateries); also "perfect for conventions", "they get pretty much everything right" so "make reservations way in advance."

Inn on Woodlake 60R   ▽ 21 | 22 | 21 | 18 | $151
705 Woodlake Rd., Kohler; (920) 452-7800; (800) 919-3600; FAX: (920) 452-6288
■ Adjacent to a shopping complex yet "charming and intimate", the Inn on Woodlake is a cheaper alternative to the American Club and offers complimentary access to the famous resort's health club along with golf at two 18-hole Pete Dye–designed courses at Blackwolf Run; rooms in the contemporary property feature Kohler bathroom fixtures, natch; there's no dining facility on-site (although continental breakfast is included), but there are plenty of restaurants in the Village of Kohler.

Lake Geneva

Grand Geneva Resort & Spa 318R (47S)   22 | 21 | 20 | 23 | $150
PO Box 130, Hwy. 50 E. & Hwy. 12, Lake Geneva; (414) 248-8811; (800) 558-3417; FAX: (414) 248-3192
■ A jump in scores since our last *Survey* reflects a "very successful renovation" that has "beautifully restored" the "elegance and comfort" of this lakeside complex; set on 1,300 "lovely" acres, it offers nearly every activity, including two "pretty" golf courses, indoor/outdoor pools and tennis courts, horseback riding, the Mountain Top Ski area, three restaurants, kids' programs, nightly entertainment, shopping and "great spa" facilities; though a few mutter about an "overrated" "yuppie playground", most applaud this "improved" family and corporate retreat.

Interlaken Resort & Country Spa 144R (84S)   18 | 19 | 19 | 20 | $131
W. 4240 State Rd. 50, Hwy. 50 W., Lake Geneva; (414) 248-9121; (800) 225-5558; FAX: (414) 248-1071
☑ While it gets a few nods as a "good place for a family vacation" (with hillside villas that keep "kids away from quieter guests"), this Lake Geneva–area getaway that's actually on neighboring Lake Como is "disappointing" to some who cite "unremarkable decor" and "confused service"; but supporters report "nice people" and "good facilities" at a year-round destination offering plenty of activities, including indoor/outdoor swimming, hiking, tennis, snowmobiling, boating, spa services and three golf courses at Geneva National only minutes away.

Milwaukee

Hilton Milwaukee 468R (32S)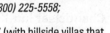
(fka Marc Plaza Hotel)
509 W. Wisconsin Ave., Milwaukee; (414) 271-7250; (800) 445-8667; FAX: (414) 271-8841
☑ Enthusiasts proclaim Downtown Milwaukee's 1925 "grande dame" "beautifully restored", especially the "old but still elegant" "classic" lobby; but while it may be "improving", surveyors disagree over rooms that are either "large" and "wonderful" or "small" and "old-fashioned" (some had yet to be upgraded at *Survey* time), with doubters claiming the remodeling "cut too many corners" and applied "too much gold on that which does not glitter"; all agree on the "perfect location" for visiting the Public Museum, Bradley Center and Grand Avenue Mall, even if some find the neighborhood iffy.

Hilton Milwaukee River 153R (11S)   20 17 18 17 $102
4700 N. Port Washington Rd., Milwaukee; (414) 962-6040; (800) 445-8667; FAX: (414) 962-6166
■ Despite "no lobby or amenities to speak of", this "more-motel-than-hotel" North Shore chainer that totally renovated in '95 is praised as a "cozy, off-the-beaten-path bargain" catering to a business clientele (Miller Brewing is nearby) and visitors attending Summerfest; guests can watch the Milwaukee River drift by while dining at Anchorage restaurant (and drift themselves in the indoor pool), but for more strenuous activity, they must hightail it to the North Shore Racquet Club or Brown Deer golf course close by.

Hyatt Regency Milwaukee 465R (19S)   18 18 17 17 $137
333 W. Kilbourn Ave., Milwaukee; (414) 276-1234; (800) 233-1234; FAX: (414) 276-6338
☑ "Clean", "efficient", "functional" – yes, it's a Hyatt, and surveyors who have "seen one, have seen them all" (which is not necessarily a negative); the "nice" if "small" guestrooms rim an 18-story atrium (caveat: sometimes its "activities can be heard in rooms") topped by the Polaris, Wisconsin's only revolving rooftop restaurant, and there's a fitness center on-site (but no pool); enclosed skywalks connect the hotel to the Wisconsin Center, Federal Plaza and Grand Avenue Mall.

Marriott Milwaukee 381R (9S)   17 19 17 16 $119
375 S. Moorland Rd., Brookfield; (414) 786-1100; (800) 228-9290; FAX: (414) 786-5210
☑ While some believe this "good road stop" with indoor/outdoor pools might top off a visit to the Zoo, County Stadium or Mayfair, others brew over "a very tired hotel" that "could improve" both its service and guestrooms; on tap is a "much-needed renovation" of public spaces and suites that could bring happier days back to a suburban hostelry that seems below Marriott's usual standards.

Pfister, The 216R (91S)   22 22 22 22 $151
424 E. Wisconsin Ave., Milwaukee; (414) 273-8222; (800) 558-8222; FAX: (414) 273-8082
■ "A native won't let you stay anywhere else" insist fans of this "classic old-world" "grande dame" with "one of the most impressive lobbies" around and "fabulous [Victorian] art in public areas"; the "lovely" "redone period rooms" in the "very cool" original 1893 eight-story section are complemented by the "very nice" newer tower rooms, and there's an indoor pool and guest use of the YMCA across the street; dining in the English Room and being "royally" treated by a staff that "knows how to run a hotel" are the final touches on this "little bit of heaven in Milwaukee."

Wyndham Milwaukee Center 219R (2S)   21 20 19 20 $126
139 E. Kilbourn Ave., Milwaukee; (414) 276-8686; (800) 996-3426; FAX: (414) 276-8007
☑ The "great location" (connected by walkway to the Repertory and Pabst Theaters and a 28-story office complex) makes this modern 10-story brick-and-stone Downtowner with "very nice public spaces" appealing as a "convention hotel", with a business center and meeting rooms for groups up to 575 and two restaurants serving American fare; the "small" rooms are "lovely" to some, and "attentive service" is another plus, but a few unenthused reviewers feel it "needs a spark."

Wisconsin Dells

Chula Vista Resort 120R (120S)   19 19 18 19 $119
4031 N. River Rd., Wisconsin Dells; (608) 254-8366; (800) 388-4782; FAX: (608) 254-7653
☑ For better or worse, "you know you're in the Dells" at this "nice but undistinguished" Southwestern theme resort in a popular family vacation area offering views of the Wisconsin River from a complex of cabins and motel units; but despite what some term "tacky at best" decor, the real news is moderate pricing for a wide array of activities, especially for children, including a water park, 18 holes of minigolf, five pools (indoor and outdoor), tennis courts, three whirlpools and hiking trails; 24 meeting rooms for groups up to 1,000 keep pencil-pushers occupied indoors.

Wyoming

	R	S	D	P	$

Jackson Hole Racquet Club Resort (120S)
20 **19** **19** **21** **$180**

3535 N. Moose-Wilson Rd., Jackson; (307) 733-3990; (800) 443-8616; FAX: (307) 733-5551
■ Nestled among aspen groves with a "spectacular view" of the Tetons, convenient to three ski areas and Yellowstone National Park, this condo resort offers "roomy" accommodations with "great facilities" (fireplace, full kitchen, washer/dryer); in summer the on-site golf course, tennis courts and athletic facility make it a favorite for corporate meetings, while in winter it's popular with families and groups skiing nearby Jackson Hole (five minutes away by free shuttle).

RUSTY PARROT LODGE 31R (1S)
25 **26** **22** **23** **$187**

PO Box 1657, 175 N. Jackson St., Jackson; (307) 733-2000; (800) 458-2004; FAX: (307) 733-5566
■ There's no squawking, just cooing about this "charming", "wonderfully cozy" Jackson Hole lodge that "looks like it was decorated by Ralph Lauren", "complete with teddy bears on the bed"; it's "a superb place to relax" after hiking, fishing or skiing in the "gorgeous" Grand Teton area, and now with the addition of a day spa and massage center it's "simply heaven" all day long, from the "great" full breakfast (included) to bedtime milk and cookies.

Snow King Resort 194R (60S)
16 **16** **15** **17** **$169**

PO Box SKI, 400 E. Snow King Ave., Jackson Hole; (307) 733-5200; (800) 522-KING; FAX: (307) 733-4086
☑ Geography trumps comfort as surveyors rave about the "great location", "gorgeous area" and "beautiful setting" of this "rustic ski lodge" at the base of Snow King Mountain, but critics claim "no king would stay" in "dark rooms" that "need upgrading"; '96 renovations (which also brought voicemail) may have helped, and other compensations include a heated outdoor pool, indoor ice skating, on-site dining, extensive meeting facilities and a free airport shuttle.

Spring Creek Resort 36R (79S)
24 **22** **23** **24** **$208**

1800 Spirit Dance Rd., Jackson; (307) 733-8833; (800) 443-6139; FAX: (307) 733-1524
■ "Divine", "beautiful", "spectacular" enthuse guests awed by the Tetons views at this resort set in "splendid isolation" north of Jackson; praise also goes to the "beautiful" accommodations, whether in hotel rooms with fireplaces and refrigerators or "neat" condos (though some condo "furnishings are dated and could use freshening up"); add "great" American food at the Granary restaurant and a year-round wealth of activities and you have a candidate for the "short list of exceptional resorts."

Teton Pines Resort 8R (8S)
23 **22** **20** **23** **$194**

3450 N. Clubhouse Dr., Jackson; (307) 733-1005; (800) 238-2223; FAX: (307) 733-2860
■ Guests soak up "wonderful Wyoming scenery" from room patios and from the Arnold Palmer–designed golf course (which turns into a x-country skiing area in winter) at this "fabulous" Western-style lodge at the foot of the Tetons; accommodations, though limited in number, are "very nice" and can be configured as single rooms or one- or two-bedroom suites; diversions include year-round tennis, swimming and fly fishing, while free perks include continental breakfast and shuttles to ski areas and the airport.

Wort Hotel 57R (3S)
18 **20** **18** **19** **$141**

50 N. Glenwood St., Jackson; (307) 733-2190; (800) THE-WORT; FAX: (307) 733-2067
☑ A real "throwback to the Wild West", from the "moose heads mounted on the wall" to the "must"-see Silver Dollar Bar (inlaid with more than 2,000 silver dollars); boosters call it a "pleasant" place to stay "in the heart" of Jackson with "cozy", "charming" rooms, but scoffers claim it "has been resting on its laurels for years"· basically it's "love it or leave it, Worts and all."

Cottonwoods Ranch 5R ⇗
– **–** **–** **–** **E**

PO Box 95, Moose; (307) 733-0945; FAX: (307) 733-1954
Accessible only by four-wheel drive, which may explain why surveyors don't know this rustic, backwoods mountain guest ranch; outstanding views of the Tetons, Fish Creek and the Gros Ventre Wilderness, on-site fishing and an almost unlimited expanse for hiking and horseback riding appeal to outdoorsy types in search of seclusion; accommodations are in five simple cabins with pine beds, but no TVs, phones or radios (bathrooms are in a modern bath house); N.B. rates include meals; no credit cards accepted.

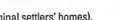
Moran

Colter Bay Village Cabins (208S) ▽ 14 | 14 | 14 | 20 | $81
PO Box 240, Grand Teton National Park, Moran; (307) 543-2811; (800) 628-9988;
FAX: (307) 543-3143
■ The log cabin lodgings are "rustic in the extreme" (some are original settlers' homes), "but with the beautiful surroundings" of Grand Teton National Park, "who cares?"; you "stay for the scenery, not the amenities", though the "basic" quarters (no phones, radios or TVs) "beat camping" (and if camping's your thing, Colter Bay Village also has tent cabins plus an RV park); the Jackson Lake locale is ideal for water sports and hiking, and you can fuel up on American fare at the Chuckwagon; open mid-May to late September.

Jackson Lake Lodge 381R (4S) 20 | 20 | 20 | 25 | $154
PO Box 240, Grand Teton National Park, Hwy. 89, Moran; (307) 543-3100; (800) 628-9988;
FAX: (307) 543-3143
■ "The setting is magnificent" at this "beautiful" resort in Grand Teton National Park offering "great views of wildlife", Jackson Lake and the mountains; nearby activities range from boating and fishing to hiking and horseback riding, and the "spectacular" Mural Room serves fine regional fare "with a view that can't be matched", but nitpickers note that rooms (in the main lodge or cottages) are "nothing special" – "like summer camp with a view, but what a view"; N.B. no TVs or radios; open mid-May to mid-October.

JENNY LAKE LODGE 31R (6S) 24 | 24 | 25 | 25 | $262
PO Box 240, Grand Teton National Park, Hwy. 89, Moran; (307) 733-4647; (800) 623-9988;
FAX: (307) 543-2869
■ Epitomizing "rustic luxury", Wyoming's top-rated property is a "gloriously underdone" resort that illustrates "how to rough it in style"; in an "incredible setting" in Grand Teton National Park, guests stay in cabins that are simple (no phones, radios or TVs) yet "elegant", enjoying "once-in-a-lifetime views", "first-rate service" and "very good food" (breakfast and dinner are included); while some find it "expensive", most agree it's well "worth it"; open mid-May to early October.

Yellowstone National Park

Lake Yellowstone Hotel 193R (103S) 18 | 19 | 18 | 22 | $124
PO Box 165, Yellowstone National Park; (307) 344-7901; FAX: (307) 344-7456
■ With a "beautiful natural setting" and "great ambiance" including evening chamber music, this "genteel" 1891 Victorian is "the place to stay" in Yellowstone National Park; some prefer the "wonderful" original building ("splurge for lake-view" rooms) rather than the annex ("verges on dumpy"), but in any case the "huge lounges" and public areas are "well maintained" and there's "surprisingly good food"; overall it's "bursting with charm", though it can also be bursting with "tour buses"; open May to October.

Mammoth Hot Springs Hotel 96R (126S) 13 | 16 | 16 | 18 | $99
PO Box 165, Yellowstone National Park; (307) 344-7901; FAX: (307) 344-7456
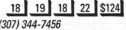 "The wildlife show right outside your window" and "the perfect location to view the Hot Springs" or enjoy fishing, hiking and horseback riding amid pretty Yellowstone scenery put some reviewers in a bubbly mood, but others boil about "dreary", "cramped rooms" at this "typical National Park lodge" built in the '30s; it's unquestionably a "bargain" though, and full breakfast is included; open May to October.

Old Faithful Inn 317R (8S) 17 | 19 | 17 | 24 | $124
PO Box 165, Yellowstone National Park; (307) 344-7901; FAX: (307) 344-7456
☑ An "American classic" in "a fascinating setting" next to Old Faithful Geyser and surrounded by "gorgeous" grounds; while admirers find the circa 1904 main building with its rustic log architecture and three-story stone fireplace "charming" ("skip the new wing" they advise), others spout off about "old", "funky" rooms and find the whole place "teeming with tourists" and "noisy"; still, most side with those who call it a "must-see-and-stay in Yellowstone"; closed May to October.

Carmel Valley: Bernardus Lodge
888 648 9463

Spas* S. BARB: BACARA

TOP 10 OVERALL

BEST OVERALL**
- **28** Golden Door/ Escondido, CA
- **26** Canyon Ranch/Tucson, AZ
  Canyon Ranch/Lenox, MA
  Givenchy/Palm Springs, CA
- **25** Spa Internazionale/Fisher Island, FL
  Spa at Doral/Miami, FL
- **24** Rancho La Puerta/Baja, Mexico
  Sonoma Mission Inn/Sonoma, CA
- **23** La Costa Spa/Carlsbad, CA
- **22** Lake Austin Spa Resort/Austin, TX

BEST VALUES
Kripalu Center/Lenox, MA
Indian Springs/Calistoga, CA
Lake Austin Spa Resort/Austin, TX
Palms/Palm Springs, CA
Sonoma Mission Inn/Sonoma, CA
Norwich Inn & Spa/Norwich, CT
Givenchy/Palm Springs, CA
Registry/Ft. Lauderdale, FL
La Costa Spa/Carlsbad, CA
New Age/Neversink, NY

R	S	D	P	$
▽ 12	20	18	19	VE

Ashram Retreat 5R
2025 N. McKain St., Calabasas, CA; (818) 222-6900
■ "You will lose weight and get fit" is the consensus from devotees and dropouts alike on this New Age "boot camp" 30 miles from LAX; a typical day includes early morning (6:30 AM) meditation followed by a challenging hike, free-weight workout, yoga class, massage and spartan low-carbo meals that match the minimalist decor; it's not for those who think a facial is life's greatest reward, but hardy celebs swear by its shared rooms and week-minimum regimen ($2,500).

---

* Most spas prohibit alcohol and smoking, many ban caffeine, and some have specific dietary restrictions, so be sure to check in advance. Minimum stays, where required, are noted, with nondiscounted rates.
** Based on overall ratings derived by averaging ratings for rooms, service, dining and public facilities; this list excludes places with low voting (▽)

Aveda Spa Retreat (15S)   - | - | - | - | E
1015 Cascade St., Osceola, WI; (800) 283-3202; FAX: (715) 294-2196
About an hour northeast of Minneapolis is this serene retreat owned by the Aveda Corp. and keyed to the same kind of environmentally aware, back-to-nature theme that marks its cosmetics products; 300 wooded acres offer hiking, biking, canoeing, x-country skiing and other activities, and there's a full menu of skin and body treatments using aromatic plant and flower essences; guestrooms are decorated with diverse antiques and Organica restaurant serves gourmet organic fare in an enclosed sun porch setting.

Birdwing Spa 9R (3S)   - | - | - | - | VE
21398 575th Ave., Litchfield, MN; (320) 693-6064; FAX: (320) 693-7026
This Tudor chalet's "great location" on a private Minnesota lakefront surrounded by 300 acres provides a year-round nature fix: guests can hike on 12 miles of trails, bike, x-country ski, skate, bird-watch and more, or head to the indoor fitness center to burn up even more of the controlled calories provided by the spa cuisine; hair and skin treatments help perk up the enervated; despite a 1995 renovation, some charge the place is "showing signs of wear."

Cal-a-Vie (24S)   ▽ 26 | 27 | 27 | 26 | VE
2249 Somerset Rd., Vista, CA; (760) 945-2055; FAX: (760) 630-0074
■ "Wow! – there are hardly enough words to describe the wonderful experience" at this elite, secluded spa in 150 woodsy and hilly acres 40 miles north of San Diego; "a fabulous week" (one-week minimum: $3,950) in the "luxurious" private villas spread around a central pool might include "great beauty treatments", "wonderful food", morning hikes, aerobics classes, weight training, stress reduction and enough hydrotherapy treatments and seaweed wraps to suit a mermaid; a few dynamos dis a "weak fitness" program.

CANYON RANCH HEALTH &   25 | 27 | 26 | 27 | VE
FITNESS RESORT 150R (40S)
8600 E. Rockcliff Rd., Tucson, AZ; (520) 749-9000; (800) 726-9900; FAX: (520) 749-7755
■ "Who cares that it costs $1,000 per pound? – it's worth it" swear supporters of this "fabulously run" "adult summer camp" (where a four-night minimum is actually $1,548) in a "beautiful" desert setting; the emphasis is on fitness but sports activities, body treatments, spiritual awareness classes and metaphysical services (dubbed "New Age nausea" by nonbelievers) are also available, along with "excellent food" and "relentlessly cheerful, friendly" staffers; P.S. rooms "vary with price – go for the best."

CANYON RANCH IN THE BERKSHIRES 96R (24S)   24 | 27 | 25 | 28 | VE
165 Kemble St., Lenox, MA; (413) 637-4100; (800) 726-9900; FAX: (413) 637-0057
■ "Life-altering", "the zenith of spas" typifies praise for this standout built around a stately Berkshires mansion; devotees deem it "classier" than its older sibling in Tucson, with "incredibly well-trained" staff and "state-of-the-art" facilities that make it "worth" the cost (three-night minimum in high season: $1,579); if rooms (in a modern New England–style inn) strike some as "pleasant but boring", the 120-acre setting ameliorates with hiking, tennis and more; as for food, big eaters claim you "starve to death", but more side with the voter who "ate like a queen."

Carmel Country Spa 22R   ▽ 24 | 23 | 24 | 25 | M
10¹ Country Club Way, Carmel, CA; (408) 659-3486; (800) KOUNTRY; FAX: (408) 659-5022
☑ "A delight" for some in an idyllic California locale, this "comfortable" if basic spa is "cheaper and more low-key than most", offering a range of wholesome activities such as hiking in the green hills, low-impact aerobics and yoga classes, swimming or aquatics in the heated pool and beauty treatments in the salon; there's a two-night minimum ($284) with special weekly packages in November and December.

Cooper Wellness Program 51R (12S)   ▽ 19 | 22 | 19 | 21 | $203
12230 Preston Rd., Dallas, TX; (972) 386-4777; (800) 444-5192; FAX: (972) 386-0039
■ At his world-renowned Cooper Aerobics Center in Dallas, aerobics pioneer Dr. Kenneth H. Cooper has designed a Wellness Program for those who want to get serious about rejuvenation, fitness and good health; guests stay in a colonial-style inn and follow a personalized program built around cardio exercise, tennis, swimming, lectures, "healthy, very good" meals and cooking demos, stop-smoking techniques and optional full medical testing; stays can be as brief as one day, but longer visits are encouraged.

Deerfield Manor Spa 22R   ▽ 18 | 23 | 22 | 21 | M
650 Resica Falls Rd., East Stroudsburg, PA; (717) 223-0160; (800) 852-4494; FAX: (717) 223-8270
■ "Friendly and low-key", this intimate spa in a white shingled house nestled in the Pocono Mountains wins praise for its "warm, supportive staff, interesting guests" and "food so good it's shocking to discover it's healthy"; a typical day might include hiking, exercise, tennis, swimming and beauty treatments; there's a minimum two-night stay ($270), plus reasonable weekend and weekly rates; open late March–mid-November.

Franklin Quest Institute of Fitness 118R ▽ 17 | 19 | 14 | 19 | M
(fka National Institute of Fitness)
202 N. Snow Canyon Rd., Ivins, UT; (801) 673-4905; (800) 407-3002; FAX: (801) 673-1363
■ "Excellent value" is a major appeal of this no-nonsense modern spa in southwest Utah where one-week-minimum stays start at $695; even those who cite "sparse accommodations" and call it "a little preachy on vegan vegetarianism" (nonvegan fare is also served) admit it's a "great place to lose weight", engage in some "serious physical conditioning" in the new fitness center or simply "recharge" via hiking in glorious Snow Canyon State Park or options like the Franklin Quest time management seminar.

GIVENCHY HOTEL & SPA 40R (70S) 25 | 26 | 26 | 26 | $290
4200 E. Palm Canyon Dr., Palm Springs, CA; (760) 770-5000; (800) 276-5000; FAX: (760) 324-7280
▣ This French Renaissance–style newcomer (with 12 luxury villas and several gardens) on 14 acres at the foot of the San Jacinto Mountains is considered "the ultimate" by most early enthusiasts who also applaud the "best restaurant in the Coachella Valley" (the Franco-Californian menu was created by two-Michelin-star chef Gérard Vié); surveyors who shape up with fitness classes, tennis, swimming and à la carte (and pricey) beauty treatments can pour the results into something new and fetching – there is, *bien sûr*, a Givenchy boutique; a few sniff "overrated" but they're a minority.

GOLDEN DOOR (39S) 28 | 28 | 27 | 28 | VE
777 Deer Springs Rd., Escondido, CA; (760) 744-5777; (800) 424-0777; FAX: (760) 471-2393
■ Once again the *Survey*'s top spa overall, this "superb, small" Japanese-style "paradise" set in landscaped gardens "does everything well" for its "fantastic clientele" (only 39 guests per week); it's "very expensive but worth it" for "personalized programs" selected from 40 classes, top spa cuisine by celebrated chef Michel Stroot and "comfortable" if spare private accommodations (each featuring a *tokonoma* – a decorative shrine with fresh flower arrangement) that provide a restful "retreat" for "privacy, fulfillment and growth"; some "wish they allowed shorter visits" (the one-week minimum stay is an all-inclusive $4,500), and it's usually women-only, but there are some coed and men-only weeks.

Greenhouse, The 33R (2S) ▽ 29 | 29 | 28 | 28 | VE
PO Box 1144, 1171 107th St., Arlington, TX; (817) 640-4000; FAX: (817) 649-0422
■ For women only, this tony suburban Dallas shrine to fitness and beauty earns top-notch ratings from the few surveyors who voted on it; attracting socialites, names in the news and career women, it offers personalized exercise and grooming regimens as well as special programs geared to changing themes; a "fantastic staff" adds to the "wonderful" experience, as do such luxuries as breakfast in bed, poolside lunch and candlelit spa cuisine dinners; needless to say, it's expensive (one-week minimum: $4,000).

Green Mountain At Fox Run 23R – | – | – | – | E
Box 164, Fox Ln., Ludlow, VT; (802) 228-8885; (800) 448-8106; FAX: (802) 228-8887
Women only come for one-week-minimum stays ($1,150) at this weight-loss, no-fad-diet spa in the Green Mountains with a "youthful, energetic staff"; some surveyors aren't energized by the lodgings ("too spartan for me", "ain't no Ritz-Carlton"), but then interior design isn't supposed to be the focus: exercise, nutrition and long-term behavior modification are; guests also enjoy jogging, biking, swimming, hiking and antiquing trips into town; massage and beauty treatments are à la carte.

Green Valley Spa & Tennis Resort (100S) ▽ 25 | 24 | 24 | 24 | VE
1871 W. Canyon View Dr., St. George, UT; (801) 628-8060; (800) 237-1068; FAX: (801) 673-4084
■ "If you love hiking over beautiful red rocks, then getting pampered" with a "good combination of exercise and spa treatments", you're likely to agree with those who call this Southwestern-style spa "heaven on earth"; set in a dazzling, remote part of Utah near Zion National Park and adorned with Native American artifacts, it offers aerobics, yoga, tennis (through the Vic Braden Tennis College), massage, meditation and more, not to mention "good value" (three-night minimum: $960).

Gurney's Inn 59R (50S) 18 | 19 | 18 | 20 | VE
Old Montauk Hwy., Montauk, NY; (516) 668-2345; (800) GURNEYS; FAX: (516) 668-3576
▣ Location, location: a "superb" oceanfront setting near the star-studded Long Island enclaves of East Hampton and Amagansett is still this veteran's major lure; some also laud the "fine" spa facilities, "great" indoor salt-water pool and "delicious" food, calling it a relaxing "getaway for NYers"; yet despite a recent renovation, we still hear complaints that "rooms aren't great" at this ex-motel and it's "time to refurbish"; there's a four-night summer minimum ($1,240).

Spas

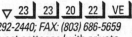

R | S | D | P | $

Heartland Spa 14R

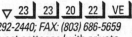

▽ | 14 | 23 | 24 | 21 | $241

Box 181, R.R. 1, Kam Lake Estate, Gilman, IL; (815) 683-2182; (800) 545-HTLD; FAX: (815) 683-2144

◧ This homey, unpretentious ex-farmhouse on 32 rural acres south of Chicago wins high marks for its heartland spa cuisine and offers a range of activities including exercise classes, x-country skiing, water bikes for the on-site lake, an adventure program designed to build self-esteem and nearby horseback riding; supporters "love it" even if they find the decor "sparse", while the less impressed say "nice, but that's all"; two-for-one deals (two-night minimum) help cut costs.

Hilton Head Health Institute (55S)

▽ | 23 | 23 | 20 | 22 | VE

14 Valencia Rd., Hilton Head Island, SC; (803) 785-7292; (800) 292-2440; FAX: (803) 686-5659

■ It's on the beautiful resort island of Hilton Head and its guest cottages (with private bedrooms and baths) adjoin a golf course, but this facility has a serious mission: helping clients achieve long-term weight control and improved overall health; the week-minimum program ($1,695) focuses on weight loss, cholesterol reduction, smoking cessation and stress management via exercise, seminars, counseling and nutritious, low-fat meals; biking, hiking and jogging are on-site and there's "good tennis" nearby.

Hippocrates Health Institute 15R (11S)

– | – | – | – | VE

1443 Palmdale Ct., West Palm Beach, FL; (407) 471-8876; (800) 842-2125; FAX: (407) 471-9464

A wholly holistic enterprise emphasizing spirituality, revitalization and maintenance rather than fitness and beauty, an approach that's "fantastic" to some voters, less appealing to others; guests stay in cottages on a 10-acre wooded estate in West Palm Beach and enjoy 100-percent vegan meals (veggie and fruit juices only for breakfast), nonstressful exercise, massage ozonated pools and other detoxifiers; one-week minimum: $1,500.

Indian Springs Resort & Spa 16R (1S)

20 | 23 | – | 21 | $147

1712 Lincoln Ave., Calistoga, CA; (707) 942-4913; FAX: (707) 942-4919

■ Admirers are afraid of "letting the secret out" about this "original", "low-key gem" located on an ancient volcanic bed in the heart of California wine country where you can sink into a mud bath made with volcanic ash (a "memorable life experience"), indulge in a mineral bath treatment or take a dip in an Olympic-size mineral pool fed by three geysers; "charming little well-appointed cabins" with kitchenettes and fireplaces appeal to most, but a few just "go for the mud bath and massage"; N.B. no restaurant on-site.

Kerr House 5R

– | – | – | – | VE

17777 Beaver St., Grand Rapids, OH; (419) 832-1733; FAX: (419) 832-4303

Breakfast in bed begins a day of exercise, body treatments and stress management in a restored 1880 Victorian mansion set near a canal south of Toledo; eight guests at a time (usually all women) check in for five-day, weekend or day programs aimed at restoring mind-body balance through yoga, aerobics, massage and the like, with fuel provided by meals low in fat, sodium and calories; while there's lots to do on-site, there's also hiking, fishing, boating and more nearby.

Kripalu Center for Yoga & Health 111R

11 | 17 | 16 | 18 | I

Box 793, West St./Rte. 183, Lenox, MA; (413) 448-3152; (800) 741-7353; FAX: (413) 448-3196

◧ "No stress from arrival to departure" and a "sense of spirituality and community" draw the dedicated to this former seminary in the Berkshires, where the "pastoral setting" yields lovely lake and mountain views, but looking inward via yoga and self-discovery programs are the star attractions; not everyone warms to "spartan, cell-like rooms" and some find the ambiance "a bit too New Agey", but vegetarians "love" the "greens and beans" food and as the Survey's best spa value it's judged "great for the price" (two-night minimum: $150).

La Costa Resort And Spa 414R (64S)

23 | 23 | 23 | 25 | $269

Costa del Mar Rd., Carlsbad, CA; (619) 438-9111; (800) 854-5000; FAX: (619) 931-7585

◧ For admirers "this must be the Garden of Eden", a pampering "paradise" on 450 acres of "beautiful" grounds north of San Diego; in addition to spa services there are nutrition, fitness and lifestyle programs, 21 tennis courts, two 18-hole golf courses, four restaurants and 15 meeting rooms – "all top drawer" to some, but "mass market" to the less enchanted; N.B. a multiphase renovation currently in the works should address repeated concerns that it's "showing its age", but watch out for "rooms that haven't been redone."

Lake Austin Spa Resort 40R

20 | 23 | 24 | 20 | $213

1705 S. Quinlan Park Rd., Austin, TX; (512) 266-2444; (800) 847-5637; FAX: (512) 266-1572

◧ A low-key lakefront resort in Texas Hill Country that posts respectable scores all-around and gets a special nod for healthy Southwestern cuisine that's "surprisingly good – you could almost say delicious"; guests can rev up with hiking, biking, swimming and exercise classes, or relax with yoga, massage and stress management techniques; nonbelievers liken it to "summer camp for big people": two-night minimum: $677.

359

Lido Spa 106R (15S) ▽ 15 17 18 17 $305

40 Island Ave., Miami Beach, FL; (305) 538-4621; (800) 327-8363; FAX: (305) 534-3680

■ Weight loss and healthy living are the goals at this relaxed spa catering to a mostly older clientele on a residential island in Biscayne Bay; exercise, massage, sauna and swimming in two saltwater pools are included in the rates but scheduled only when the guests feel up to it – no rigorous routine here; open October–May, no smoking or alcohol.

Lodge at Skylonda 15R ▽ 23 27 24 25 VE
(fka Skylonda Fitness Retreat)

16350 Skyline Blvd., Woodside, CA; (415) 851-4500; (800) 851-2222; FAX: (415) 851-5504

■ This "perfect getaway" spa in a large-scale log cabin among magnificent redwoods and madrona about an hour from San Francisco is being renovated by new management (the folks from Post Ranch Inn and San Ysidro) as we go to press, focusing on enlarging rooms and bathrooms, and adding oversized tubs and decks; previous guests lauded its emphasis on "inspirational hikes" through "beautiful scenery", with yoga, strength conditioning, meditation and aquatics classes also part of the program, as well as salon services and spa cuisine; it reopened May 1 with a two-night minimum; $790.

Mario's International Hotel & Spa 13R (1S) ▽ 18 20 19 18 $187
(aka Aurora House Spa)

35 Garfield Rd., Aurora, OH; (216) 562-9171; FAX: (216) 562-2386

■ Beauty gets equal billing with fitness at this country hotel/spa boasting a full menu of facials, scrubs, wraps, massage and grooming sessions, plus consultations by plastic surgeons from the Cleveland Clinic; relaxation and pampering are the main goals, but working out isn't ignored: there are exercise sessions, indoor and outdoor pools plus nearby tennis, waterskiing and even ice skating; tip: "if going for a day, try not to go on a weekend."

Miraval 106R (11S) ▽ 28 27 29 29 $569

5000 E. Via Estancia Miraval, Catalina, AZ; (520) 825-4000; (800) 825-4000; FAX: (520) 792-5870

■ "Awesome – the best thought-out, most relaxing spa" where "you can exercise your mind as well as your body" coo soothed initiates of this "beautiful" Santa Fe–style newcomer in the spectacular Sonoran Desert near Tucson; "very personalized" programs range from mountain hiking, horseback riding and rock climbing to quieter pursuits such as yoga, tai chi, meditation (emphasized) and body treatments ("the hot stone massage is a must"); it may still "need a little work", but stellar ratings from the limited number who've tried it mean this is one to watch.

New Age Health Spa 41R 12 17 16 16 E

Rte. 55, Neversink, NY; (914) 985-7601; (800) 682-4348; FAX: (914) 985-2467

☑ "Clean, upbeat, a good value" chant supporters of this "no-pretensions" Catskills spa with a mindset befitting its proximity to Woodstock – it's strong on yoga, tai chi and healthy (mostly Vegetarian) eating and is "always evolving and getting better" (ongoing renovations are adding a new fitness facility, Jacuzzi, solarium and more); the mantra from others is mixed: "nothing special but pleasant", "for New Agers and the emotionally needy", but most agree "you get your money's worth"; two-night minimum: $338.

Northern Pines 14R (10S) – – – – E

559 N. Rte. 85, Raymond, ME; (207) 655-7624; FAX: (207) 655-3321

A no-frills, holistic health and weight-loss spa set amid 70 acres of pine forest on a Southern Maine lakefront; it offers rooms in the main lodge, log cabins and even a yurt, Vegetarian cuisine (guests can help in the kitchen) with a special regimen for fasters, and activities that focus on stretching, yoga and massage (there's plenty of outdoor exercise too); the main season is late June–October 20, but private retreats can be arranged at other times (with x-country skiing in winter), and there's a conference center for groups up to 75.

Norwich Inn & Spa 65R (75S) 20 21 21 21 $222

607 W. Thames St./Rte. 32, Norwich, CT; (860) 886-2401; (800) 275-4772; FAX: (860) 886-9483

☑ It's "a godsend in an area bereft of spas", but even fans say this 1929 Georgian-style inn plus numerous villas on 40 "lovely" acres is "pleasant but a little tired", with some rooms in the main building "in desperate need of an upgrade" – "after refurbishment [a two-year redo and expansion is in the works] it will hopefully be restored to its former glory"; in the meantime, there's a "friendly staff", "nice mix of men and women", swimming pools, tennis, jogging trails and a choice of á la carte classes and treatments (book well ahead of time); "adequate but no raves" sums it up for now.

Spas

Oaks at Ojai 43R
15 | 20 | 18 | 18 | M

122 E. Ojai Ave., Ojai, CA; (805) 646-5573; (800) 753-OAKS; FAX: (805) 640-1504
☑ Reasonable rates (two-night minimum from $270) and "very good classes" (take your pick from 16 a day) are the draw at this "poor man's spa" where "spa is short for spartan" – as in "motel-type accommodations" and "they tried to starve me to death" cuisine; but the "staff makes all feel energized and healthy", beauty and body treatments are available on an à la carte basis, and golf, tennis, bicycling and shopping are minutes away; best of all, "you can afford it."

Palm-Aire Resort & Spa 12R (77S)
20 | 19 | 17 | 20 | $242

2601 Palm-Aire Dr. N., Pompano Beach, FL; (954) 972-3300; (800) 2-PALM-AIR; FAX: (954) 968-2711
☑ While a few chat up this "good spa with good food" in a resort condo complex (with 37 tennis courts, five golf courses, a large fitness center, racquetball and squash courts), more shrug "so-so, no big deal" and suggest it's "not what it was"; nevertheless, those who tire of the long roster of outdoor activities can enjoy hand and foot paraffin treatments, loofah body scrubs and a full range of relaxation therapy, as well as virtuous meals in the Spa Dining Room (for those who can't face another plate of vegetables, other restaurants are available.)

Palms at Palm Springs 37R
17 | 20 | 19 | 19 | E

572 N. Indian Canyon Dr., Palm Springs, CA; (760) 325-1111; (800) 753-7256; FAX: (760) 327-0867
☑ "It isn't fancy or posh" but loyalists say "the lovely people know how to pamper" at this "good-value" spa in Downtown Palm Springs; mountain hiking, skiing, golf and horseback riding complement 14 daily exercise classes and a full range of massages, facials and wraps; there's a two-night minimum ($319) plus five- and seven-night packages that include all fitness programs and spa cuisine; but despite its charms, even friends agree the "equipment is not up to date", "rooms are plain" and a "face-lift" is overdue for this old-time Hollywood favorite.

Pritikin Longevity Center 88R (12S)
▽ 16 | 21 | 17 | 17 | VE

5875 Collins Ave., Miami Beach, FL; (305) 866-2237; (800) 327-4914; FAX: (305) 866-1872
■ "Miraculous results – a real winner" enthuse slimmed-down respondents about this "clinic with individual attention paid to all by excellent health professionals"; there's intensive education in behavioral change for eating and living right to "help save your life", with meals that are low-fat and "well prepared"; not for laid-back pleasure seekers, this no alcohol, smoking or caffeine spa (with a sister branch in Santa Monica) demands serious commitment or it may feel a little regimented; one-week minimum ($3,800), with two- and three-week programs available.

Raj, The 18R (9S)
– | – | – | – | VE

1734 Jasmine Ave., Fairfield, IA; (515) 472-9580; (800) 248-9050; FAX: (515) 472-2496
"Nice views" of meadows and woods and "good rooms" please visitors to this luxuriously appointed spa set on 100 acres of Iowa countryside; dedicated to rejuvenation through modern medicine combined with natural healing techniques based on the ancient Maharishi Ayur-Veda system, it offers three-, five- and seven-day packages that place less emphasis on exercise, more on improving mind/body balance through herbal and oil treatments, vegetarian diet and more; three-day minimum is $1,611.

Rancho La Puerta 88R *TONY'S FAVOURITE*
24 | 24 | 23 | 25 | VE

Tecate, Baja Calif., Mexico; (619) 744-4222; (800) 443-7565; FAX: (619) 744-5007
■ This "comfortable", "down-to-earth" fave set on 3,000 "beautiful" acres on the Baja Peninsula rates raves for its "lovely Mexican decor, laid-back staff and interesting food" that's mostly Vegetarian and grown on-site; gung-ho guests can sign up for hiking in the high desert, weight training and aerobics, while mellower visitors can lounge in the shade or pamper their bodies at the separate Women's and Men's Health Centers; it's a sibling of the Golden Door but more "affordable", which is why many make it an "every year" habit (one-week minimum: $1,636).

Regency House Natural Health Spa 32R (30S)
▽ 16 | 19 | 19 | 16 | M

2000 S. Ocean Dr., Hallandale, FL; (954) 454-2220; (800) 454-0003; FAX: (954) 454-4637
☑ This "health-oriented, Vegetarian" spa on the beach is "not luxurious", but it suits a certain clientele that finds it "very special – one of a kind"; weight loss and fitness are the focus of a week of lectures, yoga, aerobics, aquatics, body massage, skin care treatments and walks on the beach, along with a menu that's alcohol and caffeine free (juice fasts and detox regimens are also available); although some complain that "rooms are the worst", for those into holistic health, psychic astrology and chiropractic care it's "hard to beat"; one-week minimum is $695.

R S D P $

Registry Resort & Spa 404R (96S)
19 | 20 | 19 | 21 | $223

(fka Bonaventure Resort & Spa)
250 Racquet Club Rd., Fort Lauderdale, FL; (954) 389-3300; (800) 327-8090; FAX: (954) 384-0563

▐ Under new ownership and name, the former Bonaventure is undergoing a $10-million restoration – a good thing since pre-redo patrons agreed it had "great golf" and "beautiful grounds" but needed "upgrading"; both a spa and full resort complex, it offers five restaurants (including a Spa Dining Room), children's programs, two championship golf courses, 15 tennis courts, five pools, exercise classes and an extensive array of body treatments ranging from herbal wraps to facials and massage therapy; spa packages with golf or tennis are available.

Safety Harbor Resort and Spa 173R
18 | 22 | 21 | 21 | $236

105 N. Bayshore Dr., Safety Harbor, FL; (813) 726-1161; (888) BEST-SPA; FAX: (813) 726-4268

▐ "Outstanding cuisine, beautiful scenery" and a "terrific array of classes with great teachers" have kept this venerable 22-acre complex a contender on the Tampa Bay waterfront scene since 1945; it emphasizes aqua sports and tennis (there's a tennis academy and nine courts), but doesn't skimp on exercise, offering cardiovascular and weight training classes, and for the extra-determined, programs run with Outward Bound; there's also a body care center for the requisite soothing and smoothing; but it's an "old property" and critics think there's "plenty of room for improvement on all fronts" – perhaps a '96 room redo has helped.

Shangri-La Historic Inn, Resort & Spa 56R (4S)
– | – | – | – | VE

27580 Old 41 Rd., Bonita Springs, FL; (941) 992-3811; (800) 279-3811; FAX: (941) 947-9079
There's a feel of old Florida in this Spanish-style inn on eight subtropical acres with gardens and streams near Naples; its emphasis is partly on weight loss and fitness with three meal plans (natural hygiene, Vegetarian spa and à la carte), exercise machines, classes, tennis and swimming, and partly on stress reduction with yoga, forays to the Gulf beach and a host of wraps, massages, scrubs and facials to choose from.

SONOMA MISSION INN & SPA 167R (3S)
22 | 24 | 24 | 24 | $247

18140 Sonoma Hwy. 12, Sonoma, CA; (707) 938-9000; (800) 862-4945; FAX: (707) 996-5358

▐ A "pink pleasure palace" in California wine country, this spa for hedonists "indulges the body and soul" with "superior service" and "superb restaurants" (but "forget diets"); San Franciscans have taken the waters from hot artesian wells here since the turn of the century, and today's guests can also choose from vigorous workouts in an array of classes, "stunning AM walks", swims, cycling and body treatments in a nonregimented smoke-free atmosphere; the downside: "cramped rooms" (though some were renovated in '96) and a location "too close to traffic"· two-night minimum on weekends ($510).

SPA AT DORAL (48S)
25 | 25 | 25 | 26 | VE

8755 NW 36th St., Miami, FL; (305) 593-6030; (800) 71-DORAL; FAX: (305) 591-6630

▐ "Heaven on earth", "especially if your husband prefers golf to spa activities" enthuse fans of this "beautiful" self-contained facility adjacent to a 650-acre fully equipped resort with five golf courses and 15 tennis courts; but while it may be "the last word in luxury" to some, a few dissenters complain that staff should "lose the attitude" and suggest it's "time for a makeover" (a 1996 $30-million renovation should certainly help); the list of pampering and fitness options is massive, and there's a variety of packages that include most everything; two-night minimum is $674.

Spa at Grand Lake 75R
▽ 13 | 19 | 14 | 13 | $170

1667 Exeter Rd., Lebanon, CT; (860) 642-4306; (800) 843-7721; FAX: (860) 642-4799

▐ Despite its "not fancy", "no-frills" ambiance, several patrons say this weight-loss spa in the northeastern Connecticut countryside offers "lots for your money" such as a "caring staff" and exercise classes, tennis, swimming, cooking classes and hikes in a nearby state park; the "good", "plain fare" is low-fat, no-salt, no-sugar and the "simple but clean" rooms come equipped with TVs and a/c; open April–December.

SPA INTERNAZIONALE AT THE FISHER ISLAND CLUB 12R (48S)
26 | 25 | 24 | 25 | $558

656-700)

1 Fisher Island Dr., Fisher Island, FL; (305) 535-6030; (800) 485-3708; FAX: (305) 535-6032

■ "Great spa, the closest thing to leaving the country without actually leaving" is an early take on this posh "no pressure" newcomer in a 1926 Vanderbilt estate on a private tropical island an eight-minute ferry ride from Miami; an elite international clientele feels at home in the luxurious surroundings, but the attitude toward fitness is all-American enthusiasm with state-of-the-art equipment, a menu of classes from spinning to body sculpting, pools, Jacuzzis, heart-healthy food and extensive body pampering; three- and seven-night packages available.

LHotels: 800 223 6800

Structure House, Inc. (75S)   – – – – VE
3017 Pickett Rd., Durham, NC; (919) 493-4205; (800) 553-0052; FAX: (919) 490-0191
Weight loss and long-term maintenance are the goal at this serious, medically supervised spa on 21 acres in Durham, where the meals (which meet American Heart Association guidelines) and exercise regimens (yoga, cardio training, water aerobics) are designed to help clients alter future behavior and achieve lifetime weight control; the Life Extension Center, which houses the gym, pools and more, has recently been expanded with Cybex equipment; lodgings are in private one- and two-bedroom apartments, with a one-week minimum stay of $1,599.

Ten Thousand Waves/House of the Moon (8S) – – – – M
2451 Hyde Park Rd., Santa Fe, NM; (505) 982-9304; FAX: (505) 989-5077
East meets West at this Japanese health spa just outside Santa Fe; on the menu: hot and cold baths (both communal and individual, including a pebble-bottomed Kojiro bath), massage (ranging from shiatsu, watsu and reflexology to Japanese-style group massage), aromatherapy, facials, herbal wraps and ayurvedic treatments; though primarily a day spa, accommodations (all with luxury futons, voicemail and coffeemakers, many with fireplaces) are available at the neighboring Houses of the Moon.

Vatra Mountain Valley Lodge & Spa 27R (48S) ▽ 17 19 16 17 $187
(fka Mountain Valley Health Resort)
PO Box F, Rte. 214, Hunter, NY; (518) 263-4919; (800) 232-2772; FAX: (518) 263-4994
■ "Rustic but nice", this "inexpensive" Catskill Mountains spa fulfills its pound-shedding promises with Vegetarian vittles, exercise classes, hiking, mountain biking and swimming in indoor and outdoor pools, plus nearby golf, horseback riding and skiing; the full spa program is offered from late March–mid-November, with skiing taking over as the main focus in winter; antiquing in nearby Woodstock is a bonus.

Westglow Spa 6R (2S)   – – – – VE
Hwy. 221 S., Blowing Rock, NC; (704) 295-4463; (800) 562-0807; FAX: (704) 295-5115
A pillared 1916 mansion on a 20-acre estate in the Blue Ridge Mountains is a pleasant getaway year-round and especially "super in the fall"; rooms are outfitted with period furnishings and the emphasis is on both fitness and emotional well-being, with activities ranging from hiking, biking, tennis, aerobics and indoor swimming to massage, beauty treatments, stress management counseling, cooking classes and more; there's a two-night weekend minimum ($650) and various packages.

Hotels and Resorts With Significant Spa Facilities
(Full reviews and ratings for the following can be found in the Hotels, Resorts & Inns section of this *Survey*)

Abbey Resort & Fontana Spa, Fontana, WI
Either à la carte or flexible one- to five-day plans are available at the European-style spa offering wraps, scrubs, phyto-aromatherapy body massages, fitness classes, facials and cardiovascular weight training.

Bally's Park Place – A Hilton Casino Resort, Atlantic City, NJ
Spa packages for the $28-million, 40,000-square-foot facility include tower rooms, meals and various pampering services; also available are one-on-one workouts, fitness assessments and an aerobics studio.

Broadmoor, The, Colorado Springs, CO
Try the golf or tennis packages combined with spa treatments at this European-style resort where you can take the waters of Broadmoor Falls or experience hydrotherapy, wraps, skin care and fitness classes.

Claremont Resort & Spa, The, Berkeley, CA
Year-round offerings at this fitness/beauty facility range all the way from preventive medicine and yoga to fitness classes, massages and body scrubs; overnight packages and à la carte services are available.

Coolfont Resort, Berkeley Springs, WV
The Spectrum Spa at Coolfont provides exercise and pampering including fitness classes at a 14,000-square-foot center, spa cuisine, wellness seminars, reflexology, reiki treatments, kinesiology (using biofeedback), scrubs, beauty treatments and wraps.

Fontainebleau Hilton Resort & Towers, Miami Beach, FL
Choose from pampering or fitness programs at this 30,000-square-foot beachside spa boasting individual mineral baths, personal trainers, Cybex, Nautilus and cardiovascular equipment and the Adrien Arpel Salon.

Grand Wailea Resort, Hotel & Spa, Wailea, Maui, HI
The 50,000-square-foot Spa Grande at the Grand Wailea combines Hawaiian healing techniques with European rejuvenation therapies, offering beauty and exercise options.

Greenbrier, The, White Sulphur Springs, WV
Mineral baths, beauty treatments and use of fitness equipment like Nautilus, Airdyne and Lifecycle can be combined with elaborate spa packages at the Greenbrier Spa.

Hilton Waikoloa Village Resort, Kamuela, Big Island, HI
The vast resort complex sports a 25,000-square-foot spa featuring cardiovascular and weight training rooms, yoga, tai chi and water aerobics, ocean rejuvenation retreats and a full-service beauty salon.

Hyatt Regency Kauai, Kauai, HI
The 25,000-square-foot ANARA Spa takes 'A New Age Restorative Approach' to revitalizing the mind, body and spirit, offering outdoor lava rock showers and sunrise fitness walks along with the usual array of fitness classes and equipment and beauty and body treatments, including six types of massage.

Ihilani Resort & Spa, Kapolei, HI
Hawaiian thalassotherapy spotlights this resort's holistic approach to health programs, using a 35,000-square-foot fitness center and offering tai chi, yoga, sports training, Roman pools, a Spa Cafe and a beauty salon.

Kingsmill Resort, Williamsburg, VA
Fitness is emphasized at the 7,600-square-foot center with Cybex, Keiser, Nordic Track and Stairmasters; there are also yoga, water aerobics, hair and skin treatments available.

Lodge and Spa at Cordillera, Edwards, CO
There are 37 beauty treatments to choose from at this spa offering wellness programs, aromatherapy, thalassotherapy, yoga, aerobics and packages combining golf or skiing.

Marriott Camelback Inn, Resort, Golf Club & Spa, Scottsdale, AZ
Besides Ayurvedic herbal body treatments, loofah rooms, a salon, Sprouts spa cuisine restaurant and fitness equipment, one can try aeroboxing (aerobics/boxing), fitness and lifestyle evaluations pioneered by Dallas' Institute for Aerobic Research and even adobe clay purification treatments inspired by Native American health rituals at this 27,000-square-foot spa.

MGM Grand, Las Vegas, NV
European facials, massages and herbal wraps are typical beauty treatments at this spa attached to the casino/hotel, offering weight loss programs and numerous fitness options with an economical $20-per-day charge for use of steam, sauna, whirlpools, cardiovascular and strength training equipment.

Nemacolin Woodlands Resort, Farmington, PA
The Woodlands Spa features fitness classes, a beauty salon, massages and day packages, as well as personal trainers and seasonal golf/spa packages.

PGA National Resort & Spa, Palm Beach, FL
Lifestyle enhancement programs complement the spa's full range of exercise, training, hydrotherapy, massages and body treatments, highlighted by herbal Krauter baths and craniosacral therapy.

Phoenician, The, Scottsdale, AZ
There's a combo golf-and-spa package at this year-round resort which offers lifestyle counseling at its Centre for Well-Being, part of the no smoking/no alcohol/ no caffeine regimen; on the 'yes' side of the coin, there's a full range of beauty and fitness treatments.

Spa Hotel & Casino, Palm Springs, CA
The Agua Caliente natural mineral hot springs form the basis for this resort's rejuvenation program utilizing individual sunken marble tubs as well as plenty of massages, skin treatments, body therapies and eucalyptus sauna.

Topnotch at Stowe Resort & Spa, Stowe, VT
Three exercise studios, a beauty salon and other amenities are available with tennis and golf packages as well as skiing.

Two Bunch Palms, Desert Hot Springs, CA
Any month except August you can utilize this famous spa's variety of mudbath treatments, Swiss Wassertanzen hydrotherapy, watsu (mineral water yoga), or the usual massage and body care services.

Special Features
and Appeals

Airport Convenience

Alabama
Birmingham:
Sheraton Birmingham (H)

Alaska
Anchorage:
Regal Alaskan (H)
Fairbanks:
Fairbanks Princess (H)

Arizona
Phoenix/Scottsdale:
Embassy Scottsdale (H)

California
Costa Mesa:
Country Side Inn (H)
Marriott Costa Mesa (H)
Red Lion (H)
Westin South Coast (H)
Irvine:
Hilton Orange County (H)
Hyatt Reg. Irvine (H)
Irvine Marriott (H)
Los Angeles:
Barnabey's (H)
Doubletree LAX (H)
Marriott LAX (H)
Renaissance LA (H)
Ritz Marina del Rey (H)
Wyndham LAX (H)
Newport Beach:
Four Seasons Newport (H)
Hyatt Newporter (R)
Marriott Suites (H)
Sutton Place (H)
Palm Springs:
Hilton Palm Springs (H)
Hyatt Reg. Palm Springs (H)
La Mancha (R)
Monte Vista (H)
Spa (H)
Wyndham Palm Springs (H)
San Diego:
Embassy San Diego (H)
Horton Grand (H)
Kona Kai (R)
Sheraton San Diego (H)
Westin San Diego (H)
Wyndham Emerald (H)

Florida
Fort Lauderdale:
Wyndham Ft. Lauderdale (H)
Miami/Miami Beach:
Doral Golf (R)
Hyatt Reg. Coral Gables (H)
Radisson Mart Plaza (H)
Tampa Bay:
Dbltree Tampa Bay (H)
Embassy Westshore (H)
Hyatt Reg. Westshore (H)
Marriott Tampa (H)
Sheraton Grand (H)

Georgia
Atlanta:
Hilton Atlanta Airport (H)
Marriott Atlanta Airport (H)
Sheraton Gateway (H)
Westin Atlanta (H)

Illinois
Chicago:
Hilton O'Hare (H)
Hyatt Reg. O'Hare (H)
Marriott O'Hare (H)
Rosemont O'Hare (H)
Sheraton Gateway (H)
Sofitel (H)
Westin O'Hare (H)

Kansas
Wichita:
Hilton Wichita Airport (H)

Maine
Portland:
Marriott at Sable Oaks (H)
Sheraton Portland (H)

Maryland
Stevensville:
Kent Manor (H)

Massachusetts
Boston:
Hyatt Harborside (H)

Minnesota
Minneapolis/St. Paul:
Dbltree Mall of America (H)
Radisson Plaza Tower (H)
Sofitel (H)

Missouri
St. Louis:
Harley St. Louis (H)

New York
Albany:
Marriott Albany (H)

North Carolina
Raleigh-Durham:
Marriott at Research (H)

North Dakota
Fargo:
Best Western Doublewood (H)

Oklahoma
Tulsa:
Sheraton Tulsa (H)

Puerto Rico
San Juan:
Sands (H)

South Carolina
Charleston:
Hilton Charleston (H)

Tennessee
Nashville:
Embassy Nashville (H)
Marriott Nashville Airport (H)
Sheraton Music City (H)

Texas
Austin:
Hilton Austin North (H)
Dallas/Fort Worth:
Four Seasons (R)
Omni Dallas (H)
Omni Mandalay (H)
Houston:
Sofitel (H)
Wyndham Greenspoint (H)

Washington, DC
(including nearby Maryland and Virginia)
Virginia:
Doubletree (H)
Hilton Washington (H)
Hyatt Dulles (H)
Hyatt Reg. Reston (H)
Marriott Key Bridge (H)
Morrison House (B)
Radisson Mark Ctr (H)
Ritz Pentagon City (H)

All-Suites

Arizona
Phoenix/Scottsdale:
Embassy Biltmore (H)
Embassy Scottsdale (H)
Marriott Scottsdale (H)
Orange Tree (R)
Pte Hilton S. Mountain (R)
Pte Hilton Squaw (R)
Pte Hilton Tapatio (R)

Arkansas
Eureka Springs:
Palace (B)
Hot Springs:
Lake Hamilton (R)

California
Costa Mesa:
Marriott Costa Mesa (H)
Los Angeles:
Le Parc (H)
Westwood Marquis (H)
Monterey:
Pacific (H)
Napa:
Embassy Napa Valley (H)
Silverado (R)
Newport Beach:
Marriott Suites (H)
Palm Springs:
Hyatt Grand (R)
Hyatt Reg. Palm Springs (H)
Inn at Racquet Club (B)
Rutherford:
Rancho Caymus (B)
San Diego:
Embassy San Diego (H)
Princess San Diego (R)
Rancho Valencia (R)
San Francisco:
Hyde Park (B)
Santa Monica:
Oceana (H)

Colorado
Beaver Creek:
Charter at Beaver Creek (H)
Embassy Beaver Creek (R)
Denver:
Burnsley (H)
Cambridge (H)
Embassy Denver (H)
Residence by Marriott (H)
Durango:
Wit's End (B)

Connecticut
Essex:
Griswold Inn (B)

Florida
Fort Lauderdale:
Doubletree (H)
Haines City:
Grenelefe Golf (R)
Key West:
Cuban Club (H)
Little Torch Key:
Little Palm Island (B)
Longboat Key:
Colony Beach (R)
Resort at Longboat Key (R)
Miami/Miami Beach:
Alexander (H)
Casa Grande (H)
Fisher Island (R)
La Voile Rouge (B)
Marlin (H)
Mayfair House (H)
Spa at Doral (S)
Naples:
Edgewater Beach (H)
Orlando:
Disney's Old Key West (R)
Doubletree (H)
Residence by Marriott (H)
Westgate Lakes (R)
Palm Beach:
Palm Beach Polo (R)
Sanibel Island:
Casa Ybel (R)
Sundial Beach (R)
Tampa Bay:
Dbltree Tampa Bay (H)
Embassy Westshore (H)
Innisbrook Hilton (R)
Radisson Sand Key (R)

Georgia
Atlanta:
Doubletree (H)
French Quarter (H)
Hyatt Reg. Perimeter (H)
Marriott Midtown Atlanta (H)
Summerfield (H)

Hawaii
Kauai:
Kiahuna Plantation (R)
Maui:
Kea Lani (R)
Oahu:
Aston Waikiki (H)

Illinois
Chicago:
Doubletree (H)
Marriott O'Hare (H)
Omni Chicago (H)
Rosemont O'Hare (H)
Sheraton Gateway (H)
Summerfield (H)

Indiana
Indianapolis:
Embassy Indianapolis (H)

Kansas
Lawrence:
Eldridge (H)

Kentucky
Lexington:
Hilton Lexington (H)
Louisville.
Galt House East (H)

Louisiana
St. Francisville:
Lodge at the Bluffs (H)

Maine
Cape Elizabeth:
Inn by the Sea (B)

Maryland
(see also Washington, DC)
Baltimore:
Brookshire (H)
Ocean City:
Coconut Malorie (H)
Lighthouse Club (H)

367

All-Suites

Massachusetts
Boston:
  Doubletree (H)
  Eliot (H)
Cape Cod:
  Coonamessett Inn (B)
  New Seabury (R)

Michigan
Detroit:
  Atheneum (H)

Minnesota
Minneapolis/St. Paul:
  Embassy Minneapolis (H)
Stillwater:
  Lumber Baron's (H)

Missouri
Branson:
  Clarion at Fall Creek (R)
  Red Bud Cove B&B (B)
Kansas City:
  Historic Suites of America (B)
  Sheraton Kansas City (H)
St. Louis:
  Embassy St. Louis (H)

Montana
Darby:
  Triple Creek Ranch (R)

Nevada
Las Vegas:
  Alexis Park (H)
  Frontier (H)

New Jersey
Atlantic City:
  Atlantic Palace (H)
Vernon:
  Great Gorge Village (R)

New York
Geneva:
  Geneva on the Lake (B)
New York City:
  Beekman Tower (H)
  Delmonico (H)
  Doubletree (H)
  Dumont Plaza (H)
  Eastgate Tower (H)
  Flatotel International (H)
  Lyden Gardens (H)
  Lyden House (H)
  Murray Hill East (H)
  Rihga Royal (H)
  Shelburne Murray Hill (H)
  Southgate Tower (H)
  Trump International (H)
Tarrytown:
  Castle at Tarrytown (B)

North Carolina
Fayetteville:
  Radisson Prince Charles (H)

Ohio
Cincinnati:
  Doubletree (H)
Cleveland:
  Embassy (H)
Columbus:
  Doubletree (H)
  Sheraton Columbus (H)

South Carolina
Hilton Head:
  Hilton Head Health (S)
  Hilton Hilton Head (R)
Seabrook Island:
  Seabrook Island (R)

Tennessee
Memphis:
  Embassy Memphis (H)
Nashville:
  Embassy Nashville (H)
  Hermitage (H)

Texas
Dallas/Fort Worth:
  Embassy Dallas (H)
  Sheraton Market Ctr (H)
  St. Germain (B)
Houston:
  Doubletree (H)
  Hilton Houston (H)
  La Colombe d'Or (B)
Montgomery:
  Del Lago (R)

Utah
Salt Lake City:
  Embassy (H)
St. George:
  Green Valley Spa (S)

Vermont
Barnard:
  Twin Farms (R)
Manchester:
  Inn at Willow Pond (B)

Virginia
Virginia Beach:
  Virginia Beach (R)

Washington, DC
(including nearby Maryland and Virginia)
Maryland:
  Marriott Suites Bethesda (H)
Washington, DC:
  Canterbury (H)
  Dbltree NH Avenue (H)
  Dbltree Penn Avenue (H)
  Embassy Chevy Chase (H)
  Georgetown Dutch (H)
  One Washington (H)
  River Inn (H)
  State Plaza (H)

Wisconsin
Osceola:
  Aveda Spa Retreat (S)

Beach/Water Setting

Alabama
Mobile:
Adam's Mark (H)
Orange Beach:
Perdido Beach (R)
Point Clear:
Marriott's Grand (R)

Arizona
Page:
Wahweap (H)
Phoenix/Scottsdale:
Holiday Inn SunSpree (R)
Sedona:
Garland's (R)

Arkansas
Hot Springs:
Lake Hamilton (R)
Lakeview:
Gaston's (R)
Little Rock:
Arkansas Excelsior (H)
Dbltree Little Rock (H)

California
Albion:
Albion River (B)
Big Sur:
Post Ranch (B)
Ventana Inn (B)
Capitola by the Sea:
Inn at Depot Hill (B)
Carmel:
Carmel Country Spa (S)
Cobblestone Inn (B)
Highlands Inn (B)
Cazadero:
Timberhill (B)
Dana Point:
Ritz Laguna Niguel (R)
Eureka:
Carter House (B)
Gualala:
Whale Watch Inn (B)
Laguna Beach:
Surf & Sand (H)
Lake Arrowhead:
Lake Arrowhead (R)
Little River:
Heritage House (B)
Little River Inn (B)
Long Beach:
Queen Mary (H)
Renaissance Long Beach (H)
Los Angeles:
Georgian (H)
Loews Santa Monica (H)
Malibu Beach (B)
Mansion Inn (B)
Marriott Marina Beach (H)
Miramar Sheraton (H)
Ritz Marina del Rey (H)
Shangri-La (H)
Shutters (H)
Mendocino:
Hill House Mendocino (B)
Mendocino (H)
Stanford Inn (B)
Montecito:
Montecito Inn (B)
San Ysidro (B)

Monterey:
Dbltree Fish. Wharf (H)
Monterey Plaza (H)
Spindrift Inn (B)
Morro Bay:
Inn at Morro Bay (B)
Newport Beach:
Hyatt Newporter (R)
Marriott Suites (H)
Marriott Tennis (H)
Oakland:
Waterfront Plaza (H)
Pacific Grove:
Gosby House (B)
Green Gables (B)
Martine Inn (B)
Pebble Beach:
Inn at Spanish Bay (R)
Lodge at Pebble Beach (R)
Sacramento:
Radisson Sacramento (H)
San Diego:
Catamaran (H)
del Coronado Hotel (R)
Hilton San Diego (H)
Hyatt Islandia (H)
Hyatt Reg. San Diego (H)
Kona Kai (R)
La Jolla Beach (H)
L'Auberge Del Mar (R)
La Valencia (H)
Le Meridien San Diego (H)
Princess San Diego (R)
Sea Lodge (H)
Sheraton Grande (R)
Sheraton San Diego (H)
Wyndham Emerald (H)
San Francisco:
Griffon (H)
Harbor Court (H)
Hyatt Reg. SF (H)
Park Hyatt SF (H)
Tuscan Inn (H)
Santa Barbara:
Fess Parker's (R)
Four Seasons Biltmore (R)
Santa Clara:
Westin Santa Slara (H)
Santa Monica:
Oceana (H)
Sausalito:
Casa Madrona (H)
Shell Beach:
Cliffs at Shell Beach (R)
Ventura:
Cliff House (B)
Yosemite:
Ahwahnee (H)

Colorado
Colorado Springs:
Cheyenne Mountain (R)
Durango:
Wit's End (B)
Granby:
C Lazy U Ranch (B)
Keystone:
Keystone (R)

Connecticut
Essex:
Griswold Inn (B)

Beach/Water Setting

Lebanon:
Spa at Grand Lake (S)
Mystic:
Inn at Mystic (B)
New Preston:
Boulders (B)
Inn on Lake Waramaug (B)
Norfolk:
Blackberry River (B)
Old Lyme:
Bee & Thistle (B)
Westbrook:
Water's Edge (B)
Westport:
Inn at National Hall (B)

Delaware
Bethany Beach:
Addy Sea (B)
New Castle:
Armitage Inn (B)
Rehoboth Beach:
Boardwalk Plaza (H)

Florida
Amelia Island:
Amelia Island (R)
Ritz Amelia Island (R)
Boca Raton:
Boca Raton (R)
Captiva Island:
South Seas Plantation (R)
Destin:
Hilton Sandestin (R)
Fisher Island:
Spa Internazionale (S)
Fort Lauderdale:
Hyatt Reg. Pier 66 (H)
Lago Mar (R)
Little Inn by the Sea (B)
Marriott's Harbor (R)
Radisson Bahia Mar (R)
Riverside (H)
Fort Myers:
Sanibel Harbour (R)
Gasparilla Island:
Gasparilla Inn (B)
Hallandale:
Regency House (S)
Howey-in-the-Hills:
Mission Inn (R)
Islamorada:
Cheeca Lodge (R)
Jupiter:
Jupiter Beach (R)
Key Largo:
Marriott's Key Largo (R)
Ocean Reef (R)
Key West:
Banana Bay (B)
Hyatt Key West (H)
Marriott's Casa Marina (R)
Marriott's Reach (R)
Ocean Key House (R)
Pier House (R)
Lake Wales:
Chalet Suzanne (B)
Little Torch Key:
Little Palm Island (B)
Longboat Key:
Colony Beach (R)
Resort at Longboat Key (R)
Marathon:
Hawk's Cay (R)

Marco Island:
Marco Island Hilton (R)
Marriott's Marco Island (R)
Radisson Beach (R)
Miami/Miami Beach:
Albion (H)
Alexander (H)
Astor (H)
Casa Grande (H)
Dbltree Grand (H)
Delano (H)
Eden Roc (H)
Fisher Island (R)
Fontainebleau Hilton (R)
Greenview (H)
Grove Isle Club (B)
Hyatt Reg. Miami (H)
Indian Creek (H)
Lafayette (H)
La Voile Rouge (B)
Marlin (H)
Mayfair House (H)
Miami Beach Ocean (H)
Ocean Front (H)
Park Central (H)
Pritikin Longevity (S)
Raleigh (H)
Ritz Plaza (H)
Sheraton Biscayne Bay (H)
Sonesta Beach (R)
Tides (H)
Turnberry Isle (R)
Westin Miami (R)
Naples:
Naples Bath & Tennis (R)
Naples Beach (R)
Registry (R)
Ritz Naples (R)
Orlando:
Buena Vista Palace (H)
Disney Institute (R)
Disney's Caribbean (R)
Disney's Dixie Landings (R)
Disney's Grand Floridian (R)
Disney's Port Orleans (R)
Disney's Yacht (R)
Hyatt Reg. Grand Cypress (R)
Villas of Grand Cypress (R)
Walt Disney Dolphin (R)
Walt Disney Swan (R)
Westgate Lakes (R)
Palm Beach:
Breakers (R)
Colony (H)
Four Seasons Palm Beach (H)
PGA National (R)
Ritz Palm Beach (R)
Panama City Beach:
Marriott's Bay Point (R)
Ponte Vedra Beach:
Lodge at Ponte Vedra (R)
Marriott at Sawgrass (R)
Ponte Vedra (R)
Port St. Lucie:
Club Med Sandpiper (R)
Safety Harbor:
Safety Harbor (S)
Sanibel Island:
Casa Ybel (R)
Sanibel (R)
Sundial Beach (R)
Siesta Key:
Captiva Beach (B)

Beach/Water Setting

Stuart:
Indian River Plantation (R)
Tampa Bay:
Dbltree Tampa Bay (H)
Don CeSar (R)
Holiday Inn Beachfront (R)
Hyatt Reg. Westshore (H)
Innisbrook Hilton (R)
Radisson Sand Key (R)
Renaissance Vinoy (R)
Sheraton Sand Key (R)
TradeWinds St. Pete (R)
Wyndham Harbour (H)
West Palm Beach:
Hippocrates Health (S)

Georgia
Atlanta:
Evergreen (R)
Jekyll Island:
Jekyll Island Club (R)
Lake Lanier Islands:
Renaissance Pineisle (R)
Pine Mountain:
Callaway Gardens (R)
Savannah:
Marriott Savannah (H)
Planters Inn Savannah (B)
Sea Island:
Cloister (R)
St. Simons Island:
King & Prince Beach (R)
Lodge at Little St. Simons (B)

Hawaii
Big Island:
Four Seasons Hualalai (R)
Hapuna Prince (R)
Hilton Waikoloa (R)
Kona Village (R)
Mauna Kea (R)
Orchid at Mauna Lani (R)
Royal Waikoloan (R)
Kauai:
Hyatt Reg. Kauai (R)
Kauai Coconut (R)
Kiahuna Plantation (R)
Marriott Kauai (R)
Outrigger Kauai (R)
Princeville (R)
Lanai:
Lodge at Koele (R)
Manele Bay (R)
Maui:
Aston Kaanapali (R)
Aston Wailea (R)
Four Seasons Maui (R)
Grand Wailea (R)
Hana-Maui Hotel (H)
Hyatt Reg. Maui (R)
Kapalua Bay (R)
Kea Lani (R)
Marriott Maui (R)
Maui Prince (R)
Renaissance Wailea (R)
Ritz Kapalua (R)
Royal Lahaina (R)
Sheraton Maui (R)
Westin Maui (R)
Oahu:
Ala Moana (H)
Aston Waikiki (H)
Halekulani (H)
Hawaiian Regent (H)
Hawaii Prince Waikiki (H)
Hilton Hawaiian (H)

Hyatt Reg. Waikiki (H)
Ihilani Resort (R)
Ilikai Nikko Waikiki (H)
Kahala Mandarin (R)
New Otani Kaimana (H)
Outrigger Reef (R)
Outrigger Waikiki (R)
Pacific Beach (R)
Royal Hawaiian (H)
Sheraton Moana (H)
Sheraton Waikiki (H)
Waikiki Parc (H)

Idaho
Coeur d'Alene:
Coeur d'Alene (R)
McCall:
Shore Lodge (B)
Priest Lake:
Hill's Hospitality (B)

Illinois
Chicago:
Ambassador West (H)
Drake (H)
Four Seasons Chicago (H)
La Salle Club (H)
Ritz Chicago (H)
Galena:
Eagle Ridge (R)
Gilman:
Heartland Spa (S)
Whittington:
Rend Lake (R)

Indiana
Bloomington:
Fourwinds (R)

Louisiana
New Orleans:
Westin Canal (H)

Maine
Bar Harbor:
Atlantic Oakes (B)
Bar Harbor Bluenose (B)
Bar Harbor Inn (B)
Bayview (H)
Boothbay Harbor:
Spruce Point (B)
Camden:
Norumbega Inn (B)
Cape Elizabeth:
Inn by the Sea (B)
Deer Isle:
Pilgrims Inn (B)
East Holden:
Lucerne Inn (B)
Kennebunkport:
Captain Lord Mansion (B)
Inn at Harbor Head (B)
White Barn Inn (B)
Newcastle:
Newcastle Inn (B)
Northeast Harbor:
Asticou Inn (B)
Ogunquit:
Cliff House (H)
Portland:
Radisson Portland (H)
Raymond:
Northern Pines (S)
Rockport:
Samoset (R)
Scarborough:
Black Point Inn (R)

Beach/Water Setting

Maryland

Annapolis:
   Marriott Annapolis (H)
Ocean City:
   Coconut Malorie (H)
   Dunes Manor (H)
   Lighthouse Club (H)
   Sheraton Fontainebleau (H)
Oxford:
   Robert Morris Inn (B)
St. Michaels:
   Inn at Perry Cabin (B)

Massachusetts

Boston:
   Hyatt Harborside (H)
   Marriott Long Wharf (H)
Cape Cod:
   Brass Key (B)
   Chatham Bars (B)
   Coonamessett Inn (B)
   Dunscroft by the Sea (B)
   High Brewster (B)
   New Seabury (R)
   Ocean Edge (R)
   Sea Crest (R)
   Wequassett Inn (B)
Martha's Vineyard:
   Daggett House (B)
   Harbor View (B)
   Outermost Inn (B)
   Thorncroft Inn (B)
Nantucket:
   Cliffside Beach (H)
   Summer House (B)
   Wauwinet (B)
   White Elephant (R)
Northampton:
   Northampton (H)
Rockport:
   Yankee Clipper (B)

Michigan

Acme:
   Grand Traverse (R)
Bellaire:
   Shanty Creek (R)
Detroit:
   River Place (H)
Mackinac Island:
   Grand (H)
   Iroquois (B)
   Mission Point (R)
New Buffalo:
   Harbor Grand (H)
Traverse City:
   Waterfront Inn (R)
Ypsilanti:
   Marriott Ypsilanti (R)

Minnesota

Alexandria:
   Arrowwood Radisson (R)
Brainerd:
   Madden's (R)
Litchfield:
   Birdwing Spa (S)
Lutsen:
   Lutsen (R)
Minneapolis/St. Paul:
   Whitney (H)
Red Wing:
   St. James (H)
Stillwater:
   Lumber Baron's (H)

Mississippi

Vicksburg:
   Cedar Grove (B)

Missouri

Branson:
   Red Bud Cove B&B (B)
Lake Ozark:
   Lodge at Four Seasons (R)
Osage Beach:
   Marriott's Tan-Tar-A (R)
Ridgedale:
   Big Cedar (R)

Montana

Bigfork:
   Averill's Flathead (B)

Nevada

Crystal Bay:
   Cal-Neva Resort (R)
Lake Tahoe:
   Harrah's Lake Tahoe (R)
Laughlin:
   Don Laughlin's (H)
   Flamingo Hilton (H)
   Golden Nugget (H)
   Harrah's Laughlin (H)

New Hampshire

Dixville Notch:
   Balsams Grand (R)
Holderness:
   Manor on Golden Pond (B)
Lincoln:
   Mountain Club (R)
Meredith:
   Inn at Mill Falls (B)
Waterville Valley:
   Waterville Valley (R)

New Jersey

Atlantic City:
   Atlantic Palace (H)
   Bally's Park Place (H)
   Caesar Atlantic City (H)
   Claridge Casino (H)
   Harrah's Casino (H)
   Marriott Seaview (R)
   Merv Griffin's (H)
   Sands (H)
   Showboat Casino (H)
   Tropicana Casino (H)
   Trump Plaza (H)
   Trump's Castle (H)
   Trump Taj Mahal (H)
   Trump World's Fair (H)
Beach Haven:
   Green Gables (B)
Cape May:
   Angel of the Sea (B)
   Chalfonte (H)
   Mainstay Inn (B)
   Queen Victoria (B)
   Virginia Hotel (B)
Lambertville:
   Inn at Lambertville (B)
Long Beach:
   Ocean Place Hilton (R)
Spring Lake:
   Breakers (B)
   Sea Crest by the Sea (B)
Vernon:
   Great Gorge Village (R)

Beach/Water Setting

New Mexico
Mescalero:
Inn of Mountain Gods (R)

New York
Alexandria Bay:
Riveredge (H)
Amenia:
Troutbeck (B)
Bolton Landing:
Sagamore (R)
Geneva:
Geneva on the Lake (B)
Great Neck:
Inn at Great Neck (H)
Hopewell Junction:
Le Chambord (B)
Lake Placid:
Lake Placid Lodge (B)
Mirror Lake (B)
Lew Beach:
Beaverkill Valley (B)
Montauk:
Gurney's Inn (S)
Montauk Yacht (R)
Monticello:
Kutsher's (R)
New Paltz:
Mohonk Mountain (R)
North Hudson:
Elk Lake Lodge (R)
Saranac Lake:
Point (B)
Shelter Island:
Ram's Head (B)
Stony Brook:
Three Village (B)

North Carolina
Duck:
Sanderling Inn (R)
Lake Toxaway:
Greystone Inn (B)
Nags Head:
First Colony (H)
Pinehurst:
Pinehurst (R)
Wrightsville Beach:
Blockade Runner (R)

Ohio
Huron:
Sawmill Creek (R)

Oklahoma
Kingston:
Texoma State (R)

Oregon
Eugene:
Valley River (H)
Gleneden Beach:
Salishan (R)
Gold Beach:
Tu Tu'Tun (B)
Hood River:
Columbia Gorge (H)
Lincoln City:
Inn at Spanish Head (B)
Newport:
Embarcadero (H)
Sylvia Beach (H)
Portland:
RiverPlace (H)
Warm Springs:
Kah-Nee-Ta (R)

Pennsylvania
Erwinna:
Evermay on Delaware (B)
Mt. Pocono/Pocono Manor:
Mount Airy Lodge (R)
Pittsburgh:
Sheraton Station Square (H)
South Sterling:
Sterling Inn (B)

Puerto Rico
Dorado:
Hyatt Reg. Cerromar (R)
Hyatt Reg. Dorado (R)
Fajardo:
El Conquistador (R)
Humacao:
Palmas del Mar (R)
Rincon:
Horned Dorset (B)
San Juan:
Caribe Hilton (H)
Condado Beach Trio (H)
Condado Plaza (H)
El San Juan (H)
Sands (H)

Rhode Island
Block Island:
Atlantic Inn (B)
Manisses (H)
1661 Inn (B)
Newport:
Castle Hill Inn (B)
Cliffside Inn (B)
Dbltree Newport (H)
Marriott Newport (H)
Newport Harbor (H)
Vanderbilt Hall (H)

South Carolina
Beaufort:
Rhett House (B)
Charleston:
Battery Carriage (B)
Indigo Inn (B)
Planters Inn (B)
Vendue Inn (B)
Hilton Head:
Hilton Hilton Head (R)
Hyatt Reg. Hilton Head (R)
Palmetto Dunes (R)
Sea Pines (R)
Westin (R)
Isle of Palms:
Wild Dunes (R)
Kiawah Island:
Kiawah Island (R)
Myrtle Beach:
Hilton Myrtle Beach (R)
Kingston Planation (R)
Myrtle Beach Martinique (R)
Ocean Creek (R)
Ocean Dunes (R)
Sheraton Myrtle Beach (R)
Pawleys Island:
Litchfield Beach (R)
Litchfield Plantation (B)
Seabrook Island:
Seabrook Island (R)

South Dakota
Chamberlain:
Radisson Cedar Shore (R)
Gettysburg:
Harer Lodge (B)

Beach/Water Setting

Rapid City:
Abend Haus (B)
Willow Springs (B)

Tennessee
Fairfield Glade:
Fairfield Glade (R)

Texas
Austin:
Hyatt Reg. Austin (H)
Lake Austin Spa (S)
Lakeway Inn (R)
Corpus Christi:
Omni Bayfront (H)
Dallas/Fort Worth:
Omni Mandalay (H)
Galveston:
Galvez (H)
Harbor House (B)
Montgomery:
Del Lago (R)
South Padre Island:
Radisson South Padre (R)

Utah
Park City:
Olympia Park (H)

Vermont
Chittenden:
Mountain Top (B)
Goshen:
Blueberry Hill (B)
Highgate Springs:
Tyler Place (R)
Perkinsville:
Inn at Weathersfield (B)
Plymouth:
Hawk Inn (B)
Shelburne:
Inn at Shelburne Farms (B)
Vergennes:
Basin Harbor (R)

Virginia
Irvington:
Tides Inn (R)
Tides Lodge (R)
Richmond:
Radisson (H)
Virginia Beach:
Hilton Virginia Beach (H)
Holiday Inn Sunspree (R)

Ramada Plaza (R)
Virginia Beach (R)
Williamsburg:
Kingsmill (R)

Washington
Blaine:
Inn at Semi-Ah-Moo (R)
Coupeville:
Captain Whidbey (B)
Eastsound:
Rosario Resort (R)
Lake Quinault:
Lake Quinault (B)
Port Angeles:
Domaine Madeleine (B)
Port Ludlow:
Inn at Ludlow Bay (B)
Port Ludlow (R)
Seattle:
Edgewater (H)
Woodmark (H)
Silverdale:
Silverdale on Bay (R)
Stevenson:
Skamania Lodge (R)
Winthrop:
Sun Mountain (R)

Wisconsin
Bailey's Harbor:
Gordon Lodge (B)
Bayfield:
Old Rittenhouse (B)
Delavan:
Lake Lawn Lodge (R)
Eagle River:
Chanticleer Inn (B)
Fontana:
Abbey Resort (R)
Green Lake:
Heidel House (R)
Kohler:
Inn on Woodlake (B)
Lake Geneva:
Interlaken Resort (R)
Milwaukee:
Hilton Milwaukee River (H)

Wyoming
Moran:
Colter Bay Village (R)
Yellowstone National Park:
Lake Yellowstone (H)

Beautiful Grounds

Alabama
Point Clear:
Marriott's Grand (R)

Alaska
Denali National Park:
Denali Princess (H)
North Face (B)
Gustavus:
Glacier Bay (B)

Arizona
Gold Canyon:
Gold Canyon (R)
Phoenix/Scottsdale:
Arizona Biltmore (R)
Buttes (R)
Dbltree La Posada (R)
Gardiner's (R)
Holiday Inn SunSpree (R)
Hyatt Reg. Scottsdale (R)
Marriott's Camelback (R)
Marriott's Mountain (R)
Phoenician (R)
Pte Hilton S. Mountain (R)
Pte Hilton Squaw (R)
Pte Hilton Tapatio (R)
Radisson Scottsdale (R)
Regal McCormick (R)
Scottsdale Conference (R)
Scottsdale Hilton (H)
Scottsdale Princess (R)
Sheraton San Marcos (R)
Wigwam (R)
Sedona:
Enchantment (R)
L'Auberge de Sedona (H)
Los Abrigados (R)
Tucson:
Arizona Inn (H)
Lodge Ventana (R)
Loews Ventana (R)
Omni Tucson (R)
SunCatcher B&B (B)
Westin La Paloma (R)
Westward Look (R)
Wickenburg:
Merv Griffin's (B)

Arkansas
Hot Springs:
Lake Hamilton (R)

California
Albion:
Albion River (B)
Big Sur:
Big Sur Lodge (B)
Ventana Inn (B)
Carlsbad:
La Costa (S)
Carmel:
Carmel Country Spa (S)
Carmel Valley (R)
Highlands Inn (B)
John Gardiner's (R)
La Playa (H)
Los Laureles (H)
Quail Lodge (R)
Stonepine (B)
Cazadero:
Timberhill (B)
Dana Point:
Laguna Cliff Marriott (R)
Ritz Laguna Niguel (R)

Death Valley:
Furnace Creek Inn (R)
Escondido:
Golden Door (S)
Fish Camp:
Tenaya Lodge (R)
Garberville:
Benbow Inn (B)
Gualala:
St. Orres (B)
Guerneville:
Applewood Inn (B)
Healdsburg:
Madrona Manor (B)
Little River:
Heritage House (B)
Little River Inn (B)
Los Angeles:
Bel-Air (H)
Beverly Hills (H)
Chateau Marmont (H)
Four Seasons (H)
Loews Santa Monica (H)
Miramar Sheraton (H)
New Otani (H)
Peninsula Beverly Hills (H)
Sunset Marquis (H)
Los Olivos:
Los Olivos Grand (B)
Mendocino:
Stanford Inn (B)
Montecito:
San Ysidro (B)
Monterey:
Hyatt Reg. Monterey (H)
Old Monterey Inn (B)
Pacific (H)
Morro Bay:
Inn at Morro Bay (B)
Napa:
Silverado (R)
Newport Beach:
Four Seasons Newport (H)
Hyatt Newporter (R)
Marriott Suites (H)
Marriott Tennis (H)
Sutton Place (H)
Oakhurst:
Chateau du Sureau (B)
Ojai:
Ojai Valley (R)
Olympic Valley:
Resort at Squaw Creek (R)
Pacific Grove:
Green Gables (B)
Palm Springs:
Dbltree Palm Springs (R)
Givenchy (S)
Ingleside (B)
Inn at Racquet Club (B)
La Mancha (R)
La Quinta (R)
Marriott's Desert Springs (R)
Marriott's Rancho (R)
Monte Vista (H)
Renaissance Esmeralda (R)
Ritz Rancho Mirage (R)
Shadow Mountain (R)
Westin Mission Hills (R)
Palo Alto:
Garden Court (H)

Beautiful Grounds

Pebble Beach:
Inn at Spanish Bay (R)
Lodge at Pebble Beach (R)
Rutherford:
Auberge du Soleil (B)
Rancho Caymus (B)
San Diego:
Catamaran (H)
del Coronado Hotel (R)
Hilton San Diego (H)
Inn at Rancho Santa Fe (H)
Kona Kai (R)
L'Auberge Del Mar (R)
La Valencia (H)
Le Meridien San Diego (H)
Loews Coronado (R)
Princess San Diego (R)
Rancho Bernardo (R)
Rancho Valencia (R)
Sheraton Grande (R)
Sheraton San Diego (H)
San Francisco:
Gramma's Rose Garden (B)
San Luis Obispo:
Apple Farm (B)
Santa Barbara:
El Encanto (H)
Fess Parker's (R)
Four Seasons Biltmore (R)
Santa Rosa:
Vintners Inn (B)
Solvang:
Alisal (R)
Sonoma:
Sonoma Mission (S)
St. Helena:
Harvest Inn (B)
Meadowood (R)
Tecate:
Rancho La Puerta (S)
Vista:
Cal-a-Vie (S)
Yosemite:
Ahwahnee (H)

Colorado
Aspen:
Gant (B)
Colorado Springs:
Broadmoor (R)
Durango:
Tall Timber (B)
Tamarron Hilton (R)
Granby:
C Lazy U Ranch (B)
Telluride:
Peaks at Telluride (R)

Connecticut
Ivoryton:
Copper Beech (B)
Lakeville:
Interlaken Inn (R)
Mystic:
Inn at Mystic (B)
Norfolk:
Blackberry River (B)
Norwich:
Norwich Inn (S)
Ridgefield:
Stonehenge Inn (B)
Salisbury:
White Hart (B)

Simsbury:
Simsbury Inn (H)
Washington:
Mayflower Inn (B)

Florida
Amelia Island:
Amelia Island (R)
Ritz Amelia Island (R)
Boca Raton:
Boca Raton (R)
Bonita Springs:
Shangri-La (S)
Clearwater:
Belleview Mido (R)
Destin:
Hilton Sandestin (R)
Fisher Island:
Spa Internazionale (S)
Fort Lauderdale:
Hyatt Reg. Pier 66 (H)
Registry Resort (S)
Westin Ft. Lauderdale (H)
Fort Myers:
Sanibel Harbour (R)
Haines City:
Grenelefe Golf (R)
Howey-in-the-Hills:
Mission Inn (R)
Islamorada:
Cheeca Lodge (R)
Jupiter:
Jupiter Beach (R)
Key Largo:
Ocean Reef (R)
Key West:
Marquesa (H)
Pier House (R)
Little Torch Key:
Little Palm Island (B)
Longboat Key:
Colony Beach (R)
Resort at Longboat Key (R)
Marco Island:
Marriott's Marco Island (R)
Miami/Miami Beach:
Alexander (H)
Biltmore (R)
Dbltree Coconut Grove (H)
Doral Golf (R)
Fisher Island (R)
Fontainebleau Hilton (R)
Grove Isle Club (B)
Lido Spa (S)
Sheraton Bal Harbour (H)
Turnberry Isle (R)
Westin Miami (R)
Naples:
Naples Bath & Tennis (R)
Registry (R)
Ritz Naples (R)
Orlando:
Disney's Beach Club (R)
Disney's Caribbean (R)
Disney's Dixie Landings (R)
Disney's Grand Floridian (R)
Disney's Old Key West (R)
Disney's Polynesian (R)
Disney's Port Orleans (R)
Disney's Yacht (R)
Hyatt Orlando (H)
Hyatt Reg. Grand Cypress (R)
Renaissance Orlando (R)
Residence by Marriott (H)

Beautiful Grounds

Villas of Grand Cypress (R)
Vistana (R)
Westgate Lakes (R)
Palm Beach:
Breakers (R)
Four Seasons Palm Beach (H)
Palm Beach Polo (R)
PGA National (R)
Ritz Palm Beach (R)
Panama City Beach:
Marriott's Bay Point (R)
Pompano Beach:
Palm-Aire Resort (S)
Ponte Vedra Beach:
Lodge at Ponte Vedra (R)
Marriott at Sawgrass (R)
Ponte Vedra (R)
Port St. Lucie:
Club Med Sandpiper (R)
Sanibel Island:
Casa Ybel (R)
Stuart:
Indian River Plantation (R)
Tampa Bay:
Don CeSar (R)
Hyatt Reg. Westshore (H)
Innisbrook Hilton (R)
Renaissance Vinoy (R)
Saddlebrook Tampa (R)
TradeWinds St. Pete (R)
Wyndham Harbour (H)

Georgia
Atlanta.
Evergreen (R)
Grand Hyatt Atlanta (H)
Holiday Inn Ravinia (H)
Marietta (R)
Peachtree (H)
Braselton:
Chateau Elan Winery (B)
Jekyll Island:
Jekyll Island Club (R)
Lake Lanier Islands:
Renaissance Pineisle (R)
Peachtree City:
Aberdeen Woods (H)
Pine Mountain:
Callaway Gardens (R)
Savannah:
Ballastone Inn (B)
Eliza Thompson (B)
Sea Island:
Cloister (R)
St. Simons Island:
King & Prince Beach (R)
Sea Palms (R)

Hawaii
Big Island:
Four Seasons Hualalai (R)
Hapuna Prince (R)
Hilton Waikoloa (R)
Kona Village (R)
Mauna Kea (R)
Orchid at Mauna Lani (R)
Royal Waikoloan (R)
Kauai:
Marriott Kauai (R)
Outrigger Kauai (R)
Princeville (R)
Lanai:
Lodge at Koele (R)
Manele Bay (R)

Maui:
Aston Wailea (R)
Four Seasons Maui (R)
Grand Wailea (R)
Hana-Maui Hotel (H)
Ka'anapali Beach (R)
Kapalua Bay (R)
Kea Lani (R)
Marriott Maui (R)
Maui Prince (R)
Renaissance Wailea (R)
Ritz Kapalua (R)
Royal Lahaina (R)
Westin Maui (R)
Oahu:
Halekulani (H)
Hawaiian Regent (H)
Hilton Hawaiian (H)
Hilton Turtle Bay (R)
Ihilani Resort (R)
Ilikai Nikko Waikiki (H)
Kahala Mandarin (H)
Royal Hawaiian (H)
Sheraton Moana (H)

Illinois
Galena.
Eagle Ridge (R)
Gilman:
Heartland Spa (S)
Oak Brook:
Oak Brook Hills (R)

Indiana
French Lick:
French Lick Springs (R)

Kentucky
Harrodsburg:
Beaumont Inn (B)
Inn at Shaker Village (B)

Louisiana
Napoleonville:
Madewood Plantation (B)
New Orleans:
Royal Sonesta (H)

Maine
Bar Harbor:
Bar Harbor Inn (B)
Bayview (H)
Boothbay Harbor:
Spruce Point (B)
Camden:
Norumbega Inn (B)
Cape Elizabeth:
Inn by the Sea (B)
Castine:
Castine Inn (B)
East Holden:
Lucerne Inn (B)
Kennebunkport:
Kennebunkport Inn (B)
Northeast Harbor:
Asticou Inn (B)
Ogunquit:
Cliff House (H)
Portland:
Radisson Portland (H)
Raymond:
Northern Pines (S)
Rockport:
Samoset (R)

Maryland
Baltimore:
Inn at Henderson's (B)

Beautiful Grounds

Easton:
  Tidewater Inn (B)
Ocean City:
  Lighthouse Club (H)
St. Michaels:
  Inn at Perry Cabin (B)

Massachusetts
Cape Cod:
  Coonamessett Inn (B)
  Dan'l Webster Inn (B)
  High Brewster (B)
  Ocean Edge (R)
  Wequassett Inn (B)
  Whalewalk Inn (B)
Lenox:
  Blantyre (B)
  Cranwell (R)
  Wheatleigh (B)
Martha's Vineyard:
  Charlotte Inn (B)
  Daggett House (B)
  Harbor View (B)
  Thorncroft Inn (B)
  Tuscany Inn (B)
Nantucket:
  Summer House (B)
  Wauwinet (B)
  White Elephant (R)
Rockport:
  Yankee Clipper (B)
Williamstown:
  Orchards (B)

Michigan
Acme:
  Grand Traverse (R)
Bellaire:
  Shanty Creek (R)
Harbor Springs:
  Boyne Highlands (R)
Mackinac Island:
  Bay View B&B (B)
  Iroquois (B)

Minnesota
Alexandria:
  Arrowwood Radisson (R)
Lutsen:
  Lutsen (R)
Minneapolis/St. Paul:
  Radisson Conference (H)

Mississippi
Natchez:
  Briars Inn (B)
  Dunleith (B)
  Linden B&B (B)
  Monmouth Plantation (B)
Vicksburg:
  Cedar Grove (B)

Missouri
Hannibal:
  Garth Woodside (B)
Osage Beach:
  Marriott's Tan-Tar-A (R)
Ridgedale:
  Big Cedar (R)

Montana
Gallatin Gateway:
  Gallatin Gateway (B)
  320 Guest Ranch (B)
Whitefish:
  North Forty (B)

Nevada
Lake Tahoe:
  Hyatt Reg. Lake Tahoe (R)
Las Vegas:
  Alexis Park (H)
  Desert Inn (R)
  Mirage (H)

New Hampshire
Bretton Woods:
  Mount Washington (R)
Dixville Notch:
  Balsams Grand (R)
Holderness:
  Manor on Golden Pond (B)
Jackson:
  Christmas Farm (B)
Meredith:
  Inn at Mill Falls (B)

New Jersey
Atlantic City:
  Marriott Seaview (R)
Basking Ridge:
  Olde Mill Inn (B)
Cape May:
  Mainstay Inn (B)
Princeton:
  Forrestal (H)

New Mexico
Raton:
  Vermejo Park (B)
Santa Fe:
  Bishop's Lodge (R)
  La Posada Santa Fe (H)
  Rancho Encantado (B)
Taos:
  Quail Ridge (R)

New York
Alexandria Bay:
  Bonnie Castle (R)
  Riveredge (H)
Amenia:
  Troutbeck (B)
Bolton Landing:
  Sagamore (R)
Cooperstown:
  Otesaga (H)
Dover Plains:
  Old Drovers Inn (B)
Ellenville:
  Nevele (R)
Geneva:
  Geneva on the Lake (B)
Glen Cove:
  Harrison (H)
Hopewell Junction:
  Le Chambord (B)
Hunter:
  Vatra Mountain (S)
Ithaca:
  Rose Inn (B)
Kiamesha Lake:
  Concord (R)
Lake Placid:
  Lake Placid Lodge (B)
Montauk:
  Gurney's Inn (S)
  Montauk Yacht (R)
New Paltz:
  Mohonk Mountain (R)
North Hudson:
  Elk Lake Lodge (R)

378

Beautiful Grounds

Old Chatham:
Old Chatham Inn (B)
Poughkeepsie:
Inn at the Falls (B)
Rye Brook:
Doral Arrowwood (R)
Saranac Lake:
Saranac (H)
Point (B)
Saratoga Springs:
Inn at Saratoga (B)
Shandaken:
Shandaken Inn (B)
Shelter Island:
Ram's Head (B)
Tarrytown:
Castle at Tarrytown (B)
Tarrytown House (B)

North Carolina
Blowing Rock:
Hound Ears (R)
Cashiers:
High Hampton (R)
Pinehurst:
Pinehurst (R)
Pittsboro:
Fearrington House (B)
Raleigh-Durham:
Washington Duke (H)

North Dakota
Fargo:
Bohlig's B&B (B)

Ohio
Dellroy:
Atwood Lake (R)
Grand Rapids:
Kerr House (S)
Millersburg:
Inn at Honey Run (B)
Painesville:
Quail Hollow (R)

Oregon
Gold Beach:
Tu Tu'Tun (B)
Hood River:
Columbia Gorge (H)
Lincoln City:
Inn at Spanish Head (B)

Pennsylvania
Champion:
Seven Springs (R)
Erwinna:
Evermay on Delaware (B)
Farmington:
Nemacolin Woodlands (R)
Hershey:
Hershey (H)
Lahaska:
Golden Plough (B)
Mount Joy:
Cameron Estate (B)
Mt. Pocono/Pocono Manor:
Mount Airy Lodge (R)
Pocono Manor (R)
Skytop:
Skytop Lodge (R)
South Sterling:
Sterling Inn (B)

Puerto Rico
Dorado:
Hyatt Reg. Cerromar (R)
Hyatt Reg. Dorado (R)
Fajardo:
El Conquistador (R)
Humacao:
Palmas del Mar (R)
Rincon:
Horned Dorset (B)
San Juan:
Caribe Hilton (H)
El San Juan (H)
Sands (H)

Rhode Island
Block Island:
Atlantic Inn (B)
Newport:
Castle Hill Inn (B)
Dbltree Newport (H)

South Carolina
Charleston:
Battery Carriage (B)
John Rutledge (B)
Kings Courtyard (B)
Hilton Head:
Hilton Head Health (S)
Hilton Hilton Head (R)
Palmetto Dunes (R)
Sea Pines (R)
Westin (R)
Isle of Palms:
Wild Dunes (R)
Kiawah Island:
Kiawah Island (R)
Myrtle Beach:
Kingston Planation (R)
Pawleys Island:
Litchfield Beach (R)
Litchfield Plantation (B)
Seabrook Island:
Seabrook Island (R)

Tennessee
Fairfield Glade:
Fairfield Glade (R)
Gatlinburg:
Buchhorn Inn (B)
Memphis:
Embassy Memphis (H)
Nashville:
Opryland (H)
Sheraton Music City (H)
Walland:
Inn at Blackberry Farm (B)

Texas
Arlington:
Greenhouse (S)
Austin:
Barton Creek (R)
Lakeway Inn (R)
Bandera:
Mayan Dude Ranch (B)
Dallas/Fort Worth:
Cooper Wellness (S)
Four Seasons (R)
Green Oaks Park (H)
Omni Dallas (H)
Omni Mandalay (H)
Wyndham Anatole (H)
Galveston:
Galvez (H)

Beautiful Grounds

Houston:
  Houstonian (H)
  Woodlands (R)
San Antonio:
  Hyatt Reg. Hill Country (R)
  Plaza San Antonio (H)
South Padre Island:
  Radisson South Padre (R)

Utah
Midway:
  Homestead (B)
Park City:
  Goldener Hirsch (B)
Provo:
  Sundance Resort (R)
Snowbird:
  Iron Blosam (H)
  Lodge at Snowbird (H)
Springdale:
  Zion Lodge (H)
St. George:
  Green Valley Spa (S)

Vermont
Barnard:
  Twin Farms (R)
Craftsbury Common:
  Inn on Common (H)
Essex:
  Inn at Essex (B)
Highgate Springs:
  Tyler Place (R)
Manchester:
  Inn at Manchester (B)
  Village Country (B)
  Wilburton Inn (B)
Middlebury:
  Swift House (B)
Perkinsville:
  Inn at Weathersfield (B)
Plymouth:
  Hawk Inn (B)
Shelburne:
  Inn at Shelburne Farms (B)
Smugglers' Notch:
  Smugglers' Notch (R)
Stowe:
  Topnotch at Stowe (R)
  Trapp Family (B)
Vergennes:
  Basin Harbor (R)
Woodstock:
  Woodstock Inn (R)

Virginia
Hot Springs:
  Homestead (R)
Irvington:
  Tides Inn (R)
  Tides Lodge (R)

Keswick:
  Keswick Hall (B)
Leesburg:
  Lansdowne (R)
Richmond:
  Linden Row (B)
Washington:
  Inn at Little Washington (B)
Williamsburg:
  Kingsmill (R)
Wintergreen:
  Wintergreen (R)

Washington
Coupeville:
  Captain Whidbey (B)
Lake Quinault:
  Lake Quinault (B)
Snoqualmie:
  Salish Lodge (B)
Winthrop:
  Sun Mountain (R)

West Virginia
Berkeley Springs:
  Coolfront Resort (R)
Davis:
  Canaan Valley (R)
Wheeling:
  Oglebay Resort (R)
White Sulphur Springs:
  Greenbrier (R)

Wisconsin
Bailey's Harbor:
  Gordon Lodge (B)
Delavan:
  Lake Lawn Lodge (R)
Fontana:
  Abbey Resort (R)
Green Lake:
  Heidel House (R)
Kohler:
  American Club (R)
  Inn on Woodlake (B)
Lake Geneva:
  Grand Geneva (R)
  Interlaken Resort (R)

Wyoming
Jackson:
  Rusty Parrot (B)
  Teton Pines (R)
Moran:
  Colter Bay VIllage (R)
  Jenny Lake (B)
Yellowstone National Park:
  Lake Yellowstone (H)
  Mammoth Hot Springs (H)
  Old Faithful (H)

Children's Programs

Alabama
Orange Beach:
Perdido Beach (R)

Alaska
Girdwood:
Alyeska (R)

Arizona
Phoenix/Scottsdale:
Arizona Biltmore (R)
Buttes (R)
Holiday Inn SunSpree (R)
Hyatt Reg. Scottsdale (R)
Marriott's Camelback (R)
Marriott's Mountain (R)
Phoenician (R)
Radisson Scottsdale (R)
Scottsdale Hilton (H)
Scottsdale Princess (R)
Sheraton San Marcos (R)
Wigwam (R)
Sedona:
Enchantment (R)
Tucson:
Loews Ventana (R)
Tanque Verde (B)
Westin La Paloma (R)
Westward Look (R)
Wickenburg:
Merv Griffin's (B)

Arkansas
Hot Springs:
Arlington Resort (H)
Little Rock:
Dbltree Little Rock (H)

California
Anaheim:
Hilton Anaheim (H)
Carlsbad:
La Costa (S)
Carmel:
Carmel Valley (R)
John Gardiner's (R)
Los Laureles (H)
Stonepine (B)
Dana Point:
Ritz Laguna Niguel (R)
Fish Camp:
Tenaya Lodge (R)
Irvine:
Irvine Marriott (H)
Laguna Beach:
Surf & Sand (H)
Lake Arrowhead:
Lake Arrowhead (R)
Los Angeles:
Century Plaza (H)
Loews Santa Monica (H)
Omni LA (H)
Regent Beverly Wilshire (H)
Ritz Huntington (H)
Summit Bel-Air (H)
Montecito:
San Ysidro (B)
Newport Beach:
Hyatt Newporter (R)
Sutton Place (H)
Ojai:
Ojai Valley (R)
Olympic Valley:
Resort at Squaw Creek (R)

Palm Springs:
Hilton Palm Springs (H)
Hyatt Grand (R)
Marquis Palm Springs (H)
Marriott's Desert Springs (R)
Marriott's Rancho (R)
Renaissance Esmeralda (R)
Ritz Rancho Mirage (R)
Riviera Palm Springs (R)
Shadow Mountain (R)
Westin Mission Hills (R)
San Diego:
Catamaran (H)
del Coronado Hotel (R)
Hilton San Diego (H)
Hyatt Islandia (H)
La Jolla Beach (H)
Loews Coronado (R)
Princess San Diego (R)
Rancho Bernardo (R)
Rancho Valencia (R)
Sheraton Grande (R)
San Francisco:
Clift (H)
Fairmont SF (H)
Hilton SF (H)
Rex (H)
Westin St. Francis (H)
Santa Barbara:
Four Seasons Biltmore (R)
Santa Monica:
Oceana (H)
Solvang:
Alisal (R)
Truckee:
Northstar-at-Tahoe (R)

Colorado
Aspen:
Little Nell (H)
Ritz Aspen (H)
Beaver Creek:
Hyatt Reg. Beaver Creek (H)
Breckenridge:
Village at Breckenridge (R)
Clark:
Home Ranch (R)
Colorado Springs:
Broadmoor (R)
Copper Mountain:
Copper Mountain (R)
Denver:
Hyatt Reg. Denver Tech (H)
Loews Giorgio (H)
Durango:
Tamarron Hilton (R)
Wit's End (B)
Edwards:
Lodge & Spa Cordillera (R)
Granby:
C Lazy U Ranch (B)
Keystone:
Keystone (R)
Mt. Crested Butte:
Grande Butte (H)
Snowmass Village:
Snowmass Lodge (R)
Telluride:
Peaks at Telluride (R)
Vail:
Sonnenalp of Vail (R)
Vail Athletic Club (H)

Children's Programs

Connecticut
Westbrook:
  Water's Edge (B)

Florida
Amelia Island:
  Amelia Island (R)
  Ritz Amelia Island (R)
Boca Raton:
  Boca Raton (R)
Captiva Island:
  South Seas Plantation (R)
Destin:
  Hilton Sandestin (R)
Fisher Island:
  Spa Internazionale (S)
Fort Lauderdale:
  Hyatt Reg. Pier 66 (H)
  Marriott's Harbor (R)
  Radisson Bahia Mar (R)
  Registry Resort (S)
  Westin Ft. Lauderdale (H)
Fort Myers:
  Sanibel Harbour (R)
Gasparilla Island:
  Gasparilla Inn (B)
Haines City:
  Grenelefe Golf (R)
Islamorada:
  Cheeca Lodge (R)
Jupiter:
  Jupiter Beach (R)
Key Largo:
  Marriott's Key Largo (R)
  Ocean Reef (R)
Key West:
  Hyatt Key West (H)
  Marriott's Casa Marina (R)
Longboat Key:
  Resort at Longboat Key (R)
Marathon:
  Hawk's Cay (R)
Marco Island:
  Marco Island Hilton (R)
  Marriott's Marco Island (R)
  Radisson Beach (R)
Miami/Miami Beach:
  Delano (H)
  Doral Golf (R)
  Eden Roc (H)
  Fisher Island (R)
  Fontainebleau Hilton (R)
  Hyatt Reg. Coral Gables (H)
  Sheraton Bal Harbour (H)
  Spa at Doral (S)
  Westin Miami (R)
Naples:
  Edgewater Beach (H)
  La Playa Beach (R)
  Naples Bath & Tennis (R)
  Naples Beach (R)
  Registry (R)
  Ritz Naples (R)
Orlando:
  Buena Vista Palace (H)
  Disney Institute (R)
  Disney's All-Star Music (R)
  Disney's All-Star Sports (R)
  Disney's Beach Club (R)
  Disney's Caribbean (R)
  Disney's Ft. Wilderness (R)
  Disney's Polynesian (R)
  Disney's Port Orleans (R)
  Disney's Wilderness (R)
  Disney's Yacht (R)
  Doubletree (H)
  Hilton at Walt Disney (H)
  Holiday Inn Main Gate (H)
  Holiday Inn SunSpree (R)
  Hyatt Reg. Grand Cypress (R)
  Marriott's Orl. World Ctr (H)
  Peabody Orlando (H)
  Renaissance Orlando (R)
  Residence by Marriott (H)
  Sheraton World (R)
  Villas of Grand Cypress (R)
  Vistana (R)
  Westgate Lakes (R)
Palm Beach:
  Breakers (R)
  Four Seasons Palm Beach (H)
  Palm Beach Polo (R)
  Ritz Palm Beach (R)
Panama City Beach:
  Marriott's Bay Point (R)
Pompano Beach:
  Palm-Aire Resort (S)
Ponte Vedra Beach:
  Marriott at Sawgrass (R)
  Ponte Vedra (R)
Port St. Lucie:
  Club Med Sandpiper (R)
Sanibel Island:
  Casa Ybel (R)
  Sanibel (R)
  Sundial Beach (R)
Stuart:
  Indian River Plantation (R)
Tampa Bay:
  Don CeSar (R)
  Innisbrook Hilton (R)
  Radisson Sand Key (R)
  Saddlebrook Tampa (R)
  Sheraton Sand Key (R)
  TradeWinds St. Pete (R)

Georgia
Americus:
  Windsor (H)
Atlanta:
  Evergreen (R)
  Marietta (R)
  Ritz Buckhead (H)
  Swissotel Atlanta (H)
  Westin Peachtree (H)
Braselton:
  Chateau Elan Winery (B)
Lake Lanier Islands:
  Renaissance Pineisle (R)
Pine Mountain:
  Callaway Gardens (R)
Sea Island:
  Cloister (R)
St. Simons Island:
  Lodge at Little St. Simons (B)
  Sea Palms (R)

Hawaii
Big Island:
  Four Seasons Hualalai (R)
  Hapuna Prince (R)
  Hilton Waikoloa (R)
  Kona Village (R)
  Mauna Kea (R)
  Orchid at Mauna Lani (R)
Kauai:
  Hyatt Reg. Kauai (R)
  Kauai Coconut (R)
  Kiahuna Plantation (R)

Children's Programs

Marriott Kauai (R)
Princeville (R)
Lanai:
  Lodge at Koele (R)
Maui:
  Aston Kaanapali (R)
  Aston Wailea (R)
  Four Seasons Maui (R)
  Grand Wailea (R)
  Hyatt Reg. Maui (R)
  Ka'anapali Beach (R)
  Kapalua Bay (R)
  Kea Lani (R)
  Marriott Maui (R)
  Maui Prince (R)
  Renaissance Wailea (R)
  Ritz Kapalua (R)
  Sheraton Maui (R)
  Westin Maui (R)
Oahu:
  Halekulani (H)
  Hawaiian Regent (H)
  Hilton Hawaiian (H)
  Hyatt Reg. Waikiki (H)
  Ihilani Resort (R)
  Kahala Mandarin (R)
  Pacific Beach (H)
  Royal Hawaiian (H)
  Sheraton Kaiulani (H)
  Sheraton Waikiki (H)

Idaho
Coeur d'Alene:
  Coeur d'Alene (R)
Priest Lake:
  Hill's Hospitality (B)
Sun Valley:
  Sun Valley (R)

Illinois
Chicago:
  Four Seasons Chicago (H)
  Hilton Chicago (H)
  Ritz Chicago (H)
Galena:
  Eagle Ridge (R)
St. Charles:
  Pheasant Run (R)

Indiana
Bloomington:
  Fourwinds (R)
French Lick:
  French Lick Springs (R)

Kentucky
Lexington:
  Hyatt Reg. Lexington (H)
  Marriott Griffin Gate (R)

Louisiana
New Orleans:
  Chateau Sonesta (H)
  Hilton New Orleans (H)
  Pontchartrain (H)
  Royal Sonesta (H)
  Westin Canal (H)

Maine
Rockport:
  Samoset (R)

Maryland
Annapolis:
  Loews Annapolis (H)

Massachusetts
Boston:
  Boston Harbor (H)
  Boston Park Plaza (H)
  Four Seasons Boston (H)
  Hyatt Reg. Cambridge (H)
  Omni Parker (H)
  Ritz Boston (H)
  Royal Sonesta (H)
  Swissotel (H)
Cape Cod:
  Cape Codder (B)
  Chatham Bars (B)
  New Seabury (R)
  Ocean Edge (R)
  Sea Crest (R)
  Wequassett Inn (B)
Lenox:
  Kripalu Center (S)
Martha's Vineyard:
  Harbor View (B)
Nantucket:
  Nantucket Inn (H)

Michigan
Acme:
  Grand Traverse (R)
Bellaire:
  Shanty Creek (R)
Boyne Falls:
  Boyne Mountain (R)
Detroit:
  Hyatt Reg. Dearborn (H)
Mackinac Island:
  Grand (H)
Thompsonville:
  Crystal Mountain (R)

Minnesota
Alexandria:
  Arrowwood Radisson (R)
Minneapolis/St. Paul:
  Radisson Plaza Tower (H)

Mississippi
Biloxi:
  Grand Casino (H)
Robinsonville:
  Harrah's Mardi Gras (H)

Missouri
Branson:
  Best Western Knights (H)
  Chateau on the Lake (R)
Kansas City:
  Westin Crown Ctr (H)

Montana
Bigfork:
  Averill's Flathead (B)
Big Sky:
  Lone Mountain (B)
Bozeman:
  Mountain Sky (B)

Nevada
Las Vegas:
  MGM Grand (H)
Laughlin:
  Don Laughlin's (H)
  Flamingo Hilton (H)

New Hampshire
Bretton Woods:
  1896 Bretton Arms (B)
  Mount Washington (R)
Dixville Notch:
  Balsams Grand (R)
Lincoln:
  Mountain Club (R)

Children's Programs

New Jersey
Atlantic City:
  Harrah's Casino (H)
  Marriott Seaview (R)
Cape May:
  Chalfonte (H)
Long Beach:
  Ocean Place Hilton (R)
Vernon:
  Great Gorge Village (R)

New Mexico
Albuquerque:
  Hyatt Reg. Albuquerque (H)
  Sheraton Old Town (H)
Santa Fe:
  Bishop's Lodge (R)
  Rancho Encantado (B)
Taos Ski Valley:
  Edelweiss (B)
  St. Bernard (B)

New York
Bolton Landing:
  Sagamore (R)
Kiamesha Lake:
  Concord (R)
Monticello:
  Kutsher's (R)
New York City:
  Doubletree (H)
  Essex House Nikko (H)
  Four Seasons (H)
  Grand Hyatt NY (H)
  Hilton & Towers NY (H)
  Holiday Inn Downtown (H)
  Millenium Hilton (H)
  Trump International (H)
  Westbury (H)

North Carolina
Asheville:
  Great Smokies (R)
  Grove Park Inn (R)
Blowing Rock:
  Hound Ears (R)
Charlotte:
  Hyatt Charlotte (H)
  Park (H)
  Radisson Charlotte (H)
Lake Toxaway:
  Greystone Inn (B)
Pinehurst:
  Pinehurst (R)
Wrightsville Beach:
  Blockade Runner (R)

Ohio
Cincinnati:
  Hyatt Reg. Cincinnati (H)
  Westin (H)
Cleveland:
  Ritz Cleveland (H)
Columbus:
  Hyatt on Capital Square (H)
  Hyatt Reg. Columbus (H)
Dellroy:
  Atwood Lake (R)
Huron:
  Sawmill Creek (R)

Oklahoma
Checotah:
  Fountainhead (R)
Kingston:
  Texoma State (R)

Oregon
Bend:
  Inn of Seventh Mtn (R)
Black Butte Ranch:
  Black Butte (R)
Timberline:
  Timberline (R)
Warm Springs:
  Kah-Nee-Ta (R)

Pennsylvania
Champion:
  Seven Springs (R)
Farmington:
  Nemacolin Woodlands (R)
Hershey:
  Hershey (H)
  Hershey Lodge (H)
Mt. Pocono/Pocono Manor:
  Mount Airy Lodge (R)
  Pocono Manor (R)
Philadelphia:
  Best Western Independence (H)
  Rittenhouse (H)
Skytop:
  Skytop Lodge (R)

Puerto Rico
Fajardo:
  El Conquistador (R)
San Juan:
  El San Juan (H)
  Sands (H)

South Carolina
Charleston:
  Charleston Place (H)
  Planters Inn (B)
Hilton Head:
  Hilton Hilton Head (R)
  Palmetto Dunes (R)
  Westin (R)
Kiawah Island:
  Kiawah Island (R)
Myrtle Beach:
  Hilton Myrtle Beach (R)
  Ocean Dunes (R)
  Sheraton Myrtle Beach (R)
Pawleys Island:
  Litchfield Beach (R)
Seabrook Island:
  Seabrook Island (R)

Tennessee
Nashville:
  Loews Vanderbilt (H)
  Opryland (H)

Texas
Austin:
  Lakeway Inn (R)
  Omni Austin Downtown (H)
Bandera:
  Mayan Dude Ranch (B)
Dallas/Fort Worth:
  Four Seasons (R)
  Omni Mandalay (H)
  Westin Galleria Dallas (H)
Houston:
  Houstonian (H)
  Westin Oaks (H)
South Padre Island:
  Radisson South Padre (R)

Utah
Park City:
  Stein Eriksen (R)

Children's Programs

Provo:
  Sundance Resort (R)
Snowbird:
  Cliff Lodge (R)
  Inn at Snowbird (B)
Vermont
Barnard:
  Twin Farms (R)
Brownsville:
  Ascutney Mountain (R)
Goshen:
  Blueberry Hill (B)
Highgate Springs:
  Tyler Place (R)
Killington:
  Killington Resort (R)
Plymouth:
  Hawk Inn (B)
Shelburne:
  Inn at Shelburne Farms (B)
Smugglers' Notch:
  Smugglers' Notch (R)
Stowe:
  Topnotch at Stowe (R)
  Trapp Family (B)
Stratton Mountain:
  Stratton Mtn (R)
Vergennes:
  Basin Harbor (R)
Warren:
  Sugarbush (R)
Virginia
(see also Washington, DC)
Charlottesville:
  Boar's Head Inn (R)
Hot Springs:
  Homestead (R)
Irvington:
  Tides Inn (R)
  Tides Lodge (R)
Leesburg:
  Lansdowne (R)
Virginia Beach:
  Hilton Virginia Beach (H)
  Holiday Inn Sunspree (R)
  Ramada Plaza (R)
  Virginia Beach (R)
Williamsburg:
  Kingsmill (R)
  Williamsburg Lodge (H)

Wintergreen:
  Wintergreen (R)
Washington
Blaine:
  Inn at Semi-Ah-Moo (R)
Lake Quinault:
  Lake Quinault (B)
Port Ludlow:
  Port Ludlow (R)
Seattle:
  Four Seasons Olympic (H)
Stevenson:
  Skamania Lodge (R)
Winthrop:
  Sun Mountain (R)
Washington, DC
(including nearby Maryland and Virginia)
Virginia:
  Ritz Tysons Corner (H)
Washington, DC:
  Carlton (H)
  Four Seasons (H)
  Hyatt Reg. Washington (H)
  Loews L'Enfant (H)
  Radisson Barcelo (H)
  Watergate (H)
  Westin Washington DC (H)
West Virginia
Berkeley Springs:
  Coolfront Resort (R)
Davis:
  Canaan Valley (R)
Hedgesville:
  Woods Resort (R)
White Sulphur Springs:
  Greenbrier (R)
Wisconsin
Delavan:
  Lake Lawn Lodge (R)
Green Lake:
  Heidel House (R)
Kohler:
  Inn on Woodlake (B)
Lake Geneva:
  Interlaken Resort (R)
Wyoming
Jackson:
  Spring Creek (R)

Conference Centers

Alabama
Tuskegee:
  Kellogg (H)

Arizona
Phoenix/Scottsdale:
  Scottsdale Conference (R)

California
Los Angeles:
  Sheraton Industry Hills (H)
Santa Cruz:
  Chaminade (H)

Georgia
Atlanta:
  Evergreen (R)
  Marietta (R)
  Peachtree (H)
Peachtree City:
  Aberdeen Woods (H)

Massachusetts
Boston:
  Hyatt Harborside (H)

Minnesota
Minneapolis/St. Paul:
  Radisson Conference (H)

Missouri
St. Louis:
  Doubletree (H)

New Jersey
Princeton:
  Chauncey Conference (H)
  Forrestal (H¹

New York
Glen Cove:
  Harrison (H)
Tarrytown:
  Tarrytown House (B)

Ohio
Dellroy:
  Atwood Lake (R)

Texas
Austin:
  Lakeway Inn (R)
Houston:
  Woodlands (R)

Virginia
Leesburg:
  Lansdowne (R)

Washington, DC
(including nearby Maryland and Virginia)
Virginia:
  Marriott Westfield's (H)

Corporate Retreats

Alabama
Point Clear:
 Marriott's Grand (R)
Tuskegee:
 Kellogg (H)

Alaska
Fairbanks:
 Fairbanks Princess (H)

Arizona
Gold Canyon:
 Gold Canyon (R)
Phoenix/Scottsdale:
 Arizona Biltmore (R)
 Buttes (R)
 Gardiner's (R)
 Hyatt Reg. Scottsdale (R)
 Marriott's Camelback (R)
 Phoenician (R)
 Pte Hilton S. Mountain (R)
 Pte Hilton Squaw (R)
 Pte Hilton Tapatio (R)
 Scottsdale Conference (R)
 Scottsdale Princess (R)
 Sheraton San Marcos (R)
 Wigwam (R)
Sedona:
 Enchantment (R)
 L'Auberge de Sedona (H)
Tucson:
 Lodge Ventana (R)
 Loews Ventana (R)
 Omni Tucson (R)
 Sheraton El Conquistador (R)
 Tanque Verde (B)
 Westin La Paloma (R)
 Westward Look (R)
Wickenburg:
 Merv Griffin's (B)

Arkansas
Hot Springs:
 Lake Hamilton (R)
Lakeview:
 Gaston's (R)

California
Big Sur:
 Big Sur Lodge (B)
 Post Ranch (B)
Bodega Bay:
 Inn at the Tides (B)
Borrego Springs:
 La Casa del Zorro (R)
Carlsbad:
 La Costa (S)
Carmel:
 Carmel Valley (R)
 Highlands Inn (B)
 Quail Lodge (R)
Cazadero:
 Timberhill (B)
Dana Point:
 Laguna Cliff Marriott (R)
 Ritz Laguna Niguel (R)
Death Valley:
 Furnace Creek Inn (R)
Eureka:
 Carter House (B)
Fish Camp:
 Tenaya Lodge (R)
Laguna Beach:
 Surf & Sand (H)

Little River:
 Little River Inn (B)
Los Olivos:
 Los Olivos Grand (B)
Montecito:
 Montecito Inn (B)
Monterey:
 Monterey Plaza (H)
Napa:
 Embassy Napa Valley (H)
 Silverado (R)
Newport Beach:
 Four Seasons Newport (H)
 Marriott Tennis (H)
Ojai:
 Ojai Valley (R)
Olympic Valley:
 Plumpjack's (B)
 Resort at Squaw Creek (R)
Palm Springs:
 La Quinta (R)
 Marriott's Desert Springs (R)
 Marriott's Rancho (R)
 Renaissance Esmeralda (R)
 Ritz Rancho Mirage (R)
 Westin Mission Hills (R)
Pebble Beach:
 Inn at Spanish Bay (R)
 Lodge at Pebble Beach (R)
Rutherford:
 Auberge du Soleil (B)
 Rancho Caymus (B)
San Diego:
 Inn at Rancho Santa Fe (H)
 L'Auberge Del Mar (R)
 Rancho Bernardo (R)
 Rancho Valencia (R)
 Sheraton Grande (R)
Santa Barbara:
 El Encanto (H)
Santa Rosa:
 Vintners Inn (B)
Shell Beach:
 Cliffs at Shell Beach (R)
Solvang:
 Alisal (R)
Sonoma:
 Sonoma Mission (S)
St. Helena:
 Harvest Inn (B)
 Meadowood (R)
Truckee:
 Northstar-at-Tahoe (R)
Yountville:
 Vintage Inn (H)

Colorado
Aspen:
 Inn at Aspen (H)
 Jerome (H)
 Little Nell (H)
 Ritz Aspen (H)
Beaver Creek:
 Charter at Beaver Creek (H)
 Embassy Beaver Creek (R)
 Hyatt Reg. Beaver Creek (H)
 Pines Lodge (H)
Clark:
 Home Ranch (R)
Colorado Springs:
 Broadmoor (R)
 Hearthstone Inn (B)
 Sheraton (H)

Corporate Retreats

Denver:
  Inverness (R)
Durango:
  General Palmer (H)
  Tall Timber (B)
  Tamarron Hilton (R)
  Wit's End (B)
Edwards:
  Lodge & Spa Cordillera (R)
Granby:
  C Lazy U Ranch (B)
Mt. Crested Butte:
  Grande Butte (H)
Snowmass Village:
  Snowmass Lodge (R)
Steamboat Springs:
  Sheraton Steamboat (R)
Telluride:
  Peaks at Telluride (R)
Vail:
  Lodge at Vail (H)
  Mountain Haus at Vail (H)
  Sonnenalp of Vail (R)
  Vail Cascade (H)

Connecticut
Chester:
  Inn at Chester (B)
Lakeville:
  Interlaken Inn (R)
Norfolk:
  Blackberry River (B)
Norwich:
  Norwich Inn (S)
Simsbury:
  Simsbury Inn (H)
Southbury:
  Heritage Inn (H)
Washington:
  Mayflower Inn (B)

Florida
Amelia Island:
  Amelia Island (R)
  Ritz Amelia Island (R)
Boca Raton:
  Boca Raton (R)
Captiva Island:
  South Seas Plantation (R)
Destin:
  Hilton Sandestin (R)
Haines City:
  Grenelefe Golf (R)
Howey-in-the-Hills:
  Mission Inn (R)
Islamorada:
  Cheeca Lodge (R)
Key Largo:
  Marriott's Key Largo (R)
  Ocean Reef (R)
Key West:
  Hyatt Key West (H)
  Marriott's Casa Marina (R)
  Marriott's Reach (R)
Longboat Key:
  Colony Beach (R)
  Resort at Longboat Key (R)
Marathon:
  Hawk's Cay (R)
Marco Island:
  Marco Island Hilton (R)
  Marriott's Marco Island (R)
  Radisson Beach (R)

Miami/Miami Beach:
  Doral Golf (R)
  Fisher Island (R)
  Grove Isle Club (B)
  Turnberry Isle (R)
Naples:
  Naples Bath & Tennis (R)
  Registry (R)
  Ritz Naples (R)
Orlando:
  Villas of Grand Cypress (R)
Palm Beach:
  Breakers (R)
  Four Seasons Palm Beach (H)
  PGA National (R)
  Ritz Palm Beach (R)
Panama City Beach:
  Marriott's Bay Point (R)
Ponte Vedra Beach:
  Lodge at Ponte Vedra (R)
  Marriott at Sawgrass (R)
  Ponte Vedra (R)
Stuart:
  Indian River Plantation (R)
Tampa Bay:
  Innisbrook Hilton (R)
  Saddlebrook Tampa (R)

Georgia
Atlanta:
  Evergreen (R)
  Marietta (R)
  Peachtree (H)
Braselton:
  Chateau Elan Winery (B)
Jekyll Island:
  Jekyll Island Club (R)
Lake Lanier Islands:
  Renaissance Pineisle (R)
Pine Mountain:
  Callaway Gardens (R)
Sea Island:
  Cloister (R)
St. Simons Island:
  Sea Palms (R)

Hawaii
Big Island:
  Four Seasons Hualalai (R)
  Hapuna Prince (R)
  Hilton Waikoloa (R)
  Mauna Kea (R)
  Orchid at Mauna Lani (R)
Kauai:
  Marriott Kauai (R)
  Princeville (R)
Lanai:
  Lodge at Koele (R)
  Manele Bay (R)
Maui:
  Aston Wailea (R)
  Four Seasons Maui (R)
  Grand Wailea (R)
  Kapalua Bay (R)
  Kea Lani (R)
  Marriott Maui (R)
  Maui Prince (R)
  Renaissance Wailea (R)
  Ritz Kapalua (R)
  Royal Lahaina (R)
Oahu:
  Halekulani (H)
  Hilton Hawaiian (H)
  Hilton Turtle Bay (R)
  Ihilani Resort (R)

Corporate Retreats

Ilikai Nikko Waikiki (H)
Kahala Mandarin (R)
Outrigger Prince Kuhio (H)

Idaho

Coeur d'Alene:
Coeur d'Alene (R)
Priest Lake:
Hill's Hospitality (B)
Sun Valley:
Sun Valley (R)

Illinois

Bloomingdale:
Indian Lakes (R)
Galena:
Eagle Ridge (R)
Gilman:
Heartland Spa (S)
Itasca:
Nordic Hills (R)
Lake Forest:
Deer Path (B)
Lincolnshire:
Marriott's Lincolnshire (R)
Oak Brook:
Oak Brook Hills (R)
St. Charles:
Pheasant Run (R)

Indiana

Bloomington:
Fourwinds (R)
French Lick:
French Lick Springs (R)

Kentucky

Harrodsburg:
Inn at Shaker Village (B)
Lexington:
Marriott Griffin Gate (R)

Louisiana

St. Francisville:
Lodge at the Bluffs (H)

Maine

Bar Harbor:
Atlantic Oakes (B)
Bar Harbor Inn (B)
Bayview (H)
Boothbay Harbor:
Spruce Point (B)
Cape Elizabeth:
Inn by the Sea (B)
Freeport:
Harraseeket Inn (B)
Northeast Harbor:
Asticou Inn (B)
Ogunquit:
Cliff House (H)
Rockport:
Samoset (R)
Scarborough:
Black Point Inn (R)

Maryland

Chestertown:
Imperial (B)
Easton:
Tidewater Inn (B)
Ocean City:
Sheraton Fontainebleau (H)
St. Michaels:
Inn at Perry Cabin (B)
Taneytown:
Antrim 1844 (B)

Massachusetts

Cape Cod:
Brass Key (B)
Chatham Bars (B)
New Seabury (R)
Ocean Edge (R)
Sea Crest (R)
Wequassett Inn (B)
Danvers:
Tara's Ferncroft (R)
Lenox:
Blantyre (B)
Martha's Vineyard:
Harbor View (B)
Nantucket:
Nantucket Inn (H)
Wauwinet (B)
White Elephant (R)

Michigan

Acme:
Grand Traverse (R)
Bellaire:
Shanty Creek (R)
Boyne Falls:
Boyne Mountain (R)
Harbor Springs:
Boyne Highlands (R)
Mackinac Island:
Mission Point (R)
Thompsonville:
Crystal Mountain (R)
Ypsilanti:
Marriott Ypsilanti (R)

Minnesota

Alexandria:
Arrowwood Radisson (R)
Brainerd:
Madden's (R)
Lutsen:
Lutsen (R)
Red Wing:
St. James (H)
Stillwater:
Lumber Baron's (H)

Mississippi

Natchez:
Dunleith (B)

Missouri

Lake Ozark:
Lodge at Four Seasons (R)
Osage Beach:
Marriott's Tan-Tar-A (R)

Montana

Bigfork:
Averill's Flathead (B)
Big Sky:
Lone Mountain (B)
Bozeman:
Mountain Sky (B)
Gallatin Gateway:
Gallatin Gateway (B)
Whitefish:
Grouse Mountain (R)

New Hampshire

Bretton Woods:
Mount Washington (R)
Dixville Notch:
Balsams Grand (R)
Holderness:
Manor on Golden Pond (B)

Corporate Retreats

Jackson:
Eagle Mountain (H)
Lincoln:
Mountain Club (R)
Meredith:
Inn at Mill Falls (B)
North Conway:
Four Points Sheraton (H)

New Jersey
Atlantic City:
Marriott Seaview (R)
Basking Ridge:
Olde Mill Inn (B)
Cape May:
Virginia Hotel (B)
Hope:
Inn at Millrace Pond (B)
Long Beach:
Ocean Place Hilton (R)
Princeton:
Forrestal (H)
Summit:
Grand Summit (H)

New Mexico
Chama:
Lodge at Chama (B)
Cloudcroft:
Lodge at Cloudcroft (B)
Mescalero:
Inn of Mountain Gods (R)
Raton:
Vermejo Park (B)
Santa Fe:
Bishop's Lodge (R)
Rancho Encantado (B)
Taos:
Fechin Inn (B)

New York
Alexandria Bay:
Bonnie Castle (R)
Amenia:
Troutbeck (B)
Bolton Landing:
Sagamore (R)
Geneva:
Geneva on the Lake (B)
Glen Cove:
Harrison (H)
Great Neck:
Inn at Great Neck (H)
Hopewell Junction:
Le Chambord (B)
Kiamesha Lake:
Concord (R)
Lake Placid:
Lake Placid Lodge (B)
Mirror Lake (B)
Lew Beach:
Beaverkill Valley (B)
Montauk:
Gurney's Inn (S)
Montauk Yacht (R)
New Paltz:
Mohonk Mountain (R)
Poughkeepsie:
Inn at the Falls (B)
Rye Brook:
Doral Arrowwood (R)
Saratoga Springs:
Gideon Putnam (H)
Inn at Saratoga (B)
Sheraton Saratoga (R)

Shelter Island:
Ram's Head (B)
Stony Brook:
Three Village (B)
Tarrytown:
Castle at Tarrytown (B)
Tarrytown House (B)

North Carolina
Asheville:
Grove Park Inn (R)
Richmond Hill (B)
Blowing Rock:
Hound Ears (R)
Cashiers:
High Hampton (R)
Duck:
Sanderling Inn (R)
Pittsboro:
Fearrington House (B)
Wrightsville Beach:
Blockade Runner (R)

Ohio
Dellroy:
Atwood Lake (R)
Huron:
Sawmill Creek (R)
Painesville:
Quail Hollow (R)

Oklahoma
Afton:
Shangri-La (R)
Kingston:
Texoma State (R)

Oregon
Gleneden Beach:
Salishan (R)
Gold Beach:
Tu Tu'Tun (B)
Hood River:
Columbia Gorge (H)
Lincoln City:
Inn at Spanish Head (B)
Timberline:
Timberline (R)
Welches:
Resort at Mountain (R)

Pennsylvania
Farmington:
Nemacolin Woodlands (R)
Hershey:
Hershey (H)
Hershey Lodge (H)
Malvern:
Desmond (H)
Mt. Pocono/Pocono Manor:
Pocono Manor (R)
Skytop:
Skytop Lodge (R)

Puerto Rico
Dorado:
Hyatt Reg. Cerromar (R)
Fajardo:
El Conquistador (R)
Humacao:
Palmas del Mar (R)
Old San Juan:
El Convento (H)

Rhode Island
Newport:
Dbltree Newport (H)

Corporate Retreats

South Carolina
Hilton Head:
Hilton Hilton Head (R)
Palmetto Dunes (R)
Westin (R)
Isle of Palms:
Wild Dunes (R)
Kiawah Island:
Kiawah Island (R)
Myrtle Beach:
Hilton Myrtle Beach (R)
Kingston Planation (R)
Ocean Dunes (R)
Pawleys Island:
Litchfield Beach (R)
Seabrook Island:
Seabrook Island (R)

South Dakota
Chamberlain:
Radisson Cedar Shore (R)

Tennessee
Walland:
Inn at Blackberry Farm (B)

Texas
Austin:
Barton Creek (R)
Lakeway Inn (R)
Bandera:
Mayan Dude Ranch (B)
Dallas/Fort Worth:
Four Seasons (R)
Green Oaks Park (H)
Galveston:
Tremont House (H)
Houston:
Houstonian (H)
Woodlands (R)
Montgomery:
Del Lago (R)
San Antonio:
Hyatt Reg. Hill Country (R)

Utah
Midway:
Homestead (B)
Park City:
Deer Valley (H)
Goldener Hirsch (B)
Shadow Ridge (H)
Stein Eriksen (R)
Provo:
Sundance Resort (R)

Vermont
Killington:
Cortina Inn (B)
Lower Waterford:
Rabbit Hill (B)
Manchester:
Equinox (H)
Wilburton Inn (B)
Plymouth:
Hawk Inn (B)
Stowe:
Topnotch at Stowe (R)
Stratton Mountain:
Stratton Mtn (R)
Vergennes:
Basin Harbor (R)
Wilmington:
Hermitage Inn (B)
Woodstock:
Woodstock Inn (R)

Virginia
(see also Washington, DC)
Charlottesville:
Boar's Head Inn (R)
Hot Springs.
Homestead (R)
Irvington:
Tides Lodge (R)
Leesburg:
Larsdowne (R)
Virginia Beach:
Pavilion Towers (H)
Virginia Beach (R)
Williamsburg:
Kingsmill (R)
Wintergreen:
Wintergreen (R)

Washington
Blaine:
Inr at Semi-Ah-Moo (R)
Coupeville:
Captain Whidbey (B)
Eastsound:
Rosario Resort (R)
Port Ludlow:
Port Ludlow (R)
Snoqualmie:
Salish Lodge (B)
Stevenson:
Skamania Lodge (R)
Winthrop:
Sun Mountain (R)

Washington, DC
(including nearby Maryland and Virginia)
Virginia:
Marriott Westfield's (H)

West Virginia
Berkeley Springs:
Coolfront Resort (R)
Hedgesville:
Woods Resort (R)
Shepherdstown:
Bavarian Inn (B)
Wheeling:
Oglebay Resort (R)
White Sulphur Springs:
Greenbrier (R)

Wisconsin
Delavan:
Lake Lawn Lodge (R)
Fontana:
Abbey Resort (R)
Green Lake:
Heidel House (R)
Kohler:
American Club (R)
Inn on Woodlake (B)
Lake Geneva:
Grand Geneva (R)
Interlaken Resort (R)
Wisconsin Dells:
Chula Vista (R)

Wyoming
Jackson:
Jackson Hole Racquet (R)
Spring Creek (R)
Teton Pines (R)
Moran:
Jackson Lake (B)

Dramatic Public Spaces

Alabama

Birmingham:
Tutwiler (H)
Wynfrey (H)
Mobile:
Radisson Admiral (H)
Point Clear:
Marriott's Grand (R)

Alaska

Girdwood:
Alyeska (R)

Arizona

Catalina:
Miraval (S)
Douglas:
Gadsden (H)
Phoenix/Scottsdale:
Arizona Biltmore (R)
Arizona Golf (R)
Boulders (R)
Buttes (R)
Dbltree La Posada (R)
Dbltree Paradise Valley (R)
Embassy Biltmore (H)
Gardiner's (R)
Hyatt Reg. Scottsdale (R)
Marriott's Camelback (R)
Phoenician (R)
Pte Hilton S. Mountain (R)
Pte Hilton Squaw (R)
Pte Hilton Tapatio (R)
Regal McCormick (R)
Ritz Phoenix (H)
Scottsdale Princess (R)
Sheraton Crescent (H)
Sheraton Mesa (H)
Sheraton San Marcos (R)
Prescott:
Hassayampa Inn (H)
Sedona:
Enchantment (R)
Los Abrigados (R)
Tucson:
Arizona Inn (H)
Canyon Ranch (S)
Lodge Ventana (R)
Loews Ventana (R)
Omni Tucson (R)
Sheraton El Conquistador (R)
Westin La Paloma (R)

Arkansas

Little Rock:
Capital (H)

California

Anaheim:
Dbltree Anaheim (H)
Hilton Anaheim (H)
Borrego Springs:
La Casa del Zorro (R)
Calistoga:
Indian Springs (S)
Carlsbad:
La Costa (S)
Carmel:
Carmel Valley (R)
Costa Mesa:
Red Lion (H)
Dana Point:
Laguna Cliff Marriott (R)

Irvine:
Hyatt Reg. Irvine (H)
Lafayette:
Lafayette Park (H)
Lake Arrowhead:
Lake Arrowhead (R)
Long Beach:
Queen Mary (H)
Renaissance Long Beach (H)
Los Angeles:
Argyle (H)
Barnabey's (H)
Beverly Hills (H)
Beverly Prescott (H)
Century Plaza (H)
Chateau Marmont (H)
Doubletree LAX (H)
Four Seasons (H)
Loews Santa Monica (H)
Marriott Marina Beach (H)
Marriott Warner Ctr (H)
Mondrian (H)
New Otani (H)
Nikko Beverly Hills (H)
Omni LA (H)
Park Hyatt LA (H)
Peninsula Beverly Hills (H)
Regal Biltmore (H)
Regent Beverly Wilshire (H)
Ritz Huntington (H)
Ritz Marina del Rey (H)
Sheraton Grande (H)
Shutters (H)
Westin Bonaventure (H)
Wyndham Bel Age (H)
Wyndham Checkers (H)
Wyndham LAX (H)
Monterey:
Monterey Plaza (H)
Pacific (H)
Newport Beach:
Four Seasons Newport (H)
Marriott Tennis (H)
Sutton Place (H)
Ojai:
Ojai Valley (R)
Olympic Valley:
Resort at Squaw Creek (R)
Palm Springs:
Hyatt Grand (R)
Indian Wells (R)
La Quinta (R)
Marquis Palm Springs (H)
Marriott's Desert Springs (R)
Marriott's Rancho (R)
Monte Vista (R)
Ritz Rancho Mirage (R)
Westin Mission Hills (R)
Pebble Beach:
Lodge at Pebble Beach (R)
Riverside:
Mission Inn (H)
San Diego:
del Coronado Hotel (R)
Hyatt Reg. La Jolla (H)
Hyatt Reg. San Diego (H)
La Jolla Beach (H)
La Valencia (H)
Le Meridien San Diego (H)
Loews Coronado (R)
Marriott San Diego (H)
Princess San Diego (R)

Dramatic Public Spaces

Rancho Bernardo (R)
Rancho Valencia (R)
Sheraton Grande (R)
Sheraton San Diego (H)
US Grant (H)
Westgate (H)
Wyndham Emerald (H)

San Francisco:
Campton Place (H)
Claremont (R)
Clift (H)
Parc Fifty-Five (H)
Fairmont SF (H)
Grand Hyatt SF (H)
Hilton SF (H)
Hyatt Reg. SF (H)
Majestic (H)
Mandarin Oriental (H)
Mark Hopkins (H)
Marriott SF (H)
Monaco (H)
Nikko SF (H)
Palace (H)
Pan Pacific SF (H)
Queen Anne (H)
Renaissance Stanford (H)
Rex (H)
Sir Francis Drake (H)
Westin St. Francis (H)

San Jose:
Fairmont San Jose (H)

Santa Barbara:
El Encanto (H)
Four Seasons Biltmore (R)

Santa Monica:
Oceana (H)

Shell Beach:
Cliffs at Shell Beach (R)

Solvang:
Alisal (R)

Sonoma:
Sonoma Mission (S)

Yosemite:
Ahwahnee (H)

Colorado

Aspen:
Jerome (H)
Little Nell (H)
Ritz Aspen (H)

Beaver Creek:
Hyatt Reg. Beaver Creek (H)
Pines Lodge (H)

Boulder:
Boulderado (H)

Breckenridge:
Village at Breckenridge (R)

Clark:
Home Ranch (R)

Colorado Springs:
Antlers Dlbtree (H)
Broadmoor (R)

Copper Mountain:
Copper Mountain (R)

Denver:
Brown Palace (H)
Holtze (H)
Hyatt Reg. Denver Tech (H)
Inverness (H)
Renaissance Denver (H)

Durango:
Rochester (H)
Tamarron Hilton (R)

Edwards:
Lodge & Spa Cordillera (R)

Keystone:
Keystone (R)

Telluride:
Peaks at Telluride (R)

Vail:
Sonnenalp of Vail (R)

Connecticut

Ledyard:
Foxwoods (H)

Norwich:
Norwich Inn (S)

Delaware

Wilmington:
Hotel du Pont (H)

Florida

Amelia Island:
Amelia Island (R)
Ritz Amelia Island (R)

Boca Raton:
Boca Raton (R)

Captiva Island:
South Seas Plantation (R)

Clearwater:
Belleview Mido (R)

Destin:
Hilton Sandestin (R)

Fort Lauderdale:
Hyatt Reg. Pier 66 (H)
Lago Mar (R)
Marriott's Harbor (R)
Westin Ft. Lauderdale (H)

Fort Myers:
Sanibel Harbour (R)

Haines City:
Grenelefe Golf (R)

Howey-in-the-Hills:
Mission Inn (R)

Jacksonville:
Omni Jacksonville (H)

Jupiter:
Jupiter Beach (R)

Key Largo:
Marriott's Key Largo (R)
Ocean Reef (R)

Key West:
Holiday Inn La Concha (H)
Hyatt Key West (H)
Ocean Key House (R)

Marco Island:
Radisson Beach (R)

Miami/Miami Beach:
Albion (H)
Alexander (H)
Astor (H)
Biltmore (R)
Delano (H)
Doral Golf (R)
Eden Roc (H)
Fisher Island (R)
Fontainebleau Hilton (R)
Grand Bay (H)
Inter-Continental Miami (H)
Marriott Biscayne Bay (H)
Mayfair House (H)
Miami Beach Ocean (H)
Omni Colonnade (H)
Park Central (H)
Raleigh (H)
Sheraton Bal Harbour (H)
Sheraton Biscayne Bay (H)

Dramatic Public Spaces

Spa at Doral (S)
Turnberry Isle (R)
Mount Dora:
Lakeside Inn (R)
Naples:
La Playa Beach (R)
Naples Bath & Tennis (R)
Naples Beach (R)
Registry (R)
Ritz Naples (R)
Orlando:
Buena Vista Palace (H)
Disney's Caribbean (R)
Disney's Dixie Landings (R)
Disney's Ft. Wilderness (R)
Disney's Grand Floridian (R)
Disney's Polynesian (R)
Disney's Old Key West (R)
Disney's Port Orleans (R)
Disney's Wilderness (R)
Disney's Yacht (R)
Grosvenor (R)
Hyatt Reg. Grand Cypress (R)
Hyatt Reg. Orlando (H)
Marriott's Orl. World Ctr (H)
Peabody Orlando (H)
Renaissance Orlando (R)
Vistana (R)
Walt Disney Swan (R)
Palm Beach:
Breakers (R)
Colony (H)
Four Seasons Palm Beach (H)
Palm Beach Polo (R)
PGA National (R)
Ritz Palm Beach (R)
Panama City Beach:
Marriott's Bay Point (R)
Pompano Beach:
Palm-Aire Resort (S)
Ponte Vedra Beach:
Marriott at Sawgrass (R)
Ponte Vedra (R)
Sanibel Island:
Sundial Beach (R)
Stuart:
Indian River Plantation (R)
Tampa Bay:
Don CeSar (R)
Innisbrook Hilton (R)
Saddlebrook Tampa (R)
TradeWinds St. Pete (R)

Georgia
Americus:
Windsor (H)
Atlanta:
Evergreen (R)
Four Seasons Atlanta (H)
Grand Hyatt Atlanta (H)
Hilton Atlanta (H)
Holiday Inn Ravinia (H)
Hyatt Reg. Atlanta (H)
Marietta (R)
Marriott Marquis Atlanta (H)
Renaissance Waverly (H)
Ritz Buckhead (H)
Sheraton Colony Square (H)
Westin Peachtree (H)
Jekyll Island:
Jekyll Island Club (R)
Lake Lanier Islands:
Renaissance Pineisle (R)
Pine Mountain:
Callaway Gardens (R)

Savannah:
Hyatt Reg. Savannah (H)
Marriott Savannah (H)

Hawaii
Big Island:
Four Seasons Hualalai (R)
Hapuna Prince (R)
Hilton Waikoloa (R)
Kona Village (R)
Kauai:
Hyatt Reg. Kauai (R)
Kauai Coconut (R)
Marriott Kauai (R)
Princeville (R)
Lanai:
Lodge at Koele (R)
Manele Bay (R)
Maui:
Aston Wailea (R)
Four Seasons Maui (R)
Grand Wailea (R)
Kea Lani (R)
Marriott Maui (R)
Maui Prince (R)
Renaissance Wailea (R)
Ritz Kapalua (R)
Sheraton Maui (R)
Westin Maui (R)
Oahu:
Halekulani (H)
Hawaiian Regent (H)
Hawaii Prince Waikiki (H)
Hilton Hawaiian (H)
Royal Hawaiian (H)
Sheraton Moana (H)
Sheraton Waikiki (H)

Idaho
Boise:
Owyhee Plaza (H)
Sun Valley:
Sun Valley (R)

Illinois
Chicago:
Drake (H)
Fairmont (H)
Four Seasons Chicago (H)
Hilton Chicago (H)
Hyatt Reg. Chicago (H)
Hyatt Reg. O'Hare (H)
Inter-Continental Chicago (H)
Omni Chicago (H)
Palmer Hilton (H)
Renaissance Chicago (H)
Ritz Chicago (H)
Rosemont O'Hare (H)
Sheraton Chicago (H)
Sutton Place (H)
Westin River North (H)
Galena:
Eagle Ridge (R)
Lake Forest:

Indiana
Indianapolis:
Omni Severin (H)
Westin Indianapolis (H)

Iowa

Kansas

Kentucky
Lexington:
Hyatt Reg. Lexington (H)
Marriott Griffin Gate (R)

Dramatic Public Spaces

Louisville:
Camberly Brown (H)
Hyatt Reg. Louisville (H)
Seelbach (H)

Louisiana
New Orleans:
Chateau Sonesta (H)
Fairmont New Orleans (H)
Hilton New Orleans (H)
Hyatt Reg. New Orleans (H)
Le Meridien (H)
Maison Dupuy (H)
Monteleone (H)
Omni Royal Crescent (H)
Omni Royal Orleans (H)
Royal Sonesta (H)
Westin Canal (H)
Windsor Court (H)
Wyndham Riverfront (H)

Maine
Bar Harbor:
Bayview (H)
Ogunquit:
Cliff House (H)
Portland:
Radisson Portland (H)
Rockport:
Samoset (R)
Scarborough:
Black Point Inn (R)

Maryland
Annapolis:
Loews Annapolis (H)
Baltimore:
Clarion at Mt. Vernon (H)
Dbltree Colonnade (H)
Harbor Court (H)
Omni Inner Harbor (H)
Renaissance Harborplace (H)
Ocean City:
Coconut Malorie (H)

Massachusetts
Boston:
Boston Harbor (H)
Boston Park Plaza (H)
Fairmont Copley (H)
Four Seasons Boston (H)
Hyatt Harborside (H)
Hyatt Reg. Cambridge (H)
Le Meridien (H)
Marriott Copley Place (H)
Omni Parker (H)
Regal Bostonian (H)
Renaissance Bedford (H)
Royal Sonesta (H)
Swissotel (H)
Tremont House (H)
Westin Copley Place (H)
Westin Waltham-Boston (H)
Cape Cod:
Ocean Edge (R)
Danvers:
Tara's Ferncroft (R)
Lenox:
Canyon Ranch (S)
Cranwell (R)
Nantucket:
White Elephant (R)

Michigan
Detroit:
Hyatt Reg. Dearborn (H)
Radisson Plaza (H)
Ritz Dearborn (H)
River Place (H)

Mackinac Island:
Grand (H)

Minnesota
Minneapolis/St. Paul:
Embassy Minneapolis (H)
Marriott Minneapolis (H)
Radisson Minneapolis (H)
Saint Paul (H)

Mississippi
Robinsonville:
Sam's (H)

Missouri
Kansas:
Dbltree Corporate Woods (H)
Branson:
Best Western Music (H)
Kansas City:
Radisson (H)
Ritz Kansas City (H)
Westin Crown Ctr (H)
Ridgedale:
Big Cedar (R)
St. Louis:
Adam's Mark (H)
Crowne Plaza Majestic (H)
Frontenac Hilton (H)
Hyatt Reg. St. Louis (H)
Marriott St. Louis (H)

Montana
Whitefish:
Grouse Mountain (R)

Nebraska
Omaha:
Red Lion Omaha (H)

Nevada
Crystal Bay:
Cal-Neva Resort (R)
Lake Tahoe:
Harrah's Lake Tahoe (R)
Las Vegas:
Alexis Park (H)
Bally's Las Vegas (H)
Caesars Palace (H)
Circus Circus (H)
Excalibur (H)
Flamingo Hilton (H)
Luxor Las Vegas (H)
Maxim (H)
MGM Grand (H)
Mirage (H)
NY Hotel & Casino (H)
Rio Suite (H)
Riviera (H)
Sahara (H)
Stratosphere (H)
Treasure Island (H)
Laughlin:
Golden Nugget (H)
Mesquite:
Players Island (R)
Reno:
John Ascuaga's (H)
Silver Legacy (H)

New Hampshire
Dixville Notch:
Balsams Grand (R)
Jackson:

New Jersey
Atlantic City:
Bally's Park Place (H)
Caesar Atlantic City (H)

Dramatic Public Spaces

Hilton Atlantic City (H)
Marriott Seaview (R)
Merv Griffin's (H)
Showboat Casino (H)
Tropicana Casino (H)
Trump's Castle (H)
Trump Taj Mahal (H)
Trump World's Fair (H)
Morristown:
Headquarters Plaza (H)
Princeton:
Hyatt Reg. Princeton (H)
Marriott Princeton (H)

New Mexico
Albuquerque:
Crowne Plaza (H)
Hyatt Reg. Albuquerque (H)
La Posada Albuquerque (H)
Española:
Rancho de San Juan (R)
Santa Fe:
Eldorado (H)
La Posada Santa Fe (H)
Santa Fe (H)
St. Francis (H)

New York
Albany:
Desmond (H)
Alexandria Bay:
Bonnie Castle (R)
Great Neck:
Inn at Great Neck (H)
Kiamesha Lake:
Concord (R)
Montauk:
Montauk Yacht (R)
Monticello:
Kutsher's (R)
New Paltz:
Mohonk Mountain (R)
New York City:
Algonquin (H)
Box Tree (H)
Carlyle (H)
Essex House Nikko (H)
Four Seasons (H)
Grand Hyatt NY (H)
Hilton & Towers NY (H)
Le Parker Meridien (H)
Mark (H)
Marriott Financial Ctr (H)
Marriott Marquis (H)
Marriott World Trade (H)
Millenium Hilton (H)
Millennium Broadway (H)
NY Palace (H)
Paramount (H)
Peninsula NY (H)
Plaza (H)
Plaza Athénée (H)
Renaissance NY (H)
Rihga Royal (H)
Royalton (H)
St. Regis (H)
Trump International (H)
UN Plaza Park Hyatt (H)
Waldorf Astoria (H)
Rye Brook:
Doral Arrowwood (R)

North Carolina
Asheville:
Grove Park Inn (R)

Blowing Rock:
Hound Ears (R)
Westglow Spa (S)
Charlotte:
Hyatt Charlotte (H)
Marriott Charlotte (H)
Westin Charlotte (H)
Duck:
Sanderling Inn (R)
Fayetteville:
Radisson Prince Charles (H)
Pinehurst:
Pinehurst (R)
Raleigh-Durham:
Carolina Inn (H)
Siena (H)
Wrightsville Beach:
Blockade Runner (R)

North Dakota
Fargo:
Best Western Doublewood (H)
Radisson Fargo (H)

Ohio
Cincinnati:
Cincinnatian (H)
Omni Netherland (H)
Cleveland:
Omni International (H)
Renaissance Cleveland (H)
Ritz Cleveland (H)
Wyndham Cleveland (H)
Columbus:
Hyatt Reg. Columbus (H)
Westin Columbus (H)

Oklahoma
Checotah:
Fountainhead (R)

Oregon
Black Butte Ranch:
Black Butte (R)
Eugene:
Valley River (H)
Gleneden Beach:
Salishan (R)
Hood River:
Columbia Gorge (H)
Portland:
Benson (H)
5th Avenue Suites (H)
Governor (H)
Marriott Portland (H)
Vintage Plaza (H)
Sunriver:
Sunriver (R)
Timberline:
Timberline (R)
Welches:
Resort at Mountain (R)

Pennsylvania
Hershey:
Hershey (H)
Hershey Lodge (H)
Philadelphia:
Four Seasons Philadelphia (H)
Marriott Philadelphia (H)
Omni at Independence (H)
Rittenhouse (H)
Ritz Philadelphia (H)
Warwick Philadelphia (H)
Pittsburgh:
Dbltree Pittsburgh (H)
Sheraton Station Square (H)
Westin William Penn (H)

Dramatic Public Spaces

Wayne:
Wayne (H)

Puerto Rico
Dorado:
Hyatt Reg. Cerromar (R)
Hyatt Reg. Dorado (R)
Fajardo:
El Conquistador (R)
Humacao:
Palmas del Mar (R)
San Juan:
Caribe Hilton (H)

Rhode Island
Newport:
Vanderbilt Hall (H)
Providence:
Westin Providence (H)

South Carolina
Charleston:
Charleston Place (H)
Mills House (H)
Hilton Head:
Hilton Hilton Head (R)
Westin (R)
Isle of Palms:
Wild Dunes (R)
Kiawah Island:
Kiawah Island (R)
Myrtle Beach:
Hilton Myrtle Beach (R)
Ocean Dunes (R)
Seabrook Island:
Seabrook Island (R)

South Dakota

Tennessee
Memphis:
Peabody Memphis (H)
Nashville:
Embassy Nashville (H)
Hermitage (H)
Opryland (H)
Sheraton Music City (H)
Union Station (H)

Texas
Arlington:
Greenhouse (S)
Austin:
Barton Creek (R)
Driskill (H)
Four Seasons Austin (H)
Hyatt Reg. Austin (H)
Omni Austin Downtown (H)
Renaissance Austin (H)
Dallas/Fort Worth:
Adolphus (H)
Crescent Court (H)
Fairmont (H)
Four Seasons (R)
Hyatt Reg. Dallas (H)
Le Meridien (H)
Mansion on Turtle Creek (H)
Melrose (H)
Omni Dallas (H)
Omni Mandalay (H)
Radisson Park (H)
Wyndham Anatole (H)
Galveston:
Galvez (H)
Tremont House (H)
Houston:
Adam's Mark (H)
Four Seasons Houston (H)

Omni Houston (H)
Ritz Houston (H)
Sofitel (H)
South Shore Harbour (H)
Westin Galleria (H)
Wyndham Greenspoint (H)
Wyndham Warwick (H)
Montgomery:
Del Lago (R)
San Antonio:
Fairmount (H)
Hyatt Reg. Hill Country (R)
Hyatt Reg. San Antonio (H)
Marriott Rivercenter (H)
Menger (H)

Utah
Park City:
Deer Valley (H)
Stein Eriksen (R)
Provo:
Sundance Resort (R)
Salt Lake City:
Peery (H)
Snowbird:
Lodge at Snowbird (H)
St. George:
Green Valley Spa (S)

Vermont
Barnard:
Twin Farms (R)
Highgate Springs:
Tyler Place (R)
Killington:
Killington Resort (R)
Stowe:
Topnotch at Stowe (R)
Stratton Mountain:
Stratton Mtn (R)

Virginia
(see also Washington, DC)
Hot Springs:
Homestead (R)
Richmond:
Jefferson (H)
Williamsburg:
Williamsburg Lodge (H)

Washington
Seattle:
Edgewater (H)
Four Seasons Olympic (H)
Sorrento (H)
Woodmark (H)
Stevenson:
Skamania Lodge (R)
Winthrop:
Sun Mountain (R)

Washington, DC
(including nearby Maryland and Virginia)
Virginia:
Ritz Pentagon City
Ritz Tysons Corner (H)
Washington, DC:
(including nearby Maryland and
Virginia)
Capital Hilton (H)
Carlton (H)
Four Seasons (H)
Hay-Adams (H)
Marriott JW (H)
Omni Shoreham (H)
Park Hyatt Washington (H)
Renaissance Mayflower (H)

Dramatic Public Spaces

Watergate (H)
Willard (H)

West Virginia
White Sulphur Springs:
Greenbrier (R)

Wisconsin
Fontana:
Abbey Resort (R)
Kohler:
American Club (R)
Milwaukee:
Hilton Milwaukee (H)

Hyatt Reg. Milwaukee (H)
Pfister (H)
Wyndham Milwaukee (H)

Wyoming
Jackson:
Snow King (R)
Teton Pines (R)
Yellowstone National Park:
Lake Yellowstone (H)
Old Faithful (H)

Elite Status

Alabama
Birmingham:
  Tutwiler (H)
  Wynfrey (H)

Arizona
Phoenix/Scottsdale:
  Arizona Biltmore (R)
  Gardiner's (R)
  Hyatt Reg. Scottsdale (R)
  Inn at the Citadel (B)
  Phoenician (R)
  Scottsdale Princess (R)
  Wigwam (R)
Sedona:
  Enchantment (R)
  L'Auberge de Sedona (H)
Tucson:
  Canyon Ranch (S)
  Loews Ventana (R)

Arkansas
Little Rock:
  Capital (H)

California
Big Sur:
  Post Ranch (B)
  Ventana Inn (B)
Carlsbad:
  La Costa (S)
Carmel:
  Carmel Valley (R)
  Highlands Inn (B)
  Quail Lodge (R)
  Stonepine (B)
Dana Point:
  Ritz Laguna Niguel (R)
Escondido:
  Golden Door (S)
Los Angeles:
  Bel-Air (H)
  Beverly Hills (H)
  Beverly Prescott (H)
  Four Seasons (H)
  Inter-Continental LA (H)
  Loews Santa Monica (H)
  Nikko Beverly Hills (H)
  Peninsula Beverly Hills (H)
  Regal Biltmore (H)
  Regent Beverly Wilshire (H)
  Ritz Huntington (H)
  Ritz Marina del Rey (H)
  Shutters (H)
  Wyndham Bel Age (H)
  Wyndham Checkers (H)
Montecito:
  San Ysidro (B)
Newport Beach:
  Four Seasons Newport (H)
Oakhurst:
  Chateau du Sureau (B)
Palm Springs:
  Ingleside (B)
  La Quinta (R)
  Renaissance Esmeralda (R)
  Ritz Rancho Mirage (R)
  Two Bunch Palms (B)
  Westin Mission Hills (R)
Pebble Beach:
  Inn at Spanish Bay (R)
  Lodge at Pebble Beach (R)
Rutherford:
  Auberge du Soleil (B)

San Diego:
  Hyatt Reg. La Jolla (H)
  Le Meridien San Diego (H)
  Loews Coronado (R)
  Rancho Bernardo (R)
  Rancho Valencia (R)
  Sheraton Grande (R)
  Sheraton San Diego (H)
  Westgate (H)
San Francisco:
  Archbishop's Mansion (B)
  Campton Place (H)
  Clift (H)
  Huntington (H)
  Mandarin Oriental (H)
  Nikko SF (H)
  Palace (H)
  Pan Pacific SF (H)
  Park Hyatt SF (H)
  Renaissance Stanford (H)
  Ritz SF (H)
  Sherman House (B)
Santa Barbara:
  Four Seasons Biltmore (R)
St. Helena:
  Meadowood (R)
Vista:
  Cal-a-Vie (S)

Colorado
Aspen:
  Jerome (H)
  Little Nell (H)
  Ritz Aspen (H)
Beaver Creek:
  Hyatt Reg. Beaver Creek (H)
  Pines Lodge (H)
Clark:
  Home Ranch (R)
Colorado Springs:
  Broadmoor (R)
Denver:
  Brown Palace (H)
  Loews Giorgio (H)
  Oxford (H)
Edwards:
  Lodge & Spa Cordillera (R)
Telluride:
  Peaks at Telluride (R)
Vail:
  Sonnenalp of Vail (R)

Connecticut
Washington:
  Mayflower Inn (B)
Westport:
  Inn at National Hall (B)

Delaware
Wilmington:
  Hotel du Pont (H)

Florida
Amelia Island:
  Ritz Amelia Island (R)
Boca Raton:
  Boca Raton (R)
Fisher Island:
  Spa Internazionale (S)
Little Torch Key:
  Little Palm Island (B)
Miami/Miami Beach:
  Fisher Island (R)
  Grand Bay (H)
  Mayfair House (H)

Elite Status

Spa at Doral (S)
Turnberry Isle (R)
Naples:
Registry (R)
Ritz Naples (R)
Orlando:
Disney's Grand Floridian (R)
Hyatt Reg. Grand Cypress (R)
Peabody Orlando (H)
Palm Beach:
Breakers (R)
Four Seasons Palm Beach (H)
Ponte Vedra Beach:
Ponte Vedra (R)

Georgia
Atlanta:
Four Seasons Atlanta (H)
Grand Hyatt Atlanta (H)
Ritz Atlanta (H)
Ritz Buckhead (H)
Swissotel Atlanta (H)
Macon:
1842 Inn (B)
Savannah:
Ballastone Inn (B)
Gastonian (B)
Sea Island:
Cloister (R)

Hawaii
Big Island:
Four Seasons Hualalai (R)
Hapuna Prince (R)
Hilton Waikoloa (R)
Mauna Kea (R)
Orchid at Mauna Lani (R)
Kauai:
Princeville (R)
Lanai:
Lodge at Koele (R)
Maui:
Four Seasons Maui (R)
Grand Wailea (R)
Hana-Maui Hotel (H)
Kapalua Bay (R)
Kea Lani (R)
Maui Prince (R)
Ritz Kapalua (R)
Oahu:
Halekulani (H)
Hawaii Prince Waikiki (H)
Ihilani Resort (R)
Kahala Mandarin (R)

Illinois
Chicago:
Drake (H)
Fairmont (H)
Four Seasons Chicago (H)
La Salle Club (H)
Renaissance Chicago (H)
Ritz Chicago (H)
Westin River North (H)

Indiana
Indianapolis:
Canterbury (H)

Louisiana
Napoleonville:
Madewood Plantation (B)
New Orleans:
Maison de Ville (B)
Windsor Court (H)

Maine
Kennebunkport:
White Barn Inn (B)

Maryland
Baltimore:
Harbor Court (H)
St. Michaels:
Inn at Perry Cabin (B)

Massachusetts
Boston:
Four Seasons Boston (H)
Le Meridien (H)
Regal Bostonian (H)
Ritz Boston (H)
Lenox:
Blantyre (B)
Canyon Ranch (S)
Wheatleigh (B)
Martha's Vineyard:
Charlotte Inn (B)
Nantucket:
Wauwinet (B)

Michigan
Detroit:
Ritz Dearborn (H)
Townsend (H)

Minnesota
Minneapolis/St. Paul:
Saint Paul (H)

Mississippi
Natchez:
Briars Inn (B)
Monmouth Plantation (B)

Missouri
Kansas City:
Ritz Kansas City (H)
St. Louis:
Ritz St. Louis (H)

New Hampshire
Dixville Notch:
Balsams Grand (R)

New Jersey
Cape May:
Mainstay Inn (B)
Short Hills:
Hilton at Short Hills (H)

New Mexico
Española:
Rancho de San Juan (R)
Santa Fe:
Inn of Anasazi (B)

New York
Amenia:
Troutbeck (B)
Lake Placid:
Lake Placid Lodge (B)
New York City:
Carlyle (H)
Essex House Nikko (H)
Four Seasons (H)
Kitano NY (H)
Lowell (H)
Mark (H)
Peninsula NY (H)
Pierre (H)
Plaza Athénée (H)
Regency (H)
Rihga Royal (H)
Ritz New York (H)
Stanhope (H)

Elite Status

St. Regis (H)
Trump International (H)
UN Plaza Park Hyatt (H)
Waldorf Towers (H)
Tarrytown:
Castle at Tarrytown (B)

North Carolina
Charlotte:
Park (H)
Pinehurst:
Pinehurst (R)
Pittsboro:
Fearrington House (B)
Raleigh-Durham:
Siena (H)

Ohio
Cincinnati:
Cincinnatian (H)
Cleveland:
Marriott Downtown (H)
Ritz Cleveland (H)

Oregon
Portland:
Benson (H)
Heathman (H)
RiverPlace (H)
Vintage Plaza (H)

Pennsylvania
Farmington:
Nemacolin Woodlands (R)
Philadelphia:
Four Seasons Philadelphia (H)
Park Hyatt Philadelphia (H)
Rittenhouse (H)

Puerto Rico
Fajardo:
El Conquistador (R)
Rincon:
Horned Dorset (B)
San Juan:
El San Juan (H)

Rhode Island
Providence:
Westin Providence (H)

South Carolina
Charleston:
Vendue Inn (B)
Hilton Head:
Westin (R)

Tennessee
Walland:
Inn at Blackberry Farm (B)

Texas
Arlington:
Greenhouse (S)
Austin:
Barton Creek (R)
Four Seasons Austin (H)
Dallas/Fort Worth:
Adolphus (H)
Crescent Court (H)

Four Seasons (R)
Mansion on Turtle Creek (H)
Omni Mandalay (H)
St. Germain (B)
Wyndham Anatole (H)
Houston:
La Colombe d'Or (B)
Lancaster (H)
Omni Houston (H)
Ritz Houston (H)
San Antonio:
Hyatt Reg. Hill Country (R)
Plaza San Antonio (H)

Utah
Park City:
Stein Eriksen (R)

Vermont
Essex:
Inn at Essex (B)
West Dover:
Inn at Sawmill Farm (B)

Virginia
Hot Springs:
Homestead (R)
Richmond:
Jefferson (H)
Washington:
Inn at Little Washington (B)
Williamsburg:
Williamsburg Inn (H)

Washington
Seattle:
Alexis (H)
Four Seasons Olympic (H)
Sorrento (H)
Woodmark (H)
Snoqualmie:
Salish Lodge (B)

Washington, DC
(including nearby Maryland and Virginia)
Virginia:
Morrison House (B)
Ritz Pentagon City (H)
Ritz Tysons Corner (H)
Washington, DC:
Carlton (H)
Four Seasons (H)
Hay-Adams (H)
Jefferson (H)
Park Hyatt Washington (H)
Ritz Washington DC (H)
Watergate (H)
Willard (H)

West Virginia
White Sulphur Springs:
Greenbrier (R)

Wisconsin
Kohler:
American Club (R)
Milwaukee:
Pfister (H)
Wyndham Milwaukee (H)

Family Places

Alabama
Fairhope:
 Malaga Inn (B)
Orange Beach:
 Perdido Beach (R)

Alaska
Denali National Park:
 North Face (B)
Fairbanks:
 Captain Bartlett (H)
Girdwood:
 Alyeska (R)

Arizona
Bisbee:
 Copper Queen (H)
Douglas:
 Gadsden (H)
Grand Canyon:
 El Tovar (H)
Page:
 Wahweap (H)
Phoenix/Scottsdale:
 Arizona Biltmore (R)
 Arizona Golf (R)
 Buttes (R)
 Dbltree La Posada (R)
 Dbltree Paradise Valley (R)
 Embassy Biltmore (H)
 Embassy Scottsdale (H)
 Gardiner's (R)
 Holiday Inn SunSpree (R)
 Hyatt Reg. Scottsdale (R)
 Marriott's Camelback (R)
 Marriott Scottsdale (H)
 Marriott's Mountain (R)
 Phoenician (R)
 Pte Hilton S. Mountain (R)
 Pte Hilton Squaw (R)
 Scottsdale Hilton (H)
 Scottsdale Princess (R)
 Sheraton Crescent (H)
 Sheraton San Marcos (R)
Sedona:
 Enchantment (R)
 Poco Diablo (R)
Tucson:
 Arizona Inn (H)
 Dbltree Reid Park (H)
 Lodge Ventana (R)
 Loews Ventana (R)
 Sheraton El Conquistador (R)
 Tanque Verde (B)
 Triangle L Ranch (R)
 Westin La Paloma (R)
 Westward Look (R)
Wickenburg:
 Merv Griffin's (B)

Arkansas
Hot Springs:
 Arlington Resort (H)
 Hot Springs Park (H)
 Lake Hamilton (R)
Lakeview:
 Gaston's (R)

California
Anaheim:
 Dbltree Anaheim (H)
 Disneyland (H)
 Disneyland Pacific (H)
 Hilton Anaheim (H)
 Inn at the Park (H)

Marriott Anaheim (H)
 Sheraton Anaheim (H)
Big Sur:
 Big Sur Lodge (B)
Bodega Bay:
 Inn at the Tides (B)
Carlsbad:
 La Costa (S)
Dana Point:
 Ritz Laguna Niguel (R)
Fish Camp:
 Tenaya Lodge (R)
Laguna Beach:
 Surf & Sand (H)
Lake Arrowhead:
 Lake Arrowhead (R)
Little River:
 Little River Inn (B)
Long Beach:
 Queen Mary (H)
Los Angeles:
 Beverly Prescott (H)
 Le Parc (H)
 Loews Santa Monica (H)
 Malibu Beach (B)
 Mansion Inn (B)
 Marriott Marina Beach (H)
 Miramar Sheraton (H)
 Sheraton Universal (H)
Montecito:
 San Ysidro (B)
Monterey:
 Marriott Monterey (H)
 Monterey Plaza (H)
Newport Beach:
 Four Seasons Newport (H)
 Hyatt Newporter (R)
 Marriott Suites (H)
 Marriott Tennis (H)
Ojai:
 Ojai Valley (R)
Olympic Valley:
 Plumpjack's (B)
 Resort at Squaw Creek (R)
Palm Springs:
 Dbltree Palm Springs (R)
 Hyatt Grand (R)
 Indian Wells (R)
 La Mancha (R)
 La Quinta (R)
 Marquis Palm Springs (H)
 Marriott's Desert Springs (R)
 Marriott's Rancho (R)
 Renaissance Esmeralda (R)
 Riviera Palm Springs (R)
 Shadow Mountain (R)
 Westin Mission Hills (R)
San Diego:
 Catamaran (H)
 Dbltree Del Mar (H)
 del Coronado Hotel (R)
 Embassy San Diego (H)
 Hilton San Diego (H)
 Hyatt Islandia (H)
 Kona Kai (R)
 La Jolla Beach (H)
 Lodge at Torrey Pines (H)
 Loews Coronado (R)
 Marriott San Diego (H)
 Princess San Diego (R)
 Radisson Harbor View (H)
 Rancho Bernardo (R)

Family Places

Sea Lodge (H)
Sheraton San Diego (H)

San Francisco:
Clift (H)
Hyatt Fish. Wharf (H)
Hyde Park (B)
Marriott Fish. Wharf (H)
Nikko SF (H)
Savoy (H)
Sheraton Fish. Wharf (H)

San Luis Obispo:
Apple Farm (B)

Santa Barbara:
Fess Parker's (R)
Four Seasons Biltmore (R)

Santa Monica:
Oceana (H)

Solvang:
Alisal (R)

St. Helena:
Harvest Inn (B)
Meadowood (R)

Truckee:
Northstar-at-Tahoe (R)

Yosemite:
Ahwahnee (H)

Colorado

Aspen:
Gant (B)
Inn at Aspen (H)

Beaver Creek:
Charter at Beaver Creek (H)
Embassy Beaver Creek (R)
Hyatt Reg. Beaver Creek (H)
Inn at Beaver Creek (B)
Pines Lodge (H)

Breckenridge:
Breckenridge Mtn (H)
Hilton Breckenridge (R)
Village at Breckenridge (R)

Clark:
Home Ranch (R)

Colorado Springs:
Broadmoor (R)
Sheraton (H)

Copper Mountain:
Copper Mountain (R)

Denver:
Embassy Denver (H)
Residence by Marriott (H)

Durango:
Strater (H)
Tamarron Hilton (R)
Wit's End (B)

Edwards:
Lodge & Spa Cordillera (R)

Granby:
C Lazy U Ranch (B)

Keystone:
Keystone (R)

Mt. Crested Butte:
Grande Butte (H)

Snowmass Village:
Silvertree (H)
Snowmass Lodge (R)

Steamboat Springs:
Sheraton Steamboat (R)

Telluride:
Peaks at Telluride (R)

Vail:
Christiana at Vail (H)
Sitzmark Lodge (H)

Sonnenalp of Vail (R)
Vail Athletic Club (H)

Connecticut

Essex:
Griswold Inn (B)

Lakeville:
Interlaken Inn (R)

Southbury:
Heritage Inn (H)

Westbrook:
Water's Edge (B)

Delaware

Newark:
Christiana Hilton (H)

Rehoboth Beach:
Boardwalk Plaza (H)
Corner Cupboard (B)

Florida

Amelia Island:
Amelia Island (R)
Ritz Amelia Island (R)

Boca Raton:
Boca Raton (R)

Captiva Island:
South Seas Plantation (R)

Destin:
Hilton Sandestin (R)

Fort Lauderdale:
Doubletree (H)
Lago Mar (R)
Little Inn by the Sea (B)
Marriott's Harbor (R)
Registry Resort (S)

Fort Myers:
Sanibel Harbour (R)

Gasparilla Island:
Gasparilla Inn (B)

Haines City:
Grenelefe Golf (R)

Howey-in-the-Hills:
Mission Inn (R)

Islamorada:
Cheeca Lodge (R)

Jupiter:
Jupiter Beach (R)

Key Largo:
Marriott's Key Largo (R)
Ocean Reef (R)

Key West:
Cuban Club (H)
Holiday Inn La Concha (H)
Hyatt Key West (H)
Marriott's Casa Marina (R)
Ocean Key House (R)

Longboat Key:
Colony Beach (R)
Resort at Longboat Key (R)

Marathon:
Hawk's Cay (R)

Marco Island:
Marco Island Hilton (R)
Marriott's Marco Island (R)
Radisson Beach (R)

Miami/Miami Beach:
Biltmore (R)
Doral Golf (R)
Eden Roc (H)
Fisher Island (R)
Florida Suites (H)
Fontainebleau Hilton (R)
Miami Beach Ocean (H)

Family Places

Sheraton Bal Harbour (H)
Sonesta Beach (R)
Mount Dora:
Lakeside Inn (R)
Naples:
La Playa Beach (R)
Naples Beach (R)
Registry (R)
Orlando:
Buena Vista Palace (H)
Clarion Plaza (H)
Disney Institute (R)
Disney's All-Star Music (R)
Disney's All-Star Sports (R)
Disney's Boardwalk (H)
Disney's Caribbean (R)
Disney's Contemporary (R)
Disney's Dixie Landings (R)
Disney's Ft. Wilderness (R)
Disney's Grand Floridian (R)
Disney's Old Key West (R)
Disney's Polynesian (R)
Disney's Port Orleans (R)
Disney's Wilderness (R)
Disney's Yacht (R)
Doubletree (H)
Grosvenor (R)
Hilton at Walt Disney (H)
Holiday Inn SunSpree (R)
Hyatt Reg. Grand Cypress (R)
Marriott Orl. Int'l Drive (H)
Marriott's Orl. World Ctr (H)
Peabody Orlando (H)
Radisson Twin Towers (H)
Renaissance Orlando (R)
Residence by Marriott (H)
Sheraton World (R)
Travelodge (H)
Vistana (R)
Walt Disney Dolphin (R)
Walt Disney Swan (R)
Westgate Lakes (R)
Palm Beach:
Breakers (R)
Four Seasons Palm Beach (H)
Palm Beach Polo (R)
Ritz Palm Beach (R)
Panama City Beach:
Marriott's Bay Point (R)
Pompano Beach:
Palm-Aire Resort (S)
Ponte Vedra Beach:
Lodge at Ponte Vedra (R)
Marriott at Sawgrass (R)
Ponte Vedra (R)
Port St. Lucie:
Club Med Sandpiper (R)
Sanibel Island:
Casa Ybel (R)
Sanibel (R)
Sundial Beach (R)
Siesta Key:
Captiva Beach (B)
Stuart:
Indian River Plantation (R)
Tampa Bay:
Don CeSar (R)
Holiday Inn Beachfront (R)
Innisbrook Hilton (R)
Radisson Sand Key (R)
Renaissance Vinoy (R)
TradeWinds St. Pete (R)

Georgia
Americus:
Windsor (H)
Atlanta:
Doubletree (H)
Embassy Perimeter Ctr (H)
Evergreen (H)
Hyatt Reg. Perimeter (H)
Marietta (R)
Marque of Atlanta (H)
Marriott Midtown Atlanta (H)
Summerfield (H)
Braselton:
Chateau Elan Winery (B)
Jekyll Island:
Jekyll Island Club (R)
Lake Lanier Islands:
Renaissance Pineisle (R)
Pine Mountain:
Callaway Gardens (R)
Savannah:
Mulberry Inn (H)
Sea Island:
Cloister (R)
St. Simons Island:
King & Prince Beach (R)
Lodge at Little St. Simons (B)
Sea Palms (R)

Hawaii
Big Island:
Four Seasons Hualalai (R)
Hapuna Prince (R)
Hilton Waikoloa (R)
Kona Village (R)
Mauna Kea (R)
Orchid at Mauna Lani (R)
Royal Waikoloan (R)
Kauai:
Hyatt Reg. Kauai (R)
Kauai Coconut (R)
Kiahuna Plantation (R)
Outrigger Kauai (R)
Princeville (R)
Maui:
Aston Kaanapali (R)
Aston Wailea (R)
Four Seasons Maui (R)
Grand Wailea (R)
Hyatt Reg. Maui (R)
Ka'anapali Beach (R)
Kapalua Bay (R)
Kea Lani (R)
Marriott Maui (R)
Renaissance Wailea (R)
Ritz Kapalua (R)
Royal Lahaina (R)
Sheraton Maui (R)
Westin Maui (R)
Oahu:
Ala Moana (H)
Aston Waikiki (H)
Hawaiian Regent (H)
Hilton Hawaiian (H)
Hyatt Reg. Waikiki (H)
Ihilani Resort (R)
Ilikai Nikko Waikiki (H)
Kahala Mandarin (R)
Outrigger Reef (R)
Outrigger Waikiki (R)
Pacific Beach (H)
Sheraton Kaiulani (H)

Idaho
Boise:
Red Lion Boise (H)

Family Places

Coeur d'Alene:
  Coeur d'Alene (R)
McCall:
  Shore Lodge (B)
Priest Lake:
  Hill's Hospitality (B)
Sun Valley:
  Sun Valley (R)

Illinois
Bloomingdale:
  Indian Lakes (R)
Chicago:
  Doubletree (H)
  Holiday Inn Chicago (H)
  Omni Chicago (H)
  Renaissance Chicago (H)
Galena:
  Eagle Ridge (R)
Itasca:
  Nordic Hills (R)
St. Charles:
  Pheasant Run (R)
Whittington:
  Rend Lake (R)

Indiana
Bloomington:
  Fourwinds (R)
French Lick:
  French Lick Springs (R)
Indianapolis:
  Crowne Plaza (H)
  Marriott Indianapolis (H)

Iowa
Des Moines:
  Embassy (H)
Homestead:
  Die Heimat (B)

Kansas
Fort Scott:
  Chenault Mansion (B)

Kentucky
Berea:
  Boone Tavern (H)
Harrodsburg:
  Beaumont Inn (B)
  Inn at Shaker Village (B)
Lexington:
  Hyatt Reg. Lexington (H)
  Marriott Griffin Gate (R)

Louisiana
New Orleans:
  Hilton New Orleans (H)
  Holiday Inn Le Moyne (H)
  Hyatt Reg. New Orleans (H)
  Marriott New Orleans (H)
  St. Ann (H)
  Westin Canal (H)

Maine
Bar Harbor:
  Atlantic Oakes (B)
  Bayview (H)
Boothbay Harbor:
  Spruce Point (B)
Cape Elizabeth:
  Inn by the Sea (B)
Scarborough:
  Black Point Inn (R)

Maryland
(see also Washington, DC)
Baltimore:
  Admiral Fell Inn (B)
  Cross Keys Inn (H)
  Marriott Baltimore (H)
  Omni Inner Harbor (H)
  Radisson Lord Baltimore (H)
  Renaissance Harborplace (H)
Easton:
  Tidewater Inn (B)
Ocean City:
  Dunes Manor (H)
  Sheraton Fontainebleau (H)

Massachusetts
Boston:
  Boston Park Plaza (H)
  Doubletree (H)
  Hyatt Harborside (H)
  Hyatt Reg. Cambridge (H)
  Marriott Long Wharf (H)
Cape Cod:
  Cape Codder (B)
  Chatham Bars (B)
  Dan'l Webster Inn (B)
  High Brewster (B)
  Ocean Edge (R)
  Sea Crest (R)
Danvers:
  Tara's Ferncroft (R)
Martha's Vineyard:
  Harbor View (B)
Nantucket:
  Beachside Nantucket (H)
  Nantucket Inn (H)
  White Elephant (R)
Northampton:
  Northampton (H)
Williamstown:
  Orchards (B)

Michigan
Acme:
  Grand Traverse (R)
Bellaire:
  Shanty Creek (R)
Boyne Falls:
  Boyne Mountain (R)
Mackinac Island:
  Grand (H)
Thompsonville:
  Crystal Mountain (R)
Ypsilanti:
  Marriott Ypsilanti (R)

Minnesota
Alexandria:
  Arrowwood Radisson (R)
Brainerd:
  Madden's (R)
Hibbing:
  Kahler Park (H)
Lutsen:
  Lutsen (R)
Minneapolis/St. Paul:
  Radisson Plaza Tower (H)

Mississippi
Vicksburg:
  Corners B&B (B)

Missouri
Branson:
  Best Western Knights (H)
  Best Western Mtn Oak (H)
  Best Western Music (H)
  Chateau on the Lake (R)
  Clarion at Fall Creek (R)
Kansas City:
  Sheraton Kansas City (H)
  Westin Crown Ctr (H)

Family Places

Lake Ozark:
Lodge at Four Seasons (R)
Osage Beach:
Marriott's Tan-Tar-A (R)
Ridgedale:
Big Cedar (R)
St. Louis:
Doubletree (H)
Embassy St. Louis (H)
Holiday Inn Riverfront (H)
Hyatt Reg. St. Louis (H)

Montana
Bigfork:
Averill's Flathead (B)
Big Sky:
Lone Mountain (B)
Bozeman:
Mountain Sky (B)
Gallatin Gateway:
Gallatin Gateway (B)

Nebraska
Wilber:
Wilber (B)

Nevada
Crystal Bay:
Cal-Neva Resort (R)
Lake Tahoe:
Harrah's Lake Tahoe (R)
Hyatt Reg. Lake Tahoe (R)
Las Vegas:
Alexis Park (H)
Circus Circus (H)
Excalibur (H)
Luxor Las Vegas (H)
MGM Grand (H)
Mirage (H)
Monte Carlo (H)
Stratosphere (H)

New Hampshire
Bretton Woods:
Mount Washington (R)
Dixville Notch:
Balsams Grand (R)
Franconia:
Franconia Inn (B)
Jackson:
Christmas Farm (B)
Eagle Mountain (H)
Lincoln:
Mountain Club (R)
North Conway:
Four Points Sheraton (H)
White Mountain (R)
Waterville Valley:
Snowy Owl (B)
Waterville Valley (R)

New Jersey
Atlantic City:
Atlantic Palace (H)
Marriott Seaview (R)
Showboat Casino (H)
Trump's Castle (H)
Basking Ridge:
Olde Mill Inn (B)
Cape May:
Chalfonte (H)
Long Beach:
Ocean Place Hilton (R)
Morristown:
Headquarters Plaza (H)

Princeton:
Forrestal (H)
Spring Lake:
Breakers (B)
Vernon:
Great Gorge Village (R)

New Mexico
Albuquerque:
Sheraton Old Town (H)
Mescalero:
Inn of Mountain Gods (R)
Santa Fe:
Bishop's Lodge (R)
Grant Corner (B)
Inn of Governors (B)
Inn on the Alameda (B)
La Fonda (B)
Radisson Santa Fe (H)
Rancho Encantado (B)
Santa Fe (H)
Taos:
Casa Benavides (B)
Quail Ridge (R)
Sagebrush Inn (B)
Taos Ski Valley:
Edelweiss (B)

New York
Alexandria Bay:
Bonnie Castle (R)
Bolton Landing:
Sagamore (R)
Ellenville:
Nevele (R)
Kiamesha Lake:
Concord (R)
Lake Placid:
Mirror Lake (B)
Lew Beach:
Beaverkill Valley (B)
Montauk:
Montauk Yacht (R)
Monticello:
Kutsher's (R)
New Paltz:
Mohonk Mountain (R)
New York City:
Beekman Tower (H)
Crowne Plaza (H)
Doubletree (H)
Dumont Plaza (H)
Eastgate Tower (H)
Fitzpatrick Manhattan (H)
Lyden Gardens (H)
Lyden House (H)
Marriott Marquis (H)
Millenium Hilton (H)
Murray Hill East (H)
Plaza (H)
Sheraton Manhattan (H)
Sheraton NY (H)
Poughkeepsie:
Inn at the Falls (B)
Saranac Lake:
Saranac (H)
Saratoga Springs:
Inn at Saratoga (B)
Stony Brook:
Three Village (B)

North Carolina
Asheville:
Grove Park Inn (R)

Family Places

Blowing Rock:
  Hound Ears (R)
Cashiers:
  High Hampton (R)
Charlotte:
  Hyatt Charlotte (H)
  Westin Charlotte (H)
Pinehurst:
  Pinehurst (R)
Wrightsville Beach:
  Blockade Runner (R)

North Dakota
Medora:
  Rough Rider (B)

Ohio
Aurora:
  Aurora Inn (H)
Cincinnati:
  Doubletree (H)
  Marriott Cincinnati (H)
  Vernon Manor (H)
Cleveland:
  Wyndham Cleveland (H)
Columbus:
  Doubletree (H)
  Hyatt on Capital Square (H)
Dellroy:
  Atwood Lake (R)
Huron:
  Sawmill Creek (R)

Oklahoma
Afton:
  Shangri-La (R)
Checotah:
  Fountainhead (R)
Kingston:
  Texoma State (R)

Oregon
Bend:
  Inn of Seventh Mtn (R)
Black Butte Ranch:
  Black Butte (R)
Eugene:
  Valley River (H)
Gold Beach:
  Tu Tu'Tun (B)
Lincoln City:
  Inn at Spanish Head (B)
Portland:
  5th Avenue Suites (H)
  Greenwood Inn (B)
  Marriott Portland (H)
Sunriver:
  Sunriver (R)
Timberline:
  Timberline (R)
Warm Springs:
  Kah-Nee-Ta (R)

Pennsylvania
Champion:
  Seven Springs (R)
Farmington:
  Nemacolin Woodlands (R)
Glen Mills:
  Sweetwater Farm (B)
Hershey:
  Hershey (H)
  Hershey Lodge (H)
Malvern:
  Desmond (H)

Mt. Pocono/Pocono Manor:
  Mount Airy Lodge (R)
  Pocono Manor (R)
Philadelphia:
  Park Hyatt Philadelphia (H)
Skytop:
  Skytop Lodge (R)
Strasburg:
  Historic Strasburg (B)

Puerto Rico
Dorado:
  Hyatt Reg. Cerromar (R)
  Hyatt Reg. Dorado (R)
Fajardo:
  El Conquistador (R)
Humacao:
  Palmas del Mar (R)
Old San Juan:
  El Convento (H)
San Juan:
  Caribe Hilton (H)
  El San Juan (H)

Rhode Island
Block Island:
  Atlantic Inn (B)
Newport:
  Dbltree Newport (H)
  Newport Harbor (H)

South Carolina
Charleston:
  Charleston Place (H)
Hilton Head:
  Hilton Hilton Head (R)
  Hyatt Reg. Hilton Head (R)
  Palmetto Dunes (R)
  Sea Pines (R)
  Westin (R)
Isle of Palms:
  Wild Dunes (R)
Kiawah Island:
  Kiawah Island (R)
Myrtle Beach:
  Hilton Myrtle Beach (R)
  Kingston Planation (R)
  Myrtle Beach Martinique (R)
  Ocean Creek (R)
  Ocean Dunes (R)
  Sheraton Myrtle Beach (R)
Pawleys Island:
  Litchfield Beach (R)
Seabrook Island:
  Seabrook Island (R)

South Dakota
Chamberlain:
  Radisson Cedar Shore (R)
Custer:
  State Game Lodge (R)

Tennessee
Fairfield Glade:
  Fairfield Glade (R)
Memphis:
  Crowne Plaza (H)
  Embassy Memphis (H)
Nashville:
  Embassy Nashville (H)
  Opryland (H)
  Renaissance Nashville (H)

Texas
Austin:
  Hilton Austin North (H)
  Hyatt Reg. Austin (H)

Family Places

Lakeway Inn (R)
Marriott Austin (H)
Bandera:
Mayan Dude Ranch (B)
Cat Spring:
Southwind B&B (B)
Corpus Christi:
Omni Bayfront (H)
Dallas/Fort Worth:
Four Seasons (R)
Galveston:
Galvez (H)
Houston:
Doubletree (H)
Westin Oaks (H)
Woodlands (R)
Montgomery:
Del Lago (R)
San Antonio:
Hilton Palacio del Rio (H)
Hyatt Reg. Hill Country (R)
Hyatt Reg. San Antonio (H)
Marriott Rivercenter (H)
Menger (H)
South Padre Island:
Radisson South Padre (R)

Utah
Cedar City:
Bryce Canyon (H)
Midway:
Homestead (B)
Park City:
Deer Valley (H)
1904 Imperial (H)
Olympia Park (H)
Shadow Ridge (H)
Provo:
Sundance Resort (R)
Salt Lake City:
Embassy (H)
Snowbird:
Inn at Snowbird (B)
Iron Blosam (H)
Lodge at Snowbird (H)
Springdale:
Zion Lodge (H)

Vermont
Brownsville:
Ascutney Mountain (R)
Essex:
Inn at Essex (B)
Grafton:
Old Tavern at Grafton (B)
Highgate Springs:
Tyler Place (R)
Killington:
Cortina Inn (B)
Inn of Six Mountains (B)
Killington Resort (R)
Manchester:
Equinox (H)
Inn at Willow Pond (B)
Wilburton Inn (B)
Middlebury:
Waybury Inn (B)
Plymouth:
Hawk Inn (B)
Shelburne:
Inn at Shelburne Farms (B)
Smugglers' Notch:
Smugglers' Notch (R)

Stowe:
Stowe Snowdrift (R)
Topnotch at Stowe (R)
Trapp Family (B)
Stratton Mountain:
Stratton Mtn (R)
Warren:
Sugarbush (R)
Woodstock:
Woodstock Inn (R)

Virginia
(see also Washington, DC)
Abingdon:
Camberley's (B)
Charlottesville:
Boar's Head Inn (R)
Hot Springs:
Homestead (R)
Irvington:
Tides Inn (R)
Tides Lodge (R)
Richmond:
Sheraton Park South (H)
Virginia Beach:
Cavalier (R)
Holiday Inn Sunspree (R)
Ramada Plaza (R)
Williamsburg:
Kingsmill (R)
Marriott Williamsburg (H)
Williamsburg (H)
Williamsburg Lodge (H)
Wintergreen:
Wintergreen (R)

Washington
Blaine:
Inn at Semi-Ah-Moo (R)
Eastsound:
Rosario Resort (R)
Forks:
Kalaloch Lodge (B)
Lake Quinault:
Lake Quinault (B)
Port Ludlow:
Port Ludlow (R)
Seattle:
Edgewater (H)
Westin Seattle (H)
Silverdale:
Silverdale on Bay (R)
Stevenson:
Skamania Lodge (R)
Winthrop:
Sun Mountain (R)

Washington, DC
(including nearby Maryland and Virginia)
Maryland:
Hyatt Reg. Bethesda (H)
Marriott Suites Bethesda (H)
Residence Inn Bethesda (H)
Virginia:
Hilton Washington (H)
Marriott Tysons Corner (H)
Washington, DC:
Dbltree Penn Avenue (H)
Embassy Chevy Chase (H)
Marriott JW (H)
Marriott Metro Center (H)
River Inn (H)

West Virginia
Berkeley Springs:
Coolfront Resort (R)

Family Places

Davis.
  Canaan Valley (R)
Harpers Ferry:
  Historic Hilltop House (H)
Hedgesville:
  Woods Resort (R)
Wheeling:
  Oglebay Resort (R)
White Sulphur Springs:
  Greenbrier (R)

Wisconsin
Delavan:
  Lake Lawn Lodge (R)
Eagle River:
  Chanticleer Inn (B)
Fontana:
  Abbey Resort (R)
Green Lake:
  Heidel House (R)

Kohler:
  Inn on Woodlake (B)
Lake Geneva:
  Grand Geneva (R)
  Interlaken Resort (R)
Wisconsin Dells:
  Chula Vista (R)

Wyoming
Jackson:
  Jackson Hole Racquet (R)
  Snow King (R)
Moran:
  Colter Bay VIllage (R)
  Jackson Lake (B)
Yellowstone National Park:
  Mammoth Hot Springs (H)
  Old Faithful (H)

Fireplaces (in all rooms)*

Alabama
Eutaw:
  Kirkwood B&B (B)

Arizona
Phoenix/Scottsdale:
  Boulders (R)

California
Albion:
  Albion River (B)
Big Sur:
  Post Ranch (B)
Capitola by the Sea:
  Inn at Depot Hill (B)
Carmel:
  Carmel Valley (R)
  Cobblestone Inn (B)
  Highlands Inn (B)
  John Gardiner's (R)
Cazadero:
  Timberhill (B)
Gualala:
  Whale Watch Inn (B)
Los Angeles:
  Le Parc (H)
  Malibu Beach (B)
Los Olivos:
  Los Olivos Grand (B)
Mendocino:
  Stanford Inn (B)
Montecito:
  San Ysidro (B)
Monterey:
  Pacific (H)
  Spindrift Inn (B)
Napa:
  Silverado (R)
Pebble Beach:
  Inn at Spanish Bay (R)
  Lodge at Pebble Beach (R)
Rutherford:
  Auberge du Soleil (B)
San Diego:
  Horton Grand (H)
  Rancho Valencia (R)
San Francisco:
  Sherman House (B)
  White Swan (B)
San Luis Obispo:
  Apple Farm (B)
Solvang:
  Alisal (R)
Yountville:
  Vintage Inn (H)

Colorado
Aspen:
  Gant (B)
  Little Nell (H)
Clark:
  Home Ranch (R)
Durango:
  Wit's End (B)
Telluride:
  Columbia (B)

Florida
Longboat Key:
  Colony Beach (R)

Georgia
Savannah:
  Gastonian (B)
  Kehoe House (B)

President's Quarters (B)
  17 Hundred 90 Inn (B)

Maine
East Holden:
  Lucerne Inn (B)
Kennebunkport:
  Captain Lord Mansion (B)

Minnesota
Stillwater:
  Lumber Baron's (H)

Mississippi
Natchez:
  Burn (B)
  Dunleith (B)
  Linden B&B (B)

Montana
Darby:
  Triple Creek Ranch (R)

New Mexico
Chimayo:
  Hacienda Rancho (B)
Española:
  Rancho de San Juan (R)
Santa Fe:
  Inn of Anasazi (B)
Taos:
  Quail Ridge (R)

New York
New York City:
  Box Tree (B)
  Inn at Irving Place (B)
North Hudson:
  Elk Lake Lodge (R)
Saranac Lake:
  Point (B)

Oregon
Gleneden Beach:
  Salishan (R)

Puerto Rico
San Juan:
  Sands (H)

Texas
Dallas/Fort Worth:
  St. Germain (B)

Utah
Park City:
  Deer Valley (H)

Vermont
Barnard:
  Twin Farms (R)
Wilmington:
  Hermitage Inn (B)

Virginia
Virginia Beach:
  Holiday Inn Sunspree (R)

Washington
Port Angeles.
  Domaine Madeleine (B)
Port Ludlow:
  Inn at Ludlow Bay (B)
Snoqualmie:
  Salish Lodge (B)

Wisconsin
Bayfield:
  Old Rittenhouse (B)

Wyoming
Jackson:
  Jackson Hole Racquet (R)
  Spring Creek (R)

---

* Obviously, many older hotels have a few guestrooms with fireplaces; those listed here
  have them in all rooms.

410

Golf

Alabama
Eufaula:
Kendall Manor (B)
Point Clear:
Marriott's Grand (R)

Arizona
Bisbee:
Copper Queen (H)
Douglas:
Gadsden (H)
Gold Canyon:
Gold Canyon (R)
Phoenix/Scottsdale:
Arizona Biltmore (R)
Boulders (R)
Hermosa Inn (B)
Hyatt Reg. Scottsdale (R)
Marriott's Camelback (R)
Marriott's Mountain (R)
Orange Tree (R)
Phoenician (R)
Pte Hilton S. Mountain (R)
Pte Hilton Squaw (R)
Pte Hilton Tapatio (R)
Regal McCormick (R)
Royal Palms (H)
Scottsdale Conference (R)
Scottsdale Princess (R)
Sheraton San Marcos (R)
Wigwam (R)
Prescott:
Hassayampa Inn (H)
Sedona:
Enchantment (R)
Poco Diablo (R)
Tucson:
Lodge Ventana (R)
Loews Ventana (R)
Omni Tucson (R)
Sheraton El Conquistador (R)
Tanque Verde (B)
Westin La Paloma (R)

California
Carlsbad:
La Costa (R)
Carmel:
Carmel Valley (R)
Quail Lodge (R)
Death Valley:
Furnace Creek Inn (R)
Little River:
Little River Inn (B)
Los Angeles:
Ramada W. Hollywood (B)
Sheraton Industry Hills (H)
Napa:
La Residence (B)
Silverado (R)
Newport Beach:
Hyatt Newporter (R)
Ojai:
Ojai Valley (R)
Olympic Valley:
Resort at Squaw Creek (R)
Oxnard:
Embassy Mandalay (H)
Palm Springs:
Dbltree Palm Springs (R)
Givenchy (S)
Hyatt Grand (R)
Indian Wells (R)

Marriott's Desert Springs (R)
Marriott's Rancho (R)
Renaissance Esmeralda (R)
Westin Mission Hills (R)
Pebble Beach:
Inn at Spanish Bay (R)
Lodge at Pebble Beach (R)
San Diego:
Inn at Rancho Santa Fe (H)
La Jolla Beach (H)
Le Meridien San Diego (H)
Loews Coronado (R)
Marriott San Diego (H)
Rancho Bernardo (R)
Sheraton Grande (R)
San Jose:
Hayes (H)
Santa Clara:
Westin Santa Slara (H)
Santa Monica:
Oceana (H)
Solvang:
Alisal (R)
Truckee:
Northstar-at-Tahoe (R)

Colorado
Beaver Creek:
Charter at Beaver Creek (H)
Clark:
Home Ranch (R)
Colorado Springs:
Broadmoor (R)
Cheyenne Mountain (R)
Sheraton (H)
Copper Mountain:
Copper Mountain (R)
Denver:
Inverness (R)
Durango:
Rochester (H)
Tamarron Hilton (R)
Edwards:
Lodge & Spa Cordillera (R)
Mosca:
Inn at Zapata (B)
Snowmass Village:
Snowmass Lodge (R)
Telluride:
Columbia (B)
Peaks at Telluride (R)

Connecticut
Lakeville:
Interlaken Inn (R)
Southbury:
Heritage Inn (H)

Delaware
Montchanin.
Inn at Montchanin (B)

Florida
Amelia Island:
Amelia Island (R)
Ritz Amelia Island (R)
Boca Raton:
Boca Raton (R)
Marriott Boca Raton (H)
Captiva Island:
South Seas Plantation (R)
Clearwater:
Belleview Mido (R)

Golf

Destin:
  Hilton Sandestin (R)
Fisher Island:
  Spa Internazionale (S)
Fort Lauderdale:
  Registry Resort (S)
Gasparilla Island:
  Gasparilla Inn (B)
Haines City:
  Grenelefe Golf (R)
Howey-in-the-Hills:
  Mission Inn (R)
Key West:
  Cuban Club (H)
Longboat Key:
  Resort at Longboat Key (R)
Miami/Miami Beach:
  Biltmore (R)
  Doral Golf (R)
  Fisher Island (R)
  Greenview (H)
  Turnberry Isle (R)
Naples:
  Naples Beach (R)
Orlando:
  Disney Institute (R)
  Hyatt Reg. Grand Cypress (R)
  Hyatt Reg. Orlando (H)
  Marriott's Orl. World Ctr (H)
  Villas of Grand Cypress (R)
Palm Beach:
  Breakers (R)
  Palm Beach Polo (R)
  PGA National (R)
Panama City Beach:
  Marriott's Bay Point (R)
Pompano Beach:
  Palm-Aire Resort (S)
Ponte Vedra Beach:
  Marriott at Sawgrass (R)
  Ponte Vedra (R)
Port St. Lucie:
  Club Med Sandpiper (R)
Stuart:
  Indian River Plantation (R)
Tampa Bay:
  Innisbrook Hilton (R)
  Saddlebrook Tampa (R)

Georgia
Atlanta:
  Evergreen (R)
  Marietta (R)
  Peachtree (H)
Braselton:
  Chateau Elan Winery (B)
Lake Lanier Islands:
  Renaissance Pineisle (R)
Pine Mountain:
  Callaway Gardens (R)
St. Simons Island:
  Lodge at Little St. Simons (B)
  Sea Palms (R)

Hawaii
Big Island:
  Four Seasons Hualalai (R)
  Hapuna Prince (R)
  Hawaii Naniloa (R)
  Hilton Waikoloa (R)
  Mauna Kea (R)
  Mauna Lani Bay (R)

Kauai:
  Hyatt Reg. Kauai (R)
  Marriott Kauai (R)
Lanai:
  Lodge at Koele (R)
  Manele Bay (R)
Maui:
  Aston Wailea (R)
  Embassy Maui (R)
  Hyatt Reg. Maui (R)
  Kapalua Bay (R)
  Marriott Maui (R)
  Maui Prince (R)
  Renaissance Wailea (R)
  Ritz Kapalua (R)
Oahu:
  Ihilani Resort (R)

Idaho
Coeur d'Alene:
  Coeur d'Alene (R)
Sun Valley:
  Sun Valley (R)

Illinois
Bloomingdale:
  Indian Lakes (R)
Itasca:
  Nordic Hills (R)
Lake Forest:
  Deer Path (B)
Lincolnshire:
  Marriott's Lincolnshire (R)
Oak Brook:
  Oak Brook Hills (R)
St. Charles:
  Pheasant Run (R)

Indiana
French Lick:
  French Lick Springs (R)

Kansas
Topeka:
  Heritage House (B)

Kentucky
Lexington:
  Marriott Griffin Gate (R)

Louisiana
New Orleans:
  Windsor Court (H)
St. Francisville:
  Lodge at the Bluffs (H)

Maine
Bar Harbor:
  Bar Harbor Inn (B)
Rockport:
  Samoset (R)
Scarborough:
  Black Point Inn (R)

Maryland
Berlin:
  Atlantic (H)
Ocean City:
  Coconut Malorie (H)

Massachusetts
Boston:
  Newbury (B)
Cape Cod:
  Chatham Bars (B)
  Dunscroft by the Sea (B)
  New Seabury (R)
  Ocean Edge (R)

Golf

Danvers:
Tara's Ferncroft (R)
Lenox:
Cranwell (R)

Michigan
Acme:
Grand Traverse (R)
Bellaire:
Shanty Creek (R)
Boyne Falls:
Boyne Mountain (R)
Harbor Springs:
Boyne Highlands (R)
Mackinac Island:
Grand (H)
Thompsonville:
Crystal Mountain (R)
Ypsilanti:
Marriott Ypsilanti (R)

Minnesota
Alexandria:
Arrowwood Radisson (R)
Brainerd:
Madden's (R)
Lutsen:
Lutsen (R)
Pine River:
McGuire's (B)

Mississippi
Biloxi:
Grand Casino (H)
Jackson:
Milsaps Buie House (H)
Oxford:
Barksdale-Isom (B)

Missouri
Lake Ozark:
Lodge at Four Seasons (R)
Osage Beach:
Marriott's Tan-Tar-A (R)
Ridgedale:
Big Cedar (R)
St. Louis:
Frontenac Hilton (H)

Montana
Big Sky:
Huntley Lodge (R)
Darby:
Triple Creek Ranch (R)
Red Lodge:
Pollard (B)

Nevada
Crystal Bay:
Cal-Neva Resort (R)
Lake Tahoe:
Harrah's Lake Tahoe (R)
Las Vegas:
Desert Inn (R)
Golden Nugget (H)
Hilton Las Vegas (H)
Tropicana (H)

New Hampshire
Bretton Woods:
1896 Bretton Arms (B)
Mount Washington (R)
Dixville Notch:
Balsams Grand (R)
Jackson:
Eagle Mountain (H)

North Conway:
White Mountain (R)
Waterville Valley:
Waterville Valley (R)

New Jersey
Atlantic City:
Hilton Atlantic City (H)
Spring Lake:
Sea Crest by the Sea (B)
Vernon:
Great Gorge Village (R)

New Mexico
Albuquerque:
Hyatt Reg. Albuquerque (H)
Cloudcroft:
Lodge at Cloudcroft (B)
Santa Fe:
House of the Moon (S)

New York
Cooperstown:
Otesaga (H)
Ellenville:
Nevele (R)
Kiamesha Lake:
Concord (R)
Lake Placid:
Lake Placid Lodge (B)
Monticello:
Kutsher's (R)
New Paltz:
Mohonk Mountain (R)
Rye Brook:
Doral Arrowwood (R)
Saratoga Springs:
Gideon Putnam (H)

North Carolina
Asheville:
Great Smokies (R)
Grove Park Inn (R)
Blowing Rock:
Hound Ears (R)
Cashiers:
High Hampton (R)
Edenton:
Lords Proprietors' (B)
Lake Toxaway:
Greystone Inn (B)
Pinehurst:
Holly Inn (B)
Pinehurst (R)
Pittsboro:
Fearrington House (B)
Raleigh-Durham:
Washington Duke (H)

Ohio
Dellroy:
Atwood Lake (R)
Huron:
Sawmill Creek (R)
Painesville:
Quail Hollow (R)

Oklahoma
Checotah:
Fountainhead (R)
Kingston:
Texoma State (R)
Norman:
Holmberg House (B)

413

Oregon

Black Butte Ranch:
  Black Butte (R)
Gleneden Beach:
  Salishan (R)
Gold Beach:
  Tu Tu'Tun (B)
Portland:
  5th Avenue Suites (H)
Sunriver:
  Sunriver (R)
Warm Springs:
  Kah-Nee-Ta (R)
Welches:
  Resort at Mountain (R)

Pennsylvania

Champion:
  Seven Springs (R)
Farmington:
  Nemacolin Woodlands (R)
Hershey:
  Hershey (H)
Mt. Pocono/Pocono Manor:
  Mount Airy Lodge (R)
  Pocono Manor (R)
Skytop:
  Skytop Lodge (R)

Puerto Rico

Dorado:
  Hyatt Reg. Cerromar (R)
  Hyatt Reg. Dorado (R)
Fajardo:
  El Conquistador (R)
Humacao:
  Palmas del Mar (R)
San Juan:
  Condado Plaza (H)

Rhode Island

Newport:
  Cliffside Inn (B)
  Elm Tree Cottage (B)
  Vanderbilt Hall (H)

South Carolina

Hilton Head:
  Disney's Hilton Head (R)
  Hilton Head Health (S)
  Hilton Hilton Head (R)
  Hyatt Reg. Hilton Head (R)
  Palmetto Dunes (R)
  Sea Pines (R)
  Westin (R)
Kiawah Island:
  Kiawah Island (R)
Myrtle Beach:
  Hilton Myrtle Beach (R)
Pawleys Island:
  Litchfield Beach (R)
Seabrook Island:
  Seabrook Island (R)

Tennessee

Fairfield Glade:
  Fairfield Glade (R)
Gatlinburg:
  Bent Creek (R)
Nashville:
  Opryland (H)

Texas

Austin:
  Barton Creek (R)
  Lakeway Inn (R)

Dallas/Fort Worth:
  Four Seasons (R)
Horseshoe Bay:
  Horseshoe Bay (R)
Houston:
  Red Lion (H)
  South Shore Harbour (H)
  Woodlands (R)
Montgomery:
  Del Lago (R)
Rancho Viejo:
  Rancho Viejo (R)
San Antonio:
  Hyatt Reg. Hill Country (R)

Utah

Midway:
  Homestead (B)

Vermont

Barnard:
  Maple Leaf (B)
Goshen:
  Blueberry Hill (B)
Killington:
  Killington Resort (R)
Ludlow:
  Governor's Inn (B)
  Green Mountain (S)
Manchester:
  Equinox (H)
  Reluctant Panther (B)
Middlebury:
  Waybury Inn (B)
Stratton Mountain:
  Stratton Mtn (R)
Vergennes:
  Basin Harbor (R)
Woodstock:
  Woodstock Inn (R)

Virginia

Charlottesville:
  Boar's Head Inn (R)
Hot Springs:
  Homestead (R)
Irvington:
  Tides Inn (R)
  Tides Lodge (R)
Keswick:
  Keswick Hall (B)
Leesburg:
  Lansdowne (R)
Richmond:
  Linden Row (B)
Williamsburg:
  Kingsmill (R)
  Williamsburg Inn (H)
  Williamsburg Lodge (H)
Wintergreen:
  Wintergreen (R)
Woodstock:
  Inn at Narrow Passage (B)

Washington

Blaine:
  Inn at Semi-Ah-Moo (R)
Port Ludlow:
  Port Ludlow (R)
Stevenson:
  Skamania Lodge (R)

West Virginia

Charles Town:
  Hillbrook Inn (B)

Golf

Davis:
Canaan Valley (R)
Harpers Ferry:
Historic Hilltop House (H)
Morgantown:
Lakeview Resort (R)
Parkersburg:
Blennerhassett Clarion (H)
Pipestem:
McKeever Pipestem (R)
Wheeling:
Oglebay Resort (R)
White Sulphur Springs:
Greenbrier (R)

Wisconsin
Bailey's Harbor:
Gordon Lodge (B)

Delavan:
Lake Lawn Lodge (R)
Green Lake:
Heidel House (R)
Kohler:
American Club (R)
Inn on Woodlake (B)
Lake Geneva:
Grand Geneva (R)
Osceola:
Aveda Spa Retreat (S)

Wyoming
Jackson:
Jackson Hole Racquet (R)
Teton Pines (R)
Wort (H)

Historic/Grand Dames

Alabama

Anniston:
Victoria (B)
Birmingham:
Tutwiler (H)
Fairhope:
Malaga Inn (B)
Mobile:
Radisson Admiral (H)
Point Clear:
Marriott's Grand (R)
Tuskegee:
Kellogg (H)

Arizona

Grand Canyon:
El Tovar (H)
Phoenix/Scottsdale:
Arizona Biltmore (R)
San Carlos (H)
Crowne Phoenix (H)
Sheraton San Marcos (R)
Wigwam (R)
Sedona:
Garland's (R)
Tucson:
Arizona Inn (H)
Tanque Verde (B)
Triangle L Ranch (R)

Arkansas

Eureka Springs.
Palace (B)
Hot Springs:
Arlington Resort (H)
Majestic (H)
Little Rock:
Capital (H)

California

Avalon:
Inn on Mt. Ada (B)
Big Sur:
Deetjen's Big Sur (B)
Borrego Springs:
La Casa del Zorro (R)
Calistoga:
Indian Springs (S)
Capitola by the Sea:
Inn at Depot Hill (B)
Carmel:
Highlands Inn (B)
La Playa (H)
Los Laureles (H)
Stonepine (B)
Death Valley:
Furnace Creek Inn (R)
Garberville:
Benbow Inn (B)
Guerneville:
Applewood Inn (B)
Healdsburg:
Madrona Manor (B)
Little River:
Heritage House (B)
Little River Inn (B)
Long Beach:
Queen Mary (H)
Los Angeles:
Argyle (H)
Bel-Air (H)
Beverly Hills (H)
Chateau Marmont (H)

Clarion Hollywood (H)
Miramar Sheraton (H)
Regal Biltmore (H)
Regent Beverly Wilshire (H)
Ritz Huntington (H)
Shangri-La (H)
Wyndham Checkers (H)
Mendocino:
Mendocino (H)
Stanford Inn (B)
Montecito:
Montecito Inn (B)
San Ysidro (B)
Monterey:
Old Monterey Inn (B)
Napa:
Silverado (R)
Ojai:
Oaks at Ojai (S)
Ojai Valley (R)
Pacific Grove:
Gosby House (B)
Green Gables (B)
Martine Inn (B)
Seven Gables (B)
Palm Springs:
Ingleside (B)
Monte Vista (H)
Palms (S)
Two Bunch Palms (B)
Pebble Beach:
Lodge at Pebble Beach (R)
Riverside:
Mission Inn (H)
San Diego:
del Coronado Hotel (R)
Gaslamp (H)
Horton Grand (H)
Inn at Rancho Santa Fe (H)
La Jolla Beach (H)
La Valencia (H)
US Grant (H)
San Francisco:
Archbishop's Mansion (B)
Boheme (H)
Campton Place (H)
Chancellor (H)
Claremont (R)
Clarion Bedford (H)
Clift (H)
Fairmont SF (H)
Galleria Park (H)
Gramma's Rose Garden (B)
Griffon (H)
Handlery Union Square (H)
Harbor Court (H)
Huntington (H)
Inn at the Opera (B)
Inn at Union Square (B)
Juliana (H)
Kensington Park (H)
Majestic (H)
Mansions (B)
Mark Hopkins (H)
Maxwell (H)
Milano (H)
Monaco (H)
Mosser Victorian (H)
Palace (H)
Prescott (H)
Queen Anne (H)
Renaissance Stanford (H)

Historic/Grand Dames

Rex (H)
Ritz SF (H)
Savoy (H)
Sherman House (B)
Sir Francis Drake (H)
Triton (H)
Victorian Inn (B)
Villa Florence (H)
Vintage Court (H)
Warwick Regis (H)
Washington Square (B)
Westin St. Francis (H)
White Swan (B)
York (H)
San Jose:
  de Anza (H)
  Hyatt Saint Claire (H)
Santa Barbara:
  El Encanto (H)
  Four Seasons Biltmore (R)
Santa Rosa:
  La Rose (B)
Sausalito:
  Alta Mira (H)
  Casa Madrona (H)
Sonoma:
  El Dorado (H)
  Sonoma Mission (S)
Yosemite:
  Ahwahnee (H)

Colorado

Aspen:
  Jerome (H)
  Sardy House (B)
Colorado Springs:
  Antlers Dlbtree (H)
  Broadmoor (R)
  Hearthstone Inn (B)
Denver:
  Brown Palace (H)
  Oxford (H)
Durango:
  General Palmer (H)
  Strater (H)
  Wit's End (B)
Mosca:
  Inn at Zapata (B)

Connecticut

Chester:
  Inn at Chester (B)
Essex:
  Griswold Inn (B)
Greenwich:
  Homestead Inn (B)
Hartford:
  Goodwin (H)
Ivoryton:
  Copper Beech (B)
Lakeville:
  Interlaken Inn (R)
Mystic:
  Inn at Mystic (B)
New Haven:
  Three Chimneys (B)
New Preston:
  Boulders (B)
  Inn on Lake Waramaug (B)
Norfolk:
  Blackberry River (B)
Norwich:
  Norwich Inn (S)

Old Lyme:
  Bee & Thistle (B)
  Old Lyme Inn (B)
Ridgefield:
  Stonehenge Inn (B)
Salisbury:
  White Hart (B)
Washington:
  Mayflower Inn (B)
Westport:
  Inn at National Hall (B)

Delaware

Bethany Beach:
  Addy Sea (B)
Lewes:
  New Devon (B)
New Castle:
  Armitage Inn (B)
Rehoboth Beach:
  Corner Cupboard (B)
Wilmington:
  Boulevard B&B (B)
  Hotel du Pont (H)

Florida

Boca Raton:
  Boca Raton (R)
Bonita Springs:
  Shangri-La (S)
Clearwater:
  Belleview Mido (R)
Fisher Island:
  Spa Internazionale (S)
Fort Lauderdale:
  Riverside (H)
Gasparilla Island:
  Gasparilla Inn (B)
Key West:
  Holiday Inn La Concha (H)
  Marquesa (H)
  Marriott's Casa Marina (R)
Lake Wales:
  Chalet Suzanne (B)
Miami/Miami Beach:
  Astor (H)
  Biltmore (R)
  Casa Grande (H)
  Fisher Island (R)
  Indian Creek (H)
  Lafayette (H)
  Marlin (H)
  Ocean Front (H)
  Park Central (H)
  Place St. Michel (H)
  Raleigh (H)
  Ritz Plaza (H)
Palm Beach:
  Breakers (R)
  Chesterfield (H)
Ponte Vedra Beach:
  Ponte Vedra (R)
Tampa Bay:
  Don CeSar (R)
  Renaissance Vinoy (R)
Winter Park:
  Park Plaza (B)

Georgia

Americus:
  Windsor (H)
Atlanta:
  Ansley Inn (B)
  Biltmore (H)

Historic/Grand Dames

Augusta:
 Partridge Inn (H)
Jekyll Island:
 Jekyll Island Club (R)
Macon:
 1842 Inn (B)
Savannah:
 Ballastone Inn (B)
 Eliza Thompson (B)
 Gastonian (B)
 Kehoe House (B)
 Magnolia Place (B)
 Mulberry Inn (B)
 Planters Inn Savannah (B)
 President's Quarters (B)
 17 Hundred 90 Inn (B)
Sea Island:
 Cloister (R)

Hawaii
Oahu:
 Halekulani (H)
 Royal Hawaiian (H)
 Sheraton Moana (H)

Idaho
Boise:
 Idanha (H)
 Owyhee Plaza (H)
Coeur d'Alene:
 Blackwell B&B (B)
 Gregory's McFarland B&B (B)
Sun Valley:
 Sun Valley (R)

Illinois
Chicago:
 Ambassador West (H)
 Blackstone (H)
 Claridge (H)
 Drake (H)
 Hilton Chicago (H)
 Inter-Continental Chicago (H)
 Midland (H)
 Omni Ambassador (H)
 Palmer Hilton (H)
 Raphael (H)
 Regal Knickerbocker (H)
 Tremont (H)
 Whitehall (H)
Lake Forest:
 Deer Path (B)

Indiana
French Lick:
 French Lick Springs (R)
Indianapolis:
 Canterbury (H)
 Omni Severin (H)

Iowa
Des Moines:
 Savery (H)
Dubuque:
 Redstone Inn (B)
 Richards House (B)
Fort Madison:
 Kingsley Inn (B)
Homestead:
 Die Heimat (B)
Newton:
 La Corsette Maison (B)
Walnut:
 Antique City (B)

Kansas
Council Grove:
 Cottage House (B)

Fort Scott:
 Chenault Mansion (B)
Lawrence:
 Eldridge (H)
Lindsborg:
 Swedish Country (B)
Topeka:
 Heritage House (B)
 Inn at the Park (H)
Wichita:
 Castle Inn Riverside (B)

Kentucky
Berea:
 Boone Tavern (H)
Harrodsburg:
 Beaumont Inn (B)
 Inn at Shaker Village (B)
Louisville:
 Camberly Brown (H)
 Seelbach (H)

Louisiana
Napoleonville:
 Madewood Plantation (B)
New Orleans:
 Bourbon Orleans (H)
 Chateau Sonesta (H)
 Cornstalk (B)
 Fairmont New Orleans (H)
 Lafayette (H)
 Le Pavillon (H)
 Le Richelieu (H)
 Maison de Ville (B)
 Melrose Mansion (B)
 Monteleone (H)
 Pelham (H)
 Pontchartrain (H)
 Prince Conti (H)
 Queen & Crescent (H)
 Radisson New Orleans (H)
 Soniat House (B)
White Castle:
 Nottoway Plantation (B)

Maine
Bar Harbor:
 Bayview (H)
Boothbay Harbor:
 Spruce Point (B)
Brunswick:
 Captain Daniel Stone (B)
Camden:
 Norumbega Inn (B)
Castine:
 Castine Inn (B)
Deer Isle:
 Pilgrims Inn (B)
East Holden:
 Lucerne Inn (B)
Freeport:
 Harraseeket Inn (B)
Kennebunkport:
 Captain Lord Mansion (B)
 Inn at Harbor Head (B)
 Kennebunkport Inn (B)
 White Barn Inn (B)
Newcastle:
 Newcastle Inn (B)
Northeast Harbor:
 Asticou Inn (B)
Ogunquit:
 Cliff House (H)

Historic/Grand Dames

Portland:
  Radisson Portland (H)
  Regency Portland (H)
Scarborough:
  Black Point Inn (R)

Maryland
Annapolis:
  Maryland Historic Inn (B)
Baltimore:
  Admiral Fell Inn (B)
  Ann Street B&B (B)
  Clarion at Mt. Vernon (H)
  Inn at Henderson's (B)
  Mr. Mole B&B (B)
  Radisson Lord Baltimore (H)
Berlin:
  Atlantic (H)
Chestertown:
  Imperial (B)
Oxford:
  Robert Morris Inn (B)
St. Michaels:
  Inn at Perry Cabin (B)
Taneytown:
  Antrim 1844 (B)

Massachusetts
Boston:
  Boston Park Plaza (H)
  Chandler Inn (H)
  Copley Square (H)
  Eliot (H)
  Fairmont Copley (H)
  Le Meridien (H)
  Lenox (H)
  Newbury (B)
  Omni Parker (H)
  Ritz Boston (H)
  Sheraton Commander (H)
  Tremont House (H)
Cape Cod:
  Brass Key (B)
  Chatham Bars (B)
  Coonamessett Inn (B)
  Dan'l Webster Inn (B)
  High Brewster (B)
  Wequassett Inn (B)
  Whalewalk Inn (B)
Deerfield:
  Deerfield Inn (B)
Lenox:
  Blantyre (B)
  Cranwell (R)
  Gables Inn (B)
  Wheatleigh (B)
Martha's Vineyard:
  Charlotte Inn (B)
  Daggett House (B)
  Harbor View (B)
  Thorncroft Inn (B)
  Tuscany Inn (B)
Nantucket:
  Jared Coffin House (B)
  Summer House (B)
  Wauwinet (B)
  White Elephant (R)
Northampton:
  Northampton (H)
Rockport:
  Yankee Clipper (B)
Salem:
  Hawthorne (H)
Stockbridge:
  Red Lion (B)

Sturbridge:
  Publick House (B)

Michigan
Detroit:
  Marriott Dearborn (H)
  Mayflower B&B (B)
  River Place (H)
Mackinac Island:
  Bay View B&B (B)
  Iroquois (B)
Petoskey:
  Stafford's Bay View (B)

Minnesota
Minneapolis/St. Paul:
  Saint Paul (H)
  Whitney (H)
Red Wing:
  St. James (H)
Rochester:
  Kahler (H)
Stillwater:
  Lumber Baron's (H)

Mississippi
Jackson:
  Milsaps Buie House (H)
Natchez:
  Briars Inn (B)
  Burn (B)
  Dunleith (B)
  Linden B&B (B)
  Monmouth Plantation (B)
  Natchez Eola (H)
Tupelo:
  Mockingbird B&B (B)
Vicksburg:
  Cedar Grove (B)
  Corners B&B (B)
  Duff Green (B)

Missouri
Branson:
  Branson Hotel B&B (B)
  Branson House B&B (B)
Hannibal:
  Fifth St. Mansion (B)
  Garth Woodside (B)
Kansas City:
  Radisson (H)
  Raphael (H)
  Savoy (H)
  Southmoreland (H)
St. Louis:
  Crowne Plaza Majestic (H)
  Drury Inn (H)
  Hyatt Reg. St. Louis (H)
  Seven Gables (B)

Montana
Bigfork:
  Averill's Flathead (B)
Big Sky:
  Lone Mountain (B)
Bozeman:
  Mountain Sky (B)
Gallatin Gateway:
  Gallatin Gateway (B)
  320 Guest Ranch (B)
Red Lodge:
  Pollard (B)

Nebraska
Beatrice:
  Carriage House (B)

Historic/Grand Dames

Waterloo:
 JC Robinson B&B (B)
Wilber:
 Wilber (B)

New Hampshire
Bretton Woods:
 1896 Bretton Arms (B)
 Mount Washington (R)
Dixville Notch:
 Balsams Grand (R)
Hanover:
 Hanover Inn (B)
Holderness:
 Manor on Golden Pond (B)
Jackson:
 Christmas Farm (B)
 Eagle Mountain (H)
Meredith:
 Inn at Mill Falls (B)
Portsmouth:
 Sise Inn (B)

New Jersey
Atlantic City:
 Claridge Casino (H)
 Marriott Seaview (R)
 Merv Griffin's (H)
Beach Haven:
 Green Gables (B)
Cape May:
 Abbey (B)
 Angel of the Sea (B)
 Chalfonte (H)
 Mainstay Inn (B)
 Queen Victoria (B)
 Virginia Hotel (B)
Hope:
 Inn at Millrace Pond (B)
Princeton:
 Nassau Inn (H)
Spring Lake:
 Breakers (B)
Summit:
 Grand Summit (H)

New Mexico
Albuquerque:
 La Posada Albuquerque (H)
Cloudcroft:
 Lodge at Cloudcroft (B)
Raton:
 Vermejo Park (B)
Santa Fe:
 Bishop's Lodge (R)
 La Fonda (H)
 La Posada Santa Fe (H)
 Preston House (B)
 St. Francis (H)
Taos:
 Historic Taos (B)

New York
Amenia:
 Troutbeck (B)
Bolton Landing:
 Sagamore (R)
Cooperstown:
 Otesaga (H)
Dover Plains:
 Old Drovers Inn (B)
Ellenville:
 Nevele (R)
Geneva:
 Geneva on the Lake (B)

Glen Cove:
 Harrison (H)
Hopewell Junction:
 Le Chambord (B)
Ithaca:
 Rose Inn (B)
Kiamesha Lake:
 Concord (R)
Lake Placid:
 Lake Placid Lodge (B)
Lew Beach:
 Beaverkill Valley (B)
Montauk:
 Gurney's Inn (S)
 Montauk Yacht (R)
Monticello:
 Kutsher's (R)
New Paltz:
 Mohonk Mountain (R)
New York City:
 Algonquin (H)
 Beekman Tower (H)
 Box Tree (B)
 Carlyle (H)
 Chelsea (H)
 Delmonico (H)
 Essex House Nikko (H)
 Inter-Continental NY (H)
 Lombardy (H)
 Lowell (H)
 Mansfield (H)
 Mark (H)
 NY Palace (H)
 Pierre (H)
 Plaza (H)
 Plaza Athénée (H)
 St. Moritz (H)
 St. Regis (H)
 Waldorf Astoria (H)
 Waldorf Towers (H)
 Westbury (H)
 Wyndham (H)
North Hudson:
 Elk Lake Lodge (R)
Old Chatham:
 Old Chatham Inn (B)
Rhinebeck:
 Beekman Arms (B)
Saranac Lake:
 Saranac (H)
Saratoga Springs:
 Gideon Putnam (H)
 Inn at Saratoga (B)
Shandaken:
 Shandaken Inn (B)
Shelter Island:
 Chequit Inn (B)
 Ram's Head (B)
Stony Brook:
 Three Village (B)
Tarrytown:
 Castle at Tarrytown (B)
 Tarrytown House (B)

North Carolina
Asheville:
 Grove Park Inn (R)
 Richmond Hill (B)
Blowing Rock:
 Westglow Spa (S)
Cashiers:
 High Hampton (R)
Charlotte:
 Dunhill (H)

Historic/Grand Dames

Fayetteville:
  Radisson Prince Charles (H)
Lake Toxaway:
  Greystone Inn (B)
Nags Head:
  First Colony (H)
Pinehurst:
  Holly Inn (B)
  Pinehurst (R)
Raleigh-Durham:
  Carolina Inn (H)

North Dakota
Fargo:
  Bohlig's B&B (B)
Jamestown:
  Country Charm (B)
Luverne:
  Volden Farm B&B (B)
Medora:
  Rough Rider (B)

Ohio
Aurora:
  Aurora Inn (H)
  Mario's International (S)
Cincinnati:
  Cincinnatian (H)
  Omni Netherland (H)
  Vernon Manor (H)
Cleveland:
  Baricelli Inn (B)
  Glidden House (B)
  Renaissance Cleveland (H)
Columbus:
  Westin Columbus (H)
  Worthington Inn (B)
Grand Rapids:
  Kerr House (S)
Granville:
  Granville Inn (B)
Marietta:
  Lafayette (H)

Oregon
Hood River:
  Columbia Gorge (H)
Newport:
  Sylvia Beach (H)
Portland:
  Benson (H)
  Governor (H)
  Heathman (H)
  Vintage Plaza (H)
Timberline:
  Timberline (R)

Pennsylvania
Champion:
  Seven Springs (R)
Erwinna:
  Evermay on Delaware (B)
Glen Mills:
  Sweetwater Farm (B)
Hershey:
  Hershey (H)
Lahaska:
  Golden Plough (B)
Mount Joy:
  Cameron Estate (B)
Mt. Pocono/Pocono Manor:
  Mount Airy Lodge (R)
  Pocono Manor (R)

Philadelphia:
  Best Western Independence (H)
  Chestnut Hill (H)
  Latham (H)
  Park Hyatt Philadelphia (H)
  Penn's View (B)
  Warwick Philadelphia (H)
Pittsburgh:
  Priory (B)
  Westin William Penn (H)
Skytop:
  Skytop Lodge (R)
South Sterling:
  Sterling Inn (B)
Wayne:
  Wayne (H)

Puerto Rico
Old San Juan:
  El Convento (H)
San Juan:
  Condado Beach Trio (H)

Rhode Island
Block Island:
  Atlantic Inn (B)
  Manisses (H)
  1661 Inn (B)
Newport:
  Castle Hill Inn (B)
  Inntowne Inn (B)
Providence:
  Biltmore Providence (H)

South Carolina
Beaufort:
  Rhett House (B)
Charleston:
  Battery Carriage (B)
  Fulton Lane Inn (B)
  Indigo Inn (B)
  John Rutledge (B)
  Kings Courtyard (B)
  Lodge Alley (B)
  Mills House (H)
  Planters Inn (B)
  Vendue Inn (B)
  Victoria House (B)
Pawleys Island:
  Litchfield Plantation (B)

South Dakota
Custer:
  Custer Mansion (B)
  State Game Lodge (R)
Rapid City:
  Alex Johnson (H)
Spearfish:
  Eighth St. Inn (B)
Yankton:
  Mulberry Inn (B)

Tennessee
Gatlinburg:
  Buchhorn Inn (B)
Memphis:
  Peabody Memphis (H)
Nashville:
  Hermitage (H)
  Union Station (H)
Walland:
  Inn at Blackberry Farm (B)

Texas
Austin:
  Driskill (H)

Historic/Grand Dames

Bandera:
  Mayan Dude Ranch (B)
Dallas/Fort Worth:
  Adolphus (H)
  Mansion on Turtle Creek (H)
  Melrose (H)
  Radisson Ft. Worth (H)
  St. Germain (B)
  Stockyards (H)
  Stoneleigh (H)
Galveston:
  Galvez (H)
  Tremont House (H)
Houston:
  La Colombe d'Or (B)
  Lancaster (H)
  Wyndham Warwick (H)
San Antonio:
  Crowne Plaza (H)
  Fairmount (H)
  La Mansion del Rio (H)
  Menger (H)

Utah
Cedar City:
  Bryce Canyon (H)
Midway:
  Homestead (B)
Ogden:
  Historic Radisson (H)
Park City:
  1904 Imperial (H)
  Washington School (B)
Salt Lake City:
  Inn at Temple Square (H)
  Peery (H)
Springdale:
  Zion Lodge (H)

Vermont
Barnard:
  Twin Farms (R)
Craftsbury Common:
  Inn on Common (H)
Dorset:
  Dorset Inn (B)
Goshen:
  Blueberry Hill (B)
Grafton:
  Old Tavern at Grafton (B)
Highgate Springs:
  Tyler Place (R)
Lower Waterford.
  Rabbit Hill (B)
Ludlow:
  Governor's Inn (B)
Manchester:
  Equinox (H)
  Inn at Manchester (B)
  Village Country (B)
  Wilburton Inn (B)
Middlebury:
  Middlebury Inn (B)
  Swift House (B)
Newfane:
  Four Columns (H)
Perkinsville:
  Inn at Weathersfield (B)
Quechee:
  Quechee Inn (B)
Shelburne:
  Inn at Shelburne Farms (B)
Stowe:
  Green Mountain (B)

Vergennes:
  Basin Harbor (R)
West Dover:
  Inn at Sawmill Farm (B)
Wilmington:
  Hermitage Inn (B)
Woodstock:
  Kedron Valley (B)

Virginia
Abingdon:
  Camberley's (B)
Hot Springs:
  Homestead (R)
Keswick:
  Keswick Hall (B)
Paris:
  Ashby Inn (B)
Richmond:
  Jefferson (H)
Williamsburg:
  Williamsburg Inn (H)

Washington
Lake Quinault:
  Lake Quinault (B)
Seattle:
  Alexis (H)
  Four Seasons Olympic (H)
  Mayflower Park (H)
  Roosevlet (H)
  Sorrento (H)
  Vintage Park (H)

Washington, DC
  Carlton (H)
  Hay-Adams (H)
  Henley Park (H)
  Jefferson (H)
  Morrison-Clark Inn (B)
  Omni Shoreham (H)
  Renaissance Mayflower (H)
  Ritz Washington DC (H)
  Willard (H)

West Virginia
Berkeley Springs:
  Country Inn (B)
Shepherdstown:
  Bavarian Inn (B)
White Sulphur Springs:
  Greenbrier (R)

Wisconsin
Bailey's Harbor:
  Gordon Lodge (B)
Bayfield:
  Old Rittenhouse (B)
Delavan:
  Lake Lawn Lodge (R)
Eagle River:
  Chanticleer Inn (B)
Kohler:
  American Club (R)
Milwaukee:
  Hilton Milwaukee (H)
  Pfister (H)

Wyoming
Moran:
  Jenny Lake (B)
Yellowstone National Park:
  Lake Yellowstone (H)
  Mammoth Hot Springs (H)
  Old Faithful (H)

"In" Places

Alabama
Birmingham:
Wynfrey (H)

Alaska
Anchorage:
Captain Cook (H)

Arizona
Phoenix/Scottsdale:
Arizona Biltmore (R)
Hyatt Reg. Scottsdale (R)
Phoenician (R)
Scottsdale Princess (R)
Wigwam (R)
Sedona:
Enchantment (R)
Graham B&B (B)
L'Auberge de Sedona (H)
Tucson:
Arizona Inn (H)
Canyon Ranch (S)
Lodge Ventana (R)
Loews Ventana (R)
Westin La Paloma (R)

Arkansas
Little Rock:
Capital (H)

California
Big Sur:
Post Ranch (B)
Ventana Inn (B)
Carlsbad:
La Costa (S)
Carmel:
Carmel Valley (R)
Highlands Inn (B)
John Gardiner's (R)
Quail Lodge (R)
Stonepine (B)
Cazadero:
Timberhill (B)
Dana Point:
Ritz Laguna Niguel (R)
Escondido:
Golden Door (S)
Los Angeles:
Bel-Air (H)
Beverly Hills (H)
Beverly Prescott
Four Seasons (H)
Mondrian (H)
Nikko Beverly Hills (H)
Peninsula Beverly Hills (H)
Regent Beverly Wilshire (H)
Ritz Huntington (H)
Ritz Marina del Rey (H)
Shutters (H)
Wyndham Checkers (H)
Montecito:
San Ysidro (B)
Newport Beach:
Four Seasons Newport (H)
Sutton Place (H)
Oakhurst:
Chateau du Sureau (B)
Olympic Valley:
Resort at Squaw Creek (R)
Palm Springs:
Ingleside (B)
La Quinta (R)
Marriott's Desert Springs (R)

Renaissance Esmeralda (R)
Ritz Rancho Mirage (R)
Two Bunch Palms (B)
Westin Mission Hills (R)
Pebble Beach:
Inn at Spanish Bay (R)
Lodge at Pebble Beach (R)
Riverside:
Mission Inn (H)
Rutherford:
Auberge du Soleil (B)
San Diego:
Hyatt Reg. La Jolla (H)
Hyatt Reg. San Diego (H)
Le Meridien San Diego (H)
Loews Coronado (R)
Rancho Bernardo (R)
Rancho Valencia (R)
Sheraton Grande (R)
San Francisco:
Archbishop's Mansion (B)
Boheme (H)
Campton Place (H)
Clift (H)
Huntington (H)
Mandarin Oriental (H)
Monaco (H)
Pan Pacific SF (H)
Park Hyatt SF (H)
Ritz SF (H)
Sherman House (B)
San Jose:
Fairmont San Jose (H)
Santa Barbara:
Four Seasons Biltmore (R)
St. Helena:
Meadowood (R)
Vista:
Cal-a-Vie (S)

Colorado
Aspen:
Jerome (H)
Little Nell (H)
Ritz Aspen (H)
Beaver Creek:
Hyatt Reg. Beaver Creek (H)
Clark:
Home Ranch (R)
Colorado Springs:
Broadmoor (R)
Denver:
Loews Giorgio (H)
Oxford (H)
Durango:
Tall Timber (B)
Edwards:
Lodge & Spa Cordillera (R)
Granby:
C Lazy U Ranch (B)
Telluride:
Peaks at Telluride (R)
Vail:
Sonnenalp of Vail (R)

Connecticut
Washington:
Mayflower Inn (B)
Westport:
Inn at National Hall (B)

"In" Places

Florida

Amelia Island:
  Ritz Amelia Island (R)

Boca Raton:
  Boca Raton (R)

Fort Lauderdale:
  Lago Mar (R)
  Registry Resort (S)

Key Largo:
  Ocean Reef (R)

Little Torch Key:
  Little Palm Island (B)

Miami/Miami Beach:
  Biltmore (R)
  Delano (H)
  Fisher Island (R)
  Grand Bay (H)
  Marlin (H)
  Mayfair House (H)
  Omni Colonnade (H)
  Park Central (H)
  Ritz Plaza (H)
  Spa at Doral (S)
  Turnberry Isle (R)

Naples:
  Naples Bath & Tennis (R)
  Registry (R)
  Ritz Naples (R)

Orlando:
  Disney Institute (R)
  Disney's Grand Floridian (R)
  Disney's Yacht (R)
  Hyatt Reg. Grand Cypress (R)
  Peabody Orlando (H)

Palm Beach:
  Breakers (R)
  Four Seasons Palm Beach (H)
  Palm Beach Polo (R)
  Ritz Palm Beach (R)

Ponte Vedra Beach:
  Ponte Vedra (R)

Tampa Bay:
  Renaissance Vinoy (R)

Georgia

Atlanta:
  Four Seasons Atlanta (H)
  Grand Hyatt Atlanta (H)
  Ritz Atlanta (H)
  Ritz Buckhead (H)

Sea Island:
  Cloister (R)

Hawaii

Big Island:
  Four Seasons Hualalai (R)
  Hapuna Prince (R)
  Hilton Waikoloa (R)
  Kona Village (R)
  Mauna Kea (R)
  Orchid at Mauna Lani (R)

Kauai:
  Princeville (R)

Lanai:
  Lodge at Koele (R)

Maui:
  Four Seasons Maui (R)
  Grand Wailea (R)
  Hana-Maui Hotel (H)
  Kapalua Bay (R)
  Kea Lani (R)
  Ritz Kapalua (R)

Oahu:
  Halekulani (H)
  Hawaii Prince Waikiki (H)
  Kahala Mandarin (R)

Idaho

Coeur d'Alene:
  Coeur d'Alene (R)

Ketchum:
  Knob Hill (H)

Illinois

Chicago:
  Fairmont (H)
  Four Seasons Chicago (H)
  La Salle Club (H)
  Renaissance Chicago (H)
  Ritz Chicago (H)
  Westin River North (H)

Galena:
  Eagle Ridge (R)

Indiana

Indianapolis:
  Canterbury (H)

Kentucky

Lexington:
  Marriott Griffin Gate (R)

Louisville:
  Seelbach (H)

Louisiana

New Orleans:
  Maison de Ville (B)
  Melrose Mansion (B)
  Pelham (H)
  Soniat House (B)
  Westin Canal (H)
  Windsor Court (H)
  Wyndham Riverfront (H)

Maine

Kennebunkport:
  Captain Lord Mansion (B)
  White Barn Inn (B)

Maryland

Annapolis:
  Loews Annapolis (H)

Baltimore:
  Harbor Court (H)
  Mr. Mole B&B (B)
  Renaissance Harborplace (H)

Massachusetts

Boston:
  Four Seasons Boston (H)
  Inn at Harvard (B)
  Le Meridien (H)
  Regal Bostonian (H)
  Ritz Boston (H)

Lenox:
  Blantyre (B)
  Canyon Ranch (S)
  Wheatleigh (B)

Martha's Vineyard:
  Charlotte Inn (B)

Nantucket:
  Wauwinet (B)

Williamstown:
  Orchards (B)

Michigan

Detroit:
  Ritz Dearborn (H)
  Townsend (H)

Mackinac Island:
  Iroquois (B)

"In" Places

Minnesota
Minneapolis/St. Paul:
Hilton Minneapolis (H)
Saint Paul (H)
Whitney (H)

Mississippi
Natchez:
Monmouth Plantation (B)

Missouri
Kansas City:
Raphael (H)
Ritz Kansas City (H)
St. Louis:
Ritz St. Louis (H)

Montana
Bozeman:
Mountain Sky (B)
Gallatin Gateway:
Gallatin Gateway (B)

Nevada
Las Vegas:
Caesars Palace (H)
Mirage (H)
Stratosphere (H)

New Hampshire
Dixville Notch:
Balsams Grand (R)

New Jersey
Cape May:
Mainstay Inn (B)
Short Hills:
Hilton at Short Hills (H)

New Mexico
Albuquerque:
Hyatt Reg. Albuquerque (H)
Española:
Rancho de San Juan (R)
Santa Fe:
Inn of Anasazi (B)
Taos:
Fechin Inn (B)

New York
Amenia:
Troutbeck (B)
Ithaca:
Rose Inn (B)
Lake Placid:
Lake Placid Lodge (B)
New York City:
Box Tree (B)
Carlyle (H)
Four Seasons (H)
Lowell (H)
Mark (H)
Morgans (H)
Paramount (H)
Peninsula NY (H)
Pierre (H)
Plaza Athénée (H)
Ritz New York (H)
Royalton (H)
SoHo Grand (H)
St. Regis (H)
Tarrytown:
Castle at Tarrytown (B)

North Carolina
Charlotte:
Park (H)
Pittsboro:
Fearrington House (B)

Raleigh-Durham:
Siena (H)

Ohio
Cincinnati:
Cincinnatian (H)
Cleveland:
Ritz Cleveland (H)
Wyndham Cleveland (H)
Columbus:
Hyatt on Capital Square (H)
Worthington Inn (B)

Oregon
Gleneden Beach:
Salishan (R)
Portland:
Heathman (H)
RiverPlace (H)
Vintage Plaza (H)

Pennsylvania
Farmington:
Nemacolin Woodlands (R)
Philadelphia:
Four Seasons Philadelphia (H)
Marriott Philadelphia (H)
Park Hyatt Philadelphia (H)
Rittenhouse (H)
Ritz Philadelphia (H)
Pittsburgh:
Westin William Penn (H)

Puerto Rico
Fajardo:
El Conquistador (R)
Old San Juan:
El Convento (H)
Rincon:
Horned Dorset (B)
San Juan:
El San Juan (H)

Rhode Island
Providence:
Westin Providence (H)

South Carolina
Charleston:
Charleston Place (H)
Vendue Inn (B)
Hilton Head:
Westin (R)

South Dakota
Rapid City:
Willow Springs (B)

Tennessee
Nashville:
Union Station (H)
Walland:
Inn at Blackberry Farm (B)

Texas
Arlington:
Greenhouse (S)
Austin:
Barton Creek (R)
Four Seasons Austin (H)
Dallas/Fort Worth:
Adolphus (H)
Cooper Wellness (S)
Crescent Court (H)
Four Seasons (R)
Mansion on Turtle Creek (H)
Omni Mandalay (H)
St. Germain (B)
Wyndham Anatole (H)

"In" Places

Galveston:
Tremont House (H)
Houston:
La Colombe d'Or (B)
Omni Houston (H)
Ritz Houston (H)
San Antonio:
Fairmount (H)
Hvatt Reg. Hill Country (R)

Utah
Park City:
Stein Eriksen (R)

Vermont
Barnard:
Twin Farms (R)
Stowe:
Topnotch at Stowe (R)
West Dover:
Inn at Sawmill Farm (B)

Virginia
(see also Washington, DC)
Richmond:
Jefferson (H)
Washington:
Inn at Little Washington (B)
Williamsburg:
Williamsburg Inn (H)

Washington
Seattle:
Alexis (H)
Four Seasons Olympic (H)

Inn at Market (H)
Sorrento (H)
Vintage Park (H)
Woodmark (H)
Snoqualmie:
Salish Lodge (B)

Washington, DC
(including nearby Maryland and Virginia)
Virginia:
Ritz Pentagon City (H)
Ritz Tysons Corner (H)
Washington, DC:
Four Seasons (H)
Hay-Adams (H)
Jefferson (H)
Park Hyatt Washington (H)
Ritz Washington DC (H)
Willard (H)

West Virginia
White Sulphur Springs:
Greenbrier (R)

Wisconsin
Kohler:
American Club (R)
Milwaukee:
Pfister (H)
Wyndham Milwaukee (H)

Wyoming
Jackson:
Rusty Parrot (B)
Moran:
Jenny Lake (B)

Jacuzzis (in all rooms)*

Arizona
Phoenix/Scottsdale:
  Orange Tree (R)
Sedona:
  Canyon Villa B&B (B)

Arkansas
Eureka Springs:
  Palace (B)

California
Big Sur:
  Post Ranch (B)
Carmel:
  Stonepine (B)
Los Angeles:
  Shutters (H)
Palm Springs:
  Ingleside (B)
Yountville:
  Vintage Inn (H)

Colorado
Clark:
  Home Ranch (R)

Florida
Fisher Island:
  Spa Internazionale (S)
Little Torch Key:
  Little Palm Island (B)
Longboat Key:
  Colony Beach (R)
Miami/Miami Beach:
  Mayfair House (H)
  Turnberry Isle (R)

Georgia
Atlanta:
  Ansley Inn (B)
  French Quarter (H)

Idaho
Tetonia:
  Teton Ridge (B)

Maine
East Holden:
  Lucerne Inn (B)

Maryland
Ocean City:
  Coconut Malorie (H)

Minnesota
Stillwater:
  Lumber Baron's (H)

Montana
Darby:
  Triple Creek Ranch (R)

Nevada
Lake Tahoe:
  Caesars Tahoe (R)

New York
New York City:
  Flatotel International (H)
  Trump International (H)

North Carolina
Lake Toxaway:
  Greystone Inn (B)

Ohio
Aurora:
  Mario's International (S)

South Dakota
Rapid City:
  Abend Haus (B)

Tennessee
Memphis:
  French Quarter (H)

Utah
Park City:
  Shadow Ridge (H)
  Stein Eriksen (R)

Washington
Port Ludlow:
  Inn at Ludlow Bay (B)

---

* Most hotels offer Jacuzzis in some rooms; if this feature is important, ask for one when reserving.

Kitchenettes (in all rooms)*

Arizona
Phoenix/Scottsdale:
  Arizona Golf (R)
  Embassy Biltmore (H)
  Embassy Scottsdale (H)
  Marriott Scottsdale (H)
Tucson:
  Lodge Ventana (R)

California
Calistoga:
  Indian Springs (S)
Los Angeles:
  Le Parc (H)
  Wyndham Bel Age (H)
Napa:
  Embassy Napa Valley (H)
  Silverado (R)
Palm Springs:
  Shadow Mountain (R)
  Sundance (B)
San Diego:
  Gaslamp (H)
San Francisco:
  Hyde Park (B)
Santa Monica:
  Oceana (H)

Colorado
Aspen:
  Gant (B)
Beaver Creek:
  Embassy Beaver Creek (R)
Denver:
  Burnsley (H)
  Residence by Marriott (H)
Durango:
  Tamarron Hilton (R)
Snowmass Village:
  Silvertree (H)
Vail:
  Marriott's at Vail (R)

Delaware
Montchanin:
  Inn at Montchanin (B)

Florida
Destin:
  Hilton Sandestin (R)
Fort Lauderdale:
  Doubletree (H)
Haines City:
  Grenelefe Golf (R)
Key West:
  Cuban Club (H)
Longboat Key:
  Colony Beach (R)
Miami/Miami Beach:
  Alexander (H)
  Casa Grande (H)
  Dbltree Grand (H)
  Fisher Island (R)
  Florida Suites (H)
  Marlin (H)
Naples:
  Edgewater Beach (H)
  Naples Bath & Tennis (R)
Orlando:
  Disney Institute (R)
  Holiday Inn Main Gate (H)

  Holiday Inn SunSpree (R)
  Residence by Marriott (H)
  Vistana (R)
  Westgate Lakes (R)
Palm Beach:
  Brazilian Court (H)
  Palm Beach Polo (R)
Sanibel Island:
  Casa Ybel (R)
  Sundial Beach (R)
Siesta Key:
  Captiva Beach (B)
Tampa Bay:
  Embassy Westshore (H)
  Innisbrook Hilton (R)
  TradeWinds St. Pete (R)

Georgia
Atlanta:
  Biltmore (H)
  Doubletree (H)
  Embassy Perimeter Ctr (H)
  Summerfield (H)

Hawaii
Kauai:
  Kiahuna Plantation (R)
Maui:
  Embassy Maui (R)
Oahu:
  Aston Waikiki (H)
  Outrigger Prince Kuhio (H)
  Outrigger Reef (R)
  Outrigger Waikiki (R)

Idaho
Priest Lake:
  Hill's Hospitality (B)

Illinois
Chicago:
  Sheraton Gateway (H)

Iowa
Des Moines:
  Embassy (H)

Kansas
Lawrence:
  Eldridge (H)

Maine
Cape Elizabeth:
  Inn by the Sea (B)
East Holden:
  Lucerne Inn (B)

Maryland
Baltimore:
  Brookshire (H)

Massachusetts
Cape Cod:
  New Seabury (R)

Minnesota
Minneapolis/St. Paul:
  Embassy Minneapolis (H)

Missouri
Branson:
  Clarion at Fall Creek (R)
  Red Bud Cove B&B (B)
Kansas City:
  Historic Suites of America (B)

---

* Most all-suite hotels have kitchenettes; the hotels listed here have them in all guest quarters.

Kitchenettes (in all rooms)

St. Louis:
Embassy St. Louis (H)

Montana
Darby:
Triple Creek Ranch (R)
Whitefish:
North Forty (B)

New Jersey
Atlantic City:
Atlantic Palace (H)
Vernon:
Great Gorge Village (R)

New York
Geneva:
Geneva on the Lake (B)
New York City:
Beekman Tower (H)
Dumont Plaza (H)
Eastgate Tower (H)
59th St. Bridge Apts (H)
Flatotel International (H)
Lombardy (H)
Lyden Gardens (H)
Lyden House (H)
Murray Hill East (H)
Plaza Fifty (H)
Shelburne Murray Hill (H)
Southgate Tower (H)
Surrey (H)
Trump International (H)

North Carolina
Durham:
Structure House (S)

North Dakota
Fargo:
Best Western Doublewood (H)

South Carolina
Charleston:
Victoria House (B)
Hilton Head:
Disney's Hilton Head (R)
Hilton Head Health (S)
Palmetto Dunes (R)
Seabrook Island:
Seabrook Island (R)

Tennessee
Nashville:
Embassy Nashville (H)

Texas
Cat Spring:
Southwind B&B (B)
Dallas/Fort Worth:
Embassy Dallas (H)
Houston:
Doubletree (H)
Montgomery:
Del Lago (R)

Utah
Park City:
Deer Valley (H)
Salt Lake City:
Embassy (H)
St. George:
Green Valley Spa (S)

Vermont
Smugglers' Notch:
Smugglers' Notch (R)

Virginia
Virginia Beach:
Virginia Beach (R)
Wintergreen:
Wintergreen (R)

Washington
Snoqualmie:
Salish Lodge (B)

Washington, DC
Canterbury (H)
Dbltree NH Avenue (H)
Dbltree Penn Avenue (H)
Embassy Chevy Chase (H)
Georgetown Dutch (H)
One Washington (H)
River Inn (H)
State Plaza (H)
Wyndham Bristol (H)

Wyoming
Jackson:
Jackson Hole Racquet (R)

Marina

Alabama
Orange Beach:
  Perdido Beach (R)
Point Clear:
  Marriott's Grand (R)

Alaska
Gustavus:
  Glacier Bay (B)

Arizona
Page:
  Wahweap (H)

Arkansas
Hot Springs:
  Lake Hamilton (R)
Lakeview:
  Gaston's (R)

California
Anaheim:
  Dbltree Anaheim (H)
Avalon:
  Inn on Mt. Ada (B)
Big Sur:
  Big Sur River (B)
Bodega Bay:
  Inn at the Tides (B)
Carlsbad:
  La Costa (R)
Carmel:
  Carmel Country Spa (S)
  Carmel Valley (R)
  Highlands Inn (B)
Costa Mesa:
  Country Side Inn (H)
Dana Point:
  Laguna Cliff Marriott (R)
  Ritz Laguna Niguel (R)
Eureka:
  Carter House (B)
Irvine:
  Hyatt Reg. Irvine (H)
Lake Arrowhead:
  Lake Arrowhead (R)
Little River:
  Little River Inn (B)
Long Beach:
  Queen Mary (H)
  Renaissance Long Beach (H)
  Sheraton Long Beach (H)
Los Angeles:
  Marriott Marina Beach (H)
  Ritz Marina del Rey (H)
Montecito:
  Montecito Inn (B)
  San Ysidro (B)
Monterey:
  Hyatt Reg. Monterey (H)
  Marriott Monterey (H)
  Monterey Plaza (H)
  Old Monterey Inn (B)
  Pacific (H)
  Spindrift Inn (B)
Morro Bay:
  Inn at Morro Bay (B)
Newport Beach:
  Four Seasons Newport (H)
  Hyatt Newporter (R)
  Marriott Suites (H)
  Marriott Tennis (H)
  Sutton Place (H)

Oakland:
  Waterfront Plaza (H)
Ojai:
  Oaks at Ojai (S)
  Ojai Valley (R)
Olympic Valley:
  Plumpjack's (B)
Pacific Grove:
  Gosby House (B)
  Martine Inn (B)
Palo Alto:
  Garden Court (H)
Pebble Beach:
  Inn at Spanish Bay (R)
  Lodge at Pebble Beach (R)
San Diego:
  Catamaran (H)
  del Coronado Hotel (R)
  Embassy San Diego (H)
  Horton Grand (H)
  Hyatt Islandia (H)
  Hyatt Reg. San Diego (H)
  Kona Kai (R)
  La Valencia (H)
  Le Meridien San Diego (H)
  Loews Coronado (R)
  Marriott La Jolla (H)
  Marriott Mission Valley (H)
  Marriott San Diego (H)
  Princess San Diego (R)
  Radisson Harbor View (H)
  Sheraton San Diego (H)
  US Grant (H)
  Westgate (H)
  Westin San Diego (H)
  Wyndham Emerald (H)
San Francisco:
  ANA San Francisco (H)
  Boheme (H)
  Clarion Bedford (H)
  Diva (H)
  Donatello (H)
  Fairmont SF (H)
  Galleria Park (H)
  Gramma's Rose Garden (B)
  Grand Hyatt SF (H)
  Harbor Court (H)
  Hilton SF (H)
  Hyatt Fish. Wharf (H)
  Hyatt Reg. SF (H)
  Hyde Park (B)
  Juliana (H)
  Kensington Park (H)
  Majestic (H)
  Mansions (B)
  Mark Hopkins (H)
  Marriott Fish. Wharf (H)
  Marriott SF (H)
  Maxwell (H)
  Milano (H)
  Monaco (H)
  Mosser Victorian (H)
  Nikko SF (H)
  Palace (H)
  Parc Fifty-Five (H)
  Park Hyatt SF (H)
  Petite Auberge (B)
  Phoenix (H)
  Prescott (H)
  Queen Anne (H)
  Radisson Miyako (H)
  Renaissance Stanford (H)
  Rex (H)

Marina

Ritz SF (H)
Sheraton Fish. Wharf (H)
Sherman House (B)
Tuscan Inn (H)
Victorian Inn (B)
Vintage Court (H)
Westin St. Francis (H)
White Swan (B)
York (H)
San Luis Obispo:
Apple Farm (B)
Santa Barbara:
El Encanto (H)
Fess Parker's (R)
Four Seasons Biltmore (R)
Santa Cruz:
Chaminade (H)
Santa Monica:
Oceana (H)
Sausalito:
Alta Mira (H)
Casa Madrona (H)
Shell Beach:
Cliffs at Shell Beach (R)
Truckee:
Northstar-at-Tahoe (R)

Colorado
Breckenridge:
Village at Breckenridge (R)
Copper Mountain:
Copper Mountain (R)
Durango:
Rochester (H)
Wit's End (B)
Granby:
C Lazy U Ranch (B)
Keystone:
Keystone (R)

Connecticut
Essex:
Griswold Inn (B)
Ledyard:
Foxwoods (H)
Mystic:
Inn at Mystic (B)
Norwich:
Norwich Inn (S)
Old Lyme:
Bee & Thistle (B)
Westbrook:
Water's Edge (B)

Delaware
Lewes:
New Devon (B)

Florida
Amelia Island:
Amelia Island (R)
Ritz Amelia Island (R)
Boca Raton:
Boca Raton (R)
Captiva Island:
South Seas Plantation (R)
Clearwater:
Belleview Mido (R)
Destin:
Hilton Sandestin (R)
Fisher Island:
Spa Internazionale (S)
Fort Lauderdale:
Hyatt Reg. Pier 66 (H)
Lago Mar (R)
Little Inn by the Sea (B)

Marriott Ft. Lauderdale (H)
Radisson Bahia Mar (R)
Fort Myers:
Sanibel Harbour (R)
Gasparilla Island:
Gasparilla Inn (B)
Haines City:
Grenelefe Golf (R)
Howey-in-the-Hills:
Mission Inn (R)
Islamorada:
Cheeca Lodge (R)
Jupiter:
Jupiter Beach (R)
Key Largo:
Marriott's Key Largo (R)
Ocean Reef (R)
Key West:
Banana Bay (B)
Cuban Club (H)
Holiday Inn La Concha (H)
Hyatt Key West (H)
Marquesa (H)
Pier House (R)
Lake Wales:
Chalet Suzanne (B)
Little Torch Key:
Little Palm Island (B)
Longboat Key:
Colony Beach (R)
Resort at Longboat Key (R)
Marathon:
Hawk's Cay (R)
Marco Island:
Marco Island Hilton (R)
Radisson Beach (R)
Miami/Miami Beach:
Alexander (H)
Biltmore (R)
Casa Grande (H)
Dbltree Coconut Grove (H)
Dbltree Grand (H)
Delano (H)
Eden Roc (H)
Fisher Island (R)
Florida Suites (H)
Fontainebleau Hilton (R)
Grand Bay (H)
Grove Isle Club (B)
Hyatt Reg. Coral Gables (H)
Indian Creek (H)
Inter-Continental Miami (H)
Lafayette (H)
La Voile Rouge (B)
Lido Spa (S)
Marlin (H)
Marriott Biscayne Bay (H)
Mayfair House (H)
Occidental Plaza (H)
Ocean Front (H)
Park Central (H)
Sheraton Bal Harbour (H)
Sheraton Biscayne Bay (H)
Turnberry Isle (R)
Westin Miami (R)
Mount Dora:
Lakeside Inn (R)
Naples:
Edgewater Beach (H)
La Playa Beach (R)
Naples Bath & Tennis (R)
Naples Beach (R)
Registry (R)
Ritz Naples (R)

Orlando:
Buena Vista Palace (H)
Disney's Boardwalk (H)
Disney's Caribbean (R)
Disney's Dixie Landings (R)
Disney's Grand Floridian (R)
Disney's Old Key West (R)
Disney's Polynesian (R)
Disney's Port Orleans (R)
Disney's Wilderness (R)
Disney's Yacht (R)

Palm Beach:
Breakers (R)
Chesterfield (H)
Four Seasons Palm Beach (H)
PGA National (R)

Panama City Beach:
Marriott's Bay Point (R)

Ponte Vedra Beach:
Lodge at Ponte Vedra (R)
Ponte Vedra (R)

Port St. Lucie:
Club Med Sandpiper (R)

Safety Harbor:
Safety Harbor (S)

Sanibel Island:
Casa Ybel (R)
Sundial Beach (R)

Siesta Key:
Captiva Beach (B)

Stuart:
Indian River Plantation (R)

Tampa Bay:
Hyatt Reg. Westshore (H)
Renaissance Vinoy (R)
Sheraton Sand Key (R)
TradeWinds St. Pete (R)
Wyndham Harbour (H)

West Palm Beach:
Hippocrates Health (S)

Georgia

Braselton:
Chateau Elan Winery (B)

Jekyll Island:
Jekyll Island Club (R)

Lake Lanier Islands:
Renaissance Pineisle (R)

Savannah:
Kehoe House (B)
Marriott Savannah (H)

St. Simons Island:
King & Prince Beach (R)
Lodge at Little St. Simons (B)

Hawaii

Big Island:
Four Seasons Hualalai (R)
Hilton Waikoloa (R)

Kauai:
Kauai Coconut (R)

Lanai:
Lodge at Koele (R)
Manele Bay (R)

Maui:
Aston Wailea (R)
Grand Wailea (R)
Hyatt Reg. Maui (R)
Kapalua Bay (R)
Renaissance Wailea (R)
Ritz Kapalua (R)
Sheraton Maui (R)
Westin Maui (R)

Oahu:
Ala Moana (H)

Hawaii Prince Waikiki (H)
Hyatt Reg. Waikiki (H)
Ilikai Nikko Waikiki (H)
Sheraton Kaiulani (H)
Sheraton Moana (H)
Sheraton Waikiki (H)
Waikiki Parc (H)

Idaho

Coeur d'Alene:
Blackwell B&B (B)
Coeur d'Alene (R)

McCall:
Shore Lodge (B)

Priest Lake:
Hill's Hospitality (B)

Illinois

Chicago:
Clarion (H)
Doubletree (H)
Drake (H)
Four Seasons Chicago (H)
Hilton Chicago (H)
Omni Ambassador (H)
Omni Chicago (H)
Raphael (H)

Galena:
Eagle Ridge (R)

Whittington:
Rend Lake (R)

Indiana

Bloomington:
Fourwinds (R)

French Lick:
French Lick Springs (R)

Iowa

Bettendorf:
Jumer's Castle (H)

Dubuque:
Richards House (B)

Louisiana

New Orleans:
Chateau Sonesta (H)
De La Poste (H)
Hilton New Orleans (H)
Hyatt Reg. New Orleans (H)
Le Pavillon (H)
Melrose Mansion (B)
Omni Royal Crescent (H)
Pontchartrain (H)
Royal Sonesta (H)

Maine

Bar Harbor:
Bar Harbor Inn (B)

Brunswick:
Captain Daniel Stone (B)

Camden:
Norumbega Inn (B)

Castine:
Castine Inn (B)

Deer Isle:
Pilgrims Inn (B)

Freeport:
Harraseeket Inn (B)

Kennebunkport:
Captain Lord Mansion (B)
Kennebunkport Inn (B)
White Barn Inn (B)

Portland:
Radisson Portland (H)
Regency Portland (H)

Rockport:
Samoset (R)

Marina

Scarborough:
 Black Point Inn (R)

Maryland
Annapolis:
 Loews Annapolis (H)
 Marriott Annapolis (H)
Baltimore:
 Admiral Fell Inn (B)
 Ann Street B&B (B)
 Brookshire (H)
 Celie's Waterfront B&B (B)
 Cross Keys Inn (H)
 Harbor Court (H)
 Hyatt Reg. Baltimore (H)
 Inn at Henderson's (B)
 Renaissance Harborplace (H)
 Sheraton Inner Harbor (H)
Chestertown:
 Imperial (B)
Easton:
 Tidewater Inn (B)
Ocean City:
 Dunes Manor (H)
 Sheraton Fontainebleau (H)
Oxford:
 Robert Morris Inn (B)
St. Michaels:
 Inn at Perry Cabin (B)

Massachusetts
Boston:
 Boston Harbor (H)
 Four Seasons Boston (H)
 Hilton Boston Back Bay (H)
 Hyatt Harborside (H)
 Le Meridien (H)
 Marriott Long Wharf (H)
 Tremont House (H)
Cape Cod:
 Brass Key (B)
 Chatham Bars (B)
 Coonamessett Inn (B)
 Dan'l Webster Inn (B)
 High Brewster (B)
 Sea Crest (R)
 Wequassett Inn (B)
 Whalewalk Inn (B)
Danvers:
 Tara's Ferncroft (R)
Martha's Vineyard:
 Daggett House (B)
 Harbor View (B)
 Outermost Inn (B)
 Tuscany Inn (B)
Nantucket:
 Beachside Nantucket (H)
 Cliffside Beach (H)
 Harbor House (B)
 Jared Coffin House (B)
 Nantucket Inn (H)
 Summer House (B)
 White Elephant (R)
Northampton:
 Northampton (H)

Michigan
Acme:
 Grand Traverse (R)
Bellaire:
 Shanty Creek (R)
Detroit:
 Crowne Pontchartrain (H)
 River Place (H)
 St. Regis (H)
 Westin Renaissance (H)

Mackinac Island:
 Bay View B&B (B)
 Grand (H)
 Iroquois (B)
 Mission Point (R)
New Buffalo:
 Harbor Grand (H)
Petoskey:
 Stafford's Bay View (B)
Saugatuck:
 Wickwood Country (B)
Thompsonville:
 Crystal Mountain (R)
Traverse City:
 Waterfront Inn (R)

Minnesota
Alexandria:
 Arrowwood Radisson (R)
Brainerd:
 Madden's (R)
Red Wing:
 St. James (H)
Stillwater:
 Lumber Baron's (H)

Missouri
Branson:
 Best Western Knights (H)
 Best Western Music (H)
 Branson House B&B (B)
 Chateau on the Lake (R)
 Clarion at Fall Creek (R)
 Red Bud Cove B&B (B)
Hannibal:
 Fifth St. Mansion (B)
 Garth Woodside (B)
Lake Ozark:
 Lodge at Four Seasons (R)
Osage Beach:
 Marriott's Tan-Tar-A (R)
Ridgedale:
 Big Cedar (R)

Montana
Bigfork:
 Averill's Flathead (B)
Whitefish:
 Grouse Mountain (R)

Nevada
Crystal Bay:
 Cal-Neva Resort (R)
Lake Tahoe:
 Caesars Tahoe (R)
 Harrah's Lake Tahoe (R)
Las Vegas:
 Golden Nugget (H)
Laughlin:
 Don Laughlin's (H)
 Harrah's Laughlin (H)

New Hampshire
Holderness:
 Manor on Golden Pond (B)
Meredith:
 Inn at Mill Falls (B)

New Jersey
Atlantic City:
 Atlantic Palace (H)
 Caesar Atlantic City (H)
 Claridge Casino (H)
 Harrah's Casino (H)
 Hilton Atlantic City (H)
 Marriott Seaview (R)
 Tropicana Casino (H)

Trump Plaza (H)
Trump's Castle (H)
Trump Taj Mahal (H)
Trump World's Fair (H)
Beach Haven:
Green Gables (B)
Cape May:
Abbey (B)
Chalfonte (H)
Mainstay Inn (B)
Queen Victoria (B)
Virginia Hotel (B)
Long Beach:
Ocean Place Hilton (R)
Spring Lake:
Sea Crest by the Sea (B)

New Mexico
Española:
Rancho de San Juan (R)

New York
Bolton Landing:
Sagamore (R)
Cooperstown:
Otesaga (H)
Geneva:
Geneva on the Lake (B)
Great Neck:
Inn at Great Neck (H)
Hopewell Junction:
Le Chambord (B)
Lake Placid:
Lake Placid Lodge (B)
Mirror Lake (B)
Montauk:
Montauk Yacht (R)
Monticello:
Kutsher's (R)
New York City:
Le Refuge Inn (H)
Marriott World Trade (H)
Shelter Island:
Ram's Head (B)
Stony Brook:
Three Village (B)

North Carolina
Charlotte:
Radisson Charlotte (H)
Lake Toxaway:
Greystone Inn (B)
Pinehurst:
Pinehurst (R)

North Dakota
Bismarck:
Holiday Inn Bismarck (H)

Ohio
Cincinnati:
Cincinnatian (H)
Vernon Manor (H)
Cleveland:
Ritz Cleveland (H)
Wyndham Cleveland (H)
Dellroy:
Atwood Lake (R)
Grand Rapids:
Kerr House (S)
Huron:
Sawmill Creek (R)

Oklahoma
Checotah:
Fountainhead (R)

Kingston:
Texoma State (R)

Oregon
Gleneden Beach:
Salishan (R)
Gold Beach:
Tu Tu'Tun (B)
Hood River:
Columbia Gorge (H)
Newport:
Embarcadero (H)
Sylvia Beach (H)
Portland:
Heathman (H)
RiverPlace (H)
Sunriver:
Sunriver (R)
Warm Springs:
Kah-Nee-Ta (R)

Pennsylvania
Pittsburgh:
Hilton Pittsburgh (H)

Puerto Rico
Fajardo:
El Conquistador (R)
Humacao:
Palmas del Mar (R)
Rincon:
Horned Dorset (B)

Rhode Island
Block Island:
Atlantic Inn (B)
Manisses (H)
1661 Inn (B)
Newport:
Castle Hill Inn (B)
Dbltree Newport (H)
Inntowne Inn (B)
Marriott Newport (H)
Newport Harbor (H)

South Carolina
Charleston:
Battery Carriage (B)
Charleston Place (H)
Indigo Inn (B)
Lodge Alley (B)
Mills House (H)
Planters Inn (B)
Vendue Inn (B)
Hilton Head:
Hilton Head Health (S)
Hyatt Reg. Hilton Head (R)
Palmetto Dunes (R)
Westin (R)
Isle of Palms:
Wild Dunes (R)
Kiawah Island:
Kiawah Island (R)
Myrtle Beach:
Myrtle Beach Martinique (R)
Ocean Dunes (R)
Sheraton Myrtle Beach (R)
Pawleys Island:
Litchfield Plantation (B)
Seabrook Island:
Seabrook Island (R)

South Dakota
Chamberlain:
Radisson Cedar Shore (R)

Marina

Tennessee
Fairfield Glade:
  Fairfield Glade (R)
Nashville:
  Embassy Nashville (H)

Texas
Austin:
  Barton Creek (R)
  Lake Austin Spa (S)
  Lakeway Inn (R)
Dallas/Fort Worth:
  Dbltree Lincoln Ctr (H)
Galveston:
  Galvez (H)
  Harbor House (B)
  Tremont House (H)
Horseshoe Bay:
  Horseshoe Bay (R)
Houston:
  South Shore Harbour (H)
Montgomery:
  Del Lago (R)
South Padre Island:
  Radisson South Padre (R)

Vermont
Brownsville:
  Ascutney Mountain (R)
Essex:
  Inn at Essex (B)
Manchester:
  Inn at Willow Pond (B)
Middlebury:
  Middlebury Inn (B)
  Swift House (B)
Plymouth:
  Hawk Inn (B)
Vergennes:
  Basin Harbor (R)

Virginia
Irvington:
  Tides Inn (R)
  Tides Lodge (R)
Virginia Beach:
  Hilton Virginia Beach (H)
  Holiday Inn Sunspree (R)
  Pavilion Towers (H)
Williamsburg:
  Kingsmill (R)
  Williamsburg Lodge (H)

Washington
Blaine:
  Inn at Semi-Ah-Moo (R)
Coupeville:
  Captain Whidbey (B)
Eastsound:
  Rosario Resort (R)
Lake Quinault:
  Lake Quinault (B)
Port Angeles:
  Domaine Madeleine (B)
Port Ludlow:
  Inn at Ludlow Bay (B)
Seattle:
  Dbltree Bellevue (H)
  Edgewater (H)
  Hilton Seattle (H)
  Inn at Market (H)
  Renaissance Madison (H)
  Sorrento (H)
  Woodmark (H)
Silverdale:
  Silverdale on Bay (R)
Stevenson:
  Skamania Lodge (R)

West Virginia
Morgantown:
  Lakeview Resort (R)

Wisconsin
Bayfield:
  Old Rittenhouse (B)
Delavan:
  Lake Lawn Lodge (R)
Eagle River:
  Chanticleer Inn (B)
Fontana:
  Abbey Resort (R)
Green Lake:
  Heidel House (R)
Milwaukee:
  Wyndham Milwaukee (H)

Wyoming
Moran:
  Colter Bay VIllage (R)
  Jackson Lake (B)
Yellowstone National Park:
  Lake Yellowstone (H)

Mountain Setting

Alaska

Denali National Park:
  North Face (B)
Girdwood:
  Alyeska (R)

Arizona

Gold Canyon:
  Gold Canyon (R)
Grand Canyon:
  El Tovar (H)
  Holiday Inn (H)
Phoenix/Scottsdale:
  Buttes (R)
  Marriott's Camelback (R)
  Pte Hilton Squaw (R)
  Royal Palms (H)
  Scottsdale Conference (R)
  Scottsdale Hilton (H)
  Scottsdale Princess (R)
  Sheraton Crescent (H)
Prescott:
  Hassayampa Inn (H)
Sedona:
  Enchantment (R)
  Garland's (R)
  Graham B&B (B)
  L'Auberge de Sedona (H)
  Los Abrigados (R)
Tucson:
  Canyon Ranch (S)
  Loews Ventana (R)
  Omni Tucson (R)
  Tanque Verde (B)
  Westward Look (R)
Wickenburg:
  Merv Griffin's (B)

Arkansas

Eureka Springs:
  Dairy Hollow House (B)
  Palace (B)
Hot Springs:
  Arlington Resort (H)
  Hot Springs Park (H)

California

Big Sur:
  Big Sur Lodge (B)
  Deetjen's Big Sur (B)
  Post Ranch (B)
  Ventana Inn (B)
Calabasas:
  Ashram Retreat (S)
Carlsbad:
  La Costa (R)
Carmel:
  Stonepine (B)
Cazadero:
  Timberhill (B)
Escondido:
  Golden Door (S)
Fish Camp:
  Tenaya Lodge (R)
Lake Arrowhead:
  Lake Arrowhead (R)
Montecito:
  San Ysidro (B)
Oakhurst:
  Chateau du Sureau (B)
Ojai:
  Ojai Valley (R)

Olympic Valley:
  Resort at Squaw Creek (R)
Palm Springs:
  Hyatt Grand (R)
  Hyatt Reg. Palm Springs (H)
  Inn at Racquet Club (B)
  La Quinta (R)
  Ritz Rancho Mirage (R)
Tecate:
  Rancho La Puerta (S)
Truckee:
  Northstar-at-Tahoe (R)
Woodside:
  Lodge at Skylonda (S)
Yosemite:
  Ahwahnee (H)

Colorado

Aspen:
  Gant (B)
  Jerome (H)
  Little Nell (H)
  Sardy House (B)
Beaver Creek:
  Charter at Beaver Creek (H)
  Hyatt Reg. Beaver Creek (H)
  Inn at Beaver Creek (B)
  Pines Lodge (H)
Boulder:
  Boulderado (H)
Breckenridge:
  Breckenridge Mtn (H)
  Village at Breckenridge (R)
Colorado Springs:
  Antlers Dlbtree (H)
  Broadmoor (R)
  Cheyenne Mountain (R)
  Sheraton (H)
Copper Mountain:
  Copper Mountain (R)
Durango:
  General Palmer (H)
  Rochester (H)
  Tamarron Hilton (R)
  Wit's End (B)
Edwards:
  Lodge & Spa Cordillera (R)
Granby:
  C Lazy U Ranch (B)
Keystone:
  Keystone (R)
Mosca:
  Inn at Zapata (B)
Mt. Crested Butte:
  Grande Butte (H)
Redstone:
  Redstone Inn (B)
Snowmass Village:
  Silvertree (H)
Telluride:
  Columbia (B)
  Peaks at Telluride (R)
  San Sophia (B)
Vail:
  Lodge at Vail (H)
  Mountain Haus at Vail (H)
  Sitzmark Lodge (H)
  Sonnenalp of Vail (R)
  Vail Athletic Club (H)

Mountain Setting

Connecticut
New Preston:
  Boulders (B)
Washington:
  Mayflower Inn (B)

Georgia
Atlanta:
  Evergreen (R)
Pine Mountain:
  Callaway Gardens (R)

Hawaii
Lanai:
  Lodge at Koele (R)
Maui:
  Ritz Kapalua (R)
  Westin Maui (R)
Oahu:
  Ihilani Resort (R)

Idaho
Boise:
  Idanha (H)
Coeur d'Alene:
  Coeur d'Alene (R)
Ketchum:
  Knob Hill (H)
Priest Lake:
  Hill's Hospitality (B)
Sun Valley:
  Sun Valley (R)
Tetonia:
  Teton Ridge (B)

Kentucky
Berea:
  Boone Tavern (H)

Maine
East Holden:
  Lucerne Inn (B)
Raymond:
  Northern Pines (S)

Massachusetts
Lenox:
  Blantyre (B)
  Canyon Ranch (S)
  Kripalu Center (S)
  Wheatleigh (B)
Northampton:
  Northampton (H)
Stockbridge:
  Red Lion (B)
Williamstown:
  Orchards (B)

Missouri
Branson:
  Best Western Mtn Oak (H)
  Chateau on the Lake (R)
Lake Ozark:
  Lodge at Four Seasons (R)
Ridgedale:
  Big Cedar (R)

Montana
Bigfork:
  Averill's Flathead (B)
Big Sky:
  Huntley Lodge (R)
  Lone Mountain (B)
Bozeman:
  Mountain Sky (B)
Darby:
  Triple Creek Ranch (R)

Gallatin Gateway:
  Gallatin Gateway (B)
  320 Guest Ranch (B)
Red Lodge:
  Pollard (B)
Whitefish:
  Grouse Mountain (R)

Nevada
Crystal Bay:
  Cal-Neva Resort (R)
Lake Tahoe:
  Harrah's Lake Tahoe (R)
  Hyatt Reg. Lake Tahoe (R)
Laughlin:
  Flamingo Hilton (H)
Reno:
  Flamingo Hilton (H)

New Hampshire
Dixville Notch:
  Balsams Grand (R)
Franconia:
  Franconia Inn (B)
Holderness:
  Manor on Golden Pond (B)
Jackson:
  Christmas Farm (B)
North Conway:
  Four Points Sheraton (H)
  White Mountain (R)
Waterville Valley:
  Waterville Valley (R)

New Jersey
Vernon:
  Great Gorge Village (R)

New Mexico
Chimayo:
  Hacienda Rancho (B)
Raton:
  Vermejo Park (B)
Santa Fe:
  Inn at Loretto (B)
  La Posada Santa Fe (H)
  Plaza Real (H)
  Preston House (B)
  Rancho Encantado (B)
Taos:
  Historic Taos (B)
Taos Ski Valley:
  Edelweiss (B)
  St. Bernard (B)

New York
Bolton Landing:
  Sagamore (R)
Ellenville:
  Nevele (R)
Hunter:
  Vatra Mountain (S)
Lake Placid:
  Lake Placid Lodge (B)
  Mirror Lake (B)
Lew Beach:
  Beaverkill Valley (B)
Monticello:
  Kutsher's (R)
Neversink:
  New Age Health Spa (S)
New Paltz:
  Mohonk Mountain (R)
North Hudson:
  Elk Lake Lodge (R)

Mountain Setting

Saranac Lake:
 Point (B)
 Saranac (H)
Saratoga Springs:
 Sheraton Saratoga (R)
Shandaken:
 Shandaken Inn (B)

North Carolina
Blowing Rock:
 Hound Ears (R)
 Westglow Spa (S)
Lake Toxaway:
 Greystone Inn (B)

Oregon
Bend:
 Inn of Seventh Mtn (R)
Black Butte Ranch:
 Black Butte (R)
Timberline:
 Timberline (R)

Pennsylvania
Champion:
 Seven Springs (R)
E. Stroudsburg:
 Deerfield Manor (S)
Farmington:
 Nemacolin Woodlands (R)
Mt. Pocono/Pocono Manor:
 Mount Airy Lodge (R)
 Pocono Manor (R)
Skytop:
 Skytop Lodge (R)
South Sterling:
 Sterling Inn (B)

Puerto Rico
Fajardo:
 El Conquistador (R)

South Dakota
Rapid City:
 Abend Haus (B)
 Alex Johnson (H)
 Willow Springs (B)
Spearfish:
 Eighth St. Inn (B)

Tennessee
Fairfield Glade:
 Fairfield Glade (R)
Gatlinburg:
 Buckhorn Inn (B)
Walland:
 Inn at Blackberry Farm (B)

Utah
Cedar City:
 Bryce Canyon (H)
Ivins:
 Franklin Quest (S)
Midway:
 Homestead (B)
Park City:
 Deer Valley (H)
 Goldener Hirsch (B)
 1904 Imperial (H)
 Olympia Park (H)
 Shadow Ridge (H)
 Stein Eriksen (R)
 Washington School (B)
Provo:
 Sundance Resort (R)
Salt Lake City:
 Hilton Salt Lake (H)

Snowbird:
 Cliff Lodge (R)
 Inn at Snowbird (B)
 Lodge at Snowbird (H)
Springdale:
 Zion Lodge (H)

Vermont
Barnard:
 Maple Leaf (B)
 Twin Farms (R)
Brownsville:
 Ascutney Mountain (R)
Chittenden:
 Mountain Top (B)
Craftsbury Common:
 Inn on Common (H)
Dorset:
 Dorset Inn (B)
Essex:
 Inn at Essex (B)
Goshen:
 Blueberry Hill (B)
Killington:
 Inn of Six Mountains (B)
 Killington Resort (R)
Lower Waterford:
 Rabbit Hill (B)
Ludlow:
 Governor's Inn (B)
 Green Mountain (S)
Manchester:
 Equinox (H)
 Inn at Manchester (B)
 Wilburton Inn (B)
Middlebury:
 Waybury Inn (B)
Newfane:
 Four Columns (H)
Perkinsville:
 Inn at Weathersfield (B)
Plymouth:
 Hawk Inn (B)
Smugglers' Notch:
 Smugglers' Notch (R)
Stowe:
 Green Mountain (B)
 Stowe Snowdrift (R)
 Topnotch at Stowe (R)
 Trapp Family (B)
Stratton Mountain:
 Stratton Mtn (R)
Warren:
 Sugarbush (R)
West Dover:
 Inn at Sawmill Farm (B)
Wilmington:
 Hermitage Inn (B)
Woodstock:
 Kedron Valley (B)
 Woodstock Inn (R)

Virginia
Abingdon:
 Camberley's (B)
Hot Springs:
 Homestead (R)
Paris:
 Ashby Inn (B)
Washington:
 Inn at Little Washington (B)
Wintergreen:
 Wintergreen (R)

Mountain Setting

Woodstock:
Inn at Narrow Passage (B)

Washington

Forks:
Kalaloch Lodge (B)

Port Angeles:
Domaine Madeleine (B)

Stevenson:
Skamania Lodge (R)

Winthrop:
Sun Mountain (R)

West Virginia

Berkeley Springs:
Coolfront Resort (R)
Country Inn (B)

Harpers Ferry:
Historic Hilltop House (H)

Hedgesville:
Woods Resort (R)

Pipestem:
McKeever Pipestem (R)

White Sulphur Springs:
Greenbrier (R)

Wyoming

Jackson:
Jackson Hole Racquet (R)
Rusty Parrot (B)
Snow King (R)
Spring Creek (R)
Teton Pines (R)
Wort (H)

Moose:
Cottonwoods Ranch (B)

Moran:
Colter Bay VIllage (R)
Jackson Lake (B)
Jenny Lake (B)

Yellowstone National Park:
Lake Yellowstone (H)
Mammoth Hot Springs (H)
Old Faithful (H)

No Credit Cards Accepted

Alabama
Eutaw:
  Kirkwood B&B (B)

Alaska
Denali National Park:
  North Face (B)

Arizona
Tucson:
  El Presidio B&B (B)

Colorado
Durango:
  Tall Timber (B)
Granby:
  C Lazy U Ranch (B)

Florida
Gasparilla Island:
  Gasparilla Inn (B)

Georgia
Sea Island:
  Cloister (R)

Idaho
Tetonia:
  Teton Ridge (B)

Maryland
Baltimore:
  Ann Street B&B (B)

Mississippi
Natchez:
  Linden B&B (B)

Nebraska
Waterloo:
  JC Robinson B&B (B)

New Jersey
Cape May:
  Mainstay Inn (B)

New Mexico
Raton:
  Vermejo Park (B)
Taos Ski Valley:
  St. Bernard (B)

New York
New York City:
  Hotel 17 (H)
North Hudson:
  Elk Lake Lodge (R)

North Carolina
Edenton:
  Lords Proprietors' (B)
Nags Head:
  First Colony (H)

North Dakota
Fargo:
  Bohlig's B&B (B)
Jamestown:
  Country Charm (B)
Luverne:
  Volden Farm B&B (B)

South Dakota
Custer:
  Custer Mansion (B)
Rapid City:
  Abend Haus (B)

Wyoming
Moose:
  Cottonwoods Ranch (B)

Noteworthy Newcomers

Arizona
Catalina:
  Miraval (S)
Grand Canyon:
  Holiday Inn (H)
California
Palm Springs:
  Givenchy (S)
San Francisco:
  Monaco (H)
Colorado
Denver:
  Holtze (H)
Florida
Key West:
  Banana Bay (B)
Miami/Miami Beach:
  Albion (H)
  Greenview (H)
  Tides (H)
Orlando:
  Disney's Boardwalk (H)
  Omni Rosen (H)
Georgia
Atlanta:
  Buckhead B&B (B)
  Marietta (R)
Hawaii
Big Island:
  Four Seasons Hualalai (R)
Louisiana
New Orleans:
  Chateau Sonesta (H)
  Omni Royal Crescent (H)
  Queen & Crescent (H)
  Wyndham Riverfront (H)
Michigan
New Buffalo:
  Harbor Grand (H)

Minnesota
Stillwater:
  Lumber Baron's (H)
Nevada
Las Vegas:
  Hard Rock (H)
  Monte Carlo (H)
  NY Hotel & Casino (H)
  Stratosphere (H)
Reno:
  Silver Legacy (H)
New Mexico
Taos:
  Fechin Inn (B)
New York
New York City:
  Belvedere (H)
  Best Western Manhattan (H)
  Broadway B&B (B)
  Casablanca (H)
  Chelsea Savoy (H)
  59th St. Bridge Apts. (H)
  Lucerne (H)
  Marriott World Trade (H)
  Millennium Broadway (H)
  Omni Berkshire (H)
  Quality Rockefeller Ctr. (H)
  Quality East Side (H)
  Remington (H)
  Roosevelt (H)
  SoHo Grand (H)
  Trump International (H)
Ohio
Cleveland:
  Wyndham Cleveland (H)
South Dakota
Chamberlain:
  Radisson Cedar Shore (R)

Outstanding Dining

Arizona

Phoenix/Scottsdale:
Arizona Biltmore (R)
Gardiner's (R)
Hyatt Reg. Scottsdale (R)
Marriott's Camelback (R)
Phoenician (R)
Ritz Phoenix (H)
Scottsdale Conference (R)
Scottsdale Princess (R)
Wigwam (R)

Sedona:
L'Auberge de Sedona (H)

Tucson:
Loews Ventana (R)
Westin La Paloma (R)
Westward Look (R)

California

Albion:
Albion River (B)

Anaheim:
Marriott Anaheim (H)

Big Sur:
Post Ranch (B)
Ventana Inn (B)

Carmel:
Carmel Valley (R)
Highlands Inn (B)
John Gardiner's (R)
Quail Lodge (R)
Stonepine (B)

Cazadero:
Timberhill (B)

Dana Point:
Ritz Laguna Niguel (R)

Eureka:
Carter House (B)

Gualala:
St. Orres (B)

Guerneville:
Applewood Inn (B)

Healdsburg:
Madrona Manor (B)

Laguna Beach:
Surf & Sand (H)

Little River:
Heritage House (B)

Los Angeles:
Argyle (H)
Barnabey's (H)
Bel-Air (H)
Beverly Hills (H)
Beverly Hilton (H)
Beverly Prescott (H)
Four Seasons (H)
Mondrian (H)
New Otani (H)
Nikko Beverly Hills (H)
Palos Verdes (H)
Peninsula Beverly Hills (H)
Regal Biltmore (H)
Regent Beverly Wilshire (H)
Ritz Huntington (H)
Ritz Marina del Rey (H)
Shutters (H)
Wyndham Bel Age (H)
Wyndham Checkers (H)

Montecito:
San Ysidro (B)

Newport Beach:
Four Seasons Newport (H)

Sutton Place (H)

Oakhurst:
Chateau du Sureau (B)

Palm Springs:
Ingleside (B)
La Quinta (R)
Renaissance Esmeralda (R)
Ritz Rancho Mirage (R)
Two Bunch Palms (B)

Palo Alto:
Garden Court (H)

Pebble Beach:
Inn at Spanish Bay (R)
Lodge at Pebble Beach (R)

Rutherford:
Auberge du Soleil (B)

San Diego:
Le Meridien San Diego (H)
Loews Coronado (R)
Rancho Bernardo (R)
Rancho Valencia (R)
US Grant (H)

San Francisco:
Campton Place (H)
Clift (H)
Donatello (H)
Griffon (H)
Huntington (H)
Inn at the Opera (B)
Mandarin Oriental (H)
Mark Hopkins (H)
Park Hyatt SF (H)
Prescott (H)
Renaissance Stanford (H)
Ritz SF (H)
Savoy (H)
Sherman House (B)
Villa Florence (H)
Vintage Court (H)

San Jose:
de Anza (H)
Fairmont San Jose (H)

Santa Barbara:
Four Seasons Biltmore (R)

Santa Rosa:
Vintners Inn (B)

Sonoma:
El Dorado (H)

St. Helena:
Meadowood (R)

Colorado

Aspen:
Jerome (H)
Little Nell (H)
Ritz Aspen (H)

Beaver Creek:
Hyatt Reg. Beaver Creek (H)

Boulder:
Boulderado

Clark:
Home Ranch (R)

Colorado Springs:
Broadmoor (R)

Denver:
Brown Palace (H)
Cambridge (H)
Inverness (R)
Loews Giorgio (H)
Oxford (H)
Westin Tabor Center (H)

Outstanding Dining

Edwards:
Lodge & Spa Cordillera (R)
Granby:
C Lazy U Ranch (B)
Vail:
Lodge at Vail (H)
Sitzmark Lodge (H)
Sonnenalp of Vail (R)

Connecticut
Chester:
Inn at Chester (B)
Greenwich:
Homestead Inn (B)
Hartford:
Goodwin (H)
Ivoryton:
Copper Beech (B)
Ridgefield:
Stonehenge Inn (B)
Washington:
Mayflower Inn (B)
Westport:
Inn at National Hall (B)

Delaware
Wilmington:
Hotel du Pont (H)

Florida
Amelia Island:
Ritz Amelia Island (R)
Boca Raton:
Boca Raton (R)
Key West:
Marquesa (H)
Lake Wales:
Chalet Suzanne (B)
Little Torch Key:
Little Palm Island (B)
Miami/Miami Beach:
Grand Bay (H)
Place St. Michel (H)
Turnberry Isle (R)
Naples:
Registry (R)
Ritz Naples (R)
Orlando:
Buena Vista Palace (H)
Disney's Grand Floridian (R)
Hyatt Reg. Grand Cypress (R)
Peabody Orlando (H)
Four Seasons Palm Beach (H)
Ritz Palm Beach (R)
Tampa Bay:
Don CeSar (R)
Hyatt Reg. Westshore (H)

Georgia
Atlanta:
Four Seasons Atlanta (H)
Grand Hyatt Atlanta (H)
Hilton Atlanta (H)
Ritz Atlanta (H)
Ritz Buckhead (H)
Swissotel Atlanta (H)
Sea Island:
Cloister (R)

Hawaii
Big Island:
Hilton Waikoloa (R)
Orchid at Mauna Lani (R)
Kauai:
Princeville (R)

Lanai:
Lodge at Koele (R)
Manele Bay (R)
Maui:
Four Seasons Maui (R)
Grand Wailea (R)
Hana-Maui Hotel (H)
Kapalua Bay (R)
Maui Prince (R)
Ritz Kapalua (R)
Oahu:
Halekulani (H)
Hawaii Prince Waikiki (H)
Hilton Hawaiian (H)
Kahala Mandarin (R)

Idaho
Coeur d'Alene:
Coeur d'Alene (R)
Ketchum:
Knob Hill (H)

Illinois
Chicago:
Doubletree (H)
Drake (H)
Fairmont (H)
Four Seasons Chicago (H)
Omni Ambassador (H)
Ritz Chicago (H)
Westin River North (H)

Indiana
Indianapolis:
Canterbury (H)

Kentucky
Harrodsburg:
Beaumont Inn (B)
Inn at Shaker Village (B)
Lexington:
Marriott Griffin Gate (R)
Louisville:
Seelbach (H)

Louisiana
New Orleans:
De La Poste (H)
Fairmont New Orleans (H)
Inter-Continental (H)
Lafayette (H)
Maison de Ville (B)
Omni Royal Orleans (H)
Pelham (H)
Pontchartrain (H)
Royal Sonesta (H)
Saint Louis (H)
Windsor Court (H)

Maine
Deer Isle:
Pilgrims Inn (B)
Kennebunkport:
White Barn Inn (B)
Newcastle:
Newcastle Inn (B)
Scarborough:
Black Point Inn (R)

Maryland
Baltimore:
Dbltree Colonnade (H)
Harbor Court (H)
Berlin:
Atlantic (H)
Chestertown:
Imperial (B)
Oxford:
Robert Morris Inn (B)

Outstanding Dining

St. Michaels:
  Inn at Perry Cabin (B)

Massachusetts
Boston:
  Boston Harbor (H)
  Boston Park Plaza (H)
  Charles in Harvard Square (H)
  Fairmont Copley (H)
  Four Seasons Boston (H)
  Le Meridien (H)
  Regal Bostonian (H)
  Ritz Boston (H)
Lenox:
  Blantyre (B)
  Wheatleigh (B)
Martha's Vineyard:
  Charlotte Inn (B)
  Tuscany Inn (B)
Nantucket:
  Summer House (B)
  Wauwinet (B)

Michigan
Detroit:
  Ritz Dearborn (H)
  Townsend (H)
Mackinac Island:
  Iroquois (B)

Minnesota
Minneapolis/St. Paul:
  Hyatt Reg. Minneapolis (H)
  Radisson Minneapolis (H)
  Saint Paul (H)
  Sofitel (H)
  Whitney (H)

Missouri
Kansas:
  Marriott Overland Park (H)
Kansas City:
  Adam's Mark (H)
  Hyatt Reg. Crown Ctr (H)
  Raphael (H)
  Ritz Kansas City (H)
  Savoy (H)
  Westin Crown Ctr (H)
St. Louis:
  Adam's Mark (H)
  Ritz St. Louis (H)
  Seven Gables (B)

Montana
Gallatin Gateway:
  Gallatin Gateway (B)
Whitefish:
  Grouse Mountain (R)

Nevada
Las Vegas:
  Bally's Las Vegas (H)
  Binion's Horseshoe (H)
  Caesars Palace (H)
  Circus Circus (H)
  Four Queens (H)
  MGM Grand (H)
  Mirage (H)
  Rio Suite (H)
Reno:
  Eldorado (H)

New Hampshire
Dixville Notch:
  Balsams Grand (R)
Holderness:
  Manor on Golden Pond (B)
Jackson:
  Christmas Farm (B)

New Jersey
Atlantic City:
  Bally's Park Place (H)
Beach Haven:
  Green Gables (B)
Lambertville:
  Inn at Lambertville (B)
Princeton:
  Nassau Inn (H)
Short Hills:
  Hilton at Short Hills (H)

New Mexico
Albuquerque:
  Hilton Albuquerque (H)
  Hyatt Reg. Albuquerque (H)
Española:
  Rancho de San Juan (R)
Santa Fe:
  Inn of Anasazi (B)
Taos:
  Historic Taos (B)
Taos Ski Valley:
  St. Bernard (B)

New York
Amenia:
  Troutbeck (B)
Dover Plains:
  Old Drovers Inn (B)
Garden City:
  Garden City (H)
Hopewell Junction:
  Le Chambord (B)
Lake Placid:
  Lake Placid Lodge (B)
New York City:
  Box Tree (B)
  Carlyle (H)
  Elysée (H)
  Essex House Nikko (H)
  Four Seasons (H)
  Kitano NY (H)
  Le Refuge Inn (H)
  Lexington (H)
  Lowell (H)
  Mark (H)
  Marriott Marquis (H)
  NY Palace (H)
  Peninsula NY (H)
  Pierre (H)
  Plaza (H)
  Plaza Athénée (H)
  Regency (H)
  Rihga Royal (H)
  Ritz New York (H)
  Royalton (H)
  Sherry Netherland (H)
  Shoreham (H)
  St. Regis (H)
  Surrey (H)
  Trump International (H)
  UN Plaza Park Hyatt (H)
  Waldorf Astoria (H)
  Westbury (H)
Rhinebeck:
  Beekman Arms (B)
Shelter Island:
  Ram's Head (B)

North Carolina
Asheville:
  Great Smokies (R)
  Richmond Hill (B)

Outstanding Dining

Lake Toxaway:
  Greystone Inn (B)
Pittsboro:
  Fearrington House (B)
Raleigh-Durham:
  Siena (H)

Ohio
Cincinnati:
  Cincinnatian (H)
Cleveland:
  Baricelli Inn
  Omni International (H)
  Ritz Cleveland (H)
Columbus:
  Worthington Inn (B)

Oregon
Gold Beach:
  Tu Tu'Tun (B)
Portland:
  Benson (H)
  Governor (H)
  Heathman (H)
  RiverPlace (H)
  Vintage Plaza (H)

Pennsylvania
Erwinna:
  Evermay on Delaware (B)
Philadelphia:
  Adam's Mark (H)
  Four Seasons Philadelphia (H)
  Latham (H)
  Omni at Independence (H)
  Park Hyatt Philadelphia (H)
  Penn's View (B)
  Rittenhouse (H)
  Ritz Philadelphia (H)
  Warwick Philadelphia (H)

Puerto Rico
Fajardo:
  El Conquistador (R)
Rincon:
  Horned Dorset (B)
San Juan:
  Sands (H)

Rhode Island
Block Island:
  Atlantic Inn (B)
  Manisses (H)
Providence:
  Westin Providence (H)

South Carolina
Charleston:
  Charleston Place (H)
  Vendue Inn (B)
Hilton Head:
  Westin (R)

Tennessee
Gatlinburg:
  Buchhorn Inn (B)
Nashville:
  Hermitage (H)
  Union Station (H)
Walland:
  Inn at Blackberry Farm (B)

Texas
Austin:
  Four Seasons Austin (H)
Dallas/Fort Worth:
  Adolphus (H)
  Crescent Court (H)
  Fairmont (H)

  Four Seasons (R)
  Mansion on Turtle Creek (H)
  Omni Mandalay (H)
  Sheraton Park Central (H)
  St. Germain (B)
  Stoneleigh (H)
  Westin Galleria Dallas (H)
  Worthington (H)
  Wyndham Anatole (H)
Houston:
  Four Seasons Houston (H)
  La Colombe d'Or (B)
  Lancaster (H)
  Omni Houston (H)
  Ritz Houston (H)
San Antonio:
  Fairmount (H)

Utah
Park City:
  Deer Valley (H)
  Goldener Hirsch (B)
  Stein Eriksen (R)

Vermont
Barnard:
  Twin Farms (R)
Essex:
  Inn at Essex (B)
Goshen:
  Blueberry Hill (B)
Lower Waterford:
  Rabbit Hill (B)
Ludlow:
  Governor's Inn (B)
Manchester:
  Equinox (H)
Perkinsville:
  Inn at Weathersfield (B)
West Dover:
  Inn at Sawmill Farm (B)

Virginia
(see also Washington, DC)
Richmond:
  Jefferson (H)
Washington:
  Inn at Little Washington (B)
White Post:
  L'Auberge Provencale (B)
Williamsburg:
  Williamsburg Inn (H)

Washington
Seattle:
  Alexis (H)
  Four Seasons Olympic (H)
  Sheraton Seattle (H)
  Sorrento (H)
  Vintage Park (H)
  Westin Seattle (H)
  Woodmark (H)
Snoqualmie:
  Salish Lodge (B)

Washington, DC
(including nearby Maryland and Virginia)
Virginia:
  Morrison House (B)
  Ritz Pentagon City (H)
  Ritz Tysons Corner (H)
Washington, DC:
  Carlton (H)
  Four Seasons (H)
  Hay-Adams (H)
  Henley Park (H)
  Jefferson (H)

Outstanding Dining

Latham Georgetown (H)
Morrison-Clark Inn (B)
Park Hyatt Washington (H)
Phoenix Park (H)
Ritz Washington DC (H)
Watergate (H)
Willard (H)

West Virginia
Sheperdstown:
  Bavarian Inn (B)
White Sulphur Springs:
  Greenbrier (R)

Wisconsin
Bayfield:
  Old Rittenhouse (B)
Kohler:
  American Club (R)
Milwaukee:
  Pfister (H)

Wyoming
Moran:
  Jenny Lake (B)

Power Scenes

Alabama
Birmingham:
  Sheraton Birmingham (H)
  Tutwiler (H)
  Wynfrey (H)

Arizona
Phoenix/Scottsdale:
  Arizona Biltmore (R)
  Phoenician (R)
  Scottsdale Princess (R)
Tucson:
  Loews Ventana (R)

Arkansas
Little Rock:
  Capital (H)

California
Carmel:
  Stonepine (B)
Dana Point:
  Ritz Laguna Niguel (R)
Los Angeles:
  Bel-Air (H)
  Beverly Hills (H)
  Century Plaza (H)
  Four Seasons (H)
  Inter-Continental LA (H)
  Nikko Beverly Hills (H)
  Peninsula Beverly Hills (H)
  Regent Beverly Wilshire (H)
  Ritz Marina del Rey (H)
  Sheraton Grande (H)
  Sunset Marquis (H)
  Wyndham Checkers (H)
Newport Beach:
  Four Seasons Newport (H)
Palm Springs:
  Ritz Rancho Mirage (R)
  Two Bunch Palms (B)
Pebble Beach:
  Inn at Spanish Bay (R)
San Diego:
  Hyatt Reg. San Diego (H)
  Le Meridien San Diego (H)
  Rancho Bernardo (R)
  Rancho Valencia (R)
  Sheraton Grande (R)
  Westgate (H)
  Wyndham Emerald (H)
San Francisco:
  Campton Place (H)
  Clift (H)
  Huntington (H)
  Mandarin Oriental (H)
  Nikko SF (H)
  Palace (H)
  Pan Pacific SF (H)
  Park Hyatt SF (H)
  Renaissance Stanford (H)
  Ritz SF (H)
  Sherman House (B)
  Westin St. Francis (H)
San Jose:
  Fairmont San Jose (H)
  Hyatt Saint Claire (H)
Santa Barbara:
  Four Seasons Biltmore (R)

Colorado
Aspen:
  Jerome (H)
  Little Nell (H)
  Ritz Aspen (H)

Denver:
  Brown Palace (H)
  Holtze (H)
  Hyatt Reg. Denver Dwtn (H)
  Loews Giorgio (H)

Connecticut
Hartford:
  Goodwin (H)

Delaware
Wilmington:
  Hotel du Pont (H)

Florida
Boca Raton:
  Boca Raton (R)
Miami/Miami Beach:
  Biltmore (R)
  Fisher Island (R)
  Grand Bay (H)
  Mayfair House (H)
  Turnberry Isle (R)
Naples:
  Ritz Naples (R)
Orlando:
  Peabody Orlando (H)
Palm Beach:
  Breakers (R)
  Four Seasons Palm Beach (H)
  Ritz Palm Beach (R)

Georgia
Atlanta:
  Four Seasons Atlanta (H)
  Grand Hyatt Atlanta (H)
  Ritz Atlanta (H)
  Ritz Buckhead (H)
  Swissotel Atlanta (H)
Sea Island:
  Cloister (R)

Hawaii
Maui:
  Grand Wailea (R)
Oahu:
  Halekulani (H)

Illinois
Chicago:
  Drake (H)
  Fairmont (H)
  Four Seasons Chicago (H)
  La Salle Club (H)
  Omni Chicago (H)
  Renaissance Chicago (H)
  Ritz Chicago (H)
  Westin River North (H)

Indiana
Indianapolis:
  Canterbury (H)

Kentucky
Louisville:
  Seelbach (H)

Louisiana
New Orleans:
  Le Meridien (H)
  Pontchartrain (H)
  Westin Canal (H)
  Windsor Court (H)

Maryland
Annapolis:
  Loews Annapolis (H)
Baltimore:
  Clarion at Mt. Vernon (H)
  Dbltree Colonnade (H)

Power Scenes

    Harbor Court (H)
    Renaissance Harborplace (H)

Massachusetts
Boston:
    Charles in Harvard Square (H)
    Four Seasons Boston (H)
    Inn at Harvard (B)
    Le Meridien (H)
    Regal Bostonian (H)
    Ritz Boston (H)

Michigan
Detroit:
    Ritz Dearborn (H)
    Townsend (H)
Mackinac Island:
    Bay View B&B (B)

Minnesota
Minneapolis/St. Paul:
    Saint Paul (H)
    Whitney (H)

Missouri
Kansas City:
    Hyatt Reg. Crown Ctr (H)
    Ritz Kansas City (H)
St. Louis:
    Adam's Mark (H)
    Ritz St. Louis (H)

Nevada
Las Vegas:
    Caesars Palace (H)

New Jersey
Short Hills:
    Hilton at Short Hills (H)

New Mexico
Santa Fe:
    Inn of Anasazi (B)

New York
Amenia:
    Troutbeck (B)
New York City:
    Carlyle (H)
    Four Seasons (H)
    Lowell (H)
    Mark (H)
    Millenium Hilton (H)
    Peninsula NY (H)
    Pierre (H)
    Plaza (H)
    Plaza Athénée (H)
    Regency (H)
    Ritz New York (H)
    Royalton (H)
    Stanhope (H)
    St. Regis (H)
    UN Plaza Park Hyatt (H)
    Waldorf Towers (H)
Rye Brook:
    Doral Arrowwood (R)

North Carolina
Raleigh-Durham:
    Siena (H)
    Washington Duke (H)

Ohio
Cincinnati:
    Cincinnatian (H)
    Omni Netherland (H)
Cleveland:
    Ritz Cleveland (H)
    Wyndham Cleveland (H)
Columbus:
    Westin Columbus (H)

Oregon
Portland:
    Benson (H)
    Heathman (H)
    RiverPlace (H)

Pennsylvania
Philadelphia:
    Four Seasons Philadelphia (H)
    Park Hyatt Philadelphia (H)
    Rittenhouse (H)
    Ritz Philadelphia (H)

Puerto Rico
San Juan:
    El San Juan (H)

Rhode Island
Providence:
    Westin Providence (H)

Texas
Austin:
    Four Seasons Austin (H)
Dallas/Fort Worth:
    Adolphus (H)
    Crescent Court (H)
    Four Seasons (R)
    Le Meridien (H)
    Mansion on Turtle Creek (H)
    Westin Galleria Dallas (H)
    Worthington (H)
Houston:
    Houstonian (H)
    La Colombe d'Or (B)
    Lancaster (H)
    Omni Houston (H)
    Ritz Houston (H)
    Wyndham Warwick (H)
San Antonio:
    Plaza San Antonio (H)

Virginia
(see also Washington, DC)
Hot Springs:
    Homestead (R)
Richmond:
    Jefferson (H)
Washington:
    Inn at Little Washington (B)

Washington
Seattle:
    Four Seasons Olympic (H)
    Sorrento (H)
    Woodmark (H)

Washington, DC
(including nearby Maryland and Virginia)
Virginia:
    Ritz Pentagon City (H)
    Ritz Tysons Corner (H)
Washington, DC:
    ANA (H)
    Carlton (H)
    Four Seasons (H)
    Hay-Adams (H)
    Jefferson (H)
    Park Hyatt Washington (H)
    Ritz Washington DC (H)
    Watergate (H)
    Willard (H)

West Virginia
White Sulphur Springs:
    Greenbrier (R)

Wisconsin
Kohler:
    American Club (R)
Milwaukee:
    Pfister (H)
    Wyndham Milwaukee (H)

Romantic

Alabama

Fairhope:
Malaga Inn (B)
Point Clear:
Marriott's Grand (R)

Arizona

Phoenix/Scottsdale:
Arizona Biltmore (R)
Hyatt Reg. Scottsdale (R)
Inn at the Citadel (B)
Phoenician (R)
Renaissance Cottonwoods (R)
Scottsdale Princess (R)
Wigwam (R)
Sedona:
Enchantment (R)
Graham B&B (B)
L'Auberge de Sedona (H)
Tucson:
Loews Ventana (R)
Westin La Paloma (R)

California

Albion:
Albion River (B)
Avalon:
Inn on Mt. Ada (B)
Big Sur:
Post Ranch (B)
Ventana Inn (B)
Borrego Springs:
La Casa del Zorro (R)
Carmel:
Carmel Valley (R)
Cobblestone Inn (B)
Highlands Inn (B)
John Gardiner's (R)
Quail Lodge (R)
Stonepine (B)
Cazadero:
Timberhill (B)
Dana Point:
Laguna Cliff Marriott (R)
Ritz Laguna Niguel (R)
Eureka:
Carter House (B)
Gualala:
St. Orres (B)
Guerneville:
Applewood Inn (B)
Healdsburg:
Madrona Manor (B)
Lafayette:
Lafayette Park (H)
Laguna Beach:
Surf & Sand (H)
Little River:
Heritage House (B)
Los Angeles:
Barnabey's (H)
Bel-Air (H)
Beverly Hills (H)
Four Seasons (H)
Malibu Beach (B)
Peninsula Beverly Hills (H)
Regent Beverly Wilshire (H)
Ritz Marina del Rey (H)
Shutters (H)
Wyndham Checkers (H)
Los Olivos:
Los Olivos Grand (B)

Mendocino:
Mendocino (H)
Stanford Inn (B)
Montecito:
San Ysidro (B)
Monterey:
Old Monterey Inn (B)
Spindrift Inn (B)
Newport Beach:
Four Seasons Newport (H)
Oakhurst:
Chateau du Sureau (B)
Ojai:
Ojai Valley (R)
Pacific Grove:
Gosby House (B)
Green Gables (B)
Martine Inn (B)
Seven Gables (B)
Palm Springs:
Ingleside (B)
La Mancha (R)
La Quinta (R)
Marriott's Desert Springs (R)
Marriott's Rancho (R)
Renaissance Esmeralda (R)
Ritz Rancho Mirage (R)
Westin Mission Hills (R)
Pebble Beach:
Inn at Spanish Bay (R)
Lodge at Pebble Beach (R)
Rutherford:
Auberge du Soleil (B)
Rancho Caymus (B)
San Diego:
del Coronado Hotel (R)
Horton Grand (H)
Inn at Rancho Santa Fe (H)
Le Meridien San Diego (H)
Loews Coronado (R)
Rancho Bernardo (R)
Rancho Valencia (R)
San Francisco:
Archbishop's Mansion (B)
Campton Place (H)
Clift (H)
Inn at the Opera (B)
Inn at Union Square (B)
Majestic (H)
Petite Auberge (B)
Prescott (H)
Queen Anne (H)
Ritz SF (H)
Sherman House (B)
Victorian Inn (B)
Warwick Regis (H)
White Swan (B)
San Luis Obispo:
Apple Farm (B)
Santa Barbara:
El Encanto (H)
Four Seasons Biltmore (R)
Santa Rosa:
Vintners Inn (B)
Sausalito:
Alta Mira (H)
Casa Madrona (H)
Shell Beach:
Cliffs at Shell Beach (R)
Sonoma:
Sonoma Mission (S)

Romantic

St. Helena:
  Harvest Inn (B)
  Meadowood (R)
  Wine Country (B)
Ventura:
  Cliff House (B)
Yosemite:
  Ahwahnee (H)
Yountville:
  Vintage Inn (H)

Colorado
Aspen:
  Jerome (H)
  Lenado (B)
  Little Nell (H)
  Ritz Aspen (H)
  Sardy House (B)
Beaver Creek:
  Hyatt Reg. Beaver Creek (H)
  Inn at Beaver Creek (B)
Colorado Springs:
  Hearthstone Inn (B)
Denver:
  Cambridge (H)
Durango:
  General Palmer (H)
  Strater (H)
  Tall Timber (B)
Edwards:
  Lodge & Spa Cordillera (R)
Mosca:
  Inn at Zapata (B)
Telluride:
  Peaks at Telluride (R)
  San Sophia (B)
Vail:
  Sonnenalp of Vail (R)

Connecticut
Chester:
  Inn at Chester (B)
Greenwich:
  Homestead Inn (B)
Ivoryton:
  Copper Beech (B)
Lakeville:
  Interlaken Inn (R)
Mystic:
  Inn at Mystic (B)
New Haven:
  Three Chimneys (B)
New Preston:
  Boulders (B)
Norfolk:
  Blackberry River (B)
Old Lyme:
  Bee & Thistle (B)
Salisbury:
  White Hart (B)
Washington:
  Mayflower Inn (B)
Westport:
  Inn at National Hall (B)

Delaware
Bethany Beach:
  Addy Sea (B)

Florida
Amelia Island:
  Ritz Amelia Island (R)
Boca Raton:
  Boca Raton (R)

Islamorada:
  Cheeca Lodge (R)
Key West:
  Banana Bay (B)
  Holiday Inn La Concha (H)
  Hyatt Key West (H)
  Marquesa (H)
  Marriott's Casa Marina (R)
  Pier House (R)
Lake Wales:
  Chalet Suzanne (B)
Little Torch Key:
  Little Palm Island (B)
Miami/Miami Beach:
  Biltmore (R)
  Fisher Island (R)
  Grand Bay (H)
  Mayfair House (H)
  Place St. Michel (H)
  Turnberry Isle (R)
Naples:
  Naples Bath & Tennis (R)
  Registry (R)
  Ritz Naples (R)
Orlando:
  Disney's Grand Floridian (R)
  Hyatt Reg. Grand Cypress (R)
Palm Beach:
  Breakers (R)
  Chesterfield (H)
  Four Seasons Palm Beach (H)
  Ritz Palm Beach (R)
Panama City Beach:
  Marriott's Bay Point (R)
Ponte Vedra Beach:
  Marriott at Sawgrass (R)
  Ponte Vedra (R)
Tampa Bay:
  TradeWinds St. Pete (R)
Winter Park:
  Park Plaza (B)

Georgia
Atlanta:
  Ansley Inn (B)
  Four Seasons Atlanta (H)
  Ritz Atlanta (H)
  Ritz Buckhead (H)
Macon:
  1842 Inn (B)
Savannah:
  Ballastone Inn (B)
  Eliza Thompson (B)
  Gastonian (B)
  Kehoe House (B)
  Magnolia Place (B)
  President's Quarters (B)
  17 Hundred 90 Inn (B)
Sea Island:
  Cloister (R)

Hawaii
Big Island:
  Four Seasons Hualalai (R)
  Hapuna Prince (R)
  Hilton Waikoloa (R)
  Kona Village (R)
  Mauna Kea (R)
  Orchid at Mauna Lani (R)
Kauai:
  Marriott Kauai (R)
  Princeville (R)
Lanai:
  Lodge at Koele (R)
  Manele Bay (R)

Romantic

Maui:
 Aston Wailea (R)
 Four Seasons Maui (R)
 Grand Wailea (R)
 Hana-Maui Hotel (H)
 Kapalua Bay (R)
 Kea Lani (R)
 Marriott Maui (R)
 Maui Prince (R)
 Renaissance Wailea (R)
 Ritz Kapalua (R)
 Westin Maui (R)
Oahu:
 Halekulani (H)
 Hilton Turtle Bay (R)
 Kahala Mandarin (R)
 Royal Hawaiian (H)
 Sheraton Moana (H)

Idaho
Coeur d'Alene:
 Blackwell B&B (B)
 Coeur d'Alene (R)
 Gregory's McFarland B&B (B)
Ketchum:
 Knob Hill (H)

Illinois
Chicago:
 Drake (H)
 Fairmont (H)
 Four Seasons Chicago (H)
 Ritz Chicago (H)

Indiana
Indianapolis:
 Canterbury (H)

Iowa
Dubuque:
 Redstone Inn (B)
 Richards House (B)
Fort Madison:
 Kingsley Inn (B)
Newton:
 La Corsette Maison (B)
Walnut:
 Antique City (B)

Kansas
Fort Scott:
 Chenault Mansion (B)
Topeka:
 Inn at the Park (H)
Wichita:
 Castle Inn Riverside (B)

Louisiana
Napoleonville:
 Madewood Plantation (B)
New Orleans:
 Maison de Ville (B)
 Melrose Mansion (B)
 Soniat House (B)
 Windsor Court (H)
White Castle:
 Nottoway Plantation (B)

Maine
Bar Harbor:
 Bar Harbor Inn (B)
 Bayview (H)
Camden:
 Norumbega Inn (B)
Cape Elizabeth:
 Inn by the Sea (B)
Castine:
 Castine Inn (B)

Deer Isle:
 Pilgrims Inn (B)
Kennebunkport:
 Captain Lord Mansion (B)
 Kennebunkport Inn (B)
 White Barn Inn (B)
Scarborough:
 Black Point Inn (R)

Maryland
Annapolis:
 Maryland Historic Inn (B)
Baltimore:
 Admiral Fell Inn (B)
 Celie's Waterfront B&B (B)
 Harbor Court (H)
 Inn at Henderson's (B)
 Mr. Mole B&B (B)
Berlin:
 Atlantic (H)
Chestertown:
 Imperial (B)
Ocean City:
 Lighthouse Club (H)
St. Michaels:
 Inn at Perry Cabin (B)
Taneytown:
 Antrim 1844 (B)

Massachusetts
Boston:
 Ritz Boston (H)
Cape Cod:
 Wequassett Inn (B)
Lenox:
 Blantyre (B)
 Cranwell (R)
 Gables Inn (B)
 Wheatleigh (B)
Martha's Vineyard:
 Charlotte Inn (B)
 Daggett House (B)
 Harbor View (B)
 Thorncroft Inn (B)
Nantucket:
 Beachside Nantucket (H)
 Jared Coffin House (B)
 Summer House (B)
 Wauwinet (B)
Williamstown:
 Orchards (B)

Michigan
Mackinac Island:
 Bay View B&B (B)
 Iroquois (B)

Minnesota
Minneapolis/St. Paul:
 Saint Paul (H)
Red Wing:
 St James (H)
Stillwater:
 Lumber Baron's (H)

Mississippi
Jackson:
 Milsaps Buie House (H)
Natchez:
 Briars Inn (B)
 Burn (B)
 Dunleith (B)
 Monmouth Plantation (B)
 Natchez Eola (H)
Tupelo:
 Mockingbird B&B (B)

451

Vicksburg:
Cedar Grove (B)
Corners B&B (B)

Missouri

Branson:
Branson Hotel B&B (B)
Branson House B&B (B)

Hannibal:
Garth Woodside (B)

Kansas City:
Raphael (H)
Savoy (H)
Southmoreland (H)

St. Louis:
Ritz St. Louis (H)
Seven Gables (B)

Montana

Gallatin Gateway:
Gallatin Gateway (B)

New Hampshire

Dixville Notch:
Balsams Grand (R)

Holderness:
Manor on Golden Pond (B)

Meredith:
Inn at Mill Falls (B)

Portsmouth:
Sise Inn (B)

New Jersey

Beach Haven:
Green Gables (B)

Cape May:
Abbey (B)
Angel of the Sea (B)
Mainstay Inn (B)
Queen Victoria (B)
Virginia Hotel (B)

Hope:
Inn at Millrace Pond (B)

Spring Lake:
Breakers (B)

New Mexico

Cloudcroft:
Lodge at Cloudcroft (B)

Española:
Rancho de San Juan (R)

Mescalero:
Inn of Mountain Gods (R)

Santa Fe:
Inn of Anasazi (B)
Preston House (B)
Rancho Encantado (B)

New York

Alexandria Bay:
Bonnie Castle (R)

Amenia:
Troutbeck (B)

Bolton Landing:
Sagamore (R)

Dover Plains:
Old Drovers Inn (B)

Geneva:
Geneva on the Lake (B)

Great Neck:
Inn at Great Neck (H)

Ithaca:
Rose Inn (B)

Lake Placid:
Lake Placid Lodge (B)

New Paltz:
Mohonk Mountain (R)

New York City:
Box Tree (B)
Inn at Irving Place (B)
Le Refuge Inn (H)
Lowell (H)
Plaza (H)
Plaza Athénée (H)
St. Regis (H)

North Hudson:
Elk Lake Lodge (R)

Old Chatham:
Old Chatham Inn (B)

Poughkeepsie:
Inn at the Falls (B)

Shandaken:
Shandaken Inn (B)

Shelter Island:
Chequit Inn (B)
Ram's Head (B)

Tarrytown:
Castle at Tarrytown (B)

North Carolina

Asheville:
Grove Park Inn (R)

Blowing Rock:
Hound Ears (R)

Charlotte:
Dunhill (H)
Park (H)

Duck:
Sanderling Inn (R)

Lake Toxaway:
Greystone Inn (B)

Nags Head:
First Colony (H)

Pinehurst:
Holly Inn (B)

Pittsboro:
Fearrington House (B)

North Dakota

Fargo:
Bohlig's B&B (B)

Luverne:
Volden Farm B&B (B)

Ohio

Cleveland:
Baricelli Inn (B)
Glidden House (B)

Columbus:
Worthington Inn (B)

Millersburg:
Inn at Honey Run (B)

Oregon

Gleneden Beach:
Salishan (R)

Hood River:
Columbia Gorge (H)

Lincoln City:
Inn at Spanish Head (B)

Newport:
Sylvia Beach (H)

Portland:
Benson (H)
Heathman (H)
Vintage Plaza (H)

Pennsylvania

Erwinna:
Evermay on Delaware (B)

Glen Mills:
Sweetwater Farm (B)

Romantic

Mount Joy:
Cameron Estate (B)
Philadelphia:
Best Western Independence (H)
Four Seasons Philadelphia (H)
Rittenhouse (H)
Ritz Philadelphia (H)
Pittsburgh:
Priory (B)
South Sterling:
Sterling Inn (B)

Puerto Rico
Dorado:
Hyatt Reg. Cerromar (R)
Hyatt Reg. Dorado (R)
Fajardo:
El Conquistador (R)
Humacao:
Palmas del Mar (R)
Old San Juan:
El Convento (H)
Rincon:
Horned Dorset (B)
San Juan:
Condado Plaza (H)

Rhode Island
Block Island:
Manisses (H)
1661 Inn (B)
Newport:
Elm Tree Cottage (B)

South Carolina
Charleston:
Battery Carriage (B)
Fulton Lane Inn (B)
Indigo Inn (B)
John Rutledge (B)
Kings Courtyard (B)
Lodge Alley (B)
Mills House (H)
Planters Inn (B)
Vendue Inn (B)
Victoria House (B)
Hilton Head:
Westin (R)
Pawleys Island:
Litchfield Plantation (B)
Seabrook Island:
Seabrook Island (R)

South Dakota
Gettysburg:
Harer Lodge (B)
Rapid City:
Abend Haus (B)
Willow Springs (B)

Tennessee
Gatlinburg:
Buchhorn Inn (B)
Walland:
Inn at Blackberry Farm (B)

Texas
Austin:
Barton Creek (R)
Dallas/Fort Worth:
Adolphus (H)
Crescent Court (H)
Four Seasons (R)
Mansion on Turtle Creek (H)
St. Germain (B)
Galveston:
Tremont House (H)

Houston:
La Colombe d'Or (B)
Omni Houston (H)
Ritz Houston (H)
San Antonio:
Fairmount (H)
La Mansion del Rio (H)
Plaza San Antonio (H)

Utah
Midway:
Homestead (B)
Park City:
Goldener Hirsch (B)
Stein Eriksen (R)
Washington School (B)
Salt Lake City:
Marriott Salt Lake City (H)

Vermont
Barnard:
Twin Farms (R)
Craftsbury Common:
Inn on Common (H)
Dorset:
Dorset Inn (B)
Essex:
Inn at Essex (B)
Grafton:
Old Tavern at Grafton (B)
Lower Waterford:
Rabbit Hill (B)
Ludlow:
Governor's Inn (B)
Manchester:
Village Country (B)
Wilburton Inn (B)
Middlebury:
Swift House (B)
Newfane:
Four Columns (H)
Perkinsville:
Inn at Weathersfield (B)
Shelburne:
Inn at Shelburne Farms (B)
Stowe:
Topnotch at Stowe (R)
Vergennes:
Basin Harbor (R)
West Dover:
Inn at Sawmill Farm (B)
Wilmington:
Hermitage Inn (B)
Woodstock:
Kedron Valley (B)
Woodstock Inn (R)

Virginia
(see also Washington, DC)
Hot Springs:
Homestead (R)
Keswick:
Keswick Hall (B)
Paris:
Ashby Inn (B)
Richmond:
Jefferson (H)
Washington:
Inn at Little Washington (B)
White Post:
L'Auberge Provencale (B)

Washington
Blaine:
Inn at Semi-Ah-Moo (R)

Romantic

Port Angeles:
  Domaine Madeleine (B)
Port Ludlow:
  Inn at Ludlow Bay (B)
Seattle:
  Alexis (H)
  Four Seasons Olympic (H)
  Sorrento (H)
  Vintage Park (H)
Snoqualmie:
  Salish Lodge (B)
Winthrop:
  Sun Mountain (R)

Washington, DC
(including nearby Maryland and Virginia)
Virginia:
  Morrison House (B)
Washington, DC:
  Four Seasons (H)
  Henley Park (H)
  Jefferson (H)

  Morrison-Clark Inn (B)
  Willard (H)

West Virginia
Berkeley Springs:
  Country Inn (B)
Shepherdstown:
  Bavarian Inn (B)

Wisconsin
Bayfield:
  Old Rittenhouse (B)
Kohler:
  American Club (R)
  Inn on Woodlake (B)
Milwaukee:
  Pfister (H)
  Wyndham Milwaukee (H)

Wyoming
Jackson:
  Rusty Parrot (B)
  Teton Pines (R)
Moran:
  Jenny Lake (B)

Rustic

Alaska
Cooper Landing:
  Kenai Princess (R)
Denali National Park:
  Camp Denali (H)
  Denali Princess (H)
  McKinley Chalet (R)
  North Face (B)
Gustavus:
  Glacier Bay (B)

Arizona
Grand Canyon:
  El Tovar (H)
Sedona:
  Garland's (R)
Tucson:
  Tanque Verde (B)
  Triangle L Ranch (R)

California
Big Sur:
  Big Sur Lodge (B)
  Big Sur River (B)
  Deetjen's Big Sur (B)
Calabasas:
  Ashram Retreat (S)
Cazadero:
  Timberhill (B)
Montecito:
  San Ysidro (B)
Rutherford:
  Rancho Caymus (B)
Woodside:
  Lodge at Skylonda (S)

Colorado
Beaver Creek:
  Hyatt Reg. Beaver Creek (H)
Clark:
  Home Ranch (R)
Colorado Springs:
  Cheyenne Mountain (R)
Granby:
  C Lazy U Ranch (B)
Mosca:
  Inn at Zapata (B)

Connecticut
Essex:
  Griswold Inn (B)
Norfolk:
  Blackberry River (B)

Florida
Orlando:
  Disney's Ft. Wilderness (R)
Ponte Vedra Beach:
  Marriott at Sawgrass (R)

Georgia
Pine Mountain:
  Callaway Gardens (R)
St. Simons Island:
  Lodge at Little St. Simons (B)

Hawaii
Maui:
  Royal Lahaina (R)

Idaho
McCall:
  Shore Lodge (B)
Priest Lake:
  Hill's Hospitality (B)

Tetonia:
  Teton Ridge (B)

Illinois
Gilman:
  Heartland Spa (S)
Whittington:
  Rend Lake (R)

Kentucky
Harrodsburg:
  Inn at Shaker Village (B)

Maine
Bar Harbor:
  Atlantic Oakes (B)
Boothbay Harbor:
  Spruce Point (B)
Raymond:
  Northern Pines (S)

Massachusetts
Cape Cod:
  Coonamessett Inn (B)

Minnesota
Pine River:
  McGuire's (B)

Missouri
Lake Ozark:
  Lodge at Four Seasons (R)
Ridgedale:
  Big Cedar (R)

Montana
Bigfork:
  Averill's Flathead (B)
Big Sky:
  Lone Mountain (B)
Bozeman:
  Mountain Sky (B)
Darby:
  Triple Creek Ranch (R)
Whitefish:
  North Forty (B)

Nevada
Crystal Bay:
  Cal-Neva Resort (R)
Lake Tahoe:
  Hyatt Reg. Lake Tahoe (R)

New Mexico
Chama:
  Lodge at Chama (B)
Cloudcroft:
  Lodge at Cloudcroft (B)
Santa Fe:
  Rancho Encantado (B)
Taos:
  Historic Taos (B)

New York
Bolton Landing:
  Sagamore (R)
Lake Placid:
  Lake Placid Lodge (B)
Neversink:
  New Age Health Spa (S)
North Hudson:
  Elk Lake Lodge (R)
Saranac Lake:
  Point (B)

North Carolina
Blowing Rock:
  Hound Ears (R)

Rustic

Cashiers:
High Hampton (R)

Ohio

Dellroy:
Atwood Lake (R)

Huron:
Sawmill Creek (R)

Painesville:
Quail Hollow (R)

Oklahoma

Kingston:
Texoma State (R)

Oregon

Bend:
Inn of Seventh Mtn (R)

Gold Beach:
Tu Tu'Tun (B)

Newport:
Sylvia Beach (H)

Timberline:
Timberline (R)

Pennsylvania

Champion:
Seven Springs (R)

Glen Mills:
Sweetwater Farm (B)

Mt. Pocono/Pocono Manor:
Pocono Manor (R)

Skytop:
Skytop Lodge (R)

Rhode Island

Newport:
Castle Hill Inn (B)

South Dakota

Rapid City:
Willow Springs (B)

Tennessee

Gatlinburg:
Bent Creek (R)

Texas

Austin:
Lake Austin Spa (S)

Bandera:
Mayan Dude Ranch (B)

Cat Spring:
Southwind B&B (B)

Houston:
Woodlands (R)

Utah

Cedar City:
Bryce Canyon (H)

Park City:
Shadow Ridge (H)

Provo:
Sundance Resort (R)

Springdale:
Zion Lodge (H)

Vermont

Chittenden:
Mountain Top (B)

Killington:
Killington Resort (R)

Virginia

Woodstock:
Inn at Narrow Passage (B)

Washington

Blaine:
Inn at Semi-Ah-Moo (R)

Coupeville:
Captain Whidbey (B)

Forks:
Kalaloch Lodge (B)

West Virginia

Berkeley Springs:
Coolfront Resort (R)

Davis:
Canaan Valley (R)

Hedgesville:
Woods Resort (R)

Wheeling:
Oglebay Resort (R)

Wisconsin

Bailey's Harbor:
Gordon Lodge (B)

Delavan:
Lake Lawn Lodge (R)

Eagle River:
Chanticleer Inn (B)

Fontana:
Abbey Resort (R)

Green Lake:
Heidel House (R)

Lake Geneva:
Interlaken Resort (R)

Wisconsin Dells:
Chula Vista (R)

Wyoming

Jackson:
Spring Creek (R)
Teton Pines (R)

Moose:
Cottonwoods Ranch (B)

Moran.
Colter Bay VIllage (R)
Jackson Lake (B)
Jenny Lake (B)

Sports Facilities

(**Bi** = Bicycling; **Bl** = Bowling; **Bo** = Boating;
E = Exercise Equipment; **F** = Fishing; **G** = Golf;
Hi = Hiking; **Ho** = Horseback Riding; **I** = Ice Skating;
J = Jogging; **S** = Skiing; **Sa** = Sauna/Steam/Jacuzzi;
Si = Swimming Pool – Indoors;
So = Swimming Pool – Outdoors;
T = Tennis; **W** = Water Skiing)

Alabama
Birmingham
  Radisson Birmingham (H) *(E,Sa,So)*
  Sheraton Birmingham (H) *(E,Sa,Si)*
  Wynfrey (H) *(E)*
Eufaula:
  Kendall Manor (B) *(Bi,F,G,Hi,J,So,W)*
Fairhope:
  Malaga Inn (B) *(So)*
Mobile:
  Adam's Mark (H) *(E,Sa,So)*
  Radisson Admiral (H) *(Sa,So)*
Orange Beach:
  Perdido Beach (R) *(E,F,T)*
Point Clear:
  Marriott's Grand (R) *(E,G)*
Tuscaloosa:
  Sheraton Capstone (H) *(So)*

Alaska
Anchorage:
  Anchorage Hilton (H) *(E,Sa)*
  Regal Alaskan (H) *(Bi,E,J)*
Cooper Landing:
  Kenai Princess (R) *(E,F)*
Fairbanks:
  Fairbanks Princess (H) *(F,Hi,Sa)*
Girdwood:
  Alyeska (R) *(Bi,E,Hi,I,J,S,Sa,Si)*
Gustavus:
  Glacier Bay (B) *(F,Hi)*

Arizona
Bisbee:
  Copper Queen (H) *(Bi,G,Hi,So)*
Catalina:
  Miraval (S) *(Bi,E,Hi,Ho,J,Sa,So,T)*
Douglas:
  Gadsden (H) *(Bi,E,G,Hi,Ho,J,So,T)*
Gold Canyon:
  Gold Canyon (R) *(Bi,G,Hi,Ho,Sa,So,T)*
Grand Canyon:
  El Tovar (H) *(Hi)*
Page:
  Wahweap (H) *(E,F,Hi,Sa,So,W)*
Phoenix/Scottsdale:
  Arizona Biltmore (R) *(Bi,E,G,Hi)*
  Arizona Golf (R) *(Bi,J,Sa,So,T)*
  Boulders (R) *(Bi,E,G,Hi,J,Sa,So,T)*
  Buttes (R) *(Bi,E,Hi,J,Sa,So,T)*
  Crowne Phoenix (H) *(E,Sa,So)*
  Dbltree La Posada (R) *(Bi,E,Sa,So,T)*
  Dbltree Paradise Valley (R) *(E)*
  Embassy Biltmore (H) *(E,Sa,So)*
  Embassy Scottsdale (H) *(So,T)*
  Gardiner's (R) *(E,Hi,J,Sa,So,T)*
  Hermosa Inn (B) *(G,Hi,J,Sa,So,T)*
  Holiday Inn SunSpree (R)
  (Bi,E,F,Hi,J,Sa,So,T)
  Hyatt Reg. Phoenix (H) *(E,J,Sa,So,T)*
  Hyatt Reg. Scottsdale (R)
  (Bi,E,G,J,Sa,So,T)
  Marriott's Camelback (R)
  (Bi,E,G,J,Sa,So,T)
  Marriott Scottsdale (H) *(Sa,So)*
  Marriott's Mountain (R)
  (Bi,E,G,Hi,J,Sa,So,T)
  Orange Tree (R) *(Bi,E,G,Hi,J,So)*
  Phoenician (R) *(Bi,E,G,Hi,J,Sa,So,T)*
  Pte Hilton S. Mountain (R)
  (Bi,E,G,Hi,Ho,J,Sa,So,T)
  Pte Hilton Squaw (R)
  (Bi,E,G,Hi,Ho,J,Sa,So)
  Pte Hilton Tapatio (R) *(Bi,E,G,Ho,Sa,So,T)*
  Radisson Scottsdale (R) *(Bi,E,J,Sa,So,T)*
  Regal McCormick (R) *(F,G)*
  Renaissance Cottonwoods (R)
  (Bi,J,Sa,So,T)
  Ritz Phoenix (H) *(Bi,E,Sa,So,T)*
  Royal Palms (H) *(G,So,T)*
  San Carlos (H) *(E,So)*
  Scottsdale Conference (R)
  (Bi,E,G,Ho,J,Sa,So,T)
  Scottsdale Hilton (H) *(E,Sa,So,T)*
  Scottsdale Plaza (R) *(Bi,E,J,Sa,So,T)*
  Scottsdale Princess (R) *(Bi,E,F,G,Sa,So,T)*
  Sheraton Crescent (H) *(Bi,E)*
  Sheraton Mesa (H) *(E,So)*
  Sheraton San Marcos (R)
  (Bi,E,G,J,Sa,So,T)
  Wigwam (R) *(Bi,E,G,So,T)*
Prescott:
  Hassayampa Inn (H)
  (Bi,Bo,E,F,G,Hi,Ho,So)
Sedona:
  Canyon Villa B&B (B) *(So)*
  Enchantment (R) *(Bi,E,G,Hi,Ho,J,Sa,So,T)*
  Garland's (R) *(Hi,T)*
  Graham B&B (B) *(Bi,Sa,So)*
  L'Auberge de Sedona (H) *(F,Hi,So)*
  Los Abrigados (R) *(E,Sa,So,T)*
  Poco Diablo (R) *(Bi,E,G,Hi,J,Sa,So,T)*
Tucson:
  Arizona Inn (H) *(Bi,E,T)*
  Canyon Ranch (S) *(Bi,Hi,J,Sa,Si,So,T)*
  Dbltree Reid Park (H) *(E,Sa,So,T)*
  Lodge Ventana (R) *(Bi,E,G,Sa,So,T)*
  Loews Ventana (R) *(E,G,Hi,J,Sa,So,T)*
  Omni Tucson (R) *(Bi,E,G,Sa,So,T)*
  Sheraton El Conquistador (R)
  (Bi,Bo,E,G,Hi,Ho,J,S,Sa,So,T)
  SunCatcher B&B (B) *(Hi,Ho,J,Sa,So)*
  Tanque Verde (B)
  (E,F,G,Hi,Ho,J,Sa,Si,So,T)
  Westin La Paloma (R) *(E,G,Sa,So,T)*
  Westward Look (R) *(Bi,E,Hi,Ho,J,So,T)*
Wickenburg:
  Merv Griffin's (B) *(E,Hi,Ho,J,Sa,So,T)*

Arkansas
Eureka Springs:
  Dairy Hollow House (B) *(F,Hi)*
Hot Springs:
  Arlington Resort (H) *(E,Sa,So)*
  Hot Springs Park (H) *(Sa,Si,So)*

Sports Facilities

Lake Hamilton (R) *(E,F,J,Sa,Si,So,T)*
Majestic (H) *(E,So)*
Lakeview:
Gaston's (R) *(F,Hi,J,So,T)*
Little Rock:
Arkansas Excelsior (H) *(E)*
Dbltree Little Rock (H) *(E,So)*
Little Rock Hilton (H) *(E,So)*

California
Anaheim:
Dbltree Anaheim (H) *(E,J,Sa,So,T)*
Disneyland (H) *(E,Sa,So)*
Disneyland Pacific (H) *(E,So)*
Hilton Anaheim (H) *(E,Sa,Si,So)*
Hyatt Reg. Alicante (H) *(E,Sa,So,T)*
Inn at the Park (H) *(Sa,So)*
Marriott Anaheim (H) *(E,Si,So)*
Sheraton Anaheim (H) *(E,J,Sa,So)*
Big Sur:
Big Sur Lodge (B) *(Hi,J,So)*
Big Sur River (B) *(F,Hi,J,So)*
Deetjen's Big Sur (B) *(Hi)*
Post Ranch (B) *(E,Hi,J,So)*
Ventana Inn (B) *(E,J,Sa,So)*
Bodega Bay:
Inn at the Tides (B) *(Sa,So)*
Borrego Springs:
La Casa del Zorro (R) *(Bi,E,Sa,So,T)*
Calabasas:
Ashram Retreat (S) *(E,Hi,Sa,So)*
Calistoga:
Indian Springs (S) *(Bi,E,So,T)*
Carlsbad:
La Costa (R) *(E,G,J,Sa,So,T)*
Carmel:
Carmel Country Spa (S) *(E,So)*
Carmel Valley (R) *(E,G,Hi,Ho,J,Sa,So,T)*
Cobblestone Inn (B) *(Bi)*
Highlands Inn (B) *(Bi,E,Hi,J,Sa,So)*
John Gardiner's (R) *(Sa,So,T)*
La Playa (H) *(So)*
Los Laureles (H) *(Bi,E,Hi,J,Sa,So)*
Quail Lodge (R) *(G,J,Sa,So,T)*
Stonepine (B) *(Bi,E,Hi,Ho,J,So,T)*
Cazadero:
Timberhill (B) *(Hi,J,Sa,So,T)*
Costa Mesa:
Country Side Inn (H) *(E,Sa)*
Marriott Costa Mesa (H) *(E,Sa,So)*
Red Lion (H) *(E,Sa,So)*
Westin South Coast (H) *(E,J,So,T)*
Dana Point:
Laguna Cliff Marriott (R) *(E,Sa,So,T)*
Ritz Laguna Niguel (R) *(Hi,J,Sa,So,T)*
Death Valley:
Furnace Creek Inn (R) *(E,G,Hi,Ho,Sa,So,T)*
Escondido:
Golden Door (S) *(E,Hi,Sa,So,T)*
Fish Camp:
Tenaya Lodge (R) *(Bi,E,F,Hi,Ho,Sa,Si,So)*
Fresno:
4 Points ITT Sheraton (H) *(E,Sa,So)*
Guerneville:
Applewood ınn (B) *(Sa,So)*
Healdsburg:
Madrona Manor (B) *(Sa,So)*
Irvine:
Hilton Orange County (H) *(E,So,T)*
Hyatt Reg. Irvine (H) *(Bi,E,S,Sa,So,T)*
Irvine Marriott (H) *(Bi,E,Sa,Si,So,T)*
Lafayette:
Lafayette Park (H) *(E,Sa,So)*
Laguna Beach:
Surf & Sand (H) *(J,So)*

Lake Arrowhead:
Lake Arrowhead (R) *(Bi,E,F,Hi,J,Sa,So,T)*
Little River:
Little River Inn (B) *(G,Hi,J,T)*
Long Beach:
Renaissance Long Beach (H) *(E)*
Sheraton Long Beach (H) *(E,Sa,So)*
Los Angeles:
Argyle (H) *(E,Sa,So)*
Barnabey's (H) *(Sa,So)*
Bel-Air (H) *(So)*
Beverly Hills (H) *(E,Hi,Sa,So,T)*
Beverly Hilton (H) *(E,J,So)*
Beverly Prescott (H) *(E,So)*
Century Plaza (H) *(E,Sa,So)*
Chateau Marmont (H) *(E,So)*
Clarion Hollywood (H) *(E,Sa,So)*
Doubletree LAX (H) *(E,Sa,So)*
Four Seasons (H) *(E,Sa,So)*
Hilton LAX (H) *(E,So)*
Hilton Long Beach (H) *(E,Sa,So)*
Hyatt Reg. LA (H) *(E,Sa)*
Inter-Continental LA (H) *(E,Sa,So)*
Le Parc (H) *(E,Sa,So,T)*
Loews Santa Monica (H) *(Bi,E,Sa,Si,So)*
Malibu Beach (B) *(E,J,Sa)*
Marriott LAX (H) *(E,Sa,So)*
Marriott Marina Beach (H) *(So)*
Marriott Warner Ctr (H) *(E,Sa,Si,So)*
Miramar Sheraton (H) *(E,Sa,So)*
Mondrian (H) *(Bi,E,Hi,J,Sa,So)*
New Otani (H) *(E)*
Nikko Beverly Hills (H) *(Sa,So)*
Omni LA (H) *(E,Sa,So)*
Palos Verdes (H) *(Bi,Sa,Si)*
Park Hyatt LA (H) *(E,Sa,Si,So)*
Peninsula Beverly Hills (H) *(E,Sa,So)*
Ramada W. Hollywood (B)
(E,G,Hi,Ho,So,T)
Regal Biltmore (H) *(E,Sa,Si)*
Regent Beverly Wilshire (H) *(E,Sa,So)*
Renaissance LA (H) *(E,Sa,So)*
Ritz Huntington (H) *(Bi,Bo,E,Sa,So,T)*
Ritz Marina del Rey (H) *(Bi,E,J,Sa,So,T)*
Shangri-La (H) *(E)*
Sheraton Grande (H) *(So)*
Sheraton Industry Hills (H)
(E,G,Ho,J,Sa,So,T)
Sheraton Universal (H) *(E,Sa,So)*
Shutters (H) *(Bi,E,J,Sa,So)*
Sofitel LA (H) *(E,Sa,So)*
Summit Bel-Air (H) *(E,So,T)*
Sunset Marquis (H) *(E,Sa,So)*
Westin Bonaventure (H) *(E,Si,So)*
Westwood Marquis (H) *(E,So)*
Wyndham Bel Age (H) *(E,Sa,So)*
Wyndham Checkers (H) *(E,Sa,So)*
Wyndham LAX (H) *(E,Sa,So)*
Los Olivos:
Los Olivos Grand (B) *(Bi,F,Sa,So)*
Mendocino:
Hill House Mendocino (B) *(Hi)*
Mendocino (H) *(Hi)*
Stanford Inn (B) *(Bi,E,F,Hi,J,Sa,Si)*
Montecito:
Montecito Inn (B) *(Bi,E,Sa,So)*
San Ysidro (B) *(E,Hi,So,T)*
Monterey:
Dbltree Fish. Wharf (H) *(Bi,So)*
Hyatt Reg. Monterey (H) *(E,Sa,So,T)*
Monterey Plaza (H) *(Bi,E,J)*
Pacific (H) *(Sa)*
Morro Bay:
Inn at Morro Bay (B) *(Bi,Sa,So)*

Sports Facilities

Napa:
Embassy Napa Valley (H) *(Sa,Si,So)*
La Residence (B) *(Bi,G,Hi,Ho,Sa,So,T)*
Marriott Napa Valley (H) *(E,Sa,So,T)*
Silverado (R) *(Bi,G,J,Sa,So,T)*

Newport Beach:
Four Seasons Newport (H) *(Bi,E,J,T)*
Hyatt Newporter (R) *(Bi,E,G,Sa,So)*
Marriott Suites (H) *(E,J,Sa,Si,So)*
Marriott Tennis (H) *(Bi,E,J,Sa,So,T)*
Sutton Place (H) *(Bi,E,Sa,So,T)*

Oakhurst:
Chateau du Sureau (B) *(J,So)*

Oakland:
Waterfront Plaza (H) *(E,F,Sa,So)*

Ojai:
Oaks at Ojai (S) *(E,Hi,Sa,So)*
Ojai Valley (R) *(Bi,E,G,Hi,Sa,So,T)*

Olympic Valley:
Plumpjack's (B) *(Sa,So)*
Resort at Squaw Creek (R)
(E,G,J,S,Sa,So,T)

Oxnard:
Embassy Mandalay (H) *(Bi,F,G,Sa,So,T)*

Pacific Grove:
Green Gables (B) *(J)*
Martine Inn (B) *(Bi,F,Hi,J,Sa)*

Palm Springs:
Dbltree Palm Springs (R) *(E,G,Sa,So)*
Givenchy (S) *(Bi,E,G,J,Sa,Si,So,T)*
Hilton Palm Springs (H) *(E,Sa,So,T)*
Hyatt Grand (R) *(Bi,Bo,E,G,J,Sa,So,T)*
Hyatt Reg. Palm Springs (H) *(E,Sa,So)*
Indian Wells (R) *(Bi,E,G,Sa,So,T)*
Ingleside (B) *(Sa,So)*
Inn at Racquet Club (B) *(Sa,Si,So,T)*
La Mancha (R) *(Bi,E,J,Sa,So,T)*
La Quinta (R) *(Bi,Sa,So,T)*
L'Horizon Garden (R) *(Bi,Hi,Ho,S,Sa,So,T)*
Marquis Palm Springs (H) *(E,Sa,So,T)*
Marriott's Desert Springs (R)
(E,G,Hi,Sa,So,T)
Marriott's Rancho (R) *(E,G,Sa,So,T)*
Monte Vista (H) *(Sa,So)*
Palms (S) *(E,Sa,So)*
Renaissance Esmeralda (R)
(Bi,E,G,Hi,Ho,J,Sa,So,T)
Ritz Rancho Mirage (R) *(Bi,E,J,Sa,So,T)*
Riviera Palm Springs (R) *(Bi,E,Sa,So,T)*
Shadow Mountain (R) *(E,Sa,So,T)*
Spa (H) *(E,Sa,So)*
Sundance (B) *(So,T)*
Two Bunch Palms (B) *(Bi,Hi,J,Sa,So,T)*
Westin Mission Hills (R)
(Bi,E,G,J,Sa,So,T)
Wyndham Palm Springs (H)
(Bi,E,J,Sa,So)

Palo Alto:
Garden Court (H) *(Bi,E)*

Pasadena:
Dbltree Pasadena (H) *(Sa,So)*

Pebble Beach:
Inn at Spanish Bay (R)
(Bi,E,G,Hi,Ho,Sa,So,T)
Lodge at Pebble Beach (R)
(Bi,E,G,Hi,Ho,J,Sa,So,T)

Redwood City:
Sofitel SF (H) *(J,Sa,So)*

Riverside:
Mission Inn (H) *(E,Sa,So)*

Rutherford:
Auberge du Soleil (B) *(Bi,E,Hi,Sa,So,T)*
Rancho Caymus (B) *(J)*

Sacramento:
Hyatt Reg. Sacramento (H) *(E,Sa,So)*
Radisson Sacramento (H) *(Bi,E,J,Sa,So)*

San Diego:
Catamaran (H) *(Bi,E,Sa,So)*
Dbltree Del Mar (H) *(E)*
del Coronado Hotel (R) *(Bi,E,Sa,So,T)*
Embassy San Diego (H) *(E,Sa,Si)*
Hilton San Diego (H) *(Bi,E,Sa,So,T,W)*
Hyatt Islandia (H) *(Bi,E,F,J,Sa,So,W)*
Hyatt Reg. La Jolla (H) *(Bi,E,Hi,Sa,So,T)*
Hyatt Reg. San Diego (H)
(Bi,E,F,J,Sa,So,T,W)
Inn at Rancho Santa Fe (H) *(E,G,Hi,So,T)*
Kona Kai (R) *(E,F,J,Sa,So,T)*
La Jolla Beach (H) *(Bi,E,G,J,So,T)*
L'Auberge Del Mar (R) *(E,Sa,So,T)*
La Valencia (H) *(E,Sa,So)*
Le Meridien San Diego (H)
(Bi,E,G,Ho,J,Sa,So,T)
Lodge at Torrey Pines (H) *(So)*
Loews Coronado (R)
(Bi,Bo,E,F,G,Hi,Ho,I,J,Sa,Si,So,T,W)
Marriott La Jolla (H) *(E,Sa,Si,So)*
Marriott Mission Valley (H) *(E,Sa,So,T)*
Marriott San Diego (H)
(Bi,E,F,G,Hi,Ho,I,J,Sa,So,T,W)
Princess San Diego (R)
(Bi,Bo,E,F,Sa,So,T,W)
Radisson Harbor View (H) *(E,Sa,So)*
Rancho Bernardo (R) *(Bi,E,G,Sa,So,T)*
Rancho Valencia (R) *(Bi,E,Hi,J,Sa,So,T)*
Sea Lodge (H) *(E,Sa,So,T)*
Sheraton Grande (R) *(Bi,E,G,Hi,Sa,So,T)*
Sheraton San Diego (H) *(Bi,E,Sa,So,T)*
US Grant (H) *(E)*
Westgate (H) *(E)*
Westin San Diego (H) *(E,Sa,So,T)*
Wyndham Emerald (H) *(E,Sa,So)*

San Francisco:
ANA San Francisco (H) *(E)*
Cathedral Hill (H) *(So)*
Claremont (R) *(E,Hi,J,Sa,So,T)*
Clift (H) *(E)*
Diva (H) *(E)*
Donatello (H) *(E,Sa)*
Fairmont SF (H) *(E,Sa)*
Galleria Park (H) *(J)*
Grand Hyatt SF (H) *(E)*
Griffon (H) *(E)*
Handlery Union Square (H) *(Sa,So)*
Harbor Court (H) *(E,J,Sa,Si)*
Hilton SF (H) *(E,Sa,So)*
Hyatt Fish. Wharf (H) *(E,Sa,So)*
Hyatt Reg. SF (H) *(E)*
Kensington Park (H) *(E)*
Mandarin Oriental (H) *(E)*
Marriott Fish. Wharf (H) *(E,Sa)*
Marriott SF (H) *(E,Sa,Si)*
Milano (H) *(E,Sa)*
Monaco (H) *(E,Sa)*
Nikko SF (H) *(Sa,Si)*
Palace (H) *(E,Sa,Si)*
Pan Pacific SF (H) *(E)*
Parc Fifty-Five (H) *(E)*
Park Hyatt SF (H) *(E)*
Phoenix (H) *(So)*
Prescott (H) *(E)*
Radisson Miyako (H) *(E,Sa)*
Renaissance Stanford (H) *(E)*
Ritz SF (H) *(E,Sa,Si)*
Sheraton Fish. Wharf (H) *(So)*
Sir Francis Drake (H) *(E)*
Triton (H) *(E)*
Tuscan Inn (H) *(E)*

Sports Facilities

Westin St. Francis (H) *(E)*
York (H) *(E)*
San Jose:
Fairmont San Jose (H) *(E,Sa,So)*
Hayes (H) *(G,Hi,So,T)*
San Luis Obispo:
Apple Farm (B) *(Sa,So)*
Santa Barbara:
El Encanto (H) *(So,T)*
Fess Parker's (R) *(Bi,E,Sa,So,T)*
Four Seasons Biltmore (R)
(Bi,E,J,Sa,So,T)
Santa Clara:
Westin Santa Slara (H) *(E,G,J,Sa,So,T)*
Santa Cruz:
Chaminade (H) *(E,Hi,Sa,So,T,W)*
Santa Monica:
Oceana (H) *(Bi,Bo,E,G,Hi,Ho,I,J,Sa,So,T)*
Sausalito:
Alta Mira (H) *(Bi,Hi)*
Casa Madrona (H) *(Sa)*
Shell Beach:
Cliffs at Shell Beach (R) *(E,J,Sa,So)*
Solvang:
Alisal (R) *(Bi,F,G,Hi,Ho,J,Sa,So,T)*
Sonoma:
El Dorado (H) *(Si)*
Sonoma Mission (S) *(Bi,E,Hi,Sa,So,T)*
St. Helena:
Harvest Inn (B) *(Sa,So)*
Meadowood (R) *(Bi,E,Hi,J,Sa,So,T)*
Wine Country (B) *(Sa,So)*
Tecate:
Rancho La Puerta (S) *(E,Hi,J,Sa,So,T)*
Truckee:
Northstar-at-Tahoe (R)
(Bi,E,G,Hi,Ho,J,S,Sa,So,T)
Ventura:
Cliff House (B) *(So)*
Vista:
Cal-a-Vie (S) *(E,Hi,Sa,So,T)*
Woodside:
Lodge at Skylonda (S) *(E,Hi,Sa,Si)*
Yosemite:
Ahwahnee (H) *(Hi,Ho,J,So,T)*
Yountville:
Vintage Inn (H) *(Bi,Sa,So,T)*

Colorado
Aspen:
Aspen Club (B) *(S,Sa,So)*
Gant (B) *(Sa,So,T)*
Inn at Aspen (H) *(Bi,E,Hi,J,S,Sa,So)*
Jerome (H) *(E,S,Sa,So)*
Lenado (B) *(Sa)*
Little Nell (H) *(Bi,E,Hi,J,S,Sa,So)*
Ritz Aspen (H) *(Bi,E,I,S,Sa,So)*
Sardy House (B) *(Sa,So)*
Beaver Creek:
Charter at Beaver Creek (H) *(Bi,E,F,G,Hi)*
Embassy Beaver Creek (R)
(Bi,E,Hi,Ho,S,Sa,Si,So)
Hyatt Reg. Beaver Creek (H)
(E,Hi,Ho,I,S,Sa,Si,So,T)
Inn at Beaver Creek (B) *(J,S,Sa,So)*
Pines Lodge (H) *(Bi,E,Hi,J,S,Sa,So)*
Breckenridge:
Breckenridge Mtn (H) *(So)*
Hilton Breckenridge (R) *(E,Sa,Si)*
Village at Breckenridge (R)
(Bi,E,F,Hi,I,S,Sa,Si,So)
Clark:
Home Ranch (R) *(F,G,Hi,Ho,J,S,Sa,So)*
Colorado Springs:
Antlers Dlbtree (H) *(E,Sa,Si)*

Broadmoor (R) *(Bi,E,G,Hi,Ho,J,Sa,Si,So,T)*
Cheyenne Mountain (R)
(Bi,E,F,G,J,Sa,Si,So,T)
Sheraton (H) *(E,F,G,Sa,Si,So,T)*
Copper Mountain:
Copper Mountain (R)
(Bi,E,F,G,Hi,Ho,I,J,S,Sa,Si,So,T,W)
Denver:
Brown Palace (H) *(E)*
Burnsley (H) *(So)*
Dbltree Denver SE (H) *(E)*
Embassy Denver (H) *(E)*
Hyatt Reg. Denver Dwtn (H) *(E,J,Sa,Si,T)*
Hyatt Reg. Denver Tech (H) *(Bi,E,Sa,Si,T)*
Inverness (R) *(Bi,E,G,J,Sa,Si,So,T)*
Loews Giorgio (H) *(E)*
Marriott Denver (H) *(E,Sa,Si)*
Marriott SE Denver (H) *(E,Sa,Si,So)*
Marriott Tech Denver (H) *(E,J,Sa,Si,So)*
Oxford (H) *(E)*
Renaissance Denver (H) *(E,Sa,Si,So)*
Residence by Marriott (H) *(E,Sa,So)*
Warwick (H) *(So)*
Westin Tabor Center (H) *(E,Sa,Si,So)*
Durango:
Rochester (H)
(Bi,Bo,E,F,G,Hi,Ho,J,S,So,T,W)
Strater (H) *(Sa)*
Tamarron Hilton (R)
(Bi,E,F,G,Hi,Ho,J,Sa,Si,So,T)
Wit's End (B) *(Bi,F,Hi,Ho,I,J,S,So,T)*
Edwards:
Lodge & Spa Cordillera (R)
(Bi,E,G,Hi,Ho,J,S,Sa,Si,So,T)
Granby:
C Lazy U Ranch (B)
(E,F,Hi,Ho,I,J,S,Sa,So,T)
Keystone:
Keystone (R) *(Bi,E,Hi,I,J,S,Sa,Si,So,T)*
Mosca:
Inn at Zapata (B) *(Bi,E,F,G,Hi,Ho,J,Sa,So)*
Mt. Crested Butte:
Grande Butte (H) *(E)*
Redstone:
Redstone Inn (B) *(E,F,S,So,T)*
Snowmass Village:
Silvertree (H) *(Bi,E,S,Sa,So)*
Snowmass Lodge (R) *(E,G,Hi,J,Sa,So,T)*
Steamboat Springs:
Sheraton Steamboat (R) *(E,S,Sa,So,T)*
Telluride:
Columbia (B)
(Bi,E,F,G,Hi,Ho,I,J,S,Sa,So,T)
Peaks at Telluride (R)
(Bi,E,G,Hi,J,S,Sa,Si,So,T)
San Sophia (B) *(Hi,J,Sa)*
Vail:
Christiana at Vail (H) *(Bi,Sa,So)*
Lodge at Vail (H) *(Bi,E,Hi,S,Sa,So)*
Marriott's at Vail (R) *(S,Si,So)*
Mountain Haus at Vail (H)
(E,Hi,J,S,Sa,So)
Sitzmark Lodge (H) *(J,Sa,So)*
Sonnenalp of Vail (R) *(Bi,E,Sa,Si,So)*
Vail Athletic Club (H) *(E,S,Sa,Si)*
Vail Cascade (H) *(Bi,E,F,Hi,S,Sa,So,T)*

Connecticut
Chester:
Inn at Chester (B) *(Bi,E,Hi,I,J,Sa,T)*
Hartford:
Goodwin (H) *(E)*
Lakeville:
Interlaken Inn (R) *(Bi,E,F,G,Sa,So,T)*
Lebanon:
Spa at Grand Lake (S) *(E,F,Sa,Si,So,T)*

Sports Facilities

Ledyard:
Foxwoods (H) *(E,Hi,J,Sa,Si)*

Mystic:
Inn at Mystic (B) *(F,Hi,Sa,So,T)*

New London:
Lighthouse Inn (H) *(Hi,T)*

New Preston:
Boulders (B) *(Bi,F,Hi,I,T)*
Inn on Lake Waramaug (B) *(Bi,F,I,Sa,Si,T)*

Norfolk:
Blackberry River (B) *(F,Hi,So)*

Norwich:
Norwich Inn (S) *(E,J,Sa,Si,So,T)*

Ridgefield:
Stonehenge Inn (B) *(Hi)*

Simsbury:
Simsbury Inn (H) *(E,J,Sa,Si,T)*

Southbury:
Heritage Inn (H) *(Bi,E,F,G,Hi,J,Sa,Si,So,T)*

Washington:
Mayflower Inn (B) *(E,Hi,Sa,So,T)*

Westbrook:
Water's Edge (B) *(E,Sa,Si,So,T)*

Delaware

Bethany Beach:
Addy Sea (B) *(Bi)*

Montchanin:
Inn at Montchanin (B) *(F,G,T)*

Rehoboth Beach:
Boardwalk Plaza (H) *(E,Si,So)*
Corner Cupboard (B) *(Bi)*

Wilmington:
Hotel du Pont (H) *(E,Sa)*

Florida

Amelia Island:
Amelia Island (R) *(Bi,E,F,G,Ho,J,Sa,Si,So,T)*
Ritz Amelia Island (R) *(Bi,E,F,G,Sa,Si,So,T)*

Boca Raton:
Boca Raton (R) *(Bi,E,F,G,Hi,Sa,So)*
Marriott Boca Raton (H) *(G,J,Sa,So)*

Bonita Springs:
Shangri-La (S) *(E,Sa,So,T)*

Captiva Island:
South Seas Plantation (R)
(Bi,E,F,G,J,Sa,So,T,W)

Clearwater:
Belleview Mido (R)
(Bi,Bo,E,F,G,J,Sa,Si,So,T)

Destin:
Hilton Sandestin (R) *(Bi,G,J,Sa,Si,So,T,W)*

Fisher Island:
Spa Internazionale (S)
(Bi,E,F,G,J,Sa,Si,So,T)

Fort Lauderdale:
Doubletree (H) *(Sa,So)*
Hyatt Reg. Pier 66 (H) *(E,F,J,Sa,So,T,W)*
Lago Mar (R) *(E,So,T)*
Little Inn by the Sea (B) *(Bi,So)*
Marriott Ft. Lauderdale (H) *(Sa,So,T)*
Marriott's Harbor (R) *(Bi,E,Sa,So,T)*
Radisson Bahia Mar (R) *(E,F,Si,T,W)*
Registry Resort (S) *(E,G,J,Sa,Si,So)*
Riverside (H) *(So)*
Westin Ft. Lauderdale (H) *(E,J,Sa,So)*
Wyndham Ft. Lauderdale (H) *(Sa,So,T)*

Fort Myers:
Sanibel Harbour (R)
(Bi,E,F,Hi,J,Sa,Si,So,T)

Gasparilla Island:
Gasparilla Inn (B) *(Bi,E,G,J,So,T)*

Haines City:
Grenelefe Golf (R) *(Bi,E,F,G,Hi,J,Sa,So,T)*

Hallandale:
Regency House (S) *(E,Sa,So)*

Howey-in-the-Hills:
Mission Inn (R) *(Bi,E,F,G,J,Sa,So,T)*

Islamorada:
Cheeca Lodge (R) *(Bi,E,F,J,Sa,So,T,W)*

Jacksonville:
Club Hotel by Dbltree (H) *(E,Sa,So)*
Marriott Jacksonville (H) *(E,Sa,Si,So,T)*
Omni Jacksonville (H) *(E,So)*

Jupiter:
Jupiter Beach (R) *(Bi,E,So)*

Key Largo:
Marriott's Key Largo (R) *(F,So,W)*
Ocean Reef (R) *(Bi,E,F,J,Sa,So,T)*

Key West:
Banana Bay (B) *(E,F,So)*
Cuban Club (H) *(Bi,E,F,G,J,W)*
Holiday Inn La Concha (H) *(Si)*
Hyatt Key West (H) *(Bi,E,F,Sa,So)*
Marquesa (H) *(So)*
Marriott's Casa Marina (R)
(Bi,E,Sa,So,T,W)
Marriott's Reach (R) *(E,So,W)*
Ocean Key House (R) *(Bi,F,So)*
Pier House (R) *(E,Sa,So)*

Lake Wales:
Chalet Suzanne (B) *(Bi,Hi,J,Si)*

Little Torch Key:
Little Palm Island (B) *(E,F,Sa,So,W)*

Longboat Key:
Colony Beach (R) *(Bi,E,F,Sa,So)*
Resort at Longboat Key (R)
(Bi,E,G,J,Sa,So,T)

Marathon:
Hawk's Cay (R) *(Bi,E,F,Hi,J,Sa,So,T)*

Marco Island:
Marco Island Hilton (R) *(E,Sa,So,T,W)*
Marriott's Marco Island (R)
(Bi,E,F,Sa,So,T,W)
Radisson Beach (R) *(Bi,E,F,Sa,So,T,W)*

Miami/Miami Beach:
Albion (H) *(So)*
Alexander (H) *(E,Sa,So)*
Astor (H) *(So)*
Biltmore (R) *(E,G,Sa,So,T)*
Crowne Plaza Miami (H) *(E,So)*
Dbltree Coconut Grove (H) *(E,So,T)*
Dbltree Grand (H) *(E,F,Sa,Si,W)*
Delano (H) *(E,Sa,So)*
Doral Golf (R) *(Bi,E,F,G,J,Sa,Si,So,T)*
Eden Roc (H) *(E,F,J,Sa,So,W)*
Fisher Island (R) *(Bi,E,F,G,J,Sa,Si,So,T)*
Florida Suites (H) *(E,So)*
Fontainebleau Hilton (R) *(E,J,Sa,So,T,W)*
Grand Bay (H) *(E,Sa,So)*
Greenview (H) *(G,T)*
Grove Isle Club (B) *(E,F,J,Sa,So,T,W)*
Hyatt Reg. Coral Gables (H) *(E,Sa,So)*
Hyatt Reg. Miami (H) *(E,So)*
Indian Creek (H) *(E,So)*
Inter-Continental Miami (H) *(J,So)*
La Voile Rouge (B) *(So)*
Lido Spa (S) *(E,Sa,So)*
Marriott Biscayne Bay (H) *(E,F,So)*
Miami Beach Ocean (H) *(Bi,So,W)*
Occidental Plaza (H) *(E,So)*
Omni Colonnade (H) *(E,Sa,So)*
Park Central (H) *(So)*
Pritikin Longevity (S) *(Bi,E,So)*
Radisson Mart Plaza (H) *(E,Si,So,T)*
Raleigh (H) *(E,So)*
Ritz Plaza (H) *(E,So)*
Sheraton Bal Harbour (H) *(E,J,Sa,Si,T,W)*
Sheraton Biscayne Bay (H) *(E,J,So)*
Spa at Doral (S) *(Bi,F,G,J,So,T)*
Tides (H) *(E,So)*

461

Sports Facilities

Turnberry Isle (R) *(E,F,G,J,So,T)*
Westin Miami (R) *(E,Sa,So,T)*
Naples:
Edgewater Beach (H) *(Bi,E,So)*
La Playa Beach (R) *(E,So,T)*
Naples Bath & Tennis (R)
(E,F,Hi,J,Sa,So,T)
Naples Beach (R) *(Bi,F,G,So,T)*
Registry (R) *(Bi,E,Sa,So,T)*
Ritz Naples (R) *(Bi,E,F,Sa,So,T,W)*
Orlando:
Buena Vista Palace (H) *(Bi,E,J,Sa,So,T)*
Disney Institute (R) *(Bi,E,G,Sa,Si,So,T)*
Disney's All-Star Music (R) *(So)*
Disney's All-Star Sports (R) *(Si,So)*
Disney's Beach Club (R) *(E,J,Sa,So,T)*
Disney's Boardwalk (H) *(E)*
Disney's Caribbean (R) *(Bi,J,So,W)*
Disney's Contemporary (R) *(E,Si,So)*
Disney's Dixie Landings (R) *(Bi,F,So)*
Disney's Ft. Wilderness (R)
(Bi,F,Hi,Ho,J,So,T)
Disney's Grand Floridian (R)
(E,F,J,Sa,So,T,W)
Disney's Polynesian (R) *(J,So,W)*
Disney's Port Orleans (R) *(Bi,J,So)*
Disney's Wilderness (R) *(Bi,J,So)*
Disney's Yacht (R) *(E,F,Sa,So,T)*
Doubletree (H) *(E,Sa,So,T)*
Grosvenor (R) *(E,Sa,So,T)*
Hilton at Walt Disney (H) *(E,Sa,So)*
Holiday Inn Main Gate (H) *(E,So,T)*
Holiday Inn SunSpree (R) *(E,Sa,So)*
Hyatt Orlando (H) *(E,J,Sa,So,T)*
Hyatt Reg. Grand Cypress (R)
(Bi,E,F,G,Hi,Ho,J,Sa,So,T)
Hyatt Reg. Orlando (H) *(E,G,J,Sa,So)*
Marriott Orl. Downtown (H) *(E,Sa,So)*
Marriott Orl. Int'l Drive (H) *(E,J,Sa,So,T)*
Marriott's Orl. World Ctr (H)
(E,G,J,Sa,Si,So,T)
Omni Rosen (H) *(E,Si,So,T)*
Peabody Orlando (H) *(E,Sa,So,T)*
Radisson Barcelo (H) *(E,J,Sa,Si,So,T)*
Radisson Plaza (H) *(E,J,Sa,So,T)*
Radisson Twin Towers (H) *(E,Sa,So)*
Renaissance Orlando (R) *(E,J,Sa,So,T)*
Residence by Marriott (H) *(E,Sa,So,T)*
Sheraton World (R) *(E,Sa,So,T)*
Travelodge (H) *(So)*
Villas of Grand Cypress (R)
(Bi,G,J,Sa,So,T)
Vistana (R) *(Bi,E,J,Sa,So)*
Walt Disney Dolphin (R) *(E,Sa,So,T)*
Walt Disney Swan (R) *(Bi,E,J,Sa,So,T)*
Westgate Lakes (R) *(Bi,E,F,J,Sa,So,T)*
Palm Beach:
Brazilian Court (H) *(So)*
Breakers (R) *(Bi,E,G,J,So,T)*
Chesterfield (H) *(Sa,So)*
Colony (H) *(Bi,So)*
Four Seasons Palm Beach (H)
(Bi,E,J,Sa,So,T)
Palm Beach Polo (R) *(E,G,Ho,Sa,So,T)*
PGA National (R) *(Bi,E,G,J,Sa,So,T)*
Ritz Palm Beach (R) *(Bi,E,Sa,So,T,W)*
Panama City Beach:
Marriott's Bay Point (R)
(Bi,E,F,G,J,Si,So,T,W)
Pompano Beach:
Palm-Aire Resort (S) *(E,G,J,So,T)*
Ponte Vedra Beach:
Lodge at Ponte Vedra (R) *(Bi,E,J,Sa,So)*

Marriott at Sawgrass (R)
(Bi,E,G,J,Sa,So,T)
Ponte Vedra (R) *(Bi,E,F,G,Hi,Sa,So,T)*
Port St. Lucie:
Club Med Sandpiper (R) *(E,G,So,T,W)*
Safety Harbor:
Safety Harbor (S) *(Bi,E,F,Sa,Si,So,T)*
Sanibel Island:
Casa Ybel (R) *(Bi,F,J,Sa,So,T,W)*
Sanibel (R) *(Bi,J,So,T)*
Sundial Beach (R) *(Bi,E,Hi,Sa,So,T)*
Siesta Key:
Captiva Beach (B) *(So)*
Stuart:
Indian River Plantation (R)
(Bi,E,F,G,J,So,T,W)
Tampa Bay:
Dbltree Tampa Bay (H) *(E,J,Sa,So)*
Don CeSar (R) *(E,J,Sa,So)*
Embassy Westshore (H) *(E,Sa,So)*
Holiday Inn Beachfront (R) *(E,Sa,So)*
Hyatt Reg. Tampa (H) *(E,Sa,So)*
Hyatt Reg. Westshore (H) *(E,F,J,Sa,So,T)*
Innisbrook Hilton (R)
(Bi,E,F,G,Hi,J,Sa,So,T)
Marriott Tampa (H) *(E,Sa,Si,So)*
Radisson Sand Key (R) *(Bi,E,F,Sa,So,W)*
Renaissance Vinoy (R) *(Bi,E,F,T)*
Saddlebrook Tampa (R) *(Bi,E,F,G,Sa,So,T)*
Sheraton Sand Key (R) *(Bi,E,So,T)*
TradeWinds St. Pete (R) *(E,So,T,W)*
Wyndham Harbour (H) *(E,F,J,So)*
West Palm Beach:
Hippocrates Health (S) *(E,J,Sa,So,T)*

Georgia
Atlanta:
Doubletree (H) *(Sa,Si,So)*
Embassy Perimeter Ctr (H) *(E,Sa,Si)*
Evergreen (R) *(Bi,E,F,G,Hi,J,Sa,Si,So,T)*
Four Seasons Atlanta (H) *(Sa,Si)*
French Quarter (H) *(E,Si,So)*
Grand Hyatt Atlanta (H) *(E,Sa,So)*
Hilton Atlanta (H) *(E,J,Sa,So,T)*
Hilton Atlanta Airport (H) *(E,Sa,Si,So,T)*
Holiday Inn Ravinia (H) *(E,Sa,Si,T)*
Hyatt Reg. Atlanta (H) *(E,So)*
Hyatt Reg. Perimeter (H) *(E,Sa,So)*
Marietta (R) *(E,G,Sa,So,T)*
Marque of Atlanta (H) *(Sa,So)*
Marriott Atlanta Airport (H) *(Sa,Si,So,T)*
Marriott JW Lenox (H) *(E,Sa,Si)*
Marriott Marquis Atlanta (H) *(Sa,Si,So)*
Marriott Midtown Atlanta (H) *(E,Sa,Si,So)*
Marriott N. Central Atlanta (H) *(E,J,So,T)*
Marriott NW Atlanta (H) *(J,Sa,Si,So,T)*
Marriott Perimeter Atlanta (H)
(E,Sa,Si,So,T)
Omni CNN Center (H) *(E,Si)*
Peachtree (H) *(Bi,E,G,Sa,Si,So,T,W)*
Renaissance Downtown (H) *(E,So)*
Renaissance Waverly (H) *(E,Sa,Si,So)*
Ritz Atlanta (H) *(E,Sa)*
Ritz Buckhead (H) *(E,Sa,Si)*
Sheraton Colony Square (H) *(So)*
Sheraton Gateway (H) *(E,Sa,Si,So)*
Summerfield (H) *(E,Sa,So)*
Swissotel Atlanta (H) *(E,Sa,Si)*
Terrace Buckhead (H) *(E,Sa,Si,So)*
Westin Atlanta (H) *(E,J,Sa,So)*
Westin Peachtree (H) *(E,Sa,Si,So)*
Wyndham Midtown (H) *(E)*
Wyndham Vinings (H) *(Sa,So)*
Augusta:
Partridge Inn (H) *(So)*

Sports Facilities

Braselton:
 Chateau Elan Winery (B)
 (Bi,E,G,Hi,J,Sa,Si,So,T)
Jekyll Island:
 Jekyll Island Club (R) *(Bi,E,Hi,J,So,T)*
Lake Lanier Islands:
 Renaissance Pineisle (R)
 (E,G,J,Sa,Si,So,T)
Peachtree City:
 Aberdeen Woods (H) *(Bi,E,J,Si,T)*
Pine Mountain:
 Callaway Gardens (R)
 (Bi,E,F,G,Hi,J,Si,So,T,W)
Savannah:
 Gastonian (B) *(Sa)*
 Hyatt Reg. Savannah (H) *(E,Si)*
 Marriott Savannah (H) *(E,Si,So)*
 Mulberry Inn (H) *(Sa)*
 President's Quarters (B) *(Sa)*
Sea Island:
 Cloister (R) *(Bi,E,F,Sa,So,T)*
St. Simons Island:
 King & Prince Beach (R) *(E,J,Sa,Si,So,T)*
 Lodge at Little St. Simons (B)
 (Bi,F,G,Hi,Ho,J,So)
 Sea Palms (R) *(Bi,E,G,Hi,So,T)*

Hawaii
Big Island:
 Four Seasons Hualalai (R) *(E,G,Sa,So,T)*
 Hapuna Prince (R) *(E,G,Sa,So)*
 Hawaii Naniloa (R) *(E,G,Sa,So)*
 Hilton Waikoloa (R) *(Bi,E,F,G,Hi,J,T)*
 Kona Village (R) *(E,F,Sa,So,T)*
 Mauna Kea (R) *(E,G,J,Sa,So,T)*
 Mauna Lani Bay (R) *(E,F,G,Ho,J,Sa,So,T)*
 Orchid at Mauna Lani (R) *(Bi,E,J,Sa,So.T)*
 Royal Waikoloan (R) *(Bi,E,J,Sa,So,T)*
Kauai:
 Hyatt Reg. Kauai (R) *(Bi,E,G,Sa,So,T)*
 Kauai Coconut (R) *(Bi,F,J,Sa,So,T)*
 Marriott Kauai (R) *(E,G,J,So,T)*
 Outrigger Kauai (R) *(So,T)*
 Princeville (R) *(E,Sa,So)*
Lanai:
 Lodge at Koele (R) *(Bi,E,G,Hi,Ho,J,So,T)*
 Manele Bay (R) *(E,F,G,J,Sa,So,T)*
Maui:
 Aston Kaanapali (R) *(E,Sa,So,T)*
 Aston Wailea (R) *(G,J,Sa,So,T)*
 Embassy Maui (R) *(G,So,T)*
 Four Seasons Maui (R) *(Bi,E,Sa,So,T)*
 Grand Wailea (R) *(Bi,E,J,Sa,So)*
 Hana-Maui Hotel (H) *(Bi,E,Hi,Ho,Sa,So,T)*
 Hyatt Reg. Maui (R) *(Bi,E,G,J,Sa,So,T)*
 Ka'anapali Beach (R) *(J,So)*
 Kapalua Bay (R) *(E,G,Hi,J,Si,So,T)*
 Kea Lani (R) *(Bi,E,J,Sa,So)*
 Marriott Maui (R) *(Bi,E,G,Sa,So,T)*
 Maui Prince (R) *(Bi,E,G,Sa,So,T)*
 Renaissance Wailea (R) *(E,G,J,So,T)*
 Ritz Kapalua (R) *(Bi,E,F,G,Hi,J,Sa,So,T)*
 Royal Lahaina (R) *(Sa,So,T)*
 Sheraton Maui (R) *(E,F,Sa,T)*
 Westin Maui (R) *(E,F,Sa,So)*
Oahu:
 Ala Moana (H) *(So)*
 Aston Waikiki (H) *(Sa,So)*
 Halekulani (H) *(E,So)*
 Hawaiian Regent (H) *(Sa,So,T)*
 Hawaii Prince Waikiki (H) *(E,Sa,So)*
 Hilton Hawaiian (H) *(So)*
 Hyatt Reg. Waikiki (H) *(Sa,So)*
 Ihilani Resort (R) *(E,F,G,J,Sa,So,T)*
 Ilikai Nikko Waikiki (H) *(E,So,T)*
 Kahala Mandarin (R) *(E,Sa,So)*

New Otani Kaimana (H) *(Bi,E,F,J,T)*
 Outrigger Prince Kuhio (H) *(Sa,So)*
 Outrigger Reef (R) *(E,Sa,So)*
 Outrigger Waikiki (R) *(E,Sa,So)*
 Pacific Beach (H) *(E,Sa,So,T)*
 Royal Hawaiian (H) *(So)*
 Sheraton Kaiulani (H) *(So)*
 Sheraton Moana (H) *(So)*
 Sheraton Waikiki (H) *(E,So)*
 Waikiki Parc (H) *(So)*

Idaho
Boise:
 Doubletree Club (H) *(E,So)*
 Owyhee Plaza (H) *(So)*
 Red Lion Boise (H) *(Bi,E,J,Sa,So)*
Coeur d'Alene:
 Coeur d'Alene (R)
 (Bi,Bo,E,F,G,Hi,J,Sa,Si,So,T,W)
Ketchum:
 Knob Hill (H) *(E,Sa,Si,So)*
McCall:
 Shore Lodge (B) *(E,Sa,So,T,W)*
Priest Lake:
 Hill's Hospitality (B) *(Bi,F,Hi,J,T,W)*
Sun Valley:
 Sun Valley (R) *(Bi,Bo,E,F,G,I,S,So)*
Tetonia:
 Teton Ridge (B) *(Bi,F,Hi,Ho,S)*

Illinois
Bloomingdale:
 Indian Lakes (R) *(E,G,Sa,Si,So,T)*
Chicago:
 Ambassador West (H) *(E)*
 Clarion (H) *(E)*
 Doubletree (H) *(E,Sa,Si)*
 Drake (H) *(E)*
 Four Seasons Chicago (H) *(Bi,E)*
 Hilton Chicago (H) *(E,J,So)*
 Hilton O'Hare (H) *(Si)*
 Holiday Inn Chicago (H) *(Sa,Si,So,T)*
 Hyatt on Printers Row (H) *(E)*
 Hyatt Reg. Chicago (H) *(E,J,Sa,Si)*
 Hyatt Reg. O'Hare (H) *(E,J,Sa,Si)*
 Inter-Continental Chicago (H) *(E,Sa,Si)*
 La Salle Club (H) *(E,Sa,Si,T)*
 Marriott Chicago (H) *(E,Sa,Si)*
 Marriott O'Hare (H)
 (E,E,J,Sa,Sa,Si,Si,So,T)
 Midland (H) *(E)*
 Omni Chicago (H) *(E,Sa)*
 Palmer Hilton (H) *(E,Sa,Si)*
 Radisson Chicago (H) *(E,So)*
 Renaissance Chicago (H)
 (Bi,Bo,E,J,Sa,Si)
 Ritz Chicago (H) *(E,Sa,Si)*
 Rosemont O'Hare (H) *(E,Sa,Si)*
 Sheraton Chicago (H) *(E,Sa,Si)*
 Sheraton Gateway (H) *(E,Sa,Si)*
 Sofitel (H) *(Sa,Si)*
 Sutton Place (H) *(E)*
 Tremont (H) *(E)*
 Westin Chicago (H) *(E)*
 Westin O'Hare (H) *(E,Sa,Si)*
 Westin River North (H) *(E)*
Galena:
 Eagle Ridge (R) *(Bi,Hi,Ho,I,S,Sa,T)*
Gilman:
 Heartland Spa (S) *(Bi,E,F,Hi,J,S,Sa,So,T)*
Itasca:
 Nordic Hills (R) *(Bo,E,G,Sa,Si,So,T)*
 Wyndham (H) *(E,J,Sa,T)*
Lake Forest:
 Deer Path (B) *(E,G)*

Sports Facilities

Lincolnshire:
   Marriott's Lincolnshire (R) *(E,G,Si,So,T)*
Oak Brook:
   Oak Brook Hills (R) *(E,G,Sa,Si,So,T)*
St. Charles:
   Pheasant Run (R) *(E,G,S,Sa,Si,So,T)*
Whittington:
   Rend Lake (R) *(Bi,F,Ho,So,T,W)*

Indiana
Bloomington:
   Fourwinds (R) *(F,Hi,Sa,Si,So)*
French Lick:
   French Lick Springs (R)
   (Bo,E,G,Hi,Ho,J,Sa,Si,So,T)
Indianapolis:
   Crowne Plaza (H) *(E,Sa,Si)*
   Embassy Indianapolis (H) *(E,Sa,Si)*
   Hyatt Reg. Indianapolis (H) *(E,Sa,Si)*
   Marriott Indianapolis (H) *(E,Sa,Si,So)*
   Omni Severin (H) *(E)*
   Westin Indianapolis (H) *(E,Si)*

Iowa
Bettendorf:
   Jumer's Castle (H) *(E,Sa,Si,So)*
Cedar Rapids:
   Wyndham Five Seasons (R) *(E,Sa,Si)*
Des Moines:
   Embassy (H) *(E)*
   Marriott Des Moines (H) *(E,Si)*
   Savery (H) *(E,J,Sa,Si)*
Fairfield:
   Raj (S) *(E,Hi,J)*

Kansas
Lawrence:
   Eldridge (H) *(E,Sa)*
Topeka:
   Heritage House (B) *(G,So)*
Wichita:
   Marriott Wichita (H) *(E,J,Sa,Si,So)*

Kentucky
Harrodsburg:
   Beaumont Inn (B) *(So,T)*
   Inn at Shaker Village (B) *(Hi)*
Lexington:
   Hilton Lexington (H) *(E,Sa,So)*
   Hyatt Reg. Lexington (H) *(E,Si)*
   Marriott Griffin Gate (R)
   (E,G,Hi,Sa,Si,So,T)
Louisville:
   Camberly Brown (H) *(E)*
   Club Hotel by Dbltree. (H) *(E,Sa,Si)*
   Galt House East (H) *(So)*
   Hyatt Reg. Louisville (H) *(E,Sa,Si,T)*
   Marriott E. Louisville (H) *(E)*

Louisiana
New Orleans:
   Best Western Bourbon (H) *(E)*
   Bienville House (B) *(So)*
   Chateau Sonesta (H) *(E,So)*
   Crowne Plaza New Orleans (H) *(E,So)*
   Dauphine Orleans (H) *(E,Sa,So)*
   Dbltree New Orleans (H) *(E,So)*
   De La Poste (H) *(So)*
   Fairmont New Orleans (H) *(E,J,So,T)*
   Hilton New Orleans (H) *(E,J,Sa,So,T)*
   Holiday Inn Le Moyne (H) *(So)*
   Hyatt Reg. New Orleans (H) *(E,Sa,So)*
   Inter-Continental (H) *(E,So)*
   Lafayette (H) *(J)*
   Le Meridien (H) *(Sa,So)*
   Le Pavillon (H) *(E,Sa,So)*
   Le Richelieu (H) *(So)*
   Maison de Ville (B) *(So)*
   Maison Dupuy (H) *(E,So)*

Marriott New Orleans (H) *(E,Sa,So)*
Melrose Mansion (B) *(E,So)*
Monteleone (H) *(E,So)*
Omni Royal Crescent (H) *(E,Sa,So)*
Omni Royal Orleans (H) *(E,So)*
Place d'Armes (H) *(So)*
Radisson New Orleans (H) *(Sa,So)*
Royal Sonesta (H) *(E,So)*
Sheraton New Orleans (H) *(E,Sa,So)*
St. Ann (H) *(So)*
Westin Canal (H) *(E,So)*
Windsor Court (H) *(G,Sa,So,T)*
Wyndham Riverfront (H) *(E)*
St. Francisville:
   Lodge at the Bluffs (H) *(Bi,G,Hi,So,T)*
White Castle:
   Nottoway Plantation (B) *(So)*

Maine
Bar Harbor:
   Atlantic Oakes (B) *(Si,So,T)*
   Bar Harbor Bluenose (B) *(E,Sa,Si,So)*
   Bar Harbor Inn (B)
   (Bi,E,F,G,Hi,Ho,I,J,S,Sa,So,T)
   Bayview (H) *(E,Si,So,T)*
Boothbay Harbor:
   Spruce Point (B) *(F,Sa,So,T)*
Cape Elizabeth:
   Inn by the Sea (B) *(Bi,Hi,J,So,T)*
East Holden:
   Lucerne Inn (B) *(So)*
Kennebunkport:
   Inn at Harbor Head (B) *(F,W)*
   Kennebunkport Inn (B) *(So)*
   White Barn Inn (B) *(Bi,J,S,Sa,So)*
Northeast Harbor:
   Asticou Inn (B) *(Bi,Hi)*
Ogunquit:
   Cliff House (H) *(E,Sa,Si,So,T)*
Portland:
   Marriott at Sable Oaks (H) *(E,Sa,Si)*
   Radisson Portland (H) *(E)*
   Regency Portland (H) *(E,Sa)*
   Sheraton Portland (H) *(E,Sa,Si)*
Raymond:
   Northern Pines (S) *(E,F,Hi,I,J,S,Sa)*
Rockport:
   Samoset (R) *(Bi,E,F,G,I,J,S,Sa,Si,So,T)*
Scarborough:
   Black Point Inn (R)
   (Bi,E,F,G,Hi,J,Sa,Si,So,T)

Maryland
(see also Washington, DC)
Annapolis:
   Loews Annapolis (H) *(E)*
   Marriott Annapolis (H) *(E,F,W)*
Baltimore:
   Admiral Fell Inn (B) *(J)*
   Cross Keys Inn (H) *(Bi,J,Sa,So,T)*
   Dbltree Colonnade (H) *(E,Sa)*
   Harbor Court (H) *(Sa,T)*
   Hyatt Reg. Baltimore (H) *(E,J,Sa,So,T)*
   Inn at Henderson's (B) *(Bi,E,J)*
   Marriott Baltimore (H) *(E,Sa,Si)*
   Marriott's Hunt Valley (H) *(E,Sa,Si,So,T)*
   Omni Inner Harbor (H) *(E,Si)*
   Radisson Lord Baltimore (H) *(E,Sa)*
   Renaissance Harborplace (H) *(E,J,Sa,Si)*
   Sheraton Baltimore (H) *(E,Sa,Si)*
   Sheraton Inner Harbor (H) *(E,Sa,Si)*
Berlin:
   Atlantic (H) *(G)*
Easton:
   Tidewater Inn (B) *(So)*

Sports Facilities

Ocean City:
Coconut Malorie (H) *(G,So)*
Dunes Manor (H) *(E,Sa,Si,So)*
Sheraton Fontainebleau (H) *(E,F,Sa,Si)*
St. Michaels:
Inn at Perry Cabin (B) *(Bi,E,F,Sa,Si)*
Stevensville:
Kent Manor (H) *(Bi,J,So,T)*
Taneytown:
Antrim 1844 (B) *(Sa,So,T)*

Massachusetts

Boston:
Boston Harbor (H) *(Sa,Si)*
Boston Park Plaza (H) *(E)*
Charles in Harvard Square (H) *(E,J,Sa,Si)*
Colonnade (H) *(E)*
Doubletree (H) *(E,Sa,Si)*
Eliot (H) *(E)*
Fairmont Copley (H) *(E,Sa,Si)*
Four Seasons Boston (H) *(E,Sa,Si)*
Hilton Boston Back Bay (H) *(E,Si)*
Hyatt Harborside (H) *(E,J,Sa,Si)*
Hyatt Reg. Cambridge (H) *(Bi,E,Sa,Si)*
Le Meridien (H) *(E,Sa,Si)*
Lenox (H) *(E)*
Marriott Copley Place (H) *(E,Sa,Si)*
Marriott Long Wharf (H) *(E,Sa,Si)*
Newbury (B) *(G)*
Renaissance Bedford (H) *(E,J,Sa,Si,T)*
Ritz Boston (H) *(E)*
Royal Sonesta (H) *(Bi,E,Sa,Si,So)*
Sheraton Boston (H) *(E,Sa,Si,So)*
Sheraton Commander (H) *(E)*
Swissotel (H) *(E,Sa,Si)*
Tremont House (H) *(E)*
Westin Copley Place (H) *(E,Sa,Si)*
Westin Waltham-Boston (H) *(E,Sa,Si)*
Cape Cod:
Brass Key (B) *(Sa,So)*
Cape Codder (B) *(Si,So)*
Chatham Bars (B) *(Bi,E,G,So,T)*
Dan'l Webster Inn (B) *(So)*
Dunscroft by the Sea (B) *(F,G,T)*
New Seabury (R) *(Bi,E,G,J,Sa,So,T)*
Ocean Edge (R) *(Bi,E,G,J,Sa,Si,So,T)*
Sea Crest (R) *(Bi,E,Hi,Sa,Si,So)*
Wequassett Inn (B) *(Bi,E,F,J)*
Whalewalk Inn (B) *(Bi)*
Danvers:
Tara's Ferncroft (R) *(E,G,J,S,Sa,Si,So,T,W)*
Deerfield:
Deerfield Inn (B) *(Hi,J)*
Lenox:
Blantyre (B) *(Bi,E,Hi,J,Sa,So,T)*
Canyon Ranch (S) *(Bi,E,Hi,J,S,Sa,Si,So,T)*
Cranwell (R) *(Bi,E,G,J,S,So,T)*
Gables Inn (B) *(So,T)*
Kripalu Center (S) *(Bi,F,Hi,I,J,Sa)*
Wheatleigh (B) *(E,Hi,J,So,T)*
Martha's Vineyard:
Harbor View (B) *(Sa,So,T)*
Outermost Inn (B) *(Bi,F,Hi,J)*
Nantucket:
Beachside Nantucket (H) *(Si)*
Centerboard (B) *(Bi,Hi)*
Cliffside Beach (H) *(Bi,E,F)*
Harbor House (B) *(So)*
Nantucket Inn (H) *(E,Sa,Si,So,T)*
Summer House (B) *(Sa,So)*
Wauwinet (B) *(Bi,F,Hi,T)*
White Elephant (R) *(Sa,So)*
Northampton:
Northampton (H) *(E)*
Peabody:
Marriott Peabody (H) *(E,Sa,Si)*

Rockport:
Yankee Clipper (B) *(So)*
Salem:
Hawthorne (H) *(E)*
Stockbridge:
Red Lion (B) *(E,So)*
Sturbridge:
Publick House (B) *(Hi,J,So,T)*
Williamstown:
Orchards (B) *(E,Sa,So)*

Michigan

Acme:
Grand Traverse (R)
(Bi,E,G,Hi,I,J,S,Sa,Si,So,T,W)
Bellaire:
Shanty Creek (R)
(Bi,E,F,G,Hi,I,J,S,Sa,Si,So,T,W)
Boyne Falls:
Boyne Mountain (R) *(Bi,E,F,G,Hi,I,J,S,So)*
Detroit:
Crowne Pontchartrain (H) *(E,Sa,So)*
Dbltree Detroit (H) *(E,J,Sa,Si,T)*
Hilton Novi (H) *(E)*
Hyatt Reg. Dearborn (H) *(E,Sa,Si)*
Marriott Dearborn (H) *(E,So,T)*
Marriott Southfield (H) *(Sa,Si)*
Radisson Plaza (H) *(E,Sa,Si)*
Ritz Dearborn (H) *(E,Sa,Si)*
River Place (H) *(E,Si,T)*
St. Regis (H) *(E)*
Westin Renaissance (H) *(E,J,Sa,Si)*
Grand Rapids:
Amway Grand (H) *(E,Sa,Si,T)*
Harbor Springs:
Boyne Highlands (R) *(Bi,E,F,G,I,S,Sa,So,T)*
Mackinac Island:
Grand (H) *(Bi,E,F,G,Hi,Ho,J,Sa,So,T)*
Mission Point (R) *(Bi,Sa,So,T)*
New Buffalo:
Harbor Grand (H) *(E,Si)*
Petoskey:
Stafford's Bay View (B) *(Bi)*
Thompsonville:
Crystal Mountain (R)
(Bi,E,G,Hi,I,J,S,Sa,So,T)
Traverse City:
Waterfront Inn (R) *(E,F,Sa,Si,W)*
Ypsilanti:
Marriott Ypsilanti (R) *(E,G,J,Sa,Si)*

Minnesota

Alexandria:
Arrowwood Radisson (R)
(Bi,E,F,G,Hi,Ho,I,J,S,Sa,Si,So,T,W)
Brainerd:
Madden's (R)
(Bi,Bo,E,F,G,Hi,Sa,Si,So,T,W)
Hibbing:
Kahler Park (H) *(J,S,Sa,Si)*
Litchfield:
Birdwing Spa (S) *(Bi,E,Hi,I,J,S,Sa,So)*
Lutsen:
Lutsen (R) *(F,G,Hi,J,Sa,Si,T)*
Minneapolis/St. Paul:
Dbltree Mall of America (H) *(E,Sa,Si)*
Embassy Minneapolis (H) *(Sa,Si,T)*
Hilton Minneapolis (H) *(E,Sa,Si)*
Hyatt Reg. Minneapolis (H) *(E,Sa,Si,T)*
Marquette (H) *(E,Sa)*
Marriott Minneapolis (H) *(E,Sa)*
Radisson Conference (H) *(E,Hi,J,Sa,Si,T)*
Radisson Metrodome (H) *(Bi,Hi)*
Radisson Minneapolis (H) *(Sa)*
Radisson Plaza Tower (H) *(E,Sa,Si)*
Saint Paul (H) *(E)*

Sports Facilities

Sheraton Park Place (H) *(Bi,E,Sa)*
Sofitel (H) *(E,J,Si)*
Pine River:
  McGuire's (B) *(F,G,Hi,Ho,S,So,T)*
Rochester:
  Kahler (H) *(E,Sa)*
  Kahler Plaza (H) *(E,Sa,Si)*

Mississippi
Biloxi:
  Grand Casino (H) *(Bi,E,G,Sa,So,T)*
Jackson:
  Milsaps Buie House (H) *(G,Hi)*
Natchez:
  Briars Inn (B) *(Hi,So)*
  Burn (B) *(So)*
  Monmouth Plantation (B) *(F,Hi)*
Oxford:
  Barksdale-Isom (B) *(Bi,Bo,E,F,G)*
Robinsonville:
  Harrah's Mardi Gras (H) *(E,F)*
  Hollywood Casino (H) *(Sa,Si)*
  Horseshoe Casino (H) *(So)*
  Sam's (H) *(E,J,Sa,So)*
Vicksburg:
  Cedar Grove (B) *(Bi,Sa,So,T)*

Missouri
Kansas:
  Dbltree Corporate Woods (H) *(E,J,Sa,Si)*
  Marriott Overland Park (H) *(E,Si,So)*
Branson:
  Best Western Knights (H) *(E,Sa,Si,So)*
  Best Western Mtn Oak (H) *(So)*
  Best Western Music (H) *(E,Sa,Si)*
  Chateau on the Lake (R) *(E,Si,So)*
  Clarion at Fall Creek (R) *(E,F,Si,So,T)*
  Red Bud Cove B&B (B) *(Bi,F,Hi,J)*
Hannibal:
  Garth Woodside (B) *(F)*
Kansas City:
  Adam's Mark (H) *(E,Sa,Si,So)*
  Historic Suites of America (B) *(E,Sa,So)*
  Holiday Inn Crowne Plaza (H) *(Sa,Si)*
  Hyatt Reg. Crown Ctr (H) *(E,T)*
  Marriott Downtown (H) *(E,Sa,Si)*
  Radisson (H) *(E)*
  Ritz Kansas City (H) *(E,Sa,So)*
  Sheraton Kansas City (H) *(E,Sa,Si,So)*
  Southmoreland (H) *(J,T)*
  Westin Crown Ctr (H) *(E,J,Sa,So,T)*
Lake Ozark:
  Lodge at Four Seasons (R)
  (Bi,Bo,G,Hi,Ho,Sa,Si,So,T)
Osage Beach:
  Marriott's Tan-Tar-A (R)
  (Bo,E,F,G,Ho,I,J,Sa,Si,So,T,W)
Ridgedale:
  Big Cedar (R) *(E,F,G,Hi,Ho,J,Sa,So,T,W)*
St. Louis:
  Adam's Mark (H) *(E,Sa,Si,So)*
  Cheshire Inn (H) *(Si,So)*
  Crowne Plaza Majestic (H) *(E)*
  Daniele (H) *(So)*
  Doubletree (H) *(E,J,Sa,Si,So,T)*
  Drury Inn (H) *(E,Sa,Si)*
  Embassy St. Louis (H) *(E,Sa,Si)*
  Frontenac Hilton (H) *(Bi,E,G,J,Sa,So)*
  Harley St. Louis (H) *(Sa,Si,So)*
  Holiday Inn Riverfront (H) *(So)*
  Hyatt Reg. St. Louis (H) *(E,Sa,So)*
  Marriott Pavilion (H) *(E,Sa,Si)*
  Marriott St. Louis (H) *(E,J,Si,So)*
  Ritz St. Louis (H) *(E,Sa,Si)*
  Sheraton Plaza (H) *(Sa,Si)*

Montana
Bigfork:
  Averill's Flathead (B)
  (Bi,F,Hi,Ho,J,So,T,W)
Big Sky:
  Huntley Lodge (R) *(F,G,Hi,Ho,S,Sa,Si,So,T)*
  Lone Mountain (B) *(F,Hi,Ho,S,Sa)*
Bozeman:
  Mountain Sky (B) *(F,Hi,Ho,Sa,So,T)*
Darby:
  Triple Creek Ranch (R)
  (Bi,E,F,G,Hi,Ho,J,S,So,T)
Gallatin Gateway:
  Gallatin Gateway (B) *(Bi,F,Hi,I,J,T)*
  320 Guest Ranch (B) *(F,Ho)*
Red Lodge:
  Pollard (B)
  (Bi,Bo,E,F,G,Hi,Ho,I,J,S,Sa,So,T)
Whitefish:
  Grouse Mountain (R) *(Bi,Sa,Si,T)*
  North Forty (B) *(Hi,Sa)*

Nebraska
Beatrice:
  Carriage House (B) *(Hi,J)*
Omaha:
  Marriott Omaha (H) *(E,Sa,Si,So)*
  Radisson Redick (H) *(E,Sa)*
  Red Lion Omaha (H) *(E,Sa,Si)*
Waterloo:
  JC Robinson B&B (B) *(J)*

Nevada
Crystal Bay:
  Cal-Neva Resort (R)
  (Bi,Bo,E,F,G,Hi,Ho,I,J,S,Sa,So,T,W)
Lake Tahoe:
  Caesars Tahoe (R) *(E,J,Sa,Si,T)*
  Harrah's Lake Tahoe (R) *(E,G,Hi,J,Sa,Si)*
  Hyatt Reg. Lake Tahoe (R)
  (Bi,E,F,Hi,Sa,So,T,W)
  Lake Tahoe Horizon (H) *(E,Hi,Sa,So)*
Las Vegas:
  Aladdin (H) *(So,T)*
  Alexis Park (H) *(E,Sa,So)*
  Bally's Las Vegas (H) *(E,So,T)*
  Binion's Horseshoe (H) *(So)*
  Caesars Palace (H) *(E,Sa,So,T)*
  Circus Circus (H) *(Sa,So)*
  Desert Inn (R) *(E,G,Sa,So,T)*
  Excalibur (H) *(Sa,So)*
  Flamingo Hilton (H) *(E,So,T)*
  Frontier (H) *(Sa,So,T)*
  Golden Nugget (H)
  (Bi,Bo,E,F,G,Hi,Ho,I,J,S,Sa,So,T,W)
  Hard Rock (H) *(Sa,So)*
  Harrah's Casino (H) *(E,Sa,So)*
  Hilton Las Vegas (H) *(G,Sa,So,T)*
  Lady Luck Casino (H) *(So)*
  Luxor Las Vegas (H) *(E,Sa,So)*
  Maxim (H) *(So)*
  MGM Grand (H) *(E,So,T)*
  Mirage (H) *(E,Sa,So)*
  NY Hotel & Casino (H) *(E,Sa,So)*
  Rio Suite (H) *(E,Sa,So)*
  Riviera (H) *(E,Sa,So,T)*
  Stardust (H) *(Sa,So)*
  Stratosphere (H) *(E,So)*
  Treasure Island (H) *(E,Si)*
  Tropicana (H) *(G,T)*
Laughlin:
  Don Laughlin's (H) *(So,W)*
  Flamingo Hilton (H) *(J,So,T)*
  Golden Nugget (H) *(Sa,So)*
  Harrah's Laughlin (H) *(E)*

Sports Facilities

Mesquite:
Players Island (R) *(E,Sa,So,W)*
Reno:
Eldorado (H) *(Sa,So)*
Flamingo Hilton (H) *(E)*
Harrah's & Hampton (H) *(E,Si,So)*
John Ascuaga's (H) *(E,J,Sa,Si,So)*
Peppermill (H) *(E,Sa,So)*
Silver Legacy (H) *(Sa,So)*

New Hampshire
Bretton Woods:
1896 Bretton Arms (B)
(Bi,F,G,Hi,S,Sa,Si,T)
Mount Washington (R) *(Bi,F,G,Hi,J,Si,T)*
Dixville Notch:
Balsams Grand (R) *(Bi,F,G,I,J,S,So,T)*
Franconia:
Franconia Inn (B)
(Bi,F,Hi,Ho,I,J,S,Sa,So,T)
Holderness:
Manor on Golden Pond (B) *(F,I,Sa,So)*
Jackson:
Christmas Farm (B) *(Bi,Sa,So)*
Eagle Mountain (H) *(E,F,G)*
Lincoln:
Mountain Club (R)
(Bi,E,F,Hi,Ho,I,J,S,Sa,Si,So,T)
Meredith:
Inn at Mill Falls (B) *(F,I,S,Sa,Si,W)*
North Conway:
Four Points Sheraton (H)
(E,Hi,I,Sa,Si,So,T)
White Mountain (R) *(E,G,Hi,J,Sa,So,T)*
Waterville Valley:
Waterville Valley (R) *(Bi,E,F,G,Hi,Sa,Si,T)*

New Jersey
Atlantic City:
Atlantic Palace (H) *(Sa,So)*
Bally's Park Place (H) *(E,Sa,Si)*
Caesar Atlantic City (H)
(Bi,E,F,Sa,So,T,W)
Claridge Casino (H) *(E,Si)*
Harrah's Casino (H) *(E,Sa,Si,T)*
Hilton Atlantic City (H) *(E,G,Sa,Si)*
Marriott Seaview (R) *(Bi,E,Hi,J,Sa,Si,So,T)*
Merv Griffin's (H) *(E,Sa,Si,So)*
Sands (H) *(E,Sa)*
Showboat Casino (H) *(Bo,E,Sa,So)*
Tropicana Casino (H) *(J,Si,So,T)*
Trump Plaza (H) *(E,Sa,Si,T)*
Trump's Castle (H) *(E,J,So,T)*
Trump Taj Mahal (H) *(E,Sa,Si)*
Trump World's Fair (H) *(E,Sa,Si,T)*
Basking Ridge:
Olde Mill Inn (B) *(E)*
Beach Haven:
Green Gables (B) *(Bi)*
Cape May:
Angel of the Sea (B) *(Bi)*
Hope:
Inn at Millrace Pond (B) *(Bi,T)*
Lambertville:
Inn at Lambertville (B) *(Bi,Hi)*
Long Beach:
Ocean Place Hilton (R) *(E,Sa,Si,So,T)*
Morristown:
Headquarters Plaza (H) *(E,J,Sa,Si)*
Princeton:
Chauncey Conference (H) *(Bi,E,Hi,I,J)*
Forrestal (H) *(Bi,E,J,Sa,Si,T)*
Hyatt Reg. Princeton (H) *(E,J,Sa,Si,T)*
Marriott Princeton (H) *(Si,So)*
Nassau Inn (H) *(E)*

Short Hills:
Hilton at Short Hills (H) *(E,Sa,Si,So,T)*
Spring Lake:
Breakers (B) *(Sa,So)*
Sea Crest by the Sea (B)
(Bi,Bo,F,G,Hi,Ho,I,J,Sa,So,T)
Summit:
Grand Summit (H) *(E,So)*
Vernon:
Great Gorge Village (R)
(E,F,G,Hi,S,Sa,Si,So,T)

New Mexico
Albuquerque:
Crowne Plaza (H) *(E,J,Sa,Si,So)*
Dbltree Albuquerque (H) *(E)*
Hilton Albuquerque (H) *(E,T)*
Hyatt Reg. Albuquerque (H) *(E,G,Sa,So)*
Marriott Albuquerque (H) *(E,Sa,Si,So)*
Sheraton Old Town (H) *(E,Sa,So)*
Chama:
Lodge at Chama (B) *(F,Hi,Ho,S,Sa)*
Chimayo:
Hacienda Rancho (B) *(F,Hi,S)*
Cloudcroft:
Lodge at Cloudcroft (B)
(Bi,G,Hi,J,S,Sa,So)
Española:
Rancho de San Juan (R) *(Bi,Hi,J,Sa)*
Mescalero:
Inn of Mountain Gods (R)
(Bi,F,Hi,Ho,S,Sa,So,T)
Raton:
Vermejo Park (B) *(F,Hi,Ho)*
Santa Fe:
Bishop's Lodge (R) *(E,F,Hi,Ho,Sa,So,T)*
Eldorado (H) *(E,Sa,So)*
House of the Moon (S) *(G,S,T)*
Inn at Loretto (B) *(Bi,J,So)*
Inn of Governors (B) *(So)*
Inn on the Alameda (B) *(Sa)*
La Fonda (H) *(Sa,So)*
La Posada Santa Fe (H) *(So)*
Radisson Santa Fe (H) *(E,Sa,So)*
Rancho Encantado (B) *(Hi,Ho,J,Sa,So,T)*
Santa Fe (H) *(Sa,So)*
Taos:
Casa Benavides (B) *(Sa)*
Fechin Inn (B) *(E,Sa)*
Historic Taos (B) *(Sa,So)*
Quail Ridge (R) *(E,Sa,So)*
Sagebrush Inn (B) *(Sa,So)*
Taos Ski Valley:
Edelweiss (B) *(F,Hi,Ho,J,S,Sa,T)*
St. Bernard (B) *(E,Hi,S,Sa)*

New York
Albany:
Desmond (H) *(E,Sa,Si)*
Marriott Albany (H) *(E,Sa,Si,So)*
Omni Albany (H) *(E,Sa,Si)*
Alexandria Bay:
Bonnie Castle (R) *(Sa,Si,So,T)*
Riveredge (H) *(E,F,Sa,Si,So)*
Amenia:
Troutbeck (B) *(E,F,J,Sa,Si,So,T)*
Bolton Landing:
Sagamore (R) *(Bi,E,F,Hi,I.J,S,Sa.Si,T,W)*
Cooperstown:
Otesaga (H) *(G,So,T)*
Dover Plains:
Old Drovers Inn (B) *(Bi)*
Ellenville:
Nevele (R) *(E,F,G,Hi,Ho,I,J,S,Sa,Si,So,T)*
Garden City:
Garden City (H) *(E,Sa,Si)*

467

Sports Facilities

Geneva:
  Geneva on the Lake (B) *(Bi,F,So)*
Glen Cove:
  Harrison (H) *(Bo,E,J,Sa,Si,So)*
Great Neck:
  Inn at Great Neck (H) *(E)*
Hopewell Junction:
  Le Chambord (B) *(E)*
Hunter:
  Vatra Mountain (S) *(E,Hi)*
Ithaca:
  Rose Inn (B) *(F,Hi)*
Kiamesha Lake:
  Concord (R) *(E,G,Ho,I,J,S,Sa,Si,So,T)*
Lake Placid:
  Lake Placid Lodge (B) *(Bi,F,G,Hi,J)*
  Mirror Lake (B) *(E,F,I,S,Sa,Si,So,T)*
Lew Beach:
  Beaverkill Valley (B) *(F,Hi,I,J,S,Si,T)*
Montauk:
  Gurney's Inn (S) *(E,Sa)*
  Montauk Yacht (R) *(E,Sa,Si,So,T)*
Monticello:
  Kutsher's (R)
  (Bi,E,F,G,Hi,I,J,S,Sa,Si,So,T,W)
Neversink:
  New Age Health Spa (S)
  (E,Hi,J,S,Sa,Si,So,T)
New Paltz:
  Mohonk Mountain (R)
  (E,F,G,Hi,Ho,I,J,Sa,T)
New York City:
  Beekman Tower (H) *(E,Sa)*
  Best Western Manhattan (H) *(E)*
  Carlyle (H) *(E,Sa)*
  Crowne Plaza (H) *(E,Si)*
  Doral Inn (H) *(Sa)*
  Doubletree (H) *(E)*
  Dumont Plaza (H) *(E,Sa)*
  Eastgate Tower (H) *(E)*
  Essex House Nikko (H) *(E,Sa)*
  59th St. Bridge Apts (H) *(Bi)*
  Flatotel International (H) *(E)*
  Four Seasons (H) *(E,Sa)*
  Gorham (H) *(E)*
  Hilton & Towers NY (H) *(E)*
  Inter-Continental NY (H) *(E,Sa)*
  Le Parker Meridien (H) *(E,Sa,Si)*
  Loews NY (H) *(E,Sa,T)*
  Lombardy (H) *(E)*
  Lowell (H) *(E)*
  Mark (H) *(Sa)*
  Marriott East Side (H) *(E)*
  Marriott Financial Ctr (H) *(E,Sa,Si)*
  Marriott Marquis (H) *(E,Sa)*
  Marriott World Trade (H) *(J,Sa,Si)*
  Mayflower (H) *(E)*
  Millenium Hilton (H) *(E,Sa,Si)*
  Millennium Broadway (H) *(E,Sa)*
  Novotel NY (H) *(E)*
  NY Palace (H) *(Sa)*
  Omni Berkshire (H) *(E)*
  Peninsula NY (H) *(E,Sa,Si)*
  Pierre (H) *(E)*
  Plaza (H) *(E)*
  Plaza Athénée (H) *(E)*
  Quality East Side (H) *(E)*
  Quality Rockefeller Ctr (H) *(E)*
  Ramada Milford (H) *(E)*
  Regency (H) *(E,Sa)*
  Renaissance NY (H) *(E)*
  Rihga Royal (H) *(E,Sa)*
  Ritz New York (H) *(E)*
  Roosevelt (H) *(I)*
  Royalton (H) *(E)*

  Shelburne Murray Hill (H) *(E,Sa)*
  Sheraton NY (H) *(E,Sa)*
  Sherry Netherland (H) *(E)*
  Southgate Tower (H) *(E)*
  Stanhope (H) *(E,Sa)*
  St. Regis (H) *(Sa)*
  Surrey (H) *(E)*
  Trump International (H) *(Bi,E,J,Sa,Si)*
  Tudor (H) *(E,Sa)*
  UN Plaza Park Hyatt (H) *(E,Sa,Si,T)*
  Waldorf Astoria (H) *(E,Sa)*
  Waldorf Towers (H) *(E,Sa)*
  Wales (H) *(E,J)*
  Warwick (H) *(E)*
  Washington Square (H) *(E)*
  Westbury (H) *(E,Sa)*
North Hudson:
  Elk Lake Lodge (R) *(Bi,Hi,J,So)*
Old Chatham:
  Old Chatham Inn (B) *(Bi,F,Hi)*
Rhinebeck:
  Beekman Arms (B) *(Bi,Hi,J)*
Rye Brook:
  Doral Arrowwood (R) *(E,G,Sa,Si,So,T)*
Saranac Lake:
  Point (B) *(F,Hi,I,J,T,W)*
Saratoga Springs:
  Gideon Putnam (H) *(Bi,G,Hi,So,T)*
  Sheraton Saratoga (R) *(E,Sa,Si)*
Shandaken:
  Shandaken Inn (B) *(F,Hi,I,J,So,T)*
Shelter Island:
  Chequit Inn (B) *(Bi,F,T)*
  Ram's Head (B) *(Bi,E,F,Hi,Sa,T)*
Tarrytown:
  Castle at Tarrytown (B) *(E)*
  Marriott Westchester (H) *(E,Sa,Si,So)*
  Tarrytown House (B) *(Bo,E,J,Sa,Si,So,T)*

North Carolina
Asheville:
  Great Smokies (R) *(E,G,Sa,So,T)*
  Grove Park Inn (R) *(Bi,E,G,J,Sa,Si,So,T)*
Blowing Rock:
  Hound Ears (R) *(E,G,So,T)*
  Westglow Spa (S) *(E,Hi,Sa,Si,T)*
Cashiers:
  High Hampton (R) *(Bi,E,F,G,Hi,J)*
Charlotte:
  Adam's Mark (H) *(E,Sa,Si,So)*
  Hyatt Charlotte (H) *(E,Sa,Si)*
  Marriott Charlotte (H) *(Bo,E,Si)*
  Park (H) *(E,Sa,So)*
  Radisson Charlotte (H) *(E,Sa,So)*
  Westin Charlotte (H) *(E,J,Sa,Si)*
Duck:
  Sanderling Inn (R) *(E,F,J,Sa,Si,So,T)*
Durham:
  Structure House (S) *(E,Si,So)*
Edenton:
  Lords Proprietors' (B)
  (Bi,F,G,Hi,Ho,J,So,T)
Fayetteville:
  Radisson Prince Charles (H) *(E)*
Lake Toxaway:
  Greystone Inn (B) *(Bi,F,G,Hi,Sa,So,T,W)*
Nags Head:
  First Colony (H) *(F,So,W)*
Pinehurst:
  Holly Inn (B) *(G,T)*
  Pinehurst (R) *(Bi,E,F,G,J,So,T)*
Pittsboro:
  Fearrington House (B) *(Bi,G,J,So,T)*
Raleigh-Durham:
  Four Points Raleigh (H) *(E,Si)*

Sports Facilities

Hilton North Raleigh (H) *(E,J,Sa,Si)*
Marriott at Research (H) *(E,Sa,Si)*
Marriott Crabtree (H) *(E,Sa,Si,So)*
Omni Chapel Hill (H) *(So,T)*
Washington Duke (H) *(G,J,So)*
Wrightsville Beach:
Blockade Runner (R) *(Bi,E,F,Hi,Sa,Si,So)*

North Dakota
Bismarck:
Holiday Inn Bismarck (H) *(E,Sa,Si)*
Radisson Bismarck (H) *(E,Sa,Si)*
Fargo:
Best Western Doublewood (H) *(E,Sa,Si)*
Radisson Fargo (H) *(E,Sa)*
Jamestown:
Country Charm (B) *(Bi,S)*
Luverne:
Volden Farm B&B (B) *(Bi,E,Hi,J,S)*

Ohio
Aurora:
Aurora Inn (H) *(Sa,Si,So,T)*
Mario's International (S) *(Bi,Sa,Si,So)*
Cincinnati:
Cincinnatian (H) *(E,Sa)*
Doubletree (H) *(E,Sa,Si,So)*
Hyatt Reg. Cincinnati (H) *(Sa,Si)*
Marriott Cincinnati (H) *(E,Sa,Si,So)*
Omni Netherland (H) *(E,Sa,Si)*
Regal Cincinnati (H) *(E,Sa,So)*
Westin (H) *(E,Sa,Si)*
Cleveland:
Embassy (H) *(E,Sa,Si,T)*
Renaissance Cleveland (H) *(E,Si)*
Ritz Cleveland (H) *(E,Sa,Si)*
Sheraton Cleveland (H) *(E)*
Wyndham Cleveland (H) *(E,Sa,Si)*
Columbus:
Holiday Inn (H) *(E,Sa,Si)*
Hyatt on Capital Square (H) *(E,Sa)*
Hyatt Reg. Columbus (H) *(E,Si)*
Marriott N. Columbus (H) *(E,J,Sa,Si,So)*
Renaissance Dublin (H) *(E,Sa,Si)*
Sheraton Columbus (H) *(E,Si,So)*
Dellroy:
Atwood Lake (R)
(Bi,E,F,G,Hi,J,S,Sa,Si,So,T)
Grand Rapids:
Kerr House (S) *(Sa)*
Huron:
Sawmill Creek (R) *(E,F,G,Hi,Sa,Si,So,T)*
Millersburg:
Inn at Honey Run (B) *(E,Hi)*
Painesville:
Quail Hollow (R) *(Bi,E,G,Hi,J,Sa,Si,So,T)*

Oklahoma
Afton:
Shangri-La (R) *(E)*
Checotah:
Fountainhead (R) *(G,Hi,J,Sa,Si,So,T)*
Kingston:
Texoma State (R)
(Bi,E,F,G,Hi,Ho,J,Sa,Si,So,T,W)
Norman:
Holmberg House (B) *(F,G,W)*
Oklahoma City:
Marriott Oklahoma City (H) *(E,Sa,Si,So)*
Radisson Oklahoma City (H) *(E,Sa,Si,So,T)*
Waterford (H) *(E,Sa,So)*
Tulsa:
Adam's Mark Tulsa (H) *(Si,So)*
Sheraton Tulsa (H) *(E,Si,So)*

Oregon
Bend:
Inn of Seventh Mtn (R)
(Bi,Hi,Ho,I,J,Sa,So,T)
Black Butte Ranch:
Black Butte (R)
(Bi,E,F,G,Hi,Ho,J,Sa,Si,So,T)
Eugene:
Valley River (H) *(Bi,E,J,Sa,So)*
Gleneden Beach:
Salishan (R) *(E,G,Hi,J,Sa,Si,T)*
Gold Beach:
Tu Tu'Tun (B) *(F,G,Hi,Sa,So)*
Hood River:
Columbia Gorge (H) *(Bi)*
Lincoln City:
Inn at Spanish Head (B) *(E,Sa,So)*
Newport:
Embarcadero (H) *(F,Sa,Si)*
Sylvia Beach (H) *(Hi,J)*
Portland:
Benson (H) *(E,Sa)*
5th Avenue Suites (H)
(Bi,Bo,E,F,G,Hi,Ho,I,J,S,Sa,Si,T,W)
Governor (H) *(E,Sa,Si)*
Greenwood Inn (B) *(E,Sa,So)*
Heathman (H) *(E)*
Marriott Portland (H) *(Bi,E,Sa,Si)*
Vintage Plaza (H) *(E)*
Steamboat:
Steamboat Inn (B) *(Bi,F,Hi,J,S)*
Sunriver:
Sunriver (R) *(Bi,F,G,Hi,Ho,J,S,Sa,So,T)*
Timberline:
Timberline (R) *(Hi,J,S,Sa,So)*
Warm Springs:
Kah-Nee-Ta (R) *(Bi,E,F,G,Hi,Ho,J,Sa,So,T)*
Welches:
Resort at Mountain (R) *(Bi,E,F,G,Sa,So,T)*

Pennsylvania
Champion:
Seven Springs (R)
(Bi,Bo,E,G,Hi,Ho,J,S,Sa,Si,So,T)
E. Stroudsburg:
Deerfield Manor (S) *(E,Hi,Sa,So,T)*
Erwinna:
Evermay on Delaware (B) *(Hi,J)*
Farmington:
Nemacolin Woodlands (R)
(Bi,E,F,G,Hi,Ho,J,S,Sa,Si,So,T)
Glen Mills:
Sweetwater Farm (B) *(Bi,E,F,Hi,Ho,I,J,So)*
Hershey:
Hershey (H) *(Bi,Bo,E,G,Hi,J,S,Sa,Si,So,T)*
Hershey Lodge (H) *(Bi,E,J,Sa,Si,So,T)*
King of Prussia:
Park Ridge (H) *(E,So,T)*
Sheraton Valley Forge (H) *(E,Sa,So)*
Malvern:
Desmond (H) *(E,Sa,Si,T)*
Mount Joy:
Cameron Estate (B) *(Bi,Hi)*
Mt. Pocono/Pocono Manor:
Mount Airy Lodge (R)
(Bi,E,F,G,Hi,Ho,I,J,S,Sa,Si,So,T,W)
Pocono Manor (R)
(Bi,E,F,G,Hi,Ho,I,J,S,Sa,Si,So,T)
Philadelphia:
Adam's Mark (H) *(E,Sa,Si,So)*
Dbltree Philadelphia (H) *(E,J,Sa,Si)*
Four Seasons Philadelphia (H) *(E,Sa,Si)*
Marriott Philadelphia (H) *(E,Sa,Si)*
Omni at Independence (H) *(E,Sa,Si)*
Park Hyatt Philadelphia (H) *(E,J,Sa,Si)*

Sports Facilities

Rittenhouse (H) *(E,Sa,Si)*
Ritz Philadelphia (H) *(E,Sa)*
Sheraton Society Hill (H) *(E,Sa,Si)*
Thomas Bond B&B (B) *(So)*
Warwick Philadelphia (H) *(Sa,Si)*
Wyndham Franklin (H) *(E,Sa,Si,T)*
Pittsburgh:
  Dbltree Pittsburgh (H) *(Bi,E,Sa,Si)*
  Hilton Pittsburgh (H) *(E,J)*
  Marriott City Center (H) *(E,Sa,Si)*
  Marriott Greentree (H) *(E,Sa,Si,So)*
  Radisson Pittsburgh (H) *(Si,So)*
  Sheraton Station Square (H) *(E,Sa,Si)*
  Westin William Penn (H) *(E)*
Skytop:
  Skytop Lodge (R)
  (Bi,Bo,E,F,G,Hi,I,J,S,Sa,Si,So,T)
South Sterling:
  Sterling Inn (B) *(Hi,Ho,J,Sa,Si,T)*
St. Davids:
  Radnor (H) *(E,J,So)*
Strasburg:
  Historic Strasburg (B) *(E,Sa,So)*

Puerto Rico
Dorado:
  Hyatt Reg. Cerromar (R)
  (Bi,E,F,G,J,Sa,So,T)
  Hyatt Reg. Dorado (R) *(Bi,E,G,J,So,T)*
Fajardo:
  El Conquistador (R) *(E,F,G,J,Sa,So,T,W)*
Humacao:
  Palmas del Mar (R)
  (Bi,E,F,G,Hi,Ho,Sa,So,T)
Old San Juan:
  El Convento (H) *(E,Sa,So)*
Rincon:
  Horned Dorset (B) *(So)*
San Juan:
  Caribe Hilton (H) *(E,Sa,So,T)*
  Condado Beach Trio (H) *(E,F,So)*
  Condado Plaza (H) *(F,G,So,T)*
  El San Juan (H) *(E,J,Sa,So,T,W)*
  Sands (H) *(E,So)*

Rhode Island
Block Island:
  Atlantic Inn (B) *(T)*
Newport:
  Castle Hill Inn (B) *(F)*
  Cliffside Inn (B) *(Bi,Bo,E,F,G,Ho,J,T,W)*
  Dbltree Newport (H) *(E,Si)*
  Elm Tree Cottage (B) *(F,G,Hi)*
  Marriott Newport (H) *(E,Sa,Si)*
  Newport Harbor (H) *(Sa,Si)*
  Vanderbilt Hall (H)
  (Bi,Bo,E,F,G,Ho,Sa,Si,T)
  Viking (H) *(E,Sa,Si)*
Providence:
  Biltmore Providence (H) *(E)*
  Marriott Providence (H) *(E,Sa,Si,So)*
  Westin Providence (H) *(E,Sa,Si)*

South Carolina
Beaufort:
  Rhett House (B) *(Bi)*
Charleston:
  Battery Carriage (B) *(J)*
  Charleston Place (H) *(E,Sa,Si,So)*
  Hilton Charleston (H) *(E,Sa,Si,So)*
  Mills House (H) *(So)*
  Vendue Inn (B) *(E,Sa)*
Hilton Head:
  Disney's Hilton Head (R) *(F,G,So,T)*
  Hilton Head Health (S) *(Bi,E,G,Hi,J,Sa,So)*
  Hilton Hilton Head (R) *(Bi,E,G,Sa,So,T)*

Hyatt Reg. Hilton Head (R)
  (Bi,E,G,J,Sa,Si,So,T)
Palmetto Dunes (R) *(Bi,F,G,J,Si,So,T,W)*
Sea Pines (R) *(Bi,G,Ho,J,Si,So,T)*
Westin (R) *(Bi,E,F,G,Hi,J,Sa,Si,So,T)*
Isle of Palms:
  Wild Dunes (R) *(Bi,E,F,Hi,J,Sa,Si,So)*
Kiawah Island:
  Kiawah Island (R) *(Bi,F,G,J,So,T)*
Myrtle Beach:
  Hilton Myrtle Beach (R) *(Bi,E,G,So,T)*
  Kingston Planation (R)
  (Bi,E,Hi,J,Sa,Si,So,T)
  Myrtle Beach Martinique (R) *(Sa,Si,So)*
  Ocean Creek (R) *(J,T)*
  Ocean Dunes (R) *(Bi,E,F,J,Sa,Si,So)*
  Sheraton Myrtle Beach (R) *(E,Sa,Si,So)*
Pawleys Island:
  Litchfield Beach (R) *(E,G,Sa,Si,So,T)*
  Litchfield Plantation (B) *(J,So,T)*
Seabrook Island:
  Seabrook Island (R)
  (Bi,E,F,G,Hi,Ho,J,Si,So,T)

South Dakota
Chamberlain:
  Radisson Cedar Shore (R)
  (E,F,Hi,Ho,Sa,Si,W)
Custer:
  State Game Lodge (R) *(F,Hi,J)*
Gettysburg:
  Harer Lodge (B) *(F)*
Rapid City:
  Abend Haus (B) *(Bi,F,Hi,J,Sa)*
  Willow Springs (B) *(F,Hi,Sa)*
Spearfish:
  Eighth St. Inn (B) *(Bi,Hi)*

Tennessee
Fairfield Glade:
  Fairfield Glade (R) *(E,G,Hi,Ho,Sa,Si,So)*
Fernvale:
  Lyric Springs (B) *(F,Hi,So)*
Gatlinburg:
  Bent Creek (R) *(G,Hi,Ho)*
  Buchhorn Inn (B) *(F,Hi)*
Memphis:
  Adam's Mark (H) *(So)*
  Crowne Plaza (H) *(E,Sa,Si)*
  Embassy Memphis (H) *(E,Sa,Si)*
  French Quarter (H) *(E,So)*
  Marriott Memphis (H) *(E,Sa,Si,So)*
  Peabody Memphis (H) *(E,Sa,Si)*
  Radisson Memphis (H) *(E,Sa,So)*
Nashville:
  Embassy Nashville (H) *(E,Sa,Si)*
  Loews Vanderbilt (H) *(E)*
  Marriott Nashville Airport (H) *(E)*
  Opryland (H) *(E,G,I,J)*
  Renaissance Nashville (H) *(E,Sa,Si)*
  Sheraton Music City (H) *(E,J,Sa,Si,So,T)*
Pigeon Forge:
  Grand Resort (R) *(Sa,Si,So)*
Walland:
  Inn at Blackberry Farm (B)
  (Bi,F,Hi,J,So,T)

Texas
Arlington:
  Greenhouse (S) *(E,J,Sa,Si,So,T)*
Austin:
  Barton Creek (R) *(Bi,E,G,Hi,J,Sa,Si,So,T)*
  Four Seasons Austin (H) *(Bi,E,J,Sa,Si)*
  Hilton Austin North (H) *(E,So)*
  Hyatt Reg. Austin (H) *(Bi,E,J,Sa,So)*
  Lake Austin Spa (S) *(Bi,E,F,Hi,J,Sa,Si,So,T)*

Sports Facilities

Lakeway Inn (R)
(Bi,E,F,G,Hi,Ho,J,Sa,So,T,W)
Marriott Austin (H) *(E,Si,So)*
Omni Austin Downtown (H) *(E,Sa,So)*
Omni Austin South Park (H) *(E,Si,So)*
Renaissance Austin (H) *(E,Hi,J,Si,So)*
Bandera:
  Mayan Dude Ranch (B) *(F,Ho,So,T)*
Cat Spring:
  Southwind B&B (B) *(Bi,F,Hi,J)*
Corpus Christi:
  Omni Bayfront (H) *(E,F,Si,So)*
Dallas/Fort Worth:
  Adolphus (H) *(E)*
  Cooper Wellness (S) *(E,J,Sa,So,T)*
  Crescent Court (H) *(E,Sa,So)*
  Dallas Parkway Hilton (H) *(E,Sa,Si,So)*
  Dbltree Campbell Ctr (H) *(E,Sa,T)*
  Dbltree Lincoln Ctr (H) *(E,Sa,So)*
  Embassy Dallas (H) *(E,Sa,Si)*
  Fairmont (H) *(So)*
  Four Seasons (R) *(E,G,J,Sa,Si,So,T)*
  Grand Kempinski Dallas (H)
  (E,J,Sa,Si,So,T)
  Green Oaks Park (H) *(E,Sa,So,T)*
  Hyatt Reg. Dallas (H) *(E,J,Sa,So,T)*
  Le Meridien (H) *(E,I,J,Sa,T)*
  Mansion on Turtle Creek (H) *(E,Sa,So)*
  Marriott Quorum Dallas (H) *(E,Sa,Si,So,T)*
  Omni Dallas (H) *(E,J,Sa,So)*
  Omni Mandalay (H) *(Bi,E,J,Sa,So)*
  Radisson Ft. Worth (H) *(E,Sa,So)*
  Radisson Park (H) *(E,Sa,So)*
  Renaissance Dallas (H) *(E,Sa,So)*
  Sheraton Market Ctr (H) *(E)*
  Sheraton Park Central (H) *(E,Sa,So,T)*
  Westin Galleria Dallas (H) *(So)*
  Worthington (H) *(E,Sa,Si,T)*
  Wyndham Anatole (H) *(E,Sa,Si,So,T)*
  Wyndham Garden (H) *(Sa,Si)*
Galveston:
  Galvez (H) *(Sa,So)*
  San Luis Resort (R) *(Sa,So,T)*
Horseshoe Bay:
  Horseshoe Bay (R) *(E,F,G,Ho,So,T,W)*
Houston:
  Adam's Mark (H) *(E,Sa,Si,So)*
  Crowne Plaza Galleria (H) *(E,Sa,Si)*
  Dbltree Allen Ctr (H) *(E)*
  Dbltree Post Oak (H) *(E,So)*
  Doubletree (H) *(E,Sa,So)*
  Four Seasons Houston (H) *(E,Sa,So)*
  Hilton Houston (H) *(E,J,Sa,So)*
  Houstonian (H) *(E,J,Sa,So,T)*
  Hyatt Reg. Houston (H) *(E,So)*
  Marriott JW (H) *(E,Sa,Si,So)*
  Marriott Medical Ctr (H) *(E)*
  Marriott West Loop (H) *(E,Si)*
  Omni Houston (H) *(Bi,E,Sa,So,T)*
  Red Lion (H) *(G,So)*
  Renaissance Houston (H) *(E,Sa,So)*
  Ritz Houston (H) *(E,So)*
  Sofitel (H) *(E,Sa,So)*
  South Shore Harbour (H)
  (Bi,E,F,G,J,Sa,Si,So,T,W)
  Westchase Hilton (H) *(E,Sa,So)*
  Westin Galleria (H) *(I,Sa,T)*
  Westin Oaks (H) *(J,So)*
  Woodlands (R) *(Bi,E,G,Hi,J,Sa,So,T)*
  Wyndham Greenspoint (H) *(E,Sa,So)*
  Wyndham Warwick (H) *(E,Sa,So)*
Montgomery:
  Del Lago (R) *(Bi,E,F,G,Hi,J,Sa,So,T,W)*
Rancho Viejo:
  Rancho Viejo (R) *(E,G,So,T)*

San Antonio:
  Crowne Plaza (H) *(E,So)*
  Fairmount (H) *(E)*
  Hilton Palacio del Rio (H) *(So)*
  Hyatt Reg. Hill Country (R)
  (Bi,E,G,J,Sa,So,T)
  Hyatt Reg. San Antonio (H) *(E,So)*
  La Mansion del Rio (H) *(So)*
  Marriott Rivercenter (H) *(E,Sa,Si,So)*
  Marriott San Antonio (H) *(Sa,Si,So)*
  Menger (H) *(E,Sa,So)*
  Plaza San Antonio (H) *(Bi,J,Sa,So,T)*
South Padre Island:
  Radisson South Padre (R) *(F,Sa,T)*

Utah

Ivins:
  Franklin Quest (S) *(Bi,E,Hi,J,Sa,Si,T)*
Midway:
  Homestead (B)
  (Bi,E,G,Hi,Ho,J,S,Sa,Si,So,T)
Ogden:
  Historic Radisson (H) *(E)*
Park City:
  Deer Valley (H) *(Bi,Hi,Ho,J,S,Sa,So)*
  Goldener Hirsch (B) *(E,Sa)*
  1904 Imperial (H) *(Sa)*
  Olympia Park (H) *(E,Sa,Si,So)*
  Shadow Ridge (H) *(E,So)*
  Stein Eriksen (R) *(Bi,E,Hi,Ho,J,S,Sa,So)*
  Washington School (B) *(E,Sa)*
Provo:
  Sundance Resort (R) *(Bi,E,F,Hi,Ho,J,S)*
Salt Lake City:
  Dbltree Salt Lake (H) *(E,Sa,Si)*
  Embassy (H) *(E,Sa,Si)*
  Hilton Salt Lake (H) *(E,J,Sa,So)*
  Little America (H) *(E,Sa,Si,So)*
  Marriott Salt Lake City (H) *(E,Sa,Si,So)*
  Peery (H) *(E,Sa)*
  Wyndham (H) *(E,Sa,Si)*
Snowbird:
  Cliff Lodge (R) *(Bi,E,Hi,J,S,Sa,Si,So,T)*
  Inn at Snowbird (B) *(Bi,F,Hi,J,S,Sa,So,T)*
  Iron Blosam (H) *(E,Sa,So)*
  Lodge at Snowbird (H) *(E,Hi,Sa,So,T)*
Springdale:
  Zion Lodge (H) *(Hi,Ho)*
St. George:
  Green Valley Spa (S)
  (E,Hi,Ho,J,Sa,Si,So,T)

Vermont

Barnard:
  Maple Leaf (B) *(Bi,F,G,Hi,Ho,S,T)*
  Twin Farms (R) *(Bi,E,F,Hi,I,J,S,Sa,T)*
Brownsville:
  Ascutney Mountain (R)
  (Bi,E,Hi,I,J,S,Sa,Si,So,T)
Chittenden:
  Mountain Top (B) *(Bi,F,Hi,Ho,I,S,Sa,So)*
Craftsbury Common:
  Inn on Common (H) *(Hi,S,So,T)*
Essex:
  Inn at Essex (B) *(Hi,J,So)*
Goshen:
  Blueberry Hill (B) *(Bi,F,G,Hi,I,J,S,Sa)*
Grafton:
  Old Tavern at Grafton (B)
  (Bi,F,Hi,I,J,S,So,T)
Highgate Springs:
  Tyler Place (R) *(Bi,E,F,Hi,Sa,Si,So,T,W)*
Killington:
  Cortina Inn (B) *(Bi,E,F,Hi,I,J,Sa,Si,So,T,W)*
  Inn of Six Mountains (B) *(E,Sa,Si,So,T)*

Sports Facilities

Killington Resort (R) *(Bi,G,Hi,J,S,T)*
Trio of Inns (B) *(S,Sa)*
Lower Waterford:
Rabbit Hill (B) *(Bi,F,Hi,S)*
Ludlow:
Governor's Inn (B)
(Bi,F,G,Hi,Ho,I,J,S,Sa,T)
Green Mountain (S) *(Bi,E,G,J,S,Sa,So,T)*
Manchester:
Equinox (H)
(Bi,E,F,G,Hi,Ho,I,J,S,Sa,Si,So,T)
Inn at Manchester (B) *(Bi,Hi,So)*
Inn at Willow Pond (B) *(Bi,E,Hi,J,Sa,So)*
Reluctant Panther (B)
(Bi,Bo,E,F,G,Hi,Ho,I,J,S,Sa,Si,So,T)
Village Country (B) *(Ho,S,So)*
Wilburton Inn (B) *(Bi,Hi,J,So,T)*
Middlebury:
Middlebury Inn (B) *(Bi,J,So)*
Swift House (B) *(Sa)*
Waybury Inn (B)
(Bo,E,F,G,Hi,Ho,I,J,S,Si,So,T,W)
Newfane:
Four Columns (H) *(Hi,I,J,Sa,So)*
Perkinsville:
Inn at Weathersfield (B) *(Bi,E,Hi,Ho,I,J)*
Plymouth:
Hawk Inn (B)
(Bi,E,F,Hi,Ho,I,J,S,Sa,Si,So,T)
Quechee:
Quechee Inn (B) *(Bi,F,Hi,J)*
Shelburne:
Inn at Shelburne Farms (B) *(Hi,J)*
Smugglers' Notch:
Smugglers' Notch (R)
(Bi,F,Hi,Ho,I,S,Sa,Si,So,T)
Stowe:
Green Mountain (B) *(Sa,So)*
Stowehof Inn (B) *(S,Sa,T)*
Stowe Snowdrift (R) *(Bi,F,Sa,So,T)*
Topnotch at Stowe (R)
(Bi,Hi,Ho,I,J,Sa,Si,So,T)
Trapp Family (B)
(Bi,E,Hi,Ho,I,J,S,Sa,Si,So,T)
Stratton Mountain:
Stratton Mtn (R)
(Bi,E,F,G,Hi,Ho,I,J,S,Sa,Si,So,T)
Vergennes:
Basin Harbor (R) *(Bi,E,F,G,Hi,J,So,T,W)*
Warren:
Sugarbush (R) *(E,S,Sa,Si,So,T)*
West Dover:
Inn at Sawmill Farm (B) *(F,So,T)*
Wilmington:
Hermitage Inn (B) *(Bi,F,Hi,J,S,Sa,So,T)*
Woodstock:
Kedron Valley (B) *(F,So)*
Woodstock Inn (R) *(E,G,Hi,S,Sa,Si,So,T)*

Virginia
(see also Washington, DC)
Charlottesville:
Boar's Head Inn (R) *(Bi,E,F,G,J,Sa,So,T)*
Hot Springs:
Homestead (R)
(Bi,Bo,E,G,Hi,Ho,I,J,S,Sa,Si,So,T)
Irvington:
Tides Inn (R) *(Bi,F,G,Hi,J,So,T)*
Tides Lodge (R) *(Bi,E,G,J,Sa,So,T)*
Keswick:
Keswick Hall (B) *(Bi,E,F,G,J,Sa,Si,T)*
Leesburg:
Lansdowne (R) *(Bi,G,J,Si,So,T)*
Paris:
Ashby Inn (B) *(Bi,Hi,J)*

Richmond:
Hyatt Richmond (H) *(E,J,Si,So,T)*
Jefferson (H) *(E)*
Linden Row (B) *(Bi,Bo,E,G,Ho,J,Sa,Si,T)*
Marriott Richmond (H) *(E,Sa,Si)*
Omni Richmond (H) *(Si,So)*
Radisson (H) *(Bi,E,Hi,J,Sa,Si)*
Sheraton Park South (H) *(Bi,Sa,Si,So)*
Virginia Beach:
Cavalier (R) *(Bi,E,Si,So,T)*
Founders Inn (H) *(E,Si,So,T)*
Hilton Virginia Beach (H) *(So)*
Holiday Inn Sunspree (R) *(Bi,Sa)*
Pavilion Towers (H) *(E,J,Sa,Si,T)*
Ramada Plaza (R) *(Bi,E,Sa,Si,So)*
Virginia Beach (R) *(Bi,E,Hi,J,Sa,Si,So,T)*
Washington:
Inn at Little Washington (B) *(Bi,J)*
Williamsburg:
Kingsmill (R) *(Bi,E,F,G,J,Sa,Si,So,T)*
Marriott Williamsburg (H) *(E,Sa,Si,So,T)*
Williamsburg (H) *(So)*
Williamsburg Inn (H) *(E,G,Sa,Si,T)*
Williamsburg Lodge (H)
(Bi,E,G,Hi,J,Sa,Si,So,T,W)
Wintergreen:
Wintergreen (R)
(Bi,E,F,G,Hi,Ho,J,S,Sa,Si,So,T,W)
Woodstock:
Inn at Narrow Passage (B)
(Bi,Bo,F,G,Hi,Ho,J,S,T)

Washington
Blaine:
Inn at Semi-Ah-Moo (R) *(E,G,Sa,So,T)*
Coupeville:
Captain Whidbey (B) *(F,Hi,J)*
Eastsound:
Rosario Resort (R) *(Bi,E,Sa,Si,So)*
Lake Quinault:
Lake Quinault (B) *(F,Hi,J,Sa,Si)*
Port Ludlow:
Port Ludlow (R) *(Bi,E,F,G,Sa,Si,So,T)*
Seattle:
Alexis (H) *(E,Sa)*
Dbltree Bellevue (H) *(E,Sa,So)*
Edgewater (H) *(Bi,E)*
Four Seasons Olympic (H) *(Bi,E,Sa,Si)*
Hilton Seattle (H) *(E)*
Hyatt Reg. Bellevue (H) *(Si)*
Renaissance Madison (H) *(E,Sa,Si)*
Roosevlet (H) *(E)*
Sheraton Seattle (H) *(E,Sa,Si)*
Sorrento (H) *(E)*
Warwick (H) *(E,Sa,Si)*
Westin Seattle (H) *(E,Sa,Si)*
Woodmark (H) *(E,F,J)*
Silverdale:
Silverdale on Bay (R) *(Hi,Sa,Si,T)*
Snoqualmie:
Salish Lodge (B) *(Bi,E,Hi,J,Sa,Si)*
Stevenson:
Skamania Lodge (R)
(Bi,E,G,Hi,Ho,I,J,Sa,Si,T)
Winthrop:
Sun Mountain (R)
(Bi,E,F,Hi,Ho,I,J,S,Sa,So,T)

Washington, DC
(including nearby Maryland and Virginia)
Maryland:
Hyatt Reg. Bethesda (H) *(E,Sa,Si)*
Marriott Suites Bethesda (H) *(E,Sa,Si,So)*
Virginia:
Hilton Washington (H) *(E,Sa,Si)*
Hyatt Dulles (H) *(E,Sa,Si)*

Sports Facilities

Hyatt Reg. Crystal City (H) *(Bi,E,J,Sa,So)*
Hyatt Reg. Reston (H) *(E,Sa,Si)*
Marriott Crystal Gateway (H) *(E,Si,So)*
Marriott Fairview Park (H) *(E,Si,So)*
Marriott Key Bridge (H) *(E,Sa,Si,So)*
Marriott Tysons Corner (H) *(E,Si)*
Marriott Westfield's (H) *(E,J,Sa,Si,So,T)*
Radisson Mark Ctr (H) *(E,J,Sa,Si,So,T)*
Ritz Pentagon City (H) *(E,Sa)*
Ritz Tysons Corner (H) *(E)*
Sheraton Tysons Corner (H) *(E,Sa,Si,So)*
Washington, DC:
ANA (H) *(E,Sa,Si)*
Capital Hilton (H) *(E,Sa)*
Carlton (H) *(E)*
Dbltree NH Avenue (H) *(So)*
Embassy Chevy Chase (H) *(E,Sa,Si)*
Embassy Row Hilton (H) *(E,So)*
Four Seasons (H) *(E,Hi,J,Sa,Si)*
Georgetown Inn (H) *(E)*
Grand Hyatt Washington (H) *(E,Sa,Si)*
Hyatt Reg. Washington (H) *(E,Sa,Si)*
Latham Georgetown (H) *(J,So)*
Loews L'Enfant (H) *(E,Si,So)*
Madison (H) *(E,Sa)*
Marriott JW (H) *(Bi,E,Sa,Si)*
Marriott Metro Center (H) *(E,Sa,Si)*
Marriott Washington (H) *(E,Sa,Si)*
Morrison-Clark Inn (B) *(E)*
Omni Shoreham (H) *(E,So)*
One Washington (H) *(Bi,E,So)*
Park Hyatt Washington (H) *(E,Sa,Si)*
Radisson Barcelo (H) *(Sa,So)*
Renaissance Mayflower (H) *(E)*
Renaissance Wash DC (H) *(E,Sa,Si,W)*
Ritz Washington DC (H) *(E)*
Sheraton City Ctr (H) *(E)*
Sheraton Washington (H) *(E,So)*
Sofitel (H) *(E)*
State Plaza (H) *(E)*
Washington (H) *(E,Sa)*
Washington Court (H) *(E,Sa)*
Washinton Hilton (H) *(E,Sa,So,T)*
Watergate (H) *(E,Sa,Si)*
Westin City Ctr (H) *(E,Sa)*
Westin Washington DC (H) *(E,So)*
Willard (H) *(E)*
Wyndham Bristol (H) *(E)*

West Virginia
Berkeley Springs:
Coolfront Resort (R)
(Bi,E,F,Hi,Ho,I,J,S,Sa,Si,T)
Country Inn (B) *(E)*
Charles Town:
Hillbrook Inn (B) *(F,G)*
Davis:
Canaan Valley (R)
(Bi,E,G,Hi,I,J,S,Sa,Si,So,T)
Harpers Ferry:
Historic Hilltop House (H)
(Bi,Bo,F,G,Hi,Ho,J,So)
Hedgesville:
Woods Resort (R) *(Bi,E,F,Hi,I,J,Sa,Si,So,T)*
Morgantown:
Lakeview Resort (R) *(Bi,E,G,J,Sa,Si,So,T)*

Parkersburg:
Blennerhassett Clarion (H) *(G)*
Pipestem:
McKeever Pipestem (R)
(F,G,Hi,Ho,Si,So,T,W)
Shepherdstown:
Bavarian Inn (B) *(E,Sa,So,T)*
Wheeling:
Oglebay Resort (R) *(E,F,G,Hi,Sa,Si,So,T)*
White Sulphur Springs:
Greenbrier (R)
(Bi,Bo,E,F,G,Hi,Ho,I,J,Sa,Si,So,T)

Wisconsin
Bailey's Harbor:
Gordon Lodge (B) *(Bi,E,F,G,Hi,J,So,T)*
Bayfield:
Old Rittenhouse (B) *(Sa)*
Delavan:
Lake Lawn Lodge (R)
(Bi,E,F,G,Hi,Ho,I,J,Sa,Si,So,T,W)
Eagle River:
Chanticleer Inn (B) *(Bi,F,Hi,J,T,W)*
Fontana:
Abbey Resort (R) *(Bi,E,I,J,Sa,Si,So,T,W)*
Green Lake:
Heidel House (R)
(Bi,E,F,G,Hi,I,J,S,Sa,Si,So,T,W)
Kohler:
American Club (R)
(Bi,E,F,G,Hi,Ho,I,J,S,Sa,Si,T)
Inn on Woodlake (B) *(G,J,T)*
Lake Geneva:
Grand Geneva (R)
(Bi,E,G,Hi,Ho,I,S,Sa,Si,So,T)
Interlaken Resort (R)
(Bi,E,F,Hi,I,J,S,Sa,Si,So,T,W)
Milwaukee:
Hilton Milwaukee (H) *(E,Si)*
Hilton Milwaukee River (H) *(Si)*
Hyatt Reg. Milwaukee (H) *(E)*
Marriott Milwaukee (H) *(Sa,Si,So)*
Pfister (H) *(E,Si)*
Wyndham Milwaukee (H) *(E,Sa)*
Osceola:
Aveda Spa Retreat (S)
(Bi,Bo,E,F,G,Hi,Ho,I,J,S,Sa,Si,T)
Wisconsin Dells:
Chula Vista (R) *(F,Hi,I,Sa,Si,So,T,W)*

Wyoming
Jackson:
Jackson Hole Racquet (R)
(Bi,E,F,G,J,Sa,So,T)
Rusty Parrot (B) *(Sa)*
Spring Creek (R) *(Hi,Ho,J,Sa,So,T)*
Teton Pines (R) *(F,G,So)*
Wort (H) *(Bi,E,F,G,Hi,Ho,S,T)*
Moose:
Cottonwoods Ranch (B) *(F,Hi,Ho)*
Moran:
Colter Bay VIllage (R) *(F,Hi,Ho,J)*
Jenny Lake (B) *(Bi)*
Yellowstone National Park:
Lake Yellowstone (H) *(F,Hi)*
Mammoth Hot Springs (H) *(F,Hi,Ho)*
Old Faithful (H) *(F,Hi)*

Student Budget

Alabama
Anniston:
Victoria (B)
Mobile:
Radisson Admiral (H)

Alaska
Fairbanks:
Captain Bartlett (H)

Arizona
Page:
Wahweap (H)
Phoenix/Scottsdale:
Dbltree Paradise Valley (R)
Holiday Inn SunSpree (R)
Scottsdale Hilton (H)
Sheraton Mesa (H)
Tucson:
Arizona Inn (H)

Arkansas
Eureka Springs:
Palace (B)
Hot Springs:
Arlington Resort (H)
Lake Hamilton (R)
Majestic (H)
Lakeview:
Gaston's (R)
Little Rock:
Dbltree Little Rock (H)
Little Rock Hilton (H)

California
Big Sur:
Big Sur Lodge (B)
Big Sur River (B)
Deetjen's Big Sur (B)
Fish Camp:
Tenaya Lodge (R)
Irvine:
Hilton Orange County (H)
Los Angeles:
Clarion Hollywood (H)
Mansion Inn (B)
Palos Verdes (H)
Shangri-La (H)
Summit Bel-Air (H)
Summit Rodeo Drive (H)
Mendocino:
Mendocino (H)
Ojai:
Oaks at Ojai (S)
Palm Springs:
Ingleside (B)
Inn at Racquet Club (B)
Riviera Palm Springs (R)
Spa (H)
Riverside:
Mission Inn (H)
San Diego:
Gaslamp (H)
San Francisco:
Chancellor (H)
Clarion Bedford (H)
Gramma's Rose Garden (B)
Maxwell (H)
Mosser Victorian (H)
Phoenix (H)
Queen Anne (H)
Rex (H)
Savoy (H)

San Luis Obispo:
Madonna Inn (H)
Santa Rosa:
La Rose (B)
Sausalito:
Alta Mira (H)

Colorado
Breckenridge:
Village at Breckenridge (R)
Colorado Springs:
Antlers Dlbtree (H)
Hearthstone Inn (B)
Denver:
Marriott SE Denver (H)
Vail:
Sitzmark Lodge (H)

Connecticut
Chester:
Inn at Chester (B)
Norfolk:
Blackberry River (B)
Old Lyme:
Bee & Thistle (B)
Old Lyme Inn (B)

Delaware
Dover:
Sheraton Inn (H)
Lewes:
New Devon (B)
Newark:
Christiana Hilton (H)
Wilmington:
Boulevard B&B (B)

Florida
Fort Lauderdale:
Riverside (H)
Miami/Miami Beach:
Lafayette (H)
Lido Spa (S)
Occidental Plaza (H)
Park Central (H)
Orlando:
Disney's All-Star Music (R)
Disney's All-Star Sports (R)
Disney's Caribbean (R)
Disney's Dixie Landings (R)
Disney's Ft. Wilderness (R)
Disney's Port Orleans (R)
Grosvenor (R)
Holiday Inn Main Gate (H)
Holiday Inn SunSpree (R)
Hyatt Orlando (H)
Marriott Orl. Int'l Drive (H)
Radisson Barcelo (H)
Radisson Twin Towers (H)
Westgate Lakes (R)
Safety Harbor:
Safety Harbor (S)
Siesta Key:
Captiva Beach (B)

Georgia
Americus:
Windsor (H)
Atlanta:
Biltmore (H)
Buckhead B&B (B)
Augusta:
Partridge Inn (H)
Jekyll Island:
Jekyll Island Club (R)

Student Budget

Savannah:
  Eliza Thompson (B)
Idaho
Boise:
  Idanha (H)
  Owyhee Plaza (H)
  Red Lion Boise (H)
Coeur d'Alene:
  Blackwell B&B (B)
  Gregory's McFarland B&B (B)
McCall:
  Shore Lodge (B)
Illinois
Chicago:
  Blackstone (H)
Whittington:
  Rend Lake (R)
Indiana
Bloomington:
  Fourwinds (R)
French Lick:
  French Lick Springs (R)
Iowa
Bettendorf:
  Jumer's Castle (H)
Dubuque:
  Richards House (B)
Homestead:
  Die Heimat (B)
Newton:
  La Corsette Maison (B)
Kansas
Lawrence:
  Eldridge (H)
Lindsborg:
  Swedish Country (B)
Kentucky
Berea:
  Boone Tavern (H)
Harrodsburg:
  Beaumont Inn (B)
  Inn at Shaker Village (B)
Louisiana
New Orleans:
  Cornstalk (B)
  Radisson New Orleans (H)
St. Francisville:
  Lodge at the Bluffs (H)
Maine
East Holden:
  Lucerne Inn (B)
Portland:
  Marriott at Sable Oaks (H)
  Radisson Portland (H)
Maryland
Baltimore:
  Ann Street B&B (B)
Ocean City:
  Coconut Malorie (H)
  Dunes Manor (H)
Massachusetts
Boston:
  Chandler Inn (H)
  Newbury (B)
Cape Cod:
  Sea Crest (R)
Lenox:
  Kripalu Center (S)
Sturbridge:
  Publick House (B)

Michigan
Acme:
  Grand Traverse (R)
Bellaire:
  Shanty Creek (R)
Detroit:
  Mayflower B&B (B)
Mackinac Island:
  Iroquois (B)
Thompsonville:
  Crystal Mountain (R)
Traverse City:
  Waterfront Inn (R)
Minnesota
Alexandria:
  Arrowwood Radisson (R)
Hibbing:
  Kahler Park (H)
Lutsen:
  Lutsen (R)
Minneapolis/St. Paul:
  Sheraton Park Place (H)
Red Wing:
  St. James (H)
Rochester:
  Kahler (H)
Mississippi
Natchez:
  Burn (B)
  Dunleith (B)
  Linden B&B (B)
  Natchez Eola (H)
Robinsonville:
  Harrah's Mardi Gras (H)
  Hollywood Casino (H)
  Sam's (H)
Tupelo:
  Mockingbird B&B (B)
Vicksburg:
  Corners B&B (B)
  Duff Green (B)
Missouri
Branson:
  Best Western Knights (H)
  Best Western Mtn Oak (H)
  Best Western Music (H)
  Branson Hotel B&B (B)
  Branson House B&B (B)
  Red Bud Cove B&B (B)
Hannibal:
  Fifth St. Mansion (B)
  Garth Woodside (B)
Kansas City:
  Savoy (H)
Lake Ozark:
  Lodge at Four Seasons (R)
Osage Beach:
  Marriott's Tan-Tar-A (R)
Ridgedale:
  Big Cedar (R)
St. Louis:
  Cheshire Inn (H)
  Daniele (H)
  Holiday Inn Riverfront (H)
Montana
Gallatin Gateway:
  Gallatin Gateway (B)
Nebraska
Beatrice:
  Carriage House (B)

Waterloo:
JC Robinson B&B (B)
Wilber:
Wilber (B)

Nevada
Lake Tahoe:
Lake Tahoe Horizon (H)
Las Vegas:
Aladdin (H)
Circus Circus (H)
Excalibur (H)
Harrah's Casino (H)
Lady Luck Casino (H)
Luxor Las Vegas (H)
Maxim (H)
MGM Grand (H)
Mirage (H)
Monte Carlo (H)
Rio Suite (H)
Riviera (H)
Stardust (H)
Stratosphere (H)
Treasure Island (H)
Laughlin:
Don Laughlin's (H)
Flamingo Hilton (H)
Golden Nugget (H)
Harrah's Laughlin (H)
Mesquite:
Players Island (R)
Reno:
Eldorado (H)
Flamingo Hilton (H)
Harrah's & Hampton (H)
John Ascuaga's (H)
Peppermill (H)
Silver Legacy (H)

New Hampshire
Bretton Woods:
1896 Bretton Arms (B)
Franconia:
Franconia Inn (B)
Jackson:
Eagle Mountain (H)
North Conway:
Four Points Sheraton (H)
White Mountain (R)
Waterville Valley:
Snowy Owl (B)

New Jersey
Atlantic City:
Bally's Park Place (H)
Caesar Atlantic City (H)
Claridge Casino (H)
Sands (H)
Showboat Casino (H)
Tropicana Casino (H)
Cape May:
Chalfonte (H)

New Mexico
Albuquerque:
La Posada Albuquerque (H)
Santa Fe:
La Posada Santa Fe (H)
Santa Fe (H)
Taos:
Quail Ridge (R)

New York
Alexandria Bay:
Riveredge (H)
Ithaca:
Statler (H)

New York City:
Edison (H)
Franklin (H)
Gramercy Park (H)
Holiday Inn Downtown (H)
Le Refuge Inn (H)
Pickwick Arms (H)
Ramada Milford (H)
Remington (H)
Washington Square (H)
Wolcott (H)
Wyndham (H)
Saranac Lake:
Saranac (H)
Saratoga Springs:
Inn at Saratoga (B)

North Carolina
Charlotte:
Adam's Mark (H)
Durham:
Structure House (S)
Fayetteville:
Radisson Prince Charles (H)
Raleigh-Durham:
Marriott Crabtree (H)

North Dakota
Bismarck:
Radisson Bismarck (H)
Fargo:
Best Western Doublewood (H)
Bohlig's B&B (B)
Radisson Fargo (H)
Jamestown:
Country Charm (B)
Luverne:
Volden Farm B&B (B)
Medora:
Rough Rider (B)

Ohio
Cincinnati:
Vernon Manor (H)
Columbus:
Marriott N. Columbus (H)
Dellroy:
Atwood Lake (R)
Granville:
Granville Inn (B)
Huron:
Sawmill Creek (R)
Marietta:
Lafayette (H)

Oklahoma
Bartlesville:
Phillips (H)
Kingston:
Texoma State (R)

Oregon
Newport:
Embarcadero (H)
Sylvia Beach (H)

Pennsylvania
E. Stroudsburg:
Deerfield Manor (S)
King of Prussia:
Sheraton Valley Forge (H)
Mount Joy:
Cameron Estate (B)
Mt. Pocono/Pocono Manor:
Pocono Manor (R)
Philadelphia:
Penn's View (B)

Student Budget

Pittsburgh:
Priory (B)
Strasburg:
Historic Strasburg (B)

South Carolina
Myrtle Beach:
Myrtle Beach Martinique (R)
Ocean Dunes (R)
Sheraton Myrtle Beach (R)
Pawleys Island:
Litchfield Beach (R)

South Dakota
Chamberlain:
Radisson Cedar Shore (R)
Custer:
Custer Mansion (B)
State Game Lodge (R)
Gettysburg:
Harer Lodge (B)
Rapid City:
Alex Johnson (H)
Spearfish:
Eighth St. Inn (B)
Yankton:
Mulberry Inn (B)

Tennessee
Gatlinburg:
Bent Creek (R)
Memphis:
Radisson Memphis (H)
Pigeon Forge:
Grand Resort (R)

Texas
Dallas/Fort Worth:
Green Oaks Park (H)
Radisson Park (H)

Utah
Cedar City:
Bryce Canyon (H)
Midway:
Homestead (B)
Salt Lake City:
Little America (H)
Marriott Salt Lake City (H)
Peery (H)
Springdale:
Zion Lodge (H)

Vermont
Brownsville:
Ascutney Mountain (R)
Goshen:
Blueberry Hill (B)
Highgate Springs:
Tyler Place (R)
Stowe:
Stowehof Inn (B)

Stowe Snowdrift (R)
Stratton Mountain:
Stratton Mtn (R)

Virginia
Abingdon:
Camberley's (B)
Richmond:
Linden Row (B)
Virginia Beach:
Founders Inn (H)
Holiday Inn Sunspree (R)
Williamsburg:
Williamsburg (H)

Washington
Coupeville:
Captain Whidbey (B)
Lake Quinault:
Lake Quinault (B)
Port Ludlow:
Port Ludlow (R)
Silverdale:
Silverdale on Bay (R)

Washington, DC
George Washington U. (H)
Normandy Inn (H)
Tabard Inn (H)

West Virginia
Berkeley Springs:
Coolfront Resort (R)
Country Inn (B)
Davis:
Canaan Valley (R)
Hedgesville:
Woods Resort (R)
Morgantown:
Lakeview Resort (R)
Shepherdstown:
Bavarian Inn (B)
Wheeling:
Oglebay Resort (R)

Wisconsin
Eagle River:
Chanticleer Inn (B)
Milwaukee:
Hilton Milwaukee River (H)
Wisconsin Dells:
Chula Vista (R)

Wyoming
Moran:
Colter Bay VIllage (R)
Yellowstone National Park:
Lake Yellowstone (H)
Mammoth Hot Springs (H)
Old Faithful (H)

Swimming Pools

Alabama

Birmingham:
Radisson Birmingham (H)
Sheraton Birmingham (H)
Eufaula:
Kendall Manor (B)
Fairhope:
Malaga Inn (B)
Mobile:
Adam's Mark (H)
Radisson Admiral (H)
Tuscaloosa:
Sheraton Capstone (H)

Alaska

Girdwood:
Alyeska (R)

Arizona

Bisbee:
Copper Queen (H)
Catalina:
Miraval (S)
Douglas:
Gadsden (H)
Gold Canyon:
Gold Canyon (R)
Page:
Wahweap (H)
Phoenix/Scottsdale:
Arizona Golf (R)
Boulders (R)
Buttes (R)
Crowne Phoenix (H)
Dbltree La Posada (R)
Embassy Biltmore (H)
Embassy Scottsdale (H)
Gardiner's (R)
Hermosa Inn (B)
Holiday Inn SunSpree (R)
Hyatt Reg. Phoenix (H)
Hyatt Reg. Scottsdale (R)
Marriott's Camelback (R)
Marriott Scottsdale (H)
Marriott's Mountain (R)
Orange Tree (R)
Phoenician (R)
Pte Hilton S. Mountain (R)
Pte Hilton Squaw (R)
Pte Hilton Tapatio (R)
Radisson Scottsdale (R)
Renaissance Cottonwoods (R)
Ritz Phoenix (H)
Royal Palms (H)
San Carlos (H)
Scottsdale Conference (R)
Scottsdale Hilton (H)
Scottsdale Plaza (R)
Scottsdale Princess (R)
Sheraton Mesa (H)
Sheraton San Marcos (R)
Wigwam (R)
Prescott:
Hassayampa Inn (H)
Sedona:
Canyon Villa B&B (B)
Enchantment (R)
Graham B&B (B)
L'Auberge de Sedona (H)
Los Abrigados (R)
Poco Diablo (R)
Tucson:
Canyon Ranch (S)

Dbltree Reid Park (H)
Lodge Ventana (R)
Loews Ventana (R)
Omni Tucson (R)
Sheraton El Conquistador (R)
SunCatcher B&B (B)
Tanque Verde (B)
Westin La Paloma (R)
Westward Look (R)
Wickenburg:
Merv Griffin's (B)

Arkansas

Hot Springs:
Arlington Resort (H)
Hot Springs Park (H)
Lake Hamilton (R)
Majestic (H)
Lakeview:
Gaston's (R)
Little Rock:
Dbltree Little Rock (H)
Little Rock Hilton (H)

California

Anaheim:
Dbltree Anaheim (H)
Disneyland (H)
Disneyland Pacific (H)
Hilton Anaheim (H)
Hyatt Reg. Alicante (H)
Inn at the Park (H)
Marriott Anaheim (H)
Sheraton Anaheim (H)
Big Sur:
Big Sur Lodge (B)
Big Sur River (B)
Post Ranch (B)
Ventana Inn (B)
Bodega Bay:
Inn at the Tides (B)
Borrego Springs:
La Casa del Zorro (R)
Calabasas:
Ashram Retreat (S)
Calistoga:
Indian Springs (S)
Carmel:
Carmel Country Spa (S)
Carmel Valley (R)
Highlands Inn (B)
John Gardiner's (R)
La Playa (H)
Los Laureles (H)
Quail Lodge (R)
Stonepine (B)
Cazadero:
Timberhill (B)
Costa Mesa:
Marriott Costa Mesa (H)
Red Lion (H)
Westin South Coast (H)
Dana Point:
Laguna Cliff Marriott (R)
Ritz Laguna Niguel (R)
Death Valley:
Furnace Creek Inn (R)
Escondido:
Golden Door (S)
Fish Camp:
Tenaya Lodge (R)
Fresno:
4 Points ITT Sheraton (H)

Swimming Pools

Guerneville:
Applewood Inn (B)
Healdsburg:
Madrona Manor (B)
Irvine:
Hilton Orange County (H)
Hyatt Reg. Irvine (H)
Irvine Marriott (H)
Lafayette:
Lafayette Park (H)
Laguna Beach:
Surf & Sand (H)
Lake Arrowhead:
Lake Arrowhead (R)
Long Beach:
Sheraton Long Beach (H)
Los Angeles:
Argyle (H)
Barnabey's (H)
Bel-Air (H)
Beverly Hills (H)
Beverly Hilton (H)
Beverly Prescott (H)
Century Plaza (H)
Chateau Marmont (H)
Clarion Hollywood (H)
Doubletree LAX (H)
Four Seasons (H)
Hilton LAX (H)
Hilton Long Beach (H)
Inter-Continental LA (H)
Le Parc (H)
Loews Santa Monica (H)
Marriott LAX (H)
Marriott Marina Beach (H)
Marriott Warner Ctr (H)
Miramar Sheraton (H)
Mondrian (H)
Nikko Beverly Hills (H)
Omni LA (H)
Palos Verdes (H)
Park Hyatt LA (H)
Peninsula Beverly Hills (H)
Ramada W. Hollywood (B)
Regal Biltmore (H)
Regent Beverly Wilshire (H)
Renaissance LA (H)
Ritz Huntington (H)
Ritz Marina del Rey (H)
Sheraton Grande (H)
Sheraton Industry Hills (H)
Sheraton Universal (H)
Shutters (H)
Sofitel LA (H)
Summit Bel-Air (H)
Sunset Marquis (H)
Westin Bonaventure (H)
Westwood Marquis (H)
Wyndham Bel Age (H)
Wyndham Checkers (H)
Wyndham LAX (H)
Los Olivos:
Los Olivos Grand (B)
Mendocino:
Stanford Inn (B)
Montecito:
Montecito Inn (B)
San Ysidro (B)
Monterey:
Dbltree Fish. Wharf (H)
Hyatt Reg. Monterey (H)
Morro Bay:
Inn at Morro Bay (B)

Napa:
Embassy Napa Valley (H)
La Residence (B)
Marriott Napa Valley (H)
Silverado (R)
Newport Beach:
Hyatt Newporter (R)
Marriott Suites (H)
Marriott Tennis (H)
Sutton Place (H)
Oakhurst:
Chateau du Sureau (B)
Oakland:
Waterfront Plaza (H)
Ojai:
Oaks at Ojai (S)
Ojai Valley (R)
Olympic Valley:
Plumpjack's (B)
Resort at Squaw Creek (R)
Oxnard:
Embassy Mandalay (H)
Palm Springs:
Dbltree Palm Springs (R)
Givenchy (S)
Hilton Palm Springs (H)
Hyatt Grand (R)
Hyatt Reg. Palm Springs (H)
Indian Wells (R)
Ingleside (B)
Inn at Racquet Club (B)
La Mancha (R)
La Quinta (R)
L'Horizon Garden (R)
Marquis Palm Springs (H)
Marriott's Desert Springs (R)
Marriott's Rancho (R)
Monte Vista (H)
Palms (S)
Renaissance Esmeralda (R)
Ritz Rancho Mirage (R)
Riviera Palm Springs (R)
Shadow Mountain (R)
Spa (H)
Sundance (B)
Two Bunch Palms (B)
Westin Mission Hills (R)
Wyndham Palm Springs (H)
Pasadena:
Dbltree Pasadena (H)
Pebble Beach:
Inn at Spanish Bay (R)
Lodge at Pebble Beach (R)
Redwood City:
Sofitel SF (H)
Riverside:
Mission Inn (H)
Rutherford:
Auberge du Soleil (B)
Sacramento:
Hyatt Reg. Sacramento (H)
Radisson Sacramento (H)
San Diego:
Catamaran (H)
del Coronado Hotel (R)
Embassy San Diego (H)
Hilton San Diego (H)
Hyatt Islandia (H)
Hyatt Reg. La Jolla (H)
Hyatt Reg. San Diego (H)
Inn at Rancho Santa Fe (H)
Kona Kai (R)
La Jolla Beach (H)
L'Auberge Del Mar (R)

La Valencia (H)
Le Meridien San Diego (H)
Lodge at Torrey Pines (H)
Loews Coronado (R)
Marriott La Jolla (H)
Marriott Mission Valley (H)
Marriott San Diego (H)
Princess San Diego (R)
Radisson Harbor View (H)
Rancho Bernardo (R)
Rancho Valencia (R)
Sea Lodge (H)
Sheraton Grande (R)
Sheraton San Diego (H)
Westin San Diego (H)
Wyndham Emerald (H)

San Francisco:
Cathedral Hill (H)
Claremont (R)
Handlery Union Square (H)
Harbor Court (H)
Hilton SF (H)
Hyatt Fish. Wharf (H)
Marriott SF (H)
Nikko SF (H)
Palace (H)
Phoenix (H)
Ritz SF (H)
Sheraton Fish. Wharf (H)

San Jose:
Fairmont San Jose (H)
Hayes (H)

San Luis Obispo:
Apple Farm (B)

Santa Barbara:
El Encanto (H)
Fess Parker's (R)
Four Seasons Biltmore (R)

Santa Clara:
Westin Santa Slara (H)

Santa Cruz:
Chaminade (H)

Santa Monica:
Oceana (H)

Shell Beach:
Cliffs at Shell Beach (R)

Solvang:
Alisal (R)

Sonoma:
El Dorado (H)
Sonoma Mission (S)

St. Helena:
Harvest Inn (B)
Meadowood (R)
Wine Country (B)

Tecate:
Rancho La Puerta (S)

Truckee:
Northstar-at-Tahoe (R)

Ventura:
Cliff House (B)

Vista:
Cal-a-Vie (S)

Woodside:
Lodge at Skylonda (S)

Yosemite:
Ahwahnee (H)

Yountville:
Vintage Inn (H)

Colorado
Aspen:
Aspen Club (B)
Gant (B)

Inn at Aspen (H)
Jerome (H)
Little Nell (H)
Ritz Aspen (H)
Sardy House (B)

Beaver Creek:
Embassy Beaver Creek (R)
Hyatt Reg. Beaver Creek (H)
Inn at Beaver Creek (B)
Pines Lodge (H)

Breckenridge:
Breckenridge Mtn (H)
Hilton Breckenridge (R)
Village at Breckenridge (R)

Clark:
Home Ranch (R)

Colorado Springs:
Antlers Dlbtree (H)
Broadmoor (R)
Cheyenne Mountain (R)
Sheraton (H)

Copper Mountain:
Copper Mountain (R)

Denver:
Burnsley (H)
Hyatt Reg. Denver Dwtn (H)
Hyatt Reg. Denver Tech (H)
Inverness (R)
Marriott Denver (H)
Marriott SE Denver (H)
Marriott Tech Denver (H)
Renaissance Denver (H)
Residence by Marriott (H)
Warwick (H)
Westin Tabor Center (H)

Durango:
Rochester (H)
Tamarron Hilton (R)
Wit's End (B)

Edwards:
Lodge & Spa Cordillera (R)

Granby:
C Lazy U Ranch (B)

Keystone:
Keystone (R)

Mosca:
Inn at Zapata (B)

Redstone:
Redstone Inn (B)

Snowmass Village:
Silvertree (H)
Snowmass Lodge (R)

Steamboat Springs:
Sheraton Steamboat (R)

Telluride:
Columbia (B)
Peaks at Telluride (R)

Vail:
Christiana at Vail (H)
Lodge at Vail (H)
Marriott's at Vail (R)
Mountain Haus at Vail (H)
Sitzmark Lodge (H)
Sonnenalp of Vail (R)
Vail Athletic Club (H)
Vail Cascade (H)

Connecticut
Lakeville:
Interlaken Inn (R)

Lebanon:
Spa at Grand Lake (S)

Ledyard:
Foxwoods (H)

Swimming Pools

Mystic:
Inn at Mystic (B)
New Preston:
Inn on Lake Waramaug (B)
Norfolk:
Blackberry River (B)
Norwich:
Norwich Inn (S)
Simsbury:
Simsbury Inn (H)
Southbury:
Heritage Inn (H)
Washington:
Mayflower Inn (B)
Westbrook:
Water's Edge (B)

Delaware
Rehoboth Beach:
Boardwalk Plaza (H)

Florida
Amelia Island:
Amelia Island (R)
Ritz Amelia Island (R)
Boca Raton:
Boca Raton (R)
Marriott Boca Raton (H)
Bonita Springs:
Shangri-La (S)
Captiva Island:
South Seas Plantation (R)
Clearwater:
Belleview Mido (R)
Destin:
Hilton Sandestin (R)
Fisher Island:
Spa Internazionale (S)
Fort Lauderdale:
Doubletree (H)
Hyatt Reg. Pier 66 (H)
Lago Mar (R)
Little Inn by the Sea (B)
Marriott Ft. Lauderdale (H)
Marriott's Harbor (R)
Radisson Bahia Mar (R)
Registry Resort (S)
Riverside (H)
Westin Ft. Lauderdale (H)
Wyndham Ft. Lauderdale (H)
Fort Myers:
Sanibel Harbour (R)
Gasparilla Island:
Gasparilla Inn (B)
Haines City:
Grenelefe Golf (R)
Hallandale:
Regency House (S)
Howey-in-the-Hills:
Mission Inn (R)
Islamorada:
Cheeca Lodge (R)
Jacksonville:
Club Hotel by Dbltree (H)
Marriott Jacksonville (H)
Omni Jacksonville (H)
Jupiter:
Jupiter Beach (R)
Key Largo:
Marriott's Key Largo (R)
Ocean Reef (R)
Key West:
Banana Bay (B)
Holiday Inn La Concha (H)

Hyatt Key West (H)
Marquesa (H)
Marriott's Casa Marina (R)
Marriott's Reach (R)
Ocean Key House (R)
Pier House (R)
Lake Wales:
Chalet Suzanne (B)
Little Torch Key:
Little Palm Island (B)
Longboat Key:
Colony Beach (R)
Resort at Longboat Key (R)
Marathon:
Hawk's Cay (R)
Marco Island:
Marco Island Hilton (R)
Marriott's Marco Island (R)
Radisson Beach (R)
Miami/Miami Beach:
Albion (H)
Alexander (H)
Astor (H)
Biltmore (R)
Crowne Plaza Miami (H)
Dbltree Coconut Grove (H)
Dbltree Grand (H)
Delano (H)
Doral Golf (R)
Eden Roc (H)
Fisher Island (R)
Florida Suites (H)
Fontainebleau Hilton (R)
Grand Bay (H)
Grove Isle Club (B)
Hyatt Reg. Coral Gables (H)
Hyatt Reg. Miami (H)
Indian Creek (H)
Inter-Continental Miami (H)
La Voile Rouge (B)
Lido Spa (S)
Marriott Biscayne Bay (H)
Miami Beach Ocean (H)
Occidental Plaza (H)
Omni Colonnade (H)
Park Central (H)
Pritikin Longevity (S)
Radisson Mart Plaza (H)
Raleigh (H)
Ritz Plaza (H)
Sheraton Bal Harbour (H)
Sheraton Biscayne Bay (H)
Spa at Doral (S)
Tides (H)
Turnberry Isle (R)
Westin Miami (R)
Naples:
Edgewater Beach (H)
La Playa Beach (H)
Naples Bath & Tennis (R)
Naples Beach (R)
Registry (R)
Ritz Naples (R)
Orlando:
Buena Vista Palace (H)
Disney Institute (R)
Disney's All-Star Music (R)
Disney's All-Star Sports (R)
Disney's Beach Club (R)
Disney's Caribbean (R)
Disney's Contemporary (R)
Disney's Dixie Landings (R)
Disney's Ft. Wilderness (R)
Disney's Grand Floridian (R)
Disney's Polynesian (R)

Swimming Pools

Disney's Port Orleans (R)
Disney's Wilderness (R)
Disney's Yacht (R)
Doubletree (H)
Grosvenor (R)
Hilton at Walt Disney (H)
Holiday Inn Main Gate (H)
Holiday Inn SunSpree (R)
Hyatt Orlando (H)
Hyatt Reg. Grand Cypress (R)
Hyatt Reg. Orlando (H)
Marriott Orl. Downtown (H)
Marriott Orl. Int'l Drive (H)
Marriott's Orl. World Ctr (H)
Omni Rosen (H)
Peabody Orlando (H)
Radisson Barcelo (H)
Radisson Plaza (H)
Radisson Twin Towers (H)
Renaissance Orlando (R)
Residence by Marriott (H)
Sheraton World (R)
Travelodge (H)
Villas of Grand Cypress (R)
Vistana (R)
Walt Disney Dolphin (R)
Walt Disney Swan (R)
Westgate Lakes (R)

Palm Beach:
Brazilian Court (H)
Breakers (R)
Chesterfield (H)
Colony (H)
Four Seasons Palm Beach (H)
Palm Beach Polo (R)
PGA National (R)
Ritz Palm Beach (R)

Panama City Beach:
Marriott's Bay Point (R)

Pompano Beach:
Palm-Aire Resort (S)

Ponte Vedra Beach:
Lodge at Ponte Vedra (R)
Marriott at Sawgrass (R)
Ponte Vedra (R)

Port St. Lucie:
Club Med Sandpiper (R)

Safety Harbor:
Safety Harbor (S)

Sanibel Island:
Casa Ybel (R)
Sanibel (R)
Sundial Beach (R)

Siesta Key:
Captiva Beach (B)

Stuart:
Indian River Plantation (R)

Tampa Bay:
Dbltree Tampa Bay (H)
Don CeSar (R)
Embassy Westshore (H)
Holiday Inn Beachfront (R)
Hyatt Reg. Tampa (H)
Hyatt Reg. Westshore (H)
Innisbrook Hilton (R)
Marriott Tampa (H)
Radisson Sand Key (R)
Saddlebrook Tampa (R)
Sheraton Sand Key (R)
TradeWinds St. Pete (R)
Wyndham Harbour (H)

West Palm Beach:
Hippocrates Health (S)

Georgia

Atlanta:
Doubletree (H)
Embassy Perimeter Ctr (H)
Evergreen (R)
Four Seasons Atlanta (H)
French Quarter (H)
Grand Hyatt Atlanta (H)
Hilton Atlanta (H)
Hilton Atlanta Airport (H)
Holiday Inn Ravinia (H)
Hyatt Reg. Atlanta (H)
Hyatt Reg. Perimeter (H)
Marietta (R)
Marque of Atlanta (H)
Marriott Atlanta Airport (H)
Marriott JW Lenox (H)
Marriott Marquis Atlanta (H)
Marriott Midtown Atlanta (H)
Marriott N. Central Atlanta (H)
Marriott NW Atlanta (H)
Marriott Perimeter Atlanta (H)
Omni CNN Center (H)
Peachtree (H)
Renaissance Downtown (H)
Renaissance Waverly (H)
Ritz Buckhead (H)
Sheraton Colony Square (H)
Sheraton Gateway (H)
Summerfield (H)
Swissotel Atlanta (H)
Terrace Buckhead (H)
Westin Atlanta (H)
Westin Peachtree (H)
Wyndham Vinings (H)

Augusta:
Partridge Inn (H)

Braselton:
Chateau Elan Winery (B)

Jekyll Island:
Jekyll Island Club (R)

Lake Lanier Islands:
Renaissance Pineisle (R)

Peachtree City:
Aberdeen Woods (H)

Pine Mountain:
Callaway Gardens (R)

Savannah:
Hyatt Reg. Savannah (H)
Marriott Savannah (H)

Sea Island:
Cloister (R)

St. Simons Island:
King & Prince Beach (R)
Lodge at Little St. Simons (B)
Sea Palms (R)

Hawaii

Big Island:
Four Seasons Hualalai (R)
Hapuna Prince (R)
Hawaii Naniloa (R)
Kona Village (R)
Mauna Kea (R)
Mauna Lani Bay (R)
Orchid at Mauna Lani (R)
Royal Waikoloan (R)

Kauai:
Hyatt Reg. Kauai (R)
Kauai Coconut (R)
Marriott Kauai (R)
Outrigger Kauai (R)
Princeville (R)

Swimming Pools

Lanai:
  Lodge at Koele (R)
  Manele Bay (R)
Maui:
  Aston Kaanapali (R)
  Aston Wailea (R)
  Embassy Maui (R)
  Four Seasons Maui (R)
  Grand Wailea (R)
  Hana-Maui Hotel (H)
  Hyatt Reg. Maui (R)
  Ka'anapali Beach (R)
  Kapalua Bay (R)
  Kea Lani (R)
  Marriott Maui (R)
  Maui Prince (R)
  Renaissance Wailea (R)
  Ritz Kapalua (R)
  Royal Lahaina (R)
  Westin Maui (R)
Oahu:
  Ala Moana (H)
  Aston Waikiki (H)
  Halekulani (H)
  Hawaiian Regent (H)
  Hawaii Prince Waikiki (H)
  Hilton Hawaiian (H)
  Hyatt Reg. Waikiki (H)
  Ihilani Resort (R)
  Ilikai Nikko Waikiki (H)
  Kahala Mandarin (R)
  Outrigger Prince Kuhio (H)
  Outrigger Reef (R)
  Outrigger Waikiki (R)
  Pacific Beach (H)
  Royal Hawaiian (H)
  Sheraton Kaiulani (H)
  Sheraton Moana (H)
  Sheraton Waikikı (H)
  Waikiki Parc (H)

Idaho
Boise:
  Doubletree Club (H)
  Owyhee Plaza (H)
  Red Lion Boise (H)
Coeur d'Alene:
  Coeur d'Alene (R)
Ketchum:
  Knob Hill (H)
McCall:
  Shore Lodge (B)
Sun Valley:
  Sun Valley (R)

Illinois
Bloomingdale:
  Indian Lakes (R)
Chicago:
  Doubletree (H)
  Hilton Chicago (H)
  Hilton O'Hare (H)
  Holiday Inn Chicago (H)
  Hyatt Reg. Chicago (H)
  Hyatt Reg. O'Hare (H)
  Inter-Continental Chicago (H)
  La Salle Club (H)
  Marriott Chicago (H)
  Marriott O'Hare (H)
  Marriott O'Hare (H)
  Palmer Hilton (H)
  Radisson Chicago (H)
  Renaissance Chicago (H)
  Ritz Chicago (H)
  Rosemont O'Hare (H)
  Sheraton Chicago (H)

  Sheraton Gateway (H)
  Sofitel (H)
  Westin O'Hare (H)
Gilman:
  Heartland Spa (S)
Itasca:
  Nordic Hills (R)
Lincolnshire:
  Marriott's Lincolnshire (R)
Oak Brook:
  Oak Brook Hills (R)
St. Charles:
  Pheasant Run (R)
Whittington:
  Rend Lake (R)

Indiana
Bloomington:
  Fourwinds (R)
French Lick:
  French Lick Springs (R)
Indianapolis:
  Crowne Plaza (H)
  Embassy Indianapolis (H)
  Hyatt Reg. Indianapolis (H)
  Marriott Indianapolis (H)
  Westin Indianapolis (H)

Iowa
Bettendorf:
  Jumer's Castle (H)
Cedar Rapids:
  Wyndham Five Seasons (R)
Des Moines:
  Marriott Des Moines (H)
  Savery (H)

Kansas
Topeka:
  Heritage House (B)
Wichita:
  Marriott Wichita (H)

Kentucky
Harrodsburg:
  Beaumont Inn (B)
Lexington:
  Hilton Lexington (H)
  Hyatt Reg. Lexington (H)
  Marriott Griffin Gate (R)
Louisville:
  Club Hotel by Dbltree. (H)
  Galt House East (H)
  Hyatt Reg. Louisville (H)

Louisiana
New Orleans:
  Bienville House (B)
  Chateau Sonesta (H)
  Crowne Plaza New Orleans (H)
  Dauphine Orleans (H)
  Dbltree New Orleans (H)
  De La Poste (H)
  Fairmont New Orleans (H)
  Hilton New Orleans (H)
  Holiday Inn Le Moyne (H)
  Hyatt Reg. New Orleans (H)
  Inter-Continental (H)
  Le Meridien (H)
  Le Pavillon (H)
  Le Richelieu (H)
  Maison de Ville (B)
  Maison Dupuy (H)
  Marriott New Orleans (H)
  Melrose Mansion (B)
  Monteleone (H)
  Omni Royal Crescent (H)

Omni Royal Orleans (H)
Place d'Armes (H)
Radisson New Orleans (H)
Royal Sonesta (H)
Sheraton New Orleans (H)
St. Ann (H)
Westin Canal (H)
Windsor Court (H)

St. Francisville:
Lodge at the Bluffs (H)

White Castle:
Nottoway Plantation (B)

Maine

Bar Harbor:
Atlantic Oakes (B)
Bar Harbor Bluenose (B)
Bar Harbor Inn (B)
Bayview (H)

Boothbay Harbor:
Spruce Point (B)

Cape Elizabeth:
Inn by the Sea (B)

East Holden:
Lucerne Inn (B)

Kennebunkport:
Kennebunkport Inn (B)
White Barn Inn (B)

Ogunquit:
Cliff House (H)

Portland:
Marriott at Sable Oaks (H)
Sheraton Portland (H)

Rockport:
Samoset (R)

Scarborough:
Black Point Inn (R)

Maryland

Baltimore:
Cross Keys Inn (H)
Hyatt Reg. Baltimore (H)
Marriott Baltimore (H)
Marriott's Hunt Valley (H)
Omni Inner Harbor (H)
Renaissance Harborplace (H)
Sheraton Baltimore (H)
Sheraton Inner Harbor (H)

Easton:
Tidewater Inn (B)

Ocean City:
Coconut Malorie (H)
Dunes Manor (H)
Sheraton Fontainebleau (H)

St. Michaels:
Inn at Perry Cabin (B)

Stevensville:
Kent Manor (H)

Taneytown:
Antrim 1844 (B)

Massachusetts

Boston:
Boston Harbor (H)
Charles in Harvard Square (H)
Doubletree (H)
Fairmont Copley (H)
Four Seasons Boston (H)
Hilton Boston Back Bay (H)
Hyatt Harborside (H)
Hyatt Reg. Cambridge (H)
Le Meridien (H)
Marriott Copley Place (H)
Marriott Long Wharf (H)
Renaissance Bedford (H)
Royal Sonesta (H)

Sheraton Boston (H)
Swissotel (H)
Westin Copley Place (H)
Westin Waltham-Boston (H)

Cape Cod:
Brass Key (B)
Cape Codder (B)
Chatham Bars (B)
Dan'l Webster Inn (B)
New Seabury (R)
Ocean Edge (R)
Sea Crest (R)

Danvers:
Tara's Ferncroft (R)

Lenox:
Blantyre (B)
Canyon Ranch (S)
Cranwell (R)
Gables Inn (B)
Wheatleigh (B)

Martha's Vineyard:
Harbor View (B)

Nantucket:
Beachside Nantucket (H)
Harbor House (B)
Nantucket Inn (H)
Summer House (B)
White Elephant (R)

Peabody:
Marriott Peabody (H)

Rockport:
Yankee Clipper (B)

Stockbridge:
Red Lion (B)

Sturbridge:
Publick House (B)

Williamstown:
Orchards (B)

Michigan

Acme:
Grand Traverse (R)

Bellaire:
Shanty Creek (R)

Boyne Falls:
Boyne Mountain (R)

Detroit:
Crowne Pontchartrain (H)
Dbltree Detroit (H)
Hyatt Reg. Dearborn (H)
Marriott Dearborn (H)
Marriott Southfield (H)
Radisson Plaza (H)
Ritz Dearborn (H)
River Place (H)
Westin Renaissance (H)

Grand Rapids:
Amway Grand (H)

Harbor Springs:
Boyne Highlands (R)

Mackinac Island:
Grand (H)
Mission Point (R)

New Buffalo:
Harbor Grand (H)

Thompsonville:
Crystal Mountain (R)

Traverse City:
Waterfront Inn (R)

Ypsilanti:
Marriott Ypsilanti (R)

Minnesota

Alexandria:
Arrowwood Radisson (R)

Swimming Pools

Brainerd:
  Madden's (R)
Hibbing:
  Kahler Park (H)
Litchfield:
  Birdwing Spa (S)
Lutsen:
  Lutsen (R)
Minneapolis/St. Paul:
  Dbltree Mall of America (H)
  Embassy Minneapolis (H)
  Hilton Minneapolis (H)
  Hyatt Reg. Minneapolis (H)
  Radisson Conference (H)
  Radisson Plaza Tower (H)
  Sofitel (H)
Pine River:
  McGuire's (B)
Rochester:
  Kahler Plaza (H)

Mississippi
Biloxi:
  Grand Casino (H)
Natchez:
  Briars Inn (B)
  Burn (B)
Robinsonville:
  Hollywood Casino (H)
  Horseshoe Casino (H)
  Sam's (H)
Vicksburg:
  Cedar Grove (B)

Missouri
Kansas:
  Dbltree Corporate Woods (H)
  Marriott Overland Park (H)
Branson:
  Best Western Knights (H)
  Best Western Mtn Oak (H)
  Best Western Music (H)
  Chateau on the Lake (R)
  Clarion at Fall Creek (R)
Kansas City:
  Adam's Mark (H)
  Historic Suites of America (B)
  Holiday Inn Crowne Plaza (H)
  Marriott Downtown (H)
  Ritz Kansas City (H)
  Sheraton Kansas City (H)
  Westin Crown Ctr (H)
Lake Ozark:
  Lodge at Four Seasons (R)
Osage Beach:
  Marriott's Tan-Tar-A (R)
Ridgedale:
  Big Cedar (R)
St. Louis:
  Adam's Mark (H)
  Cheshire Inn (H)
  Daniele (H)
  Doubletree (H)
  Drury Inn (H)
  Embassy St. Louis (H)
  Frontenac Hilton (H)
  Harley St. Louis (H)
  Holiday Inn Riverfront (H)
  Hyatt Reg. St. Louis (H)
  Marriott Pavilion (H)
  Marriott St. Louis (H)
  Ritz St. Louis (H)
  Sheraton Plaza (H)

Montana
Bigfork:
  Averill's Flathead (B)
Big Sky:
  Huntley Lodge (R)
Bozeman:
  Mountain Sky (B)
Darby:
  Triple Creek Ranch (R)
Red Lodge:
  Pollard (B)
Whitefish:
  Grouse Mountain (R)

Nebraska
Omaha:
  Marriott Omaha (H)
  Red Lion Omaha (H)

Nevada
Crystal Bay:
  Cal-Neva Resort (R)
Lake Tahoe:
  Caesars Tahoe (R)
  Harrah's Lake Tahoe (R)
  Hyatt Reg. Lake Tahoe (R)
  Lake Tahoe Horizon (H)
Las Vegas:
  Aladdin (H)
  Alexis Park (H)
  Bally's Las Vegas (H)
  Binion's Horseshoe (H)
  Caesars Palace (H)
  Circus Circus (H)
  Desert Inn (R)
  Excalibur (H)
  Flamingo Hilton (H)
  Frontier (H)
  Golden Nugget (H)
  Hard Rock (H)
  Harrah's Casino (H)
  Hilton Las Vegas (H)
  Lady Luck Casino (H)
  Luxor Las Vegas (H)
  Maxim (H)
  MGM Grand (H)
  Mirage (H)
  NY Hotel & Casino (H)
  Rio Suite (H)
  Riviera (H)
  Stardust (H)
  Stratosphere (H)
  Treasure Island (H)
Laughlin:
  Don Laughlin's (H)
  Flamingo Hilton (H)
  Golden Nugget (H)
Mesquite:
  Players Island (R)
Reno:
  Eldorado (H)
  Harrah's & Hampton (H)
  John Ascuaga's (H)
  Peppermill (H)
  Silver Legacy (H)

New Hampshire
Bretton Woods:
  1896 Bretton Arms (B)
  Mount Washington (R)
Dixville Notch:
  Balsams Grand (R)
Franconia:
  Franconia Inn (B)
Holderness:
  Manor on Golden Pond (B)

Swimming Pools

Jackson:
  Christmas Farm (B)
Lincoln:
  Mountain Club (R)
Meredith:
  Inn at Mill Falls (B)
North Conway:
  Four Points Sheraton (H)
  White Mountain (R)
Waterville Valley:
  Waterville Valley (R)

New Jersey
Atlantic City:
  Atlantic Palace (H)
  Bally's Park Place (H)
  Caesar Atlantic City (H)
  Claridge Casino (H)
  Harrah's Casino (H)
  Hilton Atlantic City (H)
  Marriott Seaview (R)
  Merv Griffin's (H)
  Showboat Casino (H)
  Tropicana Casino (H)
  Trump Plaza (H)
  Trump's Castle (H)
  Trump Taj Mahal (H)
  Trump World's Fair (H)
Long Beach:
  Ocean Place Hilton (R)
Morristown:
  Headquarters Plaza (H)
Princeton:
  Forrestal (H)
  Hyatt Reg. Princeton (H)
  Marriott Princeton (H)
Short Hills:
  Hilton at Short Hills (H)
Spring Lake:
  Breakers (B)
  Sea Crest by the Sea (B)
Summit:
  Grand Summit (H)
Vernon:
  Great Gorge Village (R)

New Mexico
Albuquerque:
  Crowne Plaza (H)
  Hyatt Reg. Albuquerque (H)
  Marriott Albuquerque (H)
  Sheraton Old Town (H)
Cloudcroft:
  Lodge at Cloudcroft (B)
Mescalero:
  Inn of Mountain Gods (R)
Santa Fe:
  Bishop's Lodge (R)
  Eldorado (H)
  Inn at Loretto (B)
  Inn of Governors (B)
  La Fonda (H)
  La Posada Santa Fe (H)
  Radisson Santa Fe (H)
  Rancho Encantado (B)
  Santa Fe (H)
Taos:
  Historic Taos (B)
  Quail Ridge (R)
  Sagebrush Inn (B)

New York
Albany:
  Desmond (H)
  Marriott Albany (H)
  Omni Albany (H)

Alexandria Bay:
  Bonnie Castle (R)
  Riveredge (H)
Amenia:
  Troutbeck (B)
Bolton Landing:
  Sagamore (R)
Cooperstown:
  Otesaga (H)
Ellenville:
  Nevele (R)
Garden City:
  Garden City (H)
Geneva:
  Geneva on the Lake (B)
Glen Cove:
  Harrison (H)
Kiamesha Lake:
  Concord (R)
Lake Placid:
  Mirror Lake (B)
Lew Beach:
  Beaverkill Valley (B)
Montauk:
  Montauk Yacht (R)
Monticello:
  Kutsher's (R)
Neversink:
  New Age Health Spa (S)
New York City:
  Crowne Plaza (H)
  Le Parker Meridien (H)
  Marriott Financial Ctr (H)
  Marriott World Trade (H)
  Millenium Hilton (H)
  Peninsula NY (H)
  Trump International (H)
  UN Plaza Park Hyatt (H)
North Hudson:
  Elk Lake (R)
Rye Brook:
  Doral Arrowwood (R)
Saratoga Springs:
  Gideon Putnam (H)
  Sheraton Saratoga (R)
Shandaken:
  Shandaken Inn (B)
Tarrytown:
  Marriott Westchester (H)
  Tarrytown House (B)

North Carolina
Asheville:
  Great Smokies (R)
  Grove Park Inn (R)
Blowing Rock:
  Hound Ears (R)
  Westglow Spa (S)
Charlotte:
  Adam's Mark (H)
  Hyatt Charlotte (H)
  Marriott Charlotte (H)
  Park (H)
  Radisson Charlotte (H)
  Westin Charlotte (H)
Duck:
  Sanderling Inn (R)
Durham:
  Structure House (S)
Edenton:
  Lords Proprietors' (B)
Lake Toxaway:
  Greystone Inn (B)

Swimming Pools

Nags Head:
First Colony (H)
Pinehurst:
Pinehurst (R)
Pittsboro:
Fearrington House (B)
Raleigh-Durham:
Four Points Raleigh (H)
Hilton North Raleigh (H)
Marriott at Research (H)
Marriott Crabtree (H)
Omni Chapel Hill (H)
Washington Duke (H)
Wrightsville Beach:
Blockade Runner (R)

North Dakota
Bismarck:
Holiday Inn Bismarck (H)
Radisson Bismarck (H)
Fargo:
Best Western Doublewood (H)

Ohio
Aurora:
Aurora Inn (H)
Mario's International (S)
Cincinnati:
Doubletree (H)
Hyatt Reg. Cincinnati (H)
Marriott Cincinnati (H)
Omni Netherland (H)
Regal Cincinnati (H)
Westin (H)
Cleveland:
Embassy (H)
Renaissance Cleveland (H)
Ritz Cleveland (H)
Wyndham Cleveland (H)
Columbus:
Holiday Inn (H)
Hyatt Reg. Columbus (H)
Marriott N. Columbus (H)
Renaissance Dublin (H)
Sheraton Columbus (H)
Dellroy:
Atwood Lake (R)
Huron:
Sawmill Creek (R)
Painesville:
Quail Hollow (R)

Oklahoma
Checotah:
Fountainhead (R)
Kingston:
Texoma State (R)
Oklahoma City:
Marriott Oklahoma City (H)
Radisson Oklahoma City (H)
Waterford (H)
Tulsa:
Adam's Mark Tulsa (H)
Sheraton Tulsa (H)

Oregon
Bend:
Inn of Seventh Mtn (R)
Black Butte Ranch:
Black Butte (R)
Eugene:
Valley River (H)
Gleneden Beach:
Salishan (R)
Gold Beach:
Tu Tu'Tun (B)

Lincoln City:
Inn at Spanish Head (B)
Newport:
Embarcadero (H)
Portland:
5th Avenue Suites (H)
Governor (H)
Greenwood Inn (B)
Marriott Portland (H)
Sunriver:
Sunriver (R)
Timberline:
Timberline (R)
Warm Springs:
Kah-Nee-Ta (R)
Welches:
Resort at Mountain (R)

Pennsylvania
Champion:
Seven Springs (R)
E. Stroudsburg:
Deerfield Manor (S)
Farmington:
Nemacolin Woodlands (R)
Glen Mills:
Sweetwater Farm (B)
Hershey:
Hershey (H)
Hershey Lodge (H)
King of Prussia:
Park Ridge (H)
Sheraton Valley Forge (H)
Malvern:
Desmond (H)
Mt. Pocono/Pocono Manor:
Mount Airy Lodge (R)
Pocono Manor (R)
Philadelphia:
Adam's Mark (H)
Dbltree Philadelphia (H)
Four Seasons Philadelphia (H)
Marriott Philadelphia (H)
Omni at Independence (H)
Park Hyatt Philadelphia (H)
Rittenhouse (H)
Sheraton Society Hill (H)
Thomas Bond B&B (B)
Warwick Philadelphia (H)
Wyndham Franklin (H)
Pittsburgh:
Dbltree Pittsburgh (H)
Marriott City Center (H)
Marriott Greentree (H)
Radisson Pittsburgh (H)
Sheraton Station Square (H)
Skytop:
Skytop Lodge (R)
South Sterling:
Sterling Inn (B)
St. Davids:
Radnor (H)
Strasburg:
Historic Strasburg (B)

Puerto Rico
Dorado:
Hyatt Reg. Cerromar (R)
Hyatt Reg. Dorado (R)
Fajardo:
El Conquistador (R)
Humacao:
Palmas del Mar (R)

Swimming Pools

Old San Juan:
El Convento (H)

Rincon:
Horned Dorset (B)

San Juan:
Caribe Hilton (H)
Condado Beach Trio (H)
Condado Plaza (H)
El San Juan (H)
Sands (H)

Rhode Island

Newport:
Dbltree Newport (H)
Marriott Newport (H)
Newport Harbor (H)
Vanderbilt Hall (H)
Viking (H)

Providence:
Marriott Providence (H)
Westin Providence (H)

South Carolina

Charleston:
Charleston Place (H)
Hilton Charleston (H)
Mills House (H)

Hilton Head:
Disney's Hilton Head (R)
Hilton Head Health (S)
Hilton Hilton Head (R)
Hyatt Reg. Hilton Head (R)
Palmetto Dunes (R)
Sea Pines (R)
Westin (R)

Isle of Palms:
Wild Dunes (R)

Kiawah Island:
Kiawah Island (R)

Myrtle Beach:
Hilton Myrtle Beach (R)
Kingston Planation (R)
Myrtle Beach Martinique (R)
Ocean Dunes (R)
Sheraton Myrtle Beach (R)

Pawleys Island:
Litchfield Beach (R)
Litchfield Plantation (B)

Seabrook Island:
Seabrook Island (R)

South Dakota

Chamberlain:
Radisson Cedar Shore (R)

Tennessee

Fairfield Glade:
Fairfield Glade (R)

Fernvale:
Lyric Springs (B)

Memphis:
Adam's Mark (H)
Crowne Plaza (H)
Embassy Memphis (H)
French Quarter (H)
Marriott Memphis (H)
Peabody Memphis (H)
Radisson Memphis (H)

Nashville:
Embassy Nashville (H)
Renaissance Nashville (H)
Sheraton Music City (H)

Pigeon Forge:
Grand Resort (R)

Walland:
Inn at Blackberry Farm (B)

Texas

Arlington:
Greenhouse (S)

Austin:
Barton Creek (R)
Four Seasons Austin (H)
Hilton Austin North (H)
Hyatt Reg. Austin (H)
Lake Austin Spa (S)
Lakeway Inn (R)
Marriott Austin (H)
Omni Austin Downtown (H)
Omni Austin South Park (H)
Renaissance Austin (H)

Bandera:
Mayan Dude Ranch (B)

Corpus Christi:
Omni Bayfront (H)

Dallas/Fort Worth:
Cooper Wellness (S)
Crescent Court (H)
Dallas Parkway Hilton (H)
Dbltree Lincoln Ctr (H)
Embassy Dallas (H)
Fairmont (H)
Four Seasons (R)
Grand Kempinski Dallas (H)
Green Oaks Park (H)
Hyatt Reg. Dallas (H)
Mansion on Turtle Creek (H)
Marriott Quorum Dallas (H)
Omni Dallas (H)
Omni Mandalay (H)
Radisson Ft. Worth (H)
Radisson Park (H)
Renaissance Dallas (H)
Sheraton Park Central (H)
Westin Galleria Dallas (H)
Worthington (H)
Wyndham Anatole (H)
Wyndham Garden (H)

Galveston:
Galvez (H)
San Luis Resort (R)

Horseshoe Bay:
Horseshoe Bay (R)

Houston:
Adam's Mark (H)
Crowne Plaza Galleria (H)
Dbltree Post Oak (H)
Doubletree (H)
Four Seasons Houston (H)
Hilton Houston (H)
Houstonian (H)
Hyatt Reg. Houston (H)
Marriott JW (H)
Marriott West Loop (H)
Omni Houston (H)
Red Lion (H)
Renaissance Houston (H)
Ritz Houston (H)
Sofitel (H)
South Shore Harbour (H)
Westchase Hilton (H)
Westin Oaks (H)
Woodlands (R)
Wyndham Greenspoint (H)
Wyndham Warwick (H)

Montgomery:
Del Lago (R)

Rancho Viejo:
Rancho Viejo (R)

Swimming Pools

San Antonio:
Crowne Plaza (H)
Hilton Palacio del Rio (H)
Hyatt Reg. Hill Country (R)
Hyatt Reg. San Antonio (H)
La Mansion del Rio (H)
Marriott Rivercenter (H)
Marriott San Antonio (H)
Menger (H)
Plaza San Antonio (H)

Utah
Ivins:
Franklin Quest (S)
Midway:
Homestead (B)
Park City:
Deer Valley (H)
Olympia Park (H)
Shadow Ridge (H)
Stein Eriksen (R)
Salt Lake City:
Dbltree Salt Lake (H)
Embassy (H)
Hilton Salt Lake (H)
Little America (H)
Marriott Salt Lake City (H)
Wyndham (H)
Snowbird:
Cliff Lodge (R)
Inn at Snowbird (B)
Iron Blosam (H)
Lodge at Snowbird (H)
St. George:
Green Valley Spa (S)

Vermont
Brownsville:
Ascutney Mountain (R)
Chittenden:
Mountain Top (B)
Craftsbury Common:
Inn on Common (H)
Essex:
Inn at Essex (B)
Grafton:
Old Tavern at Grafton (B)
Highgate Springs:
Tyler Place (R)
Killington:
Cortina Inn (B)
Inn of Six Mountains (B)
Ludlow:
Green Mountain (S)
Manchester:
Equinox (H)
Inn at Manchester (B)
Inn at Willow Pond (B)
Reluctant Panther (B)
Village Country (B)
Wilburton Inn (B)
Middlebury:
Middlebury Inn (B)
Waybury Inn (B)
Newfane:
Four Columns (H)
Plymouth:
Hawk Inn (B)
Smugglers' Notch:
Smugglers' Notch (R)
Stowe:
Green Mountain (B)
Stowe Snowdrift (R)
Topnotch at Stowe (R)
Trapp Family (B)

Stratton Mountain:
Stratton Mtn (R)
Vergennes:
Basin Harbor (R)
Warren:
Sugarbush (R)
West Dover:
Inn at Sawmill Farm (B)
Wilmington:
Hermitage Inn (B)
Woodstock:
Kedron Valley (B)
Woodstock Inn (R)

Virginia
Charlottesville:
Boar's Head Inn (R)
Hot Springs:
Homestead (R)
Irvington:
Tides Inn (R)
Tides Lodge (R)
Keswick:
Keswick Hall (B)
Leesburg:
Lansdowne (R)
Richmond:
Hyatt Richmond (H)
Linden Row (B)
Marriott Richmond (H)
Omni Richmond (H)
Radisson (H)
Sheraton Park South (H)
Virginia Beach:
Cavalier (R)
Founders Inn (H)
Hilton Virginia Beach (H)
Pavilion Towers (H)
Ramada Plaza (R)
Virginia Beach (R)
Williamsburg:
Kingsmill (R)
Marriott Williamsburg (H)
Williamsburg (H)
Williamsburg Inn (H)
Williamsburg Lodge (H)
Wintergreen:
Wintergreen (R)

Washington
Blaine:
Inn at Semi-Ah-Moo (R)
Eastsound:
Rosario Resort (R)
Lake Quinault:
Lake Quinault (B)
Port Ludlow:
Port Ludlow (R)
Seattle:
Dbltree Bellevue (H)
Four Seasons Olympic (H)
Hyatt Reg. Bellevue (H)
Renaissance Madison (H)
Sheraton Seattle (H)
Warwick (H)
Westin Seattle (H)
Silverdale:
Silverdale on Bay (R)
Snoqualmie:
Salish Lodge (B)
Stevenson:
Skamania Lodge (R)
Winthrop:
Sun Mountain (R)

Swimming Pools

Washington, D.C.

Maryland:
  Hyatt Reg. Bethesda (H)
  Marriott Suites Bethesda (H)
Virginia:
  Hilton Washington (H)
  Hyatt Dulles (H)
  Hyatt Reg. Crystal City (H)
  Hyatt Reg. Reston (H)
  Marriott Crystal Gateway (H)
  Marriott Fairview Park (H)
  Marriott Key Bridge (H)
  Marriott Tysons Corner (H)
  Marriott Westfield's (H)
  Radisson Mark Ctr (H)
  Sheraton Tysons Corner (H)
Washington, DC:
  ANA (H)
  Dbltree NH Avenue (H)
  Embassy Chevy Chase (H)
  Embassy Row Hilton (H)
  Four Seasons (H)
  Grand Hyatt Washington (H)
  Hyatt Reg. Washington (H)
  Latham Georgetown (H)
  Loews L'Enfant (H)
  Marriott JW (H)
  Marriott Metro Center (H)
  Marriott Washington (H)
  Omni Shoreham (H)
  One Washington (H)
  Park Hyatt Washington (H)
  Radisson Barcelo (H)
  Renaissance Wash DC (H)
  Sheraton Washington (H)
  Washinton Hilton (H)
  Watergate (H)
  Westin Washington DC (H)

West Virginia

Berkeley Springs:
  Coolfront Resort (R)
Davis:
  Canaan Valley (R)

Harpers Ferry:
  Historic Hilltop House (H)
Hedgesville:
  Woods Resort (R)
Morgantown:
  Lakeview Resort (R)
Pipestem:
  McKeever Pipestem (R)
Shepherdstown:
  Bavarian Inn (B)
Wheeling:
  Oglebay Resort (R)
White Sulphur Springs:
  Greenbrier (R)

Wisconsin

Bailey's Harbor:
  Gordon Lodge (B)
Delavan:
  Lake Lawn Lodge (R)
Fontana:
  Abbey Resort (R)
Green Lake:
  Heidel House (R)
Kohler:
  American Club (R)
Lake Geneva:
  Grand Geneva (R)
  Interlaken Resort (R)
Milwaukee:
  Hilton Milwaukee (H)
  Hilton Milwaukee River (H)
  Marriott Milwaukee (H)
  Pfister (H)
Osceola:
  Aveda Spa Retreat (S)
Wisconsin Dells:
  Chula Vista (R)

Wyoming

Jackson:
  Jackson Hole Racquet (R)
  Spring Creek (R)
  Teton Pines (R)

Teas

Alaska
Fairbanks:
Captain Bartlett (H)

Arizona
Phoenix/Scottsdale:
Phoenician (R)
Ritz Phoenix (H)
Sedona:
Garland's (R)
Graham B&B (B)
Tucson:
Loews Ventana (R)
Wickenburg:
Merv Griffin's (B)

California
Capitola by the Sea:
Inn at Depot Hill (B)
Carmel:
Quail Lodge (R)
Stonepine (B)
Costa Mesa:
Country Side Inn (H)
Dana Point:
Ritz Laguna Niguel (R)
Escondido:
Golden Door (S)
Eureka:
Carter House (B)
Guerneville:
Applewood Inn (B)
Little River:
Heritage House (B)
Los Angeles:
Beverly Hills (H)
Beverly Hilton (H)
Century Plaza (H)
Chateau Marmont (H)
Four Seasons (H)
Mondrian (H)
Regal Biltmore (H)
Regent Beverly Wilshire (H)
Ritz Huntington (H)
Shangri-La (H)
Shutters (H)
Summit Bel-Air (H)
Summit Rodeo Drive (H)
Westwood Marquis (H)
Wyndham Checkers (H)
Mendocino:
Stanford Inn (B)
Monterey:
Pacific (H)
Spindrift Inn (B)
Oakhurst:
Chateau du Sureau (B)
Pacific Grove:
Gosby House (B)
Seven Gables (B)
Palm Springs:
Givenchy (S)
La Quinta (R)
Ritz Rancho Mirage (R)
San Diego:
del Coronado Hotel (R)
Horton Grand (H)
Kona Kai (R)
La Valencia (H)
Rancho Bernardo (R)
US Grant (H)
Westgate (H)

San Francisco:
Boheme (H)
Clift (H)
Fairmont SF (H)
Harbor Court (H)
Huntington (H)
Hyde Park (B)
Inn at Union Square (B)
Juliana (H)
Kensington Park (H)
Mark Hopkins (H)
Palace (H)
Pan Pacific SF (H)
Parc Fifty-Five (H)
Park Hyatt SF (H)
Petite Auberge (B)
Queen Anne (H)
Renaissance Stanford (H)
Ritz SF (H)
Savoy (H)
Vintage Court (H)
Washington Square (B)
Westin St. Francis (H)
White Swan (B)
San Jose:
Fairmont San Jose (H)
Santa Barbara:
Four Seasons Biltmore (R)
St. Helena:
Meadowood (R)
Yountville:
Vintage Inn (H)

Colorado
Aspen:
Little Nell (H)
Colorado Springs:
Broadmoor (R)
Denver:
Brown Palace (H)
Durango:
Rochester (H)
Mosca:
Inn at Zapata (B)
Telluride:
Columbia (B)
San Sophia (B)
Vail:
Mountain Haus at Vail (H)
Sonnenalp of Vail (R)

Connecticut
Mystic:
Inn at Mystic (B)
New Haven:
Three Chimneys (B)
New Preston:
Boulders (B)
Inn on Lake Waramaug (B)
Norfolk:
Blackberry River (B)
Old Lyme:
Bee & Thistle (B)

Delaware
Bethany Beach:
Addy Sea (B)
Newark:
Christiana Hilton (H)
Wilmington:
Boulevard B&B (B)
Hotel du Pont (H)

Teas

Florida

Amelia Island:
Ritz Amelia Island (R)

Bonita Springs:
Shangri-La (S)

Fort Lauderdale:
Riverside (H)

Fort Myers:
Sanibel Harbour (R)

Key West:
Marquesa (H)

Lake Wales:
Chalet Suzanne (B)

Marco Island:
Marco Island Hilton (R)

Miami/Miami Beach:
Biltmore (R)
Grand Bay (H)
Turnberry Isle (R)

Naples:
Naples Beach (R)
Registry (R)
Ritz Naples (R)

Orlando:
Disney's Grand Floridian (R)
Peabody Orlando (H)

Palm Beach:
Chesterfield (H)
Ritz Palm Beach (R)

Georgia

Atlanta:
Ansley Inn (B)
Doubletree (H)
Four Seasons Atlanta (H)
Grand Hyatt Atlanta (H)
Ritz Atlanta (H)
Ritz Buckhead (H)

Braselton:
Chateau Elan Winery (B)

Jekyll Island:
Jekyll Island Club (R)

Lake Lanier Islands:
Renaissance Pineisle (R)

Savannah:
Ballastone Inn (B)
Gastonian (B)
Magnolia Place (B)
Mulberry Inn (H)
Planters Inn Savannah (B)
President's Quarters (B)

Sea Island:
Cloister (R)

Hawaii

Kauai:
Princeville (R)

Lanai:
Lodge at Koele (R)

Maui:
Kapalua Bay (R)
Westin Maui (R)

Oahu:
Halekulani (H)

Idaho

Coeur d'Alene:
Gregory's McFarland B&B (B)

Ketchum:
Knob Hill (H)

Tetonia:
Teton Ridge (B)

Illinois

Chicago:
Ambassador West (H)
Drake (H)
Four Seasons Chicago (H)
Inter-Continental Chicago (H)
Regal Knickerbocker (H)
Renaissance Chicago (H)
Westin River North (H)

Lincolnshire:
Marriott's Lincolnshire (R)

Oak Brook:
Oak Brook Hills (R)

Indiana

French Lick:
French Lick Springs (R)

Indianapolis:
Canterbury (H)

Iowa

Walnut:
Antique City (B)

Kansas

Fort Scott:
Chenault Mansion (B)

Kentucky

Harrodsburg:
Inn at Shaker Village (B)

Louisiana

New Orleans:
Dauphine Orleans (H)
Hyatt Reg. New Orleans (H)
Royal Sonesta (H)
Westin Canal (H)
Windsor Court (H)

White Castle:
Nottoway Plantation (B)

Maine

Freeport:
Harraseeket Inn (B)

Kennebunkport:
Captain Lord Mansion (B)
Inn at Harbor Head (B)

Newcastle:
Newcastle Inn (B)

Northeast Harbor:
Asticou Inn (B)

Scarborough:
Black Point Inn (R)

Maryland

Easton:
Tidewater Inn (B)

Ocean City:
Dunes Manor (H)

St. Michaels:
Inn at Perry Cabin (B)

Taneytown:
Antrim 1844 (B)

Massachusetts

Boston:
Boston Harbor (H)
Boston Park Plaza (H)
Copley Square (H)
Fairmont Copley (H)
Four Seasons Boston (H)

Deerfield:
Deerfield Inn (B)

Lenox:
Wheatleigh (B)

Martha's Vineyard:
Outermost Inn (B)
Thorncroft Inn (B)
Tuscany Inn (B)

Nantucket:
Jared Coffin House (B)

Williamstown:
  Orchards (B)

Michigan
Detroit:
  Townsend (H)
Mackinac Island:
  Grand (H)
Petoskey:
  Stafford's Bay View (B)

Minnesota
Minneapolis/St. Paul:
  Saint Paul (H)
Red Wing:
  St. James (H)
Stillwater:
  Lumber Baron's (H)

Mississippi
Tupelo:
  Mockingbird B&B (B)
Vicksburg:
  Corners B&B (B)

Missouri
Kansas City:
  Ritz Kansas City (H)
St. Louis:
  Adam's Mark (H)
  Ritz St. Louis (H)

Nevada
Las Vegas:
  Desert Inn (R)
Laughlin:
  Don Laughlin's (H)

New Hampshire
Hanover:
  Hanover Inn (B)
Holderness:
  Manor on Golden Pond (B)
Jackson:
  Eagle Mountain (H)
Lincoln:
  Mountain Club (R)

New Jersey
Beach Haven:
  Green Gables (B)
Cape May:
  Abbey (B)
  Mainstay Inn (B)
  Queen Victoria (B)
Short Hills:
  Hilton at Short Hills (H)
Spring Lake:
  Sea Crest by the Sea (B)
Summit:
  Grand Summit (H)

New Mexico
Santa Fe:
  Grant Corner (B)
  Preston House (B)
  St. Francis (H)
Taos:
  Casa Benavides (B)

New York
Bolton Landing:
  Sagamore (R)
Lake Placid:
  Lake Placid Lodge (B)
  Mirror Lake (B)
Lew Beach:
  Beaverkill Valley (B)

New Paltz:
  Mohonk Mountain (R)
New York City:
  Algonquin (H)
  Carlyle (H)
  Casablanca (H)
  Elysée (H)
  59th St. Bridge Apts (H)
  Fitzpatrick Manhattan (H)
  Helmsley Park Lane (H)
  Hilton & Towers NY (H)
  Inter-Continental NY (H)
  Lowell (H)
  Mark (H)
  Morgans (H)
  NY Palace (H)
  Omni Berkshire (H)
  Peninsula NY (H)
  Pierre (H)
  Plaza (H)
  Regency (H)
  Stanhope (H)
  St. Regis (H)
  Tudor (H)
  Waldorf Astoria (H)
  Waldorf Towers (H)
  Wales (H)
  Washington Square (H)
North Hudson:
  Elk Lake Lodge (R)
Old Chatham:
  Old Chatham Inn (B)
Poughkeepsie:
  Inn at the Falls (B)

North Carolina
Asheville:
  Richmond Hill (B)
Duck:
  Sanderling Inn (R)
Lake Toxaway:
  Greystone Inn (B)
Nags Head:
  First Colony (H)
Pinehurst:
  Pinehurst (R)
Pittsboro:
  Fearrington House (B)

North Dakota
Fargo:
  Bohlig's B&B (B)

Ohio
Cincinnati:
  Cincinnatian (H)
Cleveland:
  Embassy (H)
  Ritz Cleveland (H)

Oklahoma
Kingston:
  Texoma State (R)

Oregon
Gleneden Beach:
  Salishan (R)
Newport:
  Sylvia Beach (H)
Portland:
  Heathman (H)

Pennsylvania
Erwinna:
  Evermay on Delaware (B)
Farmington:
  Nemacolin Woodlands (R)

Teas

Glen Mills:
  Sweetwater Farm (B)
Hershey:
  Hershey (H)
Mt. Pocono/Pocono Manor:
  Pocono Manor (R)
Philadelphia:
  Best Western Independence (H)
  Four Seasons Philadelphia (H)
  Rittenhouse (H)
  Ritz Philadelphia (H)
  Warwick Philadelphia (H)
Pittsburgh:
  Westin William Penn (H)
Skytop:
  Skytop Lodge (R)
South Sterling:
  Sterling Inn (B)

Puerto Rico
Rincon:
  Horned Dorset (B)

Rhode Island
Block Island:
  Atlantic Inn (B)
Newport:
  Cliffside Inn (B)
  Inntowne Inn (B)
  Vanderbilt Hall (H)

South Carolina
Beaufort:
  Rhett House (B)
Charleston:
  Charleston Place (H)
  John Rutledge (B)
  Planters Inn (B)
  Vendue Inn (B)
Pawleys Island:
  Litchfield Beach (R)

South Dakota
Rapid City:
  Alex Johnson (H)
Yankton:
  Mulberry Inn (B)

Tennessee
Memphis:
  Peabody Memphis (H)
Walland:
  Inn at Blackberry Farm (B)

Texas
Austin:
  Four Seasons Austin (H)
Dallas/Fort Worth:
  Adolphus (H)
  Omni Mandalay (H)
Galveston:
  Tremont House (H)
Houston:
  Omni Houston (H)
  Ritz Houston (H)

Utah
Park City:
  1904 Imperial (H)
  Washington School (B)
Snowbird:
  Inn at Snowbird (B)
St. George:
  Green Valley Spa (S)

Vermont
Barnard:
  Twin Farms (R)

Essex:
  Inn at Essex (B)
Goshen:
  Blueberry Hill (B)
Grafton:
  Old Tavern at Grafton (B)
Killington:
  Cortina Inn (B)
Lower Waterford:
  Rabbit Hill (B)
Ludlow:
  Governor's Inn (B)
Manchester:
  Equinox (H)
  Inn at Manchester (B)
  Wilburton Inn (B)
Middlebury:
  Middlebury Inn (B)
Newfane:
  Four Columns (H)
Quechee:
  Quechee Inn (B)
Shelburne:
  Inn at Shelburne Farms (B)
Stowe:
  Topnotch at Stowe (R)
  Trapp Family (B)
West Dover:
  Inn at Sawmill Farm (B)

Virginia
(see also Washington, D.C.)
Hot Springs:
  Homestead (R)
Irvington:
  Tides Inn (R)
  Tides Lodge (R)
Keswick:
  Keswick Hall (B)
Paris:
  Ashby Inn (B)
Richmond:
  Jefferson (H)
Washington:
  Inn at Little Washington (B)

Washington
Port Angeles:
  Domaine Madeleine (B)
Seattle:
  Four Seasons Olympic (H)
  Sorrento (H)
Snoqualmie:
  Salish Lodge (B)

Washington, DC
(including nearby Maryland and Virginia)
Virginia:
  Morrison House (B)
  Ritz Pentagon City (H)
  Ritz Tysons Corner (H)
Washington, DC:
  Carlton (H)
  Four Seasons (H)
  Grand Hyatt Washington (H)
  Hay-Adams (H)
  Henley Park (H)
  Madison (H)
  Park Hyatt Washington (H)
  Radisson Barcelo (H)
  Renaissance Mayflower (H)
  Tabard Inn (H)
  Washinton Hilton (H)
  Watergate (H)
  Willard (H)

Teas

West Virginia

Berkeley Springs:
Country Inn (B)

Parkersburg:
Blennerhassett Clarion (H)

White Sulphur Springs:
Greenbrier (R)

Wisconsin

Kohler:
American Club (R)

Milwaukee:
Pfister (H)

Wyoming

Jackson:
Rusty Parrot (B)
Spring Creek (R)

Technologically Friendly

Alabama

Birmingham:
Sheraton Birmingham (H)
Tutwiler (H)
Mobile:
Adam's Mark (H)
Radisson Admiral (H)
Point Clear:
Marriott's Grand (R)
Tuskegee:
Kellogg (H)

Alaska

Anchorage:
Anchorage Hilton (H)
Sheraton Anchorage (H)

Arizona

Gold Canyon:
Gold Canyon (R)
Grand Canyon:
Holiday Inn (H)
Phoenix/Scottsdale:
Arizona Golf (R)
Buttes (R)
Crowne Phoenix (H)
Dbltree Paradise Valley (R)
Embassy Biltmore (H)
Gardiner's (R)
Holiday Inn SunSpree (R)
Hyatt Reg. Phoenix (H)
Marriott's Camelback (R)
Marriott Scottsdale (H)
Marriott's Mountain (R)
Phoenician (R)
Pte Hilton S. Mountain (R)
Pte Hilton Squaw (R)
Pte Hilton Tapatio (R)
Radisson Scottsdale (R)
San Carlos (H)
Scottsdale Conference (R)
Scottsdale Princess (R)
Sheraton Mesa (H)
Sheraton San Marcos (R)
Sedona:
Poco Diablo (R)
Tucson:
Arizona Inn (H)
Canyon Ranch (S)
Loews Ventana (R)
Sheraton El Conquistador (R)
Westin La Paloma (R)

Arkansas

Hot Springs:
Lake Hamilton (R)
Little Rock:
Arkansas Excelsior (H)
Capital (H)

California

Anaheim:
Dbltree Anaheim (H)
Hilton Anaheim (H)
Hyatt Reg. Alicante (H)
Inn at the Park (H)
Sheraton Anaheim (H)
Carmel:
Carmel Country Spa (S)
Carmel Valley (R)
Los Laureles (H)
Costa Mesa:
Country Side Inn (H)
Marriott Costa Mesa (H)
Red Lion (H)

Westin South Coast (H)
Dana Point:
Ritz Laguna Niguel (R)
Fresno:
4 Points ITT Sheraton (H)
Irvine:
Hilton Orange County (H)
Irvine Marriott (H)
Lafayette:
Lafayette Park (H)
Long Beach:
Renaissance Long Beach (H)
Los Angeles:
Argyle (H)
Barnabey's (H)
Bel-Air (H)
Century Plaza (H)
Chateau Marmont (H)
Doubletree LAX (H)
Four Seasons (H)
Georgian (H)
Hilton Long Beach (H)
Hyatt Reg. LA (H)
Inter-Continental LA (H)
Le Parc (H)
Loews Santa Monica (H)
Malibu Beach (B)
Mansion Inn (B)
Marriott LAX (H)
Marriott Marina Beach (H)
Marriott Warner Ctr (H)
Miramar Sheraton (H)
Mondrian (H)
New Otani (H)
Palos Verdes (H)
Peninsula Beverly Hills (H)
Regal Biltmore (H)
Regent Beverly Wilshire (H)
Sheraton Grande (H)
Sheraton Industry Hills (H)
Shutters (H)
Sunset Marquis (H)
Wyndham Checkers (H)
Wyndham LAX (H)
Mendocino:
Stanford Inn (B)
Montecito:
San Ysidro (B)
Monterey:
Hyatt Reg. Monterey (H)
Monterey Plaza (H)
Napa:
Marriott Napa Valley (H)
Silverado (R)
Newport Beach:
Four Seasons Newport (H)
Hyatt Newporter (R)
Marriott Suites (H)
Marriott Tennis (H)
Sutton Place (H)
Palm Springs:
Hilton Palm Springs (H)
Marquis Palm Springs (H)
Renaissance Esmeralda (R)
Westin Mission Hills (R)
Wyndham Palm Springs (H)
Palo Alto:
Garden Court (H)
Riverside:
Mission Inn (H)
Sacramento:
Hyatt Reg. Sacramento (H)

Technologically Friendly

San Diego:
del Coronado Hotel (R)
Hilton San Diego (H)
Horton Grand (H)
Hyatt Reg. La Jolla (H)
Hyatt Reg. San Diego (H)
Kona Kai (R)
Le Meridien San Diego (H)
Loews Coronado (R)
Marriott La Jolla (H)
Radisson Harbor View (H)
Rancho Bernardo (R)
Rancho Valencia (R)
Sea Lodge (H)
Sheraton Grande (R)
Sheraton San Diego (H)
US Grant (H)
Westgate (H)
Westin San Diego (H)

San Francisco:
ANA San Francisco (H)
Boheme (H)
Campton Place (H)
Chancellor (H)
Claremont (R)
Clarion Bedford (H)
Clift (H)
Fairmont SF (H)
Galleria Park (H)
Griffon (H)
Handlery Union Square (H)
Harbor Court (H)
Hilton SF (H)
Huntington (H)
Hyatt Fish. Wharf (H)
Hyatt Reg. SF (H)
Inn at the Opera (B)
Inn at Union Square (B)
Juliana (H)
Mandarin Oriental (H)
Marriott Fish. Wharf (H)
Marriott SF (H)
Maxwell (H)
Monaco (H)
Nikko SF (H)
Palace (H)
Pan Pacific SF (H)
Parc Fifty-Five (H)
Park Hyatt SF (H)
Prescott (H)
Queen Anne (H)
Radisson Miyako (H)
Ritz SF (H)
Savoy (H)
Sheraton Fish. Wharf (H)
Sir Francis Drake (H)
Triton (H)
Victorian Inn (B)
Vintage Court (H)
Westin St. Francis (H)
York (H)

San Jose:
de Anza (H)
Fairmont San Jose (H)
Hyatt Saint Claire (H)

Santa Barbara:
Four Seasons Biltmore (R)

Santa Cruz:
Chaminade (H)

Santa Rosa:
La Rose (B)
Vintners Inn (B)

Sonoma:
Sonoma Mission (S)

Woodside:
Lodge at Skylonda (S)

Yountville:
Vintage Inn (H)

Colorado

Aspen:
Gant (B)
Inn at Aspen (H)
Jerome (H)
Lenado (B)
Little Nell (H)
Ritz Aspen (H)

Beaver Creek:
Embassy Beaver Creek (R)
Inn at Beaver Creek (B)
Pines Lodge (H)

Colorado Springs:
Antlers Dlbtree (H)
Broadmoor (R)
Sheraton (H)

Denver:
Brown Palace (H)
Burnsley (H)
Hyatt Reg. Denver Tech (H)
Loews Giorgio (H)
Marriott SE Denver (H)
Renaissance Denver (H)
Residence by Marriott (H)
Warwick (H)

Mt. Crested Butte:
Grande Butte (H)

Snowmass Village:
Silvertree (H)

Vail:
Sonnenalp of Vail (R)

Connecticut

Ledyard:
Foxwoods (H)

New Haven:
Three Chimneys (B)

Westbrook:
Water's Edge (B)

Westport:
Inn at National Hall (B)

Delaware

New Castle:
Armitage Inn (B)

Newark:
Christiana Hilton (H)

Rehoboth Beach:
Boardwalk Plaza (H)

Wilmington:
Boulevard B&B (B)
Hotel du Pont (H)

Florida

Amelia Island:
Amelia Island (R)

Boca Raton:
Boca Raton (R)
Marriott Boca Raton (H)

Captiva Island:
South Seas Plantation (R)

Destin:
Hilton Sandestin (R)

Fisher Island:
Spa Internazionale (S)

Fort Lauderdale:
Doubletree (H)
Hyatt Reg. Pier 66 (H)
Riverside (H)
Westin Ft. Lauderdale (H)

Technologically Friendly

Fort Myers:
  Sanibel Harbour (R)
Hallandale:
  Regency House (S)
Howey-in-the-Hills:
  Mission Inn (R)
Key Largo:
  Marriott's Key Largo (R)
Key West:
  Hyatt Key West (H)
Marathon:
  Hawk's Cay (R)
Marco Island:
  Marco Island Hilton (R)
  Radisson Beach (R)
Miami/Miami Beach:
  Alexander (H)
  Astor (H)
  Biltmore (R)
  Eden Roc (H)
  Grove Isle Club (B)
  Hyatt Reg. Coral Gables (H)
  Hyatt Reg. Miami (H)
  Marriott Biscayne Bay (H)
  Mayfair House (H)
  Miami Beach Ocean (H)
  Ocean Front (H)
  Omni Colonnade (H)
  Radisson Mart Plaza (H)
  Raleigh (H)
  Sheraton Bal Harbour (H)
  Sheraton Biscayne Bay (H)
  Sonesta Beach (R)
  Turnberry Isle (R)
  Westin Miami (R)
Naples:
  Edgewater Beach (H)
  Naples Beach (R)
  Ritz Naples (R)
Orlando:
  Clarion Plaza (H)
  Disney's Boardwalk (H)
  Holiday Inn SunSpree (R)
  Hyatt Orlando (H)
  Marriott Orl. Int'l Drive (H)
  Marriott's Orl. World Ctr (H)
  Omni Rosen (H)
  Radisson Barcelo (H)
  Radisson Plaza (H)
  Sheraton World (R)
  Walt Disney Dolphin (R)
Palm Beach:
  Breakers (R)
  Chesterfield (H)
  Ritz Palm Beach (R)
Panama City Beach:
  Marriott's Bay Point (R)
Ponte Vedra Beach:
  Marriott at Sawgrass (R)
Tampa Bay:
  Don CeSar (R)
  Holiday Inn Beachfront (R)
  Marriott Tampa (H)
  Sheraton Grand (H)
  TradeWinds St. Pete (R)
  Wyndham Harbour (H)

Georgia

Americus:
  Windsor (H)
Atlanta:
  Ansley Inn (B)
  Buckhead B&B (B)
  Doubletree (H)
  Embassy Perimeter Ctr (H)
  Evergreen (R)
  Four Seasons Atlanta (H)
  French Quarter (H)
  Grand Hyatt Atlanta (H)
  Hilton Atlanta (H)
  Hilton Atlanta Airport (H)
  Holiday Inn Ravinia (H)
  Hyatt Reg. Atlanta (H)
  Hyatt Reg. Perimeter (H)
  Marietta (R)
  Marque of Atlanta (H)
  Marriott Atlanta Airport (H)
  Marriott N. Central Atlanta (H)
  Peachtree (H)
  Renaissance Downtown (H)
  Ritz Atlanta (H)
  Ritz Buckhead (H)
  Sheraton Gateway (H)
  Summerfield (H)
  Terrace Buckhead (H)
  Westin Atlanta (H)
  Westin Peachtree (H)
  Wyndham Midtown (H)
  Wyndham Vinings (H)
Augusta:
  Partridge Inn (H)
Braselton:
  Chateau Elan Winery (B)
Jekyll Island:
  Jekyll Island Club (R)
Lake Lanier Islands:
  Renaissance Pineisle (R)
Macon:
  1842 Inn (B)
Peachtree City:
  Aberdeen Woods (H)
Savannah:
  Hyatt Reg. Savannah (H)
  Mulberry Inn (H)
Sea Island:
  Cloister (R)

Hawaii

Big Island:
  Royal Waikoloan (R)
Maui:
  Aston Wailea (R)
  Four Seasons Maui (R)
  Kapalua Bay (R)
  Kea Lani (R)
  Renaissance Wailea (R)
  Ritz Kapalua (R)
Oahu:
  Halekulani (H)
  Hawaii Prince Waikiki (H)
  Hilton Hawaiian (H)
  Hyatt Reg. Waikiki (H)
  New Otani Kaimana (H)
  Royal Hawaiian (H)
  Sheraton Waikiki (H)
  Waikiki Parc (H)

Idaho

Boise:
  Idanha (H)
  Owyhee Plaza (H)
  Red Lion Boise (H)

Illinois

Bloomingdale:
  Indian Lakes (R)
Chicago:
  Claridge (H)
  Clarion (H)
  Drake (H)
  Fairmont (H)

Technologically Friendly

Hilton Chicago (H)
Holiday Inn Chicago (H)
Hyatt Reg. Chicago (H)
Hyatt Reg. O'Hare (H)
Inter-Continental Chicago (H)
Marriott Chicago (H)
Marriott O'Hare (H)
Marriott O'Hare (H)
Midland (H)
Omni Chicago (H)
Palmer Hilton (H)
Radisson Chicago (H)
Regal Knickerbocker (H)
Renaissance Chicago (H)
Ritz Chicago (H)
Rosemont O'Hare (H)
Sheraton Chicago (H)
Sheraton Gateway (H)
Sofitel (H)
Sutton Place (H)
Tremont (H)
Westin Chicago (H)
Westin O'Hare (H)
Westin River North (H)

Itasca:
Nordic Hills (R)
St. Charles:
Pheasant Run (R)

Indiana
Indianapolis:
Hyatt Reg. Indianapolis (H)
Marriott Indianapolis (H)
Omni Severin (H)
Radisson Indianapolis (H)
Westin Indianapolis (H)

Iowa
Cedar Rapids:
Wyndham Five Seasons (R)
Dubuque:
Richards House (B)
Newton:
La Corsette Maison (B)

Kansas
Lawrence:
Eldridge (H)
Wichita:
Marriott Wichita (H)

Kentucky
Lexington:
Hyatt Reg. Lexington (H)
Marriott Griffin Gate (R)
Louisville:
Club Hotel by Dbltree. (H)
Galt House East (H)
Hyatt Reg. Louisville (H)
Marriott E. Louisville (H)
Seelbach (H)

Louisiana
New Orleans:
Bourbon Orleans (H)
Chateau Sonesta (H)
Crowne Plaza New Orleans (H)
Dbltree New Orleans (H)
Fairmont New Orleans (H)
Holiday Inn Le Moyne (H)
Hyatt Reg. New Orleans (H)
Inter-Continental (H)
Lafayette (H)
Maison Dupuy (H)
Marriott New Orleans (H)
Monteleone (H)
Omni Royal Crescent (H)
Omni Royal Orleans (H)

Queen & Crescent (H)
Radisson New Orleans (H)
Royal Sonesta (H)
Westin Canal (H)
Wyndham Riverfront (H)

Maine
Bar Harbor:
Bar Harbor Bluenose (B)
Freeport:
Harraseeket Inn (B)
Kennebunkport:
White Barn Inn (B)
Portland:
Marriott at Sable Oaks (H)
Radisson Portland (H)
Regency Portland (H)
Sheraton Portland (H)
Rockport:
Samoset (R)
Scarborough:
Black Point Inn (R)

Maryland
(see also Washington, D.C.)
Annapolis:
Loews Annapolis (H)
Marriott Annapolis (H)
Maryland Historic Inn (B)
Baltimore:
Admiral Fell Inn (B)
Clarion at Mt. Vernon (H)
Cross Keys Inn (H)
Harbor Court (H)
Hyatt Reg. Baltimore (H)
Marriott Baltimore (H)
Marriott's Hunt Valley (H)
Omni Inner Harbor (H)
Radisson Lord Baltimore (H)
Renaissance Harborplace (H)
Sheraton Baltimore (H)
Sheraton Inner Harbor (H)
Chestertown:
Imperial (B)
Ocean City:
Sheraton Fontainebleau (H)
St. Michaels:
Inn at Perry Cabin (B)

Massachusetts
Boston:
Boston Park Plaza (H)
Charles in Harvard Square (H)
Colonnade (H)
Doubletree (H)
Eliot (H)
Fairmont Copley (H)
Four Seasons Boston (H)
Hilton Boston Back Bay (H)
Hyatt Harborside (H)
Hyatt Reg. Cambridge (H)
Inn at Harvard (B)
Le Meridien (H)
Lenox (H)
Marriott Copley Place (H)
Marriott Long Wharf (H)
Regal Bostonian (H)
Renaissance Bedford (h)
Ritz Boston (H)
Sheraton Boston (H)
Sheraton Commander (H)
Swissotel (H)
Tremont House (H)
Westin Copley Place (H)
Westin Waltham-Boston (H)

Technologically Friendly

Cape Cod:
  Brass Key (B)
  Ocean Edge (R)
  Sea Crest (R)
Danvers:
  Tara's Ferncroft (R)
Deerfield:
  Deerfield Inn (B)
Lenox:
  Canyon Ranch (S)
Martha's Vineyard:
  Thorncroft Inn (B)
Nantucket:
  White Elephant (R)
Peabody:
  Marriott Peabody (H)
Williamstown:
  Orchards (B)

Michigan
Detroit:
  Atheneum (H)
  Crowne Pontchartrain (H)
  Hyatt Reg. Dearborn (H)
  Marriott Dearborn (H)
  Marriott Southfield (H)
  Radisson Plaza (H)
  River Place (H)
  St. Regis (H)
  Townsend (H)
  Westin Renaissance (H)
Grand Rapids:
  Amway Grand (H)
Ypsilanti:
  Marriott Ypsilanti (R)

Minnesota
Alexandria:
  Arrowwood Radisson (R)
Hibbing:
  Kahler Park (H)
Minneapolis/St. Paul:
  Dbltree Mall of America (H)
  Embassy Minneapolis (H)
  Hilton Minneapolis (H)
  Marquette (H)
  Marriott Minneapolis (H)
  Radisson Conference (H)
  Radisson Minneapolis (H)
  Radisson Plaza Tower (H)
  Saint Paul (H)
  Sheraton Park Place (H)
  Sofitel (H)
  Whitney (H)

Mississippi
Natchez:
  Briars Inn (B)

Missouri
Kansas City:
  Adam's Mark (H)
  Historic Suites of America (B)
  Holiday Inn Crowne Plaza (H)
  Radisson (H)
  Ritz Kansas City (H)
  Sheraton Kansas City (H)
  Southmoreland (H)
  Westin Crown Ctr (H)
St. Louis:
  Cheshire Inn (H)
  Crowne Plaza Majestic (H)
  Daniele (H)
  Drury Inn (H)
  Embassy St. Louis (H)
  Frontenac Hilton (H)
  Holiday Inn Riverfront (H)

Hyatt Reg. St. Louis (H)
  Marriott Pavilion (H)
  Marriott St. Louis (H)
  Ritz St. Louis (H)
  Sheraton Plaza (H)

Nebraska
Beatrice:
  Carriage House (B)

Nevada
Lake Tahoe:
  Harrah's Lake Tahoe (R)
  Harvey's (H)
  Hyatt Reg. Lake Tahoe (R)
Las Vegas:
  Alexis Park (H)
  Desert Inn (R)
  Excalibur (H)
  Harrah's Casino (H)
  Rio Suite (H)
  Riviera (H)
Reno:
  Harrah's & Hampton (H)
  John Ascuaga's (H)
  Silver Legacy (H)

New Hampshire
Hanover:
  Hanover Inn (B)
Waterville Valley:
  Waterville Valley (R)

New Jersey
Atlantic City:
  Caesar Atlantic City (H)
  Marriott Seaview (R)
  Merv Griffin's (H)
  Trump World's Fair (H)
Cape May:
  Virginia Hotel (B)
Hope:
  Inn at Millrace Pond (B)
Long Beach:
  Ocean Place Hilton (R)
Morristown:
  Headquarters Plaza (H)
Princeton:
  Chauncey Conference (H)
  Forrestal (H)
  Marriott Princeton (H)
  Nassau Inn (H)
Short Hills:
  Hilton at Short Hills (H)
Summit:
  Grand Summit (H)
Vernon:
  Great Gorge Village (R)

New Mexico
Albuquerque:
  Dbltree Albuquerque (H)
  Hyatt Reg. Albuquerque (H)
Santa Fe:
  Bishop's Lodge (R)
  Inn on the Alameda (B)
  Radisson Santa Fe (H)
  Santa Fe (H)
Taos:
  Fechin Inn (B)

New York
Albany:
  Desmond (H)
  Marriott Albany (H)
  Omni Albany (H)
Garden City:
  Garden City (H)

Technologically Friendly

Geneva:
Geneva on the Lake (B)
Glen Cove:
Harrison (H)
Great Neck:
Inn at Great Neck (H)
Hopewell Junction:
Le Chambord (B)
Lake Placid:
Mirror Lake (B)
Monticello:
Kutsher's (R)
New York City:
Algonquin (H)
Barbizon (H)
Beekman Tower (H)
Carlyle (H)
Casablanca (H)
Crowne Plaza (H)
Doubletree (H)
Drake Swissotel (H)
Eastgate Tower (H)
Elysée (H)
Essex House Nikko (H)
Fitzpatrick Manhattan (H)
Flatotel International (H)
Gorham (H)
Grand Hyatt NY (H)
Helmsley NY (H)
Hilton & Towers NY (H)
Holiday Inn Downtown (H)
Inn at Irving Place (B)
Inter-Continental NY (H)
Kimberly (H)
Kitano NY (H)
Le Parker Meridien (H)
Loews NY (H)
Lowell (H)
Lyden Gardens (H)
Lyden House (H)
Mansfield (H)
Marriott East Side (H)
Marriott Financial Ctr (H)
Marriott Marquis (H)
Michelangelo (H)
Millenium Hilton (H)
Millennium Broadway (H)
Murray Hill East (H)
NY Palace (H)
Omni Berkshire (H)
Peninsula NY (H)
Pierre (H)
Plaza (H)
Plaza Athénée (H)
Plaza Fifty (H)
Radisson Empire (H)
Regency (H)
Renaissance NY (H)
Rihga Royal (H)
Ritz New York (H)
Royalton (H)
Shelburne Murray Hill (H)
Sheraton Manhattan (H)
Southgate Tower (H)
Stanhope (H)
St. Moritz (H)
St. Regis (H)
Surrey (H)
UN Plaza Park Hyatt (H)
Waldorf Astoria (H)
Waldorf Towers (H)
Wyndham (H)
Poughkeepsie:
Inn at the Falls (B)

Rye Brook:
Doral Arrowwood (R)
Saranac Lake:
Saranac (H)
Saratoga Springs:
Inn at Saratoga (B)
Sheraton Saratoga (R)
Tarrytown:
Castle at Tarrytown (B)
Tarrytown House (B)

North Carolina
Asheville:
Great Smokies (R)
Grove Park Inn (R)
Charlotte:
Adam's Mark (H)
Marriott Charlotte (H)
Park (H)
Radisson Charlotte (H)
Westin Charlotte (H)
Fayetteville:
Radisson Prince Charles (H)
Raleigh-Durham:
Carolina Inn (H)
Four Points Raleigh (H)
Hilton North Raleigh (H)
Marriott at Research (H)
Omni Chapel Hill (H)
Siena (H)

North Dakota
Bismarck:
Holiday Inn Bismarck (H)
Radisson Bismarck (H)
Fargo:
Best Western Doublewood (H)
Radisson Fargo (H)

Ohio
Aurora:
Mario's International (S)
Cincinnati:
Cincinnatian (H)
Doubletree (H)
Marriott Cincinnati (H)
Regal Cincinnati (H)
Westin (H)
Cleveland:
Embassy (H)
Glidden House (B)
Marriott Downtown (H)
Omni International (H)
Renaissance Cleveland (H)
Ritz Cleveland (H)
Sheraton Cleveland (H)
Wyndham Cleveland (H)
Columbus:
Doubletree (H)
Holiday Inn (H)
Hyatt on Capital Square (H)
Marriott N. Columbus (H)
Sheraton Columbus (H)
Westin Columbus (H)
Worthington Inn (B)
Dellroy:
Atwood Lake (R)
Huron:
Sawmill Creek (R)

Oklahoma
Bartlesville:
Phillips (H)
Kingston:
Texoma State (R)

Technologically Friendly

Oklahoma City:
  Marriott Oklahoma City (H)
Tulsa:
  Adam's Mark Tulsa (H)

Oregon
Lincoln City:
  Inn at Spanish Head (B)
Portland:
  Benson (H)
  Governor (H)
  Heathman (H)
  RiverPlace (H)
Welches:
  Resort at Mountain (R)

Pennsylvania
Erwinna:
  Evermay on Delaware (B)
Farmington:
  Nemacolin Woodlands (R)
Hershey:
  Hershey (H)
King of Prussia:
  Sheraton Valley Forge (H)
Malvern:
  Desmond (H)
Mt. Pocono/Pocono Manor:
  Pocono Manor (R)
Philadelphia:
  Chestnut Hill (H)
  Dbltree Philadelphia (H)
  Four Seasons Philadelphia (H)
  Korman (H)
  Latham (H)
  Marriott Philadelphia (H)
  Omni at Independence (H)
  Rittenhouse (H)
  Ritz Philadelphia (H)
  Warwick Philadelphia (H)
Pittsburgh:
  Dbltree Pittsburgh (H)
  Hilton Pittsburgh (H)
  Marriott City Center (H)
  Marriott Greentree (H)
  Radisson Pittsburgh (H)
  Sheraton Station Square (H)
  Westin William Penn (H)
Wayne:
  Wayne (H)

Puerto Rico
Dorado:
  Hyatt Reg. Dorado (R)
San Juan:
  Caribe Hilton (H)

Rhode Island
Providence:
  Marriott Providence (H)
  Westin Providence (H)

South Carolina
Beaufort:
  Rhett House (B)
Charleston:
  Fulton Lane Inn (B)
  Indigo Inn (B)
  John Rutledge (B)
  Kings Courtyard (B)
  Mills House (H)
  Vendue Inn (B)
  Victoria House (B)
Hilton Head:
  Hilton Hilton Head (R)
Myrtle Beach:
  Sheraton Myrtle Beach (R)

South Dakota
Chamberlain:
  Radisson Cedar Shore (R)
Rapid City:
  Alex Johnson (H)

Tennessee
Memphis:
  Crowne Plaza (H)
  French Quarter (H)
  Peabody Memphis (H)
  Radisson Memphis (H)
Nashville:
  Loews Vanderbilt (H)
  Renaissance Nashville (H)
  Sheraton Music City (H)
  Union Station (H)
Walland:
  Inn at Blackberry Farm (B)

Texas
Austin:
  Barton Creek (R)
  Driskill (H)
  Four Seasons Austin (H)
  Hyatt Reg. Austin (H)
  Lakeway Inn (R)
  Omni Austin South Park (H)
  Renaissance Austin (H)
Dallas/Fort Worth:
  Adolphus (H)
  Dallas Parkway Hilton (H)
  Dbltree Campbell Ctr (H)
  Dbltree Lincoln Ctr (H)
  Embassy Dallas (H)
  Fairmont (H)
  Four Seasons (R)
  Grand Kempinski Dallas (H)
  Hyatt Reg. Dallas (H)
  Le Meridien (H)
  Mansion on Turtle Creek (H)
  Marriott Quorum Dallas (H)
  Melrose (H)
  Omni Mandalay (H)
  Radisson Ft. Worth (H)
  Radisson Park (H)
  Sheraton Market Ctr (H)
  Sheraton Park Central (H)
  Stoneleigh (H)
  Westin Galleria Dallas (H)
  Wyndham Anatole (H)
Galveston:
  Tremont House (H)
Houston:
  Adam's Mark (H)
  Crowne Plaza Galleria (H)
  Dbltree Allen Ctr (H)
  Dbltree Post Oak (H)
  Doubletree (H)
  Houstonian (H)
  Hyatt Reg. Houston (H)
  Marriott JW (H)
  Marriott Medical Ctr (H)
  Omni Houston (H)
  Renaissance Houston (H)
  Sofitel (H)
  South Shore Harbour (H)
  Westin Galleria (H)
  Woodlands (R)
Montgomery:
  Del Lago (R)
San Antonio:
  Crowne Plaza (H)
  Fairmount (H)
  Hyatt Reg. San Antonio (H)

Technologically Friendly

La Mansion del Rio (H)
Marriott Rivercenter (H)

Utah
Park City:
Goldener Hirsch (B)
Salt Lake City:
Dbltree Salt Lake (H)
Embassy (H)
Hilton Salt Lake (H)
Inn at Temple Square (H)
Wyndham (H)

Vermont
Essex:
Inn at Essex (B)
Killington:
Cortina Inn (B)
Inn of Six Mountains (B)
Ludlow:
Green Mountain (S)
Manchester:
Inn at Willow Pond (B)
Middlebury:
Swift House (B)
Stowe:
Trapp Family (B)

Virginia
(see also Washington, D.C.)
Charlottesville:
Boar's Head Inn (R)
Irvington:
Tides Inn (R)
Tides Lodge (R)
Leesburg:
Lansdowne (R)
Richmond:
Hyatt Richmond (H)
Radisson (H)
Sheraton Park South (H)
Virginia Beach:
Founders Inn (H)
Holiday Inn Sunspree (R)
Ramada Plaza (R)
Virginia Beach (R)
Williamsburg:
Kingsmill (R)
Marriott Williamsburg (H)
Williamsburg Inn (H)
Williamsburg Lodge (H)

Washington
Blaine:
Inn at Semi-Ah-Moo (R)
Port Angeles:
Domaine Madeleine (B)
Seattle:
Alexis (H)
Dbltree Bellevue (H)
Four Seasons Olympic (H)
Roosevlet (H)
Sheraton Seattle (H)
Sorrento (H)
Vintage Park (H)
Warwick (H)
Westin Seattle (H)
Silverdale:
Silverdale on Bay (R)

Stevenson:
Skamania Lodge (R)
Washington, DC
(including nearby Maryland and Virginia)
Maryland:
Marriott Suites Bethesda (H)
Virginia:
Doubletree (H)
Hyatt Reg. Crystal City (H)
Hyatt Reg. Reston (H)
Marriott Key Bridge (H)
Marriott Westfield's (H)
Ritz Pentagon City (H)
Ritz Tysons Corner (H)
Sheraton Tysons Corner (H)
Washington, DC:
ANA (H)
Canterbury (H)
Capital Hilton (H)
Carlton (H)
Four Seasons (H)
Georgetown Dutch (H)
Georgetown Inn (H)
Grand Hyatt Washington (H)
Henley Park (H)
Hyatt Reg. Washington (H)
Jefferson (H)
Latham Georgetown (H)
Loews L'Enfant (H)
Madison (H)
Marriott Metro Center (H)
Marriott Washington (H)
Morrison-Clark Inn (B)
One Washington (H)
Park Hyatt Washington (H)
Phoenix Park (H)
Radisson Barcelo (H)
Renaissance Mayflower (H)
Sheraton City Ctr (H)
Sofitel (H)
Tabard Inn (H)
Washington Court (H)
Washinton Hilton (H)
Watergate (H)
Westin City Ctr (H)
Westin Washington DC (H)
Willard (H)

West Virginia
Shepherdstown:
Bavarian Inn (B)
White Sulphur Springs:
Greenbrier (R)

Wisconsin
Green Lake:
Heidel House (R)
Lake Geneva:
Grand Geneva (R)
Milwaukee:
Hilton Milwaukee (H)
Hilton Milwaukee River (H)
Hyatt Reg. Milwaukee (H)

Wyoming
Moran:
Jackson Lake (B)

Tennis

Alabama
Orange Beach:
  Perdido Beach (R)
Arizona
Catalina:
  Miraval (S)
Douglas:
  Gadsden (H)
Gold Canyon:
  Gold Canyon (R)
Phoenix/Scottsdale:
  Arizona Golf (R)
  Boulders (R)
  Buttes (R)
  Dbltree La Posada (R)
  Embassy Scottsdale (H)
  Gardiner's (R)
  Hermosa Inn (B)
  Holiday Inn SunSpree (R)
  Hyatt Reg. Phoenix (H)
  Hyatt Reg. Scottsdale (R)
  Marriott's Camelback (R)
  Marriott's Mountain (R)
  Phoenician (R)
  Pte Hilton S. Mountain (R)
  Pte Hilton Tapatio (R)
  Radisson Scottsdale (R)
  Renaissance Cottonwoods (R)
  Ritz Phoenix (H)
  Royal Palms (H)
  Scottsdale Conference (R)
  Scottsdale Hilton (H)
  Scottsdale Plaza (R)
  Scottsdale Princess (R)
  Sheraton San Marcos (R)
  Wigwam (R)
Sedona:
  Enchantment (R)
  Garland's (R)
  Los Abrigados (R)
  Poco Diablo (R)
Tucson:
  Arizona Inn (H)
  Canyon Ranch (S)
  Dbltree Reid Park (H)
  Lodge Ventana (R)
  Loews Ventana (R)
  Omni Tucson (R)
  Sheraton El Conquistador (R)
  Tanque Verde (B)
  Westin La Paloma (R)
  Westward Look (R)
Wickenburg:
  Merv Griffin's (B)
Arkansas
Hot Springs:
  Lake Hamilton (R)
Lakeview:
  Gaston's (R)
California
Anaheim:
  Dbltree Anaheim (H)
  Hyatt Reg. Alicante (H)
Borrego Springs:
  La Casa del Zorro (R)
Calistoga:
  Indian Springs (S)
Carmel:
  Carmel Valley (R)
  John Gardiner's (R)
  Quail Lodge (R)
  Stonepine (B)

Cazadero:
  Timberhill (B)
Costa Mesa:
  Westin South Coast (H)
Dana Point:
  Laguna Cliff Marriott (R)
  Ritz Laguna Niguel (R)
Death Valley:
  Furnace Creek Inn (R)
Escondido:
  Golden Door (S)
Irvine:
  Hilton Orange County (H)
  Hyatt Reg. Irvine (H)
  Irvine Marriott (H)
Lake Arrowhead:
  Lake Arrowhead (R)
Little River:
  Little River Inn (B)
Los Angeles:
  Beverly Hills (H)
  Le Parc (H)
  Ramada W. Hollywood (B)
  Ritz Huntington (R)
  Ritz Marina del Rey (H)
  Sheraton Industry Hills (H)
  Summit Bel-Air (H)
Montecito:
  San Ysidro (B)
Monterey:
  Hyatt Reg. Monterey (H)
Napa:
  La Residence (B)
  Marriott Napa Valley (H)
  Silverado (R)
Newport Beach:
  Four Seasons Newport (H)
  Marriott Tennis (H)
  Sutton Place (H)
Ojai:
  Ojai Valley (R)
Olympic Valley:
  Resort at Squaw Creek (R)
Oxnard:
  Embassy Mandalay (H)
Palm Springs:
  Givenchy (S)
  Hilton Palm Springs (H)
  Hyatt Grand (R)
  Indian Wells (R)
  Inn at Racquet Club (B)
  La Mancha (R)
  La Quinta (R)
  L'Horizon Garden (R)
  Marquis Palm Springs (H)
  Marriott's Desert Springs (R)
  Marriott's Rancho (R)
  Renaissance Esmeralda (R)
  Ritz Rancho Mirage (R)
  Riviera Palm Springs (R)
  Shadow Mountain (R)
  Sundance (B)
  Two Bunch Palms (B)
  Westin Mission Hills (R)
Pebble Beach:
  Inn at Spanish Bay (R)
  Lodge at Pebble Beach (R)
Rutherford:
  Auberge du Soleil (B)
San Diego:
  del Coronado Hotel (R)
  Hilton San Diego (H)
  Hyatt Reg. La Jolla (H)

Tennis

Hyatt Reg. San Diego (H)
Inn at Rancho Santa Fe (H)
Kona Kai (R)
La Jolla Beach (H)
L'Auberge Del Mar (R)
Le Meridien San Diego (H)
Loews Coronado (R)
Marriott Mission Valley (H)
Marriott San Diego (H)
Princess San Diego (R)
Rancho Bernardo (R)
Rancho Valencia (R)
Sea Lodge (H)
Sheraton Grande (R)
Sheraton San Diego (H)
Westin San Diego (H)
San Francisco:
Claremont (R)
San Jose:
Hayes (H)
Santa Barbara:
El Encanto (H)
Fess Parker's (R)
Four Seasons Biltmore (R)
Santa Clara:
Westin Santa Slara (H)
Santa Cruz:
Chaminade (H)
Santa Monica:
Oceana (H)
Solvang:
Alisal (R)
Sonoma:
Sonoma Mission (S)
St. Helena:
Meadowood (R)
Tecate:
Rancho La Puerta (S)
Truckee:
Northstar-at-Tahoe (R)
Vista:
Cal-a-Vie (S)
Yosemite:
Ahwahnee (H)
Yountville:
Vintage Inn (H)

Colorado
Aspen:
Gant (B)
Beaver Creek:
Hyatt Reg. Beaver Creek (H)
Colorado Springs:
Broadmoor (R)
Cheyenne Mountain (R)
Sheraton (H)
Copper Mountain:
Copper Mountain (R)
Denver:
Hyatt Reg. Denver Dwtn (H)
Hyatt Reg. Denver Tech (H)
Inverness (R)
Durango:
Rochester (H)
Tamarron Hilton (R)
Wit's End (B)
Edwards:
Lodge & Spa Cordillera (R)
Granby:
C Lazy U Ranch (B)
Keystone:
Keystone (R)
Redstone:
Redstone Inn (B)

Snowmass Village:
Snowmass Lodge (R)
Steamboat Springs:
Sheraton Steamboat (R)
Telluride:
Columbia (B)
Peaks at Telluride (R)
Vail:
Vail Cascade (H)

Connecticut
Chester:
Inn at Chester (B)
Lakeville:
Interlaken Inn (R)
Lebanon:
Spa at Grand Lake (S)
Mystic:
Inn at Mystic (B)
New London:
Lighthouse Inn (H)
New Preston:
Boulders (B)
Inn on Lake Waramaug (B)
Norwich:
Norwich Inn (S)
Simsbury:
Simsbury Inn (H)
Southbury:
Heritage Inn (H)
Washington:
Mayflower Inn (B)
Westbrook:
Water's Edge (B)

Delaware
Montchanin:
Inn at Montchanin (B)

Florida
Amelia Island:
Amelia Island (R)
Ritz Amelia Island (R)
Bonita Springs:
Shangri-La (S)
Captiva Island:
South Seas Plantation (R)
Clearwater:
Belleview Mido (R)
Destin:
Hilton Sandestin (R)
Fisher Island:
Spa Internazionale (S)
Fort Lauderdale:
Hyatt Reg. Pier 66 (H)
Lago Mar (R)
Marriott Ft. Lauderdale (H)
Marriott's Harbor (R)
Radisson Bahia Mar (R)
Wyndham Ft. Lauderdale (H)
Fort Myers:
Sanibel Harbour (R)
Gasparilla Island:
Gasparilla Inn (B)
Haines City:
Grenelefe Golf (R)
Howey-in-the-Hills:
Mission Inn (R)
Islamorada:
Cheeca Lodge (R)
Jacksonville:
Marriott Jacksonville (H)
Key Largo:
Ocean Reef (R)
Key West:
Marriott's Casa Marina (R)

Tennis

Longboat Key:
Resort at Longboat Key (R)
Marathon:
Hawk's Cay (R)
Marco Island:
Marco Island Hilton (R)
Marriott's Marco Island (R)
Radisson Beach (R)
Miami/Miami Beach:
Biltmore (R)
Dbltree Coconut Grove (H)
Doral Golf (R)
Fisher Island (R)
Fontainebleau Hilton (R)
Greenview (H)
Grove Isle Club (B)
Radisson Mart Plaza (H)
Sheraton Bal Harbour (H)
Spa at Doral (S)
Turnberry Isle (R)
Westin Miami (R)
Naples:
La Playa Beach (R)
Naples Bath & Tennis (R)
Naples Beach (R)
Registry (R)
Ritz Naples (R)
Orlando:
Buena Vista Palace (H)
Disney Institute (R)
Disney's Beach Club (R)
Disney's Ft. Wilderness (R)
Disney's Grand Floridian (R)
Disney's Yacht (R)
Doubletree (H)
Grosvenor (R)
Holiday Inn Main Gate (H)
Hyatt Orlando (H)
Hyatt Reg. Grand Cypress (R)
Marriott Orl. Int'l Drive (H)
Marriott's Orl. World Ctr (H)
Omni Rosen (H)
Peabody Orlando (H)
Radisson Barcelo (H)
Radisson Plaza (H)
Renaissance Orlando (R)
Residence by Marriott (H)
Sheraton World (R)
Villas of Grand Cypress (R)
Walt Disney Dolphin (R)
Walt Disney Swan (R)
Westgate Lakes (R)
Palm Beach:
Breakers (R)
Four Seasons Palm Beach (H)
Palm Beach Polo (R)
PGA National (R)
Ritz Palm Beach (R)
Panama City Beach:
Marriott's Bay Point (R)
Pompano Beach:
Palm-Aire Resort (S)
Ponte Vedra Beach:
Marriott at Sawgrass (R)
Ponte Vedra (R)
Port St. Lucie:
Club Med Sandpiper (R)
Safety Harbor:
Safety Harbor (S)
Sanibel Island:
Casa Ybel (R)
Sanibel (R)
Sundial Beach (R)
Stuart:
Indian River Plantation (R)

Tampa Bay:
Hyatt Reg. Westshore (H)
Innisbrook Hilton (R)
Renaissance Vinoy (R)
Saddlebrook Tampa (R)
Sheraton Sand Key (R)
TradeWinds St. Pete (R)
West Palm Beach:
Hippocrates Health (S)

Georgia
Atlanta:
Evergreen (R)
Hilton Atlanta (H)
Hilton Atlanta Airport (H)
Holiday Inn Ravinia (H)
Marietta (R)
Marriott Atlanta Airport (H)
Marriott N. Central Atlanta (H)
Marriott NW Atlanta (H)
Marriott Perimeter Atlanta (H)
Peachtree (H)
Braselton:
Chateau Elan Winery (B)
Jekyll Island:
Jekyll Island Club (R)
Lake Lanier Islands:
Renaissance Pineisle (R)
Peachtree City:
Aberdeen Woods (H)
Pine Mountain:
Callaway Gardens (R)
Sea Island:
Cloister (R)
St. Simons Island:
King & Prince Beach (R)
Sea Palms (R)

Hawaii
Big Island:
Four Seasons Hualalai (R)
Hilton Waikoloa (R)
Kona Village (R)
Mauna Kea (R)
Mauna Lani Bay (R)
Orchid at Mauna Lani (R)
Royal Waikoloan (R)
Kauai:
Hyatt Reg. Kauai (R)
Kauai Coconut (R)
Marriott Kauai (R)
Outrigger Kauai (R)
Lanai:
Lodge at Koele (R)
Manele Bay (R)
Maui:
Aston Kaanapali (R)
Aston Wailea (R)
Embassy Maui (R)
Four Seasons Maui (R)
Hana-Maui Hotel (H)
Hyatt Reg. Maui (R)
Kapalua Bay (R)
Marriott Maui (R)
Maui Prince (R)
Renaissance Wailea (R)
Ritz Kapalua (R)
Royal Lahaina (R)
Sheraton Maui (R)
Oahu:
Hawaiian Regent (H)
Ihilani Resort (R)
Ilikai Nikko Waikiki (H)
New Otani Kaimana (H)
Pacific Beach (H)

Tennis

Idaho

Coeur d'Alene:
Coeur d'Alene (R)
McCall:
Shore Lodge (B)
Priest Lake:
Hill's Hospitality (B)

Illinois

Bloomingdale:
Indian Lakes (R)
Chicago:
Holiday Inn Chicago (H)
La Salle Club (H)
Marriott O'Hare (H)
Galena:
Eagle Ridge (R)
Gilman:
Heartland Spa (S)
Itasca:
Nordic Hills (R)
Wyndham (H)
Lincolnshire:
Marriott's Lincolnshire (R)
Oak Brook:
Oak Brook Hills (R)
St. Charles:
Pheasant Run (R)
Whittington:
Rend Lake (R)

Indiana

French Lick:
French Lick Springs (R)

Kentucky

Harrodsburg:
Beaumont Inn (B)
Lexington:
Marriott Griffin Gate (R)
Louisville:
Hyatt Reg. Louisville (H)

Louisiana

New Orleans:
Fairmont New Orleans (H)
Hilton New Orleans (H)
Windsor Court (H)
St. Francisville:
Lodge at the Bluffs (H)

Maine

Bar Harbor:
Atlantic Oakes (B)
Bar Harbor Inn (B)
Bayview (H)
Boothbay Harbor:
Spruce Point (B)
Cape Elizabeth:
Inn by the Sea (B)
Ogunquit:
Cliff House (H)
Rockport:
Samoset (R)
Scarborough:
Black Point Inn (R)

Maryland

Baltimore:
Cross Keys Inn (H)
Harbor Court (H)
Hyatt Reg. Baltimore (H)
Marriott's Hunt Valley (H)
Stevensville:
Kent Manor (H)
Taneytown:
Antrim 1844 (B)

Massachusetts

Boston:
Renaissance Bedford (H)
Cape Cod:
Chatham Bars (B)
Dunscroft by the Sea (B)
New Seabury (R)
Ocean Edge (R)
Danvers:
Tara's Ferncroft (R)
Lenox:
Blantyre (B)
Canyon Ranch (S)
Cranwell (R)
Gables Inn (B)
Wheatleigh (B)
Martha's Vineyard:
Harbor View (B)
Nantucket:
Nantucket Inn (H)
Wauwinet (B)
Sturbridge:
Publick House (B)

Michigan

Acme:
Grand Traverse (R)
Bellaire:
Shanty Creek (R)
Detroit:
Dbltree Detroit (H)
Marriott Dearborn (H)
River Place (H)
Grand Rapids:
Amway Grand (H)
Harbor Springs:
Boyne Highlands (R)
Mackinac Island:
Grand (H)
Mission Point (R)
Thompsonville:
Crystal Mountain (R)

Minnesota

Alexandria:
Arrowwood Radisson (R)
Brainerd:
Madden's (R)
Lutsen:
Lutsen (R)
Minneapolis/St. Paul:
Embassy Minneapolis (H)
Hyatt Reg. Minneapolis (H)
Radisson Conference (H)
Pine River:
McGuire's (B)

Mississippi

Biloxi:
Grand Casino (H)
Vicksburg:
Cedar Grove (B)

Missouri

Branson:
Clarion at Fall Creek (R)
Kansas City:
Hyatt Reg. Crown Ctr (H)
Southmoreland (H)
Westin Crown Ctr (H)
Lake Ozark:
Lodge at Four Seasons (R)
Osage Beach:
Marriott's Tan-Tar-A (R)
Ridgedale:
Big Cedar (R)

Tennis

St. Louis:
  Doubletree (H)

Montana
Bigfork:
  Averill's Flathead (B)
Big Sky:
  Huntley Lodge (R)
Bozeman:
  Mountain Sky (B)
Darby:
  Triple Creek Ranch (R)
Gallatin Gateway:
  Gallatin Gateway (B)
Red Lodge:
  Pollard (B)
Whitefish:
  Grouse Mountain (R)

Nevada
Crystal Bay:
  Cal-Neva Resort (R)
Lake Tahoe:
  Caesars Tahoe (R)
  Hyatt Reg. Lake Tahoe (R)
Las Vegas:
  Aladdin (H)
  Bally's Las Vegas (H)
  Caesars Palace (H)
  Desert Inn (R)
  Flamingo Hilton (H)
  Frontier (H)
  Golden Nugget (H)
  Hilton Las Vegas (H)
  MGM Grand (H)
  Riviera (H)
  Tropicana (H)
Laughlin:
  Flamingo Hilton (H)

New Hampshire
Bretton Woods:
  1896 Bretton Arms (B)
  Mount Washington (R)
Dixville Notch:
  Balsams Grand (R)
Franconia:
  Franconia Inn (B)
Lincoln:
  Mountain Club (R)
North Conway:
  Four Points Sheraton (H)
  White Mountain (R)
Waterville Valley:
  Waterville Valley (R)

New Jersey
Atlantic City:
  Caesar Atlantic City (H)
  Harrah's Casino (H)
  Marriott Seaview (R)
  Tropicana Casino (H)
  Trump Plaza (H)
  Trump's Castle (H)
  Trump World's Fair (H)
Hope:
  Inn at Millrace Pond (B)
Long Beach:
  Ocean Place Hilton (R)
Princeton:
  Forrestal (H)
  Hyatt Reg. Princeton (H)
Short Hills:
  Hilton at Short Hills (H)
Spring Lake:
  Sea Crest by the Sea (B)

Vernon:
  Great Gorge Village (R)

New Mexico
Albuquerque:
  Hilton Albuquerque (H)
Mescalero:
  Inn of Mountain Gods (R)
Santa Fe:
  Bishop's Lodge (R)
  House of the Moon (S)
  Rancho Encantado (B)
Taos Ski Valley:
  Edelweiss (B)

New York
Alexandria Bay:
  Bonnie Castle (R)
Amenia:
  Troutbeck (B)
Bolton Landing:
  Sagamore (R)
Cooperstown:
  Otesaga (H)
Ellenville:
  Nevele (R)
Kiamesha Lake:
  Concord (R)
Lake Placid:
  Mirror Lake (B)
Lew Beach:
  Beaverkill Valley (B)
Montauk:
  Montauk Yacht (R)
Monticello:
  Kutsher's (R)
Neversink:
  New Age Health Spa (S)
New Paltz:
  Mohonk Mountain (R)
New York City:
  Loews NY (H)
  UN Plaza Park Hyatt (H)
Rye Brook:
  Doral Arrowwood (R)
Saranac Lake:
  Point (B)
Saratoga Springs:
  Gideon Putnam (H)
Shandaken:
  Shandaken Inn (B)
Shelter Island:
  Chequit Inn (B)
  Ram's Head (B)
Tarrytown:
  Tarrytown House (B)

North Carolina
Asheville:
  Great Smokies (R)
  Grove Park Inn (R)
Blowing Rock:
  Hound Ears (R)
  Westglow Spa (S)
Duck:
  Sanderling Inn (R)
Edenton:
  Lords Proprietors' (B)
Lake Toxaway:
  Greystone Inn (B)
Pinehurst:
  Holly Inn (B)
  Pinehurst (R)
Pittsboro:
  Fearrington House (B)

Tennis

Raleigh-Durham:
  Omni Chapel Hill (H)

Ohio
Aurora:
  Aurora Inn (H)
Cleveland:
  Embassy (H)
Dellroy:
  Atwood Lake (R)
Huron:
  Sawmill Creek (R)
Painesville:
  Quail Hollow (R)

Oklahoma
Checotan:
  Fountainhead (R)
Kingston:
  Texoma State (R)
Oklahoma City:
  Radisson Oklahoma City (H)

Oregon
Bend:
  Inn of Seventh Mtn (R)
Black Butte Ranch:
  Black Butte (R)
Gleneden Beach:
  Salishan (R)
Portland:
  5th Avenue Suites (H)
Sunriver:
  Sunriver (R)
Warm Springs:
  Kah-Nee-Ta (R)
Welches:
  Resort at Mountain (R)

Pennsylvania
Champion:
  Seven Springs (R)
E. Stroudsburg:
  Deerfield Manor (S)
Farmington:
  Nemacolin Woodlands (R)
Hershey:
  Hershey (H)
  Hershey Lodge (H)
King of Prussia:
  Park Ridge (H)
Malvern:
  Desmond (H)
Mt. Pocono/Pocono Manor:
  Mount Airy Lodge (R)
  Pocono Manor (R)
Philadelphia:
  Wyndham Franklin (H)
Skytop:
  Skytop Lodge (R)
South Sterling:
  Sterling Inn (B)

Puerto Rico
Dorado:
  Hyatt Reg. Cerromar (R)
  Hyatt Reg. Dorado (R)
Fajardo:
  El Conquistador (R)
Humacao:
  Palmas del Mar (R)
San Juan:
  Caribe Hilton (H)
  Condado Plaza (H)
  El San Juan (H)

Rhode Island
Block Island:
  Atlantic Inn (B)

Newport:
  Cliffside Inn (B)
  Vanderbilt Hall (H)

South Carolina
Hilton Head:
  Disney's Hilton Head (R)
  Hilton Hilton Head (R)
  Hyatt Reg. Hilton Head (R)
  Palmetto Dunes (R)
  Sea Pines (R)
  Westin (R)
Kiawah Island:
  Kiawah Island (R)
Myrtle Beach:
  Hilton Myrtle Beach (R)
  Kingston Planation (R)
  Ocean Creek (R)
Pawleys Island:
  Litchfield Beach (R)
  Litchfield Plantation (B)
Seabrook Island:
  Seabrook Island (R)

Tennessee
Nashville:
  Sheraton Music City (H)
Walland:
  Inn at Blackberry Farm (B)

Texas
Arlington:
  Greenhouse (S)
Austin:
  Barton Creek (R)
  Lake Austin Spa (S)
  Lakeway Inn (R)
Bandera:
  Mayan Dude Ranch (B)
Dallas/Fort Worth:
  Cooper Wellness (S)
  Dbltree Campbell Ctr (H)
  Four Seasons (R)
  Grand Kempinski Dallas (H)
  Green Oaks Park (H)
  Hyatt Reg. Dallas (H)
  Le Meridien (H)
  Marriott Quorum Dallas (H)
  Sheraton Park Central (H)
  Worthington (H)
  Wyndham Anatole (H)
Galveston:
  San Luis Resort (R)
Horseshoe Bay:
  Horseshoe Bay (R)
Houston:
  Houstonian (H)
  Omni Houston (H)
  South Shore Harbour (H)
  Westin Galleria (H)
  Woodlands (R)
Montgomery:
  Del Lago (R)
Rancho Viejo:
  Rancho Viejo (R)
San Antonio:
  Hyatt Reg. Hill Country (R)
  Plaza San Antonio (H)
South Padre Island:
  Radisson South Padre (R)

Utah
Ivins:
  Franklin Quest (S)
Midway:
  Homestead (B)

Tennis

Snowbird:
Cliff Lodge (R)
Inn at Snowbird (B)
Lodge at Snowbird (H)
St. George:
Green Valley Spa (S)

Vermont
Barnard:
Maple Leaf (B)
Twin Farms (R)
Brownsville:
Ascutney Mountain (R)
Craftsbury Common:
Inn on Common (H)
Grafton:
Old Tavern at Grafton (B)
Highgate Springs:
Tyler Place (R)
Killington:
Cortina Inn (B)
Inn of Six Mountains (B)
Killington Resort (R)
Ludlow:
Governor's Inn (B)
Green Mountain (S)
Manchester:
Equinox (H)
Reluctant Panther (B)
Wilburton Inn (B)
Middlebury:
Waybury Inn (B)
Plymouth:
Hawk Inn (B)
Smugglers' Notch:
Smugglers' Notch (R)
Stowe:
Stowehof Inn (B)
Stowe Snowdrift (R)
Topnotch at Stowe (R)
Trapp Family (B)
Stratton Mountain:
Stratton Mtn (R)
Vergennes:
Basin Harbor (R)
Warren:
Sugarbush (R)
West Dover:
Inn at Sawmill Farm (B)
Wilmington:
Hermitage Inn (B)
Woodstock:
Woodstock Inn (R)

Virginia
Charlottesville:
Boar's Head Inn (R)
Hot Springs:
Homestead (R)
Irvington:
Tides Inn (R)
Tides Lodge (R)
Keswick:
Keswick Hall (B)
Leesburg:
Lansdowne (R)
Richmond:
Hyatt Richmond (H)
Linden Row (B)
Virginia Beach:
Cavalier (R)
Founders Inn (H)

Pavilion Towers (H)
Virginia Beach (R)
Williamsburg:
Kingsmill (R)
Marriott Williamsburg (H)
Williamsburg Inn (H)
Williamsburg Lodge (H)
Wintergreen:
Wintergreen (R)
Woodstock:
Inn at Narrow Passage (B)

Washington
Blaine:
Inn at Semi-Ah-Moo (R)
Port Ludlow:
Port Ludlow (R)
Silverdale:
Silverdale on Bay (R)
Stevenson:
Skamania Lodge (R)
Winthrop:
Sun Mountain (R)

Washington, D.C.
Virginia:
Marriott Westfield's (H)
Radisson Mark Ctr (H)
Washington, DC:
Washinton Hilton (H)

West Virginia
Berkeley Springs:
Coolfront Resort (R)
Davis:
Canaan Valley (R)
Hedgesville:
Woods Resort (R)
Morgantown:
Lakeview Resort (R)
Pipestem:
McKeever Pipestem (R)
Shepherdstown:
Bavarian Inn (B)
Wheeling:
Oglebay Resort (R)
White Sulphur Springs:
Greenbrier (R)

Wisconsin
Bailey's Harbor:
Gordon Lodge (B)
Delavan:
Lake Lawn Lodge (R)
Eagle River:
Chanticleer Inn (B)
Fontana:
Abbey Resort (R)
Green Lake:
Heidel House (R)
Kohler:
American Club (R)
Inn on Woodlake (B)
Lake Geneva:
Grand Geneva (R)
Interlaken Resort (R)
Osceola:
Aveda Spa Retreat (S)
Wisconsin Dells:
Chula Vista (R)

Wyoming
Jackson:
Jackson Hole Racquet (R)
Spring Creek (R)
Wort (H)

Week or More Stay

Arizona

Phoenix/Scottsdale:
  Arizona Golf (R)
  Embassy Biltmore (H)
  Embassy Scottsdale (H)
  Gardiner's (R)
  Marriott Scottsdale (H)
  Regal McCormick (R)
  Renaissance Cottonwoods (R)
  Scottsdale Conference (R)
  Scottsdale Hilton (H)

Tucson:
  Canyon Ranch (S)
  Lodge Ventana (R)
  Tanque Verde (B)

Arkansas

Lakeview:
  Gaston's (R)

California

Borrego Springs:
  La Casa del Zorro (R)
Calabasas:
  Ashram Retreat (S)
Calistoga:
  Indian Springs (S)
Carmel:
  Carmel Valley (R)
  John Gardiner's (R)
Escondido:
  Golden Door (S)
Los Angeles:
  Chateau Marmont (H)
  Le Parc (H)
  Mondrian (H)
  Shangri-La (H)
  Sunset Marquis (H)
  Wyndham Bel Age (H)
Monterey:
  Pacific (H)
Napa:
  Embassy Napa Valley (H)
  Silverado (R)
Ojai:
  Oaks at Ojai (S)
Palm Springs:
  Hyatt Reg. Palm Springs (H)
  Inn at Racquet Club (B)
  Marquis Palm Springs (H)
  Monte Vista (H)
  Shadow Mountain (R)
  Sundance (B)
San Diego:
  Catamaran (H)
  Gaslamp (H)
  Inn at Rancho Santa Fe (H)
  La Jolla Beach (H)
  Princess San Diego (R)
  Rancho Valencia (R)
San Francisco:
  Hyde Park (B)
Solvang:
  Alisal (R)
Tecate:
  Rancho La Puerta (S)
Truckee:
  Northstar-at-Tahoe (R)
Vista:
  Cal-a-Vie (S)
Woodside:
  Lodge at Skylonda (S)

Colorado

Aspen:
  Gant (B)
  Inn at Aspen (H)
Beaver Creek:
  Charter at Beaver Creek (H)
  Embassy Beaver Creek (R)
Breckenridge:
  Village at Breckenridge (R)
Clark:
  Home Ranch (R)
Denver:
  Burnsley (H)
  Cambridge (H)
  Holtze (H)
  Residence by Marriott (H)
Durango:
  Tall Timber (B)
  Tamarron Hilton (R)
Granby:
  C Lazy U Ranch (B)
Snowmass Village:
  Snowmass Lodge (R)
Steamboat Springs:
  Sheraton Steamboat (R)
Vail:
  Mountain Haus at Vail (H)
  Vail Cascade (H)

Connecticut

Norwich:
  Norwich Inn (S)
Westbrook:
  Water's Edge (B)

Delaware

Rehoboth Beach:
  Boardwalk Plaza (H)

Florida

Amelia Island:
  Amelia Island (R)
Bonita Springs:
  Shangri-La (S)
Captiva Island:
  South Seas Plantation (R)
Destin:
  Hilton Sandestin (R)
Fort Lauderdale:
  Doubletree (H)
  Lago Mar (R)
  Little Inn by the Sea (B)
Fort Myers:
  Sanibel Harbour (R)
Haines City:
  Grenelefe Golf (R)
Hallandale:
  Regency House (S)
Islamorada:
  Cheeca Lodge (R)
Key West:
  Marriott's Casa Marina (R)
  Ocean Key House (R)
Longboat Key:
  Colony Beach (R)
  Resort at Longboat Key (R)
Marco Island:
  Marriott's Marco Island (R)
  Radisson Beach (R)
Miami/Miami Beach:
  Alexander (H)
  Fisher Island (R)
  Florida Suites (H)

Week or More Stay

Marlin (H)
Pritikin Longevity (S)
Naples:
 Edgewater Beach (H)
 Naples Bath & Tennis (R)
Orlando:
 Disney Institute (R)
 Disney's Boardwalk (H)
 Disney's Ft. Wilderness (R)
 Disney's Old Key West (R)
 Doubletree (H)
 Holiday Inn SunSpree (R)
 Residence by Marriott (H)
 Villas of Grand Cypress (R)
 Vistana (R)
 Westgate Lakes (R)
Palm Beach:
 Palm Beach Polo (R)
 PGA National (R)
Ponte Vedra Beach:
 Marriott at Sawgrass (R)
 Ponte Vedra (R)
Sanibel Island:
 Casa Ybel (R)
 Sanibel (R)
Siesta Key:
 Captiva Beach (B)
Stuart:
 Indian River Plantation (R)
Tampa Bay:
 Dbltree Tampa Bay (H)
 Embassy Westshore (H)
 Innisbrook Hilton (R)
 Radisson Sand Key (R)
 Saddlebrook Tampa (R)
 TradeWinds St. Pete (R)

Georgia
Atlanta:
 Biltmore (H)
 Embassy Perimeter Ctr (H)
 French Quarter (H)
 Marque of Atlanta (H)
 Marriott Midtown Atlanta (H)
 Summerfield (H)
Pine Mountain:
 Callaway Gardens (R)
Sea Island:
 Cloister (R)
St. Simons Island:
 King & Prince Beach (R)

Hawaii
Big Island:
 Hilton Waikoloa (R)
Kauai:
 Kauai Coconut (R)
Lanai:
 Lodge at Koele (R)
 Manele Bay (R)
Maui:
 Four Seasons Maui (R)
 Grand Wailea (R)
 Kapalua Bay (R)
 Kea Lani (R)
 Royal Lahaina (R)
 Westin Maui (R)
Oahu:
 Halekulani (H)

Idaho
Priest Lake:
 Hill's Hospitality (B)

512

Illinois
Chicago:
 Omni Chicago (H)
 Raphael (H)
 Rosemont O'Hare (H)
 Summerfield (H)
Galena:
 Eagle Ridge (R)

Iowa
Des Moines:
 Embassy (H)
Fairfield:
 Raj (S)

Kansas
Lawrence:
 Eldridge (H)

Louisiana
New Orleans:
 Pontchartrain (H)
 Soniat House (B)
 Windsor Court (H)
St. Francisville:
 Lodge at the Bluffs (H)

Maine
Bar Harbor:
 Bayview (H)
Cape Elizabeth:
 Inn by the Sea (B)
Northeast Harbor:
 Asticou Inn (B)
Rockport:
 Samoset (R)

Maryland
Baltimore:
 Brookshire (H)
Ocean City:
 Sheraton Fontainebleau (H)

Massachusetts
Boston:
 Eliot (H)
Cape Cod:
 New Seabury (R)
Lenox:
 Canyon Ranch (S)
Martha's Vineyard:
 Charlotte Inn (B)
 Daggett House (B)

Michigan
Acme:
 Grand Traverse (R)
Bellaire:
 Shanty Creek (R)
Detroit:
 Atheneum (H)
Harbor Springs:
 Boyne Highlands (R)
Thompsonville:
 Crystal Mountain (R)

Minnesota
Litchfield:
 Birdwing Spa (S)
Lutsen:
 Lutsen (R)
Minneapolis/St. Paul:
 Embassy Minneapolis (H)
 Whitney (H)

Missouri
Branson:
 Clarion at Fall Creek (R)
 Red Bud Cove B&B (B)

Week or More Stay

Kansas City:
  Historic Suites of America (B)
  Raphael (H)
Lake Ozark:
  Lodge at Four Seasons (R)
St. Louis:
  Embassy St. Louis (H)
  Holiday Inn Riverfront (H)

Montana
Bigfork:
  Averill's Flathead (B)
Big Sky:
  Lone Mountain (B)
Bozeman:
  Mountain Sky (B)

Nevada
Las Vegas:
  Monte Carlo (H)
  Rio Suite (H)

New Hampshire
Dixville Notch:
  Balsams Grand (R)

New Jersey
Vernon:
  Great Gorge Village (R)

New Mexico
Santa Fe:
  Radisson Santa Fe (H)
  Rancho Encantado (B)
Taos:
  Quail Ridge (R)

New York
Geneva:
  Geneva on the Lake (B)
Hunter:
  Vatra Mountain (S)
Montauk:
  Gurney's Inn (S)
New York City:
  Beekman Tower (H)
  Beverly (H)
  Carlyle (H)
  Delmonico (H)
  Doral Court (H)
  Doubletree (H)
  Eastgate Tower (H)
  Fitzpatrick Manhattan (H)
  Flatotel International (H)
  Gorham (H)
  Gramercy Park (H)
  Kimberly (H)
  Lombardy (H)
  Lowell (H)
  Lyden Gardens (H)
  Lyden House (H)
  Mark (H)
  Mayflower (H)
  Murray Hill East (H)
  Plaza Fifty (H)
  Regency (H)
  Rihga Royal (H)
  Shelburne Murray Hill (H)
  Sherry Netherland (H)
  Southgate Tower (H)
  Stanhope (H)
  Surrey (H)
  Wales (H)
  Westbury (H)
  Wyndham (H)
North Hudson:
  Elk Lake Lodge (R)

North Carolina
Pinehurst:
  Pinehurst (R)

North Dakota
Fargo:
  Best Western Doublewood (H)

Ohio
Cincinnati:
  Vernon Manor (H)

Oklahoma
Afton:
  Shangri-La (R)

Oregon
Newport:
  Embarcadero (H)
Portland:
  RiverPlace (H)
Welches:
  Resort at Mountain (R)

Pennsylvania
Champion:
  Seven Springs (R)
E. Stroudsburg:
  Deerfield Manor (S)
Farmington:
  Nemacolin Woodlands (R)

Puerto Rico
Fajardo:
  El Conquistador (R)
Humacao:
  Palmas del Mar (R)
Rincon:
  Horned Dorset (B)

Rhode Island
Block Island:
  Atlantic Inn (B)
Newport:
  Castle Hill Inn (B)

South Carolina
Charleston:
  Lodge Alley (B)
Hilton Head:
  Hilton Head Health (S)
  Palmetto Dunes (R)
  Sea Pines (R)
  Westin (R)
Isle of Palms:
  Wild Dunes (R)
Kiawah Island:
  Kiawah Island (R)
Myrtle Beach:
  Kingston Planation (R)
  Myrtle Beach Martinique (R)
  Ocean Creek (R)
  Ocean Dunes (R)
  Sheraton Myrtle Beach (R)
Pawleys Island:
  Litchfield Beach (R)
Seabrook Island:
  Seabrook Island (R)

South Dakota
Custer:
  State Game Lodge (R)

Tennessee
Memphis:
  Embassy Memphis (H)
  French Quarter (H)
Nashville:
  Embassy Nashville (H)
  Hermitage (H)

Week or More Stay

Texas
Arlington:
  Greenhouse (S)
Bandera:
  Mayan Dude Ranch (B)
Cat Spring:
  Southwind B&B (B)
Dallas/Fort Worth:
  Embassy Dallas (H)
  Sheraton Market Ctr (H)
Houston:
  Doubletree (H)
  La Colombe d'Or (B)
  Marriott Medical Ctr (H)
Montgomery:
  Del Lago (R)
Rancho Viejo:
  Rancho Viejo (R)
South Padre Island:
  Radisson South Padre (R)

Utah
Ivins:
  Franklin Quest (S)
Park City:
  Deer Valley (H)
  Shadow Ridge (H)
Provo:
  Sundance Resort (R)
Salt Lake City:
  Embassy (H)
Snowbird:
  Inn at Snowbird (B)
  Iron Blosam (H)
  Lodge at Snowbird (H)
St. George:
  Green Valley Spa (S)

Vermont
Brownsville:
  Ascutney Mountain (R)
Highgate Springs:
  Tyler Place (R)
Ludlow:
  Green Mountain (S)

Plymouth:
  Hawk Inn (B)
Smugglers' Notch:
  Smugglers' Notch (R)
Stratton Mountain:
  Stratton Mtn (R)
Vergennes:
  Basin Harbor (R)
Warren:
  Sugarbush (R)

Virginia
Wintergreen:
  Wintergreen (R)

Washington
Port Ludlow:
  Port Ludlow (R)

Washington, DC
  Canterbury (H)
  Dbltree NH Avenue (H)
  Dbltree Penn Avenue (H)
  Embassy Chevy Chase (H)
  Georgetown Dutch (H)
  George Washington U. (H)
  One Washington (H)
  Watergate (H)
  Wyndham Bristol (H)

West Virginia
Berkeley Springs:
  Coolfront Resort (R)
Hedgesville:
  Woods Resort (R)
Wheeling:
  Oglebay Resort (R)

Wisconsin
Bailey's Harbor:
  Gordon Lodge (B)
Eagle River:
  Chanticleer Inn (B)
Lake Geneva:
  Interlaken Resort (R)

Wyoming
Jackson:
  Jackson Hole Racquet (R)
  Rusty Parrot (B)

Alphabetical Page Index*

* H = Hotels, R = Resorts, S = Spas; B = Bed & Breakfasts and Inns

522

523